THE MGMT SOLUTION

STUDENT RESOURCES

- Interactive eBook
- Flashcards
- Practice Quiz Generator
- Trackable Activities:
  - Graded Quizzing
  - Media Quizzing
  - Matching Exercises
- Chapter Videos
- Games: Crossword Puzzles and Beat the Clock
- Online Glossary
- Chapter Case Studies

Students sign in at **www.cengagebrain.com**

INSTRUCTOR RESOURCES

- Access to All Student Resources
- Engagement Tracker
- Instructor Companion Site
- PowerPoint® Slides
- Updated Test Bank
- Instructor Prep Cards

Instructors log in at **www.cengage.com/login**

Print

MGMT8 delivers all the key terms and all the content for the **Principles of Management** course through a visually-engaging and easy to reference print experience.

CourseMate

CourseMate provides access to the full **MGMT8** narrative, alongside a rich assortment of quizzing, flashcards, and interactive resources for convenient reading and studying.

MGMT 8
Chuck Williams

Vice President, General Manager, 4LTR Press and the Student Experience: Neil Marquardt

Product Director, 4LTR Press: Steven E. Joos

Product Manager: Laura Redden

Content/Media Developer: Daniel Celenza

Development Services: Colin Grover, B-books

Product Assistant: Mandira Jacob

Marketing Manager: Emily Horowitz

Market Strategist: Elizabeth Rankin

Sr. Content Project Manager: Kim Kusnerak

Manufacturing Planner: Ron Montgomery

Production Service: MPS Limited

Sr. Art Director: Stacy Jenkins Shirley

Cover/Internal Designer: Red Hangar/ Joe Devine

Cover Image: Image Source/Getty Images

Monitor, back cover: ©A-R-T/Shutterstock.com

Tablet, page i: ©tele52/Shutterstock.com

Intellectual Property

Analyst: Diane Garrity

Project Manager: Sarah Shainwald

Vice President, General Manager, Social Science & Qualitative Business: Erin Joyner

Product Manager: Scott Person

Library of Congress Control Number: 2014957067

ISBN: 978-1-285-86750-2

Cengage Learning
20 Channel Center Street
Boston, MA 02210
USA

Cengage Learning is a leading provider of customized learning solutions with office locations around the globe, including Singapore, the United Kingdom, Australia, Mexico, Brazil, and Japan. Locate your local office at: **www.cengage.com/global**

Cengage Learning products are represented in Canada by Nelson Education, Ltd.

To learn more about Cengage Learning Solutions, visit **www.cengage.com**

Purchase any of our products at your local college store or at our preferred online store **www.cengagebrain.com**

Printed in the United States of America
Print Number: 01   Print Year: 2015

CHUCK WILLIAMS
MGMT⁸
Brief Contents

© Joshua Resnick/Shutterstock.com

PART 1 INTRODUCTION TO MANAGEMENT

1 Management 2
2 The History of Management 22
3 Organizational Environments and Cultures 44
4 Ethics and Social Responsibility 66

PART 2 PLANNING

5 Planning and Decision Making 88
6 Organizational Strategy 110
7 Innovation and Change 134
8 Global Management 154

PART 3 ORGANIZING

9 Designing Adaptive Organizations 178
10 Managing Teams 200
11 Managing Human Resource Systems 218
12 Managing Individuals and a Diverse Work Force 248

PART 4 LEADING

13 Motivation 268
14 Leadership 290
15 Managing Communication 312

PART 5 CONTROLLING

16 Control 334
17 Managing Information 352
18 Managing Service and Manufacturing Operations 374

Endnotes 395
Index 423

Contents

Part 1
Introduction to Management

1 Management 2

1-1 Management Is . . . 3

1-2 Management Functions 4

1-3 Kinds of Managers 6

1-4 Managerial Roles 10

1-5 What Companies Look for in Managers 13

1-6 Mistakes Managers Make 15

1-7 The Transition to Management: The First Year 17

1-8 Competitive Advantage Through People 19

2 The History of Management 22

2-1 The Origins of Management 23

2-2 Scientific Management 25

2-3 Bureaucratic and Administrative Management 30

2-4 Human Relations Management 33

2-5 Operations, Information, Systems, and Contingency Management 38

3 Organizational Environments and Cultures 44

3-1 Changing Environments 45

3-2 General Environment 48

3-3 Specific Environment 52

3-4 Making Sense of Changing Environments 57

3-5 Organizational Cultures: Creation, Success, and Change 60

4 Ethics and Social Responsibility 66

4-1 Workplace Deviance 67

4-2 U.S. Sentencing Commission Guidelines for Organizations 69

4-3 Influences on Ethical Decision Making 72

4-4 Practical Steps to Ethical Decision Making 76

4-5 To Whom Are Organizations Socially Responsible? 80

4-6 For What Are Organizations Socially Responsible? 82

4-7 Responses to Demands for Social Responsibility 84

4-8 Social Responsibility and Economic Performance 86

Part 2
Planning

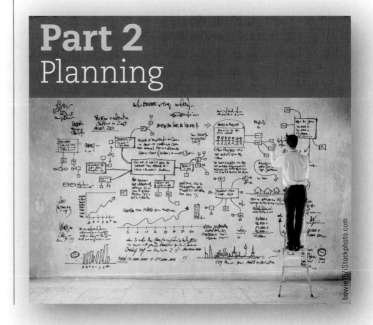

5 Planning and Decision Making 88

5-1 Benefits and Pitfalls of Planning 89

5-2 How to Make a Plan That Works 90

5-3 Planning from Top to Bottom 94

5-4 Steps and Limits to Rational Decision Making 98

5-5 Using Groups to Improve Decision Making 103

6 Organizational Strategy 110

6-1 Sustainable Competitive Advantage 111

6-2 Strategy-Making Process 113

6-3 Corporate-Level Strategies 119

6-4 Industry-Level Strategies 124

6-5 Firm-Level Strategies 128

7 Innovation and Change 134

7-1 Why Innovation Matters 135

7-2 Managing Innovation 140

7-3 Organizational Decline: The Risk of Not Changing 146

7-4 Managing Change 147

8 Global Management 154

8-1 Global Business, Trade Rules, and Trade Agreements 155

8-2 Consistency or Adaptation? 161

8-3 Forms for Global Business 163

8-4 Finding the Best Business Climate 167

8-5 Becoming Aware of Cultural Differences 172

8-6 Preparing for an International Assignment 174

Part 3
Organizing

Robert Churchill/iStockphoto.com

9 Designing Adaptive Organizations 178

9-1 Departmentalization 179

9-2 Organizational Authority 186

9-3 Job Design 189

9-4 Intraorganizational Processes 192

9-5 Interorganizational Processes 196

10 Managing Teams 200

10-1 The Good and Bad of Using Teams 201

10-2 Kinds of Teams 204

10-3 Work Team Characteristics 208

10-4 Enhancing Work Team Effectiveness 212

11 Managing Human Resource Systems 218

11-1 Employment Legislation 219

11-2 Recruiting 223

11-3 Selection 227

11-4 Training 233

11-5 Performance Appraisal   236

11-6 Compensation and Employee Separation   240

12 Managing Individuals and a Diverse Work Force   248

12-1 Diversity: Differences That Matter   249

12-2 Surface-Level Diversity   252

12-3 Deep-Level Diversity   258

12-4 Managing Diversity   260

Part 4
Leading

13 Motivation   268

13-1 Basics of Motivation   269

13-2 Equity Theory   274

13-3 Expectancy Theory   278

13-4 Reinforcement Theory   281

13-5 Goal-Setting Theory   286

13-6 Motivating with the Integrated Model   289

14 Leadership   290

14-1 Leaders versus Managers   291

14-2 Who Leaders Are and What Leaders Do   292

14-3 Putting Leaders in the Right Situation: Fiedler's Contingency Theory   296

14-4 Adapting Leader Behavior: Path-Goal Theory   299

14-5 Adapting Leader Behavior: Normative Decision Theory   303

14-6 Visionary Leadership   307

15 Managing Communication   312

15-1 Perception and Communication Problems   313

15-2 Kinds of Communication   317

15-3 Managing One-on-One Communication   323

15-4 Managing Organization-Wide Communication   328

Part 5
Controlling

16 Control   334

16-1 The Control Process   335

16-2 Control Methods   339

16-3 What to Control?   343

17 Managing Information 352

17-1 Strategic Importance of Information   353

17-2 Characteristics and Costs of Useful Information   356

17-3 Capturing, Processing, and Protecting Information   359

17-4 Accessing and Sharing Information and Knowledge   368

18 Managing Service and Manufacturing Operations 374

18-1 Productivity   375

18-2 Quality   378

18-3 Service Operations   383

18-4 Manufacturing Operations   386

18-5 Inventory   389

Endnotes   395

Index   423

1 Management

GlobalStock/iStockphoto.com

LEARNING OUTCOMES

1-1 Describe what management is.

1-2 Explain the four functions of management.

1-3 Describe different kinds of managers.

1-4 Explain the major roles and subroles that managers perform in their jobs.

1-5 Explain what companies look for in managers.

1-6 Discuss the top mistakes that managers make in their jobs.

1-7 Describe the transition that employees go through when they are promoted to management.

1-8 Explain how and why companies can create competitive advantage through people.

After you finish this chapter, go to **PAGE 21** for **STUDY TOOLS**

1-1 MANAGEMENT IS . . .

Management issues are fundamental to any organization: How do we plan to get things done, organize the company to be efficient and effective, lead and motivate employees, and put controls in place to make sure our plans are followed and our goals met? Good management is basic to starting a business, growing a business, and maintaining a business once it has achieved some measure of success.

To understand how important *good* management is, think about this mistake. Instead of recruiting better authors, improving marketing, and reducing costs (and therefore prices), Apple and five e-book publishers—Macmillan, Penguin, Hachette, HarperCollins, and Simon & Schuster—agreed to fix prices to neutralize Amazon.com's low-price leadership in the e-books marketplace. The agreement specified that the publishers, and not retailers like Amazon, would set prices, thus preventing Amazon from discounting book prices. The plan was dropped after Apple and the publishers were sued by the European Union and the US Department of Justice. In turn, Amazon again began discounting the prices of these publishers' e-books.[1]

Ah, bad managers and bad management. Is it any wonder that companies pay management consultants nearly $250 billion a year for advice on basic management issues such as how to outperform competitors to earn customers' business, lead people effectively, organize the company efficiently, and manage large-scale projects and processes?[2] This textbook will help you understand some of the basic issues that management consultants help companies resolve. (And it won't cost you billions of dollars.)

Many of today's managers got their start welding on the factory floor, clearing dishes off tables, helping customers fit a suit, or wiping up a spill in aisle 3. Similarly, lots of you will start at the bottom and work your way up. There's no better way to get to know your competition, your customers, and your business. But whether you begin your career at the entry level or as a supervisor, your job as a manager is not to do the work but to help others do theirs. **Management** is getting work done through others.

Vineet Nayar, CEO of IT services company HCL Technologies, doesn't see himself as the guy who has to do everything or have all the answers. Instead, he sees himself as "the guy who is obsessed with enabling employees to create value." Rather than coming up with

dem10/iStockphoto.com

solutions himself, Nayar creates opportunities for collaboration, for peer review, and for employees to give feedback on ideas and work processes. Says Nayar, "My job is to make sure everybody is enabled to do what they do well."[3]

Nayar's description of managerial responsibilities suggests that managers also have to be concerned with efficiency and effectiveness in the work process. **Efficiency** is getting work done with a minimum of effort, expense, or waste. Starbucks Coffee measures efficiency, or productivity, in terms of transactions per labor hour, meaning the number of coffee/food transactions it has each hour relative to the number of Starbucks employees it takes to handle those transactions. At 11.7 transactions per labor hour, Starbucks is 46% more efficient today than in 2008 when it averaged 8 transactions per labor hour.[4] Because they save an estimated 10 seconds per transaction over credit cards and 20 seconds per transaction compared to cash payments, Starbucks increased use of mobile payments is a key driver of its ability to process more customers each hour.[5] While Starbucks now handles 5 million mobile transactions per week, or 14% of all sales, efficiency is likely to rise even more as mobile transactions have more than doubled in the last year.[6]

Efficiency alone, however, is not enough to ensure success. Managers must also strive for **effectiveness,** which is accomplishing tasks that help fulfill organizational objectives such as customer service and satisfaction. After a 37% surge in last-minute holiday shopping

Management getting work done through others

Efficiency getting work done with a minimum of effort, expense, or waste

Effectiveness accomplishing tasks that help fulfill organizational objectives

(compared to the previous year) overwhelmed UPS and led to tens of thousands of late deliveries, Amazon.com began expanding its own "last-mile" delivery service to improve customer service and satisfaction, and therefore effectiveness.[7] While it typically uses UPS, FedEx, and the U.S. Postal Service for deliveries, Amazon hopes that its Amazon Fresh trucks, in use in a limited number of cities, will reduce rising shipping costs, challenge e-tail competitors such as eBay and Wal-Mart, and, if it works, allow it to fulfill the "holy grail" of online buying—same-day delivery. Analyst Ajay Agarwal, of Bain Capital Ventures, says, "In the old days, it used to be your milkman coming to your house every week. I think in five years I could imagine . . . some significant fraction of the population having an Amazon truck coming to their house every week."[8]

1-2 MANAGEMENT FUNCTIONS

Henri Fayol, who was a managing director (CEO) of a large steel company in the early 1900s, was one of the founders of the field of management. You'll learn more about Fayol and management's other key contributors when you read about the history of management in Chapter 2. Based on his twenty years of experience as a CEO, Fayol argued that "the success of an enterprise generally depends much more on the administrative ability of its leaders than on their technical ability."[9] A century later, Fayol's arguments still hold true. During a two-year study code-named Project Oxygen, Google analyzed performance reviews and feedback surveys to identify the traits of its best managers. According to Laszlo Bock, Google's vice president for people operations, "We'd always believed that to be a manager, particularly on the engineering side, you need to be as deep or deeper a technical expert than the people who work for you. It turns out that that's absolutely the least important thing." What was most important? "Be a good coach." "Empower; Don't micromanage." "Be product and results-oriented." "Be a good communicator and listen to your team." Be interested in [your] direct reports success and well being." In short, Google found what Fayol observed:

administrative ability, or management, is key to an organization's success.[10]

Managers need to perform five managerial functions in order to be successful, according to Fayol: planning, organizing, coordinating, commanding, and controlling.[11] Most management textbooks today have updated this list by dropping the coordinating function and referring to Fayol's commanding function as "leading." Fayol's management functions are thus known today in this updated form as planning, organizing, leading, and controlling. Studies indicate that managers who perform these management functions well are more successful, gaining promotions for themselves and profits for their companies. For example, the more time CEOs spend planning, the more profitable their companies are.[12] A twenty-five-year study at AT&T found that employees with better planning and decision-making skills were more likely to be promoted into management jobs, to be successful as managers, and to be promoted into upper levels of management.[13]

The evidence is clear. Managers serve their companies well when they plan, organize, lead, and control. So we've organized this textbook based on these functions of management, as shown in Exhibit 1.1.

Now let's take a closer look at each of the management functions: 1-2a planning, 1-2b organizing, 1-2c leading, and 1-2d controlling.

1-2a Planning

Planning involves determining organizational goals and a means for achieving them. As you'll learn in Chapter 5, planning is one of the best ways to improve performance. It encourages people to work harder, to work hard for

---

Planning determining organizational goals and a means for achieving them

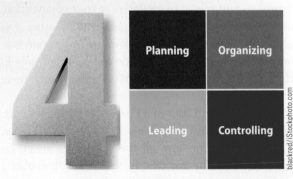

Exhibit 1.1
The Four Functions of Management

Planning Organizing

Leading Controlling

blackred/iStockphoto.com

extended periods, to engage in behaviors directly related to goal accomplishment, and to think of better ways to do their jobs. But most importantly, companies that plan have larger profits and faster growth than companies that don't plan.

For example, the question "What business are we in?" is at the heart of strategic planning. You'll learn about this in Chapter 6. If you can answer the question "What business are you in?" in two sentences or fewer, chances are you have a very clear plan for your business. But getting a clear plan is not so easy. Sometimes even very successful companies stray from their core business. Alibaba is a Chinese-based e-commerce company whose mission is, "To make it easy to do business anywhere." Like eBay, Alibaba operates online and mobile marketplaces that bring retail and wholesale buyers and sellers together. While Alibaba has 600 million customers in China, it's now expanding to the U.S. market via 11main.com, on which 1,000+ companies will sell everything from clothing to jewelry to arts and crafts. With such a clear mission and focus, it was surprising when Alibaba bought a 50% stake in China's Guangzhou Evergrande soccer team. Alibaba's Chairman Jack Ma explained, "I think not understanding soccer doesn't matter. I also didn't understand retail, e-commerce or the Internet, but that didn't stop me from doing it anyway." Ma's confidence aside, Simon Wong of the London School of Economics warns, "You should focus on what you're good at and this seems so ancillary to what they're doing today."[14]

You'll learn more about planning in Chapter 5 on planning and decision making, Chapter 6 on organizational strategy, Chapter 7 on innovation and change, and Chapter 8 on global management.

1-2b Organizing

Organizing is deciding where decisions will be made, who will do what jobs and tasks, and who will work for whom in the company. With 1,400 different computer systems; different labor unions representing pilots, flight attendants, and maintenance workers; and different ways of washing planes and boarding and feeding passengers; as well as different classes in the cabins (no first class on Continental), Continental Airlines and United Airlines faced an enormous organizing task to merge their two companies into the world's second-largest airline. Lori Gobillot, vice president of integration management at the time of the reorganization, oversaw thirty-three teams that decided the fastest way to board passengers and which computer systems to use,

United's or Continental's, for scheduling crews, routing planes, handling bags and cargo, or just basic accounting. Said Gobillot, "I tell them to be fact-based, and direct and objective, and keep the emotions out of it—and don't keep score. It's not important how many things come from United and how many come from Continental." Three years after the merger, significant challenges remain. For instance, mechanics continue to use separate information systems (one from United and one from Continental) to track and manage critical airplane maintenance and repair work. Likewise, labor agreements restrict "Continental" flight attendants to working on "Continental" planes and "United" flight attendants to "United" planes.[15] Each decision matters, as reducing costs by as little a half-cent per mile can result in a $1 billion increase in annual profits for an industry that historically loses billions each year.[16]

You'll learn more about organizing in Chapter 9 on designing adaptive organizations, Chapter 10 on managing teams, Chapter 11 on managing human resources, and Chapter 12 on managing individuals and a diverse work force.

1-2c Leading

Our third management function, **leading,** involves inspiring and motivating workers to work hard to achieve organizational goals. Eileen Martinson, CEO of software developer Sparta Systems, believes that it is important for leaders to clearly communicate what an organization's goals are. She says, "A boss taught me a long time ago that people are going to remember only two to three things." So at her first company-wide meeting, she communicated just one goal—doubling revenues over the next few years.[17] Martinson says, "The employees completely understand where we are going, and we've built a culture around that. If you have to come in and show me 45 charts and go through a lot of mumbo jumbo that neither of us understands, it's not going to work."[18]

You'll learn more about leading in Chapter 13 on motivation, Chapter 14 on leadership, and Chapter 15 on managing communication.

Organizing deciding where decisions will be made, who will do what jobs and tasks, and who will work for whom

Leading inspiring and motivating workers to work hard to achieve organizational goals

Bravely Changing Course

Video game developer Square Enix has traditionally specialized in making Japanese-style role-playing games (JRPGs). In recent years, Square began focusing on trying to develop global blockbuster titles that would appeal to a global audience. It began to struggle when sales of games like Tomb Raider, Sleeping Dogs, and Hitman: Absolution did not meet expectations. So it came as some surprise when Square released Bravely Default, a JRPG, and it sold over 200,000 copies in the US in three weeks. Square president Yosuke Matsuda took this as a cue. "In the past, when we developed console games with a worldwide premise, we lost our focus." Matsuda said. "We weren't able to see this clearly up until now, but fans of JRPGs are really spread around the world." The sales trends of its different games told Square what customers were looking for. In response, Matsuda said that Square would begin to include more JRPGs in its core stable of titles.

Source: M. Futter, "Square Enix Believes Company Has 'Lost Focus'," *Game Informer*, March 31, 2014, accessed April 9, 2014. http://www.gameinformer.com/b/news/archive/2014/03/31/square-enix-president-believes-company-has-lost-focus.aspx.

While globally appealing video games like Sleeping Dogs (pictured) have failed to meet sales expectations, Square Enix has had unexpected success with highly-targeted titles like JRPG Bravely Default.

1-2d Controlling

The last function of management, **controlling,** is monitoring progress toward goal achievement and taking corrective action when progress isn't being made. The basic control process involves setting standards to achieve goals, comparing actual performance to those standards, and then making changes to return performance to those standards. According to Michael Corbat, CEO of financial services company Citigroup, managerial and company success are contingent on setting goals, measuring performance, and making adjustments and corrections as needed. He recently stated during a meeting of executives, "You are what you measure." Therefore, a central part of his plan to restore Citigroup's financial performance is to measure how well executives perform against the plans they created. The basic idea, said one Citigroup executive, is "You said you would do this. Did you?" Corbat created a scorecard to measure the company's fifty top executives in four categories: capital, clients, culture, and controls. Scores ranging from 100 (the highest) to –40 (the lowest) will show how well each executive is performing. Corbat expects that the control process inherent in the scorecards will help Citigroup develop more accountability and discipline as it tries to recover from years of losses.[19]

You'll learn more about the control function in Chapter 16 on control, Chapter 17 on managing information, and Chapter 18 on managing service and manufacturing operations.

1-3 KINDS OF MANAGERS

Not all managerial jobs are the same. The demands and requirements placed on the CEO of Sony are significantly different from those placed on the manager of your local Wendy's restaurant.

*As shown in Exhibit 1.2, there are four kinds of managers, each with different jobs and responsibilities: **1-3a top managers**, **1-3b middle managers**, **1-3c first-line managers**, and **1-3d team leaders**.*

1-3a Top Managers

Top managers hold positions like chief executive officer (CEO), chief operating officer (COO), chief

Controlling monitoring progress toward goal achievement and taking corrective action when needed

Top managers executives responsible for the overall direction of the organization

Exhibit 1.2
What the Four Kinds of Managers Do

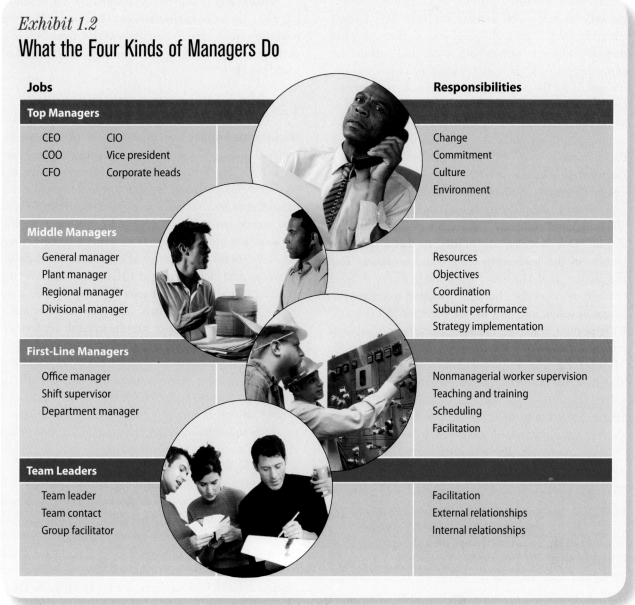

Jobs   **Responsibilities**

Top Managers

CEO	CIO
COO	Vice president
CFO	Corporate heads

Change
Commitment
Culture
Environment

Middle Managers

General manager
Plant manager
Regional manager
Divisional manager

Resources
Objectives
Coordination
Subunit performance
Strategy implementation

First-Line Managers

Office manager
Shift supervisor
Department manager

Nonmanagerial worker supervision
Teaching and training
Scheduling
Facilitation

Team Leaders

Team leader
Team contact
Group facilitator

Facilitation
External relationships
Internal relationships

---

financial officer (CFO), and chief information officer (CIO) and are responsible for the overall direction of the organization. Top managers have the following responsibilities.[20] First, they are responsible for creating a context for change. In fact, Andrew Mason, **Groupon's** founder and CEO, was fired because he had not moved fast enough to bring about significant changes needed to reverse a 77 percent decline in the stock price, an $81 million loss in the last quarter of his tenure, and an investigation from the Securities and Exchange Commission for some questionable accounting practices that may have overstated the company's value. On the day he was fired, Mason wrote to employees, "I was fired today. If you're wondering why…You haven't been paying attention. The events of the last year and a half speak for themselves. As CEO, I am accountable."[21]

Indeed, in both Europe and the United States, 35 percent of all CEOs are eventually fired because of their inability to successfully change their companies.[22] Creating a context for change includes forming a long-range vision or mission for the company. As one CEO said, "The CEO has to think about the future more than anyone."[23] Once that vision or mission is set, the second responsibility of top managers is to develop employees' commitment to and ownership of the company's performance. That is, top managers are responsible for creating employee buy-in. Third, top managers must create a positive organizational culture through language and action. Top managers impart company values, strategies, and lessons through what they do and say to others both inside and outside the company. Indeed, no matter what they communicate, it's critical for them to send and reinforce clear, consistent messages.[24] When Phil Martens became CEO of aluminum producer Novelis, he spent his first 100 days visiting plants around the world and discovered that the company, with 11,000 employees, had highly fragmented business practices, operations and strategies. To clearly communicate, "that we're going to move from a fragmented, regional company to a globally integrated company," Martens had shirts with the slogan, "One Novelis," distributed so that a symbolic picture of the leadership team could be taken. For the picture, said Martens, "We stood in a very defined triangle, very precise, because I wanted to create the image of order, and that we are together."[25] Likewise, it's important to actively manage internal organizational communication. As part of the One Novelis program, Martens created a global safety program, called Together We Are Safe, which monitored health and safety practices across Novelis' global sites, identified best practices, and then adopted and communicated them as a global standard. As a result, from 2009 to 2013, Novelis saw injuries, illnesses, and fatalities drop by over 40 percent.[26]

Finally, top managers are responsible for monitoring their business environments. This means that top managers must closely monitor customer needs, competitors' moves, and long-term business, economic, and social trends.

1-3b Middle Managers

Middle managers hold positions like plant manager, regional manager, or divisional manager. They are responsible for setting objectives consistent with top management's goals and for planning and implementing subunit strategies for achieving those objectives.[27] Or as one middle manager put it, a middle manager is, "the implementer of the company's strategy" who figures out the "how" to do the "what."[28] Middle manager Michelle Davis, an analytics director at FICO, the company that calculates credit scores, begins her day at 6:30 a.m. "when the hallways are dark" and there are few interruptions. Regular meetings, like the monthly conference call that she has with the analytics team, start at 7:30 a.m. The rest of her long days are often filled with additional meetings, training sessions that she either leads or participates in, and quick check-ins with her boss and various product management teams across the company, in which she communicates the concerns of her group about the software that banks use when applying credit scores to bank customers.[29]

One specific middle management responsibility is to plan and allocate resources to meet objectives. A second major responsibility is to coordinate and link groups, departments, and divisions within a company. Indeed, one middle manager described his job as, "A man who can discuss strategy with [the] CXO at breakfast and [then] eat lunch with workers."[30] FICO's Michelle Davis admits that coordinating and linking teams across different groups and departments can be "frustrating," but that it's a significant part of her job. Indeed, she says, "It takes time to do management right."[31]

A third responsibility of middle management is to monitor and manage the performance of the subunits and individual managers who report to them. Finally, middle managers are also responsible for implementing the changes or strategies generated by top managers. Why? Because they're closer to the managers and employees who work on a daily basis with suppliers to effectively and efficiently deliver

Middle managers responsible for setting objectives consistent with top management's goals and for planning and implementing subunit strategies for achieving these objectives

Robert Churchill/iStockphoto.com

the company's product or service. In short, they're closer to the people who can best solve problems and implement solutions. How important are middle managers to company performance? A study of nearly 400 videogame companies conducted at the University of Pennsylvania's Wharton School of Business found that middle managers' effectiveness accounted for 22% of the differences in performance across companies. In fact, middle managers were three times as important as the video game designers who develop game characters and story lines. Professor Ethan Mollick who conducted the study said that middle managers are the key to "making sure the people at the bottom and the top [of the organization] are getting what they need."[32]

1-3c First-Line Managers

First-line managers hold positions like office manager, shift supervisor, or department manager. The primary responsibility of first-line managers is to manage the performance of entry-level employees who are directly responsible for producing a company's goods and services. Thus, first-line managers are the only managers who don't supervise other managers. The responsibilities of first-line managers include monitoring, teaching, and short-term planning.

First-line managers encourage, monitor, and reward the performance of their workers. First-line managers are also responsible for teaching entry-level employees how to do their jobs. They also make detailed schedules and operating plans based on middle management's intermediate-range plans. By contrast to the long-term plans of top managers (three to five years out) and the intermediate plans of middle managers (six to eighteen months out), first-line managers engage in plans and actions that typically produce results within two weeks.[33] Consider the typical convenience store manager (e.g., 7-Eleven) who starts the day by driving past competitors' stores to inspect their gasoline prices and then checks the outside of his or her store for anything that might need maintenance, such as burned-out lights or signs, or restocking, such as windshield washer fluid and paper towels. Then comes an inside check, where the manager determines what needs to be done for that day. (Are there enough donuts and coffee for breakfast or enough sandwiches for lunch?) Once the day is planned, the manager turns to weekend orders. After accounting for the weather (hot or cold) and the sales trends at the same time last year, the manager makes sure the store will have enough beer, soft drinks, and newspapers on hand. Finally, the manager looks seven to ten days ahead for hiring needs. Because of strict hiring procedures (basic math tests, drug tests, and background checks), it can take that long to hire new employees. Said one convenience store manager, "I have to continually interview, even if I am fully staffed."[34]

1-3d Team Leaders

The fourth kind of manager is a team leader. This relatively new kind of management job developed as companies shifted to self-managing teams, which, by definition, have no formal supervisor. In traditional management hierarchies, first-line managers are responsible for the performance of nonmanagerial employees and have the authority to hire and fire workers, make job assignments, and control resources. In this new structure, the teams themselves perform nearly all of the functions performed by first-line managers under traditional hierarchies.[35]

Team leaders are primarily responsible for facilitating team activities toward accomplishing a goal. This doesn't mean team leaders are responsible for team performance. They aren't. The team is. So how do team leaders help their teams accomplish their goals? Avinoam Nowogrodski, CEO at Clarizen, a software company, says. "Great leaders ask the right questions. They recognize . . . that a team is much better at figuring out the answers."[36] Team leaders help their team members plan and schedule work, learn to solve problems, and work effectively with each other. Management consultant Franklin Jonath says, "The idea is for the team leader to be at the service of the group." It should be clear that the team members own the outcome. The leader is there to bring intellectual, emotional, and spiritual resources to the team. Through his or her actions, the leader should be able to show the others how to think about the work that they're doing in the context of their lives. It's a tall order, but the best teams have such leaders.[37]

Relationships among team members and between different teams are crucial to good team performance and must be well managed by team leaders, who are responsible for fostering good relationships and addressing problematic ones within their teams. Getting along with others is much more important in team structures

First-line managers train and supervise the performance of nonmanagerial employees who are directly responsible for producing the company's products or services

Team leaders managers responsible for facilitating team activities toward goal accomplishment

because team members can't get work done without the help of teammates. Clarizen CEO Avinoam Nowogrodski agrees, saying, "Innovation is created with people who you respect. It will never happen in a group of people who hate each other. If you want to have Innovation within your company, you need to have a culture of respect."[38] And, Nowogrodski adds, that starts with the team leader. "If you respect other people, they'll respect you."[39] Tim Clem emerged as a team leader at **GitHub**, a San Francisco–based software company that provides collaborative tools and online work spaces for people who code software. GitHub, itself, also uses team structures and team leaders to decide the software projects on which its 170 employees will work. After only a few months at the company, Clem, who had not previously led a team, convinced his GitHub colleagues to work on a new product he had designed for Microsoft Windows. Without their approval, he would not have gotten the go-ahead and the resources to hire people to do the project. By contrast, a manager, and not the team, would have likely made this decision in a traditional management structure.[40]

Team leaders are also responsible for managing external relationships. Team leaders act as the bridge or liaison between their teams and other teams, departments, and divisions in a company. For example, if a member of Team A complains about the quality of Team B's work, Team A's leader is responsible for solving the problem by initiating a meeting with Team B's leader. Together, these team leaders are responsible for getting members of both teams to work together to solve the problem. If it's done right, the problem is solved without involving company management or blaming members of the other team.[41]

In summary, because of these critical differences, team leaders who don't understand how their roles are different from those of traditional managers often struggle in their jobs.

You will learn more about teams in Chapter 10.

1-4 MANAGERIAL ROLES

Although all four types of managers engage in planning, organizing, leading, and controlling, if you were to follow them around during a typical day on the job, you would probably not use these terms to describe what they actually do. Rather, what you'd see are the various roles managers

play. Professor Henry Mintzberg followed five American CEOs, shadowing each for a week and analyzing their mail, their conversations, and their actions. He concluded that managers fulfill three major roles while performing their jobs—interpersonal, informational, and decisional.[42]

In other words, managers talk to people, gather and give information, and make decisions. Furthermore, as shown in Exhibit 1.3, these three major roles can be subdivided into ten subroles.

*Let's examine each major role—**1-4a interpersonal, 1-4b informational,** and **1-4c decisional roles**—and their ten subroles.*

1-4a Interpersonal Roles

More than anything else, management jobs are people-intensive. When asked about her experience as a first-time CEO, Kim Bowers, CEO of CST Brands, said,"We have 12,000 employees. [So,] I spend a lot of time out in the field with them."[43] Estimates vary with the level of management, but most managers spend between two-thirds and four-fifths of their time in face-to-face communication with others.[44] If you're a loner, or if you consider dealing with people a pain, then you may not be cut out for management work. In fulfilling the interpersonal role of management, managers perform three subroles: figurehead, leader, and liaison.

In the **figurehead role,** managers perform ceremonial duties like greeting company visitors, speaking at the opening of a new facility, or representing the company at a community luncheon to support local charities. When NetJets, a fractional private jet ownership company, broke ground on a new 140,000-square-foot headquarters in Columbus, Ohio, its new CEO, Jordan Hansell, presided over the ceremony.[45]

In the **leader role,** managers motivate and encourage workers to accomplish organizational objectives (see box "Nine Things to Avoid"). One way managers can act as leaders is to establish challenging goals. William Xu, the enterprise division chief of Chinese telecom equipment maker Huawei Enterprises, gave his division a 40% sales growth target for 2013. Xu said, "The (2013) target was very ambitious to motivate staff."[46]

In the **liaison role,** managers deal with people outside their units. Studies consistently indicate that managers spend as much time with outsiders as they do with their own subordinates and their own bosses. For example, CEOs often sit on other companies' boards. CEO Stephen Zarrilli, of **Safeguard Scientifics,** which invests in high-growth healthcare and technology firms, says, "When you sit on another company's board you gain perspective—not only about the company and its industry—but, more importantly, about other operating methodologies, governance, and viewpoints that can be very beneficial when you bring them back to your company."[47] Indeed, companies in low-growth, highly competitive industries whose CEOs sit on outside boards earn an average return on assets 15 percent higher than companies with CEOs who don't sit on outside boards![48]

1-4b Informational Roles

Not only do managers spend most of their time in face-to-face contact with others, they spend much of it obtaining and sharing information. Indeed, Mintzberg found that the managers in his study spent 40 percent of their time giving and getting information from others. In this regard, management can be viewed as gathering information by scanning the business environment and listening to others in face-to-face conversations,

> **Figurehead role** the interpersonal role managers play when they perform ceremonial duties
>
> **Leader role** the interpersonal role managers play when they motivate and encourage workers to accomplish organizational objectives
>
> **Liaison role** the interpersonal role managers play when they deal with people outside their units

Nine Things to Avoid

A manager is responsible not only for providing direction and guidance to employees but also for making sure to create a work environment that allows them to be the best. Author and columnist Jeff Haden identifies nine things that managers often do that create an uncomfortable and unproductive work atmosphere:

1. Pressuring employees to attend social events. When your employees are with people from work, even at some party, it might just end up feeling like "work."

2. Asking an employee to do something that you've already asked someone else to do.

3. Pressuring employees to give to charity.

4. Not giving employees time to eat during mealtime hours.

5. Asking employees to do self-evaluations.

6. Asking employees to evaluate their coworkers.

7. Revealing too much information to employees.

8. Asking employees to make sure that you stay on course during meetings.

9. Asking employees to do something that you don't want to do.

Dmitriy Shironosov/iStockphoto.com

Source: J. Haden "9 Things You Should Never Ask Employees to Do" *Inc.com*, February 22, 2012, accessed February 25, 2012, http://www.inc.com/jeff-haden/9-things-you-should-never-ask-employees-to-do.html.

processing that information, and then sharing it with people both inside and outside the company. Mintzberg described three informational subroles: monitor, disseminator, and spokesperson.

In the **monitor role,** managers scan their environment for information, actively contact others for information, and, because of their personal contacts, receive a great deal of unsolicited information. Besides receiving firsthand information, managers monitor their environment by reading local newspapers and the *Wall Street Journal* to keep track of customers, competitors, and technological changes that may affect their businesses. Now, managers can also take advantage of electronic monitoring and distribution services that track the news wires (Associated Press, Reuters, and so on) for stories related to their businesses. These services deliver customized electronic newspapers that include only stories on topics the managers specify. Business Wire (http://www.businesswire.com) monitors and distributes daily news headlines from major industries (e.g., automotive, banking and financial, health, high tech).[49] CyberAlert (http://www.cyberalert.com) keeps round-the-clock track of new stories in categories chosen by each subscriber.[50] Another site, Federal News Service (http://fednews.com), provides subscribers with daily electronic news clips from more than 5,000 online news sites.[51]

AP Images/Ted S. Warren

Because of their numerous personal contacts and their access to subordinates, managers are often hubs for the distribution of critical information. In the **disseminator role,** managers share the information they have collected with their subordinates and others in the company. At **Qualtrics**, a software company that provides sophisticated online survey research tools, CEO Ryan Smith makes sure that everyone in the company is clear on company goals and plans. Every Monday, employees are asked via email to respond to two questions: "What are you going to get done this week? And what did you get done last week that you said you were going to do?" Smith says, "Then that rolls up into one e-mail that the entire organization gets. So if someone's got a question, they can look at that for an explanation. We share other information, too—every time we have a meeting, we release meeting notes to the organization. When we have a board meeting, we write a letter about it afterward and send it to the organization." Qualtrics also uses an internal database where each quarter employees enter their plans for meeting the company's objectives. Those plans are then made visible to everyone else at Qualtrics.[52]

In contrast to the disseminator role, in which managers distribute information to employees inside the company, managers in the **spokesperson role** share information with people outside their departments or companies. One of the most common ways CEOs serve as spokespeople for their companies is at annual meetings with company shareholders or the board of directors. CEOs also serve as spokespeople to the media when their companies are involved in major news stories. For example, Amazon founder and CEO Jeff Bezos attracted worldwide attention when he announced that Amazon was actively working on ways to use airborne drones to deliver Amazon purchases to its Amazon Prime members who pay $99 a year for the privilege of unlimited 2-day delivery. Bezos said, "The Prime Air team is already flight testing our 5th and 6th generation aerial vehicles, and we are in the design phase on generations 7 and 8."[53] As with its Amazon Fresh trucks, drones would be used to speed delivery and reduce costs. While many believe that drone delivery is 5 years away or more, Bezos says, "It will work, and it will happen, and it's gonna be a lot of fun."[54]

1-4c **Decisional Roles**

Mintzberg found that obtaining and sharing information is not an end in itself. Obtaining and sharing information with people inside and outside the company is useful to managers because it helps them make good

Monitor role the informational role managers play when they scan their environment for information

Disseminator role the informational role managers play when they share information with others in their departments or companies

Spokesperson role the informational role managers play when they share information with people outside their departments or companies

decisions. According to Mintzberg, managers engage in four decisional subroles: entrepreneur, disturbance handler, resource allocator, and negotiator.

In the **entrepreneur role,** managers adapt themselves, their subordinates, and their units to change. When Peter Löscher took over as CEO of Siemens, the German manufacturer had just been fined $2.5 billion for bribing government officials throughout the world to gain favor to win contracts. As a result, Löscher knew massive change was needed. He started by replacing the company's entire executive team and eventually replaced half of Siemens's middle managers. Then, he sold Siemens's best-performing units, mobile phones and information technology, and used the proceeds to invest in sustainable projects like solar energy, wind energy, and high-efficiency electricity grids, from which Siemens now derives $38 billion in sales annually. Today, 100,000 Siemens employees are so-called green-collar workers. Despite the turnaround, Löscher maintains an entrepreneurial mindset, saying, "Being good today means you have to be better tomorrow, and even better the day after tomorrow. The biggest risk is complacency."[55]

In the **disturbance handler role,** managers respond to pressures and problems so severe that they demand immediate attention and action. In December 2013, Target, the second largest U.S. retailer, announced hackers had illegally accessed the names, home addresses, emails, and credit cards of up to 110 million Target customers. CEO Gregg Steinhafel told his leadership team that, "Target won't be defined by the breach, but how we handle the breach." Target, which could end up paying $1.1 billion to banks to cover fraudulent transactions, quickly offered all customers 10% discounts at its stores and a year's worth of free identity-theft insurance and credit monitoring. It later took out full-page newspapers advertisements all over the U.S. to apologize, saying, "Your trust is a top priority for Target, and we deeply regret the inconvenience this may cause."[56]

In the **resource allocator role,** managers decide who will get what resources and how many resources they will get. Ford's F-series truck, the best selling vehicle in the U.S. for 32 consecutive years, generates $22 billion in sales a year and accounts for 12% of Ford's global sales and 40% of its global profits. In 2009, Ford committed to a multi-billion investment to redesign the F-series, whose prices range from $24,000 to $50,000, to be built with a completely aluminum body, something found only in much more expensive cars, such as the the $70,000 Tesla Model S or the $75,000 Audi A8. Ford Chairman Bill Ford, says, "Some people might say, 'Aren't you taking a chance

with your best-selling vehicle?' But that's what you have to do." He said, "I would have had much more anxiety if they had come in with business-as-usual." The 2015 F-series is 700 lbs. lighter, which allowed Ford engineers to replace a 6.2 liter V8 with a 3.5-liter turbocharged V6. While still capable of towing 8,000 pounds, overall gas mileage rose by 16% from 19 mpg to 22 mpg, making the F-series the most fuel efficient gas-powered vehicle in its class."[57]

In the **negotiator role,** managers negotiate schedules, projects, goals, outcomes, resources, and employee raises. When Disney and Marvel Studios were determining filming locations for *Iron Man 3*, they turned to **DMG** to negotiate film rights in China for its 10,000+ theaters. Only thirty-one foreign films are imported to China each year, and film companies are limited to just 25 percent of box office revenues. However, DMG struck a deal to make *Iron Man 3* a US-China coproduction by incorporating "Chinese elements" in the script and then shooting part of the movie in China. Doing so increased the Chinese box office take from 25 percent to 38 percent. With *Iron Man 3*'s Chinese box office receipts estimated at more than $100 million, DMG's deal will earn Disney and Marvel at least $13 million more in revenues for the film.[58]

1-5 WHAT COMPANIES LOOK FOR IN MANAGERS

I didn't have the slightest idea what my job was. I walked in giggling and laughing because I had been promoted and had no idea what principles or style to be guided by. After the first day, I felt like I had run into a brick wall. (Sales Representative #1)

Entrepreneur role the decisional role managers play when they adapt themselves, their subordinates, and their units to change

Disturbance handler role the decisional role managers play when they respond to severe pressures and problems that demand immediate action

Resource allocator role the decisional role managers play when they decide who gets what resources and in what amounts

Negotiator role the decisional role managers play when they negotiate schedules, projects, goals, outcomes, resources, and employee raises

Suddenly, I found myself saying, boy, I can't be responsible for getting all that revenue. I don't have the time. Suddenly you've got to go from [taking care of] yourself and say now I'm the manager, and what does a manager do? It takes awhile thinking about it for it to really hit you . . . a manager gets things done through other people. That's a very, very hard transition to make. (Sales Representative #2)[59]

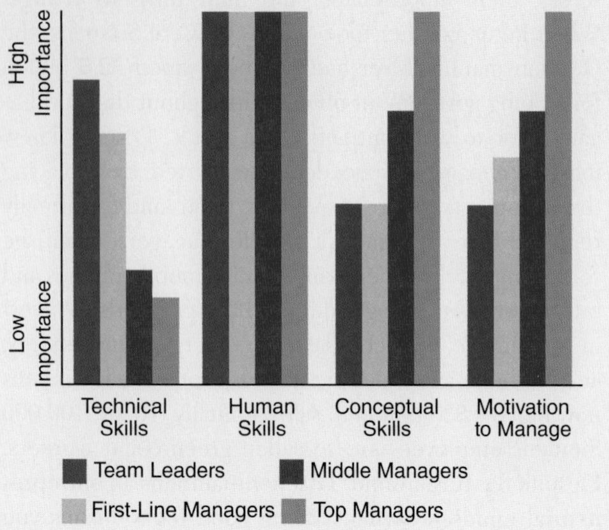

The preceding statements were made by two star sales representatives who, on the basis of their superior performance, were promoted to the position of sales manager. As their comments indicate, at first they did not feel confident about their ability to do their jobs as managers. Like most new managers, these sales managers suddenly realized that the knowledge, skills, and abilities that led to success early in their careers (and were probably responsible for their promotion into the ranks of management) would not necessarily help them succeed as managers. As sales representatives, they were responsible only for managing their own performance. But as sales managers, they were now directly responsible for supervising all of the sales representatives in their sales territories. Furthermore, they were now directly accountable for whether those sales representatives achieved their sales goals. If performance in nonmanagerial jobs doesn't necessarily prepare you for a managerial job, then what does it take to be a manager?

When companies look for employees who would be good managers, they look for individuals who have technical skills, human skills, conceptual skills, and the motivation to manage.[60] Exhibit 1.4 shows the relative importance of these four skills to the jobs of team leaders, first-line managers, middle managers, and top managers.

Technical skills are the specialized procedures, techniques, and knowledge required to get the job done. For the sales managers described above, technical

Exhibit 1.4
Management Skills

skills involve the ability to find new sales prospects, develop accurate sales pitches based on customer needs, and close sales. For a nurse supervisor, technical skills include being able to insert an IV or operate a crash cart if a patient goes into cardiac arrest.

Technical skills are most important for team leaders and lower-level managers because they supervise the workers who produce products or serve customers. Team leaders and first-line managers need technical knowledge and skills to train new employees and help employees solve problems. Technical knowledge and skills are also needed to troubleshoot problems that employees can't handle. Technical skills become less important as managers rise through the managerial ranks, but they are still important.

Human skills can be summarized as the ability to work well with others. Managers with human skills work effectively within groups, encourage others to express their thoughts and feelings, are sensitive to others' needs and viewpoints, and are good listeners and communicators. Human skills are equally important at all levels of management, from

alphaspirit/iStockphoto.com

team leaders to CEOs. However, because lower-level managers spend much of their time solving technical problems, upper-level managers may actually spend more time dealing directly with people. On average, first-line managers spend 57 percent of their time with people, but that percentage increases to 63 percent for middle managers and 78 percent for top managers.[61]

Conceptual skills are the ability to see the organization as a whole, to understand how the different parts of the company affect each other, and to recognize how the company fits into or is affected by its external environment such as the local community, social and economic forces, customers, and the competition. Good managers have to be able to recognize, understand, and reconcile multiple complex problems and perspectives. In other words, managers have to be smart! In fact, intelligence makes so much difference for managerial performance that managers with above-average intelligence typically outperform managers of average intelligence by approximately 48 percent.[62] Clearly, companies need to be careful to promote smart workers into management. Conceptual skills increase in importance as managers rise through the management hierarchy.

Good management involves much more than intelligence, however. For example, making the department genius a manager can be disastrous if that genius lacks technical skills, human skills, or one other factor known as the motivation to manage. **Motivation to manage** is an assessment of how motivated employees are to interact with superiors, participate in competitive situations, behave assertively toward others, tell others what to do, reward good behavior and punish poor behavior,

perform actions that are highly visible to others, and handle and organize administrative tasks. Managers typically have a stronger motivation to manage than their subordinates, and managers at higher levels usually have a stronger motivation to manage than managers at lower levels. Furthermore, managers with a stronger motivation to manage are promoted faster, are rated as better managers by their employees, and earn more money than managers with a weak motivation to manage.[63]

 ## MISTAKES MANAGERS MAKE

Another way to understand what it takes to be a manager is to look at the mistakes managers make. In other words, we can learn just as much from what managers shouldn't do as from what they should do. Exhibit 1.5 lists the top ten mistakes managers make.

Several studies of US and British managers have compared "arrivers," or managers who made it all the way to the top of their companies, with "derailers," or managers who were successful early in their careers

---

Conceptual skills the ability to see the organization as a whole, understand how the different parts affect each other, and recognize how the company fits into or is affected by its environment

Motivation to manage an assessment of how enthusiastic employees are about managing the work of others

but were knocked off the fast track by the time they reached the middle to upper levels of management.[64] The researchers found that there were only a few differences between arrivers and derailers. For the most part, both groups were talented and both groups had weaknesses. But what distinguished derailers from arrivers was that derailers possessed two or more fatal flaws with respect to the way they managed people. Although arrivers were by no means perfect, they usually had no more than one fatal flaw or had found ways to minimize the effects of their flaws on the people with whom they worked.

The top mistake made by derailers was that they were insensitive to others by virtue of their abrasive, intimidating, and bullying management style. The authors of one study described a manager who walked into his subordinate's office and interrupted a meeting by saying, "I need to see you." When the subordinate tried to explain that he was not available because he was in the middle of a meeting, the manager barked, "I don't give a damn. I said I wanted to see you now."[65] Not surprisingly, only 25 percent of derailers were rated by others as being good with people, compared to 75 percent of arrivers.

The second mistake was that derailers were often cold, aloof, or arrogant. Although this sounds like insensitivity to others, it has more to do with derailed managers being so smart, so expert in their areas of knowledge, that they treated others with contempt because they weren't experts, too.[66] For example, AT&T called in an industrial psychologist to counsel its vice president of human resources because she had been blamed for "ruffling too many feathers" at the company.[67] Interviews with the vice president's coworkers and subordinates revealed that they thought she was brilliant, was "smarter and faster than other people," "generates a lot of ideas," and "loves to deal with complex issues." Unfortunately, these smarts were accompanied by a cold, aloof, and arrogant management style. The people she worked with complained that she does "too much too fast," treats coworkers with "disdain," "impairs teamwork," "doesn't always show her warm side," and has "burned too many bridges."[68]

The third mistake made by derailers involved betraying a trust. Betraying a trust doesn't mean being dishonest. Instead, it means making others look bad by not doing what you said you would do when you said you would do it. That mistake, in itself, is not fatal because managers and their workers aren't machines. Tasks go undone in every company every single business day. There's always too much to do and not enough time, people, money, or resources to do it. The fatal betrayal of trust is failing to inform others when things will not be done on time. This failure to admit mistakes, quickly inform others of the mistakes, take responsibility for the mistakes, and then fix them without blaming others clearly distinguished the behavior of derailers from arrivers.

The fourth mistake was being overly political and ambitious. Managers who always have their eye on their next job rarely establish more than superficial relationships with peers and coworkers. In their haste to gain credit for successes that would be noticed by upper

Steven Robertson/iStockphoto.com

management, they make the fatal mistake of treating people as though they don't matter. An employee with an overly ambitious boss described him this way: "He treats employees coldly, even cruelly. He assigns blame without regard to responsibility, and takes all the credit for himself. I once had such a boss, and he gave me a new definition of shared risk: If something I did was successful, he took the credit. If it wasn't, I got the blame."[69]

The fatal mistakes of being unable to delegate, build a team, and staff effectively indicate that many derailed managers were unable to make the most basic transition to managerial work: to quit being hands-on doers and get work done through others. Two things go wrong when managers make these mistakes. First, when managers meddle in decisions that their subordinates should be making—when they can't stop being doers—they alienate the people who work for them. Rich Dowd, founder of Dowd Associates, an executive search firm, admits to constantly monitoring and interrupting employees because they weren't doing the job "in the way I saw fit, even when their work was outstanding." According to Richard Kilburg of Johns Hopkins University, when managers interfere with workers' decisions, "You . . . have a tendency to lose your most creative people. They're able to say, 'Screw this. I'm not staying here.'"[70] Indeed, one employee told Dowd that if he was going to do her job for her, she would quit. Second, because they are trying to do their subordinates' jobs in addition to their own, managers who fail to delegate will not have enough time to do much of anything well. An office assistant to a Washington politician came in to work every day to find a long to-do list waiting on her desk, detailing everything she was expected to get done that day, along with how to do it, who to call, and when to give her boss updates on her progress. She said, "Sometimes, this list was 3 or 4 pages long. It must have taken him at least an hour to create."[71]

1-7 THE TRANSITION TO MANAGEMENT: THE FIRST YEAR

In her book *Becoming a Manager: Mastery of a New Identity*, Harvard Business School professor Linda Hill followed the development of nineteen people in their first year as managers. Her study found that becoming a manager produced a profound psychological transition that changed the way these managers viewed themselves and others. As shown in Exhibit 1.6, the evolution of the managers' thoughts, expectations, and realities over the course of their first year in management reveals the magnitude of the changes they experienced.

Initially, the managers in Hill's study believed that their job was to exercise formal authority and to manage tasks—basically being the boss, telling others what to do, making decisions, and getting things done. One of the managers Hill interviewed said, "Being the manager means running my own office, using my ideas and thoughts." Another said, "[The office is] my

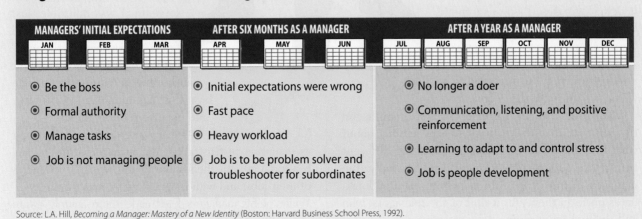

Exhibit 1.6
Stages in the Transition to Management

MANAGERS' INITIAL EXPECTATIONS	AFTER SIX MONTHS AS A MANAGER	AFTER A YEAR AS A MANAGER
JAN FEB MAR	APR MAY JUN	JUL AUG SEP OCT NOV DEC
⊙ Be the boss	⊙ Initial expectations were wrong	⊙ No longer a doer
⊙ Formal authority	⊙ Fast pace	⊙ Communication, listening, and positive reinforcement
⊙ Manage tasks	⊙ Heavy workload	⊙ Learning to adapt to and control stress
⊙ Job is not managing people	⊙ Job is to be problem solver and troubleshooter for subordinates	⊙ Job is people development

Source: L.A. Hill, *Becoming a Manager: Mastery of a New Identity* (Boston: Harvard Business School Press, 1992).

baby. It's my job to make sure it works."[72] In fact, most of the new managers were attracted to management positions because they wanted to be in charge. Surprisingly, the new managers did not believe that their job was to manage people. The only aspects of people management mentioned by the new managers were hiring and firing.

After six months, most of the new managers had concluded that their initial expectations about managerial work were wrong. Management wasn't just about being the boss, making decisions, and telling others what to do. The first surprise was the fast pace and heavy workload involved. Said one of Hill's managers, "This job is much harder than you think. It is 40 to 50 percent more work than being a producer! Who would have ever guessed?" The pace of managerial work was startling, too. Another manager said, "You have eight or nine people looking for your time . . . coming into and out of your office all day long." A somewhat frustrated manager declared that management was "a job that never ended . . . a job you couldn't get your hands around."[73]

Informal descriptions like these are consistent with studies indicating that the average first-line manager spends no more than two minutes on a task before being interrupted by a request from a subordinate, a phone call, or an email. The pace is somewhat less hurried for top managers, who spend an average of approximately nine minutes on a task before having to switch to another. In practice, this means that supervisors may perform thirty tasks per hour, while top managers perform seven tasks per hour, with each task typically different from the one that preceded it. A manager described this frenetic level of activity by saying, "The only time you are in control is when you shut your door, and then I feel I am not doing the job I'm supposed to be doing, which is being with the people."[74]

The other major surprise after six months on the job was that the managers' expectations about what they should do as managers were very different from their subordinates' expectations. Initially, the managers defined their jobs as helping their subordinates perform their jobs well. For the managers, who still defined themselves as doers rather than managers, assisting their subordinates meant going out on sales calls or handling customer complaints. One manager said, "I like going out with the rep, who may need me to lend him my credibility as manager. I like the challenge, the joy in closing. I go out with the reps and we make the call and talk about the customer; it's fun."[75] But when the managers "assisted" in this way, their subordinates were resentful and viewed their help as interference. The subordinates wanted their managers to help them by solving problems that they couldn't solve themselves. Once the managers realized this distinction, they embraced their role as problem solver and troubleshooter. Thus, they could help without interfering with their subordinates' jobs.

After a year on the job, most of the managers thought of themselves as managers and no longer as doers. In making the transition, they finally realized that people management was the most important part of their job. One of Hill's interviewees summarized the lesson that had taken him a year to learn by saying, "As many demands as managers have on their time, I think their primary responsibility is people development. Not production, but people development."[76] Another indication of how much their views had changed was that most of the managers now regretted the rather heavy-handed approach they had used in their early attempts to manage their subordinates. "I wasn't good at managing . . . , so I was bossy like a first-grade teacher." "Now I see that I started out as a drill sergeant. I was inflexible, just a lot of how-to's." By the end of the year, most of the managers had abandoned their authoritarian approach for one based on communication, listening, and positive reinforcement.

Finally, after beginning their year as managers in frustration, the managers came to feel comfortable with their subordinates, with the demands of their jobs, and with their emerging managerial styles. While being managers had made them acutely aware of their limitations and their need to develop as people, it also provided them with an unexpected reward of coaching and developing the people who worked for them. One manager said, "It gives me the best feeling to see somebody do something well after I have helped them. I get excited." Another stated, "I realize now that when I accepted the position of branch manager that it is truly an exciting vocation. It is truly awesome, even at this level; it can be terribly challenging and terribly exciting."[77]

1-8 COMPETITIVE ADVANTAGE THROUGH PEOPLE

If you walk down the aisle of the business section in your local bookstore, you'll find hundreds of books that explain precisely what companies need to do to be successful. Unfortunately, the best-selling business books tend to be faddish, changing dramatically every few years. One thing that hasn't changed, though, is the importance of good people and good management: companies can't succeed for long without them.

In his books *Competitive Advantage through People: Unleashing the Power of the Work Force* and *The Human Equation: Building Profits by Putting People First*, Stanford University business professor Jeffrey Pfeffer contends that what separates top-performing companies from their competitors is the way they treat their work forces—in other words, their management style.[78]

Pfeffer found that managers in top-performing companies used ideas like employment security, selective hiring, self-managed teams and decentralization, high pay contingent on company performance, extensive training, reduced status distinctions (between managers and employees), and extensive sharing of financial information to achieve financial performance that, on average, was 40 percent higher than that of other companies. These ideas, which are explained in detail in Exhibit 1.7, help organizations develop work forces that are smarter, better trained, more motivated, and more committed than their competitors' work forces. And—as indicated by the phenomenal growth and return on investment earned by these companies—smarter, better trained, more motivated, and more committed work forces provide superior products and service to customers. Such

---

Exhibit 1.7

Competitive Advantage Through People: Management Practices

1. Employment Security—Employment security is the ultimate form of commitment companies can make to their workers. Employees can innovate and increase company productivity without fearing the loss of their jobs.

2. Selective Hiring—If employees are the basis for a company's competitive advantage and those employees have employment security, then the company needs to aggressively recruit and selectively screen applicants in order to hire the most talented employees available.

3. Self-Managed Teams and Decentralization—Self-managed teams are responsible for their own hiring, purchasing, job assignments, and production. Self-managed teams can often produce enormous increases in productivity through increased employee commitment and creativity. Decentralization allows employees who are closest to (and most knowledgeable about) problems, production, and customers to make timely decisions. Decentralization increases employee satisfaction and commitment.

4. High Wages Contingent on Organizational Performance—High wages are needed to attract and retain talented workers and to indicate that the organization values its workers. Employees, like company founders, shareholders, and managers, need to share in the financial rewards when the company is successful. Why? Because employees who have a financial stake in their companies are more likely to take a long-run view of the business and think like business owners.

5. Training and Skill Development—Like a high-tech company that spends millions of dollars to upgrade computers or research and development labs, a company whose competitive advantage is based on its people must invest in the training and skill development of its people.

6. Reduction of Status Differences—A company should treat everyone, no matter what the job, as equal. There are no reserved parking spaces. Everyone eats in the same cafeteria and has similar benefits. The result: improved communication as employees focus on problems and solutions rather than on how they are less valued than managers.

7. Sharing Information—If employees are to make decisions that are good for the long-term health and success of the company, they need to be given information about costs, finances, productivity, development times, and strategies that was previously known only by company managers.

Source: J. Pfeffer, *The Human Equation: Building Profits by Putting People First* (Boston: Harvard Business School Press, 1996).

The CFO: Not Just A Bean Counter

Having served as CFO at ADT Corp., Nalco Holdings Co., UAL Corp., and recently having become CFO at Xerox Corp., Kathryn Mikells knows a thing or two about the challenges of being a new CFO. Mikells describes several keys that can help new CFOs be successful. One of the most important steps is taking the time to talk to senior management and get a sense of where the company is and what challenges it faces. She also believes that the CFO should involve herself in strategic planning. "Strategy tends to tie directly into resource allocation and capital allocation," she says. "It's really important that [they] all link together." She also stresses the importance of getting a good feel for your team. A new CFO wants to quickly figure out what direction the team is going and what kind of skills the members have.

Source: K. Mikells, "Xerox CFO; An Atmosphere for Transformation," Interview by N. Knox, *The Wall Street Journal*, April 4, 2014, accessed April 9, 2014. http://blogs.wsj.com /cfo/2014/04/04/xerox-cfo-an-atmosphere-for-transformation/?mod=WSJ_business_cfo.

customers keep buying and, by telling others about their positive experiences, bring in new customers.

According to Pfeffer, companies that invest in their people will create long-lasting competitive advantages that are difficult for other companies to duplicate. Indeed, other studies clearly demonstrate that sound management practices can produce substantial advantages in four critical areas of organizational performance: sales revenues, profits, stock market returns, and customer satisfaction.

In terms of sales revenues and profits, a study of nearly 1,000 US firms found that companies that use *just some* of the ideas shown in Exhibit 1.7 had $27,044 more sales per employee and $3,814 more profit per employee than companies that didn't. For a 100-person company, these differences amount to $2.7 million more in sales and nearly $400,000 more in annual profit! For a 1,000-person company, the difference grows to $27 million more in sales and $4 million more in annual profit![79]

Another study that considers the effect of investing in people on company sales found that poorly performing companies were able to improve their average return on investment from 5.1 percent to 19.7 percent and increase sales by $94,000 per employee. They did this by adopting management techniques as simple as setting performance expectations (establishing goals, results, and schedules), coaching (informal, ongoing discussions between managers and subordinates about what is being done well and what could be done better), reviewing (annual, formal discussion about results), and rewarding employee performance (adjusting salaries and bonuses based on employee performance and results).[80] Indeed, two decades of research across 92 companies indicates that the average increase in company performance from using these management practices is typically around 20%.[81] So, in addition to significantly improving the profitability of healthy companies, sound management practices can turn around failing companies.

To determine how investing in people affects stock market performance, researchers matched companies on *Fortune* magazine's list of "100 Best Companies to Work for in America" with companies that were similar in industry, size, and—this is key—operating performance. Both sets of companies were equally good performers; the key difference was how well they treated their employees. For both sets of companies, the researchers found that employee attitudes such as job satisfaction changed little from year to year. The people who worked for the "100 Best" companies were consistently much more satisfied with their jobs and employers year after year than were employees in the matched companies. More importantly, those stable differences in employee attitudes were strongly related to differences in stock market performance. Over a one-year period, an investment in the "100 Best" would have resulted in an 82 percent cumulative stock return compared with just 37 percent for the matched companies.[82] This difference is remarkable given that both sets of companies were equally good performers at the beginning of the period.

Finally, research also indicates that managers have an important effect on customer satisfaction. Many people find this surprising. They don't understand how managers, who are largely responsible for what goes on inside the company, can affect what goes on outside the company. They wonder how managers, who often interact with customers under negative conditions (when customers are angry or dissatisfied), can actually improve customer satisfaction. It turns out that managers influence customer satisfaction through employee satisfaction. When employees are satisfied with their jobs, their bosses, and the companies they work for, they provide much better service to customers.[83] In turn, customers are more satisfied, too. Indeed, customers of companies on *Fortune*'s list of "100 Best," where employees are much more satisfied with their jobs and their companies, have much higher customer satisfaction scores than do customers of comparable companies that are not on *Fortune*'s list. Over an eight-year period, that difference in customer satisfaction also resulted in a 14 percent annual stock market return for the "100 Best" companies compared to a 6 percent return for the overall stock market.[84]

You will learn more about the service-profit chain in Chapter 18 on managing service and manufacturing operations.

STUDY TOOLS 1

LOCATED AT THE BACK OF YOUR BOOK:
☐ Rip out and study the Chapter Review Card at the end of the book

LOG IN TO WWW.CENGAGEBRAIN.COM TO:
☐ Review Key Term Flashcards
☐ Complete Practice Quizzing (take up to four times without repeating the same quiz)
☐ Complete Interactive Content: Graded Quiz, Media Quiz and Fill-in-the-Blank Questions
☐ Watch Management Workplace Video on "Camp Bow Wow"

2 The History of Management

Arekmalang/iStockphoto.com

LEARNING OUTCOMES

2-1 Explain the origins of management.

2-2 Explain the history of scientific management.

2-3 Discuss the history of bureaucratic and administrative management.

2-4 Explain the history of human relations management.

2-5 Discuss the history of operations, information, systems, and contingency management.

After you finish this chapter, go to **PAGE 42** for **STUDY TOOLS**

2-1 THE ORIGINS OF MANAGEMENT

Each day, managers are asked to solve challenging problems and given only a limited amount of time, people, or resources. Yet it's still their responsibility to get things done on time and within budget. Tell today's managers to "reward workers for improved production or performance," "set specific goals to increase motivation," or "innovate to create and sustain a competitive advantage," and they'll respond, "Duh! Who doesn't know that?" A mere 125 years ago, however, business ideas and practices were so different that today's widely accepted management ideas would have been as self-evident as space travel, cell phones, and the Internet. In fact, management jobs and careers didn't exist 125 years ago, so management was not yet a field of study. Now, of course, managers and management are such an important part of the business world that it's hard to imagine organizations without them. So if there were no managers 125 years ago but you can't walk down the hall today without bumping into one, where did management come from?

Although we can find the seeds of many of today's management ideas throughout history, not until the last two centuries did systematic changes in the nature of work and organizations create a compelling need for managers.

2-1a Management Ideas and Practices Throughout History

Examples of management thought and practice can be found throughout history.[1] For example, the earliest recorded instance of information management dates to ancient Sumer (modern Iraq), *circa* 8000–3000 BCE. Sumerian businessmen used small clay tokens to calculate quantities of grain and livestock—and later, value-added goods like perfume or pottery—they owned and traded in temples and at city gates. Different shapes and sizes represented different types and quantities of goods. The tokens were also used to store data. They were kept in small clay envelopes, and the token shapes were impressed on the outside of the envelope to indicate what was inside. Eventually, someone figured out that it was easier to just write these symbols with a stylus on a tablet instead of using the tokens. In the end, the new technology of *writing* led to more efficient management of the business of Sumerian temples.[2]

A task as enormous as building the great pyramids in Egypt was bound to present practical problems that would lead to the development of management ideas. Egyptians recognized the need for planning, organizing, and controlling; for submitting written requests; and for consulting staff for advice before making decisions. The enormity of the task they faced is evident in the pyramid of King Khufu, which contains 2.3 million blocks of stone. Each block had to be quarried, cut to precise size and shape, cured (hardened in the sun), transported by boat for two to three days, moved to the construction site, numbered to identify where it would be placed, and then shaped and smoothed so that it would fit perfectly into place. It took 20,000 workers twenty-three years to complete this pyramid; more than 8,000 were needed just to quarry and transport the stones. A typical quarry expedition might include 100 army officers, fifty government and religious officials, and 200 members of the king's court to lead; 130 stonemasons to cut the stones; and 5,000 soldiers, 800 barbarians, and 2,000 bond servants to load and unload the stones from the ships.[3]

Exhibit 2.1 shows how other management ideas and practices throughout history relate to the management functions we discuss in this textbook.

2-1b Why We Need Managers Today

Working from 8:00 a.m. to 5:00 p.m., coffee breaks, lunch hours, crushing rush hour traffic, and punching a time clock are things we associate with today's working world. Work hasn't always been this way, however. In fact, the design of jobs and organizations has changed dramatically over the last 500 years. For most of humankind's history, for example, people didn't commute to work.[4] Work usually occurred in homes or on farms. In 1720, almost 80 percent of the 5.5 million people in England lived and worked in the country. And as recently as 1870, two-thirds of Americans earned their living from agriculture. Even most of those who didn't earn their living from agriculture didn't commute to work. Blacksmiths, furniture makers, leather goods makers, and other skilled tradespeople or crafts-people who formed trade guilds (the historical predecessors of labor unions) in England as early as 1093 typically worked out of shops in or next to their homes.[5] Likewise, cottage workers worked with each other out of small homes that were often built in a semicircle. A family in each cottage would complete a different production step, and work passed from one cottage to the

Exhibit 2.1
Management Ideas and Practices Throughout History

Time	Individual or Group	Planning	Organizing	Leading	Controlling	Contributions to Management Thought and Practice
5000 BCE	Sumerians				√	Written record keeping.
4000 BCE to 2000 BCE	Egyptians	√	√		√	Planning, organizing, and controlling to build the pyramids; submitting requests in writing; making decisions after consulting staff for advice.
1800 BCE	Hammurabi				√	Controls and using witnesses in legal cases.
600 BCE	Nebuchadnezzar		√	√		Wage incentives and production control.
500 BCE	Sun Tzu	√		√		Strategy and identifying and attacking opponents' weaknesses.
400 BCE	Xenophon	√	√	√		Management as separate art.
400 BCE	Cyrus		√	√	√	Human relations and motion study.
175	Cato		√			Job descriptions.
284	Diocletian		√			Delegation of authority.
900	al-Farabi			√		Leadership traits.
1100	Ghazali			√		Managerial traits.
1418	Barbarigo		√			Different organizational forms/structures.
1436	Venetians				√	Numbering, standardization, and interchangeability of parts.
1500	Sir Thomas More			√		Critique of poor management and leadership.
1525	Machiavelli		√	√		Cohesiveness, power, and leadership in organizations.

Source: C. S. George, Jr., *The History of Management Thought* (Englewood Cliffs, NJ: Prentice Hall, 1972).

next until production was complete. With small, self-organized work groups, no commute, no bosses, and no common building, there wasn't a strong need for management.

During the Industrial Revolution (1750–1900), however, jobs and organizations changed dramatically.[6] First, unskilled laborers running machines began to replace high-paid, skilled artisans. What made this possible? The availability of power (steam engines and, later, electricity) as well as numerous related inventions, including Darby's coke-smelting process and Cort's puddling and rolling process (both for making iron), as well as Hargreaves's spinning jenny and Arkwright's water frame (both for spinning cotton). Whereas artisans made entire goods by themselves by hand, this new production system was based on a division of labor: each worker, interacting with machines, performed separate, highly specialized tasks that were but a small part of all the steps required to make manufactured goods. Mass production was born as

rope- and chain-driven assembly lines moved work to stationary workers who concentrated on performing one small task over and over again. While workers focused on their singular tasks, managers were needed to coordinate the different parts of the production system and optimize its overall performance. Productivity skyrocketed at companies that understood this. At **Ford Motor Company**, where the assembly line was developed, the time required to assemble a car dropped from 12.5 work hours to just 93 minutes after switching to mass production.[7]

Second, instead of being performed in fields, homes, or small shops, jobs occurred in large, formal organizations where hundreds, if not thousands, of people worked under one roof.[8] In 1849, for example, **Chicago Harvester** (the predecessor of International Harvester) ran the largest factory in the United States with just 123 workers. Yet by 1913, Henry Ford employed 12,000 employees in his Highland Park, Michigan, factory alone. Because the number of people working in manufacturing quintupled from 1860 to 1890, and individual factories employed so many workers under one roof, companies now had a strong need for disciplinary rules to impose order and structure. For the first time, they needed managers who knew how to organize large groups, work with employees, and make good decisions.

2-2 SCIENTIFIC MANAGEMENT

Before 1880, business educators taught only basic bookkeeping and secretarial skills, and no one published books or articles about management.[9] Today you can turn to dozens of academic journals (such as the Academy of Management's *Journal* or *Review*, *Administrative Science Quarterly*, the *Strategic Management Journal*, and the *Journal of Applied Psychology*), hundreds of business school and practitioner journals (such as *Harvard Business Review*, *MIT Sloan Management Review*, and the *Academy of Management Perspectives*), and thousands of books and articles if you have a question about management. In the next four sections, you will learn about some important contributors to the field of management and how their ideas shaped our current understanding of management theory and practice.

Bosses, who were hired by the company owner or founder, used to make decisions by the seat of their pants—haphazardly, without any systematic study, thought, or collection of information. If the bosses decided that workers should work twice as fast, little or no thought was given to worker motivation. If workers resisted, the bosses often resorted to physical beatings to get workers to work faster, harder, or longer. With no incentives for bosses and workers to cooperate with one another, both groups played the system by trying to take advantage of each other. Moreover, each worker did the same job in his or her own way with different methods and different tools. In short, there were no procedures to standardize operations, no standards by which to judge whether performance was good or bad, and no follow-up to determine if productivity or quality actually improved when changes were made.[10]

This all changed, however, with the advent of **scientific management,** which involved thorough study and testing of different work methods to identify the best, most efficient ways to complete a job.

Anatoliy Babiy/iStockphoto.com

Let's find out more about scientific management by learning about 2-2a Frederick W. Taylor, the father of scientific management; 2-2b Frank and Lillian Gilbreth and motion studies; and 2-2c Henry Gantt and his Gantt charts.

2-2a Father of Scientific Management: Frederick W. Taylor

Frederick W. Taylor (1856–1915), the father of scientific management, began his career as a worker at **Midvale Steel Company**. He was promoted to patternmaker, supervisor, and then chief engineer. At Midvale, Taylor was deeply affected by his three-year struggle to get the men who worked for him to do, as he called it, "a fair day's work." Taylor, who had worked alongside the men as a co-worker before becoming their boss, said, "We who were the workmen of that shop had the quantity output carefully agreed upon for everything that was turned out in the shop. We limited the output to about, I should think, one third of what we could very well have done." Taylor explained that, as soon as he became the boss, "the men who were working under me . . . knew that I was onto the whole game of **soldiering,** or deliberately restricting output."[11] When Taylor told his workers, "I have accepted a job under the management of this company and I am on the other side of the fence . . . I am going to try to get a bigger output," the workers responded, "We warn

Scientific management   thoroughly studying and testing different work methods to identify the best, most efficient way to complete a job

Soldiering   when workers deliberately slow their pace or restrict their work output

Exhibit 2.2
Taylor's Four Principles of Scientific Management

First:	Develop a science for each element of a man's work, which replaces the old rule-of-thumb method.
Second:	Scientifically select and then train, teach, and develop the workman, whereas in the past, he chose his own work and trained himself as best he could.
Third:	Heartily cooperate with the men so as to ensure all of the work being done is in accordance with the principles of the science that has been developed.
Fourth:	There is an almost equal division of the work and the responsibility between the management and the workmen. The management take over all the work for which they are better fitted than the workmen, while in the past, almost all of the work and the greater part of the responsibility were thrown upon the men.

Source: F. W. Taylor, *The Principles of Scientific Management* (New York: Harper, 1911).

you, Fred, if you try to bust any of these rates [a **rate buster** was someone who worked faster than the group] we will have you over the fence in six weeks."[12]

Over the next three years, Taylor tried everything he could think of to improve output. By doing the job himself, he showed workers that it was possible to produce more output. He hired new workers and trained them himself, hoping they would produce more. But "very heavy social pressure" from the other workers kept them from doing so. Pushed by Taylor, the workers began breaking their machines so that they couldn't produce. Taylor responded by fining them every time they broke a machine and for any violation of the rules, no matter how small, such as being late to work. Tensions became so severe that some of the workers threatened to shoot Taylor. Looking back at the situation, Taylor reflected, "It is a horrid life for any man to live, not to be able to look any workman in the face all day long without seeing hostility there and feeling that every man around one is his virtual enemy." He said, "I made up my mind either to get out of the business entirely and go into some other line of work or to find some remedy for this unbearable condition."[13]

The remedy that Taylor eventually developed was scientific management. Taylor, who once described scientific management as "seventy-five percent science and twenty-five percent common sense," emphasized that the goal of scientific management was to use systematic study to find the "one best way" of doing each task. To do that, managers had to follow the four principles shown in Exhibit 2.2. The first principle was to "develop a science" for each element of work. Study it. Analyze it. Determine the "one best way" to do the work. For example, one of Taylor's controversial proposals at the time was to give rest breaks to factory workers doing physical labor. We take morning, lunch, and afternoon breaks for granted, but in Taylor's day, factory workers were expected to work without stopping.[14] When Taylor said that breaks would increase worker productivity, no one believed him. Nonetheless, through systematic experiments, he showed that workers receiving frequent rest breaks were able to greatly increase their daily output.

Second, managers had to scientifically select, train, teach, and develop workers to help them reach their full potential. Before Taylor, supervisors often hired on the basis of favoritism and nepotism. Who you knew was often more important than what you could do. By contrast, Taylor instructed supervisors to hire "first-class" workers on the basis of their aptitude to do a job well. In one of the first applications of this principle, physical reaction times were used to select bicycle ball-bearing inspectors, who had to be able to examine ball bearings as fast as they were produced on a production line. For similar reasons, Taylor also recommended that companies train and develop their workers—a rare practice at the time.

The third principle instructed managers to cooperate with employees to ensure that the scientific principles were actually implemented. Labor unrest was widespread at the time; the number of labor strikes against companies doubled between 1893 and 1904. As Taylor knew from personal experience, workers and management more often than not viewed each other as enemies. Taylor's advice ran contrary to the common wisdom of

Rate buster a group member whose work pace is significantly faster than the normal pace in his or her group

MGMT Trends

How do you get employees and managers on the same page? According to Frederick W. Taylor, one of the best ways to align managers and employees is to use incentives. As Taylor wrote in *The Principles of Scientific Management*:

In order to have any hope of obtaining the initiative of his workmen, the manager must give some special incentive to his men beyond that which is given to the average of the trade. This incentive can be given in several different ways, as, for example, the hope of rapid promotion or advancement; higher wages, either in the form of generous piecework prices or of a premium or bonus of some kind for good and rapid work; shorter hours of labor; better surroundings and working conditions than are ordinarily given, etc., and, above all, this special incentive should be accompanied by that personal consideration for, and friendly contact with, his workmen, which comes only from a genuine and kindly interest in the welfare of those under him. It is only by giving a special inducement or "incentive" of this kind that the employer can hope even approximately to get the "initiative" of his workmen.

Source: F. W. Taylor, *The Principles of Scientific Management* (New York: Harper, 1911).

the day. He said, "The majority of these men believe that the fundamental interests of employees and employers are necessarily antagonistic. Scientific management, on the contrary, has for its very foundation the firm conviction that the true interests of the two are one and the same; that prosperity for the employer cannot exist through a long term of years unless it is accompanied by prosperity for the employee and vice versa; and that it is possible to give the workman what he most wants—high wages—and the employer what he wants—a low labor cost for his manufactures."[15] (See the MGMT Trends box for more on this point.)

The fourth principle of scientific management was to divide the work and the responsibility equally between management and workers. Prior to Taylor, workers alone were held responsible for productivity and performance. But, said Taylor, "Almost every act of the workman should be preceded by one or more preparatory acts of the management, which enable him to do his work better and quicker than he otherwise could. And each man should daily be taught by and receive the most friendly help from those who are over him, instead of being, at

the one extreme, driven or coerced by his bosses, and at the other left to his own unaided devices."[16]

Above all, Taylor believed these principles could be used to determine a "fair day's work," that is, what an average worker could produce at a reasonable pace, day in and day out. Once that was determined, it was management's responsibility to pay workers fairly for that fair day's work. In essence, Taylor was trying to align management and employees so that what was good for employees was also good for management. In this way, he believed, workers and managers could avoid the conflicts he had experienced at Midvale Steel.

Although Taylor remains a controversial figure among some academics who believe that his ideas were bad for workers, his key ideas have stood the test of time.[17] These include using systematic analysis to identify the best methods; scientifically selecting, training, and developing workers; promoting cooperation between management and labor; developing standardized approaches and tools; setting specific tasks or goals and then rewarding workers with financial incentives; and giving workers shorter work hours and frequent breaks. In fact, his ideas are so well accepted and widely used that we take most of them for granted. As eminent management scholar Edwin Locke said, "The point is not, as is often claimed, that he was 'right in the context of his time,' but is now outdated, but that *most of his insights are still valid today*."[18]

2-2b Motion Studies: Frank and Lillian Gilbreth

The husband and wife team of Frank and Lillian Gilbreth are best known for their use of motion studies to simplify work, but they also made significant contributions to the employment of disabled workers and to the field of industrial psychology. Like Taylor, their

Tomas Bercic/iStockphoto.com

early experiences significantly shaped their interests and contributions to management.

Though admitted to MIT, Frank Gilbreth (1868–1924) began his career as an apprentice bricklayer. While learning the trade, he noticed the bricklayers using three different sets of motions—one to teach others how to lay bricks, a second to work at a slow pace, and a third to work at a fast pace.[19] Wondering which was best, he studied the various approaches and began eliminating unnecessary motions. For example, by designing a stand that could be raised to waist height, he eliminated the need to bend over to pick up each brick. Turning to grab a brick was faster and easier than bending down. By having lower-paid workers place all the bricks with their most attractive side up, bricklayers didn't waste time turning a brick over to find it. By mixing a more consistent mortar, bricklayers no longer had to tap each brick numerous times to put it in the right position. Together, Gilbreth's improvements raised productivity from 120 to 350 bricks per hour and from 1,000 bricks to 2,700 bricks per day.

As a result of his experience with bricklaying, Gilbreth and his wife, Lillian, developed a long-term interest in

---

Motion study breaking each task or job into its separate motions and then eliminating those that are unnecessary or repetitive

Time study timing how long it takes good workers to complete each part of their jobs

---

using motion study to simplify work, improve productivity, and reduce the level of effort required to safely perform a job. Indeed, Frank Gilbreth said, "The greatest waste in the world comes from needless, ill-directed, and ineffective motions."[20] **Motion study** broke each task or job into separate motions and then eliminated those that were unnecessary or repetitive. Because many motions were completed very quickly, the Gilbreths used motion-picture films, then a relatively new technology, to analyze jobs. Most film cameras at that time were hand cranked and thus variable in their film speed, so Frank invented the micro chronometer, a large clock that could record time to 1/2,000th of a second. By placing the micro chronometer next to the worker in the camera's field of vision and attaching a flashing strobe light to the worker's hands to better identify the direction and sequence of key movements, the Gilbreths could use film to detect and precisely time even the slightest, fastest movements. Motion study typically yielded production increases of 25 to 300 percent.[21]

Taylor also strove to simplify work, but he did so by managing time rather than motion as the Gilbreths did.[22] Taylor developed time study to put an end to soldiering and to determine what could be considered a fair day's work. **Time study** worked by timing how long it took a "first-class man" to complete each part of his job. A standard time was established after allowing for rest periods, and a worker's pay would increase or decrease depending on whether the worker exceeded or fell below that standard.

Nullplus/iStockphoto.com

Exhibit 2.3

Gantt Chart for Starting Construction on a New Headquarters

Tasks	Weeks	23 Sep to 29 Sep	30 Sep to 6 Oct	7 Oct to 13 Oct	14 Oct to 20 Oct	21 Oct to 27 Oct	28 Oct to 3 Nov	4 Nov to 10 Nov	11 Nov to 17 Nov	18 Nov to 25 Nov
Interview and select architectural firm		Architect by October 7								
Hold weekly planning meetings with architects				Planning with architects by November 4						
Obtain permits and approval from city						Permits and approval by November 11				
Begin preparing site for construction							Site preparation done by November 18			
Finalize loans and financing								Financing finalized by November 18		
Begin construction										Start building

Lillian Gilbreth (1878–1972) was an important contributor to management in her own right. She was the first woman to receive a PhD in industrial psychology as well as the first woman to become a member of the Society of Industrial Engineers and the American Society of Mechanical Engineers. When Frank died in 1924, she continued the work of their management consulting company (which they had shared for over a dozen years) on her own. Lillian, who was concerned with the human side of work, was one of the first contributors to industrial psychology, originating ways to improve office communication, incentive programs, job satisfaction, and management training. Her work also convinced the government to enact laws regarding workplace safety, ergonomics, and child labor.

2-2c Charts: Henry Gantt

Henry Gantt (1861–1919) was first a protégé and then an associate of Frederick W. Taylor. Gantt is best known for the Gantt chart, but he also made significant contributions to management with respect to pay-for-performance plans and the training and development of workers. As shown in Exhibit 2.3, a **Gantt chart** visually indicates what tasks must be completed at which times in order to complete a project. It accomplishes this by showing time in various units on the *x*-axis and tasks on the *y*-axis. For example, Exhibit 2.3 shows that the following tasks must be completed by the following dates: in order to start construction on a new company headquarters by the week of November 18, the architectural firm must be selected by October 7, architectural planning done by November 4, permits obtained from the city by November 11, site preparation finished by November 18, and loans and financing finalized by November 18.

Though simple and straightforward, Gantt charts were revolutionary in the era of seat-of-the-pants management because of the detailed planning information they provided. As Gantt wrote, "By using the graphical forms, its [the Gantt chart's] value is very much increased, for the general appearance of the sheet is sufficient to tell how closely the schedule is being lived up to; in other words, whether the plant is being run efficiently or not."[23] Gantt said, "Such sheets show at a glance where the delays occur, and indicate what must have our attention in order to keep up the proper

Gantt chart a graphical chart that shows which tasks must be completed at which times in order to complete a project or task output." The use of Gantt charts is so widespread today that nearly all project management software and computer spreadsheets have the capability to create charts that track and visually display the progress being made on a project.

Finally, Gantt, along with Taylor, was one of the first to strongly recommend that companies train and develop their workers.[24] In his work with companies, he found that workers achieved their best performance levels if they were trained first. At the time, however, supervisors were reluctant to teach workers what they knew for fear that they could lose their jobs to more knowledgeable workers. Gantt overcame the supervisors' resistance by rewarding them with bonuses for properly training all of their workers. Said Gantt, "This is the first recorded attempt to make it in the financial interest of the foreman to teach the individual worker, and the importance of it cannot be overestimated, for it changes the foreman from a driver of men to their friend and helper."[25] Gantt's approach to training was straightforward: "(1) A scientific investigation in detail of each piece of work, and the determination of the best method and the shortest time in which the work can be done. (2) A teacher capable of teaching the best method and the shortest time. (3) Reward for both teacher and pupil when the latter is successful."[26]

2-3 BUREAUCRATIC AND ADMINISTRATIVE MANAGEMENT

The field of scientific management developed quickly in the United States between 1895 and 1920 and focused on improving the efficiency of manufacturing facilities and their workers. At about the same time, equally important ideas about bureaucratic and administrative management were developing in Europe. German sociologist Max Weber presented a new way to run entire organizations (bureaucratic management) in *The Theory of Social and Economic Organization*, published in 1922.

Bureaucracy the exercise of control on the basis of knowledge, expertise, or experience

Henri Fayol, an experienced French CEO, published his ideas about how and what managers should do in their jobs (administrative management) in *General and Industrial Management* in 1916.

Let's find out more about the contributions Weber and Fayol made to management by learning about 2-3a bureaucratic management and 2-3b administrative management.

2-3a Bureaucratic Management: Max Weber

Today, when we hear the term *bureaucracy*, we think of inefficiency and red tape, incompetence and ineffectiveness, and rigid administrators blindly enforcing nonsensical rules. When German sociologist Max Weber (1864–1920) first proposed the idea of bureaucratic organizations, however, these problems were associated with monarchies and patriarchies rather than bureaucracies. In monarchies, where kings, queens, sultans, and emperors ruled, and patriarchies, where a council of elders, wise men, or male heads of extended families ruled, the top leaders typically achieved their positions by virtue of birthright. For example, when the queen died, her oldest son became king, regardless of his intelligence, experience, education, or desire. Likewise, promotion to prominent positions of authority in monarchies and patriarchies was based on who you knew (politics), who you were (heredity), or ancient rules and traditions.

It was against this historical background of monarchical and patriarchal rule that Weber proposed the then-new idea of bureaucracy. *Bureaucracy* comes from the French word *bureaucratie*. Because *bureau* means desk or office and *cratie* or *cracy* means to rule, *bureaucracy* literally means to rule from a desk or office. According to Weber, **bureaucracy** is "the exercise of control on the basis of knowledge."[27] Rather than ruling by virtue of favoritism or personal or family connections, people in a bureaucracy would lead by virtue of their rational-legal authority—in other words, their knowledge, expertise, or experience. Furthermore, the aim of bureaucracy is not to protect authority but to achieve an organization's goals in the most efficient way possible.

Exhibit 2.4 shows the seven elements that, according to Weber, characterize bureaucracies. First, instead of hiring people because of their family or political connections or personal loyalty, they should be hired because their technical training or education qualifies them to do the job well. Second, along the same lines, promotion within the company should no longer be based on who

Exhibit 2.4
Elements of Bureaucratic Organizations

Qualification-based hiring:	Employees are hired on the basis of their technical training or educational background.
Merit-based promotion:	Promotion is based on experience or achievement. Managers, not organizational owners, decide who is promoted.
Chain of command:	Each job occurs within a hierarchy, the chain of command, in which each position reports and is accountable to a higher position. A grievance procedure and a right to appeal protect people in lower positions.
Division of labor:	Tasks, responsibilities, and authority are clearly divided and defined.
Impartial application of rules and procedures:	Rules and procedures apply to all members of the organization and will be applied in an impartial manner, regardless of one's position or status.
Recorded in writing:	All administrative decisions, acts, rules, and procedures will be recorded in writing.
Managers separate from owners:	The owners of an organization should not manage or supervise the organization.

Source: M. Weber, *The Theory of Social and Economic Organization*, trans. A. Henderson and T. Parsons (New York: The Free Press, 1947), 329–334.

you know (politics) or who you are (heredity) but on your experience or achievements. And to further limit the influence of personal connections in the promotion process, *managers* rather than organizational owners should decide who gets promoted. Third, each position or job is part of a chain of command that clarifies who reports to whom throughout the organization. Those higher in the chain of command have the right, if they so choose, to give commands, take action, and make decisions concerning activities occurring anywhere below them in the chain. Unlike in many monarchies or patriarchies, however, those lower in the chain of command are protected by a grievance procedure that gives them the right to appeal the decisions of those in higher positions. Fourth, to increase efficiency and effectiveness, tasks and responsibilities should be separated and assigned to those best qualified to complete them. Authority is vested in these task-defined positions rather than in people, and the authority of each position is clearly defined in order to reduce confusion and conflict. If you move to a different job in a bureaucracy, your authority increases or decreases commensurate with the responsibilities of that job. Fifth, because of his strong distaste for favoritism, Weber believed that an organization's rules and procedures should apply to all members regardless of their position or status. Sixth, to ensure consistency and fairness over time and across different leaders and supervisors, all rules, procedures, and decisions should be recorded in writing. Finally, to reduce favoritism, "professional" managers rather than company owners should manage or supervise the organization.

When viewed in historical context, Weber's ideas about bureaucracy represent a tremendous improvement in how organizations should be run. Fairness supplanted favoritism, the goal of efficiency replaced the goal of personal gain, and logical rules and procedures took the place of traditions or arbitrary decision making.

Today, however, after more than a century of experience, we recognize that bureaucracy has limitations as well. Weber called bureaucracy the "iron cage" and said, "Once fully established, bureaucracy is among those social structures which are the hardest to destroy."[28] In bureaucracies, managers are supposed to influence employee behavior by fairly rewarding or punishing employees for compliance or noncompliance with organizational policies, rules, and procedures. In reality, however, most employees would argue that bureaucratic managers emphasize punishment for noncompliance much more than rewards for compliance. Ironically, bureaucratic management was created to prevent just this type of managerial behavior.

2-3b Administrative Management: Henri Fayol

Though his work was not translated and widely recognized in the United States until 1949, Frenchman Henri Fayol (1841–1925) was as important a contributor to the field of management as Taylor. Like Taylor and the Gilbreths, Fayol's work experience significantly shaped his thoughts and ideas about management. But, whereas Taylor's ideas changed companies from the shop floor up, Fayol's ideas were shaped by his experience as a managing director (CEO) and generally changed companies from the board of directors down.[29] Fayol is best known for developing five functions of managers and fourteen principles of management, as well as for his belief that management can and should be taught to others.

The most formative events in Fayol's business career came during his twenty-plus years as the managing director of Compagnie de Commentry-Fourchambault et Décazeville, commonly known as **Comambault**, a vertically integrated steel company that owned several coal and iron ore mines and employed 10,000 to 13,000 workers. Fayol was initially hired by the board of directors to shut down the "hopeless" steel company. The company was facing increased competition from English and German steel companies, which had lower costs, and from new steel mills in northern and eastern France, which were closer to major markets and thus could avoid the large shipping costs incurred by Fayol's company, located in central France.[30] In the five years before Fayol became CEO, production had dropped more than 60 percent, from 38,000 to 15,000 annual metric tons. Comambault had exhausted a key supply of coal needed for steel production, had already shut down one steel mill, and was

DOING THE RIGHT THING

The Benefits of Bureaucracy

So what is the use of bureaucracy today? At Rubbermaid's Graco, design teams send every new product through hundreds of tests and at least five design iterations. A lot of ideas get squashed through such rigorous testing. But Graco is making products like strollers and child car seats. Product flaws could result in children getting seriously injured or even killed and the company facing billions of dollars in lawsuits. So while some good ideas may not make it past brainstorming, Graco's bureaucratic processes also keep a lot of really bad ideas from getting out. Companies face the challenge of finding a balance between freedom to innovate and bureaucratic processes to ensure quality and safety.

Source: R. Fisman and T. Sullivan. "The Unsung Beauty of Bureaucracy," *The Wall Street Journal*. March 5, 2013. accessed March 17, 2013, http://online.wsj.com/news/articles/SB10001424127887324077704578360243017096714?mg=reno64-wsj#printMode.

losing money at another.[31] The company had quit paying dividends to shareholders and had no cash to invest in new technology, such as blast furnaces, that could lower its costs and increase productivity.

So the board hired Fayol as CEO to quickly dissolve and liquidate the business. But, after "four months of reflection and study," he presented the board with a plan, backed by detailed facts and figures, to save the company.[32] With little to lose, the board agreed. Fayol then began the process of turning the company around by obtaining supplies of key resources such as coal and iron ore; using research to develop new steel alloy products; carefully selecting key subordinates in research, purchasing, manufacturing, and sales and then delegating responsibility to them; and cutting costs by moving the company to a better location closer to key markets.[33] Looking back ten years later, Fayol attributed his and the company's success to changes in management practices. He wrote, "When I assumed the responsibility for the restoration of Décazeville, I did not rely on my technical superiority. . . . I relied on my ability as an organizer [and my] skill in handling men."[34]

Based on his experience as a CEO, Fayol argued that "the success of an enterprise generally depends much more on the administrative ability of its leaders than on their technical ability."[35] And, as you learned in Chapter 1, Fayol argued that managers need to perform five managerial functions if they are to be successful: planning, organizing, coordinating, commanding, and controlling.[36] Because most management textbooks have dropped the coordinating function and now refer to Fayol's commanding function as "leading," these functions are widely known as planning (determining organizational goals and a means for achieving them), organizing (deciding where decisions will be made, who will do what jobs and tasks, and who will work for whom), leading (inspiring and motivating workers to work hard to achieve organizational goals), and controlling (monitoring progress toward goal achievement and taking corrective action when needed). In addition, according to Fayol, effective management is based on the fourteen principles in Exhibit 2.5.

2-4 HUMAN RELATIONS MANAGEMENT

As we have seen, scientific management focuses on improving efficiency; bureaucratic management focuses on using knowledge, fairness, and logical rules

Michael DeLeon/iStockphoto.com

and procedures; and administrative management focuses on how and what managers should do in their jobs. The human relations approach to management focuses on *people*, particularly the psychological and social aspects of work. This approach to management sees people not as just extensions of machines but as valuable organizational resources in their own right. Human relations management holds that people's needs are important and that their efforts, motivation, and performance are affected by the work they do and their relationships with their bosses, coworkers, and work groups. In other words, efficiency alone is not enough. Organizational success also depends on treating workers well.

*Let's find out more about human relations management by learning about **2-4a Mary Parker Follett's theories of constructive conflict and coordination, 2-4b Elton Mayo's Hawthorne Studies,** and **2-4c Chester Barnard's theories of cooperation and acceptance of authority.***

2-4a Constructive Conflict and Coordination: Mary Parker Follett

Mary Parker Follett (1868–1933) was a social worker with a degree in political science who, in her fifties, after twenty-five years of working with schools and nonprofit organizations, began lecturing and writing about management and working extensively as a consultant for business and government leaders in the United States and Europe. Although her contributions were overlooked for decades, perhaps because she was a woman or perhaps because they were so different, many of today's "new" management ideas can clearly be traced to her work.

Exhibit 2.5

Fayol's Fourteen Principles of Management

1 Division of work

Increase production by dividing work so that each worker completes smaller tasks or job elements.

2 Authority and responsibility

A manager's authority, which is the "right to give orders," should be commensurate with the manager's responsibility. However, organizations should enact controls to prevent managers from abusing their authority.

3 Discipline

Clearly defined rules and procedures are needed at all organizational levels to ensure order and proper behavior.

4 Unity of command

To avoid confusion and conflict, each employee should report to and receive orders from just one boss.

5 Unity of direction

One person and one plan should be used in deciding the activities to be carried out to accomplish each organizational objective.

6 Subordination of individual interests to the general interests

Employees must put the organization's interests and goals before their own.

7 Remuneration

Compensation should be fair and satisfactory to both the employees and the organization; that is, don't overpay or underpay employees.

8 Centralization

Avoid too much centralization or decentralization. Strike a balance depending on the circumstances and employees involved.

9 Scalar chain

From the top to the bottom of an organization, each position is part of a vertical chain of authority in which each worker reports to just one boss. For the sake of simplicity, communication outside normal work groups or departments should follow the vertical chain of authority.

10 Order

To avoid confusion and conflict, order can be obtained by having a place for everyone and having everyone in his or her place; in other words, there should be no overlapping responsibilities.

11 Equity

Kind, fair, and just treatment for all will develop devotion and loyalty. This does not exclude discipline, if warranted, and consideration of the broader general interests of the organization.

12 Stability of tenure of personnel

Low turnover, meaning a stable work force with high tenure, benefits an organization by improving performance, lowering costs, and giving employees, especially managers, time to learn their jobs.

13 Initiative

Because it is a "great source of strength for business," managers should encourage the development of initiative, or the ability to develop and implement a plan, in others.

14 *Esprit de corps*

Develop a strong sense of morale and unity among workers that encourages coordination of efforts.

Sources: H. Fayol, *General and Industrial Management* (London: Pittman & Sons, 1949); M. Fells, "Fayol Stands the Test of Time," *Journal of Management History* 6 (2000): 345–360; C. Rodrigues, "Fayol's 14 Principles of Management Then and Now: A Framework for Managing Today's Organizations Effectively," *Management Decision* 39 (2001): 880–889.

Follett believed that the best way to deal with conflict was not **domination,** where one side wins and the other loses, or **compromise,** where each side gives up some of what it wants, but integration. Said Follett, "There is a way beginning now to be recognized at least, and even occasionally followed: when two desires are *integrated*, that means that a solution has been found in which both desires have found a place that neither side has had to sacrifice anything."[37] So, rather than one side dominating the other or both sides compromising, the point of **integrative conflict resolution** is to have both parties indicate their preferences and then work together to find an alternative that meets the needs of both. According to Follett, "Integration involves invention, and the clever thing is to recognize this, and not to let one's thinking stay within the boundaries of two alternatives which are mutually exclusive." Indeed, Follett's ideas about the positive use of conflict and an integrative approach to conflict resolution predate accepted thinking in the negotiation and conflict resolution literature by six decades (see the best-selling book *Getting to Yes: Negotiating Agreement without Giving In* by Roger Fisher, William Ury, and Bruce Patton).

Exhibit 2.6 summarizes Follett's contributions to management in her own words. She casts power as "with" rather than "over" others. Giving orders involves discussing instructions and dealing with resentment. Authority flows from job knowledge and experience rather than position. Leadership involves setting the tone for the team rather than being aggressive and dominating, which may be harmful. Coordination and control should be based on facts and information. In the end, Follett's contributions added significantly to our understanding of the human, social, and psychological sides of management. Peter Parker, the former chairman of the London School of Economics, said about Follett: "People often puzzle about who is the father of management. I don't know who the father was, but I have no doubt about who was the mother."[38]

2-4b Hawthorne Studies: Elton Mayo

Australian-born Elton Mayo (1880–1948) is best known for his role in the famous Hawthorne Studies at the **Western Electric Company**. The Hawthorne Studies were conducted in several stages between 1924 and 1932 at a Western Electric plant in Chicago. Although Mayo didn't join the studies until 1928, he played a significant role thereafter, writing about the results in his book *The Human Problems of an Industrial Civilization*.[39] The first stage of the Hawthorne Studies investigated the effects of lighting levels and incentives on employee productivity in the Relay Test Assembly Room, where workers took approximately a minute to put "together a coil, armature, contact springs, and insulators in a fixture and secure the parts by means of four machine screws."[40]

Two groups of six experienced female workers, five to do the work and one to supply needed parts, were separated from the main part of the factory by a ten-foot partition and placed at a standard work bench with the necessary parts and tools. Over the next five years, the experimenters introduced various levels and combinations of lighting, financial incentives, and rest pauses (work breaks) to study the effect on productivity. Curiously, however, production levels increased whether the experimenters increased or decreased the lighting, paid workers based on individual production or group production, or increased or decreased the number and length of rest pauses. In fact, Mayo and his fellow researchers were surprised that production steadily increased from 2,400 relays per day at the beginning of the study to 3,000 relays per day five years later. The question was: Why?

Mayo and his colleagues eventually concluded that two things accounted for the results. First, substantially more attention was paid to these workers than to workers in the rest of the plant. Mayo wrote, "Before every change of program [in the study], the group is consulted. Their comments are listened to and discussed; sometimes their objections are allowed to negate a suggestion. The group unquestionably develops a sense of participation in the critical determinations and becomes something of a social unit."[41]

For years, the "Hawthorne Effect" has been *incorrectly* defined as increasing productivity by paying more attention to workers.[42] But it is not simply about attention from management. The Hawthorne Effect cannot be understood without giving equal importance to the social units, which became intensely cohesive groups. Mayo said, "What actually happened was that six individuals became a team and the team gave itself wholeheartedly and spontaneously to cooperation in the experiment. The consequence was that they felt themselves to be participating freely and without afterthought, and were happy

Domination an approach to dealing with conflict in which one party satisfies its desires and objectives at the expense of the other party's desires and objectives

Compromise an approach to dealing with conflict in which both parties give up some of what they want in order to reach agreement on a plan to reduce or settle the conflict

Integrative conflict resolution an approach to dealing with conflict in which both parties indicate their preferences and then work together to find an alternative that meets the needs of both

Exhibit 2.6

On constructive conflict...

"As conflict—difference—is here in this world, as we cannot avoid it, we should, I think, use it to work for us. Instead of condemning it, we should set it to work for us."

On power...

"It seems to me that whereas power usually means power-over, the power of some person or group over some other person or group, it is possible to develop the conception of power-with, a jointly developed power, a co-active, not a coercive power."

On the giving of orders...

"An advantage of not exacting blind obedience, of discussing your instructions with your subordinates, is that if there is any resentment, any comeback, you get it out into the open, and when it is in the open, you can deal with it."

On authority...

"Authority should go with knowledge and experience, that is where obedience is due, no matter whether it is up the line or down."

On leadership...

"Of the greatest importance is the ability to grasp a total situation. . . . Out of a welter of facts, experience, desires, aims, the leader must find the unifying thread. He must see a whole, not a mere kaleidoscope of pieces. . . . The higher up you go, the more ability you have to have of this kind."

On coordination...

"The most important thing to remember about unity is—that there is no such thing. There is only unifying. You cannot get unity and expect it to last a day—or five minutes. Every man in a business should be taking part in a certain process and that process is unifying."

On control...

"Central control is coming more and more to mean the co-relation of many controls rather than a superimposed control."

Source: M. Parker Follett, *Mary Parker Follett—Prophet of Management: A Celebration of Writings from the 1920s*, ed. P. Graham (Boston: Harvard Business School Press, 1995).

Kokoroyuki/iStockphoto.com

what the researchers did, productivity dropped in the Bank Wiring Room. Again, the question was: Why?

Mayo and his colleagues found that the differences in performance were due to group dynamics. The workers in the Bank Wiring Room had been an existing work group for some time and had already developed strong negative norms that governed their behavior. For instance, despite a group financial incentive for production, the group members decided that they would wire only 6,000 to 6,600 connections a day (depending on the kind of equipment they were wiring), well below the production goal of 7,300 connections that management had set for them. Individual workers who worked at a faster pace were socially ostracized from the group or "binged" (hit on the arm) until they slowed their work pace. Thus, the group's behavior was reminiscent of the soldiering that Taylor had observed. Mayo concluded, "Work [was] done in accord with the group's conception of a day's work; this was exceeded by only one individual who was cordially disliked."[45]

In the end, the Hawthorne Studies demonstrated that the workplace was more complex than previously thought, that workers were not just extensions of machines, and that financial incentives weren't necessarily the most important motivator for workers. By highlighting the crucial role, positive or negative, that groups, group norms, and group behavior play at work, Mayo strengthened Follett's point about coordination—make just one change in an organization and others,

in the knowledge that they were working without coercion from above or limits from below."[43]

For the first time, human factors related to work were found to be more important than the physical conditions or design of the work. Together, the increased attention from management and the development of a cohesive work group led to significantly higher levels of job satisfaction and productivity. In short, the Hawthorne Studies found that workers' feelings and attitudes affected their work.

The next stage of the Hawthorne Studies was conducted in the Bank Wiring Room, where "the group consisted of nine wiremen, three solderers, and two inspectors. Each of these groups performed a specific task and collaborated with the other two in completion of each unit of equipment. The task consisted of setting up the banks of terminals side-by-side on frames, wiring the corresponding terminals from bank to bank, soldering the connections, and inspecting with a test set for short circuits or breaks in the wire. One solderman serviced the work of the three wiremen."[44] While productivity increased in the Relay Test Assembly Room no matter

DOING THE RIGHT THING

Building a Good Team

In the Hawthorne Studies, Elton Mayo revealed the importance of group dynamics and cohesion in the workplace. In trying to build cohesion, many modern managers turn to teambuilding exercises like trust falls, ropes courses, and scavenger hunts. And while these activities might be fun, they aren't particularly effective at building group cohesion and teaching workers how to work well together. When planning your department's annual retreat, skip the trust falls and get straight to work, focusing on helping the team discover how to produce great results. After all, it's only when teams work together to overcome serious obstacles that team members learn to count on each other.

Source: J. Haden. "6 Ways to Ruin a Company Offsite Meeting," *Inc.com*, February 21, 2012, accessed February 25, 2012, http://www.inc.com/jeff-haden/6-ways-to-ruin-a-company-offsite-meeting.html.

some expected and some unexpected, will occur. Thanks to Mayo and his colleagues and their work on the Hawthorne Studies, managers better understood the effect that group social interactions, employee satisfaction, and attitudes had on individual and group performance.

2-4c Cooperation and Acceptance of Authority: Chester Barnard

Like Fayol, Chester Barnard (1886–1961) had experiences as a top executive that shaped his views of management. Barnard began his career in 1909 as an engineer and translator for AT&T, becoming a general manager at Pennsylvania Bell Telephone in 1922 and then president of New Jersey Bell Telephone in 1927.[46] Barnard's ideas, published in his classic book, *The Functions of the Executive*, influenced companies from the board of directors down. He is best known for his ideas about cooperation and the acceptance of authority.

Barnard proposed a comprehensive theory of cooperation in formal organizations. In fact, he defines an **organization** as a "system of consciously coordinated activities or forces of two or more persons."[47] In other words, organization occurs whenever two people work together for some purpose, whether it be classmates working together to complete a class project, Habitat for Humanity volunteers donating their time to build a house, or managers working with subordinates to reduce costs, improve quality, or increase sales. Why did Barnard place so much emphasis on cooperation? Because cooperation is *not* the normal state of affairs: "Failure to cooperate, failure of cooperation, failure of organization, disorganization, disintegration, destruction of organization—and reorganization—are characteristic facts of human history."[48]

According to Barnard, the extent to which people willingly cooperate in an organization depends on how workers perceive executive authority and whether they're willing to accept it. Many managerial requests or directives fall within a *zone of indifference* in which acceptance of managerial authority is automatic. For example, if your supervisor asks you for a copy of the monthly inventory report, and compiling and writing that report is part of your job, you think nothing of the request and automatically send it. In general, people will be indifferent to managerial directives or orders if they (1) are understood, (2) are consistent with the purpose of the organization, (3) are compatible with the people's personal interests, and (4) can actually be carried out by those people. Acceptance of managerial authority (i.e., cooperation) is not automatic, however. Ask people to do things contrary to the organization's purpose or to their own benefit and they'll put up a fight. While many people assume that managers have the authority to do whatever they want, Barnard, referring to the "fiction of superior authority," believed that workers ultimately grant managers their authority.

2-5 OPERATIONS, INFORMATION, SYSTEMS, AND CONTINGENCY MANAGEMENT

In this last section, we review four other significant historical approaches to management that have influenced how today's managers produce goods and services on a daily basis, gather and manage the information they need to understand their businesses and make good decisions, understand how the different parts of the company work together as a whole, and recognize when and where particular management practices are likely to work.

To better understand these ideas, let's learn about 2-5a operations management, 2-5b information management, 2-5c systems management, and 2-5d contingency management.

2-5a Operations Management

In Chapter 18, you will learn about *operations management*, which involves managing the daily production of goods and services. In general, operations management uses a quantitative or mathematical approach to find ways to increase productivity, improve quality, and manage or reduce costly inventories. The most commonly used operations management tools and methods are quality control, forecasting techniques, capacity planning, productivity measurement and improvement, linear programming, scheduling systems, inventory systems, work measurement techniques (similar to the Gilbreths' motion studies), project management (similar to Gantt's charts), and cost-benefit analysis.[49]

Organization a system of consciously coordinated activities or forces created by two or more people

Since the 16th century, skilled craftspeople made the lock, stock, and barrel of a gun by hand. After each part was made, a skilled gun finisher assembled the parts into a complete gun. But the gun finisher did not simply screw the different parts of a gun together, as is done today. Instead, each handmade part required extensive finishing and adjusting so that it would fit together with the other handmade gun parts. Hand-fitting was necessary because, even when made by the same skilled craftspeople, no two parts were alike. In fact, gun finishers played a role similar to that of fine watchmakers who meticulously assembled expensive watches—without them, the product simply wouldn't work. Today, we would say that these parts were low quality because they varied so much from one part to another.

All this changed in 1791 when the US government, worried about a possible war with France, ordered 40,000 muskets from private gun contractors. All but one contractor built handmade muskets assembled by skilled gun finishers who made sure that all the parts fit together. Thus, each musket was unique. If a part broke, a replacement part had to be handcrafted. But one contractor, Eli Whitney of New Haven, Connecticut (who is better known for his invention of the cotton gin) determined that if gun parts were made accurately enough, guns could be made with standardized, interchangeable parts. So he designed machine tools that allowed unskilled workers to make each gun part the same as the next. Said Whitney, "The tools which I contemplate to make are similar to an engraving on copper plate from which may be taken a great number of impressions perceptibly alike."[50] Years passed before Whitney delivered his 10,000 muskets to the US government. But he demonstrated the superiority of interchangeable parts to President-elect Thomas Jefferson in 1801 by quickly and easily assembling complete muskets from randomly picked piles of musket parts. Today, because of Whitney's ideas, most products, from cars to toasters to space shuttles, are manufactured using standardized, interchangeable parts.

But even with this advance, manufacturers still could not produce a part unless they had seen or examined it firsthand. Thanks to Gaspard Monge, a Frenchman of modest beginnings, this soon changed. Monge's greatest achievement was his book *Descriptive Geometry*.[51] In it, he explained techniques for drawing three-dimensional objects on paper. For the first time, precise drawings permitted manufacturers to make standardized, interchangeable parts without first examining a prototype. Today, thanks to Monge, manufacturers rely on CAD (computer-aided design) and CAM (computer-aided manufacturing) to take three-dimensional designs straight from the computer to the factory floor.

Once standardized, interchangeable parts became the norm, and once parts could be made from design drawings alone, manufacturers ran into a costly problem that they had never faced before: too much inventory. *Inventory* is the amount and number of raw materials, parts, and finished products that a company has in its possession. In fact, large factories were accumulating parts inventories sufficient for two to three months, much more than they needed on a daily basis to run their manufacturing operations. A solution to this problem was found in 1905 when the Oldsmobile Motor Works in Detroit burned down.[52] Management rented a new production facility to get production up and running as quickly as possible after the fire. But because the new facility was much smaller, there was no room to store large stockpiles of inventory (which the company couldn't afford anyway as it was short on funds). Therefore, the company made do with what it called "hand-to-mouth inventories," in which each production station had only enough parts on hand to do a short production run. Because all of its parts suppliers were close by, Oldsmobile could place orders in the morning and receive them in the afternoon (even without telephones), just as with today's computerized just-in-time inventory systems. So, contrary to common belief, just-in-time inventory systems were not invented by Japanese manufacturers. Instead, they were invented out of necessity more than a century ago because of a fire.

2-5b Information Management

For most of recorded history, information has been costly, difficult to obtain, and slow to spread. Because of the immense labor and time it took to hand copy information, books, manuscripts, and written documents of any kind

Dardespot/iStockphoto.com

were rare and extremely expensive. Word of Joan of Arc's death in 1431 took eighteen months to travel from France across Europe to Constantinople (now Istanbul, Turkey).

Consequently, throughout history, organizations have pushed for and quickly adopted new information technologies that reduce the cost or increase the speed with which they can acquire, store, retrieve, or communicate information. The first technologies to truly revolutionize the business use of information were paper and the printing press. In the 14th century, water-powered machines were created to pulverize rags into pulp to make paper. Paper prices, which were already lower than those of animal-skin parchments, dropped dramatically. Less than a half-century later, Johannes Gutenberg invented the printing press, which greatly reduced the cost and time needed to copy written information. In 15th-century Florence, Italy, a scribe would charge one florin (an Italian unit of money) to hand copy one document page. By contrast, a printer would set up and print 1,025 copies of the same document for just three florins. Within fifty years of its invention, Gutenberg's printing press cut the cost of information by 99.8 percent!

What Gutenberg's printing press did for publishing, the manual typewriter did for daily communication. Before 1850, most business correspondence was written by hand and copied using the letterpress. With the ink still wet, the letter would be placed into a tissue-paper book.

A hand press would then be used to squeeze the book and copy the still-wet ink onto the tissue paper. By the 1870s, manual typewriters made it cheaper, easier, and faster to produce and copy business correspondence. Of course, in the 1980s, slightly more than a century later, typewriters were replaced by personal computers and word processing software with the same results.

Finally, businesses have always looked for information technologies that would speed access to timely information. The Medici family, which opened banks throughout Europe in the early 1400s, used post messengers to keep in contact with their more than forty branch managers. The post messengers, who predated the US Postal Service Pony Express by 400 years, could travel ninety miles per day, twice what average riders could cover, because the Medicis were willing to pay for the expense of providing them with fresh horses. This need for timely information also led companies to quickly adopt the telegraph in the 1860s, the telephone in the 1880s, and, of course, Internet technologies in the last three decades.

2-5c Systems Management

Today's companies are much more complex than they used to be. They are larger and employ more people. They most likely manufacture, service, *and* finance what they sell, not only in their home markets but in foreign markets throughout the world, too. They also operate in complex, fast-changing, competitive, global environments that can quickly turn competitive advantages into competitive disadvantages. How, then, can managers make sense of this complexity, both within and outside their organizations?

One way to deal with organizational and environmental complexity is to take a systems view of organizations. The systems approach is derived from theoretical models in biology and social psychology developed in the 1950s and 1960s.[53] A **system** is a set of interrelated elements or parts that function as a whole. Rather than viewing one part of an organization as separate from the other parts, a systems approach encourages managers to complicate their thinking by looking for connections between the different parts of the organization. Indeed, one of the more important ideas in the systems approach to management is that organizational systems are composed of parts or **subsystems**,

System a set of interrelated elements or parts that function as a whole

Subsystems smaller systems that operate within the context of a larger system

Exhibit 2.7
Systems View of Organizations

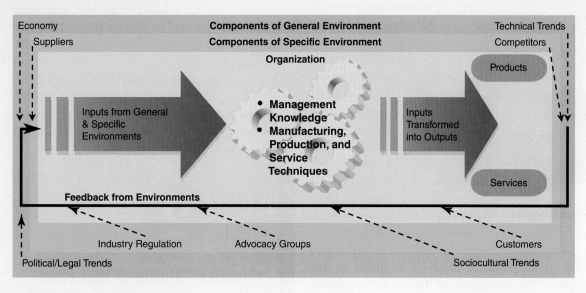

which are simply smaller systems within larger systems. Subsystems and their connections matter in systems theory because of the possibility for managers to create synergy. **Synergy** occurs when two or more subsystems working together can produce more than they can working apart. In other words, synergy occurs when 1 + 1 = 3.

Systems can be open or closed. **Closed systems** can function without interacting with their environments. But nearly all organizations should be viewed as **open systems** that interact with their environments and depend on them for survival. Therefore, rather than viewing what goes on within the organization as separate from what goes on outside it, the systems approach encourages managers to look for connections between the different parts of the organization and the different parts of its environment. Exhibit 2.7 illustrates how the elements of systems management work together.

A systems view of organizations offers several advantages. First, it forces managers to view their organizations as part of and subject to the competitive, economic, social, technological, and legal/regulatory forces in their environments.[54] Second, it forces managers to be aware of how the environment affects specific parts of the organization. Third, because of the complexity and difficulty of trying to achieve synergies among different parts of the organization, the systems view encourages managers to focus on better communication and cooperation within the organization. Finally,

it makes managers acutely aware that good internal management of the organization may not be enough to ensure survival. Survival also depends on making sure that the organization continues to satisfy critical environmental stakeholders such as shareholders, employees, customers, suppliers, governments, and local communities.

2-5d Contingency Management

Earlier, you learned that the goal of scientific management was to use systematic study to find the one best way of doing each task and then use that one best way everywhere. The problem, as you may have gathered from reading about the various approaches to management, is that no one in management seems to agree on what that one best way is. Furthermore, more than 100 years of management research has shown that

Synergy when two or more subsystems working together can produce more than they can working apart

Closed systems systems that can sustain themselves without interacting with their environments

Open systems systems that can sustain themselves only by interacting with their environments, on which they depend for their survival

there are clear boundaries or limitations to most management theories and practices. No management ideas or practices are universal. Although any theory or practice may work much of the time, none works all the time. How, then, is a manager to decide what theory to use? Well, it depends on the situation. The **contingency approach** to management clearly states that there are no universal management theories and that the most effective management theory or idea depends on the kinds of problems or situations that managers or organizations are facing at a particular time and place.[55] In short, the best way depends on the situation.

One of the practical implications of the contingency approach to management is that management is much harder than it looks. In fact, because of the clarity and obviousness of management theories (OK, most of them), students and workers often wrongly assume that a company's problems would be quickly and easily solved if management would take just a few simple steps. If this were true, few companies would have problems.

Contingency approach holds that there are no universal management theories and that the most effective management theory or idea depends on the kinds of problems or situations that managers are facing at a particular time and place

A second implication of the contingency approach is that managers need to look for key contingencies that differentiate today's situation or problems from yesterday's situation or problems. Moreover, it means that managers need to spend more time analyzing problems, situations, and employees before taking action to fix them. Finally, it means that as you read this text and learn about management ideas and practices, you need to pay particular attention to qualifying phrases such as "usually," "in these situations," "for this to work," and "under these circumstances." Doing so will help you identify the key contingencies that will help you become a better manager.

STUDY TOOLS ②

LOCATED AT THE BACK OF YOUR BOOK:

☐ Rip out and study the Chapter Review Card at the end of the book

LOG IN TO WWW.CENGAGEBRAIN.COM TO:

☐ Review Key Term Flashcards

☐ Complete Practice Quizzing (take up to four times without repeating the same quiz)

☐ Complete Interactive Content: Graded Quiz, Media Quiz, Fill-in-the-Blank Questions

☐ Work Through the What Would You Do Case on ISG Steelton

☐ Watch Management Workplace Video on "Barcelona Restaurants"

3 Organizational Environments and Cultures

Johnny Greig/iStockphoto.com

LEARNING OUTCOMES

- **3-1** Discuss how changing environments affect organizations.
- **3-2** Describe the four components of the general environment.
- **3-3** Explain the five components of the specific environment.
- **3-4** Describe the process that companies use to make sense of their changing environments.
- **3-5** Explain how organizational cultures are created and how they can help companies be successful.

After you finish this chapter, go to **PAGE 65** for **STUDY TOOLS**

3-1 CHANGING ENVIRONMENTS

This chapter examines the internal and external forces that affect business. We begin by explaining how the changes in external organizational environments affect the decisions and performance of a company. Next, we examine the two types of external organizational environment: the general environment that affects all organizations and the specific environment unique to each company. Then, we learn how managers make sense of their changing general and specific environments. The chapter finishes with a discussion of internal organizational environments by focusing on organizational culture. But first, let's see how the changes in external organizational environments affect the decisions and performance of a company.

External environments are the forces and events outside a company that have the potential to influence or affect it. In most cities, taxi prices (what's charged on the meter) and taxi licenses (for drivers and cars) are highly regulated. The taxi industry, however, is threatened by Uber, a 4-year old Internet company. After signing up as an Uber customer (name, password, credit card information), customers use the Uber app on their smartphones to order rides. Tap Uber. Enter a destination. Tap a button indicating your location. Then, the Uber app indicates the cost and how long till the car arrives. Afterwards, it sends email receipts and automatically pays the driver. No cash changes hands. Customers love Uber because it's often faster than hailing a cab on the street. Taxi drivers and companies hate it because it represents competition. Which is why 30,000 taxi drivers across London, Berlin, Madrid, and Paris parked their taxis in protest. Steve McNamara, a spokesperson for London's Licensed Taxi Driver Association, said, "We have nothing against competition. But Uber is being allowed to 'operate outside the law.'"[1] So far, London's taxi regulation agency has ruled that Uber apps and cars do not have taxi meters, therefore, they can't be regulated as taxi cabs. While London's famous black cab taxi drivers disagree, the goal of these protests is to influence regulatory agencies to prevent Uber from operating, or to force Uber to buy expensive, limited-in-number taxi licenses.

Let's examine the three basic characteristics of changing external environments: 3-1a environmental change; 3-1b environmental complexity; 3-1c resource scarcity; and 3-1d the uncertainty that environmental change, complexity, and resource scarcity can create for organizational managers.

3-1a Environmental Change

Environmental change is the rate at which a company's general and specific environments change. In **stable environments,** the rate of environmental change is slow. Apart from occasional shortages due to drought or frost, the wholesale food distribution business—where dairy items, fresh produce, baked goods, poultry, fish, and meat are processed and delivered by trucks from warehouses to restaurants, grocers, and other retailers—changes little from year to year. Distributors take shipments from farmers, food manufacturers, and food importers, consolidate them at warehouses, and then distribute them to retailers. While recent adoption of global positioning satellite (GPS) systems and radio frequency identification (RFID) devices might be seen as "change," wholesale food distributors began using them because, like the trucks they bought to replace horse-drawn carriages in the early 1900s, GPS and RFID improved the core part of their business—getting the freshest food ingredients to customers as quickly and inexpensively as possible—which has not changed in over a century.[2]

While wholesale food distribution companies have stable environments, BlackBerry competes in an extremely dynamic external environment. In **dynamic environments,** the rate of environmental change is fast. Blackberry competitors, such as Apple, Samsung, HTC, and Motorola, frequently updated models with innovative features and new technology. Over a five-year span, Apple released six different iPhone models, the 3G, the 3GS, the 4, the 4S, the 5, and the 5S, each having better features and functionality. For instance, the new iPhone 5s has a new, 64-bit processing chip, the first of its kind in a smartphone, a camera with a larger sensor that is more sensitive to light, and a fingerprint scanner on the home button that allows the user to perform multiple functions, from unlocking the phone to approving purchases from the App Store. None of Apple's competitors has these kinds of features on their phones.[3]

External environments   all events outside a company that have the potential to influence or affect it

Environmental change   the rate at which a company's general and specific environments change

Stable environment   an environment in which the rate of change is slow

Dynamic environment   an environment in which the rate of change is fast

---

Although you might think that a company's external environment would be either stable or dynamic, research suggests that companies often experience both. According to **punctuated equilibrium theory,** companies go through long periods of stability (equilibrium) during which incremental changes occur; followed by short, complex periods of dynamic, fundamental change (revolutionary periods); and finishing with a return to stability (new equilibrium).[4]

The US airline industry is a classic example of punctuated equilibrium, as three times in the last thirty years it has experienced revolutionary periods followed by a temporary return to stability. The first, from mid-1979 to mid-1982, occurred immediately after airline deregulation in 1978. Prior to deregulation, the federal government controlled where airlines could fly, how much they could charge, when they could fly, and the number of flights they could have on a particular route. After deregulation, these choices were left to the airlines. The large financial losses during this period clearly indicate that the airlines had trouble adjusting to the intense competition from new airlines that occurred after deregulation. By mid-1982, however, profits returned to the industry and held steady until mid-1989.

Then, after experiencing record growth and profits, US airlines lost billions of dollars between 1989 and 1993 as the industry went through dramatic changes. Key expenses, including jet fuel and employee salaries,

which had held steady for years, suddenly increased. Furthermore, revenues, which had grown steadily year after year, suddenly dropped because of dramatic changes in the airlines' customer base. Business travelers, who had typically paid full-price fares, comprised more than half of all passengers during the 1980s. However, by the late 1980s, the largest customer base had changed to leisure travelers, who wanted the cheapest flights they could get.[5] With expenses suddenly up and revenues suddenly down, the airlines responded to these changes in their business environment by laying off 5 to 10 percent of their workers, canceling orders for new planes, and eliminating unprofitable routes. Starting in 1993 and lasting till 1998, these changes helped the airline industry achieve profits far in excess of their historical levels. The industry began to stabilize, if not flourish, just as punctuated equilibrium theory predicts.[6]

The third revolutionary period for the US airline industry began with the terrorist attacks of September 11, 2001, in which planes were used as missiles to bring down the World Trade Center towers and damage the Pentagon. The immediate effect was a 20 percent drop in scheduled flights, a 40 percent drop in passengers, and losses so large that the US government approved a $15 billion bailout to keep the airlines in business. Heightened airport security also affected airports, the airlines themselves, and airline customers. Five years after the 9/11 attacks, United Airlines, US Airways, Delta, and American Airlines had reduced staffing by 169,000 full-time jobs to cut costs after losing a combined $42 billion.[7] Due to their financially weaker position, the airlines restructured operations to take advantage of the combined effect of increased passenger travel, a sharply reduced cost structure, and a 23 percent reduction in the fleet to return their businesses to profitability.[8] But, just as the airlines were heading toward a more stable period of equilibrium in 2006 and 2007, the price of oil jumped dramatically, doubling, if not tripling, the price of jet fuel, which prompted the airlines to charge for luggage (to increase revenues and discourage heavy baggage) and cut flights using older, fuel-inefficient jets.

In 2013, however, stability and profitability largely returned. Compared to 2007, the airlines cut total seat capacity 14 percent, filled 83 percent of seats, up from 80 percent, and with stronger demand and fewer flights saw round-trip fares rise by 4 percent, even after adjusting for inflation. In 2008, US airlines collectively lost $23.7 billion, but by the end of 2013, they had logged their fourth consecutive year of profits.[9] Multiple airline

Punctuated equilibrium theory the theory that companies go through long periods of stability (equilibrium), followed by short periods of dynamic, fundamental change (revolutionary periods), and then a new equilibrium

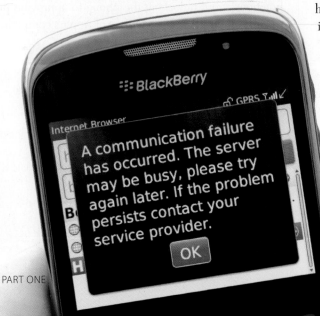

Scott Mangham/iStockphoto.com

mergers—Delta and Northwest, United and Continental, Southwest and AirTran, and US Airways and American Airlines—reduced competition and routes even further, especially at non-hub airports like Cincinnati, where the number of flights has plummeted by two-thirds since 2007. Bob Cortelyou, Delta's senior vice president for network planning, explained that the airlines are making these moves because, "We want an airline industry that is stable and profitable."[10]

3-1b Environmental Complexity

Environmental complexity refers to the number and the intensity of external factors in the environment that affect organizations. **Simple environments** have few environmental factors, whereas **complex environments** have many environmental factors. The dairy industry is an excellent example of a relatively simple external environment. Even accounting for decades-old advances in processing and automatic milking machines, milk is produced the same way today as it was 100 years ago. And although food manufacturers introduce dozens of new dairy-based products each year, US milk production has grown a meager 1.25 percent per year over the last decade. In short, producing milk is a highly competitive but simple business that has experienced few environmental changes.[11]

At the other end of the spectrum, few industries find themselves in more complex environments today than the personal computer (PC) business. Since the early 1980s, PC sales have grown spectacularly. But with consumers now spending technology dollars on tablets, e-readers, and smartphones (some as big as tablets and e-readers!), sales of Windows-based PCs dropped 14 percent from 2012 to 2013. PC manufacturers saw similar trends, with HP (−23.7 percent), Dell (−10.9 percent), Acer Group (−31.3 percent), and Asus (−19.2 percent) all posting double-digit declines. Microsoft's Windows 8 operating system, which brought touchscreen capabilities and design to the PC and Microsoft tablets and smartphones, was supposed to revive PC sales. But one year after its release, even Microsoft admitted that sales had been disappointing. David Daoud, research director at International Data Corporation, concluded, "The industry is going through a critical crossroads, and strategic choices will have to be made as to how to compete with the proliferation of alternative devices and remain relevant to the consumer."[12]

3-1c Resource Scarcity

The third characteristic of external environments is resource scarcity. **Resource scarcity** is the abundance or shortage of critical organizational resources in an organization's external environment. Chenab Ltd, a garment manufacturer in Faisalabad, Pakistan, makes fashionable sports ware for global brands, ranging from Victoria's Secret to Tommy Hilfiger. But because of severe electricity shortages in Pakistan, where demand for electricity exceeds supply by 50%, power outages occur 12 to 18 hours a day. Latif bought a $6 million generator to power the entire plant, but it goes unused because of gas shortages. Muhammad Latif, Chenab's owner, "I am asked to pay interest on my loans for 365 days a year, but I can only work my business for half that time."[13] As a result, Chenab's clothing plant runs at only one-third of its capacity and is forced to turn down orders. It's 14,000 strong workforce, likewise, has shrunk to just 4,500 employees and its sales are down 75%.

Environmental complexity the number and the intensity of external factors in the environment that affect organizations

Simple environment an environment with few environmental factors

Complex environment an environment with many environmental factors

Resource scarcity the abundance or shortage of critical organizational resources in an organization's external environment

Exhibit 3.1
Environmental Change, Environmental Complexity, and Resource Scarcity

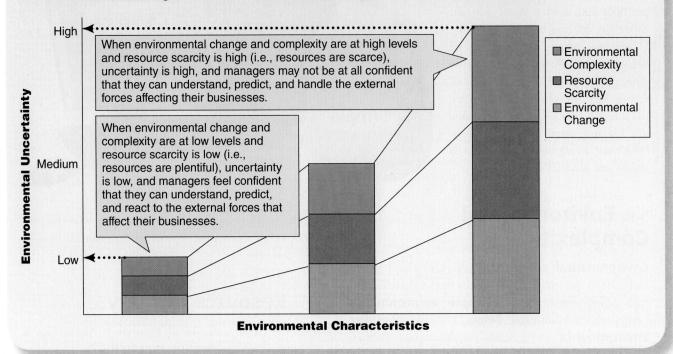

Environmental Uncertainty (y-axis): High, Medium, Low

When environmental change and complexity are at high levels and resource scarcity is high (i.e., resources are scarce), uncertainty is high, and managers may not be at all confident that they can understand, predict, and handle the external forces affecting their businesses.

When environmental change and complexity are at low levels and resource scarcity is low (i.e., resources are plentiful), uncertainty is low, and managers feel confident that they can understand, predict, and react to the external forces that affect their businesses.

Legend:
- Environmental Complexity
- Resource Scarcity
- Environmental Change

Environmental Characteristics (x-axis)

3-1d Uncertainty

As Exhibit 3.1 shows, environmental change, environmental complexity, and resource scarcity affect environmental **uncertainty**, which is how well managers can understand or predict the external changes and trends affecting their businesses. Starting at the left side of the figure, environmental uncertainty is lowest when environmental change and environmental complexity are at low levels and resource scarcity is low (i.e., resources are plentiful). In these environments, managers feel confident that they can understand, predict, and react to the external forces that affect their businesses. By contrast, the right side of the figure shows that environmental uncertainty is highest when

environmental change and complexity are extensive and resource scarcity is a problem. In these environments, managers may not be confident that they can understand, predict, and handle the external forces affecting their businesses.

3-2 GENERAL ENVIRONMENT

As Exhibit 3.2 shows, two kinds of external environments influence organizations: the general environment and the specific environment. The **general environment** consists of the economy and the technological, sociocultural, and political/legal trends that indirectly affect *all* organizations. Changes in any sector of the general environment eventually affect most organizations. For example, when the Federal Reserve lowers its prime lending rate, most businesses benefit because banks and credit card companies often lower the interest rates they charge for loans. Consumers, who can then borrow money more cheaply, might borrow more to buy homes, cars, refrigerators, and large-screen plasma or LCD TVs.

Each organization also has a **specific environment** that is unique to that firm's industry and directly affects

Uncertainty extent to which managers can understand or predict which environmental changes and trends will affect their businesses

General environment the economic, technological, sociocultural, and political/legal trends that indirectly affect all organizations

Specific environment the customers, competitors, suppliers, industry regulations, and advocacy groups that are unique to an industry and directly affect how a company does business

Exhibit 3.2
General and Specific Environments

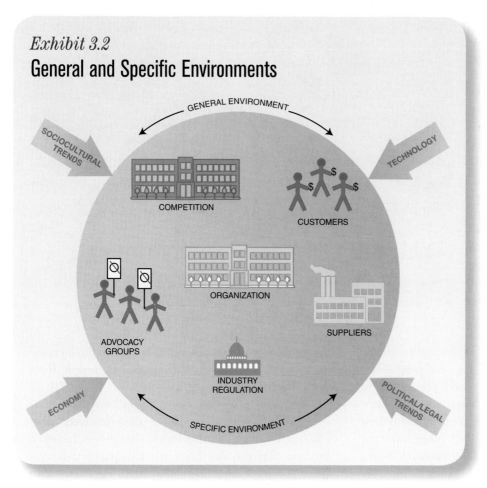

But first let's take a closer look at the four components of the general environment: **3-2a the economy** *and* **3-2b the technological,** **3-2c sociocultural,** *and* **3-2d political/legal** *trends that indirectly affect all organizations.*

3-2a Economy

The current state of a country's economy affects virtually every organization doing business there. In general, in a growing economy, more people are working and wages are growing, and therefore consumers have relatively more money to spend. More products are bought and sold in a growing economy than in a static or shrinking economy. Though an individual firm's sales will not necessarily increase, a growing economy does provide an environment favorable to business growth. In contrast, in a shrinking economy, consumers have less money to spend and relatively fewer products are bought and sold. Thus, a shrinking economy makes growth for individual businesses more difficult.

Because the economy influences basic business decisions, such as whether to hire more employees, expand production, or take out loans to purchase equipment, managers scan their economic environments for signs of significant change. Unfortunately, the economic statistics that managers rely on when making these decisions are notoriously poor predictors of *future* economic activity. The Organization for Economic Cooperation and Development (OECD), an influential, but independent non-profit organization which works with governments to improve economic and social well-being, regularly publishes country economic forecasts. Over the last 7 years, however, the OECD found that its forecasts were consistently overly optimistic and wrong.[15] So a manager who hired ten more employees because OECD forecasts data suggested future growth could very well have had to lay off those workers when forecasted economic growth did not occur.

the way it conducts day-to-day business. Yum! Brands first entered China in the late 1980s with its KFC and Pizza Hut restaurants. As the Chinese economy boomed and wealthier Chinese consumers began spending their growing discretionary income on fast food, Yum! Brands sales grew exponentially. By 2012, KFC's and Pizza Hut's Chinese sales accounted for half of Yum's global revenue. During that time, Yum relied on Chinese growth to drive overall sales and profits, and therefore made few changes to its restaurants or its menus. In the last few years, however, China's economy has cooled off, numerous competitors have entered China, building new restaurants and bringing a wider variety of menu options, especially healthier foods. Finally, because of an avian flu outbreak in spring 2013, Chinese consumers began eating much less poultry. Together, these changes have directly affected and reduced Yum! Brands' Chinese sales by 16%.[14]

The specific environment, which will be discussed in detail in Section 3-3 of this chapter, includes customers, competitors, suppliers, industry regulation, and advocacy groups.

Because economic statistics can be poor predictors, some managers try to predict future economic activity by keeping track of business confidence. **Business confidence indices** show how confident actual managers are about future business growth. For example, the Conference Board's CEO Confidence Index is a quarterly survey of 100 CEOs in large companies across a variety of different industries that examines attitudes regarding future growth in the economy or particular industries.[16] Another widely cited measure is the Small Business Research Board's Business Confidence Index, which asks 500 small-business owners and managers to express their optimism (or pessimism) about future business sales and prospects.[17] Managers often prefer business confidence indices to economic statistics because they know that other managers make business decisions that are in line with their expectations concerning the economy's future. So if the Conference Board or Small Business Research Board business confidence indices are dropping, a manager might decide against hiring new employees, increasing production, or taking out additional loans to expand the business.

3-2b Technological Component

Technology is the knowledge, tools, and techniques used to transform inputs (raw materials, information, and so on) into outputs (products and services). For example, the inputs of authors, editors, and artists (knowledge) and the use of equipment like computers and printing presses (technology) transformed paper, ink, and glue (raw materials) into this book (the finished product). In the case of a service company such as an airline, the technology consists of equipment, including airplanes, repair tools, and computers, as well as the knowledge of mechanics, ticketers, and flight crews. The output is the service of transporting people from one place to another.

Changes in technology can help companies provide better products or produce their products more efficiently. Although technological changes can benefit a business, they can also threaten it. Companies must embrace new technology and find effective ways to use it to improve their products and services or decrease costs. If they don't, they will lose out to those companies that do.

3-2c Sociocultural Component

The sociocultural component of the general environment refers to the demographic characteristics, general behavior, attitudes, and beliefs of people in a particular society. Sociocultural changes and trends influence organizations in two important ways.

First, changes in demographic characteristics, such as the number of people with particular skills or the growth of or decline in the number of people with particular population characteristics (marital status, age, gender, ethnicity) affect how companies staff their businesses. Married women with children are much more likely to work today than they were four decades ago, as illustrated in Exhibit 3.3. In 1960, only 18.6 percent of women with children under the age of six and 39 percent of women with children between the ages of six and seventeen worked. By 2010, those percentages had risen to 61.6 percent and 76.7 percent, respectively.

Second, sociocultural changes in behavior, attitudes, and beliefs also affect the demand for a business's products and services. For example, European car sales are at

Business confidence indices indices that show managers' level of confidence about future business growth

Technology the knowledge, tools, and techniques used to transform inputs into outputs

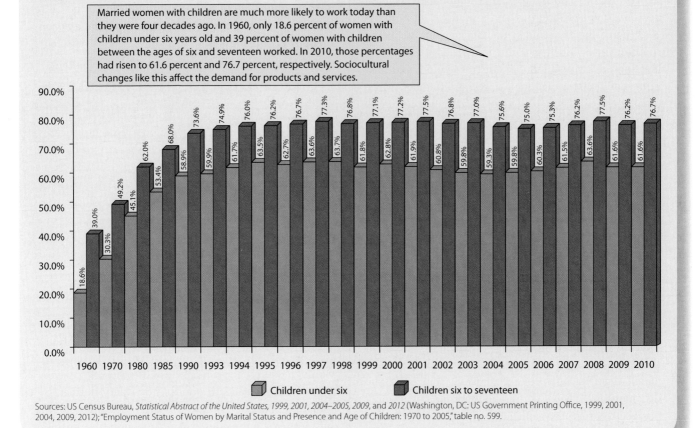

Exhibit 3.3
Demographics: Percentage of Married Women (with Children) Who Work

Married women with children are much more likely to work today than they were four decades ago. In 1960, only 18.6 percent of women with children under six years old and 39 percent of women with children between the ages of six and seventeen worked. In 2010, those percentages had risen to 61.6 percent and 76.7 percent, respectively. Sociocultural changes like this affect the demand for products and services.

Children under six   Children six to seventeen

Sources: US Census Bureau, *Statistical Abstract of the United States, 1999, 2001, 2004–2005, 2009*, and *2012* (Washington, DC: US Government Printing Office, 1999, 2001, 2004, 2009, 2012); "Employment Status of Women by Marital Status and Presence and Age of Children: 1970 to 2005," table no. 599.

their lowest point in two decades, 30% below 1990 levels. Europe's driving-age population, having peaked in 2011, is shrinking because of declining birth rates. Jean-Marc Gales, who heads an industry lobbying group for European auto suppliers, said, "Demographics . . . are not positive for most European countries."[18] Demographics alone could reduce European auto sales by 400,000 cars a year. European attitudes toward car ownership are also changing. Angus Ross, a Brit who lives in Paris, said, "Owning a car just isn't so important for my generation." With extensive public transportation in Europe, it's easier to get buy without a car. Likewise, Europe's economy remains weak, so a larger percentage of Europeans are without jobs, and those with jobs are more cautious with their spending. Indeed, forty-one year-old Sergio Felice, a Barcelona bank consultant, says he doesn't plan to buy a car until he's in his 60s. "I prefer to put the money I don't spend on a car in a retirement plan." Instead, he uses a motor cycle and rents cars for weekend trips. That way, he says, "I still get to have a car whenever I want."

3-2d Political/Legal Component

The political/legal component of the general environment includes the legislation, regulations, and court decisions that govern and regulate business behavior. New laws and regulations continue to impose additional responsibilities on companies. Unfortunately, many managers are unaware of these new responsibilities. For example, under the 1991 Civil Rights Act (http://www.eeoc.gov/policy/cra91.html), if an employee is sexually harassed by anyone at work (a supervisor, a coworker, or even a customer), the company—not just the harasser—is potentially liable for damages, attorneys' fees, and back pay.[19] Under the Family and Medical Leave Act (http://www.dol.gov /dol/topic/benefits-leave/fmla.htm), employees who have been on the job one year are guaranteed twelve weeks of unpaid leave per year to tend to their own illnesses or to their elderly parents, a newborn baby, or a newly adopted child. Employees are guaranteed the same job, pay, and benefits when they return to work.[20]

Many managers are also unaware of the potential legal risks associated with traditional managerial decisions about recruiting, hiring, and firing employees. Increasingly, businesses and managers are being sued for negligent hiring and supervision, defamation, invasion of privacy, emotional distress, fraud, and misrepresentation during employee recruitment.[21] More than 14,000 suits for wrongful termination (unfairly firing employees) are filed each year.[22] In fact, wrongful termination lawsuits increased by 77 percent during the 1990s.[23] Likewise, Equal Employment Opportunity Commission filings alleging wrongful discharge increased from 39,000 in 2005 to 55,000 in 2010.[24] One in four employers will at some point be sued for wrongful termination. It can cost $300,000 to settle such a case once it goes to court, but employers lose 50% to 70% of court cases[25], and the former employee is awarded, on average, $1 million or more.[26] On the other hand, employers who settle before going to court typically pay just $10,000 to $100,000 per case.[27]

Not everyone agrees that companies' legal risks are too severe. Indeed, many believe that the government should do more to regulate and restrict business behavior and that it should be easier for average citizens to sue dishonest or negligent corporations. From a managerial perspective, the best medicine against legal risk is prevention. As a manager, it is your responsibility to educate yourself about the laws, regulations, and potential lawsuits that could affect your business. Failure to do so may put you and your company at risk of sizable penalties, fines, or legal charges.

3-3 SPECIFIC ENVIRONMENT

As you just learned, changes in any sector of the general environment (economic, technological, sociocultural, and political/legal) eventually affect most organizations. Each organization also has a specific environment that is unique to that firm's industry and directly affects the way it conducts day-to-day business. For instance, if your customers decide to use another product, your main competitor cuts prices 10 percent, your best supplier can't deliver raw materials, federal regulators mandate reductions in pollutants in your industry, or environmental groups accuse your company of selling unsafe products, the impact from the specific environment on your business is immediate.

*Let's examine how the **3-3a customer, 3-3b competitor, 3-3c supplier, 3-3d industry regulation,** and **3-3e advocacy group components of the specific environment affect businesses.***

3-3a Customer Component

Customers purchase products and services. Companies cannot exist without customer support. Monitoring customers' changing wants and needs is critical to business success. There are two basic strategies for monitoring customers: reactive and proactive.

Reactive customer monitoring involves identifying and addressing customer trends and problems after they occur. One reactive strategy is to listen closely to customer complaints and respond to customer concerns. **Listen360** is a company that helps businesses monitor customer satisfaction and complaints by contacting their customers and asking two questions, "How likely are you to recommend this business?" followed by an open-ended question to explain why. Customer responses fall into three categories: "promoters," who would recommend the business to others; "passives," who are neither negative nor positive; and "detractors," unhappy customers who would not recommend the business. When customers are unhappy, the business receives a report detailing what products and services the customer purchased, what it would cost the company if it lost that customer's business, and a "voice of the customer" report that scans the answers to the open-ended question for key words about specific likes, dislikes, and concerns. At Macaroni Grill, an Italian restaurant chain, thanks to Listen360, servers now know whether returning customers are promoters, passives, or detractors, and can take specific actions to ensure great service and food.[28]

Companies that respond quickly to customer letters of complaint (i.e., reactive customer monitoring) are viewed much more favorably than companies that are slow to respond or never respond.[29] In particular, studies have shown that when a company sends a follow-up letter to thank the customer for writing, offers a sincere, specific response to the complaint (not a form letter, but an explanation of how the problem will be handled), and offers a small gift, coupons, or a refund to make up for the problem, customers are much more likely to purchase products or services again from that company.[30]

Proactive monitoring of customers means identifying and addressing customer needs, trends, and issues *before* they occur. Cable TV's *The Weather Channel* forecasts weather worldwide. But it changed its name to *The Weather Co.* to reflect its growing use of 75 years of weather data to predict consumer needs and behaviors *before* they occur. CEO David Kenny says, "People generally check the weather because they're planning to do something. We are getting better at knowing the kind of things people will be planning based on where and when they are checking the weather and what the weather is."[31] Michaels, a nationwide arts and crafts chain, planned to advertise on The Weather Co.'s web site and TV channel on rainy days, on which it believed customers would be more likely to buy and then do arts and crafts projects. WeatherFX, the Weather Co.'s data analytic unit, examined daily sales for each Michaels store, which it then combined with corresponding weather data. Instead of sales increasing on rainy days, WeatherFX found that sales increased three days before. In other words, people bought arts and crafts at Michaels to have something to do before rainy weather arrived. This kind of proactive monitoring has proven so valuable that WeatherFX now accounts for half of the Weather Co.'s advertising revenue.[32]

3-3b Competitor Component

Competitors are companies in the same industry that sell similar products or services to customers. Ford, Toyota, Honda, Nissan, Hyundai, and Kia all compete for automobile customers. NBC, ABC, CBS, and Fox (along with hundreds of cable channels) compete for TV viewers' attention. McDonald's, Burger King, Wendy's, Hardee's, Chick-fil-A, and a host of others compete for fast-food customers' dollars. Often the difference between business success and failure comes down to whether your company is doing a better job of satisfying customer wants and needs than the competition. Consequently, companies need to keep close track of what their competitors are doing. To do this, managers perform a **competitive analysis,** which involves deciding who your competitors are, anticipating competitors' moves, and determining competitors' strengths and weaknesses.

Surprisingly, managers often do a poor job of identifying potential competitors because they tend to focus on only two or three well-known competitors with similar goals and resources.[33]

Another mistake managers may make when analyzing the competition is to underestimate potential competitors' capabilities. When this happens, managers don't take the steps they should to continue to improve their products

or services. The result can be significant decreases in both market share and profits. For decades, TV viewers had two options—watch the four or five channels that could be picked up with an antenna or purchase a package from a local cable supplier, which almost always operated as a local monopoly. Then, a third choice came along—buy a package from a satellite provider, like DirecTV or DISH Network. In the last five years, however, the television marketplace has changed dramatically and cable TV companies now find themselves surrounded by competitors. Netflix started the process by offering an inexpensive DVD-by-mail service, which began eroding cable TV dominance. Over the last four years, however, online content providers and streaming services and devices like Netflix, Hulu, YouTube, iTunes, Roku, Apple TV, and Amazon Instant Video allow consumers to watch their favorite TV shows and movies at a fraction of the cost of a monthly cable subscription. Cable companies have been slow to respond to this rapid change in competition, however, and in 2010, for the first time since cable TV was introduced, suffered a net loss of cable subscribers. Roughly 1 million consumers canceled cable subscriptions in 2013.

Competitors companies in the same industry that sell similar products or services to customers

Competitive analysis a process for monitoring the competition that involves identifying competition, anticipating their moves, and determining their strengths and weaknesses

External Pressures

According to a recent survey by Accenture of C-level executives, the following top five external pressures are leading companies to give more emphasis to risk management.

1. Legal risks

2. Business risks

3. Regulatory requirements

4. Market risks

5. Credit risks/Operational risks/Strategic risks [tie]

As a result, 98 percent of executives surveyed said they are giving a higher priority to risk management and incorporating it more closely into decision-making.

Source: "Accenture 2013 Global Risk Management Study: Risk management for an era of greater uncertainty," *Accenture*. September 17, 2013. accessed April 11, 2014. http://www.accenture.com/us-en/Pages/insight-global-risk-management -study-2013-era-greater-uncertainty.aspx.

And, according to research firm TDG, the number of cable subscribers is estimated to fall by another 6 million subscribers over the next five years.[34]

3-3c Supplier Component

Suppliers are companies that provide material, human, financial, and informational resources to other companies. US Steel buys iron ore from suppliers to make steel products. When IBM sells a mainframe computer, it also provides support staff, engineers, and other technical consultants to the company that bought the computer. If you're shopping for desks, chairs, and office supplies, chances are that Office Depot will be glad to help your business open a revolving charge account to pay for your purchases. When a clothing manufacturer has spent $100,000 to purchase new high-pressure water drills to cut shirt and pant patterns to precise sizes, the water drill manufacturer, as part of the purchase, will usually train the workers to use the machinery.

A key factor influencing the impact and quality of the relationship between companies and their suppliers is how dependent they are on each other.[35] **Supplier dependence** is the degree to which a company relies on that supplier because of the importance of the supplier's product to the company and the difficulty of finding other sources for that product. Even though Apple and Samsung are fierce competitors when it comes to smart phones and computer tablets, and have sued and countersued each other over alleged patent infringements, for over a decade Apple has been highly dependent on Samsung for the computer chips, flash drives, and high resolution touch screens in iPhones and iPads. Stanford University professor Michael Marks said that Apple's choices for alternative suppliers, "aren't good, which is why they keep buying from Samsung."[36]

Buyer dependence is the degree to which a supplier relies on a buyer because of the importance of that buyer to the supplier's sales and the difficulty of finding other buyers of its products. While Samsung is one of Apple's key suppliers (i.e., supplier dependence), Apple, in turn, is Samsung's key buyer of computer components. Apple purchase of $10 billion of chips, flash memory drives, and touch screens in 2013 represented 17% of Samsung's $59.13 billion components business.

A high degree of buyer or seller dependence can lead to **opportunistic behavior,** in which one party benefits at the expense of the other. Apple was concerned with the possibility of opportunistic behavior when it stopped buying touch screens from Samsung in 2010. Technology analyst Hiroshi Hayase explained, "If you buy screens from your competitor, you will be sharing some key information on your next product."[37] Consequently, Apple shifted its touch screen orders to Sharp and Toshiba. This is also why Apple began working with Toshiba in 2009, to build flash memory for iPads and iPhones, and with TSMC (Taiwan Semiconductor Manufacturing Company) in 2010, to build computer chips. As of June 2014, Apple only purchases 10% of its flash memory from Samsung. TSMC started chip production for Apple in 2014, which will allow Apple to significantly reduce its reliance on Samsung over the next few years.

In contrast to opportunistic behavior, **relationship behavior** focuses on establishing a mutually beneficial, long-term relationship between buyers and suppliers.[38] DreamWorks Studios, which makes films and TV shows, has had a long-term strategic relationship with Hewlett-Packard (H-P), which makes computers and software. DreamWorks, the buyer, advises H-P, the supplier, on the advanced servers and data management it needs to produce animated films, or even traditional films, which today contain significant portions of computer generated images.[39] The average DreamWorks film is created using 300 graphics work stations, 60 million rendering hours (a rendering hour is an hour of computer time used to process an image), the simultaneous use of 17,000 computer core chips, and over 200 terabytes of storage.[40] In fact, the DreamWorks animation data center in Redwood City, California is run completely on H-P systems.

AP Images

Suppliers companies that provide material, human, financial, and informational resources to other companies

Supplier dependence the degree to which a company relies on a supplier because of the importance of the supplier's product to the company and the difficulty of finding other sources of that product

Buyer dependence the degree to which a supplier relies on a buyer because of the importance of that buyer to the supplier and the difficulty of finding other buyers for its products

Opportunistic behavior a transaction in which one party in the relationship benefits at the expense of the other

Relationship behavior the establishment of mutually beneficial, long-term exchanges between buyers and suppliers

3-3d Industry Regulation Component

Whereas the political/legal component of the general environment affects all businesses, the **industry regulation** component consists of regulations and rules that govern the practices and procedures of specific industries, businesses, and professions. To combat rising rates of obesity, New York City Mayor Michael Bloomberg passed a controversial new law requiring restaurants, movie theaters, and other food service locations in the city to limit the size of sugary drinks, such as soda, energy drinks, and even fruit smoothies, to no more than 16 ounces. Josh Lebowitz, owner of New York City's Brother Jimmy's BBQ, said, "Everything we do is big, so serving it in quaint little 16-ounce soda cups is going to look kind of odd. [But] as long as they keep allowing us to serve beer in glasses larger than 16 ounces, we'll be OK."[41]

Regulatory agencies affect businesses by creating and enforcing rules and regulations to protect consumers, workers, or society as a whole. For example, the US Department of Agriculture and the US Food and Drug Administration regulate the safety of seafood (as well as meat and poultry) through the science-based Hazard Analysis and Critical Control Points program. Seafood processors are required to identify hazards (toxins, chemicals, pesticides, and decomposition) that could cause the fish they process to be unsafe. They must also establish critical control points to control hazards both inside and outside their fish-processing plants and then establish monitoring, corrective action, and verification procedures to certify that the fish they process is safe to consume.[42]

The nearly 100 federal agencies and regulatory commissions can affect almost any kind of business. For example, when product testers at the Coca-Cola Company

> **Industry regulation** regulations and rules that govern the business practices and procedures of specific industries, businesses, and professions

Federal Regulatory Agencies and Commissions

Consumer Product Safety Commission
Reduces risk of injuries and deaths associated with consumer products, sets product safety standards, enforces product recalls, and provides consumer education **http://www.cpsc.gov**

Department of Labor
Collects employment statistics and administers labor laws concerning safe working conditions, minimum hourly wages and overtime pay, employment discrimination, and unemployment insurance **http://www.dol.gov**

Environmental Protection Agency
Reduces and controls pollution through research, monitoring, standard setting, and enforcement activities **http://www.epa.gov**

Equal Employment Opportunity Commission
Promotes fair hiring and promotion practices **http://www.eeoc.gov**

Federal Communications Commission
Regulates interstate and international communications by radio, television, wire, satellite, and cable **http://www.fcc.gov**

Federal Reserve System
As the nation's central bank, controls interest rates and money supply and monitors the US banking system to produce a growing economy with stable prices **http://www.federalreserve.gov**

Federal Trade Commission
Restricts unfair methods of business competition and misleading advertising and enforces consumer protection laws **http://www.ftc.gov**

Food and Drug Administration
Protects nation's health by making sure food, drugs, and cosmetics are safe **http://www.fda.gov**

National Labor Relations Board
Monitors union elections and stops companies from engaging in unfair labor practices **http://www.nlrb.gov**

Occupational Safety and Health Administration
Saves lives, prevents injuries, and protects the health of workers **http://www.osha.gov**

Securities and Exchange Commission
Protects investors in the bond and stock markets, guarantees access to information on publicly traded securities, and regulates firms that sell securities or give investment advice **http://www.sec.gov**

discovered trace amounts of a fungicide in orange juice imported from Brazil, the Food and Drug Administration temporarily banned importation of orange juice shipments so they could be tested for safety.[43]

3-3e Advocacy Groups

Advocacy groups are groups of concerned citizens who band together to try to influence the business practices of specific industries, businesses, and professions. The members of a group generally share the same point of view on a particular issue. For example, environmental advocacy groups might try to get manufacturers to reduce smokestack pollution emissions. Unlike the industry regulation component of the specific environment, advocacy groups cannot force organizations to change their practices. Nevertheless, they can use a number of techniques to try to influence companies, including public communications, media advocacy, web pages, blogs, and product boycotts.

The **public communications** approach relies on *voluntary* participation by the news media and the advertising industry to send out an advocacy group's message. Hydraulic fracturing, better known as fracking, is a process by which natural gas or petroleum is extracted from a layer of underground rocks. Proponents argue that fracking dramatically increases oil and gas supplies, lowers costs, and reduces dependence on foreign oil. Anti-fracking advocacy groups, such as **Artists Against Fracking** (**AAF**), however, argue that it contaminates groundwater, causes air pollution, and economically harms people who live near the mines. AAF was started by Sean Lennon and Yoko Ono to persuade New York Governor Andrew Cuomo to ban fracking in New York state. In addition to roadside billboards, petitions, and television ads, AAF released a music video called "Don't Frack My Mother," starring celebrities Susan Sarandon, Joseph Gordon-Levitt, the Black Keys, and Maggie Gyllenhaal.[44]

Media advocacy is much more aggressive than the public communications approach. A **media advocacy** approach typically involves framing the group's concerns as public issues (affecting everyone); exposing questionable, exploitative, or unethical practices; and creating controversy that is likely to receive extensive news coverage.

A **product boycott** is a tactic in which an advocacy group actively tries to persuade consumers not to purchase a company's product or service. Food in many Muslim

Advocacy groups concerned citizens who band together to try to influence the business practices of specific industries, businesses, and professions

Public communications an advocacy group tactic that relies on voluntary participation by the news media and the advertising industry to get the advocacy group's message out

Media advocacy an advocacy group tactic that involves framing issues as public issues; exposing questionable, exploitative, or unethical practices; and forcing media coverage by buying media time or creating controversy that is likely to receive extensive news coverage

Product boycott an advocacy group tactic that involves protesting a company's actions by persuading consumers not to purchase its product or service

DOING THE RIGHT THING

Walmart's "Three Strikes" Is Out for Safety; Now It's Zero Tolerance

Since Walmart clothing was found in a Bangladesh factory where a fire killed 112 workers, Walmart has adopted a much stricter policy on global sourcing standards. Formerly, Walmart had used a three-strikes approach, but after the fire, the retailer warned suppliers that there would be zero-tolerance going forward. It also said it would immediately server ties with any organizations that subcontracted to other factories without Walmart's knowledge. The retailer said it had thought the factory where the fire occurred was no longer making Walmart's clothes. It began posting names of factories that suppliers are not allowed to contract with as well as requiring pre-approval audits for new factories.

Source: S. Banjo, "Wal-Mart Toughens Supplier Policies," *The Wall Street Journal*, January 21, 2013. accessed April 11, 2014. http://online.wsj.com/news/articles /SB10001424127887323301104578256183164905720?KEYWORDS=supplier+relationship&mg=reno64-wsj.

countries is routinely tested by government agencies to make sure it is Halal, or free of traces of pork, alcohol, or other foods not allowed under Islamic law. So when the Malaysian Ministry of Heath reported that traces of pork were found in Cadbury Dairy Milk Hazelnut and Cadbury Dairy Milk Roast Almond bars, the Muslim Consumers Association of Malaysia (MCAM) called for a boycott. MCAM's research head, Sheikh Abdul Kareem Khadaied, said, "This is an issue that cuts across religion. It affects the vegetarians as much as it affects the Muslims."[45] Subsequent tests revealed no traces of pork in Cadbury products, but MCAM's Sheikh Abdul Kareem Khadaied still insisted on a boycott until the discrepancy between the tests was resolved.[46]

3-4 MAKING SENSE OF CHANGING ENVIRONMENTS

In Chapter 1, you learned that managers are responsible for making sense of their business environments. As our discussions of the general and specific environments have indicated, however, making sense of business environments is not an easy task.

Because external environments can be dynamic, confusing, and complex, managers use a three-step process to make sense of the changes in their external environments: 3-4a environmental scanning, 3-4b interpreting environmental factors, and 3-4c acting on threats and opportunities.

3-4a Environmental Scanning

Environmental scanning involves searching the environment for important events or issues that might affect an organization. Managers scan the environment to stay up to date on important factors in their industry and to reduce uncertainty. They want to know if demand will increase, prices for key components will rise, and whether competitors sales are rising or falling. Which is why Google paid $500 million to buy Skybox, a company that captures high resolution satellite images. By 2016, Skybox will have six dedicated satellites that take complete images of the earth twice daily. By 2014, it will have 24 dedicated satellites that do so three times a day and can provide real-time video of trucks moving down highways. The timeliness and resolution of its images will be so good that when traveling you'll be able to use Google maps street view see if you left the front porch light on at your house. That also means Walmart's sales can be accurately predicted by counting the number of cars in its parking lots. Want to know when the next iPhone will be release? You'll be able to monitor the number of trucks coming and going from Foxconn factories in Taiwan, where they're manufactured. Co-founder Dan Berkenstock says, "We think we are

Environmental scanning searching the environment for important events or issues that might affect an organization

SSL Headquarters

Skybox Headquarters

AP Images/PR NEWSWIRE

going to fundamentally change humanity's understanding of the economic landscape on a daily basis."[47]

Organizational strategies also affect environmental scanning. In other words, managers pay close attention to trends and events that are directly related to their company's ability to compete in the marketplace.[48] With nearly 70 percent of China's water sources polluted from industry and agriculture, consumers are understandably concerned about drinking tap water. Furthermore, water purified at Chinese treatment plants is often recontaminated by hazardous materials when transported to homes. According to Hope Lee, an analyst with Euromonitor, "You don't dare drink the tap water in China." China's water problem, however, represents a business opportunity for Nestlé's bottled water business, especially with sales flat in North America and Europe. Chinese sales of bottled water, by contrast, are expected to grow significantly from $9 billion in 2012 to $16 billion in 2017. Therefore, Nestlé is rapidly expanding in China, selling water in five-gallon jugs, often through company-owned stores that provide free delivery to consumers' homes. Nestlé's Chinese sales have jumped 27 percent from the previous year.[49]

Finally, environmental scanning is important because it contributes to organizational performance. Environmental scanning helps managers detect environmental changes and problems before they become organizational crises.[50] Furthermore, companies whose CEOs do more environmental scanning have higher profits.[51] CEOs in better-performing firms scan their firms' environments more frequently and scan more key factors in their environments in more depth and detail than do CEOs in poorer-performing firms.[52]

3-4b Interpreting Environmental Factors

After scanning, managers determine what environmental events and issues mean to the organization. Typically, managers view environmental events and issues as either threats or opportunities. When managers interpret environmental events as threats, they take steps to protect the company from further harm. For example, the influx of food trucks in major cities is prompting established, brick-and-mortar restaurants to ask cities to restrict where and when the food trucks can do business. Camy Silva, who co-owns El Gaucho Luca's Cafe in Las Vegas, complains, "They come during our busiest hours and park in front of us." "We spend a lot on advertising and promotions to bring people downtown, and the food trucks benefit from that," says her husband and co-owner Pablo Silva. Restaurant owners also complain

that food trucks play loud music and take up parking spots for their customers. As a result of restaurant owners' complaints, Chicago now requires food trucks to park at least 200 feet from restaurants. That, in turn, prompts complaints from food truck owners like Amy Le, who owns the Duck N Roll food truck. "The 200-foot buffer prohibits me from competing. It is a free market. Let the consumers decide when and where they want to eat."[53]

By contrast, when managers interpret environmental events as opportunities, they consider strategic alternatives for taking advantage of those events to improve company performance. The Panama Canal, open since 1914, handles 5% of the world's shipping traffic. Ships traveling from San Francisco to New York City, or from Asia to the U.S. east coast, sail 8,000 fewer miles compared to rounding Cape Horn at the southern tip of South America. While wide and deep enough to handle today's so-called Panamax ships with 5,000 20-foot TEU (twenty-foot equivalent unit) containers, the Panama Canal is losing business because the shipping industry is changing to larger Post Panamax ships carrying 8,000 to 18,000 TEUs. Post Panamax ships are much more fuel efficient and save on canal charges, too, which can run as much as $450,000 per ship.[54] For example, instead of sending two 4,500 TEU ships through the Panama Canal to transport goods from Asia to the U.S. east coast, the Maersk Line will send one Post Panamax ship loaded with 9,000 TEUs through the Suez Canal.[55] Faced with the loss of a significant amount of shipping traffic (Post Panamax ships will handle 65% of sea transportation by 2030), the Panama Canal Authority District began a $5.25 billion expansion to handle ships—ships with up to 13,000 TEUs. When the canal completes the addition of a parallel 50-foot wide canal in mid-2015, the Panama Canal will instantly double its cargo shipping capacity.[56]

3-4c Acting on Threats and Opportunities

After scanning for information on environmental events and issues and interpreting them as threats or opportunities, managers have to decide how to respond to these

Exhibit 3.4
Cognitive Maps

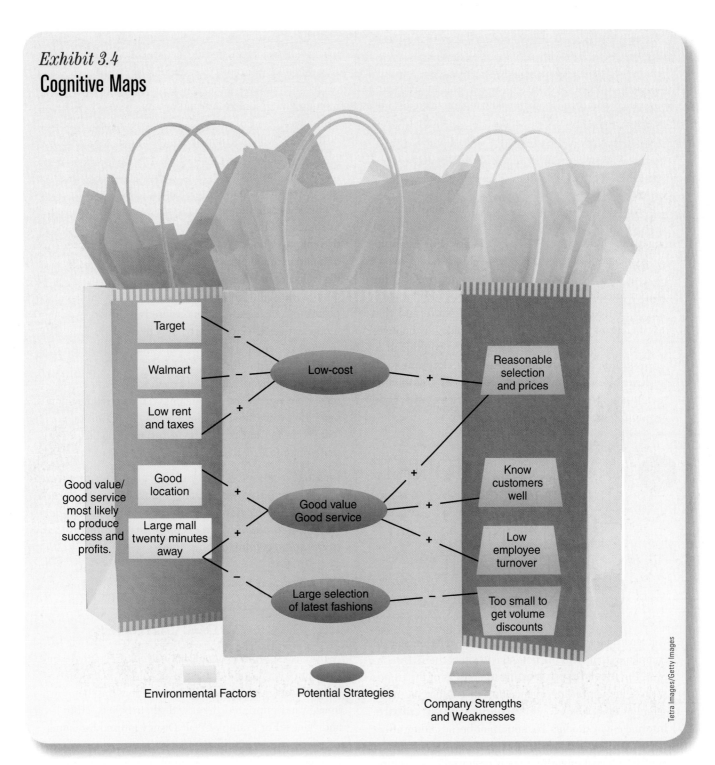

Environmental Factors · Potential Strategies · Company Strengths and Weaknesses

Tetra Images/Getty Images

environmental factors. Deciding what to do under conditions of uncertainty is always difficult. Managers can never be completely confident that they have all the information they need or that they correctly understand the information they have.

Because it is impossible to comprehend all the factors and changes, managers often rely on simplified models of external environments called cognitive maps. **Cognitive maps** summarize the perceived relationships between environmental factors and possible organizational actions. For example, the cognitive map shown in Exhibit 3.4 represents a small clothing-store owner's interpretation of her business

Cognitive maps graphic depictions of how managers believe environmental factors relate to possible organizational actions

environment. The map shows three kinds of variables. The first variables, shown as rectangles, are environmental factors, such as a Walmart or a large mall twenty minutes away. The second variables, shown in ovals, are potential actions that the store owner might take, such as a low-cost strategy; a good-value, good-service strategy; or a "large selection of the latest fashions" strategy. The third variables, shown as trapezoids, are company strengths, such as low employee turnover, and weaknesses, such as small size.

The plus and minus signs on the map indicate whether the manager believes there is a positive or negative relationship between variables. For example, the manager believes that a low-cost strategy won't work because Walmart and Target are nearby. Offering a large selection of the latest fashions would not work either—not with the small size of the store and that large nearby mall. However, the manager believes that a good-value, good-service strategy would lead to success and profits because of the store's low employee turnover, good knowledge of customers, reasonable selection of clothes at reasonable prices, and good location.

3-5 ORGANIZATIONAL CULTURES: CREATION, SUCCESS, AND CHANGE

We have been looking at trends and events outside of companies that have the potential to affect them. By contrast, the **internal environment** consists of the trends and events *within* an organization that affect the management, employees, and **organizational culture**. Internal environments are important because they affect what people think, feel, and do at work. The key component in internal environments is organizational culture, or the set of key values, beliefs, and attitudes shared by members of the organization.

Internal environment the events and trends inside an organization that affect management, employees, and organizational culture

Organizational culture the values, beliefs, and attitudes shared by organizational members

Under Armour, the sporting apparel and accessories maker, got its start two decades ago when founder and CEO Kevin Plank, a former college football player and special teams captain, sewed shorts and shirts himself in his grandmother's Baltimore, Maryland, basement. Today, Under Armour is a fast-growing—sales increased 27 percent in 2013—$2.3 billion company that competes with Nike, Reebok, and Adidas. One of the keys to its meteoric rise may be its "faster-stronger-better" internal culture. Plank says, "We as a company don't sleep much. We work harder. We have a commitment that I think would be exhausting to someone else." To sustain that hard-driving, competitive culture, Under Armour builds camaraderie and a team orientation among employees. New employees are given big welcome breakfasts. Staff members are treated to outdoor movie nights, tuition reimbursement, and discounted tickets to sporting events, and there is a club for working mothers that offers support and advice. Says Plank, "I manage the company much like a team. Coming out of school and starting the business, sales and marketing were offense, and manufacturing was defense, and finance and operations were like special teams. What I've come to find out is that when the company is the best, it's not that one team is playing and another team is winning on the side, it's that everyone is on the field together."[57]

Let's take a closer look at 3-5a how organizational cultures are created and maintained, 3-5b the characteristics of successful organizational cultures, and 3-5c how companies can accomplish the difficult task of changing organizational cultures.

3-5a Creation and Maintenance of Organizational Cultures

A primary source of organizational culture is the company founder. Founders like Walt Disney (Disney) and Steve Jobs (Apple) created organizations in their own images and imprinted them with their beliefs, attitudes, and values. For example, Walt Disney infused his animation studio with a culture of innovation and experimentation, which lead to the creation of new technologies and filmmaking techniques.[58] Dr. Ed Catmull, co-founder of Pixar Animation Studios, and President of Walt Disney and Pixar Animation Studios, said if you consider, "What happened when Walt Disney was starting his company [in 1923], you realize that at that time, the technology of filmmaking and animation was brand new. At that time, it [meaning Disney's animation] was high technology and it was pretty magical. Every time [Disney Studios created animated films] they were inventing something new.

You had color, sound, blue-screen matting, multiple-plane cameras, gyrography—all these things were brought in and absorbed and driven by the studio, so the technological change was an integral part of the mind set [at Disney]."[59] How are values, attitudes, and beliefs sustained in organizational cultures? Answer: stories and heroes.

People tell **organizational stories** to make sense of organizational events and changes and to emphasize culturally consistent assumptions, decisions, and actions.[60] Andreessen Horowitz (AH) is a venture capital (VC) firm that invests millions in high potential technology startups. AH's co-founders, Mark Andreessen and Ben Horowitz have significant experience—and success—starting high-tech companies that have sold for nearly $2 billion. Horowitz said, "When we started Andreessen Horowitz, we knew that one of the most frustrating things for entrepreneurs is that VCs do not respect their time. As entrepreneurs, every time we'd visit a VC [trying to secure funding for our companies], we'd wait in the lobby for 30 to 45 minutes. So at the core of the firm, we wanted a cultural tenet to be respect for the entrepreneur and the entrepreneurial process. But how do you get that into people's minds? The mechanism I came up with was to tell VCs that if you are late for a meeting with an entrepreneur, then the fine is $10 a minute. That is a very big fine. It is shocking to people who have to pay it. And that's the point. Because every time somebody pays a fine, *we get to tell the story* of why the person is paying so much money."[61]

A second way in which organizational culture is sustained is by recognizing and celebrating heroes. By definition, **organizational heroes** are organizational people admired for their qualities and achievements within the organization. Francisco D'Souza, CEO of Cognizant, an information technology firm with 170,000 employees, explains that, "Culture gets passed along not by writing it down, but through the rituals you have in the organization, the legends you refer to, and the heroes of the organization. So we institutionalized a set of things to create rituals, heroes and legends"[62] How does Cognizant do that? By having each regional division name an associate of the year who heroically exemplifies the company's culture. Likewise, to broaden cultural recognition beyond individuals to key teams and groups, Cognizant has each division celebrate a project of the year. D'Souza explains that, "We rent stadiums around the world and bring all the employees and their families for a celebration, with entertainment and awards."[63]

3-5b Successful Organizational Cultures

Preliminary research shows that organizational culture is related to organizational success. As shown in Exhibit 3.5,

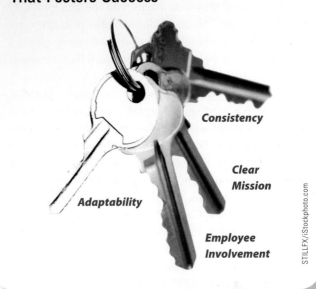

Exhibit 3.5
Keys to an Organizational Culture That Fosters Success

Consistency

Clear Mission

Adaptability

Employee Involvement

STILLFX/iStockphoto.com

cultures based on adaptability, involvement, a clear mission, and consistency can help companies achieve higher sales growth, return on assets, profits, quality, and employee satisfaction.[64]

Adaptability is the ability to notice and respond to changes in the organization's environment. Cultures need to reinforce important values and behaviors, but a culture becomes dysfunctional if it prevents change. One of the surest ways to do that is to discourage open discussion and disagreement. In cultures that promote higher levels of *employee involvement* in decision making, employees feel a greater sense of ownership and responsibility. Jim Whitehurst, the CEO of **Red Hat,** the world's largest producer of open source software, says, "To engage people, you listen to them and make sure the best ideas win." He does this by inviting employee involvement in key company decisions through something Red Hat calls Memo List. Whitehurst explains, "Basically it's just a giant email list where every employee is subscribed. Everyone can give feedback, share ideas, criticize ideas . . . just like with open-source software, the best ideas rise to the top.

Organizational stories stories told by organizational members to make sense of organizational events and changes and to emphasize culturally consistent assumptions, decisions, and actions

Organizational heroes people celebrated for their qualities and achievements within an organization

Problems are brought to light and other people can jump in to make suggestions and add detail." Memo List was used to great success to create Red Hat's mission statement. Over a five-month period, a draft of the statement was read, revised, debated, discussed, and dissected by employees until they were happy with the final product. Says Whitehurst, "All that dialogue makes your decisions better and makes execution a lot better. When employees are involved and feel they have been heard they are much more likely to execute well."[65]

Company mission is the business's purpose or reason for existing. In organizational cultures with a clear company mission, the organization's strategic purpose and direction are apparent to everyone in the company. When managers are uncertain about their business environments, the mission helps guide the discussions, decisions, and behavior of the people in the company. BPV Capital Management is a Knoxville, Tennessee mutual fund with 38 employees. Alluding to the common dream of owning a retirement home with wonderful weather and a great view, founder Mike West explains that "BPV" stands for "back porch vista" BPV exists "to help American families retire well." More specifically, its mission is, "To ensure that investors who work hard and save have the opportunity to retire comfortably, regardless of net worth." Says West, "Our values and the promise that we make to every advisor and investor are driven by that core ideology."[66]

Finally, in **consistent organizational cultures,** the company actively defines and teaches organizational values, beliefs, and attitudes (see box "At Eaton, Integration Starts Early"). Consistent with its code of conduct to "Do no harm to people. Protect the environment, and comply with all laws and regulations," when Royal Dutch Shell, the multinational energy company, buys smaller drilling companies, the first thing it does is shut down the drilling rigs for several weeks to retrain the workers in terms of safety and environmental procedures. J. R. Justus, Shell's general manager in Appalachia, says, "I don't think there's any question that the culture around safety has changed considerably since Shell came here. We've got a lot more technical resources to bring to bear than a smaller independent company would." In terms of Shell's improvements to environmental practices, Shell, unlike many smaller drilling

At Eaton, Integration Starts Early

When two companies merge, there is always the risk that the culture of one company will clash with the other, making it miserable for people to work together. As Alexander Cutler, CEO of diversified manufacturer Eaton, says, "Our rule has always been that no acquisition is better than a bad acquisition." Cutler would know too: since 2000, Eaton has acquired over 65 other companies. According to Cutler, assessment of cultural integration should start before the deal is finalized. Leadership styles and ethical standards should receive close attention. Once the deal is closed, Cutler is quick to work towards opening communication channels. The new employees will begin ethics training courses. Eaton representatives will visit sites of the acquired firm and begin discussions with management at the new firm about corporate values and operational processes. Cutler adds, "It's not a situation where the Eaton idea wins. We want to understand the best way to do things."

Source: J. Katz, "The Key to Corporate Cultures? Start Early," *IndustryWeek*, February 14, 2013. accessed April 14, 2014. http://www.industryweek.com /corporate-culture/key-merging-corporate-cultures-start-early?page=1.

companies, lines oil wells with steel pipe surrounded by cement, which fills the gaps between the pipe and surrounding earth, so that gas or fluids can't seep into rock layers or water sources. As a result, Shell is cited for environmental citations just 6.5 percent of the time compared to 14 percent for mid sized drillers and 17 percent for small ones.[67]

Having a consistent or strong organizational culture doesn't guarantee good company performance. When core beliefs are widely shared and strongly held, it is very difficult to bring about needed change. Consequently, companies with strong cultures tend to perform poorly when they need to adapt to dramatic changes in their external environments. Their consistency sometimes prevents them from adapting to those changes.[68]

3-5c Changing Organizational Cultures

As shown in Exhibit 3.6, organizational cultures exist on three levels.[69] On the first, or surface, level are the reflections of an organization's culture that can be seen and observed, such as symbolic artifacts (for example, dress codes and office layouts) and workers' and managers' behaviors. Next, just below the surface, are the values and beliefs expressed by people in the company. You can't see these values and beliefs, but they become clear

Exhibit 3.6
Three Levels of Organizational Culture

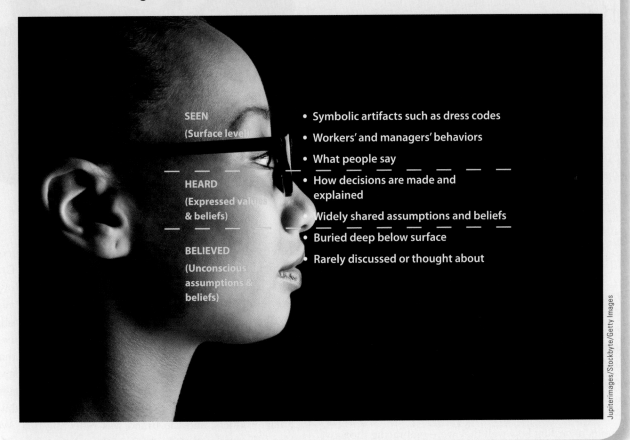

SEEN
(Surface level)

HEARD
(Expressed values & beliefs)

BELIEVED
(Unconscious assumptions & beliefs)

- Symbolic artifacts such as dress codes
- Workers' and managers' behaviors
- What people say
- How decisions are made and explained
- Widely shared assumptions and beliefs
- Buried deep below surface
- Rarely discussed or thought about

Jupiterimages/Stockbyte/Getty Images

if you carefully listen to what people say and observe how decisions are made or explained. Finally, unconsciously held assumptions and beliefs about the company are buried deep below the surface. These are the unwritten views and rules that are so strongly held and so widely shared that they are rarely discussed or even thought about unless someone attempts to change them or unknowingly violates them. Changing such assumptions and beliefs can be very difficult. Instead, managers should focus on the parts of the organizational culture they can control. These include observable surface-level items, such as workers' behaviors and symbolic artifacts, and expressed values and beliefs, which can be influenced through employee selection. Let's see how these can be used to change organizational cultures.

One way of changing a corporate culture is to use behavioral addition or behavioral substitution to establish new patterns of behavior among managers and employees. **Behavioral addition** is the process of having managers and employees perform a new behavior,

while **behavioral substitution** is having managers and employees perform a new behavior in place of another behavior. The key in both instances is to choose behaviors that are central to and symbolic of the old culture you're changing and the new culture that you want to create. When Bob Flexon became CEO of **Dynegy,** which provides wholesale energy to utilities, energy cooperatives, and municipalities, the company was losing hundreds of millions of dollars. So, he not only cut costs, he began changing the company culture by emphasizing new behaviors. The first move was to ditch his expansive corner office—with a $15,000 marble desk and Oriental

Behavioral addition the process of having managers and employees perform new behaviors that are central to and symbolic of the new organizational culture that a company wants to create

Behavioral substitution the process of having managers and employees perform new behaviors central to the new organizational culture in place of behaviors that were central to the old organizational culture

Breigouze/iStockphoto.com

rugs—for a 64-foot cubicle identical to those used by everyone else at Dynegy's new headquarters, which is now on a single floor in a cheaper building (resulting in annual savings of $5 million). In terms of culture, Flexon and his leadership team created a new set of expectations regarding management and employee behavior. To start, employees received their first performance appraisals in two years (i.e., behavioral addition), including judgments regarding how well they were embracing the new cultural norms of safety, accountability, and agility. Next, managers and employees were expected to "Be Here Now," which means no distractions when engaging with others. For example, chief administrative officer Carolyn Burke has told employees who are tapping on their smartphones in meetings, "Hey, be here now." Likewise, CEO Flexon has a "Be Here Now" plaque underneath his computer monitor to remind him to not read emails during phone calls (i.e., behavioral substitution).[70]

Another way in which managers can begin to change corporate culture is to change the **visible artifacts** of their old culture, such as the office design and layout, company dress code, and recipients (or nonrecipients) of company benefits and perks like stock options, personal parking spaces, or the private company dining room. In the 1990s, AOL was the dominant force among

Internet service and content providers. So many people had AOL accounts that its well-known "You've Got Mail" alert was the title of a Hollywood movie. However, intense competition from high-speed Internet providers, two decades of bad decisions, and a costly merger with and then split from Time Warner reduced it to a Silicon Valley dinosaur. AOL is trying to shed that image and create a new culture that emphasizes creativity, collaboration, and innovation. Brad Garlinghouse, former president of AOL, said, "AOL wasn't building great products, and the brand was reflecting that. We have to expunge the ghosts of AOL and start fresh." A key component of AOL's culture change is the tear down and complete redesign of offices in Palo Alto, California. Whereas its old offices had drab halls, cubicles, and high walls that limited employee interactions, the newly redesigned offices have an open design featuring a central space with glass-walled work rooms for team collaboration; round standalone rooms with opaque glass for quiet work that requires privacy and concentration; and public spaces with pool, Ping-Pong, and foosball tables; couches and chairs with laptop stands; and a cafeteria that's open 24/7. Consistent with its culture change, AOL also took the unusual move of opening up its redesigned offices to seventy-five employees from twenty-five start-up companies, who work with and share ideas with AOL's staffers. CEO Tim Armstrong said, "We really have tried to make our offices into centers of creativity where we can invite other people to come in and work for us. The opportunity is to take some of the world's best entrepreneurs and technologists and have them work in a deeply engaging place."[71]

Cultures can also be changed by hiring and selecting people with values and beliefs consistent with the

Visible artifacts visible signs of an organization's culture, such as the office design and layout, company dress code, and company benefits and perks, like stock options, personal parking spaces, or the private company dining room

company's desired culture. *Selection* is the process of gathering information about job applicants to decide who should be offered a job. As discussed in Chapter 11 on human resources, most selection instruments measure whether job applicants have the knowledge, skills, and abilities needed to succeed in their jobs. But companies are increasingly testing job applicants to determine how they fit with the company's desired culture (i.e., values and beliefs). In the last ten years, the Cleveland Browns football team has had only one season in which it won more than 6 games. During that time, the Browns had 7 different head coaches. When Mike Pettine became the head coach in spring 2014, he inherited a team with a culture marked by instability, losing, and inexperience; only four Browns' players had ever been to the playoffs. When he started signing new players for the upcoming season, a key qualification (in addition to talent) was experience on a team with a winning culture. Consistent with his goal of building that winning culture, five of the first seven players he signed had been to the playoffs, while three had played in the Super Bowl.[72]

The second step is to ensure that applicants fit with the culture by using selection tests, instruments, and exercises to measure these values and beliefs in job applicants. (See Chapter 11 for a complete review of applicant and managerial selection.) During the hiring process, Amazon uses a group of employees called "Bar Raisers," who interview job candidates from other areas of the company, asking difficult and unexpected questions. Bar Raisers, who spend 2-3 hours on each job candidate, conducting phone and face-to-face interviews and participating in evaluation meetings, have the power to veto any applicant they've assessed. Founder Jeff Bezos started the Bar Raiser program to create a consistent corporate culture by "raising the bar" when it came to hiring talent. Rather than hiring people for particular jobs, Bezos asks Bar Raisers to focus on hiring people who can succeed in Amazon's culture. John Vlastelica, an HR consultant who worked at Amazon in its early days, says, "You want someone who can adapt to new roles in the company, not just someone who can fill the role that's vacant." Susan Harker, Amazon's vice president of global talent acquisition, says, "We want to be as objective and scientific in our hiring as possible. The point is

to optimize our chances of having long-term employees." And, unlike many companies, that means hiring talented people who fit Amazon's culture. Human resource consultant Valerie Frederickson says, "There is no company that sticks to its process like Amazon does. They don't just hire the best of what they see; they're willing to keep looking and looking for the right talent."[73]

Corporate cultures are very difficult to change. Consequently, there is no guarantee that any one approach—changing visible cultural artifacts, using behavioral substitution, or hiring people with values consistent with a company's desired culture—will change a company's organizational culture. The best results are obtained by combining these methods. Together, these are some of the best tools managers have for changing culture because they send the clear message to managers and employees that "the accepted way of doing things" has changed.

STUDY TOOLS 3

LOCATED AT THE BACK OF YOUR BOOK:

- [ ] Rip out and study the Chapter Review Card at the end of the book

LOG IN TO WWW.CENGAGEBRAIN.COM TO:

- [ ] Review Key Term Flashcards
- [ ] Complete Practice Quizzing (take up to four times without repeating the same quiz)
- [ ] Complete Interactive Content: Graded Quiz, Media Quiz, and Fill-in-the-Blank Questions
- [ ] Complete Games: Beat the Clock and Crossword Puzzle
- [ ] Watch Management Workplace Video on "Camp Bow Wow"
- [ ] Work Through the What Would You Do Case on Waste Management Headquarters

4 Ethics and Social Responsibility

Elliotwestacott/iStockphoto.com

LEARNING OUTCOMES

4-1 Identify common kinds of workplace deviance.

4-2 Describe the US Sentencing Commission Guidelines for Organizations and explain how they both encourage ethical behavior and punish unethical behavior by businesses.

4-3 Describe what influences ethical decision making.

4-4 Explain what practical steps managers can take to improve ethical decision making.

4-5 Explain to whom organizations are socially responsible.

4-6 Explain for what organizations are socially responsible.

4-7 Explain how organizations can respond to societal demands for social responsibility.

4-8 Explain whether social responsibility hurts or helps an organization's economic performance.

After you finish

this chapter, go

to **PAGE 87** for

STUDY TOOLS

4-1 WORKPLACE DEVIANCE

Today, it's not enough for companies to make a profit. We also expect managers to make a profit by doing the right things. Unfortunately, no matter what managers decide to do, someone or some group will be unhappy with the outcome. Managers don't have the luxury of choosing theoretically optimal, win-win solutions that are obviously desirable to everyone involved. In practice, solutions to ethical and social responsibility problems aren't optimal. Often, managers must be satisfied with a solution that just makes do or does the least harm. Rights and wrongs are rarely crystal clear to managers charged with doing the right thing. The business world is much messier than that.

Ethics is the set of moral principles or values that defines right and wrong for a person or group. Unfortunately, numerous studies have consistently produced distressing results about the state of ethics in today's business world. One global ethics study reported that only 28 percent of respondents believed businesses were ethical. Another study found that just 25 percent trust business leaders to honestly correct mistakes and that less than 20 percent believed that business leaders would be truthful and make ethical decisions.[1] According to the Ethics Recourse Center's National Business Ethics Survey, 41 percent of employees observed unethical behavior at work. Twenty-four percent of unethical behavior was committed by senior managers, while 60 percent was committed by managers (of all kinds). Moreover, 9 percent of employees report being pressured to compromise ethical standards at work.[2] The good news, however, is that 63 percent of employees observing unethical behavior reported it.[3]

Other studies contain additional good news about workplace ethics. When people believe their work environment is ethical, they are six times more likely to stay with that company than if they believe they work in an unethical environment.[4] In fact, a survey by Deloitte reported that employees who were considering leaving their jobs cited "loss of trust" as the greatest factor.[5] One study asked 570 white-collar workers which of twenty-eight qualities were important in company leaders. The results? Honesty (24 percent) and integrity/morals/ethics (16 percent) ranked by far the highest. (Caring/compassion was third at 7 percent.)[6] According to Eduardo Castro-Wright, vice chairman of Walmart Stores Inc., "There's nothing that destroys credibility more than not being able to look someone in the eye and have them know that they can trust you."[7] In short, much needs to be done to make workplaces more

AVAVA//Stockphoto.com

ethical, but—and this is very important—most managers and employees want this to happen.

Ethical behavior follows accepted principles of right and wrong. Depending on which study you look at, one-third to three-quarters of all employees admit that they have stolen from their employers, committed computer fraud, embezzled funds, vandalized company property, sabotaged company projects, faked injuries to receive workers' compensation benefits or insurance, or been "sick" from work when they weren't really sick.

> **Ethics** the set of moral principles or values that defines right and wrong for a person or group
>
> **Ethical behavior** behavior that conforms to a society's accepted principles of right and wrong

Exhibit 4.1
Types of Workplace Deviance

Organizational

Production Deviance	Property Deviance
• Leaving early	• Sabotaging equipment
• Taking excessive breaks	• Accepting kickbacks
• Intentionally working slowly	• Lying about hours worked
• Wasting resources	• Stealing from company

Minor ← → **Serious**

Political Deviance	Personal Aggression
• Showing favoritism	• Sexual harassment
• Gossiping about coworkers	• Verbal abuse
• Blaming coworkers	• Stealing from coworkers
• Competing nonbeneficially	• Endangering coworkers

Interpersonal

Source: Republished with permission of Academy of Management, P.O. Box 3020, Briar Cliff Manor, NY, 10510- 8020. "A Typology of Deviant Workplace Behaviors" (Figure), S. L. Robinson and R. J. Bennett. *Academy of Management Journal*, 1995, Vol. 38. Reproduced by permission of the publisher via Copyright Clearance Center, Inc.

Experts estimate that unethical behaviors like these, which researchers call *workplace deviance*, may cost companies as much as $3.5 trillion a year, or roughly 5 percent of their revenues.[8]

Workplace deviance is unethical behavior that violates organizational norms about right and wrong. As Exhibit 4.1 shows, workplace deviance can be categorized by how deviant the behavior is, from minor to serious, and by the target of the deviant behavior, either the organization or particular people in the workplace.[9]

Company-related deviance can affect both tangible and intangible assets. One kind of workplace deviance,

called **production deviance,** hurts the quality and quantity of work produced. Examples include leaving early, taking excessively long work breaks, intentionally working slower, or wasting resources. Every spring, employees fill out their tournament brackets for March Madness in hopes of winning office betting pools (which are technically illegal) for most accurately predicting which teams advance during the NCAA basketball tournament. Outplacement firm Challenger, Gray & Christmas estimates that 50 million American office workers participate in March Madness office pools. John Challenger says, "You have employees talking about which teams made or didn't make the tournament. You have other workers setting up and managing office pools. Of course, there are the office pool participants, some of whom might take five minutes to fill out a bracket, while others spend several hours researching teams, analyzing statistics and completing multiple brackets. With 56% of those 50 million workers spending at least one hour filling out their tournament selections, the cost to employers of that lost hour nationwide is $1.9 billion. And that doesn't even consider how much more time employees will spend not working as they watch the games at work online, or get updates via Twitter or special sports apps on their smartphones.[10]

Property deviance is unethical behavior aimed at company property or products. Examples include sabotaging, stealing, or damaging equipment or products and overcharging for services and then pocketing the difference. For example, in Nigeria thieves steal 150,000 barrels a day of oil from oil company pipelines. Jacob Mandi, a diver who has grown rich stealing oil from pipelines, says, "We know which [pipeline] is gas, products, crude. We can sense whether it is hot or cold. We need nobody's help to know what's inside." Eni S.p.A., an Italian oil company, closed its production facilities in Nigeria because it was losing 60 percent of its production to thieves like Mandi.[11]

Organizational employees, however, do a significant amount of property deviance themselves. **Employee shrinkage,** when employees steal company merchandise, costs US retailers $15.2 billion a year.[12] A survey of twenty-three large retailers employing 2.8 million workers found that one out of forty employees is caught stealing each year and that a dishonet employee steals 5.5 times as much as the typical shoplifter.[13] Likewise, 58 percent of office workers acknowledge taking company property for personal use, according to a survey conducted for

Workplace deviance unethical behavior that violates organizational norms about right and wrong

Production deviance unethical behavior that hurts the quality and quantity of work produced

Property deviance unethical behavior aimed at the organization's property or products

Employee shrinkage employee theft of company merchandise

lawyers.com. "Sweethearting" occurs when employees discount or don't ring up merchandise their family or friends bring to the cash register. It's estimated that sweethearting is responsible for 35 percent of losses in supermarkets. In "dumpster diving," employees unload trucks, stash merchandise in a dumpster, and then retrieve it after work.[14]

Whereas production and property deviance harm companies, political deviance and personal aggression are unethical behaviors that hurt particular people within companies. **Political deviance** is using one's influence to harm others in the company. Examples include making decisions based on favoritism rather than performance, spreading rumors about coworkers, or blaming others for mistakes they didn't make. **Personal aggression** is hostile or aggressive behavior toward others. Examples include sexual harassment, verbal abuse, stealing from coworkers, or personally threatening coworkers. Another kind of personal aggression is workplace violence. Fortunately, like nearly all kinds of crime, workplace violence has dropped significantly since 1993, when 16 of every 1,000 employees experienced nonfatal workplace violence. Today, the rate has dropped to just 4 of every 1,000 employees. Furthermore, the rate of workplace violence is one-third the level of nonworkplace violence. So, overall you are less likely to encounter violence at work.[15] Still, between 525 and 1,100 people are actually killed at work each year.[16] For more information on workplace violence, see the Bureau of Labor Statistics website, http://www.bls.gov/iif/osh_wpvs.htm.

 4-2 # U.S. SENTENCING COMMISSION GUIDELINES FOR ORGANIZATIONS

A male supervisor is sexually harassing female coworkers. A sales representative offers a $10,000 kickback to persuade an indecisive customer to do business with his company. A company president secretly meets with the CEO of her biggest competitor, and they agree not to compete in markets where the other has already established customers. Each of these behaviors is clearly unethical (and, in these cases, also illegal). Historically, if management was unaware of such activities, the company could not be held responsible for them. Since 1991, however, when the US Sentencing Commission Guidelines for Organizations were established, companies can be prosecuted and punished *even if management didn't know about the*

unethical behavior. Penalties can be substantial, with maximum fines approaching a whopping $300 million.[17] Later changes to the Guidelines resulted in much stricter ethics training requirements and emphasized the importance of creating a legal and ethical company culture.[18]

*Let's examine **4-2a to whom the guidelines apply and what they cover** and **4-2b how, according to the guidelines, an organization can be punished for the unethical behavior of its managers and employees.***

4-2a Who, What, and Why?

Nearly all businesses are covered by the US Sentencing Commission's guidelines. This includes nonprofits, partnerships, labor unions, unincorporated organizations and associations, incorporated organizations, and even pension funds, trusts, and joint stock companies. If your organization can be characterized as a business (remember, nonprofits count, too), then it is subject to the guidelines.[19] For example, World Vision, a nonprofit Christian humanitarian aid organization, has a compliance program based on the US sentencing guidelines. The program includes regular audits, a code of conduct, ethics standards, and anti-bribery and corruption policies (since much of its humanitarian work is carried out in 3rd world countries).[20]

The guidelines cover offenses defined by federal laws such as invasion of privacy, price fixing, fraud, customs violations, antitrust violations, civil rights violations, theft, money laundering, conflicts of interest, embezzlement, dealing in stolen goods, copyright infringements, extortion, and more. But it's not enough merely to stay within the law. The purpose of the guidelines is not just to punish companies *after* they or their employees break the law but also to encourage companies to take proactive steps that will discourage or prevent white-collar crime *before* it happens. The guidelines also give companies an incentive to cooperate with and disclose illegal activities to federal authorities.[21]

4-2b Determining the Punishment

The guidelines impose smaller fines on companies that take proactive steps to encourage ethical behavior or voluntarily disclose illegal activities to federal authorities. Essentially,

Political deviance using one's influence to harm others in the company

Personal aggression hostile or aggressive behavior toward others

Exhibit 4.2

Offense Levels, Base Fines, Culpability Scores, and Possible Total Fines under the US Sentencing Commission Guidelines for Organizations

Offense Level	Base Fine	Culpability Scores					
		0.05	0.5	1.0	2.0	3.0	4.0
6 or less	$ 5,000	$ 250	$ 2,500	$ 5,000	$ 10,000	$ 15,000	$ 20,000
7	7,500	375	3,750	7,500	15,000	22,500	30,000
8	10,000	500	5,000	10,000	20,000	30,000	40,000
9	15,000	750	7,500	15,000	30,000	45,000	60,000
10	20,000	1,000	10,000	20,000	40,000	60,000	80,000
11	30,000	1,500	15,000	30,000	60,000	90,000	120,000
12	40,000	2,000	20,000	40,000	80,000	120,000	160,000
13	60,000	3,000	30,000	60,000	120,000	180,000	240,000
14	85,000	4,250	42,500	85,000	170,000	255,000	340,000
15	125,000	6,250	62,500	125,000	250,000	375,000	500,000
16	175,000	8,750	87,500	175,000	350,000	525,000	700,000
17	250,000	12,500	125,000	250,000	500,000	750,000	1,000,000
18	350,000	17,500	175,000	350,000	700,000	1,050,000	1,400,000
19	500,000	25,000	250,000	500,000	1,000,000	1,500,000	2,000,000
20	650,000	32,500	325,000	650,000	1,300,000	1,950,000	2,600,000
21	910,000	45,500	455,000	910,000	1,820,000	2,730,000	3,640,000
22	1,200,000	60,000	600,000	1,200,000	2,400,000	3,600,000	4,800,000
23	1,600,000	80,000	800,000	1,600,000	3,200,000	4,800,000	6,400,000
24	2,100,000	105,000	1,050,000	2,100,000	4,200,000	6,300,000	8,400,000
25	2,800,000	1,40,000	1,400,000	2,800,000	5,600,000	8,400,000	11,200,000
26	3,700,000	185,000	1,850,000	3,700,000	7,400,000	11,100,000	14,800,000
27	4,800,000	240,000	2,400,000	4,800,000	9,600,000	14,400,000	19,200,000
28	6,300,000	315,000	3,150,000	6,300,000	12,600,000	18,900,000	25,200,000
29	8,100,000	405,000	4,050,000	8,100,000	16,200,000	24,300,000	32,400,000
30	10,500,000	525,000	5,250,000	10,500,000	21,000,000	31,500,000	42,000,000
31	13,500,000	675,000	6,750,000	13,500,000	27,000,000	40,500,000	54,000,000
32	17,500,000	875,000	8,750,000	17,500,000	35,000,000	52,500,000	70,000,000
33	22,000,000	1,100,000	11,000,000	22,000,000	44,000,000	66,000,000	88,000,000
34	28,500,000	1,425,000	14,250,000	28,500,000	57,000,000	85,500,000	114,000,000
35	36,000,000	1,800,000	18,000,000	36,000,000	72,000,000	108,000,000	144,000,000
36	45,500,000	2,275,000	22,750,000	45,500,000	91,000,000	136,500,000	182,000,000
37	57,500,000	2,875,000	28,750,000	57,500,000	115,000,000	172,500,000	230,000,000
38 or more	72,500,000	3,625,000	36,250,000	72,500,000	145,000,000	217,500,000	290,000,000

Source: US Sentencing Commission, *Guidelines Manual*, §3E1.1 (Nov. 2009), 509–531, accessed June 4, 2010, http://www.ussc.gov/2009guid/GL2009.pdf.

Terry Hankins//iStockphoto.com

the law uses a carrot-and-stick approach. The stick is the threat of heavy fines that can total millions of dollars. The carrot is a greatly reduced fine, but only if the company has started an effective compliance program (discussed below) to encourage ethical behavior *before* the illegal activity occurs.[22] The method used to determine a company's punishment illustrates the importance of establishing a compliance program, as illustrated in Exhibit 4.2.

The first step is to compute the *base fine* by determining what *level of offense* (i.e., its seriousness) has occurred. The level of the offense varies depending on the kind of crime, the loss incurred by the victims, and how much planning went into the crime. For example, simple fraud is a level 6 offense (there are thirty-eight levels in all). But if the victims of that fraud lost more than $5 million, that level 6 offense becomes a level 22 offense. Moreover, anything beyond minimal planning to commit the fraud results in an increase of two levels to a level 24 offense. How much difference would this make to a company? As Exhibit 4.2 shows, crimes at or below level 6 incur a base fine of $5,000, whereas the base fine for level 24 is $2.1 million, a difference of $2.095 million! The base fine for level 38, the top-level offense, is a hefty $72.5 million.

After assessing a *base fine*, the judge computes a culpability score, which is a way of assigning blame to the company. The culpability score can range from 0.05 to 4.0. The greater the corporate responsibility in conducting, encouraging, or sanctioning illegal or unethical activity, the higher the culpability score. A company that already has a compliance program and voluntarily reports the offense to authorities will incur a culpability score of 0.05. By contrast, a company whose management secretly plans, approves, and participates in illegal or unethical activity will receive the maximum score of 4.0.

The culpability score is critical because the total fine is computed by multiplying the base fine by the culpability score. Going back to our level 24 fraud offense, the left point of the upper arrow in Exhibit 4.2 shows that a company with a compliance program that turns itself in will be fined only $105,000 ($2,100,000 × 0.05). In contrast, a company that secretly planned, approved, and participated in illegal activity will be fined $8.4 million ($2,100,000 × 4.0), as shown by the right point of the upper arrow. The difference is even greater for level 38 offenses. As shown by the left point of the bottom arrow, a company with a compliance program and a 0.05 culpability score is fined only $3.625 million, whereas a company with the maximum 4.0 culpability score is fined a whopping $290 million, as indicated by the right point of the bottom arrow. These differences clearly show the importance of having a compliance program in place. Over the last decade, 1,494 companies have been charged under the US Sentencing Guidelines. Seventy-six percent of those charged were fined, with the average fine exceeding $2 million. Company fines are on average

twenty times larger now than before the implementation of the guidelines in 1991.[23]

Fortunately for companies that want to avoid paying these stiff fines, the US Sentencing Guidelines clearly spell out the seven necessary components of an effective compliance program.[24] Exhibit 4.3 lists those components. Caremark International, a managed-care service provider in Delaware, pleaded guilty to criminal charges related to its physician contracts and improper patient referrals. When shareholders sued the company for negligence and poor management, the Delaware court dismissed the case, ruling that the company's ethics compliance program, built on the components described in Exhibit 4.3, was a good-faith attempt to monitor employees and that the company did not knowingly allow illegal and unethical behavior to occur. The court went on to rule that a compliance program based on the US Sentencing Guidelines was enough to shield the company from liability.[25]

Exhibit 4.3

Compliance Program Steps from the US Sentencing Commission Guidelines for Organizations

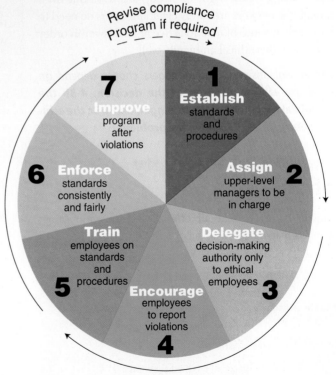

Source: D. R. Dalton, M. B. Metzger, and J. W. Hill, "The 'New' US Sentencing Commission Guidelines: A Wake-up Call for Corporate America," *Academy of Management Executive* 8 (1994): 7–16.

INFLUENCES ON ETHICAL DECISION MAKING

As the senior human resources executive at United Parcel Service (UPS), you're facing an ethical dilemma. With health care costs rising 11.25 percent this year, or nearly five times the rate of inflation, plus implementation of the federal Affordable Care Act, which has added significant additional expenses, fees, and rules that must be followed (or you're in violation of the law), it's becoming increasingly difficult for UPS to maintain the affordability of its current healthcare coverage. The CEO and the executive team have asked you to consider a range of scenarios, from no price changes coupled with reduced coverage to significant price increases but no changes in coverage to something in the middle with moderate price changes and some changes in coverage.[26] As the senior human resources executive at UPS, what would be the ethical thing for you to do? With 322,000 US employees, any changes you recommend will have a huge impact, both at the corporate and individual levels.

Although some ethical issues are easily solved, many do not have clearly right or wrong answers. But even though the answers are rarely clear, managers do need to have a clear sense of *how* to arrive at an answer in order to manage this ethical ambiguity well.

The ethical answers that managers choose depend on 4-3a the ethical intensity of the decision, 4-3b the moral development of the manager, and 4-3c the ethical principles used to solve the problem.

4-3a Ethical Intensity of the Decision

Managers don't treat all ethical decisions the same. The UPS manager who has to decide how changes in healthcare prices and coverage might affect 322,000 employees is going to treat that decision much more seriously than the decision of how to deal with an assistant who has been taking paper home for personal use. These decisions differ in their **ethical intensity**, or the degree of concern people have about an ethical issue. When addressing an issue of high ethical intensity, managers are more aware of the impact their decision will have on others. They are more likely to view the decision as an ethical or moral decision than as an economic decision. They are also more likely to worry about doing the right thing.

Six factors must be taken into account when determining the ethical intensity of an action, as shown in Exhibit 4.4. **Magnitude of consequences** is the total harm or benefit derived from an ethical decision. The more people who are harmed or the greater the harm to those people, the larger the consequences. **Social consensus** is agreement on whether behavior is bad or good. **Probability of effect** is the chance that something will happen that results in harm to others. If we combine these factors, we can see the effect they can have on ethical intensity. For example, if there is *clear agreement* (social consensus) that a managerial decision or action is *certain* (probability of effect) to have *large negative consequences* (magnitude of consequences) in some way, then people will be highly concerned about that managerial decision or action, and ethical intensity will be high.

Ethical intensity the degree of concern people have about an ethical issue

Magnitude of consequences the total harm or benefit derived from an ethical decision

Social consensus agreement on whether behavior is bad or good

Probability of effect the chance that something will happen that results in harm to others

---

Exhibit 4.4

Six Factors That Contribute to Ethical Intensity

Magnitude of consequences
Social consensus
Probability of effect
Temporal immediacy
Proximity of effect
Concentration of effect

Source: Republished with permission of Academy of Management; P.O. Box 3020, Briar Cliff Manor, NY, 10510-8020. T.M. Jones, "Ethical Decision Making by Individuals in Organizations: An Issue Contingent Model," *Academy of Management Review 16* (1991) 366–395; Reproduced by permission of the publisher via Copyright Clearance Center, Inc.

Trevor Hunt/iStockphoto.com

Temporal immediacy is the time between an act and the consequences the act produces. Temporal immediacy is stronger if a manager has to lay off workers next week as opposed to three months from now. **Proximity of effect** is the social, psychological, cultural, or physical distance of a decision maker from those affected by his or her decisions. Thus, proximity of effect is greater when a manager lays off employees he knows than when he lays off employees he doesn't know. Finally, whereas the magnitude of consequences is the total effect across all people, **concentration of effect** is how much an act affects the average person. For instance, eliminating healthcare coverage for 100 employees has a greater concentration of effect than reducing the healthcare benefits for 1,000 employees by 10 percent.

Which of these six factors has the most impact on ethical intensity? Studies indicate that managers are much more likely to view decisions as ethical issues when the magnitude of consequences (total harm) is high and there is a social consensus (agreement) that a behavior or action is bad.[27]

4-3b Moral Development

It's Friday. Another long week of classes and studying is over, and all you want to do is sit down and relax. "A movie sounds good," you think to yourself, but you don't want to spend $12 to trek down to the megaplex. And, while it would cost less than a $1.50 to rent a DVD, you're too tired to make the short trip down to the corner drugstore's Redbox machine. Your roommate says he's got the perfect solution and gives you the URL of a website that streams all the latest blockbuster movies and TV shows for free. The writers, actors, and producers won't earn a dime if you watch the pirated copy of the movie. Furthermore, it's illegal to download or watch streamed copies of pirated shows. But how will the movie studios ever find out? Are the cops going to come through your door because you watched a pirated copy of *Avengers 2*? Will you watch the movie? What are you going to do?

In part, according to psychologist Lawrence Kohlberg, your decision will be based on your level of moral development. Kohlberg identified three phases of moral development, with two stages in each phase (see Exhibit 4.5).[28] At the **preconventional level of moral development,** people decide based on selfish reasons. For example, if you are in Stage 1, the punishment and obedience stage,

Temporal immediacy the time between an act and the consequences the act produces

Proximity of effect the social, psychological, cultural, or physical distance between a decision maker and those affected by his or her decisions

Concentration of effect the total harm or benefit that an act produces on the average person

Preconventional level of moral development the first level of moral development, in which people make decisions based on selfish reasons

Conventional level of moral development the second level of moral development, in which people make decisions that conform to societal expectation

your primary concern will be to avoid trouble for yourself. So you won't watch the pirated movie, because you are afraid of being caught and punished. Yet, in Stage 2, the instrumental exchange stage, you worry less about punishment and more about doing things that directly advance your wants and needs. So you will watch the pirated movie.

People at the **conventional level of moral development** make decisions that conform to societal expectations. In other words, they look outside themselves to others for guidance on ethical issues. In Stage 3, the "good boy, nice girl" stage, you normally do what the other "good boys" and "nice girls" are doing. If everyone else is watching the pirated movie, you will, too. But if they aren't, you won't either. In the law and order stage, Stage 4, you again look for

POSTCONVENTIONAL LEVEL OF MORAL DEVELOPMENT

CONVENTIONAL LEVEL OF MORAL DEVELOPMENT

PRECONVENTIONAL LEVEL OF MORAL DEVELOPMENT

Exhibit 4.5
Kohlberg's Stages of Moral Development

Stage 1	Stage 2	Stage 3	Stage 4	Stage 5	Stage 6
Punishment and Obedience	Instrumental Exchange	Good Boy, Nice Girl	Law and Order	Social Contract	Universal Principle
Preconventional		**Conventional**		**Postconventional**	
Self-Interest		**Societal Expectations**		**Internalized Principles**	

external guidance and do whatever the law permits, so you won't watch the movie.

People at the **postconventional level of moral development** use internalized ethical principles to solve ethical dilemmas. In Stage 5, the social contract stage, you will refuse to watch the pirated movie because, as a whole, society is better off when the rights of others—in this case, the rights of actors, producers, directors, and writers—are not violated. In Stage 6, the universal principle stage, you might or might not watch the pirated movie, depending on your principles of right and wrong. Moreover, you will stick to your principles even if your decision conflicts with the law (Stage 4) or what others believe is best for society (Stage 5). For example, those with socialist or communist beliefs would probably choose to watch the pirated movie, because they believe goods and services should be owned by society rather than by individuals and corporations.

Kohlberg believed that people would progress sequentially from earlier stages to later stages as they became more educated and mature. But only 20 percent of adults ever reach the postconventional stage of moral development, where internal principles guide their decisions. Most adults are in the conventional stage of moral development, in which they look outside themselves to others for guidance on ethical issues. This means that most people in the workplace look to and need leadership when it comes to ethical decision making.[29]

Postconventional level of moral development the third level of moral development, in which people make decisions based on internalized principles

Principle of long-term self-interest an ethical principle that holds that you should never take any action that is not in your or your organization's long-term self-interest

4-3c Principles of Ethical Decision Making

Beyond an issue's ethical intensity and a manager's level of moral maturity, the particular ethical principles that managers use will also affect how they solve ethical dilemmas. Unfortunately, there is no one ideal principle to use in making ethical business decisions.

According to professor LaRue Hosmer, a number of different ethical principles can be used to make business decisions: long-term self-interest, religious injunctions, government requirements, individual rights, personal virtue, distributive justice, and utilitarian benefits.[30] All of these ethical principles encourage managers and employees to take others' interests into account when making ethical decisions. At the same time, however, these principles can lead to very different ethical actions, as we can see by using these principles to decide what UPS might do regarding its employees' healthcare coverage.

According to the **principle of long-term self-interest,** you should never take any action that is not in your or your organization's long-term self-interest. Although this sounds as if the principle promotes selfishness, it doesn't. What we do to maximize our long-term interests (save more, spend less, exercise every day, watch what we eat) is often very different from what we do to maximize short-term interests (max out our credit cards, be couch potatoes, eat whatever we want). Healthcare costs at UPS have nearly doubled in the last 8 years. Furthermore, they are expected to rise 11.25 percent this year, nearly 5 times faster than the rate of inflation.[31] On one hand, reducing healthcare costs would be in UPS's long-term self-interest. So, UPS might choose to to significantly reduce or eliminate healthcare coverage for as many employees as possible. On the other hand, cutting health care benefits might make it much more difficult for UPS to attract and retain good employees, and it would most certainly lead to much more difficult contract negotiations with the labor unions that represent its non-managerial employees. So, based on those concerns, UPS would absorb the cost increases itself, thus maintaining current healthcare coverage levels for its employees. In this instance, the principle of long-term self-interest doesn't provide clear guidance.

According to the **principle of religious injunctions,** you should never take an action that is unkind or that harms a sense of community, such as the positive feelings that come from working together to accomplish a commonly accepted goal. Using this principle, and knowing how contentious these changes would be, UPS would absorb the 11.25 percent increase and maintain current levels of health benefits.

According to the **principle of government requirements,** the law represents the minimal moral standards of society, so you should never take any action that violates the law. According to the Affordable Care Act, companies with more than 50 employees can be fined for not providing adequate coverage to employees and their children (up to the age of 26). However, the law does not require that spouses be covered. So, based on the law, you could recommend that everyone else but employees' spouses maintain healthcare benefits.[32]

The **principle of individual rights** holds that you should never take an action that infringes on others' agreed-upon rights. With a large unionized workforce, any changes that UPS makes to its healthcare coverage must be consistent with existing labor union contracts. Since union contracts covering 250,000 workers specify that spouses are entitled to healthcare benefits, UPS would only be able to change healthcare benefits and costs for non-union workers and managers at this time.[33] However, it could attempt to change unionized workers benefits when their contract comes open for renegotiation, typically every three years.

The **principle of personal virtue** holds that you should never do anything that is not honest, open, and truthful and that you would not be glad to see reported in the newspapers or on TV. Using the principle of personal virtue, UPS would have quietly absorbed the increased costs of healthcare coverage and maintained current benefit levels. Had it done so, it could have avoided the publication of a *Wall Street Journal* article on this topic.

Under the **principle of distributive justice,** you should never take any action that harms the least fortunate among us in some way. This principle is designed to protect the poor, the uneducated, and the unemployed. Because UPS cannot change healthcare benefits for its unionized workers (until the next contract is negotiated), it is limited to changing healthcare benefits for its managers and office workers. But because healthcare coverage is mandatory under the Affordable Care Act for companies with more than 50 employees, UPS can only make significant changes to the spouses of managerial employees. Given that UPS pays competitive wages and benefits, is it likely that those spouses can be characterized as poor? Probably not? Might those spouses be uneducated, meaning without a college or high school degree? Perhaps, but probably not in most cases. Unemployed? Certainly, there could be spouses who are out of a job or who have chosen to stay at home to care for children. But would UPS want to be seen as cutting health care benefits of unemployed spouses? The principle of distributive justices says they would not.

The Affordable Care Act (ACA) has created additional expenses, fees, and rules for companies like UPS. In this April 2014 photo, President Barack Obama speaks in Washington about ACA signups crossing the 8-million mark.

AP Images/J. Scott Applewhite

Principle of religious injunctions an ethical principle that holds that you should never take any action that is not kind and that does not build a sense of community

Principle of government requirements an ethical principle that holds that you should never take any action that violates the law, for the law represents the minimal moral standard

Principle of individual rights an ethical principle that holds that you should never take any action that infringes on others' agreed-upon rights

Principle of personal virtue an ethical principle that holds that you should never do anything that is not honest, open, and truthful and that you would not be glad to see reported in the newspapers or on TV

Principle of distributive justice an ethical principle that holds that you should never take any action that harms the least fortunate among us: the poor, the uneducated, the unemployed

Finally, the **principle of utilitarian benefits** states that you should never take an action that does not result in greater good for society. In short, you should do whatever creates the greatest good for the greatest number. At first, this principle seems to suggest that UPS should absorb the higher costs and not change healthcare benefits. After all, it can be argued that maintaining healthcare benefits for 330,000 employees contributes to the greater good. If UPS did this with any regularity, however, the costs would be enormous (remember that healthcare costs have doubled in the last 8 years and are increasing much faster than the rate of inflation), profits would shrink, and UPS would have to cut its stock dividend and the price of its stock would drop, harming countless shareholders, many of whom rely on UPS stock price appreciation and dividend growth for retirement income. Likewise, reduced profitability could lead to even more severe cost cutting, such as layoffs, which could produce more harm than reduced benefits. In this case, the principle does not lead to a clear choice.

So, what did UPS decide to do? Management factored in many of the concerns raised by these ethical principles and announced that it would no longer provide healthcare benefits for employed spouses of non-unionized workers who already had health benefits from their employers. No one else was affected.[34] Do you think UPS's decision was ethical? Some of you might believe that UPS is not fulfilling the commitments it made to its managerial employees and their families and that as a large corporation, it can afford the increase. Others might argue that UPS's decision was legal, that it honored existing contracts, and that ultimately cuts of some kind would be required given the exponential rise in costs. Indeed, a UPS spokesperson explained that this decision was the best way to continue offering health coverage premiums at current levels for the largest number of UPS employees.

Principle of utilitarian benefits an ethical principle that holds that you should never take any action that does not result in greater good for society

Overt integrity test a written test that estimates job applicants' honesty by directly asking them what they think or feel about theft or about punishment of unethical behaviors

Personality-based integrity test a written test that indirectly estimates job applicants' honesty by measuring psychological traits, such as dependability and conscientiousness

---

 ## 4-4 PRACTICAL STEPS TO ETHICAL DECISION MAKING

Companies are putting more emphasis on ethical decision making. Eighty-one percent now provide ethics training. Sixty-seven percent include ethical conduct as a standard part of performance evaluations. And, seventy-four percent communicate internally about disciplinary actions that are taken when unethical behavior occurs.[35]

*Managers can encourage more ethical decision making in their organizations by **4-4a carefully selecting and hiring ethical employees, 4-4b establishing a specific code of ethics, 4-4c training employees to make ethical decisions,** and **4-4d creating an ethical climate.***

4-4a Selecting and Hiring Ethical Employees

As an employer, how can you increase your chances of hiring honest employees, the kind who would return a wallet filled with money to its rightful owner? **Overt integrity tests** estimate job applicants' honesty by asking them directly what they think or feel about theft or about punishment of unethical behaviors.[36] For example, an employer might ask an applicant, "Would you ever consider buying something from somebody if you knew the person had stolen the item?" or "Don't most people steal from their companies?" Surprisingly, unethical people will usually answer "yes" to such questions, because they believe that the world is basically dishonest and that dishonest behavior is normal.[37]

Personality-based integrity tests indirectly estimate job applicants' honesty by measuring psychological traits such as dependability and conscientiousness. For example, prison inmates serving time for white-collar crimes (counterfeiting, embezzlement, and fraud) scored much lower than a comparison group of middle-level managers on scales measuring reliability, dependability, honesty, conscientiousness, and abiding by rules.[38] These results show that companies can selectively hire and promote people who will be more ethical.[39]

4-4b Codes of Ethics

Today, almost all large corporations have an ethics code in place. Even if a company has a code of ethics, two

Company Code of Ethics
1. Uphold the law.
2. Respect your coworkers.
3. Be accountable to your clients.
4. Build trust and credibility.
5. Avoid conflicts of interest.

Squaredpixels/iStockphoto.com

4-4c Ethics Training

In addition to establishing ethical standards for the company, managers must sponsor and be involved in ethics and compliance training in order to create an ethical company culture.[42] The first objective of ethics training is to develop employees' awareness of ethics.[43] This means helping employees recognize which issues are ethical issues and then avoiding rationalizing unethical behavior by thinking, "This isn't really illegal or immoral" or "No one will ever find out." Several companies have created board games, produce videos, or invite special speakers to improve awareness of ethical issues.[44] Howard Winkler, project manager for ethics and compliance at Southern Co., an Atlanta-based energy provider, uses a wide range of tools to educate and engage its employees on ethics. Like many companies, Southern's mandatory ethics training requires employees to go online, read the code of ethics, and certify they have done so. Says Winkler, "When its put online, it usually has all the charm and engagement of a software licensing agreement."[45] So Winkler replaced it with a 10 minute video where actors explained the company's policies. He varies delivery methods to keep employees interested, using videos, contests, and internal social media to communicate important ethics issues. Winkler even had a convicted felon come in to talk about how small ethical compromises eventually lead to bigger unethical behavior, such as fraud, that charges that sent him to jail for five years. "It created an enormous impression," Winkler says, as, "This person didn't start out his career looking to commit fraud. The main message was that once you make the first ethical compromise, you are embarking on a path that can lead all the way to a prison cell."[46] Winkler also regularly creates opportunities for senior executives to speak with employees about ethics issues. This multifaceted approach appears to be working, as internal surveys indicate that 93 percent of employees recognize that their continued career at Southern "depends on my ethical behavior."

The second objective for ethics training programs is to achieve credibility with employees. Not surprisingly, employees can be highly suspicious of management's

things must still happen if those codes are to encourage ethical decision making and behavior.[40] First, a company must communicate its code to others both inside and outside the company.

Second, in addition to having an ethics code with general guidelines like "do unto others as you would have others do unto you," management must also develop practical ethical standards and procedures specific to the company's line of business. Hershey's, the leading producer of chocolate and confectionary goods in North America, also does business in ninety countries. Visitors to Hershey's website can download the company's "Code of Ethical Business Conduct" in eight languages. The code sets specific ethical standards on topics ranging from treatment of coworkers to protecting the environment to maintenance of financial records. For example, the code states specifically, "If management, our auditors or government investigators request information or documentation from us, we must cooperate. This means we may not conceal, alter or destroy such information. Falsifying business records, destroying documents or lying to auditors, investigators or government officials is a serious offense." Likewise, Hershey's code states that information about competitors can only be obtained in legal and ethical ways and that it is wrong to attempt to pry confidential information from others. "If a coworker, customer or business partner has competitive information that they are required to keep confidential, we must not encourage them to disclose it."[41] Specific codes of ethics such as this make it much easier for employees to decide what to do when they want to do the right thing.

Some of America's biggest companies are using volunteerism to help make the world a better place. IBM's Corporate Service Corps has sent employees to Kenya to improve the country's postal service and to India to create an online education system. All told, IBM employees have given 3.2 million hours to volunteer service. At Campbell Soup Company, employees are given time in the workday to help schools design more nutritious menus and to expand the availability of fresh produce in local grocery stores. The company also allows a food bank to take from its assembly lines product that would otherwise be discarded and use it to feed the needy. Employees at AT&T, meanwhile, have spent 270,000 hours mentoring high school students, and the company has donated $100 million to various education programs.

Source: D. Brady, "Volunteerism as a Core Competency," *Bloomberg Businessweek*, November 8, 2012, http://www.businessweek.com/articles/2012-11-08/volunteerism-as -a-core-competency.

reasons for offering ethics training. Some companies have hurt the credibility of their ethics programs by having outside instructors and consultants conduct the classes.[47] Employees often complain that outside instructors and consultants are teaching theory that has nothing to do with their jobs and the practical dilemmas they actually face on a daily basis. CA Technologies made its ethics training practical and relevant by creating a series of comical training videos with a fictional manager, Griffin Peabody, who is shown facing a series of ethics issues, such as conflicts of interest, competitive intelligence, workplace harassment, client expenses, and conduct outside of the workplace (search "Griffin Peabody" at YouTube.com). Chief ethics officer Joel Katz says, "It's easy for it [i.e., ethics training] to become a check-the-box exercise. We use Griffin's escapades to teach compliance lessons in a funny way." For instance, since CA Technologies acquires lots of companies—a common practice in technology industries—it's critical, and required by law, that its employees keep potential acquisitions confidential to prevent insider trading. Chief compliance officer Gary Brown says, "They think they can tell a friend, 'Guess what I was working on today.' They have to realize it is a much bigger problem." To reinforce this point, Griffin Peabody is visited by Securities and Exchange Commission investigators after publicly disclosing information about a company that is being acquired.[48]

Ethics training becomes even more credible when top managers teach the initial ethics classes to their subordinates who in turn teach their subordinates.[49]

At Intuitive Research and Technology Corp., an engineering services company in Huntsville, Alabama, Howard "Hal" Brewer, the company's co-founder and president, is the company's ethics champion. Every new employee attends a session called "Let's Talk Ethics with Hal," led by Brewer and the director of human resources, Juanita Phillips. Brewer explains how employees' decisions impact the company, situations they will likely encounter with outside organizations they do business with, and then how to respond. What effect does having the co-founder and president talk to every employee about ethics? Philips says about Hal, "He makes it clear that he is the ethics officer. His strength is that he means every word of it, and he shows it in how he lives every day in terms of running the company."[50] Michael Hoffman, executive director for the Center for Business Ethics at Bentley University, says that having managers teach ethics courses greatly reinforces the seriousness with which employees treat ethics in the workplace.[51]

The third objective of ethics training is to teach employees a practical model of ethical decision making. A basic model should help them think about the consequences their choices will have on others and consider how they will choose between different solutions. Exhibit 4.6 presents a basic model of ethical decision making.

4-4d Ethical Climate

Organizational culture is key to fostering ethical decision making. The 2013 National Business Ethics Survey reported that only 20 percent of employees who work at companies with a strong ethical culture (where core beliefs are widely shared and strongly held) have observed others engaging in unethical behavior, whereas 88 percent of those who work in organizations with weak ethical cultures (where core beliefs are not widely shared or strongly held) have observed others engaging in unethical behavior.[52] Companies with strong ethical cultures are also less likely to experience ongoing misconduct (10 percent versus 35 percent in weak ethical cultures).[53]

The first step in establishing an ethical climate is for managers, especially top managers, to act ethically themselves. It's no surprise that in study after study, when researchers ask, "What is the most important influence on your ethical behavior at work?" the answer comes back, "My manager."

A second step in establishing an ethical climate is for top management to be active in and committed to the company ethics program.[54] Top managers who consistently talk about the importance of ethics and back up that talk by participating in their companies' ethics programs send the clear message that ethics matter. When management engages and communicates about

Exhibit 4.6
A Basic Model of Ethical Decision Making

1. **Identify the problem.** What makes it an ethical problem? Think in terms of rights, obligations, fairness, relationships, and integrity. How would you define the problem if you stood on the other side of the fence?

2. **Identify the constituents.** Who has been hurt? Who could be hurt? Who could be helped? Are they willing players, or are they victims? Can you negotiate with them?

3. **Diagnose the situation.** How did it happen in the first place? What could have prevented it? Is it going to get worse or better? Can the damage now be undone?

4. **Analyze your options.** Imagine the range of possibilities. Limit yourself to the two or three most manageable. What are the likely outcomes of each? What are the likely costs? Look to the company mission statement or code of ethics for guidance.

5. **Make your choice.** What is your intention in making this decision? How does it compare with the probable results? Can you discuss the problem with the affected parties before you act? Could you disclose without qualm your decision to your boss, the CEO, the board of directors, your family, or society as a whole?

6. **Act.** Do what you have to do. Don't be afraid to admit errors. Be as bold in confronting a problem as you were in causing it.

Source: L. A. Berger, "Train All Employees to Solve Ethical Dilemmas," *Best's Review—Life-Health Insurance Edition* 95 (1995): 70–80.

ethical issues, employees are less likely to break rules and more likely to report ethical violations.[55] Business writer Dayton Fandray says, "You can have ethics offices and officers and training programs and reporting systems, but if the CEO doesn't seem to care, it's all just a sham. It's not surprising to find that the companies that really do care about ethics make a point of including senior management in all of their ethics and compliance programs."[56]

A third step is to put in place a reporting system that encourages managers and employees to report potential ethics violations. **Whistleblowing,** that is, reporting others' ethics violations, is a difficult step for most people to take.[57] Managers who have been interviewed about whistleblowing have said, "In every organization, someone's been screwed for standing up." "If anything, I figured that by taking a strong stand I might get myself in trouble. People might look at me as a goody two-shoes. Someone might try to force me out."[58] Indeed, 41 percent of workers have observed unethical behavior, 63 percent of those have reported the misconduct, and 21 percent of those who reported the unethical behavior experienced some kind of retaliation.[59]

An AirTran Airways pilot, for example, was removed from "flight status," meaning he was ineligible to fly, after filing ten safety reports in two days, all concerning an unbalanced tire on one of AirTran's passenger jets. Three weeks later, following a seventeen-minute hearing, he was fired for allegedly not satisfactorily answering questions at the hearing. However, the Occupational Safety and Health Administration (OSHA) ruled that the firing was retaliatory, that AirTran violated whistleblower protection laws, and that AirTran should reinstate the pilot and pay him more than $1 million in back pay and compensatory damages. OSHA Assistant Secretary of Labor Dr. David Michaels said, "Airline workers must be free to raise safety and security concerns, and companies that diminish those rights through intimidation or retaliation must be held accountable. Airline safety is of vital importance, not only to the workers, but to the millions of Americans who use our airways."[60]

A 2014 ruling by the U.S. Supreme Court greatly expands protections for whistleblowers. The Court declared that the strong whistleblower protections built into the 2002 Sarbanes-Oxley Act, which apply to employees of publicly traded companies, should also apply to the employees of contractors and subcontractors that work with those public companies. This ruling extends whistleblower protection laws beyond the 5,000 publicly traded companies covered by Sarbanes-Oxley to an additional 6 million private companies.[61]

To encourage employees to report ethics violations, that is, to act as whistleblowers, many companies have installed confidential ethics hotlines. The information obtained from the hotline at Paychex, a multibillion dollar payroll services firm in Rochester, New York, is reported directly to the company's board of directors and audit committee, which can then trigger an investigation independent of company management.[62]

The factor that does the most to discourage whistleblowers from reporting problems is lack of company

Whistleblowing reporting others' ethics violations to management or legal authorities

action on their complaints.[63] Thus, the final step in developing an ethical climate is for management to fairly and consistently punish those who violate the company's code of ethics. The key, says Paychex CEO Martin Mucci, is "to deal with it quickly, severely, and publicize it."[64] Says Mucci, "I learned early in my career you have to deal with it quickly, severely, and publicize it. Our employees know that if they are caught cheating in any way, even if only to make a few dollars or improve their scores, they will most likely be terminated. Then we review that with the entire management team. We have done that with managers of locations, top sales representatives—we don't treat anyone differently."[65] Amazingly, though, not all companies fire ethics violators. In fact, 8 percent of surveyed companies admit that they would promote top performers even if they violated ethical standards.[66]

4-5 TO WHOM ARE ORGANIZATIONS SOCIALLY RESPONSIBLE?

Social responsibility is a business's obligation to pursue policies, make decisions, and take actions that benefit society.[67] Unfortunately, because there are strong disagreements over to whom and for what in society organizations are responsible, it can be difficult for managers to know what is or will be perceived as socially responsible corporate behavior. In a recent McKinsey & Company study of 1,144 top global executives, 79 percent predicted that at least some responsibility for dealing with future social and political issues would fall on corporations, but only 3 percent said they themselves do a

good job of dealing with these issues.[68] So what should managers and corporations do to be socially responsible?

There are two perspectives regarding to whom organizations are socially responsible: the shareholder model and the stakeholder model. According to the late Nobel Prize–winning economist Milton Friedman, the only social responsibility that organizations have is to satisfy their owners, that is, company shareholders. This view—called the **shareholder model**—holds that the only social responsibility that businesses have is to maximize profits. By maximizing profit, the firm maximizes shareholder wealth and satisfaction. More specifically, as profits rise, the company stock owned by shareholders generally increases in value.

Friedman argued that it is socially irresponsible for companies to divert time, money, and attention from maximizing profits to social causes and charitable organizations. The first problem, he believed, is that organizations cannot act effectively as moral agents for all company shareholders. Although shareholders are likely to agree on investment issues concerning a company, it's highly unlikely that they have common views on what social causes a company should or should not support.

The second major problem, Friedman said, is that the time, money, and attention diverted to social causes undermine market efficiency.[69] In competitive markets, companies compete for raw materials, talented workers, customers, and investment funds. A company that spends money on social causes will have less money to purchase quality materials or to hire talented workers who can produce a valuable product at a good price. If customers find the company's product less desirable, its sales and profits will fall. If profits fall, the company's stock price will decline, and the company will have difficulty attracting investment funds that could be used to fund long-term growth. In the end, Friedman argues, diverting the firm's money, time, and resources to social causes hurts customers, suppliers, employees, and shareholders. Russell Roberts, an economist at George Mason University, agrees, saying, "Doesn't it make more sense to have companies do what they do best, make good products at fair prices, and then let consumers use the savings for the charity of their choice?"[70]

By contrast, under the **stakeholder model,** management's most important responsibility is the firm's long-term survival (not just maximizing profits), which is achieved by satisfying the interests of multiple corporate stakeholders (not just shareholders).[71] **Stakeholders** are persons or groups with a legitimate interest in a company.[72] Since stakeholders are interested in and affected by the organization's actions, they have a stake in what those actions are. In 2013, when an environmental group, As You Sow, along with company shareholders, asked

Exxon Mobile via a formal shareholder proposal to provide detailed information about the impact of fracking, a technique in which water is injected at high pressure into oil shale deposits to force lose oil and natural gas, at Exxon's annual shareholder meeting. Exxon declined to answer, stating, "the minimal environmental impacts of hydraulic fracturing have been well-documented." But, in the face of increased concerns about fracking, the company agreed in April 2014 to provide a report on fracking's impact on air quality, water, and chemical usage at Exxon sites. A company spokesperson said the agreement was, "a productive evolution of our relationship with some of these shareholder groups." After formally withdrawing its shareholder proposal, As You Sow president Danielle Fugere, commented that, "It does feel like Exxon is changing the way it's doing business. [But if the report doesn't provide much information], "we did reserve the right to bring a [shareholder] resolution next year."[73]

Stakeholder groups may try to influence the firm to act in their own interests. Exhibit 4.7 shows the various stakeholder groups that the organization must satisfy to assure its long-term survival. Being responsible to multiple stakeholders raises two basic questions. First, how does a company identify organizational stakeholders? Second, how does a company balance the needs of different stakeholders? Distinguishing between primary and secondary stakeholders can help answer these questions.[74]

Some stakeholders are more important to the firm's survival than others. **Primary stakeholders** are groups on which the organization depends for its long-term survival; they include shareholders, employees, customers, suppliers, governments, and local communities. When managers are struggling to balance the needs of different stakeholders, the stakeholder model suggests that the needs of primary stakeholders take precedence over the needs of secondary stakeholders. But among primary stakeholders, are some more important than others? According to the life-cycle theory of organizations, the answer is yes. In practice, the answer is also yes, as CEOs typically give somewhat higher priority to shareholders, employees, and customers than to suppliers, governments, and local communities, no matter what stage of the life cycle a company

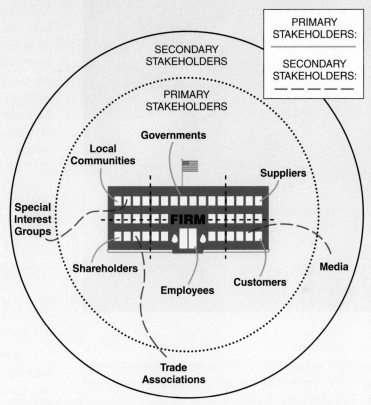

Exhibit 4.7
Stakeholder Model of Corporate Social Responsibility

Source: Republished with permission of Academy of Management, P.O. Box 3020, Briar Cliff Manor, NY, 10510-8020. "The Stakeholder Theory of the Corporation: Concepts, Evidence and Implications" (Figure), T. Donaldson and L. E. Preston, *Academy of Management Review* 20 (1995). Reproduced by permission of the publisher via Copyright Clearance Center, Inc.

is in.[75] Addressing the concerns of primary stakeholders is important, because if a stakeholder group becomes dissatisfied and terminates its relationship with the company, the company could be seriously harmed or go out of business.

Secondary stakeholders, such as the media and special interest groups, can influence or be influenced by the company. Unlike the primary stakeholders, however, they do not engage in regular transactions with the company and are not critical to its long-term survival. Meeting the needs of primary stakeholders is therefore usually

Primary stakeholder any group on which an organization relies for its long-term survival

Secondary stakeholder any group that can influence or be influenced by a company and can affect public perceptions about the company's socially responsible behavior

nesjerry/iStockphoto.com

more important than meeting the needs of secondary stakeholders. Nevertheless, secondary stakeholders are still important because they can affect public perceptions and opinions about socially responsible behavior.

The Keystone XL pipeline, proposed by Trans-Canada Corporation, would carry 800,000 barrels of crude oil per day from the tar sands in Alberta, Canada to oil refineries in Texas and Louisiana. Even though the project is approved by 75 percent of Americans and 68 percent of Canadians and would create tens of thousands of jobs, environmental groups are trying to kill or delay the project. The Natural Resources Defense Council, for example, argues that the pipeline will increase oil sands production, which they argue is one of the most energy and carbon-intensive methods of retrieving oil. Another environmental advocacy group, 350.org, which sponsors grassroots protests against projects that increase carbon production, held a 40,000-person rally in the nation's capital against the Keystone XL pipeline. It also supported the Do The Math Tour, which traveled to twenty cities, arguing that governments and energy companies should leave the oil sands in the ground.[76]

> **Economic responsibility** a company's social responsibility to make a profit by producing a valued product or service

So, to whom are organizations socially responsible? Many commentators, especially economists and financial analysts, continue to argue that organizations are responsible only to shareholders. Increasingly, however, top managers have come to believe that they and their companies must be socially responsible to their stakeholders. Today, surveys show that as many as 80 percent of top-level managers believe that it is unethical to focus just on shareholders. Twenty-nine states have changed their laws to allow company boards of directors to consider the needs of employees, creditors, suppliers, customers, and local communities, as well as those of shareholders.[77] Although there is not complete agreement, a majority of opinion makers would argue that companies must be socially responsible to their stakeholders.

4-6 FOR WHAT ARE ORGANIZATIONS SOCIALLY RESPONSIBLE?

If organizations are to be socially responsible to stakeholders, what are they to be socially responsible *for*? Companies can best benefit their stakeholders by fulfilling their economic, legal, ethical, and discretionary responsibilities.[78] Economic and legal responsibilities are at the bottom of the pyramid because they play a larger part in a company's social responsibility than do ethical and discretionary responsibilities. However, the relative importance of these various responsibilities depends on society's expectations of corporate social responsibility at a particular point in time.[79] A century ago, society expected businesses to meet their economic and legal responsibilities and little else. Today, when society judges whether businesses are socially responsible, ethical and discretionary responsibilities are considerably more important than they used to be (see box "The Sea of Green").

Historically, **economic responsibility,** or making a profit by producing a product or service valued by society, has been a business's most basic social responsibility. Organizations that don't meet their financial and economic expectations come under tremendous pressure. For example, company boards are quick these days to fire CEOs. Typically, all it takes is two or three bad quarters in a row. Ron Johnson, who left Apple to become CEO at JCPenney, was fired after just a year on the job. When Johnson started, JCPenney had sales of

The Sea of Green

Hong Kong is a business hub in Asia but also one of the most polluted cities in the world. According to a local environmental group, more than 3,000 people die from smog each year, and the city has never met air quality standards it set in 1987. To help Hong Kong become greener, Maersk Line, the largest container-shipping company in the world, has used a special type of fuel on its ships that travel to Hong Kong. This fuel has just 0.5 percent sulphur, a level one-seventh lower than what the Hong Kong government requires. This environmental move does not come cheap to Maersk. The low-sulphur fuel costs the company an extra $2 million per year!

Source: J. Wang, K. Park, and N. Kahn, "Shipper Maersk Wants Hong Kong to Require Clean Fuel," *Bloomberg Businessweek*, January 10, 2013, http://www.businessweek.com/articles/2013-01-10/shipper-maersk-wants-hong-kong-to-require-clean-fuel.

$17.5 billion a year, had 150,000 employees, and was financially stable. When he was fired, the company had sales of $13 billion, had only 116,000 employees, and was at risk of running out of cash within a year.[80] Likewise, when Symmantec, the software virus company fired its second CEO in less than two years, the explanation was, "We weren't making enough progress in product innovation. We were not seeing revenue growth."[81] William Rollnick, who became acting chairman of Mattel after the company fired its previous CEO, says, "There's zero forgiveness. You screw up and you're dead."[82] According to the Conference Board, approximately 25 percent of CEOs of large companies are fired each year.[83]

Legal responsibility is a company's social responsibility to obey society's laws and regulations as it tries to meet its economic responsibilities. For instance, companies award stock options so that managers and employees are rewarded when the company does well. Stock options give you the right to purchase shares of stock at a set price. Let's say that on June 1, the company awards you the right (or option) to buy 100 shares of stock, which, on that day, sell for $10 a share. If the stock price falls below $10, the options are worthless. But, if the stock price rises above $10, the options have value. Specifically, if the stock price rises to $15 a share, you can exercise your option by paying the company $1,000 (100 shares at $10 a share). But because the stock is selling for $15, you can sell your 100 shares for $1,500 and make $500. But what if you could go back in time to, say, January 1 when the stock was selling for $5? You'd make $1,000 instead of $500. It would be unethical and illegal, however, to "backdate" your option to when the stock sold for a lower price. Doing so would illegally increase the value of your option. Over the last 8 years, 151 lawsuits have been filed over allegations of backdating Despite public denials of wrongdoing, companies paid out 7.3 billion in legal settlements.[84]

Ethical responsibility is a company's social responsibility to not violate accepted principles of right and wrong when conducting its business. Bribery is specifically prohibited in most ethics codes, particularly when conducting global business, and is illegal under the U.S. Foreign Corrupt Practices act. Walmart executives in Mexico are alleged to have used $24 million in bribes to Mexican authorities to earn quick approval for construction projects as it rapidly expanded the number of Walmart and Sam's Club stores in Mexico.[85] Walmart informed the U.S. Securities and Exchange Commission

Legal responsibility a company's social responsibility to obey society's laws and regulations

Ethical responsibility a company's social responsibility not to violate accepted principles of right and wrong when conducting its business

that it was conducting a formal investigation after a New York Times article indicated that Walmart's top leaders in Mexico not only knew about the payments, but facilitated and hid them from Walmart headquarters in Bentonville, Arkansas.[86] In a company statement, Walmart said, "If these allegations are true, it is not a reflection of who we are or what we stand for. We are deeply concerned by these allegations and are working aggressively to determine what happened."[87] The company then took the step of removing Jose Luis Rodriguezmacedo Rivera, its Mexican general counsel "effective immediately…," and, "… in the interests of the investigation." The company has since directly linked executive pay and bonuses to "overhauling" its ethics compliance program.[88]

Discretionary responsibilities pertain to the social roles that businesses play in society beyond their economic, legal, and ethical responsibilities. Hurricane Sandy, the largest Atlantic hurricane ever recorded, caused approximately $75 billion in damage—New York state and New Jersey taking the brunt of the 1,100 mile-wide storm. As recovery efforts began, many companies stepped in with donations, contributions, and other forms of valuable assistance. J.P. Morgan, for example, pledged $2 million to the Red Cross, $1 million to local agencies, and $5 billion in special loans to small and mid-sized businesses. The bank also allowed storm-affected customers to skip mortgage payments for ninety days and suspended all of its foreclosure activity in storm-damaged areas. Entertainment companies Time Warner, News Corporation, Walt Disney, and Viacom each pledged to donate $1–$2 million. Meanwhile, Adidas, the sporting goods company, donated $600,000 worth of jackets, while Terramar Sports, which makes outdoor clothing and gear, donated $500,000 worth of long underwear and thermal clothing to people displaced from their homes by the storm.[89]

Carrying out discretionary responsibilities such as these is voluntary. Companies are not considered unethical if they don't perform them. Today, however, corporate stakeholders expect companies to do much more than in the past to meet their discretionary responsibilities.

4-7 RESPONSES TO DEMANDS FOR SOCIAL RESPONSIBILITY

Social responsiveness refers to a company's strategy to respond to stakeholders' economic, legal, ethical, or discretionary expectations concerning social responsibility. A social responsibility problem exists whenever company actions do not meet stakeholder expectations. One model of social responsiveness identifies four strategies for responding to social responsibility problems: reactive, defensive, accommodative, and proactive. These strategies differ in the extent to which the company is willing to act to meet or exceed society's expectations.

A company using a **reactive strategy** will do less than society expects. In Spring 2014, General Motors (GM) publicly acknowledged that since 2001 it had knowingly produced 1.6 million GM cars with faulty ignition switches. The issue, which is linked to 12 auto-related deaths, could happen when turning the ignition key from "off" to "accessory" (used to power accessories, like radios, without the engine running) and then back "on."[90] The car would start, but the ignition switch, which was only partially engaged, could switch off, causing car engines to unexpectedly stop. Service technicians first documented the issue in 2001. Engineers knew in 2004. GM management found out in 2011.[91] Despite knowing about the problem for so long, GM did not issue a safety recall because engineering managers thought drivers could still maintain control of their cars even if their motors suddenly turned off. The defective

Discretionary responsibilities the social roles that a company fulfills beyond its economic, legal, and ethical responsibilities

Social responsiveness a company's strategy to respond to stakeholders' economic, legal, ethical, or discretionary expectations concerning social responsibility

Reactive strategy a social responsiveness strategy in which a company does less than society expects

switches were not redesigned until 2007 and the first vehicle recall was not issued until February 2013. Ironically, the problem is easily fixed with a $5 replacement part that takes minutes to install. GM is offering to either repair the switches or give customers a $500 allowance toward the purchase or lease of a new GM vehicle. It's estimated that GM will spend $1.3 billion just to fix affected vehicles.[92] The Center for Auto Safety, a non-profit organization, has called for GM to waive legal immunity from lawsuits, which it obtained via its 2009 bankruptcy, and to set aside an additional $1 billion as a dedicated fund for victims.[93]

By contrast, a company using a **defensive strategy** would admit responsibility for a problem but would do the least required to meet societal expectations. Foxconn is a Taiwanese electronics manufacturing company that operates Chinese factories that produce 40 percent of the world's consumer electronic products. Over the last four years, at the Foxconn factories that make iPhones and iPads, eighteen employees attempted suicide, most by leaping to their deaths. After the eleventh suicide, the company placed suicide nets that reach twenty feet out around the perimeter of each building. An extensive *New York Times* investigation found that employees often worked seven days a week, were exposed to dangerous chemicals, and lived in crowded, company-supplied dorm rooms, some with as many as twenty people per three-bedroom apartment. However, Apple, which had been conducting audits of its suppliers' manufacturing facilities for many years, was slow to respond. A consultant with Business for Social Responsibility, a company Apple hired for advice on labor issues, said, "We've spent years telling Apple there are serious problems and recommending changes. They don't want to pre-empt problems, they just want to avoid embarrassments." A former Apple executive said, "If you see the same pattern of problems, year after year, that means the company's ignoring the issue rather than solving it. Noncompliance is tolerated, as long as the suppliers promise to try harder next time. If we meant business, core violations would disappear." After the *New York Times* story, Apple began working with the Fair Labor Association, a nonprofit organization that promotes and monitors safe working conditions. Four years after the problems began, following the Fair Labor Association's report, Apple and Foxconn agreed to increase pay, limit workers to a maximum of forty-nine hours a week, build more dormitories, and hire thousands of additional workers. [94]

A company using an **accommodative strategy** will accept responsibility for a problem and take a progressive approach by doing all that could be expected to solve the problem. Novartis, a Swiss drug maker, experienced a series of scandals in its Japanese clinical research trials, such as data being altered to indicate more positive results for an experimental blood pressure drug, and covering up the severe side effects associated with a potential leukemia treatment. An independent panel commissioned by the company found Japanese sales staff had "ethically inappropriate" links to clinical researchers. Novartis's global pharmaceuticals head, David Epstein, apologized to Japanese regulators, saying, that the link between sales and research came as a "complete shock" and that, because sales staff had made attempts to influence research results,"We fully expect to find other clinical trials that are problematic." Stating that,"Our company culture and the way we do business in Japan needs to change urgently, he announced the immediate resignation of their Japanese division's top three executives, along with a freeze on all doctor-led clinical trials in Japan until a complete investigation could be conducted."[95] Novartis would furthermore begin training programs in its Japanese division to make clear what was and was not acceptable in the context of sales and clinical research.[96]

Finally, a company using a **proactive strategy** will anticipate responsibility for a problem before it occurs, do more than expected to address the problem, and lead the industry in its approach. Recently, Unilever announced that it would no longer use microplastic beads in its soap products. The beads, about one-third of a millimeter in size, function like a gentle abrasive to remove dead skin.[97] A single bottle of facial cleanser can contain as many as 360,000 microbeads. While it's not yet known with scientific certainty that microbeads are harmful, there is potential because they absorb chemicals and are easily ingested by sea animals because of their minuscule size. Rather than waiting for conclusive evidence, Unilever announced that it is completely eliminating microbeads from its products because, "We believe we can provide consumers with products that deliver a similar exfoliating performance without the need to use plastics. We expect to complete this phase-out globally by 1 January 2015 and are currently exploring which suitable alternatives can best match the sensory experience that the plastic scrub beads provide."[98]

Defensive strategy a social responsiveness strategy in which a company admits responsibility for a problem but does the least required to meet societal expectations

Accommodative strategy a social responsiveness strategy in which a company accepts responsibility for a problem and does all that society expects to solve that problem

Proactive strategy a social responsiveness strategy in which a company anticipates a problem before it occurs and does more than society expects to take responsibility for and address the problem

In India Social Responsibility Is the Law

In India, a new law has changed the landscape for social responsibility; India's largest companies are now required to contribute 2 percent of profits to charity. The law applies to companies worth more than 5 billion rupees ($83 million) with either annual turnover greater than 10 billion rupees or 50 million rupees in profits. Issues that contributions can be directed toward include hunger, poverty, education, women's rights, child mortality, disease, and environmental issues. It has yet to be seen how effective this measure will be, and many companies may simply see the law as another tax burden. According to Dasra, a company from Mumbai that connects corporate donors with non-profit organizations, many companies favor the opportunity to determine where their money goes, rather than just being taxed by the government. Deval Sanghavi, a partner at Dasra, says, "The government thinks corporations might have a greater impact if they decide how to spend the money themselves." Still, many Indian charities will have to improve their administrative capabilities to be able to handle the volume of donations that are now forthcoming.

Source: S. Seervai, "Indian Companies and Charities Aren't Ready for New Giving Law," *The Wall Street Journal*, April 11, 2014. accessed April 17, 2014. http://blogs.wsj.com /indiarealtime/2014/04/11/indian-companies-and-charities-arent-ready-for-new-giving-law /?KEYWORDS=social+responsibility.

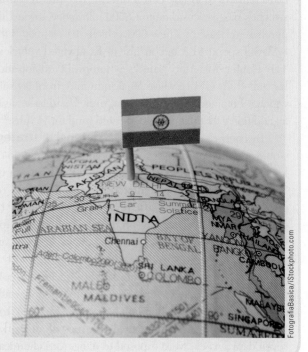

FotografiaBasica/iStockphoto.com

4-8 SOCIAL RESPONSIBILITY AND ECONOMIC PERFORMANCE

One question that managers often ask is, "Does it pay to be socially responsible?" In previous editions of this textbook, the answer was no, as early research indicated that there was not an inherent relationship between social responsibility and economic performance.[99] Recent research, however, leads to different conclusions. There is no trade-off between being socially responsible and economic performance.[100] And there is a small, positive relationship between being socially responsible and economic performance that strengthens with corporate reputation.[101] Let's explore what each of these results means.

First, as noted earlier, there is no trade-off between being socially responsible and economic performance.[102] Being socially responsible usually won't make a business less profitable. What this suggests is that the costs of being socially responsible—and those costs can be high, especially early on—can be offset by a better product or corporate reputation, which results in stronger sales or higher profit margins. When businesses enhance their reputations by being socially responsible, they hope to maximize *willingness to pay*, that is, customers paying more for products and services that are socially responsible. Patagonia sells expensive outdoor gear and clothing to customers who are willing to pay a higher price because of the company's environmental focus. For example, two decades ago, it switched to organic cotton, which costs three times as much as traditional cotton because it is grown without chemicals and irrigation. Just two years ago, Patagonia created the Common Threads Partnership, in which it pledges "to build useful things that last, to repair what breaks and recycle what comes to the end of its useful life," and in which customers are asked "to buy only what I need (and will last), repair what breaks, reuse (share) what I no longer need and recycle everything else."[103] Patagonia promotes the Common Threads Partnership with advertisements proclaiming, "Don't Buy This Jacket." Of course, because environmental consumers are willing to pay more, sales jumped after this ad, presumably taking market share from Patagonia's competitors.[104]

Second, it usually *does* pay to be socially responsible, and that relationship becomes stronger particularly when a company or its products have a strong reputation for social responsibility.[105] Finally, even if there is generally a small positive relationship between social responsibility and economic performance that becomes stronger when a company or its products have a positive reputation for social responsibility, and even if there is no trade-off between being socially responsible and economic performance, there is no guarantee that socially responsible companies will be profitable. Simply put, socially responsible companies experience the same ups and downs in economic performance that traditional businesses do. General Motors' Chevy Volt features a plug-in hybrid engine, producing outstanding fuel efficiency of 60 miles per gallon and the ability to drive 800 miles between fill-ups. The Volt is a tremendous technological and environmental product, but it's been a disaster for GM's bottom line. GM's investment in the Volt, so far, is estimated at $1.2 billion. But, because of the technology involved, the Volt is difficult and expensive to assemble, so much so that Reuters estimates that GM loses $50,000 per Volt! Sales have been incredibly disappointing. Priced at $39,995, GM has sold only 58,000 Volts in four years, far short of its goal of 60,000 per year. Sales picked up slightly only after GM offered a 25 percent discount on top of the Volt's already steep price discounts, which are three to four times higher than the rest of the auto industry. GM's attempt at building a highly fuel-efficient, environmentally friendly car may have been good for the planet, but it has been a drag on GM's profits and finances.[106]

Being socially responsible may be the right thing to do, and it is usually associated with increased profits, but it doesn't guarantee business success.

STUDY TOOLS 4

LOCATED AT THE BACK OF YOUR BOOK:
☐ Rip out and study the Chapter Review Card at the end of the book

LOG IN TO WWW.CENGAGEBRAIN.COM TO:
☐ Review Key Term Flashcards
☐ Complete Practice Quizzing (take up to four times without repeating the same quiz)
☐ Complete Interactive Content: Graded Quiz, Media Quiz, and Fill-in-the-Blank Questions
☐ Complete Games: Beat the Clock and Crossword Puzzle
☐ Watch Management Workplace Video on "Theo Chocolate"
☐ Work Through the What Would You Do Case on American Express Headquarters

5 Planning and Decision Making

LEARNING OUTCOMES

5-1 Discuss the benefits and pitfalls of planning.

5-2 Describe how to make a plan that works.

5-3 Discuss how companies can use plans at all management levels, from top to bottom.

5-4 Explain the steps and limits to rational decision making.

5-5 Explain how group decisions and group decision-making techniques can improve decision making.

After you finish

this chapter, go

to **PAGE 108** for

STUDY TOOLS

5-1 BENEFITS AND PITFALLS OF PLANNING

Even inexperienced managers know that planning and decision making are central parts of their jobs. Figure out what the problem is. Generate potential solutions or plans. Pick the best one. Make it work. Experienced managers, however, know how hard it really is to make good plans and decisions. One seasoned manager says: "I think the biggest surprises are the problems. Maybe I had never seen it before. Maybe I was protected by my management when I was in sales. Maybe I had delusions of grandeur, I don't know. I just know how disillusioning and frustrating it is to be hit with problems and conflicts all day and not be able to solve them very cleanly."[1]

Planning is choosing a goal and developing a method or strategy to achieve that goal. Having succeeded in the United States, where it is now the second-largest foreign carmaker, selling 1.1 million low-priced, high-quality, feature-rich cars per year, Hyundai and its Kia subsidiary are planning to expand in Europe. With a 5.1 percent share of the European market, it plans to expand sales by 25 percent to 500,000 cars per year by 2013. To accomplish the plan, Hyundai will introduce new models, like the i40, Veloster, and i30, all of which have been designed and styled specifically to suit European consumer tastes. The company will also add a third shift to its factory in the Czech Republic and expand annual production there by 100,000 cars. Stefan Bratzel, director of the Center of Automotive Management at the University of Applied Sciences in Bergisch Gladbach, Germany, says, "Hyundai is one of VW's most serious challengers. The mix of good value, quality, and design is a solid basis, and they've been getting more innovative every year."[2]

Are you one of those naturally organized people who always makes a daily to-do list, writes everything down so you won't forget, and never misses a deadline because you keep track of everything with your handy time-management notebook, iPhone, or PC? Or are you one of those flexible, creative, go-with-the-flow people who dislikes planning and organizing because it restricts your freedom, energy, and performance? Some people are natural planners. They love it and can see only its benefits. Others dislike planning and can see only its disadvantages. It turns out that *both* views have real value.

*Planning has advantages and disadvantages. Let's learn about **5-1a the benefits** and **5-1b the pitfalls of planning.***

5-1a Benefits of Planning

Planning offers several important benefits: intensified effort, persistence, direction, and creation of task strategies.[3] First, managers and employees put forth greater effort when following a plan. Take two workers. Instruct one to "do your best" to increase production, and instruct the other to achieve a 2 percent increase in production each month. Research shows that the one with the specific plan will work harder.[4]

Second, planning leads to persistence, that is, working hard for long periods. In fact, planning encourages persistence even when there may be little chance of short-term success.[5] McDonald's founder Ray Kroc, a keen believer in the power of persistence, had this quotation from President Calvin Coolidge hung in all of his executives' offices: "Nothing in the world can take the place of persistence. Talent will not; nothing is more common than unsuccessful men with talent. Genius will not; unrewarded genius is almost a proverb. Education will not; the world is full of educated derelicts. Persistence and determination alone are omnipotent."[6]

The third benefit of planning is direction. Irving Wladawsky-Berger of the Institute for Data Driven Design explains that planning through goal setting is especially important when organizations experience major transitions. "A major way of rallying the organization to embrace the needed transformation is to have a compelling target to shoot for, a kind of promised land everyone can aim for instead of wandering in the desert without a clear path forward," Wladawsky-Berger says.[7]

The fourth benefit of planning is that it encourages the development of task strategies. In other words, planning not only encourages people to work hard for extended periods and to engage in behaviors directly related to goal accomplishment, it also encourages them to think of better ways to do their jobs. Finally, perhaps the most compelling benefit of planning is that it has been proved to work for both companies and individuals. On average, companies with plans have larger profits and grow much faster than companies without plans.[8] The same holds true for individual managers and employees: There is no better way to improve the performance of the people who work in a company than to have them set goals and develop strategies for achieving those goals.

Planning choosing a goal and developing a strategy to achieve that goal

5-1b Pitfalls of Planning

Despite the significant benefits associated with planning, it is not a cure-all. Plans won't fix all organizational problems. In fact, many management authors and consultants believe that planning can harm companies in several ways.[9]

The first pitfall of planning is that it can impede change and prevent or slow needed adaptation. Sometimes companies become so committed to achieving the goals set forth in their plans or on following the strategies and tactics spelled out in them that they fail to see that their plans aren't working or that their goals need to change. For nearly a century, Kodak dominated the photography business, as it was world famous for its photo paper, its cameras, and especially its film. However, its commitment to film ultimately proved disastrous as its business turned digital. The tragic irony, of course, is that Kodak engineers invented digital photography in 1975 but didn't pursue the technology out of fear that it would destroy its highly profitable film business. So while other photo companies were busy remaking themselves for the digital age (Canon, for example, stopped selling its last film camera in 2004), Kodak still dedicated most of its resources to the film market, resulting in huge losses. Since 2003, Kodak has closed thirteen factories and laid off 47,000 employees at a cost of $3.4 billion. With a debt of $6.8 billion and losses in six of the past seven years, Kodak was forced to declare Chapter 11 bankruptcy. Don Strickland, a former Kodak vice president for digital imaging, said, "Out of the bankruptcy proceedings, a much smaller company can emerge. But I really don't believe that there's going to be another Kodak moment."[10]

The second pitfall is that planning can create a false sense of certainty. Planners sometimes feel that they know exactly what the future holds for their competitors, their suppliers, and their companies. However, all plans are based on assumptions: "The price of gasoline will increase by 4 percent per year"; "Exports will continue to rise." For plans to work, the assumptions on which they are based must hold true. If the assumptions turn out to be false, then the plans based on them are likely to fail.

The third potential pitfall of planning is the detachment of planners. In theory, strategic planners and top-level managers are supposed to focus on the big picture and not concern themselves with the details of implementation (i.e., carrying out the plan). According to management professor Henry Mintzberg, detachment leads planners to plan for things they don't understand.[11] Plans are meant to be guidelines for action, not abstract theories. Consequently, planners need to be familiar with the daily details of their businesses if they are to produce plans that can work.

British-based **Tesco,** the third-largest retailer in the world, spent five years researching and planning before it spent $1.6 billion to enter the U.S. grocery business by building 199 Fresh & Easy stores. Former CEO Terry Leahy said, "Our team went over to live in the U.S. We stayed in people's homes. We went through their fridges. We did all our research, and we're good at research." Unfortunately, because they had never competed in the U.S. grocery business, Tesco's research and planning failed to account for Americans' different tastes. For example, at 10,000 square feet, or 20 percent of the size of a typical American supermarket, Fresh & Easy stores were too small and had too limited a selection, and, at first, didn't have bakeries, which Americans like. Tesco relied heavily on its Fresh & Easy brand of premade meals, popular in England but unknown in the United States, where shoppers prefer brand-name products. According to Natalie Berg, director of Planet Retail, "The main thing is that they underestimated how Americans shop."[12]

5-2 HOW TO MAKE A PLAN THAT WORKS

Planning is a double-edged sword. If done right, planning brings about tremendous increases in individual and organizational performance. If planning is done wrong, however, it can have just the opposite effect and harm individual and organizational performance.

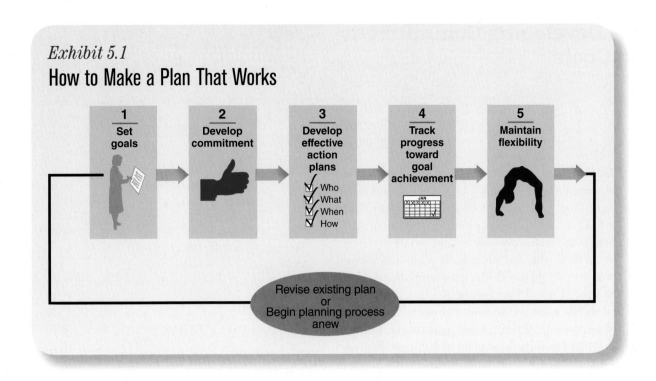

Exhibit 5.1

How to Make a Plan That Works

1 Set goals

2 Develop commitment

3 Develop effective action plans
☑ Who
☑ What
☑ When
☑ How

4 Track progress toward goal achievement

5 Maintain flexibility

Revise existing plan or Begin planning process anew

In this section, you will learn how to make a plan that works. As depicted in Exhibit 5.1, planning consists of **5-2a setting goals, 5-2b developing commitment to the goals, 5-2c developing effective action plans, 5-2d tracking progress toward goal achievement,** *and* **5-2e maintaining flexibility in planning.**

5-2a Setting Goals

The first step in planning is to set goals. To direct behavior and increase effort, goals need to be specific and challenging.[13] For example, deciding to "increase sales this year" won't direct and energize workers as much as deciding to "increase North American sales by 4 percent in the next six months." Specific, challenging goals provide a target for which to aim and a standard against which to measure success.

One way of writing effective goals for yourself, your job, or your company is to use the S.M.A.R.T. guidelines. **S.M.A.R.T. goals** are **S**pecific, **M**easurable, **A**ttainable, **R**ealistic, and **T**imely.[14] Atlanta-based Novelis is the biggest recycler of aluminum beverage cans in the world. It recycles 40 billion cans a year into "can sheets" that are used to make new beverage cans and other products. In 2010, 33 percent of the materials it used to roll aluminum can sheets were recycled. The company's goal is to increase that share to 50 percent by 2015 and 80 percent by 2020.[15] Let's see how Novelis's objectives measure up to the S.M.A.R.T. guidelines for goals.

First, is the goal **S**pecific? Yes, as opposed to saying they simply want to increase the percentage of recycled material it uses, Novelis has clearly specified the percentages, 50 percent by 2015 and 80 percent by 2020. Is the goal **M**easurable? Again the answer is yes, since Novelis can easily track and compare the percentage of recycled material it uses now to what it used before. Whether the goal is **A**ttainable or not depends on many factors. One challenge is that beverage cans are made from two types of aluminum: one for the sides of the can and another that is stiffer and stronger and used to make can tops and bottoms. Melting recycled cans combines these two kinds of aluminum which, once mixed together, are not suitable for making cans. However, Novelis developed a production method that overcomes this problem, which will allow it to greatly increase the amount of recycled material it uses.[16] Time will tell if the goal is **R**ealistic. But Novelis has made solid progress, increasing the percentage of recycled materials it uses from 33 percent in 2010 to 43 percent in 2013.[17] Finally, while its goals are ambitious, they are **T**imely. When it set the goals in 2011, it gave itself four years to increase the recycled percentage to 50 percent in 2015 and nine years to increase the percentage to 80 percent in 2020.

S.M.A.R.T. goals goals that are specific, measurable, attainable, realistic, and timely

5-2b Developing Commitment to Goals

Just because a company sets a goal doesn't mean that people will try to accomplish it. If workers don't care about a goal, that goal won't encourage them to work harder or smarter. Thus, the second step in planning is to develop commitment to goals.[18]

Goal commitment is the determination to achieve a goal. Commitment to achieve a goal is not automatic. Managers and workers must choose to commit themselves to a goal. Edwin Locke, professor emeritus of management at the University of Maryland and the foremost expert on how, why, and when goals work, tells a story about an overweight friend who lost seventy-five pounds. Locke says, "I asked him how he did it, knowing how hard it was for most people to lose so much weight." His friend responded, "Actually, it was quite simple. I simply decided that I *really wanted* to do it."[19] Put another way, goal commitment is really wanting to achieve a goal.

So how can managers bring about goal commitment? The most popular approach is to set goals participatively. Rather than assigning goals to workers ("Johnson, you've got till Tuesday of next week to redesign the flux capacitor so it gives us 10 percent more output"), managers and employees choose goals together. The goals are more likely to be realistic and attainable if employees participate in setting them. Another technique for gaining commitment to a goal is to make the goal public. For example, college students who publicly communicated their semester grade goals ("This semester, I'm shooting for a 3.5") to important people in their lives (usually a parent or sibling) were much more committed to achieving their grades than those who did not. Still another way to increase goal commitment is to obtain top management's support. Top management can show support for a plan or program by providing funds, speaking publicly about the plan, or participating in the plan itself.

5-2c Developing Effective Action Plans

The third step in planning is to develop effective action plans. An **action plan** lists the specific steps (how),

Goal commitment the determination to achieve a goal

Action plan a plan that lists the specific steps, people, resources, and time period needed to attain a goal

Proximal goals short-term goals or subgoals

Planning for Your Staff Needs

Creating work schedules can require extensive planning. For instance, how many waitpersons will you need to staff your restaurant during peak hours from 11:00 to 2:30, and how do you manage a shift change at 12:00 right in the middle? Many technology companies have developed software programs and apps that can help managers handle a wide range of scheduling related issues. Workforce Ready, created by Kronos Inc., allows managers to start with a basic scheduling app and add on additional features like tracking acquired vacation time and managing payroll. Workforce Central, a more advanced suite from Kronos, can help firms keep track of changes to laws that might affect reporting and tracking time and payroll. Dayforce, by Ceridian Corp., allows employees access to scheduling information online, where they can check schedules, exchange time slots with coworkers, and report on their availability to fill slots.

Source: L. Weber, "The Best New Apps for Workplace Scheduling," *The Wall Street Journal*, September 15, 2013, accessed April 18, 2014.

people (who), resources (what), and time period (when) for accomplishing a goal. For its first eight years in business, Facebook focused on growth, but now its top leadership team, known as the "M team," is developing specific action plans to hold Facebook managers and employees accountable for increasing profit and, ultimately, its stock price. For example, software engineers who write code for Facebook's website and mobile apps were challenged to solve revenue-related issues. Andrew Bosworth, heading the new department of advertising engineering, worked with software engineers to write code so that ads could be run for the first time on mobile phones and tablets. However, instead of the ads being on the right side of the screen, the ads appear in the center, where they're impossible to miss. That step, along with nine other action plans that Facebook is pursuing, helped increase revenue to $1.46 billion, up 38 percent from $1.06 billion a year earlier. Twenty-five percent of Facebook's overall revenue now comes from mobile ads.[20]

5-2d Tracking Progress

The fourth step in planning is to track progress toward goal achievement. There are two accepted methods of tracking progress. The first is to set proximal goals and distal goals. **Proximal goals** are short-term goals or

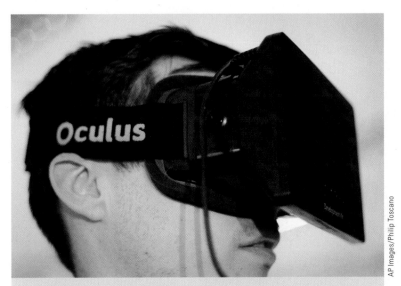

Facebook has undertaken a number of new ventures to grow its presence and increase profits. For example, in March 2014, Facebook announced plans to purchase Oculus VR, maker of the Oculus Rift virtual reality headset.

subgoals, whereas **distal goals** are long-term or primary goals.[21]

The second method of tracking progress is to gather and provide performance feedback. Regular, frequent performance feedback allows workers and managers to track their progress toward goal achievement and make adjustments in effort, direction, and strategies.[22] Exhibit 5.2 shows the impact of feedback on safety behavior at a large bakery company with a worker safety record that was two-and-a-half times worse than the industry average. During the baseline period, workers in the wrapping department, who measure and mix ingredients, roll the bread dough, and put it into baking pans, performed their jobs safely about 70 percent of the time (see 1 in Exhibit 5.2). The baseline safety record for workers in the makeup department, who bag and seal baked bread and assemble, pack, and tape cardboard cartons for shipping, was somewhat better at 78 percent (see 2). The company then gave workers thirty minutes of safety training, set a goal of 90 percent safe behavior, and then provided daily feedback (such as a chart similar to Exhibit 5.2). Performance improved dramatically. During the intervention period, safely performed behaviors rose to an average of 95.8 percent for wrapping workers (see 3) and 99.3 percent for workers in the makeup department (see 4), and never fell below 83 percent. Thus, the combination of training, a challenging goal, and feedback led to a dramatic increase in performance. The importance of feedback alone can be seen in the reversal stage, when the company quit posting daily feedback on safe behavior. Without daily feedback, the percentage of safely performed behaviors returned to baseline levels—70.8 percent for the wrapping department (see 5) and 72.3 percent for the makeup department (see 6). For planning to be effective, workers need both a specific, challenging goal and regular feedback to track their progress. Indeed, additional research indicates that the effectiveness of goal setting can be doubled by the addition of feedback.[23]

5-2e Maintaining Flexibility

Because action plans are sometimes poorly conceived and goals sometimes turn out not to be achievable, the last step in developing an effective plan is to maintain flexibility. One method of maintaining flexibility while planning is to adopt an options-based approach.[24] The goal of **options-based planning** is to keep options open by making small, simultaneous investments in many alternative plans. Then, when one or a few of these plans emerge as likely winners, you invest even more in these plans while discontinuing or reducing investment in the others.

In part, options-based planning is the opposite of traditional planning. Whereas the purpose of an action plan is to commit people and resources to a particular course of action, the purpose of options-based planning is to leave those commitments open by maintaining **slack resources**—that is, a cushion of resources, such as extra time, people, money, or production capacity, that can be used to address and adapt to unanticipated changes, problems, or opportunities.[25] Holding options open gives you choices. And choices, combined with slack resources, give you flexibility. The winter of

Distal goals long-term or primary goals

Options-based planning maintaining planning flexibility by making small, simultaneous investments in many alternative plans

Slack resources a cushion of extra resources that can be used with options-based planning to adapt to unanticipated changes, problems, or opportunities

Exhibit 5.2
Effects of Goal Setting, Training, and Feedback on Safe Behavior in a Bread Factory

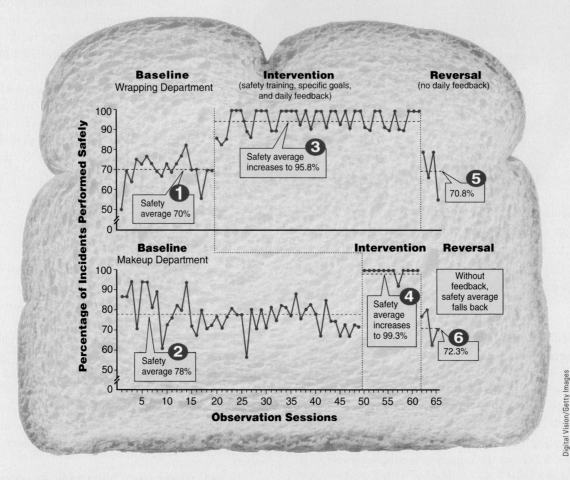

Source: Komaki, J., Barwick K. D., & Scott, L. R. "A Behavioral Approach to Occupational Safety: Pinpointing and Reinforcing Safe Performance in a Food Manufacturing Plant."
Journal of Applied Psychology 63 (1978).

2014, which broke records nationwide for record cold and snow, forced railroad companies to run and staff more trains with shorter loads that are easier to start and stop in bad weather. Unlike its competitors, Union Pacific railroad had already created "surge capacity," or slack resources, to handle the situation. Instead of selling or scrapping old locomotives when it bought new ones, Union Pacific "retired" them to long-term storage. So when the severe weather hit, it had 600 extra locomotives ready to go, including 550 extra workers on furlough or standby who were immediately ready to work. That winter, CSX Corp., a competitor, saw its operating ratio, a measure of operational efficiency, drop more than 4 percent, whereas thanks to slack resources, Union Pacific's rose 2 percent.[26]

 5-3 # PLANNING FROM TOP TO BOTTOM

Planning works best when the goals and action plans at the bottom and middle of the organization support the goals and action plans at the top of the organization. In other words, planning works best when everybody pulls in the same direction. Exhibit 5.3 illustrates this planning continuity, beginning at the top with a clear definition of the company purpose and ending at the bottom with the execution of operational plans.

*Let's see how **5-3a top managers create the organization's purpose statement and strategic objective, 5-3b***

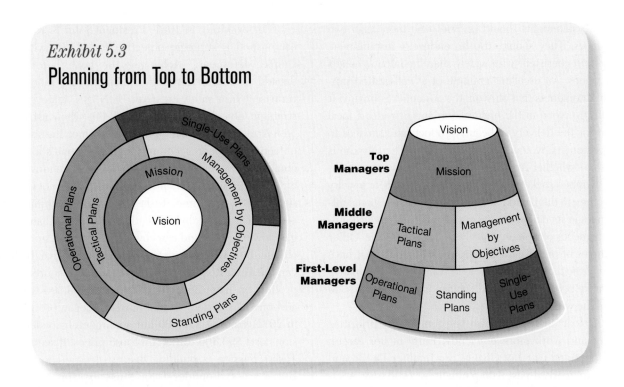

Exhibit 5.3

Planning from Top to Bottom

middle managers develop tactical plans and use management by objectives to motivate employee efforts toward the overall purpose and strategic objective, and 5-3c first-level managers use operational, single-use, and standing plans to implement the tactical plans.

5-3a Starting at the Top

Top management is responsible for developing long-term **strategic plans** that make clear how the company will serve customers and position itself against competitors in the next two to five years. Although its U.S.-based Chrysler division has been earning strong profits, Fiat's European sales are down 16.7 percent from a year ago; its debt, now at about $8.7 billion, is rising; and its factories are running at just 45 percent of capacity. Instead of layoffs and factory closings to cut costs, CEO Sergio Marchionne hopes to boost sales of its premium-priced small cars by following a long-term strategy that shifts Fiat's focus from selling cars in Europe to exporting them to fast-growing markets in Asia and the Americas. Over the next five years, Fiat will introduce five new cars and three new light trucks under the Fiat brand, nine new Alfa Romeos, and six new Maseratis. In Europe, Fiat's new cars will be based on its compact 500 and Panda models, while its larger cars will be sold

in North America, South America, and Asia. Fiat spent nearly $5 billion in 2013 and 2014 to develop these new cars and trucks.[27]

Strategic planning begins with the creation of an organizational purpose. A **purpose statement,** which is often referred to as an organizational mission or vision, is a statement of a company's purpose or reason for existing.[28]

> **Strategic plans** overall company plans that clarify how the company will serve customers and position itself against competitors over the next two to five years
>
> **Purpose statement** a statement of a company's purpose or reason for existing

Purpose statements should be brief—no more than two sentences. They should also be enduring, inspirational, clear, and consistent with widely shared company beliefs and values. An excellent example of a well-crafted purpose statement is that of Avon, the cosmetics company. It guides everyone in the organization and provides a focal point for the delivery of beauty products and services to the customers, women around the world. The purpose is the same whether Avon is selling lipstick to women in India, shampoo packets to women in the Amazon, or jewelry to women in the United States. Despite these regional differences in specific strategy, the overall goal—understanding the needs of women globally—does not change. Other examples of organizational purpose statements that have been particularly effective include Walt Disney Company's "to make people happy" and Schlage Lock Company's "to make the world more secure."[29]

A clear mission can also help employees prioritize better and work more efficiently. Early in her career, president and COO of Change.org Jennifer Dulski and her team worked past 9:00 p.m. almost every day. A supervisor took notice and told her she was working too hard. His advice: "Write down at the top of a piece of paper the mission you're trying to accomplish. Now take your entire to-do list and check every item against the mission."[30]

The **strategic objective**, which flows from the purpose, is a more specific goal that unifies company-wide efforts, stretches and challenges the organization, and possesses a finish line and a time frame.[31] Collins and Porras define an organization's mission: "A mission is a clear and compelling goal that serves to unify an organization's efforts. An effective mission must stretch and challenge the organization, yet be achievable." However, many others define *mission* as an organization's purpose. In this edition, to be more specific and avoid confusion, we use Collins and Porras's term *purpose statement*, meaning a clear statement of an organization's purpose or reason for existence. Furthermore, we will continue to use Collins and Porras's definition of a mission (i.e., "a clear and compelling goal . . .") but instead call it "the strategic objective."

For example, in 1961, President John F. Kennedy established a strategic objective for NASA with this simple statement: "Achieving the goal, before this decade is out, of landing a man on the moon and returning him safely to earth."[32] NASA achieved this strategic objective on July 20, 1969, when astronaut Neil Armstrong walked on the moon. Once the strategic objective has been accomplished, a new one should be chosen. However, the new strategic objective must grow out of the organization's purpose, which does not change significantly over time. Tesla Motors builds completely electric cars—not hybrids—that are faster than most gas-powered cars and can cover over 300 miles on a full charge. But, Teslas are extraordinarily expensive. Its first car, the Tesla Roadster, a high performance sports car in production from 2008 to 2012, cost $109,000 without add-ons. The 4-door Model S, which began production in 2012, starts at $70,000 but a completely loaded version costs $93,400. Based on those prices, it seems that Tesla's mission is building luxury, electric sports cars. But, it's not. Founder Elon Musk explains that, "the strategy at Tesla is to enter at the high end of the market, where customers are prepared to pay a premium, and then drive down market as fast as possible to high volume and lower prices with each successive model."[33] In other words, Musk says, "When someone buys the Tesla Roadster sports car, they are actually helping pay for development of the low cost family car."[34] Tesla's Model X, a smaller sedan with gull-wing rear doors, is estimated to sell for $70,000 when it debuts in 2015. But at a technology conference in 2013, Musk said that Tesla's goal was to release an electric car for under $30,000 in the next five years, thus eventually fulfilling the company's mission.[35]

5-3b Bending in the Middle

Middle management is responsible for developing and carrying out tactical plans to accomplish the organization's strategic objective. **Tactical plans** specify how a company will use resources, budgets, and people to accomplish specific goals related to its strategic objective for the next five years. Whereas strategic plans and objectives are used to focus company efforts over the next two to five years, tactical plans and objectives are used to direct behavior, efforts, and attention over the next six months to two years. Target, for example, recently announced that it is undertaking its first foreign expansion in Canada by opening 124 stores there over the next year. The first twenty-four stores are in Ontario, with the remaining stores located in Quebec and

Strategic objective a more specific goal that unifies company-wide efforts, stretches and challenges the organization, and possesses a finish line and a time frame

Tactical plans plans created and implemented by middle managers that specify how the company will use resources, budgets, and people over the next six months to two years to accomplish specific goals within its mission

Canada's western provinces. One of the key tactical steps to making this happen was a $1.81 billion purchase of Zellers discount store leases throughout Canada. Like Target, Zellers positioned itself as a more fashionable, chic alternative to Walmart. Buying the store leases gave Target immediate entry to the Canadian market. However, it will spend another $3 billion to redesign and enlarge Zellers stores into Target stores.[36]

Management by objectives is a management technique often used to develop and carry out tactical plans. **Management by objectives** is a four-step process in which managers and their employees (1) discuss possible goals; (2) collectively select goals that are challenging, attainable, and consistent with the company's overall goals; (3) jointly develop tactical plans that lead to the accomplishment of tactical goals and objectives; and (4) meet regularly to review progress toward accomplishment of those goals. In Chapter 1, we learned that on Mondays, **Qualtrics,** which sells online survey research tools, sends out a company-wide email describing each employee's goals for the coming week and whether they met their prior week's goals. Those weekly goals, however, are derived from quarterly goals containing detailed, measurable objectives and key results, such as revenue and customer satisfaction. Similar to the weekly email, Qualtrics's internal database, which is open to all who work there, shows each employee's quarterly goals and results, individual weekly goals, performance reviews and bonuses, successes and failures from which others can learn, and full career histories.[37] CEO Adam Bryant says, "When everyone's rowing together toward the same objective, it's extremely powerful. We're trying to execute at a very high level, and we need to make sure everyone knows where we're going."[38]

5-3c Finishing at the Bottom

Lower-level managers are responsible for developing and carrying out **operational plans,** which are the day-to-day plans for producing or delivering the organization's products and services. Operational plans direct the behavior, efforts, and priorities of operative employees for periods ranging from thirty days to six months. There are three kinds of operational plans: single-use plans, standing plans, and budgets.

Single-use plans deal with unique, one-time-only events. After a devastating earthquake and tsunami critically disabled a nuclear power plant, several Japanese electric companies warned that they might not be able to provide enough power for businesses and residents. The Japanese government then required heavy power users to cut their consumption by 15 percent, which required many businesses to enact conservation plans. Sony, for example, announced that it would encourage all workers to leave their offices by 5:00 p.m., one hour earlier than usual, and shut off the air conditioning promptly at 6:00 p.m. The company also decided to extend summer holidays at several factories in order to reduce power consumption. Komatsu, a manufacturer of heavy machinery, announced that it would close two stories of its ten-story headquarters building and give employees one day off per week. Nissan, meanwhile, installed power meters at its factories so that it could stop its operations when its daily power consumption target was exceeded.[39]

Unlike single-use plans that are created, carried out once, and then never used again, **standing plans** save managers time because once the plans are created, they can be used repeatedly to handle frequently recurring events. If you encounter a problem that you've seen before, someone in your company has probably written a standing plan that explains how to address it. Using this plan rather than reinventing the wheel will save you time. There are three kinds of standing plans: policies, procedures, and rules and regulations.

Policies indicate the general course of action that company managers should take in response to a particular event or situation. A well-written policy will also specify why the policy exists and what outcome the policy is intended to produce. Absenteeism means missing work, while "presenteeism" is coming to work when you're sick.[40] Ann Stevens at ClearRock, a leadership and career consulting company says, "People get really, really ticked off at co-workers who spread germs in the workplace." So why do people come to work sick? Because of policies that reward people for good attendance. Or, because of policies with a limited number of sick days. Use them up and you're stuck if you're sick again. Both reasons are

Management by objectives a four-step process in which managers and employees discuss and select goals, develop tactical plans, and meet regularly to review progress toward goal accomplishment

Operational plans day-to-day plans, developed and implemented by lower-level managers, for producing or delivering the organization's products and services over a thirty-day to six-month period

Single-use plans plans that cover unique, one-time-only events

Standing plans plans used repeatedly to handle frequently recurring events

Policies standing plans that indicate the general course of action that should be taken in response to a particular event or situation

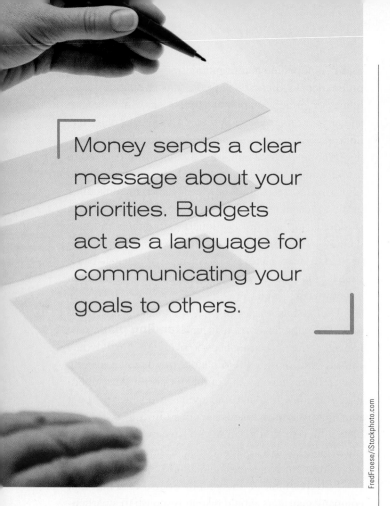

Money sends a clear message about your priorities. Budgets act as a language for communicating your goals to others.

why more companies are using paid-time-off policies that don't distinguish between sick days, personal days, or vacation days. This give employees maximum flexibility and discourages them from coming to work sick. Carol Sladek, at Aon Hewitt, a human resource consulting firm, says, "If you have the flu, stay home. Just stay home . . ."[41]

Procedures are more specific than policies because they indicate the series of steps that should be taken in response to a particular event. A manufacturer's

---

procedure for handling defective products might include the following steps.

▸ Step 1: Rejected material is locked in a secure area with "reject" documentation attached.

▸ Step 2: Material Review Board (MRB) identifies the defect and notes how far outside the standard the rejected products are.

▸ Step 3: MRB determines the disposition of the defective product as either scrap or rework.

▸ Step 4: Scrap is either discarded or recycled, and rework is sent back through the production line to be fixed.

▸ Step 5: If delays in delivery will result, an MRB member notifies customer.[42]

Rules and regulations are even more specific than procedures because they specify what must happen or not happen. They describe precisely how a particular action should be performed. For instance, many companies have rules and regulations forbidding managers from writing job reference letters for employees who have worked at their firms because a negative reference may prompt a former employee to sue for defamation of character.[43]

After single-use plans and standing plans, budgets are the third kind of operational plan. **Budgeting** is quantitative planning because it forces managers to decide how to allocate available money to best accomplish company goals. According to Jan King, author of *Business Plans to Game Plans*, "Money sends a clear message about your priorities. Budgets act as a language for communicating your goals to others."

 STEPS AND LIMITS TO RATIONAL DECISION MAKING

Decision making is the process of choosing a solution from available alternatives.[44] **Rational decision making** is a systematic process in which managers define problems, evaluate alternatives, and choose optimal solutions that provide maximum benefits to their organizations. Thus, for example, your boss comes to you requesting that you define and evaluate the various options for the company's social media strategy; after all, you tweet and use Facebook, Google+, Instagram, Groupon, etc., and he doesn't even know how to

---

Procedures standing plans that indicate the specific steps that should be taken in response to a particular event

Rules and regulations standing plans that describe how a particular action should be performed or what must happen or not happen in response to a particular event

Budgeting quantitative planning through which managers decide how to allocate available money to best accomplish company goals

Decision making the process of choosing a solution from available alternatives

Rational decision making a systematic process of defining problems, evaluating alternatives, and choosing optimal solutions

reboot his computer. Furthermore, your solution has to be optimal. Because budgets and expertise are limited, the company gets one, maybe two tries to make their social media strategy work. If you choose incorrectly, the company's investment will just go to waste, without increasing sales and market share. What would you recommend?

*Let's learn more about each of these: **5-4a define the problem, 5-4b identify decision criteria, 5-4c weigh the criteria, 5-4d generate alternative courses of action, 5-4e evaluate each alternative,** and **5-4f compute the optimal decision.** Then we'll consider **5-4g limits to rational decision making.***

5-4a Define the Problem

The first step in decision making is identifying and defining the problem. A **problem** exists when there is a gap between a desired state (what is wanted) and an existing state (the situation you are actually facing). You're the VP of HR for Guitar Center, a music instrument retailer with 240 U.S. locations. Each store has a combination of full time and part time employees, each of whom wants a schedule that fits their personal lives and gives them the most hours. Furthermore, daily customer flow is steady on the weekends. But during the work week it's inconsistent—light in the morning (stores open at 10:00 a.m. to 11:00 a.m), heavier around lunch, then lighter till about 3:00 p.m. Customer flow becomes heavier again between 3:00 p.m and 6:00 p.m. (after school and people getting off of work), and then heaviest in the evening from 6:00 p.m. till stores close at 8:00 p.m. or 9:00 p.m. Your problem, and it's not easy, is how to match employees' schedules and wishes to lighter and heavier parts of the day throughout the week so that there are enough employees to help customers, but not so many so that stores are overstaffed.[45]

The presence of a gap between an existing state and a desired state is no guarantee that managers will make decisions to solve problems. Three things must occur for this to happen.[46] First, managers have to be aware of the gap. They have to know there is a problem before they can begin solving it. For example, after noticing that people were spending more money on their pets, a new dog food company created an expensive, high-quality dog food. To emphasize its quality, the dog food was sold in cans and bags with gold labels, red letters, and detailed information about its benefits and nutrients. Yet the product did not sell very well, and the company went out of business in less than a year. Its founders didn't understand why. When they asked a manager at a competing dog food company what their biggest mistake had been, the answer was "Simple. You didn't have a picture of a dog on the package."[47] This problem would have been easy to solve if management had only been aware of it.

Being aware of a problem isn't enough to begin the decision-making process. Managers have to be motivated to reduce the gap between a desired and an existing state. For almost a decade, managers at Borders Books were aware of the gap between its struggling performance and the strong sales, market share, and profits it desired. Moreover, they knew that its poor performance resulted from not embracing online, electronic sales like its competitors Amazon, Barnes & Noble, and Netflix did. Amazingly, Borders actually outsourced its online presence to Amazon, strengthening its rival and weakening its own position. Why? So it could invest more money in its brick-and-mortar stores. In its 2000 annual report the company explained: "Our online investment will be channeled to support our in-store platform, while Borders.com [run by Amazon for Borders] will continue to be utilized as a convenience retail channel." And, instead of viewing online sales as a growth opportunity, Borders "targeted loss reduction as a major goal in this area." Likewise, Borders's e-book reader, the Kobo, was introduced almost four years after Amazon's Kindle and Barnes & Noble's Nook. Even though Borders's leadership was aware of these problems, it did not take action to resolve them until it was too late to save the failing company, which was liquidated and then closed.[48]

Finally, it's not enough to be aware of a problem and be motivated to solve it. Managers must also have

Problem a gap between a desired state and an existing state

the knowledge, skills, abilities, and resources to fix the problem. So how did Guitar Center solve its scheduling problem? By replacing the Excel spreadsheets that it had been using to manually manage schedules with powerful Dayforce scheduling software from Ceridian Corporation. Guitar Centers' Chris Salles says that, "We load [customer traffic and transactions] in 15-minute intervals into Dayforce, and it generates labor-demand curves that let each store know how many people they should staff for every 15 minutes." Plus, employees can go online to indicate their weekly availability, to see their schedules, and to swap and cover shifts with co-workers.[49]

5-4b Identify Decision Criteria

Decision criteria are the standards used to guide judgments and decisions. Typically, the more criteria a potential solution meets, the better that solution will be. Again, imagine your boss asks you to determine the best options for the company's social media strategy. What general factors would be important when selecting one social media tool over another? Are you trying to increase your search rankings? Provide customer support? Are you trying to reach a particular target market? Is it young single women ages eighteen to twenty-five or, perhaps, married women ages twenty-five to thirty-five? Are you reaching out directly to consumers or to businesses (i.e., business-to-business)? Will your strategy focus on visual content, demonstrations, or detailed, complex knowledge? Answering questions like these will help you identify the criteria that will guide the social media strategy you recommend.

5-4c Weigh the Criteria

After identifying decision criteria, the next step is deciding which criteria are more or less important. Although there are numerous mathematical models for weighing decision criteria, all require the decision maker to provide an initial ranking of the criteria. Some use **absolute comparisons,** in which each

---

Exhibit 5.4
Absolute Weighting of Decision Criteria for a Car Purchase

5 critically important
4 important
3 somewhat important
2 not very important
1 completely unimportant

1. Predicted reliability	1	2	3	4	(5)
2. Owner satisfaction	1	(2)	3	4	5
3. Predicted depreciation	(1)	2	3	4	5
4. Avoiding accidents	1	2	3	(4)	5
5. Fuel economy	1	2	3	4	(5)
6. Crash protection	1	2	3	(4)	5
7. Acceleration	(1)	2	3	4	5
8. Ride	1	2	(3)	4	5
9. Front seat comfort	1	2	3	4	(5)

---

criterion is compared with a standard or ranked on its own merits. For example, *Consumer Reports* uses nine criteria when it rates and recommends new cars: predicted reliability, current owners' satisfaction, predicted depreciation (the price you could expect if you sold the car), ability to avoid an accident, fuel economy, crash protection, acceleration, ride, and front seat comfort.[50]

Different individuals will rank these criteria differently, depending on what they value or require in a car. Exhibit 5.4 shows the absolute weights that someone buying a car might use. Because these weights are absolute, each criterion is judged on its own importance using a five-point scale, with 5 representing "critically important" and 1 representing "completely unimportant." In this instance, predicted reliability, fuel economy, and front seat comfort were rated most important, and acceleration and predicted depreciation were rated least important.

Another method uses **relative comparisons,** in which each criterion is compared directly with every other criterion.[51] Exhibit 5.5 shows six criteria that someone might use when buying a house. Moving down the first column of Exhibit 5.5, we see that the time of the daily commute has been rated less important (−1) than

---

Exhibit 5.5
Relative Comparison of Home Characteristics

Home Characteristics	L	SSQ	IP	SR	QS	NBH
Daily commute (L)		+1	−1	−1	−1	0
School system quality (SSQ)	−1		−1	−1	−1	−1
In-ground pool (IP)	+1	+1		0	0	+1
Sun room (SR)	+1	+1	0		0	0
Quiet street (QS)	+1	+1	0	0		0
Newly built house (NBH)	0	+1	−1	0	0	
Total weight	+2	+5	−3	−2	−2	0

5-4e Evaluate Each Alternative

The next step is to systematically evaluate each alternative against each criterion. Because of the amount of information that must be collected, this step can take much longer and be much more expensive than other steps in the decision-making process. When selecting a European city for your office, you could contact economic development offices in each city, systematically interview businesspeople or executives who operate there, retrieve and use published government data on each location, or rely on published studies such as Cushman & Wakefield's *European Cities Monitor*, which conducts an annual survey of more than five hundred senior European executives who rate thirty-four European cities on twelve business-related criteria.[52]

No matter how you gather the information, once you have it, the key is to use that information systematically to evaluate each alternative against each criterion. Exhibit 5.6 shows how each of the ten cities on your staff's list fared with respect to each of the twelve criteria (higher scores are better), from qualified staff to freedom from pollution. Although London has the most qualified staff, the best access to markets and telecommunications, and is the easiest city to travel to and from, it is also one of the most polluted and expensive cities on the list. Paris offers excellent access to markets and clients, but if your staff is multilingual, Brussels may be a better choice.

school system quality; more important (+1) than having an in-ground pool, a sun room, or a quiet street; and just as important as the house being brand new (0). Total weights, which are obtained by summing the scores in each column, indicate that the school system quality and daily commute are the most important factors to this home buyer, while an in-ground pool, sun room, and a quiet street are the least important. So with relative comparison, criteria are directly compared with each other.

5-4d Generate Alternative Courses of Action

After identifying and weighting the criteria that will guide the decision-making process, the next step is to identify possible courses of action that could solve the problem. In general, at this step, the idea is to generate as many alternatives as possible. Let's assume that you're trying to select a city in Europe to be the location of a major office. After meeting with your staff, you generate a list of possible alternatives: Amsterdam, the Netherlands; Barcelona or Madrid, Spain; Berlin, Dusseldorf, Frankfurt, or Munich, Germany; Brussels, Belgium; London, England; and Paris, France.

5-4f Compute the Optimal Decision

The final step in the decision-making process is to compute the optimal decision by determining the optimal value of each alternative. This is done by multiplying the rating for each criterion (Step 5-4e) by the weight for that criterion (Step 5-4c), and then summing those scores for each alternative course

Jason Walton/iStockphoto.com

Exhibit 5.6
Criteria Ratings Used to Determine the Best Location for a New Office

Criteria Weights:	Access to Markets 0.60	Qualified Staff 0.53	Telecom- munications 0.52	Easy to Travel to/from City 0.42	Cost & Value of Office Space 0.33	Cost of Staff 0.32	Available Office Space 0.25	Languages Spoken 0.21	Business Cli- mate 0.20	Travel within City 0.20	Quality of Life 0.16	Freedom from Pollution 0.16	Weighted Average	Ranking
Amsterdam	0.42	0.40	0.39	0.68	0.30	0.19	0.30	0.96	0.47	0.34	0.44	0.63	1.72	5
Barcelona	0.23	0.32	0.16	0.29	0.52	0.59	0.52	0.23	0.31	0.47	1.08	0.42	1.45	8
Berlin	0.44	0.39	0.41	0.35	0.78	0.40	0.79	0.50	0.34	0.78	0.38	0.29	1.85	4
Brussels	0.46	0.43	0.37	0.48	0.44	0.17	0.42	0.98	0.37	0.29	0.41	0.27	1.65	7
Dusseldorf	0.30	0.30	0.23	0.21	0.37	0.14	0.28	0.18	0.17	0.22	0.20	0.26	0.97	10
Frankfurt	0.68	0.57	0.70	1.17	0.38	0.11	0.44	0.57	0.38	0.35	0.17	0.18	2.16	3
London	1.50	1.36	1.27	1.79	0.27	0.10	0.42	1.48	0.55	1.26	0.46	0.15	4.03	1
Madrid	0.45	0.46	0.27	0.41	0.52	0.61	0.67	0.22	0.29	0.53	0.67	0.13	1.70	6
Munich	0.34	0.47	0.48	0.37	0.18	0.03	0.18	0.30	0.22	0.47	0.62	0.57	1.36	9
Paris	1.09	0.84	0.89	1.36	0.22	0.10	0.37	0.58	0.30	1.07	0.52	0.12	2.83	2

Source: "European Cities Monitor 2011," Cushion & Wakefield, 2011, accessed 27 May 2013, http://www.berlin-partner.de/fileadmin/chefredaktion/pdf/studien-rankings/2011_en_European-Cities-Monitor.pdf.

of action that you generated (Step 5-4d). For example, the five hundred executives participating in Cushman & Wakefield's survey of the best European cities for business rated the twelve decision criteria in terms of importance, as shown in the first row of Exhibit 5.6. Access to markets, qualified staff, telecommunications, and easy travel to and from the city were the four most important factors, while quality of life and freedom from pollution were the least important factors. To calculate the optimal value for Paris, the weight for each category is multiplied by its score in each category (.53 × .84 in the qualified staff category, for example). Then all of these scores are added together to produce the optimal value, as follows:

$$(.60 \times 1.09) + (.53 \times .84) + (.52 \times .89) +$$
$$(.42 \times 1.36) + (.33 \times .22) + (.32 \times .10) +$$
$$(.25 \times .37) + (.21 \times .58) + (.20 \times .30) +$$
$$(.20 \times 1.07) + (.16 \times .52) + (.16 \times .12) = 2.83$$

Since London has a weighted average of 4.03 compared to 2.83 for Paris and 2.16 for Frankfurt (the cities with the next-best ratings), London clearly ranks as the best location for your company's new European office because of its large number of qualified staff; easy access to markets; outstanding ease of travel to, from, and within the city; excellent telecommunications; and top-notch business climate.

5-4g Limits to Rational Decision Making

In general, managers who diligently complete all six steps of the rational decision-making model will make better decisions than those who don't. So, when they can, managers should try to follow the steps in the rational decision-making model, especially for big decisions with long-range consequences.

To make completely rational decisions, managers would have to operate in a perfect world with no real-world constraints. Of course, it never actually works like that in the real world. Managers face time and money constraints. They often don't have time to make extensive lists of decision criteria. And they often don't have the resources to test all possible solutions against all possible criteria.

In theory, fully rational decision makers **maximize** decisions by choosing the optimal solution. In practice, however, limited resources along with attention, memory, and expertise problems make it nearly impossible for managers to maximize decisions. Consequently, most managers don't maximize—they satisfice. Whereas maximizing is choosing the best alternative, **satisficing** is choosing a "good-enough" alternative.

In the opening to this section, your boss comes to you asking for a recommendation on the best options for the company's social media strategy. With so many options and the fast pace of change, deciding isn't easy. In other words, there's no optimal solution that will satisfy all criteria. For instance, if you're trying to increase your search rankings, you should use Google+ and YouTube, both of which are owned and linked to Google and its search results. If you're interested in providing customer support, then pay close attention to what your customers are saying on Facebook and Twitter, and reach out to them when they're having problems or are dissatisfied. If your target market is young single women ages eighteen to twenty-five, use Twitter and Facebook, but if it's married women ages twenty-five to thirty-five, use Pinterest. If reaching out directly to consumers, use Pinterest and Facebook, but if reaching out to businesses, use LinkedIn and Twitter. Finally, if your strategy focuses on visual content, use Pinterest; if your intent is to demonstrate what your product or service does, use YouTube; and if you've got detailed, complex knowledge, use Twitter and blogs.[53] Your decision will be complete when you find a "good-enough alternative" that does the best job of meeting your decision criteria.

5-5 USING GROUPS TO IMPROVE DECISION MAKING

A survey of 2,044 human resources and organizational leaders found that 84 percent of companies used teams for special projects, while 74 percent used teams to address departmental issues and innovation.[54] In other words, groups were used to solve problems and make decisions. Why do so companies rely so heavily on groups to make decisions? Because when done properly, group decision making can lead to much better decisions than those typically made by individuals. In fact, numerous studies show that groups consistently outperform individuals on complex tasks.

*Let's explore the **5-5a advantages and pitfalls of group decision making** and see how the following group decision-making methods—**5-5b structured conflict, 5-5c the nominal group technique, 5-5d the Delphi technique**, and **5-5e electronic brainstorming**—can be used to improve decision making.*

5-5a Advantages and Pitfalls of Group Decision Making

Groups can do a much better job than individuals in two important steps of the decision-making process: defining the problem and generating alternative solutions. Still, group decision making is subject to some pitfalls that can quickly erase these gains. One possible pitfall is groupthink. **Groupthink** occurs in highly cohesive groups when group members feel intense pressure to agree with each other so that the group can approve a proposed solution.[55] Because groupthink leads to consideration of a limited number of solutions and restricts discussion of any considered solutions, it usually results in poor decisions. Groupthink is most likely to occur under the following conditions:

▶ The group is insulated from others with different perspectives.

▶ The group leader begins by expressing a strong preference for a particular decision.

▶ The group has no established procedure for systematically defining problems and exploring alternatives.

▶ Group members have similar backgrounds and experiences.[56]

A second potential problem with group decision making is that it takes considerable time. Reconciling schedules so that group members can meet takes time.

Maximize choosing the best alternative

Satisficing choosing a "good-enough" alternative

Groupthink a barrier to good decision making caused by pressure within the group for members to agree with each other

Furthermore, it's a rare group that consistently holds productive, task-oriented meetings to effectively work through the decision-making process. Some of the most common complaints about meetings (and thus group decision making) are that the meeting's purpose is unclear, participants are unprepared, critical people are absent or late, conversation doesn't stay focused on the problem, and no one follows up on the decisions that were made.

A third possible pitfall to group decision making is that sometimes one or two people, perhaps the boss or a strong-willed, vocal group member, can dominate group discussions and limit the group's consideration of different problem definitions and alternative solutions. And, unlike individual decisions where people feel personally responsible for making a good choice, another potential problem is that group members may not feel accountable for the decisions made and actions taken by the group.

C-type conflict (cognitive conflict) disagreement that focuses on problem- and issue-related differences of opinion

Although these pitfalls can lead to poor decision making, this doesn't mean that managers should avoid using groups to make decisions. When done properly, group decision making can lead to much better decisions. The pitfalls of group decision making are not inevitable. Managers can overcome most of them by using the various techniques described next.

5-5b Structured Conflict

Most people view conflict negatively. Yet the right kind of conflict can lead to much better group decision making. **C-type conflict,** or "cognitive conflict," focuses on problem- and issue-related differences of opinion.[57] In c-type conflict, group members disagree because their different experiences and expertise lead them to view the problem and its potential solutions differently. C-type conflict is also characterized by a willingness to examine, compare, and reconcile those differences to produce the best possible solution. Douglas Merrill, CEO of big-data firm ZestFinance, says, "Without conflict of some sort, you can't get to better answers. The challenge is to build a culture that enables conflict without the kind of painful

A-type conflict: When disagreements become personal rather than professional.

PaulaConnelly/iStockphoto.com

conflict that some companies thrive on."[58] According to Ray Dalio, founder and CEO of Bridgewater Associates, the world's largest hedge fund, says anyone in the company can say that what the firm is doing doesn't make sense to them. At most investment firms, he says, "people keep that [kind of criticism] to themselves." But at Bridgewater, "you have a right and an obligation to say 'I think this is terrible' and explore whether or not that's true." Ultimately, he believes that, "if you can't have independent thinking, you can't know what your weaknesses are, and sort those things out, you're not going to be successful."[59]

By contrast, **a-type conflict,** meaning "affective conflict," refers to the emotional reactions that can occur when disagreements become personal rather than professional. A-type conflict often results in hostility, anger, resentment, distrust, cynicism, and apathy. Unlike c-type conflict, a-type conflict undermines team effectiveness by preventing teams from engaging in the activities characteristic of c-type conflict that are critical to team effectiveness. Examples of a-type conflict statements are "your idea," "our idea," "my department," "you don't know what you are talking about," or "you don't understand our situation." Rather than focusing on issues and ideas, these statements focus on individuals.[60]

The **devil's advocacy** approach can be used to create c-type conflict by assigning an individual or a subgroup the role of critic. The following five steps establish a devil's advocacy program:

1. Generate a potential solution.
2. Assign a devil's advocate to criticize and question the solution.
3. Present the critique of the potential solution to key decision makers.
4. Gather additional relevant information.
5. Decide whether to use, change, or not use the originally proposed solution.[61]

When properly used, the devil's advocacy approach introduces c-type conflict into the decision-making process. Contrary to the common belief that conflict is bad, studies show that these methods lead not only to less a-type conflict but also to improved decision quality and greater acceptance of decisions once they have been made.[62]

Another method of creating c-type conflict is **dialectical inquiry,** which creates c-type conflict by forcing decision makers to state the assumptions of a proposed solution (a thesis) and then generate a solution that is the opposite (antithesis) of the proposed solution. The following are the five steps of the dialectical inquiry process:

1. Generate a potential solution.
2. Identify the assumptions underlying the potential solution.
3. Generate a conflicting counterproposal based on the opposite assumptions.
4. Have advocates of each position present their arguments and engage in a debate in front of key decision makers.
5. Decide whether to use, change, or not use the originally proposed solution.

5-5c Nominal Group Technique

Nominal means "in name only." Accordingly, the **nominal group technique** received its name because it begins with a quiet time in which group members independently write down as many problem definitions and alternative solutions as possible. In other words, the nominal group technique begins by having group members act as individuals. After the quiet time, the group leader asks each member to share one idea at a time with the group. As they are read aloud, ideas are posted on flip charts or wallboards for all to see. This step continues until all ideas have been shared. In the next step, the group discusses the advantages and disadvantages of the ideas. The nominal group technique closes with a second quiet time in which group members independently rank the ideas presented. Group members then read their rankings aloud, and the idea with the highest average rank is selected.[63]

A-type conflict (affective conflict) disagreement that focuses on individuals or personal issues

Devil's advocacy a decision-making method in which an individual or a subgroup is assigned the role of critic

Dialectical inquiry a decision-making method in which decision makers state the assumptions of a proposed solution (a thesis) and generate a solution that is the opposite (antithesis) of that solution

Nominal group technique a decision-making method that begins and ends by having group members quietly write down and evaluate ideas to be shared with the group

The nominal group technique improves group decision making by decreasing a-type conflict. But it also restricts c-type conflict. Consequently, the nominal group technique typically produces poorer decisions than the devil's advocacy and dialectical inquiry approaches. Nonetheless, more than eighty studies have found that nominal groups produce better ideas than those produced by traditional groups.[64]

5-5d Delphi Technique

In the **Delphi technique,** the members of a panel of experts respond to questions and to each other until reaching agreement on an issue. The first step is to assemble a panel of experts. Unlike other approaches to group decision making, however, it isn't necessary to bring the panel members together in one place. Because the Delphi technique does not require the experts to leave their offices or disrupt their schedules, they are more likely to participate.

The second step is to create a questionnaire consisting of a series of open-ended questions for the group. In the third step, the group members' written responses are analyzed, summarized, and fed back to the group for reactions until the members reach agreement. Asking group members why they agree or disagree is important because it helps uncover their unstated assumptions and beliefs. Again, this process of summarizing panel feedback and obtaining reactions to that feedback continues until the panel members reach agreement.

sb-borg/iStockphoto.com

5-5e Electronic Brainstorming

Brainstorming, in which group members build on others' ideas, is a technique for generating a large number of alternative solutions. Brainstorming has four rules:

1. The more ideas, the better.

2. All ideas are acceptable, no matter how wild or crazy they might seem.

3. Other group members' ideas should be used to come up with even more ideas.

4. Criticism or evaluation of ideas is not allowed.

Although brainstorming is great fun and can help managers generate a large number of alternative solutions, it does have a number of disadvantages. Fortunately, **electronic brainstorming,** in which group members use computers to communicate and generate alternative solutions, overcomes the disadvantages associated with face-to-face brainstorming.[65]

The first disadvantage that electronic brainstorming overcomes is **production blocking,** which occurs when you have an idea but have to wait to share it because someone else is already presenting an idea to the group. During this short delay, you may forget your idea or decide that it really wasn't worth sharing. Production blocking doesn't happen with electronic brainstorming. All group members are seated at computers, so everyone can type in ideas whenever they occur. There's no waiting your turn to be heard by the group.

The second disadvantage that electronic brainstorming overcomes is **evaluation apprehension,**

Delphi technique a decision-making method in which members of a panel of experts respond to questions and to each other until reaching agreement on an issue

Brainstorming a decision-making method in which group members build on each others' ideas to generate as many alternative solutions as possible

Electronic brainstorming a decision-making method in which group members use computers to build on each others' ideas and generate as many alternative solutions as possible

Production blocking a disadvantage of face-to-face brainstorming in which a group member must wait to share an idea because another member is presenting an idea

Evaluation apprehension fear of what others will think of your ideas

that is, being afraid of what others will think of your ideas. For example, Robert Murphy, an online marketing representative, had prepared for a meeting with his boss and six coworkers by conducting research and bringing detailed notes to the meeting. Then, when the discussion began, his evaluation apprehension regarding what his boss and colleagues would say about his ideas overwhelmed his preparation. Says Murphy, "I just sat there like a lump, fixated on the fact that I was quiet."[66]

With electronic brainstorming, all ideas are anonymous. When you type in an idea and hit the Enter key to share it with the group, group members see only the idea. Furthermore, many brainstorming software programs also protect anonymity by displaying ideas in random order. So if you laugh maniacally when you type "Cut top management's pay by 50 percent!" and then hit the Enter key, it won't show up immediately on everyone's screen. This makes it doubly difficult to determine who is responsible for which comments.

In the typical layout for electronic brainstorming, all participants sit in front of computers around a U-shaped table. This configuration allows them to see their computer screens, the other participants, a large main screen, and a meeting leader or facilitator. Step 1 in electronic brainstorming is to anonymously generate as many ideas as possible. Groups commonly generate one hundred ideas in a half-hour period. Step 2 is to edit the generated ideas, categorize them, and eliminate redundancies. Step 3 is to rank the categorized ideas in terms of quality. Step 4, the last step, has three parts: generate a series of action steps, decide the best order for accomplishing these steps, and identify who is responsible for each step. All four steps are accomplished with computers and electronic brainstorming software.[67]

Studies show that electronic brainstorming is much more productive than face-to-face brainstorming. Four-person electronic brainstorming groups produce 25 to 50 percent more ideas than four-person regular brainstorming groups, and twelve-person electronic brainstorming groups produce 200 percent more ideas than regular groups of the same size! In fact, because production blocking (having to wait your turn) is not a problem in electronic brainstorming, the number and quality of ideas generally increase with group size.[68]

Even though it works much better than traditional brainstorming, electronic brainstorming has disadvantages, too. An obvious problem is the expense of computers, networks, software, and other equipment. As these costs continue to drop, however, electronic brainstorming will become cheaper.

Purpose in Transition

Under Steve Jobs, Apple's purpose was often not difficult to determine. As Jobs once said, "We want to make great products." While the departure of an iconic figure like Jobs can greatly impact the vision and direction of a company, Apple's "Think Different" campaign reaffirmed many of the values Jobs instilled in the company. In 1997, Jobs declared, "Innovation is saying no to 1,000 things." The Think Different campaign restated this, saying, "There are a thousand nos for every yes." Today, Apple continues to strive for perfection in its products as it did under Steve Jobs. Apple's Think Different ethos still resonates—it drives the company to question all of its ideas: How will [the idea] make someone feel? Will it make life better? Does it deserve to exist? These questions provide a foundation and purpose for Apple as it strives to create and perfect new innovative products.

AP Images/Marcio Jose Sanchez

Source: J. Paczkowski, "Apple's Declaration of Values: Simplify, Perfect, Delight," *All Things D*, June 11, 2013, accessed April 21, 2014, http://allthingsd.com/20130611 /apples-declaration-of-values-simplify-perfect-delight/?KEYWORDS=company+mission+statement.

Another problem is that the anonymity of ideas may bother people who are used to having their ideas accepted by virtue of their position (i.e., the boss). On the other hand, one CEO said, "Because the process is anonymous, the sky's the limit in terms of what you can say, and as a result it is more thought-provoking. As a CEO, you'll probably discover things you might not want to hear but need to be aware of."[69]

A third disadvantage is that outgoing individuals who are more comfortable expressing themselves verbally may find it difficult to express themselves in writing. Finally, the most obvious problem is that participants have to be able to type. Those who can't type, or who type slowly, may be easily frustrated and find themselves at a disadvantage compared to experienced typists.

STUDY TOOLS 5

LOCATED AT THE BACK OF YOUR BOOK:

☐ Rip out and study the Chapter Review Card at the end of the book

LOG IN TO WWW.CENGAGEBRAIN.COM TO:

☐ Review Key Term Flashcards

☐ Complete Practice Quizzing (take up to four times without repeating the same quiz)

☐ Complete Games: Beat the Clock and Crossword Puzzle

☐ Watch Management Workplace Video on "Plant Fantasies"

☐ Work Through the What Would You Do Case on DuPont

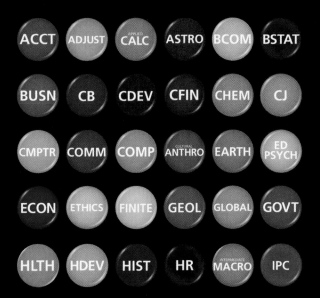

ONE APPROACH.
70 UNIQUE SOLUTIONS.

www.cengage.com/4ltrpress

6 Organizational Strategy

GlobalStock/iStockphoto.com

LEARNING OUTCOMES

6-1 Specify the components of sustainable competitive advantage, and explain why it is important.

6-2 Describe the steps involved in the strategy-making process.

6-3 Explain the different kinds of corporate-level strategies.

6-4 Describe the different kinds of industry-level strategies.

6-5 Explain the components and kinds of firm-level strategies.

After you finish this chapter, go to **PAGE 132** for

STUDY TOOLS

SUSTAINABLE COMPETITIVE ADVANTAGE

Just four years ago, there was no market for tablet computers. A number of computer makers sold touch-screen laptops, but other than some programs that allowed users to handwrite notes, there was little to distinguish these machines from traditional laptops. All of that changed when Apple released its iPad, a tablet computer that is controlled by a multitouch display and can run hundreds of thousands of applications that allow users to read books, watch movies, listen to music, check the weather, or play games. With its innovative product, Apple in effect created a new market for por-table, touch-based tablet computers. The iPad is not without its competitors, however. There is, for example, the Amazon Kindle Fire, Barnes & Noble's Nook HD, and Samsung's Android-based Galaxy Tab. The latest competitor is the Microsoft Surface, which comes with a touch screen, a combination cover/detachable keyboard, and two versions of the Windows operating system. The Surface, however, has done little to dim enthusiasm for the iPad. Critics complain about the lack of apps, just 47,000 compared to over 300,000 for the iPad, the higher price ($999 for a 256 gb Surface Pro with an Intel i7chip versus $929 for a 64 gb iPad with an A7 chip and a high-definition screen), and that the Windows 8 touch interface on the Surface is more difficult to learn and use than the iPad's. Despite these competitors, Apple still dominates tablet sales with 33.8 percent of the market, selling 26 million iPads in the fourth quarter of 2013 compared to just 1.5 million Surfaces, 14.5 million Samsung Galaxies, and 8 million Amazon Kindles.

Sales of Microsoft's Surface tablets was too small to be broken out in industry reports.[1] Likewise, a report on web usage, meaning the percentage of tablet web traf-fic (i.e., surfing the web with your tablet rather than a PC or your smartphone) found that Apple generated 75 percent of all tablet web traffic in North America compared to just 6.7 percent for Microsoft's Surface.[2]

How can a company like Apple, which dominates a particular industry, maintain its competitive advantage as strong, well-financed competitors enter the market? What steps can Apple and other companies take to bet-ter manage their strategy-making process?

Resources are the assets, capabilities, processes, employee time, information, and knowledge that an or-ganization controls. Firms use their resources to improve organizational effectiveness and efficiency. Resources are critical to organizational strategy because they can help companies create and sustain an advantage over competitors.[3]

Organizations can achieve a **competitive advantage** by using their resources to provide greater value for customers than competitors can. For example, the iPad's competitive advantage came partly from its sleek, attractive design and partly from the reputation of Apple's iPod and iPhone as innovative, easy-to-use products.

The goal of most organizational strategies is to create and then sustain a competitive advantage. A competitive

Resources the assets, capabilities, processes, employee time, information, and knowledge that an organization uses to improve its effectiveness and efficiency and create and sustain competitive advantage

Competitive advantage providing greater value for customers than competitors can

francesco riccardo iacomino/iStockphoto.com

advantage becomes a **sustainable competitive advantage** when other companies cannot duplicate the value a firm is providing to customers. Sustainable competitive advantage is *not* the same as a long-lasting competitive advantage, though companies obviously want a competitive advantage to last a long time. Instead, a competitive advantage is *sustained* if competitors have tried unsuccessfully to duplicate the advantage and have, for the moment, stopped trying to duplicate it. It's the corporate equivalent of your competitors saying, "We give up. You win. We can't do what you do, and we're not even going to try to do it anymore." Four conditions must be met if a firm's resources are to be used to achieve a sustainable competitive advantage. The resources must be valuable, rare, imperfectly imitable, *and* nonsubstitutable.

Valuable resources allow companies to improve their efficiency and effectiveness. Unfortunately, changes in customer demand and preferences, competitors' actions, and technology can make once-valuable resources much less valuable. Before the iPad was introduced, netbooks appeared to be the next big thing in mobile computing. These laptops were small and light, making them ultra portable, were very affordable, averaging anywhere from $200 to $500, and let users run basic programs like Web browsing and word processing on the go. At first sales were brisk—in 2009, 7.5 million netbooks were sold in the United States and more than 34 million worldwide. But all that changed. The iPad had a touch screen, an intuitive operating system, and a large selection of app software, while netbooks were often criticized for having small, hard-to-use keyboards, a slow operating system, and a lack of software options. While it took only twenty-eight days for Apple to sell its first 1 million iPads, netbook sales fell by 40 percent in one year.[4] Only one year after netbook sales peaked, tablet sales passed them, and netbook sales have been steadily declining ever since.[5]

For sustained competitive advantage, valuable resources must also be rare resources. Think about it: How can a company sustain a competitive advantage if all of its competitors have similar resources and capabilities? Consequently, **rare resources,** resources that are not controlled or possessed by many competing firms, are necessary to sustain a competitive advantage. One of Apple's truly rare resources is its ability to reconfigure existing technology into a package that is easy to use, elegantly designed, and therefore highly desired by customers. Apple used its wealth of experience from developing the iPod, iPod touch, and iPhone to create an operating system for the iPad that was easy to use and, more importantly, basically identical to what was found on its other products. In other words, it created a single platform that would give users the same experience across multiple devices. An iPhone user who just purchased an iPad will have little difficulty learning how to use it. This is not the case with the iPad's chief competitors, tablets powered by Google's Android. Because it is open source, meaning that manufacturers can alter the basic operating system in different ways, there is little uniformity across various Android devices. Simply put, one Android tablet might look and work differently than another, and one company might offer an app that will not work on another Android device.[6]

As this example shows, valuable and rare resources can create temporary competitive advantage. For sustained competitive advantage, however, other firms must be unable to imitate or find substitutes for those valuable, rare resources. **Imperfectly imitable resources** are those resources that are impossible or extremely costly or difficult to duplicate. Both Google and Amazon operate online app stores that are in some way similar to Apple's App Store. Users can log on to the sites, browse for programs, and purchase and download them to their devices. There is a big difference, however, in security. Apple's App Store is a closed platform, meaning that if a software developer wants to sell an app on Apple's site, the company first puts it through a review process to check for content and security issues. As noted above, however, Android is an open platform, which means that Google does not prescreen apps before publishing them. This makes it far easier for developers with bad intentions to create and sell applications that can harm devices or steal personal information. According to a study by Juniper Networks, by 2013, Android devices were targeted for 92 percent of all mobile malware threats, up from 47 percent in 2011 and 24 percent in 2010.[7]

Valuable, rare, imperfectly imitable resources can produce sustainable competitive advantage only if they are also **nonsubstitutable resources,** meaning

Sustainable competitive advantage a competitive advantage that other companies have tried unsuccessfully to duplicate and have, for the moment, stopped trying to duplicate

Valuable resource a resource that allows companies to improve efficiency and effectiveness

Rare resource a resource that is not controlled or possessed by many competing firms

Imperfectly imitable resource a resource that is impossible or extremely costly or difficult for other firms to duplicate

Nonsubstitutable resource a resource that produces value or competitive advantage and has no equivalent substitutes or replacements that no other resources can replace them and produce similar value or competitive advantage. This is most evident in the dominance of Apple's iTunes software. The industry has tried to produce equivalent substitutes for iTunes, but competitors have had to experiment with different business models to get customers to accept them. For example, Amazon MP3 not only gives consumers access to 20 million digital songs, it allows consumers to store their files on Amazon's cloud servers. In essence, this means that users can buy a song from Amazon and stream it to any device they own, from their desktop computer to their Android tablet. Apple responded by introducing its own cloud-based service called iCloud, which, combined with a service called iTunes Match, provides consumers with an online locker in which they can store music, video, or photo files, as well as apps, to access from multiple devices, whether they bought them from Apple or not. In addition, iCloud lets users synchronize other data, like appointments, email, and documents, between their iPhone, iPad, and Mac computers.[8] Likewise, iTunes faces growing competition from music streaming services, like Spotify, that provide basic free services for a limited number of hours per month and sell premium subscriptions for about $10 a month. Spotify has over 25 million users, a quarter of whom are premium subscribers, providing roughly $576 million a year in revenues. By contrast, iTunes has 575 million users worldwide and earns Apple $9.3 billion a year in revenue. Apple has responded to Spotify and other music streaming companies by adding fifty-six new countries to the iTunes store for a total of 155 worldwide. Furthermore, Apple launched iTunes Radio, its own streaming music service, and then paid $3 billion to acquire Beats Music, a music subscription service also known for its high end headphones.[9]

In summary, Apple has reaped the rewards of a first-mover advantage when it introduced the iPad. The company's history of developing customer-friendly software, the innovative capabilities of the iPad, the uniformity of experience, and the security of the App Store provide customers with a service that has been valuable, rare, relatively nonsubstitutable, and, in the past, imperfectly imitable. Past success is, however, no guarantee of future success: Apple needs to continually change and develop its offerings or risk being unseated by a more nimble competitor whose products are more relevant and have higher perceived value to the consumer.

6-2

STRATEGY-MAKING PROCESS

In order to create a sustainable competitive advantage, a company must have a strategy.[10] Exhibit 6.1 displays the three steps of the strategy-making process:

6-2a assess the need for strategic change, 6-2b conduct a situational analysis, and then **6-2c choose strategic alternatives.** Let's examine each of these steps in more detail.

6-2a Assessing the Need for Strategic Change

The external business environment is much more turbulent than it used to be. With customers' needs constantly growing and changing, and with competitors working harder, faster, and smarter to meet those needs,

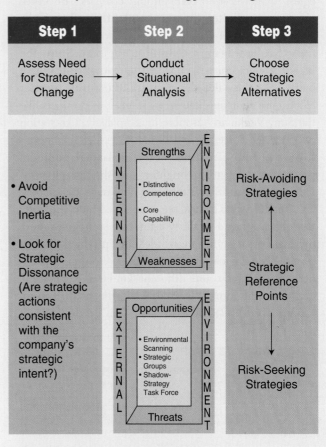

Exhibit 6.1

Three Steps of the Strategy-Making Process

the first step in creating a strategy is determining the need for strategic change. In other words, the company should determine whether it needs to change its strategy to sustain a competitive advantage.[11]

Determining the need for strategic change might seem easy to do, but it's really not. There's a great deal of uncertainty in strategic business environments. Furthermore, top-level managers are often slow to recognize the need for strategic change, especially at successful companies that have created and sustained competitive advantages. Because they are acutely aware of the strategies that made their companies successful, they continue to rely on those strategies, even as the competition changes. In other words, success often leads to **competitive inertia**—a reluctance to change strategies or competitive practices that have been successful in the past. **Sony,** the Japanese electronics firm, is an example of competitive inertia. For three decades, Sony was the world's premier electronics company, known for innovative products like the Sony Walkman (portable music player), PlayStation (video game console), and CyberShot (digital camera). Likewise, Sony Trinitron TVs commanded premium prices for their much brighter and sharper pictures. During this time, Sony's different divisions—computers, TVs, media, video games, etc.—operated independently from each other. For thirty years that strategy worked, producing innovative market-leading products. But it eventually led each division to produce too many products, for instance, ten different kinds of camcorders and thirty different TVs. And, when the product innovations stopped—Sony hasn't had a hit product in half

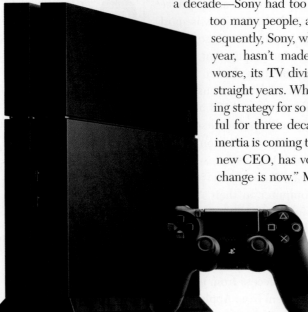

The PlayStation 4 video game console, released in November 2013, is a cornerstone of Sony's efforts to enact strategic change.

a decade—Sony had too many high-priced products, too many people, and extraordinary costs. Consequently, Sony, which will lose $6.5 billion this year, hasn't made a profit since 2008. Even worse, its TV division has lost money for nine straight years. Why did Sony stick with this losing strategy for so long? Because it was successful for three decades. But Sony's competitive inertia is coming to an end. Kazuo Hirai, Sony's new CEO, has vowed, "The time for Sony to change is now." Moving forward, Sony will focus on three areas: mobile products (smartphones and tablets), cameras and camcorders, and games. It plans to cut costs in the TV division by 60 percent.[12]

Besides being aware of the dangers of competitive inertia, what can managers do to improve the speed and accuracy with which they determine the need for strategic change? One method is to actively look for signs of strategic dissonance. **Strategic dissonance** is a discrepancy between a company's intended strategy and the strategic actions managers take when actually implementing that strategy.[13] With Japan's shrinking population, little economic growth, stiff competition from Japan's high-speed railways, and airline deregulation leading to new low-cost airlines, **All Nippon Airways (ANA),** Japan's largest airline, needed to cut costs and move quickly to respond to competitors. However, that intended strategy was at odds (i.e., strategic dissonance) with its long-standing high-price, high-quality service strategy. So, it started two low-cost airlines, Peach Aviation and AirAsia Japan. While that provided low-cost flights to customers, an unintended benefit for ANA was seeing how Peach and AirAsia made faster decisions to respond to competition and lower costs. For example, AirAsia's top management decided to expand service to Nagoya, Japan, three months faster than planned but got the work done in one-third of the planned time! At ANA, that decision would have taken six months and involved fifty people from across the company in multiple discussions. Yoshinori Odagiri, a long-time ANA executive who became AirAsia's CEO, said, "I was taken aback by the decision-making speed." So, to overcome strategic dissonance and make sure that its new low-cost, speed-to-market strategy is infused through the entire company, ANA

Competitive inertia a reluctance to change strategies or competitive practices that have been successful in the past

Strategic dissonance a discrepancy between a company's intended strategy and the strategic actions managers take when implementing that strategy

has now brought Peach and AirAsia directly into its organizational structure.[14]

Note, however, that strategic dissonance is not the same thing as when a strategy does not produce the results that it's supposed to. While most toy and game makers make big profits during the holidays, Hasbro, the maker of games like Monopoly and Scrabble, saw profits fall 15 percent during a disastrous Christmas season. This sharp decline is due primarily to Hasbro's strategy of focusing on movies and television. Rather than producing innovative board game offerings or investing in the rapidly growing online gaming market, Hasbro has spent most of its resources on trying to develop movies and TV shows based on its toys and games, such as the *Transformers* movie franchise and, most recently, *Battleship*.[15]

The Washington Post/Getty Images

6-2b Situational Analysis

A situational analysis can also help managers determine the need for strategic change. A **situational analysis**, also called a **SWOT analysis,** for *strengths*, *weaknesses*, *opportunities*, and *threats*, is an assessment of the strengths and weaknesses in an organization's internal environment and the opportunities and threats in its external environment.[16] Ideally, as shown in Step 2 of Exhibit 6.1, a SWOT analysis helps a company determine how to increase internal strengths and minimize internal weaknesses while maximizing external opportunities and minimizing external threats.

An analysis of an organization's internal environment, that is, a company's strengths and weaknesses, often begins with an assessment of its distinctive competencies and core capabilities. A **distinctive competence** is something that a company can make, do, or perform better than its competitors. For example, *Consumer Reports* magazine consistently ranks Honda and Subaru cars as tops in quality and reliability.[17] Similarly, *PC Magazine* readers ranked Apple's desktop and laptop computers best in terms of service and reliability.[18]

Whereas distinctive competencies are tangible— for example, a product or service is faster, cheaper, or better—the core capabilities that produce distinctive competencies are not. **Core capabilities** are the less visible, internal decision-making routines, problem-solving processes, and organizational cultures that determine how efficiently inputs can be turned into outputs. Distinctive competencies cannot be sustained for long without superior core capabilities.

For years, large retail stores like Walmart and Target have been trying to open stores in New York City only to be met with protests. Aldi, however, recently opened two stores in the city, not only with no protests but even with some politicians in attendance. The reason that Aldi faces little opposition as it opens stores in dense, urban settings is that it is able to make money in small, high-rent stores that are dictated by location. It operates with a business model that focuses on selling a limited number of groceries and household items in a small setting; its typical stores are just 16 percent the size of a typical Walmart store and carry just 1,500 or so items, compared to 100,000 items in a superstore. Furthermore, most of its items are private brands, that is, goods that Aldi buys and packages itself. All of this means that Aldi can offer prices that are 20 percent less than Walmart's, making it an attractive place for city dwellers to shop.[19]

After examining internal strengths and weaknesses, the second part of a situational analysis is to look outside the company and assess the opportunities and threats in the external environment. In Chapter 3, you learned that *environmental scanning* involves searching the environment for important events or issues that might affect the organization, such as pricing trends or new products and technology. In a situational analysis, however, managers use environmental scanning to identify specific opportunities and threats that can either improve or harm the company's ability to sustain its competitive

Situational (SWOT) analysis an assessment of the strengths and weaknesses in an organization's internal environment and the opportunities and threats in its external environment

Distinctive competence what a company can make, do, or perform better than its competitors

Core capabilities the internal decision-making routines, problem-solving processes, and organizational cultures that determine how efficiently inputs can be turned into outputs

advantage. Identification of strategic groups and formation of shadow-strategy task forces are two ways to do this (see box "Shadow-Strategy Task Force").

Strategic groups are not groups that actually work together. They are companies—usually competitors—that managers closely follow. More specifically, a **strategic group** is a group of other companies within an industry against which top managers compare, evaluate, and benchmark their company's strategic threats and opportunities.[20] (*Benchmarking* involves identifying outstanding practices, processes, and standards at other companies and adapting them to your own company.) Typically, managers include companies as part of their strategic group if they compete directly with those companies for customers or if those companies use strategies similar to theirs. The U.S. home improvement industry has annual sales in excess of $275 billion.[21] It's likely that the managers at Home Depot, the largest U.S. home improvement and hardware retailer, assess strategic threats and opportunities

by comparing their company to a strategic group consisting of the other major home improvement supply companies. Exhibit 6.2 shows the number of stores, the size of the typical new store, and the overall geographic distribution (states, countries) of Home Depot stores compared with Lowe's, Ace Hardware, and 84 Lumber.

In fact, when scanning the environment for strategic threats and opportunities, managers tend to categorize the different companies in their industries as core, secondary, and transient firms.[22] **Core firms** are the central companies in a strategic group. Home Depot operates more than 2,200 stores covering all fifty states, Puerto Rico, the U.S. Virgin Islands, Guam, Mexico, and Canada. The company has more than 300,000 employees and annual revenues of $78.8 billion. By comparison, Lowe's has more than 1,830 stores and 260,000 employees in fifty states and twelve provinces in Canada, stocks more than 40,000 products in each store, and has annual revenues of $53.4 billion.[23] Clearly, Lowe's is the closest competitor to Home Depot and is the core firm in Home Depot's strategic group. Even though Ace Hardware has more stores (4,600) than Home Depot and appears to be a bigger multinational player (seventy different countries), Ace's different franchise structure and small, individualized stores (10,000 to 14,000 square feet, with each store laid out differently with a different mix of products) keep it from being a core firm in Home Depot's strategic group.[24] Likewise, Home Depot's management probably doesn't include Aubuchon Hardware in its core strategic group, because Aubuchon has only 125 stores in New England and upstate New York.[25]

When most managers scan their environments for strategic threats and opportunities, they concentrate on the strategic actions of core firms, not unrelated firms like Aubuchon. Where does a firm like Ace Hardware fit in? Ace's 20/20 vision employs a customer-focused strategy to grow Ace's brand and improve store performance.[26]

Secondary firms are firms that use strategies related to but somewhat different from those of core firms. 84 Lumber has more than 250 stores in thirty states, but even though its stores are open to the public, the company focuses on supplying professional contractors, to whom it sells 85 percent of its products. Without the wide variety of products on the shelves or assistance available to the average consumer, people without expertise in building or remodeling probably don't find 84 Lumber stores very accessible. Home Depot would most likely classify 84 Lumber as a secondary firm in its strategic group analysis.[27] Managers need to be aware of the potential threats and opportunities posed

Exhibit 6.2
Core and Secondary Firms in the Home Improvement Industry

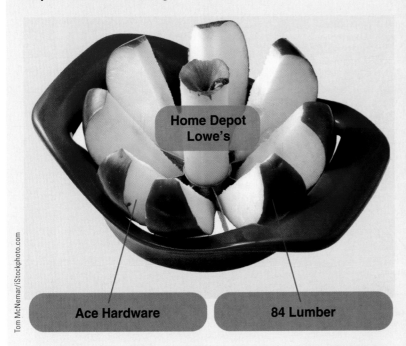

Home Depot
Lowe's

Ace Hardware

84 Lumber

Tom McNemar/iStockphoto.com

	# of Stores	# of States	Countries	Size of Typical Store (sq. feet)
Home Depot	2,257	50	4	130,000
Lowe's	1,750	50	2	117,000
Ace Hardware	4,700	50	70	10,000 to 14,000
84 Lumber	265	35	1	33,000

strategy that aims to extend or create a sustainable competitive advantage.

The choice to seek risk or avoid risk typically depends on whether top management views the company as falling above or below strategic reference points. **Strategic reference points** are the targets that managers use to measure whether their firm has developed the core competencies that it needs to achieve a sustainable competitive advantage. If a hotel chain decides to compete by providing superior quality and service, then top management will track the success of this strategy through customer surveys or published hotel ratings such as those provided by the prestigious *Mobil Travel Guide*. If a hotel chain decides to compete on price, it will regularly conduct market surveys to check the prices of other hotels. The competitors' prices are the hotel managers' strategic reference points against which to compare their own pricing strategy. If competitors can consistently underprice them, then the managers need to determine whether their staff and resources have the core competencies to compete on price.

As shown in Exhibit 6.3, when a company is performing above or better than its strategic reference points, top management will typically be satisfied with the company's strategy. Ironically, this satisfaction tends to make top management conservative and risk-averse. Since the company already has a sustainable competitive advantage, the worst thing that could happen would be to lose it, so new issues or changes in the company's external environment are viewed as threats. By contrast, when a company is performing below or worse than its strategic reference points, top management will typically be dissatisfied with the company's strategy. In this instance, managers are much more likely to choose a daring, risk-taking strategy. If the current strategy is producing substandard results, the company has nothing to lose by switching to risky new strategies in the hope that it can create a sustainable competitive advantage.

by secondary firms, but they usually spend more time assessing the threats and opportunities associated with core firms.

6-2c Choosing Strategic Alternatives

After determining the need for strategic change and conducting a situational analysis, the last step in the strategy-making process is to choose strategic alternatives that will help the company create or maintain a sustainable competitive advantage. According to *strategic reference point theory*, managers choose between two basic alternative strategies. They can choose a conservative, *risk-avoiding strategy* that aims to protect an existing competitive advantage. Or they can choose an aggressive, *risk-seeking*

Strategic reference points the strategic targets managers use to measure whether a firm has developed the core competencies it needs to achieve a sustainable competitive advantage

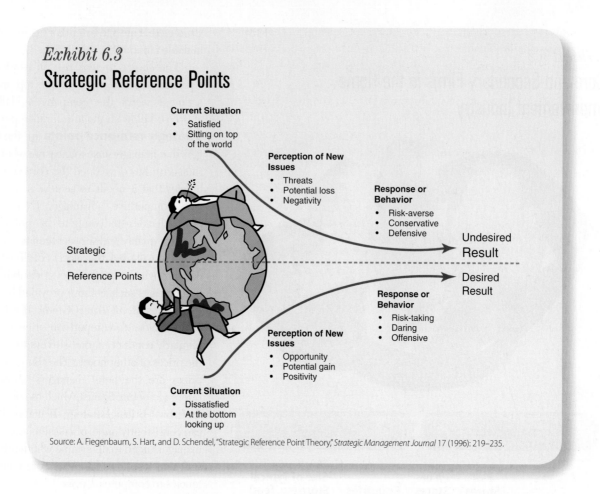

Exhibit 6.3

Strategic Reference Points

Current Situation
- Satisfied
- Sitting on top of the world

Perception of New Issues
- Threats
- Potential loss
- Negativity

Response or Behavior
- Risk-averse
- Conservative
- Defensive

Undesired **Result**

Strategic

Reference Points

Desired **Result**

Response or Behavior
- Risk-taking
- Daring
- Offensive

Perception of New Issues
- Opportunity
- Potential gain
- Positivity

Current Situation
- Dissatisfied
- At the bottom looking up

Source: A. Fiegenbaum, S. Hart, and D. Schendel, "Strategic Reference Point Theory," *Strategic Management Journal* 17 (1996): 219–235.

Managers of companies in this situation view new issues or changes in the external environment as opportunities for potential gain.

Strategic reference point theory is not deterministic, however. Managers are not predestined to choose risk-averse or risk-seeking strategies for their companies. Indeed, one of the most important elements of the theory is that managers *can* influence the strategies chosen by their company by *actively changing and adjusting* the strategic reference points they use to judge strategic performance. If a company has become complacent after consistently surpassing its strategic reference points, then top management can change from a risk-averse to a risk-taking orientation by raising the standards of performance (i.e., the strategic reference points). This is just what happened at eBay.

When John Donahoe first joined eBay, Amazon was growing, Google helped shoppers find what they wanted on other websites, and eBay's auction business was shrinking dramatically. But, few at eBay saw the problem. According to the *Wall Street Journal*, employees "became so absurdly self-congratulatory that people clapped at the end of meetings, even after discussions over declining customer satisfaction."[28] Founder Pierre Omidyar said, "They didn't seem to see what was going on outside the company

in terms of competition. They had lost their ability to innovate, to create new things."[29] In other words, success had made eBay complacent and risk averse.

When Donahoe later became eBay's CEO, he raised standards, thus changing the strategic reference points eBay had been using to assess its strategic performance. His first week on the job he told everyone that eBay needed a major turnaround. Said Donahoe, "Our sellers hated that word. Our employees hated it. Investors hated it. But it was the first step … we had to confront reality."[30] To encourage a daring, offensive-minded strategy, he funded a mobile app team that produced the eBay Red-Laser (barcode price scanning that finds products locally and online) and eBay Motors apps, which have been downloaded 120 million times; he told his team to find a way to deliver purchased products in one day (called eBay Now); and he sent a design team offsite to create a fresh graphics-based look to its aging text-based website. His ultimate challenges, however, were to double eBay's active users to 225 million, increase revenue from $14 billion to $23.5 billion, and increase customer payments from $145 billion to $300 billion, all within the next three years. Says CEO Donahoe, "The turnaround is behind us, and we are now playing offense."[31]

So even when (perhaps *especially* when) companies have achieved a sustainable competitive advantage, top managers must adjust or change strategic reference points to challenge themselves and their employees to develop new core competencies for the future. In the long run, effective organizations will frequently revise their strategic reference points to better focus managers' attention on the new challenges and opportunities that occur in their ever-changing business environments.

6-3 CORPORATE-LEVEL STRATEGIES

To formulate effective strategies, companies must be able to answer these three basic questions:

▶ What business are we in?

▶ How should we compete in this industry?

▶ Who are our competitors, and how should we respond to them?

These simple but powerful questions are at the heart of corporate-, industry-, and firm-level strategies.

Corporate-level strategy is the overall organizational strategy that addresses the question "What business or businesses are we in or should we be in?"

There are two major approaches to corporate-level strategy that companies use to decide which businesses they should be in: 6-3a portfolio strategy and 6-3b grand strategies.

6-3a Portfolio Strategy

One of the standard strategies for stock market investors is **diversification,** or owning stocks in a variety of companies in different industries. The purpose of this strategy is to reduce risk in the overall stock portfolio (the entire collection of stocks). The basic idea is simple: if you invest in ten companies in ten different industries, you won't lose your entire investment if one company performs poorly. Furthermore, because they're in different industries, one company's losses are likely to be offset by another company's gains. Portfolio strategy is based on these same ideas. We'll start by taking a look at the theory and ideas behind portfolio strategy and then proceed with a critical review that suggests that some of the key ideas behind portfolio strategy are *not* supported.

Portfolio strategy is a corporate-level strategy that minimizes risk by diversifying investment among

various businesses or product lines.[32] Just as a diversification strategy guides an investor who invests in a variety of stocks, portfolio strategy guides the strategic decisions of corporations that compete in a variety of businesses. For example, portfolio strategy could be used to guide the strategy of a company like 3M, which makes 55,000 products for five different business groups: Consumer (Post-its, Scotch tape); Electronics and Energy (electronic devices, telecoms equipment, renewable energy solutions); Health Care (medical, surgical, and dental products, health information systems); Industrial (tapes, abrasives, adhesives, specialty materials, filtration systems); and Safety and Graphics (safety and security products, track and trace solutions, graphic solutions).[33]

Just as investors consider the mix of stocks in their stock portfolio when deciding which stocks to buy or sell, managers following portfolio strategy try to acquire companies that fit well with the rest of their corporate portfolio and to sell those that don't. Procter & Gamble used to be a big name in the food business, as it sold everything from cake mixes to juice. However, the company decided that it wanted to focus its resources on its core business of household, beauty, and healthcare items. It thus began selling off products and brands that did not relate to the core business, a process that was completed when P&G sold the Pringles line of potato chips to Kellogg for $2.7 billion.[34]

First, according to portfolio strategy, the more businesses in which a corporation competes, the smaller its overall chances of failing. Think of a corporation as a stool and its businesses as the legs of the stool. The more legs or businesses added to the stool, the less likely it is to tip over. Using this analogy, portfolio strategy reduces 3M's risk of failing because the corporation's survival depends on essentially five different business sectors. Managers employing portfolio strategy can either develop new businesses internally or look for **acquisitions,** that is, other companies to buy. Either way, the goal is to add legs to the stool.

Second, beyond adding new businesses to the corporate portfolio, portfolio strategy predicts that companies

Corporate-level strategy the overall organizational strategy that addresses the question "What business or businesses are we in or should we be in?"

Diversification a strategy for reducing risk by buying a variety of items (stocks or, in the case of a corporation, types of businesses) so that the failure of one stock or one business does not doom the entire portfolio

Portfolio strategy a corporate-level strategy that minimizes risk by diversifying investment among various businesses or product lines

Acquisition the purchase of a company by another company

can reduce risk even more through **unrelated diversification**—creating or acquiring companies in completely unrelated businesses (more on the accuracy of this prediction later). According to portfolio strategy, when businesses are unrelated, losses in one business or industry should have minimal effect on the performance of other companies in the corporate portfolio. General Electric, which was founded in part by Thomas Edison, is the largest conglomerate in the world and has a presence in a wide range of businesses. Its appliances division produces refrigerators, ovens, and dishwashers. Its consumer electronics divisions make everything from computer mice to digital cameras to portable generators. Its lighting division, of course, sells light bulbs, as well as traffic signals and specialty lighting. Its aviation division, meanwhile, is one of the world leaders in making jet engines. GE also has divisions in energy distribution, energy, business and consumer finance, health care, oil and gas, rail, software and services, and water.[35]

Because most internally grown businesses tend to be related to existing products or services, portfolio strategy suggests that acquiring new businesses is the preferred method of unrelated diversification.[36]

Third, investing the profits and cash flows from mature, slow-growth businesses into newer, faster-growing businesses can reduce long-term risk. The best-known portfolio strategy for guiding investment in a

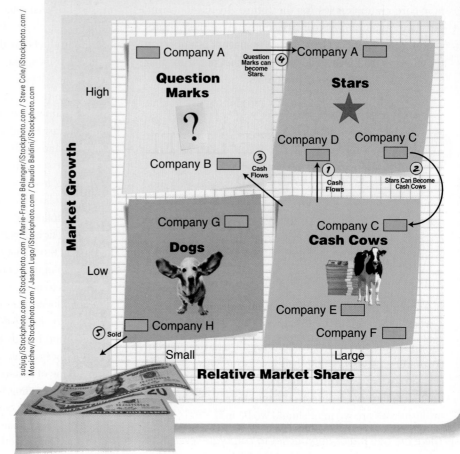

Exhibit 6.4
Boston Consulting Group Matrix

corporation's businesses is the Boston Consulting Group (BCG) matrix.[37] The **BCG matrix** is a portfolio strategy that managers use to categorize their corporation's businesses by growth rate and relative market share, which helps them decide how to invest corporate funds. The matrix, shown in Exhibit 6.4, separates businesses into four categories based on how fast the market is growing (high growth or low growth) and the size of the business's share of that market (small or large). **Stars** are companies that have a large share of a fast-growing market. To take advantage of a star's fast-growing market and its strength in that market (large share), the corporation must invest substantially in it. The investment is usually worthwhile, however, because many stars produce sizable future profits. **Question marks** are companies that have a small share of a fast-growing market. If the corporation invests in these companies, they may eventually become stars, but their relative weakness in the market (small share) makes investing in question marks more risky than investing in stars. **Cash cows** are companies that have a large share of a slow-growing

---

Unrelated diversification creating or acquiring companies in completely unrelated businesses

BCG matrix a portfolio strategy developed by the Boston Consulting Group that categorizes a corporation's businesses by growth rate and relative market share and helps managers decide how to invest corporate funds

Star a company with a large share of a fast-growing market

Question mark a company with a small share of a fast-growing market

Cash cow a company with a large share of a slow-growing market

market. Companies in this situation are often highly profitable, hence the name "cash cow." Finally, **dogs** are companies that have a small share of a slow-growing market. As the name suggests, having a small share of a slow-growth market is often not profitable.

Since the idea is to redirect investment from slow-growing to fast-growing companies, the BCG matrix starts by recommending that while the substantial cash flows from cash cows last, they should be reinvested in stars (see 1 in Exhibit 6.4) to help them grow even faster and obtain even more market share. Using this strategy, current profits help produce future profits. Over time, as their market growth slows, some stars may turn into cash cows (see 2). Cash flows should also be directed to some question marks (see 3). Though riskier than stars, question marks have great potential because of their fast-growing market. Managers must decide which question marks are most likely to turn into stars (and therefore warrant further investment) and which ones are too risky and should be sold. Over time, managers hope some question marks will become stars as their small markets become large ones (see 4). Finally, because dogs lose money, the corporation should "find them new owners" or "take them to the pound." In other words, dogs should either be sold to other companies or closed down and liquidated for their assets (see 5).

Although the BCG matrix and other forms of portfolio strategy are relatively popular among managers, portfolio strategy has some drawbacks. The most significant? Contrary to the predictions of portfolio strategy, the evidence suggests that acquiring unrelated businesses is *not* useful. As shown in Exhibit 6.5, there is a U-shaped relationship between diversification and risk. The left side of the curve shows that single businesses with no diversification are extremely risky (if the single business fails, the entire business fails). So, in part, the portfolio strategy of diversifying is correct—competing in a variety of different businesses can lower risk. However, portfolio strategy is partly wrong, too—the right side of the curve shows that conglomerates composed of completely unrelated businesses are even riskier than single, undiversified businesses.[38]

A second set of problems with portfolio strategy has to do with the dysfunctional consequences that can occur when companies are categorized as stars, cash cows, question marks, or dogs. Contrary to expectations, the BCG matrix often yields incorrect judgments about a company's potential. In other words, managers using the BCG matrix aren't very good at accurately determining which companies should be categorized as stars, cash cows, questions marks, or dogs. The most common mistake is simply miscategorizing highly

Exhibit 6.5

U-Shaped Relationship between Diversification and Risk

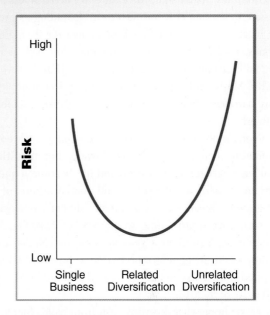

Source: M. Lubatkin & P.J. Lane, "Psst! . . . The Merger Mavens Still Have It Wrong," *Academy of Management Executive* 10 (1996) 21–39.

profitable companies as dogs.[39] In part, this is because the BCG matrix relies on past performance (previous market share and previous market growth), which is a notoriously poor predictor of future company performance. More worrisome, however, is research that indicates that the BCG matrix actually makes managers worse at judging the future profitability of a business. A study conducted in six countries over five years gave managers and business students clear information about the current and future profits (i.e., slow or fast growth) of three companies and asked them to select the one that would be most successful in the future. Although not labeled this way, one company was clearly a star, another was a dog, and the last was a cash cow. Just exposing people to the ideas in the BCG matrix led them to incorrectly categorize less profitable businesses as the most successful businesses 64 percent of the time, while actually *using* the BCG matrix led to making the same mistake 87 percent of the time.[40]

> **Dog** a company with a small share of a slow-growing market

Furthermore, using the BCG matrix can also weaken the strongest performer in the corporate portfolio: the cash cow. As funds are redirected from cash cows to stars, corporate managers essentially take away the resources needed to take advantage of the cash cow's new business opportunities. As a result, the cash cow becomes less aggressive in seeking new business or in defending its present business. While Nokia is best known for its mobile phones, it also has separate companies for Web mapping and location services and software (HERE Drive+, HERE Maps, and HERE Transit), and telecommunications hardware, software, and services (Nokia Siemens Networks).[41]

Nokia's phones were once the company cash cow, dominating cell phone sales worldwide, but now that business is struggling to survive and has become a question mark, with a relatively small market share of a fast-growing business. Today, Nokia Siemens is clearly the cash cow, representing 46 percent of Nokia's sales and yielding $3 billion a year in cash that Nokia uses to support its struggling mobile phone business, which dropped from a 22 percent world market share in 2012 to 16.6 percent in 2013.[42]

Nokia hopes that diverting cash from Nokia Siemens will turn its mobile phone business from a question mark back into a star and, eventually, a cash cow. Diverting cash from Nokia Siemens, however, may make it less able to defend its current business or to grow by seeking new business. Furthermore, cutting 17,000 jobs the last two years to increase Nokia Siemens's profits and cash flow may indicate that Nokia is "over milking" their cash cow in support of the struggling phone business.[43]

Finally, labeling a top performer as a cash cow can harm employee morale. Cash-cow employees realize that they have inferior status and that instead of working for themselves, they are now working to fund the growth of stars and question marks.

So, what kind of portfolio strategy does the best job of helping managers decide which companies to buy or sell? The U-shaped curve in Exhibit 6.5 indicates that, contrary to the predictions of portfolio strategy, the best approach is probably **related diversification,** in which the different business units share similar products, manufacturing, marketing, technology, or cultures. The key to related diversification is to acquire or create new companies with core capabilities that complement the core capabilities of businesses already in the corporate portfolio. Hormel Foods is an example of related diversification in the food business. The company both manufactures and markets a variety of foods, from deli meats to salsa to the infamous SPAM.

We began this section with the example of 3M and its 55,000 products sold in five different business groups. While seemingly different, most of 3M's product divisions are based in some fashion on its distinctive competencies in adhesives and tape (e.g., wet or dry sandpaper, Post-it notes, Scotchgard fabric protector, transdermal skin patches, and reflective material used in traffic signs). Furthermore, all of 3M's divisions share its strong corporate culture that promotes and encourages risk taking and innovation. In sum, in contrast to a single, undiversified business or unrelated diversification, related diversification reduces risk because the different businesses can work as a team, relying on each other for needed experience, expertise, and support.

6-3b Grand Strategies

A **grand strategy** is a broad strategic plan used to help an organization achieve its strategic goals.[44] Grand strategies guide the strategic alternatives that managers of individual businesses or subunits may use in deciding what businesses they should be in. There are three kinds of grand strategies: growth, stability, and retrenchment/recovery.

The purpose of a **growth strategy** is to increase profits, revenues, market share, or the number of places (stores, offices, locations) in which the company does business. Companies can grow in several ways. They can grow externally by merging with or acquiring other companies in the same or different businesses. AT&T is growing slowly at 3 percent per year. DirecTV, a satellite TV service, is growing at less than 1 percent a year. In hopes of accelerating growth for both companies, AT&T agreed to buy DirecTV for $48.5 billion. CBS News business analyst Jill Schlesinger says, "AT&T wants content. DirecTV has content."[45] AT&T is also interested in selling phone services to DirecTV's 18 million customers in Latin America. But the primary benefit that could accelerate growth for both companies is the ability to combine and discount their services for consumers. For example, instead of paying more to buy separate

---

Related diversification creating or acquiring companies that share similar products, manufacturing, marketing, technology, or cultures

Grand strategy a broad corporate-level strategic plan used to achieve strategic goals and guide the strategic alternatives that managers of individual businesses or subunits may use

Growth strategy a strategy that focuses on increasing profits, revenues, market share, or the number of places in which the company does business

The Dangers of Diversification

Diversification can have its advantages, but managers must be cautious when considering possible mergers. History is littered with failed mega mergers. Jeffrey Pfeffer of Stanford's Graduate Business School points out that an acquisition can often be a tempting go-to strategy when the way forward isn't obvious. He says that when managers "can't figure out what to do, they go buy something, particularly when they have a lot of cash. It seldom works." Juan Alcarcer of Harvard Business School added to this sentiment when speaking about Microsoft's proposed acquisition of Nokia's handset unit: "Two bad companies don't make a good company." When a company has small market share, there's usually a reason for it, and combining two of them rarely fixes that.

Source: S. Thurm, "History Isn't on Side of Microsoft-Nokia Tie Up," *The Wall Street Journal*, September 4, 2013, B4.

AP Images/Eric Risberg

Microsoft CEO Satya Nadella (left) is greeted by Stephen Elop, executive vice president of Nokia, during the keynote address of the 2014 Build Conference in San Francisco, California.

Internet, TV (subscription and pay TV packages), and wireless phone services, DirecTV's 20 million customers and AT&T's 107 million customers would then be able to buy those services together in a discounted bundle.[46]

Another way to grow is internally, directly expanding the company's existing business or creating and growing new businesses. Nestlé, the largest food company in the world, faced a serious challenge—it had to find a way to grow while having to deal with record-high prices for cocoa and sugar, two key ingredients for its chocolate products. To boost growth, Nestlé spent $24 million to promote Aero, a chocolate bar that is filled with bubbles of air. While the bubbles give the chocolate a creamier texture, they also help bulk up the candy bar without adding more ingredients, quite helpful at a time of high commodity costs. Thanks to the company's promotional emphasis, sales of Aero increased by 20 percent from the previous year, which helped the company as a whole earn a profit of $10.3 billion and sales growth of 7.5 percent.[47]

The purpose of a **stability strategy** is to continue doing what the company has been doing, just doing it better. Companies following a stability strategy try to improve the way in which they sell the same products or services to the same customers. Since its inception in 1909 as a window washing company in San Francisco, **ABM Industries** has focused on providing facility

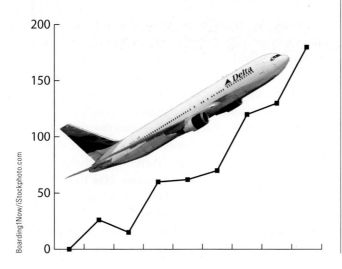

Boarding1Now/iStockphoto.com

Stability strategy a strategy that focuses on improving the way in which the company sells the same products or services to the same customers

services to businesses. Today, ABM's 100,000 employees in the United States and twenty other countries offer facility services management for electrical and lighting solutions, energy management, building maintenance and repair, janitorial services, landscape and ground maintenance, security, and parking services. In short, for over 100 years, ABM has reduced costs by keeping businesses' facilities safe, clean, comfortable, and energy efficient.[48] Companies often choose a stability strategy when their external environment doesn't change much or after they have struggled with periods of explosive growth.

The purpose of a **retrenchment strategy** is to turn around very poor company performance by shrinking the size or scope of the business or, if a company is in multiple businesses, by closing or shutting down different lines of the business. The first step of a typical retrenchment strategy might include making significant cost reductions: laying off employees; closing poorly performing stores, offices, or manufacturing plants; or closing or selling entire lines of products or services.[49] Barclays Plc, a London-based bank for over 300 years, got its start in 1690 when founders John Freame and Thomas Gould served as goldsmith bankers that, much like today's banks, stored gold and money, made loans, transferred deposits from account to account, and handled foreign exchange currencies.[50] By 2008, Barclays aspired to become a global bank serving customers, businesses, and investors worldwide. In 2014, however, following numerous financial scandals and poor financial performance, Barclays began an aggressive retrenchment strategy. Chairman Michael Rake said, "It's just no longer doable for us to be a global, universal bank."[51] Following a strategy that Rake termed "bold simplification," Barclays will cut 19,000 employees by 2016, exit commodities trading, sell half of its investment bank, and sell its retail banking operations in France, Spain, and Italy. Rake explained that, "In the future, Barclays will be leaner, stronger, much better balanced and well positioned to deliver lower volatility, higher returns and growth. My goal is unchanged: to create a Barclays that does business in the right way, with the right values, and delivers the returns that our shareholders deserve. However, the way in which we will achieve this is different."[52]

After cutting costs and reducing a business's size or scope, the second step in a retrenchment strategy is recovery. **Recovery** consists of the strategic actions that a company takes to return to a growth strategy. This two-step process of cutting and recovery is analogous to pruning roses. Prior to each growing season, roses should be cut back to two-thirds their normal size. Pruning doesn't damage the roses; it makes them stronger and more likely to produce beautiful, fragrant flowers. The retrenchment-and-recovery process is similar.

Like pruning, the cuts are made as part of a recovery strategy intended to allow companies to eventually return to a successful growth strategy. When company performance drops significantly, a strategy of retrenchment and recovery may help the company return to a successful growth strategy.

6-4 INDUSTRY-LEVEL STRATEGIES

Industry-level strategy addresses the question "How should we compete in this industry?"

*Let's find out more about industry-level strategies by discussing **6-4a the five industry forces that determine overall levels of competition in an industry** as well as **6-4b the positioning strategies** and **6-4c adaptive strategies that companies can use to achieve sustained competitive advantage and above-average profits.***

6-4a Five Industry Forces

According to Harvard professor Michael Porter, five industry forces determine an industry's overall attractiveness and potential for long-term profitability. These include the character of the rivalry, the threat of new entrants, the threat of substitute products or services, the bargaining power of suppliers, and the bargaining power of buyers. The stronger these forces, the less attractive the industry becomes to corporate investors because it is more difficult for companies to be profitable. Porter's industry forces are illustrated in Exhibit 6.6. Let's examine how these forces are bringing changes to several kinds of industries.

Character of the rivalry is a measure of the intensity of competitive behavior among companies in an industry. Is the competition among firms aggressive

Retrenchment strategy a strategy that focuses on turning around very poor company performance by shrinking the size or scope of the business

Recovery the strategic actions taken after retrenchment to return to a growth strategy

Industry-level strategy a corporate strategy that addresses the question "How should we compete in this industry?"

Character of the rivalry a measure of the intensity of competitive behavior between companies in an industry

Exhibit 6.6
Porter's Five Industry Forces

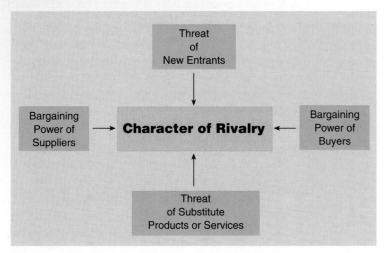

Source: Based on the Simon & Schuster, Inc. Porter, M. E. Competitive Strategy: Techniques for Analyzing Industries and Competitors. New York: Free Press, 1980.

and cutthroat, or do competitors focus more on serving customers than on attacking each other? Both industry attractiveness and profitability decrease when rivalry is cutthroat. For example, selling cars is a highly competitive business. Pick up a local newspaper on Friday, Saturday, or Sunday morning, and you'll find dozens of pages of car advertising ("Anniversary Sale-A-Bration," "Ford March Savings!" and "$99 Down, You Choose!"). In fact, competition in new-car sales is so intense that if it weren't for used-car sales, repair work, and replacement parts, many auto dealers would actually lose money.

The **threat of new entrants** is a measure of the degree to which barriers to entry make it easy or

difficult for new companies to get started in an industry. If new companies can enter the industry easily, then competition will increase and prices and profits will fall. Altos Research provides real-time statistics and analysis of real estate markets for investors and news services such as Bloomberg Financial. Because its business relies on access to terabytes of market data, it leases computing power and data storage from Amazon Web Services (AWS), the market leader in cloud services. Without any negotiation, AWS cut its costs in half, enough to pay for two new programmers. Altos' CEO Michael Simonsen said, "Nobody ever gives you a 40% price break overnight."[53] If so, why did AWS—and Microsoft and Google—all cut their prices by a third or more in the last six months? Because of the threat of new entrants.[54] In addition to new competitors over the last few years, such as Box.com, GoDaddy.com, and ZenBox, Oracle, and Salesforce.com, both Hewlett-Packard, which makes personal and network computers, and Cisco Systems, which makes the routers, switches, and systems that drive the Internet and corporate networks, are each investing $1 billion to develop cloud software and data centers.[55] On the other hand, if there are sufficient barriers to entry, such as large capital requirements to buy expensive equipment or plant facilities or the need for specialized knowledge, then competition will be weaker and prices and profits will generally be higher.

The **threat of substitute products or services** is a measure of the ease with which customers can find substitutes for an industry's products or services. If customers can easily find substitute products or services, the competition will be greater and profits will be lower. If there are few or no substitutes, competition will be weaker and profits will be higher. In many cities, hailing a cab can be frustrating. Enter **Uber**, a smartphone app that connects people needing rides with drivers who will take them where they want to go. Open Uber, choose your

Threat of new entrants a measure of the degree to which barriers to entry make it easy or difficult for new companies to get started in an industry

Threat of substitute products or services a measure of the ease with which customers can find substitutes for an industry's products or services

preferred vehicle (taxi, town car, or SUV), position the pin on the map in the app showing where you'd like to be picked up, do the same for your destination, and then Uber's app estimates the cost, charges your credit card, emails the receipt, indicates on the map how far away the car is, and then lets you know when the driver has arrived to pick you up. Average wait time is only three to ten minutes. Uber maintains quality control by using social media to gather feedback on drivers' timeliness, politeness, and service. Drivers with negative feedback lose the chance to drive for Uber. Taxi services, not surprisingly, are not happy about competing with Uber, and its drivers have sued Uber—unsuccessfully—in San Francisco, New York, and Washington, DC, to shield themselves from competition.[56]

Bargaining power of suppliers is a measure of the influence that suppliers of parts, materials, and services to firms in an industry have on the prices of these inputs. When companies can buy parts, materials, and services from numerous suppliers, the companies will be able to bargain with the suppliers to keep prices low. On the other hand, if there are few suppliers, or if a company is dependent on a supplier with specialized skills and knowledge, then the suppliers will have the bargaining power to dictate price levels.

Bargaining power of buyers is a measure of the influence that customers have on the firm's prices. If a company sells a popular product or service to multiple buyers, then the company has more power to set prices. By contrast, if a company is dependent on just a few high-volume buyers, those buyers will typically have enough bargaining power to dictate prices. Most agricultural commodities, such as beef and soybeans, are sold by farmers to commodity traders who then sell them to buyers around the world. Australian farmers, who are generally the world's second-largest growers of wheat, beef, cotton, and sugar, typically sell their agricultural produce to Archer Daniels Midland, Bunge Ltd., Cargill, and Dreyfus, the "ABCD" trading houses, who control 60 percent of the wheat bought and shipped from Australia. Consequently, the trading houses have incredible bargaining power, which means that Australian farmers end up with much smaller prices for their agriculture products. Some Aussie farmers are trying to counter this bargaining power by selling directly to global buyers. Glen Rogan, who farms cotton in Queensland, Australia, says, "To make a reasonable living as a farmer under current prices was becoming untenable." So he sold 6,500 bales of cotton directly to Asian cotton mills, getting 30 percent more than he would have through the trading houses. Says Rogan, selling directly to cotton mills "was the only way I could see to stay relevant and viable."[57]

6-4b Positioning Strategies

After analyzing industry forces, the next step in industry-level strategy is to protect your company from the negative effects of industry-wide competition and to create a sustainable competitive advantage. According to Michael Porter, there are three positioning strategies: cost leadership, differentiation, and focus.

Cost leadership means producing a product or service of acceptable quality at consistently lower production costs than competitors so that the firm can offer the product or service at the lowest price in the industry. Cost leadership protects companies from industry forces by deterring new entrants, who will have to match low costs and prices. Cost leadership also forces down the prices of substitute products and services, attracts bargain-seeking buyers, and increases bargaining power with suppliers, who have to keep their prices low if they want to do business with the cost leader. But Burt Flickinger, a retail consultant with the Strategic Resource Group (SRG), believes that Idaho-based WinCo, which brands itself as "The Supermarket Low Price Leader," "may be the best retailer in the western U.S. WinCo is really unstoppable at this point."[58] Super Market News' Jon Springer says, "While many supermarkets strive to keep within a few percentage points of Walmart Stores' prices, WinCo Foods often undersells the massive discount chain."[59] How? With minimalist stores, having customers bag their groceries, not accepting credit cards (which saves 3 percent per transaction), limiting selection within product categories, and by buying directly from farms and factories, thereby cutting out food distributors who mark up prices and sell more expensive brands. WinCo's prices are so much better than Walmart's that SRG's Flickinger says, "They're Walmart's worst nightmare."[60]

Differentiation means making your product or service sufficiently different from competitors' offerings

---

Bargaining power of suppliers a measure of the influence that suppliers of parts, materials, and services to firms in an industry have on the prices of these inputs

Bargaining power of buyers a measure of the influence that customers have on a firm's prices

Cost leadership the positioning strategy of producing a product or service of acceptable quality at consistently lower production costs than competitors can, so that the firm can offer the product or service at the lowest price in the industry

Differentiation the positioning strategy of providing a product or service that is sufficiently different from competitors' offerings that customers are willing to pay a premium price for it

that customers are willing to pay a premium price for the extra value or performance that it provides. Differentiation protects companies from industry forces by reducing the threat of substitute products. It also protects companies by making it easier to retain customers and more difficult for new entrants trying to attract new customers. Would you pay $113 for a mop? Or $26.99 for a polishing cloth? Norway-based Norwex makes premium-priced cleaning products that clean your house with water and no chemicals or cleaning agents. For instance, a Norwex Microfiber cloth contains microfibers that are 1/200th the thickness of a human hair.[61] The microfibers capture and can hold seven times their weight, which means that they capture dirt, grease, and moisture. Does it work? Microbiologist Kristen Gibson says, "A damp microfiber cloth is a really good tool for removing microorganisms, including viruses and bacteria."[62] Her research, funded by the U.S. Department of Agriculture, found that microfibers removed viruses, unlike typical cloth towels that simply spread viruses from one surface to another. Norwex advises using the cloths dry to dust and wet (with water) to clean. And while its products are expensive, with the average family spending $600–800 a year on cleaning supplies and chemicals, Norwex claims that consumers save time and money because its products are reusable.[63]

With a **focus strategy,** a company uses either cost leadership or differentiation to produce a specialized product or service for a limited, specially targeted group of customers in a particular geographic region or market segment. Focus strategies typically work in market niches that competitors have overlooked or have difficulty serving. **Axe** began selling body spray in the United States in 2002. In just five short years, it grew into a $2.5 billion global brand and the dominant force in the

men's body spray market, with a 72 percent market share (58 points higher than its nearest competitor, Old Spice). Axe accomplished this with a relentless focus on its key demographic—men ages twenty to twenty-five. It does not target its products or its marketing campaigns to a younger audience, and it does not try to follow its customers as they age to their late twenties and beyond. Accordingly, Axe's products, campaigns, and marketing research are completely focused on men ages twenty to twenty-five, with whom it conducts extensive research in college towns and urban settings.[64]

6-4c Adaptive Strategies

Adaptive strategies are another set of industry-level strategies. Whereas the aim of positioning strategies is to minimize the effects of industry competition and build a sustainable competitive advantage, the purpose of adaptive strategies is to choose an industry-level strategy that is best suited to changes in the organization's external environment. There are four kinds of adaptive strategies: defenders, prospectors, analyzers, and reactors.[65]

Defenders seek moderate, steady growth by offering a limited range of products and services to a well-defined set of customers. In other words, defenders aggressively "defend" their current strategic position by doing the best job they can to hold on to customers in a particular market segment.

Prospectors seek fast growth by searching for new market opportunities, encouraging risk taking, and being the first to bring innovative new products to market. Prospectors are analogous to gold miners who "prospect" for gold nuggets (i.e., new products) in hope that the nuggets will lead them to a rich deposit of gold (i.e., fast growth). 3M has long been known for its innovative products, particularly in the area of adhesives. Since 1904, it has invented sandpaper; masking, cellophane, electrical, and Scotch tapes; the first commercially available audio and videotapes; and its most famous invention, Post-it notes. Lately, 3M has invented a film that increases the brightness of LCD displays on laptop computers; developed a digital system for construction companies to detect underground telecommunication, gas, water, sewer, or electrical lines without digging; and created a pheromone spray that, by preventing harmful insects from mating, will protect apple, walnut, tomato, cranberry, and grape crops. For more on 3M's innovative products, see the 3M innovation archive (http://solutions.3m.com/innovation/en_US/).

Focus strategy the positioning strategy of using cost leadership or differentiation to produce a specialized product or service for a limited, specially targeted group of customers in a particular geographic region or market segment

Defenders companies using an adaptive strategy aimed at defending strategic positions by seeking moderate, steady growth and by offering a limited range of high-quality products and services to a well-defined set of customers

Prospectors companies using an adaptive strategy that seeks fast growth by searching for new market opportunities, encouraging risk taking, and being the first to bring innovative new products to market

Analyzers are a blend of the defender and prospector strategies. They seek moderate, steady growth and limited opportunities for fast growth. Analyzers are rarely first to market with new products or services. Instead, they try to simultaneously minimize risk and maximize profits by following or imitating the proven successes of prospectors. Netflix has achieved growth not only through its mail-order DVD service but also through its video streaming service, which allows users to watch a variety of movies and TV shows almost instantly. In fact, the streaming service has been so successful that Netflix has nearly two times more streaming customers than DVD customers. Motivated by Netflix's success, Redbox (with Verizon) and Amazon now offer similar streaming services. Redbox, the DVD rental kiosk operator, and Verizon, the wireless carrier, teamed up to offer Redbox Instant. Nonsubscribers can reserve movies and games at Redbox kiosks or rent or buy individual movies via streaming services. Subscribers, who pay $8 a month, also get four DVD credits to use at Redbox kiosks and access to Redbox's entire streaming library. Amazon Prime members, who pay $99 a year, get free two-day shipping on Amazon products, can borrow one Kindle book free each month, and have access to 41,000 TV shows and movies on Amazon's Instant Video.[66] After Netflix tried to differentiate itself by developing exclusive, original shows like *House of Cards* and *Orange Is the New Black*, Amazon followed suit by offering its own original series, *Alpha House and Betas*.[67]

Finally, unlike defenders, prospectors, or analyzers, **reactors** do not follow a consistent strategy. Rather than anticipating and preparing for external opportunities and threats, reactors tend to react to changes in their external environment after they occur. Not surprisingly, reactors tend to be poorer performers than defenders, prospectors, or analyzers. A reactor approach is inherently unstable, and firms that fall into this mode of operation must change their approach or face almost certain failure.

Analyzers companies using an adaptive strategy that seeks to minimize risk and maximize profits by following or imitating the proven successes of prospectors

Reactors companies that do not follow a consistent adaptive strategy but instead react to changes in the external environment after they occur

Amazon Coming Back to Earth?

For years, online and brick-and-mortar retailers have had to compete with cost leader Amazon's prices. It appears, however, that Amazon might be losing its edge and that other retailers are gaining ground. BB&T Capital Markets has been tracking the prices on a basket of 30 goods from Amazon and Bed, Bath, & Beyond since 2012. When it began, Amazon's prices were 9 percent lower. However, the price of the Bed, Bath, & Beyond basket recently dropped to 6.5 percent below the price of the Amazon basket for the first time ever. Much of Amazon's pricing advantage comes from its razor thin profit margins. Other retailers are beginning to see that to compete, they may have to drop their profit margins as well. Some retailers, like Best Buy, have begun to fight fire with fire by offering to match Amazon prices on all in-store items.

Source: T. Gara, "Amazon Losing its Price Edge," *The Wall street Journal*, August 20, 2013, B2.

6-5 FIRM-LEVEL STRATEGIES

Microsoft unveils its Xbox One video-game console; Sony counters with its PlayStation 4. Sprint Nextel drops prices and increases monthly cell phone minutes; Verizon strikes back with better reception and even lower prices and more minutes. FedEx, the overnight delivery company, buys Kinko's copying and printing stores and turns

AP Images/Wendy's Co

Casual dining restaurants like Chipotle and Panera offer better quality foods and more sophisticated atmospheres for slightly higher prices. Wendy's push to remake itself as a higher-end hamburger chain is starting to pay off, with key sales figures rising for the sixth straight quarter. This photo shows the improved interior of a recently remodeled Wendy's restaurant.

them into FedEx Kinko's Office and Print Centers to provide a convenient place for businesspeople to drop off and pick up packages; UPS buys Mail Boxes, Etc. and turns its outlets into UPS Stores for exactly the same purpose. Starbucks Coffee opens a store, and nearby locally run coffeehouses respond by improving service, increasing portions, and holding the line on prices. Attack and respond, respond and attack. **Firm-level strategy** addresses the question "How should we compete against a particular firm?"

*Let's find out more about the firm-level strategies (direct competition between companies) by reading about **6-5a the basics of direct competition** and **6-5b the strategic moves involved in direct competition between companies.***

6-5a Direct Competition

Although Porter's five industry forces indicate the overall level of competition in an industry, most companies do not compete directly with all the firms in their industry. For example, McDonald's and Red Lobster are both in the restaurant business, but no one would characterize them as competitors. McDonald's offers low-cost, convenient fast food in a seat-yourself restaurant, while Red Lobster offers mid-priced seafood dinners complete with servers and a bar.

Instead of competing with an entire industry, most firms compete directly with just a few companies within it. **Direct competition** is the rivalry between two companies offering similar products and services that acknowledge each other as rivals and take offensive and defensive positions as they act and react to each other's strategic actions.[68] Two factors determine the extent to which firms will be in direct competition with each other: market commonality and resource similarity. **Market commonality** is the degree to which two companies have overlapping products, services, or customers in multiple markets. The more markets in which there is product, service, or customer overlap, the more intense the direct competition between the two companies. **Resource similarity** is the extent to which a competitor has similar amounts and kinds of resources, that is, similar assets, capabilities, processes, information, and knowledge used to create and sustain an advantage over competitors. From a competitive

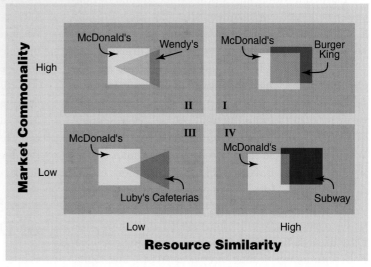

Exhibit 6.7
A Framework of Direct Competition

Source: M. Chen, "Competitor Analysis and InterFirm Rivalry: Toward a Theoretical Integration," *Academy of Management Review* 21 (1996): 100–134.

standpoint, resource similarity means that your direct competitors can probably match the strategic actions that your company takes.

Exhibit 6.7 shows how market commonality and resource similarity interact to determine when and where companies are in direct competition.[69] The overlapping area in each quadrant (between the triangle and the rectangle, or between the differently colored rectangles) depicts market commonality. The larger the overlap, the greater the market commonality. Shapes depict resource similarity, with rectangles representing one set of competitive resources and triangles representing another. Quadrant I shows two companies in direct competition because they have similar resources at their disposal

Firm-level strategy a corporate strategy that addresses the question "How should we compete against a particular firm?"

Direct competition the rivalry between two companies that offer similar products and services, acknowledge each other as rivals, and act and react to each other's strategic actions

Market commonality the degree to which two companies have overlapping products, services, or customers in multiple markets

Resource similarity the extent to which a competitor has similar amounts and kinds of resources

and a high degree of market commonality. These companies try to sell similar products and services to similar customers. McDonald's and Burger King would clearly fit here as direct competitors. For example, Burger King has partnered with Seattle's Best Coffee, owned by Starbucks, to add premium coffee, lattes, hot chocolate, and iced coffee drinks to its breakfast menu to compete with McDonald's McCafé specialty coffees and drinks.[70]

In Quadrant II, the overlapping parts of the triangle and rectangle show two companies going after similar customers with some similar products or services but doing so with different competitive resources. McDonald's and Wendy's restaurants would fit here. Wendy's is after the same lunchtime and dinner crowds that McDonald's is. Nevertheless, with its more expensive hamburgers, fries, shakes, and salads, Wendy's is less of a direct competitor to McDonald's than Burger King is. For example, Wendy's has recently rebranded itself more like a casual dining restaurant, redesigning its locations with lounge seating, fireplaces, Wi-Fi, and digital menu boards.[71] Wendy's goal is to convert 85 percent of its company-owned locations and 35 percent of its franchised stores by 2017.[72] Nonetheless, because there is some customer overlap, Wendy's has added a new Right Price, Right Size value menu with items such as burgers, fries, chicken wraps and sandwiches, and a small Frosty to compete directly with McDonald's value menu.[73]

In Quadrant III, the very small overlap shows two companies with different competitive resources and little market commonality. McDonald's and Luby's cafeterias fit here. Although both are in the fast-food business, there's almost no overlap in terms of products and customers. Luby's sells baked chicken, turkey, roasts, meat loaf, and vegetables, none of which are available at McDonald's. Furthermore, Luby's customers aren't likely to eat at McDonald's. In fact, Luby's is not really competing with other fast-food restaurants, but with eating at home. Company surveys show that close to half of its customers would have eaten at home, not at another restaurant, if they hadn't come to Luby's.[74]

Finally, in Quadrant IV, the small overlap between the two rectangles shows that McDonald's and Subway compete with similar resources but with little market commonality. In terms of resources, sales at McDonald's are much larger, but Subway has grown substantially in the last decade and now has 47,101 stores in 105 countries, compared to McDonald's with more than 35,000 in more than 100 countries.[75]

Though Subway and McDonald's compete, they aren't direct competitors in terms of market commonality in the way that McDonald's and Burger King are because Subway, unlike McDonald's, sells itself as a provider of healthy fast food. Thus, the overlap is much smaller in Quadrant IV than in Quadrant I. With its advertising featuring Jared, who lost 245 pounds eating at Subway, the detailed nutritional information available in its stores, and its close relationship with the American Heart Association, Subway's goal "is to emphasize that the Subway brand represents all that is good about health and well-being."[76]

6-5b Strategic Moves of Direct Competition

While corporate-level strategies help managers decide what business to be in and industry-level strategies help them determine how to compete within an industry, firm-level strategies help managers determine when, where, and what strategic actions should be taken against a direct competitor. Firms in direct competition can make two basic strategic moves: attack and response. These moves occur all the time in virtually every industry, but they are most noticeable in industries where multiple large competitors are pursuing customers in the same market space.

An **attack** is a competitive move designed to reduce a rival's market share or profits. For example, the two leaders in the e-reader market, Amazon and Barnes & Noble, have been engaged in a lengthy battle over prices. The Amazon's Kindle Paperwhite was designed to compete with Barnes & Noble's Nook Touch with Glowlight, a black and white e-reader with a built-in light for night reading.[77] When the Paperwhite was released, Barnes & Noble cut the price on the Nook Touch by $20 to match Paperwhite's price.[78]

A **response** is a countermove, prompted by a rival's attack, that is designed to defend or improve a company's market share or profit. There are two kinds of responses.[79] The first is to match or mirror your competitor's move. This is what Barnes & Noble did when it lowered the price of its Nook Simple Touch, which had been selling for $139, to $99.[80]

The second kind of response, however, is to respond along a different dimension from your competitor's move or attack. Wireless carriers, such at AT&T, Verizon, and Sprint, have typically responded to competitors' attacks by cutting prices, expanding coverage, or speeding up

Attack a competitive move designed to reduce a rival's market share or profits

Response a competitive countermove, prompted by a rival's attack, to defend or improve a company's market share or profit

their networks. T-Mobile, the smallest of the major wireless carriers, faired poorly on those dimensions and lost 2 million customers as a result two years ago.[81] In the last 18 months, however, T-Mobile has taken 3.3 million customers from its competitors by responding with an "uncarrier" strategy that removes key restrictions found in its competitors' wireless services.[82] Overage charges? Not at T-Mobile, which offers unlimited minutes, texts and data (go beyond your data "cap" and T-Mobile slows down your data rather than charge you). Exorbitant roaming charges for international plans? T-Mobile charges a meager 20 cents per minute for international calls, while providing unlimited international data and texts at no extra charge in 120 countries. Streaming music on your phone? Thirty minutes a day uses 900 megabytes a month against the typical 1 or 2 gigabyte data plan. At T-Mobile, though, streaming music does NOT count against data usage. Upgrade your phone just once every two years? At T-Mobile, upgrade whenever you want by trading in your old phone and receiving credits for remaining payments (up to half of the original cost). Finally, termination fees to keep you locked into in a 2-year contract? Not at T-Mobile, where you can quit at any time. In fact, T-Mobile will pay your termination fee if you leave your current carrier to sign with it.[83]

Market commonality and resource similarity determine the likelihood of an attack or response, that is, whether a company is likely to attack a direct competitor or to strike back with a strong response when attacked. When market commonality is large and companies have overlapping products, services, or customers in multiple markets, there is less motivation to attack and more motivation to respond to an attack. The reason for this is straightforward: when firms

are direct competitors in a large number of markets, they have a great deal at stake. For instance, GE makes 70 percent of the freight locomotive rail cars in the North American market, with the remaining 30 percent sold by Caterpillar, which bought EMD, a locomotive manufacturer, in 2010. To become more competitive with GE, Caterpillar closed EMD's unionized locomotive manufacturing plant in London, Ontario, Canada, replacing it with brand-new non-unionized plants in Muncie, Indiana, and Brazil. Bill Ainsworth, who leads Caterpillar's railroad business, says the new Muncie plant "will be the most efficient locomotive-manufacturing plant in the world."[84]

In response to Caterpillar's cost-cutting moves, GE eliminated 950 jobs at its unionized plant in Pennsylvania, shifting production work to a new, non-unionized manufacturing plant in Texas. With GE's union wages running $25 to $36 an hour compared to $14.50 an hour at Caterpillar's non-unionized Muncie plant, GE had to respond by finding a way to lower costs.[85]

Whereas market commonality affects the likelihood of an attack or a response to an attack, resource similarity largely affects response capability, that is, how quickly and forcefully a company can respond to an attack. When resource similarity is strong, the responding firm will generally be able to match the strategic moves of the attacking firm. Consequently, a firm is less likely to attack firms with similar levels of resources because it is unlikely to gain any sustained advantage when the responding firms strike back. On the other hand, if one firm is substantially stronger than another (i.e., there is low resource similarity), then a competitive attack is more likely to produce sustained competitive advantage.

In general, the more moves (i.e., attacks) a company initiates against direct competitors, and the greater a company's tendency to respond when attacked, the better its performance. More specifically, attackers and early responders (companies that are quick to launch a retaliatory attack) tend to gain market share and profits at the expense of late responders. This is not to suggest that a full-attack strategy always works best. In fact, attacks can provoke harsh retaliatory responses.

Amazon outraged competing retailers by promoting its new Price Check mobile app with a 5 percent discount that could only be applied on items found at brick-and-mortar stores. When shoppers scanned a product's bar code or took a picture of the product, Amazon's app displayed the same item from Amazon's website with a coupon good for free shipping and 5 percent off Amazon's already low price.[86]

AP Images/Jae C. Hong

fifty store closings in 2012. Consequently, when deciding when, where, and what strategic actions to take against a direct competitor, managers should always consider the possibility of retaliation.[87]

Best Buy is the world's largest electronics retailer. Today, 60 percent of its consumers "showroom shop," looking at products in Best Buy stores and then checking their smartphones to find prices at online stores like Amazon. Best Buy responded aggressively to Amazon's Price Check app by matching online prices year round in its stores and by offering deep Black Friday discounts the day after Thanksgiving (typically the heaviest shopping day of the year). Best Buy's retaliatory responses, however, have come at a steep cost, with profits dropping over 90 percent and the announcement of more than

STUDY TOOLS 6

LOCATED AT THE BACK OF YOUR BOOK:

☐ Rip out and study the Chapter Review Card at the end of the book

LOG IN TO WWW.CENGAGEBRAIN.COM TO:

☐ Review Key Term Flashcards

☐ Complete Practice Quizzing (take up to four time without repeating the same quiz)

☐ Complete Games: Beat the Clock and Crossword Puzzle

☐ Watch Management Workplace Video on "Theo Chocolate"

☐ Work Through the What Would You Do Case on The Walt Disney Company

USE THE TOOLS.

- Rip out the Review Cards in the back of your book to study.

Or Visit CourseMate to:

- Read, search, highlight, and take notes in the Interactive eBook
- Review Flashcards (Print or Online) to master key terms
- Test yourself with Auto-Graded Quizzes
- Bring concepts to life with Games, Videos, and Animations!

Go to CourseMate for **MGMT8** to begin using these tools.
Access at **www.cengagebrain.com**

Complete the Speak Up
survey in CourseMate at
www.cengagebrain.com

Follow us at
www.facebook.com/4ltrpress

A-Digit/iStockphoto.com

7 Innovation and Change

STEEX//iStockphoto.com

LEARNING OUTCOMES

7-1 Explain why innovation matters to companies.

7-2 Discuss the different methods that managers can use to effectively manage innovation in their organizations.

7-3 Discuss why not changing can lead to organizational decline.

7-4 Discuss the different methods that managers can use to better manage change as it occurs.

After you finish this chapter, go to **PAGE 153** for **STUDY TOOLS**

7-1 WHY INNOVATION MATTERS

At age fifty-seven, composer Richard Einhorn lost his hearing and feared he would never hear music again. So when he went to New York's Metropolitan Opera and was given special headphones to amplify the music, he was hopeful, but the sound quality was poor and filled with background noise, static, and interference. However, when he attended a performance of *Wicked* at the Kennedy Center in Washington, DC, he said, "For the first time since I lost most of my hearing, live music was perfectly clear, perfectly clean and incredibly rich. There I was at 'Wicked' weeping uncontrollably—and I don't even like musicals." The superb sound at the Kennedy Center was due to a device called a hearing loop, in which a copper wire around the edges of a room broadcasts signals to special receivers built directly into most hearing aids. But unlike other such devices, hearing loops filter background noise and only broadcast sounds coming directly from strategically placed microphones. Janice Schacter Lintz, of the Hearing Access Program, which advocates for the installation of hearing loops in public places, says that with 10,000 baby boomers turning sixty-five every day and with one-third of people over sixty-five experiencing hearing loss, "This isn't just about disability rights—it's about good customer service. That's a big group of customers who won't go to museums or theaters or restaurants where they can't hear. Put in a loop, and they can hear clearly without any of the bother or embarrassment of wearing a special headset."[1] **Organizational innovation** is the successful implementation of creative ideas, like the hearing loop at the Kennedy Center in Washington, DC.

We can only guess what changes technological innovations will bring in the next twenty years. Will we carry computers in our pockets? Today's iPhones and Android phones are a step in that direction. Will solar power and wind power get cheap and efficient enough so that your home can have a stand-alone power source off the main electrical grid? Will fully automated, self-driving cars chauffeur you (working in the back seat on a computing tablet via high-speed Internet) to work in the next decade? Who knows? The only thing we do know about the next twenty years is that innovation will continue to change our lives.

Let's begin our discussion of innovation by learning about 7-1a technology cycles and 7-2b innovation streams.

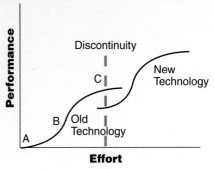

Exhibit 7.1
S-Curves and Technological Innovation

Source: R. N. Foster, *Innovation: The Attacker's Advantage* (New York: Summitt, 1986).

7-1a Technology Cycles

In Chapter 3, you learned that technology consists of the knowledge, tools, and techniques used to transform inputs (raw materials and information) into outputs (products and services). A **technology cycle** begins with the birth of a new technology and ends when that technology reaches its limits and dies as it is replaced by a newer, substantially better technology.[2] For example, technology cycles occurred when air conditioners supplanted fans, when Henry Ford's Model T replaced horse-drawn carriages, when planes replaced trains as a means of cross-country travel, when vaccines that prevented diseases replaced medicines designed to treat them, and when battery-powered wristwatches replaced mechanically powered, stem-wound wristwatches.

From Gutenberg's invention of the printing press in 1448 to the rapid advance of the Internet, studies of hundreds of technological innovations have shown that nearly all technology cycles follow the typical **S-curve pattern of innovation** shown in Exhibit 7.1.[3] Early in a technology cycle, there is still much to learn, so progress is slow, as depicted by point A on the S-curve.

Organizational innovation the successful implementation of creative ideas in organizations

Technology cycle a cycle that begins with the birth of a new technology and ends when that technology reaches its limits and is replaced by a newer, substantially better technology

S-curve pattern of innovation a pattern of technological innovation characterized by slow initial progress, then rapid progress, and then slow progress again as a technology matures and reaches its limits

The flat slope indicates that increased effort (in terms of money or research and development) brings only small improvements in technological performance.

Fortunately, as the new technology matures, researchers figure out how to get better performance from it. This is represented by point B of the S-curve in Exhibit 7.1. The steeper slope indicates that small amounts of effort will result in significant increases in performance. At point C, the flat slope again indicates that further efforts to develop this particular technology will result in only small increases in performance. More importantly, however, point C indicates that the performance limits of that particular technology are being reached. In other words, additional significant improvements in performance are highly unlikely.

Intel's technology cycles have followed this pattern. Intel spends billions to develop new computer chips and to build new facilities to produce them. Intel has found that the technology cycle for its integrated circuits is about three years. In each three-year cycle, Intel spends billions to introduce a new chip, improves the chip by making it a little bit faster each year, and then replaces that chip at the end of the cycle with a brand-new, different chip that is substantially faster than the old chip. At first, though (point A), the billions Intel spends typically produce only small improvements in performance. But after six months to a year with a new chip design, Intel's engineering and production people typically figure out how to make the new chips much faster than they were initially (point B). Yet, despite impressive gains in performance, Intel is unable to make a particular computer chip run any faster because the chip reaches its design limits.

After a technology has reached its limits at the top of the S-curve, significant improvements in performance usually come from radical new designs or new performance-enhancing materials. In Exhibit 7.1, that new technology is represented by the second S-curve. The changeover or discontinuity between the old and new technologies is represented by the dotted line. At first, the old and new technologies will likely coexist. Eventually, however, the new technology will replace the old technology. When that happens, the old technology cycle will be complete, and a new one will have started. The changeover between newer and older computer chip designs typically takes about one year. Over time, improving existing technology (tweaking the performance of the current technology cycle), combined with replacing old technology with new technology cycles (i.e., new, faster computer chip designs replacing older ones), has increased the speed of Intel's computer processors by a factor of 300. Today's super-powerful 64-bit processors, which provide instantaneous processing and results, have 1.4 billion transistors compared to 3.1 million transistors for 1990s 32-bit processors, 275,000 transistors for the earliest 1980s 32-bit processors, or just 4,500 transistors for the 8-bit processors, which began personal computing in the 1970s.[4]

Though the evolution of Intel's chips has been used to illustrate S-curves and technology cycles, it's important to note that technology cycles and technological innovation don't necessarily involve faster computer chips or cleaner-burning automobile engines. Remember, *technology* is simply the knowledge, tools, and techniques used to transform inputs into outputs. So a technology cycle occurs whenever there are major advances or changes in the *knowledge*, *tools*, and *techniques* of a field or discipline, whatever it may be.

For example, one of the most important technology cycles in the history of civilization occurred in 1859, when 1,300 miles of central sewer line were constructed throughout London to carry human waste to the sea more than eleven miles away. This extensive sewer system replaced the widespread practice of dumping raw sewage directly into streets, where people walked through it and where it drained into public wells that supplied drinking water. Though the relationship between raw sewage and cholera wasn't known at the time, preventing waste runoff from contaminating water supplies stopped the spread of that disease, which had killed millions of people for centuries in cities throughout the world.[5] Safe water supplies immediately translated into better health and longer life expectancies. Indeed, the water you drink today is safe thanks to this technological breakthrough. So, when you think about technology cycles, don't automatically think "high technology." Instead, broaden your perspective by considering advances or changes in *any* kind of knowledge, tools, and techniques.

7-1b Innovation Streams

In Chapter 6, you learned that organizations can create *competitive advantage* for themselves if they have a *distinctive competence* that allows them to make, do, or perform something better than their competitors. A competitive advantage becomes sustainable if other companies cannot duplicate the benefits obtained from that distinctive competence. Technological innovation, however, can enable competitors to duplicate the benefits obtained from a company's distinctive advantage. It can also quickly turn a company's competitive advantage into a competitive disadvantage.

Twenty-five years ago, digital cameras replaced film-based technology. But with digital camera sales down 40 percent in four years (and still dropping), digital camera makers are losing their competitive advantage to smartphones with HD photo and video capabilities far better than basic digital cameras. Shigenobu Nagamori, CEO of Nidec, which makes electric motors used in consumer electronics, says that thanks to smartphones we should, "assume that the inexpensive cameras are dead, just like PCs."[6] Tsugio Tsuchiya, a general manager at Tamron which makes lenses for more advanced DSLRS (digital single-lens reflex cameras), worries that "Smartphones pose a threat not just to compact cameras but entry-level DSLRS," which start at $400 and use interchangeable lenses, such as telescoping zooms.[7] But even that advantage may soon be lost. HTC's Symon Whitehorn says, "I think we're looking at about 18 months to two years until that [zoom] lens barrier begins breaking down and it becomes much harder to justify buying a dedicated camera outside of specialist or nostalgia reasons."[8]

Companies that want to sustain a competitive advantage must understand and protect themselves from the strategic threats of innovation. Over the long run, the best way for a company to do that is to create a stream of its own innovative ideas and products year after year. Consequently, we define **innovation streams** as patterns of innovation over time that can create sustainable competitive advantage.[9] Exhibit 7.2 shows a typical innovation consisting of a series of technology cycles. Recall that a technology cycle begins with a new technology and ends when that technology is replaced by a newer, substantially better technology. The innovation stream in Exhibit 7.2 shows three such technology cycles.

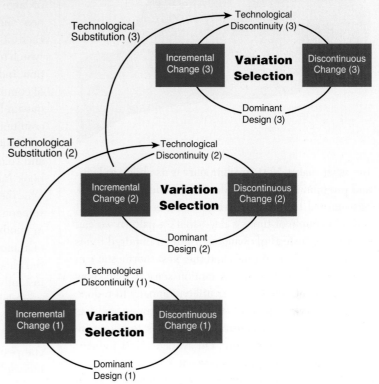

Exhibit 7.2
Innovation Streams: Technology Cycles over Time

Source: Adapted from M. L. Tushman, P. C. Anderson, and C. O'Reilly, "Technology Cycles, Innovation Streams and Ambidextrous Organizations: Organization Renewal Through Innovation Streams and Strategic Change," On Managing Strategic Innovation and Change, eds. M. L. Tushman and P. C. Anderson (New Oxford Press, 1997) 3–23.

An innovation stream begins with a **technological discontinuity,** in which a scientific advance or a unique combination of existing technologies creates a significant breakthrough in performance or function. Most home thermostats simply raise or lower the temperature. Advanced models can change the temperature when you leave for work and come home, but because they're difficult to program, most people just set the temperature manually, greatly reducing energy efficiency. The **Nest** thermostat, designed by the people who created the iPod, has a digital screen showing the temperature and a silver control ring that turns to adjust the temperature.

Innovation streams patterns of innovation over time that can create sustainable competitive advantage

Technological discontinuity the phase of an innovation stream in which a scientific advance or unique combination of existing technologies creates a significant breakthrough in performance or function

AP Images

But what makes Nest revolutionary is its ability to learn and program itself. Cofounder Tony Fadell says, "Think of a normal thermostat. Everyone turns it up, turns it down, a couple of times a day—that's a pattern we can infer from. Instead of changing it fifteen hundred times a year, do it 10 or 20 times and the Nest thermostat can learn from that."[10] Nest has motion sensors that know if you're home; links to your utility company to reduce power usage at expensive, peak energy times; and has smartphone apps to control your home's temperature even when you're not there. On average, Nest reduces energy usage a whopping 15 percent.[11]

Technological discontinuities are followed by a **discontinuous change,** which is characterized by technological substitution and design competition. **Technological substitution** occurs when customers purchase new technologies to replace older technologies. For example, just twenty years ago, nearly all phone calls were made via hardwired landline telephones. But, according to the U.S. National Health Information Survey, 39.4 percent of U.S. homes don't have landline phones.[12] That's up from 17 percent in 2008.[13] Furthermore, another 15.7 percent of U.S. homes get almost all of their calls on wireless phones, despite having a landline.[14] Finally, with AT&T and Verizon announcing the replacement of their old cable-based phone system with wireless IP-based networks, landline phones won't even be an option within several years.[15]

Discontinuous change the phase of a technology cycle characterized by technological substitution and design competition

Technological substitution the purchase of new technologies to replace older ones

Design competition competition between old and new technologies to establish a new technological standard or dominant design

Dominant design a new technological design or process that becomes the accepted market standard

Discontinuous change is also characterized by **design competition,** in which the old technology and several different new technologies compete to establish a new technological standard or dominant design. Because of large investments in old technology and because the new and old technologies are often incompatible with each other, companies and consumers are reluctant to switch to a different technology during a design competition. Indeed, the telegraph was so widely used as a means of communication in the late 1800s that at first almost no one understood why telephones would be a better way to communicate. It's hard to envision today, with everyone constantly checking cell phones for email, texts, tweets, and voice mail, but as Edwin Schlossberg explains in his book *Interactive Excellence*: "People could not imagine why they would want or need to talk immediately to someone who was across town or, even more absurdly, in another town. Although people could write letters to one another, and some could send telegraph messages, the idea of sending one's voice to another place and then instantly hearing another voice in return was simply not a model that existed in people's experience. They also did not think it was worth the money to accelerate sending or hearing a message."[16] In addition, during design competition, the older technology usually improves significantly in response to the competitive threat from the new technologies; this response also slows the changeover from older to newer technologies.

Discontinuous change is followed by the emergence of a **dominant design,** which becomes the new accepted market standard for technology.[17] Dominant designs emerge in several ways. One is critical mass, meaning that a particular technology can become the dominant design simply because most people use it, for example, Blu-ray beating out HD-DVD. Critical mass will likely determine the dominant design for wireless device charging, where instead of plugging in your device to recharge you simply place it on top of a recharging station containing magnetic charging coils. A year ago, three different wireless technologies were trying to become the dominant standard: the Power Matters Alliance (PMA) backing Duracell's Powermat, a Duracell and Procter & Gamble joint venture supported by Google, AT&T, Starbucks, and McDonald's; the Alliance for Wireless Power (A4WP) and its Rezence charging mats, backed by Samsung, Broadcom, Deutsche Telekom, and Texas Instruments; and the Wireless Power Consortium (WPC) and its Qi charging mats, supported by LG Electronics, Energizer, and Nokia. However, PMA and A4WP joined forces to created a new, combined standard for wireless charging devices.[18] Again, why does this matter? Because the market for wireless charging, estimated at $785 million, is projected to increase to $8.5 billion by 2018. In other words, becoming the dominant standard is worth billions to the winner.[19]

The best technology doesn't always become the dominant design because a number of other factors come into play. For instance, a design can become dominant if it solves a practical problem. The QWERTY keyboard (named for the top left line of letters) became the dominant design for typewriters because it slowed typists who, by typing too fast, caused mechanical typewriter keys to jam. Though computers can easily be switched to the Dvorak keyboard layout, which doubles typing speed and cuts typing errors in half, QWERTY lives on as the standard keyboard. In this instance, the QWERTY keyboard solved a problem that, with computers, is no longer relevant. Yet it remains the dominant design not because it is the best technology, but because most people learned to type that way and continue to use it.

Dominant designs can also emerge through independent standards bodies. The International Telecommunication Union (ITU) (http://www.itu.ch) is an independent organization that establishes standards for the communications industry. The ITU was founded in Paris in 1865 because European countries all had different telegraph systems that could not communicate with each other. Messages crossing borders had to be transcribed from one country's system before they could be coded and delivered on another. After three months of negotiations, twenty countries signed the International Telegraph Convention, which standardized equipment and instructions, enabling telegraph messages to flow seamlessly from country to country. Today, as in 1865, various standards are proposed, discussed, negotiated, and changed until agreement is reached on a final set of standards that communication industries (Internet, telephony, satellites, radio) will follow worldwide.

For example, the ITU has agreed on the new standard for 4G, or fourth-generation, service on mobile phones. "True" 4G, according to the ITU, allows larger amounts of data to be sent over smaller cellular bandwidth and will be much faster than the 4G LTE (or 4G Light) now offered by mobile phone companies. According to Hamadoun Touré, the ITU's secretary general, true 4G "will make the present day smartphone feel like an old dial-up Internet connection." François Rancy, who directs ITU's Radiocommunication Bureau, says that true 4G "would be like putting a fiber optic broadband connection on your mobile phone, making your phone at least 500 times faster than today's 3G smartphones."[20]

No matter how it happens, the emergence of a dominant design is a key event in an innovation stream. First, the emergence of a dominant design indicates that

The Patent Trial and Appeal Board

The Patent Trial and Appeal Board was launched in September 2012 as part of a congressional overhaul of the patent system. Created primarily to rule on patent lawsuit findings, the new regulatory body is overseen by 181 judges, all of whom have deep experience in intellectual property and technical fields. Companies in patent infringement lawsuits may appeal to the board to challenge whether a patent should have been issued in the first place. Of its twenty-five rulings issued so far, only a handful have upheld any portion of the challenged patent. Many advocates have cheered the board, saying that it both helps corporations fight back against cases based on vague and flawed patents and defends against groups that collect large patent portfolios to use solely for infringement cases. Opponents have complained, however, that the board makes it difficult for patent holders, especially small inventors, to hold onto patents that they could barely afford to secure in the first place. This could disincentivize work on technological advancement, they argue. The board has proven controversial, but it certainly promises to influence the way innovations are made going forward.

Source: A. Jones, "New Weapon in Corporate Patent Wars," *The Wall Street Journal*, March 10, 2014, accessed April 25, 2014, http://online.wsj.com/news/articles/SB10001424052702304020104579431393308282698?KEYWORDS=new+weapon+in+corporate+patent+wars&mg=reno64-wsj.

there are winners and losers. Technological innovation is both competence enhancing and competence destroying. Companies that bet on the now-dominant design usually prosper. By contrast, when companies bet on the wrong design or the old technology, they may experience **technological lockout,** which occurs when a new dominant design (i.e., a significantly better technology) prevents a company from competitively selling its products or makes it difficult to do so.[21] For example, while 85 percent of U.S. movie theatres (totaling 34,161 screens) use digital technology, 1,000 small theaters may go out of business because they can't afford the $60,000 cost to buy digital projectors. Patrick Corcoran, spokesman for the National Association of Theatre Owners, says, "When you have a business and technology that has always worked for you, it's hard to imagine it going away. Some [theatres] are looking at the money they have to lay out. Some are scrambling to try to raise funds."[22]

Technological lockout the inability of a company to competitively sell its products because it relies on old technology or a nondominant design

In fact, more companies are likely to go out of business in a time of discontinuous change and changing standards than in an economic recession or slowdown.

Second, the emergence of a dominant design signals a shift from design experimentation and competition to **incremental change,** a phase in which companies innovate by lowering the cost and improving the functioning and performance of the dominant design. For example, manufacturing efficiencies enable Intel to cut the cost of its chips by one-half to two-thirds during a technology cycle, while doubling or tripling their speed. This focus on improving the dominant design continues until the next technological discontinuity occurs.

7-2 MANAGING INNOVATION

One consequence of technology cycles and innovation streams is that managers must be equally good at managing innovation in two very different circumstances. First, during discontinuous change, companies must find a way to anticipate and survive the technological changes that can

Incremental change the phase of a technology cycle in which companies innovate by lowering costs and improving the functioning and performance of the dominant technological design

suddenly transform industry leaders into losers and industry unknowns into powerhouses. Companies that can't manage innovation following technological discontinuities risk quick organizational decline and dissolution. Second, after a new dominant design emerges following discontinuous change, companies must manage the very different process of incremental improvement and innovation. Companies that can't manage incremental innovation slowly deteriorate as they fall further behind industry leaders.

Unfortunately, what works well when managing innovation during discontinuous change doesn't work well when managing innovation during periods of incremental change (and vice versa).

Consequently, to successfully manage innovation streams, companies need to be good at three things: ***7-2a managing sources of innovation, 7-2b managing innovation during discontinuous change,*** *and* ***7-2c managing innovation during incremental change.***

7-2a Managing Sources of Innovation

Innovation comes from great ideas. So a starting point for managing innovation is to manage the sources of innovation, that is, where new ideas come from. One place where new ideas originate is with brilliant inventors. But only a few companies have the likes of a Thomas Edison or Alexander Graham Bell. Given that great thinkers and inventors are in short supply, what might companies do to ensure a steady flow of good ideas?

Toyota Addresses Environmental Threat from Hybrid Car Batteries

Hybrid engines have been great for consumers and the environment. Using less gas helps prevent pollution and saves drivers money at the pump. However, the batteries represent a significant environmental danger when the car is no longer useful. Each hybrid battery pack contains nickel, which can cause irritation and cancer, and give off toxic fumes as well. To prevent the potential harm of this toxic metal, Toyota has created an Electricity Management System, a back-up energy system that is made from batteries recycled from its old hybrid vehicles. According to Toyota engineers, the systems will store up to 10 kilowatt hours of energy and will provide backup or supplemental power as needed.

Source: D. King, "Toyota Recycling Old Hybrid Batteries into Energy Storage Systems for Dealers," *AutoBlogGreen*, February 2, 2013, accessed June 2, 2013, http://green.autoblog.com/2013/02/02/toyota-recycling-old-hybrid-batteries-into-energy-storage-system/.

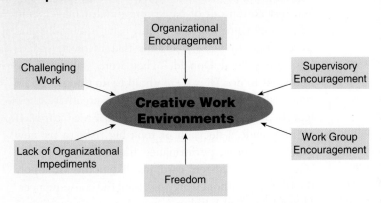

Exhibit 7.3
Components of Creative Work Environments

Organizational Encouragement

Challenging Work

Supervisory Encouragement

Creative Work Environments

Lack of Organizational Impediments

Work Group Encouragement

Freedom

Source: T. M. Amabile, R. Conti, H. Coon, J. Lazenby, and M. Herron, "Assessing the Work Environment for Creativity," *Academy of Management Journal* 39 (1996): 1154–1184.

Well, when we say that innovation begins with great ideas, we're really saying that innovation begins with creativity. As we defined it at the beginning of this chapter, creativity is the production of novel and useful ideas.[23] Although companies can't command employees to be creative ("You *will* be more creative!"), they can jump-start innovation by building **creative work environments** in which workers perceive that creative thoughts and ideas are welcomed and valued. As Exhibit 7.3 shows, creative work environments have six components that encourage creativity: challenging work, organizational encouragement, supervisory encouragement, work group encouragement, freedom, and a lack of organizational impediments.[24]

Work is *challenging* when it requires effort, demands attention and focus, and is perceived as important to others in the organization. According to researcher Mihaly Csikszentmihalyi (pronounced ME-high-ee CHICK-sent-me-high-ee), challenging work promotes creativity because it creates a rewarding psychological experience known as "flow." **Flow** is a psychological state of effortlessness, in which you become completely absorbed in what you're doing and time seems to fly. When flow occurs, who you are and what you're doing become one. Csikszentmihalyi first encountered flow when studying artists: "What struck me by looking at artists at work was their tremendous focus on the work, this enormous involvement, this forgetting of time and body. It wasn't justified by expectation of rewards, like, 'Aha, I'm going to sell this painting.'"[25] Csikszentmihalyi has found that chess players, rock climbers, dancers, surgeons, and athletes regularly experience flow, too. A key part of

creating flow experiences, and thus creative work environments, is to achieve a balance between skills and task challenge. Workers become bored when they can do more than is required of them and anxious when their skills aren't sufficient to accomplish a task. When skills and task challenge are balanced, however, flow and creativity can occur.

A creative work environment requires three kinds of encouragement: organizational, supervisory, and work group. *Organizational encouragement* of creativity occurs when management encourages risk taking and new ideas, supports and fairly evaluates new ideas, rewards and recognizes creativity, and encourages the sharing of new ideas throughout different parts of the company. When David Richter became the VP of information technology at **Kimberly-Clark**, the division had just had a round of layoffs in which nearly everyone was fired. A year later, 200 IT engineers were hired back. He said, "We had very low morale and very low employee engagement. . . . People were in a self-preservation mode." Creativity, innovation, and risk taking were at a standstill because people were afraid they would lose their jobs again. He said, "There was a palpable fear that if you tried something and failed, it would damage your career forever." So Richter encouraged creativity by rewarding creative ideas with "start-up" funding. Anyone with an idea could pitch it to him in thirty minutes or less. They didn't need a PowerPoint presentation. The only requirement before the pitch was a one-page form asking for an explanation regarding the benefit, the resources it would take, and the scope of the idea. Richter said, "It's as simple as that. Make me a pitch. And, if it's good. Let's proceed." If pilot trial of the idea succeeded, then Richter provided significant resources to implement it throughout the division. Finally, to celebrate and encourage risk taking, he shared all employees' ideas, whether they worked or not, on the division's intranet. Says Richter, "Failure is simply the opportunity to begin again, this time more intelligently. It's about what we learn from the failure. Not the failure itself. We celebrate that learning."[26]

Creative work environments workplace cultures in which workers perceive that new ideas are welcomed, valued, and encouraged

Flow a psychological state of effortlessness, in which you become completely absorbed in what you're doing and time seems to pass quickly

Supervisory encouragement of creativity occurs when supervisors provide clear goals, encourage open interaction with subordinates, and actively support development teams' work and ideas. When it comes to clear goals, MIT's Andrew McAfee says be specific. He says goals like, "We need to figure out why so many people are leaving our site before completing a transaction," or, "How can we increase sales to women in their 30s?" are much better at generating innovations than broad goals like, "What should our next great idea be?"[27] Burberry, the luxury British brand, on the other hand, has innovated by fostering open interaction across all levels. Former CEO Angela Ahrendts says that Burberry's "Strategic Innovation Council," is "a monthly forum for our next generation of great thinkers, chaired by our chief creative officers. And the remit of the council is simple: to dream."[28] Likewise, Burberry took a social media platform used for working with customers and turned it into "Burberry Chat," which allows everyone in the company to participate in broad and targeted discussions, ensuring, she says, that "everyone has a voice and every voice is heard."[29]

Work group encouragement occurs when group members have diverse experience, education, and backgrounds and the group fosters mutual openness to ideas; positive, constructive challenge to ideas; and shared commitment to ideas. *Freedom* means having autonomy over one's day-to-day work and a sense of ownership and control over one's ideas. Numerous studies have indicated that creative ideas thrive under conditions of freedom.

To foster creativity, companies may also have to *remove impediments* to creativity from their work environments. Internal conflict and power struggles, rigid management structures, and a conservative bias toward the status quo can all discourage creativity. They create the perception that others in the organization will decide which ideas are acceptable and deserve support. Like Richter at Kimberly-Clark, when Jim Donald became CEO at **Extended Stay America**, the company had just gotten out of bankruptcy, and managers and employees were worried about losing their jobs and were afraid to make decisions that involved spending money. Said Donald, "They were waiting to be told what to do. They were afraid to do things." So he removed the greatest impediment to creativity, their fear, by handing out "Get Out of Jail, Free," cards. If anyone made a decision or took big risks to try new things or improve performance, they could "play" their "Get Out of Jail, Free" card, just like in the Monopoly board game, without worrying about the consequences. Donald says that hotel managers have been sending in the cards, along with brief notes explaining what they tried. For instance, a New Jersey manager heard that a movie production crew would be filming in the area, so she cold-called them and struck a deal that resulted in a lengthy stay for the crew resulting in $250,000 in revenue for her hotel.[30]

7-2b Experiential Approach: Managing Innovation during Discontinuous Change

A study of seventy-two product-development projects (i.e., innovation) in thirty-six computer companies across the United States, Europe, and Asia sheds light on how to manage innovation. Companies that succeeded in periods of discontinuous change (characterized by technological substitution and design competition, as described earlier) typically followed an experiential approach to innovation.[31] The **experiential approach to innovation** assumes that innovation is occurring within a highly uncertain environment and that the key to fast product innovation is to use intuition, flexible options, and hands-on experience to reduce uncertainty and accelerate learning and

RT images/iStockphoto.com

understanding. The experiential approach to innovation has five aspects: design iterations, testing, milestones, multifunctional teams, and powerful leaders.[32]

An *iteration* is a repetition. So a **design iteration** is a cycle of repetition in which a company tests a prototype of a new product or service, improves on the design, and then builds and tests the improved product or service prototype. A **product prototype** is a full-scale working model that is being tested for design, function, and reliability. For example, Facebook-owned Oculus VR designed virtual reality headsets (i.e., goggles) to be used in simulations and digital games. Oculus shipped 60,000 units of its first product prototype, and using the resulting product feedback to develop its second prototype, the DK2, which it pre-sold to game developers who will not only test the DK2, but how well the digital games they're designing perform using the DK2.[33]

Testing is a systematic comparison of different product designs or design iterations. Companies that want to create a new dominant design following a technological discontinuity quickly build, test, improve, and retest a series of different product prototypes. One of Oculus Rift's key concerns during prototype testing was "simulator sickness," the nausea or disorientation caused by "motion blur." Thanks to testing and feedback from game developers, Oculus improved the DK2 with a faster, higher resolution display that provides greater

clarity and contrast, and reduces motion blur and judder (jagged, stuttering movement), both of which are major contributors to simulator sickness.[34]

By trying a number of very different designs or making successive improvements and changes in the same design, frequent design iterations reduce uncertainty and improve understanding. Simply put, the more prototypes you build, the more likely you are to learn what works and what doesn't. Also, when designers and engineers build a number of prototypes, they are less likely to fall in love with a particular prototype. Instead, they'll be more concerned with improving the product or technology as much as they can. Testing speeds up and improves the innovation process, too. When two very different design prototypes are tested against each other or the new design iteration is tested against the previous iteration, product design strengths and weaknesses quickly become apparent. Likewise, testing uncovers errors early in the design process when they are easiest to correct. Finally, testing accelerates learning and understanding by forcing engineers and product designers to examine hard data about product performance. When there's hard evidence that prototypes are testing well, the confidence of the design team grows. Also, personal conflict between design team members is less likely when testing focuses on hard measurements and facts rather than on personal hunches and preferences.

Milestones are formal project review points used to assess progress and performance. For example, a company that has put itself on a twelve-month schedule to complete a project might schedule milestones at the three-month, six-month, and nine-month points on the schedule. At Pixar and Disney Animation Studios, there are fourteen steps involved in creating a full-length animated film, from pitching story ideas, to drawing storyboards, to recording character voices, to using "digital light" (the equivalent of stage lighting) to light each scene in the movie. When it comes time to animate each scene in the movie, Pixar's animation team is always

---

DOING THE RIGHT THING

Creative Work

Stealing ideas is never a good idea. By taking credit for other people's great work, you're totally disregarding the efforts that they put into thinking of and developing the next great idea that will fuel your company's success. But, did you know that stealing ideas is also bad for the entire organization? When you steal ideas from others, it actually squelches the creative powers in your company. After all, if someone else is just going to take credit for all of your creative work and get all of the benefits, then what's the point? Why even bother thinking of anything innovative? So do the right thing, and don't steal others' ideas; it will help keep the creative juices flowing.

Source: S. Carson, "Plagiarism and Its Effect on Creative Work," *Psychology Today*, October 16, 2010, http://www.psychologytoday.com/blog/life-art/201010/plagiarism-and-its-effect-creative-work.

Design iteration a cycle of repetition in which a company tests a prototype of a new product or service, improves on that design, and then builds and tests the improved prototype

Product prototype a full-scale, working model that is being tested for design, function, and reliability

Testing the systematic comparison of different product designs or design iterations

Milestones formal project review points used to assess progress and performance

on a short, tight schedule. As a result, the film director uses daily milestones to review progress and keep the film on budget and on schedule. Ed Catmull, president of Pixar and Disney Animation Studios, explains that at the end of each day's work, the artists performing the computerized animation will "show work in an incomplete state to the whole animation crew, and although the director makes decisions, everyone is encouraged to comment." The benefits from these reviews, which Pixar calls "dailies," are tremendous. Says Catmull, "First, once people get over the embarrassment of showing work still in progress, they become more creative. Second, the director or creative leads guiding the review process can communicate important points to the entire crew at the same time. Third, people learn from and inspire each other; a highly creative piece of animation will spark others to raise their game. Finally, there are no surprises at the end: When you're done, you're done. People's overwhelming desire to make sure their work is 'good' before they show it to others increases the possibility that their finished version won't be what the director wants. The dailies process avoids such wasted efforts."[35]

By making people regularly assess what they're doing, how well they're performing, and whether they need to take corrective action, milestones provide structure to the general chaos that follows technological discontinuities. Milestones also shorten the innovation process by creating a sense of urgency that keeps everyone on task. Finally, milestones are beneficial for innovation because meeting regular milestones builds momentum by giving people a sense of accomplishment.

Multifunctional teams are work teams composed of people from different departments. Multifunctional teams accelerate learning and understanding by mixing and integrating technical, marketing, and manufacturing activities. By involving all key departments in development from the start, multifunctional teams speed innovation through early identification of new ideas or problems that would typically not have been generated or addressed until much later. **The Sealy Company**, a leading mattress manufacturer, had to find a way to revive its high-end Stearns & Foster brand, whose sales were declining. Sealy's solution was to redesign the entire brand through collaboration teams, or jokingly,

"getting in bed together." So it brought its engineering, sales, and marketing staff together to find out what customers wanted by visiting stores in New York, Chicago, and Atlanta. The message? Focus on quality. Don't cut costs. Allen Platek, VP of new product development, said, "Prior to this, what we did was in silos. Sales did their thing, marketing did their promotions and ads, R&D developed innovation, and then it was all thrown to operations. We had a disjointed effort." Sealy's multifunctional teams got the job done. Even though the redesigned Stearns & Foster mattresses cost 40 percent more, the changes produced record sales.[36]

Powerful leaders provide the vision, discipline, and motivation to keep the innovation process focused, on time, and on target. Powerful leaders are able to get resources when they are needed, are typically more experienced, have high status in the company, and are held directly responsible for the products' success or failure. On average, powerful leaders can get innovation-related projects done nine months faster than leaders with little power or influence.

7-2c Compression Approach: Managing Innovation during Incremental Change

Whereas the experiential approach is used to manage innovation in highly uncertain environments during periods of discontinuous change, the compression approach is used to manage innovation in more certain environments during periods of incremental change. Whereas the goals of the experiential approach are significant improvements in performance and the establishment of a *new* dominant design, the goals of the compression approach are lower costs and incremental improvements in the performance and function of the *existing* dominant design.

The general strategies in each approach are different, too. With the experiential approach, the general strategy is to build something new, different, and substantially better. Because there's so much uncertainty—no one knows which technology will become the market leader—companies adopt a winner-take-all approach by trying to create the market-leading, dominant design. With the compression approach, the general strategy is to compress the time and steps needed to bring about small, consistent improvements in performance and functionality. Because a dominant technology design already exists, the general strategy is to continue improving the existing technology as rapidly as possible.

In short, a **compression approach to innovation** assumes that innovation is a predictable

Multifunctional teams work teams composed of people from different departments

Compression approach to innovation an approach to innovation that assumes that incremental innovation can be planned using a series of steps and that compressing those steps can speed innovation

process, that incremental innovation can be planned using a series of steps, and that compressing the time it takes to complete those steps can speed up innovation. The compression approach to innovation has five aspects: planning, supplier involvement, shortening the time of individual steps, overlapping steps, and multifunctional teams.[37]

In Chapter 5, *planning* was defined as choosing a goal and a method or strategy to achieve that goal. When *planning for incremental innovation*, the goal is to squeeze or compress development time as much as possible, and the general strategy is to create a series of planned steps to accomplish that goal. Planning for incremental innovation helps avoid unnecessary steps and enables developers to sequence steps in the right order to avoid wasted time and delays between steps. Planning also reduces misunderstandings and improves coordination.

Most planning for incremental innovation is based on the idea of generational change. **Generational change** occurs when incremental improvements are made to a dominant technological design such that the improved version of the technology is fully backward compatible with the older version.[38] Most computers, for instance, have USB (universal serial bus) input slots to connect and power USB thumb drives, monitors, or external hard drives used for backup storage. USB 3.1, the latest USB standard, can transfer more than 10 Gbps (gigabytes per second), compared to USB 3.0 devices, which operate at 5 Gbps, or USB 2.0 devices, which operate at roughly 1/2 Gbps.[39] What happens if you buy a new computer with USB 3.1 slots, but still own a USB 3.0 external hard drive and a USB 2.0 thumb drive? Both will work because they are backward compatible with USB 3.1, but at slower speeds.

Because the compression approach assumes that innovation can follow a series of preplanned steps, one of the ways to shorten development time is *supplier involvement*. Delegating some of the preplanned steps in the innovation process to outside suppliers reduces the amount of work that internal development teams must do. Plus, suppliers provide an alternative source of ideas and expertise that can lead to better designs.

Another way to shorten development time is simply to *shorten the time of individual steps* in the innovation process. A common way to do that is through computer-aided design (CAD). CAD speeds up the design process by allowing designers and engineers to make and test design changes using computer models rather than physically testing expensive prototypes. CAD also speeds innovation by making it easy to see how design changes affect engineering, purchasing, and production. For example, 3-D design software reduces the time and cost involved in creating new products. **Ansys** simulation software

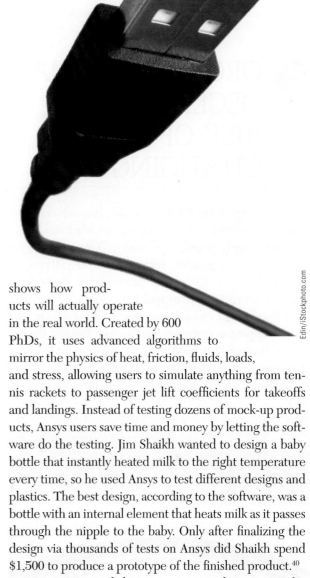

Edin/iStockphoto.com

shows how products will actually operate in the real world. Created by 600 PhDs, it uses advanced algorithms to mirror the physics of heat, friction, fluids, loads, and stress, allowing users to simulate anything from tennis rackets to passenger jet lift coefficients for takeoffs and landings. Instead of testing dozens of mock-up products, Ansys users save time and money by letting the software do the testing. Jim Shaikh wanted to design a baby bottle that instantly heated milk to the right temperature every time, so he used Ansys to test different designs and plastics. The best design, according to the software, was a bottle with an internal element that heats milk as it passes through the nipple to the baby. Only after finalizing the design via thousands of tests on Ansys did Shaikh spend $1,500 to produce a prototype of the finished product.[40]

In a sequential design process, each step must be completed before the next step begins. But sometimes multiple development steps can be performed at the same time. *Overlapping steps* shorten the development process by reducing delays or waiting time between steps. Summit Entertainment used overlapping steps to great success in producing the *Twilight* movie franchise. While it used the same actors and screenwriters throughout the series, by using new directors and

> **Generational change** change based on incremental improvements to a dominant technological design such that the improved technology is fully backward compatible with the older technology

production crews for each film Summit was able to begin production on each film while the previous film was in post-production. This allowed the studio to release films at regular intervals in order to capitalize on the surprising success of the first film in a timely manner.[41]

Chris Lamphear/iStockphoto.com

ORGANIZATIONAL DECLINE: THE RISK OF NOT CHANGING

In the 1990s, **Slim-Fast**, a low-fat, low-calorie drink that dieters drank instead of eating breakfast and lunch, became hugely popular, promising "Give us a week, we'll take off the weight!" With sales growing 20 percent a year, Unilever, the global consumer products company (maker of Lifebuoy and Dove soaps, Lipton tea, and Pond's cold cream), purchased Slim-Fast for $2.4 billion hoping to grow revenue fivefold. But just the opposite happened; while the meal replacement business has grown by 27 percent since 2002, Slim-Fast sales, by contrast, are 81 percent lower. Dieters and the diet

Organizational decline a large decrease in organizational performance that occurs when companies don't anticipate, recognize, neutralize, or adapt to the internal or external pressures that threaten their survival

marketplace changed, but Slim-Fast did not. Going on a crash diet and drinking two "meals" per day is no longer attractive. Melissa Wood, a British marketing executive, says, "It's a quick fix and not the right thing for me. The fake flavoring and sugar are not part of healthy living in the 21st century." Moreover, despite encouragement from its customers on Slim-Fast message boards, the company missed an incredible opportunity by not developing a diet app for smartphones and tablets. Indeed, it's estimated that half a billion people will use diet apps this year. Global sales have been so disappointing that Unilever pulled Slim-Fast out of France last year. Finally, Slim-Fast's product innovation has slowed to just seven new products in 2012, down from seventy-seven in 2005. Research analyst Andrew Wood wonders, "Perhaps they [Unilever] are just letting it die quickly."[42]

Businesses operate in a constantly changing environment. Recognizing and adapting to internal and external changes can mean the difference between continued success and going out of business. Companies that fail to change run the risk of organizational decline.[43] **Organizational decline** occurs when companies don't anticipate, recognize, neutralize, or adapt to the internal or external pressures that threaten their survival. In other words, decline occurs when organizations don't recognize the need for change. There are five stages of organizational decline: blinded, inaction, faulty action, crisis, and dissolution.

In the *blinded stage*, decline begins because key managers fail to recognize the internal or external changes that will harm their organizations. This blindness may be due to a simple lack of awareness about changes or an inability to understand their significance. It may also come from the overconfidence that can develop when a company has been successful.

In the *inaction stage*, as organizational performance problems become more visible, management may recognize the need to change but still take no action. The managers may be waiting to see if the problems will correct themselves. Or, they may find it difficult to change the practices and policies that previously led to success. Possibly, too, they wrongly assume that they can easily correct the problems, so they don't feel the situation is urgent.

In the *faulty action stage*, faced with rising costs and decreasing profits and market share, management will announce belt-tightening plans designed to cut costs, increase efficiency, and restore profits. In other words, rather than recognizing the need for fundamental changes, managers assume that if they just run a tighter ship, company performance will return to previous levels.

In the *crisis stage*, bankruptcy or dissolution (breaking up the company and selling its parts) is likely to occur unless the company completely reorganizes the way it does business. At this point, however, companies typically lack the resources to fully change how they run their businesses. Cutbacks and layoffs will have reduced the level of talent among employees. Furthermore, talented managers who were savvy enough to see the crisis coming will have found jobs with other companies, often with competitors.

In the *dissolution stage*, after failing to make the changes needed to sustain the organization, the company is dissolved through bankruptcy proceedings or by selling assets in order to pay suppliers, banks, and creditors. At this point, a new CEO may be brought in to oversee the closing of stores, offices, and manufacturing facilities, the final layoff of managers and employees, and the sale of assets. It is important to note that decline is reversible at each of the first four stages and that not all companies in decline reach final dissolution.

7-4 MANAGING CHANGE

According to social psychologist Kurt Lewin, change is a function of the forces that promote change and the opposing forces that slow or resist change.[44] **Change forces** lead to differences in the form, quality, or condition of an organization over time. In contrast to change forces, **resistance forces** support the status quo, that is, the existing conditions in an organization. Change is difficult under any circumstances. Production schedules on movie sets have changed dramatically as a result of directors having switched from film to digital recordings. When shooting with film, a new film reel has to be loaded every 10 minutes, creating frequent breaks when stars would return to their trailers to read, rehearse, or rest. Because there are no film reels with digital recording, shooting can occur continuously, significantly reducing film production time and costs. A number of famous actors, however, don't like the change. Actor Robert Downey, Jr. complained, "I can't work like this. I never get to go to my trailer … I'm on my feet 14 hours a day. I'm shooting all the time."[45]

Resistance to change is caused by self-interest, misunderstanding and distrust, and a general intolerance

for change.[46] People resist change out of *self-interest* because they fear that change will cost or deprive them of something they value. Resistance might stem from a fear that the changes will result in a loss of pay, power, responsibility or even perhaps one's job. The Mayo Clinic, the world-renowned medical facility in Rochester, Minnesota, announced a new uniform policy for its 900 desk staff and clinical assistants. Rather than wearing scrubs like the doctors and nurses do, they would instead be required to wear black pants and light blue shirts. Because the $400 expense for the new uniforms came out of their paychecks, employees reacted with angry comments on an in-house discussion board, calling themselves "LPEs," or low-paid employees. One wrote, "I think this is an incredible elitist and insensitive decision," while another wrote, "It just seems like none of our opinions matter."[47]

People also resist change because of *misunderstanding and distrust*; they don't understand the change or the reasons for it, or they distrust the people—typically management—behind the change. Resistance isn't always visible at first. In fact, some of the strongest resisters may initially support the changes in public, nodding and smiling their agreement, but then ignore the changes in private and do their jobs as they always have. Management consultant Michael Hammer calls this deadly form of resistance the "Kiss of Yes."[48]

Resistance may also come from a generally low tolerance for change. Some people are simply less capable of handling change than others. People with a *low tolerance for change* feel threatened by the uncertainty associated with change and worry that they won't be able to learn the new skills and behaviors needed to successfully negotiate change in their companies.

Because resistance to change is inevitable, successful change efforts require careful management.

Viorika Prikhodko/iStockphoto.com

"The Kiss of Yes": Some of the strongest resisters may support the changes in public but then ignore them in private.

Change forces forces that produce differences in the form, quality, or condition of an organization over time

Resistance forces forces that support the existing conditions in organizations

Resistance to change opposition to change resulting from self-interest, misunderstanding and distrust, and a general intolerance for change

7-4a Managing Resistance to Change

According to psychologist Kurt Lewin, managing organizational change is a basic process of unfreezing, change intervention, and refreezing. **Unfreezing** is getting the people affected by change to believe that change is needed. During the **change intervention** itself, workers and managers change their behavior and work practices. **Refreezing** is supporting and reinforcing the new changes so that they stick.

Resistance to change is an example of frozen behavior. Given the choice between changing and not changing, most people would rather not change. Because resistance to change is natural and inevitable, managers need to unfreeze resistance to change to create successful change programs. The following methods can be used to manage resistance to change: education and communication, participation, negotiation, top-management support, and coercion.[49]

When resistance to change is based on insufficient, incorrect, or misleading information, managers should *educate* employees about the need for change and *communicate* change-related information to them. Managers must also supply the information and funding, or other support employees need to make changes. For example, resistance to change can be particularly strong when one company buys another company. This is because one company in the merger usually has a higher status due to its size or its higher profitability or the fact that it is the acquiring company. These status differences are important to managers and employees, particularly if they're in the lower-status company, who worry about retaining their jobs or influence after the merger. That fear or concern can greatly increase resistance to change.[50] When PMA Companies, an insurance risk management firm, was acquired by Old Republic International, an insurance company, PMA's CEO Vince Donnelly communicated frequently with PMA's employees about the merger. Four months before the acquisition became official, he traveled to each of the company's twenty offices and gave employees a detailed description of how their day-to-day operations would change and why the acquisition was good for everyone involved. He also held quarterly updates with employees via videoconference. Said Donnelly, "It's not just one and done. Communication needs to be continual. You need to continue to reinforce the messages that you want people to internalize. So you need to understand that communication is a continuous process and not something that you do just once." He went on to say, "What you are asking people to do is trust you, [trust] that you have the best interest of everybody in mind, and [trust that] when there is news to tell, you're going to hear it directly from the CEO—good, bad or indifferent."[51]

Another way to reduce resistance to change is to have those affected by the change *participate in planning and implementing the change process.* Employees who participate have a better understanding of the change and the need for it. Furthermore, employee concerns about change can be addressed as they occur if employees participate in the planning and implementation process. When United Airlines and Continental Airlines merged to form one of the world's largest airlines, there were thousands of decisions to be made to integrate the two companies, such as combining websites, ticketing systems, pay and promotion policies, etc. They even had to decide which coffee to serve, as Continental served coffee from Fresh Brew, and United served Starbucks. While seemingly a small decision, United and Continental served a combined 62 million cups of coffee in 2011. Sandra Pineau-Boddison, the vice president of food services, picked a fourteen-member team consisting of people from flight operations, finance, food service, and marketing to make the decision, even asking them to blindly taste twelve different coffees to identify which tasted best. Then, she took the committee's selection and asked the company's board of directors, as well as 1,100 flight attendants who also tried the new brew, for input.[52]

Employees are also less likely to resist change if they are allowed *to discuss and agree on who will do what* after change occurs. Craig Durosko, founder of **Sun Design Home Remodeling Specialists** in Burke, Virginia, says, "Unfortunately, the way most employees find out when a company isn't doing well is when their paychecks bounce or when they show up and the front doors are locked. When changes go down and they don't know about it, they can't do anything about it." So, when Sun

Unfreezing getting the people affected by change to believe that change is needed

Change intervention the process used to get workers and managers to change their behaviors and work practices

Refreezing supporting and reinforcing new changes so that they stick

Design's business shrank dramatically during the recession, Durosko explained the problem, sharing detailed financial information, and then asked his employees what could be done to minimize losses. He says, "No less than 20 employees gave line-by-line specific *things they could do* to make a difference."[53]

Resistance to change also decreases when change efforts receive *significant managerial support*. Managers must do more than talk about the importance of change, though. They must provide the training, resources, and autonomy needed to make change happen. Finally, resistance to change can be managed through **coercion,** or the use of formal power and authority to force others to change. Because of the intense negative reactions it can create (e.g., fear, stress, resentment, sabotage of company products), coercion should be used only when a crisis exists or when all other attempts to reduce resistance to change have failed.

7-4b What Not to Do When Leading Change

So far, you've learned about the basic change process (unfreezing, change intervention, refreezing) and managing resistance to change. Harvard Business School professor John Kotter argues that knowing what *not* to do is just as important as knowing what to do when it comes to achieving successful organizational change.[54]

Managers commonly make certain errors when they lead change. The first two errors occur during the unfreezing phase, when managers try to get the people affected by change to believe that change is really needed. The first and potentially most serious error is *not establishing a great enough sense of urgency*. Indeed, Kotter estimates that more than half of all change efforts fail because the people affected are not convinced that change is necessary. People will feel a greater sense of urgency if a leader in the company makes a public, candid assessment of the company's problems and weaknesses.

Nokia went from being the world's largest cell phone company in 2007 to nearly going out of business and then selling off its handset division to Microsoft in 2013. Frank Nuovo, who designed several of Nokia's most successful mobile phones, notes that Nokia was working on innovations, like tablet computers and touch-screen devices, long before Apple's iPad or iPhone came to market. Nuovo said, "We realized at Nokia that touch [screen technology] was increasingly important and were working towards doing it, but when a company is really busy holding on to what it has built, it is difficult to put enough of a push towards something so drastically new and engender urgency in it." He further explained that instead of a sense of urgency,

AP Images/Invision for Nokia/Diane Bondareff

Stephen Elop (right) with Microsoft CEO Steve Ballmer

"There was a real sense of saying 'we will get to that eventually.'"[55] Nokia sacrificed innovation in favor of supporting existing customers and technology. As a result, companies like Apple began releasing new game-changing products, and Nokia was left behind.[56]

The second mistake that occurs in the unfreezing process is *not creating a powerful enough coalition*. Change often starts with one or two people. But change has to be supported by a critical and growing group of people to build enough momentum to change an entire department, division, or company. Besides top management, Kotter recommends that key employees, managers, board members, customers, and even union leaders be members of a *core change coalition* that guides and supports organizational change. Celestica Inc., located in Toronto, Canada, is an electronics manufacturing services company that produces complex printed circuit assemblies, such as PC motherboards and networking cards, flat-screen TVs, and Xbox video game systems for Microsoft. Celestica's CEO Craig Muhlhauser says, "In a turnaround, there are three kinds of employees, those on your side, those on the fence, and those who will never buy in. The latter have to be let go and those on the fence should be persuaded to contribute or leave." Says Muhlhauser, "We have to make change, change is difficult and as we make change, it is important to realize that there are people who are going to resist that change. In talking

Coercion the use of formal power and authority to force others to change

to those people, the objective is to move everybody into the column of supporters. But that is probably unachievable."[57] It's also important to strengthen this core change coalition's resolve by periodically bringing its members together for off-site retreats.

The next four errors that managers make occur during the change phase, when a change intervention is used to try to get workers and managers to change their behavior and work practices. *Lacking a vision* for change is a significant error at this point. As you learned in Chapter 5, a *vision* (defined as a *purpose statement* in Chapter 5) is a statement of a company's purpose or reason for existing. A vision for change makes clear where a company or department is headed and why the change is occurring. Change efforts that lack vision tend to be confused, chaotic, and contradictory. By contrast, change efforts guided by visions are clear and easy to understand and can be effectively explained in five minutes or less.

Undercommunicating the vision by a factor of ten is another mistake in the change phase. According to Kotter, companies mistakenly hold just one meeting to announce the vision. Or, if the new vision receives heavy emphasis in executive speeches or company newsletters, senior management then undercuts the vision by behaving in ways contrary to it. Successful communication of the vision requires that top managers link everything the company does to the new vision and that they "walk the talk" by behaving in ways consistent with the vision. Furthermore, even companies that begin change with a clear vision sometimes make the mistake of *not removing obstacles to the new vision*. They leave formidable barriers to change in place by failing to redesign jobs, pay plans, and technology to support the new way of doing things. One of the biggest obstacles that Nokia CEO Stephen Elop removed soon after joining the company was Symbian, the core operating software on over 400 million Nokia phones. Killing Symbian saved Nokia $1.4 billion a year in software maintenance and research and development costs. The software was out of date and buggy, and Nokia's computer software engineers had not delivered a new smartphone on schedule or on budget since 2009. Plus, app developers hated programming for Symbian. Tuomas Artman, who used to work at Nokia, said, "Developing for Symbian could make you want to slice your wrists."[58]

Killing Symbian not only saved billions in costs, it also allowed Nokia to strike an exclusive deal with Microsoft to use Microsoft's Windows Phone 7 software on its phones. Microsoft agreed to allow Nokia to innovate by creating new features for Windows Phone and injected hundreds of millions of dollars of marketing funds to support Nokia's efforts to sell new Windows-based smartphones. The change helped both companies, as Microsoft only had a 4 percent share of the smartphone market by itself, whereas in May 2013 Nokia and Microsoft had a combined 15 percent market share.[59]

Another error in the change phase is *not systematically planning for and creating short-term wins*. Most people don't have the discipline and patience to wait two years to see if the new change effort works. Change is threatening and uncomfortable, so people need to see an immediate payoff if they are to continue to support it. Kotter recommends that managers create short-term wins by actively picking people and projects that are likely to work extremely well early in the change process. Celestica's Craig Muhlhauser understood the importance of short-term wins. Said Muhlhauser, "My approach was to look at the first thirty days, then at the first three months, then at the first twelve months and then I took a look at the three years. In a turnaround, you have to take hold very quickly. You have to show relatively quick hits [i.e., short-term wins] to show your turnaround strategy is working—and then you deal with a multitude of issues in a very focused way that will allow you to continue to show improvement."[60]

The last two errors that managers make occur during the refreezing phase, when attempts are made to support and reinforce changes so that they stick. *Declaring victory too soon* is a tempting mistake in the refreezing phase. Managers typically declare victory right after the first large-scale success in the change process. Declaring success too early has the same effect as draining the gasoline out of a car: it stops change efforts dead in their tracks. With success declared, supporters of the change process stop pushing to make change happen. After all, why push when success has been achieved? Rather than declaring victory, managers should use the momentum from short-term wins to push for even bigger or faster changes. This maintains urgency and prevents change supporters from slacking off before the changes are frozen into the company's culture.

The last mistake that managers make is *not anchoring changes in the corporation's culture*. An *organization's culture* is the set of key values, beliefs, and attitudes shared by organizational members that determines the accepted way of doing things in a company. As you learned in Chapter 3, changing cultures is extremely difficult and slow. According to Kotter, two things help anchor changes in a corporation's culture. The first is directly showing people that the changes have actually improved

William Howell/iStockphoto.com

performance. The second is to make sure that the people who get promoted fit the new culture. If they don't, it's a clear sign that the changes were only temporary.

7-4c Change Tools and Techniques

Imagine that your boss came to you and said, "All right, genius, you wanted it. You're in charge of turning around the division." Where would you begin? How would you encourage change-resistant managers to change? What would you do to include others in the change process? How would you get the change process off to a quick start? Finally, what approach would you use to promote long-term effectiveness and performance? Results-driven change, the General Electric workout, and organizational development are different change tools and techniques that can be used to address these issues.

One of the reasons that organizational change efforts fail is that they are activity oriented rather than results oriented. In other words, they focus primarily on changing company procedures, management philosophy, or employee behavior. Typically, there is much buildup and preparation as consultants are brought in, presentations are made, books are read, and employees and managers are trained. There's a tremendous emphasis on doing things the new way. But, with all the focus on "doing," almost no attention is paid to *results*, to seeing if all this activity has actually made a difference.

By contrast, **results-driven change** supplants the emphasis on activity with a laser-like focus on quickly

measuring and improving results.[61] When Ben van Beurden became CEO of Royal Dutch Shell, one of the world's largest oil companies, he put everyone in the company on notice by proclaiming that oil refining profits were "simply too low," and that Shell needed, "better operational discipline." Furthermore, he changed managers' focus from "professional excellence," which served Shell well after a serious financial scandal, to specific results-driven goals. So Beurden split Shell into 150 performance units, each to be evaluated on its profitability, with profitable units continuing, and unprofitable units closing or being sold. Likewise, managers now had to compete for additional funds for their units by submitting formal requests to a central committee, which in turn had its spending recommendations reviewed by a "challenge committee."[62]

Another advantage of results-driven change is that managers introduce changes in procedures, philosophy, or behavior only if they are likely to improve measured performance. In other words, managers and workers actually test to see if changes make a difference. A third advantage of results-driven change is that quick, visible improvements motivate employees to continue to make additional changes to improve measured performance. Exhibit 7.4 describes the basic steps of results-driven change.

Exhibit 7.4
How to Create a Results-Driven Change Program

1. Set measurable, short-term goals to improve performance.
2. Make sure your action steps are likely to improve measured performance.
3. Stress the importance of immediate improvements.
4. Solicit help from consultants and staffers to achieve quick improvements in performance.
5. Test action steps to see if they actually yield improvements. If they don't, discard them and establish new ones.
6. Use resources you have or that can be easily acquired. It doesn't take much.

Source: R. H. Schaffer and H. A. Thomson, "Successful Change Programs Begin with Results," *Harvard Business Review on Change* (Boston: Harvard Business School Press, 1998), 189–213.

Results-driven change change created quickly by focusing on the measurement and improvement of results

The **General Electric workout** is a special kind of results-driven change. The "workout" involves a three-day meeting that brings together managers and employees from different levels and parts of an organization to quickly generate and act on solutions to specific business problems.[63] On the first morning, the boss discusses the agenda and targets specific business problems that the group will solve. Then, the boss leaves and an outside facilitator breaks the group (typically thirty to forty people) into five or six teams and helps them spend the next day and a half discussing and debating solutions.

On day three, in what GE calls a "town meeting," the teams present specific solutions to their boss, who has been gone since day one. As each team's spokesperson makes specific suggestions, the boss has only three options: agree on the spot, say no, or ask for more information so that a decision can be made by a specific, agreed-on date. GE boss Armand Lauzon sweated his way through a town meeting. To encourage him to say yes, his workers set up the meeting room to put pressure on Lauzon. He says, "I was wringing wet within half an hour. They had 108 proposals, I had about a minute to say yes or no to each one, and I couldn't make eye contact with my boss without turning around, which would show everyone in the room that I was chicken."[64] In the end, Lauzon agreed to all but eight suggestions. Furthermore, once those decisions were made, no one at GE was allowed to overrule them.

Organizational development is a philosophy and collection of planned change interventions designed to improve an organization's long-term health and performance. Organizational development takes a long-range approach to change; assumes that top-management support is necessary for change to succeed; creates change by educating workers and managers to change ideas, beliefs, and behaviors so that problems can be solved in new ways; and emphasizes employee participation in diagnosing, solving, and evaluating problems.[65] As shown in Exhibit 7.5, organizational development interventions begin with the recognition of a problem. Then, the company designates a **change agent** to be formally in charge of guiding the change effort. This person can be someone from within the company or a professional consultant. The change agent clarifies the problem, gathers information, works with decision makers to create and implement an action plan, helps to evaluate the plan's effectiveness, implements the plan throughout the company, and then leaves (if from outside the company) after making sure the change intervention will continue to work.

Organizational development interventions are aimed at changing large systems, small groups, or people.[66] More specifically, the purpose of *large-system*

General Electric workout a three-day meeting in which managers and employees from different levels and parts of an organization quickly generate and act on solutions to specific business problems

Organizational development a philosophy and collection of planned change interventions designed to improve an organization's long-term health and performance

Change agent the person formally in charge of guiding a change effort

Exhibit 7.5
General Steps for Organizational Development Interventions

1. Entry	A problem is discovered and the need for change becomes apparent. A search begins for someone to deal with the problem and facilitate change.
2. Startup	A change agent enters the picture and works to clarify the problem and gain commitment to a change effort.
3. Assessment & feedback	The change agent gathers information about the problem and provides feedback about it to decision makers and those affected by it.
4. Action planning	The change agent works with decision makers to develop an action plan.
5. Intervention	The action plan, or organizational development intervention, is carried out.
6. Evaluation	The change agent helps decision makers assess the effectiveness of the intervention.
7. Adoption	Organizational members accept ownership and responsibility for the change, which is then carried out through the entire organization.
8. Separation	The change agent leaves the organization after first ensuring that the change intervention will continue to work.

Source: W. J. Rothwell, R. Sullivan, and G. M. McLean, *Practicing Organizational Development: A Guide for Consultants* (San Diego: Pfeiffer & Co., 1995).

Exhibit 7.6
Different Kinds of Organizational Development Interventions

Large-System Interventions

Sociotechnical systems	An intervention designed to improve how well employees use and adjust to the work technology used in an organization.
Survey feedback	An intervention that uses surveys to collect information from the members of the system, reports the results of that survey to the members, and then uses those results to develop action plans for improvement.

Small-Group Interventions

Team building	An intervention designed to increase the cohesion and cooperation of work group members.
Unit goal setting	An intervention designed to help a work group establish short- and long-term goals.

Person-Focused Interventions

Counseling/coaching	An intervention designed so that a formal helper or coach listens to managers or employees and advises them on how to deal with work or interpersonal problems.
Training	An intervention designed to provide individuals with the knowledge, skills, or attitudes they need to become more effective at their jobs.

Source: W. J. Rothwell, R. Sullivan, and G. M. McLean, *Practicing Organizational Development: A Guide for Consultants* (San Diego: Pfeiffer & Co., 1995).

interventions is to change the character and performance of an organization, business unit, or department. *Small-group intervention* focuses on assessing how a group functions and helping it work more effectively to accomplish its goals. *Person-focused intervention* is intended to increase interpersonal effectiveness by helping people to become aware of their attitudes and behaviors and to acquire new skills and knowledge. Exhibit 7.6 describes the most frequently used organizational development interventions for large systems, small groups, and people.

STUDY TOOLS 7

LOCATED AT THE BACK OF YOUR BOOK:

☐ Rip out and study the Chapter Review Card at the end of the book

LOG IN TO WWW.CENGAGEBRAIN.COM TO:

☐ Review Key Term Flashcards

☐ Complete Practice Quizzing (take up to four times without repeating the same quiz)

☐ Complete Games: Beat the Clock and Crossword Puzzle

☐ Watch Management Workplace Video on "Holden"

☐ Work Through the What Would You Do Case on 3M Headquarters

8 Global Management

velkol/iStockphoto.com

LEARNING OUTCOMES

8-1 Discuss the impact of global business and the trade rules and agreements that govern it.

8-2 Explain why companies choose to standardize or adapt their business procedures.

8-3 Explain the different ways that companies can organize to do business globally.

8-4 Explain how to find a favorable business climate.

8-5 Discuss the importance of identifying and adapting to cultural differences.

8-6 Explain how to successfully prepare workers for international assignments.

After you finish

this chapter, go

to **PAGE 177** for

STUDY TOOLS

8-1 GLOBAL BUSINESS, TRADE RULES, AND TRADE AGREEMENTS

Business is the buying and selling of goods or services. Buying this textbook was a business transaction. So was selling your first car. So was getting paid for babysitting or for mowing lawns. **Global business** is the buying and selling of goods and services by people from different countries. The Timex watch that I wore while I was writing this chapter was purchased at a Walmart in Texas. But since it was made in the Philippines, I participated in global business when I wrote Walmart a check. Walmart, for its part, had already paid Timex, which had paid the company that employs the Filipino managers and workers who made my watch. Of course, there is more to global business than buying imported products at Walmart.

Global business presents its own set of challenges for managers. How can you be sure that the way you run your business in one country is the right way to run that business in another? This chapter discusses how organizations answer that question. We will start by examining global business in two ways: first exploring its impact on U.S. businesses and then reviewing the basic rules and agreements that govern global trade. Next, we will examine how and when companies go global by examining the tradeoff between consistency and adaptation and discussing how to organize a global company. Finally, we will look at how companies decide where to expand globally, including finding the best business climate, adapting to cultural differences, and better preparing employees for international assignments.

If you want a simple demonstration of the impact of global business, look at the tag on your shirt, the inside of your shoes, and the inside of your digital camera (take out your battery). Chances are all of these items were made in different places around the world. As I write this, my shirt, shoes, and cell phone were made in Thailand, China, and Korea. Where were yours made?

*Let's learn more about **8-1a the impact of global business, 8-1b how tariff and nontariff trade barriers have historically restricted global business, 8-1c how today global and regional trade agreements are reducing those trade barriers worldwide**, and **8-1d how consumers are responding to those changes in trade rules and agreements.***

8-1a The Impact of Global Business

Multinational corporations are corporations that own businesses in two or more countries. In 1970, more than half of the world's 7,000 multinational corporations were headquartered in just two countries: the United States and the United Kingdom. Today, there are roughly 103,000 multinational corporations, more than fourteen times as many as in 1970, and 9,692, or 9.4 percent, are based in the United States.[1] Today, 73,144 multinationals, or 71 percent, are based in other developed countries (e.g., Germany, Italy, Canada, and Japan), while 30,209, or 29.3 percent, are based in developing countries (e.g., Colombia and South Africa). So, today, multinational companies can be found by the thousands all over the world!

Another way to appreciate the impact of global business is by considering direct foreign investment. **Direct foreign investment** occurs when a company builds a new business or buys an existing business in a foreign country. Apollo Tyres Ltd., a tire manufacturer based in India, made a direct foreign investment in the U.S. when it bought Cooper Tire & Rubber company, the second largest tire manufacturer in the U.S., for $2.5 billion.[2]

Of course, companies from many other countries also own businesses in the United States. As Exhibit 8.1 shows, companies from the United Kingdom, Japan, the Netherlands, Canada, France, Switzerland, Germany, and Luxembourg have the largest direct foreign investment in the United States. Overall, foreign companies invest more than $2.5 trillion a year to do business in the United States.

But direct foreign investment in the United States is only half the picture. U.S. companies also have made large direct foreign investments in countries throughout the world. Ford Motor Company recently announced that it will build two factories in Chongqing, China, in order to better compete in the world's largest automobile market. A new $350 million factory will supply 400,000 transmission units for Ford's joint venture in

---

Global business the buying and selling of goods and services by people from different countries

Multinational corporation a corporation that owns businesses in two or more countries

Direct foreign investment a method of investment in which a company builds a new business or buys an existing business in a foreign country

Exhibit 8.1
Direct Foreign Investment in the United States

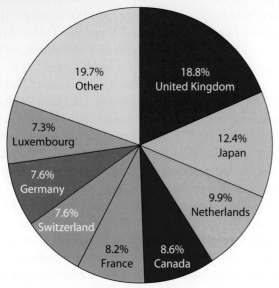

Source: K. Barefoot and M. Ibarra-Caton, "Direct Investment Positions for 2011: Country and Industry Detail," *Bureau of Economic Analysis,* July 2013, accessed June 10, 2013, http://blog.bea.gov/2014/06/25/direct-investment-positions-for-2013-now-available/.

8-1b Trade Barriers

Although today's consumers usually don't care where the products they buy come from (more on this in Section 8-1d), national governments have traditionally preferred that consumers buy domestically made products in hopes that such purchases would increase the number of domestic businesses and workers. Indeed, governments have done much more than hope that you will buy from domestic companies. Historically, governments have actively used **trade barriers** to make it much more expensive or difficult (or sometimes impossible) for consumers to buy or consume imported goods. For example, the Chinese government adds a 25 percent tariff to cars imported to China (compared to a 5 percent tariff on car imports in the United States).[4] Likewise, the U.S. government imposes a 37.5 percent to 67.5 percent tariff on imported shoes.[5] By establishing these restrictions and taxes, the Chinese and U.S. governments are engaging in **protectionism,** which is the use of trade barriers to protect local companies and their workers from foreign competition.

Governments have used two general kinds of trade barriers: tariff and nontariff barriers. A **tariff** is a direct tax on imported goods. Tariffs increase the cost of imported goods relative to that of domestic goods. The U.S. import tax on Chinese solar panels is 24 percent to 36 percent.[6]

China, while a second $500 million factory will produce engines. Joe Hinrichs, Ford's president for Asia Pacific and Africa, said, "Together with prior investments announced in the past few years, this new plant demonstrates Ford's unprecedented commitment to the China market."[3]

As Exhibit 8.2 shows, U.S. companies have made their largest direct foreign investments in the Netherlands, the United Kingdom, Luxembourg, Canada, and Bermuda. Overall, U.S. companies invest more than $4.6 trillion a year to do business in other countries.

So, whether foreign companies invest in the United States or U.S. companies invest abroad, direct foreign investment is an increasingly important and common method of conducting global business.

Trade barriers government-imposed regulations that increase the cost and restrict the number of imported goods

Protectionism a government's use of trade barriers to shield domestic companies and their workers from foreign competition

Tariff a direct tax on imported goods

Exhibit 8.2
U.S. Direct Foreign Investment Abroad

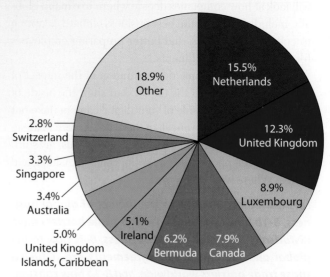

Source: K. Barefoot and M. Ibarra-Caton, "Direct Investment Positions for 2011: Country and Industry Detail," *Bureau of Economic Analysis,* July 2013, accessed June 10, 2013, http://blog.bea.gov/2014/06/25/direct-investment-positions-for-2013-now-available/.

Nontariff barriers are nontax methods of increasing the cost or reducing the volume of imported goods. There are five types of nontariff barriers: quotas, voluntary export restraints, government import standards, government subsidies, and customs valuation/classification. Because there are so many different kinds of nontariff barriers, they can be an even more potent method of shielding domestic industries from foreign competition.

Quotas are specific limits on the number or volume of imported products. For example, Indonesia only allows 32,000 tons of processed beef and 267,000 live cattle to be imported each year.[7]

Like quotas, **voluntary export restraints** limit the amount of a product that can be imported annually. The difference is that the exporting country rather than the importing country imposes restraints. Usually, however, the "voluntary" offer to limit exports occurs because the importing country has implicitly threatened to impose quotas. For example, to protect Brazilian auto manufacturers from less expensive Mexican-made cars, the Brazilian government convinced Mexico to "voluntarily" restrict auto exports to Brazil to no more than $1.55 billion a year for three years.[8] According to the World Trade Organization (see the discussion in Section 8-1c), however, voluntary export restraints are illegal and should not be used to restrict imports.[9]

In theory, **government import standards** are established to protect the health and safety of citizens. In reality, such standards are often used to restrict or ban imported goods. For example, Russia bans the importation of U.S. beef, pork, and turkey, claiming that the meat is contaminated by a commonly used food additive, ractopamine, which the United Nations Codex Alimentarius, establisher of worldwide food standards, says is not a health threat. A Western food-trade analyst regards the ban as "part of the protectionist measures they are taking against all imports."[10]

Many nations also use **subsidies,** such as long-term, low-interest loans, cash grants, and tax deferments, to develop and protect companies in special industries. As part of the 1934 Sugar Act and the 2008 Farm Bill, American sugar processors, who employ 142,000 people, receive government guaranteed loans and a government subsidized price of 21 cents per pound, roughly twice the price of sugar outside the U.S. Furthermore, when U.S. sugar producers aren't able to sell all of their sugar, the U.S. Department of Agriculture buys it and then sells it at a loss to ethanol producers.[11] The Competitive Enterprise Institute estimates the annual cost of subsidies at $3.5 billion a year.[12] Phillip Hayes of the U.S. Sugar Alliance says, "Other countries subsidize their sugar industries." Indeed, Brazilian sugar processors, which provide half of the world's sugar, receive $2.5 billion a year in subsidies from their government.

The last type of nontariff barrier is **customs classification.** As products are imported into a country, they are examined by customs agents, who must decide which of nearly 9,000 categories they should be classified into (see the Official Harmonized Tariff Schedule of the United States at http://www.usitc.gov/tata/hts/index.htm for more information). The category assigned by customs agents can greatly affect the size of the tariff and whether the item is subject to import quotas. For example, the U.S. Customs Service has several customs classifications for imported shoes. Tariffs on imported leather or "nonrubber" shoes are about 10 percent, whereas tariffs on imported rubber shoes, such as athletic footwear, range from 20 to 84 percent. The difference is large enough that some importers try to make their rubber shoes look like leather in hopes of receiving the nonrubber customs classification and lower tariff.

8-1c **Trade Agreements**

Thanks to the trade barriers described above, buying imported goods has often been much more expensive and difficult than buying domestic goods. During the

Nontariff barriers nontax methods of increasing the cost or reducing the volume of imported goods

Quota a limit on the number or volume of imported products

Voluntary export restraints voluntarily imposed limits on the number or volume of products exported to a particular country

Government import standard a standard ostensibly established to protect the health and safety of citizens but, in reality, is often used to restrict imports

Subsidies government loans, grants, and tax deferments given to domestic companies to protect them from foreign competition

Customs classification a classification assigned to imported products by government officials that affects the size of the tariff and the imposition of import quotas

1990s, however, the regulations governing global trade were transformed. The most significant change was that 124 countries agreed to adopt the **General Agreement on Tariffs and Trade (GATT).** GATT, which existed from 1947 to 1995, was an agreement to regulate trade among (eventually) more than 120 countries, the purpose of which was "substantial reduction of tariffs and other trade barriers and the elimination of preferences."[13] GATT members engaged in eight rounds of trade negotiations, with the Uruguay Round signed in 1994 and going into effect in 1995. Although GATT itself was replaced by the **World Trade Organization (WTO)** in 1995, the changes that it made continue to encourage international trade. Today, the WTO and its member countries are negotiating what's known as the Doha Round, which seeks to advance trade opportunities for developing countries in areas ranging from agriculture to services to intellectual property rights. The WTO, headquartered in Geneva, Switzerland, administers trade agreements, provides a forum for trade negotiations, handles trade disputes, monitors national trade policies, and offers technical assistance and training for developing countries for its 159 member countries.

Through tremendous decreases in tariff and nontariff barriers, the Uruguay round of GATT made it much easier and cheaper for consumers in all countries to buy foreign products. First, tariffs were cut 40 percent on average worldwide by 2005. Second, tariffs were eliminated in ten specific industries: beer, alcohol, construction equipment, farm machinery, furniture, medical equipment, paper, pharmaceuticals, steel, and toys. Third, stricter limits were put on government subsidies. For example, the Uruguay round of GATT put limits on how much national governments can subsidize private research in electronic and high-technology industries (see the discussion of subsidies in Section 8-1b). Fourth, the Uruguay round of GATT established protections for intellectual property, such as trademarks, patents, and copyrights.

Protection of intellectual property has become an increasingly important issue in global trade because of widespread product piracy. For example, the International Federation of the Phonographic Industry estimates that one-third of all Internet users download music from illegal access sites.[14] The Information Technology & Innovation Foundation found that 24 percent of global Internet traffic is used to download pirated music, movies, and other copyrighted content.[15] Likewise, according to BSA | The Software Alliance, 42 percent of all software used in the world is pirated, costing companies $63 billion in lost sales.[16]

Product piracy is also costly to the movie industry, as movie studios, distributors, and theaters, as well as video/DVD distributors, lose $18 billion each year to pirates. Indeed, digital sales of movies rose 6 percent to 10 percent for two movie studios after Megaupload, an illegal site for downloading movies, was closed.[17]

Finally, trade disputes between countries now are fully settled by arbitration panels from the WTO. In the past, countries could use their veto power to cancel a panel's decision. For instance, the French government routinely vetoed rulings that its large cash grants to French farmers constituted unfair subsidies. Now, however, countries that are members of the WTO no longer have veto power. Thus, WTO rulings are complete and final. Exhibit 8.3 provides a brief overview of the WTO and its functions.

The second major development that has reduced trade barriers has been the creation of **regional trading zones,** or zones in which tariff and nontariff barriers are reduced or eliminated for countries within the trading zone. The largest and most important trading zones are in Europe (the Maastricht Treaty), North America (the North American Free Trade Agreement, or NAFTA), Central America (Dominican Republic-Central America Free Trade Agreement, or CAFTA-DR), South America (Union of South American Nations, or USAN), and Asia (the Association of Southeast Asian Nations, or ASEAN, and Asia-Pacific Economic Cooperation, or APEC). The map

General Agreement on Tariffs and Trade (GATT) a worldwide trade agreement that reduced and eliminated tariffs, limited government subsidies, and established protections for intellectual property

World Trade Organization (WTO) the successor to GATT; the only international organization dealing with the global rules of trade between nations; its main function is to ensure that trade flows as smoothly, predictably, and freely as possible

Regional trading zones areas in which tariff and nontariff barriers on trade between countries are reduced or eliminated

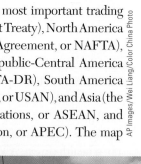

AP Images/Wei Liang/Color China Photo

Exhibit 8.3
World Trade Organization

☑ FACT FILE

WORLD TRADE
ORGANIZATION

Location: Geneva, Switzerland
Established: January 1, 1995
Created by: Uruguay Round negotiations (1986–1994)
Membership: 159 countries (on March 2, 2013)
Budget: 196 million Swiss francs for 2011
Secretariat staff: 640
Head: Pascal Lamy (Director-General)

Functions:
- Administering WTO trade agreements
- Forum for trade negotiations
- Handling trade disputes
- Monitoring national trade policies
- Technical assistance and training for developing countries
- Cooperation with other international organizations

Source: "Fact File: What Is the WTO?" *World Trade Organization*, accessed June 10, 2013, http://www.wto.org /english/thewto_e/thewto_e.htm.

in Exhibit 8.4 shows the extent to which free-trade agreements govern global trade.

In 1992, Belgium, Denmark, France, Germany, Greece, Ireland, Italy, Luxembourg, the Netherlands, Portugal, Spain, and the United Kingdom adopted the **Maastricht Treaty of Europe.** The purpose of this treaty was to transform their twelve different economies and twelve currencies into one common economic market, called the European Union (EU), with one common currency. On January 1, 2002, a single common currency, the euro, went into circulation in twelve of the EU's members (Austria, Belgium, Finland, France, Germany, Greece, Ireland, Italy, Luxembourg, the Netherlands, Portugal, and Spain). Austria, Finland, and Sweden joined the EU in 1995, followed by Cyprus, the Czech Republic, Estonia, Hungary, Latvia, Lithuania, Malta, Poland, Slovakia, and Slovenia in 2004; Bulgaria and Romania in 2007; and Croatia in 2013, bringing the total membership to twenty-eight countries.[18] Macedonia, Iceland, Montenegro, Serbia, and Turkey have applied and are being considered for membership.

Prior to the treaty, trucks carrying products were stopped and inspected by customs agents at each border. Furthermore, since the required paperwork, tariffs, and government product specifications could be radically different in each country, companies often had to file twelve different sets of paperwork, pay twelve different tariffs, produce twelve different versions of their basic product to meet various government specifications, and exchange money in twelve different currencies. Likewise, open business travel, which we take for granted in the United States, was complicated by inspections at each border crossing. If you lived in Germany but worked in Luxembourg, your car was stopped and your passport was inspected twice every day as you traveled to and from work. Also, every business transaction required a currency exchange, for example, from German deutsche marks to Italian lira, or from French francs to Dutch guilders. Imagine all of this happening to millions of trucks, cars, and workers each day, and you can begin to appreciate the difficulty and cost of conducting business across Europe before the Maastricht Treaty. For more information about the Maastricht Treaty, the EU, and the euro, see http://europa.eu/index_en.htm.

NAFTA, the **North American Free Trade Agreement** between the United States, Canada, and Mexico, went into effect on January 1, 1994. More than any other regional trade agreement, NAFTA has liberalized trade between countries so that businesses can plan for one market (North America) rather than for three separate markets. One of NAFTA's most important achievements was to eliminate most product tariffs *and* prevent the three countries from increasing existing tariffs or introducing new ones. Overall, Mexican and Canadian exports to the United States are up 596 percent and 192 percent, respectively, since NAFTA went into effect. U.S. exports to Mexico and Canada are up 420 percent and 191 percent, growing twice as fast as U.S. exports to any other part of the world. In fact, Mexico and Canada now account for 32 percent of all U.S. exports.[19]

Maastricht Treaty of Europe a regional trade agreement between most European countries

North American Free Trade Agreement (NAFTA) a regional trade agreement between the United States, Canada, and Mexico

Exhibit 8.4
Global Map of Regional Trade Agreements

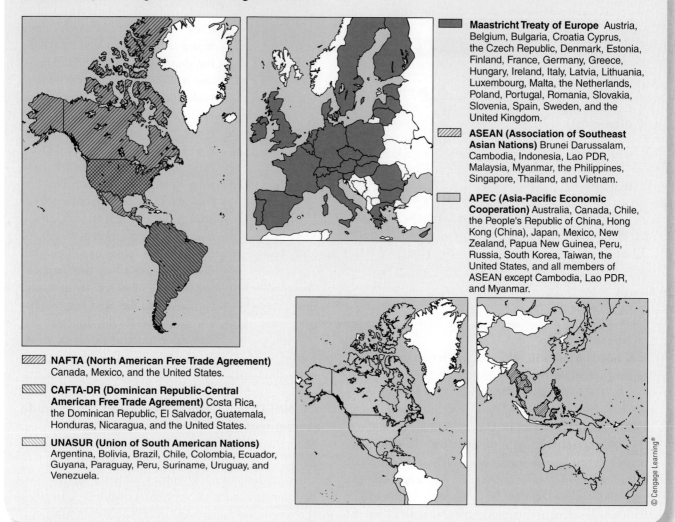

Maastricht Treaty of Europe Austria, Belgium, Bulgaria, Croatia Cyprus, the Czech Republic, Denmark, Estonia, Finland, France, Germany, Greece, Hungary, Ireland, Italy, Latvia, Lithuania, Luxembourg, Malta, the Netherlands, Poland, Portugal, Romania, Slovakia, Slovenia, Spain, Sweden, and the United Kingdom.

ASEAN (Association of Southeast Asian Nations) Brunei Darussalam, Cambodia, Indonesia, Lao PDR, Malaysia, Myanmar, the Philippines, Singapore, Thailand, and Vietnam.

APEC (Asia-Pacific Economic Cooperation) Australia, Canada, Chile, the People's Republic of China, Hong Kong (China), Japan, Mexico, New Zealand, Papua New Guinea, Peru, Russia, South Korea, Taiwan, the United States, and all members of ASEAN except Cambodia, Lao PDR, and Myanmar.

NAFTA (North American Free Trade Agreement) Canada, Mexico, and the United States.

CAFTA-DR (Dominican Republic-Central American Free Trade Agreement) Costa Rica, the Dominican Republic, El Salvador, Guatemala, Honduras, Nicaragua, and the United States.

UNASUR (Union of South American Nations) Argentina, Bolivia, Brazil, Chile, Colombia, Ecuador, Guyana, Paraguay, Peru, Suriname, Uruguay, and Venezuela.

© Cengage Learning®

CAFTA-DR, the **Dominican Republic-Central America Free Trade Agreement** between the United States, the Dominican Republic, and the Central American countries of Costa Rica, El Salvador, Guatemala, Honduras, and Nicaragua went into effect in August 2005. With a combined population of

51.1 million, the CAFTA-DR countries together are the twelfth-largest U.S. goods trading partner in the world and the third-largest U.S. export market in Latin America, after Mexico and Brazil. U.S. companies export more than $20 billion in goods each year to the CAFTA-DR countries.[20]

On May 23, 2008, twelve South American countries signed the **Union of South American Nations (UNASUR)** Constitutive Treaty, which united the countries of the former Mercosur (Argentina, Brazil, Paraguay, Uruguay, and Venezuela) and the countries of the Andean Community (Bolivia, Colombia, Ecuador, and Peru) with Guyana, Suriname, and Chile. UNASUR aims to create a unified South America by permitting free movement between nations, creating a common infrastructure that includes an interoceanic

Dominican Republic-Central America Free Trade Agreement (CAFTA-DR) a regional trade agreement between Costa Rica, the Dominican Republic, El Salvador, Guatemala, Honduras, Nicaragua, and the United States

Union of South American Nations (UNASUR) a regional trade agreement between Argentina, Brazil, Paraguay, Uruguay, Venezuela, Bolivia, Colombia, Ecuador, Peru, Guyana, Suriname, and Chile

highway, and establishing the region as a single market by eliminating all tariffs by 2019. UNASUR is one of the largest trading zones in the world, encompassing 361 million people in South America with a combined gross domestic product of nearly $973 billion.[21]

ASEAN, the **Association of Southeast Asian Nations,** and **APEC,** the **Asia-Pacific Economic Cooperation,** are the two largest and most important regional trading groups in Asia. ASEAN is a trade agreement between Brunei Darussalam, Cambodia, Indonesia, Lao PDR, Malaysia, Myanmar, the Philippines, Singapore, Thailand, and Vietnam, which form a market of more than 616 million people with a combined GDP of $2.3 trillion.[22] U.S. trade with ASEAN countries exceeds $200 billion a year.

In fact, the United States is ASEAN's fourth-largest trading partner (China is its largest), and ASEAN's member nations constitute the fifth-largest trading partner of the United States. An ASEAN free-trade area will be established in 2015 for the six original countries (Brunei Darussalam, Indonesia, Malaysia, the Philippines, Singapore, and Thailand) and in 2018 for the newer member countries (Cambodia, Lao PDR, Myanmar, and Vietnam).[23]

APEC is a broad agreement that includes Australia, Canada, Chile, the People's Republic of China, Hong Kong, Japan, Mexico, New Zealand, Papua New Guinea, Peru, Russia, South Korea, Taiwan, the United States, and all the members of ASEAN except Cambodia, Lao PDR, and Myanmar. APEC's twenty-one member countries contain 2.79 billion people, account for 44 percent of all global trade, and have a combined gross domestic product of over $41 trillion.[24]

APEC countries began reducing trade barriers in 2000, though all the reductions will not be completely phased in until 2020.[25]

8-1d Consumers, Trade Barriers, and Trade Agreements

The average worker earns nearly $80,950 a year in Switzerland, $102,610 in Norway, $46,140 in Japan, and $53,670 in the United States.[26] Yet, after adjusting these incomes for how much they can buy, the Swiss income is equivalent to just $53,920, the Norwegian income to $66,520, and the Japanese income to $37,630.[27] This is the same as saying that $1 of income can buy only $0.66 worth of goods in Switzerland, $0.65 worth in Norway, and $0.82 worth in Japan. In other words, Americans can buy much more with their incomes than those in other countries can.

One reason that Americans get more for their money is that the U.S. marketplace is the most competitive in the world and has been one of the easiest for foreign companies to enter.[28] Although some U.S. industries, such as textiles, have been heavily protected from foreign competition by trade barriers, for the most part, American consumers (and businesses) have had plentiful choices among American-made and foreign-made products. More important, the high level of competition between foreign and domestic companies that creates these choices helps keep prices low in the United States. Furthermore, it is precisely the lack of choice and the low level of competition that keep prices higher in countries that have not been as open to foreign companies and products. For example, Japanese trade barriers are estimated to cost Japanese consumers more than $100 billion a year. In fact, Japanese trade barriers amount to a 51 percent tax on food for the average Japanese family.[29]

So why do trade barriers and free-trade agreements matter to consumers? They're important because free-trade agreements increase choices, competition, and purchasing power and thus decrease what people pay for food, clothing, necessities, and luxuries. Accordingly, today's consumers rarely care where their products and services come from. From seafood to diamonds, people don't care where products are from—they just want to know which brand or kind is cheaper. And why do trade barriers and free-trade agreements matter to managers? The reason, as you're about to read, is that while free-trade agreements create new business opportunities, they also intensify competition, and addressing that competition is a manager's job.

8-2 CONSISTENCY OR ADAPTATION?

Once a company has decided that it *will* go global, it must decide *how* to go global. For example, if you decide to sell in Singapore, should you try to find a local business partner

---

Association of Southeast Asian Nations (ASEAN)
a regional trade agreement between Brunei Darussalam, Cambodia, Indonesia, Laos, Malaysia, Myanmar, the Philippines, Singapore, Thailand, and Vietnam

Asia-Pacific Economic Cooperation (APEC) a regional trade agreement between Australia, Canada, Chile, the People's Republic of China, Hong Kong, Japan, Mexico, New Zealand, Papua New Guinea, Peru, Russia, South Korea, Taiwan, the United States, and all the members of ASEAN except Cambodia, Laos, and Myanmar

who speaks the language, knows the laws, and understands the customs and norms of Singapore's culture? Or should you simply export your products from your home country? What do you do if you are also entering Eastern Europe, perhaps starting in Hungary? Should you use the same approach in Hungary that you use in Singapore?

In this section, we return to a key issue: How can you be sure that the way you run your business in one country is the right way to run that business in another? In other words, how can you strike the right balance between global consistency and local adaptation?

Global consistency means that a multinational company with offices, manufacturing plants, and distribution facilities in different countries uses the same rules, guidelines, policies, and procedures to run all of those offices, plants, and facilities. Managers at company headquarters value global consistency because it simplifies decisions. By contrast, a company following a policy of **local adaptation** modifies its standard operating procedures to adapt to differences in foreign customers, governments, and regulatory agencies. Local adaptation is typically preferred by local managers who are charged with making the international business successful in their countries.

Global consistency when a multinational company has offices, manufacturing plants, and distribution facilities in different countries and runs them all using the same rules, guidelines, policies, and procedures

Local adaptation modifying rules, guidelines, policies, and procedures to adapt to differences in foreign customers, governments, and regulatory agencies

If companies lean too much toward global consistency, they run the risk of using management procedures poorly suited to particular countries' markets, cultures, and employees (i.e., a lack of local adaptation). Home Depot became the biggest hardware and home improvement retailer in the United States thanks to its big-box model featuring huge stores, thousands of suburban locations, a vast range of products, and strong customer service. But, after eight years, Home Depot closed its seven Chinese stores. Unlike Americans, who are do-it-yourselfers when it comes to home improvement because it saves money, the widespread availability of low-cost labor makes China more of a "do-it-for-me culture," says a Home Depot spokesperson. Furthermore, unlike the U.S., where completing DIY projects is admired, there's a stigma associated with performing manual labor in China. A Chinese middle-class customer said, "Poor people are the only group in China who would bother taking on a DIY project, because they cannot afford to hire others."[30] And, unlike in the United States, where a much higher percentage of people own their homes, most Chinese, especially those with the discretionary income to afford home projects, rent small apartments in cities, which further diminished Home Depot's opportunities in China.[31]

If, however, companies focus too much on local adaptation, they run the risk of losing the cost effectiveness and productivity that result from using standardized rules and procedures throughout the world. Because its French stores are nearly identical to its U.S. stores, Starbucks has never been profitable in France. As a result, says Parisian Marion Bayod, "I never go into Starbucks; it's impersonal, the coffee is mediocre, and it's expensive. For us, it's like another planet." Likewise, Parisian Laurent Pauzié says Starbucks stores, "are only here to comfort tourists when they're lost." Canadian Kate Menzies, who lives in Paris, concedes that while Starbucks may not be popular for its coffee, it "is one of the few places with public toilets and free WiFi in the city."[32] Starbucks, however, is now embracing local adaptation. Rather than offering strong coffee in paper cups as in the United States, its French stores will offer a lighter-tasting "blonde" espresso in glass coffee cups (because the French prefer to sit and drink) in larger redesigned stores with sumptuous wooden bars, bright chandeliers, and velvet couches, similar to traditional Parisian cafés. While Starbucks hopes these changes will attract French customers, spending tens of millions more to adapt its stores to French tastes may also sacrifice the cost effectiveness and productivity that make it profitable in the United States.[33]

A Company That Exports Companies

Export Now, founded by former U.S. Ambassador to Singapore Frank Lavin, specializes in exports. The Ohio-based company doesn't sell anything, however. Instead, it sets up an infrastructure that other companies can use for exports. For an annual fee and a percentage of sales, Export Now will handle all of the customs and legal issues involved in exporting and provide an online retail space for their customers' products. According to Lavin, his service allows clients to avoid wholesalers, middlemen, or distributors, meaning that they can charge consumers in China the same prices they do in the United States. So far, the items available on Export Now's virtual mall include Osprey backpacks, singing toothbrushes from Brush Buddies, and hearing aid products from McKeon Products.

Source: N. Leiber, "Ex-U.S. Ambassador Helps Companies Break into China," *Bloomberg Businessweek*, September 13, 2012, accessed June 10, 2013, http://www.businessweek.com/articles/2012-08-23/making-it-easier-to-sell-made-in-usa-in-china.

AP Images/PRNewsFoto/Brush Buddies

8-3 FORMS FOR GLOBAL BUSINESS

Besides determining whether to adapt organizational policies and procedures, a company must also determine how to organize itself for successful entry into foreign markets.

*Historically, companies have generally followed the phase model of globalization, in which a company makes the transition from a domestic company to a global company in the following sequential phases: **8-3a exporting, 8-3b cooperative contracts, 8-3c strategic alliances,** and **8-3d wholly owned affiliates.** At each step, the company grows much larger, uses those resources to enter more global markets, is less dependent on home-country sales, and is more committed in its orientation to global*

*business. Some companies, however, do not follow the phase model of globalization. Some skip phases on their way to becoming more global and less domestic. Others don't follow the phase model at all. These are known as **8-3e global new ventures.** This section reviews these forms of global business.[34]*

8-3a Exporting

When companies produce products in their home countries and sell those products to customers in foreign countries, they are **exporting.** Exporting as a form of global business offers many advantages. It makes the company less dependent on sales in its home market and provides a greater degree of control over research, design, and production decisions. For example, while auto sales in Europe dropped 8.2 percent in 2012, the largest single-year decline in two decades, sales of Jaguars and Land Rovers, built in the United Kingdom, were up 32 percent due largely to exports to China and Asia.[35] Though advantageous in a number of ways, exporting also has its disadvantages. The primary disadvantage is that many exported goods are subject to tariff and nontariff barriers that can substantially increase their final cost to consumers. A second disadvantage is that transportation costs can significantly increase the price of an exported product. For example, when the price of crude oil was approaching $150 a barrel, manufacturers who made everything from batteries to sofas to industrial parts started bringing manufacturing production from overseas back to North America. Jeff Rubin, chief economist at CIBC World Markets in Toronto, said, "In a world of triple-digit oil prices, distance costs money."[36] There is a third disadvantage of exporting: companies that export depend on foreign importers for product distribution. If, for example, the foreign importer makes a mistake on the paperwork that accompanies a shipment of imported goods, those goods can be returned to the foreign manufacturer at the manufacturer's expense.

8-3b Cooperative Contracts

When an organization wants to expand its business globally without making a large financial commitment to do so, it may sign a **cooperative contract** with a

Exporting selling domestically produced products to customers in foreign countries

Cooperative contract an agreement in which a foreign business owner pays a company a fee for the right to conduct that business in his or her country

foreign business owner who pays the company a fee for the right to conduct that business in his or her country. There are two kinds of cooperative contracts: licensing and franchising.

Under a **licensing** agreement, a domestic company, the *licensor*, receives royalty payments for allowing another company, the *licensee*, to produce its product, sell its service, or use its brand name in a particular foreign market. For example, in Turkey,

> **Licensing** an agreement in which a domestic company, the licensor, receives royalty payments for allowing another company, the licensee, to produce the licensor's product, sell its service, or use its brand name in a specified foreign market
>
> **Franchise** a collection of networked firms in which the manufacturer or marketer of a product or service, the franchisor, licenses the entire business to another person or organization, the franchisee

Desperate Women, a Turkish adaptation of *Desperate Housewives*, is produced by MBC Group (the licensee) under a license from the Walt Disney Company (the licensor), which owns ABC, the network that produced *Desperate Housewives*. Similar licensing agreements are behind *Married with Children* being remade and adapted with local actors in twelve countries and *Glee* being remade and broadcast in China with Chinese actors.[37]

One of the most important advantages of licensing is that it allows companies to earn additional profits without investing more money. As foreign sales increase, the royalties paid to the licensor by the foreign licensee increase. Moreover, the licensee, not the licensor, invests in production equipment and facilities to produce the product. Licensing also helps companies avoid tariff and nontariff barriers. Since the licensee manufactures the product within the foreign country, tariff and nontariff barriers don't apply.

The biggest disadvantage associated with licensing is that the licensor gives up control over the quality of the product or service sold by the foreign licensee. Unless the licensing agreement contains specific restrictions, the licensee controls the entire business from production to marketing to final sales. Many licensors include inspection clauses in their license contracts, but closely monitoring product or service quality from thousands of miles away can be difficult. An additional disadvantage is that licensees can eventually become competitors, especially when a licensing agreement includes access to important technology or proprietary business knowledge.

A **franchise** is a collection of networked firms in which the manufacturer or marketer of a product or service, the *franchisor*, licenses the entire business to another person or organization, the *franchisee*. For the price of an initial franchise fee plus royalties, franchisors provide franchisees with training, assistance with marketing and advertising, and an exclusive right to conduct business in a particular location. Most franchise fees run between $5,000 and $35,000. Franchisees pay McDonald's, one of the largest franchisors in the world, an initial franchise fee of $45,000. Another $959,450 to $2,110,700 is needed beyond that to pay for food inventory, kitchen equipment, construction, landscaping, and other expenses (the cost varies by location). While franchisees typically borrow part of this cost from a bank, McDonald's requires applicants to have over $750,000 in non-borrowed assets and requires a

40 percent down payment in cash for the initial investment.[38] Typical royalties are around 8.5 percent of gross sales, but sometimes go as high as 12 percent.[39] So franchisors are well rewarded for the help they provide to franchisees. More than 400 U.S. companies franchise their businesses to foreign franchise partners.

Despite franchising's many advantages, franchisors face a loss of control when they sell businesses to franchisees who are thousands of miles away. Franchising specialist Cheryl Scott says, "One franchisor I know was wondering why the royalties coming from India were so small when he knew the shop was always packed. It was because the franchisee wasn't putting all of the sales through the cash register."[40]

Although there are exceptions, franchising success may be somewhat culture-bound. Because most global franchisors begin by franchising their businesses in similar countries or regions (Canada is by far the first choice for U.S. companies taking their first step into global franchising), and because 65 percent of franchisors make absolutely no change in their business for overseas franchisees, that success may not generalize to cultures with different lifestyles, values, preferences, and technological infrastructures. Customizing menus to local tastes is one of the primary ways that fast-food companies can succeed in international markets. With a 40 percent market share, 3,000 locations in 650 cities, and a new restaurant opening every eighteen hours, U.S.-based KFC, which is part of Yum! Brands, is the most successful foreign restaurant chain in China, even outperforming McDonald's, which has 16 percent of the market. Unlike McDonald's, which largely sells the same food in China that it does in the United States, KFC China, which is run by Chinese managers hired by Yum! Brands, has focused instead on providing Chinese-flavored dishes, such as the Dragon Twister, a chicken wrap with duck sauce, and tofu chicken rice, designed to reflect the spicy food found in China's Sichuan province. And, while Chinese customers will find some Western menu items like chicken and corn on the cob, they'll also find Chinese favorites like fried dough sticks, congee (rice porridge), preserved eggs, and other dishes that cater to more local tastes.[41]

8-3c Strategic Alliances

Companies forming **strategic alliances** combine key resources, costs, risks, technology, and people. Hewlett-Packard, the world's largest electronics manufacturer, with a 28 percent share of the computer server market, and Foxconn, the Taiwanese firm that assembles some of the world's most popular electronic devices, such as the iPhone and iPad, have formed a strategic alliance to co-develop large servers that can handle cloud computing and process "big data" for multinational firms.[42] The most common strategic alliance is a **joint venture**, which occurs when two existing companies collaborate to form a third company. The two founding companies remain intact and unchanged, except that together they now own the newly created joint venture.

One of the advantages of global joint ventures is that, like licensing and franchising, they help companies avoid tariff and nontariff barriers to entry. Another advantage is that companies participating in a joint venture bear only part of the costs and the risks of that business. Many companies find this attractive because of the expense of entering foreign markets or developing new products. Starbucks established a fifty-fifty joint venture with Tata Global Beverages, which is part of the Tata Group, the largest conglomerate in India. Starbucks-Tata plans to open fifty stores within a year, eventually establishing 3,000 in India. John Culver, president of Starbucks Asia, said, "We are going to move as fast as we possibly can to take advantage of the opportunity that exists in India. It's an economy that is moving very quickly, and the consumer is evolving very quickly."[43]

Global joint ventures can be especially advantageous to smaller local partners who link up with larger, more experienced foreign firms that can bring advanced management, resources, and business skills to the joint venture.

Global joint ventures are not without problems, though. Because companies share costs and risks with their joint venture partners, they must also share profits. Managing global joint ventures can also be difficult because they represent a merging of four cultures: the country and the organizational culture of the first partner, and the country and the organizational culture of the second partner. Often, to be fair to all involved, each partner in the global joint venture will have equal ownership and power. But this can result in power struggles and a lack of leadership. Because of these problems, companies forming global joint ventures should carefully develop detailed contracts that specify the obligations of each party.

Strategic alliance an agreement in which companies combine key resources, costs, risks, technology, and people

Joint venture a strategic alliance in which two existing companies collaborate to form a third, independent company

8-3d Wholly Owned Affiliates (Build or Buy)

Approximately one-third of multinational companies enter foreign markets through wholly owned affiliates. In 2013, Japan-based Lixil, a maker of household kitchen and bathroom products, entered the North American and European markets by purchasing two long-established companies, American Standard Brands, a U.S.-based maker of toilets, as well as bathroom and kitchen fixtures, and Germany's GROHE Group, a maker of luxury bathroom and kitchen metal fittings.[44] Unlike licensing arrangements, franchises, or joint ventures, **wholly owned affiliates,** like American Standard Brands and GROHE, are 100 percent owned by their parent company, in this case, Lixil.

The primary advantage of wholly owned businesses is that the parent company receives all of the profits and has complete control over the foreign facilities. The biggest disadvantage is the expense of building new operations or buying existing businesses. Although the payoff can be enormous if wholly owned affiliates succeed, the losses can be immense if they fail, because the parent company assumes all of the risk. London-based Standard Chartered PLC is a banking and financial services company with 87,000 employees who work at branches in 70 countries. Ninety percent of its business comes from its wholly owned affiliates in Africa, the Middle East, and Asia. While still profitable overall, Standard Chartered lost $200 million last year at its South Korean units, which are now being sold at a sizable loss to a Japanese bank.[45]

8-3e Global New Ventures

Companies used to evolve slowly from small operations selling in their home markets to large businesses selling to foreign markets. Furthermore, as companies went global, they usually followed the phase model of globalization. Recently, however, three trends have combined to allow companies to skip the phase model when going global. First, quick, reliable air travel can transport people to nearly any point in the world within one day. Second, low-cost communication technologies such as email, teleconferencing and phone conferencing via the Internet, and cloud computing make it easier to communicate with global customers, suppliers, managers, and employees.

> **Wholly owned affiliates** foreign offices, facilities, and manufacturing plants that are 100 percent owned by the parent company

Third, there is now a critical mass of businesspeople with extensive personal experience in all aspects of global business.[46] This combination of developments has made it possible to start companies that are global from inception. With sales, employees, and financing in different countries, **global new ventures** are companies that are founded with an active global strategy.[47]

Although there are several different kinds of global new ventures, all share two common factors. First, the company founders successfully develop and communicate the company's global vision from inception. Second, rather than going global one country at a time, new global ventures bring a product or service to market in several foreign markets at the same time. **MakerBot** 3-D printers "print" items made of rigid plastic based on specifications from computer-aided design software like AutoDesk. NASA's Jet Propulsion Laboratory uses MakerBot's Replicator 2 (hat tip to *Star Trek*) to print prototype parts cheaply and quickly. Cofounder Bre Pettis believes that MakerBot can fundamentally disrupt global manufacturing and replace "two centuries of mass production" by giving anyone with an idea the tools to design their own products without a factory. Though just four years old, MakerBot, which has been global since inception, has distributors in fourteen countries, including Australia, Brazil, China, Germany, Japan, and the United Kingdom.[48]

8-4 FINDING THE BEST BUSINESS CLIMATE

When deciding where to go global, companies try to find countries or regions with promising business climates.

*An attractive global business climate **8-4a positions the company for easy access to growing markets, 8-4b is an effective but cost-efficient place to build an office or manufacturing facility, and 8-4c minimizes the political risk to the company.***

8-4a Growing Markets

The most important factor in an attractive business climate is access to a growing market. For example, no product is known and purchased by as many people throughout the world as Coca-Cola. Yet even Coke, which is available in over 200 countries, still has tremendous potential for further global growth. Coca-Cola gets 79 percent of its sales outside of North America, and emerging markets, where it

has seen its fastest growth, now account for half of Coke's sales worldwide.[49]

Two factors help companies determine the growth potential of foreign markets: purchasing power and foreign competitors. **Purchasing power** is measured by comparing the relative cost of a standard set of goods and services in different countries. For example, a twenty-ounce Coke costs $3.79 in Oslo, Norway. Because that same twenty-ounce Coke costs only $1.50 in the United States, the average American would have more purchasing power than the average Norwegian.[50] Purchasing power is growing in countries like India and China, which have low average levels of income. This is because basic living expenses such as food, shelter, and transportation are very inexpensive in those countries, so consumers still have money to spend after paying for necessities, especially as salaries increase thanks to demand from international trade (see box "Paying for a 'Mac Attack'").

Consequently, countries with high and growing levels of purchasing power are good choices for companies looking for attractive global markets. As Exhibit 8.5 shows, Coke has found that the per capita consumption of Coca-Cola, or the number of Cokes a person drinks per year, rises directly with purchasing power. For example, in China, Brazil, and Australia, where the average person earns, respectively, $8,390, $11,420, and $40,270 annually, the number of Coca-Cola soft drinks consumed per year increases, respectively, from 39 to 241 to 315. The more purchasing power people have, the more likely they are to purchase soft drinks. And the Coca-Cola Company expects strong growth to continue in these markets, stating in its annual report, "To measure our growth potential, we look to our per capita consumption—the average number of eight-ounce servings of our beverages consumed each year in a given market. It is predicted that by the year 2020, the world will have nearly 1 billion more people whose disposable incomes will afford them choices and opportunities unthinkable a generation ago. We must discover innovative ways to connect with our traditional consumer base and this emerging global middle class—by creating new products and packaging formats for all lifestyles and occasions."[51]

The second part of assessing the growth potential of global markets involves analyzing the degree of global competition, which is determined by the number and

Global new ventures new companies that are founded with an active global strategy and have sales, employees, and financing in different countries

Purchasing power the relative cost of a standard set of goods and services in different countries

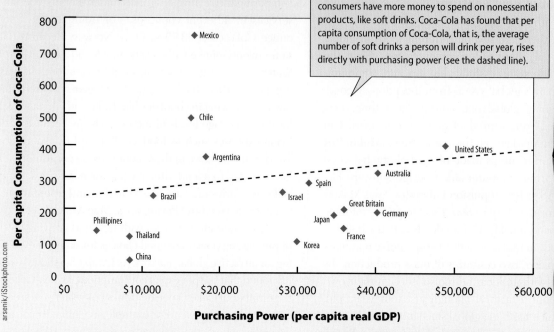

Exhibit 8.5

How Consumption of Coca-Cola Varies with Purchasing Power Around the World

Typically, the higher the purchasing power in a country, the better that country will be for doing business. Why? Because higher purchasing power means that consumers have more money to spend on nonessential products, like soft drinks. Coca-Cola has found that per capita consumption of Coca-Cola, that is, the average number of soft drinks a person will drink per year, rises directly with purchasing power (see the dashed line).

Sources: "Coca-Cola 2012 Annual Review," *Coca-Cola Company*, accessed June 10, 2013, http://www.coca-colacompany.com/annual-review/2012/year_in_review .html; "GNI Per Capita Ranking, Atlas Method and PPP Based," *The World Bank*, April 15, 2013, accessed June 10, 2013, http://data.worldbank.org/data-catalog /GNI-per-capita-Atlas-and-PPP-table.

Even Coca-Cola, which is available in more than 200 countries, still has tremendous potential for further global growth. Currently, the Coca-Cola Company gets about 80 percent of its sales from its sixteen largest markets.

quality of companies that already compete in a foreign market. As the Tata-Starbucks joint venture begins opening stores in India, one of its primary competitors is Café Coffee Day, India's most popular coffee chain, which in the last few years has grown from a dozen stores to more than 1,200 locations in 175 cities. Café Coffee Day, like most of India's coffee shops, charges about $1 for a small cappuccino, which is about one-third the cost of the same drink in U.S. stores. By contrast, Starbucks plans to focus on selling premium coffee, tea, and food.[52]

8-4b Choosing an Office/ Manufacturing Location

Companies do not have to establish an office or manufacturing location in each country they enter. They can license, franchise, or export to foreign markets, or they can serve a larger region from one country. But there are many reasons why a company might choose to establish

a location in a foreign country. Some foreign offices are established through global mergers and acquisitions, and some are established because of a commitment to grow in a new market. StarChip is a French semiconductor company that makes smart cards—plastic cards with embedded chips that transmit information to devices (like ATM machines), protect the data stored on the card (as with credit cards), or provide extra data storage (on identification cards, for example). StarChip opened a new office in Shanghai as part of its plan to expand its manufacturing and sales network in China. According to COO Christian Dupuy, "Expanding our operation to have engineers based in Shanghai is the logical first step to sustain the growing activity with our manufacturing partners in China."[53]

Other companies choose locations by seeking a tax haven (although this is more difficult for U.S. companies due to legal concerns) or as part of creating a global brand. Ireland is a popular location to establish a

Paying for a "Mac Attack"

Every year, *The Economist* magazine produces the Big Mac Index to illustrate differences in purchasing power across countries. By comparing the price of a single item, in this case a Big Mac from McDonald's, the index shows how much (or how little) consumers in each country get for their money. According to the latest index, a Big Mac costs an average of $4.62 in the United States, $5.01 in Canada, $5.25 in Brazil, and $7.14 in Switzerland, meaning that residents of those countries get far less for their money than U.S. residents do. Conversely, consumers in Russia only have to pay $2.62 for their Big Mac, while consumers in Turkey pay $3.76 and consumers in India pay only $1.54.

Source: "The Big Mac Index," *Economist*, January 23, 2014, accessed April 29, 2014, http://www.economist.com/content/big-mac-index.

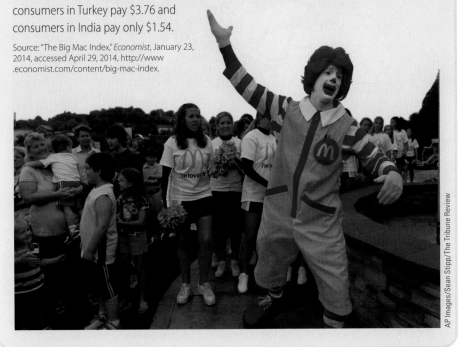

AP Images/Sean Stipp/The Tribune Review

company headquarters because of its corporate tax rate of 12.5 percent, which is much lower than the United Kingdom (25 percent), Germany (30.2 percent), or the United States (35 percent), which has the second highest corporate tax rate in the world.[54]

The criteria for choosing an office/manufacturing location are different from the criteria for entering a foreign market. Rather than focusing on costs alone, companies should consider both qualitative and quantitative factors. Two key qualitative factors are work force quality and company strategy. Work force quality is important because it is often difficult to find workers with the specific skills, abilities, and experience that a company needs to run its business. Work force quality is one reason that many companies doing business in Europe locate their customer call centers in the Netherlands. Workers in the Netherlands are the

most linguistically gifted in Europe, with 73 percent speaking two languages, 44 percent speaking three languages, and 12 percent speaking more than three. Another advantage of locating a call center in the Netherlands is that 60 percent of call center workers have university or advanced degrees in technology or management.[55]

A company's strategy is also important when choosing a location. For example, a company pursuing a low-cost strategy may need plentiful raw materials, low-cost transportation, and low-cost labor. A company pursuing a differentiation strategy (typically a higher-priced, better product or service) may need access to high-quality materials and a highly skilled and educated work force.

Quantitative factors such as the kind of facility being built, tariff and nontariff barriers, exchange rates, and transportation and labor costs should also be considered when choosing an office/manufacturing location. A real estate specialist in company location decisions explains how things change with different types of facility: "If it's an assembly plant, a company might be inclined to look for incentives that would subsidize its hiring. With a distribution facility, an adequate transportation network will likely be critical. A corporate headquarters will need a good communications network, a multilingual labor force, and easy access by air. On the other hand, a research and development operation will require proximity to a high-tech infrastructure and access to good universities."[56] Companies rely on studies such as Cushman & Wakefield's annually published "European Cities Monitor" to compare business climates throughout Europe.[57] Similar studies are available for other parts of the world. Exhibit 8.6 offers a quick overview of the best cities for business based on a variety of criteria. This information is a good starting point if your

corkcof/iStockphoto.com

Exhibit 8.6
World's Best Cities for Business

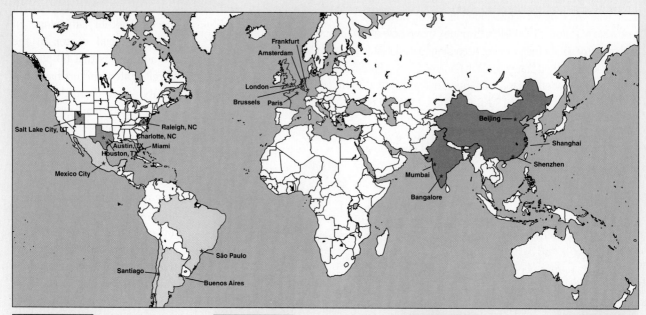

North America	Latin America	Europe	Asia Pacific
1. Raleigh, NC	1. São Paulo	1. London	1. Shanghai
2. Austin, TX	2. Santiago	2. Paris	2. Beijing
3. Salt Lake City, UT	3. Miami	3. Frankfurt	3. Shenzhen
4. Houston, TX	4. Mexico City	4. Amsterdam	4. Bangalore
5. Charlotte, NC	5. Buenos Aires	5. Brussels	5. Mumbai

Sources: "The Top 10 Large Cities for Doing Business," *Inc.*, accessed June 14, 2009, http://www.inc.com; "Where Are the Best Cities to Do Business?" *Inc.*, July 2008, accessed July 14, 2009, http://www.inc .com; "El Sitio de los Negocios Globales de América Latina 2009," *AméricaEconomía*, accessed June 14, 2009, http://www.americaeconomia .com/Multimedios/Otros/7783.pdf; "European Cities Monitor," *Cushman & Wakefield*, 2008, accessed May 30, 2009, http://www.cushwake.com/cwglobal/docviewer/2008 _European_Cities_Monitor.pdf; "Shanghai, Beijing, Shenzhen Top 3 in Best City Survey," *Fortune China*, accessed February 13, 2007, http://www.fortunechina.com/pdf /Best%20Cities%20Press%20Release%20(English)%202004.12.01.pdf.

company is trying to decide where to put an international office or manufacturing plant.

8-4c Minimizing Political Risk

When managers think about political risk in global business, they envision burning factories and riots in the streets. Although political events such as these receive dramatic and extended coverage in the media, the political risks that most companies face usually are not covered as breaking stories on Fox News or CNN. Nonetheless, the negative consequences of ordinary political risk can be just as devastating to companies that fail to identify and minimize that risk.[58]

When conducting global business, companies should attempt to identify two types of political risk: political uncertainty and policy uncertainty.[59] **Political uncertainty** is associated with the risk of major changes in political regimes that can result from war, revolution, death of political leaders, social unrest, or other influential events. **Policy uncertainty** refers to the risk associated with changes in laws and government policies that directly affect the way foreign companies conduct business.

Policy uncertainty is the most common—and perhaps most frustrating—form of political risk in global business, especially when changes in laws and government policies directly undercut sizable investments

Political uncertainty the risk of major changes in political regimes that can result from war, revolution, death of political leaders, social unrest, or other influential events

Policy uncertainty the risk associated with changes in laws and government policies that directly affect the way foreign companies conduct business

made by foreign companies. India is the third-largest retail market in the world behind the United States and China. The Indian government has long protected Indian retail stores by preventing foreign retailers from entering India unless they had a joint venture partner. So when India changed that policy, global retailers like Walmart (United States), Carrefour (France), and Tesco (United Kingdom) began making plans to enter India on their own. The Indian government, however, reversed that decision following large protests from small-business owners and politicians who feared that huge retail stores would put locally owned mom-and-pop shops out of business. Kamlesh Gupta and her husband own such a shop, the Radha Krisna Store in Central Delhi. She said that if large retailers are allowed into India, "Everything will be over. If they sell goods cheaper than us, who will come here? Already, we have lost 20 percent of our business since Big Bazaar and Reliance [two other Indian retailers] started operating in the last two years." As a result, the only option for foreign retailers like Walmart, and it's not an attractive one, is to form joint ventures to establish "cash-and-carry" stores that sell to businesses but not consumers.[60]

Several strategies can be used to minimize or adapt to the political risk inherent in global business. An *avoidance strategy* is used when the political risks associated with a foreign country or region are viewed as too great. If firms are already invested in high-risk areas, they may divest or sell their businesses. If they have not yet invested, they will likely postpone their investment until the risk shrinks. While U.S.-based **Honeywell International** employs 12,500 people in India who earn the company $600 million in annual revenues, a new law that requires foreign firms to own no more than a 75 percent share of their business in India is forcing many businesses to avoid India or perhaps postpone further investment. Honeywell CEO David Cote says, "Foreign companies are starting to become scared here. They are starting to say,

'What am I doing here?' I'll hire people here but I'll be a lot more reticent about investing, including acquisitions. I am a lot less keen on expanding our presence by putting money into the country—it's not a smart thing for me to be doing."[61]

Exhibit 8.7 shows the long-term political stability of various countries in the Middle East (higher scores indicate less political risk). The following factors, which were used to compile these ratings, indicate greater political risk: government instability, poor socioeconomic conditions, internal or external conflict, military involvement in politics, religious and ethnic tensions, high foreign debt as a percentage of gross domestic product, exchange rate instability, and high inflation.[62] An avoidance strategy would likely be used for the riskiest countries shown in Exhibit 8.7, such as Iran and Saudi Arabia, but might not be needed for the less risky countries, such as Israel or Oman. Risk conditions and factors change, so be sure to make risk decisions with the latest available information from resources such as the PRS Group, http://www.prsgroup.com, which supplies information about political risk to 80 percent of *Fortune* 500 companies.

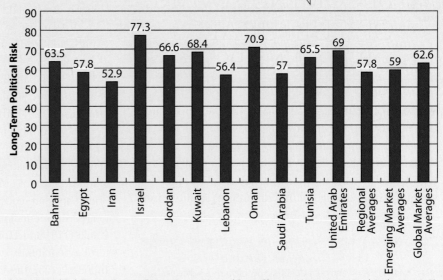

Exhibit 8.7
Overview of Political Risk in the Middle East

Higher scores indicate less long-term political risk, which is calculated by estimating government instability, socioeconomic conditions, internal or external conflicts, military involvement in politics, religious and ethnic tensions, foreign debt as a percent of gross domestic product, exchange rate instability, and whether there is high inflation.

Source: "United Arab Emirates Business Forecast Report, 2014 2nd Quarter," Business Monitor International, April 1, 2014, 1–50.

Control is an active strategy to prevent or reduce political risks. Firms using a control strategy lobby foreign governments or international trade agencies to change laws, regulations, or trade barriers that hurt their business in that country. Seattle-based Amazon.com, the world's largest Internet retailer, is lobbying the Indian government to change laws that prevent foreign companies from selling directly to Indian consumers. Amazon's Junglee.com is used by Indian consumers to compare prices, but it only links to Indian retailers. Ankur Bisen of Technopak, an Indian-based retail consulting firm, says, "Amazon's intent in launching Junglee.com was to have a presence in the Indian market till rules are changed to allow them to do business here." Amazon is eager to expand in India, where retail Internet sales are predicted to increase from $600 million today to $70 billion in 2020.[63]

Another method for dealing with political risk is *cooperation*, which involves using joint ventures and collaborative contracts, such as franchising and licensing. Although cooperation does not eliminate the political risk of doing business in a country, it can limit the risk associated with foreign ownership of a business. For example, a German company forming a joint venture with a Chinese company to do business in China may structure the joint venture contract so that the Chinese company owns 51 percent or more of the joint venture. Doing so qualifies the joint venture as a Chinese company and exempts it from Chinese laws that apply to foreign-owned businesses. However, cooperation cannot always protect against *policy risk* if a foreign government changes its laws and policies to directly affect the way foreign companies conduct business.

8-5 BECOMING AWARE OF CULTURAL DIFFERENCES

National culture is the set of shared values and beliefs that affects the perceptions, decisions, and behavior of the people from a particular country. The first step in dealing with culture is to recognize that there are meaningful differences. Professor Geert Hofstede spent twenty years studying cultural differences in fifty-three

different countries. His research shows that there are five consistent cultural dimensions across countries: power distance, individualism, masculinity, uncertainty avoidance, and short-term versus long-term orientation.[64]

Power distance is the extent to which people in a country accept that power is distributed unequally in society and organizations. In countries where power distance is weak, such as Denmark and Sweden, employees don't like their organization or their boss to have power over them or tell them what to do. They want to have a say in decisions that affect them. As Exhibit 8.8 shows, Russia and China, with scores of 95 and 80, respectively, are much stronger in power distance than Germany (35), the Netherlands (38), and the United States (40).

Individualism is the degree to which societies believe that individuals should be self-sufficient. In individualistic societies, employees put loyalty to themselves first and loyalty to their company and work group second. In Exhibit 8.8, the United States (91), the Netherlands (80), France (71), and Germany (67) are the strongest in individualism, while Indonesia (14), West Africa (20), and China (20) are the weakest.

Masculinity and *femininity* capture the difference between highly assertive and highly nurturing cultures. Masculine cultures emphasize assertiveness, competition, material success, and achievement; whereas feminine cultures emphasize the importance of relationships, modesty, caring for the weak, and quality of life. In Exhibit 8.8, Japan (95), Germany (66), and the United States (62) have the most masculine orientations, while the Netherlands (14) has the most feminine orientation.

The cultural difference of *uncertainty avoidance* is the degree to which people in a country are uncomfortable with unstructured, ambiguous, unpredictable situations. In countries with strong uncertainty avoidance, like Greece and Portugal, people tend to be aggressive and emotional and seek security rather than uncertainty. In Exhibit 8.8, Japan (92), France (86), West Africa (90), and Russia (90) are strongest in uncertainty avoidance, while Hong Kong (29) is the weakest.

The cultural dimension of *short-term/long-term orientation* addresses whether cultures are oriented to the present and seek immediate gratification or to the future and defer gratification. Not surprisingly, countries with short-term orientations are consumer-driven, whereas countries with long-term orientations are savings-driven. In Exhibit 8.8, China (118) and Hong Kong (96) have very strong long-term orientations, while Russia (10), West Africa (16), Indonesia (25), the United States (29), and Germany (31) have very strong short-term orientations. To generate a graphical comparison of two different countries' cultures,

Exhibit 8.8
Hofstede's Five Cultural Dimensions

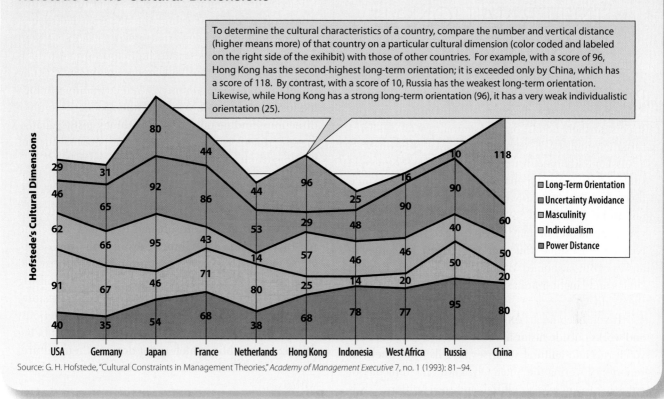

To determine the cultural characteristics of a country, compare the number and vertical distance (higher means more) of that country on a particular cultural dimension (color coded and labeled on the right side of the exihibit) with those of other countries. For example, with a score of 96, Hong Kong has the second-highest long-term orientation; it is exceeded only by China, which has a score of 118. By contrast, with a score of 10, Russia has the weakest long-term orientation. Likewise, while Hong Kong has a strong long-term orientation (96), it has a very weak individualistic orientation (25).

Source: G. H. Hofstede, "Cultural Constraints in Management Theories," *Academy of Management Executive* 7, no. 1 (1993): 81–94.

go to http://www.geert-hofstede.com/countries.html. Select a "country"; then select a "comparison country." A graph comparing the countries on each of Hofstede's five cultural differences will automatically be generated.

Cultural differences affect perceptions, understanding, and behavior. Recognizing cultural differences is critical to succeeding in global business. Nevertheless, as Hofstede pointed out, descriptions of cultural differences are based on averages—the average level of uncertainty avoidance in Portugal, the average level of power distance in Argentina, and so forth. Accordingly, says Hofstede, "If you are going to spend time with a Japanese colleague, you shouldn't assume that overall cultural statements about Japanese society automatically apply to this person."[65] Similarly, cultural beliefs may differ significantly from one part of a country to another.[66]

After becoming aware of cultural differences, the second step is deciding how to adapt your company to those differences. Unfortunately, studies investigating the effects of cultural differences on management practices point more to difficulties than to easy solutions. One problem is that different cultures will probably perceive management policies and practices

differently. For example, blue-collar workers in France and Argentina, all of whom performed the same factory jobs for the same multinational company, perceived its company-wide safety policy differently.[67] French workers perceived that safety wasn't very important to the company, but Argentine workers thought that it was. The fact that something as simple as a safety policy can be perceived differently across cultures shows just how difficult it can be to standardize management practices across different countries and cultures.

Another difficulty is that cultural values are changing, albeit slowly, in many parts of the world. The fall of communism in Eastern Europe and the former Soviet Union and the broad economic reforms in China have produced sweeping changes on two continents in the last two decades. Thanks to increased global trade resulting from free-trade agreements, major economic transformations are also under way in India, China, Central America, and South America. Consequently, when trying to adapt management practices to cultural differences, companies must ensure that they are not basing their adaptations on outdated and incorrect assumptions about a country's culture.

8-6 PREPARING FOR AN INTERNATIONAL ASSIGNMENT

During the 2014 Winter Olympics in Sochi, Russia, American reporters discovered that Russians on the streets, at their hotels, or in restaurants, would not return their smiles. When one reporter asked why this was, a Russian told him, "In Russia, only two types of people smile: idiots and rich people." In Russia, you only smile if you have a particularly good reason. And if you smile just to be friendly, like Americans, Russians will think you're insincere, or maybe a bit crazy. Also, Russians typically don't smile while working because, well, they're at work. But, at home, with friends and family, Russian smiles and laughter are as big and hearty as anyplace in the world.[68]

If you become an **expatriate,** someone who lives and works outside his or her native country, chances are you'll run into cultural surprises just like the American reporters covering the Sochi Olympics. The difficulty of adjusting to language, cultural, and social differences is the primary reason for expatriate failure in overseas assignments. For example, although there have recently been disagreements among researchers about these numbers, it is probably safe to say that 5 to 20 percent of American expatriates sent abroad by their companies will return to the United States before they have successfully completed their assignments.[69] Of those who do complete their international assignments, about one-third are judged by their companies to be no better than marginally effective.[70] Since even well-planned international assignments can cost as much as three to five times an employee's annual salary, failure in those assignments can be extraordinarily expensive.[71] Furthermore, while it is difficult to find reliable indicators, studies typically show that 8 to 25 percent of expatriate managers leave their companies following an international assignment.[72]

The chances for a successful international assignment can be increased through 8-6a language and cross-cultural training and 8-6b consideration of spouse, family, and dual-career issues.

Expatriate someone who lives and works outside his or her native country

8-6a Language and Cross-Cultural Training

Predeparture language and cross-cultural training can reduce the uncertainty that expatriates feel, the misunderstandings that take place between expatriates and natives, and the inappropriate behaviors that expatriates unknowingly commit when they travel to a foreign country. Indeed, simple things like using a phone, locating a public toilet, asking for directions, finding out how much things cost, exchanging greetings, or understanding what people want can become tremendously complex when expatriates don't know a foreign language or a country's customs and cultures. For example, Bing, the name of Microsoft's search engine, means "illness" or "pancake" in Mandarin Chinese, so Microsoft had to change the name to "Biying" from the Chinese expression "you qui bi ying," which means, more appropriately, "seek and you shall find." Likewise, in Indonesia, an oil rig supervisor yelled to a worker to take a boat to shore. While the boss thought he was sharing instructions, the Indonesian and his workers thought he was being criticized in public, which is not done in their culture. Outraged at this behavior, they chased the supervisor with axes.[73]

Expatriates who receive predeparture language and cross-cultural training make faster adjustments to foreign cultures and perform better on their international

Expatriates are still citizens of their native countries.

assignments.[74] Unfortunately, only a third of the managers who go on international assignments are offered any kind of predeparture training, and only half of those actually participate in the training![75] Suzanne Bernard, director of international mobility at Bombardier Aerospace in Canada, says, "We always offer cross-cultural training, but it's very seldom used by executives leaving in a rush at the last minute."[76] This is somewhat surprising given the failure rates for expatriates and the high cost of those failures. Furthermore, with the exception of some language courses, predeparture training is not particularly expensive or difficult to provide. Three methods can be used to prepare workers for international assignments: documentary training, cultural simulations, and field experiences.

Documentary training focuses on identifying specific critical differences between cultures. For example, when sixty workers at Axcelis Technologies in Beverly, Massachusetts, were preparing to do business in India, they learned that while Americans make eye contact and shake hands firmly when greeting others, Indians, as a sign of respect, do just the opposite, avoiding eye contact and shaking hands limply.[77]

After learning specific critical differences through documentary training, trainees can participate in *cultural simulations*, in which they practice adapting to cultural differences. EMC, a global provider of information storage solutions, uses cultural simulations to train its people. In its early days, EMC was largely based in the United States, but with research labs, offices, and customers on every continent, cross-cultural interactions are a daily part of business. EMC's cultural simulations use photos and audio and video clips to present real-world situations. EMC employees must decide what to do and then learn what happened as a result of their choices. Whether it's interacting with customers or dealing with EMC employees from other countries, at every step they have the opportunity to learn good and bad methods of responding to cultural differences. EMC requires its worldwide work force of 40,500 people to regularly use the cultural simulations. Louise Korver-Swanson, EMC's global head of executive development, said, "This is about ensuring that we're truly a global company. We need everyone in the organization to be tuned in."[78]

Finally, *field simulation* training, a technique made popular by the U.S. Peace Corps, places trainees in an ethnic neighborhood for three to four hours to talk to residents about cultural differences. For example, a U.S. electronics manufacturer prepared workers for assignments in South Korea by having trainees explore a nearby South Korean neighborhood and talk to shopkeepers and people on the street about South Korean politics, family orientation, and day-to-day living.

8-6b Spouse, Family, and Dual-Career Issues

Not all international assignments are difficult for expatriates and their families, but the evidence clearly shows that how well an expatriate's spouse and family adjust to the foreign culture is the most important factor in determining the success or failure of an international assignment.[79] Indeed, a Harvard Business Review study found that 32 percent of those offered international assignments turned them down because they did not want their families to have to relocate, while 28 percent turned them down "to protect their marriages."[80] Unfortunately, despite its importance, there has been little systematic research on what does and does not help expatriates' families successfully adapt. A number of companies, however, have found that adaptability screening and intercultural training for families can lead to more successful overseas adjustment.

Adaptability screening is used to assess how well managers and their families are likely to adjust to foreign cultures. For example, Prudential Relocation Management's international division has developed an "Overseas Assignment Inventory" (OAI) to assess a spouse and family's open-mindedness, respect for others' beliefs, sense of humor, and marital communication. The OAI was initially used to help the U.S. Peace Corps, the U.S. Navy, and the Canadian International Development Agency select people who could adapt well in foreign cultures. Success there led to its use in helping companies assess whether managers and their spouses were good candidates for international assignments.[81] Likewise, Pennsylvania-based AMP, a worldwide producer of electrical connectors, conducts extensive psychological screening of expatriates and their spouses when making international assignments. But adaptability screening does not just involve a company assessing an employee; it can also involve an employee screening international assignments for desirability. Since more employees are becoming aware of the costs of international assignments (spouses having to give up or change jobs, children having to change schools, everyone having to learn a new language), some companies are willing to pay for a preassignment trip so the employee and his or her spouse can investigate the country *before* accepting the international assignment.[82]

Only 40 percent of expatriates' families receive language and cross-cultural training, yet such training is just as important for the families of expatriates as for the expatriates themselves.[83] In fact, it may be more important because, unlike expatriates, whose professional jobs often shield them from the full force of a country's culture, spouses and children are fully immersed in foreign neighborhoods and schools. Households must be run, shopping must be done, and bills must be paid. Unfortunately, expatriate spouse Laurel Larsen, despite two hours of Chinese lessons a week, hasn't learned enough of the language to communicate with the family's babysitter. She has to phone her husband, who became fluent in Chinese in his teens, to translate. Expatriates' children must deal with different cultural beliefs and practices, too. While the Larsens' three daughters love the private, international school that they attend, they still have had difficulty adapting to, from their perspective, the incredible differences in inner China. Six-year-old Emma taped this poem to her

Farmers Against Free Trade

The great benefit of free trade is that it reduces or eliminates tariffs, lowering prices for consumers and increasing demand for products. There are, however, many who are opposed to free trade in any form. One of these groups is Japanese farmers. Japan is currently in negotiations with several other Pacific nations, like the United States, Canada, and Singapore, to craft a free trade agreement. Japanese farmers, however, fear that such an agreement will put them out of business and push them off their lands. Currently, the only way they are able to stay competitive is through the tariffs imposed on imported beef, rice, vegetables, etc. It is estimated that if free trade were to begin and the tariffs were removed, nearly all of the wheat, sugar, and beef production in Japan would end.

Source: A. Tacked and Y. Humber, "Japan Wants Free Trade. Its Farmers Don't," *Bloomberg Businessweek*, August 2, 2012, accessed June 10, 2013, http://www.businessweek.com/articles/2012-08-02/japan-wants-free-trade-dot-its-farmers-dont.

parents' nightstand: "Amarica is my place! I love Amarica. It was fun. It was so fun. I miss it."[84] In addition to helping families prepare for the cultural differences they will encounter, language and cross-cultural training can help reduce uncertainty about how to act and decrease misunderstandings between expatriates and their families and locals.

STUDY TOOLS 8

LOCATED AT THE BACK OF YOUR BOOK:

☐ Rip out and study the Chapter Review Card at the end of the book

LOG IN TO WWW.CENGAGEBRAIN.COM TO:

☐ Review Key Term Flashcards

☐ Complete Practice Quizzing (take up to four times without repeating the same quiz)

☐ Complete Games: Beat the Clock and Crossword Puzzle

☐ Complete Interactive Content: Graded Quiz, Media Quiz, and Fill-in-the-Blank Questions

☐ Watch Management Workplace Video on "Holden"

☐ Work Through the What Would You Do Case on Groupon Headquarters

9 Designing Adaptive Organizations

Robert Churchill/iStockphoto.com

LEARNING OUTCOMES

- **9-1** Describe the departmentalization approach to organizational structure.
- **9-2** Explain organizational authority.
- **9-3** Discuss the different methods for job design.
- **9-4** Explain the methods that companies are using to redesign internal organizational processes (i.e., intraorganizational processes).
- **9-5** Describe the methods that companies are using to redesign external organizational processes (i.e., interorganizational processes).

After you finish this chapter, go to **PAGE 199** for **STUDY TOOLS**

9-1 DEPARTMENTALI-ZATION

Organizational structure is the vertical and horizontal configuration of departments, authority, and jobs within a company. Organizational structure is concerned with questions such as "Who reports to whom?" and "Who does what?" and "Where is the work done?"

Thomson Reuters, which provides critical information for businesses and professionals, has restructured from divisions to four separate business units: Financial & Risk ($6.6 billion in annual revenues), which provides information to traders, investors, and marketplaces; Legal ($3.4 billion), which provides information to global businesses, law firms, governments, and universities; Tax & Accounting ($1.2 billion), which provides information to tax professionals, companies, and governments; and Intellectual Property & Science ($982 million), which provides information to life sciences companies, scientific and scholarly researchers, and those in need of intellectual property solutions. The company's former CEO Thomas Glocer said that these changes will "streamline our organization and enable us to work better across business units to achieve growth and capture operating efficiencies from scale. The professional markets in which we operate are marked by increasing collaboration among

Organizational structure the vertical and horizontal configuration of departments, authority, and jobs within a company

Organizational process the collection of activities that transform inputs into outputs that customers value

specialists and Thomson Reuters must operate with the speed and agility needed to serve these demanding professionals."[1]

You can see Thomson Reuters's organizational structure in Exhibit 9.1. In the first half of the chapter, you will learn about the traditional vertical and horizontal approaches to organizational structure, including departmentalization, organizational authority, and job design.

An **organizational process** is the collection of activities that transform inputs into outputs that customers value.[2] Organizational process asks "How do things get done?" For example, Microsoft uses basic internal and external processes, shown in Exhibit 9.2, to write computer software. The process starts when Microsoft gets feedback from customers through Internet newsgroups, email, phone calls, or letters. This information helps Microsoft understand customers' needs and problems and identify important software issues and needed changes and functions. Microsoft then rewrites the software, testing it internally at the company and then externally through its beta testing process, in which customers who volunteer or are selected by Microsoft give the company extensive feedback. The feedback is then used to make improvements to the software. Indeed, Microsoft made Windows 8 available for a public beta test before releasing it for sale. Consumers and businesses downloaded the beta, installed it on their computers, and then posted the bugs or errors they found on Microsoft's forums. Microsoft hoped the beta test for Windows 8 went as well as the beta test for Windows 7, during which users found and reported 2,000 bugs, all of which Microsoft corrected before releasing the software.[3] The beta testing process may take as long as a year and involve thousands of

Exhibit 9.1
Thomson Reuters's Organizational Chart

Thomson Reuters CEO

VP Financial & Risk
- Governance, Risk & Compliance
- Marketplaces
- Investors
- Trading

VP Legal
- Global Businesses
- Corporate, Government & Academic
- US Law Firm Solutions

VP Tax & Accounting
- Government
- Knowledge Solutions
- Corporate
- Professional

VP IP & Science
- Scientific & Scholarly Research
- Life Sciences
- Intellectual Property Solutions

The organizational chart displays Thomson Reuters's horizontal and vertical dimensions.
Source: "About Us," Thompson Reuters, accessed October 27, 2013, http://thomsonreuters.com/about-us/.

Exhibit 9.2
Process View of Microsoft's Organization

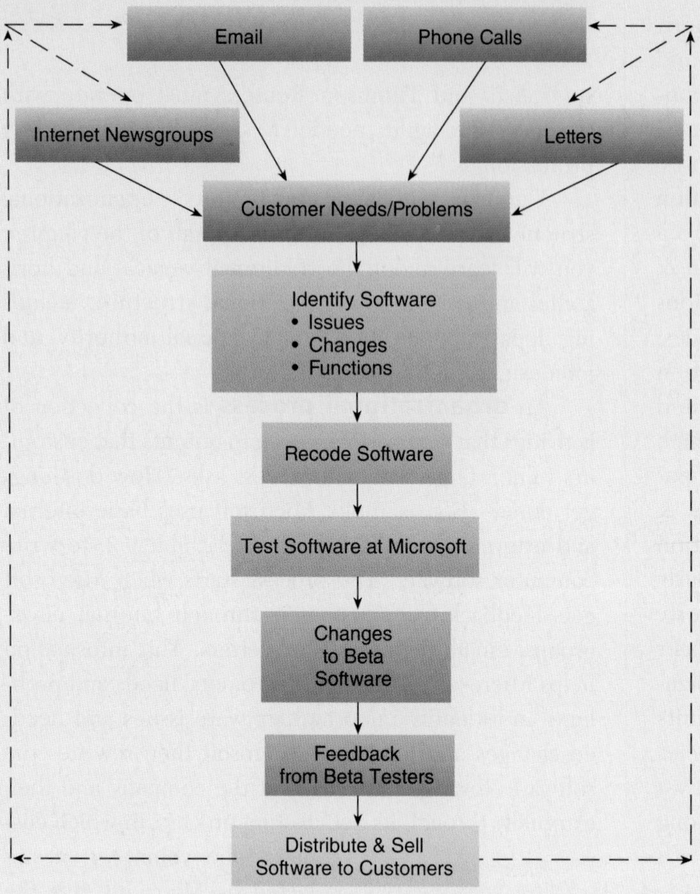

```
Email          Phone Calls

Internet Newsgroups              Letters

        Customer Needs/Problems

           Identify Software
             • Issues
             • Changes
             • Functions

           Recode Software

        Test Software at Microsoft

             Changes
             to Beta
             Software

            Feedback
         from Beta Testers

          Distribute & Sell
        Software to Customers
```

their internal organizational processes. The chapter ends with a discussion about the ways in which companies are redesigning their external processes, that is, how they are changing to improve their interactions with those outside the company. In that discussion, you will explore the basics of modular and virtual organizations.

Traditionally, organizational structures have been based on some form of departmentalization. **Departmentalization** is a method of subdividing work and workers into separate organizational units that take responsibility for completing particular tasks.[4] Bayer, a Germany-based company, has separate departments or divisions for health care, crop science, material science, and services.[5]

Traditionally, organizational structures have been created by departmentalizing work according to five methods: **9-1a functional, 9-1b product, 9-1c customer, 9-1d geographic, and 9-1e matrix.**

9-1a Functional Departmentalization

The most common organizational structure is functional departmentalization. Companies tend to use this structure when they are small or just starting out. **Functional departmentalization** organizes work and workers into separate units responsible for particular business functions or areas of expertise. A common functional structure might have individuals organized into accounting, sales, marketing, production, and human resources departments.

Not all functionally departmentalized companies have the same functions. The insurance company and the advertising agency shown in Exhibit 9.3 both have sales, accounting, human resources, and information systems departments, as indicated by the pale orange boxes. The purple and green boxes indicate the functions that are different. As would be expected, the insurance company has separate departments for life, auto, home, and health insurance. The advertising agency has departments for artwork, creative work, print advertising, and Internet advertising. So the functional departments in a company that uses functional structure depend, in part, on the business or industry a company is in.

Functional departmentalization has some advantages. First, it allows work to be done by highly qualified

knowledgeable people. After final corrections are made to the software, the company distributes and sells it to customers. They start the process again by giving Microsoft more feedback.

This process view of Microsoft, which focuses on how things get done, is very different from the hierarchical view of Thomson Reuters, which focuses on accountability, responsibility, and positions within the chain of command. In the second half of the chapter, you will learn how companies use reengineering and empowerment to redesign

Departmentalization subdividing work and workers into separate organizational units responsible for completing particular tasks

Functional departmentalization organizing work and workers into separate units responsible for particular business functions or areas of expertise

Exhibit 9.3
Functional Departmentalization

Insurance Company

Sales — Information Systems

Accounting — Human Resources

Life Insurance — Auto Insurance

Home Insurance — Health Insurance

Advertising Agency

Sales — Information Systems

Accounting — Human Resources

Art Department — Print Advertising

Creative Department — Internet Advertising

specialists. While the accountants in the accounting department take responsibility for producing accurate revenue and expense figures, the engineers in research and development can focus their efforts on designing a product that is reliable and simple to manufacture. Second, it lowers costs by reducing duplication. When the engineers in research and development come up with a fantastic new product, they don't have to worry about creating an aggressive advertising campaign to sell it. That task belongs to the advertising experts and sales representatives in marketing. Third, with everyone in the same department having similar work experience or training, communication and coordination are less problematic for departmental managers.

At the same time, functional departmentalization has a number of disadvantages. To start, cross-department coordination can be difficult. Managers and employees are often more interested in doing what's right for their function than in doing what's right for the entire organization. A good example is the traditional conflict between marketing and manufacturing. Marketing typically

pushes for spending more money to make more products with more capabilities to meet customer needs. By contrast, manufacturing pushes for fewer products with simpler designs so that manufacturing facilities can ship finished products on time and keep costs within expense budgets. As companies grow, functional departmentalization may also lead to slower decision making and produce managers and workers with narrow experience and expertise.

9-1b Product Departmentalization

Product departmentalization organizes work and workers into separate units responsible for producing particular products or services. Exhibit 9.4 shows the product departmentalization structure used by United Technologies Corporation (UTC), which is organized along four different areas with five major product lines: UTC Climate, Controls & Security (heating, ventilating, and air-conditioning; fire safety; and security products and services), UTC Propulsion and Aerospace Systems consisting of UTC Aerospace (aircraft power, controls and sensing systems) and Pratt & Whitney (commercial and military jet aircraft engines), Otis (design, manufacture, installation, maintenance, and servicing of elevators and escalators), and Sikorsky (military and commercial helicopters).[6]

One of the advantages of product departmentalization is that, like functional departmentalization, it allows managers and workers to specialize in one area of expertise. Unlike the narrow expertise and experiences in functional departmentalization, however, managers and workers develop a broader set of experiences and expertise related to an entire product line. Likewise, product departmentalization makes it easier for top managers to assess work-unit performance. Because of the clear separation of their five different product divisions, UTC's top managers can easily compare the performance of the Otis elevators division and the Pratt & Whitney aircraft engines division. In 2013, Pratt & Whitney had a $2 billion advantage over Otis in net sales ($14.5 billion versus $12.5 billion). However, Otis had a profit of $2.6 billion (a 20.8 percent margin) compared to a profit of $1.9 billion (13.1 percent margin) for Pratt & Whitney.[7]

Finally, decision making should be faster because managers and workers are responsible for the entire product line rather than for separate functional departments;

Product departmentalization organizing work and workers into separate units responsible for producing particular products or services

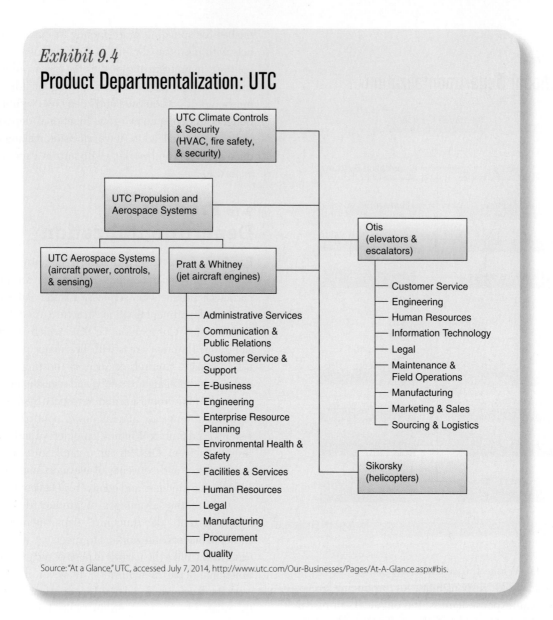

Exhibit 9.4
Product Departmentalization: UTC

UTC Climate Controls & Security (HVAC, fire safety, & security)

UTC Propulsion and Aerospace Systems

UTC Aerospace Systems (aircraft power, controls, & sensing)

Pratt & Whitney (jet aircraft engines)
- Administrative Services
- Communication & Public Relations
- Customer Service & Support
- E-Business
- Engineering
- Enterprise Resource Planning
- Environmental Health & Safety
- Facilities & Services
- Human Resources
- Legal
- Manufacturing
- Procurement
- Quality

Otis (elevators & escalators)
- Customer Service
- Engineering
- Human Resources
- Information Technology
- Legal
- Maintenance & Field Operations
- Manufacturing
- Marketing & Sales
- Sourcing & Logistics

Sikorsky (helicopters)

Source: "At a Glance," UTC, accessed July 7, 2014, http://www.utc.com/Our-Businesses/Pages/At-A-Glance.aspx#bis.

in other words, there are fewer conflicts compared to functional departmentalization.

The primary disadvantage of product departmentalization is duplication. You can see in Exhibit 9.4 that UTC's Otis and Pratt & Whitney divisions both have customer service, engineering, human resources, legal, manufacturing, and procurement (similar to sourcing and logistics) departments. Duplication like this often results in higher costs. If UTC were instead organized by function, one lawyer could handle matters related to both elevators and aircraft engines rather than working on only one or the other.

A second disadvantage is the challenge of coordinating across the different product departments. UTC would probably have difficulty standardizing its policies and procedures in product departments as different as the Carrier (heating, ventilating, and air-conditioning) and Sikorsky (military and commercial helicopters) divisions.

9-1c Customer Departmentalization

Customer departmentalization organizes work and workers into separate units responsible for particular kinds of customers. For example, as Exhibit 9.5 shows, Swisscom AG, Switzerland's leading telecommunications provider, is organized into departments by type of customer: residential customers (fixed line and voice, mobile and voice, broadband Internet, and digital TV), small- and medium-sized businesses (fixed line and voice, mobile line and voice, Internet and data

Customer departmentalization organizing work and workers into separate units responsible for particular kinds of customers

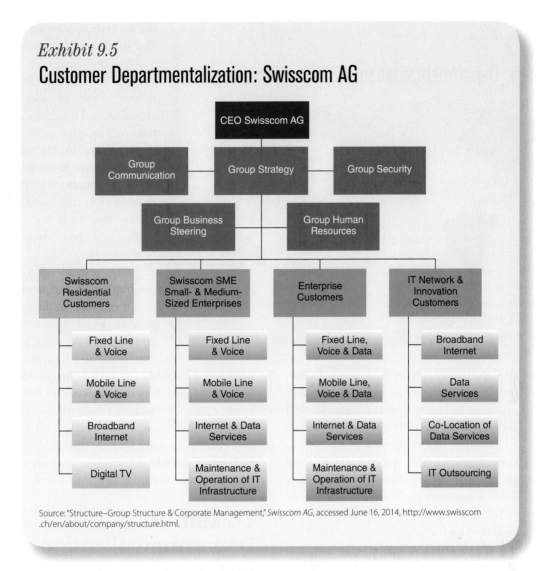

Exhibit 9.5
Customer Departmentalization: Swisscom AG

```
                        CEO Swisscom AG

    Group              Group Strategy            Group
Communication                                  Security

            Group Business        Group Human
              Steering             Resources

  Swisscom          Swisscom SME         Enterprise         IT Network &
  Residential       Small- & Medium-     Customers          Innovation
  Customers         Sized Enterprises                       Customers

  Fixed Line        Fixed Line          Fixed Line,        Broadband
  & Voice           & Voice             Voice & Data       Internet

  Mobile Line       Mobile Line         Mobile Line,       Data
  & Voice           & Voice             Voice & Data       Services

  Broadband         Internet & Data     Internet & Data    Co-Location of
  Internet          Services            Services           Data Services

  Digital TV        Maintenance &       Maintenance &      IT Outsourcing
                    Operation of IT     Operation of IT
                    Infrastructure      Infrastructure
```

Source: "Structure–Group Structure & Corporate Management," *Swisscom AG*, accessed June 16, 2014, http://www.swisscom.ch/en/about/company/structure.html.

services, and maintenance and operation of IT infrastructure), enterprise customers (fixed line, voice and data; mobile line and tablets, voice and data; Internet and data services; and maintenance and operation of IT infrastructure), and IT network and innovation (broadband Internet, data services, co-location of data services, and storage to wholesale customers).[8]

The primary advantage of customer departmentalization is that it focuses the organization on customer needs rather than on products or business functions. Furthermore, creating separate departments to serve specific kinds of customers allows companies to specialize and adapt their products and services to customer needs and problems. The primary disadvantage of customer departmentalization is that, like product departmentalization, it leads to duplication of resources. This is why Swisscom AG also has five "group" functions—communication, strategy, security, business steering, and human resources—that support each of its four customer departments, and avoids the disadvantage of

duplication common to customer departmentalization structures. It can be difficult to achieve coordination across different customer departments, as is also the case with product departmentalization. Finally, the emphasis on meeting customers' needs may lead workers to make decisions that please customers but hurt the business.

9-1d Geographic Departmentalization

Geographic departmentalization organizes work and workers into separate units responsible for doing business in particular geographic areas. Exhibit 9.6 shows

Geographic departmentalization organizing work and workers into separate units responsible for doing business in particular geographic areas

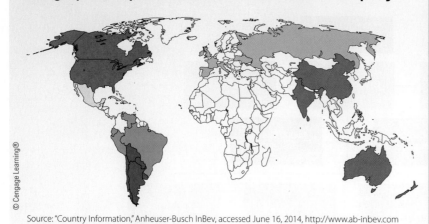

Exhibit 9.6
Geographic Departmentalization: AB InBev Company

Source: "Country Information," Anheuser-Busch InBev, accessed June 16, 2014, http://www.ab-inbev.com
/go/about_abinbev/country_information.

the geographic departmentalization used by **AB InBev,** the largest beer brewer in the world. AB InBev has 151 brewing facilities in twenty-four countries, 150,000 employees, and annual revenue of $43.2 billion.[9] As shown in Exhibit 9.6, AB InBev has six regional groups: North America, Mexico, Latin America North, Latin America South, Europe, and Asia Pacific. Each of these regions would be a sizable company by itself. The smallest region, Mexico, for instance, sold 22.4 million hectoliters of beverages for annual revenue of $2.8 billion.

The primary advantage of geographic departmentalization is that it helps companies respond to the demands of different markets. This can be especially important when the company sells in different countries. For example, while AB InBev has three brands sold worldwide (Budweiser, Stella Artois, and Corona), and three sold in multiple countries (Beck's, Hoegaarden, and Leffe), most of its brands are local. You'll find the Antarctica and Bohemia brands in Brazil, the Belle-Vue and Jupiler brands in Belgium, and

Matrix departmentalization a hybrid organizational structure in which two or more forms of departmentalization, most often product and functional, are used together

the Sibirskaya Korona and Tolstiak brands in Russia.[10]

Another advantage is that geographic departmentalization can reduce costs by locating unique organizational resources closer to customers. For instance, it is cheaper in the long run for AB InBev to build bottling plants in each region than to, for example, transport beer to Belgium, where it has four beverage plants, after it has been brewed and bottled in Russia, where it has eight beverage plants.[11]

The primary disadvantage of geographic departmentalization is that it can lead to duplication of resources. For example, while it may be necessary to adapt products and marketing to different geographic locations, it's doubtful that AB InBev needs significantly different inventory tracking systems from location to location. Also, even more than with the other forms of departmentalization, it can be difficult to coordinate departments that are literally thousands of miles from each other and whose managers have very limited contact with each other.

9-1e Matrix Departmentalization

Matrix departmentalization is a hybrid structure in which two or more forms of departmentalization are used together. The most common matrix combines the product and functional forms of departmentalization, but other forms may also be used. Exhibit 9.7 shows the matrix structure used by Procter & Gamble, which has 121,000 employees working in seventy different countries.[12] Across the top of Exhibit 9.7, you can see that the company uses a product structure where it groups its billion-dollar brands into four global business units: global beauty (beauty care, retail hair color, salon professional, and prestige); global baby, feminine, and family care (baby care, family care, and feminine care); global health and grooming (shave care, Braun, oral care, health care,

Exhibit 9.7
Matrix Departmentalization: Procter & Gamble

	Global Business Units														
	Global Beauty			Global Baby, Feminine, & Family Care			Global Health & Grooming					Global Fabric & Home Care		
	Beauty Care	Retail Hair Color	Salon Professional & Prestige	Baby Care	Family Care	Feminine Care	Braun	Shave Care	Oral Care	Health Care	Pet Care	Fabric Care	Home Care	Power
Market Development Organizations	Cover Girl	Nice 'n Easy	Wella	Pampers	Bounty	Tampax	Braun	Gillette	Crest	Vicks	Iams	Bounce	Swiffer	Duracel
Global Business Services														
Corporate Functions														

Sources: Business Wire, "Procter & Gamble Announces Organization Changes," *Motley Fool*, June 5, 2013, accessed July 7, 2014, http://www.fool.com/investing/businesswire/2013/06/05/procter-gamble-announces-organization-changes.aspx; "2013 Annual Report, P&G," Procter & Gamble, accessed July 7, 2014, http://www.pg.com/en_US/downloads/investors/annual_reports/2013/2013_AnnualReport.pdf.

Matrix structures are notorious for confusion and conflict between project bosses in different parts of the matrix.

jfmdesign/iStockphoto.com

and pet care); and global fabric and home care (fabric care, home care, and power). Global business units are responsible for product initiatives or upgrades, which are typically launched simultaneously with a worldwide marketing campaign. The left side of the figure, however, shows that the company is also using a functional structure based on three functions: market development, which makes sure that a product is adapted to and sells well within a particular region of the world (market development regions include North America, Asia/India/Australia, Northeast Asia, Greater China, Central-Eastern Europe/Middle East Africa, Western Europe, and Latin America); global business services, which enable the company to operate efficiently, work effectively with business partners, and increase employee productivity; and corporate functions, which provide global business units with the functional business assistance (i.e., finance, accounting, human resources, information technology, etc.) they need.[13]

The boxes in the figure represent the matrix structure created by the combination of the product and functional structures. For example, P&G's Gillette Group (Gillette is global brand for men's grooming products within the Shave Care segment of the Global Health & Grooming unit) would work with market development to adapt and sell Gillette products worldwide, use

global business services to work with suppliers and keep costs down, and then rely on corporate functions for assistance in hiring employees and billing customers and paying suppliers. Similar matrix combinations are shown for Cover Girl, Nice 'n Easy, Wella, Pampers, Bounty, Tampax, Braun, Crest, Vicks, Iams, Bounce, Swiffer, and Duracell within each of the segments of P&G's four global business units.

Several things distinguish matrix departmentalization from the other traditional forms of departmentalization.[14] First, most employees report to two bosses, one from each core part of the matrix. For example, in Exhibit 9.7 a manager on the Pampers team responsible for marketing would report to a boss in the baby care segment of the Global Baby, Feminine, & Family global business unit as well as to a manager in the market development function. Second, by virtue of their hybrid design, matrix structures lead to much more cross-functional interaction than other forms of departmentalization. In fact, while matrix workers are typically members of only one functional department (based on their work experience and expertise), they are also commonly members of several ongoing project, product, or customer groups. Third, because of the high level of cross-functional interaction, matrix departmentalization requires significant coordination between managers in the different parts of the matrix. In particular, managers have the complex job of tracking and managing the multiple demands (project, product, customer, or functional) on employees' time.

The primary advantage of matrix departmentalization is that it allows companies to manage in an efficient manner large, complex tasks like researching, developing, and marketing pharmaceuticals or carrying out complex global businesses. Efficiency comes from avoiding duplication. For example, rather than having an entire marketing function for each project, the company simply assigns and reassigns workers from the marketing department (or market development at P&G) as they are needed at various stages of product completion. More specifically, an employee may simultaneously be part of five different ongoing projects but may be actively completing work on only a few projects at a time. Another advantage is the pool of resources available to carry out large, complex tasks. Because of the ability to quickly pull in expert help from all the functional areas of the company, matrix project managers have a much more diverse set of expertise and experience at their disposal than managers in the other forms of departmentalization.

The primary disadvantage of matrix departmentalization is the high level of coordination required to manage the complexity involved in running large, ongoing projects at various levels of completion. Matrix structures are notorious for confusion and conflict between project bosses in different parts of the matrix. Disagreements or misunderstandings about schedules, budgets, available resources, and the availability of employees with particular functional expertise are common in matrix structures. Because of these problems, many matrix structures evolve from a **simple matrix,** in which managers in different parts of the matrix negotiate conflicts and resources directly, to a **complex matrix,** in which specialized matrix managers and departments are added to the organizational structure. In a complex matrix, managers from different parts of the matrix might report to the same matrix manager, who helps them sort out conflicts and problems.

Simple matrix a form of matrix departmentalization in which managers in different parts of the matrix negotiate conflicts and resources

Complex matrix a form of matrix departmentalization in which managers in different parts of the matrix report to matrix managers, who help them sort out conflicts and problems

Authority the right to give commands, take action, and make decisions to achieve organizational objectives

Chain of command the vertical line of authority that clarifies who reports to whom throughout the organization

9-2 ORGANIZATIONAL AUTHORITY

The second part of traditional organizational structures is authority. **Authority** is the right to give commands, take action, and make decisions to achieve organizational objectives.[15]

*Traditionally, organizational authority has been characterized by the following dimensions: **9-2a chain of command, 9-2b line versus staff authority, 9-2c delegation of authority,** and **9-2d degree of centralization.***

9-2a Chain of Command

Consider again Thomson Reuters's organizational structure. A manager in any of the corporation's divisions ultimately reports to the head of that division. That division head, in turn, reports to the corporation's Kazuo Hirai, who took over as CEO when Howard Stringer retired. This line, which vertically connects every job in the company to higher levels of management, represents the chain of command. The **chain of command** is the vertical line of authority that clarifies who reports to whom throughout the organization. People higher in the chain of command have the right, *if they so choose*, to give commands, take action, and make decisions concerning activities occurring anywhere below them in the chain. In the following discussion about delegation and decentralization, you will learn that managers don't always choose to exercise their authority directly.[16]

One of the key assumptions underlying the chain of command is **unity of command,** which means that workers should report to just one boss.[17] In practical terms, this means that only one person can be in charge at a time. Matrix organizations, in which employees have two bosses, automatically violate this principle. This is one of the primary reasons that matrix organizations are difficult to manage. Unity of command serves an important purpose: to prevent the confusion that might arise when an employee receives conflicting commands from two different bosses. From 2010 to May 2014, SAP, a global leader in enterprise software, had co-CEOs. Aware of the problems associated with violations of unity of command, co-CEO Bill McDermott worked at SAP's headquarters in Philadelphia and handled sales, while co-CEO Jim Snabe worked in SAP offices in Denmark and handled development. Despite these steps, SAP decided to return to just one CEO, Bill McDermott, as of June 2014 to achieve quicker decision making.[18]

9-2b Line versus Staff Authority

A second dimension of authority is the distinction between line and staff authority. **Line authority** is the right to command immediate subordinates in the chain of command. For example, Thomson Reuters CEO James C. Smith has line authority over the president of Thomson Reuters's Financial & Risk Information division. Smith can issue orders to that division president and expect them to be carried out. In turn, the president of the Financial & Risk Information division can issue orders to his subordinates, who run the trading, investors, marketplaces, and governance, risk, and compliance divisions, and expect them to be carried out. By contrast, **staff authority** is the right to advise but not command others who are not subordinates in the chain of command. For example, a manager in human resources at Thomson Reuters might advise the manager in charge of Thomson Reuters's Tax & Accounting group on a hiring decision but cannot order him or her to hire a certain applicant.

The terms *line* and *staff* are also used to describe different functions within the organization. A **line function** is an activity that contributes directly to creating or selling the company's products. So, for example, activities that take place within the manufacturing and marketing departments would be considered line functions. A **staff function,** such as accounting, human resources, or legal services, does not contribute directly to creating or selling the company's products but instead supports line activities. For example, marketing managers might consult with the legal staff to make sure the wording of a particular advertisement is legal.

9-2c Delegation of Authority

Managers can exercise their authority directly by completing tasks themselves, or they can choose to pass on some of their authority to subordinates. **Delegation of authority** is the assignment of direct authority and responsibility to a subordinate to complete tasks for which the manager is normally responsible.

When a manager delegates work, three transfers occur, as illustrated in Exhibit 9.8. First, the manager transfers full responsibility for the assignment to the subordinate. At Apple, when you've been delegated to a certain task, you become the DRI, or the "directly responsible individual." As a former Apple employee explains, "Any effective meeting at Apple will have an action list. Next to each action item will be the DRI," who of course, is responsible for completing that delegated responsibility. Furthermore, when you're trying to figure out who to contact to get something done in Apple's corporate structure, people simply ask, "Who's the DRI on that?"[19]

Many managers, however, find giving up full responsibility somewhat difficult. Helen Gayle, CEO of CARE U.S.A., a non-profit dedicated to reducing poverty, admits that early in her career she tried to do too much by herself without delegating. She says, "For me, it wasn't a question of not being willing to delegate, it was switching from being on the technical side as an individual contribuor—where the way you prove yourself is to be smart—to focusing on how you actually make a team work and bring out others' contributions."[20] One reason it is difficult for some managers to delegate is that they often fear that the task won't be done as well

Unity of command a management principle that workers should report to just one boss

Line authority the right to command immediate subordinates in the chain of command

Staff authority the right to advise, but not command, others who are not subordinates in the chain of command

Line function an activity that contributes directly to creating or selling the company's products

Staff function an activity that does not contribute directly to creating or selling the company's products but instead supports line activities

Delegation of authority the assignment of direct authority and responsibility to a subordinate to complete tasks for which the manager is normally responsible

Exhibit 9.8
Delegation: Responsibility, Authority, and Accountability

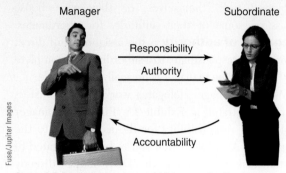

Manager   Subordinate

Responsibility →

Authority →

← Accountability

Source: C. D. Pringle, D. F. Jennings, and J. G. Longenecker, *Managing Organizations: Functions and Behaviors.*

as if they did it themselves. However, one CEO says, "If you can delegate a task to somebody who can do it 75 percent to 80 percent as well as you can today, you delegate it immediately." Why? Many tasks don't need to be done perfectly; they just need to be *done*. And delegating tasks that someone else can do frees managers to assume other important responsibilities. Delegating authority can generate a related problem: micromanaging. Sometimes managers delegate only to interfere later with how the employee is performing the task. But delegating full responsibility means that the employee—not the manager—is now completely responsible for task completion. Good managers need to trust their subordinates to do the job.

The second transfer that occurs with delegation is that the manager gives the subordinate full authority over the budget, resources, and personnel needed to do the job. To do the job effectively, subordinates must have the same tools and information at their disposal that managers had when they were responsible for the same task. In other words, for delegation to work, delegated authority must be commensurate with delegated responsibility.

The third transfer that occurs with delegation is the transfer of accountability. The subordinate now has the

authority and responsibility to do the job and, in return, is accountable for getting the job done. In other words, managers delegate their managerial authority and responsibility to subordinates in exchange for results.

9-2d Degree of Centralization

If you've ever called a company's toll-free number with a complaint or a special request and been told by the customer-service representative, "I'll have to ask my manager" or "I'm not authorized to do that," you know that centralization of authority exists in that company. **Centralization of authority** is the location of most authority at the upper levels of the organization. In a centralized organization, managers make most decisions, even the relatively small ones. That's why the customer-service representative you called couldn't make a decision without first asking the manager.

If you are lucky, however, you may have talked to a customer-service representative at another company who said, "I can take care of that for you right now." In other words, the person was able to handle your problem without any input from or consultation with company management. **Decentralization** is the location of a significant amount of authority in the lower levels of the organization. An organization is decentralized if it has a high degree of delegation at all levels. In a decentralized organization, workers closest to problems are authorized to make the decisions necessary to solve the problems on their own.

Decentralization has a number of advantages. It develops employee capabilities throughout the company and leads to faster decision making and more satisfied customers and employees. Furthermore, a study of 1,000 large companies found that companies with a high degree of decentralization outperformed those with a low degree of decentralization in terms of return on

Centralization of authority the location of most authority at the upper levels of the organization

Decentralization the location of a significant amount of authority in the lower levels of the organization

assets (6.9 percent versus 4.7 percent), return on investment (14.6 percent versus 9.0 percent), return on equity (22.8 percent versus 16.6 percent), and return on sales (10.3 percent versus 6.3 percent). Surprisingly, the same study found that few large companies actually are decentralized. Specifically, only 31 percent of employees in these 1,000 companies were responsible for recommending improvements to management. Overall, just 10 percent of employees received the training and information needed to support a truly decentralized approach to management.[21]

With results like these, the key question is no longer *whether* companies should decentralize, but *where* they should decentralize. One rule of thumb is to stay centralized where standardization is important and to decentralize where standardization is unimportant. **Standardization** is solving problems by consistently applying the same rules, procedures, and processes. Toyota became the largest auto manufacturer in the world by producing highly reliable cars at competitive costs. But as the company grew, it significantly increased the number of kinds of parts used in its cars, for example, using 100 different radiators in the cars it made around the world. Using that many varieties for the same part not only increased costs, it decreased quality, which then reduced Toyota sales. Toyota's leadership addressed this issue by using standardization to significantly reduce the variety of kinds of basic parts. For example, it now uses just 21 different kinds of radiators in its cars rather than 100, as before. This leads to greater volume for each part and thus less cost; higher quality because Toyota awarded increased production to its best suppliers; and fewer suppliers to manage overall, therefore reducing complexity. Standardization has proved so successful that Takeshi Uchiyamada, Toyota's executive vice president of research and development, said, "We won't feel we've succeeded until we raise the use of standardized parts to about 50 percent among similar-size vehicles in our lineup."[22]

9-3 JOB DESIGN

Could you stand to do the same simple tasks an average of 50 times per hour, 400 times per day, 2,000 times per week, 8,000 times per month? Few can. Fast-food workers rarely stay on the job more than six months. Indeed, McDonald's and other fast-food restaurants have well over 100 percent employee turnover each year.[23]

1. "Welcome to McDonald's. May I have your order please?"

2. Listen to the order. Repeat it for accuracy. State the total cost. "Please drive to the second window."

3. Take the money. Make change.

4. Give customers drinks, straws, and napkins.

5. Give customers food.

6. "Thank you for coming to McDonald's."

In this section, you will learn about **job design**— the number, kind, and variety of tasks that individual workers perform in doing their jobs.

You will learn **9-3a why companies continue to use specialized jobs like the McDonald's drive-through job** *and* **9-3b how job rotation, job enlargement, job enrichment,** *and* **9-3c the job characteristics model are being used to overcome the problems associated with job specialization.**

9-3a Job Specialization

Job specialization occurs when a job is composed of a small part of a larger task or process. Specialized jobs are characterized by simple, easy-to-learn steps, low variety, and high repetition, like the McDonald's drive-through window job just described. One of the clear disadvantages of specialized jobs is that, being so easy to learn, they quickly become boring. This, in turn, can lead to low job satisfaction and high absenteeism and employee turnover, all of which are very costly to organizations.

Why, then, do companies continue to create and use specialized jobs? The primary reason is that specialized jobs are very economical. As we learned from Frederick W. Taylor and Frank and Lillian Gilbreth in Chapter 2, once a job has been specialized, it takes little time to learn and master. Consequently, when experienced workers quit or are absent, the company can replace them with new employees and lose little productivity. For example, next time you're at McDonald's, notice the pictures of the food on the cash registers. These pictures make it easy for McDonald's trainees to quickly learn to take orders. Likewise, to simplify and speed operations, the drink dispensers behind the counter are set to automatically fill drink cups. Put a medium cup below the

Standardization solving problems by consistently applying the same rules, procedures, and processes

Job design the number, kind, and variety of tasks that individual workers perform in doing their jobs

Job specialization a job composed of a small part of a larger task or process

dispenser. Punch the medium drink button. The soft-drink machine then fills the cup to within a half-inch of the top, while the worker goes to get your fries. At McDonald's, every task has been simplified in this way. Because the work is designed to be simple, wages can remain low, since it isn't necessary to pay high salaries to attract highly experienced, educated, or trained workers.

9-3b Job Rotation, Enlargement, and Enrichment

Because of the efficiency of specialized jobs, companies are often reluctant to eliminate them. Consequently, job redesign efforts have focused on modifying jobs to keep the benefits of specialized jobs while reducing their obvious costs and disadvantages. Three methods—job rotation, job enlargement, and job enrichment—have been used to try to improve specialized jobs.[24]

Job rotation attempts to overcome the disadvantages of job specialization by periodically moving workers from one specialized job to another to give them more variety and the opportunity to use different skills. For example, an office receptionist who does nothing but answer phones could be systematically rotated to a different job, such as typing, filing, or data entry, every day or two. Likewise, the "mirror attacher" in an automobile plant might attach mirrors in the first half of the work shift and then install bumpers during the second half. Because employees simply switch from one specialized job to another, job rotation allows companies to retain the economic benefits of specialized work. At the same time, the greater variety of tasks makes the work less boring and more satisfying for workers.

Another way to counter the disadvantages of specialization is to enlarge the job. **Job enlargement** increases the number of different tasks that a worker

performs within one particular job. Instead of being assigned just one task, workers with enlarged jobs are given several tasks to perform. For example, an enlarged "mirror attacher" job might include attaching the mirror, checking to see that the mirror's power adjustment controls work, and then cleaning the mirror's surface. Though job enlargement increases variety, many workers report feeling more stress when their jobs are enlarged. Consequently, many workers view enlarged jobs as simply more work, especially if they are not given additional time to complete the additional tasks.

Job enrichment attempts to overcome the deficiencies in specialized work by increasing the number of tasks *and* by giving workers the authority and control to make meaningful decisions about their work.[25]

9-3c Job Characteristics Model

In contrast to job rotation, job enlargement, and job enrichment, which focus on providing variety in job tasks, the **job characteristics model (JCM)** is an approach to job redesign that seeks to formulate jobs in ways that motivate workers and lead to positive work outcomes.[26]

As shown in Exhibit 9.9, the primary goal of the model is to create jobs that result in positive personal and work outcomes, such as internal work motivation, satisfaction with one's job, and work effectiveness. Of these, the central concern of the JCM is internal motivation. **Internal motivation** is motivation that comes from the job itself rather than from outside rewards such as a raise or praise from the boss. If workers feel that performing the job well is itself rewarding, then the job has internal motivation. Statements such as "I get a nice sense of accomplishment" or "I feel good

Job rotation periodically moving workers from one specialized job to another to give them more variety and the opportunity to use different skills

Job enlargement increasing the number of different tasks that a worker performs within one particular job

Job enrichment increasing the number of tasks in a particular job and giving workers the authority and control to make meaningful decisions about their work

Job characteristics model (JCM) an approach to job redesign that seeks to formulate jobs in ways that motivate workers and lead to positive work outcomes

Internal motivation motivation that comes from the job itself rather than from outside rewards

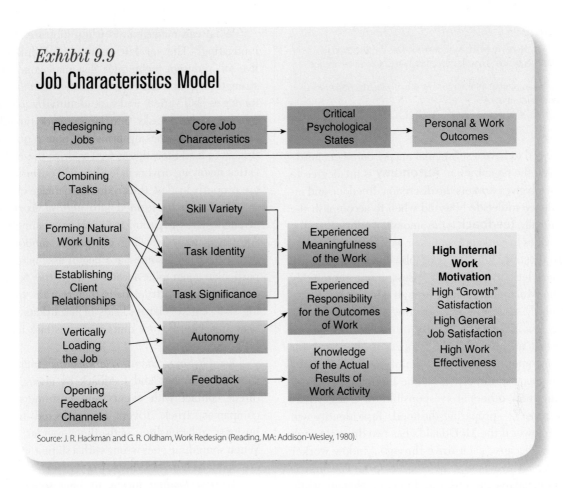

Exhibit 9.9
Job Characteristics Model

Source: J. R. Hackman and G. R. Oldham, Work Redesign (Reading, MA: Addison-Wesley, 1980).

about myself and what I'm producing" are examples of internal motivation.

In Exhibit 9.9 you can see that the JCM specifies three critical psychological states that must occur for work to be internally motivating. First, workers must *experience the work as meaningful*; that is, they must view their job as being important. Second, they must *experience responsibility for work outcomes*—they must feel personally responsible for the work being done well. Third, workers must have *knowledge of results*; that is, they must know how well they are performing their jobs. All three critical psychological states must occur for work to be internally motivating.

For example, grocery store cashiers usually have knowledge of results. When you're slow, your checkout line grows long. If you make a mistake, customers point it out: "No, I think that's on sale for $2.99, not $3.99." Likewise, cashiers experience responsibility for work outcomes. At the end of the day, the register is totaled and the money is counted. Ideally, the money matches the total sales in the register. If the money in the till is less than what's recorded in the register, most stores make the cashier pay the difference. Consequently, most cashiers are very careful to avoid being caught short at the end of the day. Nonetheless, despite knowing the results

and experiencing responsibility for work outcomes, most grocery store cashiers (at least where I shop) aren't internally motivated, because they don't experience the work as meaningful. With scanners, it takes little skill to learn or do the job. Anyone can do it. In addition, cashiers have few decisions to make, and the job is highly repetitive.

What kinds of jobs produce the three critical psychological states? Moving another step to the left in Exhibit 9.9, you can see that these psychological states arise from jobs that are strong on five core job characteristics: skill variety, task identity, task significance, autonomy, and feedback. **Skill variety** is the number of different activities performed in a job. **Task identity** is the degree to which a job, from beginning to end, requires completion of a whole and identifiable piece of work. **Task significance** is the degree to which a job

Skill variety the number of different activities performed in a job

Task identity the degree to which a job, from beginning to end, requires the completion of a whole and identifiable piece of work

Task significance the degree to which a job is perceived to have a substantial impact on others inside or outside the organization

is perceived to have a substantial impact on others inside or outside the organization. **Autonomy** is the degree to which a job gives workers the discretion, freedom, and independence to decide how and when to accomplish the work. Finally, **feedback** is the amount of information the job provides to workers about their work performance.

To illustrate how the core job characteristics work together, let's use them to assess more thoroughly why the McDonald's drive-through window job is not particularly satisfying or motivating. To start, skill variety is low. Except for the size of an order or special requests ("no onions"), the process is the same for each customer. At best, task identity is moderate. Although you take the order, handle the money, and deliver the food, others are responsible for a larger part of the process—preparing the food. Task identity will be even lower if the McDonald's has two drive-through windows, because each drive-through window worker will have an even more specialized task. The first is limited to taking the order and making change, while the second just delivers the food.

Task significance, the impact you have on others, is probably low. Autonomy is also very low: McDonald's has strict rules about dress, cleanliness, and procedures. But the job does provide immediate feedback such as positive and negative customer comments, car horns honking, the amount of time it takes to process orders, and the number of cars in the drive-through. With the exception of feedback, the low levels of the core job characteristics show why the drive-through window job is not internally motivating for many workers.

What can managers do when jobs aren't internally motivating? The far left column of Exhibit 9.9 lists five job redesign techniques that managers can use to strengthen a job's core characteristics. *Combining tasks* increases skill variety and task identity by joining separate, specialized tasks into larger work modules. For example, some trucking firms are now requiring truck drivers to load their rigs as well as drive them. The hope is that involving drivers in loading will ensure that trucks are properly loaded, thus reducing damage claims.

Work can be formed into *natural work units* by arranging tasks according to logical or meaningful groups. Although many trucking companies randomly assign drivers to trucks, some have begun assigning drivers to particular geographic locations (e.g., the Northeast or Southwest) or to truckloads that require special driving skill (e.g., oversized loads or hazardous chemicals). Forming natural work units increases task identity and task significance.

Establishing client relationships increases skill variety, autonomy, and feedback by giving employees direct contact with clients and customers. In some companies, truck drivers are expected to establish business relationships with their regular customers. When something goes wrong with a shipment, customers are told to call drivers directly.

Vertical loading means pushing some managerial authority down to workers. For truck drivers, this means that they have the same authority as managers to resolve customer problems. In some companies, if a late shipment causes problems for a customer, the driver has the authority to fully refund the cost of that shipment without first obtaining management's approval.

The last job redesign technique offered by the model, *opening feedback channels*, means finding additional ways to give employees direct, frequent feedback about their job performance. For example, with advances in electronics, many truck drivers get instantaneous data as to whether they're on schedule and driving their rigs in a fuel-efficient manner. Likewise, the increased contact with customers also means that many drivers now receive monthly data on customer satisfaction.

9-4 INTRAORGANIZATIONAL PROCESSES

More than forty years ago, Tom Burns and G. M. Stalker described how two kinds of organizational designs, mechanistic and organic, are appropriate for

toddmedia/iStockphoto.com

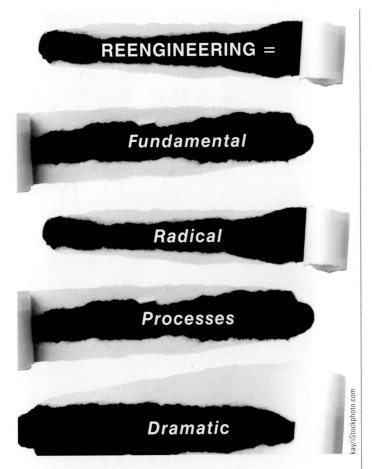

REENGINEERING =

Fundamental

Radical

Processes

Dramatic

kay/iStockphoto.com

different kinds of organizational environments.[27] **Mechanistic organizations** are characterized by specialized jobs and responsibilities; precisely defined, unchanging roles; and a rigid chain of command based on centralized authority and vertical communication. This type of organization works best in stable, unchanging business environments. By contrast, **organic organizations** are characterized by broadly defined jobs and responsibilities; loosely defined, frequently changing roles; and decentralized authority and horizontal communication based on task knowledge. This type of organization works best in dynamic, changing business environments.

The organizational design techniques described in the first half of this chapter—departmentalization, authority, and job design—are better suited for mechanistic organizations and the stable business environments that were more prevalent before 1980. By contrast, the organizational design techniques discussed next, in the second part of the chapter, are more appropriate for organic organizations and the increasingly dynamic environments in which today's businesses compete. The key difference between these approaches is that mechanistic organizational designs focus on organizational structure, whereas organic organizational designs are concerned with organizational

process, or the collection of activities that transform inputs into outputs valued by customers.

An **intraorganizational process** is the collection of activities that take place within an organization to transform inputs into outputs that customers value.

*Let's take a look at how companies are using **9-4a reengineering** and **9-4b empowerment** to redesign intraorganizational processes like these.*

9-4a Reengineering

In their best-selling book *Reengineering the Corporation*, Michael Hammer and James Champy define **reengineering** as "the *fundamental* rethinking and *radical* redesign of business *processes* to achieve *dramatic* improvements in critical, contemporary measures of performance, such as cost, quality, service and speed."[28] Hammer and Champy further explained the four key words shown in italics in this definition. The first key word is *fundamental*. When reengineering organizational designs, managers must ask themselves, "Why do we do what we do?" and "Why do we do it the way we do?" The usual answer is "Because that's the way we've always done it." The second key word is *radical*. Reengineering is about significant change, about starting over by throwing out the old ways of getting work done. The third key word is *processes*. Hammer and Champy noted that "most business people are not process oriented; they are focused on tasks, on jobs, on people, on structures, but not on processes." The fourth key word is *dramatic*. Reengineering is about achieving quantum improvements in company performance.

An example from IBM Credit's operation illustrates how work can be reengineered.[29] IBM Credit lends businesses money to buy IBM computers. Previously, the loan process began when an IBM salesperson called the home

Mechanistic organization an organization characterized by specialized jobs and responsibilities; precisely defined, unchanging roles; and a rigid chain of command based on centralized authority and vertical communication

Organic organization an organization characterized by broadly defined jobs and responsibilities; loosely defined, frequently changing roles; and decentralized authority and horizontal communication based on task knowledge

Intraorganizational process the collection of activities that take place within an organization to transform inputs into outputs that customers value

Reengineering fundamental rethinking and radical redesign of business processes to achieve dramatic improvements in critical measures of performance, such as cost, quality, service, and speed

Saks' Omnichannels

The department store company Saks Fifth Avenue is looking to create a united, holistic approach to its retail business. A major step in this strategy is to give senior managers responsibilities across multiple divisions. Rather than having separate managers for men's wares, women's accessories, and the like, Saks is appointing omnichannel managers who are tasked with guiding several divisions at once. So, for example, a newly named manager will now oversee the designer and contemporary businesses, while another's duties will combine the men's line and home accessories divisions. By giving managers cross-divisional authority, Saks hopes to create a unified approach to its business throughout the company. The company feels that the omnichannel managers will help create a dynamic synergy between the retail, Internet, and outlet stores, presenting shoppers with a unified Saks experience.

Source: D. Moin, "Saks Creates Omni-Management," *WWD*, February 8, 2013, 2, 13.

office to obtain credit approval for a customer's purchase. The first department involved in the process took the credit information over the phone from the salesperson and recorded it on the credit form. The credit form was sent to the credit checking department, then to the pricing department (where the interest rate was determined), and on through a total of five departments. In all, it took the five departments six days to approve or deny the customer's loan. Of course, this delay cost IBM business. Some customers got their loans elsewhere. Others, frustrated by the wait, simply canceled their orders.

Finally, two IBM managers decided to walk a loan straight through each of the departments involved in the process. At each step, they asked the workers to stop what they were doing and immediately process their loan application. They were shocked by what they found. From start to finish, the entire process took just ninety minutes!

The six-day turnaround time was almost entirely due to delays in handing off the work from one department to another. The solution: IBM redesigned the process so that one person, not five people in five separate departments, now handles the entire loan approval process without any handoffs. The results were indeed dramatic. Reengineering the credit process reduced approval time from six days to four hours and allowed IBM Credit to increase the number of loans it handled by a factor of 100!

Reengineering changes an organization's orientation from vertical to horizontal. Instead of taking orders from upper management, lower- and middle-level managers and workers take orders from a customer who is at the beginning and end of each process. Instead of running independent functional departments, managers and workers in different departments take ownership of cross-functional processes. Instead of simplifying work so that it becomes increasingly specialized, reengineering complicates work by giving workers increased autonomy and responsibility for complete processes.

In essence, reengineering changes work by changing **task interdependence,** the extent to which collective

Task interdependence the extent to which collective action is required to complete an entire piece of work

action is required to complete an entire piece of work. As shown in Exhibit 9.10, there are three kinds of task interdependence.[30] In **pooled interdependence,** each job or department contributes to the whole independently. In **sequential interdependence,** work must be performed in succession, as one group's or job's outputs become the inputs for the next group or job. Finally, in **reciprocal interdependence,** different jobs or groups work together in a back-and-forth manner to complete the process. By reducing the handoffs between different jobs or groups, reengineering decreases sequential interdependence. Likewise, reengineering decreases pooled interdependence by redesigning work so that formerly independent jobs or departments now work together to complete processes. Finally, reengineering increases reciprocal interdependence by making groups or individuals responsible for larger, more complete processes in which several steps may be accomplished at the same time.

As an organizational design tool, reengineering promises big rewards, but it has also come under severe criticism. The most serious complaint is that because it allows a few workers to do the work formerly done by many, reengineering is simply a corporate code word for cost cutting and worker layoffs.[31] For this reason, detractors claim that reengineering hurts morale and performance. Even though ordering times were reduced from three weeks to three days, Levi Strauss ended an $850 million reengineering project because of the fear and turmoil it created in the company's work force. One low point occurred when Levi management, encouraged by its reengineering consultants, told 4,000 workers that they would have to "reapply for their jobs" as the company shifted from its traditional vertical structure to a process-based form of organizing. Thomas Kasten, Levi Strauss's vice president for reengineering and customer service, says, "We felt the pressure building up [over reengineering efforts], and we were worried about the business."[32] Today, even reengineering gurus Hammer and Champy admit that roughly 70 percent of all reengineering projects fail because of the effects on people in the workplace. Says Hammer, "I wasn't smart enough about that [the people issues]. I was reflecting my engineering background and was insufficiently appreciative of the human dimension. I've [now] learned that's critical."[33]

9-4b Empowerment

Another way of redesigning intraorganizational processes is through empowerment. **Empowering workers** means permanently passing decision-making authority and responsibility from managers to workers. For workers to be fully empowered, companies must give them the information and resources they need to make and carry out good decisions and then

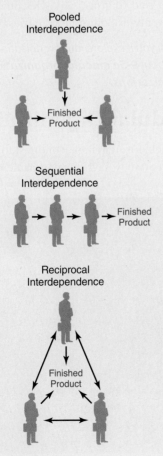

Exhibit 9.10
Reengineering and Task Interdependence

Pooled Interdependence

Finished Product

Sequential Interdependence

Finished Product

Reciprocal Interdependence

Finished Product

Pooled interdependence work completed by having each job or department independently contribute to the whole

Sequential interdependence work completed in succession, with one group's or job's outputs becoming the inputs for the next group or job

Reciprocal interdependence work completed by different jobs or groups working together in a back-and-forth manner

Empowering workers permanently passing decision-making authority and responsibility from managers to workers by giving them the information and resources they need to make and carry out good decisions

reward them for taking individual initiative.[34] In other words, employees won't feel very empowered if they constantly have someone looking over their shoulders. French-based Carrefour, the second largest retailer in the world, has seen its profits and market share consistently shrink over the last decade. New CEO Georges Plassat feels that Carrefour had "excess centralization preventing it from delivering results." The clearest sign of that was Carrefour headquarters determining which products to sell at what prices in each store worldwide. Today, however, Plassat says, "There is a change in culture" to empower local store managers to make these decisions. For example, the store manager, not headquarters, decides how much floor space to use to sell TVs, how many kinds of TVs to sell (a full range or only the best sellers), and how the TVs are priced. Says Plassat, "We have specialists in the store[s] who know what is selling," and top management now listens to them.[35]

When workers are given the proper information and resources and are allowed to make good decisions, they experience strong feelings of empowerment. **Empowerment** is a feeling of intrinsic motivation in which workers perceive their work to have meaning and perceive themselves to be competent, having an impact, and capable of self-determination.[36] Work has meaning when it is consistent with personal standards and beliefs. Workers feel competent when they believe they can perform an activity with skill. The belief that they are having an impact comes from a feeling that they can affect work outcomes. A feeling of self-determination arises from workers' belief that they have the autonomy to choose how best to do their work.

Empowerment can lead to changes in organizational processes because meaning, competence, impact, and self-determination produce empowered employees who take active rather than passive roles in their work. At Ritz-Carlton hotels, all employees are empowered to spend up to $2,000 to solve customer service issues. That's not $2,000 per year or $2,000 per day, it's $2,000 per incident. And, employees can spend that $2,000 without asking for managerial approval. Carmine Gallo, president of Gallo Communications Group, and his wife

were eating at a particularly busy Ritz-Carlton restaurant, which meant the service was slow. Gallo says, "During one especially busy time at the hotel's restaurant, the waiter apologized for the wait, gave us complimentary appetizers, and paid for our desserts. When I asked him why he did so he said, 'I'm empowered to keep my guests happy.'"[37]

9-5 INTERORGANIZATIONAL PROCESSES

An **interorganizational process** is a collection of activities that occur *among companies* to transform inputs into outputs that customers value. In other words, many companies work together to create a product or service that keeps customers happy. Nutella, the chocolate and hazelnut spread, is headquartered in Italy, has five factories in Europe, two in South America, and one each in Russia, North America, and Australia. Those factories work with suppliers in Turkey (hazelnuts), Malaysia (palm oil), Nigeria (cocoa), Brazil (sugar), and France (vanilla). The 250,000 tons of Nutella produced each year are then sold to grocers by sales offices and sales brokers in seventy-five different countries.[38]

In this section, you'll explore interorganizational processes by learning about 9-5a modular organizations and 9-5b virtual organizations.

9-5a Modular Organizations

Stephen Roach, former chief economist for investment bank Morgan Stanley, says that companies increasingly

Empowerment feeling of intrinsic motivation in which workers perceive their work to have impact and meaning and perceive themselves to be competent and capable of self-determination

Interorganizational process a collection of activities that take place among companies to transform inputs into outputs that customers value

Ridofranz/iStockphoto.com

want to take "functions that aren't central to their core competency" and outsource them.[39] Except for the core business activities that they can perform better, faster, and cheaper than others, **modular organizations** outsource all remaining business activities to outside companies, suppliers, specialists, or consultants. The term *modular* is used because the business activities purchased from outside companies can be added and dropped as needed, much like adding pieces to a three-dimensional puzzle. Exhibit 9.11 depicts a modular organization in which the company has chosen to keep training, human resources, sales, product design, manufacturing, customer service, research and development, and information technology as core business activities but has outsourced the noncore activities of product distribution, web page design, advertising, payroll, accounting, and packaging.

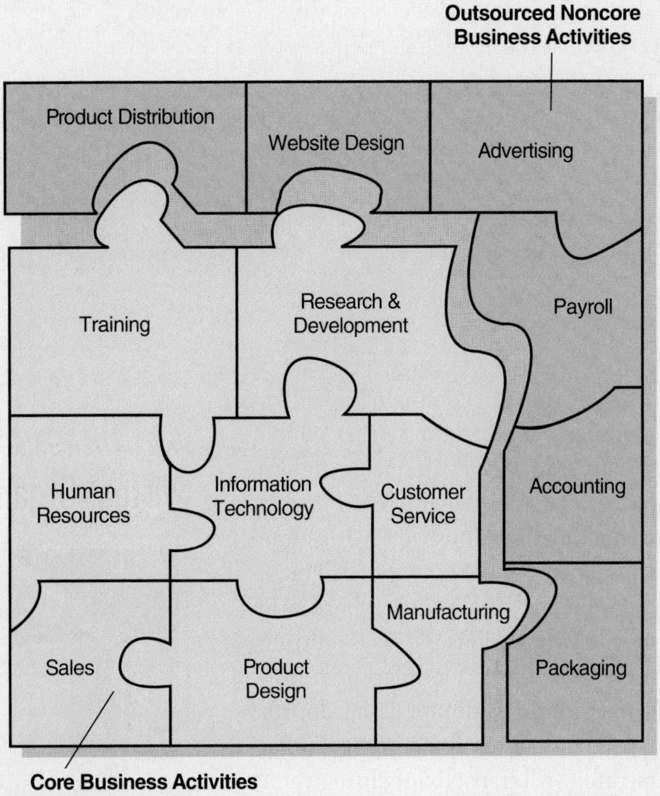

The primary advantage of modular organizations is that they can cost significantly less to run than traditional organizations because they pay for outsourced labor, expertise, or manufacturing capabilities only when needed. Merck, one of the world's leading pharmaceutical companies, is transforming into a modular organization. As little as two years ago, two-thirds of Merck's research budget was spent on in-house scientists and research labs that conducted expensive clinical research trials to test the drugs that Merck had in development. Today, Merck spends only one-third of its research budget on in-house clinical research. It outsources the rest to Quintiles, a company with 29,000 employees in 100 countries, that specializes in conducting large-scale clinical research trials for pharmaceutical companies like Merck.[40] To obtain cost advantages, however, modular organizations need reliable partners—vendors and suppliers with whom they can work closely and can trust.

Modular organizations have disadvantages, too. The primary disadvantage is the loss of control that occurs when key business activities are outsourced to other companies. Also, companies may reduce their competitive advantage in two ways if they mistakenly outsource a core business activity. First, as a result of competitive and technological change, the noncore business activities a company has outsourced may suddenly become the basis for competitive advantage. Second, related to

Exhibit 9.11
Modular Organization

that point, suppliers to whom work is outsourced can sometimes become competitors.

9-5b Virtual Organizations

In contrast to modular organizations, in which the interorganizational process revolves around a central company, a **virtual organization** is part of a network in which many companies share skills, costs, capabilities, markets, and customers with each other. Exhibit 9.12 shows a virtual organization in which, for today, the parts of a virtual company consist of product design, purchasing, manufacturing, advertising,

Modular organization an organization that outsources noncore business activities to outside companies, suppliers, specialists, or consultants

Virtual organization an organization that is part of a network in which many companies share skills, costs, capabilities, markets, and customers to collectively solve customer problems or provide specific products or services

and information technology. Unlike modular organizations, in which the outside organizations are tightly linked to one central company, virtual organizations work with some companies in the network alliance, but not with all. So, whereas a puzzle with various pieces is a fitting metaphor for a modular organization, a potluck dinner is an appropriate metaphor for a virtual organization. All participants bring their finest food dish but eat only what they want.

Another difference is that the working relationships between modular organizations and outside companies tend to be more stable and longer lasting than the shorter, often temporary relationships found among the virtual companies in a network alliance. The composition of a virtual organization is always changing. The combination of network partners that a virtual corporation has at any one time depends on the expertise needed to solve a particular problem or provide a specific product or service. For instance, today the business might need to focus on advertising and product design, as shown in Exhibit 9.12, but tomorrow, the business could want something completely different. In this sense, the term virtual organization means the organization that exists "at the moment."

Virtual organizations have a number of advantages. They let companies share costs, and because members

Exhibit 9.12
Virtual Organizations

Mike Powell/Photodisc/Getty Images

can quickly combine their efforts to meet customers' needs, they are fast and flexible. Finally, because each member of the network alliance is the best at what it does, virtual organizations should in theory provide better products and services in all respects.

As with modular organizations, a disadvantage of virtual organizations is that once work has been outsourced, it can be difficult to control the quality of work done by network partners. The greatest disadvantage, however, is that tremendous managerial skills are required to make a network of independent organizations work well together, especially since their relationships tend to be short and based on a single task or project. Virtual organizations are using two methods to solve this problem. The first is to use a *broker*. In traditional, hierarchical organizations, managers plan, organize, and control. But with the horizontal, interorganizational processes that characterize virtual organizations, the job of a broker is to create and assemble the knowledge, skills, and resources from different companies for outside parties, such as customers.[41] The second way to make networks of virtual organizations more manageable is to use a *virtual organization agreement* that, somewhat like a contract, specifies the schedules, responsibilities, costs, payouts, and liabilities for participating organizations.[42]

STUDY TOOLS 9

LOCATED AT THE BACK OF YOUR BOOK:

☐ Rip out and study the Chapter Review Card at the end of the book

LOG IN TO WWW.CENGAGEBRAIN.COM TO:

☐ Review Key Term Flashcards

☐ Complete Practice Quizzing (take up to four times without repeating the same quiz)

☐ Complete Games: Beat the Clock and Crossword Puzzle

☐ Complete Interactive Content: Graded Quiz, Media Quiz, and Fill-in-the-Blank Questions

☐ Watch Management Workplace Video on "Modern Shed"

☐ Work Through the What Would You Do Case on Eli Lilly Headquarters

10 Managing Teams

Yuri_Stockphoto.com

LEARNING OUTCOMES

10-1 Explain the good and bad of using teams.

10-2 Recognize and understand the different kinds of teams.

10-3 Understand the general characteristics of work teams.

10-4 Explain how to enhance work team effectiveness.

After you finish this chapter, go to **PAGE 217** for **STUDY TOOLS**

10-1 THE GOOD AND BAD OF USING TEAMS

Ninety-one percent of organizations are significantly improving their effectiveness by using work teams.[1] Procter & Gamble and Cummins Engine began using teams in 1962 and 1973, respectively. Boeing, Caterpillar, Champion International, Ford Motor Company, 3M, and General Electric established work teams in the mid- to late-1980s. Today, most companies use teams to tackle a variety of issues.[2] "Teams are ubiquitous. Whether we are talking about software development, Olympic hockey, disease outbreak response, or urban warfare, teams represent the critical unit that 'gets things done' in today's world."[3]

Work teams consist of a small number of people with complementary skills who hold themselves mutually accountable for pursuing a common purpose, achieving performance goals, and improving interdependent work processes.[4] By this definition, computer programmers working on separate projects in the same department of a company would not be considered a team. To be a team, the programmers would have to be interdependent and share responsibility and accountability for the quality and amount of computer code they produced.[5] Teams are becoming more important in many industries because they help organizations respond to specific problems and challenges. Though work teams are not the answer for every situation or organization, if the right teams are used properly and in the right settings, teams can dramatically improve company performance over more traditional management approaches while also instilling a sense of vitality in the workplace that is otherwise difficult to achieve.

*Let's begin our discussion of teams by learning about **10-1a the advantages of teams, 10-1b the disadvantages of teams,** and **10-1c when to use and not use teams.***

10-1a The Advantages of Teams

Companies are making greater use of teams because teams have been shown to improve customer satisfaction, product and service quality, speed and efficiency in product development, employee job satisfaction, and decision making.[6] For example, one survey indicated that 80 percent of companies with more than one hundred employees use teams, and 90 percent of all U.S. employees work part of their day in a team.[7]

Teams help businesses increase *customer satisfaction* in several ways. One way is to create work teams that are trained to meet the needs of specific customers. After financial scandals tarnished London-based Barclays Bank's reputation, it hired a director of customer experience to lead teams that were directly responsible for making sure, "the voice of the customer is heard."[8] One of those customers is business consultant and blogger Maz Iqbal. When Iqbal moved his business's bank accounts to Barclays from another bank, he blogged that his initial interactions were "frustrating." When he subsequently changed his company's registered name, he expected more paperwork, inefficiency, and frustration. Instead, before he visited his local branch, Barclays mailed him new checks and credit cards already imprinted with his company's new name. Said an obviously satisfied Iqbal, "I feel grateful. Why? Because Barclays Bank helped me out—saved me time, effort, concern—without me even asking them to help me out. They anticipated a need and met it."[9]

Teams also help firms improve *product and service quality* in several ways.[10] In contrast to traditional organizational structures, in which management is responsible for organizational outcomes and performance, teams take direct responsibility for the quality of the products and service they produce and sell. Oriental Trading Company (OTC) sells party supplies, arts and crafts, toys and games, and teaching supplies on the Internet. Like most retail websites, OTC's site allows customers to write comments about the products they buy. When customers complained about its Inflatable Solar System, giving it two stars out of five, members of OTC's

> **Work team** a small number of people with complementary skills who hold themselves mutually accountable for pursuing a common purpose, achieving performance goals, and improving interdependent work processes

intradepartmental teams sprang to action. A team member from the quality department worked directly with the manufacturer to improve quality. Another from copy writing worked with a team member from merchandising to post new photos of the improved product along with a more accurate product description. Other members of the team contacted dissatisfied customers to tell them that OTC had listened and had taken steps to address their concerns. Seven weeks after the first negative comment appeared on OTC's website, the improved product was available for sale. Customers consistently rate the new version at four out of five stars.[11]

Another reason for using teams is that teamwork often leads to increased *job satisfaction*.[12] One reason that teamwork can be more satisfying than traditional work is that it gives workers a chance to improve their skills. This is often accomplished through **cross-training,** in which team members are taught how to do all or most of the jobs performed by the other team members. The advantage for the organization is that cross-training allows a team to function normally when one member is absent, quits, or is transferred. The advantage for workers is that cross-training broadens their skills and increases their capabilities while also making their work more varied and interesting.

A second reason that teamwork is satisfying is that work teams often receive proprietary business information that typically is available only to managers. The

Great Little Box Company (GLBC), which makes corrugated boxes, custom product displays, and flexible and protective packaging for manufacturers, has an "open books" philosophy, where team members are given full access to the company's financial information. Founder Robert Meggy says, "It makes people feel more a part of the company. It instills a sense of trust. Regardless of whether the news is good or bad, people want to know and, ultimately, will try harder to make the company more profitable." After all, he says, "We want employees to run the company like their own business." Team member and customer-service representative Sandra Fung says, "If we have been profitable that month, it makes me feel good to learn that I have contributed to that." Finally, to drive home the importance of teams and teamwork, everyone receives equal monthly profit sharing checks. Says Meggy, "When it comes to teamwork, everyone is equal here. The truck drivers, the controller, office staff, plant supervisor—everybody gets the same amount."[13]

Team members also gain job satisfaction from unique leadership responsibilities that are not typically available in traditional organizations. Finally, teams share many of the advantages of group decision making discussed in Chapter 5. For instance, because team members possess different knowledge, skills, abilities, and experiences, a team is able to view problems from multiple perspectives. This diversity of viewpoints increases the odds that team decisions will solve the underlying causes of problems and not just address the symptoms. The increased knowledge and information available to teams also make it easier for them to generate more alternative solutions, a critical part of improving the quality of decisions.

Cross-training training team members to do all or most of the jobs performed by the other team members

Building Cohesiveness by Eating Lunch Together

At Ocean Spray, the cranberry juice company, no one is allowed to set a meeting during lunchtime. Why? The company sets this time aside so that employees can eat lunch together. But it's not just about eating, it's about giving everyone in the company some time to get to know each other. Leaders at Ocean Spray believe that there is no better way to find out about what is going on at work, and perhaps even to discover ways to work together, than to sit and have a conversation over lunch. It's better than emails, it's better than conference calls, and it's definitely better than cramming everyone into a conference room for five hours in the middle of the day. By encouraging everyone to eat together, the company gives people a comfortable, informal, and organic setting where they can build relationships, share knowledge and ideas, and find out what makes other people tick. And really, what's a better way to learn to trust someone—to talk to them one-on-one over lunch or to sit through another boring seminar together?

Source: M. Heffernan, "To-Do Today: Eat Lunch with a Colleague," *Inc.*, September 25, 2012, accessed June 13, 2013, http://www.inc.com/margaret-heffernan/team-building-eat-lunch-with-a-colleague.html.

Elenathewise/iStockphoto.com

Because team members are involved in decision-making processes, they are also likely to be more committed to making those decisions work. In short, teams can do a much better job than individuals in two important steps of the decision-making process: defining the problem and generating alternative solutions.

10-1b The Disadvantages of Teams

Although teams can significantly improve customer satisfaction, product and service quality, speed and efficiency in product development, employee job satisfaction, and decision making, using teams does not guarantee these positive outcomes. In fact, if you've ever participated in team projects in your classes, you're probably already aware of some of the problems inherent in work teams. Despite all of their promise, teams and teamwork are also prone to these significant disadvantages: initially high turnover, social loafing, and the problems associated with group decision making.

The first disadvantage of work teams is *initially high turnover*. Teams aren't for everyone, and some workers balk at the responsibility, effort, and learning required in team settings.

Social loafing is another disadvantage of work teams. **Social loafing** occurs when workers withhold their efforts and fail to perform their share of the work.[14] A nineteenth-century French engineer named Maximilian Ringlemann first documented social loafing when he found that one person pulling on a rope alone exerted an average of 139 pounds of force on the rope. In groups of three, the average force dropped to 117 pounds per person. In groups of eight, the average dropped to just 68 pounds per person. Ringlemann concluded that the larger the team, the smaller the individual effort. In fact, social loafing is more likely to occur in larger groups where identifying and monitoring the efforts of individual team members can be difficult.[15] In other words, social loafers count on being able to blend into the background, where their lack of effort isn't easily spotted.

From team-based class projects, most students already know about social loafers or "slackers," who contribute poor, little, or no work whatsoever. Not surprisingly, a study of 250 student teams found that the most talented students are typically the least satisfied with teamwork because of having to carry slackers and do a disproportionate share of their team's work.[16] Perceptions of fairness are negatively related to the extent of social loafing within teams.[17]

Finally, teams share many of the *disadvantages of group decision making* discussed in Chapter 5, such as

groupthink. In *groupthink*, members of highly cohesive groups feel intense pressure not to disagree with each other so that the group can approve a proposed solution. Because groupthink restricts discussion and leads to consideration of a limited number of alternative solutions, it usually results in poor decisions. Also, team decision making takes considerable time, and team meetings can often be unproductive and inefficient. Another possible pitfall is *minority domination*, where just one or two people dominate team discussions, restricting consideration of different problem definitions and alternative solutions. Minority domination is especially likely to occur when the team leader talks so much during team discussions, effectively discouraging other team members from speaking up. When that happens, team performance drops significantly.[18] Finally, team members may not feel accountable for the decisions and actions taken by the team.

10-1c When to Use Teams

As the two previous subsections made clear, teams have significant advantages *and* disadvantages. Therefore, the question is not whether to use teams, but *when* and *where* to use teams for maximum benefit and minimum cost. As Doug Johnson, associate director at the Center for Collaborative Organizations at the University of North Texas, puts it, "Teams are a means to an end, not an end in themselves. You have to ask yourself questions first. Does the work require interdependence? Will the team philosophy fit company strategy? Will management make a long-term commitment to this process?"[19] Exhibit 10.1 provides some additional guidelines on when to use or not use teams.[20]

First, teams should be used when there is a clear, engaging reason or purpose for using them. Too many companies use teams because they're popular or because the companies assume that teams can fix all problems. Teams are much more likely to succeed if they know why they exist and what they are supposed to accomplish, and more likely to fail if they don't.

Second, teams should be used when the job can't be done unless people work together. This typically means that teams are needed when tasks are complex, require multiple perspectives, or require repeated interaction with others to complete. Because of the enormous complexity of today's cars, you would think that auto companies routinely use interconnected design teams.

Social loafing behavior in which team members withhold their efforts and fail to perform their share of the work

Exhibit 10.1
When to Use and When Not to Use Teams

Use Teams When . . .

✓ there is a clear, engaging reason or purpose.

✓ the job can't be done unless people work together.

✓ rewards can be provided for teamwork and team performance.

✓ ample resources are available.

Don't Use Teams When . . .

✗ there isn't a clear, engaging reason or purpose.

✗ the job can be done by people working independently.

✗ rewards are provided for individual effort and performance.

✗ the necessary resources are not available.

Serdar Yagci/iStockphoto.com

Source: R. Wageman, "Critical Success Factors for Creating Superb Self-Managing Teams," *Organizational Dynamics* 26, no. 1 (1997): 49–61.

After all, the typical car has 30,000 parts, eighty different computer modules, indicators sensing how close other cars are when parking or going 70 mph, and the ability to automatically adjust braking, cornering, gas mileage, and acceleration. But auto companies don't routinely use interconnected design teams, as most designers are responsible for separate sections or parts of the car. Achim Badstübner, head of **Audi Group** exterior design, says, "We tend to make the mistake that we have an exterior department, an interior department and a technology department, and they all know what they're doing but the connection is not so good." Audi, however, takes a team approach. Badstübner says, "I think it's very important to basically lock them in one room, literally speaking. Then there is an interaction: you talk to the guy who does seats and he tells you something about his expertise and you might take something from him that helps you to develop a new wheel, for example." Badstübner says by connecting the teams, "you get a different result because through this method you get the best of every brain. I think you can't survive if you just depend on one brain to do a complex thing like [design] a car."[21]

Third, teams should be used when rewards can be provided for teamwork and team performance. Rewards that depend on team performance rather than individual performance are the key to rewarding team behaviors and efforts. You'll read more about team rewards later in the chapter, but for now it's enough to know that if the type of reward (individual versus team) is not matched to the type of performance (individual versus team), teams won't work.

10-2 KINDS OF TEAMS

Let's continue our discussion of teams by learning about the different kinds of teams that companies like Google and Maytag use to make themselves more competitive. We look first at **10-2a how teams differ in terms of autonomy, which is the key dimension that makes one team different from another,** *and then at* **10-2b some special kinds of teams.**

10-2a Autonomy, the Key Dimension

Teams can be classified in a number of ways, such as permanent or temporary, or functional or cross-functional. However, studies indicate that the amount of autonomy possessed by a team is the key difference among teams.[22] *Autonomy* is the degree to which workers have the discretion, freedom, and independence to decide how and when to accomplish their jobs. Exhibit 10.2 shows how five kinds of teams differ in terms of autonomy. Moving left to right across the autonomy continuum at the top of the exhibit, traditional work groups and employee involvement groups have the least autonomy, semi-autonomous work groups have more autonomy, and, finally, self-managing teams and self-designing teams have the most autonomy. Moving from bottom to top along the left side of the exhibit, note that the number of responsibilities given to each kind of team increases directly with its autonomy. Let's review each of these kinds of teams and their autonomy and responsibilities in more detail.

Exhibit 10.2
Team Autonomy Continuum

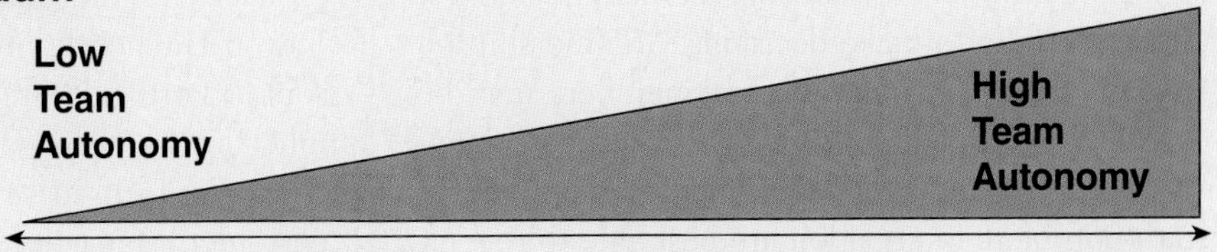

Responsibilities	Traditional Work Groups	Employee Involvement Groups	Semi-Autonomous Work Groups	Self-Managing Teams	Self-Designing Teams
Control Design of					
Team					✓
Tasks					✓
Membership					✓
Production/Service Tasks					
Make Decisions				✓	✓
Solve Problems				✓	✓
Major Production/Service Tasks					
Make Decisions			✓	✓	✓
Solve Problems			✓	✓	✓
Information			✓	✓	✓
Give Advice/Make Suggestions		✓	✓	✓	✓
Execute Task	✓	✓	✓	✓	✓

Low Team Autonomy — High Team Autonomy

Sources: R. D. Banker, J. M. Field, R. G. Schroeder, and K. K. Sinha, "Impact of Work Teams on Manufacturing Performance: A Longitudinal Field Study," *Academy of Management Journal* 39 (1996): 867–890; J. R. Hackman, "The Psychology of Self-Management in Organizations," in *Psychology and Work: Productivity, Change, and Employment*, ed. M. S. Pallak and R. Perlof (Washington, DC: American Psychological Association), 85–136.

The smallest amount of autonomy is found in **traditional work groups,** where two or more people work together to achieve a shared goal. In these groups, workers are responsible for doing the work or executing the task, but they do not have direct responsibility or control over their work. Workers report to managers, who are responsible for their performance and have the authority to hire and fire them, make job assignments, and control resources. For instance, suppose that an experienced worker blatantly refuses to do his share of the work, saying, "I've done my time. Let the younger employees do the work." In a team with high autonomy, the responsibility of getting this employee to put forth his fair share of effort would belong to his teammates. But, in a traditional work group, that responsibility belongs to the boss or supervisor. The supervisor in this situation calmly confronted the employee and told him, "We need your talent, [and] your knowledge of these machines. But if you won't work, you'll have to go elsewhere." Within days, the employee's behavior improved.[23]

Employee involvement teams, which have somewhat more autonomy, meet on company time on a

Traditional work group a group composed of two or more people who work together to achieve a shared goal

Employee involvement team team that provides advice or makes suggestions to management concerning specific issues

weekly or monthly basis to provide advice or make suggestions to management concerning specific issues such as plant safety, customer relations, or product quality.[24] Though they offer advice and suggestions, they do not have the authority to make decisions. Membership on these teams is often voluntary, but members may be selected because of their expertise. The idea behind employee involvement teams is that the people closest to the problem or situation are best able to recommend solutions. For more than three years, production of Boeing's 787 Dreamliner was delayed by multiple problems—parts shortages, improper installation, failed test flights, and more. Because of production delays, Boeing must build ten planes per month, up from the typical two and a half planes. To meet this aggressive goal, it established nearly 200 employee involvement teams to analyze the way 787s are assembled and make changes to maximize efficiency. For example, one employee involvement team found that ducts already installed in the plane were being damaged because workers were kicking and stepping on them while doing other work. The damaged ducts then had to be removed and replaced. The team recommended that temporary covers be placed over the ducts, thus eliminating delays and increased costs.[25]

Semi-autonomous work groups not only provide advice and suggestions to management but also have the authority to make decisions and solve problems related to the major tasks required to produce a product or service. Semi-autonomous groups regularly receive information about budgets, work quality and performance, and competitors' products. Furthermore, members of semi-autonomous work groups are typically cross-trained in a number of different skills and tasks. In short, semi-autonomous work groups give employees the authority to make decisions that are typically made by supervisors and managers.

That authority is not complete, however. Managers still play a role, though one that is much reduced compared with traditional work groups, in supporting the work of semi-autonomous work groups. The role a manager plays on a team usually evolves over time. "It may start with helping to transition problem-solving responsibilities to the team, filling miscellaneous requests for the team, and doing ad hoc tasks," says Steven Hitchcock, president of Axis Performance Advisors in Portland, Oregon. Later, the team may develop into a mini-enterprise, and the former manager becomes externally focused—sort of an account manager for the customer. Managers have to adjust what they do based on the sophistication of the team.[26] A lot of what managers of semi-autonomous work groups do is ask good questions, provide resources, and facilitate performance of group goals.

Self-managing teams are different from semi-autonomous work groups in that team members manage and control *all* of the major tasks *directly related* to production of a product or service without first getting approval from management. This includes managing and controlling the acquisition of materials, making a product or providing a service, and ensuring timely delivery. At Connecticut Spring & Stamping, a precision manufacturing firm, self-managing teams determine the master schedule that controls the order in which parts will flow from machines to workers, the location and proximity of machines and work stations, when and who gets overtime work (and how much), and how teams will be rewarded. For example, the teams designed a three-stage program in which constant improvement in on-time delivery is required in order to receive rewards. All of these decisions are made without management's input or approval.[27]

The use of self-managing teams has significantly increased productivity at a number of other companies, increasing quality by 12 percent at AT&T, reducing errors by 13 percent at FedEx, and helping 3M increase production by 300 percent at one of its manufacturing plants.[28] Seventy-two percent of *Fortune* 1,000 companies have at least one self-managing team, up from 28 percent in 1987.[29]

Self-designing teams have all the characteristics of self-managing teams, but they can also control and change the design of the teams themselves, the tasks they do and how and when they do them, and the membership of the teams.

10-2b Special Kinds of Teams

Companies are also increasingly using several other kinds of teams that can't easily be categorized in terms of autonomy: cross-functional teams, virtual teams, and project teams. Depending on how these teams are designed, they can be either low- or high-autonomy teams.

Semi-autonomous work group a group that has the authority to make decisions and solve problems related to the major tasks of producing a product or service

Self-managing team a team that manages and controls all of the major tasks of producing a product or service

Self-designing team a team that has the characteristics of self-managing teams but also controls team design, work tasks, and team membership

Cross-functional teams are intentionally composed of employees from different functional areas of the organization.[30] Because their members have different functional backgrounds, education, and experience, cross-functional teams usually attack problems from multiple perspectives and generate more ideas and alternative solutions, all of which are especially important when trying to innovate or solve problems creatively.[31] Cross-functional teams can be used almost anywhere in an organization and are often used in conjunction with matrix and product organizational structures (see Chapter 9). They can also be used either with part-time or temporary team assignments or with full-time, long-term teams.

Virtual teams are groups of geographically and/or organizationally dispersed coworkers who use a combination of telecommunications and information technologies to accomplish an organizational task.[32] Virtual teams are increasingly common, and are used by 28 percent of U.S.-based corporations and 66 percent of multinational firms.[33] Members of virtual teams rarely meet face-to-face; instead, they use email, videoconferencing, and group communication software.[34] Virtual teams can be employee involvement teams, self-managing teams, or nearly any kind of team discussed in this chapter. Virtual teams are often (but not necessarily) temporary teams that are set up to accomplish a specific task.[35]

The principal advantage of virtual teams is their flexibility. Employees can work with each other regardless of physical location, time zone, or organizational affiliation. Because the team members don't meet in a physical location, virtual teams also find it much easier to include other key stakeholders such as suppliers and customers. Plus, virtual teams have certain efficiency advantages over traditional team structures. Because the teammates do not meet face-to-face, a virtual team typically requires a smaller time commitment than a traditional team does. Moreover, employees can fulfill the responsibilities of their virtual team membership from the comfort of their own offices without the travel time or downtime typically required for face-to-face meetings.[36]

A drawback of virtual teams is that the team members must learn to express themselves in new contexts.[37] Indeed, over half of those participating in virtual teams find that building relationships with virtual team members is difficult.[38] The give-and-take that naturally occurs in face-to-face team meetings is more difficult to achieve through videoconferencing or other methods of virtual teaming. Indeed several studies have shown that the physical proximity of team members in non-virtual teams

enhances information processing.[39] Therefore, some companies bring virtual team members together on a regular basis to try to minimize these problems.

Project teams are created to complete specific, one-time projects or tasks within a limited time.[40] Project teams are often used to develop new products, significantly improve existing products, roll out new information systems, or build new factories or offices. The project team is typically led by a project manager who has the overall responsibility for planning, staffing, and managing the team, which usually includes employees from different functional areas. Effective project teams demand both individual and collective responsibility.[41] One advantage of project teams is that drawing employees from different functional areas can reduce or eliminate communication

Cross-functional team a team composed of employees from different functional areas of the organization

Virtual team a team composed of geographically and/or organizationally dispersed coworkers who use telecommunication and information technologies to accomplish an organizational task

Project team a team created to complete specific, one-time projects or tasks within a limited time

killerbayer/iStockphoto.com

barriers. In turn, as long as team members feel free to express their ideas, thoughts, and concerns, free-flowing communication encourages cooperation among separate departments and typically speeds up the design process.[42] Another advantage of project teams is their flexibility. When projects are finished, project team members either move on to the next project or return to their functional units. For example, publication of this book required designers, editors, page compositors, and Web designers, among others. When the task was finished, these people applied their skills to other textbook projects. Because of this flexibility, project teams are often used with the matrix organizational designs discussed in Chapter 9.

10-3 WORK TEAM CHARACTERISTICS

"Why did I ever let you talk me into teams? They're nothing but trouble."[43] Lots of managers have this reaction after making the move to teams. Many don't realize that this reaction is normal, both for them and for workers. In fact, such a reaction is characteristic of the *storming* stage of team development (discussed in Section 10-3e). Managers who are familiar with these stages and with the other important characteristics of teams will be better prepared to manage the predictable changes that occur when companies make the switch to team-based structures.

*Understanding the characteristics of work teams is essential for making teams an effective part of an organization. Therefore, in this section you'll learn about **10-3a team norms, 10-3b team cohesiveness, 10-3c team size, 10-3d team conflict,** and **10-3e the stages of team development.***

10-3a Team Norms

Over time, teams develop **norms,** which are informally agreed-on standards that regulate team behavior.[44] Norms are valuable because they let team members know what is expected of them. While leading Orbis International, a nonprofit organization in which a DC-10 jet, converted to a "Flying Eye Hospital," transports volunteer doctors and nurses to treat eye disease throughout the world, Jilly

Stephens noticed a problem with punctuality. She said, "When I first got to the field, you would have the nurses, engineers, whoever, waiting, and you would maybe have one [person] who just couldn't drag himself out of bed and everybody's waiting." So she simply decided that there would be a new norm for the team: they leave on time. "If they aren't there [on time], the bus leaves. You get to the airport yourself. If we were in Tunisia, that meant finding a bike and cycling across the desert to get to the airport." Says Stephens, "We saw behaviors change fairly rapidly."[45]

Studies indicate that norms are one of the most powerful influences on work behavior because they regulate the everyday actions that allow teams to function effectively. Team norms are often associated with positive outcomes such as stronger organizational commitment, more trust in management, and stronger job and organizational satisfaction.[46] Effective work teams develop norms about the quality and timeliness of job performance, absenteeism, safety, and honest expression of ideas and opinions.

Surgeon Atul Gawande, author of *The Checklist Manifesto*, says that with 6,000 drugs, 4,000 medical procedures, and doctors and nurses specializing in hundreds of medical subfields, "The complexity of what we [in modern medicine] have to deliver on exceeds our abilities as experts partly because the volume of knowledge has exceeded what training can possibly provide."[47] So, in his operating rooms, Gawande and his surgical teams use and review checklists to make sure each small but critical step is completed. Before administering anesthesia, the nurse and anesthetist will determine if the site of the surgery is marked, whether the anesthesia machine and medication check have been completed, and whether the patient has a difficult airway or is at risk of aspiration (vomiting into the airway). Likewise, before the first incision takes place, all team members will be asked to introduce themselves and the roles they'll be performing, and the surgeon will be asked to state where the incision will be made and what kind of critical, nonroutine steps might be taken if things don't go as planned.[48] The review checklists are a powerful way of making sure that all members of the surgical team do what they're supposed to, that is, follow agreed-on standards of behavior or norms.

Norms can also influence team behavior in negative ways. For example, most people would agree that damaging organizational property; saying or doing something to hurt someone at work; intentionally doing one's work badly, incorrectly, or slowly; griping about coworkers; deliberately bending or breaking rules; and doing something to harm the company or boss are negative

Norms informally agreed-on standards that regulate team behavior

behaviors. A study of workers from thirty-four teams in twenty different organizations found that teams with negative norms strongly influenced their team members to engage in these negative behaviors. In fact, the longer individuals were members of a team with negative norms and the more frequently they interacted with their teammates, the more likely they were to perform negative behaviors. Since team norms typically develop early in the life of a team, these results indicate how important it is for teams to establish positive norms from the outset.[49]

10-3b Team Cohesiveness

Cohesiveness is another important characteristic of work teams. **Cohesiveness** is the extent to which team members are attracted to a team and motivated to remain in it.[50] What can be done to promote team cohesiveness? First, make sure that all team members are present at team meetings and activities. Team cohesiveness suffers when members are allowed to withdraw from the team and miss team meetings and events.[51] Second, create additional opportunities for teammates to work together by rearranging work schedules and creating common workspaces. Bank of America discovered the value of cohesive teams when it did a study tracking employee behavior. When Bank of America experimented by having call center employees wear sensors monitoring their movements throughout the office, it found that the most productive employees were in cohesive teams that communicated frequently. So, to encourage more interaction, it scheduled team members to all have breaks at the same time, rather than solo breaks. As a result, worker productivity rose 10 percent.[52] When task interdependence is high and team members have lots of chances to work together, team cohesiveness tends to increase.[53] Third, engaging in nonwork activities as a team can help build cohesion. Finally, companies build team cohesiveness by making employees feel that they are part of an organization.

10-3c Team Size

The relationship between team size and performance appears to be curvilinear. Very small or very large teams may not perform as well as moderately sized teams. For most teams, the right size is somewhere between six and nine members.[54] A team of this size is small enough for the team members to get to know each other and for each member to have an opportunity to contribute in a meaningful way to the success of the team. At the same

time, the team is large enough to take advantage of team members' diverse skills, knowledge, and perspectives. It is also easier to instill a sense of responsibility and mutual accountability in teams of this size.[55]

When teams get too large, team members find it difficult to get to know one another, and the team may splinter into smaller subgroups. When this occurs, subgroups sometimes argue and disagree, weakening overall team cohesion. As teams grow, there is also a greater chance of *minority domination*, where just a few team members dominate team discussions. Even if minority domination doesn't occur, larger groups may not have time for all team members to share their input. And when team members feel that their contributions are unimportant or not needed, the result is less involvement, effort, and accountability to the team.[56] Large teams also face logistical problems such as finding an appropriate time or place to meet. Finally, the incidence of social loafing, discussed earlier in the chapter, is much higher in large teams.

Just as team performance can suffer when a team is too large, it can also be negatively affected when a team is too small. Teams with just a few people may lack the diversity of skills and knowledge found in larger teams. Also, teams that are too small are unlikely to gain the advantages of team decision making (multiple perspectives, generating more ideas and alternative solutions, and stronger commitment) found in larger teams.

What signs indicate that a team's size needs to be changed? If decisions are taking too long, if the team has difficulty making decisions or taking action, if a few members dominate the team, or if the commitment or efforts of team members are weak, chances are the team is too big.

Cohesiveness the extent to which team members are attracted to a team and motivated to remain in it

In contrast, if a team is having difficulty coming up with ideas or generating solutions, or if the team does not have the expertise to address a specific problem, chances are the team is too small.

10-3d Team Conflict

Conflict and disagreement are inevitable in most teams. But this shouldn't surprise anyone. From time to time, people who work together are going to disagree about what and how things get done. What causes conflict in teams? Although almost anything can lead to conflict—casual remarks that unintentionally offend a team member or fighting over scarce resources—the primary cause of team conflict is disagreement over team goals and priorities.[57] Other common causes of team conflict include disagreements over task-related issues, interpersonal incompatibilities, and simple fatigue.

Though most people view conflict negatively, the key to dealing with team conflict is not avoiding it, but rather making sure that the team experiences the right kind of conflict. In Chapter 5, you learned about *c-type conflict*, or *cognitive conflict*, which focuses on problem-related differences of opinion, and *a-type conflict*, or *affective conflict*, which refers to the emotional reactions that can occur when disagreements become personal rather than professional.[58] Cognitive conflict is strongly associated with improvements in team performance, whereas affective conflict is strongly associated with decreases in team performance.[59] Why does this happen? With cognitive conflict, team members disagree because their different experiences and expertise lead them to different views of the problem and solutions. Indeed, managers who participated on teams that emphasized cognitive conflict described their teammates as "smart," "team players," and "best in the business." They described their teams as "open," "fun," and "productive." One manager summed up the positive attitude that team members had about cognitive conflict by saying, "We scream a lot, then laugh, and then resolve the issue."[60] Thus, cognitive conflict is also characterized by a willingness to examine, compare, and reconcile differences to produce the best possible solution.

By contrast, affective conflict often results in hostility, anger, resentment, distrust, cynicism, and apathy. Managers who participated on teams that experienced affective conflict described their teammates as "manipulative," "secretive," "burned out," and "political."[61] Not surprisingly, affective conflict can make people uncomfortable and cause them to withdraw and decrease their commitment to a team.[62] Affective conflict also lowers the satisfaction of team members, may lead to personal hostility between coworkers, and can decrease team cohesiveness.[63] So, unlike cognitive conflict, affective conflict undermines team performance by preventing teams from engaging in the kinds of activities that are critical to team effectiveness.

So, what can managers do to manage team conflict? First, they need to realize that emphasizing cognitive conflict alone won't be enough. Studies show that cognitive and affective conflicts often occur together in a given team activity! Sincere attempts to reach agreement on a difficult issue can quickly deteriorate from cognitive to affective conflict if the discussion turns personal and tempers and emotions flare. While cognitive conflict is clearly the better approach to take, efforts to engage in cognitive conflict should be managed well and checked before they deteriorate and the team becomes unproductive.

Can teams disagree and still get along? Fortunately, they can. In an attempt to study this issue, researchers examined team conflict in twelve high-tech companies. In four of the companies, work teams used cognitive conflict to address work problems but did so in a way that minimized the occurrence of affective conflict.

There are several ways teams can have a good fight.[64] First, work with more, rather than less, information. If data are plentiful, objective, and up-to-date, teams will focus on issues, not personalities. Second, develop multiple alternatives to enrich debate. Focusing on multiple solutions diffuses conflict by getting the team to keep searching for a better solution. Positions and opinions are naturally more flexible with five alternatives than with just two. Third, establish common goals. Remember, most team conflict arises from disagreements over team goals and priorities. Therefore, common goals encourage collaboration and minimize conflict over a team's purpose. The late Steve Jobs, former CEO of Apple, explained it this way: "It's okay to spend a lot of time arguing about which route to take to San Francisco when everyone wants to end up there, but a lot of time gets wasted in such arguments if one person wants to go to San Francisco and another secretly wants to go to

Su Min-Hsuan/iStockphoto.com

Harvey Mackay, who has been writing about teamwork for nearly two decades, says that no matter what the industry, no matter how simple or complex tasks are, no matter if the company is failing or succeeding, teamwork always begins at hiring. Leaders who want to cultivate effective, efficient, productive teams must first ask the right questions during a job interview. They need to make sure that the applicant loves to collaborate, is fair and honest about giving credit to others, and shows eagerness to share knowledge with others. An individual who talks about nothing but himself and what he's accomplished by himself might sound downright heroic, but he will stifle whatever teamwork exists in the organization. To find the right person for teamwork, Mackay suggests asking the following questions:

Why do you want to join this team?

What teamwork experience do you have?

What's the most important thing about teamwork?

How have you handled conflicts in teams?

Source: H. Mackay, "Successful Teamwork Starts at the Hiring Stage," *Star Tribune*, July 8, 2012, accessed June 13, 2013, http://www.startribune.com /business/161566145.html?refer=y.

San Diego."[65] Fourth, inject humor into the workplace. Humor relieves tension, builds cohesion, and just makes being in teams fun. Fifth, maintain a balance of power by involving as many people as possible in the decision process. And, sixth, resolve issues without forcing a consensus. Consensus means that everyone must agree before decisions are finalized. Effectively, requiring consensus gives everyone on the team veto power. Nothing gets done until everyone agrees, which, of course, is nearly impossible. As a result, insisting on consensus usually promotes affective rather than cognitive conflict. If team members can't agree after constructively discussing their options, it's better to have the team leader make the final choice. Most team members can accept the team leader's choice if they've been thoroughly involved in the decision process.

10-3e Stages of Team Development

As teams develop and grow, they pass through four stages of development. As shown in Exhibit 10.3, those stages are forming, storming, norming, and performing.[66] Although not every team passes through each of these stages, teams that do tend to be better performers.[67] This holds true even for teams composed of seasoned executives. After a period of time, however, if a team is not managed well, its performance may start to deteriorate as the team begins a process of decline and progresses through the stages of de-norming, de-storming, and de-forming.[68]

Forming is the initial stage of team development. This is the getting-acquainted stage in which team members first meet each other, form initial impressions, and try to get a sense of what it will be like to be part of the team. Some of the first team norms will be established during this stage as team members begin to find out what behaviors will and won't be accepted by the team. During this stage, team leaders should allow time for team members to get to know each other, set early ground rules, and begin to set up a preliminary team structure.

Conflicts and disagreements often characterize the second stage of team development, **storming**. As team members begin working together, different personalities and work styles may clash. Team members become more assertive at this stage and more willing to state opinions. This is also the stage when team members jockey for position and try to establish a favorable role for themselves on the team. In addition, team members are likely to disagree about what the group should do and how it should do it. Team performance is still relatively low, given that team cohesion is weak and team members are still reluctant to support each other. Since teams that get stuck in the storming stage are almost always ineffective, it is important for team leaders to focus the team on team goals and on improving team performance. Team members need to be particularly patient and tolerant with each other in this stage.

During **norming,** the third stage of team development, team members begin to settle into their roles as team members. Positive team norms will have developed by this stage, and teammates should know what to expect from each other. Petty differences should have been resolved, friendships will have developed, and group cohesion will be relatively strong. At this point, team members will have accepted team goals, be operating as a unit, and, as indicated by the increase in performance, be working together

Forming the first stage of team development, in which team members meet each other, form initial impressions, and begin to establish team norms

Storming the second stage of development, characterized by conflict and disagreement, in which team members disagree over what the team should do and how it should do it

Norming the third stage of team development, in which team members begin to settle into their roles, group cohesion grows, and positive team norms develop

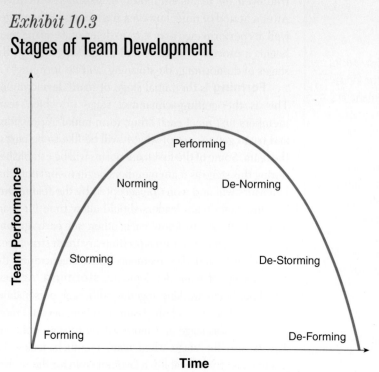

Exhibit 10.3
Stages of Team Development

Team Performance (vertical axis)
Time (horizontal axis)

Forming → Storming → Norming → Performing → De-Norming → De-Storming → De-Forming

Sources: J. F. McGrew, J. G. Bilotta, and J. M. Deeney, "Software Team Formation and Decay: Extending the Standard Model for Small Groups," *Small Group Research* 30, no. 2 (1999): 209–234; B. W. Tuckman, "Development Sequence in Small Groups," *Psychological Bulletin* 63, no. 6 (1965): 384–399.

and think of themselves as members of a team and not just employees. Team members often become intensely loyal to one another at this stage and feel mutual accountability for team successes and failures. Trivial disagreements, which can take time and energy away from the work of the team, should be rare. At this stage, teams get a lot of work done, and it is fun to be a team member.

The team should not become complacent, however. Without effective management, its performance may begin to decline as the team passes through the stages of **de-norming**, **de-storming**, and **de-forming**.[69] Indeed, John Puckett, manufacturing vice president for circuit-board manufacturer XEL Communications, says, "The books all say you start in this state of chaos and march through these various stages, and you end up in this state of ultimate self-direction, where everything is going just great. They never tell you it can go back in the other direction, sometimes just as quickly."[70]

effectively. This stage can be very short and is often characterized by someone on the team saying, "I think things are finally coming together." Note, however, that teams may also cycle back and forth between storming and norming several times before finally settling into norming.

In the last stage of team development, **performing**, performance improves because the team has finally matured into an effective, fully functioning team. At this point, members should be fully committed to the team

Performing the fourth and final stage of team development, in which performance improves because the team has matured into an effective, fully functioning team

De-norming a reversal of the norming stage, in which team performance begins to decline as the size, scope, goal, or members of the team change

De-storming a reversal of the storming phase, in which the team's comfort level decreases, team cohesion weakens, and angry emotions and conflict may flare

De-forming a reversal of the forming stage, in which team members position themselves to control pieces of the team, avoid each other, and isolate themselves from team leaders

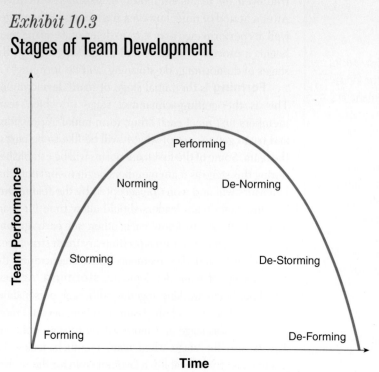

10-4 ENHANCING WORK TEAM EFFECTIVENESS

*Making teams work is a challenging and difficult process. Nonetheless, companies can increase the likelihood that teams will succeed by carefully managing **10-4a the setting of team goals and priorities** and **10-4b how work team members are selected, 10-4c trained, and 10-4d compensated.**[71]*

10-4a Setting Team Goals and Priorities

In Chapter 5, you learned that having specific, measurable, attainable, realistic, and timely (S.M.A.R.T.) goals is one of the most effective means for improving individual job performance. Fortunately, team goals also improve team performance. In fact, team goals lead to much higher team performance 93 percent of the time.[72]

To effectively motivate teams:

1. Teams must have a high degree of autonomy
2. Teams must be empowered with control of resources
3. Teams need structural accommodation
4. Teams need bureaucratic immunity

RoscoPhoto/iStockphoto.com

Why is setting *specific* team goals so critical to team success? One reason is that increasing a team's performance is inherently more complex than just increasing one individual's job performance. For instance, consider that any team is likely to involve at least four different kinds of goals: each member's goal for the team, each member's goal for himself or herself on the team, the team's goal for each member, and the team's goal for itself.[73] In other words, without a specific goal for the team itself (the last of the four goals listed), team members may head off in all directions at once pursuing these other goals. Consequently, setting a specific goal *for the team* clarifies team priorities by providing a clear focus and purpose.

Challenging team goals affect how hard team members work. In particular, they greatly reduce the incidence of social loafing. When faced with difficult goals, team members necessarily expect everyone to contribute. Consequently, they are much more likely to notice and complain if a teammate isn't doing his or her share. In fact, when teammates know each other well, when team goals are specific, when team communication is good, and when teams are rewarded for team performance (discussed later in this section), there is only a one in sixteen chance that teammates will be social loafers.[74]

What can companies and teams do to ensure that team goals lead to superior team performance? One increasingly popular approach is to give teams stretch goals. *Stretch goals* are extremely ambitious goals that workers don't know how to reach.[75] The world's largest auto company, GM, went bankrupt in 2009. Now, just six years later, GM wants to be "the world's most valuable automotive company." How big a stretch is this goal? Pretty big. GM's value (i.e., market capitalization) when this was written was $44 billion, sixth among the world's top nine auto companies and well behind market leader Toyota, which has a market cap of $151 billion. So, GM will have to more than triple its stock price relative to Toyota to achieve this goal. GM spokesman Jim Cain explains, "It's a way to get people focused around a couple of issues. We don't have competitive [profit] margins. If we can get competitive [profit] margins, it'll drive the stock price." And how will GM do that? It's not clear.[76]

Four things must occur for stretch goals to effectively motivate teams.[77] First, teams must have a high degree of autonomy or control over how they achieve their goals. Second, teams must be empowered with control of resources, such as budgets, workspaces, computers, or whatever else they need to do their jobs. Third, teams need structural accommodation. **Structural accommodation** means giving teams the ability to change organizational structures, policies, and practices if doing so helps them meet their stretch goals. Finally, teams need bureaucratic immunity. **Bureaucratic immunity** means that teams no longer have to go through the frustratingly slow process of multilevel reviews and sign-offs to get management approval before making changes. Once granted bureaucratic immunity, teams are immune from the influence of various organizational groups and are accountable only to top management. Research teams at Google X, Google's research lab, work on "moonshots," meaning hard to accomplish projects like self-driving cars and Google Glass, eye glasses that display email and can record videos and photos. Google X's teams work in two buildings half a mile from Google's main campus to separate and free them from Google's main business. With bureaucratic immunity, teams can act quickly, and even experiment,

Structural accommodation the ability to change organizational structures, policies, and practices in order to meet stretch goals

Bureaucratic immunity the ability to make changes without first getting approval from managers or other parts of an organization with little fear of failure. Richard DeVaul, who heads the Rapid Evaluation and Design Kitchen teams at Google X, says, "Google X is very consciously looking at things that Google in its right mind wouldn't do. They build the rocket pad far away from the widget factory, so if the rocket blows up, it's hopefully not disrupting the core business."[78]

10-4b Selecting People for Teamwork

University of Southern California management professor Edward Lawler says, "People are very naive about how easy it is to create a team. Teams are the Ferrari of work design. They're high performance but high maintenance and expensive."[79] It's almost impossible to have an effective work team without carefully selecting people who are suited for teamwork or for working on a particular team. A focus on teamwork (individualism-collectivism), team level, and team diversity can help companies choose the right team members.[80]

> **Individualism-collectivism** the degree to which a person believes that people should be self-sufficient and that loyalty to one's self is more important than loyalty to team or company

Are you more comfortable working alone or with others? If you strongly prefer to work alone, you may not be well suited for teamwork. Indeed, studies show that job satisfaction is higher in teams when team members prefer working with others.[81] An indirect way to measure someone's *preference for teamwork* is to assess the person's degree of individualism or collectivism. **Individualism-collectivism** is the degree to which a person believes that people should be self-sufficient and that loyalty to one's self is more important than loyalty to one's team or company.[82] *Individualists*, who put their own welfare and interests first, generally prefer independent tasks in which they work alone. In contrast, *collectivists*, who put group or team interests ahead of self-interests, generally prefer interdependent tasks in which they work with others. Collectivists would also rather cooperate than compete and are fearful of disappointing team members or of being ostracized from teams. Given these differences, it makes sense to select team members who are collectivists rather than individualists. Indeed, many companies use individualism-collectivism as an initial screening device for team members. If team diversity is desired, however, individualists may also be appropriate, as discussed below. To determine your preference for teamwork, take the Team Player Inventory shown in Exhibit 10.4.

Exhibit 10.4
The Team Player Inventory

		Strongly Disagree				Strongly Agree
1.	I enjoy working on team/group projects.	1	2	3	4	5
2.	Team/group project work easily allows others to not pull their weight.	1	2	3	4	5
3.	Work that is done as a team/group is better than work done individually.	1	2	3	4	5
4.	I do my best work alone rather than in a team/group.	1	2	3	4	5
5.	Team/group work is overrated in terms of the actual results produced.	1	2	3	4	5
6.	Working in a team/group gets me to think more creatively.	1	2	3	4	5
7.	Teams/groups are used too often when individual work would be more effective.	1	2	3	4	5
8.	My own work is enhanced when I am in a team/group situation.	1	2	3	4	5
9.	My experiences working in team/group situations have been primarily negative.	1	2	3	4	5
10.	More solutions/ideas are generated when working in a team/group situation than when working alone.	1	2	3	4	5

Reverse score items 2, 4, 5, 7, and 9. Then add the scores for items 1 to 10. Higher scores indicate a preference for teamwork, whereas lower total scores indicate a preference for individual work.

Source: T. J. B. Kline, "The Team Player Inventory: Reliability and Validity of a Measure of Predisposition Toward Organizational Team-Working Environments," *Journal for Specialists in Group Work* 24, no. 1 (1999): 102–112.

Team level is the average level of ability, experience, personality, or any other factor on a team. For example, a high level of team experience means that a team has particularly experienced team members. This does not mean that every member of the team has considerable experience, but that enough team members do to significantly raise the average level of experience on the team. Team level is used to guide selection of teammates when teams need a particular set of skills or capabilities to do their jobs well. For example, at GE's Aerospace Engines manufacturing plant in Durham, North Carolina, only applicants who have an FAA-certified mechanic's license are considered for hire. Following that, all applicants are tested in eleven different areas, only one of which involves technical skills. Keith McKee, who works at the plant, says, "You have to be above the bar in all eleven of the areas: helping skills, team skills, communication skills, diversity, flexibility, coaching ability, work ethic, and so forth. Even if just one thing out of the eleven knocks you down, you don't come to work here."[83]

Whereas team level represents the average level or capability on a team, **team diversity** represents the variances or differences in ability, experience, personality, or any other factor on a team.[84] From a practical perspective, why is team diversity important? Andy Zynga, CEO of NineSigma International, an innovation consulting firm, says, "Technologists, engineers, and designers not only have their own expertise, they have their own way of applying their expertise. Ironically, the more success they've had with their approach to a solution, the harder it is to imagine a different one."[85] Team diversity ensures that strong teams not only have talented members (that is, a high team level), but those talented members also have different abilities, experiences, and personalities from which to view and solve problems.

Once the right team has been put together in terms of individualism-collectivism, team level, and team diversity, it's important to keep the team together as long as practically possible. Interesting research by the National Transportation Safety Board shows that 73 percent of serious mistakes made by jet cockpit crews are made the very first day that a crew flies together as a team and that 44 percent of serious mistakes occur on their very first flight together that day (pilot teams fly two to three flights per day). Moreover, research has shown that fatigued pilot crews who have worked together before make significantly fewer errors than rested crews who have never worked together.[86] Their experience working together helps them overcome their fatigue and outperform new teams that have not worked together before. So, once you've created effective teams, keep them together as long as possible.

10-4c Team Training

After selecting the right people for teamwork, you need to train them. To be successful, teams need significant training, particularly in interpersonal skills, decision-making and problem-solving skills, conflict resolution skills, and technical training. Organizations that create work teams *often underestimate the amount of training* required to make teams effective. This mistake occurs frequently in successful organizations where managers assume that if employees can work effectively on their own, they can work effectively in teams. In reality, companies that successfully use teams provide thousands of hours of training to make sure that teams work. Stacy Myers, a consultant who helps companies implement teams, says, "When we help companies move to teams, we also require that employees take basic quality and business knowledge classes as well. Teams must know how their work affects the company, and how their success will be measured."[87]

Most commonly, members of work teams receive training in interpersonal skills. **Interpersonal skills** such as listening, communicating, questioning, and providing feedback enable people to have effective

Pixsooz/iStockphoto.com

Team level the average level of ability, experience, personality, or any other factor on a team

Team diversity the variances or differences in ability, experience, personality, or any other factor on a team

Interpersonal skills skills, such as listening, communicating, questioning, and providing feedback, that enable people to have effective working relationships with others

working relationships with others. Consultant Peter Grazier, founder of Teambuilding Inc., says, "Teams have told us that if they had to do it over again they would have more of the people skills upfront. They don't struggle with the technical stuff. They tend to struggle with the people skills."[88] Because of teams' autonomy and responsibility, many companies also give team members training in *decision-making and problem-solving skills* to help them do a better job of cutting costs and improving quality and customer service. Many organizations also teach teams *conflict resolution skills*. Teambuilding Inc.'s Grazier explains that "the diversity of values and personalities makes a team powerful, but it can be the greatest source of conflict. If you're a detail person and I'm not, and we get on a team, you might say that we need more analysis on a problem before making a decision, [while I] may want to make a decision [right away]." But, if I've been trained in problem-solving and conflict resolution, "then I look at your detail [focus] as something that is needed in a team because it's a shortcoming of mine."[89] Taine Moufarrige, executive director of Servcorp, a global company hosting serviced and virtual offices for about 12,000 clients, agrees. Says Moufarrige, "It's not just about disagreements, it's about working through problems, managing differences of opinion, and that's vital for moving forward."[90]

Firms must also provide team members with the *technical training* they need to do their jobs, particularly if they are being cross-trained to perform all of the different jobs on the team. Before teams were created at Milwaukee Mutual Insurance, separate employees performed the tasks of rating, underwriting, and processing insurance policies. After extensive cross-training, however, each team member can now do all three jobs.[91] Cross-training is less appropriate for teams of highly skilled workers. For instance, it is unlikely that a group of engineers, computer programmers, and systems analysts would be cross-trained for each other's jobs.

Team leaders need training, too, as they often feel unprepared for their new duties. New team leaders face myriad problems ranging from confusion about their new roles as team leaders (compared with their old jobs as managers or employees) to not knowing where to go for help when their teams have problems. The solution is extensive training. Overall, does team training work? One recent study found that across a wide variety of settings, tasks, team types, and 2,650 teams in different organizations, team training was positively related to team performance outcomes.[92]

10-4d Team Compensation and Recognition

Compensating teams correctly is very difficult. For instance, one survey found that only 37 percent of companies were satisfied with their team compensation plans and even fewer, just 10 percent, reported being "very positive."[93] One of the problems, according to Susan Mohrman of the Center for Effective

pavlen/iStockphoto.com

Organizations at the University of Southern California, is that "there is a very strong set of beliefs in most organizations that people should be paid for how well they do. So when people first get put into team-based organizations, they really balk at being paid for how well the team does. It sounds illogical to them. It sounds like their individuality and their sense of self-worth are being threatened."[94] Consequently, companies need to carefully choose a team compensation plan and then fully explain how teams will be rewarded. One basic requirement for team compensation to work is that the level of rewards (individual versus team) must match the level of performance (individual versus team).

Employees can be compensated for team participation and accomplishments in three ways: skill-based pay, gainsharing, and nonfinancial rewards. **Skill-based pay** programs pay employees for learning additional skills or knowledge.[95] These programs encourage employees to acquire the additional skills they will need to perform multiple jobs within a team and to share knowledge with others within their work groups.[96] For example, at the Patience & Nicholson (P&N) drill bit factory in Kaiapoi, New Zealand, workers produce 50,000 drill bits a day for export to Australia, Taiwan, Thailand, and other locations primarily in Asia. P&N uses a skill-based pay system. As employees learn how to run the various machines required to produce drill bits, their pay increases. According to operations manager Rick Smith, workers who are dedicated to learning can increase their pay by $6 an hour over the course of three or four years.[97]

In **gainsharing** programs, companies share the financial value of performance gains, such as productivity increases, cost savings, or quality improvements, with their workers.[98] *Nonfinancial rewards* are another way to reward teams for their performance. These rewards, which can range from vacations to T-shirts, plaques, and coffee mugs, are especially effective when coupled with management recognition, such as awards, certificates, and praise.[99] Nonfinancial awards tend to be most effective when teams or team-based interventions, such as total quality management (see Chapter 18), are first introduced.[100]

Which team compensation plan should your company use? In general, skill-based pay is most effective for self-managing and self-directing teams performing complex tasks. In these situations, the more each team member knows and can do, the better the whole team performs. By contrast, gainsharing works best in relatively stable environments where employees can focus on improving productivity, cost savings, or quality.

Skill-based pay compensation system that pays employees for learning additional skills or knowledge

Gainsharing a compensation system in which companies share the financial value of performance gains, such as increased productivity, cost savings, or quality, with their workers

STUDY TOOLS 10

LOCATED AT THE BACK OF YOUR BOOK:

☐ Rip out and study the Chapter Review Card at the end of the book

LOG IN TO WWW.CENGAGEBRAIN.COM TO:

☐ Review Key Term Flashcards

☐ Complete Practice Quizzing (take up to four times without repeating the same quiz)

☐ Complete Games: Beat the Clock and Crossword Puzzle

☐ Complete Interactive Content: Graded Quiz, Media Quiz, and Fill-in-the-Blank Questions

☐ Watch Management Workplace Video on "Holden"

☐ Work Through the What Would You Do Case on Cessna Headquarters

11 Managing Human Resource Systems

svetikd/iStockphoto.com

LEARNING OUTCOMES

11-1 Explain how different employment laws affect human resource practice.

11-2 Explain how companies use recruiting to find qualified job applicants.

11-3 Describe the selection techniques and procedures that companies use when deciding which applicants should receive job offers.

11-4 Describe how to determine training needs and select the appropriate training methods.

11-5 Discuss how to use performance appraisal to give meaningful performance feedback.

11-6 Describe basic compensation strategies and discuss the four kinds of employee separations.

After you finish

this chapter, go

to **PAGE 246** for

STUDY TOOLS

11-1 EMPLOYMENT LEGISLATION

Human resource management (HRM), or the process of finding, developing, and keeping the right people to form a qualified work force, is one of the most difficult and important of all management tasks. This chapter is organized around the three parts of the human resource management process shown in Exhibit 11.1: attracting, developing, and keeping a qualified work force.

This chapter will walk you through the steps of the HRM process. We explore how companies use recruiting and selection techniques to attract and hire qualified employees to fulfill human resource needs. The next part of the chapter discusses how training and performance appraisal can develop the knowledge, skills, and abilities of the work force. The chapter concludes with a review of compensation and employee separation; that is, how companies can keep their best workers through effective compensation practices and how they can manage the separation process when employees leave the organization.

Before we explore how human resource systems work, you need to understand better the complex legal environment in which they exist. So we'll begin the chapter by reviewing the federal laws that govern human resource management decisions.

When Justin Bassett, a statistician, applied for a job, he was asked to answer questions, list references, and provide the interviewer with his Facebook username and password. Astounded by the request, he withdrew his application, not wanting to work for a company that would ask for such information. Orin Kerr, a law professor at George Washington University, says it's "an egregious privacy violation" and "akin to requiring someone's house keys." Law enforcement agencies, such as police departments and correctional agencies, commonly ask new recruits for Facebook login information to check for gang affiliations. Robert Collins was asked for his Facebook login information just to be able to return to his job as a correctional officer after a leave following his mother's death. He provided the information but said, "To me, that's still invasive. I can appreciate the desire to learn more about the applicant, but it's still a violation of people's personal privacy." Rather than asking for log-in information, some companies will ask applicants to "friend" the interviewer. And, some companies, like Sears, ask applicants to log in to Facebook at the interview, after which it uses software to extract and search for information, including friend lists. Is it legal to ask job applicants for their Facebook log-in information? To ask them to log in on company computers? To friend the job interviewer?[1]

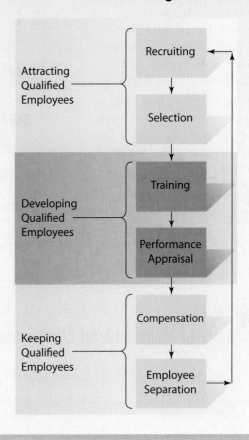

Exhibit 11.1
The Human Resource Management Process

As the Facebook example illustrates, the human resource planning process occurs in a very complicated legal environment.

*Let's explore employment legislation by reviewing **11-1a** the major federal employment laws that affect human resource practice, **11-1b** how the concept of adverse impact is related to employment discrimination,** and **11-1c** the laws regarding sexual harassment in the workplace.*

11-1a Federal Employment Laws

Exhibit 11.2 lists the major federal employment laws and their websites, where you can find more detailed

Human resource management (HRM) the process of finding, developing, and keeping the right people to form a qualified work force

information. Except for the Family and Medical Leave Act and the Uniformed Services Employment and Reemployment Rights Act, which are administered by the Department of Labor (http://www.dol.gov), all of these laws are administered by the EEOC (http://www.eeoc.gov). The general effect of this body of law, which is still evolving through court decisions, is that employers may not discriminate in employment decisions on the basis of sex, age, religion, color, national origin, race, disability, or genetic history.[2] The intent is to make these factors irrelevant in employment decisions. Stated another way, employment decisions should be based on factors that are "job related," "reasonably necessary," or a "business necessity" for successful job performance. The only time that sex, age, religion, and the like can be used to make employment decisions is when they are considered a bona fide occupational qualification. Title VII of the 1964 Civil Rights Act says that it is legal to hire and employ someone on the

Username: _____

Password: _____

© viviamo/iStockphoto.com

Exhibit 11.2

Summary of Major Federal Employment Laws

Law	URL	Description
■ Genetic Information Nondiscrimination Act of 2008	http://www.eeoc.gov/laws/types/genetic.cfm	Prohibits discrimination on the basis of genetic information.
■ Equal Pay Act of 1963	http://www.eeoc.gov/laws/statutes/epa.cfm	Prohibits unequal pay for males and females doing substantially similar work.
■ Title VII of the Civil Rights Act of 1964	http://www.eeoc.gov/laws/statutes/titlevii.cfm	Prohibits employment discrimination on the basis of race, color, religion, gender, or national origin.
■ Age Discrimination in Employment Act of 1967	http://www.eeoc.gov/laws/statutes/adea.cfm	Prohibits discrimination in employment decisions against persons age forty and older.
■ Pregnancy Discrimination Act of 1978	http://www.eeoc.gov/laws/statutes/pregnancy.cfm	Prohibits discrimination in employment against pregnant women.
■ Americans with Disabilities Act of 1990	http://www.eeoc.gov/laws/statutes/ada.cfm	Prohibits discrimination on the basis of physical or mental disabilities.
■ Civil Rights Act of 1991	http://www.eeoc.gov/laws/statutes/cra-1991.cfm	Strengthened the provisions of the Civil Rights Act of 1964 by providing for jury trials and punitive damages.
■ Family and Medical Leave Act of 1993	http://www.dol.gov/whd/fmla/index.htm	Permits workers to take up to twelve weeks of unpaid leave for pregnancy and/or birth of a new child, adoption or foster care of a new child, illness of an immediate family member, or personal medical leave.
■ Uniformed Services Employment and Reemployment Rights Act of 1994	http://www.dol.gov/compliance/laws/comp-userra.htm	Prohibits discrimination against those serving in the armed forces reserve, the National Guard, or other uniformed services; guarantees that civilian employers will hold and then restore civilian jobs and benefits for those who have completed uniformed service.

© spirit of america/Shutterstock.com

basis of sex, religion, or national origin when there is a **bona fide occupational qualification (BFOQ)** that is "reasonably necessary to the normal operation of that particular business." A Baptist church hiring a new minister can reasonably specify that being a Baptist rather than a Catholic or Presbyterian is a BFOQ for the position. However, it's unlikely that the church could specify race or national origin as a BFOQ. In general, the courts and the EEOC take a hard look when a business claims that sex, age, religion, color, national origin, race, or disability is a BFOQ. For instance, consistent with the company's marketing theme, the female waitstaff at Hooters restaurants wear short nylon shorts and cutoff T-shirts that show their midriffs. When a Chicago man alleged that he had applied for a server's job at a Hooters restaurant and was rejected because of his sex, Hooters claimed that it was "in the business of providing vicarious sexual recreation" and that "female sexuality was a bona fide occupational qualification for its waitstaff."[3] The EEOC, however, rejected that argument.

It is important to understand, however, that these laws apply to the entire HRM process and not just to selection decisions (e.g., hiring or promotion). These laws also cover all training and development activities, performance appraisals, terminations, and compensation decisions. Employers who use sex, age, race, or religion to make employment-related decisions when those factors are unrelated to an applicant's or employee's ability to perform a job may face charges of discrimination from employee lawsuits or the EEOC.

In addition to the laws presented in Exhibit 11.2, there are two other important sets of federal laws: labor laws and laws and regulations governing safety standards. Labor laws regulate the interaction between management and labor unions that represent groups of employees. These laws guarantee employees the right to form and join unions of their own choosing. For more information about labor laws, see the National Labor Relations Board at http://www.nlrb.gov.

The Occupational Safety and Health Act (OSHA) requires that employers provide employees with a workplace that is "free from recognized hazards that are causing or are likely to cause death or serious physical harm." This law is administered by the Occupational Safety and Health Administration (which, like the act, is referred to as OSHA). OSHA sets safety and health standards for employers and conducts inspections to determine whether those standards are being met. Employers who do not meet OSHA standards may be fined.[4] Even though it's well known that asbestos fiber causes cancer, AMD Industries in Cicero, Illinois, used untrained employees to remove asbestos from one of its facilities and did not provide safety training, protective gear, or a vacuum system to limit exposure to asbestos dust. Because of these egregious safety violations, OSHA fined the company $1.2 million.[5]

For more information about OSHA, see http://www.osha.gov.

11-1b Adverse Impact and Employment Discrimination

The EEOC has investigatory, enforcement, and informational responsibilities. Therefore, it investigates charges of discrimination, enforces the employment discrimination laws in federal court, and publishes guidelines that organizations can use to ensure they are in compliance with the law. One of the most important guidelines, jointly issued by the EEOC, the U.S. Department of Labor, the U.S. Department of Justice, and the federal Office of Personnel Management, is the *Uniform Guidelines on Employee Selection Procedures*, which can be read in their entirety at http://www.uniformguidelines.com/uniformguidelines.html. These guidelines define two important criteria, disparate treatment and adverse impact, which are used in determining whether companies have engaged in discriminatory hiring and promotion practices.

Disparate treatment, which is *intentional* discrimination, occurs when people, despite being qualified, are *intentionally* not given the same hiring, promotion, or membership opportunities as other employees because of their race, color, age, sex, ethnic group, national origin, or religious beliefs.[6] Bobby Nickel, a former facilities manager at Staples, the office supply retailer, was awarded $26 million by a jury which found Staples guilty of harassing him by calling him an "old coot" and an "old goat" and firing him because he was an older employee with a higher salary.[7]

Legally, a key element of discrimination lawsuits is establishing motive, meaning that the employer intended to discriminate. If no motive can be established, then a claim of disparate treatment may actually be

Bona fide occupational qualification (BFOQ) an exception in employment law that permits sex, age, religion, and the like to be used when making employment decisions, but only if they are "reasonably necessary to the normal operation of that particular business." BFOQs are strictly monitored by the Equal Employment Opportunity Commission

Disparate treatment intentional discrimination that occurs when people are purposely not given the same hiring, promotion, or membership opportunities because of their race, color, sex, age, ethnic group, national origin, or religious beliefs

a case of adverse impact. **Adverse impact,** which is *unintentional* discrimination, occurs when members of a particular race, sex, or ethnic group are *unintentionally* harmed or disadvantaged because they are hired, promoted, or trained (or any other employment decision) at substantially lower rates than others. The courts and federal agencies use the **four-fifths (or 80 percent) rule** to determine if adverse impact has occurred. Adverse impact occurs if the decision rate for a protected group of people is less than four-fifths (or 80 percent) of the decision rate for a nonprotected group (usually white males). So, if one hundred white applicants and one hundred black applicants apply for entry-level jobs, and sixty white applicants are hired (60/100 = 60 percent), but only twenty black applicants are hired (20/100 = 20 percent), adverse impact has occurred (0.20/0.60 = 0.33). The criterion for the four-fifths rule in this situation is 0.48 (0.60 × 0.80 = 0.48). Since 0.33 is less than 0.48, the four-fifths rule has been violated.

Violation of the four-fifths rule is not an automatic indication of discrimination, however. If an employer can demonstrate that a selection procedure or test is valid, meaning that the test accurately predicts job performance or that the test is job related because it assesses applicants on specific tasks actually used in the job, then the organization may continue to use the test. If validity cannot be established, however, then a violation of the four-fifths rule may likely result in a lawsuit brought by employees, job applicants, or the EEOC itself.

11-1c Sexual Harassment

According to the EEOC, **sexual harassment** is a form of discrimination in which unwelcome sexual advances, requests for sexual favors, or other verbal or physical conduct of a sexual nature occurs. From a legal perspective, there are two kinds of sexual harassment, quid pro quo and hostile work environment.[8]

Quid pro quo sexual harassment occurs when employment outcomes, such as hiring, promotion, or simply keeping one's job, depend on whether an individual submits to being sexually harassed. For example, in a quid pro quo sexual harassment lawsuit against First Student, a company that provides school bus transportation, four females alleged that a supervisor made explicit comments about their bodies and what he wanted to do to them. He was also alleged to have touched a female worker's breasts, exposed himself, and then rubbed himself against her. When his sexual advances were refused, he punished the women by cutting their work hours, while promising longer hours to the other women if they would do what he asked. This made it a quid pro quo case by linking sexual acts to economic outcomes.[9]

A **hostile work environment** occurs when unwelcome and demeaning sexually related behavior creates an intimidating, hostile, and offensive work environment. In contrast to quid pro quo cases, a hostile work environment may not result in economic injury. However, it can lead to psychological injury when the work environment becomes stressful. A federal court jury found Mercy General Hospital in Sacramento, California, guilty of creating a sexually hostile work environment for Ani Chopourian, a cardiac surgery physician assistant. Chopourian was awarded $125 million in punitive damages, $3.5 million for lost wages and benefits, and $39 million for mental anguish. Chopourian was frequently subjected to touching and sex talk in the operating room. She says, "One harasser told me one day, 'You'll give in to me.' I'd look at

RapidEye/iStockphoto.com

him [and say], 'I'll never give in to you.' I'd look at my supervisor and say, 'Do something.' They'd just laugh."[10] She was fired after filing 18 complaints in two years. Mercy General is appealing the decision.

Finally, what should companies do to make sure that sexual harassment laws are followed and not violated?[11] First, respond immediately when sexual harassment is reported. A quick response encourages victims of sexual harassment to report problems to management rather than to lawyers or the EEOC. Furthermore, a quick and fair investigation may serve as a deterrent to future harassment. A lawyer for the EEOC says, "Worse than having no sexual harassment policy is a policy that is not followed. It's merely window dressing. You wind up with destroyed morale when people who come forward are ignored, ridiculed, retaliated against, or nothing happens to the harasser."[12]

Then take the time to write a clear, understandable sexual harassment policy that is strongly worded, gives specific examples of what constitutes sexual harassment, spells outs sanctions and punishments, and is widely publicized within the company. This lets potential harassers and victims know what will not be tolerated and how the firm will deal with harassment should it occur.

Next, establish clear reporting procedures that indicate how, where, and to whom incidents of sexual harassment can be reported. The best procedures ensure that a complaint will receive a quick response, that impartial parties will handle the complaint, and that the privacy of the accused and accuser will be protected. At DuPont, Avon, and Texas Industries, employees can call a confidential hotline 24 hours a day, 365 days a year.[13]

Finally, managers should also be aware that most states and many cities or local governments have their own employment-related laws and enforcement agencies. So compliance with federal law is often not enough. In fact, organizations can be in full compliance with federal law and at the same time be in violation of state or local sexual harassment laws.

11-2 RECRUITING

Gail Hyland-Savage, CEO of the real estate and marketing firm Michaelson, Connor & Boul, says, "Staffing is absolutely critical to the success of every company. To be competitive in today's economy, companies need the best people to create ideas and execute them for the organization. Without a competent and talented workforce, organizations will stagnate and eventually perish. The right employees are the most important resources of companies today."[14]

Recruiting is the process of developing a pool of qualified job applicants.

*Let's examine **11-2a what job analysis is and how it is used in recruiting, 11-2b how companies use internal recruiting**, and **11-2c external recruiting** to find qualified job applicants.*

11-2a Job Analysis and Recruiting

Job analysis is a "purposeful, systematic process for collecting information on the important work-related aspects of a job."[15] A job analysis typically collects four kinds of information:

▶ Work activities such as what workers do and how, when, and why they do it.

▶ The tools and equipment used to do the job.

▶ The context in which the job is performed, such as the actual working conditions or schedule.

▶ The personnel requirements for performing the job, meaning the knowledge, skills, and abilities needed to do a job well.[16]

Job analysis information can be collected by having job incumbents and/or supervisors complete questionnaires about their jobs, by direct observation, by interviews, or by filming employees as they perform their jobs.

Job descriptions and job specifications are two of the most important results of a job analysis. A **job description** is a written description of the basic tasks, duties, and responsibilities required of an employee holding a particular job. **Job specifications,** which are often included as a separate section of a job description, are a summary of the qualifications needed to successfully

Recruiting the process of developing a pool of qualified job applicants

Job analysis a purposeful, systematic process for collecting information on the important work-related aspects of a job

Job description a written description of the basic tasks, duties, and responsibilities required of an employee holding a particular job

Job specifications a written summary of the qualifications needed to successfully perform a particular job

perform the job. Exhibit 11.3 shows a job description for a firefighter for the city of Portland, Oregon.

Because a job analysis specifies what a job entails as well as the knowledge, skills, and abilities that are needed to do the job well, companies must complete a job analysis *before* beginning to recruit job applicants. Job analysis, job descriptions, and job specifications are the foundation on which all critical human resource activities are built. They are used during recruiting and selection to match applicant qualifications with the requirements of the job. Reddit, a news consolidation website where readers vote on which stories and discussions are the most important, wanted to hire a new programmer, but it didn't want to sort through thousands of applications from people who had no coding skills but thought it would be cool to work for the popular website. So it used the job description as a test to make sure the company would only receive applications from highly skilled programmers. Applications for the job were to be sent to S@reddit .com, with "S" representing a real email address that applicants had to figure out by solving a series of problems and equations. If you couldn't figure it out, you couldn't send in your job application. This puzzle helped Reddit match applicant qualifications to the requirements of the job.[17]

Job descriptions are also used throughout the staffing process to ensure that selection devices and the decisions based on these devices are job related. For example, the questions asked in an interview should be based on the most important work activities identified by a job analysis. Likewise, during performance appraisals, employees should be evaluated in areas that a job analysis has identified as the most important in a job.

Job analyses, job descriptions, and job specifications also help companies meet the legal requirement that their human resource decisions be job related. To be judged *job related*, recruitment, selection, training, performance appraisals, and employee separations must be valid and be directly related to the important aspects of the job, as identified by a careful job analysis. In fact, in *Griggs v. Duke Power Co.* and *Albemarle Paper Co. v. Moody*, the U.S. Supreme Court stated that companies should use job analyses to help establish the job relatedness of their human resource procedures.[18] The EEOC's *Uniform Guidelines on Employee Selection Procedures* also recommend that companies base their human resource procedures on job analysis.

11-2b Internal Recruiting

Internal recruiting is the process of developing a pool of qualified job applicants from people who already work in the company. Internal recruiting, sometimes called "promotion from within," improves employee commitment, morale, and motivation. Recruiting current employees also reduces recruitment start-up time and costs, and because employees are already familiar with the company's culture and procedures, they are more likely to succeed in new jobs. Internal recruitment "provides a higher level of employee satisfaction, so certainly it can be a retention driver," says Maureen Henson, vice president of human resources at Henry Ford Bi-County Hospital in Warren, Michigan. Internal applicants represent a "known commodity," relieving some of the risk of making a bad hiring decision.[19] Job posting and career paths are two methods of internal recruiting.

Job posting is a procedure for advertising job openings within the company to existing employees. A job description and requirements are typically posted on a bulletin board, in a company newsletter, or in an internal computerized job bank that is accessible only to employees. Job posting helps organizations discover hidden talent, allows employees to take responsibility for career planning, and makes it easier for companies to retain talented workers who are dissatisfied in their current jobs and would otherwise leave the company.[20] Indeed, a LinkedIn survey of workers who changed jobs found that 42 percent would have stayed with their former employers if a relevant position had been available.[21] LinkedIn vice president Parker Barrile says it's often the case that, "People quit their job, not the company."[22] Booz Allen

iofoto/iStockphoto.com

Internal recruiting the process of developing a pool of qualified job applicants from people who already work in the company

Exhibit 11.3

Job Description for a Firefighter for the City of Portland, Oregon

Yes, as a Firefighter you will fight fire and provide emergency medical services to your community. But it doesn't end there: your firefighting career offers you the opportunity to expand your skills to include Hazardous Materials Response, Specialty Response Teams (dive, rope rescue, confined space, etc.), Paramedic Care, Public Education and Information, Fire Investigation, and Fire Code Enforcement.

Teamwork

Professional Firefighters work as a team at emergency scenes. The work day also includes training, fire station and equipment maintenance, fire prevention activities, and public education. As a Firefighter, you must be in excellent physical condition to meet the demands of the job; this means you must work quickly, handling heavy equipment for long periods of time while wearing special protective gear in hot and hazardous environments. If you can meet the challenge of strenuous work and like the idea of helping people, consider applying for the position of Firefighter.

Work Schedule

Portland Fire & Rescue Firefighters work a 24-on/48-off shift. This means that Firefighters report to work at 8:00 a.m. the day of their shift and continue working until 8:00 a.m. the following morning. Our Firefighters then have the following two days (48 hours) off. Firefighters are required to work shifts on holidays and weekends. Portland Fire & Rescue also has 40-hour-a-week firefighters who work in Training, Inspections/Investigations, Public Education, Logistics, and Emergency Management. These positions are usually filled after a Firefighter has met the minimum requirements for these positions.

Source: Portland Fire and Rescue, accessed August 13, 2008, http://www.portlandonline.com/fire/index.cfm?a=haea&c=cgbil.

Kendall Griffin/iStockphoto.com

Hamilton, an international consulting firm, uses an internal recruiting platform called Inside First, which lists job openings and current employee profiles indicating skills, experience, languages spoken, and willingness to relocate. Thirty percent of its positions are now filled with internal hires thanks to Inside First, compared to 10 percent before.[23]

A study of seventy large global companies found that organizations that formalize internal recruiting and job posting have a lower average rate of turnover (11 percent) compared to companies that don't (15 percent turnover).[24] Likewise, a University of Pennsylvania study found external hires generally are more costly, less reliable hires. Specifically, external hires get paid 18 percent to 20 percent more than internal hires, are 61 percent more likely to be fired, and are 21 percent more likely to quit their jobs.[25]

A *career path* is a planned sequence of jobs through which employees may advance within an organization. Virginia Rometty, IBM's CEO, started as a systems engineer after studying computer science in college, worked in IBM's consulting division, became general manager for IBM's Global Insurance and Financial Services sector, and then became senior vice president of IBM Global Business Services. Immediately prior to being named CEO, she served as the senior vice president of IBM's Global Sales and Distribution division and was responsible for overseeing sales in 170 global markets.[26]

Career paths help employees focus on long-term goals and development while also helping companies increase employee retention. As you can see in Virginia Rometty's case, career paths can also help employees gain a broad range of experience, which is especially useful at higher levels of management.

11-2c External Recruiting

External recruiting is the process of developing a pool of qualified job applicants from outside the company.

> **External recruiting** the process of developing a pool of qualified job applicants from outside the company

AP Images/Amy Sancetta

Walmart will guarantee a job over the next five years to any veteran who applies for a job within twelve months of being honorably discharged. Walmart estimates it will hire 100,000 veterans during that time. William Simon, CEO and president of Walmart USA, says, "Let's be clear: Hiring a veteran can be one of the best decisions any of us can make. These are leaders with discipline, training and a passion for service." The focus on veterans—company outsiders—is a critical part of Walmart's recruiting strategy in all parts of the company.[27]

External recruitment methods include advertising (newspapers, magazines, direct mail, radio, or television), employee referrals (asking current employees to recommend possible job applicants), walk-ins (people who apply on their own), outside organizations (universities, technical/trade schools, professional societies), employment services (state or private employment agencies, temporary help agencies, and professional search firms), special events (career conferences or job fairs), and Internet job sites. Which external recruiting method should you use? Studies show that employee referrals, walk-ins, newspaper advertisements, and state employment agencies tend to be used most frequently for office/clerical and production/service employees. By contrast, newspaper advertisements and college/university recruiting are used most frequently for professional/technical employees. When recruiting managers, organizations tend to rely most heavily on newspaper advertisements, employee referrals, and search firms.[28]

In the last decade, the biggest change in external recruiting has been the increased use of the Internet. Some companies now recruit applicants through Internet job sites such as Monster.com, HotJobs.com, Hire.com, and CareerBuilder.com. Companies can post job openings for thirty days on one of these sites for about half the cost of running an advertisement just once in a Sunday newspaper. Plus, Internet job listings generate nine times as many résumés as one ad in the Sunday newspaper.[29] And because these sites attract so many applicants and offer so many services, companies save by finding qualified applicants without having to use more expensive recruitment and search firms, which typically charge one-third or more of a new hire's salary.[30]

Some companies are even hosting virtual job fairs, where job applicants click on recruiting booths to learn about the company, see the kinds of available jobs, and speak with company representatives via video chat or instant message. Because they don't need to send HR representatives on long trips and can interact with potential hires from all over the world, Boeing, Progressive, Citibank, and Amazon.com have found virtual job fairs to be an efficient, cost-effective way to find qualified candidates. When Procter & Gamble conducted a virtual career fair, 900 participants from Eastern Europe, including Turkey, Russia, and Romania, interacted with twenty specialized recruiting booths to learn about jobs in finance, sales, or local P&G offices. Ioannis Boukas learned about the career fair on LinkedIn and logged in from Athens, Greece. His next step was an in-person career fair, which led to three on-site interviews and a job in Geneva, Switzerland, as an assistant brand manager.[31]

11-3 SELECTION

Once the recruitment process has produced a pool of qualified applicants, the selection process is used to determine which applicants have the best chance of performing well on the job. When hiring programmers, Jocelyn Golden, Facebook's engineering director, says, "I'd rather have the top student out of U.T. or University of Central Florida than the 30th best from Stanford." Anyone who successfully completes a timed online coding challenge gets a phone interview. Phone interviews involve discussion of applicants' résumés but finish with programming exercises. Applicants invited to Facebook's campus for onsite interviews must solve more difficult coding problems, including a take-home "hack." Facebook engineer Carlos Bueno says, "If it says 'expert in X' [on your résumé], we will try to schedule you with a proven expert in X, so be prepared. If you are not, leave it off."[32]

As this example illustrates, **selection** is the process of gathering information about job applicants to decide who should be offered a job. To make sure that selection decisions are accurate and legally defendable, the EEOC's *Uniform Guidelines on Employee Selection Procedures* recommend that all selection procedures be validated. **Validation** is the process of determining how well a selection test or procedure predicts future job performance. The better or more accurate the prediction of future job performance, the more valid a test is said to be.

*Let's examine common selection procedures such as **11-3a application forms and résumés, 11-3b references and background checks, 11-3c selection tests**, and **11-3d interviews**.*

11-3a Application Forms and Résumés

The first selection devices that most job applicants encounter when they seek a job are application forms and résumés. Both contain similar information about an applicant, such as name, address, job and educational history, and so forth. Though an organization's application form often asks for information already provided by the applicant's résumé, most organizations prefer to collect this information in their own format for entry into a **human resource information system (HRIS)**.

Employment laws apply to application forms just as they do to all selection devices. Application forms may ask applicants only for valid, job-related information. Nonetheless, application forms commonly ask applicants for non-job-related information such as marital status, maiden name, age, or date of high school graduation. Indeed, one study found that 73 percent of organizations had application forms that violated at least one federal or state law.[33] Likewise, interviewers may not ask about medical histories or genetics, religious beliefs, or citizenship. Exhibit 11.4 provides a more detailed explanation and list of the kinds of information that companies may *not* request in application forms, during job interviews, or in any other part of the selection process.

Courts will assume that you consider all of the information you request of applicants even if you actually don't. Be sure to ask only those questions that relate directly to the candidate's ability and motivation to perform the job. Furthermore, using social media like Facebook and LinkedIn at the initial stage of the hiring process can give employers access to information they're not allowed to obtain directly from applicants. Attorney James McDonald says, "I advise employers that it's not a good idea to use social media as a screening tool. You need to control the information you receive so you're only getting information that is legal for you to take into accounting."[34]

Résumés also pose problems for companies, but in a different way. Accu-Screen Inc. has kept records for fourteen years on résumé falsification data and reports that approximately 43 percent of résumés and job applications contain false information. According to a study conducted by J. J. Keller & Associates Inc., the nation's leading provider of risk and regulatory management solutions, 55 percent of human resource professionals have discovered lies on résumés or applications when conducting pre-employment background or reference

---

Selection the process of gathering information about job applicants to decide who should be offered a job

Validation the process of determining how well a selection test or procedure predicts future job performance; the better or more accurate the prediction of future job performance, the more valid a test is said to be

Human resource information system (HRIS) a computerized system for gathering, analyzing, storing, and disseminating information related to the HRM process

checks.[35] Therefore, managers should verify the information collected via résumés and application forms by comparing it with additional information collected during interviews and other stages of the selection process, such as references and background checks, which are discussed next.

11-3b References and Background Checks

Nearly all companies ask an applicant to provide **employment references,** such as the names of previous employers or coworkers, whom they can contact to learn more about the candidate. **Background checks** are used to verify the truthfulness and accuracy of information that applicants provide about themselves and to uncover negative, job-related background information not provided by applicants. Background checks are conducted by contacting "educational institutions, prior employers, court records, police and governmental agencies, and other informational sources, either by telephone, mail, remote computer access, or through in-person investigations."[36]

Unfortunately, previous employers are increasingly reluctant to provide references or background check information for fear of being sued by previous employees for defamation.[37] If former employers provide potential employers with unsubstantiated information that damages applicants' chances of being hired, applicants can (and do) sue for defamation. As a result, 54 percent of employers will not provide information about previous employees.[38] Many provide only dates of employment, positions held, and date of separation.

When previous employers decline to provide meaningful references or background information, they put other employers at risk of *negligent hiring* lawsuits, in which an employer is held liable for the actions of an employee who would not have been hired if the employer had conducted a thorough reference search and background check.[39] Heyl Logistics hired Washington Transportation, a trucking firm, to deliver bottled water, but its driver took drugs, fell asleep, hit a truck, and killed another driver. The killed driver's family sued

Employment references sources such as previous employers or coworkers who can provide job-related information about job candidates

Background checks procedures used to verify the truthfulness and accuracy of information that applicants provide about themselves and to uncover negative, job-related background information not provided by applicants

Exhibit 11.4
Don't Ask! Topics to Avoid in an Interview

1. **Children.** Don't ask applicants if they have children, plan to have them, or have or need child care. Questions about children can unintentionally single out women.

2. **Age.** Because of the Age Discrimination in Employment Act, employers cannot ask job applicants their age during the hiring process. Since most people graduate high school at the age of eighteen, even asking for high school graduation dates could violate the law.

3. **Disabilities.** Don't ask if applicants have physical or mental disabilities. According to the Americans with Disabilities Act, disabilities (and reasonable accommodations for them) cannot be discussed until a job offer has been made.

4. **Physical characteristics.** Don't ask for information about height, weight, or other physical characteristics. Questions about weight could be construed as leading to discrimination toward overweight people, and studies show that they are less likely to be hired in general.

5. **Name.** Yes, you can ask an applicant's name, but you cannot ask a female applicant for her maiden name because it indicates marital status. Asking for a maiden name could also lead to charges that the organization was trying to establish a candidate's ethnic background.

6. **Citizenship.** Asking applicants about citizenship could lead to claims of discrimination on the basis of national origin. However, according to the Immigration Reform and Control Act, companies may ask applicants if they have a legal right to work in the United States.

7. **Lawsuits.** Applicants may not be asked if they have ever filed a lawsuit against an employer. Federal and state laws prevent this to protect whistleblowers from retaliation by future employers.

8. **Arrest records.** Applicants cannot be asked about their arrest records. Arrests don't have legal standing. However, applicants can be asked whether they have been convicted of a crime.

9. **Smoking.** Applicants cannot be asked if they smoke. Smokers might be able to claim that they weren't hired because of fears of higher absenteeism and medical costs. However, they can be asked if they are aware of company policies that restrict smoking at work.

10. **AIDS/HIV.** Applicants can't be asked about AIDS, HIV, or any other medical condition, including genetics. Questions of this nature would violate the Americans with Disabilities Act, as well as federal and state civil rights laws.

11. **Religion.** Applicants can't be asked about religious beliefs. Questions of this nature would violate federal and state civil rights laws.

12. **Genetic information.** Employers should avoid asking about genetic test results or family medical history. This would violate the Genetic Information Nondiscrimination Act, or GINA, which was designed to help encourage people to get more genetic screening done without the fear of employers or insurers using that information to deny employment or coverage.

Sources: J. S. Pouliot, "Topics to Avoid with Applicants," *Nation's Business* 80, no. 7 (1992): 57; M. Trottman, "Employers Beware When Asking about Workers' Health," *Wall Street Journal,* July 22, 2013, accessed July 9, 2014, http://blogs.wsj.com/atwork/2013/07/22/employers-beware-when-asking-about-workers-health/; L. Weber, "Hiring Process Just Got Dicer," *Wall Street Journal,* July 3, 2014, accessed July 9, 2014, http://online.wsj.com/articles/hiring-process-just-got-dicier-1404255998.

Dan Tero/iStockphoto.com

Heyl Logistics for negligent hiring, alleging it should have known that Washington Transportation operated without a license, did not test its drivers for drug use, and carried no insurance. Heyl was found guilty, Washington Transportation's driver was sent to prison for negligent homicide and driving under the influence, and the family was awarded $5.2 million in punitive damages.[40]

With previous employers generally unwilling to give full, candid references and with negligent hiring lawsuits awaiting companies that don't get such references and background information, what can companies do? They can conduct criminal record checks, especially if the job for which the person is applying involves money, drugs, control over valuable goods, or access to the elderly, people with disabilities, or people's homes.[41] According to the Society for Human Resource Management, 96 percent of companies conduct background checks and 80 percent of companies go further and conduct criminal record checks.[42] Now that companies provide criminal record checks for $10 an applicant, pulling data from 3,100 court systems nationwide, there's no excuse to not check. Louis DeFalco, corporate director of safety, security, and investigations at ABC Fine Wine & Spirits, which has 175 stores in Florida, makes the case for criminal record checks: "If I have a guy with four arrests and bad credit versus someone who has never been in trouble in his life, who am I going to hire? It's not rocket science."[43]

Another option is to use public networking sites like LinkedIn to identify and contact the colleagues, customers, and suppliers who are linked or connected to job applicants. LinkedIn's former CEO Dan Nye says that the company called twenty-three of his LinkedIn connections without his knowledge before offering him a face-to-face interview. With the growing use and popularity of social networking websites, Nye says such practices are "fair game." One downside to this approach is that it could unintentionally alert an applicant's current employer that the person is seeking another job. As a result, says Chuck Wardell, managing director at Korn/Ferry International, an executive recruitment firm, "You have to be careful referencing people who have jobs because you might blow them out of their jobs."[44]

After doing a background check, dig deeper for more information. Ask references to provide additional references. Next, ask applicants to sign a waiver that permits you to check references, run a background check, or contact anyone else with knowledge of their work performance or history. Likewise, ask applicants if there is anything they would like the company to know or if they expect you to hear anything unusual when contacting references.[45] This in itself is often enough to get applicants to share information they typically withhold. When you've finished checking, keep the findings confidential to minimize the chances of a defamation charge. Always document all reference and background checks, noting who was called and what information was obtained. Document everything, not just information you received. To reduce the likelihood that negligent hiring lawsuits will succeed, it's particularly important to document even which companies and people refused to share reference checks and background information.

Finally, consider hiring private investigators to conduct background checks, which can often uncover information missed by traditional background checks. For example, while traditional background checks should be able to verify applicants' academic credentials, a private investigator hired by the *Wall Street Journal* found that seven out of 358 senior executives at publicly traded firms had falsified claims regarding the college degrees they had earned.[46] Likewise, private investigators can potentially identify when applicants hire companies that provide fake references from fake bosses (to avoid negative references from previous employers). Indeed, one such business claims, "We can replace a supervisor with a fictitious one, alter your work history, provide you with a positive employment reputation, and give you the glowing reference you need."[47]

11-3c Selection Tests

Selection tests give organizational decision makers a chance to know who will likely do well in a job and who won't. The basic idea behind selection testing is to have applicants take a test that measures something directly or indirectly related to doing well on the job. The selection tests discussed here are specific ability tests, cognitive ability tests, biographical data, personality tests, work sample tests, and assessment centers.

Specific ability tests measure the extent to which an applicant possesses the particular kind of ability needed to do a job well. Specific ability tests are also called **aptitude tests** because they measure aptitude for doing a particular task well. For example, if you took the SAT to get into college, then you've taken the aptly named Scholastic Aptitude Test, which is one of the best predictors of how well students will do in college

Specific ability tests (aptitude tests) tests that measure the extent to which an applicant possesses the particular kind of ability needed to do a job well

Kali Nine LLC/iStockphoto.com

(i.e., scholastic performances).[48] Specific ability tests also exist for mechanical, clerical, sales, and physical work. For example, clerical workers have to be good at accurately reading and scanning numbers as they type or enter data. Exhibit 11.5 shows items similar to the Minnesota Clerical Test, in which applicants have only a short time to determine if the two columns of numbers and letters are identical. Applicants who are good at this are likely to do well as clerical or data entry workers.

Cognitive ability tests measure the extent to which applicants have abilities in perceptual speed, verbal comprehension, numerical aptitude, general reasoning, and spatial aptitude. In other words, these tests indicate how quickly and how well people understand words, numbers, logic, and spatial dimensions. Whereas specific ability tests predict job performance in only particular types of jobs, cognitive ability tests accurately predict job performance in almost all kinds of jobs.[49] Why is this so? The reason is that people with strong cognitive or mental abilities are usually good at learning new things, processing complex information, solving problems, and making decisions, and these abilities are important in almost all jobs.[50] In fact, cognitive ability tests are almost always the best predictors of job performance. Consequently, if you were allowed to use just one selection test, a cognitive ability test would be the one to use.[51] (In practice, though, companies use a battery of different tests because doing so leads to much more accurate selection decisions.)

Biographical data, or **biodata,** are extensive surveys that ask applicants questions about their personal backgrounds and life experiences. The basic idea behind biodata is that past behavior (personal background and life experience) is the best predictor of future behavior. For example, during World War II, the U.S. Air Force had to test tens of thousands of men without flying experience to determine who was likely to be a good pilot. Since flight training took several months and was very expensive, quickly selecting the right people for training was important. After examining extensive biodata, the air force found that one of the best predictors of success in flight school was whether students had ever built model airplanes that actually flew. This one biodata item was almost as good a predictor as the entire set of selection tests that the air force was using at the time.[52]

Most biodata questionnaires have over one hundred items that gather information about habits and attitudes, health, interpersonal relations, money, what it was like growing up in your family (parents, siblings, childhood years, teen years), personal habits, current home (spouse,

Cognitive ability tests tests that measure the extent to which applicants have abilities in perceptual speed, verbal comprehension, numerical aptitude, general reasoning, and spatial aptitude

Biographical data (biodata) extensive surveys that ask applicants questions about their personal backgrounds and life experiences

Exhibit 11.5
Clerical Test Items Similar to Those Found on the Minnesota Clerical Test

	Numbers/Letters		Same	
1.	3468251	3467251	Yes	No
			O	O
2.	4681371	4681371	Yes	No
			O	O
3.	7218510	7218520	Yes	No
			O	O
4.	ZXYAZAB	ZXYAZAB	Yes	No
			O	O
5.	ALZYXMN	ALZYXNM	Yes	No
			O	O
6.	PRQZYMN	PRQZYMN	Yes	No
			O	O

Source: N. W. Schmitt and R. J. Klimoski, Research Methods in Human Resource Management (Mason, OH: South-Western, 1991).

children), hobbies, education and training, values, preferences, and work.[53] In general, biodata are very good predictors of future job performance, especially in entry-level jobs.

You may have noticed that some of the information requested in biodata surveys is related to those topics employers should avoid in applications, interviews, or other parts of the selection process. This information can be requested in biodata questionnaires provided that the company can demonstrate that the information is job related (i.e., valid) and does not result in adverse impact against protected groups of job applicants. Biodata surveys should be validated and tested for adverse impact before they are used to make selection decisions.[54]

Work sample tests, also called *performance tests*, require applicants to perform tasks that are actually done on the job. So, unlike specific ability tests, cognitive ability tests, biographical data surveys, and personality tests, which are indirect predictors of job performance, work sample tests directly measure job applicants' capability to do the job. For example, a computer-based work sample test for potential real estate agents has applicants assume the role of a real estate agent who must decide how to interact with virtual clients in a game-like scenario. As in real life, the clients can be frustrating, confusing, demanding, or indecisive. In one situation, the wife loves the virtual house, but the husband hates it. The applicants, just like actual real estate agents, must demonstrate what they would do in these realistic situations.[55] This work sample simulation gives real estate companies direct evidence of whether applicants can do the job if they are hired. Work sample tests are generally very good at predicting future job performance; however, they can be expensive to administer and can be used for only one kind of job. For example, an auto dealership could not use a work sample test for mechanics as a selection test for sales representatives.

Assessment centers use a series of job-specific simulations that are graded by multiple trained observers to determine applicants' ability to perform managerial work. Unlike the previously described selection tests that are commonly used for specific jobs or entry-level jobs, assessment centers are most often used to select applicants who have high potential to be good managers. Assessment centers often last two to five days and require participants to complete a number of tests and exercises that simulate managerial work.

Exhibit 11.6
In-Basket Item for an Assessment Center for Store Managers

February 28
Sam & Dave's Discount Warehouse
Orange, California

Dear Store Manager,

Last week, my children and I were shopping in your store. After doing our grocery shopping, we stopped in the electronics department and asked the clerk, whose name is Donald Block, to help us find a copy of the latest version of the *Madden NFL* video game. Mr. Block was rude, unhelpful, and told us to find it for ourselves as he was busy.

I've been a loyal customer for over six years and expect you to immediately do something about Mr. Block's behavior. If you don't, I'll start doing my shopping somewhere else.

Sincerely,
Margaret Quinlan

Source: Adapted from N. W. Schmitt and R. J. Klimoski, *Research Methods in Human Resource Management* (Mason, OH: South-Western 1991).

Some of the more common assessment center exercises are in-basket exercises, role-plays, small-group presentations, and leaderless group discussions. An *in-basket exercise* is a paper-and-pencil test in which an applicant is given a manager's in-basket containing memos, phone messages, organizational policies, and other communications normally received by and available to managers. Applicants have a limited time to read through the in-basket, prioritize the items, and decide how to deal with each item. Experienced managers then score the applicants' decisions and recommendations. Exhibit 11.6 shows an item that could be used in an assessment center for evaluating applicants for a job as a store manager.

In a *leaderless group discussion*, another common assessment center exercise, a group of six applicants is given approximately two hours to solve a problem, but no one is put in charge (hence the name *leaderless* group discussion). Trained observers watch and score each participant on the extent to which he or she facilitates

Work sample tests tests that require applicants to perform tasks that are actually done on the job

Assessment centers a series of managerial simulations, graded by trained observers, that are used to determine applicants' capability for managerial work

discussion, listens, leads, persuades, and works well with others.

Are tests perfect predictors of job performance? No, they aren't. Some people who do well on selection tests will do poorly in their jobs. Likewise, some people who do poorly on selection tests (and therefore weren't hired) would have been very good performers. Nonetheless, valid tests will minimize selection errors (hiring people who should not have been hired and not hiring people who should have been hired) while maximizing correct selection decisions (hiring people who should have been hired and not hiring people who should not have been hired). In short, tests increase the chances that you'll hire the right person for the job, that is, someone who turns out to be a good performer. So, although tests aren't perfect, almost nothing predicts future job performance as well as the selection tests discussed here.

11-3d Interviews

In **interviews,** company representatives ask job applicants job-related questions to determine whether they are qualified for the job. Interviews are probably the most frequently used and relied on selection device. There are several basic kinds of interviews: unstructured, structured, and semistructured.

In **unstructured interviews,** interviewers are free to ask applicants anything they want, and studies show that they do. Because interviewers often disagree about which questions should be asked during interviews, different interviewers tend to ask applicants very different questions.[56] Furthermore, individual interviewers even seem to have a tough time asking the same questions from one interview to the next. This high level of variety can make things difficult. As a result, while unstructured interviews do predict job performance with some success, they are about half as accurate as structured interviews at predicting which job applicants should be hired.[57]

By contrast, with **structured interviews,** standardized interview questions are prepared ahead of time so that all applicants are asked the same job-related

questions.[58] Structuring interviews also ensures that interviewers ask only for important, job-related information. Not only are the accuracy, usefulness, and validity of the interview improved, but the chances that interviewers will ask questions about topics that violate employment laws (see Exhibit 11.4) are reduced.

The primary advantage of structured interviews is that comparing applicants is much easier because they are all asked the same questions. Four kinds of questions are typically asked in structured interviews. Situational questions ask applicants how they would respond in a hypothetical situation ("What would you do if . . .?"). These questions are more appropriate for hiring new graduates, who are unlikely to have encountered real-work situations because of their limited work experience. Behavioral questions ask applicants what they did in previous jobs that were similar to the job for which they are applying ("In your previous jobs, tell me about . . ."). These questions are more appropriate for hiring experienced individuals. Background questions ask applicants about their work experience, education, and other qualifications ("Tell me about the training you received at . . ."). Job-knowledge questions ask applicants to demonstrate their job knowledge (e.g., nurses might be asked, "Give me an example of a time when one of your patients had a severe reaction to a medication. How did you handle it?").[59]

Semistructured interviews lie between structured and unstructured interviews. A major part of the semistructured interview (perhaps as much as 80 percent) is based on structured questions, but some time is set aside for unstructured interviewing to allow the interviewer to probe into ambiguous or missing information uncovered during the structured portion of the interview.

How well do interviews predict future job performance? Contrary to what you've probably heard, recent evidence indicates that even unstructured interviews do a fairly good job.[60] When conducted properly, however, structured interviews can lead to much more accurate hiring decisions than unstructured interviews. In some cases, the validity of structured interviews can rival that of cognitive ability tests.

But even more important, because interviews are especially good at assessing applicants' interpersonal skills, they work particularly well with cognitive ability tests. Combining the two—using structured interviews together with cognitive ability tests to identify smart people who work well with others—leads to even better selection decisions than using either alone.[61] Exhibit 11.7 provides a set of guidelines for conducting effective structured employment interviews.

Exhibit 11.7
Guidelines for Conducting Effective Structured Interviews

Interview Stage	What to Do
Planning the Interview	• Identify and define the knowledge, skills, abilities, and other (KSAO) characteristics needed for successful job performance. • For each essential KSAO, develop key behavioral questions that will elicit examples of past accomplishments, activities, and performance. • For each KSAO, develop a list of things to look for in the applicant's responses to key questions.
Conducting the Interview	• Create a relaxed, nonstressful interview atmosphere. • Review the applicant's application form, résumé, and other information. • Allocate enough time to complete the interview without interruption. • Put the applicant at ease; don't jump right into heavy questioning. • Tell the applicant what to expect. Explain the interview process. • Obtain job-related information from the applicant by asking those questions prepared for each KSAO. • Describe the job and the organization to the applicant. Applicants need adequate information to make a selection decision about the organization.
After the Interview	• Immediately after the interview, review your notes and make sure they are complete. • Evaluate the applicant on each essential KSAO. • Determine each applicant's probability of success and make a hiring decision.

Source: B. M. Farrell, "The Art and Science of Employment Interviews," *Personnel Journal* 65 (1986): 91–94.

11-4 TRAINING

According to the American Society for Training and Development, a typical investment in training increases productivity by an average of 17 percent, reduces employee turnover, and makes companies more profitable.[62] Giving employees the knowledge and skills they need to improve their performance is just the first step in developing employees, however. The second step—and not enough companies do this—is giving employees formal feedback about their actual job performance.

Training means providing opportunities for employees to develop the job-specific skills, experience, and knowledge they need to do their jobs or improve their performance. American companies spend an estimated $164 billion a year on training.[63]

To make sure those training dollars are well spent, companies need to **11-4a determine specific training needs, 11-4b select appropriate training methods,** and **11-4c evaluate training.**

11-4a Determining Training Needs

Needs assessment is the process of identifying and prioritizing the learning needs of employees. Needs

> **Training** developing the skills, experience, and knowledge employees need to perform their jobs or improve their performance
>
> **Needs assessment** the process of identifying and prioritizing the learning needs of employees

You Quit? Here's a Bonus

Employees receive a bonus for a lot of different reasons—meeting (or exceeding) goals, saving company money, or coming up with a great new idea. At the online shoe seller Zappos.com, however, employees get a very different kind of bonus—new employees are given $2,000 to quit their jobs. This offer is made about one week into a four-week training program that all new hires have to go through. The reason behind the unusual bonus is to make sure that whoever takes a job at Zappos does so because of their commitment to company values. And while it may seem like such an offer can be abused, only about 2 percent or 3 percent of new hires actually take the money and run. Amazon.com recently adopted a similar policy whereby full-time employees are offered $2,000 to quit after their first year. Each subsequent year, the offer is raised $1,000, up to $5,000. Says Amazon CEO Jeff Bezos, "In the long-run, an employee staying somewhere they don't want to be isn't healthy for the employee or the company."

Source: E. V. Holtzclaw, "Bounce Back From a Bad Hire: 10 Tips," *Inc.*, November 19, 2012, accessed May 24, 2013, http://www.inc.com/eric-v-holtzclaw/bad-hire-tips-to-bounce-back.html; E. Cohn, "Why Amazon Pays Some Workers Up To $5,000 To Quit," *The Huffington Post*, April 10, 2014, accessed May 5, 2014, http://www.huffingtonpost.com/2014/04/10/amazon-pay-to-quit_n_5128035.html.

assessments can be conducted by identifying performance deficiencies, listening to customer complaints, surveying employees and managers, or formally testing employees' skills and knowledge.

Note that training should never be conducted without first performing a needs assessment. Sometimes, training isn't needed at all or isn't needed for all employees. Unfortunately, however, many organizations simply require all employees to attend training whether they need to or not. As a result, employees who are not interested or don't need the training may react negatively during or after training. Likewise, employees who should be sent for training but aren't may also react negatively. Consequently, a needs assessment is an important tool for deciding who should or should not attend training. In fact, employment law restricts employers from discriminating on the basis of age, sex, race, color, religion, national origin, or disability when selecting training participants. Just like hiring decisions, the selection of training participants should be based on job-related information.

11-4b Training Methods

Assume that you're a training director for a major oil company and that you're in charge of making sure all employees know how to respond effectively in case of an oil spill.[64] Exhibit 11.8 lists a number of training methods you could use: films and videos, lectures, planned readings, case studies, coaching and mentoring, group discussions, on-the-job training, role-playing, simulations and games, vestibule training, and computer-based learning. Which method would be best?

To choose the best method, you should consider a number of factors, such as the number of people to be trained, the cost of training, and the objectives of the training. For instance, if the training objective is to impart information or knowledge to trainees, then you should use films and videos, lectures, and planned readings. In our example, trainees might read a manual or attend a lecture about how to protect a shoreline to keep it from being affected by the spill.

If developing analytical and problem-solving skills is the objective, then use case studies, coaching and mentoring, and group discussions. In our example, trainees might view a video documenting how a team handled exposure to hazardous substances, talk with first responders, and discuss what they would do in a similar situation.

If practicing, learning, or changing job behaviors is the objective, then use on-the-job training, role-playing, simulations and games, and vestibule training. Employees at Caterpillar's Georgia training center are taught how to assemble tractors using computers and welding tools in a facility identical to the factory floor, including colored lights showing whether trainees are maintaining the pace of the production line Caterpillar uses in its factories.[65]

Exhibit 11.8
Training Objectives and Methods

Training Objective	Training Methods
Impart Information and Knowledge	■ *Films and videos.* Films and videos present information, illustrate problems and solutions, and effectively hold trainees' attention.
	■ *Lectures.* Trainees listen to instructors' oral presentations.
	■ *Planned readings.* Trainees read about concepts or ideas before attending training.
Develop Analytical and Problem-Solving Skills	■ *Case studies.* Cases are analyzed and discussed in small groups. The cases present a specific problem or decision, and trainees develop methods for solving the problem or making the decision.
	■ *Coaching and mentoring.* Coaching and mentoring of trainees by managers involves informal advice, suggestions, and guidance. This method is helpful for reinforcing other kinds of training and for trainees who benefit from support and personal encouragement.
	■ *Group discussions.* Small groups of trainees actively discuss specific topics. The instructor may perform the role of discussion leader.
Practice, Learn, or Change Job Behaviors	■ *On-the-job training.* New employees are assigned to experienced employees. The trainee learns by watching the experienced employee perform the job and eventually by working alongside the experienced employee. Gradually, the trainee is left on his or her own to perform the job.
	■ *Role-playing.* Trainees assume job-related roles and practice new behaviors by acting out what they would do in job-related situations.
	■ *Simulations and games.* Experiential exercises place trainees in realistic job-related situations and give them the opportunity to experience a job-related condition in a relatively low-cost setting. The trainee benefits from hands-on experience before actually performing the job, where mistakes may be more costly.
	■ *Vestibule training.* Procedures and equipment similar to those used in the actual job are set up in a special area called a "vestibule." The trainee is then taught how to perform the job at his or her own pace without disrupting the actual flow of work, making costly mistakes, or exposing the trainee and others to dangerous conditions.
Impart Information and Knowledge; Develop Analytical and Problem-Solving Skills; and Practice, Learn, or Change Job Behaviors	■ *Computer-based learning.* Interactive videos, software, CD-ROMs, personal computers, teleconferencing, and the Internet may be combined to present multimedia-based training.

Source: A. Fowler, "How to Decide on Training Methods," *People Management* 25, no. 1 (1995): 36.

If training is supposed to meet more than one of these objectives, then your best choice may be to combine one of the previous methods with computer-based training. Siemens, which makes everything from power plants to electronic scanners, developed an online video game called Plantville, in which users take on the role of Pete, the plant manager. The goal is to revitalize three old factories by hiring new workers, redesigning factory layouts, and replacing old machines with new ones from Siemens. Raj Batra, president of Siemens's Industry Automation division, says, "The virtual activity in Plantville mimics the real-world environment where plant managers continually watch key performance indicators and strive to maximize productivity and efficiency." Plantville's "hands-on" experience helps employees and outsiders better understand the intricacies of running a factory and serves not only as a training tool for employees but also as a recruiting tool for outsiders. Sign up to play and join 21,000 gamers from 160 countries at Plantville.com.[66]

These days, many companies are adopting Internet training, or "computer-based learning." E-learning can

be a good way to impart information, but it isn't always as effective for changing job behaviors or developing problem-solving and analytical skills. Second, e-learning requires a significant investment in computers and high-speed Internet and network connections for all employees. Finally, though e-learning can be faster, many employees find it so boring and unengaging that they may choose to do their jobs rather than complete e-learning courses when sitting alone at their desks. E-learning may become more interesting, however, as more companies incorporate game-like features such as avatars and competition into their e-learning courses.

offer several advantages. Because employees don't need to leave their jobs, travel costs are greatly reduced. Also, because employees can take training modules when it is convenient (i.e., they don't have to fall behind at their jobs to attend week-long training courses), workplace productivity should increase and employee stress should decrease. And, if a company's technology infrastructure can support it, e-learning can be much faster than traditional training methods. Westinghouse Electric, which provides technology, services, and equipment for the nuclear electric power industry, had difficulty hiring managers and workers with prior nuclear experience. Former director of talent management Jim Ice says, "We were bringing in first-line employees and even managers that hadn't been in the nuclear industry before." So it invested "tens of millions" of dollars to create Westinghouse University, which has 100 percent of its classes online and organized into seven "colleges": project management, nuclear, technical, leadership, business, behavioral, and manufacturing. For example, employees take Westinghouse University courses where they learn to analyze air samples and conduct radiation surveys.[67]

There are, however, several disadvantages to e-learning. First, despite its increasing popularity, it's not always the appropriate training method. E-learning can

11-4c Evaluating Training

After selecting a training method and conducting the training, the last step is to evaluate the training. Training can be evaluated in four ways: on *reactions* (how satisfied trainees were with the program), on *learning* (how much employees improved their knowledge or skills), on *behavior* (how much employees actually changed their on-the-job behavior because of training), or on *results* (how much training improved job performance, such as increased sales or quality, or decreased costs).[68] In general, training provides meaningful benefits for most companies if it is done well. For example, a study by the American Society for Training and Development shows that a training budget as small as $680 per employee can increase a company's total return on investment by 6 percent.[69] Chuck Runyon, CEO of Anytime Fitness, which has 2,500 locations, says, "The only thing worse than training people and having them leave is not training people and having them stay."[70]

11-5 PERFORMANCE APPRAISAL

Performance appraisal is the process of assessing how well employees are doing their jobs. Most employees and managers intensely dislike the performance appraisal process. Samuel Culbert, professor of management at

Performance appraisal the process of assessing how well employees are doing their jobs

UCLA, says there is nothing constructive about performance appraisals and calls them a "dysfunctional pretense." Culbert says, "It's a negative to corporate performance, an obstacle to straight-talk relationships, and a prime cause of low morale at work."[71]

Many people share this view. In fact, 70 percent of employees are dissatisfied with the performance appraisal process in their companies. Likewise, according to the Society for Human Resource Management, 90 percent of human resource managers are dissatisfied with the performance appraisal systems used by their companies.[72]

Performance appraisals are used for four broad purposes: making administrative decisions (e.g., pay increase, promotion, retention), providing feedback for employee development (e.g., performance, developing career plans), evaluating human resource programs (e.g., validating selection systems), and for documentation purposes (e.g., documenting performance ratings and decisions based on those ratings).[73]

Let's explore how companies can avoid some of these problems with performance appraisals by **11-5a accurately measuring job performance** *and* **11-5b effectively sharing performance feedback with employees**.

11-5a Accurately Measuring Job Performance

Workers often have strong doubts about the accuracy of their performance appraisals—and they may be right. For example, it's widely known that assessors are prone to errors when rating worker performance. Three of the most common rating errors are central tendency, halo, and leniency. *Central tendency error* occurs when assessors rate all workers as average or in the middle of the scale. *Halo error* occurs when assessors rate all workers as performing at the same level (good, bad, or average) in all parts of their jobs. *Leniency error* occurs when assessors rate all workers as performing particularly well. One of the reasons managers make these errors is that they often don't spend enough time gathering or reviewing performance data. Winston Connor, the former vice president of human resources at Huntsman Chemical, says, "Most of the time, it's just a ritual that managers go through. They pull out last year's review, update it and do it quickly."[74] What can be done to minimize rating errors and improve the accuracy with which job performance is measured? In general, two approaches have been used: improving performance appraisal measures themselves and training performance raters to be more accurate.

One of the ways companies try to improve performance appraisal measures is to use as many objective performance measures as possible. **Objective performance measures** are measures of performance that are easily and directly counted or quantified. Common objective performance measures include output, scrap, waste, sales, customer complaints, and rejection rates.

But when objective performance measures aren't available (and frequently they aren't), subjective performance measures have to be used instead. **Subjective performance measures** require that someone judge or assess a worker's performance. The most common kind of subjective performance measure is the graphic rating scale (GRS) shown in Exhibit 11.9. Graphic rating scales are most widely used because they are easy to construct, but they are very susceptible to rating errors.

A popular alternative to graphic rating scales is the **behavior observation scale (BOS)**. BOSs requires raters to rate the frequency with which workers perform specific behaviors representative of the job dimensions that are critical to successful job performance. Exhibit 11.9 shows a BOS for two important job dimensions for a retail salesperson: customer service and money handling. Notice that each dimension lists several specific behaviors characteristic of a worker who excels in that dimension of job performance. (Normally, the scale would list seven to twelve items per dimension, not three, as in the exhibit.) Notice also that the behaviors are good behaviors, meaning they indicate good performance, and the rater is asked to judge how frequently an employee engaged in those good behaviors. The logic behind the BOS is that better performers engage in good behaviors more often.

Not only do BOSs work well for rating critical dimensions of performance, but studies also show that managers strongly prefer BOSs for giving performance feedback; accurately differentiating between poor, average, and good workers; identifying training needs; and accurately measuring performance. And in response to the statement "If I were defending a company, this rating format would be an asset to my case," attorneys strongly preferred BOSs over other kinds of subjective performance appraisal scales.[75]

Objective performance measures measures of job performance that are easily and directly counted or quantified

Subjective performance measures measures of job performance that require someone to judge or assess a worker's performance

Behavior observation scales (BOSs) rating scales that indicate the frequency with which workers perform specific behaviors that are representative of the job dimensions critical to successful job performance

Exhibit 11.9
Subjective Performance Appraisal Scales

Graphic Rating Scale

Example 1: Quality of work performed is

	Very poor	Poor	Average	Good	Very good
	1	2	3	4	5

Example 2: Quality of work performed is

	Very poor (20% errors)	Poor (15% errors)	Average (10% errors)	Good (5% errors)	Very good (less than 5% errors)
	1	2	3	4	5

Behavioral Observation Scale

Dimension: Customer Service

	Almost Never				Almost Always
1. Greets customers with a smile and a "hello."	1	2	3	4	5
2. Calls other stores to help customers find merchandise that is not in stock.	1	2	3	4	5
3. Promptly handles customer concerns and complaints.	1	2	3	4	5

Dimension: Money Handling

	Almost Never				Almost Always
1. Accurately makes change from customer transactions.	1	2	3	4	5
2. Accounts balance at the end of the day, no shortages or surpluses.	1	2	3	4	5
3. Accurately records transactions in computer system.	1	2	3	4	5

The second approach to improving the measurement of workers' job performance is **rater training**. The most effective is frame-of-reference training, in which a group of trainees learn how to do performance appraisals by watching a videotape of an employee at work. Next, they evaluate the performance of the person in the videotape. A trainer (an expert in the subject matter) then shares his or her evaluations, and trainees' evaluations are compared with the expert's. The expert then explains the rationales behind his or her evaluations. This process is repeated until the differences in evaluations given by trainees and evaluations by the expert are minimized. The underlying logic behind the frame-of-reference training is that by adopting the frame of reference used by an expert, trainees will be able to accurately observe, judge, and use relevant appraisal scales to evaluate the performance of others.[76]

11-5b Sharing Performance Feedback

After gathering accurate performance data, the next step is to share performance feedback with employees. Unfortunately, even when performance appraisal ratings are accurate, the appraisal process often breaks down at the feedback stage. Employees become defensive and dislike hearing any negative assessments of their work, no matter how small. Managers become defensive, too, and dislike giving appraisal feedback

Rater training training performance appraisal raters in how to avoid rating errors and increase rating accuracy

as much as employees dislike receiving it. One manager says, "I myself don't go as far as those who say performance reviews are inherently destructive and ought to be abolished, but I agree that the typical annual-review process does nothing but harm. It creates divisions. It undermines morale. It makes people angry, jealous, and cynical. It unleashes a whole lot of negative energy, and the organization gets nothing in return."[77]

What can be done to overcome the inherent difficulties in performance appraisal feedback sessions? Since performance appraisal ratings have traditionally been the judgments of just one person, the boss, one possibility is to use **360-degree feedback**. In this approach, feedback comes from four sources: the boss, subordinates, peers and coworkers, and the employees themselves. The data, which are obtained anonymously (except for the boss's), are compiled into a feedback report comparing the employee's self-ratings with those of the boss, subordinates, and peers and coworkers. Usually, a consultant or human resource specialist discusses the results with the employee. The advantage of 360-degree programs is that negative feedback ("You don't listen") is often more credible when it comes from several people.

Herbert Meyer, who has been studying performance appraisal feedback for more than thirty years, recommends a list of topics to discuss in performance appraisal feedback sessions (see Exhibit 11.10).[78] Furthermore, managers can do three different things to make performance reviews more comfortable and productive. First, they should separate developmental feedback, which is designed to improve future performance, from administrative feedback, which is used as a reward for past performance, such as for raises. When managers give developmental feedback, they're acting as coaches, but when they give administrative feedback, they're acting as judges. These roles, coaches and judges, are clearly incompatible. As coaches, managers encourage, pointing out opportunities for growth and improvement, and employees are typically open and receptive to feedback. But as judges, managers are evaluative, and employees are typically defensive and closed to feedback.

Second, Meyer suggests that performance appraisal feedback sessions be based on self-appraisals, in which employees carefully assess their own strengths, weaknesses, successes, and failures in writing. Because employees play an active role in the review of their performance, managers can be coaches rather than judges. Also, because the focus is on future goals and development, both employees and managers are likely to be more satisfied with the process and more committed to future plans and changes. And, because the focus is on development and not administrative assessment, studies show that self-appraisals lead to more candid self-assessments than traditional supervisory reviews.[79]

Finally, what people do with the performance feedback they receive really matters. A study of 1,361 senior managers found that managers who reviewed their 360-degree feedback with an executive coach (hired by the company) were more likely to set specific goals for improvement, ask their bosses for ways to improve, and subsequently improve their performance.[80]

A five-year study of 252 managers found that their performance improved dramatically if they met with their subordinates to discuss their 360-degree

Neustockimages/iStockphoto.com

360-degree feedback a performance appraisal process in which feedback is obtained from the boss, subordinates, peers and coworkers, and the employees themselves

Exhibit 11.10
What to Discuss in a Performance Appraisal Feedback Session

- ✔ Overall progress—an analysis of accomplishments and shortcomings.
- ✔ Problems encountered in meeting job requirements.
- ✔ Opportunities to improve performance.
- ✔ Long-range plans and opportunities— for the job and for the individual's career.
- ✔ General discussion of possible plans and goals for the coming year.

Source: H. H. Meyer, "A Solution to the Performance Appraisal Feedback Enigma," *Academy of Management Executive* 5, no. 1 (1991): 68–76.

A New Way of Onboarding

For many, the first day of work is often the worst. Many companies are trying to change this by mixing up the typical onboarding process of stacks of paperwork and orientation meetings. According to Harvard Business School associate professor Francesca Gino, people find greater satisfaction and perform better when they're able to bring more of themselves to the job. Studies indicate that activities emphasizing autonomy and learning contribute to greater employee satisfaction and retention. Dog-boarding site Rover.com tries to help employees experience this from day one, allowing them to jump into projects immediately. Business process outsourcer Wipro experimented with an employee-centric onboarding program whereby new hires discussed their strengths and were given personalized sweatshirts. After six months, they discovered that those who went through the employee-centric program were 32 percent more likely to stay with the company.

Source: R.E. Silverman, "'Companies Try to Make the First Day for New Hires More Fun," *Wall Street Journal*, May 28, 2013, accessed May 8, 2014, http://online.wsj .com/news/articles/SB10001424127887323336104578501631475934850 ?KEYWORDS=companies+try+to+make+the+first+day&mg=reno64-wsj.

11-6 COMPENSATION AND EMPLOYEE SEPARATION

---

feedback ("You don't listen") and how they were going to address it ("I'll restate what others have said before stating my opinion"). Performance was dramatically lower for managers who never discussed their 360-degree feedback with subordinates and for managers who did not routinely do so. Why is discussing 360-degree feedback with subordinates so effective? These discussions help managers understand their weaknesses better, force them to develop a plan to improve, and demonstrate to the subordinates the managers' public commitment to improving.[81] In short, it helps to have people discuss their performance feedback with others, but it particularly helps to have them discuss their feedback with the people who provided it. This is why HCL Technologies, an outsourcer of technology services, not only has employees rate their bosses but also posts each manager's ratings on the company intranet for everyone to see, in order to hold top managers accountable.[82]

Compensation the financial and nonfinancial rewards that organizations give employees in exchange for their work

While China has more than a billion people, 80 percent of its manufacturers are having difficulty finding and keeping workers. Employers are responding by hiking wages, which have increased 74 percent in four years. **Pacific Resources International**, which has ten Chinese factories, pays its workers 20 percent more than minimum wage, provides insurance and free meals, and only asks employees to work forty to forty-five hours a week, which is low in China. Still, it loses employees to the insurance industry, where salaries are 40 percent larger.[83] Factories, which have already raised pay, are now addressing nonfinancial issues in hopes of becoming more attractive places to work. **Flextronics International** sponsors company picnics, talent shows (karaoke), speed-dating for unmarried workers, sports facilities for soccer and basketball, and hair salons. Chief procurement officer Tom Linton says, "If you are able to get employees connected socially, they're more likely to stay."[84]

Compensation includes both the financial and the nonfinancial rewards that organizations give employees in exchange for their work. **Employee separation** is a broad term covering the loss of an employee for any reason. *Involuntary separation* occurs when employers terminate or lay off employees. *Voluntary separation* occurs when employees quit or retire. Because employee separations affect recruiting, selection, training, and compensation, organizations should forecast the number of employees they expect to lose through terminations, layoffs, turnover, or retirements when doing human resource planning.

Let's learn more about compensation by examining the 11-6a compensation decisions that managers must make as well as 11-6b termination, 11-6c downsizing, 11-6d retirement, and 11-6e turnover.

11-6a Compensation Decisions

There are three basic kinds of compensation decisions: pay level, pay variability, and pay structure.[85] *Pay-level decisions* are decisions about whether to pay workers at a level that is below, above, or at current market wages. Companies use job evaluation to set their pay structures. **Job evaluation** determines the worth of each job by determining the market value of the knowledge, skills, and requirements needed to perform it. After conducting a job evaluation, most companies try to pay the going rate, meaning the current market wage. There are always companies, however, whose financial situation causes them to pay considerably less than current market wages.

Some companies choose to pay above-average wages to attract and keep employees. *Above-market wages* can attract a larger, more qualified pool of job applicants, increase the rate of job acceptance, decrease the time it takes to fill positions, and increase the time that employees stay.[86] While the average U.S. grocery store cashier makes $20,000 per year, entry-level cashiers at **QuikTrip**, a chain of convenience stores and gas stations, make $40,000 per year. Despite paying employees twice as much as its competitors, QuikTrip is profitable and growing. Compared to other convenience stores, its sales per square foot are 50 percent higher and its sales per labor hour are 66 percent larger.

Furthermore, QuikTrip trains new workers for two weeks before putting them in stores, teaching them everything from the right way to clean bathrooms to ordering merchandise and tracking inventory. Finally, because the company pays well and invests in its workers, most of its managers work their way up from entry-level cashier jobs. QuikTrip's Mike Thornbrugh says, "They can see that if you work hard, if you're smart, the opportunity to grow within the company is very, very good."[87]

Pay-variability decisions concern the extent to which employees' pay varies with individual and organizational performance. Linking pay to performance is intended to increase employee motivation, effort, and job performance. Piecework, sales commissions, profit sharing, employee stock ownership plans, and stock options are common pay-variability options. For instance, under **piecework** pay plans, employees are paid a set rate for each item produced up to some standard (e.g., thirty-five cents per item produced for output up to one hundred units per day). Once productivity exceeds the standard, employees are paid a set amount for each unit of output over the standard (e.g., forty-five cents for each unit above one hundred units). Under a sales **commission** plan, salespeople are paid a percentage of the purchase price of items they sell. The more they sell, the more they earn. At Installation & Services Technologies, which sells point-of-sales systems (high-tech cash registers), a salesperson's pay is determined in large part by how much he or she sells. All members of the sales staff receive a small base salary (about 35 percent of total pay) and a commission based on how much gross profit they make on sales—17 percent for $1 to $50,000, 24 percent for $50,001 to $100,000, and 30 percent over $100,000. Plus, every time a salesperson reaches a new profit level, he or she receives an extra $1,000.[88]

Because pay plans such as piecework and commissions are based on individual performance, they can reduce the incentive that people have to work together. Therefore, companies also use group incentives (discussed in Chapter 10) and organizational incentives, such

samxmeg/iStockphoto.com

Employee separation the voluntary or involuntary loss of an employee

Job evaluation a process that determines the worth of each job in a company by evaluating the market value of the knowledge, skills, and requirements needed to perform it

Piecework a compensation system in which employees are paid a set rate for each item they produce

Commission a compensation system in which employees earn a percentage of each sale they make

as profit sharing, employee stock ownership plans, and stock options, to encourage teamwork and cooperation.

With **profit sharing,** employees receive a portion of the organization's profits over and above their regular compensation. Southwest Airlines posted a profit of $754 million in 2013. Thirty percent of those profits, $228 million, will go to its employees as a result of the company's profit sharing plan.[89]

Employee stock ownership plans (ESOPs) compensate employees by awarding them shares of the company stock in addition to their regular compensation. Central States Manufacturing, a steel cutting firm in Lowell, Arkansas, is 100 percent owned by its 517 employees. Six and a half percent of each employee's annual pay goes into a tax-deferred ESOP account. Aaron King, a 60-year old truck driver with the company for twenty-three years, has accumulated $1.25 million in his ESOP account. Because of the ESOP, he says, "We hold one another accountable. Somebody leaving a bundle of metal where it could be run over— a $3,000 bundle—we go and get that guy and talk to him. [Because] It's going to come out of all of our paychecks."[90]

Stock options give employees the right to purchase shares of stock at a set price. Options work like this. Let's say you are awarded the right (or option) to buy one hundred shares of stock from the company for $5 a share. If the company's stock price rises to $15 a share, you can exercise your options, sell the stock for $15 a share, come out with $1,000. When you exercise your options, you pay the company $500 (one hundred shares at $5 a share), but because the stock is selling for $15 in the stock market, you can sell your one hundred shares for $1,500 and make $1,000. Of course, as the company's profits and share values increase, stock options become even more valuable to employees. Stock options have no value, however, if the company's stock falls below the option "grant price," the price at which the options have been issued to you. The options you have on one hundred shares of stock with a grant price of $5 aren't going to do you a lot of good if the company's stock is worth $2.50. Proponents of stock options argue that this gives employees and managers a strong incentive to work hard

Former Independent Steelworkers Union president and retired steelworker Walter Bish stands near steel coils at the Weirton Steel plant in Weirton, West Virginia. In 1994, Weirton Steel Corp. became the first major manufacturer and the largest company in America to be owned 100 percent by employees. Its early success inspired United Airlines, Avis, and Polaroid, among others, to adopt ESOPs.

to make the company successful. If they do, the company's profits and stock price increase, and their stock options increase in value. If they don't, profits stagnate or turn into losses, and their stock options decrease in value or become worthless. To learn more about ESOPs and stock options, see the National Center for Employee Ownership (http://www.nceo.org).

The incentive has to be more than just a piece of paper, however. It has to motivate employees with the real opportunity to grow the value of the company and their wealth. **Adworkshop**, a digital marketing agency that does website design and development, search marketing, media buying, and creative work, became an employee-owned company in 2007. Account supervisor Kelly Frady says the ESOP has energized employee commitment. She says, "Everyone knows that you do well and your stock will rise. It's a driving factor in making the company succeed in the long term." In the United States, 10,900 employee-owned businesses, worth $860 billion, are owned by 10 million employees.[91]

Pay-structure decisions are concerned with internal pay distributions, meaning the extent to which people in the company receive very different levels of pay.[92] With *hierarchical pay structures*, there are big differences from one pay level to another. The highest pay levels are for people near the top of the pay distribution. The basic idea behind hierarchical pay structures is that large differences in pay between jobs or organizational levels should motivate people to work harder to obtain those higher-paying jobs. Many publicly owned companies have hierarchical pay structures, paying huge salaries to their top managers and CEOs. For example, CEOs of Fortune 500 companies, the 500 largest U.S. firms, now make an average of $12.3 million per year, which is 354 times the average employee salary of $34,645.[93]

By contrast, *compressed pay structures* typically have fewer pay levels and smaller differences in pay between levels. Pay is less dispersed and more similar across jobs in the company. The basic idea behind compressed pay structures is that similar pay levels should lead to higher levels of cooperation, feelings of fairness and a common purpose, and better group and team performance.

So should companies choose hierarchical or compressed pay structures? The evidence isn't straightforward, but studies seem to indicate that there are significant problems with the hierarchical approach. The most damaging finding is that there appears to be little link between organizational performance and the pay of top managers.[94] Furthermore, studies of professional athletes indicate that hierarchical pay structures (e.g., paying superstars forty to fifty times as much as the lowest-paid athlete on the team) hurt the performance of teams and individual players.[95] Likewise, managers are twice as likely to quit their jobs when their companies have very strong hierarchical pay structures (i.e., when they're paid dramatically less than the people above them).[96] For now, it seems that hierarchical pay structures work best for independent work, where it's easy to determine the contributions of individual performers and little coordination with others is needed to get the job done. In other words, hierarchical pay structures work best when clear links can be drawn between individual performance and individual rewards. By contrast, compressed pay structures, in which everyone receives similar pay, seem to work best for interdependent work, which requires employees to work together. Some companies are pursuing a middle ground: combining hierarchical and compressed pay structures by giving ordinary workers the chance to earn more through ESOPs, stock options, and profit sharing.

11-6b Terminating Employees

The words "You're fired!" may have never been directed at you, but lots of people hear them, as more than 400,000 people a year get fired from their jobs. Getting fired is a terrible thing, but many managers make it even worse by bungling the firing process, needlessly provoking the person who was fired and unintentionally inviting lawsuits.

Manager Craig Silverman had to fire the head of a company whom his organization had just acquired. He was specifically instructed to invite her to a meeting, which would require her to travel halfway across the country, and then fire her immediately on arrival. He said, "I literally had to tell the car service to wait. I don't think it ever entered [her] mind that [she] would be terminated."[97] When Zynga terminated almost all of the employees from OMGPOP, a startup company it had acquired a year before, one of the employees tweeted, "I learned via Facebook I was laid off today and @omgpop office is closed. Thanks @zynga for again reminding me how not to operate a business."[98] A computer systems engineer was fired on "Take Your Daughter to Work Day," with his eight-year-old daughter sitting next to him in the human resource manager's office. He and his daughter were both escorted from the building.[99] How would you feel if you had been fired in one of these ways? Though firing is never pleasant (and managers hate firings nearly as much as employees do), managers can do several things to minimize the problems inherent in firing employees.

To start, in most situations, firing should not be the first option. Instead, employees should be given a chance to change their behavior. When problems arise, employees should have ample warning and must be specifically informed as to the nature and seriousness of the trouble they're in. After being notified, they should be given sufficient time to change their behavior. Ron Cohen is CEO and founder of **Acorda Therapeutics**, a company that develops therapies to restore neurological function for people with multiple sclerosis and spinal cord injuries. Cohen first fired an employee when he was thirty-one years old. He says it was painful, and "I wound up hugging the employee and she was crying on my shoulder." Since then, however, when he fires someone, they've had plenty of opportunities to address performance issues. Says Cohen, "I've learned over the years that if the employee doesn't expect it and know it's coming, you're not doing your job as a manager."[100]

If problems continue, the employees should again be counseled about their job performance, what could be done to improve it, and the possible consequences if things don't change (such as a written reprimand, suspension without pay, or firing). Sometimes this is enough to solve the problem. If the problem isn't corrected after several rounds of warnings and discussions, however, the employee may be terminated.[101]

Second, employees should be fired only for a good reason. Employers used to hire and fire employees under the legal principle of employment at will, which allowed them to fire employees for a good reason, a bad reason, or no reason at all. (Employees could also quit

for a good reason, a bad reason, or no reason whenever they desired.) As employees began contesting their firings in court, however, the principle of wrongful discharge emerged. **Wrongful discharge** is a legal doctrine that requires employers to have a job-related reason to terminate employees. In other words, like other major human resource decisions, termination decisions should be made on the basis of job-related factors such as violating company rules or consistently poor performance. And with former employees winning 68 percent of wrongful discharge cases and the average wrongful termination award at $532,000 and climbing, managers should record the job-related reasons for the termination, document specific instances of rule violations or continued poor performance, and keep notes and documents from the counseling sessions held with employees.[102]

11-6c Downsizing

Downsizing is the planned elimination of jobs in a company (see box "How to Conduct Layoffs"). Whether it's because of cost cutting, declining market share, previous overaggressive hiring and growth, or outsourcing, companies typically eliminate 1 million to 1.9 million jobs a year.[103] Two-thirds of companies that downsize will downsize a second time within a

year.[104] In 2012, Cisco cut 8,000 employees—about 9 percent of its workforce—in an effort to cut costs. In March 2013, it cut another 500 workers. Then, just five months later, Cisco cut 4,000 more employees—around 5 percent of its workforce—despite meeting earnings expectations.[105]

Does downsizing work? In theory, downsizing is supposed to lead to higher productivity and profits, better stock performance, and increased organizational flexibility. However, numerous studies demonstrate that it doesn't. For instance, a fifteen-year study of downsizing found that downsizing 10 percent of a company's work force produced only a 1.5 percent decrease in costs; that firms that downsized increased their stock price by only 4.7 percent over three years, compared with 34.3 percent for firms that didn't; and that profitability and productivity were generally not improved by downsizing. Downsizing can also result in the loss of skilled workers who would be expensive to replace when the company grows again. These results make it clear that the best strategy is to conduct effective human resource planning and avoid downsizing altogether. Indeed, downsizing should always be a last resort.[106]

If companies do find themselves in financial or strategic situations where downsizing is required for survival, however, they should train managers in how to break the news to downsized employees, have senior managers explain in detail why downsizing is necessary, and time the announcement so that employees hear it from the company and not from other sources, such as TV or newspaper reports.[107] Finally, companies should do everything they can to help downsized employees find other jobs. One of the best ways to do this is to use **outplacement services** that provide employment counseling for employees faced with downsizing. Outplacement services often include advice and training in preparing résumés, getting ready for job interviews, and even identifying job opportunities in other companies. Sixty-nine percent of companies provide outplacement services for laid-off employees, 61 percent provide extended health coverage, and most offer up to 26 weeks of severance payments.[108] Offering this kind of assistance can soften the blow from being laid off, preserve goodwill, and lower the risk of future lawsuits.[109]

Companies also need to pay attention to the survivors, the employees remaining after layoffs have occurred. University of Pennsylvania management professor Peter Cappelli says that survivors "may feel like they could just as easily be the next person laid off."[110] Lori Stewart

Wrongful discharge a legal doctrine that requires employers to have a job-related reason to terminate employees

Downsizing the planned elimination of jobs in a company

Outplacement services employment-counseling services offered to employees who are losing their jobs because of downsizing

Coletti, director of client services at Elaine Construction, a Newton, Massachusetts–based firm, said, "The general feeling is, 'Could I be next?' That's the level of uncertainty that you really have to combat."[111] The key to working with layoff survivors, according to Barry Nickerson, president of Dallas-based Marlow Industries, which downsized from 800 to 200 employees, is "Communicate. Communicate. Communicate." Nickerson says, "Every time we had a change we had a meeting to explain exactly what we were doing. We were very open with our employees about where we were financially. We would explain exactly the current status and where we were."[112]

11-6d Retirement

Early retirement incentive programs (ERIPs) offer financial benefits to employees to encourage them to retire early. Companies use ERIPs to reduce the number of employees in the organization, to lower costs by eliminating positions after employees retire, to lower costs by replacing high-paid retirees with lower-paid, less-experienced employees, or to create openings and job opportunities for people inside the company. For example, the state of Wyoming offered its employees a lump-sum bonus, additional insurance benefits, and increased monthly retirement payments to encourage early retirement. Its ERIP must have been fairly attractive, because 56 percent of the state employees eligible for early retirement

accepted. Thirty percent of the 437 positions vacated by the early retirees remained empty, saving the state $23.2 million over the first forty-six months of the program and a projected $65 million over eight years. After accounting for the costs of the increased early retirement benefits, the predicted savings came to more than $148,000 per retiree.[113]

Although ERIPs can save companies money, they can pose a big problem for managers if they fail to accurately predict which employees—the good performers or the poor performers—and how many will retire early. Consultant Ron Nicol says, "The thing that doesn't work is just asking for volunteers. You get the wrong volunteers. Some of your best people will feel they can get a job anywhere. Or you have people who are close to retirement and are a real asset to the company."[114] When Progress Energy, in Raleigh, North Carolina, identified 450 jobs it wanted to eliminate with an ERIP, it carefully shared the list of jobs with employees, indicated that layoffs would follow if not enough people took early retirement, and then held eighty meetings with employees to answer questions. Despite this care, an extra 1,000 employees, for a total of 1,450, took the ERIP offer and applied for early retirement![115]

Early retirement incentive programs (ERIPs) programs that offer financial benefits to employees to encourage them to retire early

Because of the problems associated with ERIPs, many companies are now offering **phased retirement,** in which employees transition to retirement by working reduced hours over a period of time before completely retiring. The advantage for employees is that they have more free time but continue to earn salaries and benefits without changing companies or careers. The advantage for companies is that it allows them to reduce salaries and hiring and training costs and retain experienced, valuable workers.[116]

11-6e Employee Turnover

Employee turnover is the loss of employees who voluntarily choose to leave the company. In general, most companies try to keep the rate of employee turnover low to reduce recruiting, hiring, training, and replacement costs. Not all kinds of employee turnover are bad for organizations, however. In fact, some turnover can actually be good. **Functional turnover** is the loss of poor-performing employees who choose to leave the organization.[117] Functional turnover gives the organization a chance to replace poor performers with better workers. In fact, one study found that simply replacing poor-performing workers with average workers would increase the revenues produced by retail salespeople in an upscale department store by $112,000 per person per year.[118] By contrast, **dysfunctional turnover,** the loss of high performers who choose to leave, is a costly loss to the organization. To avoid dysfunctional turnover, Netflix uses the "Keeper Test," asking its managers, "Which of my people, if they told me they were leaving, for a similar job at a peer company, would I fight hard to keep at Netflix?" The top performers identified via the keeper test receive annual, "top of market" salary increases to encourage them to stay.[119]

Employee turnover should be carefully analyzed to determine whether good or poor performers are choosing to leave the organization. If the company is losing too many high performers, managers should determine the reasons and find ways to reduce the loss of valuable employees. The company may have to raise salary levels, offer enhanced benefits, or improve working conditions to retain skilled workers. One of the best ways to influence functional and dysfunctional turnover is to link pay directly to performance. A study of four sales forces found that when pay was strongly linked to performance via sales commissions and bonuses, poor performers were much more likely to leave (that is, functional turnover). By contrast, poor performers were much more likely to stay when paid large, guaranteed monthly salaries and small sales commissions and bonuses.[120]

STUDY TOOLS 11

LOCATED AT THE BACK OF YOUR BOOK:

☐ Rip out and study the Chapter Review Card at the end of the book

LOG IN TO WWW.CENGAGEBRAIN.COM TO:

☐ Review Key Term Flashcards

☐ Complete Practice Quizzing (take up to four times without repeating the same quiz)

☐ Complete Games: Beat the Clock and Crossword Puzzle

☐ Complete Interactive Content: Graded Quiz, Media Quiz, and Fill-in-the-Blank Questions

☐ Watch Management Workplace Video on "Barcelona Restaurant"

☐ Work Through the What Would You Do Case on Nick's Pizza & Pub

Phased retirement employees transition to retirement by working reduced hours over a period of time before completely retiring

Employee turnover loss of employees who voluntarily choose to leave the company

Functional turnover loss of poor-performing employees who voluntarily choose to leave a company

Dysfunctional turnover loss of high-performing employees who voluntarily choose to leave a company

WHY CHOOSE?

Every 4LTR Press solution comes complete with a visually engaging textbook in addition to an interactive eBook. Go to CourseMate for **MGMT8** to begin using the eBook. Access at **www.cengagebrain.com**

Complete the Speak Up survey in CourseMate at **www.cengagebrain.com**

 Follow us at **www.facebook.com/4ltrpress**

A-Digit/iStockphoto.com

12 Managing Individuals and a Diverse Work Force

LEARNING OUTCOMES

12-1 Describe diversity and explain why it matters.

12-2 Understand the special challenges that the dimensions of surface-level diversity pose for managers.

12-3 Explain how the dimensions of deep-level diversity affect individual behavior and interactions in the workplace.

12-4 Explain the basic principles and practices that can be used to manage diversity.

After you finish

this chapter, go

to **PAGE 266** for

STUDY TOOLS

12-1 DIVERSITY: DIFFERENCES THAT MATTER

Workplace diversity as we know it is changing. Exhibit 12.1 shows predictions from the U.S. Census Bureau of how the U.S. population will change over the next forty years. The percentage of white, non-Hispanic Americans in the general population is expected to decline from 61.8 percent in 2015 to 42.6 percent by 2060. By contrast, the percentage of black Americans will increase (from 12.4 percent to 13.2 percent), as will the percentage of Asian Americans (from 5.1 percent to 7.9 percent). Meanwhile, the proportion of Native Americans will hold steady at 0.7 percent. The fastest-growing group by far, though, will be Hispanics, who are expected to increase from 17.8 percent of the total population in 2015 to 30.6 percent by 2060. Other significant changes have already occurred. For example, today women hold 46.8 percent of the jobs in the United States, up from 38.2 percent in 1970.[1] Furthermore, white males, who composed 63.9 percent of the work force in 1950, hold just 35.8 percent of today's jobs.[2]

These rather dramatic changes have taken place in a relatively short time. And, as these trends clearly show, the work force of the near future will be increasingly Hispanic, Asian American, and female. It will also be older, as the average baby boomer approaches the age of seventy around 2020. Since many boomers are likely to postpone retirement and work well into their seventies to offset predicted reductions in social security and Medicare benefits, the work force may become even older than expected. For instance, between 1992 and 2022, sixteen- to twenty-four-year-olds (16.9 percent to 11.3 percent), twenty-five- to thirty-four-year-olds (27.6 percent to 22.5 percent), and thirty-five- to forty-four-year-olds (26.5 percent to 21.3 percent) will have become a smaller part of the U.S. labor force. By contrast, those forty-five to fifty-four years old (17.3 percent to 19.3 percent), fifty-five to sixty-four years old (9.0 percent to 17.3 percent), and sixty-five years and older (2.7 percent to 6.7 percent) will all have become larger parts of the U.S. labor force.[3]

Diversity means variety. Therefore, **diversity** exists in organizations when there is a variety of demographic, cultural, and personal differences among the people who work there and the customers who do business there. With 34,000 locations in 118 countries, few businesses have the diversity of locations and customers that McDonald's has.[4]

Diversity a variety of demographic, cultural, and personal differences among an organization's employees and customers

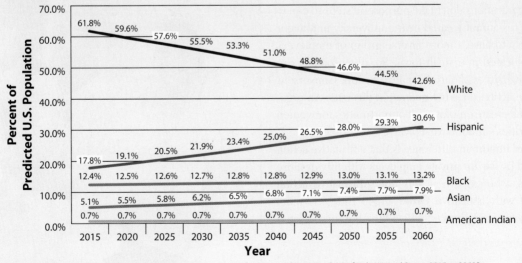

Exhibit 12.1

Percent of the Projected Population by Race and Hispanic Origin for the United States: 2015 to 2060

Source: "Table 6. Percent Distribution of the Projected Population by Race, and Hispanic Origin for the United States: 2015 to 2060," U.S. Census Bureau, accessed July 10, 2014, http://www.census.gov/population/projections/data/national/2012/summarytables.html.

Thanks to its global footprint, McDonald's has 160 global menu items, ranging from a Rice Burger (chicken or beef between two rice cakes) in Taiwan, to a Paneer Salsa Wrap (flatbread stuffed with fried paneer cheese, lettuce, red cabbage, celery, mayo, cheddar cheese and salsa) in India, to McMollettes (English muffins covered with refried beans, cheese, and pico de gallo) in Mexico.[5] McDonald's CEO Don Thompson says that diversity is not about "chasing the number, but chasing the insight, the experience, the background. Diversity fuels innovation, and innovation fuels success. You don't get products like what we've done, you don't create some of the newer products without having the insight." Thompson recognizes, however, that progress still needs to be made, saying, "We still have a long way to go, especially as we become a more global company."[6]

*You'll begin your exploration of diversity by learning **12-1a** that diversity is not affirmative action and **12-1b** that diversity makes good business sense.*

12-1a Diversity Is Not Affirmative Action

A common misconception is that workplace diversity and affirmative action are the same, yet these concepts differ in several critical ways, including their purpose, how they are practiced, and the reactions they produce. To start, **affirmative action** refers to purposeful steps taken by an organization to create employment opportunities for minorities and women.[7] By contrast, diversity has a broader focus that includes demographic, cultural, and personal differences.

A second difference is that affirmative action is a policy for actively creating diversity, but diversity can exist even if organizations don't take purposeful steps to create it. A local restaurant located near a university in a major city is likely to have a more diverse group of employees than one located in a small town. So, organizations can achieve diversity without affirmative action. Conversely, affirmative action does not guarantee diversity. An organization can create employment opportunities for women and minorities yet not have a diverse work force.

A third important difference is that affirmative action is required by law for private employers with fifty or more employees, whereas diversity is not. Affirmative action originated with Executive Order 11246 (http://www.dol.gov/ofccp/regs/compliance/fs11246.htm) but is also related to the 1964 Civil Rights Act, which bans discrimination in voting, public places, federal government programs, federally supported public education, and employment. Title VII of the Civil Rights Act (http://www.eeoc.gov/laws/statutes/titlevii.cfm) requires that workers have equal employment opportunities when being hired or promoted. More specifically, Title VII prohibits companies from discriminating on the basis of race, color, religion, sex, or national origin. Title VII also created the Equal Employment Opportunity Commission, or EEOC (http://www.eeoc.gov), to administer these laws. By contrast, there is no federal law or agency to oversee diversity. Organizations that pursue diversity goals and programs do so voluntarily.

Fourth, affirmative action programs and diversity programs have different purposes. The purpose of affirmative action programs is to compensate for past discrimination, which was widespread when legislation was introduced in the 1960s; to prevent ongoing discrimination; and to provide equal opportunities to all, regardless of race, color, religion, sex, or national origin. Organizations that fail to uphold affirmative action laws may be required to

▶ hire, promote, or give back pay to those not hired or promoted;

▶ reinstate those who were wrongly terminated;

▶ pay attorneys' fees and court costs for those who bring charges against them; or

Affirmative action purposeful steps taken by an organization to create employment opportunities for minorities and women

take other actions that make individuals whole by returning them to the condition or place they would have been had it not been for discrimination.[8]

Consequently, affirmative action is basically a punitive approach.[9] By contrast, the general purpose of diversity programs is to create a positive work environment where no one is advantaged or disadvantaged, where "we" is everyone, where everyone can do his or her best work, where differences are respected and not ignored, and where everyone feels comfortable.[10] So, unlike affirmative action, which punishes companies for not achieving specific sex and race ratios in their work forces, diversity programs seek to benefit both organizations and their employees by encouraging organizations to value all kinds of differences.

Despite the overall success of affirmative action in making workplaces much fairer than they used to be, many people argue that some affirmative action programs unconstitutionally offer preferential treatment to females and minorities at the expense of other employees, a view accepted by some courts.[11] The American Civil Rights institute successfully campaigned via state ballot initiatives to ban race- and sex-based affirmative action in college admissions, government hiring, and government contracting programs in California (1996), Washington (1998), and Michigan (2006). Led by Ward Connerly, the institute backed similar efforts in Arizona, Colorado, Missouri, Nebraska, and Oklahoma in 2008. In an April 2014 decision, the U.S. Supreme Court ruled 6-2 that state ballot initiatives banning race- and sex-based action

are constitutional.[12] Opponents of affirmative action, like Connerly, believe that affirmative action policies establish only surface-level diversity and, ironically, promote preferential treatment.[13]

Furthermore, research shows that people who have gotten a job or promotion as a result of affirmative action are frequently viewed as unqualified, even when clear evidence of their qualifications exists.[14] So, while affirmative action programs have created opportunities for minorities and women, those same minorities and women are frequently presumed to be unqualified when others believe they obtained their jobs as a result of affirmative action.[15]

12-1b Diversity Makes Good Business Sense

Those who support the idea of diversity in organizations often ignore its business aspects altogether, claiming instead that diversity is simply the right thing to do. Yet diversity actually makes good business sense in several ways: cost savings, attracting and retaining talent, and driving business growth.[16]

Diversity helps companies with *cost savings* by reducing turnover, decreasing absenteeism, and avoiding expensive lawsuits.[17] Because of lost productivity and the cost of recruiting and selecting new workers, companies lose substantial amounts of money when employees quit their jobs. In fact, turnover costs typically amount to more than 90 percent of employees' salaries. By this estimate, if an executive who makes $200,000 leaves, the organization will have to spend approximately $180,000 to find a replacement; even the lowest-paid hourly workers can cost the company as much as $10,000 when they quit. Since turnover rates for African Americans average 40 percent higher than for whites, and since women quit their jobs at twice the rate men do, companies that manage diverse work forces well can cut costs by reducing the turnover rates of these employees.[18] And, with women absent from work 60 percent more often than men, primarily because of family responsibilities, diversity programs that address the needs of female workers can also reduce the substantial costs of absenteeism.

Diversity programs also save companies money by helping them avoid discrimination lawsuits, which have increased by a factor of twenty since 1970 and quadrupled just since 1995. In one survey conducted by the Society for Human Resource Management, 78 percent of respondents reported that diversity efforts helped them avoid lawsuits and litigation costs.[19] Indeed, because companies lose two-thirds of all discrimination cases that go to trial, the best strategy from a business perspective is

Skynesher/iStockphoto.com

not to be sued for discrimination at all. When companies lose, the average individual settlement amounts to more than $600,000.[20] And settlement costs can be substantially higher in class-action lawsuits, in which individuals join together to sue a company as a group. Investment brokerage firm Merrill Lynch faced a class-action lawsuit alleging it denied 1,400 African American stock brokers promotions, bonus-based compensation, and fair access to client accounts and resources. Merrill Lynch settled the case for $160 million and agreed to changes that "will enhance opportunities for financial advisors in the future," which will be monitored by a committee of African American brokers who work at the firm.[21]

Diversity also makes business sense by helping companies *attract and retain talented workers*.[22] Indeed, diversity-friendly companies tend to attract better *and* more diverse job applicants. Very simply, diversity begets more diversity. Companies that make *Fortune* magazine's list of the fifty best companies for minorities or are recognized by *Working Women* and *Diversity Inc.* magazine have already attracted a diverse and talented pool of job applicants. But, after being recognized for their efforts, they subsequently experience big increases in both the quality and the diversity of people who apply for jobs. Research shows that companies with acclaimed diversity programs not only attract more talented workers but also have higher performance in the stock market.[23]

The third way that diversity makes business sense is by *driving business growth*. In the United States today, there are 45 million African Americans, 55.8 million Hispanic Americans, and 19.4 million Asian Americans with, respectively, $1 trillion, $1.2 trillion, and $713 billion in purchasing power. Given the size of those markets, it shouldn't be surprising that a survey conducted by the Society for Human Resource Management found that tapping into "diverse customers and markets" was the number-one reason managers gave for implementing diversity programs.[24] Kimberly-Clark, maker of well-known household brands like Kotex, Depend, Kleenex, Huggies, and Scott paper products, has a customer base that is 83 percent female. But, from first-level managers to the boardroom, women are strongly in the minority. So, from China to the U.S. to Latin America, Kimberly-Clark is implementing more generous maternity leave and flexible working schedules in hopes of growing and

retaining promising female leaders who understand the company's customers.[25] Likewise, with an increasingly large share of global sales outside of their home countries, multinational firms are putting key leaders or divisions closer to global customers. Procter & Gamble moved its global cosmetics and personal-care division to Singapore from Cincinnati. GE relocated its X-ray unit to Beijing from Wisconsin. And German-based Daimler-Benz is now requiring that young managers tapped for its "high potential" training and development program must be from outside of Germany.[26] When companies have diverse work forces, they are better able to understand the needs of their increasingly diverse customer bases.

Diversity also helps companies grow through higher-quality problem solving. Though diverse groups initially have more difficulty working together than homogeneous groups, diverse groups eventually establish a rapport and do a better job of identifying problems and generating alternative solutions, the two most important steps in problem solving.[27] When Novartis CEO David Epstein ran Novartis Oncology earlier in his career, he was given the opportunity to build his leadership team from scratch. The division at that time was heavily staffed with Americans and Europeans. But because the team was responsible for products and customers in seventy different countries, he picked his leaders based on career successes and diverse experiences. Says Epstein, "I ended up with a team that came from all over the world. We had phenomenally productive discussions. At the beginning, it was very difficult because we had different cultural backgrounds and the norms within which we communicated were different, but after a while I saw the power of people with different backgrounds and what they could contribute to business ideas. Once we got that group working as a high-performing team, we were able to accomplish feats that nobody thought were possible."[28]

12-2 SURFACE-LEVEL DIVERSITY

A survey that asked managers "What is meant by diversity to decision-makers in your organization?" found that they most frequently mentioned race, culture, sex, national origin, age, religion, and regional origin.[29] When managers describe workers this way, they are focusing on surface-level diversity. **Surface-level diversity** consists of differences that are immediately observable, typically unchangeable, and easy to measure.[30] In other words,

Surface-level diversity differences such as age, sex, race/ethnicity, and physical disabilities that are observable, typically unchangeable, and easy to measure

Alexey Fiodorov/iStockphoto.com

independent observers can usually agree on dimensions of surface-level diversity, such as another person's age, sex, race/ethnicity, or physical capabilities.

Most people start by using surface-level diversity to categorize or stereotype other people. But those initial categorizations typically give way to deeper impressions formed from knowledge of others' behaviors and psychological characteristics such as personality and attitudes.[31] When you think of others this way, you are focusing on deep-level diversity. **Deep-level diversity** consists of differences that are communicated through verbal and nonverbal behaviors and are learned only through extended interaction with others.[32] Examples of deep-level diversity include personality differences, attitudes, beliefs, and values. In other words, as people in diverse workplaces get to know each other, the initial focus on surface-level differences such as age, race/ethnicity, sex, and physical capabilities is replaced by deeper, more complex knowledge of coworkers.

If managed properly, the shift from surface- to deep-level diversity can accomplish two things.[33] First, coming to know and understand each other better can result in reduced prejudice and conflict. Second, it can lead to stronger social integration. **Social integration** is the degree to which group members are psychologically attracted to working with each other to accomplish a common objective, or, as one manager put it, "working together to get the job done."

Because age, sex, race/ethnicity, and disabilities are usually immediately observable, many managers and workers use these dimensions of surface-level diversity to form initial impressions and categorizations of coworkers, bosses, customers, or job applicants. Whether intentionally or not, sometimes those initial categorizations and impressions lead to decisions or behaviors that discriminate. Consequently, these dimensions of surface-level diversity pose special challenges for managers who are trying to

create positive work environments where everyone feels comfortable and no one is advantaged or disadvantaged.

Let's learn more about those challenges and the ways that 12-2a age, 12-2b sex, 12-2c race/ethnicity, and 12-2d mental or physical disabilities can affect decisions and behaviors in organizations.

12-2a Age

Age discrimination is treating people differently (e.g., in hiring and firing, promotion, and compensation decisions) because of their age. The victims of age discrimination are almost always older workers, and the discrimination is based on the assumption that "you can't teach an old dog new tricks." It's commonly believed that older workers are less motivated, less productive, more prone to illness and accidents, not interested in learning new things, cost more, and make greater—more expensive—use of health care benefits.[34] One manager explains his preference for younger workers over older workers this way: "The way I look at it, for $40,000 or $50,000, I can get a smart, raw kid right out of undergrad who's going to work seven days a week for me for the next two years. I'll train him the way I want him, he'll grow with me, and I'll pay him long-term options so I own him, for lack of a better word. He'll do exactly what I want—and if he doesn't, I'll fire him. . . . The alternative is to pay twice as much for some forty-year-old who does half the amount of work, has been trained improperly, and doesn't listen to what I say."[35] The increasing cost of age discrimination lawsuits—up from $72.1 million a year 2009 to $97.9 million in 2013—suggests that discriminatory attitudes like this still exist.[36]

So, what's reality and what's myth? Do older employees actually cost more? In some ways, they do. The older people are and the longer they stay with a company, the more the company pays for salaries, pension plans, and vacation time. But older workers cost companies less, too, because they show better judgment, care more about the quality of their work, and are less likely to quit, show up late, or be absent, the cost of which can

Deep-level diversity differences such as personality and attitudes that are communicated through verbal and nonverbal behaviors and are learned only through extended interaction with others

Social integration the degree to which group members are psychologically attracted to working with each other to accomplish a common objective

Age discrimination treating people differently (e.g., in hiring and firing, promotion, and compensation decisions) because of their age

Walgreens Increases Safety and Productivity by Hiring Disabled

The national pharmacy chain Walgreens has found a reliable, dedicated, and efficient work force that is largely untapped—the disabled. Just about half of its employees at the warehouse in Windsor, Connecticut, have some form of physical or mental disability. But even so, the Windsor facility is the safest, most productive warehouse throughout the entire company. No doubt it's due to the fact that disabled workers have a 48 percent lower turnover rate, 67 percent lower medical costs, and 73 percent lower time-off costs compared to the nondisabled. The disabled employees have been so great for Walgreens that it plans to increase the percentage of disabled employees throughout its warehouses to 20 percent.

Source: S. Cann, "The Debate behind Disability Hiring," *Fast Company*, November 26, 2012, accessed June 16, 2013, http://www.fastcompany.com/3002957/disabled-employee-amendment.

ivanastar/iStockphoto.com

---

be substantial.[37] A meta-analysis combining the results of 118 individual studies also found that older workers are more likely to help others at work and are much less likely to use drugs or alcohol at work, engage in workplace aggression, or be involved in accidents. The authors of this study concluded, "The stereotype of older workers as difficult colleagues, then, seems largely unfounded."[38]

As for the widespread belief that job performance declines with age, the scientific evidence clearly refutes this stereotype. Performance does not decline with age, regardless of the type of job.[39]

What can companies do to reduce age discrimination?[40] To start, managers need to recognize that age discrimination is much more pervasive than they probably think. Whereas "old" used to mean mid-fifties, in today's workplace "old" is closer to forty. When 773 CEOs were asked, "At what age does a worker's productivity peak?" the average age they gave was forty-three. Thus, age discrimination may be affecting more workers because perceptions about age have changed. In addition, with the aging of the baby boomers, age discrimination is more likely to occur simply because there are millions more older workers than there used to be. And, because studies show that interviewers rate younger job candidates as more qualified (even when they aren't), companies need to train managers and recruiters to make hiring and promotion decisions on the basis of qualifications, not age.

Companies also need to monitor the extent to which older workers receive training. The U.S. Bureau of Labor Statistics found that the number of training courses and number of hours spent in training drop dramatically after employees reach the age of forty-four.[41] Finally, companies need to ensure that younger and older workers interact with each other. One study found that younger workers generally hold positive views of older workers and that the more time they spent working with older coworkers, the more positive their attitudes became.[42]

12-2b Sex

Sex discrimination occurs when people are treated differently because of their sex. Sex discrimination and racial/ethnic discrimination (discussed in the next section) are often associated with the so-called **glass ceiling,** the invisible barrier that prevents women and minorities from advancing to the top jobs in organizations.

To what extent do women face sex discrimination in the workplace? Almost every year, the EEOC receives between 23,000 and 30,000 charges of sex-based discrimination.[43] In some ways, there is much less sex discrimination than there used to be. For example, whereas women held only 17 percent of managerial jobs in 1972, today they hold 43.1 percent of managerial jobs, 51.4 percent of managerial and professional jobs, and 47 percent of all jobs in the workplace.[44] Likewise, women own 40 percent of all U.S. businesses. Whereas women owned 700,000 businesses in 1977 and 4.1 million businesses in 1987, today they own 8.6 million businesses, generating $1.3 trillion in sales and employing 7.8 million people![45] Finally, though women still earn less than men on average, the differential is narrowing, as Exhibit 12.2 shows. Women earned 80.9 percent of what men did in 2012, up from 63 percent in 1979.[46]

Sex discrimination   treating people differently because of their sex

Glass ceiling   the invisible barrier that prevents women and minorities from advancing to the top jobs in organizations

Exhibit 12.2
Women's Earnings as a Percentage of Men's, 1979–2012

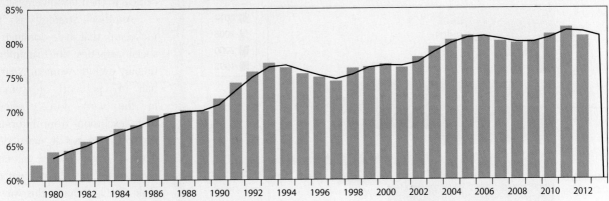

Source: "Women's Earnings, 1979–2012 : The Editor's Desk," U.S. Bureau of Labor Statistics, November 4, 2013, accessed July 12, 2014, http://www.bls.gov/opub/ted/2013/ted_20131104.htm.

Although progress is being made, sex discrimination continues to operate via the glass ceiling at higher levels in organizations, as shown in Exhibit 12.3. For instance, while the trends are going upward, women were the top earners in just 8.1 percent of companies in

Bad Edits

IKEA is often praised for its efforts for diversity. It has won a series of awards and recognitions for its commitment to hiring minorities and for making large contributions to organizations like UNICEF and Save the Children to improve the lives of marginalized children. All of that makes what it did in Saudi Arabia quite curious, perhaps even infuriating. The company released a catalog that shows its furniture laid out in fashionable ways and being enjoyed by happy looking people. In the Saudi Arabian version of the catalog, all of the women from the photos were removed. So, instead of a happy family of four brushing their teeth over an IKEA sink, Saudi customers would see just a son, a daughter, and their father. Critics railed against IKEA for making such edits, claiming that the company violated its own commitment to equality and fairness to avoid offending men in a culture where women have very little freedom. IKEA, meanwhile, apologized for the catalogs and claimed that the editorial decisions were made by an independent franchisee.

Source: T. Hz, "IKEA's Saudi Arabia Catalog Erases Women; Company Expresses Regret," *Los Angeles Times*, October 1, 2012, accessed June 16, 2013, http://www.latimes.com/business/money/la-fi-mo-ikea-women-saudi-catalog-20121001,0,579448.story.

2014.[47] Likewise, only 14.6 percent of corporate officers (i.e., top management) were women, and the numbers were even lower for women of color. Indra K. Nooyi, PepsiCo's CEO, and Ursula Burns, Xerox's CEO, are the only women of color heading *Fortune* 500 companies.[48] Indeed, only twenty-four of the 500 largest companies in the United States have women CEOs.[49] Similarly, only 16.9 percent of the members of U.S. corporate boards of directors are women.[50]

Is sex discrimination the sole reason for the slow rate at which women have been promoted to middle and upper levels of management and corporate boards? Some studies indicate that it's not.[51] In some instances, the slow progress appears to be due to career and job choices. Whereas men's career and job choices are often driven by the search for higher pay and advancement, women are more likely to choose jobs or careers that also give them a greater sense of accomplishment, more control over their work schedules, and easier movement in and out of the workplace.[52] For instance, 82 percent of women without children are interested in being promoted to the next level compared to 73 percent of women with two or more children.[53] As those numbers suggest, women are historically much more likely than men to prioritize family over work at some time in their careers. For example, 96 percent of 600 female Harvard MBAs held jobs while they were in their twenties. That dropped to 71 percent in their late thirties when they had children but then increased to 82.5 percent in their late forties as their children became older.[54] Even Indra Nooyi, PepsiCo's CEO, says, "My observation . . . is that the biological clock and the career clock are in total conflict

Exhibit 12.3

Women at *Fortune* 500 and 1000 Companies

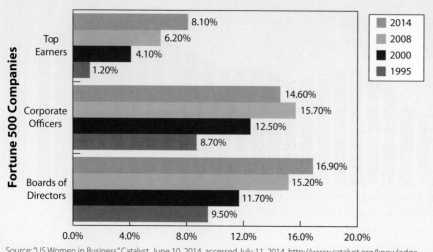

Source: "US Women in Business," Catalyst, June 10, 2014, accessed July 11, 2014, http://www.catalyst.org/knowledge/us-women-business-0.

with each other. Total, complete conflict. When you have to have kids you have to build your career. Just as you're rising to middle management your kids need you because they're teenagers, they need you for the teenage years . . . And as you grow even more, your parents need you because they're aging. So . . . we cannot have it all."[55]

Beyond these reasons, however, it's likely that sex discrimination does play a role in women's slow progress into the higher levels of management. And even if you don't think so, many of the women you work with probably do. Indeed, studies indicate that 90 percent of women believe the glass ceiling hurts their careers, 80 percent said they left their last job because of the glass ceiling, and that starting a business allows them to avoid the career limitations of the glass ceiling.[56] In fact, discrimination is believed to be the most significant factor behind the lack of women at top levels of management.[57]

So, what can companies do to make sure that women have the same opportunities for development and advancement as men? One strategy is mentoring, or pairing promising female executives with senior executives from whom they can seek advice and support.[58] A vice president at a utility company says, "I think it's the single most critical piece to women advancing careerwise. In my experience you need somebody to help guide

you and . . . go to bat for you."[59] In fact, 91 percent of female executives had a mentor at some point and feel their mentor was critical to their advancement.

Another strategy is to make sure that male-dominated social activities don't unintentionally exclude women. Nearly half (47 percent) of women in the work force believe that "exclusion from informal networks" makes it more difficult to advance their careers. By contrast, just 18 percent of male CEOs thought this was a problem. Another is to designate a go-to person other than their supervisors that women can talk to if they believe that they are being held back or discriminated against because of their sex. Make sure this person has the knowledge and authority to conduct a fair, confidential internal investigation.

12-2c Race/Ethnicity

Racial and ethnic discrimination occurs when people are treated differently because of their race or ethnicity. To what extent is racial and ethnic discrimination a factor in the workplace? Every year, the EEOC receives between 26,000 and 36,000 charges of racial discrimination, which is more than any other type of charge of discrimination.[60] However, it is true that since the passage of the 1964 Civil Rights Act and Title VII, there is much less racial and ethnic discrimination than there used to be. For example, twenty-five *Fortune* 500 firms had an African American (6), Hispanic (10), or Asian (9) CEO in 2014, whereas none did in 1988.[61] Nonetheless, strong racial and ethnic disparities still exist. For instance, whereas 11.2 percent of employed Americans are black, only 6.5 percent of managers and 2.9 percent of CEOs are black. Similarly, 15.6 percent of employed Americans are Hispanic, but only 8.5 percent are managers and 4.3 percent are CEOs. By contrast, Asians, who constitute 5.7 percent of employed workers, are better represented, holding 5.4 percent of management jobs and 4.8 percent of CEO jobs.[62]

What accounts for the disparities between the percentages of minority groups in the general population and their smaller representation in management positions? Some studies have found that the disparities are due to preexisting differences in training, education, and skills.

Racial and ethnic discrimination treating people differently because of their race or ethnicity

When African Americans, Hispanics, Asian Americans, and whites have similar skills, training, and education, they are much more likely to have similar jobs and salaries.[63]

Other studies, however, provide increasingly strong direct evidence of racial or ethnic discrimination in the workplace. For example, one study directly tested hiring discrimination by sending pairs of black and white males and pairs of Hispanic and non-Hispanic males to apply for the same jobs. Each pair had résumés with identical qualifications, and all were trained to present themselves in similar ways to minimize differences during interviews. The researchers found that the white males got three times as many job offers as the black males, and that the non-Hispanic males got three times as many offers as the Hispanic males.[64] Another study, which used similar methods to test hiring procedures at 149 different companies, found that whites received 10 percent more interviews than blacks. Half of the whites interviewed then received job offers, but only 11 percent of the blacks. And when job offers were made, blacks were much more likely to be offered lower-level positions, while whites were more likely to be offered jobs at higher levels than the jobs they had applied for.[65]

Critics of these studies point out that it's nearly impossible to train different applicants to give identical responses in job interviews and that differences in interviewing skills may have somehow accounted for the results. However, British researchers found similar kinds of discrimination just by sending letters of inquiry to prospective employers. As in the other studies, the letters were identical except for the applicant's race. Employers frequently responded to letters from Afro-Caribbean, Indian, or Pakistani applicants by indicating that the positions had been filled. By contrast, they often responded to white, Anglo-Saxon applicants by inviting them to face-to-face interviews. Similar results were found with Vietnamese and Greek applicants in Australia.[66] In short, the evidence indicates that there is strong and persistent racial and ethnic discrimination in the hiring processes of many organizations.

What can companies do to make sure that people of all racial and ethnic backgrounds have the same opportunities?[67] Start by looking at the numbers. Compare the hiring rates of whites with the hiring rates for racial and ethnic applicants. Do the same thing for promotions within the company. See if nonwhite workers quit the company at higher rates than white workers. Also, survey employees to compare white and nonwhite employees' satisfaction with jobs, bosses, and the company as well as their perceptions concerning equal treatment. Next, if the numbers indicate racial or ethnic disparities, consider employing a private firm to test your hiring system by having applicants of different races with identical qualifications apply for jobs in your company.[68] Although disparities aren't proof of discrimination, it's much better to investigate hiring and promotion disparities yourself than to have the EEOC or a plaintiff's lawyer do it for you.

Another step companies can take is to eliminate unclear selection and promotion criteria. Vague criteria allow decision makers to focus on non-job-related characteristics that may unintentionally lead to employment discrimination. Instead, selection and promotion criteria should spell out the specific knowledge, skills, abilities, education, and experience needed to perform a job well. Finally, as explained in Chapter 11, "Managing Human Resource Systems," it is also important to train managers and others who make hiring and promotion decisions.

12-2d Mental or Physical Disabilities

According to the Americans with Disabilities Act (http://www.ada.gov), a **disability** is a mental or physical impairment that substantially limits one or more major life activities.[69] Approximately 38 million Americans—12.1 percent of the population—are disabled.[70] **Disability discrimination** occurs when people are treated differently because of their disabilities. To what extent is disability discrimination a factor in the workplace? While 76.3 percent of the U.S. population was employed in 2012, only 33.5 percent of disabled people had jobs. Individuals with sensory disabilities, such as blindness (37.7 percent) or deafness (50.2 percent), had the highest employment rates; those with self-care disabilities (16.2 percent), who can't dress or bathe themselves, or with independent living disabilities (15.7 percent), who can't do basic errands such as shopping or go to the doctor without assistance, were the least likely to work.[71] Likewise, 28.4 percent of disabled people are in poverty, compared to 11.9 percent of those without disabilities.[72] Numerous studies also indicate that managers and the general public believe that discrimination against people with disabilities is common and widespread.[73]

What accounts for the disparities between those with and without disabilities? Contrary to popular opinion, it has nothing to do with how well people with disabilities can do their jobs. Studies show that as long as companies make reasonable accommodations for disabilities (e.g., changing procedures or equipment), people with disabilities perform their jobs just as well as people without disabilities.

Disability a mental or physical impairment that substantially limits one or more major life activities

Disability discrimination treating people differently because of their disabilities

Mike Groleau, 39, stocks soft drinks at the Scioto Downs Racino in Columbus, Ohio. Mike is one of nine developmentally disabled employees hired at Scioto Downs in 2014 as part of the state's push to get workers out of sheltered workshops and into community jobs.

Furthermore, they have better safety records and are not any more likely to be absent or quit their jobs.[74]

What can companies do to make sure that people with disabilities have the same opportunities as everyone else? Beyond educational efforts to address incorrect stereotypes and expectations, a good place to start is to commit to reasonable workplace accommodations such as changing work schedules, reassigning jobs, acquiring or modifying equipment, or providing assistance when needed. Accommodations for disabilities needn't be expensive. According to the Job Accommodation Network, 58 percent of accommodations don't cost anything at all, while those with costs are typically just $500.[75]

At Laser Soft Info Systems, an India-based software developer, 15 percent of the staff has some disability, with causes ranging from hearing, speech, and sight impairment to cerebral palsy, polio, or accidents, and work throughout the company. "We don't have any rule that teams must take a minimum or maximum number of people with disabilities in their roles. They are recruited like any other associate," says Suresh Kamath, Laser Soft's founder and president. Laser Soft's accommodations include wheelchair ramps, wider office aisles, elevators with audio controls for the blind, and facilitators to provide physical assistance when an employee asks for it. The company also allows employees to work from home should it become difficult to make it into the office.[76]

Some of the accommodations just described involve *assistive technology* that gives workers with disabilities the tools they need to overcome their disabilities. Providing workers with assistive technology is also an effective strategy to recruit, retain, and enhance the productivity of people with disabilities. According to the National Council on Disability, 92 percent of workers with disabilities who use assistive technology report that it helps them work faster and better, 81 percent indicate that it helps them work longer hours, and 67 percent say that it is critical to getting a job.[77] To learn about assistive technologies that can help workers with disabilities, see AbleData (http://www.abledata.com), which lists 40,000 products, or the National Rehabilitation Information Center (http://www.naric.com), which provides information for specific disabilities.

Finally, companies should actively recruit qualified workers with disabilities. Numerous organizations, such as Mainstream, Kidder Resources, the American Council of the Blind (http://www.acb.org), the National Federation of the Blind (http://nfb.org), the National Association of the Deaf (http://www.nad.org), the Epilepsy Foundation (http://www.epilepsy.com), and the National Amputation Foundation (http://www.nationalamputation.org), actively work with employers to find jobs for qualified people with disabilities. Companies can also place advertisements in publications, such as *Careers and the disABLED*, that specifically target workers with disabilities.[78]

12-3 DEEP-LEVEL DIVERSITY

As you learned in Section 12-2, people often use the dimensions of surface-level diversity to form initial impressions about others. Over time, however, as people have a chance to get to know each other, initial impressions based on age, sex, race/ethnicity, and mental or physical disabilities give way to deeper impressions based on behavior and psychological characteristics. When we think of others this way, we are focusing on deep-level diversity. *Deep-level diversity* represents differences that can be learned only through extended interaction with others. Examples of deep-level diversity include differences in personality, attitudes, beliefs, and values. In short, recognizing deep-level diversity requires getting to know and understand one another better. And that matters, because it can result in less prejudice, discrimination, and conflict in the workplace. These changes can then lead to better *social integration*, the degree to which organizational or group members are psychologically attracted to working with each other to accomplish a common objective.

Stop for a second and think about your boss (or the boss you had in your last job). What words would you use to describe him or her? Is your boss introverted or extraverted? Emotionally stable or unstable? Agreeable or disagreeable? Organized or disorganized? Open or closed to new experiences? When you describe your boss or others in this way, what you're really doing is describing dispositions and personality.

A **disposition** is the tendency to respond to situations and events in a predetermined manner. **Personality** is the relatively stable set of behaviors, attitudes, and emotions displayed over time that makes people different from each other.[79] For example, which of your aunts or uncles is a little offbeat, a little out of the ordinary? What was that aunt or uncle like when you were small? What is she or he like now? Chances are that she or he is pretty much the same wacky person. In other words, the person's core personality hasn't changed. For years, personality researchers studied hundreds of different ways to describe people's personalities. In the last decade, however, personality research conducted in different cultures, different settings, and different languages has shown that five basic dimensions of personality account for most of the differences in peoples' behaviors, attitudes, and emotions (or for why your boss is the way he or she is!). The *Big Five Personality Dimensions* are extraversion, emotional stability, agreeableness, conscientiousness, and openness to experience.[80]

Extraversion is the degree to which someone is active, assertive, gregarious, sociable, talkative, and energized by others. In contrast to extraverts, introverts are less active, prefer to be alone, and are shy, quiet, and reserved. For the best results in the workplace, introverts and extraverts should be correctly matched to their jobs.

Emotional stability is the degree to which someone is not angry, depressed, anxious, emotional, insecure, or excitable. People who are emotionally stable respond well to stress. In other words, they can maintain a calm, problem-solving attitude in even the toughest situations (e.g., conflict, hostility, dangerous conditions, or extreme time pressures). By contrast, emotionally unstable people find it difficult to handle the most basic demands of their jobs under only moderately stressful situations and become distraught, tearful, self-doubting, and anxious. Emotional stability is particularly important for high-stress jobs such as police work, fire fighting, emergency medical treatment, piloting planes, or commanding rockets.

Agreeableness is the degree to which someone is cooperative, polite, flexible, forgiving, good-natured,

The Big Five Personality Dimensions:
- Extraversion
- Emotional stability
- Agreeableness
- Conscientiousness
- Openness to experience

tolerant, and trusting. Basically, agreeable people are easy to work with and be around, whereas disagreeable people are distrusting and difficult to work with and be around. A number of companies have made general attitude or agreeableness the most important factor in their hiring decisions. Small-business owner Roger Cook says, "Hire nice people. I'm looking for personal—not professional—traits. I want a good or nice person. I can teach the skills. I call their references and ask, 'Is he or she a nice person?' I take a close look at how applicants answer questions and carry themselves. Why nice people? Because they're trustworthy; they get along with other crew members: they are good with customers and they are usually hard workers."[81]

Conscientiousness is the degree to which someone is organized, hardworking, responsible, persevering, thorough, and achievement oriented. One management consultant wrote about his experiences with a conscientious employee: "He arrived at our first meeting with a typed copy of his daily schedule, a sheet bearing his home and office phone numbers, addresses, and his email address. At his request, we established a timetable for meetings for the next four months. He showed up on

Disposition the tendency to respond to situations and events in a predetermined manner

Personality the relatively stable set of behaviors, attitudes, and emotions displayed over time that makes people different from each other

Extraversion the degree to which someone is active, assertive, gregarious, sociable, talkative, and energized by others

Emotional stability the degree to which someone is not angry, depressed, anxious, emotional, insecure, and excitable

Agreeableness the degree to which someone is cooperative, polite, flexible, forgiving, good-natured, tolerant, and trusting

Conscientiousness the degree to which someone is organized, hardworking, responsible, persevering, thorough, and achievement oriented

The Introvert as Manager

Can introverts be effective managers? Sixty-five percent of senior managers believe that introversion prevents people from being promoted to higher management levels. But research shows that both introverts and extraverts can be successful managers. While extraverts may be more effective (and comfortable) in public roles, introverts are effective in one-on-one interactions and in involving others in decision making. Colgate-Palmolive's CEO, Ian Cook, says his listening skills helped him advance in the company. Says Cook, "I listen intently. I am extremely attentive to language and body cues." Subordinates can mistakenly view their boss's introversion as aloofness, particularly if they're quiet during meetings. When Campbell Soup Company CEO Douglas Conant was president of a division at Nabisco, "People were drawing [inaccurate] conclusions about my behavior." So, he shared with his coworkers and subordinates that it takes him time to formulate his thoughts and responses. Conant said that helped, and "the more transparent I became, the more engaged people became."

Source: J. Lublin, "Introverted Execs Find Ways to Shine," *Wall Street Journal*, April 14, 2011, accessed May 29, 2011, http://online.wsj.com/article/SB10001424052748703983104576263053775879800.html.

time every time, day planner in hand, and carefully listed tasks and due dates. He questioned me exhaustively if he didn't understand an assignment and returned on schedule with the completed work or with a clear explanation as to why it wasn't done."[82] Conscientious employees are also more likely to engage in positive behaviors, such as helping new employees, coworkers, and supervisors, and are less likely to engage in negative behaviors, such as verbally or physically abusing coworkers or stealing.[83]

Openness to experience is the degree to which someone is curious, broadminded, and open to new ideas, things, and experiences; is spontaneous; and has a high tolerance for ambiguity. Most companies need people who are strong in terms of openness to experience to fill certain positions, but for other positions, this dimension is less important. People in marketing, advertising, research, or other creative jobs need to be curious, open to new ideas, and spontaneous. By contrast, openness to experience is not particularly important to accountants, who need to apply stringent rules and formulas consistently to make sense out of complex financial information.

Which of the Big Five Personality Dimensions has the largest impact on behavior in organizations? The

cumulative results of multiple studies indicate that conscientiousness is related to job performance across five different occupational groups (professionals, police, managers, salespeople, and skilled or semiskilled workers).[84] In short, people "who are dependable, persistent, goal directed, and organized tend to be higher performers on virtually any job; viewed negatively, those who are careless, irresponsible, low achievement striving, and impulsive tend to be lower performers on virtually any job."[85] The results also indicate that extraversion is related to performance in jobs, such as sales and management, that involve significant interaction with others. In people-intensive jobs like these, it helps to be sociable, assertive, and talkative and to have energy and be able to energize others. Finally, people who are extraverted and open to experience seem to do much better in training. Being curious and open to new experiences as well as sociable, assertive, talkative, and full of energy helps people perform better in learning situations.[86]

12-4 MANAGING DIVERSITY

How much should companies change their standard business practices to accommodate the diversity of their workers? What do you do when a talented top executive has a

Openness to experience the degree to which someone is curious, broad-minded, and open to new ideas, things, and experiences; is spontaneous; and has a high tolerance for ambiguity

drinking problem that seems to affect his behavior only at company business parties (for entertaining clients), where he has made inappropriate advances toward female employees? What do you do when, despite aggressive company policies against racial discrimination, employees continue to tell racist jokes and publicly post cartoons displaying racist humor? And, since many people confuse diversity with affirmative action, what do you do to make sure that your company's diversity practices and policies are viewed as benefiting all workers and not just some workers?

No doubt about it, questions like these make managing diversity one of the toughest challenges that managers face.[87] Nonetheless, there are steps companies can take to begin to address these issues.

As discussed earlier, diversity programs try to create a positive work environment where no one is advantaged or disadvantaged, where "we" is everyone, where everyone can do his or her best work, where differences are respected and not ignored, and where everyone feels comfortable.

Let's begin to address those goals by learning about 12-4a different diversity paradigms, 12-4b diversity principles, and 12-4c diversity training and practices.

12-4a Diversity Paradigms

There are several different methods or paradigms for managing diversity: the discrimination and fairness paradigm, the access and legitimacy paradigm, and the learning and effectiveness paradigm.[88]

The *discrimination and fairness paradigm*, which is the most common method of approaching diversity, focuses on equal opportunity, fair treatment, recruitment of minorities, and strict compliance with the equal employment opportunity laws. Under this approach, success is usually measured by how well companies achieve recruitment, promotion, and retention goals for women, people of different racial/ethnic backgrounds, or other underrepresented groups. According to a recent workplace diversity practices survey conducted by the Society for Human Resource Management, 66 percent to 91 percent of companies use specialized strategies to recruit, retain, and promote talented women and minorities. The percentages increase with company

size, and companies of more than 500 employees are the most likely to use these strategies. Seventy-seven percent of companies with more than 500 employees systematically collect measurements on diversity-related practices.[89] One manager says, "If you don't measure something, it doesn't count. You measure your market share. You measure your profitability. The same should be true for diversity. There has to be some way of measuring whether you did, in fact, cast your net widely and whether the company is better off today in terms of the experience of people of color than it was a few years ago. I measure my market share and my profitability. Why not this?"[90] The primary benefit of the discrimination and fairness paradigm is that it generally brings about fairer treatment of employees and increases demographic diversity. The primary limitation is that the focus of diversity remains on the surface-level diversity dimensions of sex, race, and ethnicity.[91]

The *access and legitimacy paradigm* focuses on the acceptance and celebration of differences to ensure that the diversity within the company matches the diversity found among primary stakeholders, such as customers, suppliers, and local communities. This is similar to the *business growth* advantage of diversity discussed earlier in the chapter. The basic idea behind this approach is to create a demographically diverse work force that attracts a broader customer base. For example, the diversity strategy at OshKosh, a maker of specialty trucks and truck bodies, states, "We operate and sell our products and services in over 100 countries on six continents, each with its own culture, customs, and business practices. We seek employees who are passionate about serving customers and who reflect our diverse customer base so that we can truly understand our customers to better serve and delight them."[92]

The primary benefit of this approach is that it establishes a clear business reason for diversity. Like the discrimination and fairness paradigm, however, it focuses only on the surface-level diversity dimensions of sex, race, and ethnicity. Furthermore, employees who are assigned responsibility for customers and stakeholders on the basis of their sex, race, or ethnicity may eventually feel frustrated and exploited.

Whereas the discrimination and fairness paradigm focuses on assimilation (having a demographically representative work force) and the access and legitimacy paradigm focuses on differentiation (having demographic differences inside the company match those of key customers and stakeholders), the *learning and effectiveness paradigm* focuses on integrating deep-level diversity differences, such as personality, attitudes, beliefs, and values, into the actual work of the organization. One sign that a company hasn't yet created a learning and effectiveness paradigm is that people withhold their opinions for fear of being seen as different. For example, while Helena Morrissey is the CEO of Newton Investment Management, a London firm that invests $71 billion for its clients, she admits to sometimes keeping her business opinions to herself for fear of being seen as "the annoying" woman at the table. She says, "At a recent meeting I wasn't comfortable with a controversial point and I spoke up, but I also had a different view on the next item on the agenda but instead of speaking up I held back." Says Morrissey, "I have been conscious of feeling that where I did have different views from the rest of the [all-male] group, I may be being perceived as the 'difficult woman' rather than being listened to for

Organizational plurality a work environment where (1) all members are empowered to contribute in a way that maximizes the benefits to the organization, customers, and themselves, and (2) the individuality of each member is respected by not segmenting or polarizing people on the basis of their membership in a particular group

what I was saying." She felt this way despite there being "no evidence that the men were actually feeling that."[93]

The learning and effectiveness paradigm is consistent with achieving organizational plurality. **Organizational plurality** is a work environment where (1) all members are empowered to contribute in a way that maximizes the benefits to the organization, customers, and themselves and (2) the individuality of each member is respected by not segmenting or polarizing people on the basis of their membership in a particular group.[94]

The learning and effectiveness diversity paradigm offers four benefits.[95] First, it values common ground. David Thomas of the Harvard Business School explains, "Like the fairness paradigm, it promotes equal opportunity for all individuals. And like the access paradigm, it acknowledges cultural differences among people and recognizes the value in those differences. Yet this new model for managing diversity lets the organization internalize differences among employees so it learns and grows because of them. Indeed, with the model fully in place, members of the organization can say, 'We are all on the same team, with our differences—not despite them.'"[96]

Second, this paradigm makes a distinction between individual and group differences. When diversity focuses only on differences between groups, such as females versus males, large differences within groups are ignored.[97] For example, think of the women you know at work. Now, think for a second about what they have in common. After that, think about how they're different. If your situation

"We are all on the same team

is typical, the list of differences should be just as long as the list of commonalties, if not longer. In short, managers can achieve a greater understanding of diversity and their employees by treating them as individuals and by realizing that not all African Americans, Hispanics, women, or white males want the same things at work.[98]

Third, because the focus is on individual differences, the learning and effectiveness paradigm is less likely to encounter the conflict, backlash, and divisiveness sometimes associated with diversity programs that focus only on group differences. Taylor Cox, one of the leading management writers on diversity, says, "We are concerned here with these more destructive forms of conflict which may be present with diverse work forces due to language barriers, cultural clash, or resentment by majority-group members of what they may perceive as preferential and unwarranted treatment of minority-group members."[99] And Ray Haines, a consultant who has helped companies deal with the aftermath of diversity programs that became divisive, says, "There's a large amount of backlash related to diversity training. It stirs up a lot of hostility, anguish, and resentment but doesn't give people tools to deal with [the backlash]. You have people come in and talk about their specific ax to grind."[100] Not all diversity programs are divisive or lead to conflict. But by focusing on individual rather than group differences, the learning and effectiveness paradigm helps to minimize these potential problems.

Finally, unlike the other diversity paradigms that simply focus on surface-level diversity, the learning and effectiveness paradigm focuses on bringing different talents and perspectives (i.e., deep-level diversity) *together* to make the best organizational decisions and to produce innovative, competitive products and services.

12-4b Diversity Principles

Diversity paradigms are general approaches or strategies for managing diversity. Whatever diversity paradigm a manager chooses, diversity principles will help managers do a better job of *managing company diversity programs*.[101]

Swift Punishment

When two Asian men ordered meals at their local Chick-Fil-A, the cashier did not ask for their names, which are usually printed on the receipts. Instead, she typed in two derogatory words about the customers' Asian heritage, which then showed up on the receipts. When the restaurant manager found out what happened, he acted quickly by firing the employee. What's more, the company rushed to issue a detailed apology in which it fully admitted to what the employee had done and pledged to serve all customers with respect.

Source: "Chick-fil-A Cashier Fired for Racist Receipts Mocking Asians" *MSNBC.com*, December 14, 2011, accessed March 15, 2012, http://usnews.msnbc.msn.com/_news/2011/12/14/9444087-chick-fil-a-cashier-fired-for-racist-receipts-mocking-asians.

with our differences—not despite them."

Robert Churchill/iStockphoto.com

Begin by *carefully and faithfully following and enforcing federal and state laws regarding equal opportunity employment*. Diversity programs can't and won't succeed if the company is being sued for discriminatory actions and behavior. Faithfully following the law will also reduce the time and expense associated with EEOC investigations or lawsuits. Start by learning more at the EEOC website (http://www.eeoc.gov). Following the law also means strictly and fairly enforcing company policies.

Treat group differences as important but not special. Surface-level diversity dimensions such as age, sex, and race/ethnicity should be respected but should not be treated as more important than other kinds of differences (i.e., deep-level diversity). Remember, the shift in focus from surface- to deep-level diversity helps people know and understand each other better, reduces prejudice and conflict, and leads to stronger social integration with people wanting to work together and get the job done. Also, *find the common ground*. Although respecting differences is important, it's just as important, especially with diverse work forces, to actively find ways for employees to see and share commonalties.

Tailor opportunities to individuals, not groups. Special programs for training, development, mentoring, or promotion should be based on individual strengths and weaknesses, not on group status. Instead of making mentoring available for just one group of workers, create mentoring opportunities for everyone who wants to be mentored. DuPont Corporation's mentoring program, for example, is voluntary and open to all employees. Through candid and confidential conversations, DuPont's mentors help younger workers and managers with problem solving and career and leadership development.[102]

Maintain high standards. Companies have a legal and moral obligation to make sure that their hiring and promotion procedures and standards are fair to all. At the same time, in today's competitive markets, companies should not lower standards to promote diversity. This not only hurts the organizations but also feeds the stereotype that applicants who are hired or promoted in the name of affirmative action or diversity are less qualified. Chrysler's executive director of diversity, Monica Emerson, says, "As a diversity executive, I not only have to have solid business capabilities, I need to be very knowledgeable of the different businesses in my organization to align diversity initiatives to support the needs of the businesses. Maintaining high standards when making employment decisions and involving the top management and the board in diversity initiatives is critical to the success of workplace diversity practices."[103]

Solicit negative as well as positive feedback. Diversity is one of the most difficult management issues. No company or manager gets it right from the start. Consequently, companies should aggressively seek positive and negative feedback about their diversity programs. One way to do that is to use a series of measurements to see if progress is being made. Jaya Bohlmann, a vice president at Sodexo, a food services and facilities management company, says, "We measure our progress systematically, using an objective scorecard that ties 15 percent of managers' compensation and 25 percent of our executives' compensation to their success [to ensure that] we continue to attract, develop and retain a diverse and highly skilled workforce. We report on our diversity progress annually, posting the reports on our website."[104]

Set high but realistic goals. Just because diversity is difficult doesn't mean that organizations shouldn't try to accomplish as much as possible. The general purpose of diversity programs is to try to create a positive work environment where no one is advantaged or disadvantaged, where "we" is everyone, where everyone can do his or her best work, where differences are respected and not ignored, and where everyone feels comfortable. Even if progress is slow, companies should not shrink from these goals.

12-4c Diversity Training and Practices

Organizations use diversity training and several common diversity practices to manage diversity. There are two basic types of diversity training programs, skills-based and awareness. **Skills-based diversity training** teaches employees the practical skills they need for managing a diverse work force, skills such as flexibility and adaptability, negotiation, problem solving, and conflict resolution.[105] By contrast, **awareness training** is designed to raise employees' awareness of diversity issues and to challenge underlying assumptions or stereotypes we may have about others. Some companies use the Implicit Association Test (IAT) for awareness training.[106] The IAT measures the extent to which people associate positive or negative thoughts (i.e.,

Skills-based diversity training training that teaches employees the practical skills they need for managing a diverse work force, such as flexibility and adaptability, negotiation, problem solving, and conflict resolution

Awareness training training that is designed to raise employees' awareness of diversity issues and to challenge the underlying assumptions or stereotypes they may have about others

underlying assumptions or stereotypes) with blacks or whites, men or women, homosexuals or heterosexuals, young or old, or other groups. For the race IAT (versions also exist for weight, age, sexuality, and other ethnic groups), test takers are shown black or white faces that they must instantly pair with various words. Response times (shorter responses generally indicate stronger associations) and the pattern of associations indicate the extent to which people are biased. Most people are, and strongly so. For example, 88 percent of whites have a more positive mental association toward whites than toward blacks but, surprisingly, 48 percent of blacks show the same bias. Do the strong biases measured by the IAT mean we're likely to discriminate against others? Thankfully, no.[107] But they indicate the importance of becoming aware of our potential biases and then monitoring our workplace behavior and decision making. So, taking the IAT is a good way to increase awareness of diversity issues. To take the IAT and to learn more about the decade of research behind it, go to https://implicit.harvard.edu/implicit/demo.

Companies also use diversity audits, diversity pairing, and minority experiences for top executives to better manage diversity. **Diversity audits** are formal assessments that measure employee and management attitudes, investigate the extent to which people are advantaged or disadvantaged with respect to hiring and promotions, and review companies' diversity-related policies and procedures. At Intel, the world's leading computer chip manufacturer, diversity is a key part of its competitive strategy and vision. Accordingly, Intel's managers develop annual diversity action plans with specific measures and indicators that are reviewed every three months. For example, since the creation of Intel's Women's Initiative in 2004, the percentage of women in technical middle-level to senior-level jobs has increased by 24 percent.[108]

Intel also assesses its diversity practices through an annual survey about the company's policies and their effectiveness at creating a supportive environment. The survey results are shared with all employees and used to create or revise action plans consistent with its annual diversity action plans.[109]

Earlier in the chapter you learned that *mentoring*, pairing a junior employee with a senior employee, is a common strategy for creating learning and promotional opportunities for women. Diversity pairing is a special kind of mentoring. In **diversity pairing**, people of different cultural backgrounds, sexes, or races/ethnicities are paired for mentoring. The hope is that stereotypical beliefs and attitudes will change as people get to know each other as individuals.[110] Consultant Tom McGee, who has set up mentoring programs for numerous companies, supports diversity pairing, saying, "The assumption that people participating in diversity mentoring programs are looking for someone of the same race or gender has been proved wrong in many cases."[111]

For more than twenty years, Xerox has been fostering a culture where women and minorities are prepared and considered for top positions. CEO Ursula Burns, the first African American woman to lead a major U.S. company, worked as special assistant to Xerox's president of marketing and customer operations, Wayland Hicks. Reginald Brown, Jr., CEO of Brown Technology Group, who worked with Burns at Xerox, said, "These [appointments as special assistants] were jobs in the company that division presidents put their best people in. Most of them were white males, so to have an African American female in such a position of power, you knew early on she had great potential." Burns was then given a similar role with former Xerox CEO Paul A. Allaire. When Anne Mulcahy became CEO in 2001, Burns was gradually given control of day-to-day operations while Mulcahy repaired Xerox's financial position and customer service. David Thomas, a Harvard Business School professor, says that because of steps (such as diversity pairing) to promote diversity at Xerox, "you have a culture where having women and people of color as candidates for powerful jobs has been going on for two decades."[112]

Dean Mitchell/iStockphoto.com

Diversity audits formal assessments that measure employee and management attitudes, investigate the extent to which people are advantaged or disadvantaged with respect to hiring and promotions, and review companies' diversity-related policies and procedures

Diversity pairing a mentoring program in which people of different cultural backgrounds, sexes, or races/ethnicities are paired together to get to know each other and change stereotypical beliefs and attitudes

Finally, because top managers are still overwhelmingly white and male, a number of companies believe that it is worthwhile to *have top executives experience what it is like to be in the minority*. This can be done by having top managers go to places or events where nearly everyone else is of a different sex or racial/ethnic background. For example, managers at Raytheon are required to spend an entire day in the office in a wheelchair so that they have a better understanding of the challenges faced by their disabled colleagues. Managers and executives at Sodexho Alliance are asked to spend time working with organizations that represent minorities. One male manager became the sponsor of a women employees group at Sodexho and accompanied a female colleague to a meeting of the Women's Food Service Forum. The manager called the experience, in which he was at a conference with 1,500 women, "profound" and said that it taught him what it feels like to be different. He also describes how his experiences working with women made him more sensitive to women's feelings and even led him to change the social activities that he plans with coworkers from golf to dinner cruises. Rohini Anand, Sodexho's chief diversity officer, endorses this experiential approach, saying, "To really engage people, you have to create a series of epiphanies and take leaders through those epiphanies."[113]

STUDY TOOLS 12

LOCATED AT THE BACK OF YOUR BOOK:

☐ Rip out and study the Chapter Review Card at the end of the book

LOG IN TO WWW.CENGAGEBRAIN.COM TO:

☐ Review Key Term Flashcards

☐ Complete Practice Quizzing (take up to four times without repeating the same quiz)

☐ Complete Games: Beat the Clock and Crossword Puzzle

☐ Complete Interactive Content: Graded Quiz, Media Quiz, and Fill-in-the-Blank Questions

☐ Watch Management Workplace Video on "Mitchell Gold and Bob Williams Company"

☐ Work Through the What Would You Do Case on the Circuit Court of Macomb County

ONE APPROACH.
70 UNIQUE SOLUTIONS.

CENGAGE
Learning

www.cengage.com/4ltrpress

PART 4

13 Motivation

LEARNING OUTCOMES

13-1 Explain the basics of motivation.

13-2 Use equity theory to explain how employees' perceptions of fairness affect motivation.

13-3 Use expectancy theory to describe how workers' expectations about rewards, effort, and the link between rewards and performance influence motivation.

13-4 Explain how reinforcement theory works and how it can be used to motivate.

13-5 Describe the components of goal-setting theory and how managers can use them to motivate workers.

13-6 Discuss how the entire motivation model can be used to motivate workers.

After you finish this chapter, go to **PAGE 289** for **STUDY TOOLS**

13-1 BASICS OF MOTIVATION

What makes people happiest and most productive at work? Is it money, benefits, opportunities for growth, interesting work, or something else altogether? And if people desire different things, how can a company keep everyone motivated? It takes insight and hard work to motivate workers to join the company, perform well, and then stay with the company. Indeed, a 2013 worldwide study by Gallup found that only 13 percent of employees are "engaged" or motivated at work. Sixty-three percent are "not engaged," meaning they are unmotivated and not interested in organizational goals or outcomes. Even worse, 24 percent of employees are "actively disengaged" and are "unhappy, unproductive, and liable to spread negativity."[1]

So what is motivation? **Motivation** is the set of forces that initiates, directs, and makes people persist in their efforts to accomplish a goal.[2] *Initiation of effort* is concerned with the choices that people make about how much effort to put forth in their jobs. ("Do I really knock myself out for these performance appraisals or just do a decent job?") *Direction of effort* is concerned with the choices that people make in deciding where to put forth effort in their jobs. ("I should be spending time with my high-dollar accounts instead of learning this new computer system!") *Persistence of effort* is concerned with the choices that people make about how long they will put forth effort in their jobs before reducing or eliminating those efforts. ("I'm only halfway through the project, and I'm exhausted. Do I plow through to the end, or just call it quits?") Initiation, direction, and persistence are at the heart of motivation.

At 37signals, a Chicago software company, founder Jason Fried has avoided using promotions to reward his thirty employees. Says Fried, "We revere 'horizontal' ambition—in which employees who love what they do are encouraged to dig deeper, expand their knowledge, and become better at it. We always try to hire people who yearn to be master craftspeople, that is, designers who want to be great designers, not managers of designers; developers who want to master the art of programming, not management."[3]

Which would motivate you more, the chance to become a master craftsperson or the opportunity for promotion and management responsibilities? Or, in Gallup's terms, are you engaged at work? Are your co-workers? If you and your co-workers are "disengaged" or "actively disengaged," why? Are there parts of the job that interest and energize you? If so, what are they

Exhibit 13.1
A Basic Model of Work Motivation and Performance

and why? Answering questions like these is at the heart of figuring out how best to motivate people at work.

Let's learn more about motivation by building a basic model of motivation out of 13-1a effort and performance, 13-1b need satisfaction, and 13-1c extrinsic and intrinsic rewards and then discussing 13-1d how to motivate people with this basic model of motivation.

13-1a Effort and Performance

When most people think of work motivation, they think that working hard (effort) should lead to a good job (performance). Exhibit 13.1 shows a basic model of work motivation and performance, displaying this process. The first thing to notice about Exhibit 13.1 is that this is a basic model of work motivation *and* performance. In practice, it's almost impossible to talk about one without mentioning the other. Not surprisingly, managers often assume motivation to be the only determinant of performance, saying things such as "Your performance was really terrible last quarter. What's the matter? Aren't you as motivated as you used to be?" In fact, motivation is just one of three primary determinants of job performance. In industrial psychology, job performance is frequently represented by this equation:

**Job Performance =
Motivation × Ability × Situational Constraints**

In this formula, *job performance* is how well someone performs the requirements of the job. *Motivation*, as defined above, is effort, the degree to which someone

Motivation the set of forces that initiates, directs, and makes people persist in their efforts to accomplish a goal

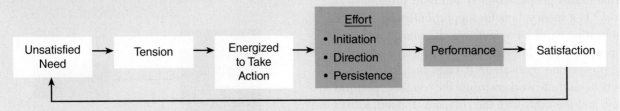

Exhibit 13.2

A Basic Model of Work Motivation and Performance

Unsatisfied Need → Tension → Energized to Take Action → Effort (• Initiation • Direction • Persistence) → Performance → Satisfaction

As shown on the left side of this exhibit, a person's unsatisfied need creates an uncomfortable internal state of tension that must be resolved. So, according to needs theories, people are motivated by unmet needs. But once a need is met, it no longer motivates. When this occurs, people become satisfied, as shown on the right side of the exhibit.

works hard to do the job well. *Ability* is the degree to which workers possess the knowledge, skills, and talent needed to do a job well. And *situational constraints* are factors beyond the control of individual employees, such as tools, policies, and resources that have an effect on job performance.

Since job performance is a multiplicative function of motivation times ability times situational constraints, job performance will suffer if any one of these components is weak. Does this mean that motivation doesn't matter? No, not at all. It just means that all the motivation in the world won't translate into high performance when an employee has little ability and high situational constraints. So, even though we will spend this chapter developing a model of work motivation, it is important to remember that ability and situational constraints affect job performance as well.

13-1b Need Satisfaction

In Exhibit 13.1 we started with a very basic model of motivation in which effort leads to job performance. But managers want to know, "What leads to effort?" Determining employee needs is the first step to answering that question.

Needs are the physical or psychological requirements that must be met to ensure survival and well-being.[4] As shown on the left side of Exhibit 13.2, a person's unmet need creates an uncomfortable, internal state of tension that must be resolved. For example, if you normally skip breakfast but then have to work through lunch, chances are you'll be so hungry by late afternoon that the only thing you'll be motivated to do is find something

to eat. So, according to needs theories, people are motivated by unmet needs. But a need no longer motivates once it is met. When this occurs, people become satisfied, as shown on the right side of Exhibit 13.2.

Note: Throughout the chapter, as we build on this basic model, the parts of the model that we've already discussed will appear shaded in color. For example, since we've already discussed the effort → performance part of the model, those components are shown with a colored background. When we add new parts to the model, they will have a white background. Since we're adding need satisfaction to the model at this step, the need-satisfaction components of unsatisfied need, tension, energized to take action, and satisfaction are shown with a white background. This shading convention should make it easier to understand the work motivation model as we add to it in each section of the chapter.

Since people are motivated by unmet needs, managers must learn what those unmet needs are and address them. This is not always a straightforward task, however, because different needs theories suggest different needs categories. Consider three well-known needs theories. Maslow's Hierarchy of Needs suggests that people are motivated by *physiological* (food and water), *safety* (physical and economic), *belongingness* (friendship, love, social interaction), *esteem* (achievement and recognition), and *self-actualization* (realizing your full potential) needs.[5] Alderfer's ERG Theory collapses Maslow's five needs into three: *existence* (safety and physiological needs), *relatedness* (belongingness), and *growth* (esteem and self-actualization).[6] McClelland's Learned Needs Theory suggests that people are motivated by the need

Needs the physical or psychological requirements that must be met to ensure survival and well-being

for *affiliation* (to be liked and accepted), the need for *achievement* (to accomplish challenging goals), or the need for *power* (to influence others).[7]

Things become even more complicated when we consider the different predictions made by these theories. According to Maslow, needs are arranged in a hierarchy from low (physiological) to high (self-actualization). Within this hierarchy, people are motivated by their lowest unsatisfied need. As each need is met, they work their way up the hierarchy from physiological to self-actualization needs. By contrast, Alderfer says that people can be motivated by more than one need at a time. Furthermore, he suggests that people are just as likely to move down the needs hierarchy as up, particularly when they are unable to achieve satisfaction at the next higher need level. McClelland argues that the degree to which particular needs motivate varies tremendously from person to person, with some people being motivated primarily by achievement and others by power or affiliation. Moreover, McClelland says that needs are learned, not innate. For instance, studies show that children whose parents own a small business or hold a managerial position are much more likely to have a high need for achievement.[8]

So, with three different sets of needs and three very different ideas about how needs motivate, how do we provide a practical answer to managers who just want to know what leads to effort? Fortunately, the research evidence simplifies things a bit. To start, studies indicate that there are two basic kinds of needs categories.[9] *Lower-order needs* are concerned with safety and with physiological and existence requirements, whereas *higher-order needs* are concerned with relationships (belongingness, relatedness, and affiliation), challenges and accomplishments (esteem, self-actualization, growth, and achievement), and influence (power). Studies generally show that higher-order needs will not motivate people as long as lower-order needs remain unsatisfied.[10]

For example, imagine that you graduated from college six months ago and are still looking for your first job. With money running short (you're probably living on your credit cards) and the possibility of having to move back in with your parents looming (if this doesn't motivate you, what will?), your basic needs for food, shelter, and security drive your thoughts, behavior, and choices at this point. But once you land that job, find a great place (of your own!) to live, and put some money in the bank, these basic needs should decrease in importance as you begin to think about making new friends and taking on challenging work assignments. In fact, once lower-order needs are satisfied, it's difficult for managers to predict which higher-order needs will motivate behavior.[11] Some people will be motivated by affiliation, while others will be motivated by growth or esteem. Also,

the relative importance of the various needs may change over time but not necessarily in any predictable pattern. So, what leads to effort? In part, needs do. After we discuss rewards in Subsection 13-1c, in Subsection 13-1d we discuss how managers can use what we know from need-satisfaction theories to motivate workers.

13-1c Extrinsic and Intrinsic Rewards

No discussion of motivation would be complete without considering rewards. Let's add two kinds of rewards, extrinsic and intrinsic, to the model in Exhibit 13.3.[12]

Extrinsic rewards are tangible and visible to others and are given to employees contingent on the performance of specific tasks or behaviors.[13] External agents (managers, for example) determine and control the distribution, frequency, and amount of extrinsic rewards, such as pay, company stock, benefits, and promotions. For example, 80 percent of 1,000 large- and medium-sized U.S. companies surveyed by Hewitt Associates, a consulting company based in Lincolnshire, Illinois, offer incentives or bonuses to reward employees.[14]

Lincoln Electric, a manufacturer of arc welding tools and technology, has paid annual profit sharing bonuses to its factory workers for 80 straight years. In 2013, Lincoln paid out one-third of its pre-tax profits, $100.7 million, to employees who received bonuses of $33,029 each, worth 62 percent of total wages. In the 80 years in which Lincoln has paid profit sharing bonuses, the percentage has never dropped below 25 percent of total wages and has been as high as 120 percent. Over the last decade, bonuses have averaged 40 percent of total salary.[15]

Why do companies need to offer extrinsic rewards? To get people to do things they wouldn't otherwise do. Companies use extrinsic rewards to motivate people to perform four basic behaviors: join the organization, regularly attend their jobs, perform their jobs well, and stay with the organization.[16] Think about it. Would you show up at work every day to do the best possible job that you could just out of the goodness of your heart? Very few people would.

Intrinsic rewards are the natural rewards associated with performing a task or activity for its own sake.

Extrinsic reward a reward that is tangible, visible to others, and given to employees contingent on the performance of specific tasks or behaviors

Intrinsic reward a natural reward associated with performing a task or activity for its own sake

Exhibit 13.3

Adding Rewards to the Model

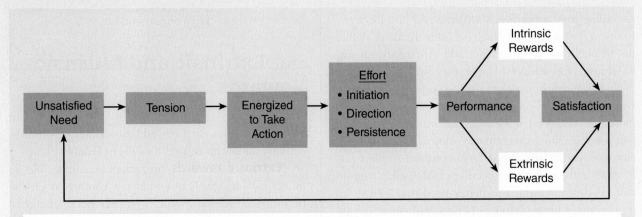

Performing a job well can be rewarding intrinsically (the job itself is fun, challenging, or interesting) or extrinsically (as you receive better pay, promotions, etc.). Intrinsic and extrinsic rewards lead to satisfaction of various needs.

For example, aside from the external rewards management offers for doing something well, employees often find the activities or tasks they perform interesting and enjoyable. Examples of intrinsic rewards include a sense of accomplishment or achievement, a feeling of responsibility, the chance to learn something new or interact with others, or simply the fun that comes from performing an interesting, challenging, and engaging task.

With 183 million active gamers (playing one to two hours a day on average) and 5 million "extreme" gamers (playing more than forty-five hours a week), video games are a $21.5 billion industry in the United States. Overall, we spend 3 billion hours a week on video games! Why? Because they're interesting, challenging, and engaging (i.e., intrinsically rewarding).[17] Companies are now beginning to apply "gamification"— meaning levels, points, time limits, and friendly competition—to organizational tasks like training, data entry, sales leads, car pooling, etc. Gabe Zichermann, who organizes the Gamification Summit conference, says, "The reason why gamification is so hot is that most people's jobs are really freaking boring." Does it work? Well, if you play *Guitar Hero* you're more likely to actually learn to play a real guitar. Likewise,

at work, people trained via video games learn more information, remember it longer, and progress to higher skill levels.[18]

Which types of rewards are most important to workers in general? A number of surveys suggest that both extrinsic and intrinsic rewards are important and that employee preferences for either intrinsic or extrinsic rewards are relatively stable.[19] A 2014 Society for Human Resource Management national survey found that over the last six years, three extrinsic factors, pay, benefits, and job security/organizational financial stability, and two intrinsic factors, the work itself and opportunities to use one's skills and abilities, have consistently been among the top five factors rated as "very important" by employees.[20]

13-1d Motivating with the Basics

So, given the basic model of work motivation in Exhibit 13.3, what practical steps can managers take to motivate employees to increase their effort?

The first step is to *start by asking people what their needs are.* Jonathan Robinson, the CEO of **Freetextbooks.com**, an online college textbook seller

dra_schwartz/iStockphoto.com

What's Better than Cash? Try a Vacation

While no employee is going to turn down a cash bonus if offered, other incentives are worth considering. When given the choice between cash and noncash rewards, the *Journal of Economic Psychology* reports that employees will take cash when offered in the abstract. However, when specific noncash rewards are offered, employees tend to choose those. So what's the best incentive? According to one study, 96 percent of employees are motivated by travel, and 72 percent who received a travel bonus expressed increased loyalty to the company. Studies also show that a good health insurance package is both a strong motivator and a good way to attract new talent.

Source: The Build Network, "What Motivates Employees Better than Cash? A Break." *Inc.*, December 31, 2013, accessed May 14, 2014, http://www.inc.com/the-build-network/what-motivates-employees-better -than-cash.

Cdwheatley/iStockphoto.com

(sorry, the textbooks aren't really free), says the key to motivating employees is finding out what they like and then giving them the rewards they want. To do that, Robinson gives each new hire a brief survey asking them about their favorite candy, restaurant, hobby, or music. Says Robinson, "You just have to know your team. We're pretty small so I have to stay in tune with the preferences and pulse of our employees. The perks are in the details." As a result, he recently gave one employee a free round of golf, another $100 to be used at a great restaurant, and another IMAX theater tickets. Because he asked, all got what they wanted.[21] So, if you want to meet employees' needs, just ask.

Next, *satisfy lower-order needs first*. Since higher-order needs will not motivate people as long as lower-order needs remain unsatisfied, companies should satisfy lower-order needs first. In practice, this means providing the equipment, training, and knowledge to create a safe workplace free of physical risks, paying employees well enough to provide financial security, and offering a benefits package that will protect employees and their families through good medical coverage and health and disability insurance. Indeed, the Society for Human Resource Management study mentioned above found that three of the five most important factors in 2013—compensation/pay (60 percent), job security (59 percent), and benefits (53 percent)—were all lower-order needs.[22] Consistent with the idea of satisfying lower-order needs first, a survey of 12,000 employees found that inadequate compensation is the number-one reason employees leave organizations.

Third, managers should *expect people's needs to change*. As some needs are satisfied or situations change,

what motivated people before may not motivate them now. Likewise, what motivates people to accept a job may not necessarily motivate them once they have the job. For instance, David Stum, president of the Loyalty Institute, says, "The [attractive] power of pay and benefits is only [strong] during the recruitment stage. After employees take the job, pay and benefits become entitlements to them. They think: 'Now that I work here, you owe me that.'"[23] Managers should also expect needs to change as people mature. For older employees, benefits are as important as pay, which is always ranked as more important by younger employees. Older employees also rank job security as more important than personal and family time, which is more important to younger employees.[24]

Finally, *as needs change and lower-order needs are satisfied, create opportunities for employees to satisfy higher-order needs*. Recall that intrinsic rewards such as accomplishment, achievement, learning something new, and interacting with others are the natural rewards associated with performing a task or activity for its own sake. And, with the exception of influence (power), intrinsic rewards correspond very closely to higher-order needs that are concerned with relationships (belongingness, relatedness, and affiliation) and challenges and accomplishments (esteem, self-actualization, growth, and achievement). Therefore, one way for managers to meet employees' higher-order needs is to create opportunities for employees to experience intrinsic rewards by providing challenging work, encouraging employees to take greater responsibility for their work, and giving employees the freedom to pursue tasks and projects they find naturally interesting.

13-2 EQUITY THEORY

We've seen that people are motivated to achieve intrinsic and extrinsic rewards. However, if employees don't believe that rewards are fairly awarded or don't believe that they can achieve the performance goals the company has set for them, they won't be very motivated.

Fairness, or what people perceive to be fair, is also a critical issue in organizations. **Equity theory** says that people will be motivated at work when they *perceive* that they are being treated fairly. In particular, equity theory stresses the importance of perceptions. So, regardless of the actual level of rewards people receive, they must also perceive that, relative to others, they are being treated fairly. For example, you learned in Chapter 11 that the CEOs of the largest U.S. firms now make $12.3 million per year, which is 354 times their average employee salary of $34,645.[25] The ten highest paid CEOs averaged earnings of $61.6 million per year, led by John H. Hammergren, the CEO of McKesson Corporation, who made $131.19 million.[26] By contrast, in most companies with less than $1 billion a year in revenues, CEOs typically make 2.3 to 12.5 times what the average employee makes.[27]

Many people believe that CEO pay is obscenely high and unfair. Others believe that CEO pay is fair because the supply and demand for executive talent largely determine what CEOs are paid. They argue that if it were easier to find good CEOs, then CEOs would be paid much less. Equity theory doesn't focus on objective equity (that is, that CEOs make 354 times more than blue-collar workers). Instead, equity theory says that equity, like beauty, is in the eye of the beholder.

Equity theory a theory that states that people will be motivated when they perceive that they are being treated fairly

Inputs in equity theory, the contributions employees make to the organization

Outcomes in equity theory, the rewards employees receive for their contributions to the organization

Referents in equity theory, others with whom people compare themselves to determine if they have been treated fairly

Outcome/input (O/I) ratio in equity theory, an employee's perception of how the rewards received from an organization compare with the employee's contributions to that organization

Underreward a form of inequity in which you are getting fewer outcomes relative to inputs than your referent is getting

---

*Let's learn more about equity theory by examining **13-2a the components of equity theory, 13-2b how people react to perceived inequity,** and **13-2c how to motivate people using equity theory.***

13-2a Components of Equity Theory

The basic components of equity theory are inputs, outcomes, and referents. **Inputs** are the contributions employees make to the organization. They include education and training, intelligence, experience, effort, number of hours worked, and ability. **Outcomes** are what employees receive in exchange for their contributions to the organization. They include pay, fringe benefits, status symbols, and job titles and assignments. And, since perceptions of equity depend on comparisons, **referents** are other people with whom people compare themselves to determine if they have been treated fairly. The referent can be a single person (comparing yourself with a coworker), a generalized other (comparing yourself with "students in general," for example), or even yourself over time ("I was better off last year than I am this year"). Usually, people choose to compare themselves with referents who hold the same or similar jobs or who are otherwise similar in gender, race, age, tenure, or other characteristics.[28] For example, 1,300 employees at Amazon's eight German distribution centers have gone on strike in pursuit of higher pay. The workers want to be paid 12 euros an hour, similar to employees (i.e., their referents) at German retail and catalog-order companies. Amazon, however, argues that the employees, who are paid 9.30 euros an hour plus bonuses and shares of Amazon stock (after two years), are paid at the top end of the range for logistical employees who work in distribution warehouses. So, with clearly different referents, it's no surprise they disagree on what constitutes fair pay.[29]

According to equity theory, employees compare their outcomes (the rewards they receive from the organization) with their inputs (their contributions to the organization). This comparison of outcomes with inputs is called the **outcome/input (O/I) ratio.** After an internal comparison in which they compare their outcomes with their inputs, employees then make an external comparison in which they compare their O/I ratio with the O/I ratio of a referent.[30]

When people perceive that their O/I ratio is equal to the referent's O/I ratio, they conclude that they are being treated fairly. But when people perceive that their O/I ratio is different from their referent's O/I ratio, they conclude that they have been treated inequitably or unfairly.

Inequity can take two forms, underreward and overreward. **Underreward** occurs when a referent's O/I ratio is better than your O/I ratio. In other words, you are getting fewer outcomes relative to your inputs than the referent you compare yourself with is getting. When people perceive that they have been underrewarded, they tend to experience anger or frustration. Auto assembly workers at Toyota's two Indian facilities went on strike out of frustration that they were being paid unfairly. Toyota is offering 3,050 rupees ($51) a month, but workers want to be paid 4,000 rupees a month ($67) and have more holidays and company-provided housing. Satish Rangaswamy, the general secretary of the union representing the workers, said, "Whenever it makes a good profit in a year, it [Toyota] shifts all the profit to the headquarters, that is [in] Japan. Why can't they share it with our employees?"[31]

By contrast, **overreward** occurs when a referent's O/I ratio is worse than your O/I ratio. In this case, you are getting more outcomes relative to your inputs than your referent is. In theory, when people perceive that they have been overrewarded, they experience guilt. But, not surprisingly, people have a very high tolerance for overreward. It takes a tremendous amount of overpayment before people decide that their pay or benefits are more than they deserve.

13-2b How People React to Perceived Inequity

So what happens when people perceive that they have been treated inequitably at work? Exhibit 13.4 shows that perceived inequity affects satisfaction. In the case of underreward, this usually translates into frustration or anger; with overreward, the reaction is guilt. These reactions lead to tension and a strong need to take action to restore equity in some way. At first, a slight inequity may not be strong enough to motivate an employee to take immediate action. If the inequity continues or there are multiple inequities, however, tension may build over time until a point of intolerance is reached and the person is energized to take action.[32]

Dejan Karabasevic, a programmer at American Superconductor, an energy technologies company, had access to the company's proprietary computer code that provided its key competitive advantage. After the company demoted him, Karabasevic sold the code to Sinovel, a Chinese power company and key customer. After Sinovel received the proprietary computer code,

it canceled all of its orders, refusing to pay American Superconductor for products it had already received. Because of Karabasevic's actions, which he took in response to being demoted, American Superconductor lost $6.5 million and saw its stock price drop a staggering 86 percent.[33]

When people perceive that they have been treated unfairly, they may try to restore equity by reducing inputs, increasing outcomes, rationalizing inputs or outcomes, changing the referent, or simply leaving. We will discuss these possible responses in terms of the inequity associated with underreward, which is much more common than the inequity associated with overreward.

People who perceive that they have been underrewarded may try to restore equity by *decreasing or withholding their inputs (that is, effort)*. After filing for bankruptcy and seeking sizable pay and benefits cuts, American Airlines pilots engaged in a sick-out that cancelled hundreds of flights. Furthermore, pilots who showed for work allegedly delayed flights by filing maintenance requests that required mechanics to inspect planes before departure. While the pilots' union denied the slowdown, its president said, "The pilots of American Airlines are angry. While AMR management continues paying lip service to needing a consensual agreement with us, their punitive approach of extracting far more value than they need is hardly conducive to reaching a consensual agreement."[34]

Increasing outcomes is another way people try to restore equity. This might include asking for a raise or pointing out the inequity to the boss and hoping that he or she takes care of it. Sometimes, however, employees may go to external organizations such as labor unions, federal agencies, or the courts for help in increasing outcomes to restore equity. For instance, the U.S. Department of Labor estimates that 10 percent of workers are not getting the extra overtime pay they deserve when they work more than forty hours a week. These are known as Fair Labor Standards Act (FLSA) violations.[35] After a U.S. Department of Labor ruling, Walmart paid $5.26 million in back wages to 4,500 security guards who were at first denied overtime pay after incorrectly being classified as exempt employees (who are ineligible for overtime).[36]

REFERENT'S OUTCOME/INPUT RATIO

MY OUTCOME/INPUT RATIO

ZargonDesign/iStockphoto.com

Exhibit 13.4

Adding Equity Theory to the Model

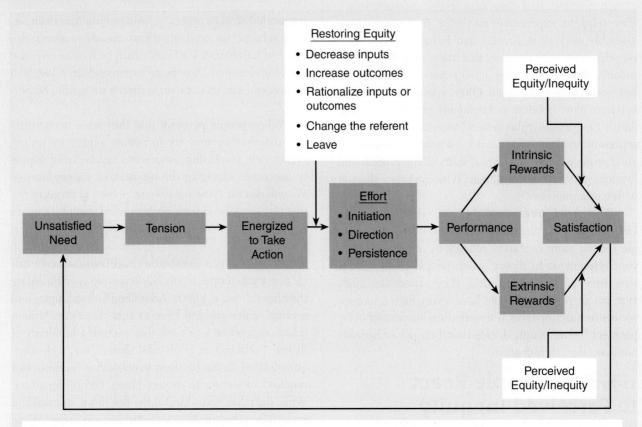

Restoring Equity
- Decrease inputs
- Increase outcomes
- Rationalize inputs or outcomes
- Change the referent
- Leave

When people perceive that they have been treated inequitably at work because of the intrinsic or extrinsic rewards they receive relative to their efforts, they are dissatisfied (or frustrated or angry), their needs aren't met, and those reactions lead to tension and a strong need to take action to restore equity in some way.

Somewhere between 25,000 and 30,000 FLSA cases are brought each year, and employees win two-thirds of them.[37] From 2001 to 2011, the number of FLSA filings in federal court rose by nearly 500 percent.[38]

Another method of restoring equity is to *rationalize or distort inputs or outcomes*. Instead of decreasing inputs or increasing outcomes, employees restore equity by making mental or emotional adjustments in their O/I ratios or the O/I ratios of their referents. For example, suppose that a company downsizes 10 percent of its work force. It's likely that the people who still have jobs will be angry or frustrated with company management because of the layoffs. If alternative jobs are difficult to find, however, these survivors may rationalize or distort their O/I ratios and conclude, "Well, things could be worse. At least I still have my job." Rationalizing or distorting outcomes may be used when other ways to restore equity aren't available.

Changing the referent is another way of restoring equity. In this case, people compare themselves with someone other than the referent they had been using for previous O/I ratio comparisons. Since people usually choose to compare themselves with others who hold the same or similar jobs or who are otherwise similar (i.e., friends, family members, neighbors who work at other companies), they may change referents to restore equity when their personal situations change, such as a decrease in job status or pay.[39]

13-2c Motivating with Equity Theory

What practical steps can managers take to use equity theory to motivate employees? They can *start by looking*

People who perceive that they have been underrewarded may try to restore equity by decreasing or withholding their efforts.

for and correcting major inequities. Among other things, equity theory makes us aware that an employee's sense of fairness is based on subjective perceptions. What one employee considers grossly unfair may not affect another employee's perceptions of equity at all. Although these different perceptions make it difficult for managers to create conditions that satisfy all employees, it's critical that they do their best to take care of major inequities that can energize employees to take disruptive, costly, or harmful actions such as decreasing inputs or leaving. So, whenever possible, managers should look for and correct major inequities.

For example, with Chinese wages rising between 10—15 percent per year on average and 30 percent a year where demand is high, the average factory worker in China, who makes between $317 and $350 a month, is generally underpaid.[40] So for two consecutive years, Lenovo CEO Yang Yuanqing has given his annual bonus to Lenovo's 10,000 employees. Approximately 90 percent of his 2013 $3.25 million bonus will go to factory employees in China, each of whom will receive about $325 dollars, roughly a month's salary. Lenovo spokeswoman Angela Lee said, "As you can imagine, an extra $300 [or more] in a manufacturing environment in China does make an impact, especially to employees supporting families."[41] Lenovo's communication to employees stated, "This payment is personally funded by Yuanqing. He believes that he has the responsibility as an owner of the company, and the opportunity as our leader, to ensure all of our employees understand the impact they have on building Lenovo."[42]

Second, managers can *reduce employees' inputs*. Increasing outcomes is often the first and only strategy that companies use to restore equity, yet reducing employee inputs is just as viable a strategy. In fact, with dual-career couples working fifty-hour weeks, more and more employees are looking for ways to reduce stress and restore a balance between work and family. Consequently, it may make sense to ask employees to do less, not more; to have them identify and eliminate the 20 percent of their jobs that doesn't increase productivity or add value for customers; and to eliminate company-imposed requirements that really aren't critical to the performance of managers, employees, or the company (for example, unnecessary meetings and reports). According to Chinese labor laws, employees may not work more than thirty-six hours of overtime per month, or no more than nine overtime hours per week. However, after a catastrophic plant explosion and a series of employee suicides disrupted production at a Foxconn factory in China, factory workers, who assemble everything from iPads to laptop computers, worked 80 to 100 overtime hours each month on top of their 174 regular hours to make up for the production shortfalls. During this time, employees regularly worked twelve-hour shifts, six days a week, or sixty hours a month over the legal limit. As a result of pressure from Apple and from international workers' rights groups, Foxconn has agreed to immediately increase pay as much as 25 percent and limit the number of hours an employee works to forty-nine per week.[43]

Finally, managers should *make sure decision-making processes are fair*. Equity theory focuses on **distributive justice,** the perceived degree to which outcomes and rewards are fairly distributed or allocated. However, **procedural justice,** the perceived fairness of the procedures used to make reward allocation decisions, is just as important.[44] Procedural justice matters because even when employees are unhappy with their outcomes (that is, low pay), they're much less likely to be unhappy with company management if they believe that the procedures used to allocate outcomes were fair. For example, employees who are laid off tend to be hostile toward their employer when they perceive that the procedures leading to the layoffs were unfair. By contrast, employees who perceive layoff procedures to be fair tend to continue to support and trust their employers.[45] Also, if employees perceive that their outcomes are unfair (that is, distributive

Distributive justice the perceived degree to which outcomes and rewards are fairly distributed or allocated

Procedural justice the perceived fairness of the process used to make reward allocation decisions

xrrr/iStockphoto.com

Four Ways to Fail

Author and speaker Minda Zetlin warns managers that there are four motivational tactics that are sure to fail. The first is money. Sure, employees love getting cash bonuses, but the motivation to work hard for cash bonuses usually does not last long unless employees feel that the work they are doing is important and that their hard work is recognized. The second is fear. An employee who is afraid of your tantrums and yelling will have zero loyalty to you and will most certainly avoid being innovative or creative. The third is competition. Which would you rather have, employees working collaboratively in smooth operating teams or lone-wolf individuals working against each other? The fourth is praise, which should only be given out when employees do something truly special. Giving too much praise too often, and making it too general, will just make it seem cheap.

Source: M. Zetlin, "4 Employee 'Motivators' That Can Backfire," *Inc.*, March 1, 2013, accessed June 17, 2013, http://www.inc.com/minda-zetlin/4-employee-motivators-that-can-backfire.html?nav=river.

injustice) but that the decisions and procedures leading to those outcomes were fair (that is, procedural justice), they are much more likely to seek constructive ways of restoring equity, such as discussing these matters with their manager. By contrast, if employees perceive both distributive and procedural injustice, they may resort to more destructive tactics, such as withholding effort, absenteeism, tardiness, or even sabotage and theft.[46]

Expectancy theory the theory that people will be motivated to the extent to which they believe that their efforts will lead to good performance, that good performance will be rewarded, and that they will be offered attractive rewards

Valence the attractiveness or desirability of a reward or outcome

Expectancy the perceived relationship between effort and performance

13-3 # EXPECTANCY THEORY

One of the hardest things about motivating people is that not everyone is attracted to the same rewards. **Expectancy theory** says that people will be motivated to the extent to which they believe that their efforts will lead to good performance, that good performance will be rewarded, and that they will be offered attractive rewards.[47]

*Let's learn more about expectancy theory by examining **13-3a the components of expectancy theory** and **13-3b how to use expectancy theory as a motivational tool.***

13-3a Components of Expectancy Theory

Expectancy theory holds that people make conscious choices about their motivation. The three factors that affect those choices are valence, expectancy, and instrumentality.

Valence is simply the attractiveness or desirability of various rewards or outcomes. Expectancy theory recognizes that the same reward or outcome—say, a promotion—will be highly attractive to some people, will be highly disliked by others, and will not make much difference one way or the other to still others. Accordingly, when people are deciding how much effort to put forth, expectancy theory says that they will consider the valence of all possible rewards and outcomes that they can receive from their jobs. The greater the sum of those valences, each of which can be positive, negative, or neutral, the more effort people will choose to put forth on the job. Consultant Carol Schultz spent nine years working for a company where the boss rewarded top-performing employees with five-day trips to expensive resorts, with the company paying for the flight, the hotel, and one dinner, leaving employees to pay for the rest of their food and all of their drinks and resort activities. Said Schultz, "It always irked me that they'd fly us to some expensive resort and expect us to pay for everything outside of our flight and hotel room. To me, this was no 'reward.'" In other words, when Schultz added up all of the valences, the positive valence of rewarding her with an expensive resort trip could not overcome the negative valence of getting stuck with large food, drink, and resort expenses.[48]

Expectancy is the perceived relationship between effort and performance. When expectancies are strong,

278 PART FOUR

employees believe that their hard work and efforts will result in good performance, so they work harder. By contrast, when expectancies are weak, employees figure that no matter what they do or how hard they work, they won't be able to perform their jobs successfully, so they don't work as hard.

Instrumentality is the perceived relationship between performance and rewards. When instrumentality is strong, employees believe that improved performance will lead to better and more rewards, so they choose to work harder. When instrumentality is weak, employees don't believe that better performance will result in more or better rewards, so they choose not to work as hard.

Expectancy theory holds that for people to be highly motivated, all three variables—valence, expectancy, and instrumentality—must be high. Thus, expectancy theory can be represented by the following simple equation:

Motivation =
Valence × Expectancy × Instrumentality

If any one of these variables (valence, expectancy, or instrumentality) declines, overall motivation will decline, too.

Exhibit 13.5 incorporates the expectancy theory variables into our motivation model. Valence and instrumentality combine to affect employees' willingness to put forth effort (i.e., the degree to which they are energized to take action), while expectancy transforms intended effort ("I'm really going to work hard in this job") into actual effort. If you're offered rewards that you desire and you believe that you will in fact receive these rewards for good performance, you're highly likely to be energized to take action. However, you're not likely to actually exert effort unless you also believe that you can do the job (i.e., that your efforts will lead to successful performance).

13-3b Motivating with Expectancy Theory

What practical steps can managers take to use expectancy theory to motivate employees? First, they can *systematically gather information to find out what employees want from their jobs*. In addition to individual managers directly asking employees what they want from their jobs (see Subsection 13-1d, "Motivating with the Basics"), companies need to survey their employees regularly to determine their wants, needs, and dissatisfactions. Since people consider the valence of all the possible rewards and outcomes that they can receive from their jobs, regular identification of wants, needs, and dissatisfactions gives companies the chance to turn negatively valent rewards and outcomes into positively valent rewards and outcomes, thus raising overall motivation and effort. Mark Peterman, vice president of client solutions at Maritz Incentives, says that individual employees are motivated in vastly different ways: "For some, being honored in front of one's peers is a great award, but for others, the thought of being put

Instrumentality the perceived relationship between performance and rewards

Exhibit 13.5
Adding Expectancy Theory to the Model

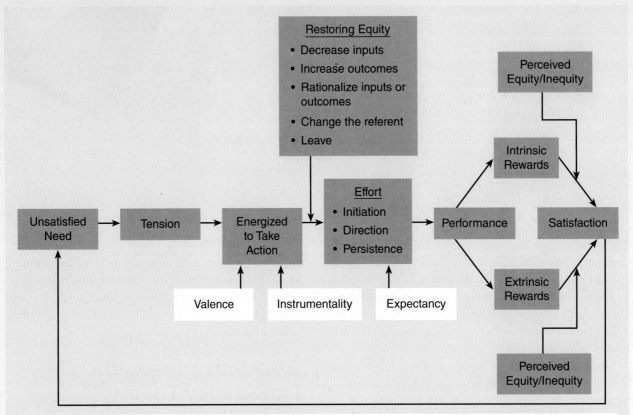

Restoring Equity
- Decrease inputs
- Increase outcomes
- Rationalize inputs or outcomes
- Change the referent
- Leave

Perceived Equity/Inequity

Intrinsic Rewards

Effort
- Initiation
- Direction
- Persistence

Unsatisfied Need → Tension → Energized to Take Action → Performance → Satisfaction

Valence · Instrumentality · Expectancy

Extrinsic Rewards

Perceived Equity/Inequity

If rewards are attractive (valence) and linked to performance (instrumentality), then people are energized to take action. In other words, good performance gets them rewards that they want. Intended effort (i.e., becoming energized to take action) turns into actual effort when people expect that their hard work and efforts will result in good performance. After all, why work hard if that hard work is wasted?

Use Expectancy Theory to Motivate by:
- ❑ surveying employees to identify preferred rewards
- ❑ ensuring that employees see the connection between pay and performance
- ❑ motivating employees to take active rather than passive roles

on display in front of peers embarrasses them." And companies have a long way to go to ensure that their employees feel valued, Peterman says. A Maritz survey found that only 27 percent of employees who want to be recognized by nonmonetary incentives are recognized that way.[49] Such findings suggest that employers should routinely survey employees to identify not only the range of rewards that are valued by most employees but also to understand the preferences of specific employees.

Second, managers can *take specific steps to link rewards to individual performance in a way that is clear and understandable to employees.* Unfortunately, most employees are extremely dissatisfied with the link between pay and performance in their organizations, and their companies are, too. Mercer's 2013 Pay for Performance

Survey found that while 55 percent of firms say they link rewards to performance, only 42 percent measure to make sure that happens and 48 percent say that programs linking performance to rewards need improvement.[50]

One way to establish a clear connection between pay and performance (see Chapter 11 for a discussion of compensation strategies) is for managers to publicize the way in which pay decisions are made. This is especially important given that only 41 percent of employees know how their pay increases are determined.[51] At Fog Creek Software, founder Joel Spolsky addresses this issue by using experience (years of full-time experience in your area), scope of responsibilities (Do you manage others, a department, a product or product line?), and programming skills (from new programmer to an expert critical to project success) to categorize each employee into one of nine different levels. Then, to make sure that the connection between pay and performance is clear, Fog Creek does two things. People with higher levels get more pay. And, everyone at the same level gets the same pay. Spolsky says, "Once a year, my management team sits down, reviews every employee's work, and recalculates every employee's level." And, if your responsibilities and experience and programming skills increase, your level and your pay do, too.[52]

Finally, managers should *empower employees to make decisions if management really wants them to believe that their hard work and effort will lead to good performance*. If valent rewards are linked to good performance, people should be energized to take action. However, this works only if they also believe that their efforts will lead to good performance. One of the ways that managers destroy the expectancy that hard work and effort will lead to good performance is by restricting what employees can do or by ignoring employees' ideas. In Chapter 9, you learned that *empowerment* is a feeling of intrinsic motivation in which workers perceive their work to have meaning and perceive themselves to be competent, to have an impact, and to be capable of self-determination.[53] So, if managers want workers to have strong expectancies, they should empower them to make decisions. Doing so will motivate employees to take active rather than passive roles in their work.

13-4 REINFORCEMENT THEORY

When used properly, rewards motivate and energize employees. But when used incorrectly, they can demotivate, baffle, and even anger them. Goals are supposed to motivate employees. But leaders who focus blindly on meeting goals at all costs often find that they destroy motivation.

Reinforcement theory says that behavior is a function of its consequences, that behaviors followed by positive consequences (i.e., reinforced) will occur more frequently, and that behaviors either followed by negative consequences or not followed by positive consequences will occur less frequently.[54] United Airlines employees get a $50 monthly bonus if 80 percent of domestic or international flights arrive on time. The bonus increases to $100 when both domestic and international flights arrive on time 80 percent of the time. Motivated by the bonuses, United employees achieved on-time rates of 85.5 percent for domestic flights and 81.2 percent for international flights in November 2012, the second-best performance in five years. And during the Thanksgiving holiday, arguably the busiest travel season, United averaged 88.3 percent on-time arrivals.[55] More specifically, **reinforcement** is the process of changing behavior by changing the consequences that follow behavior.[56]

Reinforcement has two parts: reinforcement contingencies and schedules of reinforcement. **Reinforcement contingencies** are the cause-and-effect relationships between the performance of specific behaviors and specific consequences. For example, if you get docked an hour's pay for being late to work, then a reinforcement contingency exists between a behavior (being late to work) and a consequence (losing an hour's pay). A **schedule of reinforcement** is the set of rules regarding reinforcement contingencies such as which behaviors will be reinforced, which consequences will follow those behaviors, and the schedule by which those consequences will be delivered.[57]

Exhibit 13.6 incorporates reinforcement contingencies and reinforcement schedules into our motivation model. First, notice that extrinsic rewards and the schedules of reinforcement used to deliver them are the

Reinforcement theory the theory that behavior is a function of its consequences, that behaviors followed by positive consequences will occur more frequently, and that behaviors followed by negative consequences, or not followed by positive consequences, will occur less frequently

Reinforcement the process of changing behavior by changing the consequences that follow behavior

Reinforcement contingencies cause-and-effect relationships between the performance of specific behaviors and specific consequences

Schedule of reinforcement rules that specify which behaviors will be reinforced, which consequences will follow those behaviors, and the schedule by which those consequences will be delivered

Exhibit 13.6
Adding Reinforcement Theory to the Model

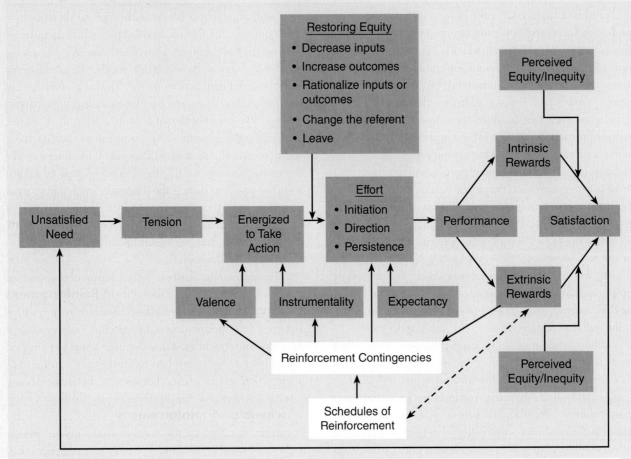

Extrinsic rewards and the schedules of reinforcement used to deliver them are the primary methods for creating reinforcement contingencies in organizations. In turn, those reinforcement contingencies directly affect valence (the attractiveness of rewards), instrumentality (the perceived link between rewards and performance), and effort (how hard employees will work).

primary method for creating reinforcement contingencies in organizations. In turn, those reinforcement contingencies directly affect valences (the attractiveness of rewards), instrumentality (the perceived link between rewards and performance), and effort (how hard employees will work).

Let's learn more about reinforcement theory by examining **13-4a the components of reinforcement theory, 13-4b the different schedules for delivering reinforcement, and 13-4c how to motivate with reinforcement theory.**

Positive reinforcement reinforcement that strengthens behavior by following behaviors with desirable consequences

13-4a Components of Reinforcement Theory

As just described, *reinforcement contingencies* are the cause-and-effect relationships between the performance of specific behaviors and specific consequences. There are four kinds of reinforcement contingencies: positive reinforcement, negative reinforcement, punishment, and extinction.

Positive reinforcement strengthens behavior (i.e., increases its frequency) by following behaviors with desirable consequences. While some companies are penalizing unhealthy behaviors, others have chosen to reward employees who practice healthy behaviors. At Whole

Foods, for example, nonsmoking employees receive larger discounts on merchandise than smoking employees. Humana, a health insurance provider, has a program called HumanaVitality, in which people with Humana-provided healthcare coverage earn points for things ranging from exercising regularly, reaching and maintaining a healthy weight, giving up smoking, and getting annual checkups and preventive care screenings to taking health education classes. Those points, in turn, can be used to buy electronics and hotel stays or used toward discounts on over 600,000 items. As part of that program, Humana has partnered with game developer Ubisoft on an Xbox 360 game, *Your Shape: Fitness Evolved 2012*. HumanaVitality members can earn fifteen Vitality points each day they play and burn 200 calories.[58]

Negative reinforcement strengthens behavior by withholding an unpleasant consequence when employees perform a specific behavior. Negative reinforcement is also called *avoidance learning* because workers perform a behavior to *avoid* a negative consequence. With the cost of healthcare averaging $12,136 annually per employee, companies are linking positive health actions and outcomes to the avoidance of negative consequences. At **Michelin**, the tire company, employees who keep their waist size below thirty-five inches for women and forty inches for men and their blood pressure, glucose, and cholesterol below particular levels will avoid a $1,000 increase in their healthcare deductibles. Likewise, employees of CVS Caremark, the pharmacy chain, avoid a $600 penalty when they report their health information, such as blood pressure, cholesterol, and blood sugar to the firm's healthcare provider. Finally, after Mohawk Industries, which makes flooring, instituted a $100 fine for employees who did not participate in its health-risk assessment process, 97 percent of employees decided to participate. Prior rewards to participate had little effect.[59]

By contrast, **punishment** weakens behavior (i.e., decreases its frequency) by following behaviors with undesirable consequences. For example, the standard disciplinary or punishment process in most companies is an oral warning ("Don't ever do that again"), followed by a written warning ("This letter is to discuss the serious problem you're having with . . ."), followed by three days off without pay ("While you're at home not being paid, we want you to think hard about . . ."),

followed by being fired ("That was your last chance"). Though punishment can weaken behavior, managers have to be careful to avoid the backlash that sometimes occurs when employees are punished at work.

Extinction is a reinforcement strategy in which a positive consequence is no longer allowed to follow a previously reinforced behavior. By removing the positive consequence, extinction weakens the behavior, making it less likely to occur. Based on the idea of positive reinforcement, most companies give company leaders and managers substantial financial rewards when the company performs well. Based on the idea of extinction, you would then expect that leaders and managers would not be rewarded (i.e., the positive consequence would be removed) when companies perform poorly. This is *not* what happened at Staples, the office supply retailer. With two years of declining revenue and store sales, and a below-the-industry average stock price, top managers didn't hit the performance goals required in the company's compensation plan. But instead of seeing their compensation drop, the Staples board of directors awarded top managers a new "Reinvention Cash Award," which resulted in a bonus of $300,000 to the CEO, whose total pay was $10.8 million, and a bonus of $49,000 to the CFO, whose total pay was $2.2 million.[60] If companies really want pay to reinforce the right kinds of behaviors then, unlike at Staples, rewards have to be removed when company management doesn't produce successful performance.

13-4b Schedules for Delivering Reinforcement

As mentioned earlier, a *schedule of reinforcement* is the set of rules regarding reinforcement contingencies, such as which behaviors will be reinforced,

Negative reinforcement reinforcement that strengthens behavior by withholding an unpleasant consequence when employees perform a specific behavior

Punishment reinforcement that weakens behavior by following behaviors with undesirable consequences

Extinction reinforcement in which a positive consequence is no longer allowed to follow a previously reinforced behavior, thus weakening the behavior

Exhibit 13.7
Intermittent Reinforcement Schedules

	Fixed	Variable
INTERVAL (TIME)	Consequences follow behavior after a fixed time has elapsed.	Consequences follow behavior after different times, some shorter and some longer, that vary around a specific average time.
RATIO (BEHAVIOR)	Consequences follow a specific number of behaviors.	Consequences follow a different number of behaviors, sometimes more and sometimes less, that vary around a specified average number of behaviors.

which consequences will follow those behaviors, and the schedule by which those consequences will be delivered. There are two categories of reinforcement schedules: continuous and intermittent.

With **continuous reinforcement schedules,** a consequence follows every instance of a behavior. For example, employees working on a piece-rate pay system earn money (consequence) for every part they manufacture (behavior). The more they produce, the more they earn. By contrast, with **intermittent reinforcement schedules,** consequences are delivered after a specified or average time has elapsed or after a specified or average number of behaviors has occurred. As Exhibit 13.7 shows, there are four types of intermittent reinforcement schedules. Two of these are based on time and are called *interval reinforcement*

schedules; the other two, known as *ratio schedules*, are based on behaviors.

With **fixed interval reinforcement schedules,** consequences follow a behavior only after a fixed time has elapsed. For example, most people receive their paychecks on a fixed interval schedule (e.g., once or twice per month). As long as they work (behavior) during a specified pay period (interval), they get a paycheck (consequence). With **variable interval reinforcement schedules,** consequences follow a behavior after different times, some shorter and some longer, that vary around a specified average time. On a ninety-day variable interval reinforcement schedule, you might receive a bonus after eighty days or perhaps after 100 days, but the average interval between performing your job well (behavior) and receiving your bonus (consequence) would be ninety days.

With **fixed ratio reinforcement schedules,** consequences are delivered following a specific number of behaviors. For example, car salesperson might receive a $1,000 bonus after every ten sales. Therefore, a salesperson with only nine sales would not receive the bonus until he or she finally sold a tenth car.

With **variable ratio reinforcement schedules,** consequences are delivered following a different number of behaviors, sometimes more and sometimes less, that vary around a specified average number of behaviors. With a ten-car variable ratio reinforcement schedule, a salesperson might receive the bonus after seven car sales, or after twelve, eleven, or nine sales, but the average number of cars sold before receiving the bonus would be ten cars.

Which reinforcement schedules work best? In the past, the standard advice was to use continuous reinforcement when employees were learning new behaviors because reinforcement after each success leads to faster learning. Likewise, the standard advice

Continuous reinforcement schedule a schedule that requires a consequence to be administered following every instance of a behavior

Intermittent reinforcement schedule a schedule in which consequences are delivered after a specified or average time has elapsed or after a specified or average number of behaviors has occurred

Fixed interval reinforcement schedule an intermittent schedule in which consequences follow a behavior only after a fixed time has elapsed

Variable interval reinforcement schedule an intermittent schedule in which the time between a behavior and the following consequences varies around a specified average

Fixed ratio reinforcement schedule an intermittent schedule in which consequences are delivered following a specific number of behaviors

Variable ratio reinforcement schedule an intermittent schedule in which consequences are delivered following a different number of behaviors, sometimes more and sometimes less, that vary around a specified average number of behaviors

was to use intermittent reinforcement schedules to maintain behavior after it is learned because intermittent rewards are supposed to make behavior much less subject to extinction.[61] Research shows, however, that except for interval-based systems, which usually produce weak results, the effectiveness of continuous reinforcement, fixed ratio, and variable ratio schedules differs very little.[62] In organizational settings, all three consistently produce large increases over noncontingent reward schedules. So managers should choose whichever of these three is easiest to use in their companies.

13-4c Motivating with Reinforcement Theory

What practical steps can managers take to use reinforcement theory to motivate employees? University of Nebraska business professor Fred Luthans, who has been studying the effects of reinforcement theory in organizations for more than a quarter of a century, says that there are five steps to motivating workers with reinforcement theory: *identify*, *measure*, *analyze*, *intervene*, and *evaluate* critical performance-related behaviors.[63]

Identify means singling out critical, observable, performance-related behaviors. These are the behaviors that are most important to successful job performance. In addition, they must also be easily observed so that they can be accurately measured. *Measure* means determining the baseline frequencies of these behaviors. In other words, find out how often workers perform them. *Analyze* means studying the causes and consequences of these behaviors. Analyzing the causes helps managers create the conditions that produce these critical behaviors, and analyzing the consequences helps them determine if these behaviors produce the results that they want. *Intervene* means changing the organization by using positive and negative reinforcement to increase the frequency of these critical behaviors. *Evaluate* means assessing the extent to which the intervention actually changed workers' behavior. This is done by comparing behavior after the intervention to the original baseline of behavior before the intervention.

In addition to these five steps, managers should remember three other key things when motivating with reinforcement theory. First, *Don't reinforce the wrong behaviors*. Although reinforcement theory sounds simple, it's actually very difficult to put into practice. One of the most common mistakes is accidentally reinforcing the wrong behaviors. Sometimes managers reinforce behaviors that they don't want! If you want to become a merit-based company, stop rewarding behavior that is not exceptional, says Dave Anderson, a management consultant. According to him, "the average car salesperson in the United States sells ten cars per month, but many pay plans begin to pay bonuses at seven, eight, nine, or ten cars. Under a typical plan, an employee who sells eight cars gets a $200 bonus, another $250 for selling two additional cars, and $300 for selling two more cars. The total bonus for selling twelve cars in a month is $750." Anderson notes, "Based on national averages, such a pay plan financially rewards average and below-average results." Many of his clients have revised their system and only pay an $800 bonus to an employee *after* he or she has sold twelve cars, thus ending bonus payments for employees who sell fewer than the target amount of cars.[64] In this system, you pay more for better performance but don't fall into the trap of rewarding and endorsing the wrong things—that is, rewarding below-average performance.

Managers should also *correctly administer punishment at the appropriate time*. Many managers believe that punishment can change workers' behavior and help them improve their job performance. Furthermore, managers believe that fairly punishing workers also lets other workers know what is or isn't acceptable.[65] A danger of using punishment is that it can produce a backlash against managers and companies. But, if administered properly, punishment can weaken the frequency of undesirable behaviors without creating a backlash.[66] To be effective, the punishment must be strong enough to stop the undesired behavior and must be administered objectively (same rules applied to everyone), impersonally (without emotion or anger), consistently and contingently (each time improper behavior occurs), and quickly (as soon as possible following the undesirable behavior). In addition, managers should clearly explain what the appropriate behavior

Cmannphoto/iStockphoto.com

is and why the employee is being punished. Employees typically respond well when punishment is administered this way.[67]

Finally, managers should *choose the simplest and most effective schedule of reinforcement*. When choosing a schedule of reinforcement, managers need to balance effectiveness against simplicity. In fact, the more complex the schedule of reinforcement, the more likely it is to be misunderstood and resisted by managers and employees. For example, a forestry and logging company experimented with a unique variable ratio schedule. When tree-planters finished planting a bag of seedlings (about 1,000 seedlings per bag), they got to flip a coin. If they called the coin flip correctly (heads or tails), they were paid $4, double the regular rate of $2 per bag. If they called the coin flip incorrectly, they got nothing. The company began having problems when several workers and a manager, who was a part-time minister, claimed that the coin flip was a form of gambling. Then another worker found that the company was taking out too much money for taxes from workers' paychecks. Since the workers didn't really understand the reinforcement schedule, they blamed the payment plan associated with it and accused the company of trying to cheat them out of their money. After all of these problems, the researchers who implemented the variable ratio schedule concluded that "the results of this study may not be so much an indication of the relative effectiveness of different schedules of reinforcement as they are an indication of the types of problems that one encounters when applying these concepts in an industrial setting."[68] In short, choose the simplest, most effective schedule of reinforcement. Since continuous reinforcement, fixed ratio, and variable ratio schedules are about equally effective, continuous reinforcement schedules may be the best choice in many instances by virtue of their simplicity.

Goal a target, objective, or result that someone tries to accomplish

Goal-setting theory the theory that people will be motivated to the extent to which they accept specific, challenging goals and receive feedback that indicates their progress toward goal achievement

Goal specificity the extent to which goals are detailed, exact, and unambiguous

Goal difficulty the extent to which a goal is hard or challenging to accomplish

Goal acceptance the extent to which people consciously understand and agree to goals

Performance feedback information about the quality or quantity of past performance that indicates whether progress is being made toward the accomplishment of a goal

13-5 GOAL-SETTING THEORY

The basic model of motivation with which we began this chapter showed that individuals feel tension after becoming aware of an unfulfilled need. Once they experience tension, they search for and select courses of action that they believe will eliminate this tension. In other words, they direct their behavior toward something. This something is a goal. A **goal** is a target, objective, or result that someone tries to accomplish. **Goal-setting theory** says that people will be motivated to the extent to which they accept specific, challenging goals and receive feedback that indicates their progress toward goal achievement.

Let's learn more about goal setting by examining **13-5a the components of goal-setting theory** *and* **13-5b how to motivate with goal-setting theory**.

13-5a Components of Goal-Setting Theory

The basic components of goal-setting theory are goal specificity, goal difficulty, goal acceptance, and performance feedback.[69] **Goal specificity** is the extent to which goals are detailed, exact, and unambiguous. Specific goals, such as "I'm going to have a 3.0 average this semester," are more motivating than general goals, such as "I'm going to get better grades this semester."

Goal difficulty is the extent to which a goal is hard or challenging to accomplish. Difficult goals, such as "I'm going to have a 3.5 average and make the dean's list this semester," are more motivating than easy goals, such as "I'm going to have a 2.0 average this semester."

Goal acceptance, which is similar to the idea of goal commitment discussed in Chapter 5, is the extent to which people consciously understand and agree to goals. Accepted goals, such as "I really want to get a 3.5 average this semester to show my parents how much I've improved," are more motivating than unaccepted goals, such as "My parents really want me to get a 3.5 average this semester, but there's so much more I'd rather do on campus than study!"

Performance feedback is information about the quality or quantity of past performance and indicates whether progress is being made toward the accomplishment of a goal. To improve employees' health and lower healthcare costs, Accenture, a global consulting company, gave 3,000 employees pedometers to record how many steps they took per day. More steps earned employees more points toward an electronic game from which they could earn cash awards. Linking awards to the feedback from pedometers led to employees walking 500 more steps per day. But employees walked an additional 664 steps per day on average after a Facebook-like "friends" feature allowed them to compare their daily steps to their friends'. In short, in this case, performance feedback led to larger improvements than rewards. Stanford researcher Balaji Prabhakar said, "Money gets the ball rolling, but we know from the data that having friends has a big effect."[70]

How does goal setting work? To start, challenging goals focus employees' attention (i.e., direction of effort) on the critical aspects of their jobs and away from unimportant areas. Goals also energize behavior. When faced with unaccomplished goals, employees typically develop plans and strategies to reach those goals. Goals also create tension between the goal, which is the desired future state of affairs, and where the employee or company is now, meaning the current state of affairs. This tension can be satisfied only by achieving or abandoning the goal. Finally, goals influence persistence. Since goals only go

away when they are accomplished, employees are more likely to persist in their efforts in the presence of goals, especially with performance feedback. Exhibit 13.8 incorporates goals into the motivation model by showing how goals directly affect tension, effort, and the extent to which employees are energized to take action.

13-5b Motivating with Goal-Setting Theory

What practical steps can managers take to use goal-setting theory to motivate employees? Managers can do three things, beginning with *assign specific, challenging goals*. One of the simplest, most effective ways to motivate workers is to give them specific, challenging goals. **Morning Star**, in Woodland, California, which bills itself as the "world's leading tomato ingredient processor," runs its business with self-managed teams (see Chapter 10 on teams) and CLOUs ("collegial letters of understanding") that spell out specific, challenging goals. Fortune columnist Geoff Colvin explains, "Every employee negotiates a 'letter of understanding' with the colleagues who are most affected by

Viafilms/iStockphoto.com

Exhibit 13.8
Adding Goal-Setting Theory to the Model

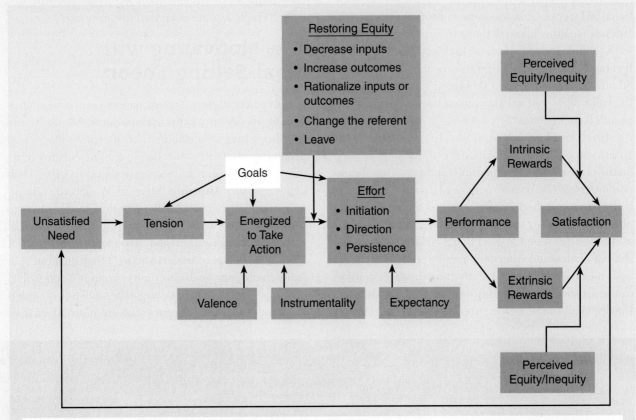

Goals create tension between the goal, which is the desired future state of affairs, and where the employee or company is now, meaning the current state of affairs. This tension can be satisfied only by achieving or abandoning the goal. Goals also energize behavior. When faced with unaccomplished goals, employees typically develop plans and strategies to reach those goals. Finally, goals influence persistence.

his or her work. It's highly specific, detailing how the employee's performance will be measured in up to 30 activity areas. When every member finishes the exercise, that team knows precisely what it's on the hook to accomplish." At year-end, peer review committees compare actual performance in those activity areas against the specific, challenging goals set out in the CLOU.[71]

Second, managers should *make sure workers truly accept organizational goals*. Specific, challenging goals won't motivate workers unless they really accept, understand, and agree to the organization's goals. For this to occur, people must see the goals as fair and reasonable. Employees must also trust management and believe that managers are using goals to clarify what is expected from them rather than to exploit or

threaten them ("If you don't achieve these goals . . ."). Participative goal setting, in which managers and employees generate goals together, can help increase trust and understanding and thus acceptance of goals. Furthermore, providing workers with training can help increase goal acceptance, particularly when workers don't believe they are capable of reaching the organization's goals.[72]

Finally, managers should *provide frequent, specific, performance-related feedback*. Once employees have accepted specific, challenging goals, they should receive frequent performance-related feedback so that they can track their progress toward goal completion. Feedback leads to stronger motivation and effort in three ways.[73] Receiving specific feedback about the quality of their performance can encourage employees who don't have specific, challenging goals to set goals to improve their performance. Once people meet goals, performance feedback often encourages them to set higher, more difficult goals. And feedback lets people know whether they need to increase their efforts or change strategies in order to accomplish their goals.

13-6 MOTIVATING WITH THE INTEGRATED MODEL

We began this chapter by defining motivation as the set of forces that initiates, directs, and makes people persist in their efforts to accomplish a goal. We also asked the basic question that managers ask when they try to figure out how to motivate their workers: What leads to effort? The answer to that question is likely to be somewhat different for each employee. So, if you're having difficulty figuring out why people aren't motivated where you work, check your Review Card for a useful, theory-based starting point.

STUDY TOOLS 13

LOCATED AT THE BACK OF YOUR BOOK:
☐ Rip out and study the Chapter Review Card at the end of the book

LOG IN TO WWW.CENGAGEBRAIN.COM TO:
☐ Review Key Term Flashcards
☐ Complete Practice Quizzing (take up to four times without repeating the same quiz)
☐ Complete Games: Beat the Clock and Crossword Puzzle
☐ Complete Interactive Content: Graded Quiz, Media Quiz, and Fill-in-the-Blank Questions
☐ Watch Management Workplace Video on "Urban Escapes" and "LivingSocial Escapes"
☐ Work Through the What Would You Do Case on SAS World Headquarters

14 Leadership

LEARNING OUTCOMES

14-1 Explain what leadership is.

14-2 Describe who leaders are and what effective leaders do.

14-3 Explain Fiedler's contingency theory.

14-4 Describe how path-goal theory works.

14-5 Explain the normative decision theory.

14-6 Explain how visionary leadership (i.e., charismatic or transformational leadership) helps leaders achieve strategic leadership.

After you finish
this chapter, go
to **PAGE 311** for
STUDY TOOLS

14-1 LEADERS VERSUS MANAGERS

If you've ever been in charge, or even just thought about it, chances are you've considered questions like: Do I have what it takes to lead? What are the most important things leaders do? How can I transform a poorly performing department, division, or company? Do I need to adjust my leadership depending on the situation and the employee? Why doesn't my leadership inspire people? If you feel overwhelmed at the prospect of being a leader, you're not alone—millions of leaders in organizations across the world struggle with these fundamental leadership issues on a daily basis.

The most common view of leaders is that they are "in charge." But leadership is about more than just making decisions and giving orders. Bill Flemming, president of **Skanska USA Building**, a division of one of the world's largest construction companies, notes, "When people [I lead] ask me a question [about solving a problem], I don't always answer it with, 'Yes, this is what I want you to do,' or, 'This is what I'd do.'" He goes on, "I've seen organizations where the boss makes all the decisions. That's not leadership; that's a boss. I don't want to be the boss, I want to be the leader. So I want to get you to help me figure out what we've got to do here. Because if you're deeply immersed in the problem or the issue, you probably know a lot more about it than I'm going to know. So what do you think is going to work?"[1]

Whether you construct buildings, create and innovate to bring new products to markets, or simply help a company gain competitive advantage and thereby increase profits, **leadership** is the process of influencing others to achieve group or organizational goals. The knowledge and skills you'll learn in this chapter won't make the task of leadership less daunting, but they will help you navigate your journey as a leader.

According to University of Southern California business professor Warren Bennis, the primary difference between leaders and managers is that leaders are concerned with doing the right thing, while managers are concerned with doing things right.[2] In other words, leaders begin with the question "What should we be doing?" while managers start with "How can we do what we're already doing better?" Leaders focus on vision, mission, goals, and objectives, while managers focus on productivity and efficiency. Managers see themselves as preservers of the status quo, while leaders see themselves as promoters of change and challengers of the status quo in that they encourage creativity and risk taking. Virginia Rometty, IBM's CEO, plans to keep her $100 billion company growing and innovating

by doing one thing—pressing managers and employees to take risks and embrace change. Rometty believes that risk-taking and change will provide the fuel for future growth, just like fifteen years ago when IBM changed from manufacturing and selling mainframe and personal computers to providing technology services and consulting. Rometty says, "I don't believe in the inevitable, or in thinking that things have to and will turn out in a certain way. Whatever business you're in, it's going to commoditize over time, so you have to keep moving it to a higher value and change.... Growth and comfort do not coexist."[3]

Another difference is that managers have a relatively short-term perspective, while leaders take a long-term view. Managers are concerned with control and limiting the choices of others, while leaders are more concerned with expanding people's choices and options.[4] Managers also solve problems so that others can do their work, while leaders inspire and motivate others to find their own solutions.

Finally, managers are also more concerned with *means*, how to get things done, while leaders are more concerned with *ends*, what gets done. Today, Samsung is a global market leader in smartphones and a dozen other industries, but twenty years ago its successes were largely in South Korea. Frustrated with Samsung's lack of success after a visit to the United States, the company's chairman, Lee Kun Hee, stopped in Frankfurt, Germany, where he had hundreds of company leaders join him. Over three days, he declared that Samsung would become a globally dominant company by 2000. He urged Samsung's leaders to "change everything but your wife and children," but change Samsung into a global powerhouse. Several years later, Lee gave out Samsung phones as New Year's presents, only to find that they quit working. He assembled 2,000 employees and had them watch as he set an enormous pile of these defective phones on fire, saying, "If you continue to make poor quality products like these, I'll come back and do the same thing." Through these symbolic acts of leadership, Lee jumpstarted Samsung's efforts that eventually produced today's class-leading phones like its Galaxy S3 and S4.[5]

Although leaders are different from managers, organizations need them both. Managers are critical to getting out the day-to-day work, and leaders are critical to inspiring employees and setting the organization's long-term direction. The key issue for any organization is the extent to which it is properly led and properly managed. As Bennis said in summing up the difference

Leadership the process of influencing others to achieve group or organizational goals

between leaders and managers, "American organizations (and probably those in much of the rest of the industrialized world) are underled and overmanaged. They do not pay enough attention to doing the right thing, while they pay too much attention to doing things right."[6]

14-2 WHO LEADERS ARE AND WHAT LEADERS DO

Indra Nooyi, PepsiCo's CEO, talks straight, has a sharp sense of humor, and sings in the hallways wherever she is. Nooyi is an extrovert. By contrast, Douglas Conant, former CEO of Campbell Soup Company, is an introvert who says that he feels exhausted after spending time in large groups of people he doesn't know.[7]

Which one is likely to be successful as a CEO? According to a survey of 1,542 senior managers, it's the extrovert. Forty-seven percent of those 1,542 senior managers felt that extroverts make better CEOs, while 65 percent said that being an introvert hurts a CEO's chances of success.[8] So clearly, senior managers believe that extroverted CEOs are better leaders. But are they? Not necessarily. In fact, a relatively high percentage of CEOs, 40 percent, are introverts. Former Sara Lee CEO Brenda Barnes said, "I've always been shy. ... People wouldn't call me that [an introvert], but I am."[9] Indeed, as CEO, Barnes turned down all speaking requests and rarely gave interviews.

So, what makes a good leader? Does leadership success depend on who leaders are, such as introverts or extroverts, or on what leaders do and how they behave?

*Let's learn more about who leaders are by investigating **14-2a leadership traits** and **14-2b leadership behaviors**.*

14-2a Leadership Traits

Trait theory is one way to describe who leaders are. **Trait theory** says that effective leaders possess a similar set of traits or characteristics. **Traits** are relatively stable characteristics such as abilities, psychological motives, or consistent patterns of behavior. For example, trait theory holds that leaders are taller and more confident and have greater physical stamina (i.e., higher energy levels) than nonleaders. In fact, studies show we perceive those in authority as being taller than they actually are, and that taller people see themselves as more qualified to lead.[10] Indeed, while just 14.5 percent of men are six feet tall, 58 percent of *Fortune* 500 CEOs are six feet or taller. Author Malcolm Gladwell says, "We have a sense, in our minds, of what a leader is supposed to look like, and that stereotype is so powerful that when someone fits it, we simply become blind to other considerations."[11] Trait theory is also known as the "great person" theory because early versions of the theory stated that leaders are born, not made. In other words, you either have the right stuff to be a leader, or you don't. And if you don't, there is no way to get it.

For some time, it was thought that trait theory was wrong and that there are no consistent trait differences between leaders and nonleaders, or between effective and ineffective leaders. However, more recent evidence shows that "successful leaders are not like other people," that successful leaders are indeed different from the rest of us.[12] More specifically, leaders are different from nonleaders in the following traits: drive, the desire to lead, honesty/integrity, self-confidence, emotional stability, cognitive ability, and knowledge of the business.[13]

Drive refers to high levels of effort and is characterized by achievement, motivation, initiative, energy, and tenacity. In terms of achievement and ambition, leaders always try to make improvements or achieve success in what they're doing. Because of their initiative, they have strong desires to promote change or solve problems. Leaders typically have more energy—they have to, given the long hours they put in and followers' expectations that they be positive and upbeat. Thus, leaders must have physical, mental, and emotional vitality. Leaders are also more tenacious than nonleaders and are better at overcoming obstacles and problems that would deter most of us.

Successful leaders also have a stronger *desire to lead*. They want to be in charge and think about ways to influence or convince others about what should or shouldn't be done. *Honesty/integrity* is also important to leaders. *Honesty*, being truthful with others, is a cornerstone of leadership. Without it, leaders won't be trusted. When leaders are honest, subordinates are willing to overlook other flaws. For example, one follower said this about the leadership qualities of his manager: "I don't like a lot of the things he does, but he's basically honest. He's a genuine article, and you'll forgive a lot of things because of that. That goes a long way in how much I trust him."[14] *Integrity* is the extent to which leaders do what they say they will do. Leaders may be honest and have good intentions, but if they don't consistently deliver on what they promise, they won't be trusted.

Self-confidence, or believing in one's abilities, also distinguishes leaders from nonleaders. Self-confident leaders are more decisive and assertive and are more likely to gain others' confidence. Moreover, self-confident leaders will admit mistakes because they view them as learning opportunities rather than as refutations of their leadership capabilities. LinkedIn CEO Jeff Weiner admits how challenging it can be for managers to recognize their mistakes. One of the most difficult mistakes, he says, can be accepting when new hires don't work out. "It's not easy to admit this to yourself. After all, as the CEO or owner, you're largely responsible for the fact that the employee is now in over his or her head," Weiner says. "Plus, admitting the mistake means that you'll have to overcome your internal wiring to 'finish the job' and 'not give up.' Persistence is often an admirable trait, but not when it prevents you from making a necessary midcourse adjustment."[15]

Leaders also have *emotional stability*. Even when things go wrong, they remain even-tempered and consistent in their outlook and in the way they treat others. Leaders who can't control their emotions, who anger quickly or attack and blame others for mistakes, are unlikely to be trusted.

LEADERS ARE DIFFERENT FROM NONLEADERS IN THE FOLLOWING TRAITS: DRIVE, THE DESIRE TO LEAD, HONESTY/INTEGRITY, SELF-CONFIDENCE, EMOTIONAL STABILITY, COGNITIVE ABILITY, AND KNOWLEDGE OF THE BUSINESS.

Long-Term Succession at GE

Some companies seem to cycle through CEOs on a yearly basis. At General Electric, however, employees can safely assume that their CEO will be around for a while. Indeed, five of GE's last eleven chiefs have held the post for more than thirteen years. So when current CEO Jeff Immelt took over for twenty-year veteran Jack Welch, many expected that Immelt would run the company for twenty years as well. Immelt himself has lead several board discussions suggesting a shorter fifteen-year timeframe. According to one GE insider, "To maintain the energy that is required to these jobs that are so broad and deep, twenty years is a really long time." While GE routinely engages in early-stage succession planning, the board hopes to avoid the last succession situation. Succession planning began seven years before Jack Welch's retirement, pitting top talent against each other. When Immelt was given the job, several competing candidates immediately left the company for outside positions.

Jeff Immelt, CEO of General Electric

Source: J.S. Lublin, T. Mann, and K. Linebaugh, "GE Rethinks the 20-year CEO," *Wall Street Journal*, April 15, 2014, accessed May 19, 2014, http://online.wsj.com/news/articles/SB10001424052702304572204579501640452285598?mod=WSJ_hp_RightTopStories&mg=reno64-wsj.

Leaders are also smart—they typically have strong *cognitive abilities*. This doesn't mean that leaders are necessarily geniuses—far from it. But it does mean that leaders have the capacity to analyze large amounts of seemingly unrelated, complex information and see patterns, opportunities, or threats where others might not see them. Finally, leaders also know their stuff, which means they have superior technical knowledge about the businesses they run. Leaders who have a good *knowledge of the business* understand the key technological decisions and concerns facing their companies. More often than not, studies indicate that effective leaders have long, extensive experience in their industries. Kevin Tsujihara, **Warner Bros. Entertainment** CEO, has been in the moviemaking business twenty years, starting as manager of Ernst & Young's (an accounting firm) entertainment division. He joined Warner Bros. in Finance, then served as executive vice president, overseeing efforts in streaming and social media, then became executive vice president of Corporate Business Development and Strategy. Before his promotion to CEO, Tsujihara served as the president of Warner Bros. Home Entertainment, in charge of home video, distribution, video games, and anti-piracy operations.[16]

14-2b Leadership Behaviors

Thus far, you've read about who leaders *are*. But traits alone are not enough to make a successful leader. They are, however, a precondition for success. After all, it's hard to imagine a truly successful leader who lacks most of these qualities. Leaders who have these traits (or many of them) must then take actions that encourage people to achieve group or organizational goals.[17] Accordingly, we now examine what leaders *do*, meaning the behaviors they perform or the actions they take to influence others to achieve group or organizational goals.

Researchers at the University of Michigan, Ohio State University, and the University of Texas examined the specific behaviors that leaders use to improve subordinate satisfaction and performance. Hundreds of studies were conducted and hundreds of leader behaviors were examined. At all three universities, two basic leader behaviors emerged as central to successful leadership: initiating structure (called *job-centered leadership* at the University of Michigan and *concern for production* at

GlobalStock//iStockphoto.com

the University of Texas) and considerate leader behavior (called *employee-centered leadership* at the University of Michigan and *concern for people* at the University of Texas).[18] These two leader behaviors form the basis for many of the leadership theories discussed in this chapter.

Initiating structure is the degree to which a leader structures the roles of followers by setting goals, giving directions, setting deadlines, and assigning tasks. A leader's ability to initiate structure primarily affects subordinates' job performance. CEO Carlos Ghosn has decreed that by 2016 Nissan will obtain an 8 percent global market share and an 8 percent profit. This unusually specific strategic plan, called "Nissan Power 88," has clear deadlines, direction, and tasks. It specifies that by 2016 Nissan will deliver an all-new car "every six weeks for six years," for a total of sixty-six different models worldwide, it will launch ninety new technologies (fifteen per year) for its cars, sell 1.56 million electric cars, and its Infiniti brand will sell 10 percent of all luxury cars worldwide. Said Ghosn, "Nissan Power 88 is a demanding business plan, but our company has a proven track record of achieving challenging objectives."[19]

Consideration is the extent to which a leader is friendly, approachable, and supportive and shows concern for employees. Consideration primarily affects subordinates' job satisfaction. Specific leader consideration behaviors include listening to employees' problems and concerns, consulting with employees before making decisions, and treating employees as equals. Marian Salzman, the CEO of Euro RSCG Worldwide PR, a New York City–based public relations firm with 233 offices worldwide, spends a lot of time listening to her staff, most of whom are millennials (i.e., born after 1980). While she hasn't provided them free food, a juice bar, or reimbursement for using

Initiating structure the degree to which a leader structures the roles of followers by setting goals, giving directions, setting deadlines, and assigning tasks

Consideration the extent to which a leader is friendly, approachable, and supportive and shows concern for employees

personal trainers, all of which they've asked for, she allows casual dress in the office—even flip-flops!—hosts happy hours on the roof of the building three times a week, and allows employees to take time off to do volunteer work. Why? Because, she says, "They want the workplace to recognize that they're not 9 to 5 people. They're not people [who are] ever going to wear gray flannel suits." It makes sense, she believes, to not play the "boss card" with millennials. Salzman says, "You're not the smartest person in the room anymore. You may be the most experienced, you may be the wisest. You're not the smartest." The payoff? Euro RSCG Worldwide PR attracts and keeps a highly motivated staff that is propelling its work in digital communications and social media.[20]

Although researchers at all three universities generally agreed that initiating structure and consideration were basic leader behaviors, their interpretation differed on how these two behaviors are related to one another and which are necessary for effective leadership. The University of Michigan studies indicated that initiating structure and consideration were mutually exclusive behaviors on opposite ends of the same continuum. In other words, leaders who wanted to be more considerate would have to do less initiating of structure (and vice versa). The University of Michigan studies also indicated that only considerate leader behaviors (i.e., employee-centered behaviors) were associated with successful leadership. By contrast, researchers at Ohio State University and the University of Texas found that initiating structure and consideration were independent behaviors, meaning that leaders can be considerate and initiate structure at the same time. Additional evidence confirms this finding.[21] The same researchers also concluded that the most effective leaders were strong on both initiating structure and considerate leader behaviors.

This "high-high" approach can be seen in the upper right corner of the Blake/Mouton leadership grid, shown in Exhibit 14.1. Blake and Mouton used two leadership behaviors, concern for people (i.e., consideration) and concern

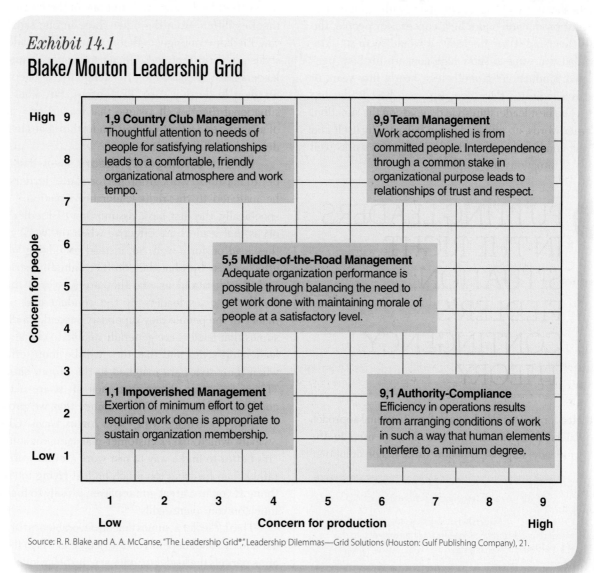

Exhibit 14.1
Blake/Mouton Leadership Grid

High 9

1,9 Country Club Management
Thoughtful attention to needs of people for satisfying relationships leads to a comfortable, friendly organizational atmosphere and work tempo.

9,9 Team Management
Work accomplished is from committed people. Interdependence through a common stake in organizational purpose leads to relationships of trust and respect.

5,5 Middle-of-the-Road Management
Adequate organization performance is possible through balancing the need to get work done with maintaining morale of people at a satisfactory level.

1,1 Impoverished Management
Exertion of minimum effort to get required work done is appropriate to sustain organization membership.

9,1 Authority-Compliance
Efficiency in operations results from arranging conditions of work in such a way that human elements interfere to a minimum degree.

Low 1

Concern for people (vertical axis, 1–9)

1 2 3 4 5 6 7 8 9
Low   **Concern for production**   **High**

Source: R. R. Blake and A. A. McCanse, "The Leadership Grid®," Leadership Dilemmas—Grid Solutions (Houston: Gulf Publishing Company), 21.

for production (i.e., initiating structure), to categorize five different leadership styles. Both behaviors are rated on a 9-point scale, with 1 representing "low" and 9 representing "high." Blake and Mouton suggest that a "high-high," or 9,9, leadership style is the best. They call this style *team management* because leaders who use it display a high concern for people (9) and a high concern for production (9).

By contrast, leaders use a 9,1 *authority-compliance* leadership style when they have a high concern for production and a low concern for people. A 1,9 *country club* style occurs when leaders care about having a friendly, enjoyable work environment but don't really pay much attention to production or performance. The worst leadership style, according to the grid, is the 1,1 *impoverished* leader, who shows little concern for people or production and does the bare minimum needed to keep his or her job. Finally, the 5,5 *middle-of-the-road* style occurs when leaders show a moderate amount of concern for both people and production.

Is the team management style, with a high concern for production and a high concern for people, the best leadership style? Logically, it would seem so. Why wouldn't you want to show high concern for both people and production? Nonetheless, nearly fifty years of research indicates that there isn't one best leadership style. The best leadership style depends on the situation. In other words, no one leadership behavior by itself and no one combination of leadership behaviors works well across all situations and employees.

14-3 PUTTING LEADERS IN THE RIGHT SITUATION: FIEDLER'S CONTINGENCY THEORY

After leader traits and behaviors, the situational approach to leadership is the third major method used in the study of leadership. We'll review three major situational approaches to leadership—Fiedler's contingency theory, path-goal theory, and Vroom, Yetton, and Jago's normative decision model. All assume that the effectiveness of any **leadership style,** the way a leader generally behaves toward followers, depends on the situation.[22] A study of 130 restaurants in a pizza franchise examined the interaction between how extroverted store managers were and how involved employees were in trying "to bring about improved procedures [in the store.]" Profits were 16 percent *above* average in stores with extroverted managers and less involved employees. In those instances the strengths of the more outgoing boss fit well with the less involved employees. By contrast, profits were 14 percent *below* average in stores with extroverted leaders and highly involved employees. Why? Because the extroverted leaders were less comfortable with employees who wanted a say in making improvements. Again, leadership success depends on the situation.[23]

According to situational leadership theories, there is no one best leadership style. But one of these situational theories differs from the other three in one significant way. Fiedler's contingency theory assumes that leadership styles are consistent and difficult to change. Therefore, leaders must be placed in or matched to a situation that fits their leadership style. By contrast, the other three situational theories all assume that leaders are capable of adapting and adjusting their leadership styles to fit the demands of different situations.

Fiedler's **contingency theory** states that in order to maximize work group performance, leaders must be matched to the right leadership situation.[24] More specifically, the first basic assumption of Fiedler's theory is that leaders are effective when the work groups they lead perform well. So, instead of judging leaders' effectiveness by what they do (i.e., initiating structure and consideration) or who they are (i.e., trait theory), Fiedler assesses leaders by the conduct and performance of the people they supervise. Second, Fiedler assumes that leaders are generally unable to change their leadership styles and that they will be more effective when their styles are matched to the proper situation. "There are some things that each of us are naturally good at, and there are some things that we probably are going to struggle with," says Angus Davis, CEO of Swipely, which makes customer-management software. "It's better to find a way to just work around your flaws rather than focusing too much on just trying to correct them. If you're a great guitar player, it's silly to focus too much on your piano skills."[25]

Third, Fiedler assumes that the favorableness of a situation for a leader depends on the degree to which the situation permits the leader to influence the behavior of group

Leadership style the way a leader generally behaves toward followers

Contingency theory a leadership theory that states that in order to maximize work group performance, leaders must be matched to the situation that best fits their leadership style

members. Fiedler's third assumption is consistent with our definition of leadership as the process of influencing others to achieve group or organizational goals. In other words, in addition to traits, behaviors, and a favorable situation to match, leaders have to be allowed to lead.

*Let's learn more about Fiedler's contingency theory by examining **14-3a the least preferred coworker and leadership styles, 14-3b situational favorableness,** and **14-3c how to match leadership styles to situations.***

14-3a Leadership Style: Least Preferred Coworker

When Fiedler refers to *leadership style*, he means the way that leaders generally behave toward their followers. Do the leaders yell and scream and blame others when things go wrong? Or do they correct mistakes by listening and then quietly but directly make their point? Do they take credit for others' work when things go right? Or do they make sure that those who did the work receive the credit they rightfully deserve? Do they let others make their own decisions and hold them accountable for the results? Or do they micromanage, insisting that all decisions be approved first by them? Fiedler also assumes that leadership styles are tied to leaders' underlying needs and personalities. Since personalities and needs are relatively stable, he assumes that leaders are generally incapable of changing their leadership styles. In other words, the way that leaders treat people now is probably the way they've always treated others. So, according to Fiedler, if your boss's first instinct is to yell and scream and blame others, chances are he or she has always done that.

Fiedler uses a questionnaire called the Least Preferred Coworker (LPC) scale to measure leadership style. When completing the LPC scale, people are instructed to consider all of the people with whom they have ever worked and then to choose the one person with whom they have worked *least* well. Fiedler explains, "This does not have to be the person you liked least well, but should be the one person with whom you have the most trouble getting the job done."[26]

Would you describe your LPC as pleasant, friendly, supportive, interesting, cheerful, and sincere? Or would you describe the person as unpleasant, unfriendly, hostile, boring, gloomy, and insincere? People who describe their LPC in a positive way (scoring 64 and above) have *relationship-oriented* leadership styles. After all, if they can still be positive about their least preferred coworker, they must be people-oriented. By contrast, people who describe their LPC in a negative way (scoring 57 or below) have *task-oriented* leadership styles. Given a choice, they'll focus first on getting the job done and second on making sure everyone gets along. Finally, those with moderate scores (from 58 to 63) have a more *flexible* leadership style and can be somewhat relationship-oriented or somewhat task-oriented.

14-3b Situational Favorableness

Fiedler assumes that leaders will be more effective when their leadership styles are matched to the proper situation. More specifically, Fiedler defines **situational favorableness** as the degree to which a particular situation either permits or denies a leader the chance to influence the behavior of group members.[27] In highly favorable situations, leaders find that their actions influence followers. But in highly unfavorable situations, leaders have little or no success influencing the people they are trying to lead.

Three situational factors determine the favorability of a situation: leader-member relations, task structure, and position power. The most important situational factor is **leader-member relations,** which refers to how well followers respect, trust, and like their leaders. When leader-member relations are good, followers trust the leader and there is a friendly work atmosphere. **Task structure** is the degree to which the requirements of a subordinate's tasks are clearly specified. With highly structured tasks,

Situational favorableness the degree to which a particular situation either permits or denies a leader the chance to influence the behavior of group members

Leader-member relations the degree to which followers respect, trust, and like their leaders

Task structure the degree to which the requirements of a subordinate's tasks are clearly specified

Hatman12/iStockphoto.com

Exhibit 14.2
Situational Favorableness

Leader-Member Relations	Good	Good	Good	Good	Poor	Poor	Poor	Poor
Task Structure	High	High	Low	Low	High	High	Low	Low
Position Power	Strong	Weak	Strong	Weak	Strong	Weak	Strong	Weak
Situation	I	II	III	IV	V	VI	VII	VIII
	Favorable			**Moderately Favorable**			**Unfavorable**	

employees have clear job responsibilities, goals, and procedures. **Position power** is the degree to which leaders are able to hire, fire, reward, and punish workers. The more influence leaders have over hiring, firing, rewards, and punishments, the greater their power.

Exhibit 14.2 shows how leader-member relations, task structure, and position power can be combined into eight situations that differ in their favorability to leaders. In general, Situation I, on the left side of Exhibit 14.2, is the most favorable leader situation. Followers like and trust their leaders and know what to do because their tasks are highly structured. Also, the leaders have the formal power to influence workers through hiring, firing, rewarding, and punishing them. Therefore, it's relatively easy for a leader to influence followers in Situation I. By

Position power the degree to which leaders are able to hire, fire, reward, and punish workers

contrast, Situation VIII, on the right side of Exhibit 14.2, is the least favorable situation for leaders. Followers don't like or trust their leaders. Plus, followers are not sure what they're supposed to be doing, given that their tasks or jobs are highly unstructured. Finally, leaders find it difficult to influence followers because they don't have the ability to hire, fire, reward, or punish the people who work for them. In short, it's very difficult to influence followers given the conditions found in Situation VIII.

14-3c Matching Leadership Styles to Situations

After studying thousands of leaders and followers in hundreds of different situations, Fiedler found that the performance of relationship- and task-oriented leaders followed the pattern displayed in Exhibit 14.3.

Relationship-oriented leaders with high LPC scores were better leaders (i.e., their groups performed more

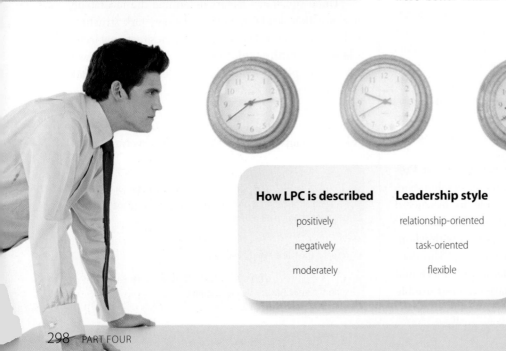

How LPC is described	Leadership style
positively	relationship-oriented
negatively	task-oriented
moderately	flexible

Exhibit 14.3
Matching Leadership Styles to Situations

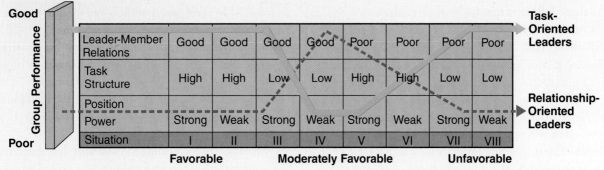

Leader-Member Relations	Good	Good	Good	Good	Poor	Poor	Poor	Poor	Task-Oriented Leaders
Task Structure	High	High	Low	Low	High	High	Low	Low	
Position Power	Strong	Weak	Strong	Weak	Strong	Weak	Strong	Weak	Relationship-Oriented Leaders
Situation	I	II	III	IV	V	VI	VII	VIII	
	Favorable			Moderately Favorable			Unfavorable		

effectively) under moderately favorable situations. In moderately favorable situations, the leader may be liked somewhat, tasks may be somewhat structured, and the leader may have some position power. In this situation, a relationship-oriented leader improves leader-member relations, which is the most important of the three situational factors. In turn, morale and performance improve.

By contrast, as Exhibit 14.3 shows, task-oriented leaders with low LPC scores are better leaders in highly favorable and unfavorable situations. Task-oriented leaders do well in favorable situations where leaders are liked, tasks are structured, and the leader has the power to hire, fire, reward, and punish. In these favorable situations, task-oriented leaders effectively step on the gas of a well-tuned car. Their focus on performance sets the goal for the group, which then charges forward to meet it. But task-oriented leaders also do well in unfavorable situations where leaders are disliked, tasks are unstructured, and the leader doesn't have the power to hire, fire, reward, and punish. In these unfavorable situations, the task-oriented leader sets goals, which focus attention on performance and clarify what needs to be done, thus overcoming low task structure. This is enough to jump-start performance even if workers don't like or trust the leader.

Finally, though not shown in Exhibit 14.3, people with moderate LPC scores, who can be somewhat relationship-oriented or somewhat task-oriented, tend to do fairly well in all situations because they can adapt their behavior. Typically, though, they don't perform quite as well as relationship-oriented or task-oriented leaders whose leadership styles are well matched to the situation.

Recall, however, that Fiedler assumes leaders to be incapable of changing their leadership styles. Accordingly, the key to applying Fiedler's contingency theory in the workplace is to accurately measure and match leaders to

situations or to teach leaders how to change situational favorableness by changing leader-member relations, task structure, or position power. Though matching or placing leaders in appropriate situations works particularly well, practicing managers have had little luck reengineering situations to fit their leadership styles. The primary problem, as you've no doubt realized, is the complexity of the theory.

In a study designed to teach leaders how to reengineer their situations to fit their leadership styles, Fiedler found that most of the leaders simply did not understand what they were supposed to do to change their situations. Furthermore, if they didn't like their LPC profile (perhaps they felt they were more relationship-oriented than their scores indicated), they arbitrarily changed it to better suit their view of themselves. Of course, the theory won't work as well if leaders are attempting to change situational factors to fit their perceived leadership style rather than their real leadership style.[28]

 # 14-4 ADAPTING LEADER BEHAVIOR: PATH-GOAL THEORY

Just as its name suggests, **path-goal theory** states that leaders can increase subordinate satisfaction and performance by clarifying and clearing the paths to goals

Path-goal theory a leadership theory that states that leaders can increase subordinate satisfaction and performance by clarifying and clearing the paths to goals and by increasing the number and kinds of rewards available for goal attainment and by increasing the number and kinds of rewards available for goal attainment. Said another way, leaders need to clarify how followers can achieve organizational goals, take care of problems that prevent followers from achieving goals, and then find more and varied rewards to motivate followers to achieve those goals.[29]

Leaders must meet two conditions for path clarification, path clearing, and rewards to increase followers' motivation and effort. First, leader behavior must be a source of immediate or future satisfaction for followers. The things you do as a leader must either please your followers today or lead to activities or rewards that will satisfy them in the future. One of the key cultural principles followed by Charlie Kim, CEO of New York-based Next Jump, which runs web-based reward programs for 90,000 companies, is "Better Me + Better You = Better Us." Kim says, "The culture we're building is predicated on the concept of long-term, sustained happiness."[30] Which is why Next Jump's leadership frequently asks its people what *would* make them happier. Because of the long hours they put in, employees were spending half a day per weekend in a NYC laundromat doing their laundry. So they asked if washers and dryers could be installed at work to be used (and which they would pay for) when working late hours. Recognizing the problem (not laundry, but the secondary effect of long hours resulting in lost weekend time), Next Jump now pays for laundry service. Employees bring in laundry on Fridays and it returns done on Mondays in a bag with Next Jump's logo and this phrase: "My company gets my laundry. I get my weekends back."[31] Next Jump's culture is so positive, rewarding, and satisfying that 18,000 people applied for thirty-five openings last year. Furthermore, while the quit rate in the tech industry is 22 percent per year, Next Jump has an incredibly low 1 percent quit rate.

Second, while providing the coaching, guidance, support, and rewards necessary for effective work performance, leader behaviors must complement and not duplicate the characteristics of followers' work environments. Thus, leader behaviors must offer something unique and valuable to followers beyond what they're already experiencing as they do their jobs or what they can already do for themselves.

In contrast to Fiedler's contingency theory, path-goal theory assumes that leaders *can* change and adapt their leadership styles. Exhibit 14.4 illustrates this process, showing that leaders change and adapt their leadership styles contingent on their subordinates or the environment in which those subordinates work.

Let's learn more about path-goal theory by examining **14-4a the four kinds of leadership styles that leaders use, 14-4b the subordinate and environmental contingency factors that determine when different leader styles are effective,** *and* **14-4c the outcomes of path-goal theory in improving employee satisfaction and performance.**

14-4a Leadership Styles

As illustrated in Exhibit 14.4, the four leadership styles in path-goal theory are directive, supportive, participative, and achievement oriented.[32] **Directive leadership** involves letting employees know precisely what is expected of them, giving them specific guidelines for performing tasks, scheduling work, setting standards of performance, and making sure that

> **Directive leadership** a leadership style in which the leader lets employees know precisely what is expected of them, gives them specific guidelines for performing tasks, schedules work, sets standards of performance, and makes sure that people follow standard rules and regulations

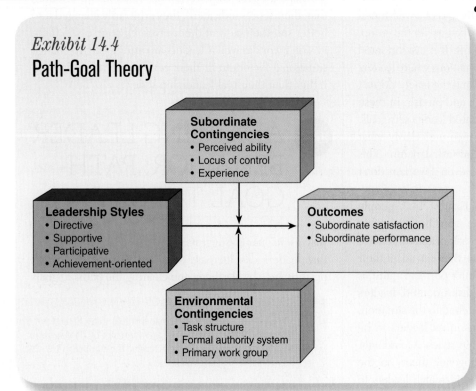

Exhibit 14.4
Path-Goal Theory

Subordinate Contingencies
- Perceived ability
- Locus of control
- Experience

Leadership Styles
- Directive
- Supportive
- Participative
- Achievement-oriented

Outcomes
- Subordinate satisfaction
- Subordinate performance

Environmental Contingencies
- Task structure
- Formal authority system
- Primary work group

people follow standard rules and regulations. Directive leadership is very similar to initiating structure.

Supportive leadership involves being approachable and friendly to employees, showing concern for them and their welfare, treating them as equals, and creating a friendly climate. Supportive leadership is very similar to considerate leader behavior. Supportive leadership often results in employee satisfaction with the job and with leaders. This leadership style may also result in improved performance when it increases employee confidence, lowers employee job stress, or improves relations and trust between employees and leaders.[33]

Participative leadership involves consulting employees for their suggestions and input before making decisions. Participation in decision making should help followers understand which goals are most important and clarify the paths to accomplishing them. Furthermore, when people participate in decisions, they become more committed to making them work. In Domino's Pizza's "Failure Is an Option" advertising campaign, Scott Hinshaw, Domino's EVP of operations, says, "In order to get better, in order to move ahead, you're going to make mistakes."[34] Chief Marketing Officer Russell Weiner explains, "Not every risk we have taken has turned out to be successful, but as a brand we have learned that sometimes you have to fail in order to be great."[35] Andy Wetzel, Director of Product and Brand Innovation, uses the cookie pizza—an idea that never made it out of the test kitchens—as an example. Participative leadership is at the heart of Domino's innovation culture, because everyone in the company, down to franchisees and entry-level employees, is encouraged to test new ideas. Patrick Doyle, Domino's CEO, says, "At a big company, new ideas don't typically come from the local store level. But a great idea can come from anywhere."[36] Indeed, some of Domino's best ideas, like Parmesan Bread Bites which were created by a franchise manager in Findlay, Ohio, come straight from Domino's stores.[37]

Achievement-oriented leadership means setting challenging goals, having high expectations of employees, and displaying confidence that employees will assume responsibility and put forth extraordinary effort. **Asustek**, a Taiwanese computer and phone maker, is the world's largest producer of computer motherboards and the fifth-largest producer of laptop computers (sold under the Asus brand). CEO Jerry Shen has challenged his managers and employees to make Asustek the world's largest supplier of touchscreen notebooks and the world's second-largest seller of tablets, just behind Apple. Chen believes its Nexus 7, a $199 Android tablet with a 7-inch screen, and its VivoBook, a $500 Android tablet with an 11.6-inch screen, combined with its plans to offer an inexpensive 7-inch Windows 8 tablet will help Asustek achieve this challenging goal. One year after announcing the goal, Asustek had moved ahead of Amazon's Kindle tablets to third place behind Samsung and Apple.[38]

14-4b Subordinate and Environmental Contingencies

As shown in Exhibit 14.4, path-goal theory specifies that leader behaviors should be adapted to subordinate characteristics. The theory identifies three kinds of subordinate contingencies: perceived ability, experience, and locus of control. *Perceived ability* is simply how much ability subordinates believe they have for doing their jobs well. Subordinates who perceive that they have a great deal of ability will be dissatisfied with directive leader behaviors. Experienced employees are likely to react in a similar way. Since they already know how to do their jobs (or perceive that they do), they don't need or want close supervision. By contrast, subordinates with little experience or little perceived ability will welcome directive leadership.

Locus of control is a personality measure that indicates the extent to which people believe that they have control over what happens to them in life. *Internals* believe that

> **Supportive leadership** a leadership style in which the leader is friendly and approachable to employees, shows concern for employees and their welfare, treats them as equals, and creates a friendly climate
>
> **Participative leadership** a leadership style in which the leader consults employees for their suggestions and input before making decisions
>
> **Achievement-oriented leadership** a leadership style in which the leader sets challenging goals, has high expectations of employees, and displays confidence that employees will assume responsibility and put forth extraordinary effort

what happens to them, good or bad, is largely a result of their choices and actions. *Externals*, on the other hand, believe that what happens to them is caused by external forces beyond their control. Accordingly, externals are much more comfortable with a directive leadership style, whereas internals greatly prefer a participative leadership style because they like to have a say in what goes on at work.

Path-goal theory specifies that leader behaviors should complement rather than duplicate the characteristics of followers' work environments. There are three kinds of environmental contingencies: task structure, the formal authority system, and the primary work group. As in Fiedler's contingency theory, *task structure* is the degree to which the requirements of a subordinate's tasks are clearly specified. When task structure is low and tasks are unclear, directive leadership should be used because it complements the work environment. When task structure is high and tasks are clear, however, directive leadership is not needed because it duplicates what task structure provides. Alternatively, when tasks are stressful, frustrating, or dissatisfying, leaders should respond with supportive leadership.

The *formal authority system* is an organization's set of procedures, rules, and policies. When the formal authority system is unclear, directive leadership complements the situation by reducing uncertainty and increasing clarity. But when the formal authority system is clear, directive leadership is redundant and should not be used.

Primary work group refers to the amount of work-oriented participation or emotional support that is provided by an employee's immediate work group. Participative leadership should be used when tasks are complex and there is little existing work-oriented participation in the primary work group. When tasks are stressful, frustrating, or repetitive, supportive leadership is called for.

Finally, since keeping track of all of these subordinate and environmental contingencies can get a bit confusing, Exhibit 14.5 provides a summary of when directive, supportive, participative, and achievement-oriented leadership styles should be used.

14-4c Outcomes

Does following path-goal theory improve subordinate satisfaction and performance? Preliminary evidence suggests that it does.[39] In particular, people who work for supportive leaders are much more satisfied with their jobs and their bosses. Likewise, people who work for directive leaders are more satisfied with their jobs and bosses (but not quite as much as when their bosses are supportive) and perform their jobs better, too. Does adapting one's leadership style to subordinate and environmental characteristics improve subordinate satisfaction and performance? At this point, because it is difficult to completely test this complex theory, it's too early to tell.[40] However, since the data clearly show that it makes sense for leaders to be both supportive *and* directive, it also makes sense that leaders could improve subordinate satisfaction and performance by adding participative and achievement-oriented leadership styles to their capabilities as leaders.

Exhibit 14.5

Path-Goal Theory: When to Use Directive, Supportive, Participative, or Achievement-Oriented Leadership

Directive Leadership	Supportive Leadership	Participative Leadership	Achievement-Oriented Leadership
Unstructured tasks	Structured, simple, repetitive tasks Stressful, frustrating tasks	Complex tasks	Unchallenging tasks
Workers with external locus of control	Workers lack confidence	Workers with internal locus of control	
Unclear formal authority system	Clear formal authority system	Workers not satisfied with rewards	
Inexperienced workers		Experienced workers	
Workers with low perceived ability		Workers with high perceived ability	

14-5 ADAPTING LEADER BEHAVIOR: NORMATIVE DECISION THEORY

Many people believe that making tough decisions is at the heart of leadership. Yet experienced leaders will tell you that deciding *how* to make decisions is just as important. The **normative decision theory** (also known as the *Vroom-Yetton-Jago model*) helps leaders decide how much employee participation (from none to letting employees make the entire decision) should be used when making decisions.[41]

*Let's learn more about normative decision theory by investigating **14-5a decision styles** and **14-5b decision quality and acceptance**.*

14-5a Decision Styles

Unlike nearly all of the other leadership theories discussed in this chapter, which have specified *leadership* styles, that is, the way a leader generally behaves toward followers, the normative decision theory specifies five different *decision* styles, or ways of making decisions. (See Chapter 5 for a more complete review of decision making in organizations.) As shown in Exhibit 14.6, those styles vary from *autocratic decisions* (AI or AII) on the left, in which leaders make the decisions by themselves, to *consultative decisions* (CI or CII), in which leaders share problems with subordinates but still make

the decisions themselves, to *group decisions* (GII) on the right, in which leaders share the problems with subordinates and then have the group make the decisions.

GE Aircraft Engines in Durham, North Carolina, uses a similar approach when making decisions. According to *Fast Company* magazine, "At GE/Durham, every decision is either an 'A' decision, a 'B' decision, or a 'C' decision. An 'A' decision is one that the plant manager makes herself, without consulting anyone."[42] Plant manager Paula Sims says, "I don't make very many of those, and when I do make one, everyone at the plant knows it. I make maybe ten or twelve a year."[43] "B" decisions are also made by the plant manager but with input from the people affected. "C" decisions, the most common type, are made by consensus, by the people directly involved, with plenty of discussion. With "C" decisions, the view of the plant manager doesn't necessarily carry more weight than the views of those affected.[44]

14-5b Decision Quality and Acceptance

Management consultant John Canfield says, "Leaders are responsible for improving the performance of organizations. Two significant components of [a leader's] decisions are the quality of the decision and the level of buy-in associated with it. Effective leaders want them both."[45] According to the normative decision

> **Normative decision theory** a theory that suggests how leaders can determine an appropriate amount of employee participation when making decisions

Bad Bonuses

Imagine for a minute that you have an employee who doesn't do his job particularly well. He's almost always late, always misses deadlines, and frequently complains about, well, everything, from clients to coworkers. Would you give an employee like this a bonus? Probably not. And yet, many companies are giving lavish bonuses to CEOs who don't meet performance goals. In 2011, Kevin Crutchfield, CEO of Alpha Natural Resources, was given a $528,000 bonus, even though the company experienced its biggest annual loss ever. CEO Robert Coury received a bonus of $900,000 from drugmaker Mylan even though his company missed several earnings goals. And while such practices might be intended to encourage CEOs to continue being adventurous in looking for growth, they could threaten to turn the whole idea of performance-based bonuses into a fixed game.

Source: Z. R. Mider and J. Green, "Heads or Tails, Some CEOs Win the Pay Game," *Bloomberg Businessweek*, October 4, 2012, accessed June 19, 2013, http://www.businessweek.com/articles/2012-10-04/heads-or-tails-some-ceos-win-the-pay-game.

Exhibit 14.6
Normative Theory, Decision Styles, and Levels of Employee Participation

Leader solves the problem or makes the decision

Leader is willing to accept any decision supported by the entire group

AI	AII	CI	CII	GII
Using information available at the time, the leader solves the problem or makes the decision.	The leader obtains necessary information from employees and then selects a solution to the problem. When asked to share information, employees may or may not be told what the problem is.	The leader shares the problem and gets ideas and suggestions from relevant employees on an individual basis. Individuals are not brought together as a group. Then the leader makes the decision, which may or may not reflect their input.	The leader shares the problem with employees as a group, obtains their ideas and suggestions, and then makes the decision, which may or may not reflect their input.	The leader shares the problem with employees as a group. Together, the leader and employees generate and evaluate alternatives and try to reach an agreement on a solution. The leader acts as a facilitator and does not try to influence the group. The leader is willing to accept and implement any solution that has the support of the entire group.

Source: Table 2.1, Decision Methods for Group and Individual Problems, from Leadership and Decision-Making, by V. H. Vroom and P. W. Yetton.

theory, using the right degree of employee participation improves the quality of decisions and the extent to which employees accept and are committed to decisions (i.e., buy-in). Exhibit 14.7 lists the decision rules that normative decision theory uses to increase the quality of a decision and the degree to which employees accept and commit to it.

The quality, leader information, subordinate information, goal congruence, and problem structure rules are used to increase decision quality. For example, the leader information rule states that if a leader doesn't have enough information to make a decision on his or her own, then the leader should not use an autocratic decision style. The commitment probability, subordinate conflict, and commitment requirement rules shown in Exhibit 14.7 are used to increase employee acceptance and commitment to decisions. For example, the commitment requirement rule says that if decision acceptance and commitment are important and the subordinates share the organization's goals, then you shouldn't use an autocratic or consultative style. In other words, if followers want to do what's best for the company and you need their acceptance and commitment to make a decision work, then use a group decision style and let them make the decision. As you can see, these decision rules help leaders improve decision quality and follower acceptance and commitment by

eliminating decision styles that don't fit the particular decision or situation they're facing. Normative decision theory, like path-goal theory, is situational in nature. The abstract decision rules in Exhibit 14.7 are framed as yes/no questions, which makes the process of applying these rules more concrete. These questions are shown in the decision tree displayed in Exhibit 14.8. You start at the left side of the tree and answer the first question, "How important is the technical quality of this decision?" by choosing "high" or "low." Then you continue by answering each question as you proceed along the decision tree until you get to a recommended decision style.

Let's use the model to make the decision of whether to change from a formal business attire policy to a casual wear policy. The problem sounds simple, but it is actually more complex than you might think. Follow the yellow line in Exhibit 14.8 as we work through the decision in the following discussion.

PROBLEM: CHANGE TO CASUAL WEAR?

1. *Quality requirement: How important is the technical quality of this decision?* **High.** This question has to do with whether there are quality differences in the alternatives and whether those quality differences

Exhibit 14.7
Normative Theory Decision Rules

Decision Rules to Increase Decision Quality

Quality Rule. If the quality of the decision is important, then don't use an autocratic decision style.

Leader Information Rule. If the quality of the decision is important, and if the leader doesn't have enough information to make the decision on his or her own, then don't use an autocratic decision style.

Subordinate Information Rule. If the quality of the decision is important, and if the subordinates don't have enough information to make the decision themselves, then don't use a group decision style.

Goal Congruence Rule. If the quality of the decision is important, and subordinates' goals are different from the organization's goals, then don't use a group decision style.

Problem Structure Rule. If the quality of the decision is important, the leader doesn't have enough information to make the decision on his or her own, and the problem is unstructured, then don't use an autocratic decision style.

Decision Rules to Increase Decision Acceptance

Commitment Probability Rule. If having subordinates accept and commit to the decision is important, then don't use an autocratic decision style.

Subordinate Conflict Rule. If having subordinates accept the decision is important and critical to successful implementation and subordinates are likely to disagree or end up in conflict over the decision, then don't use an autocratic or consultative decision style.

Commitment Requirement Rule. If having subordinates accept the decision is absolutely required for successful implementation and subordinates share the organization's goals, then don't use an autocratic or consultative style.

Sources: Adapted from V. H. Vroom, "Leadership," in *Handbook of Industrial and Organizational Psychology*, ed. M. D. Dunnette (Chicago: Rand McNally, 1976); V. H. Vroom and A. G. Jago, *The New Leadership: Managing Participation in Organizations* (Englewood Cliffs, NJ: Prentice Hall, 1988).

matter. In other words: Is there a lot at stake in this decision? Although most people would assume that quality isn't an issue here, it really is, given the incredibly strong reactions that people have regarding the rules for casual wear at their companies.

2. *Commitment requirement: How important is subordinate commitment to the decision?* High. Changes in culture, like dress codes, require subordinate commitment or they fail.

3. *Leader's information: Do you have sufficient information to make a high-quality decision?* Yes. Let's assume that you've done your homework. Much has been written about casual wear, from how to make the change to the effects it has in companies (almost all positive).

4. *Commitment probability: If you were to make the decision by yourself, is it reasonably certain that your subordinate(s) would be committed to the decision?* No. Studies of casual wear find that employees' reactions are almost uniformly positive. Nonetheless, employees are likely to be angry if you change something as personal as clothing policies without consulting them.

5. *Goal congruence: Do subordinates share the organizational goals to be attained in solving this problem?* Yes. The goals that usually accompany a change to casual dress policies are a more informal culture, better communication, and less money spent on business attire.

6. *Subordinate information: Do subordinates have sufficient information to make a high-quality decision?* No. Most employees know little about casual wear policies or even what constitutes casual wear in most companies. Consequently, most companies have to educate employees about casual wear practices and policies before making a decision.

7. *CII is the answer:* With a CII, or consultative decision process, the leader shares the problem with employees as a group, obtains their ideas and suggestions, and then makes the decision, which may or may not reflect their input. So, given the answers to these questions (remember, different managers won't necessarily answer these questions the same way), the normative decision theory recommends that leaders consult with their subordinates before deciding whether to change to a casual wear policy.

Exhibit 14.8
Normative Decision Theory Tree for Determining the Level of Participation in Decision Making

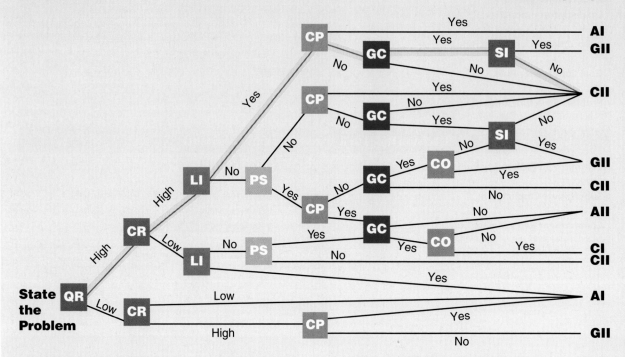

Problem Attributes

QR — Quality requirement: How important is the technical quality of this decision?

CR — Commitment requirement: How important is subordinate commitment to the decision?

LI — Leader's information: Do you have sufficient information to make a high-quality decision?

PS — Problem structure: Is the problem well structured?

CP — Commitment probability: If you were to make the decision by yourself, are you reasonably certain that your subordinate(s) would be committed to the decision?

GC — Goal congruence: Do subordinates share the organizational goals to be attained in solving this problem?

CO — Subordinate conflict: Is conflict among subordinates over preferred solutions likely?

SI — Subordinate information: Do subordinates have sufficient information to make a high-quality decision?

Source: Figure 9.3, Decision-Process Flow Chart for Both Individual and Group Problems, from Leadership and Decision-Making, by V. H. Vroom and P. W. Yetton.

How well does the normative decision theory work? A prominent leadership scholar has described it as the best supported of all leadership theories.[46] In general, the more managers violate the decision rules in Exhibit 14.7, the less effective their decisions are, especially with respect to subordinate acceptance and commitment.[47]

14-6 VISIONARY LEADERSHIP

Strategic leadership is the ability to anticipate, envision, maintain flexibility, think strategically, and work with others to initiate changes that will create a positive future for an organization.[48] During the recession, American retailers marked luxury goods down by as much as 70 percent, hoping to stimulate sales. Luxury brands, like Prada, were angry, fearing that cost cutting damaged their brands and profits. To prevent drastic markdowns from happening again, Prada is now insisting that all U.S. department stores change to a concession-based model that it uses in the rest of the world. For example, under this store-within-a-store system, **Prada** rents retail floor space from, say, KaDeWe in Berlin, the largest retail store in Europe, and pays approximately 20 percent of sales to the retailer. Prada, not KaDeWe, then runs the "store"—Prada at the KaDeWe—on its own, deciding what to sell, whom to hire, and what goes on sale when. Under the concession model, luxury goods makers lose more money when products don't sell but are much more profitable when products do sell. More important to Prada, however, is that the concession model prevents severe price markdowns and protects its luxury brand. When Barneys, which sells luxury products, refused to accept the concession model, Prada pulled its goods from Barneys stores. Prada may lose substantial business if other retailers follow Barneys's lead. However, Bloomingdales's Manhattan store and Neiman Marcus's Las Vegas store have signed on to the concession model.[49] Thus, strategic leadership captures how leaders inspire their companies to change and their followers to give extraordinary effort to accomplish organizational goals.

In Chapter 5, we defined a purpose statement, which is often referred to as an organizational mission or vision, as a statement of a company's purpose or reason for existing. Similarly, **visionary leadership** creates a positive image of the future that motivates organizational members and provides direction for future planning and goal setting.[50]

*Two kinds of visionary leadership are **14-6a charismatic leadership** and **14-6b transformational leadership**.*

14-6a Charismatic Leadership

Charisma is a Greek word meaning "divine gift." The ancient Greeks saw people with charisma as inspired by the gods and capable of incredible accomplishments. German sociologist Max Weber viewed charisma as a special bond between leaders and followers.[51] Weber wrote that the special qualities of charismatic leaders enable them to strongly influence followers. Weber also noted that charismatic leaders tend to emerge in times of crisis and that the radical solutions they propose enhance the admiration that followers feel for them. Indeed, charismatic leaders tend to have incredible influence over followers who may be inspired by their leaders and become fanatically devoted to them. From this perspective, charismatic leaders are often seen as larger-than-life or more special than other employees of the company.

Charismatic leaders have strong, confident, dynamic personalities that attract followers and enable the leaders to create strong bonds with their followers. Followers trust charismatic leaders, are loyal to them, and are inspired to work toward the accomplishment of the leader's vision. Followers who become devoted to charismatic leaders may go to extraordinary lengths to please them. Therefore, we can define **charismatic leadership** as the behavioral tendencies and personal characteristics of leaders that create an exceptionally strong relationship between them and their followers. Charismatic leaders also

▸ Articulate a clear vision for the future that is based on strongly held values or morals;

▸ Model those values by acting in a way consistent with the vision;

▸ Communicate high performance expectations to followers; and

▸ Display confidence in followers' abilities to achieve the vision.[52]

Does charismatic leadership work? Studies indicate that it often does. In general, the followers of charismatic

Strategic leadership the ability to anticipate, envision, maintain flexibility, think strategically, and work with others to initiate changes that will create a positive future for an organization

Visionary leadership leadership that creates a positive image of the future that motivates organizational members and provides direction for future planning and goal setting

Charismatic leadership the behavioral tendencies and personal characteristics of leaders that create an exceptionally strong relationship between them and their followers

leaders are more committed and satisfied, are better performers, are more likely to trust their leaders, and simply work harder.[53] Nonetheless, charismatic leadership also has risks that are at least as large as its benefits. The problems are likely to occur with ego-driven charismatic leaders who take advantage of fanatical followers.

In general, there are two kinds of charismatic leaders, ethical charismatics and unethical charismatics.[54] **Ethical charismatics** provide developmental opportunities for followers, are open to positive and negative feedback, recognize others' contributions, share information, and have moral standards that emphasize the larger interests of the group, organization, or society. Twenty years ago, J. J. Irani, CEO of Tata Steel, had to close down a money-losing steel plan in Jamshedpur, India. Given that Tata not only guaranteed all employees' jobs but also jobs for their children (once you had worked at Tata twenty-five years), this was the first time that any Tata employees would lose their jobs. Rather than doing only what was best for Tata, Irani decided that laid-off employees, age forty or under, would receive full salaries for the remainder of their working lives. Laid-off employees over forty would get salaries plus a 20 percent to 50 percent bonus, depending on how close they were to retirement. Moreover, workers' families would receive the payments even if the workers died prior to retiring. Tata benefitted, too, because it no longer had to pay payroll taxes, and part of the deal was that workers' payments would not increase over time. Over time, its labor costs shrunk, but its reputation as a caring employer among Indian managers and workers persisted.[55] As you would expect, ethical charismatics like Irani produce stronger commitment, higher satisfaction, more effort, better performance, and greater trust.

By contrast, **unethical charismatics** control and manipulate followers, do what is best for themselves instead of their organizations, want to hear only positive feedback, share information that is only beneficial to themselves, and have moral standards that put their interests before everyone else's. Russell Wasendorf, Sr., CEO and founder of Peregrine Financial Group, a commodities trading firm, stole $215 million over the course of twenty years from his clients and the company. Wasendorf printed false bank statements to hide his theft, used some of the stolen money to falsely boost Peregrine's financial performance, and used the money to live well above his means, "hiring a 'four-star chef' to run Peregrine's cafeteria, building an expansive house with a swimming pool, and sinking investor money into ventures like an Italian restaurant—the staff of which he once flew to Italy for a vacation." The sixty-five-year-old Wasendorf was sentenced to fifty years in prison.[56]

Ethical charismatics charismatic leaders who provide developmental opportunities for followers, are open to positive and negative feedback, recognize others' contributions, share information, and have moral standards that emphasize the larger interests of the group, organization, or society

Unethical charismatics charismatic leaders who control and manipulate followers, do what is best for themselves instead of their organizations, want to hear only positive feedback, share only information that is beneficial to themselves, and have moral standards that put their interests before everyone else's

Because followers can become just as committed to unethical charismatics as to ethical charismatics, unethical characteristics pose a tremendous risk for companies. Professor Diane Chandler explains, "By being greatly influenced by charismatic leaders, followers are apt to agree with, feel affection for, and obey them. With charismatic leaders fostering a sense of strong identification with followers, they may likewise curry followers' inordinate allegiance to them in the face of unethical or moral leadership indiscretion."[57]

Exhibit 14.9 shows the stark differences between ethical and unethical charismatics on several leader behaviors: exercising power, creating the vision, communicating with followers, accepting feedback, stimulating followers intellectually, developing followers, and living by moral standards. For example, ethical charismatics account for the concerns and wishes of their followers when creating a vision by having followers participate in the development of the company vision. By contrast, unethical charismatics develop a vision by themselves solely to meet their personal agendas. One unethical charismatic said, "The key thing is that it is my idea; and I am going to win with it at all costs."[58]

14-6b Transformational Leadership

While charismatic leadership involves articulating a clear vision, modeling values consistent with that vision, communicating high performance expectations, and establishing very strong relationships with followers, **transformational leadership** goes further by generating awareness and acceptance of a group's purpose and mission and by getting employees to see beyond their own needs and self-interest for the good of the group.[59] Like charismatic leaders, transformational

> **Transformational leadership** leadership that generates awareness and acceptance of a group's purpose and mission and gets employees to see beyond their own needs and self-interests for the good of the group

---

Exhibit 14.9
Ethical and Unethical Charismatics

Charismatic Leader Behaviors	Ethical Charismatics . . .	Unethical Charismatics . . .
Exercising power	. . . use power to serve others.	. . . use power to dominate or manipulate others for personal gain.
Creating the vision	. . . allow followers to help develop the vision.	. . . are the sole source of vision, which they use to serve their personal agendas.
Communicating with followers	. . . engage in two-way communication and seek out viewpoints on critical issues.	. . . engage in one-way communication and are not open to suggestions from others.
Accepting feedback	. . . are open to feedback and willing to learn from criticism.	. . . have inflated egos, thrive on attention and admiration of sycophants, and avoid candid feedback.
Stimulating followers intellectually	. . . want followers to think and question status quo as well as leader's views.	. . . don't want followers to think but instead want uncritical acceptance of leader's ideas.
Developing followers	. . . focus on developing people with whom they interact, express confidence in them, and share recognition with others.	. . . are insensitive and unresponsive to followers' needs and aspirations.
Living by moral standards	. . . follow self-guided principles that may go against popular opinion and have three virtues: courage, a sense of fairness or justice, and integrity.	. . . follow standards only if they satisfy immediate self-interests, manipulate impressions so that others think they are doing the right thing, and use communication skills to manipulate others to support their personal agendas.

Source: J. M. Howell and B. J. Avolio, "The Ethics of Charismatic Leadership: Submission or Liberation?" *Academy of Management Executive 6*, no. 2 (1992): 43–54.

leaders are visionary, but they transform their organizations by getting their followers to accomplish more than they intended and even more than they thought possible.

Transformational leaders are able to make their followers feel that they are a vital part of the organization and help them see how their jobs fit with the organization's vision. By linking individual and organizational interests, transformational leaders encourage followers to make sacrifices for the organization because they know that they will prosper when the organization prospers. Transformational leadership has four components: charismatic leadership or idealized influence, inspirational motivation, intellectual stimulation, and individualized consideration.[60]

Charismatic leadership or idealized influence means that transformational leaders act as role models for their followers. According to Professor Roger Martin, P&G's two-time CEO A.G. Lafley acts as a strong role model in a number of ways. According to Martin, "When P&G CEO A.G. Lafley insisted that in-home visits with consumers be arranged for him in whatever city he visited in the P&G worldwide network, executives throughout P&G realized that if the CEO wasn't too busy to do in-home consumer visits, neither were they. When he worked with the board to get his stock-based compensation to vest in one-tenth

Yuri Arcurs/iStockphoto.com

increments in each of the 10 years following his retirement from P&G [he has since returned as CEO], his organization got the unmistakable impression that P&G was focused on the very long term and that obsessing about one's own short-term compensation wasn't very CEO-like."[61]

Because transformational leaders put others' needs ahead of their own and share risks with their followers, they are admired, respected, and trusted, and followers want to emulate them. When Whole Foods' profit dropped 10 percent and the company needed to trim costs, CEO John Mackey voluntarily cut his pay by 67 percent. Likewise, the Tonight Show's Jay Leno voluntarily took a $15 million cut in pay when NBC announced that it needed to cut $20 million in costs for the show. While twenty employees were let go, Leno's voluntary pay cut absorbed 75 percent of the needed cost reduction so that many other long-time staffers on the show could keep their jobs.[62] Thus, in contrast to purely charismatic leaders (especially unethical charismatics), transformational leaders can be counted on to do the right thing and maintain high standards for ethical and personal conduct.

Inspirational motivation means that transformational leaders motivate and inspire followers by providing meaning and challenge to their work. By clearly communicating expectations and demonstrating commitment to goals, transformational leaders help followers envision future states, such as the organizational vision or mission. In turn, this leads to greater enthusiasm and optimism about the future.

Intellectual stimulation means that transformational leaders encourage followers to be creative and innovative, to question assumptions, and to look at problems and situations in new ways even if their ideas are different from those of leaders. Imagine a software product that lets people who speak thirty-five different languages text chat with each other in real time, providing instant translations from one language to another. Type in English, it appears in Mandarin Chinese. Type back in Mandarin, it appears in English. If asked which tech company came up with this, you'd say Apple? No. Google? No. Microsoft? No. Wait, yes, Microsoft. Microsoft engineer Harry Emil developed this software in his spare time in Microsoft's "Garage," a two-year old program that encourages Microsoft employees to create, innovate, try, and test new ideas and potential products. Or, as Microsoft calls it, "Do epic s--t." Matt Jubelirer, senior product manager, says, "The Garage has taken on a broader context within Microsoft. It's created a forum where it feels OK to tinker." The Garage, inspired by the many tech companies that started with the founders working out of someone's garage, holds "science fairs," where thirty to fifty projects are presented with poster boards. Microsoft held six last year. Harry Emil, who created the translation software at Microsoft's Garage, says, "If you succeed, we're go to celebrate that. And if you fail, we've got that covered."[63]

Individualized consideration means that transformational leaders pay special attention to followers' individual needs by creating learning opportunities, accepting and tolerating

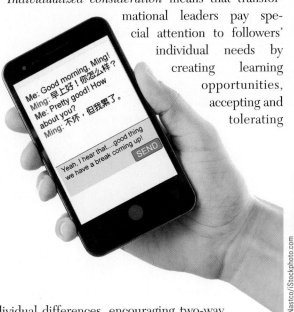

Nastco/iStockphoto.com

individual differences, encouraging two-way communication, and being good listeners.

Finally, a distinction needs to be drawn between transformational leadership and transactional leadership. While transformational leaders use visionary and inspirational appeals to influence followers, **transactional leadership** is based on an exchange process in which followers are rewarded for good performance and punished for poor performance. When leaders administer rewards fairly and offer followers the rewards that they want, followers will often reciprocate with effort. A problem, however, is that transactional leaders often rely too heavily on discipline or threats to bring performance up to standards. This may work in the short run, but it's much less effective in the long run. Also, as discussed in Chapters 11 and 13, many leaders and organizations have difficulty successfully linking pay practices to individual performance. As a result,

Transactional leadership leadership based on an exchange process in which followers are rewarded for good performance and punished for poor performance

studies consistently show that transformational leadership is much more effective on average than transactional leadership. In the United States, Canada, Japan, and India and at all organizational levels, from first-level supervisors to upper-level executives, followers view transformational leaders as much better leaders and are much more satisfied when working for them. Furthermore, companies with transformational leaders have significantly better financial performance.[64]

STUDY TOOLS 14

LOCATED AT THE BACK OF YOUR BOOK:

☐ Rip out and study the Chapter Review Card at the end of the book

LOG IN TO WWW.CENGAGEBRAIN.COM TO:

☐ Review Key Term Flashcards

☐ Complete Practice Quizzing (take up to four times without repeating the same quiz)

☐ Complete Games: Beat the Clock and Crossword Puzzle

☐ Complete Interactive Content: Graded Quiz, Media Quiz, and Fill-in-the-Blank Questions

☐ Watch Management Workplace Video on "Camp Bow Wow"

☐ Work Through the What Would You Do Case on Apple Headquarters

PART

4

15 Managing Communication

LEARNING OUTCOMES

15-1 Explain the role that perception plays in communication and communication problems.

15-2 Describe the communication process and the various kinds of communication in organizations.

15-3 Explain how managers can manage effective one-on-one communication.

15-4 Describe how managers can manage effective organization-wide communication.

After you finish

this chapter, go

to **PAGE 333** for

STUDY TOOLS

PERCEPTION AND COMMUNICATION PROBLEMS

15-1

It's estimated that managers spend over 80 percent of their day communicating with others.[1] Indeed, much of the basic management process—planning, organizing, leading, and controlling—cannot be performed without effective communication. If this weren't reason enough to study communication, consider that effective oral communication—achieved by listening, following instructions, conversing, and giving feedback—is the most important skill for college graduates who are entering the workforce.[2] **Communication** is the process of transmitting information from one person or place to another. While some bosses sugarcoat bad news, smart managers understand that effective, straightforward communication between managers and employees is essential for success.

One study found that when *employees* were asked whether their supervisor gave recognition for good work, only 13 percent said their supervisor gave a pat on the back, and a mere 14 percent said their supervisor gave sincere and thorough praise. But when the *supervisors* of these employees were asked if they gave recognition for good work, 82 percent said they gave pats on the back, while 80 percent said that they gave sincere and thorough praise.[3] Given that these managers and employees worked closely together, how could they have had such different perceptions of something as simple as praise?

*Let's learn more about perception and communication problems by examining **15-1a the basic perception process, 15-1b perception problems, 15-1c how we perceive others,** and **15-1d how we perceive ourselves.** We'll also consider how all of these factors make it difficult for managers to communicate effectively.*

15-1a Basic Perception Process

As shown in Exhibit 15.1, **perception** is the process by which individuals attend to, organize, interpret, and retain information from their environments. And since communication is the process of transmitting information from one person or place to another, perception is obviously a key part of communication. Yet perception can also be a key obstacle to communication.

As people perform their jobs, they are exposed to a wide variety of informational stimuli such as emails, direct conversations with the boss or coworkers, rumors heard over lunch, stories about the company in the press,

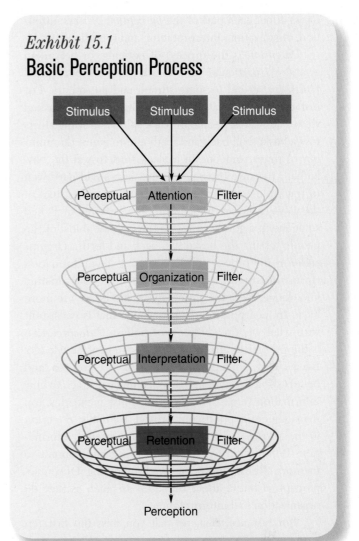

Exhibit 15.1
Basic Perception Process

Stimulus   Stimulus   Stimulus

Perceptual   Attention   Filter

Perceptual   Organization   Filter

Perceptual   Interpretation   Filter

Perceptual   Retention   Filter

Perception

or a video broadcast of a speech from the CEO to all employees. Just being exposed to an informational stimulus, however, is no guarantee that an individual will pay attention or attend to that stimulus. People experience stimuli through their own **perceptual filters**—the personality-, psychology-, or experience-based differences that influence them to ignore or pay attention to particular stimuli. Because of filtering, people exposed to the same information will often disagree about what they saw or heard. As shown in Exhibit 15.1, perceptual

---

Communication the process of transmitting information from one person or place to another

Perception the process by which individuals attend to, organize, interpret, and retain information from their environments

Perceptual filters the personality-, psychology-, or experience-based differences that influence people to ignore or pay attention to particular stimuli

filters affect each part of the *perception process*: attention, organization, interpretation, and retention.

Attention is the process of noticing, or becoming aware of, particular stimuli. Because of perceptual filters, we attend to some stimuli and not others. For instance, a study at the University of Illinois asked viewers to watch people in black shirts and white shirts toss a basketball back and forth and to count the number of times someone in a black shirt tossed the basketball. Because their perceptual filters had narrowed to track the activities of people in black shirts, half of the viewers did not notice when the experimenters had someone in a gorilla suit walk through the midst of the people tossing the basketball back and forth.[4] *Organization* is the process of incorporating new information (from the stimuli that you notice) into your existing knowledge. Because of perceptual filters, we are more likely to incorporate new knowledge that is consistent with what we already know or believe. *Interpretation* is the process of attaching meaning to new knowledge. Because of perceptual filters, our preferences and beliefs strongly influence the meaning we attach to new information (e.g., "This decision must mean that top management supports our project"). Finally, *retention* is the process of remembering interpreted information. Retention affects what we recall and commit to memory after we have perceived something. Of course, perceptual filters affect retention as much as they do organization and interpretation.

For instance, imagine that you miss the first ten minutes of a TV show and turn on your TV to see two people talking to each other in a living room. As they talk, they walk around the room, picking up and putting down various items. Some items, such as a ring, watch, and credit card, appear to be valuable, while others appear to be drug-related, such as a water pipe for smoking marijuana. In fact, this situation was depicted on videotape in a well-known study that manipulated people's perceptual filters.[5] Before watching the video, one-third of the study participants were told that the people were there to rob the apartment. Another third were told that police were on their way to conduct a drug raid and that the people in the apartment were getting rid of incriminating evidence. The remaining third of the participants were told that the people were simply waiting for a friend.

After watching the video, participants were asked to list all of the objects from the video that they could remember. Not surprisingly, the different perceptual filters (theft, drug raid, and waiting for a friend) affected what the participants attended to, how they organized the information, how they interpreted it, and ultimately which objects they remembered. Participants who thought a theft was in progress were more likely to remember the valuable objects in the video. Those who thought a drug raid was imminent were more likely to remember the drug-related objects. There was no discernible pattern to the items remembered by those who thought that the people in the video were simply waiting for a friend.

In short, because of perception and perceptual filters, people are likely to pay attention to different things, organize and interpret what they pay attention to differently, and, finally, remember things differently. Consequently, even when people are exposed to the same communications (e.g., organizational memos, discussions with managers or customers), they can end up with very different perceptions and understandings. This is why communication can be so difficult and frustrating for managers. Let's review some of the communication problems created by perception and perceptual filters.

15-1b Perception Problems

Perception creates communication problems for organizations because people exposed to the same communication and information can end up with completely different ideas and understandings. Two of the most common perception problems in organizations are selective perception and closure.

At work, we are constantly bombarded with sensory stimuli: phones ringing, people talking in the background, computers dinging as new email arrives, people calling our names, and so forth. As limited processors of information, we cannot possibly notice, receive, and interpret all of this information. As a result, we attend to and accept some stimuli but screen out and reject others. This isn't a random process.

Selective perception is the tendency to notice and accept objects and information consistent with our values, beliefs, and expectations, while ignoring or screening out inconsistent information. For example, in a research study pedestrians are stopped on a sidewalk by a man who asks for directions. Ten seconds into giving directions, two people carrying a door walk between the man who asked for directions, on the left, and the pedestrian, on the right. When the door goes by, the man who asked for directions quickly switches places with one of the young men carrying the door. The pedestrian, however, doesn't see this switch because the

Selective perception the tendency to notice and accept objects and information consistent with our values, beliefs, and expectations, while ignoring or screening inconsistent information

Andrey Popov/iStockphoto.com

did, you perceived the person through an external attribution known as the defensive bias. The **defensive bias** is the tendency for people to perceive themselves as personally and situationally similar to someone who is having difficulty or trouble.[8] When we identify with the person in a situation, we tend to use external attributions (i.e., features related to the situation) to explain the person's behavior. For instance, since flat tires are common, it's easy to perceive ourselves in that same situation and put the blame on external causes such as running over a nail.

door blocks the view. Like the invisible gorilla example above, 50 percent of the time people don't even notice that they're talking to a different man and go right back to giving directions. Selective perception, is one of the biggest contributors to misunderstandings and miscommunication, because it strongly influences what people see, hear, read, and understand at work.[6]

Once we have initial information about a person, event, or process, **closure** is the tendency to fill in the gaps where information is missing, that is, to assume that what we don't know is consistent with what we already do know. If employees are told that budgets must be cut by 10 percent, they may automatically assume that 10 percent of employees will lose their jobs, too, even if that isn't the case. Not surprisingly, when closure occurs, people sometimes fill in the gaps with inaccurate information, which can create problems for organizations.

15-1c Perceptions of Others

Attribution theory says that we all have a basic need to understand and explain the causes of other people's behavior.[7] In other words, we need to know why people do what they do. According to attribution theory, we use two general reasons or attributions to explain people's behavior: an *internal attribution*, in which behavior is thought to be voluntary or under the control of the individual; and an *external attribution*, in which behavior is thought to be involuntary and outside of the control of the individual.

Have you ever seen someone changing a flat tire on the side of the road and thought to yourself, "What rotten luck—somebody's having a bad day"? If you

Now, let's assume a different situation, this time in the workplace:

A utility company worker puts a ladder on a utility pole and then climbs up to do his work. As he's doing his work, he falls from the ladder and seriously injures himself.[9]

Answer this question: Who or what caused the accident? If you thought, "It's not the worker's fault. Anybody could fall from a tall ladder," then you interpreted the incident with a defensive bias in which you saw yourself as personally and situationally similar to someone who is having difficulty or trouble. In other words, you made an external attribution by attributing the accident to an external cause or some feature of the situation.

Most accident investigations, however, initially blame the worker (i.e., an internal attribution) and not the situation (i.e., an external attribution). Typically, 60 to 80 percent of workplace accidents each year are blamed on "operator error," that is, on the employees themselves. In reality, more complete investigations usually show that workers are responsible for only 30 to 40 percent of all workplace accidents.[10] Why are accident investigators so quick to blame workers? The reason is that they are committing the

Closure the tendency to fill in gaps of missing information by assuming that what we don't know is consistent with what we already know

Attribution theory the theory that we all have a basic need to understand and explain the causes of other people's behavior

Defensive bias the tendency for people to perceive themselves as personally and situationally similar to someone who is having difficulty or trouble

Exhibit 15.2
Defensive Bias and Fundamental Attribution Error

The Coworker	The Employee	The Boss

Defensive Bias—
the tendency for people to perceive themselves as personally and situationally similar to someone who is having difficulty or trouble

Defensive Bias—
the tendency for people to perceive themselves as personally and situationally similar to someone who is having difficulty or trouble

Fundamental Attribution Error—
the tendency to ignore external causes of behavior and to attribute other people's actions to internal causes

fundamental attribution error, which is the tendency to ignore external causes of behavior and to attribute other people's actions to internal causes.[11] In other words, when investigators examine the possible causes of an accident, they're much more likely to assume that the accident is a function of the person and not the situation.

Which attribution—the defensive bias or the fundamental attribution error—are workers likely to make when something goes wrong? In general, as shown in Exhibit 15.2, employees and coworkers are more likely to perceive events and explain behavior from a defensive bias. Because they do the work themselves and see themselves as similar to others who make mistakes, have accidents, or are otherwise held responsible for things that go wrong at work, employees and coworkers are likely to attribute problems to external causes such as failed machinery, poor support, or inadequate training.

By contrast, because they are typically observers (who don't do the work themselves) and see themselves as situationally and personally different from workers, managers tend to commit the fundamental attribution error and blame mistakes, accidents, and other things that go wrong on workers (i.e., an internal attribution).

Consequently, workers and managers in most workplaces can be expected to take opposite views when things go wrong. Therefore, the defensive bias, which is typically used by workers, and the fundamental attribution error, which is typically made by managers, together present a significant challenge to effective communication and understanding in organizations.

15-1d Self-Perception

The **self-serving bias** is the tendency to overestimate our value by attributing successes to ourselves (internal causes) and attributing failures to others or the environment (external causes).[12] The self-serving bias can make it especially difficult for managers to talk to employees about performance problems. In general, people have a need to maintain a positive self-image. This need is so strong that when people seek feedback at work, they typically want verification of their worth (rather than information about performance deficiencies) or

---

Fundamental attribution error the tendency to ignore external causes of behavior and to attribute other people's actions to internal causes

Self-serving bias the tendency to overestimate our value by attributing successes to ourselves (internal causes) and attributing failures to others or the environment (external causes)

assurance that mistakes or problems weren't their fault.[13] People can become defensive and emotional when managerial communication threatens their positive self-image. They quit listening, and communication becomes ineffective. In the second half of the chapter, which focuses on improving communication, we'll explain ways in which managers can minimize this self-serving bias and improve effective one-on-one communication with employees.

15-2 KINDS OF COMMUNICATION

There are many kinds of communication—formal, informal, coaching/counseling, and nonverbal—but they all follow the same fundamental process.

*Let's learn more about the different kinds of communication by examining **15-2a the communication process, 15-2b formal communication channels, 15-2c informal communication channels, 15-2d coaching and counseling, or one-on-one communication,** and **15-2e nonverbal communication.***

15-2a The Communication Process

At the beginning of this chapter, we defined *communication* as the process of transmitting information from one person or place to another. Exhibit 15.3 displays a model of the communication process and its major components: the sender (message to be conveyed, encoding the message, transmitting the message); the receiver (receiving message, decoding the message, and

the message that was understood); and noise, which interferes with the communication process.

The communication process begins when a *sender* thinks of a message he or she wants to convey to another person. For example, you had a flu shot and a pneumonia shot, and yet you've had an unexplainable fever for nine days, so you visit the doctor. The doctor asks a series of questions regarding your appetite, fatigue, tenderness in your abdomen, and whether your fever comes and goes during the day. The doctor, the sender, runs some tests and then has you, the receiver, come back the next day to provide a diagnosis and recommend a treatment.

The next step is to encode the message. **Encoding** means putting a message into a written, verbal, or

> **Encoding** putting a message into a written, verbal, or symbolic form that can be recognized and understood by the receiver

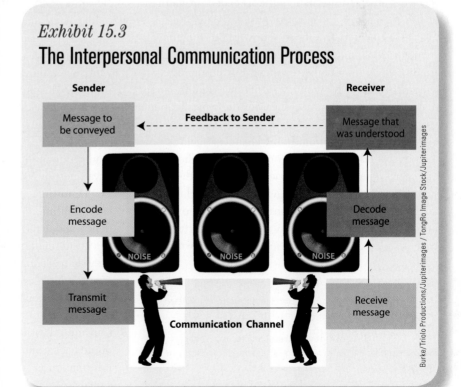

Exhibit 15.3
The Interpersonal Communication Process

Sender   **Receiver**

Message to be conveyed → *Feedback to Sender* → Message that was understood

Encode message   Decode message

NOISE   NOISE   NOISE

Transmit message   **Communication Channel**   Receive message

Burke/Triolo Productions/Jupiterimages / TongRo Image Stock/Jupiterimages

symbolic form that can be recognized and understood by the receiver. In our example, this means the doctor has to take the technical language of medicine and lab test results and communicate it in a way that patients can understand. This is not easy to do. And the difficulty of doing this well is compounded by the average doctor's visit lasting less than fifteen minutes. And, while your visit might be fifteen minutes, you're not getting a full fifteen minutes to talk to the doctor. Not surprisingly, 60 percent of patients feel as if their doctor is rushing through their exam. Despite this, 58 percent of surveyed patients say their doctors do a good job of explaining things to them. But, as we'll see in a few steps, that doesn't mean communication has been effective.[14]

The sender then *transmits the message* via *communication channels*. The traditional communication channel for doctors and patients is face-to-face discussion in the doctor's office. Ironically, though, the introduction of electronic health records may be interfering with that. Dr. Rita Redberg, at the University of California San Francisco Medical Center, says, "The recent introduction of electronic health records in the office, for example, requires many doctors to spend much of a patient exam looking at a computer screen instead of the patient in order to record information." Indeed, studies show that one-third of the time, doctors forget to give patients critical information. Another critical study found that across thirty different medical conditions, patients only received all the information they needed from their doctors about 55 percent of the time.[15] Why? Because in an average fifteen-minute doctor's visit, the doctor will spend just 1.3 minutes telling the patient about his or her condition, prognosis, and treatment. Furthermore, as we will see below, that 1.3 minutes is filled with information that is too complex and technical for the typical patient to understand.[16]

With some communication channels such as the telephone and face-to-face communication, the sender receives immediate feedback, whereas with others such as email (or text messages and file attachments), fax, beepers, voice mail, memos, and letters, the sender must wait for the receiver to respond. Unfortunately, because of technical difficulties (e.g., fax down, dead battery in the mobile phone, inability to read email attachments) or people-based transmission problems (e.g., forgetting to pass on the message), messages aren't always transmitted.

If the message is transmitted and received, however, the next step is for the receiver to decode it. **Decoding** is the process by which the receiver translates the verbal or symbolic form of the message into an understood message. Surveys indicate that many patients clearly do not understand what their doctors are telling them. Up to 85 percent of hospitalized patients don't even know the name of the doctor in charge of their treatment. As many as 58 percent don't know why they were admitted to the hospital. Likewise, in a typical fifteen-minute doctor's appointment, half of patients will leave without understanding what their doctor has told to them to do to get better.[17] Unfortunately, even when patients seem to understand what their doctors are telling them in that fifteen-minute visit, it turns out that they immediately forget 80 percent of that medical information, and then half of what they remember is wrong![18]

The last step of the communication process occurs when the receiver gives the sender feedback. **Feedback to sender** is a return message to the sender that indicates the receiver's understanding of the message (of what the receiver was supposed to know, to do, or not to do). Feedback makes senders aware of possible miscommunications and enables them to continue communicating until the receiver understands the intended message. Because of the difficulties of communicating complex medical information in too little time, many doctors now employ the "teach-back" method at the end of a patient visit, where they ask patients to explain in their own words what they've heard the doctor say regarding their problem (diagnosis), whether they'll get better (prognosis), and what the patient is supposed to do once they leave the doctor's office (i.e., treatment plan and managing medications).[19] Even so, much progress needs to be made as about half of patients are not even asked if they have questions.[20]

Unfortunately, feedback doesn't always occur in the communication process. Complacency and overconfidence about the ease and simplicity of communication can lead senders and receivers to simply assume that they share a common understanding of the message and, consequently, to not use feedback to improve the effectiveness of their communication. This is a serious mistake, especially since messages and feedback are always transmitted with and against a background of noise. Part of the background noise in medicine is how well medical information is communicated between medical professionals. After all, medicine is a "team sport" involving

Decoding the process by which the receiver translates the written, verbal, or symbolic form of a message into an understood message

Feedback to sender in the communication process, a return message to the sender that indicates the receiver's understanding of the message

various doctors, physician assistants, nurses, and other care professionals for each patient. Medical mistakes kill 500 people per day, and 80 percent of those deaths are caused by miscommunication that occurs when patients are transferred from one set of caregivers to another, for instance, the night-shift nurses not communicating key information to the day-shift nurses, or one doctor not being aware of the diagnosis and treatment plan of another doctor on a case.[21]

Noise is anything that interferes with the transmission of the intended message. Noise can occur in any of the following situations:

▸ The sender isn't sure what message to communicate.

▸ The message is not clearly encoded.

▸ The wrong communication channel is chosen.

▸ The message is not received or decoded properly.

▸ The receiver doesn't have the experience or time to understand the message.

Jargon, which is vocabulary particular to a profession or group, is another form of noise that interferes with communication in the workplace. Any idea what "rightsizing," "unsiloing," "pain points," "drilling down," and "sync up" mean? Rightsizing means laying off workers. Unsiloing means getting workers in different parts of the company (i.e., different vertical silos) to work with others outside their own areas. Pain points are customer problems that represent opportunities for businesses to fix. Drilling down is moving from a general analysis to a more specific, in-depth focus with greater detail. Finally, sync up means making sure everyone knows what is happening.[22] Unfortunately, the business world is rife with jargon. Carol Hymowitz of the *Wall Street Journal* points out, "A new crop of buzzwords usually sprouts every three to five years, or about the same length of time many top executives have to prove themselves. Some can be useful in swiftly communicating, and spreading, new business concepts. Others are less useful, even devious."[23]

15-2b Formal Communication Channels

An organization's **formal communication channel,** is the system of official channels that carry organizationally approved messages and information. Organizational objectives, rules, policies, procedures, instructions, commands, and requests for information are all transmitted via the formal communication system or channel. There are three formal communication channels: downward communication, upward communication, and horizontal communication.[24]

Downward communication flows from higher to lower levels in an organization. Downward communication is used to issue orders down the organizational hierarchy, to give organizational members job-related information, to give managers and workers performance reviews from upper managers, and to clarify organizational objectives and goals.[25] Michael Beer, professor

Noise anything that interferes with the transmission of the intended message

Jargon vocabulary particular to a profession or group that interferes with communication in the workplace

Formal communication channel the system of official channels that carry organizationally approved messages and information

Downward communication communication that flows from higher to lower levels in an organization

emeritus at Harvard Business School, says, "You can never over communicate. When you think you've communicated well, go out three or four more times and communicate again." Beer's consulting firm, TruePoint, studied forty CEOs whose companies have been above-average performers for over a decade. He found that those remarkable leaders spend an enormous amount of time in communicating downward. They have a simple story, and that story gets out every place they go."[26]

Upward communication flows from lower levels to higher levels in an organization. Upward communication is used to give higher-level managers feedback about operations, issues, and problems; to help higher-level managers assess organizational performance and effectiveness; to encourage lower-level managers and employees to participate in organizational decision making; and to give those at lower levels the chance to share their concerns with higher-level authorities. Scott Moorehead, CEO of **The Cellular Connection**, which with 800 stores is the largest Verizon wireless retailer in the United States, found a unique way to facilitate upward communication. Moorehead says, "I was sitting in front of my computer, trying to come up with something I could tell all these smart people in my company that would help them do their job better . . . and I realized that what I really should be doing is asking them what I should do." So he sent them all a message saying, "Today, you're the CEO. What would you do to make the company better?" Many people answered that they wanted the business to feel like a family again, which, with 800 locations, it had lost. Says Moorehead, "I hadn't recognized that. I still saw us as a mom and pop, but they saw us as a giant bureaucratic company. So I immediately changed my mindset from growing the company to fixing who we are."[27]

Horizontal communication flows among managers and workers who are at the same organizational level, such as when a day shift nurse comes in at 7:30 a.m. for a half-hour discussion with the midnight nurse supervisor who leaves at 8:00 a.m. Horizontal communication helps facilitate coordination and cooperation between different parts of a company and allows coworkers to

Hacked!

Social media sites like Twitter and Facebook are great tools for communicating with people inside and outside of the company. But these sites can also leave companies vulnerable to ill-minded people who want to spread false information. A group calling itself the Syrian Economic Army hacked the Twitter site of the Associated Press, leaving a message that there were explosions at the White House and that President Barack Obama was injured. Before the Associated Press and White House officials could deny the "report," investors on Wall Street panicked, and the Dow Jones Industrial Average fell 1 percent in less than thirty minutes.

Source: A. Sherter, "Fake AP Tweet Sends Stocks Briefly Plunging," *CBS MoneyWatch*, April 23, 2013, accessed June 20, 2013, http://www.cbsnews.com/8301-505123 _162-57580979/fake-ap-tweet-sends-stocks-briefly-plunging/.

share relevant information. It also helps people at the same level resolve conflicts and solve problems without involving high levels of management. At Square, the mobile credit card payment company, founder and CEO Jack Dorsey encourages horizontal communication among Square's 600 employees by requiring that in all meetings with three or more people someone must take notes and distribute them afterwards to everyone in the company. This applies at all levels, including board meetings. Says Dorsey, "It's just the simple thing to do. It's very hard to keep secrets. It's very easy to give information."[28]

In general, what can managers do to improve formal communication? First, decrease reliance on downward communication. Second, increase chances for upward communication by increasing personal contact with lower-level managers and workers. Third, like Square's Jack Dorsey, encourage much better use of horizontal communication.

15-2c Informal Communication Channels

An organization's **informal communication channel,** sometimes called the **grapevine,** is the transmission of messages from employee to employee outside of formal communication channels. The grapevine arises out of curiosity, that is, the need to know what is going on in an organization and how it might affect you or others. To satisfy this curiosity, employees need a consistent supply of relevant, accurate, in-depth information about what is going on in the company and why. At **Net Optics,**

Upward communication communication that flows from lower to higher levels in an organization

Horizontal communication communication that flows among managers and workers who are at the same organizational level

Informal communication channel (grapevine) the transmission of messages from employee to employee outside of formal communication channels

a manufacturer of computer networking equipment, CEO Bob Shaw understands the importance of the grapevine to better communication. He says, "If there's something out there that the organization's not clear on, my role and responsibility is to make sure I fill it in with the right information." So Net Optics has a rumor jar in which employees can insert anonymous notes about the rumors they've heard. Then, at the monthly company meeting, Shaw pulls out the notes, reads them to the employees, and addresses each one. Shaw says, "I never know what's going to be in there, so it's as much a surprise for me as it is for the audience." After two employees lost their jobs (for performance reasons), notes asked if the rumor that the company was going to have layoffs was true. Shaw explained that not only was Net Optics not downsizing, it was quite successful and growing.[29]

Grapevines arise out of informal communication networks such as the gossip or cluster chains shown in Exhibit 15.4. In a *gossip chain*, one highly connected individual shares information with many other managers and workers. By contrast, in a *cluster chain*, numerous people simply tell a few of their friends. The result in both cases is that information flows freely and quickly through the organization. Some believe that grapevines are a waste of employees' time, that they promote gossip and rumors that fuel political speculation, and that they are sources of highly unreliable, inaccurate information. Yet studies clearly show that grapevines are highly accurate sources of information for a number of reasons.[30] First, because grapevines typically carry "juicy" information that is interesting and timely, information spreads rapidly. During Allstate's annual Leaders Forum, a

> "THE MAIN FOCUS OF RUMOR IS TO FIGURE OUT THE TRUTH. IT'S THE GROUP TRYING TO MAKE SENSE OF SOMETHING THAT'S IMPORTANT TO THEM."

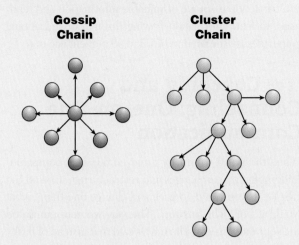

Exhibit 15.4
Grapevine Communication Networks

Gossip Chain   **Cluster Chain**

Source: K. Davis and J. W. Newstrom, Human Behavior at Work: Organizational Behavior, 8th ed. (New York: McGraw-Hill, 1989).

gathering of 2,000 agents and employees, CEO Thomas Wilson announced plans for reducing the company's sales force and changing sales commission rates. Later that evening, a group of employees were at the hotel bar, complaining about the changes and about Wilson, when Joseph Lacher, the president of Allstate's home and auto insurance division, was allegedly overheard using two expletives in reference to Wilson. By the next day, nearly all conference attendees had heard about Lacher's critical remarks. Lacher was abruptly let go just a few weeks later.[31]

Second, since information is typically spread by face-to-face conversation, receivers can send feedback to make sure they understand the message that is being communicated. This reduces misunderstandings and increases accuracy. Third, since most of the information in a company moves along the grapevine rather than through formal communication channels, people can usually verify the accuracy of information by checking it out with others.

What can managers do to manage organizational grapevines? The very worst thing they can do is withhold information or try to punish those who share information with others. The grapevine abhors a vacuum, so rumors and anxiety will flourish in the absence of information from company management. Why does this occur? According to workplace psychologist Nicholas DiFonzo, "The main focus of rumor is to figure out the truth. It's the group trying to make sense of something that's important to them."[32] A better strategy is to embrace the grapevine

John Lund/Blend Images/Getty Images

and keep employees informed about possible changes and strategies. Failure to do so will just make things worse. And, in addition to using the grapevine to communicate with others, managers should not overlook the grapevine as a tremendous source of valuable information and feedback. In fact, information flowing through organizational grapevines is estimated to be 75 to 95 percent accurate.[33]

15-2d Coaching and Counseling: One-on-One Communication

When the Wyatt Company surveyed 531 U.S. companies undergoing major changes and restructuring, it asked the CEOs, "If you could go back and change one thing, what would it be?" The answer: "The way we communicated with our employees." The CEOs said that instead of flashy videos, printed materials, or formal meetings, they would make greater use of one-on-one communication, especially with employees' immediate supervisors instead of with higher-level executives whom employees didn't know.[34]

Coaching and counseling are two kinds of one-on-one communication. **Coaching** is communicating with someone for the direct purpose of improving the person's on-the-job performance or behavior.[35] Managers tend to make several mistakes when coaching employees. First, they wait for a problem to arise before coaching. Jim Concelman, manager for leadership development at Development Dimensions International, says, "Of course, a boss has to coach an employee if a mistake has been made, but they shouldn't be waiting for the error. While it is a lot easier to see a mistake and correct it, people learn more through success than through failure, so bosses should ensure that employees are experiencing as many successes as possible. Successful employees lead to a more successful organization."[36] Second, when mistakes *are* made, managers wait much too long before talking to the employee about the problem. Management professor Ray Hilgert says, "A manager must respond as soon as possible after an incident of poor performance. Don't bury your head. … When employees are told nothing, they assume everything is okay."[37] Jack Welch, who was CEO at GE for two decades, says, "I've spoken to more than 500,000 people around the world and I always ask audiences, 'How many of you know where you stand in your organization?'" He says, "Typically no more than 10% raise their hands. That's criminal! As a manager, you owe candor to your people. They must not be guessing about what the organization thinks of them. My experience is that most employees appreciate this reality check, and today's 'Millenials' practically demand it."[38] In short, says Welch, "You have no right to be a leader if someone who works for you doesn't know where they stand."[39] So coach your employees about their job performance.

In contrast to coaching, **counseling** is communicating with someone about non-job-related issues such as stress, child care, health issues, retirement planning, or legal issues that may be affecting or interfering with the person's performance. But counseling does not mean that managers should try to be clinicians, even though an estimated 20 percent of employees are dealing with personal problems at any one time. Dana Kiel, who works for Cigna Behavioral Health, says, "We call it the quicksand. If you're a good supervisor, you do care about your employees, but it's not your job to be a therapist."[40] Instead, managers should discuss specific performance problems, listen if the employee chooses to share personal issues, and then recommend that the employee call the company's *Employee Assistance Program (EAP)*. EAPs are typically free when provided as part of a company's benefit package. In emergencies or times of crisis, EAPs can offer immediate counseling and support; they can also provide referrals to organizations and professionals that can help employees and their family members address personal issues. Apparel maker Levi Strauss, for example, established an EAP called HIV Connect, which aims to improve employees' access to HIV/AIDS education, testing, treatment, and care. Paurvi Bhatt, senior director of strategic health initiatives and the employee HIV/AIDS program at Levi Strauss, says, "How we make [HIV] relevant is [by] understanding the importance of prevention and how it affects people at work. Addressing HIV isn't just addressing the health side, but learning how to manage the issue at work. This, like a lot of issues, can affect teamwork and collaboration." HIV Connect is a part of Levi Strauss's larger EAP program.[41]

15-2e Nonverbal Communication

Nonverbal communication is any communication that doesn't involve words. Nonverbal communication almost always accompanies verbal communication and may either support and reinforce the verbal message

Coaching communicating with someone for the direct purpose of improving the person's on-the-job performance or behavior

Counseling communicating with someone about non-job-related issues that may be affecting or interfering with the person's performance

Nonverbal communication any communication that doesn't involve words

or contradict it. The importance of nonverbal communication is well established. Researchers have estimated that as much as 93 percent of any message is transmitted nonverbally, with 55 percent coming from body language and facial expressions and 38 percent coming from the tone and pitch of the voice.[42] Since many nonverbal cues are unintentional, receivers often consider nonverbal communication to be a more accurate representation of what senders are thinking and feeling than the words they use. If you have ever asked someone out on a date and been told "yes," but realized that the real answer was "no," then you understand the importance of paying attention to nonverbal communication.

Kinesics and paralanguage are two kinds of nonverbal communication.[43] **Kinesics** (from the Greek word *kinesis*, meaning "movement") are movements of the body and face.[44] These movements include arm and hand gestures, facial expressions, eye contact, folding arms, crossing legs, and leaning toward or away from another person. For example, people tend to avoid eye contact when they are embarrassed or unsure of the message they are sending. Crossed arms or legs usually indicate defensiveness or that the person is not receptive to the message or the sender. Also, people tend to smile frequently when they are seeking someone's approval.

It turns out that kinesics play an incredibly important role in communication. Studies of married couples' kinesic interactions can predict whether they will stay married with 93 percent accuracy.[45] The key is the ratio of positive to negative kinesic interactions between husbands and wives as they communicate. Negative kinesic expressions such as eye rolling suggest contempt, whereas positive kinesic expressions such as maintaining eye contact and nodding suggest listening and caring. When the ratio of positive to negative interactions drops below 5 to 1, the chances for divorce quickly increase. Kinesics operate similarly in the workplace, providing clues about people's true feelings, over and above what they say (or don't say). Unfortunately, not making or maintaining eye contact is an increasingly frequent occurrence in today's workplace. To form positive connections when speaking to others, you should maintain eye contact 60 to 70 percent of the time. But, because of habit, insecurities, or perhaps smartphones and tablets, most of us do so only 30 to 60 percent of the time. Consultant Suzanne Bates, author of "Speak Like a CEO," says that some of her CEO clients check their phones so much during appointments that, "it's the equivalent of not showing up for half of the meeting." And that, she says, breeds resentment in others who think, "I'm just as busy as the CEO. I just have different things to juggle."[46]

Paralanguage includes the pitch, rate, tone, volume, and speaking pattern (use of silences, pauses, or hesitations) of one's voice. When people are unsure of what to say, for example, they tend to decrease their communication effectiveness by speaking softly. When people are nervous, they tend to speak faster and louder. How much does paralanguage matter? A study in which 1,000 people listened to 120 different speeches found that the tone of the speaker's voice accounted for 23 percent of the difference in listener's evaluations of the speech, compared to speech content, which accounted for only 11 percent.[47] So paralanguage was twice as important as what was actually said.

In short, because nonverbal communication is so informative, especially when it contradicts verbal communication, managers need to learn how to monitor and control their nonverbal behaviors.

15-3 MANAGING ONE-ON-ONE COMMUNICATION

When it comes to improving communication, managers face two primary tasks, managing one-on-one communication and managing organization-wide communication.

On average, first-line managers spend 57 percent of their time with people, middle managers spend

Kinesics movements of the body and face

Paralanguage the pitch, rate, tone, volume, and speaking pattern (i.e., use of silences, pauses, or hesitations) of one's voice

63 percent of their time directly with people, and top managers spend as much as 78 percent of their time dealing with people.[48] These numbers make it clear that managers spend a great deal of time in one-on-one communication with others.

*Let's learn more about managing one-on-one communication by reading how to **15-3a choose the right communication medium, 15-3b be a good listener,** and **15-3c give effective feedback.***

15-3a Choosing the Right Communication Medium

Sometimes messages are poorly communicated simply because they are delivered using the wrong **communication medium,** which is the method used to deliver a message. For example, the wrong communication medium is being used when an employee returns from lunch, picks up the note left on her office chair, and learns she has been fired. The wrong communication medium is also being used when an employee pops into your office every ten minutes with a simple request. (An email would be better.)

There are two general kinds of communication media: oral and written communication. *Oral communication* includes face-to-face interactions and group meetings through telephone calls, videoconferencing, or any other means of sending and receiving spoken messages. Studies show that managers generally prefer oral communication over written because it provides the opportunity to ask questions about parts of the message that they don't understand. Oral communication is also a rich communication medium because it allows managers to receive and assess the nonverbal communication that accompanies spoken messages (i.e., body language, facial expressions, and the voice characteristics associated with paralanguage).

Furthermore, you don't need a personal computer and an Internet connection to conduct oral communication. Simply schedule an appointment, track someone down in the hall, or catch someone on the phone. In fact, *Wall Street Journal* columnist Jason Fry worries that voice mail and email have made managers less willing to engage in meaningful, face-to-face oral communication than before. In fact, 67 percent of managers admit to using email as a substitute for face-to-face conversations. While there are advantages to email (e.g., it creates a record of what's been said), it's often better to talk to people instead of just emailing them. Fry writes, "If you're close enough that the person you're emailing uses the plonk of your return key as a cue to look for the little Outlook envelope, [it's] best [to] think carefully about whether you should be typing instead of talking."[49] But the oral medium should not be used for *all* communication. In general, when the message is simple, such as a quick request or a presentation of straightforward information, a memo or email is often the better communication medium.

Written communication includes letters, email, and memos. Although most managers still like and use oral communication, email in particular is changing how they communicate with workers, customers, and each other. Email is the fastest-growing form of communication in organizations primarily because of its convenience and speed. For instance, because people read six times faster than they can listen, they usually can read thirty email messages in ten to fifteen minutes.[50] By contrast, dealing with voice messages can take a considerable amount of time.

Written communication such as email is well suited for delivering straightforward messages and information. Furthermore, with email accessible at the office, at home, and on the road (by laptop computer, cell phone, or web-based email), managers can use email to stay in touch from anywhere at almost any time. And, since email and other written communications don't have to be sent and received simultaneously, messages can be sent and stored for reading at any time. Consequently, managers can send and receive many more messages using email than by using oral communication, which requires people to get together in person or by phone or videoconference.

Email has its own drawbacks, however. One is that it lacks the formality of paper memos and letters. It is easy to fire off a rushed email that is not well written or fully thought through. Another drawback to email is that it lacks nonverbal cues, making emails very easy to misinterpret. Kristin Byron, assistant professor of management at Syracuse University, says, "People perceive emails as more negative than they are intended to be, and even emails that are intended to be positive can be misinterpreted as more neutral. You get an email that's really short, with no greeting, no closing; it's probably because they were very rushed, or maybe they're not very good typists. But because of those things, people have a tendency to perceive the message as negative."[51]

Although written communication is well suited for delivering straightforward messages and information, it is not well suited to complex, ambiguous, or emotionally laden messages, which are better delivered through oral communication.

Communication medium the method used to deliver an oral or written message

15-3b Listening

Are you a good listener? You probably think so. In fact, most people, including managers, are terrible listeners. Indeed, a recent study from Stanford Graduate School of Business showed that listening was among the least mentioned strengths in CEO performance evaluations.[52] You qualify as a poor listener if you frequently interrupt others, jump to conclusions about what people will say before they've said it, hurry the speaker to finish his or her point, are a passive listener (not actively working at your listening), or simply don't pay attention to what people are saying.[53] On this last point—attentiveness—college students were periodically asked to record their thoughts during a psychology course. On average, 20 percent of the students were paying attention (only 12 percent were actively working at being good listeners), 20 percent were thinking about sex, 20 percent were thinking about things they had done before, and the remaining 40 percent were thinking about other things unrelated to the class (e.g., worries, religion, lunch, daydreaming).[54]

How important is it to be a good listener? In general, about 45 percent of the total time you spend communicating with others is spent listening. Furthermore, listening is important for managerial and business success, even for those at the top of an organization. Bill Marriott, executive chairman of Marriott International hotels, says, "The most important thing a successful executive can do—is to listen and learn." Marriott learned the importance of listening when U.S.

President Dwight D. Eisenhower visited the Marriott family farm. It was a cold day, and the president was trying to decide whether to go hunting. Marriott, then a teenager, explains, "I was standing off in the corner, hiding, and the president looked at me and said, 'What do you want to do, Bill? What do you think we should do?' And I've never forgotten that. No wonder he could deal with [Generals] Montgomery and Patton and all those people he dealt with in the Second World War." He "made them feel important. He showed respect for them. He showed interest in what their beliefs were, and he asked that very important question: 'What do you think?'"[55]

Listening is a more important skill for managers than ever, since Generation X and Millennial employees tend to expect a high level of interaction with their supervisors. They want feedback on their performance, but they also want to offer feedback and know that it is heard. In fact, managers with better listening skills are rated more highly by their employees and are much more likely to be promoted.[56]

So, what can you do to improve your listening ability? First, understand the difference between hearing and listening. According to *Webster's New World Dictionary*, **hearing** is the "act or process of perceiving sounds," whereas **listening** is "making a conscious

Hearing the act or process of perceiving sounds

Listening making a conscious effort to hear

effort to hear." In other words, we react to sounds, such as bottles breaking or music being played too loud, because hearing is an involuntary physiological process. By contrast, listening is a voluntary behavior. So, if you want to be a good listener, you have to choose to be a good listener. Typically, that means choosing to be an active, empathetic listener.[57]

Active listening means assuming half the responsibility for successful communication by actively giving the speaker nonjudgmental feedback that shows you've accurately heard what he or she said. Active listeners make it clear from their behavior that they are listening carefully to what the speaker has to say. Active listeners put the speaker at ease, maintain eye contact, and show the speaker that they are attentively listening by nodding and making short statements.

Several specific strategies can help you be a better active listener. First, *clarify responses* by asking the speaker to explain confusing or ambiguous statements. Second, when there are natural breaks in the speaker's delivery, use this time to paraphrase or summarize what has been said. *Paraphrasing* is restating what has been said in your own words. *Summarizing* is reviewing the speaker's main points or emotions. Paraphrasing and summarizing give

the speaker the chance to correct the message if the active listener has attached the wrong meaning to it. Paraphrasing and summarizing also show the speaker that the active listener is interested in the speaker's message. Exhibit 15.5 lists specific statements that listeners can use to clarify responses, paraphrase, or summarize what has been said.

Active listeners also avoid evaluating the message or being critical until the message is complete. They recognize that their only responsibility during the transmission of a message is to receive it accurately and derive the intended meaning from it. Evaluation and criticism can take place after the message is accurately received. Finally, active listeners recognize that a large portion of any message is transmitted nonverbally and thus pay very careful attention to the nonverbal cues transmitted by the speaker.

Empathetic listening means understanding the speaker's perspective and personal frame of reference and giving feedback that conveys that understanding to the speaker. Empathetic listening goes beyond active listening because it depends on our ability to set aside our own attitudes or relationships to be able to see and understand things through someone else's eyes. Empathetic listening is just as important as active listening, especially for managers, because it helps build rapport and trust with others. When Cheryl Bachelder became CEO of Popeyes Louisiana Kitchen, a fast food franchise famous for its fried chicken, trust between headquarters and its 1,600 franchised restaurants was low. She says, "During the first meeting I had with franchisees, they wanted a palace coup—they wanted everyone replaced, and they didn't trust anyone. You only trust people you know, and that was the problem."[58] Bachelder improved things by listening. She says, "We started listening to them. I know that sounds simplistic, but we were at a stage where, in our quarterly meetings with franchisees, the company told them stuff and didn't listen. When we told them we wanted to remodel the restaurants, the first thing they said was, 'No, we need to get our sales up so we have cash to invest.' We were disappointed, but we waited. We showed them our first design and they hated it and thought it cost too much. We came back with a new store design

"THE MOST IMPORTANT THING A SUCCESSFUL EXECUTIVE CAN DO—IS TO LISTEN AND LEARN."
—MARRIOTT INTERNATIONAL CEO BILL MARRIOTT

AP Images/Marriott International Inc.

Exhibit 15.5

Clarifying, Paraphrasing, and Summarizing Responses for Active Listeners

Clarifying Responses	Paraphrasing Responses	Summarizing Responses
Could you explain that again?	What you're really saying is	Let me summarize . . . .
I don't understand what you mean.	If I understand you correctly	Okay, your main concerns are . . . .
I'm not sure how	In other words	To recap, what you've said . . . .
I'm confused. Would you run through that again?	So your perspective is that	Thus far, you've discussed . . . .
	Tell me if I'm wrong, but what you seem to be saying is	

Source: E. Atwater, *I Hear You*, rev. ed. (New York: Walker, 1992).

that was more cost-effective, and we built 12 new stores in New Orleans that they could go and see and touch, and we laid out all the costs. We got our sales up . . . and had a new design they loved, and they started getting excited about remodeling."[59] As a result of listening to and then addressing franchisees concerns, Popeyes will have remodeled 80 percent of its restaurants by the end of 2014.

The key to being a more empathetic listener is to show your desire to understand and to reflect people's feelings. You can *show your desire to understand* by listening, that is, asking people to talk about what's most important to them and then by giving them sufficient time to talk before responding or interrupting.

Reflecting feelings is also an important part of empathetic listening because it demonstrates that you understand the speaker's emotions. Unlike active listening, in which you restate or summarize the informational content of what has been said, the focus is on the affective part of the message. As an empathetic listener, you can use the following statements to *reflect the speaker's emotions*:

▶ So, right now it sounds like you're feeling . . . .

▶ You seem as if you're . . . .

▶ Do you feel a bit . . . ?

▶ I could be wrong, but I'm sensing that you're feeling . . . .

In the end, says management consultant Terry Pearce, empathetic listening can be boiled down to these three steps. First, wait ten seconds before you respond. It will seem an eternity, but waiting prevents you from interrupting others and rushing your response. Second, to be sure you understand what the speaker wants, ask

questions to clarify the speaker's intent. Third, only then should you respond first with feelings and then facts (notice that facts *follow* feelings).[60]

A word of caution, however: not everyone appreciates having what they said repeated back to them. Manager Candy Friesen says that whenever she did that, "I seemed to engender animosity or hostility. . . . the person to whom you're speaking may not appreciate having his thoughts paraphrased one little bit."[61] So, when applying these listening techniques, pay attention to the body language and tone of voice of the person you're communicating with to make sure they appreciate your attempts to be a better listener.

15-3c Giving Feedback

In Chapter 11, you learned that performance appraisal feedback (i.e., judging) should be separated from developmental feedback (i.e., coaching).[62] We can now focus on the steps needed to communicate feedback one-on-one to employees.

To start, managers need to recognize that feedback can be constructive or destructive. **Destructive feedback** is disapproving without any intention of being helpful and almost always causes a negative or defensive reaction in the recipient. By contrast, **constructive feedback** is intended to be helpful, corrective, and/or

Destructive feedback feedback that disapproves without any intention of being helpful and almost always causes a negative or defensive reaction in the recipient

Constructive feedback feedback intended to be helpful, corrective, and/or encouraging

encouraging. It is aimed at correcting performance deficiencies and motivating employees. Business author Tim Harford says the problem with constructive feedback is that it's given like a sandwich—something nice to start with, some constructive feedback in the middle, and then something positive at the end. Harford says, "We say [to the people we're managing], 'That was a great piece of work, there was just a small problem.'" "What we tend to hear," he says, is, "That was a great piece of work."[63]

For feedback to be constructive rather than destructive, it must be immediate, focused on specific behaviors, and problem-oriented. *Immediate feedback* is much more effective than delayed feedback because manager and worker can recall the mistake or incident more accurately and discuss it in detail. For example, if a worker is rude to a customer and the customer immediately reports the incident to management, and if the manager, in turn, immediately discusses the incident with the employee, there should be little disagreement over what was said or done. By contrast, it's unlikely that either the manager or the worker will be able to accurately remember the specifics of what occurred if the manager waits several weeks to discuss the incident. When that happens, it's usually too late to have a meaningful conversation.

Specific feedback focuses on particular acts or incidents that are clearly under the control of the employee. For instance, instead of telling an employee that he or she is "always late for work," it's much more constructive to say, "In the last three weeks, you have been thirty minutes late on four occasions and more than an hour late on two others." Furthermore, specific feedback isn't very helpful unless employees have control over the problems that

the feedback addresses. Giving negative feedback about behaviors beyond someone's control is likely to be seen as unfair. Similarly, giving positive feedback about behaviors beyond someone's control may be viewed as insincere.

Last, *problem-oriented feedback* focuses on the problems or incidents associated with the poor performance rather than on the worker or the worker's personality. Giving feedback does not give managers the right to personally attack workers. Although managers may be frustrated by a worker's poor performance, the point of problem-oriented feedback is to draw attention to the problem in a nonjudgmental way so that the employee has enough information to correct it. For example, if an employee has body odor, a surprisingly common workplace problem, don't leave deodorant, soap, or shampoo on the person's desk (for all to see) or say, "You stink." *HR Magazine* advises handling the problem this way: "Because this is a sensitive issue and the employee will likely be uncomfortable and embarrassed in discussing it, keep the meeting private and confidential. Be compassionate but direct. Treat it as you would handle any other job-related performance issue. Explain the problem and the need to correct it. Be specific about expectations. . . . If the employer has a dress and grooming policy, refer to the policy and provide the employee with a copy."[64]

15-4 MANAGING ORGANIZATION-WIDE COMMUNICATION

Although managing one-on-one communication is important, managers must also know how to communicate effectively with a larger number of people throughout an organization.

*Learn more about organization-wide communication by reading the following sections about **15-4a improving transmission by getting the message out** and **15-4b improving reception by finding ways to hear what others feel and think**.*

15-4a Improving Transmission: Getting the Message Out

Several methods of electronic communication—email, collaborative discussion sites, televised/videotaped speeches and conferences, and broadcast voice mail—now make it easier for managers to communicate with people throughout the organization and get the message out.

Although we normally think of email, the transmission of messages via computers, as a means of one-on-one communication, it also plays an important role in organization-wide communication. With the click of a button, managers can send an email to everyone in the company via distribution lists. When Microsoft announced it would be laying off 18,000 employees, 14 percent of its workforce, CEO Satya Nadella announced the news in a speech to Microsoft employees, accompanied by a long, detailed email, in which he said, "Nothing is off the table in how we think about shifting our culture to deliver on this core strategy [to become a mobile-first, cloud-first company]. Organizations will change. Mergers and acquisitions will occur. Job responsibilities will evolve. New partnerships will be formed. Tired traditions will be questioned. Our priorities will be adjusted. New skills will be built. New ideas will be heard. New hires will be made. Processes will be simplified. And if you want to thrive at Microsoft and make a world impact, you and your team must add numerous more changes to this list that you will be enthusiastic about driving."[65] He finished by saying, "Culture change means we will do things differently. Often people think that means everyone other than them. In reality, it means all of us taking a new approach and working together to make Microsoft better."[66]

Collaborative websites are another means of electronically promoting organization-wide communication. **Online discussion forums** use web- or software-based discussion tools to allow employees across the company to easily ask questions and share knowledge with each other. The point is to share expertise and not duplicate solutions already discovered by others in the company. Furthermore, because collaborative discussion sites remain online, they provide a historical database for people who are dealing with particular problems for the first time.

Collaborative discussion sites are typically organized by topic, project, or person and can take the shape of blogs that allow readers to post comments, wikis to allow collaborative discussions, document sharing and editing, or traditional discussion forums (see Chapter 17 on managing information for further explanation). Red Hat is the leading provider of Linux operating systems. CEO and president Jim Whitehurst says, "Your most creative ideas are going to come from people on the front lines who see a different way of doing the jobs they do every day. You have to create vehicles for those ideas to be heard. So the question is, how do you make that happen? How do you engage your employees?" One way in which Red Hat does that is through an internal collaborative discussion site called the Memo List. Says Whitehurst, "We have about 4,000 employees, but on average you'll see a couple hundred posts a day. And I go through it every single day. I would say probably three-quarters of the people are on it every day, either reading or posting." What's the value of the Memo List to Red Hat? Whitehurst argues, "Engaging people in how decisions are getting made means it can take forever to get decisions made. But once you make a decision, you get flawless execution because everybody's engaged. They know what you're doing and they know why you're doing it."[67]

Exhibit 15.6 lists the steps companies need to take to establish successful collaborative discussion sites. First, pinpoint your company's top intellectual assets through a knowledge audit and spread that knowledge throughout the organization. Second, create an online directory detailing the expertise of individual workers and make it available to all employees. Third, set up collaborative discussion sites on the intranet so that managers and workers can collaborate on problem solving. Finally, reward information sharing by making the online sharing of knowledge a key part of performance ratings.

Televised/videotaped speeches and meetings are a third electronic method of organization-wide communication. **Televised/videotaped speeches and meetings** are simply speeches and meetings originally made to a small audience that are either simultaneously broadcast to other locations in the company or videotaped for subsequent distribution and viewing by a broader audience.

Voice messaging, or voice mail, is a telephone answering system that records audio messages. In one

---

Online discussion forums the in-house equivalent of Internet newsgroups. By using web- or software-based discussion tools that are available across the company, employees can easily ask questions and share knowledge with each other

Televised/videotaped speeches and meetings speeches and meetings originally made to a smaller audience that are either simultaneously broadcast to other locations in the company or videotaped for subsequent distribution and viewing

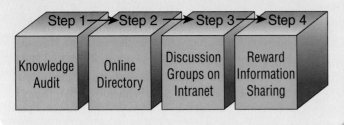

Exhibit 15.6
Establishing Collaborative Discussion Sites

Step 1 → Step 2 → Step 3 → Step 4

| Knowledge Audit | Online Directory | Discussion Groups on Intranet | Reward Information Sharing |

survey, 89 percent of respondents said that voice messaging is critical to business communication, 78 percent said that it improves productivity, and 58 percent said they would rather leave a message on a voice messaging system than with a receptionist.[68] Nonetheless, most people are unfamiliar with the ability to *broadcast voice mail* by sending a recorded message to everyone in the company. Broadcast voice mail gives top managers a quick, convenient way to address their work forces via oral communication—but only if people actually listen to the message, and that turns out to be a challenge with today's workers, who are much more likely to use their smartphones for social media rather than phone calls. Consequently, company leaders are increasingly using tools like Yammer, a Facebook-like social media platform for companies, or Lync, a version of Skype for companies, to broadcast text or video-based messages to their workforces. Ryan Holmes, CEO of HootSuite, a social media measurement and monitoring system for companies, says, "I believe that social media is the new water cooler, in the sense that more and more people are talking, sharing stories, and generally bonding through social channels like Facebook and Twitter. In this way, social media is like an ongoing team building exercise. When C-Suite members join that conversation, they become more in touch with their employees and only then can they use those channels to drive internal engagement."[69]

Organizational silence when employees withhold information about organizational problems or issues

Company hotlines phone numbers that anyone in the company can call anonymously to leave information for upper management

15-4b Improving Reception: Hearing What Others Feel and Think

When people think of "organization-wide" communication, they think of the CEO and top managers getting their message out to people in the company. But organization-wide communication also means finding ways to hear what people throughout the organization are thinking and feeling. This is important because most employees and managers are reluctant to share their thoughts and feelings with top managers. Surveys indicate that only 29 percent of first-level managers feel that their companies encourage employees to express their opinions openly. Another study of twenty-two companies found that 70 percent of the people surveyed were afraid to speak up about problems they knew existed at work.

Withholding information about organizational problems or issues is called **organizational silence.** Organizational silence occurs when employees believe that telling management about problems won't make a difference or that they'll be punished or hurt in some way for sharing such information.[70] A survey of executives found that 85 percent had at some point kept quiet when they saw a serious problem at work.[71] At Jetstar Airways, an Australia-based airline, pilots were afraid to speak up about fatigue from flying too many hours. Captain Richard Woodward, vice president of the Australian and International Pilots Association, said that his organization had received dozens of complaints from Jetstar pilots, but that the pilots were afraid to complain to Jetstar management because "there was a culture of fear and intimidation at that airline."[72] One pilot scheduler told his pilots, "Toughen up princesses! You aren't fatigued, you are tired and can't be bothered to go into work." A report from Australia's Civil Aviation Safety Authority concluded, "There remains reluctance from a number of flight crew to report fatigue risk and/or to say no to an extension of duty based on the perceived punitive nature of taking such actions."[73]

Company hotlines, survey feedback, frequent informal meetings, surprise visits, and blogs are additional ways of overcoming organizational silence. **Company hotlines** are phone numbers that anyone in the company can call anonymously to leave information for upper management. Company hotlines are incredibly useful, as 47 percent of the calls placed to them result in an investigation and some form of corrective action

Google™ | Official Blog

Insights from Googlers into our products, technology and the Google culture

Search

Introducing the Knowledge Graph: things, not strings

May 16, 2012 at 1:00 PM

g +1 695

Cross-posted on the Inside Search Blog

Search is a lot about discovery—the basic human need to learn and broaden your horizons. But searching still requires a lot of hard work by you, the user. So today I'm really excited to launch the Knowledge Graph, which will help you discover new information quickly and easily.

Take a query like [taj mahal]. For more than four decades, search has essentially been about matching keywords to queries. To a search engine the words [taj mahal] have been just that—two words.

But we all know that [taj mahal] has a much richer meaning. You might think of one of the world's most beautiful monuments, or a Grammy Award-winning musician, or possibly even a casino in Atlantic City, NJ. Or, depending on when you last ate, the nearest Indian restaurant. It's why we've been working on an intelligent model—in geek-speak, a "graph"—that understands real-world entities and their relationships to one another: things, not strings.

The Knowledge Graph enables you to search for things, people or places that Google knows about—landmarks, celebrities, cities, sports teams, buildings, geographical features, movies, celestial objects, works of art and more—and instantly get information that's relevant to your query. This is a critical first step towards building the next generation of search, which taps into the collective intelligence of the web and understands the world a bit more like people do.

Google's Knowledge Graph isn't just rooted in public sources such as Freebase, Wikipedia and the CIA World Factbook. It's also augmented at a much larger scale—because we're focused on comprehensive breadth and depth. It currently contains more than 500 million objects, as well as more than 3.5 billion facts about and relationships between these different objects. And it's tuned based on what people search for, and what we find out on the web.

The Knowledge Graph enhances Google Search in three main ways to start:

1. Find the right thing

Language can be ambiguous—do you mean Taj Mahal the monument, or Taj Mahal

Connect with us
Subscribe to this blog:

FeedBurner

RSS Feed

Browse all of Google's blogs for specific interests & topics:

Blog Directory

Follow Google alerts and news on Twitter:

@Google

We'd love to hear your feedback — discuss Google's products with others:

Product Forums

Follow

More blogs from Google

© Google

A corporate blog is an effective way of overcoming organizational silence.

within the organization. Anonymity is critical, too, because as those investigations proceeded, 54 percent of the callers did not want their identities revealed.[74]

Survey feedback is information that is collected by survey from organization members and then compiled, disseminated, and used to develop action plans for improvement. Many organizations make use of survey feedback by surveying their managers and employees several times a year. **Wolfchase Toyota-Scion** in Cordova,

Tennessee, which has been recognized as one of the best car dealerships to work for, conducts an employee survey once a year, which it combines with employee feedback lunches two times a year. General Manager Tyler Heard

Survey feedback information that is collected by surveys from organizational members and then compiled, disseminated, and used to develop action plans for improvement

Having Trouble Making Your Point? Tell a Story

Even with the wide range of electronic tools available for sending messages and presenting information, many managers still have trouble communicating their ideas to colleagues, bosses, and clients. Often, the problem is in the data. People tend to believe that data is persuasive, but for many, data by itself is not enough to get attention or captivate—much less inspire. According to communication consultant Cliff Atkinson, narratives that connect with listeners are more memorable than raw data. Atkinson says, "You have to step back and put yourself into their shoes and take them through the process of understanding." Atkinson suggests presenting the story in a way that makes an emotional connection with the listener. For example, a single mother's story about the trade-offs she had to make to support her children convinced Procter & Gamble executives to lower the company's prices on shortening. Atkinson also suggests presenting your story in three parts. First, establish the conflict and main characters. Second, show how the characters fight to resolve the conflict. Finally, present your listeners with a call to action.

Source: D. Nishi, "To Persuade People, Tell Them a Story," *Wall Street Journal*, November 9, 2013, accessed May 21, 2014, http://online.wsj.com/news/articles/SB10001424052702303482504579177651982683162?KEYWORDS=to+persuade+people&mg=reno64-wsj.

says, "The whole point is to get feedback from our employees on ways to improve business practices and increase employee satisfaction." For example, the workers who clean and detail cars before they're put on the lot and delivered to customers complained that poor lighting was making it difficult to do their jobs well. Likewise, service technicians complained that shadows from poor lighting made it difficult to see what they were doing under car hoods. As a result of employee feedback from their annual survey, Heard spent several thousand dollars per work bay to improve the lighting.[75]

Frequent *informal meetings* between top managers and lower-level employees are one of the best ways for top managers to hear what others think and feel. Many people assume that top managers are at the center of everything that goes on in organizations, but top managers commonly feel isolated from most of their lower-level managers and employees.[76] Consequently, more and more top managers are scheduling frequent informal meetings with people throughout their companies.

Mazor Robotics, an Israeli-based medical technology company, has facilities in the United States, Asia, and Europe. With employees scattered worldwide, maintaining good communication is critical. CEO Ori Hadomi says, "I think that the most constructive and the most productive way to communicate is informal communication."

So once a week he has a joint one-hour phone call with people in all of the offices. With no set agenda, employees take turns explaining what is going on in their division, what was accomplished in the past few days, and what kind of issues are coming up in the near future. Says Hadomi, "So in one hour, everyone is synchronized. And when I talk with many of the employees I hear that it's a very important meeting for them because it gives them the opportunity to hear about the business."[77]

Have you ever been around when a supervisor learns that upper management is going to be paying a visit? First, there's shock. Next, there's anxiety. And then there's panic, as everyone is told to drop what he or she is doing to polish, shine, and spruce up the workplace so that it looks perfect for the visit. Of course, when visits are conducted under these conditions, top managers don't get a realistic look at what's going on in the company. Consequently, one of the ways to get an accurate picture is to pay *surprise visits* to various parts of the organization. These visits should not just be surprise inspections but should also be used as opportunities to encourage meaningful upward communication from those who normally don't get a chance to communicate with upper management.

Blogs are another way to hear what people are thinking and saying, both inside and outside the organization.

A **blog** is a personal website that provides personal opinions or recommendations, news summaries, and reader comments. When the recession hit, **GTE Financial**, a Florida-based credit union with twenty-one locations, saw its assets shrink from $2.2 billion to $1.5 billion and had to lay off 245 of its 690 employees. When new CEO Joe Brancucci came on board, he reduced check and ATM fees that were frustrating customers, reduced bad loans from 4.06 percent to 3.58 percent, and, after cutting employees' pay, created pay incentives linked to growth in loans and new members. But, from a communication standpoint, the most important thing he did was start an internal blog to which he posted updates to all of GTE's employees. Brancucci says he never "sugar coated anything. I talked about what we were going through, the situations we faced, why we faced them, and why we were making changes." Now quarterly financial statements are posted on the blog. "Our membership knows exactly what's going on. We don't hide anything," adds Brancucci.[78]

External blogs and *Twitter sites* (micro blogs where entries are limited to 140 characters) written by people outside the company can be a good way to find out what others are saying or thinking about your organization or its products or actions. But keeping up with these communication media requires someone in the firm to actively monitor what is being said on web, blog, and Twitter sites. At its Texas headquarters, Dell operates a Social Media Listening Command Center, where staff members track what is being said about Dell on a variety of social media sites like Facebook, Twitter, and YouTube, as well as blogs. When they see that a Dell customer posts a problem with a Dell product, they quickly contact the customer and take steps to address the issue. Nearly two-thirds of Dell consumers contacted through the Social Media Listening Command Center report positive service experiences.

Manish Mehta, Dell's then–vice president for social media and community, says, "Customers were thrilled and elated that Dell was reaching out to them. It changed their perception of the company."[79]

> **Blog** a personal website that provides personal opinions or recommendations, news summaries, and reader comments

STUDY TOOLS 15

LOCATED AT THE BACK OF YOUR BOOK:

☐ Rip out and study the Chapter Review Card at the end of the book

LOG IN TO WWW.CENGAGEBRAIN.COM TO:

☐ Review Key Term Flashcards

☐ Complete Practice Quizzing (take up to four times without repeating the same quiz)

☐ Complete Games: Beat the Clock and Crossword Puzzle

☐ Complete Interactive Content: Graded Quiz, Media Quiz, and Fill-in-the-Blank Questions

☐ Watch Management Workplace Video on "Plant Fantasies"

☐ Work Through the What Would You Do Case on Google Headquarters

16 Control

Skynesher/iStockphoto.com

LEARNING OUTCOMES

16-1 Describe the basic control process.

16-2 Discuss the various methods that managers can use to maintain control.

16-3 Describe the behaviors, processes, and outcomes that today's managers are choosing to control in their organizations.

After you finish this chapter, go to **PAGE 351** for **STUDY TOOLS**

THE CONTROL PROCESS

For all companies, past success is no guarantee of future success. Even successful companies fall short or face challenges and thus have to make changes. **Control** is a regulatory process of establishing standards to achieve organizational goals, comparing actual performance to the standards, and taking corrective action when necessary to restore performance to those standards. Control is achieved when behavior and work procedures conform to standards and when company goals are accomplished.[1] Control is not just an after-the-fact process, however. Preventive measures are also a form of control.

The French Open grand slam tennis tournament at Roland Garros Stadium in Paris uses birds of prey, specifically raptors, to prevent—and thus control—pigeon problems, such as pigeon droppings and play interrupted by pigeons landing on the courts. With nearly 430,000 people in attendance during the two-week tournament, Roland Garros is the equivalent of a Parisian corner cafe for pigeons thanks to all the food served and thrown away. But with raptors circling the skies, "It creates a sense of danger for the pigeons and they won't dare to land," says Raptor trainer Ludwig Verschatse.[2] While the raptors can't be airborne when crowds are in attendance during the day, they circle high over Roland Garros each morning before play starts and in the evening as play ends for the day. To avoid protests from animal rights groups, the raptors are fed 10 percent of their body weight each day so they aren't tempted to catch and eat the pigeons. Similar prevention or control strategies are used at the Australian Open, which uses eagles, and at Wimbledon, which uses a hawk named Rufus.

*The basic control process **16-1a begins with the establishment of clear standards of performance; 16-1b involves a comparison of performance to those standards; 16-1c takes corrective action, if needed, to repair performance deficiencies; 16-1d is a dynamic, cybernetic process; and 16-1e consists of three basic methods: feedback control, concurrent control, and feedforward control.** However, as much as managers would like, **16-1f control isn't always worthwhile or possible.***

16-1a Standards

The control process begins when managers set goals such as satisfying 90 percent of customers or increasing sales by 5 percent. Companies then specify the performance standards that must be met to accomplish those goals. **Standards** are a basis of comparison for measuring the extent to which organizational performance is satisfactory or unsatisfactory. For example, many pizzerias use thirty to forty minutes as the standard for delivery time. Since anything longer is viewed as unsatisfactory, they'll typically reduce the price if they can't deliver a hot pizza to you within that time period.

So how do managers set standards? How do they decide which levels of performance are satisfactory and which are unsatisfactory? The first criterion for a good standard is that it must enable goal achievement. If you're meeting the standard but still not achieving company goals, then the standard may have to be changed. Apple's iPhone 5 has an aluminum body crafted to be stronger, lighter, thinner, and more stylish than previous models. However, after only a few days of light use, the back and sides of the phone can end up scratched or dented. Even worse, early customers reported finding scratches on brand-new phones right out of the box. Apple responded by asking its iPhone manufacturer, Foxconn, to implement stricter quality-control standards in the manufacture and handling of iPhone 5s in its factories, as well as more rigorous inspections so that iPhones with scratches do not get shipped to customers.[3]

Companies also determine standards by listening to

Mutlu Kurtbas/iStockphoto.com

Control a regulatory process of establishing standards to achieve organizational goals, comparing actual performance against the standards, and taking corrective action when necessary

Standards a basis of comparison for measuring the extent to which various kinds of organizational performance are satisfactory or unsatisfactory

customers' comments, complaints, and suggestions or by observing competitors. Sarah Beatty started Green Depot, which sells environmentally responsible construction materials, because "greenwashing"—representing products as green when they're not—was widespread among competitors. Beatty hired engineers to help Green Depot develop CLEAR standards, for **C**onservation (recycled, reclaimed, reused, or rapidly renewable resources), **L**ocal (low-carbon footprint), **E**nergy (energy-conserving or renewable resources), **A**ir quality (nontoxic, nonallergenic, or no gases or particulates), and **R**esponsibility (green jobs, worker protection, and truthful marketing). When the standards were developed, Beatty and her team sent out ten-page questionnaires to manufacturers, asking for detailed explanations regarding product production and materials. Each product is measured on each of the five standards. If a standard has been met, Green Depot displays an icon for that standard on the product's page on GreenDepot.com. As Green Depot's website explains, "Our Green Depot Icon System is designed to show at a glance why we call a particular item green."[4]

Standards can also be determined by benchmarking other companies. **Benchmarking** is the process of determining how well other companies (though not just competitors) perform business functions or tasks. In other words, benchmarking is the process of determining other companies' standards. When setting

Benchmarking the process of identifying outstanding practices, processes, and standards in other companies and adapting them to your company

standards by benchmarking, the first step is to determine what to benchmark. Companies can benchmark anything from cycle time (how fast) to quality (how well) to price (how much). For example, based on national benchmarking studies of thousands of fire departments, many firefighters are expected to respond to an alarm within fifteen seconds 95 percent of the time. Additionally, 90 percent of the time it should take no more than sixty seconds to leave the firehouse, and then no more than four minutes to arrive at the scene.[5]

After setting standards, the next step is to identify the companies *against which* to benchmark those standards. The last step is to collect data to determine other companies' performance standards. Intuit, maker of financial software and Web sites such as QuickBooks, Intuit Payroll, and Turbotax, gets nearly 40 percent of its revenues by selling its products and services to tens of thousands of small- to medium-sized businesses in different industries. Fred Shilmover, CEO of InsightSquared, which sells data-analytic tools to those businesses, says, "Intuit figured out how to leverage its internal data team for their customers, when those companies couldn't gather enough data on their own to understand the bigger [industry and business] trends."[6] And because Intuit also sells add-on products and services to help manage payroll, inventory, financing, customers, point of sale trends, and online/social media marketing, he says those businesses "Can now benchmark their costs [and organizational performance in all of those areas] against each other." This benchmarking shows them whether they perform at, above, or below thousands of other companies on a number of critical dimensions.

16-1b Comparison to Standards

The next step in the control process is to compare actual performance to performance standards. Although this sounds straightforward, the quality of the comparison depends largely on the measurement and information systems a company uses to keep track of performance. The better the system, the easier it is for companies to track their progress and identify problems that need to be fixed.

On average, 5 percent of hospital patients catch an infection at the hospital. It costs an average of $15,000 per incident to treat such infections, and 100,000 patients will die each year from them. Why? Because in most hospitals, health care workers wash their hands only 50 percent of the time before examining or touching a patient. Because of the risks, the Center for Disease Control created a video, "Hand Hygiene Saves Lives," to be shown to patients admitted to hospitals. In the video, a patient's wife asks her husband's doctor, on entering the hospital room, to wash his hands before beginning the medical exam.[7]

So, how can a hospital measure the rate at which its employees wash their hands so it can compare the actual rate of hand washing to its goal for hand washing? Some hospitals measure how much soap and alcohol are used in each hospital area. Of course, that's not very accurate. By contrast, at North Shore University Hospital in Manhasset, New York, cameras in the ceiling pointing toward sinks and hand sanitizer dispensers are activated by an electronic door monitor each time someone enters a room. Employees then have ten seconds to wash their hands. Arrowsight Medical, which runs the monitoring system, calculates hand washing rates by having employees in India observe video snippets to determine whether hands were washed or not. Unfortunately, using this video system, North Shore found out that intensive care unit (ICU) workers were washing their hands only an abysmally low 6.5 percent of the time![8]

16-1c Corrective Action

The next step in the control process is to identify performance deviations, analyze those deviations, and then develop and implement programs to correct them. This is similar to the planning process discussed in Chapter 5. Regular, frequent performance feedback allows workers and managers to track their performance and make adjustments in effort, direction, and strategies.

After discovering that its ICU staff were washing their hands only 6.5 percent of the time, North Shore University Hospital decided that frequent feedback was the best way to change its health care workers' hand washing behavior. So, it provided feedback in two ways. First, an LED display by the nurses' station shows that shift's hand washing percentage and an evaluation, such as "Great Shift!!" Second, the nursing shift manager receives an email with the shift's hand washing rates three hours into the shift and then again at the shift's conclusion. Since this system was installed, hand washing rates at North Shore's ICU have risen from 6.5 percent to 81 percent.[9]

16-1d Dynamic, Cybernetic Process

As shown in Exhibit 16.1, control is a continuous, dynamic, cybernetic process. Control begins by setting standards, measuring performance, and then comparing performance to the standards. If the performance deviates from the standards, then managers and

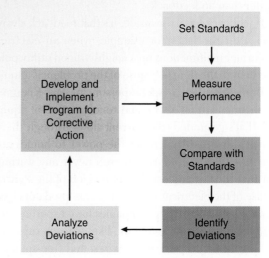

Exhibit 16.1
Cybernetic Control Process

Source: From *Business Horizons*, June 1972, H. Koontz and R. W. Bradspies, "Managing through Feedforward Control: A Future Directed View," pp. 25–36.

employees analyze the deviations and develop and implement corrective programs that (they hope) achieve the desired performance by meeting the standards. Managers must repeat the entire process again and again in an endless feedback loop (a continuous process). Thus, control is not a one-time achievement or result. It continues over time (i.e., it is dynamic) and requires daily, weekly, and monthly attention from managers to maintain performance levels at the standard (i.e., it is cybernetic). **Cybernetic** derives from the Greek word *kubernetes*, meaning "steersman," that is, one who steers or keeps on course.[10] The control process shown in Exhibit 16.1 is cybernetic because constant attention to the feedback loop is necessary to keep the company's activity on course.

16-1e Feedback, Concurrent, and Feedforward Control

The three basic control methods are feedback control, concurrent control, and feedforward control. **Feedback control** is a mechanism for gathering information about performance deficiencies *after* they occur.

Cybernetic the process of steering or keeping on course

Feedback control a mechanism for gathering information about performance deficiencies after they occur

This information is then used to correct or prevent performance deficiencies. Study after study has clearly shown that feedback improves both individual and organizational performance. In most instances, any feedback is better than no feedback.

If feedback has a downside, it's that feedback always comes after the fact. For example, when an electrical transformer malfunctions on a neighborhood utility pole, 90 percent of the time the cause of the problem is a squirrel. Brian Manthey, a spokesperson for We Energies, says, "If they are on a wire and touch a piece of equipment that's grounded, the current flows through them. They're killed and sometimes the power to homes and businesses goes out."[11] And, there's never any warning until after the fact and usually nothing left of the squirrel because of the electrical surge or because predators have taken the remains. Utility companies have experimented with a wide range of solutions, like arrester caps and brushing covers to protect the wires, and free-spinning baffles that make squirrels fall off the wires. But a foolproof method has yet to be invented.[12] The city of Austin, Texas, estimates that squirrels cause 300 power outages a year. Squirrel-related power outages cost California's economy up to $317 million per year.[13]

Concurrent control addresses the problems inherent in feedback control by gathering information about performance deficiencies *as* they occur. Thus, it is an improvement over feedback because it attempts to eliminate or shorten the delay between performance and feedback about the performance. Concussions represent one of the biggest health concerns for football players. Sometimes, however, it can be difficult to tell whether a player has suffered a concussion. And, because they don't want to come out of the game, players won't always be honest with doctors about their symptoms. Other times, teams, especially high school and small college teams, don't have staff who have been properly trained to diagnose concussions. To address this problem, Battle Sports Science created the Impact Indicator, a helmet chin strap equipped with an accelerometer that instantly measures the force that a player experiences when hit. When sensors detect a hit so hard that there is a 50 percent chance or better of injury, an indicator light flashes, letting sideline medical personnel know that they should further examine the player for possible signs of a concussion.[14]

Feedforward control is a mechanism for gathering information about performance deficiencies *before* they occur. In contrast to feedback and concurrent control, which provide feedback on the basis of outcomes and results, feedforward control provides information about performance deficiencies by monitoring inputs rather than outputs. Thus, feedforward control seeks to prevent or minimize performance deficiencies before they happen.

16-1f Control Isn't Always Worthwhile or Possible

Control is achieved when behavior and work procedures conform to standards and goals are accomplished. By contrast, **control loss** occurs when behavior and work procedures do not conform to standards.[15] At an egg production facility run by Michael Foods, repairs to machinery in a packaging room accidentally contaminated eggs with listeria, bacteria that can cause fever, muscle aches, nausea, abdominal pain, and sometimes death. As a result, Michael Foods was forced to recall more than 1 million eggs sold in thirty-four states.[16]

Maintaining control is important because control loss prevents organizations from achieving their goals. When control loss occurs, managers need to find out what, if anything, they could have done to prevent it. Usually, that means identifying deviations from standard performance, analyzing the causes of those deviations, and taking corrective action. Even so, implementing controls isn't always worthwhile or possible. Let's look at regulation costs and cybernetic feasibility to see why this is so.

To determine whether control is worthwhile, managers need to carefully assess **regulation costs,** that is, whether the costs and unintended consequences of control exceed its benefits. If a control process costs more than it benefits, it may not be worthwhile. Rosedale Estates North, a Minneapolis apartment complex, has started DNA testing of residents' dogs whose owners were not cleaning up after them. Dog owner Melody Pomerenke says, "It was bad. I would have to have a separate pair of shoes to go outside." DNA swabs are taken from the dogs' mouths and sent to BioPet Vet Lab (see PooPrints.com). Then, if dog poop is not picked up, it

Concurrent control a mechanism for gathering information about performance deficiencies as they occur, thereby eliminating or shortening the delay between performance and feedback

Feedforward control a mechanism for monitoring performance inputs rather than outputs to prevent or minimize performance deficiencies before they occur

Control loss the situation in which behavior and work procedures do not conform to standards

Regulation costs the costs associated with implementing or maintaining control

is sent to the lab to identify the dog and its owner, who then pays a $100 fine. Property manager Cheryl Gallo says, "It's been positive after that initial laughter" and that with the DNA testing "there is no denying" whose dog did it. But from a control perspective, is the cost of the lab tests and the DNA swabs worth it, especially when the DNA testing costs $150?[17]

Another factor to consider is **cybernetic feasibility,** the extent to which it is possible to implement each of the three steps in the control process. If one or more steps cannot be implemented, then maintaining effective control may be difficult or impossible.

16-2 CONTROL METHODS

In January 2010, a gallon of diesel fuel cost $2.95. By May 2014, the price had climbed 34 percent to $3.95.[18] Consequently, companies with truck fleets have become much more aggressive in exploring ways to reduce fuel costs and increase gas mileage. For example, in May 2014, Kroger bought forty natural gas-powered trucks that use a state-of-the-art cold natural gas tank (for increased driving range). Natural gas costs $1.50 less per gallon than diesel fuel.[19] UPS, on the other hand, is controlling fuel costs by using composite materials in trucks that are 1,000 pounds lighter than its standard steel and aluminum trucks. Combined with 13 percent better aerodynamics, UPS's composite trucks use 40 percent less diesel fuel. Dale Spencer, director of engineering for UPS, says, "This technology is available to us today. We don't have to worry about plugging it in or getting propane or CNG (compressed natural gas)."[20]

Managers can use five different methods to achieve control in their organizations: 16-2a bureaucratic, 16-2b objective, 16-2c normative, 16-2d concertive, and 16-2e self-control.

ryasick/iStockphoto.com

16-2a Bureaucratic Control

When most people think of managerial control, what they have in mind is bureaucratic control. **Bureaucratic control** is top-down control, in which managers try to influence employee behavior by rewarding or punishing employees for compliance or noncompliance with organizational policies, rules, and procedures. Most employees, however, would argue that bureaucratic managers emphasize punishment for noncompliance much more than rewards for compliance.

As you learned in Chapter 2, bureaucratic management and control were created to prevent just this type of managerial behavior. By encouraging managers to apply well-thought-out rules, policies, and procedures in an impartial, consistent manner to everyone in the organization, bureaucratic control is supposed to make companies more efficient, effective, and fair. Ironically, it frequently has just the opposite effect. Managers who use bureaucratic control often emphasize following the rules above all else.

Another characteristic of bureaucratically controlled companies is that, due to their rule- and policy-driven decision making, they are highly resistant to change and slow to respond to customers and competitors. Recall from Chapter 2 that even Max Weber, the German philosopher who is largely credited with popularizing bureaucratic ideals in the late nineteenth century, referred to bureaucracy as the "iron cage." He said, "Once fully established, bureaucracy is among those social structures which are the hardest to destroy."[21] Of course, the national government, with hundreds of bureaus, agencies, and departments, is typically the largest bureaucracy in most countries. Under new U.S. Department of Transportation rules for long-haul truckers, drivers can now drive only seventy hours per week, down from eighty-two. And, they must take a thirty-four hour break over two nights between work weeks. Intended to increase safety by preventing tired truck drivers from getting behind the wheel, the changes are instead increasing driver turnover (ironically putting less experienced drivers on the road), putting more trucks on the road during rush hour, and forcing drivers

Cybernetic feasibility the extent to which it is possible to implement each step in the control process

Bureaucratic control the use of hierarchical authority to influence employee behavior by rewarding or punishing employees for compliance or noncompliance with organizational policies, rules, and procedures

to try to sleep when they're not tired and to drive when they are. Manny Hernandez, who has driven trucks for three decades, says the new rules prevent him from getting home to see his family. Wherever he is when the seventy hour limit kicks in, he has to stop for thirty-four hours over two nights. Says Hernandez, "It can be a nightmare of having to sit for forty-eight hours, tired, when all you want to do is get home.... Who made up these rules?" he asks. "Did they have any experience in driving truck[s], and traffic and dealing with customers and [the time lost from] your [truck] breakdowns? Sometimes I think they're trying to choke out the trucking industry."[22]

16-2b Objective Control

In many companies, bureaucratic control has evolved into **objective control,** which is the use of observable measures of employee behavior or output to assess performance and influence behavior. Whereas bureaucratic control focuses on whether policies and rules are followed, objective control focuses on observing and measuring worker behavior or output. The Angus Barn, a steakhouse in Raleigh, North Carolina, has a strict privacy policy because it is visited by numerous celebrities—employees and managers are to keep all guests' dining experiences private. A waiter was fired for violating the policy after uploading a copy of NFL quarterback Peyton Manning's dinner receipt, following Manning's dinner at the restaurant. The picture, which quickly went viral, showed that Manning had left a generous tip of $200, on top of an 18 percent gratuity that the restaurant had already added to the bill. Speaking about the incident and the firing, Van Eure, the owner of the Angus Barn, said, "This goes against every policy we have. It's just horrible."[23]

There are two kinds of objective control: behavior control and output control. **Behavior control** is regulating behaviors and actions that workers perform on the job. The basic assumption of behavior control is that if you do the right things (i.e., the right

behaviors) every day, then those things should lead to goal achievement. Behavior control is still management-based, however, which means that managers are responsible for monitoring and rewarding or punishing workers for exhibiting desired or undesired behaviors.

Instead of measuring what managers and workers do, **output control** measures the results of their efforts. Whereas behavior control regulates, guides, and measures how workers behave on the job, output control gives managers and workers the freedom to behave as they see fit as long as they accomplish prespecified, measurable results. Output control is often coupled with rewards and incentives.

Three things must occur for output control to lead to improved business results. First, output control measures must be reliable, fair, and accurate. Second, employees and managers must believe that they can produce the desired results. If they don't, then the output controls won't affect their behavior. Third, the rewards or incentives tied to output control measures must truly be dependent on achieving established standards of performance. The "Drive Safe & Save" program at State Farm Insurance is based on output control. Using a device that plugs into your car's diagnostic port, State Farm tracks when you drive, and your braking, acceleration, left and right turns, and whether you exceed 80 mph. Drivers who participate are eligible for discounts up to 50 percent, with their driving scores determining the size of the discount. Ed Scharlau of Austin, Texas, says, "How I drive should affect my insurance premium." Moreover, he says the program's daily feedback has him and his wife talking, "about our own driving and what we see around us: 'Oops, did we just lose points?'"[24]

16-2c Normative Control

Rather than monitoring rules, behavior, or output, another way to control what goes on in organizations is to use normative control to shape the beliefs and values of the people who work there. With **normative controls,** a company's widely shared values and beliefs guide workers' behavior and decisions.

Philip Rosedale, the founder and CEO of LoveMachine, an information technology firm, runs his company entirely on one value—transparency. He applies transparency to everything at the company. Every employee, contractor, and freelancer who works for the company has access to information about everything that others are working on, what others are earning, or what other freelancers are charging and how many hours it took them to complete a project. Even Rosedale's salary

---

Objective control the use of observable measures of worker behavior or outputs to assess performance and influence behavior

Behavior control the regulation of the behaviors and actions that workers perform on the job

Output control the regulation of workers' results or outputs through rewards and incentives

Normative control the regulation of workers' behavior and decisions through widely shared organizational values and beliefs

and benefits are openly available to everyone. Rosedale believes that this extreme level of transparency is vital for creating an open, collaborative environment in which there is a free exchange of information from one person to another.[25]

Normative controls are created in two ways. First, companies that use normative controls are very careful about who they hire. While many companies screen potential applicants on the basis of their abilities, normatively controlled companies are just as likely to screen potential applicants based on their attitudes and values. Four Seasons hotels, a luxury five-star brand, are renowned for their exceptional guest service. Founder Isadore Sharp says, "Competence we can teach. Attitude is ingrained."[26] Executive vice-president of HR, Nick Mutton agrees, saying, "Job skills can be taught later. The quality of our people—their attitude, professionalism, personal growth—is actually what we are as a business. Our focus on attitude is paramount because engaged employees who care about our customers create our product, and that clearly contributes directly to our bottom line."[27]

Second, with normative controls, managers and employees learn what they should and should not do by observing experienced employees and by listening to the stories they tell about the company. We learned the importance of storytelling and organizational culture in Chapter 3. For normative controls to work, however, managers must not only select the right people, they must reward employees who honor those attitudes and values, and deal with those who don't. Elite SEM is a New York City-based search engine marketing firm that helps Fortune 500 companies increase their profile when potential customers do web searches. Elite SEM values hiring people with advanced technical skills and cooperative attitudes. More specifically, Elite SEM prides itself on being a "jerk-free workplace." So, there are consequences for employees and managers who, as CEO Ben Kirshner says, "don't embrace our core values." When a new employee refused to work late his first week on the job, he was let go. Kirshner says, "He was a bad seed!" And, because of the long hours people put in to meet client needs, Elite SEM has a free meal policy. So when another new employee ordered himself groceries and $30 breakfasts, Kirshner says, "Everyone jumped on him."[28]

16-2d Concertive Control

Whereas normative controls are based on beliefs that are strongly held and widely shared throughout a company, **concertive controls** are based on beliefs

that are shaped and negotiated by work groups.[29] Whereas normative controls are driven by strong organizational cultures, concertive controls usually arise when companies give work groups complete autonomy and responsibility for task completion (see Chapter 10, "Managing Teams," for a complete discussion of the role of autonomy in teams and groups). The most autonomous groups operate without managers and are completely responsible for controlling work group processes, outputs, and behavior. Such groups do their own hiring, firing, worker discipline, scheduling, materials ordering, budget making and meeting, and decision making.

Concertive control is not established overnight. Highly autonomous work groups evolve through two phases as they develop concertive control. In phase one, group members learn to work with each other, supervise each other's work, and develop the values and beliefs that will guide and control their behavior. And because they develop these values and beliefs themselves, work group members feel strongly about following them.

In the steel industry, Nucor was long considered an upstart compared with the "biggies," U.S. Steel and Bethlehem Steel. Today, however, not only has Nucor managed to outlast many other mills, the company has bought out thirteen other mills in the past five years. Nucor has a unique culture that gives real power to employees on the line and fosters teamwork throughout the organization. This type of teamwork can be a difficult thing for a newly acquired group of employees to get used to. For example, at Nucor's first big acquisition in Auburn, New York, David Hutchins is a frontline supervisor or "lead man" in the rolling mill, where steel from the furnace is spread thin enough to be cut into sheets. When the plant was under the previous ownership, if the guys doing the cutting got backed up, the guys doing the rolling—including Hutchins—would just take a break. He says, "We'd sit back, have a cup of coffee, and complain: 'Those guys stink.'" It took six months to convince the employees at the Auburn plant that the Nucor teamwork way was better than the old way. Now, Hutchins says: "At Nucor, we're not 'you guys' and 'us guys.' It's all of us guys. Wherever the bottleneck is, we go there, and everyone works on it."[30]

The second phase in the development of concertive control is the emergence and formalization of objective rules to guide and control behavior. The beliefs and

Concertive control the regulation of workers' behavior and decisions through work group values and beliefs

values developed in phase one usually develop into more objective rules as new members join teams. The clearer those rules, the easier it becomes for new members to figure out how and how not to behave.

Ironically, concertive control may lead to even more stress for workers to conform to expectations than bureaucratic control. Under bureaucratic control, most workers only have to worry about pleasing the boss. But with concertive control, their behavior has to satisfy the rest of their team members. For example, one team member says, "I don't have to sit there and look for the boss to be around; and if the boss is not around, I can sit there and talk to my neighbor or do what I want. Now the whole team is around me and the whole team is observing what I'm doing."[31] Plus, with concertive control, team members have a second, much more stressful role to perform: that of making sure that their team members adhere to team values and rules.

16-2e Self-Control

Self-control, also known as **self-management,** is a control system in which managers and workers control their own behavior.[32] Self-control does not result in anarchy, in which everyone gets to do whatever he or she wants. In self-control, or self-management, leaders and managers provide workers with clear boundaries

AP Images/The Decatur Daily/Gary Cosby Jr.

> **Self-control (self-management)** a control system in which managers and workers control their own behavior by setting their own goals, monitoring their own progress, and rewarding themselves for goal achievement

within which they may guide and control their own goals and behaviors.[33] Leaders and managers also contribute to self-control by teaching others the skills they need to maximize and monitor their own work effectiveness. In turn, individuals who manage and lead themselves establish self-control by setting their own goals, monitoring their own progress, rewarding or punishing themselves for achieving or for not achieving their self-set goals, and constructing positive thought patterns that remind them

We Need More Garbage

Sweden has a big problem—it needs more trash. Since the 1940s, Swedish utilities have been incinerating trash and converting the energy into electricity. However, citizens have become so efficient at recycling and reusing that they now throw away only 4 percent of their waste, meaning that Swedish power plants that run on garbage don't have enough garbage. To continue providing electricity, the Swedish government has begun importing trash from its neighbor Norway, about 800,000 tons per year. Sweden is not paying for the trash; however, Norway is paying Sweden to take its garbage and incinerate it.

Sources: L. Clark, "Sweden to Import 800,000 Tonnes of Trash to Burn for Energy," *Wired UK*, October 29, 2012, accessed June 21, 2013, http://www.wired.co.uk /news/archive/2012-10/29/sweden-imports-garbage-for-energy; D. Stone, "Sweden Needs More Trash," *National Geographic*, January 4, 2013, accessed June 21, 2013, http://newswatch.nationalgeographic .com/2013/01/04/sweden-needs -more-trash/.

Imagestock/iStockphoto.com

of the importance of their goals and their ability to accomplish them.[34]

For example, let's assume you need to do a better job of praising and recognizing the good work that your staff does for you. You can use goal setting, self-observation, and self-reward to manage this behavior on your own. For self-observation, write "praise/recognition" on a three-by-five-inch card. Put the card in your pocket. Put a check on the card each time you praise or recognize someone. (Wait until the person has left before you do this.) Keep track for a week. This serves as your baseline, or starting point. Simply keeping track will probably increase how often you do this. After a week, assess your baseline, or starting point, and then set a specific goal. For instance, if your baseline was twice a day, you might set a specific goal to praise or recognize others' work five times a day. Continue monitoring your performance with your cards. Once you've achieved your goal every day for a week, give yourself a reward (perhaps a movie or lunch with a friend at a new restaurant) for achieving your goal.[35]

As you can see, the components of self-management, self-set goals, self-observation, and self-reward have their roots in the motivation theories you read about in Chapter 13. The key difference, though, is that the goals, feedback, and rewards originate from employees themselves and not from their managers or organizations.

16-3 WHAT TO CONTROL?

In the first section of this chapter, we discussed the basics of the control process and the fact that control isn't always worthwhile or possible. In the second section, we looked at the various ways in which control can be achieved. In this third and final section, we address an equally important issue: What should managers control? Costs? Quality? Customer satisfaction? The way managers answer this question has critical implications for most businesses.

If you control for just one thing, such as costs, as many grocers have done in their meat departments, then other dimensions like marketing, customer service, and quality are likely to suffer. But if you try to control for too many things, then managers and employees become confused about what's really important. In the end, successful companies find a balance that comes from doing three or four things right, like managing costs, providing value, and keeping customers and employees satisfied.

After reading this section, you should be able to explain **16-3a the balanced scorecard approach to control** and how companies can achieve balanced control of company performance by choosing to control **16-3b budgets, cash flows, and economic value added; 16-3c customer defections; 16-3d quality;** and **16-3e waste and pollution.**

16-3a The Balanced Scorecard

Most companies measure performance using standard financial and accounting measures such as return on capital, return on assets, return on investments, cash flow, net income, and net margins. The **balanced scorecard** encourages managers to look beyond such traditional financial measures to four different perspectives on company performance. How do customers see us (the customer perspective)? At what must we excel (the internal perspective)? Can we continue to improve and create value (the innovation and learning perspective)? How do we look to shareholders (the financial perspective)?[36]

The balanced scorecard has several advantages over traditional control processes that rely solely on financial measures. First, it forces managers at each level of the company to set specific goals and measure performance in each of the four areas. For example, Exhibit 16.2 shows that Southwest Airlines uses nine different measures in its balanced scorecard in order to determine whether it is meeting the standards it has set for itself in the control process. Of those, only three—market value, seat revenue, and plane lease costs (at various compounded annual growth rates, or CAGR)—are standard financial measures of performance. In addition, Southwest measures its Federal Aviation Administration (FAA) on-time arrival rating and the cost of its airfares compared with those of competitors (customer perspective); how much time each plane spends on the ground after landing and the percentage of planes that depart on time (internal business perspective); and the percentage of its ground crew workers, such as mechanics and luggage handlers, who own company stock and have received job training (learning perspective).

The second major advantage of the balanced scorecard approach to control is that it minimizes the chances of **suboptimization**, which occurs when

Balanced scorecard measurement of organizational performance in four equally important areas: finances, customers, internal operations, and innovation and learning

Suboptimization performance improvement in one part of an organization but only at the expense of decreased performance in another part

Exhibit 16.2
Southwest Airlines's Balanced Scorecard

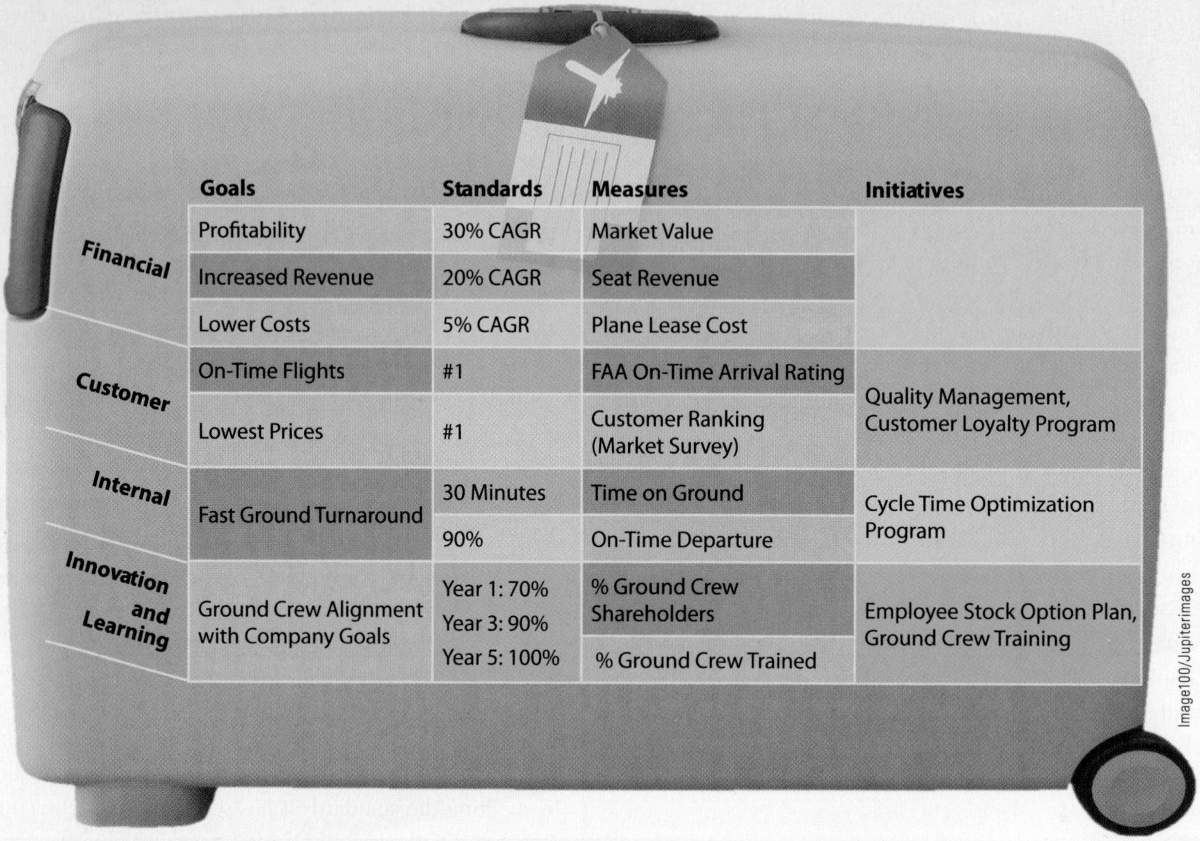

	Goals	Standards	Measures	Initiatives
Financial	Profitability	30% CAGR	Market Value	
	Increased Revenue	20% CAGR	Seat Revenue	
	Lower Costs	5% CAGR	Plane Lease Cost	
Customer	On-Time Flights	#1	FAA On-Time Arrival Rating	Quality Management, Customer Loyalty Program
	Lowest Prices	#1	Customer Ranking (Market Survey)	
Internal	Fast Ground Turnaround	30 Minutes	Time on Ground	Cycle Time Optimization Program
		90%	On-Time Departure	
Innovation and Learning	Ground Crew Alignment with Company Goals	Year 1: 70% Year 3: 90% Year 5: 100%	% Ground Crew Shareholders	Employee Stock Option Plan, Ground Crew Training
			% Ground Crew Trained	

Image100/Jupiterimages

Source: G. Anthes, "ROI Guide: Balanced Scorecard," *Computer World,* February 17, 2003, accessed September 5, 2008, http://www.computerworld.com/action/article.do?command=viewArticleBasic&articleId=78512&intsrc=article_pots_bot.

performance improves in one area at the expense of decreased performance in others. Jon Meliones, chief medical director at Duke Children's Hospital, says, "We explained the [balanced scorecard] theory to clinicians and administrators like this: if you sacrifice too much in one quadrant to satisfy another, your organization as a whole is thrown out of balance. We could, for example, cut costs to improve the financial quadrant by firing half the staff, but that would hurt quality of service, and the customer quadrant would fall out of balance. Or we could increase productivity in the internal business quadrant by assigning more patients to a nurse, but doing so would raise the likelihood of errors—an unacceptable trade-off."[37]

Cash flow analysis a type of analysis that predicts how changes in a business will affect its ability to take in more cash than it pays out

Let's examine some of the ways in which companies are controlling the four basic parts of the balanced scorecard: the financial perspective (budgets, cash flows, and economic value added), the customer perspective (customer defections), the internal perspective (total quality management), and the innovation and learning perspective (waste and pollution).

16-3b The Financial Perspective: Controlling Budgets, Cash Flows, and Economic Value Added

The traditional approach to controlling financial performance focuses on accounting tools such as cash flow analysis, balance sheets, income statements, financial ratios, and budgets. **Cash flow analysis** predicts how changes in a business will affect its ability to take in more cash than it pays out. **Balance sheets** provide a snapshot of a company's financial position at a particular time (but not the future). **Income statements,** also called profit and loss statements, show what has happened to an organization's income, expenses, and net profit (income less expenses) over a period of time. **Financial ratios** are typically used to track a business's liquidity (cash), efficiency, and profitability over time compared with other businesses in its industry. Finally, **budgets** are used to project costs and revenues, prioritize and control spending, and ensure that expenses don't exceed available funds and revenues.

By themselves, none of these tools—cash flow analyses, balance sheets, income statements, financial ratios, or budgets—tell the whole financial story of a business. They must be used together when assessing a company's financial performance. Since these tools are reviewed in detail in your accounting and finance classes, only a brief overview is provided here. Still, these are necessary tools for controlling organizational finances and expenses, and they should be part of your business toolbox. Unfortunately, most managers don't have a good understanding of these accounting tools even though they should.[38] When Boeing's new chief financial officer attended her first company retreat with other Boeing executives, she assumed that her discussion of financial ratios would be a boring review for everyone present. Afterward, she was shocked when dozens of the 280 executives attending the retreat told her that for the very first time they finally understood what the formulas meant.[39]

Though no one would dispute the importance of cash flow analyses, balance sheets, income statements, financial ratios, or budgets for determining the financial health of a business, accounting research also indicates that the complexity and sheer amount of information contained in these accounting tools can shut down the brain and glaze over the eyes of even the most experienced manager.[40] Sometimes there's simply too much information to make sense of. The balanced scorecard simplifies things by focusing on one simple question when it comes to finances: How do we look to shareholders? One way to answer that question is through something called economic value added.

Conceptually, **economic value added (EVA)** is not the same thing as profits. It is the amount by which profits exceed the cost of capital in a given year. It is based on the simple idea that capital is necessary to run a business and that capital comes at a cost. Although most people think of capital as cash, once it is invested (i.e., spent), capital is more likely to be found in a business in the form of computers, manufacturing plants, employees, raw materials, and so forth. And just like the interest that a homeowner pays on a mortgage or that a college student pays on a student loan, there is a cost to that capital.

The most common costs of capital are the interest paid on long-term bank loans used to buy all those resources, the interest paid to bondholders (who lend organizations their money), and the dividends (cash payments) and growth in stock value that accrue to shareholders. EVA is positive when company profits (revenues minus expenses minus taxes) exceed the cost of capital in a given year. In other words, if a business is to truly grow, its revenues must be large enough to cover both short-term costs (annual expenses and taxes) and long-term costs (the cost of borrowing capital from bondholders and shareholders). If you're a bit confused, the late Roberto Goizueta, the former CEO of Coca-Cola, explained it this way: "You borrow money at a certain rate and invest it at a higher rate and pocket the difference. It is simple. It is the essence of banking."[41]

Exhibit 16.3 shows how to calculate EVA. First, starting with a company's income statement, you calculate the net operating profit after taxes (NOPAT) by subtracting taxes owed from income from operations. (Remember, a quick review of an income statement is on the Financial Review Card found at the back of your book.) The NOPAT shown in Exhibit 16.3 is $3,500,000. Second, identify how much capital the company has invested (i.e., spent). Total liabilities (what the company owes) less accounts payable and less accrued expenses, neither of which you pay interest on, provides a rough approximation of this amount. In Exhibit 16.3, total capital invested is $16,800,000. Third, calculate the cost (i.e., rate) paid for capital by determining the interest paid to bondholders (who lend organizations their money), which is usually somewhere between 5 and

Balance sheets accounting statements that provide a snapshot of a company's financial position at a particular time

Income statements accounting statements, also called "profit and loss statements," that show what has happened to an organization's income, expenses, and net profit over a period of time

Financial ratios calculations typically used to track a business's liquidity (cash), efficiency, and profitability over time compared to other businesses in its industry

Budgets quantitative plans through which managers decide how to allocate available money to best accomplish company goals

Economic value added (EVA) the amount by which company profits (revenues minus expenses minus taxes) exceed the cost of capital in a given year

Exhibit 16.3
Calculating Economic Value Added (EVA)

1.	Calculate net operating profit after taxes (NOPAT).	$ 3,500,000
2.	Identify how much capital the company has invested (i.e., spent).	$16,800,000
3.	Determine the cost (i.e., rate) paid for capital (usually between 5 percent and 13 percent).	10%
4.	Multiply capital used (Step 2) times cost of capital (Step 3).	(10% × $16,800,000) = $1,680,000
5.	Subtract the total dollar cost of capital from net profit after taxes.	$3,500,000 NOPAT − $1,680,000 Total cost of capital $1,820,000 EVA

8 percent, and the return that stockholders want in terms of dividends and stock price appreciation, which is historically about 13 percent. Take a weighted average of the two to determine the overall cost of capital. In Exhibit 16.3, the cost of capital is 10 percent. Fourth, multiply the total capital ($16,800,000) from Step 2 by the cost of capital (10 percent) from Step 3. In Exhibit 16.3, this amount is $1,680,000. Fifth, subtract the total dollar cost of capital in Step 4 from the NOPAT in Step 1. In Exhibit 16.3, this value is $1,820,000, which means that our example company has created economic value or wealth this year. If our EVA number had been negative, meaning that the company didn't make enough profit to cover the cost of capital from bondholders and shareholders, then the company would have destroyed economic value or wealth by taking in more money than it returned.[42]

Why is EVA so important? First and most importantly, because it includes the cost of capital, it shows whether a business, division, department, profit center, or product is really paying for itself. The key is to make sure that managers and employees can see how their choices and behaviors affect the company's EVA. For example, because of EVA training and information systems, factory workers at Herman Miller, a leading office furniture manufacturer, understand that using more efficient materials, such as less expensive wood-dust board instead of real wood sheeting, contributes an extra dollar of EVA from each desk the company makes. On its website, Herman Miller explains, "Under the terms of the EVA plan, we shifted our focus from budget performance to long-term continuous improvements and the creation of economic value. When we make plans for improvements around here, we include an EVA analysis. When we make decisions to add or cut programs, we look at the impact on EVA. Every month we study our performance in terms of EVA, and this measurement system is one of the first things new recruits to the company learn."[43] "The result is a highly motivated and business-literate workforce that challenges convention and strives to create increasingly greater value for both customers and owners. Every month the company and all employees review performance in terms of EVA, which has proven to be a strong corollary to shareholder value."[44]

Second, because EVA can easily be determined for subsets of a company such as divisions, regional offices, manufacturing plants, and sometimes even departments, it makes managers and workers at all levels pay much closer attention to their segment of the business. In other words, EVA motivates managers and workers to think like small-business owners who must scramble to contain costs and generate enough business to meet their bills each month. And, unlike many kinds of financial controls, EVA doesn't specify what should or should not be done to improve performance. Thus, it encourages managers and workers to be creative in looking for ways to improve EVA performance.

Remember that EVA is the amount by which profits exceed the cost of capital in a given year. So the more that EVA exceeds the total dollar cost of capital, the better a company has used investors' money that year. For example, Apple had an EVA of $28 billion in 2012, by far the largest EVA in the world. The next-closest company was Google at $5.28 billion. To put Apple's 2012 EVA performance in perspective, note that its EVA grew by an astronomical 74 percent per year between 2010 and 2012 and that 2012's EVA of $28 billion is 16.5 times Apple's average EVA of "just" $1.7 billion a year from 2005 to 2009. Apple's EVA financial performance in 2013 was truly extraordinary and the largest ever achieved by any company.[45]

16-3c The Customer Perspective: Controlling Customer Defections

The second aspect of organizational performance that the balanced scorecard helps managers monitor is customers. It does so by forcing managers to address the question "How do customers see us?" Unfortunately, most companies try to answer this question through customer satisfaction surveys, but these are often misleadingly positive. Most customers are reluctant to talk about their problems because they don't know who to complain to or think that complaining will not do any good. Indeed, a study by the federal Office of Consumer Affairs found that 96 percent of unhappy customers never complain to anyone in the company.[46]

One reason that customer satisfaction surveys can be misleading is that sometimes even very satisfied customers will leave to do business with competitors. Rather than poring over customer satisfaction surveys from current customers, studies indicate that companies may do a better job of answering the question "How do customers see us?" by closely monitoring **customer defections,** that is, by identifying which customers are leaving the company and measuring the rate at which they are leaving. Unlike the results of customer satisfaction surveys,

customer defections and retention have a great effect on profits.

For example, very few managers realize that obtaining a new customer costs ten times as much as keeping a current one. In fact, the cost of replacing old customers with new ones is so great that most companies could double their profits by increasing the rate of customer retention by just 5 to 10 percent per year.[47] Retaining customers obviously means having more customers, but how many more? Consider two companies starting with a customer base of 100,000 customers and an acquisition rate of 20 percent (i.e., yearly each company's customer base grows by 20 percent). Assuming company B has a higher retention rate of just 5 percent (90 percent retention rate for company B versus an 85 percent retention rate for company A), company B will double its customer base around the ninth year, while it will take company A slightly more than fifteen years to double its customer base. On average, this means company B also profited by a higher percentage.[48] And if a company can keep a customer for life, the benefits are even larger. According to Stew Leonard, owner of the Connecticut-based Stew Leonard's grocery store chain: "The lifetime value of a customer in a supermarket is about $246,000. Every time a customer comes through our front door I see, stamped on their forehead in big red numbers, '$246,000.' I'm never going to make that person unhappy with me. Or lose her to the competition."[49]

Beyond the clear benefits to the bottom line, the second reason to study customer defections is that customers who have left are much more likely than current customers to tell you what you are doing wrong. Perhaps the best way to tap into this source of good feedback is to have top-level managers from various departments talk directly to customers who have left. It's also worthwhile to have top managers talk to dissatisfied customers who are still with the company. Finally, companies that understand why customers leave cannot only take steps to fix ongoing problems but can also identify which customers are likely to leave and can make changes to prevent them from leaving.

Customer defections a performance assessment in which companies identify which customers are leaving and measure the rate at which they are leaving

16-3d The Internal Perspective: Controlling Quality

The third part of the balanced scorecard, the internal perspective, consists of the processes, decisions, and actions that managers and workers make within the organization. In contrast to the financial perspective of EVA and the outward-looking customer perspective, the internal perspective focuses on internal processes and systems that add value to the organization. For McDonald's, it could be processes and systems that enable the company to provide consistent, quick, low-cost food. For Toyota, it could be reliability—when you turn on your car it starts, no matter whether the car has 20,000 or 200,000 miles on it. Yet, no matter what area a company chooses, the key is to excel in that area. Consequently, the internal perspective of the balanced scorecard usually leads managers to a focus on quality.

Quality is typically defined and measured in three ways: excellence, value, and conformance to expectations.[50] When the company defines its quality goal as *excellence*, managers must try to produce a product or service of unsurpassed performance and features. *Condé Nast Traveler* magazine has been ranking global airlines for twenty-six years. For twenty-five of those years, Singapore Airlines was named the best airline in the world.[51] Whereas many airlines try to cram passengers into every available inch on a plane, Singapore Airlines delivers creature comforts to encourage repeat business and lure customers willing to pay premium prices. On its newer planes, the first-class cabin is divided into eight private mini-rooms, each with an unusually wide leather seat that folds down flat for sleeping, a twenty-three-inch LCD TV that doubles as a computer monitor, and an adjustable table.

These amenities and services are common for private jets but truly unique in the commercial airline industry.[52] Singapore Airlines was the first airline, in the 1970s, to introduce a choice of meals, complimentary drinks, and earphones in coach class. It was the first to introduce worldwide video, news, telephone, and fax services and the first to feature personal video monitors for movies, news, documentaries, and games. Singapore Airlines has had AC power for laptop computers for some time, and recently it became the first airline to introduce on-board high-speed Internet access.

Value is the customer perception that the product quality is excellent for the price offered. At a higher price, for example, customers may perceive the product to be less of a value. When a company emphasizes value as its quality goal, managers must simultaneously control excellence, price, durability, and any other features of a product or service that customers strongly associate with value. The Kia Optima was recently recognized by *Kiplinger's Personal Finance* as a Best New Car Value. It has a turbocharged engine with not only the highest horsepower in its class but also the highest fuel efficiency as well. Standard equipment includes Bluetooth connectivity, power seats, satellite radio, a cooled glove box, and a voice-controlled entertainment system. The car is also backed by a five-year warranty, as well as a five-year roadside assistance program. With all these features and a $25,000 to $30,000 price that is several thousand dollars cheaper than the Toyota Camry and Honda Accord, sales have jumped 131 percent.[53]

When a company defines its quality goal as conformance to specifications, employees must base decisions and actions on whether services and products measure up to the standard. In contrast to excellence and value-based definitions of quality that can be somewhat ambiguous, measuring whether products and services are "in spec" is relatively easy. Furthermore, while conformance to specifications (e.g., precise tolerances for a part's weight or thickness) is usually associated with manufacturing, it can be used equally well to control quality in nonmanufacturing jobs. Exhibit 16.4 shows a checklist that a cook or restaurant owner would use to ensure quality when buying fresh fish.

The way in which a company defines quality affects the methods and measures that workers use to control quality. Accordingly, Exhibit 16.5 shows the advantages and disadvantages associated with the excellence, value, and conformance to specification definitions of quality.

16-3e The Innovation and Learning Perspective: Controlling Waste and Pollution

The last part of the balanced scorecard, the innovation and learning perspective, addresses the question "Can we continue to improve and create value?" Thus, the innovation and learning perspective involves continuous improvement in ongoing products and services (discussed in Chapter 18), as well as relearning and redesigning the processes by which products and services are created (discussed in Chapter 7). Since these are discussed in more detail elsewhere in the text, this section reviews an increasingly important topic, waste and pollution minimization.

Value customer perception that the product quality is excellent for the price offered

Exhibit 16.4
Conformance to Specifications Checklist for Buying Fresh Fish

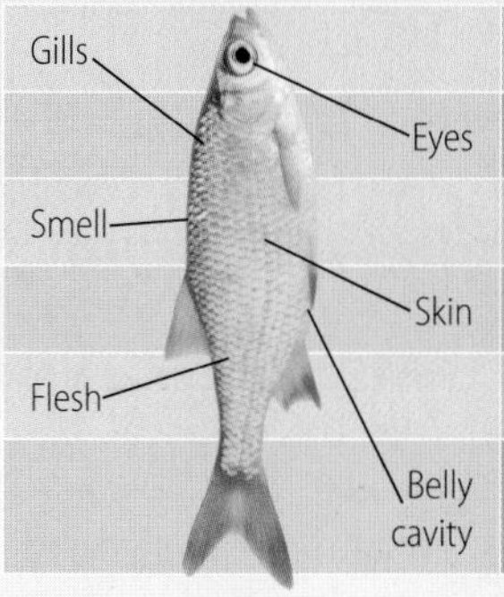

Fresh Whole Fish	Acceptable	Not Acceptable
Gills	✓ bright red, free of slime, clear mucus	✗ brown to grayish, thick, yellow mucus
Eyes	✓ clear, bright, bulging, black pupils	✗ dull, sunken, cloudy, gray pupils
Smell	✓ inoffensive, slight ocean smell	✗ ammonia, putrid smell
Skin	✓ opalescent sheen, scales adhere tightly to skin	✗ dull or faded color, scales missing or easily removed
Flesh	✓ firm and elastic to touch, tight to the bone	✗ soft and flabby, separating from the bone
Belly cavity	✓ no viscera or blood visible, lining intact, no bone protruding	✗ incomplete evisceration, cuts or protruding bones, off-odor

Sources: "A Closer Look: Buy It Fresh, Keep It Fresh," *Consumer Reports Online*, accessed June 20, 2005, http://www.seagrant.sunysb.edu/SeafoodTechnology /SeafoodMedia/CR02-2001/CR-SeafoodII020101.htm; "How to Purchase: Buying Fish," *AboutSeaFood*, accessed June 20, 2005, http://www.aboutseafood.com/faqs /purchase1.html.

Valeriy Evlakhov/iStockphoto.com

Exhibit 16.5
Advantages and Disadvantages of Different Measures of Quality

Quality Measure	Advantages	Disadvantages
Excellence	Promotes clear organizational vision.	Provides little practical guidance for managers.
	Being/providing the "best" motivates and inspires managers and employees.	Excellence is ambiguous. What is it? Who defines it?
Value	Appeals to customers who know excellence "when they see it."	Difficult to measure and control.
	Customers recognize differences in value.	Can be difficult to determine what factors influence whether a product/service is seen as having value.
	Easier to measure and compare whether products/ services differ in value.	Controlling the balance between excellence and cost (i.e., affordable excellence) can be difficult.
Conformance to Specifications	If specifications can be written, conformance to specifications is usually measurable.	Many products/services cannot be easily evaluated in terms of conformance to specifications.
	Should lead to increased efficiency.	Promotes standardization, so may hurt performance when adapting to changes is more important.
	Promotes consistency in quality.	May be less appropriate for services, which are dependent on a high degree of human contact.

Source: Briar Cliff Manor, NY, 10510-8020; C. A. Reeves and D. A. Bednar, "Defining Quality: Alternatives and Implications," *Academy of Management Review* 19 (1994): 419–445.

Exhibit 16.6 shows the four levels of waste minimization, ranging from waste disposal, which produces the smallest minimization of waste, to waste prevention and reduction, which produces the greatest minimization.[54]

The goals of the top level, *waste prevention and reduction*, are to prevent waste and pollution before they occur or to reduce them when they do occur. In its new $1.2 billion stadium in Santa Clara, California, the National Football League's San Francisco 49ers installed Bander Bermuda Grass on the field because it uses half the water of regular sports turf. The stadium has an 18,000 square-foot garden on top of the luxury box suites to provide insulation and reduce energy use, 1,000 solar panels to generate energy, and a rainwater collection system for cooling and irrigation. In all, the stadium is energy neutral, meaning it generates all of its own energy for home games. 49ers President Paraag Marathe says, "Where we are in Silicon Valley it's sort of our mandate. If it wasn't environmentally responsible, we wouldn't be as successful."[55]

There are three strategies for waste prevention and reduction:

AP Images/Eric Risberg

1. *Good housekeeping*—performing regularly scheduled preventive maintenance for offices, plants, and equipment. Examples of good housekeeping include fixing leaky valves quickly to prevent wasted water and making sure machines are running properly so that they don't use more fuel than necessary. Procter & Gamble, the largest consumer product company in the world, produces 1 million metric tons of waste per year. That amount was cut in half over the last decade, and 63 percent of its waste was recycled or reused in 2010. P&G has had great success with preventive maintenance in its manufacturing facilities. For example, it was able to reduce energy use from steam production by 43 percent in a baby-care product factory by simply changing how it cleaned equipment. That energy savings reduced CO_2 emissions by 610 tons a year and reduced water usage by 170,000 liters a year.[56]

2. *Material/product substitution*—replacing toxic or hazardous materials with less harmful materials.

3. *Process modification*—changing steps or procedures to eliminate or reduce waste.

At the second level of waste minimization, *recycle and reuse*, wastes are reduced by reusing materials as long as possible or by collecting materials for on- or off-site recycling. H&M, a worldwide clothing retailer, uses recycled polyester from more than 9.5 million PET water bottles in its products and has an in-store recycling program through which it has collected more than 5,000 metric tons of used clothing that it either donates to charities, recycles into rags, or uses to make new jeans. H&M sells five new kinds of denim clothing made with at least 20 percent recycled cotton and 28 percent recycled polyester. Henrik Lampa, H&M's sustainability manager, says, "We don't want clothes to become waste; we want them to become a resource instead."[57]

A growing trend in recycling is *design for disassembly*, where products are designed from the start for easy disassembly, recycling, and reuse once they are no longer usable. Japan-based Kyocera used design for disassembly principles to create laser printers that are cartridge-free (because of their complexity, printer cartridges are difficult to recycle). To make its printers easy to take apart at the end of their life cycle, Kyocera designed them with just five parts, down from seventy, used plastic clips instead of metal fasteners,

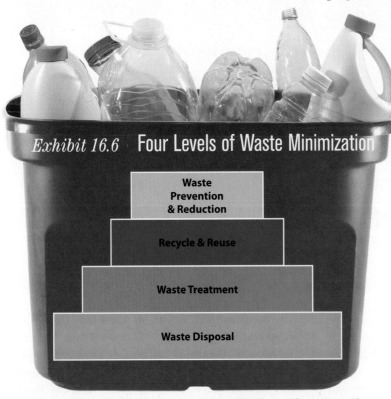

Exhibit 16.6 **Four Levels of Waste Minimization**

- Waste Prevention & Reduction
- Recycle & Reuse
- Waste Treatment
- Waste Disposal

Source: Business Horizons, September–October 1995, D. R. May and B. L. Flannery, "Cutting Waste with Employee Involvement Teams," pp. 28–38.

0g-Vision/iStockphoto.com

A New Can for a New Goal

Recall from Chapter 5 that aluminum maker Novelis pledged to increase the percentage of recycled materials used in its manufacturing process from 33 percent to 80 percent by 2020. The company has already taken a number of steps to help make this happen. For example, it invested nearly $500 million to double its recycling capacity by 2015. Novelis is also working to invent a new type of beverage can called the evercan. The evercan will be the first can of its kind to be made from 100 percent recycled materials. Novelis currently has a body sheet made from 90 percent recycled material, so when combined with can tops (typically made from a different alloy than can bodies), complete Novelis cans weigh in at 70 percent recycled materials.

Sources: Novelis, "Sustainability Through Disruptive Innovation: Novelis Sustainability Report 2013," Novelis, 2013. p. 12, 61. accessed May 27, 2014, http://www.novelis.com/Documents/Sustainability/2013_Novelis_Sustainability_Report_En.pdf.

and marked each part with codes explaining how they should be recycled. Kyocera's careful designs have reduced carbon footprints by 55 percent, waste by 85 percent, and costs by 54 percent.[58]

At the third level of waste minimization, waste treatment, companies use biological, chemical, or other processes to turn potentially harmful waste into harmless compounds or useful by-products. Usually supermarkets throw away the food they don't sell, but in the United Kingdom, several supermarket chains are using warm water and bacteria to convert food waste to a methane-rich biogas that powers electricity plants. Because the supermarkets are taxed $98 for every ton of trash that goes into landfills, Marks & Spencer now sends 89 percent of its food waste for biogas conversion, saving the company $163 million a year.[59]

The fourth and lowest level of waste minimization is *waste disposal*. Wastes that cannot be prevented, reduced, recycled, reused, or treated should be safely disposed of in processing plants or in environmentally secure landfills that prevent leakage and contamination of soil and underground water supplies. Contrary to common belief, all businesses, not just manufacturing firms, have waste disposal problems. For example, with the average computer lasting just three years, approximately 60 million computers come out of service each year, creating disposal problems for offices all over the world. But organizations can't just throw old computers away, since they have lead-containing cathode ray tubes in the monitors, toxic metals in the circuit boards, paint-coated plastic, and metal coatings that can contaminate groundwater.[60] Many companies give old computers and computer equipment to local computer recycling centers that distribute usable computers to nonprofit organizations or safely dispose of lead and other toxic materials. A number of retailers and electronics manufacturers operate recycling programs to keep electronics out of landfills. For example, customers can drop off computers, TVs, DVD players, batteries,

and other items at Best Buy stores. There is a $10 recycling fee for anything with a screen, but Best Buy offsets that with a $10 gift card. Best Buy will recycle 80 million pounds of electronics this year. But for those items that still function, Costco and Newegg.com work with Gazelle.com, which buys, refurbishes, and resells 250,000 items overseas and on eBay. College student Bobby Lozano sold his used iPod Nano and LG EnV Touch phone to Gazelle, because he says, "I got an iPhone, so I no longer needed the other two." Gazelle wiped the devices of personal information and put $70 into his PayPal account.[61]

STUDY TOOLS 16

LOCATED AT THE BACK OF YOUR BOOK:

☐ Rip out and study the Chapter Review Card at the end of the book

LOG IN TO WWW.CENGAGEBRAIN.COM TO:

☐ Review Key Term Flashcards

☐ Complete Practice Quizzing (take up to four times without repeating the same quiz)

☐ Complete Games: Beat the Clock and Crossword Puzzle

☐ Complete Interactive Content: Graded Quiz, Media Quiz, and Fill-in-the-Blank Questions

☐ Watch Management Workplace Video on "Barcelona Restaurant Group"

☐ Work Through the What Would You Do Case On Caterpillar Headquarters

17 Managing Information

LEARNING OUTCOMES

17-1 Explain the strategic importance of information.

17-2 Describe the characteristics of useful information (i.e., its value and costs).

17-3 Explain the basics of capturing, processing, and protecting information.

17-4 Describe how companies can access and share information and knowledge.

After you finish this chapter, go to **PAGE 372** for **STUDY TOOLS**

17-1 STRATEGIC IMPORTANCE OF INFORMATION

A generation ago, computer hardware and software had little to do with managing business information. Rather than storing information on hard drives, managers stored it in filing cabinets. Instead of uploading daily sales and inventory levels by satellite to corporate headquarters, they mailed hard-copy summaries to headquarters at the end of each month. Instead of word processors, reports were typed on electric typewriters. Instead of spreadsheets, calculations were made on adding machines. Managers communicated by sticky notes, not email. Phone messages were written down by assistants and coworkers, not forwarded in your email as a sound file with the message converted to text. Workers did not use desktop, laptop, or tablet computers or smartphones as daily tools to get work done. Instead, they scheduled limited access time to run batch jobs on the mainframe computer (and prayed that the batch job computer code they wrote would work).

Today, a generation later, computer hardware and software are an integral part of managing business information. This is due mainly to something called **Moore's law**. Gordon Moore is one of the founders of Intel Corporation, which makes 75 percent of the integrated processors used in personal computers. In 1965, Moore predicted that computer-processing power would double and that its cost would drop by 50 percent every two years.[1] As Exhibit 17.1 shows, Moore was right. Computer power, as measured by the number of transistors per computer chip, *has* more than doubled every few years, as have hard drive sizes and pixel density (i.e., screen resolution). Consequently, the computer sitting in your lap or on your desk (or in your hand!) is not only

> **Moore's law** the prediction that about every two years, computer processing power would double and its cost would drop by 50 percent

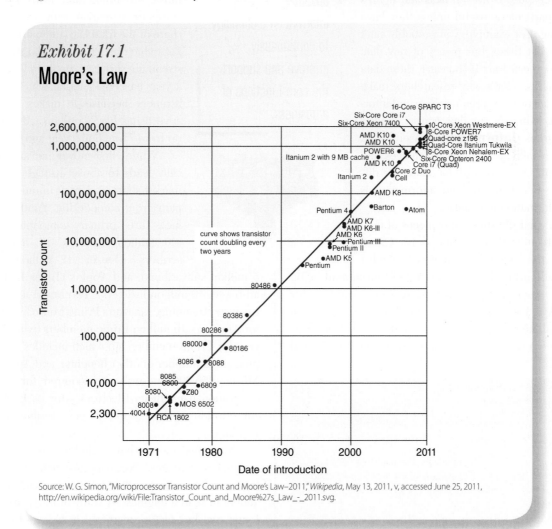

Exhibit 17.1
Moore's Law

Source: W. G. Simon, "Microprocessor Transistor Count and Moore's Law–2011," *Wikipedia*, May 13, 2011, v, accessed June 25, 2011, http://en.wikipedia.org/wiki/File:Transistor_Count_and_Moore%27s_Law_-_2011.svg.

smaller but also much cheaper and more powerful than the large mainframe computers used by *Fortune* 500 companies thirty years ago. For instance, your iPhone replaces 13 of the 15 items, such as a desktop computer, mobile phone, CD player, camcorder, etc., commonly sold by Radio Shack in 1991, items that would have cost you $3,071.21 then, or, after adjusting for inflation, $5,374.46 today. So your $600 iPhone not only replaces a trunkful of 1991 electronics gear, it does so for only 11 percent of the cost.[2] That's Moore's law in action. Will Moore's law eventually fail and technological progress eventually slow? Perhaps, but it's not likely in your lifetime. Intel's vice president of Technology and Manufacturing, Mike Mayberry, says, "If you're only using the same technology, then in principle you run into limits. The truth is we've been modifying the technology every five or seven years for forty years, and there's no end in sight for being able to do that."[3]

Raw data are facts and figures. For example, 11, $762, 32, and 26,100 are some data that I used the day I wrote this section of the chapter. However, facts and figures aren't particularly useful unless they have meaning. For example, you probably can't guess what these four pieces of raw data represent, can you? If you can't, these data are useless. That's why researchers make the distinction between raw data and information. Whereas raw data consist of facts and figures, **information** is useful data that can influence someone's choices and behavior. One way to think about the difference between data and information is that information has context.

So what did those four pieces of data mean to me? Well, 11 stands for Channel 11, the local CBS affiliate on which I watched part of the men's PGA golf tournament; $762 is how much it would cost me to rent a minivan for a week if I go skiing over spring break; 32 is for the 32-gigabyte storage card that I want to add to my digital camera (prices are low, so I'll probably buy it); and

26,100 means that it's time to get the oil changed in my car.

In today's hyper competitive business environments, information is as important as capital (i.e., money) for business success, whether it's about product inventory, pricing, or costs. It takes money to get businesses started, but businesses can't survive and grow without the right information.

Information has strategic importance for organizations because it can be used to **17-1a obtain first-mover advantage** *and* **17-1b sustain competitive advantage once it has been created.**

17-1a First-Mover Advantage

First-mover advantage is the strategic advantage that companies earn by being the first in an industry to use new information technology to substantially lower costs or to differentiate a product or service from that of competitors. Pandora, for example, pioneered music streaming and leads this highly competitive market with a 9.13 percent share of the total U.S. radio listening market (which includes all radio stations and streaming services), up from 7.29 percent a year earlier. Pandora, which is free to listeners because it makes money via advertising, has 77 million active listeners, up from 71 million a year ago.[4]

While first-mover advantage typically leads to above average profits and market share, it doesn't immunize a company from competition. Pandora already faces three primary competitors: Spotify (40 million listeners, 10 million subscribers), Deezer (12 million listeners, 5 million subscribers), and Apple's iTunes Radio (free/ad-based, 40 million listeners). Two brand-new entrants to music streaming, Amazon's Prime Music, which is free for Amazon's 10 million Prime members (who pay $99 a year for Prime membership which includes 2-day shipping and a number of other benefits), and Apple's Beats Music (250,000 subscribers), acquired for $3 billion acquisition from Beats Electronics for its Beats Music subscription service, represent new, serious threats to Pandora.[5]

Many first-movers have failed to capitalize on their strategic advantages.[6] Netscape lost first-mover advantage in web browsers, as did MySpace in social media, and Yahoo! in search engines.[7] A study of thirty first-movers found two key factors mattered in terms of sustaining

The key to sustaining a competitive advantage is using information technology to continuously improve and support the core functions of a business.

©MichaelJayBerlin/Shutterstock.com

first-mover advantage: the pace at which product technology is changing and how fast the market is growing.[8] Indeed, as these examples show, if better technology is quickly being introduced by new market entrants, and the market is quickly growing (which attracts new competitors who want a share of that growing market), it can be difficult to sustain first-mover advantage.

17-1b Sustaining Competitive Advantage

As described, companies that use information technology to establish first-mover advantage usually have higher market shares and profits. According to the resource-based view of information technology shown in Exhibit 17.2, companies need to address three critical questions in order to sustain a competitive advantage through information technology. First, does the information technology create value for the firm by lowering costs or providing a better product or service? If an information technology doesn't add value, then investing in it would put the firm at a competitive disadvantage relative to companies that choose information technologies that do add value.

Second, is the information technology the same or different across competing firms? If all the firms have access to the same information technology and use it in the same way, then no firm has an advantage over another (i.e., there is competitive parity).

Third, is it difficult for another company to create or buy the information technology used by the firm? If so, then the firm has established a sustainable competitive advantage over competitors through information technology. If not, then the competitive advantage is just temporary, and competitors should eventually be able to duplicate the advantages the

Exhibit 17.2
Using Information Technology to Sustain a Competitive Advantage

Does the information technology create value?

No → Competitive Disadvantage

Yes → Is the information technology different across competing firms?

No → Competitive Parity

Yes → Is it difficult for another firm to create or buy the information technology?

No → Temporary Competitive Advantage

Yes → Sustained Competitive Advantage

Source: Adapted from F. J. Mata, W. L. Fuerst, and J. B. Barney, "Information Technology and Sustained Competitive Advantage: A Resource-Based Analysis," MIS Quarterly 19, no. 4 (December 1995): 487–505.

leading firm has gained from information technology.

In short, the key to sustaining a competitive advantage is not faster computers, more memory, or larger hard drives. The key is using information technology to continuously improve and support the core functions of a business. While American Airlines was the first airline to issue tablet computers to pilots to replace manuals and navigation charts (previously held in binders in forty-pound carry-on bags), British Airways is using iPads to improve a core part of its business—the level of customer service flight attendants deliver to high-value business- and first-class travelers. Previously, prior to each departure, flight attendants read through stacks of printouts to memorize key passengers' preferences. Now, however, with iPads automatically updated hours before flights depart and available discreetly in the cabin throughout the flight, attendants have immediate access to passengers' likes and dislikes, special meal requests, and even medical needs. Furthermore, the iPads contain seating charts showing where loyalty club members are seated, so attendants can greet them personally when they board. Flight attendant Daljit Kaur says, "I'm ahead of myself in knowing where our corporate and high-value customers are sitting, and who needs help." Because flight attendants can attend to them so well, "They look at you and say 'have you been on a special course?'" Finally, flight attendants use the iPads to submit customer complaints. Pippa Grech, who manages British Airways' iPad program, says, "The crew does it so that passengers don't have to run around on holiday trying to do it themselves. Otherwise, by the time they get off the plane, they think 'oh, I won't bother about it.'"[9]

17-2 CHARACTERISTICS AND COSTS OF USEFUL INFORMATION

The first thing an NFL player does after being cut from a team is turn in his thick three-ring playbook binder. A third of NFL teams, however, now use **PlayerLync**, an electronic platform revolutionizing information delivery to players. **PlayerLync** lets players and coaches view the entire playbook on iPads, with ten built-in layers of security and the ability to remotely wipe an iPad if a player is cut or traded. Players can study game film anywhere. Denver Broncos tight end Jacob Tamme says, "It changes the way you prepare. You can come off the practice field, get in the cold tub and watch film…on your iPad." Before, says Russ Trainor, the Broncos's vice president of information technology, "They had to come in, sit down at a computer and look at video that way. Or they had to look at tape and they had to be at a big machine to look at that tape. Now, it's right on the iPad." Plus, new plays or changes to existing plays are pushed out to coaches and players with a click.[10]

*As the NFL's new PlayerLync system demonstrates, information is useful when it is **17-2a accurate, 17-2b complete,***

*17-2c relevant, and 17-2d timely.** However, there can be significant **17-2e acquisition, 17-2f processing, 17-2g storage, 17-2h retrieval,** and **17-2i communication costs** associated with useful information.*

17-2a Accurate Information

Information is useful when it is accurate. Before relying on information to make decisions, you must know that the information is correct. But what if it isn't? Many retailers use customer satisfaction surveys to determine what they need to improve, and checkout wait times are always near the top of the list. But asking customers about checkout wait times can produce inaccurate data. Shoppers accurately estimate wait times of three minutes or less but overestimate four-minute waits, which they report as five or six minutes, and completely misestimate five-minute waits, which they report as ten minutes. Typically, retailers relying on these data overestimate checkout wait time and can end up hiring too many cashiers to solve the problem.[11]

Kroger, instead, gets more accurate data from infrared cameras that count the number of customers in the store and waiting at checkout registers. These data showed Kroger that its stores had many customers at lunch and in the morning buying just a few items, who would be better served by express lanes, so Kroger added 2,000 more to its stores. As a result of these changes, made on the basis of more accurate information, the average wait at Kroger has dropped from four minutes to twenty-six seconds.[12]

17-2b Complete Information

Information is useful when it is complete. Incomplete or missing information makes it difficult to recognize problems and identify potential solutions. Following an airplane crash, investigators recover critical information from the plane's black box recordings. If the black box is lost or damaged, then investigators may never understand what happened. "Everyone talks about the black box on an airplane," says Vic Charlebois, vice president of flight operations at Canadian airline First Air, "but it is permanently installed on an airplane, and if the airplane goes missing so does the black box."[13] Indeed, when Malaysia Airlines Flight 370 disappeared en route from Kuala Lumpur to Beijing in March 2014, investigators were left guessing as to the cause because the plane and its black box were still missing after a four-month search.[14]

Regulators have long suggested putting live data systems on planes to transmit real time in-flight data, but airlines have hesitated because of costs estimated at $100,000 per plane.[15] Canadian-based First Air is installing a live data streaming service that can provide much more complete and useful information. Made by Canadian-based Flyht, First Air's FLYHTStream system can be preprogrammed to automatically transmit live data under certain conditions, or it can be manually activated by the pilot or ground-based flight controllers. First Air's Vic Charlebois says, "Let's take the case of the Malaysian aircraft. If it was being monitored through satellites and a dispatcher did see it wander off course somewhere, the procedure would be to activate the FLYHTStream and then contact the crew to see what was going on."[16]

17-2c Relevant Information

You can have complete, accurate information, but it's not very useful if it doesn't pertain to the problems you're facing. For instance, if you're unlucky enough to contract bullous pemphigoid, a rare skin condition resulting in large, watery blisters on your inner thighs and upper arms, chances are the dermatologist you visit won't have any relevant experience with this condition to be able to recognize and treat it. And that's exactly what happened to Dr. Kavita Mariwalla, who was stumped when a patient came in with these problems. So she turned to Modernizing Medicine, an iPad-based medical records system to obtain the relevant information needed to determine what was wrong. Modernizing Medicine is a web-based database, containing information from more than 14 million patient visits compiled by 3,700 doctors, that uses the same kind of data mining and artificial intelligence used by web sites like Amazon.com. Dr. Eric Horvitz, Microsoft's managing director of research, says, "Electronic health records [are] like large quarries where there's lots of gold, and we're just beginning to mine them."[17] Dr. Mariwalla was able to quickly access similar cases on Modernizing Medicine's database and find other drugs that had been effective in those cases. Mariwalla said that Modernizing Medicine, "Gives you access to data, and data is king. It's been very helpful, especially in clinically challenging situations."[18]

17-2d Timely Information

Finally, information is useful when it is timely. To be timely, the information must be available when needed to define a problem or to begin to identify possible solutions. If you've ever thought, "I wish I had known that earlier," then you understand the importance of timely information and the opportunity cost of not having it.

Maple syrup used to come from buckets hanging from taps bored into trees to extrude maple sap. Instead of buckets, modern maple syrup production uses long flexible plastic tubes to transport the sap miles away to sugar-storage houses. When the sap stops flowing because of leaks, it can take workers days to walk the lines to locate them. And with a short 4–6 week season, fixing leaks quickly is critical. Meadowbrook Maple Syrup, in Vermont, has 5,000 taps and 18 miles of tubes spread out over 100 acres. To reduce the time spent looking for leaks, Meadowbrook installed a Tap Track system that uses solar-powered sensors to monitor line pressure at each tree. When the system detects a drop in pressure (indicating a leak), it sends an alert to company computers and smartphones. Eric Sorkin of Thunder Basin Maple Works, described how the Tap Track system directed his workers to a porcupine-caused leak. Just as they fixed that leak, the system alerted them to one nearby. Sorkin said, "You could follow the porcupine right to the next line where he'd cut it. Otherwise, it would have been a few more days before we found those two lines."[19]

17-2e Acquisition Costs

Acquisition cost is the cost of obtaining data that you don't have. Acxiom, a billion-dollar company, gathers and processes data for direct-mail marketing companies. If you've received an unsolicited, "preapproved" credit card application recently (and who hasn't?), chances are

Pjohnson1/iStockphoto.com

| **Acquisition cost** the cost of obtaining data that you don't have |

Acxiom helped the credit card company gather information about you. Where does Acxiom get that information? The first place it turns is to companies that sell consumer credit reports at a wholesale cost of $1 each. Acxiom also obtains information from retailers. Each time you use your credit card, websites and retailers' checkout scanners gather information about your spending habits and product preferences. Acxiom also uses publicly available information such as motor vehicle and real estate records, as well as website traffic.

So why pay for this information? Acquiring it can help credit card companies better identify who will mail back a signed credit card application and who will rip the credit card application in half and toss it in the trash. Likewise, Acxiom's information helps retailers by categorizing consumers into seventy demographic groups. For example, Nordstrom, an upscale department store, would find it worthwhile to advertise to "Apple Pie Families," married homeowners between the ages of forty-six and sixty-five who live in urban areas, earn $100,000 to $500,000, and have school-age children. Likewise, Walmart is better off advertising to "Trucks and Trailers," people between the ages of thirty and forty-five who earn less than $100,000 and live in rural areas. Paying Acxiom to acquire this kind of data significantly increases the return that retailers and credit card companies get from advertising and direct marketing.

Processing cost the cost of turning raw data into usable information

Storage cost the cost of physically or electronically archiving information for later retrieval and use

17-2f Processing Costs

Companies often have massive amounts of data but not in the form or combination they need. **Processing cost** is the cost of turning raw data into usable information. While Google offers a wide range of online services, most of its revenues come from search-related ads. But those ads are effective only when Google serves up accurate searches that help people find what they're looking for. In an effort to provide more precise searches, Google is now connecting and linking the information that users "leave behind" as they use Google search, YouTube, Gmail, other Google services, and their Android phones. For example, Google says that these additional data can help it determine if a user searching for "jaguar" is looking for a cat or a car. Of course, turning all of that data into meaningful information to improve search accuracy requires massive computing power. Thus, Google operates ten extraordinarily expensive data centers around the world. Google's data center in Finland, for example, cost $273 million; the one in Hong Kong, $300 million; and the one in Singapore, $120 million. And that is just the up-front cost; the cost of staffing and maintaining the centers for years to come will be millions more.[20]

17-2g Storage Costs

Storage cost is the cost of physically or electronically archiving information for later retrieval and use. While your Facebook account is free, Facebook spends billions so that its more than 1 billion users worldwide can connect with their friends, play online games, and share photos. In addition to existing data centers in Oregon, North Carolina, and Sweden, Facebook is building a 476,000 sq. ft. $300 million data center in

Jaguar

OR

Jaguar

Ammit/iStockphoto.com / Paolo Cipriani/iStockphoto.com

Altoona, Iowa. Jay Parikh, Facebook's vice president of Infrastructure Engineering, says, "When complete, Altoona will be among the most advanced and energy efficient facilities of its kind." Tom Furlong, Facebook's vice president of Site Operations, says, "This location had fiber, power, and a shovel-ready site." Facebook has plans to triple its initial investment in Iowa to more than a billion.[21]

17-2h Retrieval Costs

Retrieval cost is the cost of accessing already-stored and processed information. One of the most common misunderstandings about information is that it is easy and cheap to retrieve once the company has it. Not so. First, you have to find the information. Then, you've got to convince whoever has it to share it with you. Then the information has to be processed into a form that is useful for you. By the time you get the information you need, it may not be timely anymore.

For example, as companies move toward paperless office systems, how will employees quickly and easily retrieve archived emails, file records, website information, word processing documents, or images? Likewise, how will managers and employees quickly and easily retrieve information about costs, inventory, and sales?

One solution is broadly known as *business intelligence software* (BIS), which transforms stored, unstructured data in real time into meaningful information for business analysis and decision making. For example, retailers now commonly use sensors, video, and bluetooth cell phone tracking to count and monitor the flow of shoppers throughout their stores. These sensors track which entrances and exits are most commonly used, where customers spend most of their time in the store, how long they stay in a particular location, etc. During the holiday season when stores were crowded, Sunhee Moon, a San Francisco retailer, was surprised to learn that customers spent more time at tables near the back of the store, and not the entrance. So holiday scarves were moved to the back where more customers would see them.[22] Likewise, through bluetooth tracking of your phone, retailers could, for instance, see that you've been to the store four times without buying. The tracking system could then be programmed to send your phone a mobile coupon on entering the store. Since mobile coupons are used 10 times more than paper coupons, and since smartphone users are 14 percent more likely than those without smartphones to use those mobile coupons while in the store, BIS monitoring gives retailers powerful new tools to track store performance and increase sales.[23]

17-2i Communication Costs

Communication cost is the cost of transmitting information from one place to another. For example, a small business with twenty people needing phone lines, a hosted website, and high-speed Internet access pays Comcast about $1,300 a month for that access. Google, Microsoft, and Facebook do the same for their employees. But because of the size of the data flowing from their websites to customers, they pay millions more in access fees to Comcast and Time Warner Cable, which provide the backbone through which Internet data run. While such payments are rare, it makes sense that generators of heavy Internet traffic pay more, especially since Comcast's Internet traffic is growing at 55 percent per year. Netflix, which accounts for 15 to 20 percent of all traffic on the Internet because of video streaming, has also begun paying Comcast and other Internet providers so that its streaming services are prioritized in network traffic to customers' homes.[24]

17-3 CAPTURING, PROCESSING, AND PROTECTING INFORMATION

In 1907, Metropolitan Life Insurance built a huge office building in New York City for its brand-new, state-of-the-art information technology system. What was this great breakthrough in information management? Card files. That's right, the same card file system that every library in America used before computers. Metropolitan Life's information technology consisted of 20,000 separate file drawers that sat in hundreds of file cabinets more than fifteen feet tall. This filing system held 20 million insurance applications, 700,000 accounting books, and 500,000 death certificates. Metropolitan Life employed sixty-one workers who did nothing but sort, file, and climb ladders to pull files as needed.[25]

How we get and share information has clearly changed. The cost, inefficiency, and ineffectiveness of

Retrieval cost the cost of accessing already-stored and processed information

Communication cost the cost of transmitting information from one place to another

using this formerly state-of-the-art system would put an insurance company out of business within months. Today, if storms, fire, or accidents damage policyholders' property, insurance companies write checks on the spot to cover the losses. When policyholders buy a car, they call their insurance agent from the dealership to activate their insurance before driving off in their new cars. And now, insurance companies are marketing their products and services to customers directly from the Internet. From card files to Internet files in just under a century, the rate of change in information technology is spectacular.

In this section, you will learn about the information technologies that companies use to **17-3a capture, 17-3b process,** *and* **17-3c protect information.**

Anatoliy Babiy/iStockphoto.com

17-3a Capturing Information

There are two basic methods of capturing information: manual and electronic. Manual capture of information is a slow, costly, labor-intensive, and often inaccurate process, which entails recording and entering data by hand into a data storage device. For example, when you applied for a driver's license, you probably recorded personal information about yourself by filling out a form. Then, after you passed your driver's test, someone typed your handwritten information into the department of motor vehicles' computer database so that local and state police could access it from their patrol cars in the event they pulled you over for speeding. (Isn't information great?) To avoid the problems inherent in such a system, companies are relying more on electronic capture. They use electronic storage devices such as bar codes, radio frequency identification tags, and document scanners to capture and record data electronically.

Bar codes represent numerical data by varying the thickness and pattern of vertical bars. The primary advantage of bar codes is that the data they represent can be read and recorded in an instant with a handheld or pen-type scanner. One pass of the scanner (okay, sometimes several) and "beep!" the information has been captured. Bar codes cut checkout times in half, reduce data entry errors by 75 percent, and save stores money because stockers don't have to go through the labor-intensive process of putting a price tag on each item in the store.[26] And, with mobile phone apps, bar codes are becoming ubiquitous in travel (mobile boarding passes), for customer loyalty and payment programs (Starbucks), and in entertainment, such as movies (Fandango) and live events (LiveNation or TicketMaster). *QR (quick response) codes* are bar codes with black and white patterns that you scan with your smartphone. While they've been used in Japan for a decade, QR codes are now becoming more popular in the U.S. Twenty percent of American shoppers scan a QR code each month, usually to get a coupon or in-store promotion or to learn more information about a company or its products.[27] Customers at Dick's Sporting Goods stores can scan QR codes when shopping to learn about athletic training tools. For example, scanning a QR code for a 12 lb. medicine ball shows customers a video that demonstrates how to perform a lunge, pushups, and a squat toss, all while incorporating the medicine ball in the exercise.[28]

Radio frequency identification (RFID) tags contain minuscule microchips and antennas that transmit information via radio waves.[29] Unlike bar codes, which require direct line-of-sight scanning, RFID tags are read by turning on an RFID reader that, like a radio, tunes into a specific frequency to determine the number *and* location of products, parts, or anything else to which the RFID tags are attached. Turn on an RFID reader, and every RFID tag within the reader's range (from several hundred to several thousand feet) is accounted for.

Bar code a visual pattern that represents numerical data by varying the thickness and pattern of vertical bars

Radio frequency identification (RFID) tags tags containing minuscule microchips that transmit information via radio waves and can be used to track the number and location of the objects into which the tags have been inserted

Because they are now so inexpensive, RFID tags and readers are being put to thousands of uses in all kinds of businesses. Disney World is using RFID sensors to offer guests an efficient, personalized vacation experience through RFID-equipped wristbands. MagicBands, as Disney calls them, allow customers to enter the park with a quick wrist swipe instead of using paper tickets, and can be linked to visitors' payment information, which means not having to carry cash or credit cards to pay for a third plate of Mickey waffles. MagicBands also facilitate a personalized experience by sharing names, birthdays and preferences with park employees (at the parents' discretion, of course) so that a birthday girl meeting Cinderella, her favorite princess, is greeted by name and with special wishes for a happy birthday. None of this could happen without RFID.[30]

Electronic scanners, which convert printed text and pictures into digital images, have become an increasingly popular method of capturing data electronically because they are inexpensive and easy to use. The first requirement for a good scanner is a document feeder that automatically feeds document pages into the scanner or turns the pages (often with a puff of air) when scanning books or bound documents. Text that has been digitized cannot be searched or edited like the regular text in your word processing software, however; so the second requirement for a good scanner is **optical character recognition** software to scan and convert original or digitized documents into ASCII (American Standard Code for Information Interchange) text or Adobe PDF documents. ASCII text can be searched, read, and edited with standard word processing, email, desktop publishing, database management, and spreadsheet software, and PDF documents can be searched and edited with Adobe's Acrobat software.

17-3b Processing Information

Processing information means transforming raw data into meaningful information that can be applied to business decision making. Evaluating sales data to determine the best- and worst-selling products, examining repair records to determine product reliability, and monitoring the cost of long-distance phone calls are all examples of processing raw data into meaningful information. And with automated, electronic capture of data, increased processing power, and cheaper and more plentiful ways to store data, managers no longer worry about getting data. Instead, they scratch their heads about how to use the overwhelming amount of data that pours into their businesses every day. Furthermore, most managers know little about statistics and

Airport Biometrics

So really, who isn't sick of waiting in line at the airport or showing your ticket and your driver's license two or three (or more) times to prove that you're just a harmless passenger and not a global threat? If Silicon Valley–based AOptix Technologies has its way, those long lines and endless ID checks may soon be a thing of the past. The company has developed a scanner that is unlike anything currently in use anywhere. Whereas other iris scanners require people to stand less than a foot away from a scanner without moving for several minutes, AOptix's scanners can take a picture from eight feet away in just seconds. The software then converts the iris scan into a code, compares it to existing codes in a central database, and confirms the identity of the passenger in just two seconds.

Source: A. Vance, "Through Airport Security in the Blink of an Eye," *Bloomberg Businessweek*, August 22, 2012, accessed June 22, 2013, http://www.businessweek .com/articles/2012-08-22/through-airport-security-in-the-blink-of-an-eye.

have neither the time nor the inclination to learn how to use them to analyze data.

One promising tool to help managers dig out from under the avalanche of data is data mining. **Data mining** is the process of discovering patterns and relationships in large amounts of data.[31] Data mining is carried out using complex algorithms such as neural networks, rule induction, and decision trees. If you don't know what those are, that's okay. With data mining, you don't have to. Most managers only need to know that data mining looks for patterns that are already in the data but are too complex for them to spot on their own. Netflix is a subscription-based service for streaming movies and TV shows and renting DVDs, so many felt it was taking a risk by producing its first series, *House of Cards*, a political drama featuring Kevin Spacey. However, with 33 million subscribers hitting "play" 30 million times a day, adding 4 million ratings each day to what they watch, and searching its website

Electronic scanner an electronic device that converts printed text and pictures into digital images

Optical character recognition the ability of software to convert digitized documents into ASCII (American Standard Code for Information Interchange) text that can be searched, read, and edited by word processing and other kinds of software

Processing information transforming raw data into meaningful information

Data mining the process of discovering unknown patterns and relationships in large amounts of data

3 million times per day, Netflix had data to mine that most entertainment businesses don't have. Those data showed that customers liked actor Kevin Spacey, the original British version of *House of Cards*, and films by director David Fincher. Chief communications officer Jonathan Friedland says, "Because we have a direct relationship with consumers, we know what people like to watch and that helps us understand how big the interest is going to be for a given show. It gave us some confidence that we could find an audience for a show like 'House of Cards.'"[32]

Data mining typically splits a data set in half, finds patterns in one half, and then tests the validity of those patterns by trying to find them again in the second half of the data set. The data typically come from a **data warehouse,** which stores huge amounts of data that have been prepared for data mining analysis by being

cleaned of errors and redundancy. The data in a data warehouse can then be analyzed using two kinds of data mining. **Supervised data mining** usually begins with the user telling the data mining software to look and test for specific patterns and relationships in a data set. Typically, this is done through a series of "what-if?" questions or statements. For instance, a grocery store manager might instruct the data mining software to determine if coupons placed in the Sunday paper increase or decrease sales. By contrast, with **unsupervised data mining,** the user simply tells the data mining software to uncover whatever patterns and relationships it can find in a data set. For example, because New York City (NYC) experiences about 3,000 major fires a year, analysts at the NYC Fire Department use data mining to predict which of the 330,000 buildings in New York are at most risk of catching fire. The data mining program checks for sixty different risk factors commonly correlated with fires, such as the building's age, elevators (which allow smoke and super heated air to move from floor to floor), and whether the building is vacant, abandoned, or has had electrical problems, and then generates a risk score for each building, allowing fire inspectors to prioritize high-risk buildings for on-site inspections.[33] Unsupervised data mining is particularly good at identifying association or affinity patterns, sequence patterns, and predictive patterns. It can also identify what data mining technicians call data clusters.[34]

Association or affinity patterns occur when two or more database elements tend to occur together

Data warehouse   a database that stores huge amounts of data that have been prepared for data mining analysis by being cleaned of errors and redundancy

Supervised data mining   the process when the user tells the data mining software to look and test for specific patterns and relationships in a data set

Unsupervised data mining   the process when the user simply tells the data mining software to uncover whatever patterns and relationships it can find in a data set

Association or affinity patterns   when two or more database elements tend to occur together in a significant way

in a significant way. Most retailers send flyers and coupons about baby products after a woman has given birth (after the birth announcement is made public), but Target wanted to act earlier, sometime around the first twenty weeks of pregnancy, when mothers-to-be start buying items to get ready for their new baby. So it turned to association and affinity patterns to see if there was a way to identify through purchasing patterns when a woman was pregnant. Target's Guest Marketing Analytics department analyzed consumer data from Target's baby registry and found that around the beginning of their second trimester, pregnant women often bought lotion, mineral and vitamin supplements, unscented soap, hand sanitizer, and washcloths. Target found a pattern of twenty-five products that identified pregnant customers with such accuracy that the company could even estimate a due date. For example, if you're female, are twenty-three years old, and have bought cocoa-butter lotion, a large purse that doubles as a diaper bag, zinc and magnesium supplements (taken by pregnant women), and a blue or pink throw rug, there's an 87 percent chance that you are pregnant. Why? Because those purchases are almost always associated with being pregnant.[35]

Sequence patterns appear when two or more database elements occur together in a significant pattern in which one of the elements precedes the other. **Zynga**, which makes the popular online game *FarmVille*, pulls down twenty-five terabytes of data per day, the equivalent of 1,000 Blu-ray discs. In the first version of *FarmVille*, animals were primarily decorative. But data mining uncovered a sequence pattern where, surprisingly, users interacted with farm animals (database element #1) and used in-game currency (database element #2), which is paid for with Facebook credits, PayPal accounts, or FarmCash, (all linked to users' credit cards), to buy and sell the animals. As a result, Zynga made animals much more important in *FarmVille 2*, where, for instance, if you sold cakes in your *FarmVille 2* virtual business, you'd have to buy a cow for milk and chickens for eggs.[36]

Predictive patterns are just the opposite of association or affinity patterns. Whereas association or affinity patterns look for database elements that seem to go together, **predictive patterns** help identify database elements that are different. Banks and credit card companies use data mining to find predictive patterns that distinguish customers who are good credit risks from those who are poor credit risks and less likely to pay their loans and monthly bills. Likewise, InterContinental Hotels Group uses data mining to customize marketing messages for different kinds of customers. A typical marketing campaign will have seven to fifteen marketing messages aimed at the typical InterContinental customer. But thanks to data mining, InterContinental's marketing campaigns now have 1,500 marketing messages for twelve different customer groups, each defined thanks to clear differences across 4,000 variables or attributes. For instance, one customer group looking for bargains uses reward points and tends to stay on weekends. So they only get marketing messages about weekend packages and events, in contrast to business travelers who are less price sensitive, pay with corporate credit cards, and stay during the week.[37]

Data clusters are the last kind of pattern found by data mining. **Data clusters** occur when three or more database elements occur together (i.e., cluster) in a significant way. For example, after analyzing several years' worth of repair and warranty claims, Ford Motor Company might find that, compared with cars built in its Chicago plant, the cars it builds in Kansas City (first element) are more likely to have problems with over-tightened fan belts (second element) that break (third element) and result in overheated engines (fourth element), ruined radiators (fifth element), and payments for tow trucks (sixth element), which are paid for by Ford's five-year, 60,000-mile power train warranty.

Traditionally, data mining has been very expensive and very complex. Today, however, data mining services and analyses are much more affordable and within reach of most companies' budgets. And, if it follows the path of most technologies, data mining will become even easier and cheaper to use in the future.

17-3c Protecting Information

Protecting information is the process of ensuring that data are reliably and consistently retrievable in a usable format for authorized users but no one else. Unfortunately, that didn't happen at Target in December 2013 when hackers entered Target's information systems by obtaining authorization credentials from a Target vendor (Fazio Mechanical Services, which installs supermarket refrigeration systems). Hacker-installed malware

Sequence patterns when two or more database elements occur together in a significant pattern in which one of the elements precedes the other

Predictive patterns patterns that help identify database elements that are different

Data clusters when three or more database elements occur together (i.e., cluster) in a significant way

Protecting information the process of ensuring that data are reliably and consistently retrievable in a usable format for authorized users but no one else

stole 40 million credit and debit card numbers via card swipes at Target checkout lanes, and 70 million phone numbers and email addresses from Target's internal databases.[38] Sales transactions dropped 3–4 percent after Target announced its systems had been compromised. To restore goodwill, it offered a 10 percent discount on all store items and gave all affected customers a free year of credit monitoring protection. Customers did not have to pay for any fraudulent transactions on their cards.[39]

People inside and outside companies can steal or destroy company data in various ways, including denial-of-service web server attacks that can bring down some of the busiest and best-run sites on the Internet; viruses and spyware/adware that spread quickly and can result in data loss and business disruption; keystroke monitoring, in which every mouse click and keystroke you make is monitored, stored, and sent to unauthorized users; password-cracking software that steals supposedly secure passwords; and phishing, where fake but real-looking emails and websites trick users into sharing personal information (user names, passwords, account numbers) leading to unauthorized account access. On average, 19 percent of computers are infected with viruses, 80 percent have spyware, and only one-third are running behind a protected firewall (discussed shortly). Studies show that the threats listed in Exhibit 17.3 are so widespread that automatic attacks will begin on an unprotected computer just fifteen seconds after it connects to the Internet.[40]

As shown in the right-hand column of Exhibit 17.3, numerous steps can be taken to secure data and data networks. Some of the most important are authentication and authorization, firewalls, antivirus software for PCs and email servers, data encryption, and virtual private networks.[41] We will review those steps and then finish this section with a brief review of the dangers of wireless networks.

Two critical steps are required to make sure that data can be accessed by authorized users and no one else. One is **authentication,** that is, making sure users are who they claim to be.[42] The other is **authorization,** that is,

Authentication making sure potential users are who they claim to be

Authorization granting authenticated users approved access to data, software, and systems

No More Passwords?

Passwords are one of the biggest inconveniences when going online. If you pick a password that's too simple, you might get hacked. If you pick a complicated password, it's too hard to remember. Many technology companies are looking for new ways to improve security, such as the use of biometrics. Many laptops have built-in fingerprint readers, and Apple's iPhone 5S introduced a fingerprint sensor to Apple's smartphones. Microsoft designed Windows 8.1 with a finger-print-based biometric ID system as well. Some analysts believe that smartphones and other mobile devices could actually help provide better security, as most of them have built-in cameras and microphones that could be used for voice- and facial-recognition applications. "We think that biometric authentication is going to be significantly more popular," says Ant Allan, research vice president at Gartner Inc., "and the driver and enabler of this is mobile computing." Allan explains that for large companies, installing new hardware for every employee would be very expensive. Using existing technologies that everyone already has, Allan says, could have great economic advantages.

Source: A. Blackman, "Say Goodbye to the Password," *Wall Street Journal*, September 15, 2013, accessed June 6, 2014, http://online.wsj.com/news/articles/SB10001424127887323585604579008620509295960?mg=reno64-wsj.

Exhibit 17.3
Security Threats to Data and Data Networks

Security Problem	Source	Affects	Severity	The Threat	The Solution
Denial of service; web server attacks and corporate network attacks	Internet hackers	All servers	High	Loss of data, disruption of service, and theft of service.	Implement firewall, password control, server-side review, threat monitoring, and bug fixes; turn PCs off when not in use.
Password cracking software and unauthorized access to PCs	Local area network, Internet	All users, especially digital subscriber line and cable Internet users	High	Hackers take over PCs. Privacy can be invaded. Corporate users' systems are exposed to other machines on the network.	Close ports and firewalls, disable file and print sharing, and use strong passwords.
Viruses, worms, Trojan horses, and rootkits	Email, downloaded and distributed software	All users	Moderate to high	Monitor activities and cause data loss and file deletion; compromise security by sometimes concealing their presence.	Use antivirus software and firewalls; control Internet access.
Spyware, adware, malicious scripts and applets	Rogue web pages	All users	Moderate to high	Invade privacy, intercept passwords, and damage files or file system.	Disable browser script support; use security, blocking, and spyware/adware software.
Email snooping	Hackers on your network and the Internet	All users	Moderate to high	People read your email from intermediate servers or packets, or they physically access your machine.	Encrypt messages, ensure strong password protection, and limit physical access to machines.
Keystroke monitoring	Trojan horses, people with direct access to PCs	All users	High	Records everything typed at the keyboard and intercepts keystrokes before password masking or encryption occurs.	Use antivirus software to catch Trojan horses, control Internet access to transmission, and implement system monitoring and physical access control.
Phishing	Hackers on your network and the Internet	All users, including customers	High	Fake but real-looking emails and websites that trick users into sharing personal information on what they wrongly think is a company's website. This leads to unauthorized account access.	Educate and warn users and customers about the dangers. Encourage both not to click on potentially fake URLs, which might take them to phishing websites. Instead, have them type your company's URL into the web browser.
Spam	Email	All users and corporations	Mild to high	Clogs and overloads email servers and inboxes with junk mail. HTML-based spam may be used for profiling and identifying users.	Filter known spam sources and senders on email servers; have users create further lists of approved and unapproved senders on their personal computers.
Cookies	Websites you visit	Individual users	Mild to moderate	Trace web usage and permit the creation of personalized web pages that track behavior and interest profiles.	Use cookie managers to control and edit cookies, and use ad blockers.

Sources: K. Bannan, "Look Out: Watching You, Watching Me," *PC Magazine*, July 2002, 99; A. Dragoon, "Fighting Phish, Fakes, and Frauds," *CIO*, September 1, 2004, 33; B. Glass, "Are You Being Watched?" *PC Magazine*, April 23, 2002, 54; K. Karagiannis, "DDoS: Are You Next?" *PC Magazine*, January 2003, 79; B. Machrone, "Protect & Defend," *PC Magazine*, June 27, 2000, 168–181; "Top 10 Security Threats," *PC Magazine*, April 10, 2007, 66; M. Sarrel, "Master End-User Security," *PC Magazine*, May 2008, 101.

granting authenticated users approved access to data, software, and systems.[43] When an ATM prompts you to enter your personal identification number (PIN), the bank is authenticating that you are you. Once you've been authenticated, you are authorized to access your funds and no one else's. Of course, as anyone who has lost a PIN or password or had one stolen knows, user authentication systems are not foolproof. In particular, users create security risks by not changing their default account passwords (such as birth dates) or by using weak passwords such as names ("Larry") or complete words ("football") that are quickly guessed by password-cracking software.[44]

This is why many companies are now turning to **two-factor authentication,** which is based on what users know, such as a password, and what they have, in their possession have, such as a secure ID card, their phones, or unique information that only they would know.[45] When logging in, users are first asked for their passwords. But then they must provide a second authentication factor, such as an answer to a security question (i.e., unique information) or a validation code that has been sent to their mobile phone. Google, for example, requires two-factor authentication for its Google Apps (Gmail, Calendar, Drive, Docs, etc.). After entering their passwords, users can either use the code sent via text to their phone, or a code generated by Google's Authenticator app. Google Authenticator works via your mobile phone connection or Wi-Fi, gives you the ability to generate authentication codes for multiple accounts (including non-Google accounts), and generates codes that are only good for 60 seconds.[46]

Unfortunately, stolen or cracked passwords are not the only way for hackers and electronic thieves to gain access to an organization's computer resources. Unless special safeguards are put in place, every time corporate users are online there's literally nothing between their personal computers and the Internet (home users with high-speed DSL or cable Internet access face the same risks).

Two-factor authentication authentication based on what users know, such as a password and what they have in their possession, such as a secure ID card or key

Firewall a protective hardware or software device that sits between the computers in an internal organizational network and outside networks, such as the Internet

Virus a program or piece of code that, without your knowledge, attaches itself to other programs on your computer and can trigger anything from a harmless flashing message to the reformatting of your hard drive to a system-wide network shutdown

Data encryption the transformation of data into complex, scrambled digital codes that can be decrypted only by authorized users who possess unique decryption keys

Hackers can access files, run programs, and control key parts of computers if precautions aren't taken. To reduce these risks, companies use **firewalls,** hardware or software devices that sit between the computers in an internal organizational network and outside networks such as the Internet. Firewalls filter and check incoming and outgoing data. They prevent company insiders from accessing unauthorized sites or from sending confidential company information to people outside the company. Firewalls also prevent outsiders from identifying and gaining access to company computers and data. Indeed, if a firewall is working properly, the computers behind the company firewall literally cannot be seen or accessed by outsiders.

A **virus** is a program or piece of code that, without your knowledge, attaches itself to other programs on your computer and can trigger anything from a harmless flashing message to the reformatting of your hard drive to a system-wide network shutdown. You used to have to do something or run something to get a virus, such as double-clicking an infected email attachment. Today's viruses are much more threatening. In fact, with some viruses, just being connected to a network can infect your computer. *Antivirus software for personal computers* scans email, downloaded files, and computer hard drives, disk drives, and memory to detect and stop computer viruses from doing damage. However, this software is effective only to the extent that users of individual computers have and use up-to-date versions. With new viruses appearing all the time, users should update their antivirus software weekly or, even better, configure their virus software to automatically check for, download, and install updates. By contrast, *corporate antivirus software* automatically scans email attachments such as Microsoft Word documents, graphics, or text files as they come across the company email server. It also monitors and scans all file downloads across company databases and network servers. So, while antivirus software for personal computers prevents individual computers from being infected, corporate antivirus software for email servers, databases, and network servers adds another layer of protection by preventing infected files from multiplying and being sent to others.

Another way of protecting information is to encrypt sensitive data. **Data encryption** transforms data into complex, scrambled digital codes that can be decrypted only by authorized users who possess unique decryption keys. One method of data encryption is to use products by Symantec (http://buy.symantec.com/estore/mf/category HomePage) to encrypt the files stored on personal computers or network servers and databases. This is especially important with laptop computers, which are easily stolen. With people increasingly gaining unauthorized access to email messages—email snooping—it's also important to encrypt sensitive email messages and file attachments. You can use a system called "public key encryption" to do so. First, give copies of your "public key" to anyone who sends you files or email. Have the sender use the public key, which is actually a piece of software, to encrypt files before sending them to you. The only way to decrypt the files is with a companion "private key" that you keep to yourself.

Although firewalls can protect personal computers and network servers connected to the corporate network, people away from their offices (e.g., salespeople, business travelers, telecommuters) who interact with their company networks via the Internet face a security risk. Because Internet data are not encrypted, "packet sniffer" software easily allows hackers to read everything sent or received except files that have been encrypted before sending. Previously, the only practical solution was to have employees dial in to secure company phone lines for direct access to the company network. Of course, with international and long-distance phone calls, the costs quickly added up. Now, **virtual private networks (VPNs)** have solved this problem by using software to encrypt all Internet data at both ends of the transmission process. Instead of making long-distance calls, employees connect to the Internet. But, unlike typical Internet connections in which data packets are decrypted, the VPN encrypts the data sent by employees outside the company computer network, decrypts the data when they arrive within the company network, and does the same when data are sent back to the computer outside the network. VPN connections provide secure access to everything on a company's network. If your employer or university doesn't provide a VPN, you can purchase VPN services for personal use and protection from well known providers, such as AnchorFree Hotspot Shield (www.anchorfree.com) or Cloak VPN (www.getcloak.com), for about $3 a month. VPN services should be used when connected to public Wi-Fi systems, such as in hotels, airports, or coffee shops, where anyone on the public network can monitor or spy on what you're doing.

Alternatively, many companies are now adopting web-based **secure sockets layer (SSL) encryption** to provide secure off-site access to data and programs. If you've ever entered your credit card in a web browser to make an online purchase, you've used SSL technology to encrypt and protect that information.

You can tell if SSL encryption is being used on a website if you see a padlock icon (gold in Internet Explorer or Firefox, green in Google Chrome, silver in Safari) or if the URL begins with "https." SSL encryption works the same way in the workplace. Managers and employees who aren't at the office simply connect to the Internet, open a web browser, and then enter a user name and password to gain access to SSL-encrypted data and programs.

Hiding from Big Data

You may have heard that Target once figured that a woman was pregnant—even before she knew it herself—using data collections. Assistant professor of sociology at Princeton University Janet Vertesi decided to try an experiment: she endeavored to keep her own pregnancy secret from big data for as long as possible. Vertesi censored what she did and said on social media, and asked her friends to do the same. She conducted all baby-related web browsing using a traceless browser and made all baby-related purchases with cash or Amazon gift cards bought with cash. She even had orders mailed to an anonymous drop box so that they wouldn't be linked to her home address. "I didn't expect it to be as hard as it was," Vertesi says. "It was extremely impractical and inconvenient." She discovered it was much more expensive, too; avoiding loyalty cards meant missing out on a lot of deals. Vertesi noted that many of the things she had to do, taken together at face value, made it appear like she was doing something illegal. Her final verdict: "I wouldn't recommend [opting out]." Spreading activity over different servers is more effective and less inconvenient.

Source: J. Goldstein, "Meet The Woman Who Did Everything in Her Power To Hide Her Pregnancy From Big Data," *ThinkProgress*, April 29, 2014, accessed June 2, 2014, http://thinkprogress.org/culture/2014/04/29/3432050/can-you-hide-from-big-data/.

Finally, many companies now have wireless networks, which make it possible for anybody with a laptop and a wireless card to access the company network from anywhere in the office. Though wireless networks come equipped with security and encryption capabilities that, in theory, permit only authorized users to access the wireless network, those capabilities are easily bypassed with the right tools. Compounding the problem, many wireless networks are shipped with their security and encryption capabilities turned off for ease of installation.[47] Caution is important even when encryption is turned on, because the WEP (Wired Equivalent Privacy) security protocol is easily compromised. If you work at home or are working on the go, extra care is critical because Wi-Fi networks in homes and public places like hotel lobbies are among

Virtual private network (VPN) software that securely encrypts data sent by employees outside the company network, decrypts the data when they arrive within the company computer network, and does the same when data are sent back to employees outside the network

Secure sockets layer (SSL) encryption Internet browser–based encryption that provides secure off-site web access to some data and programs

the most targeted by hackers.[48] See the Wi-Fi Alliance site at http://www.wi-fi.org for the latest information on wireless security and encryption protocols that provide much stronger protection for your company's wireless network.

Finally, companies are combating security threats by hiring *white hat hackers*, so-called good guys, who test security weak points in information systems so that they can be fixed. While this is typically done using traditional hacking tools, as discussed in Exhibit 17.3, white hat hackers also test security via *social engineering*, in which they trick people into giving up passwords and authentication protocols or unknowingly providing unauthorized access to company computers. One test involves emailing a picture of a cat with a purple mohawk and this subject line, "Check out these kitties!" to employees with a link to more cute kitty photos. When you click an embedded link to "more cute kitty photos," you're taken to a company website warning about the dangers of phishing scams. Think that you wouldn't fall for this? Forty-eight percent of employees receiving this email click the link.[49] Another test involves "lost or left-behind" USB thumb drives, ostensibly belonging to competitors. Inserting the thumb drive into a computer installs software that uses the webcam to snap a picture of the employee, who then receives a visit from the IT security team.[50]

17-4 ACCESSING AND SHARING INFORMATION AND KNOWLEDGE

Today, information technologies are letting companies communicate data, share data, and provide data access to workers, managers, suppliers, and customers in ways that were unthinkable just a few years ago.

After reading this section, you should be able to explain how companies use information technology to improve **17-4a internal access and sharing of information, 17-4b external access and sharing of information,** *and* **17-4c the sharing of knowledge and expertise.**

Executive information system (EIS) a data processing system that uses internal and external data sources to provide the information needed to monitor and analyze organizational performance

Intranets private company networks that allow employees to easily access, share, and publish information using Internet software

17-4a Internal Access and Sharing

Executives, managers, and workers inside the company use three kinds of information technology to access and share information: executive information systems, intranets, and portals. An **executive information system (EIS)** uses internal and external sources of data to provide managers and executives the information they need to monitor and analyze organizational performance.[51] The goal of an EIS is to provide accurate, complete, relevant, and timely information to managers. With just a few mouse clicks and basic commands such as *find*, *compare*, and *show*, the EIS displays costs, sales revenues, and other kinds of data in color-coded charts and graphs. Managers can drill down to view and compare data by global region, country, state, time period, and product. Managers at Colgate-Palmolive, which makes dental (Colgate toothpastes), personal (Irish Spring soap and Speed Stick antiperspirants), and home care (Palmolive dish soaps) products, as well as pet nutrition (Hill's Science Diet), use their EIS, which they call their "dashboard," to see how well the company is running. Ruben Panizza, Colgate's global IT director of business intelligence, says, "These real-time dashboards are a change for people who are used to seeing a lot of numbers with their data. But they quickly realize they can use the information as it's presented in the dashboards to make faster decisions. In the past, executives relied on other people to get custom reports and data. Now, they can look at the information themselves. They see the real data as it is in the system much more easily and quickly. For the first time, many of the company's business leaders are running BI [business intelligence] tools—in this case, dashboards—to monitor the business to see what's going on at a high level."[52]

Intranets are private company networks that allow employees to easily access, share, and publish information using Internet software. Intranet websites are just like external websites, but the firewall separating the internal company network from the Internet permits only authorized internal access.[53] Companies typically use intranets to share information (e.g., about benefits) and to replace paper forms with online forms. Many company intranets are built on the web model as it existed a decade ago. Intranets are evolving to include:

▸ collaboration tools, such as wikis, where team members can post all relevant information for a project they're working on together

▸ customizable email accounts

- presence awareness (information on whether someone you are looking for on the network is in the office, in a meeting, working from home, etc.)

- instant messaging

- simultaneous access to files for virtual team members

Acorda Therapeutics, which develops drugs for neurological conditions, operates a company intranet called Synapse that was recognized as one of the world's ten best intranet sites. Acorda, which doubled in size over the last five years, "needed to develop a tool that would help our associates remain connected to the Company's culture and values, and keep pace with the growing business needs of our organization," says CEO Ron Cohen, MD. One section of Synapse hosts documents that employees might need, from human resources policies and forms to research and development projects and updates. Another feature, called Chatter, functions like Twitter, allowing employees to share photos, documents, and news. Chatter also shows a live feed, where employees respond to Chatter comments, news, and documents, which has the effect of collaboratively shaping ideas. Synapse also has a company-wide seating chart showing where everyone's office is and enables communication by automatically dialing a person's office phone when you click on their profile on Synapse.[54]

Finally, **corporate portals** are a hybrid of executive information systems and intranets. While an EIS provides managers and executives with the information they need to monitor and analyze organizational performance, and intranets help companies distribute and publish information and forms within the company, corporate portals allow company managers and employees to access customized information *and* complete specialized transactions using a web browser.

17-4b External Access and Sharing

Historically, companies have been unable or reluctant to let outside groups have access to corporate information. Now, however, a number of information technologies—electronic data interchange, extranets, web services, and the Internet—are making it easier to share company data with external groups like suppliers and customers. They're also reducing costs, increasing productivity by eliminating manual information processing (70 percent of the data output from one company, like a purchase order, ends up as data input at another company, such as a sales invoice or shipping order), reducing data entry errors, improving customer service, and speeding communications. As a result, managers are scrambling to adopt these technologies.

With **electronic data interchange, or EDI,** two companies convert purchase and ordering information to a standardized format to enable direct electronic transmission of that information from one company's computer system to the other company's system. For example, when a Walmart checkout clerk drags an Apple iPod across the checkout scanner, Walmart's computerized inventory system automatically reorders another iPod through the direct EDI connection that its computer has with Apple's manufacturing and shipping computer. No one at Walmart or Apple fills out paperwork. No one makes phone calls. There are no delays to wait to find out whether Apple has the iPod in stock. The transaction takes place instantly and automatically because the data from both companies were translated into a standardized, shareable, compatible format.

Web services are another way for companies to directly and automatically transmit purchase and ordering data from one company's computer system to another company's computer system. **Web services** use standardized protocols to describe and transfer data from one company in such a way that those data can automatically be read, understood, transcribed, and processed by different computer systems in another company.[55] Route One, which helps automobile dealers process loans for car buyers, was started by the financing companies of DaimlerChrysler, Ford, General Motors, and Toyota. Not surprisingly, each auto company had a different computer system with different operating systems, different programs, and different data structures. RouteOne relies on web services to connect these different computer systems to the wide variety of different databases and software used by various auto dealers, credit bureaus, banks, and other auto financing companies. Without web services, there's no way these different companies and systems could share information.[56]

Corporate portal a hybrid of executive information systems and intranets that allows managers and employees to use a web browser to gain access to customized company information and to complete specialized transactions

Electronic data interchange (EDI) when two companies convert their purchase and ordering information to a standardized format to enable the direct electronic transmission of that information from one company's computer system to the other company's computer system

Web services software that uses standardized protocols to describe data from one company in such a way that those data can automatically be read, understood, transcribed, and processed by different computer systems in another company

Now, what's the difference between web services and EDI? For EDI to work, the data in different companies' computer, database, and network systems must adhere to a particular set of standards for data structure and processing. For example, company X, which has a seven-digit parts numbering system, and company Y, which has an eight-digit parts numbering system, would agree to convert their internal parts numbering systems to identical ten-digit parts numbers when their computer systems talk to each other. By contrast, the tools underlying web services such as extensible markup language (or XML) automatically do the describing and transcribing so that data with different structures can be shared across very different computer systems in different companies. (Don't worry if you don't understand how this works, just appreciate what it does.) As a result, by automatically handling those differences, web services allow organizations to communicate data without special knowledge of each other's computer information systems.

In EDI and web services, the different purchasing and ordering applications in each company interact automatically without any human input. No one has to lift a finger to click a mouse, enter data, or hit the return key. An **extranet,** by contrast, allows companies to exchange information and conduct transactions by purposely providing outsiders with direct, password-protected, web browser–based access to authorized parts of a company's intranet or information system.[57]

In an attempt to improve the marketing efforts of the contractors that it works with, Mitsubishi Electric Cooling & Heating developed its Creative Center extranet. The site provides a host of tools that contractors can use to grow their business. These include a range of company-approved marketing tools like newspaper ads, posters, and banners that each contractor can customize to his or her preference and use to promote both the contractor's business and the Mitsubishi Electric Cooling & Heating brand.[58]

Finally, companies are reducing paperwork and manual information processing by using the Internet to electronically automate transactions with customers; this is similar to the way in which extranets are used to handle transactions with suppliers and distributors. For example, most airlines have automated the ticketing process by eliminating paper tickets altogether. Simply buy

Chris Hondros/Getty Images

an e-ticket via the Internet, and then check yourself in online by printing your boarding pass from your personal computer or from a kiosk at the airport. Internet purchases, ticketless travel, and automated check-ins have together fully automated the purchase of airline tickets. Use of self-service kiosks is expanding, too.

At Hertz Rent-a-Car locations, self-service kiosks come equipped with two monitors. Customers can use one monitor to go through the entire rental process, from verifying identity and insurance to making a payment with a credit card. Customers who need help with the process, especially the first time, can use the other monitor to video chat with a customer service agent who guides them through the process. When done, the kiosk distributes a card with an RFID chip to unlock the customer's rental car. The kiosks allow Hertz to offer 24-hour rentals in nontraditional locations, like car repair shops or centrally located parking lots, without hiring agents for each location.[59]

In the long run, the goal is to link customer Internet sites with company intranets (or EDI) and extranets so that everyone—all the employees and managers within a company as well as the suppliers and distributors outside the company—involved in providing a service or making a product for a customer is automatically notified when a purchase is made. Companies that use EDI, web services, extranets, and the Internet to share data with customers and suppliers achieve increases in productivity 2.7 times larger than those that don't.[60]

17-4c Sharing Knowledge and Expertise

At the beginning of the chapter, we distinguished between raw data, which consist of facts and figures, and information, which consists of useful data that influence someone's choices and behavior. One more important distinction needs to be made, namely, that data and information are not the same as knowledge. **Knowledge** is the understanding that one gains from information. Importantly, knowledge does not reside in information. Knowledge resides in people. That's why companies hire consultants and why family doctors refer patients to specialists. Unfortunately, it can be quite expensive to employ consultants, specialists, and experts. So companies have begun using two information technologies to capture and share the knowledge of consultants, specialists, and experts with other managers and workers: decision support systems and expert systems.

Whereas an executive information system speeds up and simplifies the acquisition of information, a **decision support system (DSS)** helps managers understand problems and potential solutions by acquiring and analyzing information with sophisticated models and tools.[61] Furthermore, whereas EIS programs are broad in scope and permit managers to retrieve all kinds of information about a company, DSS programs are usually narrow in scope and targeted toward helping managers solve specific kinds of problems. DSS programs have been developed to help managers pick the shortest and most efficient routes for delivery trucks, select the best combination of stocks for investors, and schedule the flow of inventory through complex manufacturing facilities.

It's important to understand that DSS programs don't replace managerial decision making; they *improve* it by furthering managers' and workers' understanding of the problems they face and the solutions that might work. Though used by just 2 percent of physicians, medical DSS programs hold the promise of helping doctors make more accurate patient diagnoses. A British study of eighty-eight cases misdiagnosed or initially misdiagnosed (to be correctly diagnosed much later) found that a medical DSS made the right diagnosis 69 percent of the time.[62] With a medical DSS, doctors enter patient data such as age, gender, weight, and medical symptoms. The medical DSS then produces a list of diseases and conditions, ranked by probability, low or high, or by medical specialty, such as cardiology or oncology. For instance, when emergency room physician Dr. Harold Cross treated a ten-year-old boy who had been ill with nausea and dizziness for two weeks, he wasn't sure what was wrong because the boy had a healthy appetite, no abdominal pain, and just one brief headache. However, when the medical DSS that Dr. Cross used suggested a possible problem in the back of the boy's brain, Cross ordered an MRI scan that revealed a tumor, which was successfully removed two days later. Says Dr. Cross, "My personal knowledge of the literature and physical findings would not have prompted me to suspect a brain tumor."[63]

Expert systems are created by capturing the specialized knowledge and decision rules used by experts and experienced decision makers. They permit nonexpert employees to draw on this expert knowledge base to make

Knowledge the understanding that one gains from information

Decision support system (DSS) an information system that helps managers understand specific kinds of problems and potential solutions

Expert system an information system that contains the specialized knowledge and decision rules used by experts and experienced decision makers so that nonexperts can draw on this knowledge base to make decisions

Mobile Payment Scams

Juniper Research, which conducts research on mobile technologies, estimates that by 2015, consumers will use their phones and tablets to buy $1.3 trillion worth of goods. But while the mobile payment marketplace is about to explode, it remains critically vulnerable to hackers and thieves. For example, almost 70 percent of phones have no password protection on them, making it easy for thieves to steal whatever payment information is stored there. There are numerous malware programs sent to consumers' email that could be used to hack into a phone. And, in quite an ingenious demonstration, a security expert showed how he could steal credit card information just by waving his smartphone near a person's pants pocket or purse. Banks, credit card companies, and wireless phone carriers are all investing heavily to find a defense that is formidable enough to keep out hackers but which still allows for the convenience of mobile payment.

Source: O. Kharif, "Mobile Payments: A New Frontier for Criminals," *Bloomberg Businessweek*, October 4, 2012, accessed June 22, 2013, http://www.businessweek.com/articles/2012-10-04/mobile-payments-a-new-frontier-for-criminals.

decisions. Most expert systems work by using a collection of "if–then" rules to sort through information and recommend a course of action. For example, let's say that you're using your American Express card to help your spouse celebrate a promotion. After dinner and a movie, the two of you stroll by a travel office with a Las Vegas poster in its window. Thirty minutes later, caught up in the moment, you find yourselves at the airport ticket counter trying to purchase last-minute tickets to Vegas. But there's just one problem. American Express didn't approve your purchase. In fact, the ticket counter agent is now on the phone with an American Express customer service agent. So what put a temporary halt to your weekend escape to Vegas? An expert system that American Express calls Authorizer's Assistant.[64]

The first "if–then" rule that prevented your purchase was the rule "*if* a purchase is much larger than the cardholder's regular spending habits, *then* deny approval of the purchase." This if–then rule, just one of 3,000, is built into American Express's transaction-processing system that handles thousands of purchase requests per second. Now that the American Express customer service agent is on the line, he or she is prompted by the Authorizer's Assistant to ask the ticket counter agent to examine your identification. You hand over your driver's license and another credit card to prove you're you. Then the ticket agent asks for your address, phone number, Social Security number, and your mother's maiden name and relays the information to American Express. Finally, your ticket purchase is approved. Why? Because you met the last series of

"if–then" rules. *If* the purchaser can provide proof of identity and *if* the purchaser can provide personal information that isn't common knowledge, *then* approve the purchase.

STUDY TOOLS 17

LOCATED AT THE BACK OF YOUR BOOK:

☐ Rip out and study the Chapter Review Card at the end of the book

LOG IN TO WWW.CENGAGEBRAIN.COM TO:

☐ Review Key Term Flashcards

☐ Complete Practice Quizzing (take up to four times without repeating the same quiz)

☐ Complete Games: Beat the Clock and Crossword Puzzle

☐ Complete Interactive Content: Graded Quiz, Media Quiz, and Fill-in-the-Blank Questions

☐ Watch Management Workplace Video on "Numi Organic Tea"

☐ Work Through the What Would You Do Case on Delta Airlines Headquarters

4LTR Press solutions are designed for today's learners through the continuous feedback of students like you. Tell us what you think about **MGMT8** and help us improve the learning experience for future students.

YOUR FEEDBACK MATTERS.

Complete the Speak Up survey in CourseMate at
www.cengagebrain.com

 Follow us at
www.facebook.com/4ltrpress

18 Managing Service and Manufacturing Operations

Fuse/Getty Images

LEARNING OUTCOMES

18-1 Discuss the kinds of productivity and their importance in managing operations.

18-2 Explain the role that quality plays in managing operations.

18-3 Explain the essentials of managing a service business.

18-4 Describe the different kinds of manufacturing operations.

18-5 Explain why and how companies should manage inventory levels.

After you finish this chapter, go to **PAGE 394** for **STUDY TOOLS**

PRODUCTIVITY

Furniture manufacturers, hospitals, restaurants, automakers, airlines, and many other kinds of businesses struggle to find ways to produce quality products and services efficiently and then deliver them in a timely manner. Managing the daily production of goods and services, or **operations management,** is a key part of a manager's job. But an organization depends on the quality of its products and services as well as its productivity.

At 18.6 million cars and trucks per year, 50 percent more than in the United States, China is the largest and fastest-growing auto market in the world, with huge potential for even more growth as hundreds of millions of new middle-class Chinese families want to buy a car. But since Chinese consumers earn only about $7,500 a year, auto manufacturers will have to significantly cut development costs, which normally run about $1 billion per car model. Since that's far too expensive for a $7,500 car, automakers are slashing development costs and time by reusing designs from previously built cars. General Motors' Chinese brand, Baojun, is built on platform designs that GM had already used in other countries. Likewise, Honda's Chinese brand, Linian, is based on a previous generation of Honda's City model, while Nissan uses a recently retired car, the Tiida, for its new Chinese brand, Qichen. Reusing older designs cuts development time, largely eliminates development costs, and enables automakers to sell cars at prices that middle-class Chinese families can afford.[1]

At their core, organizations are production systems. Companies combine inputs such as labor, raw materials, capital, and knowledge to produce outputs in the form of finished products or services. **Productivity** is a measure of performance that indicates how many inputs it takes to produce or create an output.

$$\text{Productivity} = \frac{\text{Outputs}}{\text{Inputs}}$$

The fewer inputs it takes to create an output (or the greater the output from one input), the higher the productivity. For example, ArcellorMittal, which owns steel factories all over the world, measures productivity in terms of man-hours per ton of steel. The fewer man-hours it takes to produce a ton of steel, the higher the productivity. In the U.S., average productivity in steel mills is two man-hours per ton of steel. ArcellorMittal's best plant, in Gent, Belgium, is 35 percent more efficient than that as it makes a ton of steel using only 1.3 man-hours.[2]

*Let's examine **18-1a why productivity matters** and **18-1b the different kinds of productivity.***

18-1a Why Productivity Matters

Why does productivity matter? For companies, higher productivity—that is, doing more with less—results in lower costs for the company, lower prices, faster service, higher market share, and higher profits. Boeing has incorporated a series of changes to its assembly line to increase the rate at which it produces its wide-body 777 jets. For example, since each airline configures the floor layout of the planes it buys from Boeing a little differently, the floor panels had to be drilled by hand (to attach seats, kitchens, walls, lavatories, etc.) to accommodate those design differences. Boeing, however, bought automated floor-drilling equipment, which completes each airplane floor three to four times faster while also increasing quality. Jason Clark, Boeing's director of manufacturing for the 777, says, "The day we opened the box [for automated floor drilling equipment] and put it on the airplane…we got a 93-percent improvement in hole quality."[3]

Likewise, Boeing switched from hand-spraying its wings, which only sprays paint in four-foot widths, to an automated nineteen-axis painting process that sprays paint in eighteen-foot widths. As a result, the amount of time it takes to spray a 777 wing has dropped from four-and-a-half hours to just twenty-four minutes. Likewise, the quality and consistency with which the paint is applied to the wing has reduced the weight of each pair of wings by fifty to sixty pounds. Together, changes like this have increased productivity at Boeing's 777 production line from eighty-four 777s per year to 100 per year. With the average 777 selling for $288 million, the extra sixteen planes that Boeing can make every year thanks to higher productivity yields an additional $4.6 billion in revenue.[4]

Productivity matters because it results in a higher standard of living in terms of higher wages, charitable giving, and making products more affordable. When companies can do more with less, they can raise employee wages without increasing prices or sacrificing normal profits. For instance, recent government economic data indicated that U.S. companies were paying workers 1.7 percent more than in the previous year. But since workers were producing 2.3 percent more than they had the year before, real labor costs actually declined.[5]

The average American family earned approximately $62,241 in 2012. If productivity grows 1 percent

---

Operations management managing the daily production of goods and services

Productivity a measure of performance that indicates how many inputs it takes to produce or create an output

per year, that family's income will increase to $79,820 in 2037. But if productivity grows 2 percent per year, their income in 2037 will be $102,113, an increase of $22,293, and that's without working longer hours.[6]

Thanks to long-term increases in business productivity, the average American family today earns 11.6 percent more than the average family in 1980 and 30.5 percent more than the average family in 1967—and that's after accounting for inflation.[7] Productivity increased an average of 2.2 percent between 1997 and 2006, and then slowed to an average of 1.2 percent from 2007 to 2012.[8] And, from 2002 to 2012, the U.S. economy created nearly 10.1 million new jobs.[9]

And when more people have jobs that pay more, they give more to charity. For example, in 2013, Americans donated over $335 billion to charities, compared to 230 billion in 2000.[10] Did Americans become more thoughtful, caring, conscientious, and giving? Probably not. Yet, because of increases in productivity during this time, the average American's income increased by 46 percent, from $36,450 in 2000 to $53,101 in 2013.[11]

Because people earned more money, they were able to share their good fortune with others by giving more to charity.[12]

Another benefit of productivity is that it makes products more affordable or better. One way to demonstrate this is by comparing how many work hours it would take to earn enough money to buy a product now versus in the past. For instance, in 1958 when the average U.S. wage was $1.98 an hour, a toaster cost $12.95. But in 2012, when the average hourly wage was $19.19, a toaster cost $25.99. The 2012 toaster is not only better (it is, take my word for it), it's cheaper because it took only 1.35 hours of work to pay for it compared to 6.54 hours in 1958. Likewise, a 1958 24-inch black and white TV (prime time TV shows weren't broadcast in color until 1965) cost $270 and 136.3 work hours compared to a 2012 26-inch LCD HDTV which cost $250 and 13.03 work hours. Finally, a 1958 stereo phonograph that played vinyl records (look in the attic, your grandparents might still have some) cost $84.95 and 43 work hours, while a 2012 iPod Classic cost $235 and just 12.25 work hours.[13] People like to reminisce about the "good 'ol days," when things were "cheaper." But, mostly, they really weren't. Thanks to steady increases in productivity, most goods become more affordable over time.

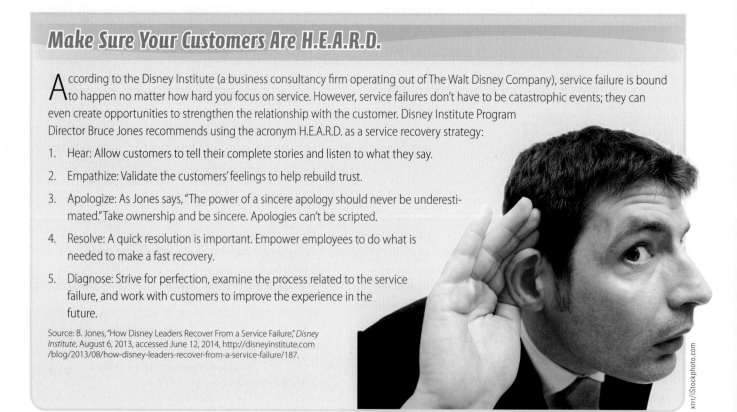

Make Sure Your Customers Are H.E.A.R.D.

According to the Disney Institute (a business consultancy firm operating out of The Walt Disney Company), service failure is bound to happen no matter how hard you focus on service. However, service failures don't have to be catastrophic events; they can even create opportunities to strengthen the relationship with the customer. Disney Institute Program Director Bruce Jones recommends using the acronym H.E.A.R.D. as a service recovery strategy:

1. Hear: Allow customers to tell their complete stories and listen to what they say.

2. Empathize: Validate the customers' feelings to help rebuild trust.

3. Apologize: As Jones says, "The power of a sincere apology should never be underestimated." Take ownership and be sincere. Apologies can't be scripted.

4. Resolve: A quick resolution is important. Empower employees to do what is needed to make a fast recovery.

5. Diagnose: Strive for perfection, examine the process related to the service failure, and work with customers to improve the experience in the future.

Source: B. Jones, "How Disney Leaders Recover From a Service Failure," *Disney Institute*, August 6, 2013, accessed June 12, 2014, http://disneyinstitute.com /blog/2013/08/how-disney-leaders-recover-from-a-service-failure/187.

18-1b Kinds of Productivity

Two common measures of productivity are partial productivity and multifactor productivity. **Partial productivity** indicates how much of a particular kind of input it takes to produce an output.

$$\text{Partial Productivity} = \frac{\text{Outputs}}{\text{Single Kind of Input}}$$

Labor is one kind of input that is frequently used when determining partial productivity. *Labor productivity* typically indicates the cost or number of hours of labor it takes to produce an output. In other words, the lower the cost of the labor to produce a unit of output, or the less time it takes to produce a unit of output, the higher the labor productivity. Labor cost as a percentage of revenue is a basic measure of labor productivity used in the airline industry. The lower the percentage of revenue attributable to labor costs, the more productively an airline uses labor to generate a unit of revenue (i.e., dollars, euros, etc.). In Europe, for example, Wizz Air (6.5 percent), Ryanair (9.5 percent), and easyJet (12.4 percent) have some of the lowest labor costs per unit of revenue, especially when compared to major carriers like British Airways

Partial productivity a measure of performance that indicates how much of a particular kind of input it takes to produce an output

Multifactor productivity an overall measure of performance that indicates how much labor, capital, materials, and energy it takes to produce an output

(21.7 percent), Lufthansa (23.4 percent), Air France (29.9 percent), and Scandinavian Airlines (32.1 percent).[14]

Partial productivity assesses how efficiently companies use only one input, such as labor, when creating outputs. Multifactor productivity is an overall measure of productivity that assesses how efficiently companies use all the inputs it takes to make outputs. More specifically, **multifactor productivity** indicates how much labor, capital, materials, and energy it takes to produce an output.[15]

$$\text{Multifactor Productivity} = \frac{\text{Outputs}}{(\text{Labor} + \text{Capital} + \text{Materials} + \text{Energy})}$$

Exhibit 18.1 shows the trends in multifactor productivity across a number of U.S. industries since 1987.

With a 58 percent increase between 2005 (scaled at 100) and 2011 (when it reached a level of 159) and a nine

Exhibit 18.1
Multifactor Productivity Growth Across Industries

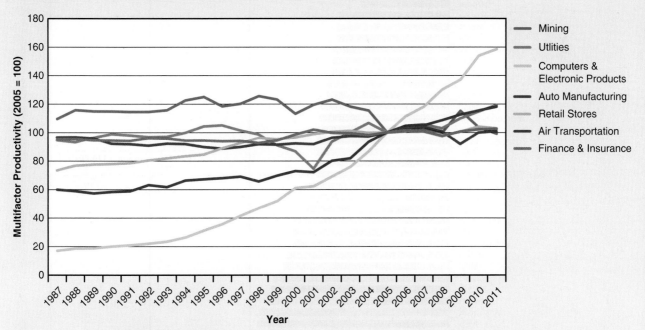

Source: "Nonmanufacturing Sectors and NIPA-level Nonmanufacturing Industries KLEMS Multifactor Productivity Tables by Industry: Table Multifactor Productivity and Related KLEMS Measures from the NIPA Industry Database, 1987 to 2011," Bureau of Labor Statistics, Division of Industry Productivity Studies, April 1, 2013, accessed July 27, 2014, http://www.bls.gov/mfp/special_requests/klemsmfpxg.zip; "Manufacturing Sector and NIPA-level Manufacturing Industries KLEMS Multifactor Productivity Tables by Industry: Table Multifactor Productivity and Related KLEMS Measures from the NIPA Industry Database, 1987 to 2011," Bureau of Labor Statistics, Division of Industry Productivity Studies, June 19, 2013, accessed July 27, 2014, http://www.bls.gov/mfp/special_requests/prod3.klemsmfp.zip.

fold increase since 1987, the growth in multifactor productivity in the computer and electronic products industry far exceeded the productivity growth in mining, utilities, auto manufacturing, retail stores, air transportation, and financial and insurance services, as well as most other industries tracked by the U.S. government.

Should managers use multiple or partial productivity measures? In general, they should use both. Multifactor productivity indicates a company's overall level of productivity relative to its competitors. In the end, that's what counts most. However, multifactor productivity measures don't indicate the specific contributions that labor, capital, materials, or energy make to overall productivity. To analyze the contributions of these individual components, managers need to use partial productivity measures. Doing so can help them determine what factors need to be adjusted or in what areas adjustment can make the most difference in overall productivity.

QUALITY

With the average car costing $31,252, car buyers want to make sure that they're getting good quality for their money.[16] Fortunately, as indicated by the number of problems per 100 cars (PP100), today's cars are of much higher quality than earlier models. In 1981, Japanese cars averaged 240 PP100. GM's cars averaged 670, Ford's averaged 740, and Chrysler's averaged 870 PP100! In other words, as measured by PP100, the quality of American cars was two to three times worse than that of Japanese cars. By 1992, however, U.S. carmakers had made great strides, significantly reducing the number of problems to an average of 155 PP100. Japanese vehicles had improved, too, averaging just 125 PP100. According to the 2013 J. D. Power and Associates survey of initial car quality, as shown in Exhibit 18.2, however, overall quality improved to 116 problems per 100 vehicles,

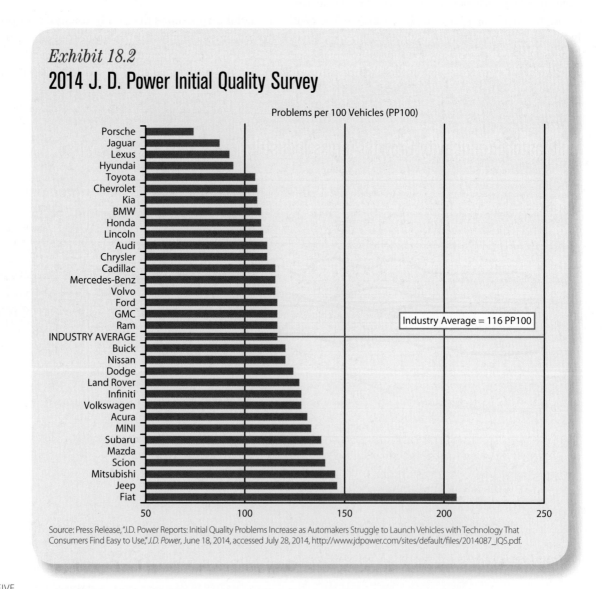

Exhibit 18.2
2014 J. D. Power Initial Quality Survey

Problems per 100 Vehicles (PP100)

Industry Average = 116 PP100

Source: Press Release, "J.D. Power Reports: Initial Quality Problems Increase as Automakers Struggle to Launch Vehicles with Technology That Consumers Find Easy to Use," *J.D. Power*, June 18, 2014, accessed July 28, 2014, http://www.jdpower.com/sites/default/files/2014087_IQS.pdf.

and even the worst rated cars beat the scores of the Japanese cars of decades ago. Category leaders like Porsche, Jaguar, Lexus, and Hyundai came in with scores under 100. That means there's fewer than one problem per car![17]

The American Society for Quality gives two meanings for **quality**. It can mean a product or service free of deficiencies, such as the number of problems per 100 cars, or it can mean the characteristics of a product or service that satisfy customer needs.[18] Today's cars are of higher quality than those produced twenty years ago in both senses. Not only do they have fewer problems per 100 cars, they also have a number of additional standard features (power brakes and steering, stereo/CD/MP3 player, power windows and locks, air bags, cruise control).

In this part of the chapter, you will learn about 18-2a quality-related characteristics for products and services, 18-2b ISO 9000 and 14000, 18-2c the Baldrige National Quality Award, and 18-2d total quality management.

18-2a Quality-Related Characteristics for Products and Services

Quality products usually possess three characteristics: reliability, serviceability, and durability.[19] A breakdown occurs when a product quits working or doesn't do what it was designed to do. The longer it takes for a product to break down, or the longer the time between breakdowns, the more reliable the product. Consequently, many companies define *product reliability* in terms of the average time between breakdowns. *Serviceability* refers to how easy or difficult it is to fix a product. The easier it is to maintain a working product or fix a broken product, the more serviceable that product is.

A product breakdown assumes that a product can be repaired. However, some products don't break down; they fail. *Product failure* means products can't be repaired. They can only be replaced. *Durability* is defined as the mean time to failure. A typical incandescent light bulb, for example, has a mean time of failure of 1,000 hours. By contrast, LED bulbs, which use the same technology that lights up HDTVs and cell phone screens, have a mean time to failure of between twenty and twenty-five years. Furthermore, the energy savings from one $10 LED bulb means it will pay for itself within two years and then provide twenty more years of lighting while saving $149 in energy costs over the longer lifetime of the bulb.[20]

While high-quality products are characterized by reliability, serviceability, and durability, services are different. There's no point in assessing the durability of a service because services don't last but are consumed the minute they're performed. For example, once a lawn service has mowed your lawn, the job is done until the mowers come back next week to do it again. Services also don't have serviceability. You can't maintain or fix a service. If a service wasn't performed correctly, all you can do is perform it again. Rather than serviceability and durability, the quality of service interactions often depends on how the service provider interacts with the customer. Was the service provider friendly, rude, or helpful? Five characteristics typically distinguish a quality service: reliability, tangibles, responsiveness, assurance, and empathy.[21]

Service reliability is the ability to consistently perform a service well. Studies clearly show that reliability matters more to customers than anything else when buying services. When you take your clothes to the dry cleaner, you don't want them returned with cracked buttons or wrinkles down the front. If your dry cleaner gives you back perfectly clean and pressed clothes every time, it's providing a reliable service.

Also, although services themselves are not tangible (you can't see or touch them), services are provided in tangible places. Thus, *tangibles* refer to the appearance of the offices, equipment, and personnel involved with the delivery of a service. One of the best examples of the effect of tangibles on the perception of quality is the restroom. When you eat at a fancy restaurant, you expect clean, upscale restrooms. How different is your perception of a business, say a gas station, if it has clean restrooms rather than filthy ones?

Quality a product or service free of deficiencies, or the characteristics of a product or service that satisfy customer needs

Responsiveness is the promptness and willingness with which service providers give good service. *Assurance* is the confidence that service providers are knowledgeable, courteous, and trustworthy. *Empathy* is the extent to which service providers give individual attention and care to customers' concerns and problems.

When Apple first launched its retail stores, they were widely predicted to fail given all of the locations already available where consumers could buy computer and electronics equipment. Those predictions were wrong, however, as 395 million people visited Apple's 416 stores in 2013.[22] Why? Because the stores are great at delivering responsiveness, assurance, and empathy.

At Apple stores, responsiveness manifests itself in a sales philosophy of not selling. Instead, Apple store employees are trained to help customers solve problems. An Apple training manual says, "Your job is to understand all of your customers' needs—some of which they may not even realize they have." David Ambrose, a former Apple store employee, says, "You were never trying to close a sale. It was about finding solutions for a customer and finding their pain points."

Apple store employees demonstrate assurance through the high level of training that they receive. Apple "geniuses," who staff the Genius Bar in each Apple store, are trained at Apple headquarters and, according to Apple's website, "can take care of everything from troubleshooting your problems to actual repairs." Geniuses are regularly tested on their knowledge and problem-solving skills to maintain their certification. Other Apple store employees are highly trained, too, and are not allowed to help customers until they've spent two to four weeks shadowing experienced store employees.

The acronym APPLE instructs employees on how to empathetically engage with customers: "Approach customers with a personalized warm welcome," "Probe politely to understand all the customer's needs," "Present a solution for the customer to take home today," "Listen for and resolve any issues or concerns," and "End with a fond farewell and an invitation to return." And when customers are frustrated and become emotional, the advice is to "listen and limit your responses to simple reassurances that you are doing so. 'Uh-huh,' 'I understand,' etc."

The results from Apple's retail approach speak for themselves, as Apple retail sales average $4,551 per square foot, higher than Tiffany & Co. jewelry stores ($3,043), Coach luxury retail ($1,532), or Deckers Outdoor ($1,246), a function-oriented footwear company.[23]

18-2b ISO 9000 and 14000

ISO, pronounced *eye-so*, comes from the Greek word *isos*, meaning "equal, similar, alike, or identical" and is also an acronym for the International Organization for Standardization, which helps set standards for 163 countries. The purpose of this agency is to develop and publish standards that facilitate the international exchange of goods and services.[24] **ISO 9000** is a series of five international standards, from ISO 9000 to ISO 9004, for achieving consistency in quality management and quality assurance in companies throughout the world. **ISO 14000** is a series of international standards for managing, monitoring, and minimizing an organization's harmful effects on the environment.[25] (For more on environmental quality and issues, see subsection 16-3e of Chapter 16 on controlling waste and pollution.)

The ISO 9000 and 14000 standards publications, which are available from the American National Standards Institute (see the end of this section), are general and can be used for manufacturing any kind of product or delivering any kind of service. Importantly, the ISO 9000 standards don't describe how to make a better-quality car, computer, or widget. Instead, they describe how companies can extensively document (and thus standardize) the steps they take to create and improve the quality of their products. Why should companies go to the trouble to achieve ISO 9000 certification? Because their customers increasingly want them to. In fact, studies show that customers clearly prefer to buy from companies that are ISO 9000 certified. Companies, in turn, believe that being ISO 9000 certified helps them keep customers who might otherwise switch to an ISO 9000–certified competitor.[26]

To become ISO certified, a process that can take months, a company must show that it is following its own procedures for improving production, updating design plans and specifications, keeping machinery in top condition, educating and training workers, and satisfactorily dealing with customer complaints.[27] An accredited third party oversees the ISO certification

ISO 9000 a series of five international standards, from ISO 9000 to ISO 9004, for achieving consistency in quality management and quality assurance in companies throughout the world

ISO 14000 a series of international standards for managing, monitoring, and minimizing an organization's harmful effects on the environment

process, just as a certified public accountant verifies that a company's financial accounts are up-to-date and accurate. Once a company has been certified as ISO 9000 compliant, the accredited third party will issue an ISO 9000 certificate that the company can use in its advertising and publications. This is the quality equivalent of the *Good Housekeeping* Seal of Approval. But continued ISO 9000 certification is not guaranteed. Accredited third parties typically conduct periodic audits to make sure the company is still following quality procedures. If it is not, its certification is suspended or canceled.

To get additional information on ISO 9000 guidelines and procedures, see the American National Standards Institute (http://www.webstore.ansi.org; the ISO 9000 and ISO 14000 standards publications are available here for about $550 and $599, respectively), the American Society for Quality (http://www.asq.org), and the IOS (http://www.iso.org).

18-2c Baldrige National Quality Award

The Baldrige National Quality Award, which is administered by the U.S. government's National Institute for Standards and Technology, is given "to recognize U.S. companies for their achievements in quality and business performance and to raise awareness about the importance of quality and performance excellence as a competitive edge."[28] Each year, up to three awards

may be given in the categories of manufacturing, education, health care, service, small business, and nonprofit.

The cost of applying for the Baldrige Award includes a $360 eligibility fee, an application fee of $18,000 for manufacturing firms and $9,600 for small businesses, and a site visitation fee of $50,000 to $60,000 for manufacturing firms and $30,000 to $35,000 for small businesses.[29] Why does it cost so much? Because you get a great deal of useful information about your business even if you don't win. At a minimum, each company that applies receives an extensive report based on 300 hours of assessment from at least eight business and quality experts. At $10 an hour for small businesses and about $20 an hour for manufacturing and service businesses, the *Journal for Quality and Participation* called the Baldrige feedback report "the best bargain in consulting in America."[30] Arnold Weimerskirch, former chair of the Baldrige Award panel of judges and vice president of quality at Honeywell, says, "The application and review process for the Baldrige Award is the best, most cost-effective and comprehensive business health audit you can get."[31]

Businesses that apply for the Baldrige Award are judged on a 1,000-point scale based on the seven criteria shown in Exhibit 18.3: leadership; strategic planning; customer focus; measurement, analysis, and knowledge management; workforce focus; process management; and results.[32] Results are clearly the most important category, as it takes up 450 out of 1,000 points. In other words, in addition to the six other criteria, companies

The Challenge of All-Day Breakfast

What's worse than walking into McDonald's expecting a hot, delicious Egg McMuffin, only to find that your watch is running slow and that you missed the 10:30 a.m. cutoff for breakfast sandwiches? Well, soon you may never have to face that struggle again, as McDonald's is considering offering its complete breakfast menu throughout day. Fans of the Egg McMuffin may rejoice at the news, but McDonald's faces some pretty big operational issues if it wants to serve breakfast all day. One big problem is the grill. There may not be enough space on current grills to cook both eggs and hamburgers. Not to mention that burgers need to be cooked at a higher temperature than eggs. What's more, the sausage and bacon used in breakfast sandwiches are cooked ahead of time in the morning, something that may not be possible during a busy lunch rush. These issues may not be insurmountable, but until McDonald's figures out some viable solutions, it'll still be breakfast in the morning.

Source: S. Berfield and L. Patton, "McDonald's All-Day Breakfast: Why the Delay?" *Bloomberg Businessweek*, April 29, 2013, accessed June 23, 2013, http://www.businessweek.com/articles/2013-04-29/an-afternoon-mcmuffin-mcdonalds-is-still-considering-it.

Exhibit 18.3
Criteria for the Baldrige National Quality Award

2007 Categories/Items	Point Values
1 Leadership	**120**
1.1 Senior Leadership	70
1.2 Governance and Social Responsibilities	50
2 Strategic Planning	**85**
2.1 Strategy Development	40
2.2 Strategy Deployment	45
3 Customer Focus	**85**
3.1 Customer Engagement	40
3.2 Voice of the Customer	45
4 Measurement, Analysis, and Knowledge Management	**90**
4.1 Measurement, Analysis, and Improvement of Organizational Performance	45
4.2 Management of Information, Information Technology, and Knowledge	45
5 Workforce Focus	**85**
5.1 Workforce Engagement	45
5.2 Workforce Environment	40
6 Process Management	**85**
6.1 Work Systems	35
6.2 Work Processes	50
7 Results	**450**
7.1 Product Outcomes	100
7.2 Customer-Focused Outcomes	70
7.3 Financial and Market Outcomes	70
7.4 Workforce-Focused Outcomes	70
7.5 Process Effectiveness Outcomes	70
7.6 Leadership Outcomes	70
Total Points 1,000	

Source: "Criteria for Performance Excellence," *Baldrige National Quality Program 2007*, accessed September 15, 2008, http://www.quality.nist.gov/PDF_files/2008_Business_Nonprofit_Criteria.pdf.

Total quality management (TQM) an integrated, principle-based, organization-wide strategy for improving product and service quality

Customer focus an organizational goal to concentrate on meeting customers' needs at all levels of the organization

Customer satisfaction an organizational goal to provide products or services that meet or exceed customers' expectations

must show that they have achieved superior quality when it comes to products and services, customers, financial performance and market share, treatment of employees, work systems and processes, and leadership and social responsibility. This emphasis on results is what differentiates the Baldrige Award from the ISO 9000 standards. The Baldrige Award indicates the extent to which companies have actually achieved world-class quality. The ISO 9000 standards simply indicate whether a company is following the management system it put into place to improve quality. In fact, ISO 9000 certification covers less than 10 percent of the requirements for the Baldrige Award.[33]

Why should companies go to the trouble of applying for the Baldrige Award? Baldrige program examiner Betsy Beam explains that it's not just about winning the award; it's about the opportunity to improve. "Ritz-Carlton has won the Baldrige Award twice," Beam says. "Even in … the years they won, there were 35 opportunities for improvement identified. This is a very difficult journey for any organization, but it's well worth it as changes [that are needed] become obvious."[34]

18-2d Total Quality Management

Total quality management (TQM) is an integrated, organization-wide strategy for improving product and service quality.[35] TQM is not a specific tool or technique. Rather, TQM is a philosophy or overall approach to management that is characterized by three principles: customer focus and satisfaction, continuous improvement, and teamwork.[36]

Although most economists, accountants, and financiers argue that companies exist to earn profits for shareholders, TQM suggests that customer focus and customer satisfaction should be a company's primary goals. **Customer focus** means that the entire organization, from top to bottom, should be focused on meeting customers' needs. The result of that customer focus should be **customer satisfaction,** which occurs when the company's products or services meet or exceed customers' expectations.

At companies where customer satisfaction is taken seriously, such as **Alaska Airlines**, paychecks depend on keeping customers satisfied. Everyone at Alaska Airlines, from the CEO to pilots to people who handle baggage, gets a monthly bonus, 70 percent of which is based on earnings, with the remaining 30 percent split among costs, safety, and customer satisfaction. J.D. Power and Associates rates Alaska Airlines as the highest in customer satisfaction among traditional U.S. airlines from 2008 to 2013. Likewise, Alaska Airlines was the best airline in terms of on-time arrivals, a key issue in terms of customer satisfaction, in 2010 and 2011, and was third best in 2012.[37]

Continuous improvement is an ongoing commitment to increase product and service quality by constantly assessing and improving the processes and procedures used to create those products and services. How do companies know whether they're achieving continuous improvement? Besides higher customer satisfaction, continuous improvement is usually associated with a reduction in variation. **Variation** is a deviation in the form, condition, or appearance of a product from the quality standard for that product. The less a product varies from the quality standard, or the more consistently a company's products meet a quality standard, the higher the quality. Beyond safety, the quality standard for an airline is on-time departure and arrival. Variation from that standard means delays, and even worse, cancellations. On average, 1.7 percent of flights are cancelled each year, sometimes because of weather, but often times because of poor management decisions. Delta Airlines, however, cancels only 0.3 percent of its flights because it stocks extra parts (engine starters) that often cause delays, maintains twenty extra planes which are brought into service when a jet encounters mechanical problems, and gets around flight hour limitations for flight crews (typically eight hours within twenty-four hours) by having planes make interim stops (meaning less than eight hours) with new crews taking over. With 15,000 daily flights, Delta cancels just forty-five flights per day. But if Delta had an average cancellation rate, it would cancel 255 flights per day, or more than five times as many.[38]

The third principle of TQM is teamwork. **Teamwork** means collaboration between managers and nonmanagers, across business functions, and between the company and its customers and suppliers. In short, quality improves when everyone in the company is given the incentive to work together and the responsibility and authority to make improvements and solve problems. At the beginning of the chapter, you learned that ArcellorMittal's Gent, Belgium plant needs only needs 1.3 man-hours to make a ton of steel, or one-third less than average. One of ArcellorMittal's practices is to "twin" its best plants, such as Gent, with its poor performing plants, such as its Burns Harbor, Indiana, plant. Then, it uses teamwork—and competition—to improve both. So it flew 100 Burns Harbor engineers and managers to Gent and told them, "Do as the Belgians do," whereas the Belgians were told to maintain their advantage. Founder Lakshmi Mittal

says, "The process doesn't change: melt iron, cast, roll [steel]. But there are always incremental improvements you can make. We wanted Burns Harbor to be more like Gent."[39] Teamwork comes into play as teams from both plants meet regularly to discuss plant performance and share the steps they're taking to improve it. Following practices at Gent, Burns Harbor began using a different high pressure water nozzle to remove flakes (i.e., imperfections) from super-heated steel. Not only did steel quality improve, the nozzle used less water and power, saving $1.4 million in annual energy costs. Likewise, Burns Harbor workers began trimming less steel off the sides of steel coils, saving 725 coils of steel per year, the equivalent of 17,000 cars. Today, thanks to twinning and teamwork, Burns Harbor now produces 900 tons of steel per employee each year, close to Gent's 950.

Customer focus and satisfaction, continuous improvement, and teamwork mutually reinforce each other to improve quality throughout a company. Customer-focused, continuous improvement is necessary to increase customer satisfaction. At the same time, continuous improvement depends on teamwork from different functional and hierarchical parts of the company.

18-3 SERVICE OPERATIONS

At the start of this chapter, you learned that operations management means managing the daily production of goods and services. Then you learned that to manage production, you must oversee the factors that affect productivity and quality. In this half of the chapter, you will learn about managing operations in service and manufacturing businesses. The chapter ends with a discussion of inventory management, a key factor in a company's profitability.

Imagine that your trusty TiVo digital video recorder (DVR) breaks down as you try to record your favorite TV show. You've got two choices. You can run to

Continuous improvement an organization's ongoing commitment to constantly assess and improve the processes and procedures used to create products and services

Variation a deviation in the form, condition, or appearance of a product from the quality standard for that product

Teamwork collaboration between managers and nonmanagers, across business functions, and between companies, customers, and suppliers

Walmart and spend $250 to purchase a new DVR, or you can spend less (you hope) to have it fixed at a repair shop. Either way, you end up with the same thing, a working DVR. However, the first choice, getting a new DVR, involves buying a physical product (a good), while the second, dealing with a repair shop, involves buying a service.

Services differ from goods in several ways. First, goods are produced or made, but services are performed. In other words, services are almost always labor-intensive: Someone typically has to perform the service for you. A repair shop could give you the parts needed to repair your old DVR, but you're still going to have a broken DVR without the technician to perform the repairs. Second, goods are tangible, but services are intangible. You can touch and see that new DVR, but you can't touch or see the service provided by the technician who fixed your old DVR. All you can "see" is that the DVR works. Third, services are perishable and unstorable. If you don't use them when they're available, they're wasted. For example, if your DVR repair shop is backlogged on repair jobs, then you'll just have to wait until next week to get your DVR repaired. You can't store an unused service and use it when you like. By contrast, you can purchase a good, such as motor oil, and store it until you're ready to use it.

Because services are different from goods, managing a service operation is different from managing a manufacturing or production operation.

*Let's look at **18-3a the service-profit chain** and **18-3b service recovery and empowerment.***

18-3a The Service-Profit Chain

One of the key assumptions in the service business is that success depends on how well employees—that is, service providers—deliver their services to customers. But success actually begins with how well management treats service employees, as the service-profit chain, depicted in Exhibit 18.4, demonstrates.[40]

The key concept behind the service-profit chain is **internal service quality,** meaning the quality of treatment that employees receive from a company's internal service providers, such as management, payroll and benefits, human resources, and so forth. For example, employees at Clif Bar, a maker of organic energy bars and drinks, get 2.5 hours a week to work out at the company's fitness center, which is equipped with a climbing wall and everything from yoga to spin classes to free sessions with trainers and nutritionists; have a concierge that provides car washes, laundry, dry cleaning, and other services; are eligible for incentives for car pools (up to $960 a year), buying a biodiesel car ($6,500) or a commuter bike ($500), or making eco-improvements in their homes ($1,000); and are enrolled in the employee stock ownership plan, which vests after three years, at which point the employee receives full ownership shares of the company. These extraordinary benefits are clearly a sign of a company with an internal service quality orientation.[41]

Internal service quality the quality of treatment employees receive from management and other divisions of a company

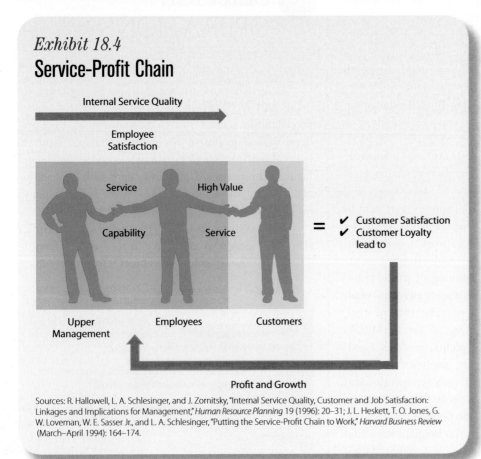

Exhibit 18.4
Service-Profit Chain

Internal Service Quality

Employee Satisfaction

Service

Capability

High Value

Service

Upper Management

Employees

Customers

= ✔ Customer Satisfaction
✔ Customer Loyalty lead to

Profit and Growth

Sources: R. Hallowell, L. A. Schlesinger, and J. Zornitsky, "Internal Service Quality, Customer and Job Satisfaction: Linkages and Implications for Management," *Human Resource Planning* 19 (1996): 20–31; J. L. Heskett, T. O. Jones, G. W. Loveman, W. E. Sasser Jr., and L. A. Schlesinger, "Putting the Service-Profit Chain to Work," *Harvard Business Review* (March–April 1994): 164–174.

The New Industrial Revolution

Additive manufacturing, commonly known as 3D printing, is changing the process by which products are created. Additive manufacturing can dramatically reduce the need for assembly, improve the consistency of each part produced, and reduce material waste and labor costs. General Electric's next-generation jet engine, the LEAP, has a fuel nozzle that would require the assembly of 18 separate parts if produced using traditional casting methods. Using 3D printing technology, however, GE can create the nozzle in a single piece, which both saves on costs and makes it five times more durable. Nike has also begun applying these technologies to the shoemaking process. Shoe assembly is typically a serial process, whereby workers along an assembly line put shoes together one piece at a time. Nike's Flyknit shoe,

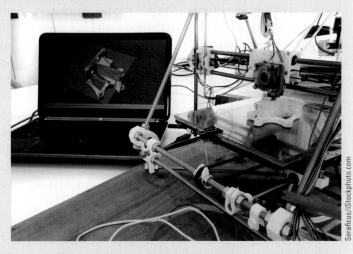

however, is made by a single machine. This machine knits the upper portion of the shoe in a single piece; design software instructs it to change materials or perform specific adjustments as it goes. The shoe is constructed using only a few pieces and a few steps, and waste is cut down by 80 percent. In addition to changing the manufacturing process, additive manufacturing could also change where companies locate their manufacturing operations. Since additive manufacturing is reducing labor costs, it could become increasingly advantageous for companies to build manufacturing facilities closer to end markets rather than in places where labor costs are low.

Source: J. Koten, "A Revolution in the Making," *Wall Street Journal*, June 10, 2013, accessed June 11, 2014, http://online.wsj.com/news/articles/SB10001424127887324063304578522812684722382?KEYWORDS=advanced+manufacturing+new+industrial&mg=reno64-wsj.

As depicted in Exhibit 18.4, good internal service leads to employee satisfaction and service capability. *Employee satisfaction* occurs when companies treat employees in a way that meets or exceeds their expectations. In other words, the better employees are treated, the more satisfied they are, and the more likely they are to give high-value service that satisfies customers. How employers treat employees is important because it affects service capability. *Service capability* is an employee's perception of his or her ability to serve customers well. When an organization serves its employees in ways that help them to do their jobs well, employees, in turn, are more likely to believe that they can and ought to provide high-value service to customers.

Finally, according to the service-profit chain shown in Exhibit 18.4, *high-value service* leads to *customer satisfaction* and *customer loyalty*, which, in turn, lead to *long-term profits and growth*.[42] What's the link between customer satisfaction and loyalty and profits? To start, the average business keeps only 70 to 90 percent of its existing customers each year. No big deal, you say? Just replace leaving customers with new customers. Well, there's one significant problem with that solution. It costs ten times as much to find a new customer as it does to keep an existing customer. Also, new customers typically buy only 20 percent as much as established customers. In fact, keeping existing customers is so cost-effective that most businesses could double their profits by simply keeping 5 percent more customers per year![43] How does this work? Imagine that keeping more of your customers turns some of those customers into customers for life. How much of a difference would that make to company profits? Consider that just one lifetime customer spends $8,000 on pizza and over $330,000 on luxury cars![44]

18-3b Service Recovery and Empowerment

When mistakes are made, when problems occur, and when customers become dissatisfied with the service they've received, service businesses must switch from the process of service delivery to the process of **service recovery,** or restoring customer satisfaction to strongly dissatisfied customers.[45] Or as business

Service recovery restoring customer satisfaction to strongly dissatisfied customers

consultant Barry Moltz explains, "When a customer says they are dissatisfied, the company gets a chance to fix it and turn them into a more loyal customer."[46] Service recovery sometimes requires service employees to not only fix whatever mistake was made but also perform heroic service acts that delight highly dissatisfied customers by far surpassing their expectations of fair treatment. Jason Friend, co-founder of 37signals.com, which provides web-based collaboration software such as Basecamp and Campfire, bought a custom bike via the web from Mission Bicycle Company in San Francisco. When the bike arrived, he found a large gash on the side of the bike's frame. He described what happened when he contacted Mission: "They said sending the whole bike back would be overkill since the only thing that was damaged was the frame. Further, the bike was rideable—it was just a paint problem—so sending the bike back would mean I didn't have a bike for a week or so. They didn't feel good about that. So here's what they did: They called up a local shop (On The Route) and arranged to ship a new frame to them. Then one of their bike techs would drive down to my office and swap the frames and reassemble the bike for me while I waited. All of this at Mission's expense." He concluded by saying, "That's incredible customer service. I'm a happy customer for life. If you're in the market for a great custom bike, check out the good people and products at Mission Bicycle Company."[47]

Unfortunately, when mistakes occur, service employees often don't have the discretion to resolve customer complaints. Customers who want service employees to correct or make up for poor service are frequently told, "I'm not allowed to do that," "I'm just following company rules," or "I'm sorry, only managers are allowed to make changes of any kind." In other words, company rules prevent them from engaging in acts of service recovery meant to turn dissatisfied customers back into satisfied customers. The result is frustration for customers and service employees and lost customers for the company.

Now, however, many companies are empowering their service employees.[48] In Chapter 9, you learned that *empowering workers* means permanently passing decision-making authority and responsibility from managers to workers. With respect to service recovery, empowering workers means giving service employees

the authority and responsibility to make decisions that immediately solve customer problems.[49] For example, when customers call into Nicor National, an energy utility, to ask for credits to their accounts, they are not transferred to a billing department. They are not put on hold while the operator looks for a supervisor or manager. Instead, the operator, who is empowered to make this decision, simply awards the credit without having to check with anyone. According to Barbara Porter, the company's vice president of business development and customer service, empowering the call centers in this way is a quick, easy resolution. "They're professionals and we trust them to make the right decisions," says Porter.[50]

When things go wrong for customers, how well does service recovery work? Sixty-nine percent of customers see quick resolution of their problems as central to good customer service. Furthermore, about half of customers will stop buying from a company when bad customer service is not resolved. Either way, roughly 9 out of 10 customers will tell others about their poor customer service or how you fixed their problem.[51]

18-4 ● MANUFACTURING OPERATIONS

Ford makes cars and Dell does computers. BP produces gasoline, whereas Sherwin-Williams makes paint. Boeing makes jet planes, but Budweiser makes beer. Maxtor makes hard drives, and Maytag makes appliances. The *manufacturing operations* of these companies all produce physical goods. But not all manufacturing operations, especially these, are the same.

Let's learn how various manufacturing operations differ in terms of 18-4a the amount of processing that is done to produce and assemble a product and 18-4b the flexibility to change the number, kind, and characteristics of products that are produced.

18-4a Amount of Processing in Manufacturing Operations

Manufacturing operations can be classified according to the amount of processing or assembly that occurs after a customer order is received. The highest degree of processing occurs in **make-to-order operations**. A make-to-order operation does not start processing or assembling products until it receives a customer order. In fact, some

Make-to-order operation a manufacturing operation that does not start processing or assembling products until a customer order is received

make-to-order operations may not even order parts until a customer order is received. Not surprisingly, make-to-order operations produce or assemble highly specialized or customized products for customers (see box "Electric Cars, Made to Order"). The John Deere 8R tractor, for example, comes with thousands of options that can be customized to the needs of a corn farmer in Kansas or a rice farmer in India. Buyers choose from six types of axles, five transmissions, thirteen types of rear hitches, and fifty-four different wheel and tire configurations. There are 354 option bundles for the basic tractor and 114 option bundles for attachments. Thanks to so many option combinations, Deere produced 7,800 unique 8R tractors in the last year. On average, each tractor configuration was built just 1.5 times, and over half of the configurations were built just once—truly a make-to-order operation.[52]

A moderate degree of processing occurs in **assemble-to-order operations**. A company using an assemble-to-order operation divides its manufacturing or assembly process into separate parts or modules. The company orders parts and assembles modules ahead of customer orders. Then, based on actual customer orders or on research forecasting what customers will want, those modules are combined to create semicustomized products. For example, when a customer orders a new car, GM may have already ordered the basic parts or modules

it needs from suppliers. In other words, based on sales forecasts, GM may already have ordered enough tires, air-conditioning compressors, brake systems, and seats from suppliers to accommodate nearly all customer orders on a particular day. Special orders from customers and car dealers are then used to determine the final assembly checklist for particular cars as they move down the assembly line.

The lowest degree of processing occurs in **make-to-stock operations** (also called build-to-stock). Because the products are standardized, meaning each product is exactly the same as the next, a company using a make-to-stock operation starts ordering parts and assembling finished products before receiving customer orders. Customers then purchase these standardized products—such as Rubbermaid storage containers, microwave ovens, and vacuum cleaners—at retail stores or directly from the manufacturer. Because parts are ordered and products are assembled before customers

Assemble-to-order operation a manufacturing operation that divides manufacturing processes into separate parts or modules that are combined to create semicustomized products

Make-to-stock operation a manufacturing operation that orders parts and assembles standardized products before receiving customer orders

Electric Cars, Made to Order

Typically, when consumers purchase cars, they have to go to a dealer and choose one from the inventory that the dealer has on hand. To sell its new Focus Electric, however, Ford is using a build-to-order model, similar to what Dell has used successfully to sell computers. Instead of a big inventory of cars, dealers will only carry one demonstration model of the Focus Electric. After trying out the model, customers can then place an order for their own Focus Electric, selecting whatever colors, interior fabric, options, and accessories they wish. So, if someone wants a silver Focus Electric with a dark gray leather interior, rear-view camera, Bluetooth connectivity, and a power sunroof, all he has to do is order one, instead of hope that the dealer has one in the inventory. In about six weeks, the car will be delivered straight from the factory.

Source: J. Murray, "Ford Focus Electric Will Use 'Build-to-Order, Sales Model," *The Guardian*, March 29, 2012, accessed April 9, 2012, http://www.guardian.co.uk/environment/2012/mar/29/ford-focus-electric-dell-build.

Built-to-order just for YOU!

order the products, make-to-stock operations are highly dependent on the accuracy of sales forecasts. If sales forecasts are incorrect, make-to-stock operations may end up building too many or too few products, or they may make products with the wrong features or without the features that customers want.

18-4b Flexibility of Manufacturing Operations

A second way to categorize manufacturing operations is by **manufacturing flexibility,** meaning the degree to which manufacturing operations can easily and quickly change the number, kind, and characteristics of products they produce. Flexibility allows companies to respond quickly to changes in the marketplace (i.e., respond to competitors and customers) and to reduce the lead time between ordering and final delivery of products. There is often a trade-off between flexibility and cost, however, with the most flexible manufacturing operations frequently having higher costs per unit and the least flexible operations having lower costs per unit. Some common manufacturing operations, arranged in order from the least flexible to the most flexible, are continuous-flow production, line-flow production, batch production, and job shops.

Most production processes generate finished products at a discrete rate. A product is completed, and then—perhaps a few seconds, minutes, or hours later—another is completed, and so on. For instance, if you stood at the end of an automobile assembly line, nothing much would seem to be happening for fifty-five seconds of every minute. In that last five seconds, however, a new car would be started and driven off the assembly line, ready for its new owner. By contrast, in **continuous-flow production,** products are produced continuously rather than at a discrete rate. Like a water hose that is never turned off and just keeps on flowing, production of the final product never stops. Liquid chemicals and petroleum products are examples of continuous-flow production. If you're still struggling with this concept, think of Play-Doh. Continuous-flow production is similar to squeezing Play-Doh into a toy press and watching the various shapes ooze out of the Play-Doh machine. With continuous-flow production, the Play-Doh machine would never stop oozing or producing rectangle- or triangle-shaped Play-Doh. Because of their complexity, continuous-flow production processes are the most standardized and least flexible manufacturing operations.

Line-flow production processes are preestablished, occur in a serial or linear manner, and are dedicated to making one type of product. In this way, the ten different steps required to make product X can be completed in a separate manufacturing process (with separate machines, parts, treatments, locations, and workers) from the twelve different steps required to make product Y. Line-flow production processes are inflexible because they are typically dedicated to manufacturing one kind of product. For example, the production process for Tesla Motors' Model S car starts with large rolls of aluminum, which are flattened, cut, and then stamped into the shapes of the car's body panels (i.e, roof, trunk, left front, etc.). Stamped panels are then moved to the body shop, where the car's underbody, sides, and front are joined via robotic welding machines. Once the shell of the car is formed, it is primed, painted, and moved to the assembly line. There, 3,000 workers and 160 robots install the battery, motor, wiring, interior, seats, and the rest of the car's 30,000-plus parts. The assembly process for a car takes three to five days. In total, Tesla's Model S factory produces about 400 cars per week.[53]

The next most flexible manufacturing operation is **batch production,** which involves the manufacture of large batches of different products in standard lot sizes. A worker in a batch production operation will perform the same manufacturing process on one hundred copies of product X, followed by two hundred copies of product Y, and then fifty copies of product Z. Furthermore, these batches move through each manufacturing department or process in identical order. So, if the paint department follows chemical treatment, and chemical treatment is now processing a batch of fifty copies of product Z, then the paint department's next task will be to paint fifty copies of product Z. Batch production is finding increasing use among restaurant chains. To ensure consistency in the taste and quality of their products, many restaurant chains have central kitchens, or commissaries, that produce batches of food such as mashed potatoes, stuffing, macaroni and cheese, rice, quiche filling, and chili, in volumes ranging from 10 to 200 gallons. These batches are then delivered to the individual restaurant locations, which in turn serve the food to customers.

Manufacturing flexibility the degree to which manufacturing operations can easily and quickly change the number, kind, and characteristics of products they produce

Continuous-flow production a manufacturing operation that produces goods at a continuous, rather than a discrete, rate

Line-flow production manufacturing processes that are preestablished, occur in a serial or linear manner, and are dedicated to making one type of product

Batch production a manufacturing operation that produces goods in large batches in standard lot sizes

Next in terms of flexibility is the job shop. **Job shops** are typically small manufacturing operations that handle special manufacturing processes or jobs. In contrast to batch production, which handles large batches of different products, job shops typically handle very small batches, some as small as one product or process per batch. Basically, each job in a job shop is different, and once a job is done, the job shop moves on to a completely different job or manufacturing process for, most likely, a different customer. For example, **Grauch Enterprises** in Philipsburg, Pennsylvania, is a job shop that mills, turns, drills, paints, and finishes everything from plastics, such as nylon, polycarbonates, and laminates, to metals, such as brass, aluminum, stainless and alloy steels, titanium, and cast iron. It made 650 different parts for one customer alone and received one order to make 5,000 units out of 20,000 individual parts. When it comes to making different parts for different customers, owner Fred Grauch says, "There's very little we won't try."[54]

18-5 INVENTORY

Inventory is the amount and number of raw materials, parts, and finished products that a company has in its possession. **Evonik Industries AG** in Marl, Germany, makes a rare resin that is a key component used to make fuel lines and brake lines in cars. An explosion at its factory killed two employees, stopping resin production for three months. Arkema SA, which also produces the resin, depends on Evonik for a key chemical whose production was also stopped by the explosion. The auto industry, in turn, is at risk of widespread production delays because it only has a one-month supply of the resin in its manufacturing facilities. As a result, 200 auto executives from different companies held a special meeting to hopefully uncover additional amounts of the resin and to look for other companies that could manufacture it to cover the shortage over the next few months.[55]

In this section, you will learn about 18-5a the different types of inventory, 18-5b how to measure inventory levels, 18-5c the costs of maintaining an inventory, and 18-5d the different systems for managing inventory.

18-5a Types of Inventory

Exhibit 18.5 shows the four kinds of inventory a manufacturer stores: raw materials, component parts, work-in-process, and finished goods. The flow of inventory through a manufacturing plant begins when the purchasing department buys raw materials from vendors.

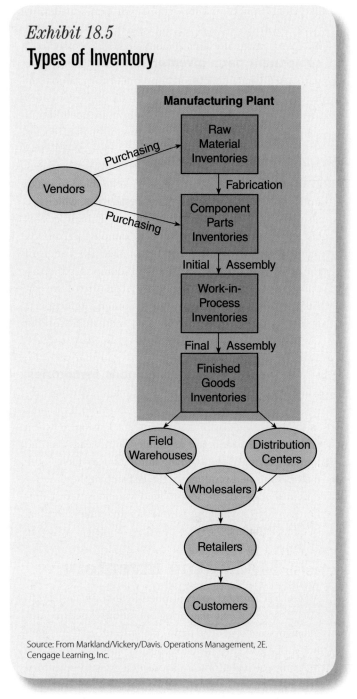

Exhibit 18.5
Types of Inventory

Source: From Markland/Vickery/Davis. Operations Management, 2E. Cengage Learning, Inc.

Raw material inventories are the basic inputs in the manufacturing process. For example, to begin making a car, automobile manufacturers purchase raw materials

Job shops manufacturing operations that handle custom orders or small batch jobs

Inventory the amount and number of raw materials, parts, and finished products that a company has in its possession

Raw material inventories the basic inputs in a manufacturing process like steel, iron, aluminum, copper, rubber, and unprocessed plastic.

Next, raw materials are fabricated or processed into **component parts inventories,** meaning the basic parts used in manufacturing a product. For example, in an automobile plant, steel is fabricated or processed into a car's body panels, and steel and iron are melted and shaped into engine parts like pistons or engine blocks. Some component parts are purchased from vendors rather than fabricated in-house.

The component parts are then assembled to make unfinished **work-in-process inventories,** which are also known as partially finished goods. This process is also called *initial assembly*. For example, steel body panels are welded to each other and to the frame of the car to make a "unibody," which comprises the unpainted interior frame and exterior structure of the car. Likewise, pistons, camshafts, and other engine parts are inserted into the engine block to create a working engine.

Next, all the work-in-process inventories are assembled to create **finished goods inventories,** which are the final outputs of the manufacturing process. This process is also called *final assembly*. For a car, the engine, wheels, brake system, suspension, interior, and electrical system are assembled into a car's painted unibody to make the working automobile, which is the factory's finished product. In the last step in the process, the finished goods are sent to field warehouses, distribution centers, or wholesalers, and then to retailers for final sale to customers.

18-5b Measuring Inventory

As you'll learn next, uncontrolled inventory can lead to huge costs for a manufacturing operation. Consequently, managers need good measures of inventory to prevent inventory costs from becoming too large. Three basic measures of inventory are average aggregate inventory, weeks of supply, and inventory turnover.

If you've ever worked in a retail store and had to take inventory, you probably weren't too excited about the process of counting every item in the store and storeroom. It's an extensive task that's a bit easier today because of bar codes that mark items and computers that can count and track them. Nonetheless, inventories still differ from day to day. An inventory count taken at the beginning of the month will likely be different from a count taken at the end of the month. Similarly, an inventory count taken on a Friday will differ from a count taken on a Monday. Because of such differences, companies often measure **average aggregate inventory,** which is the average overall inventory during a particular time period. Average aggregate inventory for a month can be determined by simply averaging the inventory counts at the end of each business day for that month. One way companies know whether they're carrying too much or too little inventory is to compare their average aggregate inventory with the industry average for aggregate inventory. For example, seventy-two days of inventory is the average for the automobile industry.

The automobile industry records inventory in terms of days of supply, but most other industries measure inventory in terms of *weeks of supply*, meaning the number of weeks it would take for a company to run out of its current supply of inventory. In general, there is an acceptable number of weeks of inventory for a particular kind of business. Too few weeks of inventory on hand, and a company risks a **stockout**—running out of inventory. Valtech makes Magna-Tiles, colorful geometric shapes that connect with magnets and children use to make plastic houses, rockets, pets, or anything else they can imagine. When Thailand was struck by floods, six feet of water destroyed the machines that make Magna-Tiles, as well as months of inventory waiting to ship for the holiday buying season, which makes up 35 percent of Valtech's annual

"In theory, make-to-order companies have no inventory. In fact, they've got inventory, but you have to measure it in hours."

Component parts inventories the basic parts used in manufacturing that are fabricated from raw materials

Work-in-process inventories partially finished goods consisting of assembled component parts

Finished goods inventories the final outputs of manufacturing operations

Average aggregate inventory average overall inventory during a particular time period

Stockout the point when a company runs out of finished product

sales. The shortage caused stockouts and a huge run on the few Magna-Tiles left in stores, which doubled or tripled in price.[56]

Another common inventory measure, **inventory turnover,** is the number of times per year that a company sells, or "turns over," its average inventory. For example, if a company keeps an average of one hundred finished widgets in inventory each month, and it sold one thousand widgets this year, then it turned its inventory ten times this year.

In general, the higher the number of inventory turns, the better. In practice, a high turnover means that a company can continue its daily operations with just a small amount of inventory on hand. For example, let's take two companies, A and B, which have identical inventory levels (520,000 widget parts and raw materials) over the course of a year. If company A turns its inventories twenty-six times a year, it will completely replenish its inventory every two weeks and have an average inventory of 20,000 widget parts and raw materials. By contrast, if company B turns its inventories only two times a year, it will completely replenish its inventory every twenty-six weeks and have an average inventory of 260,000 widget parts and raw materials. So, by turning its inventory more often, company A has 92 percent less inventory on hand at any one time than company B.

The average number of inventory turns across all kinds of manufacturing plants is approximately eight per year, although the average can be higher or lower for different industries.[57] For example, whereas the average auto company turns its entire inventory thirteen times per year, some of the best auto companies more than double that rate, turning their inventory 27.8 times per year, or once every two weeks.[58] Turning inventory more frequently than the industry average can cut an auto company's costs by several hundred million dollars per year. Finally, it should be pointed out that even make-to-order companies like Dell turn their inventory. In theory, make-to-order companies have no inventory. In fact, they've got inventory, but you have to measure it in hours. For example, Dell turns the inventory in its facilities 35.6 times a year, which means that on average it has ten days of inventory on hand in its factories.[59]

18-5c Costs of Maintaining an Inventory

Maintaining an inventory incurs four kinds of costs: ordering, setup, holding, and stockout. **Ordering cost** is not the cost of the inventory itself but the costs associated with ordering the inventory. It includes the

artag_lab/iStockphoto.com

costs of completing paperwork, manually entering data into a computer, making phone calls, getting competing bids, correcting mistakes, and simply determining when and how much new inventory should be reordered. For example, ordering costs are relatively high in the restaurant business because 80 percent of foodservice orders (in which restaurants reorder food supplies) are processed manually. A report, *Enabling Profitable Growth in the Food-Prepared-Away-From-Home Industries*, estimated that the food industry could save $14.3 billion if all restaurants converted to electronic data interchange (see Chapter 17), in which purchase and ordering information from one company's computer system is automatically relayed to another company's computer system. Toward that end, an industry-wide effort, Efficient Foodservice Response (EFR), is underway to improve efficiencies in the foodservice supply chain.[60]

Setup cost is the cost of changing or adjusting a machine so that it can produce a different kind of inventory.[61] For example, 3M uses the same production machinery to make several kinds of industrial tape,

Inventory turnover the number of times per year that a company sells, or "turns over," its average inventory

Ordering cost the costs associated with ordering inventory, including the cost of data entry, phone calls, obtaining bids, correcting mistakes, and determining when and how much to order

Setup cost the costs of downtime and lost efficiency that occur when a machine is changed or adjusted to produce a different kind of inventory

but it must adjust the machines whenever it switches from one kind of tape to another. There are two kinds of setup costs: downtime and lost efficiency. *Downtime* occurs whenever a machine is not being used to process inventory. If it takes five hours to switch a machine from processing one kind of inventory to another, then five hours of downtime have occurred. Downtime is costly because companies earn an economic return only when machines are actively turning raw materials into parts or parts into finished products. The second setup cost is *lost efficiency*. Recalibrating a machine to its optimal settings after a switchover typically takes some time. It may take several days of fine-tuning before a machine finally produces the number of high-quality parts that it is supposed to. So, each time a machine has to be changed to handle a different kind of inventory, setup costs (downtime and lost efficiency) rise.

Holding cost, also known as *carrying* or *storage cost*, is the cost of keeping inventory until it is used or sold. Holding cost includes the cost of storage facilities, insurance to protect inventory from damage or theft, inventory taxes, the cost of obsolescence (holding inventory that is no longer useful to the company), and the opportunity cost of spending money on inventory that could have been spent elsewhere in the company. For example, it's estimated that U.S. airlines have a total of $44 billion worth of airplane parts in stock at any one time for maintenance, repair, and overhauling of their planes. The holding cost for managing, storing, and purchasing these parts is nearly $11 billion—or roughly one-fourth of the cost of the parts themselves.[62]

Stockout cost is the cost incurred when a company runs out of a product. There are two basic kinds of stockout costs. First, the company incurs the transaction costs of overtime work, shipping, and the like in trying to quickly replace out-of-stock inventories with new inventories. The second and perhaps more damaging cost is the loss of customers' goodwill when a company cannot deliver the products it promised. Stockouts occur more often than you might think. In the United States, the supermarket industry's average out-of-stock rate (the percentage of items that are unavailable at a given time) is 7.9 percent, according to research firm Market6. Highly promoted items have, as would be expected, a higher average out-of-stock rate of 13.1 percent. How costly is it for stores to run out of stock? Market6 estimates that running out of stock on the twenty-five best-selling product categories reduces a grocery store's revenue by an average of $200,000 per year, per store.[63] In general, retailers can increase sales 4 percent if they never run out of stock.

18-5d Managing Inventory

Inventory management has two basic goals. The first is to avoid running out of stock and thus angering and dissatisfying customers. This goal seeks to increase inventory to a safe level that won't risk stockouts. The second is to efficiently reduce inventory levels and costs as much as possible without impairing daily operations. This goal seeks a minimum level of inventory. The following inventory management techniques—economic order quantity (EOQ), just-in-time inventory (JIT), and materials requirement planning (MRP)—are different ways of balancing these competing goals.

Economic order quantity (EOQ) is a system of formulas that helps determine how much and how often inventory should be ordered. EOQ takes into account the overall demand (D) for a product while trying to minimize ordering costs (O) and holding costs (H). The formula for EOQ is

$$EOQ = \sqrt{\frac{2DO}{H}}$$

For example, if a factory uses 40,000 gallons of paint a year (D), ordering costs (O) are $75 per order, and holding costs (H) are $4 per gallon, then the optimal quantity to order is 1,225 gallons:

$$EOQ = \sqrt{\frac{2(40,000)(75)}{4}} = 1,225$$

Holding cost the cost of keeping inventory until it is used or sold, including storage, insurance, taxes, obsolescence, and opportunity costs

Stockout cost the cost incurred when a company runs out of a product, including transaction costs to replace inventory and the loss of customers' goodwill

Economic order quantity (EOQ) a system of formulas that minimizes ordering and holding costs and helps determine how much and how often inventory should be ordered

Luis Carlos Torres/iStockphoto.com

With 40,000 gallons of paint being used per year, the factory uses approximately 110 gallons per day:

$$\frac{4,000 \text{ gallons}}{365 \text{ days}} = 110$$

Consequently, the factory would order 1,225 new gallons of paint approximately every eleven days:

$$\frac{1,225 \text{ gallons}}{110 \text{ gallons per day}} = 11.1 \text{ days}$$

In general, EOQ formulas do a good job of letting managers know what size or amount of inventory they should reorder to minimize ordering and holding costs. Mark Lore, CEO of Diapers.com, explains how his company uses EOQ formulas to decide precisely how much inventory to keep on hand. He says, "We built software with computational algorithms to determine what the optimal number of boxes to have in the warehouse is and what the sizes of those boxes should be. Should we stock five different kinds of boxes to ship product in? Twenty kinds? Fifty kinds? And what size should those boxes be? Right now, it's twenty-three box sizes, given what we sell, in order to minimize the cost of dunnage (those little plastic air-filled bags or peanuts), the cost of corrugated boxes, and the cost of shipping. We rerun the simulation every quarter."[64] As this example makes clear, EOQ formulas and models can become much more complex as adjustments are made for price changes, quantity discounts, setup costs, and many other factors.[65]

While EOQ formulas try to minimize holding and ordering costs, the just-in-time (JIT) approach to inventory management attempts to eliminate holding costs by reducing inventory levels to near zero. With a **just-in-time (JIT) inventory system,** component parts arrive from suppliers just as they are needed at each stage of production. By having parts arrive just in time, the manufacturer has little inventory on hand and thus avoids the costs associated with holding inventory. Thanks to its strict JIT inventory system, Apple carries the smallest amount of inventory among technology companies, averaging just five days of inventory of iPhones, iPads, and MacBook Pros waiting to be shipped. That five days of inventory is equivalent to an inventory turn of 74.1 times a year (remember, more turns is better). Dell was next with 35.6 turns a year, followed by Samsung with 17.1 turns a year and Amazon by 10.[66]

To have just the right amount of inventory arrive at just the right time requires a tremendous amount of coordination between manufacturing operations and suppliers. One way to promote tight coordination under JIT is close proximity. Most parts suppliers for Toyota's JIT system at its Georgetown, Kentucky, plant are located within two hundred miles of the plant. Furthermore, parts are picked up from suppliers and delivered to Toyota as often as sixteen times a day.[67] A second way to promote close coordination under JIT is to have a shared information system that allows a manufacturer and its suppliers to know the quantity and kinds of parts inventory the other has in stock. Generally, factories and suppliers facilitate information sharing by using the same part numbers and names. Ford's seat supplier accomplishes this by sticking a bar code on each seat, and Ford then uses the sticker to route the seat through its factory.

Manufacturing operations and their parts suppliers can also facilitate close coordination by using the system of kanban. **Kanban,** which is Japanese for "sign," is a simple ticket-based system that indicates when it is time to reorder inventory. Suppliers attach kanban cards to batches of parts. Then, when an assembly-line worker uses the first part out of a batch, the kanban card is removed. The cards are then collected, sorted, and quickly returned to the supplier, who begins resupplying the factory with parts that match the order information on the kanban cards. Glenn Uminger, manager of production control and logistics at Toyota's Georgetown, Kentucky, plant, says, "We are placing orders for new parts as the first part is used out of a box." Because prices and batch sizes are typically agreed to ahead of time, kanban tickets greatly reduce paperwork and ordering costs.[68]

A third method for managing inventory is **materials requirement planning (MRP)**. MRP is a production and inventory system that, from beginning to end, precisely determines the production schedule, production batch sizes, and inventories needed to complete final products. The three key parts of MRP systems are the master production schedule, the bill of materials, and inventory records. The *master production schedule* is a detailed schedule that indicates the quantity of

Just-in-time (JIT) inventory system an inventory system in which component parts arrive from suppliers just as they are needed at each stage of production

Kanban a ticket-based JIT system that indicates when to reorder inventory

Materials requirement planning (MRP) a production and inventory system that determines the production schedule, production batch sizes, and inventory needed to complete final products

each item to be produced, the planned delivery dates for those items, and the time by which each step of the production process must be completed in order to meet those delivery dates. Based on the quantity and kind of products set forth in the master production schedule, the *bill of materials* identifies all the necessary parts and inventory, the quantity or volume of inventory to be ordered, and the order in which the parts and inventory should be assembled. *Inventory records* indicate the kind, quantity, and location of inventory that is on hand or that has been ordered. When inventory records are combined with the bill of materials, the resulting report indicates what to buy, when to buy it, and what it will cost to order. Today, nearly all MRP systems are available in the form of powerful, flexible computer software.[69]

Which inventory management system should you use? Economic order quantity (EOQ) formulas are intended for use with **independent demand systems,** in which the level of one kind of inventory does not depend on another. For example, because inventory levels for automobile tires are unrelated to the inventory levels of women's dresses, Sears could use EOQ formulas to calculate separate optimal order quantities for dresses and tires. By contrast, JIT and MRP are used with **dependent demand systems,** in which the level of inventory depends on the number of finished units to be produced. For example, if Yamaha makes one thousand motorcycles a day, then it will need one thousand seats, one thousand gas tanks, and two thousand wheels and tires each day. So, when optimal inventory levels depend on the number of products to be produced, use a JIT or MRP management system.

Independent demand system an inventory system in which the level of one kind of inventory does not depend on another

Dependent demand system an inventory system in which the level of inventory depends on the number of finished units to be produced

STUDY TOOLS 18

LOCATED AT THE BACK OF YOUR BOOK:
☐ Rip out and study the Chapter Review Card at the end of the book

LOG IN TO WWW.CENGAGEBRAIN.COM TO:
☐ Review Key Term Flashcards
☐ Complete Practice Quizzing (take up to four times without repeating the same quiz)
☐ Complete Games: Beat the Clock and Crossword Puzzle
☐ Complete Interactive Content: Graded Quiz, Media Quiz, and Fill-in-the-Blank Questions
☐ Watch Management Workplace Video on "Barcelona Restaurant Group"
☐ Work Through the What Would You Do Case on Louis Vuitton Headquarters

Endnotes

1

1. S. Mlot, "Macmillan, DOJ Settle E-Book Price-Fixing Case," *PC Magazine*, February 8, 2013, accessed May 13, 2013, http://www.pcmag.com/article2/0,2817,2415244,00.asp; F. Robinson and C. Thomas, "Apple, Publishers Settle With EU," *Wall Street Journal*, September 20, 2012, B6.

2. "Business Services: Global Industry Guide," *Data Monitor*, January 21, 2010, accessed April 18, 2009, http://www.marketresearch.com.

3. "What do Managers do?" Adapted from "The Wall Street Journal Guide to Management" by Alan Murray. *Wall Street Journal*, accessed June 3, 2014, http://guides.wsj.com/management/developing-a-leadership-style/what-do-managers-do/?mod=WSJBlog.

4. M. Phillips, "Starbucks Is Now Selling 46% More Things an Hour Than It Was Five Years Ago," Quartz, November 22, 2013, http://qz.com/149995/starbucks-is-now-selling-46-more-things-an-hour-than-it-was-five-years-ago/.

5. Admin, "How Mobile Payments and IoT Can Save Starbucks $1 Million Per Day," Journal of Things, July 16, 2013, accessed June 11, 2014, http://journalofthings.com/how-mobile-payments-and-internet-of-things-saves-starbucks-mone/.

6. T. Soper, "More Than 14% of Starbucks Transactions Are Now Made with a Mobile Device," GeekWire, March 19, 2014, accessed June 11, 2014, http://www.geekwire.com/2014/starbucks-annual-meeting/.

7. S. Banzo, S. Kapner, S. Ng, & L. Stevens, "Late Surge in Web Buying Blindsides UPS, Retailers," *Wall Street Journal*, December 25, 2013, accessed June 11, 2014, http://online.wsj.com/news/articles/SB10001424052702304753504579280194287430208.

8. G. Bensinger & L. Stevens, "Amazon, in Threat to US, Tries Its Own Deliveries," *Wall Street Journal*, April 24, 2014, accessed June 11, 2014, http://online.wsj.com/news/articles/SB10001424052702304788404579521522792859890; M. Wohlsen, "Amazon's Drones are Useless. But Its Trucks Could Crush UPS," *Wired*, December 11, 2013, accessed June 12, 2014, http://www.wired.com/2013/12/amazon-fresh-trucks/.

9. D. A. Wren, A. G. Bedeian, and J. D. Breeze, "The Foundations of Henri Fayol's Administrative Theory," *Management Decision* 40 (2002): 906–918.

10. A. Bryant, "Google's Quest to Build a Better Boss," *New York Times*, March 12, 2011, accessed February 23, 2012, http://www.nytimes.com/2011/03/13/business/13hire.html?adxnnl=1&adxnnlx=1330002058-Rqx1lDmdrAh0++W48oHbRA#; B. Hall, "Google's Project Oxygen Pumps Fresh Air into Management," The Street, February 11, 2014, accessed June 11, 2014, http://www.thestreet.com/story/12328981/1/googles-project-oxygen-pumps-fresh-air-into-management.html.

11. H. Fayol, *General and Industrial Management* (London: Pittman & Sons, 1949).

12. R. Stagner, "Corporate Decision Making," *Journal of Applied Psychology* 53 (1969): 1–13.

13. D. W. Bray, R. J. Campbell, and D. L. Grant, *Formative Years in Business: A Long-Term AT&T Study of Managerial Lives* (New York: Wiley, 1993).

14. P. Mozur, "Deal-Hungry Alibaba Enters New Field: the Soccer Pitch," *Wall Street Journal*, June 6, 2014, accessed June 12, 2014, http://online.wsj.com/articles/alibaba-buys-stake-in-chinese-soccer-team-guangzhou-evergrande-1401940574.

15. S. Carey, "United Continental: One Sick Bird," *Wall Street Journal*, June 8, 2014, accessed June 12, 2014, http://online.wsj.com/articles/united-continental-struggles-to-stabilize-1402263534.

16. M. J. Credeur, "Making United and Continental Fly in Formation," *Bloomberg Businessweek*, June 30, 2011, accessed February 23, 2012, http://www.businessweek.com/magazine/making-united-and-continental-fly-information-07012011.html.

17. E. Martinson, "Corner Office: Eileen Martinson of Sparta Systems on Clarity of Leadership," interview by A. Bryant, *New York Times*, January 9, 2014, accessed June 3, 2014. http://www.nytimes.com/2014/01/10/business/eileen-martinson-of-sparta-systems-on-clarity-of-leadership.html?_r=0.

18. Ibid.

19. S. Kapner, "Citi's CEO Is Keeping Score—New Chief Plans Broad Benchmarks for Executives," *Wall Street Journal*, March 5, 2013, C1.

20. H. S. Jonas III, R. E. Fry, and S. Srivastva, "The Office of the CEO: Understanding the Executive Experience," *Academy of Management Executive* 4 (1990): 36–47.

21. S. Gustin, "Groupon Fires CEO Andrew Mason: The Rise and Fall of Tech's Enfant Terrible," *Time*, March 1, 2013, accessed May 13, 2013, http://business.time.com/2013/03/01/groupon-fires-ceo-andrew-mason-the-rise-and-fall-of-techs-enfant-terrible/.

22. Jonas et al., "The Office of the CEO."

23. Ibid.

24. M. Porter, J. Lorsch, and N. Nohria, "Seven Surprises for New CEOs," *Harvard Business Review* (October 2004): 62.

25. P. Martens, "Corner Office: Phil Martens of Novelis, on Consistent Leadership," interview by A. Bryant, *New York Times*, October 26, 2013, accessed June 3, 2014, http://www.nytimes.com/2013/10/27/business/phil-martens-of-novelis-on-consistent-leadership.html?adxnnl=1&adxnnlx=1401825619-DKFEW1MYXzF6OGl16ZbXgg.

26. Novelis, "Sustainability Through Disruptive Innovation: Sustainability Report 2013," 2013, p. 44. accessed June 3. 2014, http://www.novelis.com/Documents/Sustainability/2013_Novelis_Sustainability_Report_En.pdf.

27. Q. Huy, "In Praise of Middle Managers," *Harvard Business Review* (September 2001): 72–79.

28. No author, "Using Their Own Words, Middle Managers Describe the Nature of Their Jobs," *Wall Street Journal*, August 6, 2013, accessed June 12, 2014, http://online.wsj.com/news/articles/SB10001424127887323420604578652110485397972?mg=reno64-wsj.

29. M. Korn, "What It's Like Being a Middle Manager Today," *Wall Street Journal*, August 5, 2013, accessed June 3, 2014, http://online.wsj.com/news/articles/SB10001424127887323420604578650074170664066?KEYWORDS=what+it%27s+like+being+a+middle+manager&mg=reno64-wsj.

30. No author, "Using Their Own Words, Middle Managers Describe the Nature of Their Jobs," *Wall Street Journal*, August 6, 2013, accessed June 12, 2014, http://online.wsj.com/news/articles/SB10001424127887323420604578652110485397972?mg=reno64-wsj.

31. Ibid.

32. R. Silverman, "Some Tech Firms Ask: Who Needs Managers?" *Wall Street Journal*, August 6, 2013, accessed June 12, 2014, http://online.wsj.com/news/articles/SB10001424127887323420604578652051466314748.

33. S. Tully, "What Team Leaders Need to Know," *Fortune*, February 20, 1995, 93.

34. B. Francella, "In a Day's Work," *Convenience Store News*, September 25, 2001, 7.

35. L. Liu and A. McMurray, "Frontline Leaders: The Entry Point for Leadership Development in the Manufacturing Industry," *Journal of European Industrial Training* 28, no. 2–4 (2004): 339–352.

36. A. Nowogrodski, "Corner Office: Avinoam Nowogrodski of Clarizen, on the Rewards of Listening," interview by A. Bryant, *New York Times*, March 13, 2014, accessed June 3, 2014, http://www.nytimes.com/2014/03/14/business/avinoam-nowogrodski-of-clarizen-on-the-rewards-of-listening.html.

37. K. Hultman, "The 10 Commandments of Team Leadership," *Training & Development*, February 1, 1998, 12–13.

38. A. Nowogrodski, "Corner Office: Avinoam Nowogrodski of Clarizen, on the Rewards of Listening," interview by A. Bryant, *New York Times*, March 13, 2014, accessed June 3, 2014, http://www.nytimes.com/2014/03/14/business/avinoam-nowogrodski-of-clarizen-on-the-rewards-of-listening.html.

39. Ibid.

40. R. Silverman, "Who's the Boss? There Isn't One," *Wall Street Journal*, June 20, 2012, B1.

41. N. Steckler and N. Fondas, "Building Team Leader Effectiveness: A Diagnostic Tool," *Organizational Dynamics* (Winter 1995): 20–34.

42. H. Mintzberg, *The Nature of Managerial Work* (New York: Harper & Row, 1973).

43. K. Bowers, "Corner Office: Kim Bowers of CST Brands, on Managing Up vs. Managing Down," interview by A. Bryant, *New York Times*, April 5, 2014, accessed June 3, 2014, http://www.nytimes.com/2014/04/06/business/kim-bowers-of-cst-brands-on-managing-up-vs-managing-down.html.

44. C. P. Hales, "What Do Managers Do? A Critical Review of the Evidence," *Journal of Management Studies* 23, no. 1 (1986): 88–115.

45. S. Hendren, "NetJets Holds Headquarters Groundbreaking," WOSU, April 5, 2011, accessed February 23, 2012, http://beta.wosu.org/news/2011/04/05/netjets-holds-headquarters-groundbreaking/.

46. A. Preuschat, "Huawei Enterprise Business Grew More In Europe Than Home Last Year," *Wall Street Journal*, March 10, 2014, accessed June 3, 2014, http://online.wsj.com/news/articles/SB10001424052702304704504579431302282650692?KEYWORDS=motivate&mg=reno64-wsj.

47. M. Murphy and E. Chasan, "A Boardroom with a View—Outside Directorships Can Offer CFOs Fresh Perspective, Add to Financial Toolbox," *Wall Street Journal*, May 7, 2013, B7.

48. J. Light, "Study Points to Benefits of Outside Board Seats," *Wall Street Journal*, May 23, 2011, B6.

49. "News by Industry," *Business Wire*, accessed March 11, 2009, http://www .businesswire.com /portal/site/home/news/industries/.

50. "Media Monitoring," *CyberAlert*, accessed March 11, 2009, http://www.cyberalert.com.

51. "What Is FNS News Clips Online?" *FNS NewsClips*, accessed March 11, 2009, http://www .news-clips.com.

52. A. Bryant, "Transparency Is Much More Than a Buzzword," *New York Times*, March 2, 2013, accessed May 14, 2013, http://www.nytimes .com/2013/03/03/business/ryan-smith-of-qualtrics -on-building-a-transparent-culture.html?_r=0.

53. M. Wohlsen, "Jeff Bezos Says Amazon Is Seriously Serious about Drone Deliveries," Wired, April 11, 2014, accessed June 13, 2014, http://www .wired.com/2014/04/amazon-delivery-drones/.

54. No author, "Amazon Tests Drones for Same -Day Parcel Delivery, Bezos Says," *Bloomberg News*, December 2, 2013, accessed June 13, 2014, http://www.bloomberg.com/news/2013-12-02 /amazon-testing-octocopters-for-delivery-ceo-tells -60-minutes-.html.

55. R. Weis and B. Kammel, "How Siemens Got Its Mojo Back," *Bloomberg Businessweek*, January 27, 2011, accessed February 25, 2012, http://www .businessweek.com/magazine/content/11_06 /b4214018593359.htm.

56. M. Langley, "Holiday Cyberheist: Inside Target, CEO Struggles to Regain Shoppers' Trust," *Wall Street Journal*, February 19, 2014, A1.

57. M. Ramsey, "Fuel Goal Tests Ford's Mettle," *Wall Street Journal*, January 13, 2014, B1.

58. S. Brown, "'Iron Man 3 Gets Remixed for China," *CNN*, May 3, 2013, accessed May 14, 2013, http://edition.cnn.com/2013/05/03/business/iron -man-china; S. Montlake, "Hollywood's China Fixer," *Forbes*, November 19, 2012, 127–130.

59. L. A. Hill, *Becoming a Manager: Mastery of a New Identity* (Boston: Harvard Business School Press, 1992).

60. R. L. Katz, "Skills of an Effective Administrator," *Harvard Business Review* (September–October 1974): 90–102.

61. C. A. Bartlett and S. Ghoshal, "Changing the Role of Top Management: Beyond Systems to People," *Harvard Business Review* (May–June 1995): 132–142.

62. F. L. Schmidt and J. E. Hunter, "Development of a Causal Model of Process Determining Job Performance," *Current Directions in Psychological Science* 1 (1992): 89–92.

63. J. B. Miner, "Sentence Completion Measures in Personnel Research: The Development and Validation of the Miner Sentence Completion Scales," in *Personality Assessment in Organizations*, ed. H. J. Bernardin and D. A. Bownas (New York: Praeger, 1986), 145–176.

64. M. W. McCall, Jr., and M. M. Lombardo, "What Makes a Top Executive?" *Psychology Today*, February 1983, 26–31; E. van Velsor and J. Brittain, "Why Executives Derail: Perspectives Across Time and Cultures," *Academy of Management Executive* (November 1995): 62–72.

65. Ibid.

66. J. Lublin, "How to Delegate the Right Way," *Wall Street Journal*, March 13, 2014, accessed June 3, 2014, http://online.wsj.com/news/articles/SB1000142

40527023041851045794356408033345898 ?KEYWORDS=rewards&mg=reno64-wsj.

67. A. K. Naj, "Corporate Therapy: The Latest Addition to Executive Suite Is Psychologist's Couch," *Wall Street Journal*, August 29, 1994, A1.

68. Ibid.

69. P. Wallington, "Leadership: How to Spot a Toxic Boss," CIO, April 26, 2006, accessed June 13, 2014, http://www.cio.com/article/20139/Leadership _How_to_Spot_a_Toxic_Boss; P. Wallington, "Management2 Toxic!" *Financial Mail*, July 28, 2006, 48.

70. J. Sandberg, "Overcontrolling Bosses Aren't Just Annoying; They're Also Inefficient," *Wall Street Journal*, March 30, 2005, B1.

71. P. Drexler, "Managing Up: When Your Boss Is an Obsessive Micromanager," *Forbes*, June 13, 2013, accessed June 3, 2014, http://www.forbes .com/sites/peggydrexler/2013/06/13/managing-up -when-your-boss-is-an-obsessive-micromanager/.

72. Hill, *Becoming a Manager*, p. 17.

73. Ibid., p. 55.

74. Ibid., p. 57.

75. Ibid., p. 64.

76. Ibid., p. 67.

77. Ibid., p. 161.

78. J. Pfeffer, *The Human Equation: Building Profits by Putting People First* (Boston: Harvard Business School Press, 1996); *Competitive Advantage Through People: Unleashing the Power of the Work Force* (Boston: Harvard Business School Press, 1994).

79. M. A. Huselid, "The Impact of Human Resource Management Practices on Turnover, Productivity, and Corporate Financial Performance," *Academy of Management Journal* 38 (1995): 635–672.

80. D. McDonald and A. Smith, "A Proven Connection: Performance Management and Business Results," *Compensation & Benefits Review* 27, no. 6 (January 1, 1995): 59.

81. J. Combs, Y. Liu, A. Hall, and D. Ketchen, "How Much Do High-Performance Work Practices Matter? A Meta-Analyis of Their Effects on Organizational Performance," *Personnel Psychology*, 2006, 59, 501–528.

82. I. Fulmer, B. Gerhart, and K. Scott, "Are the 100 Best Better? An Empirical Investigation of the Relationship Between Being a 'Great Place to Work' and Firm Performance," *Personnel Psychology* (Winter 2003): 965–993.

83. B. Schneider and D. E. Bowen, "Employee and Customer Perceptions of Service in Banks: Replication and Extension," *Journal of Applied Psychology* 70 (1985): 423–433; B. Schneider, J. J. Parkington, and V. M. Buxton, "Employee and Customer Perceptions of Service in Banks," *Administrative Science Quarterly* 25 (1980): 252–267.

84. "How Investing in Intangibles—Like Employee Satisfaction—Translates into Financial Returns," *Knowledge@Wharton*, January 9, 2008, accessed January 24, 2010, http://knowledge .wharton.upenn.edu/article.cfm ?articleid=1873.

2

1. C. S. George, Jr., *The History of Management Thought* (Englewood Cliffs, NJ: Prentice-Hall, 1972).

2. D. Schmandt-Besserat, *How Writing Came About* (Austin: University of Texas Press, 1997).

3. A. Erman, *Life in Ancient Egypt* (London: Macmillan & Co., 1984).

4. J. Burke, *The Day the Universe Changed* (Boston: Little, Brown, 1985).

5. S. A. Epstein, *Wage Labor and Guilds in Medieval Europe* (Chapel Hill: University of North Carolina Press, 1991).

6. R. Braun, *Industrialization and Everyday Life*, trans. S. Hanbury-Tenison (Cambridge: Cambridge University Press, 1990).

7. J. B. White, "The Line Starts Here: Mass-Production Techniques Changed the Way People Work and Live Throughout the World," *Wall Street Journal*, January 11, 1999, R25.

8. R. B. Reich, *The Next American Frontier* (New York: Time Books, 1983).

9. J. Mickelwait and A. Wooldridge, *The Company: A Short History of a Revolutionary Idea* (New York: Modern Library, 2003).

10. H. Kendall, "Unsystematized, Systematized, and Scientific Management," in *Scientific Management: A Collection of the More Significant Articles Describing the Taylor System of Management*, ed. C. Thompson (Easton, PA: Hive Publishing, 1972), 103–131.

11. United States Congress, House, Special Committee, *Hearings to Investigate the Taylor and Other Systems of Shop Management*, vol. 3 (Washington, DC: Government Printing Office, 1912).

12. Ibid.

13. Ibid.

14. A. Derickson, "Physiological Science and Scientific Management in the Progressive Era: Frederic S. Lee and the Committee on Industrial Fatigue," *Business History Review* 68 (1994): 483–514.

15. United States Congress, House, Special Committee, 1912.

16. Taylor, *The Principles of Scientific Management*.

17. C. D. Wrege and R. M. Hodgetts, "Frederick W. Taylor's 1899 Pig Iron Observations: Examining Fact, Fiction, and Lessons for the New Millennium," *Academy of Management Journal*, 43 (December 2000): 1283; J. R. Hough and M. A. White, "Using Stories to Create Change: The Object Lesson of Frederick Taylor's 'Pig-tale,'" *Journal of Management*, 27, no. 5 (October 2001): 585–601; E. A. Locke, "The Ideas of Frederick W. Taylor: An Evaluation," *Academy of Management Review* 7, no. 1(1982) 14–24.

18. Locke, "The Ideas of Frederick W. Taylor."

19. George, *The History of Management Thought*.

20. F. Gilbreth and L. Gilbreth, "Applied Motion Study," in *The Writings of the Gilbreths*, ed. W. R. Spriegel and C. E. Myers (1917; reprint, Homewood, IL: Irwin, 1953), 207–274.

21. Ibid.

22. D. Ferguson, "Don't Call It 'Time and Motion Study,'" *IIE Solutions* 29, no. 5 (1997): 22–23.

23. H. Gantt, "A Graphical Daily Balance in Manufacture," *Transactions of the American Society of Mechanical Engineers* 24 (1903): 1325.

24. P. Peterson, "Training and Development: The View of Henry L. Gantt (1861–1919)," *SAM Advanced Management Journal* (Winter 1987): 20–23.

25. H. Gantt, "Industrial Efficiency," *National Civic Federation Report of the 11th Annual Meeting*, New York, January 12, 1991, 103.

26. Ibid.

27. M. Weber, *The Theory of Social and Economic Organization*, trans. A. Henderson and T. Parsons (New York: Free Press, 1947).

28. M. Weber, *The Protestant Ethic and the Spirit of Capitalism* (New York: Scribner's, 1958).

29. George, *The History of Management Thought*.

30. D. A. Wren, "Henri Fayol as Strategist: A Nineteenth Century Corporate Turnaround," *Management Decision*, 39, no. 6 (2001): 475–487; D. Reid, "Fayol: From Experience to Theory," *Journal of Management History* (Archive) 1, no. 3 (1995): 21–36.

31. Ibid.

32. Ibid.

33. Ibid.

34. F. Blancpain, "Les cahiers inédits d'Henri Fayol," trans. D. Wren, *Extrait du bulletin de l'institut international d'administration publique* 28–29 (1974): 1–48.

35. D. A. Wren, A. G. Bedeian, and J. D. Breeze, "The Foundations of Henri Fayol's Administrative Theory," *Management Decision* 40 (2002): 906–918.

36. H. Fayol, *General and Industrial Management* (London: Pittman & Sons, 1949); Wren, Bedeian, and Breeze, "Foundations."

37. P. Graham, ed., *Mary Parker Follett—Prophet of Management: A Celebration of Writings from the 1920s* (Boston: Harvard Business School Press, 1995).

38. D. Linden, "The Mother of Them All," *Forbes*, January 16, 1995, 75.

39. J. H. Smith, "The Enduring Legacy of Elton Mayo," *Human Relations* 51, no. 3 (1998): 221–249.

40. E. Mayo, *The Human Problems of an Industrial Civilization* (New York: Macmillan, 1933).

41. Ibid.

42. "Hawthorne Revisited: The Legend and the Legacy," *Organizational Dynamics* (Winter 1975): 66–80.

43. E. Mayo, *The Social Problems of an Industrial Civilization* (Boston: Harvard Graduate School of Business Administration, 1945).

44. "Hawthorne Revisited: The Legend and the Legacy."

45. Mayo, *The Social Problems of an Industrial Civilization*, 45.

46. George, *The History of Management Thought*.

47. C. I. Barnard, *The Functions of the Executive* (Cambridge, MA: Harvard University Press, 1938), 4.

48. C. I. Barnard, *The Functions of the Executive: 30th Anniversary Edition* (Cambridge, MA: Harvard University Press, 1968), 5.

49. J. Fuller and A. Mansour, "Operations Management and Operations Research: A Historical and Relational Perspective," *Management Decision* 41 (2003): 422–426.

50. D. Wren and R. Greenwood, "Business Leaders: A Historical Sketch of Eli Whitney," *Journal of Leadership & Organizational Studies* 6 (1999): 131.

51. "Monge, Gaspard, comte de Péluse," *Britannica Online*, accessed January 9, 2005, http://www.eb.com.

52. M. Schwartz and A. Fish, "Just-in-Time Inventories in Old Detroit," *Business History* 40, no. 3 (July 1998): 48.

53. D. Ashmos and G. Huber, "The Systems Paradigm in Organization Theory: Correcting the Record and Suggesting the Future," *Academy of Management Review* 12 (1987): 607–621; F. Kast and J. Rosenzweig, "General Systems Theory: Applications for Organizations and Management," *Academy of Management Journal* 15 (1972): 447–465; D. Katz and R. Kahn, *The Social Psychology of Organizations* (New York: Wiley, 1966).

54. R. Mockler, "The Systems Approach to Business Organization and Decision Making," *California Management Review* 11, no. 2 (1968): 53–58.

55. F. Luthans and T. Stewart, "A General Contingency Theory of Management," *Academy of Management Review* 2, no. 2 (1977): 181–195.

3

1. L. Fleisher, "Thousands of Taxi Drivers Protest Uber Across Europe," *Wall Street Journal*, June 12, 2014, B2; C. Matlack, "Europe's Cabbies, Fed Up with Uber, Plan a Day of Traffic Chaos," *Bloomberg Businessweek*, June 10, 2014, accessed June 15, 2014, http://www.businessweek.com/articles /2014-06-10/europes-cabbies-fed-up-with-uber -plan-a-day-of-traffic-chaos.

2. "Industry Profile: Food Distributors," First Research, January 24, 2011, accessed February 2, 2011, http://www.firstresearch.com/Focus-Research /Food-Distributors.html.

3. S. Stein, "iPhone 5s Review: Same Look, Small Screen, Big Potential," CNET.com, September 17, 2013, accessed September 24, 2013, http://reviews .cnet.com/iphone-5s/.

4. E. Romanelli and M. L. Tushman, "Organizational Transformation as Punctuated Equilibrium: An Empirical Test," *Academy of Management Journal* 37 (1994): 1141–1166.

5. H. Banks, "A Sixties Industry in a Nineties Economy," *Forbes*, May 9, 1994, 107–112.

6. L. Cowan, "Cheap Fuel Should Carry Many Airlines to More Record Profits for 1st Quarter," *Wall Street Journal*, April 4, 1998, B17A.

7. "Annual Revenues and Earnings: US Airlines—All Services," Air Transport Association, accessed January 15, 2005, http://www.airlines.org; S. Carey, "Carrier Makes Deeper Cuts as It Seeks Federal Backing Needed to Exit Chapter 11," *Wall Street Journal*, November 27, 2002, A3; S. Carey, "UAL Will Lay Off 1,500 Workers as Part of Cost-Cutting Strategy," *Wall Street Journal*, January 6, 2003, A3; D. Carty, "Oral Testimony of Mr. Donald J. Carty, Chairman and CEO, American Airlines: United States Senate, Committee on Commerce, Science, and Transportation," accessed January 9, 2003, http://www.amrcorp .com; S. McCartney, M. Trottman, and S. Carey, "Northwest, Continental, America West Post Losses as Delta Cuts Jobs," *Wall Street Journal*, November 18, 2002, B4.

8. "Airlines Still in Upheaval, 5 Years after 9/11," CNNMoney.com, September 8, 2006, accessed July 25, 2008, http://money.cnn.com/2006/09/08 /news/companies/airlines_sept11/?postversion =2006090813&eref=yahoo.

9. T. Maxon, "American-US Airways merger is airline industry's biggest story of 2013," *Dallas News*, December 30, 2013, accessed June 4, 2014, http://www.dallasnews.com/business/airline -industry/20131230-american-us-airways-merger-is -airline-industrys-biggest-story-of-2013.ece.

10. S. Carey and J. Nicas, "Leaner Airlines, Meaner Routes," *Wall Street Journal*, May 8, 2013, B1.

11. B. Jones, "The Changing Dairy Industry," Department of Agricultural & Applied Economics & Center for Dairy Profitability, accessed July 25, 2008, http://www.aae.wisc.edu/jones/Presentations /Wisc&TotalDairy Trends.pdf.

12. Press Release, "PC Shipments Post the Steepest Decline Ever in a Single Quarter, According to IDC," International Data Corporation, April 10, 2013, accessed May 14, 2013, http://www.idc.com /getdoc.jsp?containerId=prUS24065413.

13. S. Shah, "Power Outages Hobble Pakistan's Biggest Exporters," *Wall Street Journal*, November 29, 2013, accessed June 4, 2014, http://online.wsj .com/news/articles/SB10001424052702304795804 579097620793610020?KEYWORDS=power+outages +hobble&mg=reno64-wsj.

14. T. Stynes, "Yum's Sales in China Still Struggling," *Wall Street Journal*, January 13, 2014, accessed June 4, 2014, http://online.wsj.com/news /articles/SB1000142405270230404970457931902023 2064980?KEYWORDS=yum+brands&mg =reno64-wsj.

15. OECD (2014), "OECD Forecasts During and After the Financial Crisis: A Post Mortem," OECD Economics Department Policy Notes, No. 23, February 2014.

16. "CEO Confidence Survey," The Conference Board, April 9, 2009, accessed April 27, 2009, http://www.conference-board.org.

17. "Despite Recession, US Small Business Confidence Index Increases Six Points; Small Business Research Board Study Finds Increase in Key Indicators," US Business Confidence, February 23, 2009, accessed April 27, 2009, http://www.ipasbrb.net.

18. V. Fuhrmans, "Europe's Car Makers Spin Their Wheels," *Wall Street Journal*, September 30, 2013, accessed June 4, 2014, http://online.wsj.com/news /articles/SB1000142412788732362330457905722204 51906010?KEYWORDS=europe%27s+car+makers +spin&mg=reno64-wsj.

19. "The Civil Rights Act of 1991," US Equal Employment Opportunity Commission, accessed July 25, 2008, http://www.eeoc.gov/policy/cra91.html.

20. "Compliance Assistance—Family and Medical Leave Act (FMLA)," US Department of Labor: Employment Standards Administration, Wage and Hour Division, accessed July 25, 2005, http://www.dol.gov/.

21. R. J. Bies and T. R. Tyler, "The Litigation Mentality in Organizations: A Test of Alternative Psychological Explanations," *Organization Science* 4 (1993): 352–366.

22. M. Orey, "Fear of Firing," *BusinessWeek*, April 23, 2007, 52–62.

23. S. Gardner, G. Gomes, and J. Morgan, "Wrongful Termination and the Expanding Public Policy Exception: Implications and Advice," *SAM Advanced Management Journal* 65 (2000): 38.

24. L. Haider and S. Plancich, "Table 1. EEOC Filings Alleging Wrongful Discharge," in "Damage Estimation in Wrongful Termination Cases: Impact of the Great Recession," NERA Economic Consulting, March 29, 2012, accessed June 16, 2014, http://www.nera.com/nera-files/PUB _Wrongful_Termination_0312.pdf.

25. J. Mundy, "Wrongful Termination Lawsuits on the Rise," *LawyersandSettlements.com*, January 5, 2011, accessed June 4, 2014, http://www .lawyersandsettlements.com/articles/wrongful -termination/wrongful-termination-law-11-15747 .html#.U48_GvldWSp.

26. Orey, "Fear of Firing."

27. Ibid.

28. "Macaroni Grill Case Study," Listen360, accessed May 15, 2013, http://www.listen360.com /assets/macaronigrill_listen360casestudy_07.24.12 .pdf; "Constructive Criticism," *Entrepreneur*, April 2012, 112.

29. R. Johnston and S. Mehra, "Best-Practice Complaint Management," Academy of Management Experience 16 (November 2002): 145–154.

30. D. Smart and C. Martin, "Manufacturer Responsiveness to Consumer Correspondence: An Empirical Investigation of Consumer Perceptions," *Journal of Consumer Affairs* 26 (1992): 104.

31. K. Rosman, "Weather Channel Now Also Forecasts What You'll Buy," *Wall Street Journal*, August 14, 2013, accessed June 16, 2014, http://online.wsj .com/news/articles/SB10001424127887323639704579012674092402660.

32. Ibid.

33. S. A. Zahra and S. S. Chaples, "Blind Spots in Competitive Analysis," Academy of Management Executive 7 (1993): 7–28.

34. J. Wolford, "Cordcutting on the Rise? Cable Subscriptions Projected to Shrink Over the Next Few Years," WebProNews, January 11, 2013, accessed May 15, 2013, http://www.webpronews.com /cordcutting-on-the-rise-cable-subscriptions-projected -to-shrink-over-the-next-few-years-2013-01.

35. K. G. Provan, "Embeddedness, Interdependence, and Opportunism in Organizational Supplier-Buyer Networks," *Journal of Management* 19 (1993): 841–856.

36. J. Lessin, L. Luk, and J. Osawa, "Apple Finds It Difficult to Divorce Samsung," *Wall Street Journal*, June 29, 2013, A1.

37. Ibid.

38. S. Parker and C. Axtell, "Seeing Another Viewpoint: Antecedents and Outcomes of Employee Perspective Taking," *Academy of Management Journal* 44 (2001): 1085–1100; B. K. Pilling, L. A. Crosby, and D. W. Jackson, "Relational Bonds in Industrial Exchange: An Experimental Test of the Transaction Cost Economic Framework," *Journal of Business Research* 30 (1994): 237–251.

39. M. Hickins, "CIO Journal: H-P Reinvent Itself," *Wall Street Journal*, April 25, 2013, B5.

40. K. O'Brien, "DreamWorks Animation Data Center On-Site," Storage Review, October 24, 2012, accessed June 16, 2014, http://www.storagereview .com/dreamworks_animation_data_center_onsite.

41. Associated Press, "NYC Businesses Brace for Soda Regulations," *Washington Times*, March 9, 2013, accessed May 15, 2013, http://www .washingtontimes.com/news/2013/mar/9/nyc -businesses-brace-soda-regulations/?utm_source =feedburner &utm_medium=feed& utm_campaign =Feed%3A+Nation-TheWashingtonTimesAmericas Newspaper+(Nation%2FPolitics+-+The+Washington +Times).

42. "Seafood HACCP," US Food and Drug Administration Center for Food Safety & Applied Nutrition, accessed March 12, 2009, http://www .cfsan.fda.gov/~comm/haccpsea.html.

43. S. Armour, "FDA Suspends Orange Juice Imports to Examine for Fungicide," *Bloomberg Businessweek*, January 11, 2012, accessed February 26, 2012, http://www.bloomberg.com/news/2012 -01-11/fda-halts-orange-juice-imports-to-check-for -banned-fungicide-carpendazim.html.

44. "Sean Lennon, Yoko Ono Recruit Famous Friends for Anti-Fracking Clip," *Rolling Stone*, March 11, 2013, accessed May 15, 2013, http:// www.rollingstone.com/music/videos/sean-lennon -yoko-ono-recruit-celebrity-friends-for-anti-fracking -clip-20130311.

45. D. Kline, "Cadbury Recall Threatens Its Business in the Muslim World," Motley Fool, May 30, 2014, accessed June 17, 2014, http://www.fool .com/investing/general/2014/05/30/cadbury-recall -threatens-its-business-in-the-musli.aspx.

46. No author, "Cadbury Chocolate Pork Free, Says Malaysian Islamic Body," BBC News, June 2, 2014, accessed June 17, 2014, http://www.bbc.com /news/business-27663857.

47. C. Mims, "Amid Stratospheric Valuations, Google Unearths a Deal with Skybox," *Wall Street Journal*, June 15, 2014, http://online.wsj.com /articles/amid-stratospheric-valuations-google -unearths-a-deal-with-skybox-1402864823 ?KEYWORDS=google+acquisition+satellite.

48. D. F. Jennings and J. R. Lumpkin, "Insights Between Environmental Scanning Activities and Porter's Generic Strategies: An Empirical Analysis," *Journal of Management* 4 (1992): 791–803.

49. "China's Unsafe Water Is Nestlé's Opportunity," *Bloomberg Businessweek*, January 28–February 3, 2013, 19–20.

50. E. Jackson and J. E. Dutton, "Discerning Threats and Opportunities," *Administrative Science Quarterly* 33 (1988): 370–387.

51. B. Thomas, S. M. Clark, and D. A. Gioia, "Strategic Sensemaking and Organizational Performance: Linkages Among Scanning, Interpretation, Action, and Outcomes," *Academy of Management Journal* 36 (1993): 239–270.

52. R. Daft, J. Sormunen, and D. Parks, "Chief Executive Scanning, Environmental Characteristics, and Company Performance: An Empirical Study," *Strategic Management Journal* 9 (1988): 123–139; V. Garg, B. Walters, and R. Priem, "Chief Executive Scanning Emphases, Environmental Dynamism, and Manufacturing Firm Performance," *Strategic Management Journal* 24 (2003): 725–744; D. Miller and P. H. Friesen, "Strategy-Making and Environment: The Third Link," *Strategic Management Journal* 4 (1983): 221–235.

53. S. Needleman, "Street Fight: Food Trucks vs. Restaurants," *Wall Street Journal*, August 9, 2012, B8.

54. "Modernization of the Panama Canal," *The Washington Post*, accessed June 17, 2014, http:// www.washingtonpost.com/wp-srv/special/world /modernization-of-panama-canal/index.html.

55. K. Park, "Maersk Line to Dump Panama Canal for Suez as Ships Get Bigger," Bloomberg, March 11, 2013, accessed June 17, 2014, http://www.bloomberg .com/news/2013-03-11/maersk-line-to-dump-panama -canal-for-suez-as-ships-get-bigger.html.

56. "Frequently Asked Questions," Official Website for the Panama Canal Expansion, accessed June 17, 2014, http://micanaldepanama.com/expansion /faq/#prettyPhoto.

57. R. Feitelberg, "Building a Winning Culture," WWD, December 1, 2011, SR12; Under Armour, Inc., "2013 Under Armour Annual Report," February 21, 2014. p. 4.

58. E. Catmull, "An Interview with Disney/Pixar President Dr. Ed Catmull," interview by R. Zahed, *Animation Magazine*, April 2, 2012, accessed June 4, 2014, http://www.animationmagazine.net/people/an -interview-with-disneypixar-president-dr-ed-catmull/.

59. R. Zahed, "An Interview with Disney/Pixar President Dr. Ed Catmul," *Animation Magazine*, April 2, 2012, accessed June 18, 2014, http://www .animationmagazine.net/people/an-interview-with -disneypixar-president-dr-ed-catmull/.

60. D. M. Boje, "The Storytelling Organization: A Study of Story Performance in an Office-Supply Firm," *Administrative Science Quarterly* 36 (1991): 106–126.

61. B. Horowitz, "6 Questions for: Nobody Said Startups Would Be Easy," *Inc.*, April 2014, 39–40.

62. F. D'Souza, "Corner Office: Francisco D'Souza of Cognizant, on Finding Company Heroes," interview by A. Bryant, *New York Times*, August 31, 2013, accessed June 4, 2014, http://www.nytimes .com/2013/09/01/business/francisco-dsouza-of -cognizant-on-finding-company-heroes.html?_r=0.

63. F. D'Souza, "Corner Office: Francisco D'Souza of Cognizant, on Finding Company Heroes."

64. D. R. Denison and A. K. Mishra, "Toward a Theory of Organizational Culture and Effectiveness," *Organization Science* 6 (1995): 204–223.

65. A. Bryant, "The Memo List: Where Everyone Has an Opinion," *New York Times*, March 10, 2012, accessed June 17, 2014, http://www.nytimes.com /2012/03/11/business/jim-whitehurst-of-red-hat-on -merits-of-an-open-culture.html?pagewanted=all; J. Haden, "Red Hat CEO: How Great Leaders Inspire Followers," Inc.com, July 2, 2012, http:// www.inc.com/jeff-haden/red-hat-ceo-jim-whitehurst -how-great-leaders-inspire-followers.html.

66. "Our Philosophy," BPV Capital Management, June 18, 2014, accessed June 18, 2014, http://www .backporchvista.com/about-bpv/our-philosophy/.

67. D. Gilbert and R. Gold, "As Big Drillers Move In, Safety Goes Up," *Wall Street Journal*, April 2, 2013, A1; "Shell Code of Conduct: How to Live by the Shell General Business Principles," Shell, accessed May 16, 2013, http://s06.static-shell.com /content/dam/shell/static/public/downloads /corporate-pkg/code-of-conduct-english.pdf.

68. A. Zuckerman, "Strong Corporate Cultures and Firm Performance: Are There Tradeoffs?" Academy of Management Executive, November 2002, 158–160.

69. E. Schein, Organizational Culture and Leadership, 2nd ed. (San Francisco: Jossey-Bass, 1992).

70. J. Lublin, "This CEO Used to Have an Office—At Dynegy, Boss's Drive for a 'Winning' Culture Means More Cubicles and Fewer Emails," *Wall Street Journal*, March 13, 2013, B1.

71. D. MacMillan, "AOL Tries for Some Silicon Valley Cred," *Bloomberg Businessweek*, March 24, 2011, accessed February 26, 2012, http://www .businessweek.com/magazine/content/11_14 /b4222043205512.htm.

72. T. Pluto, "Terry's Talkin' about Cleveland Browns free agency and quarterbacks, Tribe's pitching, Cavs guards," March 29, 2014, accessed June 17, 2014, http://www.cleveland.com/pluto/index .ssf/2014/03/terrys_talkin_about_the_clevel_5.html.

73. G. Bensinger, "Amazon Recruits Face 'Bar Raisers,'" *Wall Street Journal,* January 8, 2014, B1.

4

1. "2014 Edelman Trust Barometer Annual Global Study," Edelman Berland, accessed June 19, 2014, http://www.edelman.com/insights/intellectual -property/2014-edelman-trust-barometer/; D. Meinhert, "Creating an Ethical Workplace," *HR Magazine* 59 (April 2014): 4, https://www.shrm .org/Publications/hrmagazine/EditorialContent /2014/0414/Pages/0414-ethical-workplace-culture .aspx (accessed June 4, 2014).

2. "2013 National Business Ethics Survey of the U.S. Workforce," Ethics Resource Center, 2014, accessed June 4, 2014, http://www.ethics.org /downloads/2013NBESFinalWeb.pdf.

3. "2013 National Business Ethics Survey of the U.S. Workforce," Ethics Resource Center.

4. C. Smith, "The Ethical Workplace," *Association Management* 52 (2000): 70–73.

5. "Trust in the Workplace: 2010 Ethics & Workplace Survey," Deloitte LLP, 2010, accessed June 4, 2014, http://www.deloitte.com/assets/Dcom-United -States/Local%20Assets/Documents/us_2010_Ethics _and_Workplace_Survey_report_071910.pdf.

6. D. Jones, "More Workers Do Now Than Before Recent Big Scandals," *USA Today*, February 12, 2003, B7.

7. A. Bryant, "In a Word, He Wants Simplicity," *New York Times*, May 23, 2009, accessed August 15, 2010, http://www.nytimes.com/2009/05/24 /business/24corner.html?_r=2&pagewanted=1.

8. Association of Certified Fraud Examiners, "Report to the Nation on Occupational Fraud and Abuse: 2012 Global Fraud Study," accessed May 20, 2013, http://www.acfe.com/uploadedFiles/ACFE _Website/Content/rttn/2012-report-to-nations.pdf; K. Gibson, "Excuses, Excuses: Moral Slippage in the Workplace," *Business Horizons* 43, no. 6 (2000): 65; S. L. Robinson and R. J. Bennett, "A Typology of Deviant Workplace Behaviors: A Multidimensional Scaling Study," *Academy of Management Journal* 38 (1995): 555–572.

9. Harvard Management Update, "Learn by 'Failing Forward,'" *Globe & Mail*, October 31, 2000, B17.

10. "Challenger March Madness Report," Challenger, Gray & Christmas, Inc., March 11, 2014, accessed June 19, 2014, https://www.challengergray.com/press/press-releases/march-madness-could-cost-employers-12b.

11. B. Falcon, "Oil Thieves Plague Shell in Nigeria," *Wall Street Journal*, April 12, 2013, B1.

12. K. Grannis, "National Retail Security Survey: Retail Shrinkage Totaled $34.5 Billion in 2011," National Retail Federation, June 22, 2012, accessed May 20, 2013, http://blog.nrf.com/2012/06/22/national-retail-security-survey-retail-shrinkage-totaled-34-5-billion-in-2011/.

13. More Shoplifters and Dishonest Employees Are Stealing Profits from U.S. Retailers According to 25th Annual Retail Theft Survey by Jack L. Hayes International," Jack L. Hayes International press release, June 2013, accessed June 4, 2014, http://hayesinternational.com/wp-content/uploads/2013/06/SURVEY-2013-25th-Annual-Retail-Theft-Survey-Hayes-International-Thoughts-Behind-Numbers-Final.pdf.

14. J. Norman, "Cultivating a Culture of Honesty," The Orange County [California] Register, October 23, 2006.

15. D. Amato-McCoy, "The 'Not-So-Sweet' Side of Retail Loss," *Chain Store Age*, July 2009, 38-39; M. Pressler, "Cost and Robbers; Shoplifting and Employee Thievery Add Dollars to Price Tag," *Washington Post*, February 16, 2003, H05.

16. E. Harrell, "Workplace Violence, 1993–2009: National Crime Victimization Survey and the Census of Fatal Occupational Injuries," US Department of Justice, Office of Justice Programs, Bureau of Justice Statistics, March 2011, accessed May 21, 2013, http://bjs.gov/content/pub/pdf/wv09.pdf.

17. "Workplace Safety & Health Topics: Occupational Violence," Centers for Disease Control and Prevention, March 27, 2013, accessed May 21, 2013, http://www.cdc.gov/niosh/topics/violence.

18. D. Palmer and A. Zakhem, "Bridging the Gap Between Theory and Practice: Using the 1991 Federal Sentencing Guidelines as a Paradigm for Ethics Training," *Journal of Business Ethics* 29, no. 1/2 (2001): 77–84.

19. K. Tyler, "Do the Right Thing: Ethics Training Programs Help Employees Deal with Ethical Dilemmas," *HR Magazine*, February 2005, accessed March 13, 2009, http://moss07.shrm.org/Publications/hrmagazine/EditorialContent/Pages/0205tyler.aspx.

20. D. R. Dalton, M. B. Metzger, and J. W. Hill, "The 'New' US Sentencing Commission Guidelines: A Wake-up Call for Corporate America," *Academy of Management Executive* 8 (1994): 7–16.

21. G. Marcias, "Q&A: Gayle Macias, World Vision," interview by B. DiPietro, *Wall Street Journal*, June 12, 2013, accessed June 4, 2014, http://blogs.wsj.com/riskandcompliance/2013/06/12/qa-gayle-macias-world-vision/?KEYWORDS=ethics+training.

22. B. Ettore, "Crime and Punishment: A Hard Look at White-Collar Crime," *Management Review* 83 (1994): 10–16.

23. F. Robinson and C. C. Pauze, "What Is a Board's Liability for Not Adopting a Compliance Program?" *Healthcare Financial Management* 51, no. 9 (1997): 64.

24. D. Murphy, "The Federal Sentencing Guidelines for Organizations: A Decade of Promoting Compliance and Ethics," *Iowa Law Review* 87 (2002): 697–719.

25. Robinson and Pauze, "What Is a Board's Liability?"

26. B. Schwartz, "The Nuts and Bolts of an Effective Compliance Program," *HR Focus* 74, no. 8 (1997): 13–15.

27. T. Martin, B. Morris, and S. Thurm, "UPS to End Health Benefits for Some Working Spouses of Employees," *Wall Street Journal*, August 21, 2013, accessed June 4, 2014, http://online.wsj.com/news/articles/SB10001424127887323980604579027082775945544?KEYWORDS=UPS+to+end+health&mg=reno64-wsj.

28. S. Morris and R. McDonald, "The Role of Moral Intensity in Moral Judgments: An Empirical Investigation," *Journal of Business Ethics* 14 (1995): 715–726; B. Flannery and D. May, "Environmental Ethical Decision Making in the US Metal-Finishing Industry," *Academy of Management Journal* 43 (2000): 642–662.

29. L. Kohlberg, "Stage and Sequence: The Cognitive-Developmental Approach to Socialization," in *Handbook of Socialization Theory and Research*, ed. D. A. Goslin (Chicago: Rand McNally, 1969); L. Trevino, "Moral Reasoning and Business Ethics: Implications for Research, Education, and Management," *Journal of Business Ethics* 11 (1992): 445–459.

30. L. Trevino and M. Brown, "Managing to Be Ethical: Debunking Five Business Ethics Myths," *Academy of Management Executive* 18 (May 2004): 69–81.

31. L. T. Hosmer, "Trust: The Connecting Link Between Organizational Theory and Philosophical Ethics," *Academy of Management Review* 20 (1995): 379–403.

32. T. Martin, et.al., "UPS to End Health Benefits for Some Working Spouses of Employees."

33. Ibid.

34. Ibid.

35. Ibid.

36. "2013 National Business Ethics Survey of the U.S. Workforce," Ethics Resource Center.

37. H. J. Bernardin, "Validity of an Honesty Test in Predicting Theft Among Convenience Store Employees," *Academy of Management Journal* 36 (1993): 1097–1108.

38. J. M. Collins and F. L. Schmidt, "Personality, Integrity, and White Collar Crime: A Construct Validity Study," *Personnel Psychology* (1993): 295–311.

39. W. C. Borman, M. A. Hanson, and J. W. Hedge, "Personnel Selection," *Annual Review of Psychology* 48 (1997).

40. P. E. Murphy, "Corporate Ethics Statements: Current Status and Future Prospects," *Journal of Business Ethics* 14 (1995): 727–740.

41. "Code of Ethical Business Conduct," The Hershey Company, no date, accessed February 26, 2012, http://www.thehersheycompany.com/investors/corporate-governance/code-of-conduct.aspx.

42. "More Corporate Boards Involved in Ethics Programs; Ethics Training Becoming Standard Practice," *PR Newswire*, October 16, 2006.

43. S. J. Harrington, "What Corporate America Is Teaching about Ethics," *Academy of Management Executive* 5 (1991): 21–30.

44. L. A. Berger, "Train All Employees to Solve Ethical Dilemmas," *Best's Review–Life-Health Insurance Edition* 95 (1995): 70–80.

45. D. Meinhert, "Creating an Ethical Workplace."

46. Ibid.

47. L. Trevino, G. Weaver, D. Gibson, and B. Toffler, "Managing Ethics and Legal Compliance: What Works and What Hurts," *California Management Review* 41, no. 2 (1999): 131–151.

48. M. Swanton, "Compliance Comedy," *Inside Counsel* 22 (2011): 56.

49. "Leader's Guide: A Culture of Trust 2008," Lockheed Martin, accessed July 17, 2008, http://www.lockheedmartin.com/data/assets/corporate/documents/ethics/2008_EAT_Leaders_Guide.pdf.

50. D. Meinhert, "Creating an Ethical Workplace."

51. E. White, "Theory & Practice: What Would You Do? Ethics Courses Get Context; Beyond Checking Boxes, Some Firms Start Talking about Handling Gray Areas," *Wall Street Journal*, June 12, 2006, B3.

52. "2013 National Business Ethics Survey of the U.S. Workforce," Ethics Resource Center.

53. Ibid.

54. G. Weaver and L. Trevino, "Integrated and Decoupled Corporate Social Performance: Management Commitments, External Pressures, and Corporate Ethics Practices," *Academy of Management Journal* 42 (1999): 539–552; Trevino, Weaver, Gibson, and Toffler, "Managing Ethics and Legal Compliance."

55. "2013 National Business Ethics Survey of the U.S. Workforce," Ethics Resource Center.

56. J. Salopek, "Do the Right Thing," *Training & Development* 55 (July 2001): 38–44.

57. M. Gundlach, S. Douglas, and M. Martinko, "The Decision to Blow the Whistle: A Social Information Processing Framework," *Academy of Management Executive* 17 (2003): 107–123.

58. "Retaliation: When Whistleblowers Become Victims: A Supplemental Report of the 2011 National Business Ethics Survey," Ethics Resource Center, 2012, accessed May 21, 2013, http://www.ethics.org/nbes/files/RetaliationFinal.pdf.

59. "2013 National Business Ethics Survey of the U.S. Workforce," Ethics Resource Center.

60. "OSHA Found Airline Violated Whistleblower Protection Provision of AIR21," OSHA News Release: 11-1814-ATL, January 17, 2012, accessed May 22, 2013, http://www.osha.gov/pls/oshaweb/owadisp.show_document?p_id=21651&p_table=NEWS_RELEASES; J. Incas, "Ex-AirTran Pilot Ordered Reinstated," *Wall Street Journal*, January 18, 2012, B2.

61. J. Deschenaux, "High Court Extends Employee Whistle-blower Protections," *Society for Human Resource Management*, March 5, 2014, accessed June 4, 2014, http://www.shrm.org/LegalIssues/FederalResources/Pages/High-Court-Extends-Employee-Whistle-blower-Protections.aspx.

62. M. Mucci, "Compliance Without Compliance Officer: Q&A with Martin Mucci of Paychex," interview by G. Millman, *Wall Street Journal*, February 6, 2014, accessed June 4, 2014, http://blogs.wsj.com/riskandcompliance/2014/02/06/compliance-without-a-chief-compliance-officer-qa-with-martin-mucci-of-paychex/?KEYWORDS=ethics+training.

63. M. P. Miceli and J. P. Near, "Whistleblowing: Reaping the Benefits," *Academy of Management Executive* 8 (1994): 65–72.

64. M. Mucci, "Compliance Without Compliance Officer: Q&A with Martin Mucci of Paychex."

65. Ibid.

66. M. Master and E. Heresniak, "The Disconnect in Ethics Training," *Across the Board* 39 (September 2002): 51–52.

67. H. R. Bower, *Social Responsibilities of the Businessman* (New York: Harper & Row, 1953).

68. "Beyond the Green Corporation," *BusinessWeek*, January 29, 2007.

69. S. L. Wartick and P. L. Cochran, "The Evolution of the Corporate Social Performance Model," *Academy of Management Review* 10 (1985): 758–769.

70. J. Nocera, "The Paradox of Businesses as Do-Gooders," *New York Times*, November 11, 2006, C1.

71. S. Waddock, C. Bodwell, and S. Graves, "Responsibility: The New Business Imperative," *Academy of Management Executive* 16 (2002): 132–148.

72. T. Donaldson and L. E. Preston, "The Stakeholder Theory of the Corporation: Concepts, Evidence, and Implications," *Academy of Management Review* 20 (1995): 65–91.

73. D. Gilbert, "Exxon Agrees to Disclose Fracking Risks," *Wall Street Journal*, April 3, 2014, accessed, http://online.wsj.com/news/articles/SB10001424 052702303847804579479640318263438?mod =WSJ_hps_sections_management&mg=reno64-wsj.

74. M. B. E. Clarkson, "A Stakeholder Framework for Analyzing and Evaluating Corporate Social Performance," *Academy of Management Review* 20 (1995): 92–117.

75. B. Agle, R. Mitchell, and J. Sonnenfeld, "Who Matters to CEOs? An Investigation of Stakeholder Attributes and Salience, Corporate Performance, and CEO Values," *Academy of Management Journal* 42 (1999): 507–525.

76. M. Handley, "Keystone Still Faces Delays, Fierce Opposition from Green Groups," *US News & World Report*, March 7, 2013, accessed May 22, 2013, http://www.usnews.com/news /articles/2013/03/07/keystone-still-faces-delays -fierce-opposition-from-green-groups; P. Vieira, "Survey Finds Majority Backs Keystone Pipeline," *Wall Street Journal*, April 22, 2013, accessed May 22, 2013, http://online.wsj.com/article/SB10001424127 88732373560457843847163512061.html.

77. E. W. Orts, "Beyond Shareholders: Interpreting Corporate Constituency Statutes," *George Washington Law Review* 61 (1992): 14–135.

78. A. B. Carroll, "A Three-Dimensional Conceptual Model of Corporate Performance," *Academy of Management Review* 4 (1979): 497–505.

79. Ibid.

80. D. Mattel, J. Lublin, and E. Glazer, "Penney Wounded by Deep Staff Cuts," *Wall Street Journal*, April 15, 2013, B1.

81. D. Yadron and J. Lublin, "Symantec Fires Another CEO—Struggling Antivirus Software Maker Boots Second Chief in Less than Two Years," *Wall Street Journal*, March 21, 2014, B1.

82. J. Lublin and M. Murrary, "CEOs Leave Faster Than Ever Before as Boards, Investors Lose Patience," *Wall Street Journal Interactive*, October 27, 2000.

83. "Fewer CEOs of Large U.S. Companies Lost Their Job in 2013, Contributing to Record Tenure," The Conference Board, April 9, 2014, accessed June 22, 2014, https://www.conference-board.org /press/pressdetail.cfm?pressid=5152.

84. E. Chasan, "Corporate News: The Big Number," *Wall Street Journal*, November 26, 2013, B5.

85. S. Banjo, "Wal-Mart will Tie Executive Pay to Compliance Overhaul," *Wall Street Journal*, April 23, 2014, B8.

86. D. Barstow, "Wal-Mart Hushed Up a Vast Mexican Bribery Case," *The New York Times*, April 21, 2012, accessed June 22, 2014, http://www.nytimes .com/2012/04/22/business/at-wal-mart-in-mexico -a-bribe-inquiry-silenced.html?pagewanted=all.

87. M. Bustillo, "Wal-Mart Faces Risk In Mexican Bribe Probe," *Wall Street Journal*, April 23, 2012, B1.

88. S. Banjo, "Wal-Mart will Tie Executive Pay to Compliance Overhaul," *Wall Street Journal*, April 23, 2014, B8.

89. "JPMorgan Chase Offers Relief Following Hurricane Sandy," *Business Wire*, November 1, 2012, accessed May 22, 2013, http://www.businesswire .com/news/home/20121101006246/en/JPMorgan -Chase-Offers-Relief-Hurricane-Sandy; G. Szalai, "Time Warner to Donate $1 Million for Hurricane Sandy Relief Efforts," *The Hollywood Reporter*, November 2, 2012, accessed May 22, 2013, http:// www.hollywood reporter.com/news/hurricane-sandy -time-warner-donates-million-401982; A. Stonich, "How Outdoor Gear Companies Helped Hurricane Sandy Relief Efforts," *Beyond the Edge-National Geographic Adventure Blog*, December 13, 2012, accessed May 22, 2013, http://adventureblog .nationalgeographic.com/2012/12/13/how-outdoor -gear-companies-helped-hurricane-sandy-relief -efforts/.

90. J. Bennett, "GM Now Says It Detected Ignition Switch Problem Back in 2001," *Wall Street Journal*, March 12, 2014, accessed June 4, 2014, http://online.wsj.com/news/articles/SB10001424052 7023049149045794351710047637240?KEYWORDS.

91. Ibid.; J. Bennett, "GM Now Says It Detected Ignition Switch Problem Back in 2001," *Wall Street Journal*, March 12, 2014, accessed June 4, 2014, http://online.wsj.com/news/articles/SB100014240527 0230491490457943517104763740?KEYWORDS.

92. J. Bennett and S. Hughes, "New Details Emerge in GM Cobalt Recall," *Wall Street Journal*, March 24, 2014, accessed June 4, 2014, http:// online.wsj.com/news/articles/SB1000142405270230 3949704579459783108376974?KEYWORDS=jeff +bennett&mg=reno64-wsj.

93. J. Bennett, "GM Now Says It Detected Ignition Switch Problem Back in 2001," *Wall Street Journal*, March 12, 2014, accessed June 4, 2014, http://online.wsj.com/news/articles/SB10001424052 7023049149045794351710047637240?KEYWORDS; J. White and J. Bennett, "Some at GM Brass Told of Cobalt Woe," *Wall Street Journal*, April 11, 2014, accessed June 4, 2014, http://online.wsj.com /news/articles/SB10001424052702303873604579494 95592901143598?KEYWORDS=jeff+bennett&mg =reno64-wsj.

94. C. Duhigg, "In China, Human Costs Are Built into an iPad," *New York Times*, January 25, 2012, accessed February 28, 2012, http://www.nytimes .com/2012/01/26/business/ieconomy-apples-ipad -and-the-human-costs-for-workers-in-china.html? pagewanted=all; H. Perlberg and T. Culpan, "Apple Says Fair Labor Association Began Foxconn Inspection," *Bloomberg Businessweek*, February 14, 2012, accessed February 28, 2012, http://www.bloomberg .com/news/2012-02-13/apple-says-fair-labor -association-will-inspect-suppliers-including-foxconn .html; J. Stern, "Foxconn, Apple, and the Fair Labor Association Respond to ABC News' Exclusive Report," *ABCNews*, February 22, 2012, accessed February 28, 2012, http://abcnews.go.com/blogs /technology/2012/02/foxconn-apple-and-the-fair-labor -association-respond-to-abc-news-exclusive-report/.

95. M. Negishi and M. Falconi, "Novartis Replaces Top Management in Japan," *Wall Street Journal*, April 3, 2014, accessed June 4, 2014, http://online .wsj.com/news/articles/SB100014240527023035327 0457947862055866527270?mod=WSJ_hps_sections _management&mg=reno64-wsj.

96. Ibid.

97. E. Landau, " 'Plastic micro beads' to be removed from soap," *CNN*, January 8, 2013, accessed June 4, 2014, http://www.cnn.com/2013/01/07/health /microplastics-soap-unilever.

98. "Micro-Plastics," Unilever, accessed June 22, 2014, http://www.unilever.com/sustainable-living -2014/our-approach-to-sustainability/responding-to -stakeholder-concerns/micro-plastics/index.aspx.

99. A. McWilliams and D. Siegel, "Corporate Social Responsibility: A Theory of the Firm Perspective," *Academy of Management Review* 26, no.1 (2001): 117–127; H. Haines, "Noah Joins Ranks of Socially Responsible Funds," *Dow Jones News Service*, October 13, 1995. A meta-analysis of 41 different studies also found no relationship between corporate social responsibility and profitability. Though not reported in the meta-analysis, when confidence intervals are placed around its average sample-weighted correlation of .06, the lower confidence interval includes zero, leading to the conclusion that there is no relationship between corporate social responsibility and profitability. See M. Orlitzky, "Does Firm Size Confound the Relationship Between Corporate Social Responsibility and Firm Performance?" *Journal of Business Ethics* 33 (2001): 167–180; S. Ambec and P. Lanoie, "Does It Pay to Be Green? A Systematic Overview," *Academy of Management Perspectives*, 22 (2008): 45–62.

100. M. Orlitzky, "Payoffs to Social and Environmental Performance," *Journal of Investing* 14 (2005): 48–51.

101. M. Orlitzky, F. Schmidt, and S. Rynes, "Corporate Social and Financial Performance: A Meta-analysis," *Organization Studies* 24 (2003): 403–441.

102. Orlitzky, "Payoffs to Social and Environmental Performance."

103. "Patagonia's Common Threads Partnership to Reduce our Environmental Footprint," Patagonia, accessed May 24, 2013, http://www.patagonia.com /us/common-threads.

104. S. Stevenson, "Patagonia's Founder Is America's Most Unlikely Business Guru," *WSJ Magazine*, April 26, 2012, accessed May 24, 2013, http://online.wsj.com/article/SB10001424052702303 51340457735221465986612.html.

105. Orlitzky, Schmidt, and Rynes, "Corporate Social and Financial Performance."

106. "GM Offers Big Discounts to Boost Volt Sales," Fox News, September 24, 2012, accessed May 24, 2013, http://www.foxnews.com/leisure/2012 /09/24/gm-offers-big-discounts-to-boost-volt-sales; P. Lienert & B. Woodall, "GM Planning Lower-Priced Version of 2016 Chevy Volt," *Reuters*, April 8, 2014, accessed June 22, 2014, http://www.reuters .com/article/2014/04/08/us-autos-gm-volt-idUSBREA371XW20140408; M. Maynard, "Stunner: GM May Be Losing $50,000 on Each Chevrolet Volt," *Forbes*, September 10, 2012, accessed May 24, 2013, http://www.forbes.com/sites/michelinemaynard/2012 /09/10/stunner-gm-may-be-losing-50000-on-each -chevrolet-volt/; B. Woodall, P. Lienert, and B. Klayman, "Insight: GM's Volt: The Ugly Math of Low Sales, High Costs," *Reuters*, September 10, 2012, accessed May 24, 2013, http://www.reuters.com/article /2012/09/10/us-generalmotors-autos-volt -idUSBRE88904J20120910.

5

1. L. A. Hill, *Becoming a Manager: Master a New Identity* (Boston: Harvard Business School Press, 1992).

2. C. Reiter, "Having Thrived in America, Hyundai Takes On Europe," *Bloomberg Businessweek*, January 26, 2012, accessed February 28, 2012, http://www.businessweek.com/magazine /having-thrived-in-america-hyundai-takes-on -europe-01262012.html.

3. E. A. Locke and G. P. Latham, *A Theory of Goal Setting & Task Performance* (Englewood Cliffs, NJ: Prentice Hall, 1990).

4. M. E. Tubbs, "Goal-Setting: A Meta-Analytic Examination of the Empirical Evidence," *Journal of Applied Psychology* 71 (1986): 474–483.

5. J. Bavelas and E. S. Lee, "Effect of Goal Level on Performance: A Trade-Off of Quantity and Quality," *Canadian Journal of Psychology* 32 (1978): 219–240.

6. D. Turner, "Ability, Aspirations Fine, But Persistence Is What Gets Results," *Seattle Times*, February 13, 2005, http://community.seattletimes.nwsource.com/archive/?date =20030215&slug =dale15m.

7. I. Wladawsky-Berger, "Managing Innovation Requires Unique Leaders and Goals," *Wall Street Journal*, August 25, 2013, accessed June 5, 2014, http://blogs.wsj.com/cio/2013/08/25/managing -innovation-requires-unique-leaders-and-goals /?KEYWORDS=achieving+goals.

8. C. C. Miller, "Strategic Planning and Firm Performance: A Synthesis of More Than Two Decades of Research," *Academy of Management Performance* 37 (1994): 1649–1665.

9. H. Mintzberg, "Rethinking Strategic Planning: Part I: Pitfalls and Fallacies," *Long Range Planning* 27 (1994): 12–21, and "Part II: New Roles for Planners," 22–30; H. Mintzberg, "The Pitfalls of Strategic Planning," *California Management Review* 36 (1993): 32–47.

10. D. McCarty and B. Jinks, "Kodak Files for Bankruptcy as Digital Era Spells End to Film," *Bloomberg Businessweek*, January 25, 2012, accessed February 28, 2012, http://www.businessweek.com /news/2012-01-25/kodak-files-for-bankruptcy-as -digital-era-spells-end-to-film.html.

11. Mintzberg, "The Pitfalls of Strategic Planning."

12. P. Sonne and P. Evans, "The $1.6 Billion Grocery Flop: Tesco Poised to Quit US," *Wall Street Journal*, December 6, 2012, accessed May 24, 2013, http://online.wsj.com/article/SB1000142412788732 4640104578160514192695162.html.

13. Locke and Latham, *A Theory of Goal Setting & Task Performance*.

14. A. King, B. Oliver, B. Sloop, and K. Vaverek, *Planning & Goal Setting for Improved Performance: Participant's Guide* (Cincinnati, OH: Thomson Executive Press, 1995).

15. "AMM Aluminum Award Winners Announced for 2012," *AMM*, accessed June 5, 2014, http://www.amm.com/Magazine/3080639/Features/AMM -aluminum-award-winners-announced-for-2012.html.

16. M. Wald, "Toward a Greener Soda Can," *New York Times*, June 12, 2012, accessed June 5, 2014, http://green.blogs.nytimes.com/2012/06/12/toward -a-greener-soda-can/?_php=true&_type=blogs& _php=true&_type=blogs&_r=1.

17. Novelis, "Sustainability Through Disruptive Innovation: Sustainability Report 2013," 2013, p. 6, accessed June 5, 2014, http://www.novelis.com/Documents/Sustainability/2013_Novelis _Sustainability_Report_En.pdf.

18. C. Loomis, J. Schlosser, J. Sung, M. Boyle, and P. Neering, "The 15% Delusion: Brash Predictions about Earnings Growth Often Lead to Missed Targets, Battered Stock, and Creative Accounting— and That's When Times Are Good," *Fortune*, February 5, 2001, 102; H. Paster, "Manager's Journal: Be Prepared," *Wall Street Journal*, September 24, 2001, A24; P. Sellers, "The New Breed: The Latest Crop of CEOs Is Disciplined, Deferential, Even a Bit Dull," *Fortune*, November 18, 2002, 66; H. Klein and M. Wesson, "Goal and Commitment and the Goal-Setting Process: Conceptual Clarification and Empirical Synthesis," *Journal of Applied Psychology* 84 (1999): 885–896.

19. Locke and Latham, *A Theory of Goal Setting & Task Performance*.

20. J. Light, "Facebook's Early Buyers Burned, Too," *Wall Street Journal*, June 7, 2012, accessed May 24, 2013, http://online.wsj.com/article/SB1000 1424052702303506404577448651877204794.html; E. Rustle, "The Facebook IPO, One Year Later," *Wall Street Journal*, May 17, 2013, B1.

21. A. Bandura and D. H. Schunk, "Cultivating Competence, Self-Efficacy, and Intrinsic Interest Through Proximal Self-Motivation," *Journal of Personality & Social Psychology* 41 (1981): 586–598.

22. Locke and Latham, *A Theory of Goal Setting & Task Performance*.

23. M. J. Neubert, "The Value of Feedback and Goal Setting over Goal Setting Alone and Potential Moderators of This Effect: A Meta-Analysis," *Human Performance* 11 (1998): 321–335.

24. E. H. Bowman and D. Hurry, "Strategy Through the Option Lens: An Integrated View of Resource Investments and the Incremental-Choice Process," *Academy of Management Review* 18 (1993): 760–782.

25. M. Lawson, "In Praise of Slack: Time Is of the Essence," *Academy of Management Executive* 15 (2000): 125–135.

26. B. Morris, "Union Pacific's Full Steam Ahead," *Wall Street Journal*, April 18, 2014, accessed June 5, 2014, http://blogs.wsj.com/corporate -intelligence/2014/04/18/union-pacifics-full-steam -ahead/?mod=WSJBlog&mod=WSJ_corp_intel.

27. G. Castonguay, "Corporate News: Marchionne Maps Out Fiat Revamp," *Wall Street Journal*, October 31, 2012, B2.

28. J. C. Collins and J. I. Porras, "Organizational Vision and Visionary Organizations," *California Management Review* (Fall 1991): 30–52.

29. Ibid.

30. J. Dulski, "Jennifer Dulski of Change.org, on Problem-Solving," interview by A. Bryant, *New York Times*, November 30, 2013, accessed June 5, 2014, http://www.nytimes.com/2013/12/01/business /jennifer-dulski-of-changeorg-on-problem-solving .html?ref=business.

31. Collins and Porras, "Organizational Vision and Visionary Organizations"; J. A. Pearce II, "The Company Mission as a Strategic Goal," *Sloan Management Review* (Spring 1982): 15–24.

32. "President Bush Announces New Vision for Space Exploration Program," The White House, accessed April 17, 2005, http://www.whitehouse .gov/news/releases/2004/01/20040114-1.html.

33. E. Musk, "The Secret Tesla Motors Master Plan (just between you and me)," *Tesla Motors* (blog), August 2, 2006, accessed June 5, 2014, http://www.teslamotors.com/blog/secret-tesla -motors-master-plan-just-between-you-and-me.

34. J. Boudreau, "Tesla Motors begins delivering Model S electric cars in a Silicon Valley milestone," *San Jose Mercury News*, June 22, 2012, accessed June 5, 2014, http://www.mercurynews.com /business/ci_20919722/silicon-valley-milestone -tesla-motors-begins-delivering-model?refresh=no.

35. D. Choy, "Tesla Model X Release Date Early 2015: Price Estimated Just Under $70,000," *LA Times*, June 17, 2014, accessed June 23, 2014, http://www.latintimes.com/tesla-model-x-release -date-early-2015-price-estimated-just-under-70000 -report-182247; N. Bilton, "Disruptions: The Echo Chamber of Silicon Valley," *New York Times*, June 2, 2013, accessed June 5, 2014, http://bits.blogs .nytimes.com/2013/06/02/disruptions-the-echo -chamber-of-silicon-valley/.

36. A. Zimmerman and K. Johnson, "Target Looks North for a Lift," *Wall Street Journal*, February 28, 2013, B6; A. Zimmerman and K. Talley, "Target Is Going Abroad—To Canada," *Wall Street Journal*, January 14, 2011, B1.

37. R. Smith and G. Tabbing, "Why Radical Transparency is Good Business," *HBR Blog Network*, October 11, 2012, accessed May 25, 2013, http://blogs.hbr.org/cs/2012/10/why_radical_transparency _Is_good_business.html.

38. A. Bryant, "Transparency Is Much More Than a Buzzword," *New York Times*, March 2, 2013, accessed May 14, 2013, http://www.nytimes .com/2013/03/03/business/ryan-smith-of-qualtrics -on-building-a-transparent-culture.html?_r=0.

39. Y. Okada and M. Suga, "Sony, Toyota Cut Electricity Usage as Mandatory Savings Start," *Bloomberg Businessweek*, June 30, 2011, accessed February 26, 2012, http://www.bloomberg.com /news/2011-07-01/sony-toyota-cut-electricity-usage -as-mandatory-savings-start.html.

40. J. Paterson, "Presenteeism on the Rise Among UK Workforce," Employee Benefits, May 2013, 3.

41. S. Shellenbarger, "The Art of Calling in Sick— Or Not," *Wall Street Journal*, October 12, 2012, D1.

42. Adapted from quality procedure at G & G Manufacturing, Cincinnati, Ohio.

43. N. Humphrey, "References a Tricky Issue for Both Sides," *Nashville Business Journal* 11 (May 8, 1995): 1A.

44. K. R. MacCrimmon, R. N. Taylor, and E. A. Locke, "Decision Making and Problem Solving," in *Handbook of Industrial & Organizational Psychology*, ed. M. D. Dunnette (Chicago: Rand McNally, 1976), 1397–1453.

45. L. Weber, "Businesses Use New Apps for Workplace Scheduling," *Wall Street Journal*, September 15, 2013, accessed June 23, 2014, http://online.wsj.com/news/articles/SB10001424127887324 13940457901719372450268&?mg=reno64-wsj.

46. MacCrimmon, Taylor, and Locke, "Decision Making and Problem Solving."

47. G. Kress, "The Role of Interpretation in the Decision Process," *Industrial Management* 37 (1995): 10–14.

48. A. Lowrey, "Readers Without Borders," July 20, 2011, *Slate Magazine*, accessed February 29, 2012, http://www.slate.com/articles/business/moneybox /2011/07/readers_without_borders.html.

49. L. Weber, "Businesses Use New Apps for Workplace Scheduling," *Wall Street Journal*, September 15, 2013, accessed June 23, 2014, http://online.wsj.com/news/articles/SB10001424127887324 13940457901719372450268&?mg=reno64-wsj.

50. "New-Vehicle Ratings Comparison by Car Category," *ConsumerReports.org*, February 19, 2005, http://www.consumerreports.org/cro/cars /index.htm.

51. P. Djang, "Selecting Personal Computers," *Journal of Research on Computing in Education* 25 (1993): 327.

52. "European Cities Monitor," *Cushman & Wakefield*, 2010, http://www.europeancitiesmonitor .eu/wp-content/uploads/2010/10/ECM-2010-Full -Version.pdf.

53. J. Stiff, "6 Tips to Build Your Social Media Strategy," *CIO*, May 8, 2013, accessed May 26, 2013, http://www.cio.com/article/732975/6_Tips _to_Build_Your_Social_Media_Strategy.

54. "The Critical Role of Teams," *The Ken Blanchard Companies*, March 23, 2006, accessed June 5, 2014, http://www.kenblanchard.com/img /pub/pdf_critical_role_teams.pdf.

55. I. L. Janis, *Groupthink* (Boston: Houghton Mifflin, 1983).

56. C. P. Neck and C. C. Manz, "From Groupthink to Teamthink: Toward the Creation of Constructive Thought Patterns in Self-Managing Work Teams," *Human Relations* 47 (1994): 929–952; J. Schwartz

and M. L. Wald, "'Groupthink' Is 30 Years Old, and Still Going Strong," *New York Times*, March 9, 2003, 5.

57. A. Mason, W.A. Hochwarter, K.R. Thompson, "Conflict: An Important Dimension in Successful Management Teams," *Organizational Dynamics* 24 (1995): 20.

58. D. Merrill, "Corner Office: Douglas Merrill of ZestFinance: Steer Clear of What You Can't Measure," interview by A. Bryant, March 20, 2014, accessed June 5, 2014, http://www.nytimes.com /2014/03/21/business/douglas-merrill-of-zestfinance -steer-clear-of-what-you-cant-measure.html.

59. J. Freeman, "The Soul of a Hedge Fund 'Machine,'" *Wall Street Journal*, June 6, 2014, accessed June 24, 2014, http://online.wsj.com /articles/james-freeman-the-soul-of-a-hedge-fund -machine-1402094722.

60. A. Mason, W.A. Hochwarter, and K.R. Thompson, "Conflict: An Important Dimension in Successful Management Teams," *Organizational Dynamics* 24 (1995): 20.

61. R. Cosier and C. R. Schwenk, "Agreement and Thinking Alike: Ingredients for Poor Decisions," *Academy of Management Executive* 4 (1990): 69–74.

62. K. Jenn and E. Mannix, "The Dynamic Nature of Conflict: A Longitudinal Study of Intragroup Conflict and Group Performance," *Academy of Management Journal* 44, no. 2 (2001): 238–251; R. L. Priem, D. A. Harrison, and N. K. Muir, "Structured Conflict and Consensus Outcomes in Group Decision Making," *Journal of Management* 21 (1995): 691–710.

63. A. Van De Ven and A. L. Delbecq, "Nominal versus Interacting Group Processes for Committee Decision Making Effectiveness," *Academy of Management Journal* 14 (1971): 203–212.

64. A. R. Dennis and J. S. Valicich, "Group, Sub -Group, and Nominal Group Idea Generation: New Rules for a New Media?" *Journal of Management* 20 (1994): 723–736.

65. R. B. Gallupe, W. H. Cooper, M. L. Grise, and L. M. Bastianutti, "Blocking Electronic Brainstorms," *Journal of Applied Psychology* 79 (1994): 77–86.

66. E. Bernstein, "Speaking Up Is Hard to Do: Researchers Explain Why," *Wall Street Journal*, February 7, 2012, accessed May 27, 2013, http:// online.wsj.com/article/SB1000142405297020413640 4577207020525853492.html.

67. R. B. Gallupe and W. H. Cooper, "Brainstorming Electronically," *Sloan Management Review*, Fall 1993, 27–36.

68. Ibid.

69. G. Kay, "Effective Meetings through Electronic Brainstorming," *Management Quarterly* 35 (1995): 15.

6

1. "Microsoft Surface Usage Share Takes Slight Dip in Early 2014," Chitika, May 20, 2014, accessed June 24, 2014, http://chitika.com/insights/2014 /surface-over-time.

2. Press Release, "A Strong Holiday Quarter for the Worldwide Tablet Market, But Signs of Slower Growth Are Clear, According to IDC," IDC, January 29, 2014, accessed June 24, 2014, http:// www.idc.com/getdoc.jsp?containerId=prUS24650614.

3. J. Barney, "Firm Resources and Sustained Competitive Advantage," *Journal of Management* 17 (1991): 99–120; J. Barney, "Looking Inside for Competitive Advantage," *Academy of Management Executive* 9 (1995): 49–61.

4. D. Bailey, "Is It Time to Say Goodbye to Net-books?" *The Motley Fool*, April 30, 2011, accessed March 1, 2012, http://www.fool.com/investing /general/2011/04/30/is-it-time-to-say-goodbye-to -netbooks.aspx; S. Lohr, "Netbooks Lose Status as Tablets Like the iPad Rise," *New York Times*, February 13, 2011, accessed March 1, 2012, http:// www.nytimes.com/2011/02/14/technology/14netbook .html?pagewanted=all.

5. C. Arther, "Netbooks plummet while tablets and smartphones soar, says Canalys," *The Guardian* (technology blog), February 3, 2012 (5:38), accessed June 5, 2014, http://www.theguardian .com/technology/blog/2012/feb/03/netbooks-pc -canalys-tablet.

6. D. Pogue, "Just How Many Android Tablet Apps Are There?" *New York Times*, July 1, 2011, accessed March 2, 2012, http://pogue.blogs.nytimes.com /2011/07/01/mystery-how-many-android-tablet-apps/.

7. Juniper Networks Mobile Threat Center, "Third Annual Mobile Threats Report," *Juniper Networks*, June 3, 2013, accessed June 5, 2014, http://www .juniper.net/us/en/local/pdf/additional-resources /3rd-jnpr-mobile-threats-report-exec-summary.pdf.

8. J. Newman, "In Defense of Google Music," *Time*, February 24, 2012, accessed March 1, 2012, http://techland.time.com/2012/02/24/in-defense -of-google-music/; D. Pogue, "A Look at Apple's iCloud," *New York Times*, October 13, 2011, accessed March 1, 2012, http://pogue.blogs.nytimes .com/2011/10/13/a-look-at-icloud/; B. Stone, "Will Amazon's Cloud Music Service Fly?" *Bloomberg Businessweek*, March 31, 2011, accessed March 1, 2012, http://www.businessweek.com/magazine /content/11_15/b4223043644684.htm.

9. S. Grundberg, "Apple Expands iTunes, Adding 56 New Countries," *Wall Street Journal*, December 4, 2012, accessed May 29, 2013, http://online.wsj .com/article/SB100014241278873243559045781591 61050072602.html; Spotify, "Information," accessed June 5, 2014, http://press.spotify.com/us/information/; P. Sweeting, "Spotify revenue up, profits down," *GigaOm Research*, August 1, 2013, accessed June 5, 2014, http://research.gigaom.com/2013/08/spotify -revenue-up-profits-down/; D. MacMillan and D. Wakabayashi, "Apple Pushes Deeper into Mobile Payments," *Wall Street Journal*, January 24, 2014, accessed June 5, 2014, http://online.wsj.com/news /articles/SB1000142405270203044820457934312903 95762338?KEYWORDS=itunes&mg=reno64-wsj; Apple, Inc., "2013 Apple Inc. Annual Report: Form 10-K," October 30, 2013, p. 29; E. Smith, D. Wakabayashi, and H. Karp, "Apple Looks to Amp Up Music Scene with Beats Deal," *Wall Street Journal*, May 9, 2014, A1.

10. S. Hart and C. Banbury, "How Strategy-Making Processes Can Make a Difference," *Strategic Management Journal* 15 (1994): 251–269.

11. R. A. Burgelman, "Fading Memories: A Process Theory of Strategic Business Exit in Dynamic Environments," *Administrative Science Quarterly* 39 (1994): 24–56; R. A. Burgelman and A. S. Grove, "Strategic Dissonance," *California Management Review* 38 (Winter 1996): 8–28.

12. H. Tabuchi, "How the Tech Parade Passed Sony By," *New York Times*, April 14, 2012, accessed May 30, 2013, http://www.nytimes.com/2012/04/15 /technology/how-sony-fell-behind-in-the-tech -parade.html?pagewanted=all&_r=0; Associated Press, "Sony Struggles to Regain Edge," *CBS News*, February 7, 2013, accessed May 30, 2013, http:// www.cbsnews.com/8301-505124_162-57568124 /sony-struggles-to-regain-edge/.

13. R. A. Burgelman and A. S. Grove, "Strategic Dissonance," *California Management Review* 38 (Winter 1996): 8–28.

14. Y. Koh, "Airline Learns to Be Nimble—Starting Up Budget Carriers Helped All Nippon Restructure Its Own Operations," *Wall Street Journal*, May 23, 2013, B8.

15. A. Zimmerman, "Hasbro Falls Prey to 'Angry Birds,'" *Wall Street Journal*, December 15, 2011, accessed March 1, 2012, http://online.wsj.com /article/SB1000142405297020484450457709878062 56830196.html.

16. A. Fiegenbaum, S. Hart, and D. Schendel, "Strategic Reference Point Theory," *Strategic Management Journal* 17 (1996): 219–235.

17. "Consumer Reports Automaker Report Cards 2012: Subaru Drives into Top Spot as Honda Slips," *Sacramento Bee*, March 1, 2012, accessed March 1, 2012, http://www.sacbee.com/2012/02/28/4297509 /consumer-reports-automaker-report.html.

18. B. Gottesman, "The Tech Brands You Trust Most," *PC Magazine*, October 2011, 30–43.

19. S. Clifford, "Where Wal-Mart Failed, Aldi Succeeds," *New York Times*, March 29, 2011, accessed March 1, 2012, http://www.nytimes.com/2011/03/30 /business/30aldi.html?pagewanted=all.

20. A. Fiegenbaum and H. Thomas, "Strategic Groups as Reference Groups: Theory, Modeling and Empirical Examination of Industry and Competitive Strategy," *Strategic Management Journal* 16 (1995): 461–476.

21. "March 2013 Home Improvement Market Sales Forecast," Home Improvement Research Institute, March 2013, accessed May 31, 2013, http://www.hiri.org/?page=Media.

22. R. K. Reger and A. S. Huff, "Strategic Groups: A Cognitive Perspective," *Strategic Management Journal* 14 (1993): 103–124.

23. "Corporate and Financial Overview," Home Depot, accessed April 23, 2014, https://corporate .homedepot.com/MediaCenter/PressKit/Documents /Corp_Financial_Overview.pdf; "About Lowe's," Lowe's, accessed April 23, 2014, http://media .lowes.com/about-lowes/; "Investor Relations: Corporate Profile," Home Depot, accessed June 5, 2014, http://phx.corporate-ir.net/phoenix. zhtml?c=63646&p=irol-IRHome.

24. "Frequently Asked Questions," Ace Hardware, accessed May 31, 2013, http://www.acehardware .com/corp/index.jsp?page=faq.

25. "About Aubuchon Hardware," Aubuchon Hardware, accessed April 6, 2011, http://www .hardwarestore.com/about-aubuchon-hardware.aspx.

26. "Frequently Asked Questions," Ace Hardware, accessed July 29, 2008, http://www.acehardware .com/corp/index.jsp?page=faq; "Company History: 2010s," Ace Hardware, accessed June 5, 2014, http://www.acehardware.com/category/index .jsp?categoryId=34641526.

27. 84 Lumber, accessed July 29, 2008, http://www .84lumber.com.

28. J. Mangalindan, "eBay's Back!" *Fortune*, February 5, 2013, 58–65.

29. Ibid.

30. Ibid.

31. G. Bensinger, "eBay's New Goal: Double Its Users," *Wall Street Journal*, March 29, 2013, B5.

32. M. Lubatkin, "Value-Creating Mergers: Fact or Folklore?" *Academy of Management Executive* 2 (1988): 295–302; M. Lubatkin and S. Chatterjee, "Extending Modern Portfolio Theory into the Domain of Corporate Diversification: Does It Apply?" *Academy of Management Journal* 37 (1994): 109–136; M. H. Lubatkin and P. J. Lane, "Psst... The Merger Mavens Still Have It Wrong!" *Academy of Management Executive* 10 (1996): 21–39.

33. "Company Information: About Us," 3M, accessed June 5, 2014, http://solutions.3m.com/wps /portal/3M/en_US/3M-Company/Information /AboutUs/Businesses/; "Culture of Innovation," 3M (brochure), accessed June 5, 2014, http:// solutions.3m.com/3MContentRetrievalAPI/BlobSer vlet?lmd=1349327166000&locale=en_WW& assetType=MMM_Image&assetId=1319209959040 &blobAttribute=ImageFile.

34. D. Holthaus, "Pringles Sale Allows Procter & Gamble to Keep Its Focus," Cincinnati.com, April 5, 2011, accessed March 1, 2012, http://news .cincinnati.com/article/20110405/BIZ/304050039 /Pringles-sale-allows-Procter-Gamble-keep-its -focus; M. Geller and J. Wohl, "Kellogg to Buy Pringles for $2.7 Billion," Reuters, February 15, 2012, accessed March 1, 2012, http://www.reuters .com/article/2012/02/15/us-kellogg-pringles -idUSTRE81E0S620120215.

35. "Products & Services," General Electric, no date, accessed March 1, 2012, http://www.ge.com /products_services/index.html.

36. "Affiliated Companies," Samsung, accessed April 7, 2011, http://www.samsung.com/hk_en /aboutsamsung/samsunggroup/affiliatedcompanies /SAMSUNGGroup_Affiliated Companies.html.

37. http://www.this_is_BCG/bcg_history /bcg_history_2005.html; http:www.wikipedia.org.

38. D. Hambrick, I. MacMillan, and D. Day, "Strategic Attributes and Performance in the BCG Matrix—A PIMS-based Analysis of Industrial Product Businesses," Academy of Management Journal 25 (1982): 510–531.

39. J. Armstrong and R. Brodie, "Effects of Portfolio Planning Methods on Decision Making: Experimental Results," International Journal of Research in Marketing 11 (1994): 73–84.

40. K. Brooker, "Plugging the Leaks at P&G: A First-Year Report Card for CEO Durk Jager," Fortune, February 21, 2000, 44; "R&D's Formula for Success," Procter & Gamble, accessed March 17, 2009, http://www.pg.com/science/rd_formula _success.jhtml.

41. "About Us: Our Structure," Nokia, accessed May 31, 2013, http://www.nokia.com/global/about -nokia/about-us/our-structure/.

42. Z. Epstein, "Samsung Extends Mobile Market Lead as Nokia Dwindles, Apple Stalls," BGR, April 26, 2013, accessed May 31, 2013, http://bgr .com/2013/04/26/cell-phone-market-share-q1-2013 -467162/.

43. C. Lawton, "Corporate News: Nokia Siemens to Cut 17,000 Jobs," Wall Street Journal, November 25, 2011, B3; J. Rossi, "Nokia Nears Decision Time for Venture with Siemens," Wall Street Journal, March 31, 2013, accessed May 31, 2013, http://online.wsj.com/article/SB10001424127 887323501004578390430192117780.html.

44. J. A. Pearce II, "Selecting among Alternative Grand Strategies," California Management Review (Spring 1982): 23–31.

45. No author, "AT&T to Buy DirecTV for $48.5 Billion," CBS News, May 18, 2014, accessed June 24, 2014, http://www.cbsnews.com/news/at -t-to-buy-directv-for-49-billion/.

46. M. Reardon, "AT&T Defends Benefits of Proposed DirecTV Merger," cNet, June 24, 2014, accessed June 24, 2014, http://www.cnet.com/news /at-t-defends-benefits-of-proposed-directv-merger/.

47. M. Laycock, "Aero Sales Help York Nestle Factory in Tough Year," The Press, December 31, 2011, accessed March 2, 2012, http://www.yorkpress .co.uk/news/9446032.Aero_sales_help_York_factory _in_tough_year/; T. Mulier, "Breathing More Profit into Chocolate Bars," Bloomberg Businessweek, February 24, 2011, accessed March 2, 2012, http://

www.businessweek.com/magazine/content/11_10 /b4218021563564.htm; "Nestle Reports £6.5bn Annual Profit," The Independent, February 16, 2012, accessed March 2, 2012, http:// www.independent .co.uk/news/business/news/nestle-reports-65bn -annual-profit-6977817.html.

48. "ABM Launches New Brand," ABM Industries, accessed May 31, 2013, http://www.abm.com/about -abm/pages/our-new-brand.aspx.

49. J. A. Pearce II, "Retrenchment Remains the Foundation of Business Turnaround," Strategic Management Journal 15 (1994): 407–417.

50. "Goldsmith Bankers," Encyclopedia of Money, accessed June 25, 2014, http://encyclopedia-of -money.blogspot.com/2010/03/goldsmith-bankers .html; "Timeline | 1690: The Start of Barclays," Barclays Plc, accessed June 25, 2014, history, http:// www.barclays.com/about-barclays/history.html.

51. M. Colchester and D. Enrich, "Barclays Dashes Its Global Dreams—U.K. Lender to Cut Investment Bank Nearly in Half as Expansion Efforts Falter; 'Bold Simplification,'" Wall Street Journal, May 9, 2014, C1.

52. M. Berry, "Barclays to Axe 14,000 Jobs and Create 'Bad Bank,'" FundWeb, May 8, 2014, accessed June 25, 2014, http://www.fundweb.co.uk /news-and-analysis/uk/barclays-to-axe-14000-jobs -and-create-bad-bank/2009986.article.

53. S. Ovide, "A Price War Erupts in Cloud Services," Wall Street Journal, April 15, 2014, accessed June 25, 2014, http://online.wsj.com/news /articles/SB10001424052702303887804579503713 914245756.

54. D. Gallagher, "Cloud Investing Beyond Amazon, Google and Microsoft," Wall Street Journal, April 15, 2014, accessed June 25, 2014, http:// online.wsj.com/news/articles/SB1000142405270230 3887804579503903597265752#printMode.

55. S. Ovide, "Cisco Set to Take on Amazon in the Cloud," Wall Street Journal, March 24, 2014, B1; A. Spencer, "H-P Sets $1 Billion for 'Cloud' Investment," Wall Street Journal, May 7, 2014, B6.

56. A. Kessler, "The Weekend Interview with Travis Kalanick: The Transportation Trustbuster," Wall Street Journal, January 26, 2013, A13.

57. C. Henshaw, "Australia Farmers Look to Bypass Trading Companies," Wall Street Journal, May 30, 2013, accessed June 1, 2013, http://online .wsj.com/article/SB1000142412788732441260457857 14740822671524.html.

58. B. Tuttle, "Meet the Low-Key, Low-Cost Grocery Chain Being Called 'Walmart's Worst Nightmare,'" Time, August 7, 2013, accessed June 25, 2014, http://business.time.com/2013/08/07 /meet-the-low-key-low-cost-grocery-chain-being -called-wal-marts-worst-nightmare/.

59. J. Springer, "Pricing: WinCo Keeps Costs Down and Velocity High," Super Market News, April 29, 2013, accessed June 25, 2014, http:// supermarketnews.com/retail-amp-financial/pricing -winco-keeps-costs-down-and-velocity-high.

60. B. Tuttle, "Meet the Low-Key, Low-Cost Grocery Chain Being Called 'Walmart's Worst Nightmare,'" Time, August 7, 2013, accessed June 25, 2014, http://business.time.com/2013/08/07 /meet-the-low-key-low-cost-grocery-chain-being- called-wal-marts-worst-nightmare/.

61. "Norweb Microfiber," Norwex, accessed June 26, 2014, http://www.norwex.biz/pws/home 2999999/tabs/microfiber.aspx.

62. E. Byron, "It Cleans, Polishes and Scrubs: It's a $27 Cloth and Water," Wall Street Journal, June 25, 2014, D1.

63. "'Our Purpose' Can One Person Change the World? At Norwex—We Think We Can," Norwex,

accessed June 26, 2014, http://www.norwex.biz/pws /home2999999/tabs/our-purpose.aspx.

64. J. Fifer, "How Axe Built a Highly Scientific, Totally Irresistible Marketing Machine Built on Lust," Fast Company, August 8, 2012, June 1, 2013, http://www.fastcompany.com/3000041/axes-highly -scientific-typically-outrageous-and-totally-irresistible -selling-lust.

65. R. E. Miles and C. C. Snow, Organizational Strategy, Structure, & Process (New York: McGraw-Hill, 1978); S. Zahra and J. A. Pearce, "Research Evidence on the Miles-Snow Typology," Journal of Management 16 (1990): 751–768; W. L. James and K. J. Hatten, "Further Evidence on the Validity of the Self Typing Paragraph Approach: Miles and Snow Strategic Archetypes in Banking," Strategic Management Journal 16 (1995): 161–168.

66. L. Carlozo, "How Does Walmart's VUDU Movie Streaming Service Stack Up?" Deal News, August 3, 2012, accessed June 1, 2013, http://dealnews.com /features/How-Does-Walmarts-VUDU-Movie -Streaming-Service-Stack-Up-/598146.html; D. Kerr, "Redbox Instant Launches Video Streaming to the Public," cNet, March 14, 2013, accessed June 1, 2013, http://news.cnet.com/8301-1023_3-57574480 -93/redbox-instant-launches-video-streaming-to-the -public; D. Pogue, "Potluck for the Eyeballs: Amazon's Streaming Service," New York Times, August 29, 2012, accessed June 1, 2013, http://www.nytimes .com/2012/08/30/technology/personaltech/amazons -streaming-movie-service-offers-its-own-potluck -state-of-the-art.html?pagewanted=all.

67. C. Katje, "Amazon vs. Netflix: Battle to Become Streaming King Heats Up," Variety, August 2, 2013, accessed June 5, 2014. http:// variety.com/2013/biz/news/amazon-turning-svod -space-into-a-two-company-race-1200571585/; M. Shields and D. MacMillan, "Yahoo Makes New Push into Video Content," Wall Street Journal, April 6, 2014, accessed June 5, 2014, http://online .wsj.com/news/articles/SB10001424052702304819 0457948582061082406 0?mg=reno64-wsj.

68. M. Chen, "Competitor Analysis and Interfirm Rivalry: Toward a Theoretical Integration," Academy of Management Review 21 (1996): 100–134; J. C. Baum and H. J. Korn, "Competitive Dynamics of Interfirm Rivalry," Academy of Management Journal 39 (1996): 255–291.

69. M. Chen, "Competitor Analysis and Interfirm Rivalry: Toward a Theoretical Integration," Academy of Management Review 21 (1996): 100–134.

70. A. Gasparro, "Corporate News: Burger King Steps Up Its Coffee Offerings," Wall Street Journal, February 13, 2013, B7.

71. J. White, "Wendy's Wendy Gets a Makeover," Wall Street Journal, October 11, 2012, accessed June 5, 2014. http://blogs.wsj.com/corporate -intelligence/2012/10/11/wendy/?KEYWORDS =wendy%27s+strategy.

72. "Wendy's Plans to Double Pace of Image Activation Reimages in 2014," Yahoo! Finance, February 27, 2014, accessed June 5, 2014, http:// finance.yahoo.com/news/wendys-plans-double -pace-image-123613973.html.

73. A. Gasparro, "McDonald's Cranks Up the Volume on 'Value'; Chain Fights Traffic Declines as Consumer Spending Idles, Rivals Copy Strategy and Menu," Wall Street Journal, April 14, 2013, accessed June 1, 2013, http://online.wsj.com/article /SB10001424127887324240804578419163938337 8 02.html.

74. L. Lavelle, "The Chickens Come Home to Roost, and Boston Market Is Prepared to Expand," The Record, October 6, 1996.

75. "Getting to Know Us," McDonald's, accessed June 1, 2013, http://www.aboutmcdonalds.com

/mcd/our_company.html; "About Us: Subway FAQs," Subway, accessed June 1, 2013, http://www.subway.com/ContactUs/CustServFAQs.aspx.

76. "Frequently Asked Questions," Subway Restaurants, accessed March 18, 2009, http://www.subway.com/subwayroot/AboutSubway/subwayFaqs.aspx.

77. B. Heater, "Amazon Kindle Paperwhite Hands-on (Update: video)," *Engadget*, September 6, 2012, accessed June 5, 2014, http://www.engadget.com/2012/09/06/amazon-kindle-paperwhite-hands-on/.

78. S. Buckley, "Nook Simple Touch with GlowLight gets another $20 price drop, undercuts competition," *Engadget*, August 18, 2013, accessed June 5, 2014, http://www.engadget.com/2013/08/18/nook-simple-touch-with-glowlight-gets-another-20-price-drop/.

79. J. Volpe, "E Ink's new higher contrast Carta display is the secret behind Amazon's refreshed Kindle Paperwhite," *Engadget*, September 4, 2013, accessed June 5, 2014, http://www.engadget.com/2013/09/04/e-ink-new-higher-contrast-carta-display-amazon-kindle-paperwhite/.

80. D. Ketchen, Jr., C. Snow, and V. Street, "Improving Firm Performance by Matching Strategic Decision-Making Processes to Competitive Dynamics," *Academy of Management Executive* 18 (2004): 29–43.

81. M. Gottfried, "T-Mobile's Shine Dims Sprint's Deal Hopes," *Wall Street Journal*, March 1, 2014, B14.

82. M. Gottfried, "T-Mobile Takes Toll on Verizon," *Wall Street Journal*, April 25, 2014, C8; E. Mason, "T-Mobile's Loss Widens as Costs Press Higher," *Wall Street Journal*, February 26, 2014, B4; T Gryta & B. Rubin, "T-Mobile Posts Big Gain in Subscribers," *Wall Street Journal*, May 1, 2014, accessed June 26, 2014, http://online.wsj.com/news/articles/SB10001424052702304677904579535291254065308.

83. Z. Epstein, "The Most Important Wireless Carrier in America," *BGR*, October 10, 2013, accessed June 26, 2014, http://bgr.com/2013/10/10/t-mobile-free-international-roaming-analysis/; T. Gryta, "T-Mobile will Waive Data Fees for Music Services," *Wall Street Journal*, June 18, 2014, accessed June 26, 2014, http://online.wsj.com/articles/t-mobile-will-waive-data-fees-for-music-service-1403142678.

84. J. Hagerty and K. Linebaugh, "GE, Caterpillar Face Off in Hot Locomotive Market," *Wall Street Journal*, April 11, 2012, accessed June 1, 2013, http://online.wsj.com/article/SB10001424052702304177710457730766329 2911878.html.

85. K. Linebaugh, "GE to Cut Back Trains," *Wall Street Journal*, April 9, 2013, accessed June 1, 2013, http://online.wsj.com/article/SB100014241278873245047045784130341363984 90.html.

86. A. Loten, "Why Amazon.com's New App Is Creating a Stir," *Wall Street Journal*, December 21, 2011, accessed June 1, 2013, http://online.wsj.com/article/SB1000142405297020402680457710103243 0362056.html.

87. Associate Press, "Best Buy's Store Closing List: Is Yours on It?" *CBS News*, April 16, 2012, accessed June 1, 2013, http://www.cbsnews.com/8301-505144_162-57414517/best-buys-store-closing-list-is-yours-on-it/; G. Bensinger, "When Apps Attack: Industries Under Pressure," *Wall Street Journal*, March 27, 2013, accessed June 1, 2013, http://online.wsj.com/article/SB100014241278873243928 04578358793409826294.html; M. Bustle, "Best Buy Pays Price to Rival Amazon," *Wall Street Journal*, December 14, 2011, accessed June 1, 2013, http://online.wsj.com/article/SB10001424052970203518404577096160252527328.html; A. Zimmerman,

"Can Electronics Stores Survive?" *Wall Street Journal*, August 20, 2012, accessed June 1, 2013, http://online.wsj.com/article/SB1000087239639044477280457762158173 9401906.html.

7

1. J. Tierney, "A Hearing Aid That Cuts Out All the Clatter," *New York Times*, October 23, 2011, accessed May 2, 2012, http:// www.nytimes.com/2011/10/24/science/24loops.html.

2. P. Anderson and M. L. Tushman, "Managing Through Cycles of Technological Change," *Research/Technology Management*, May–June 1991, 26–31.

3. R. N. Foster, *Innovation: The Attacker's Advantage* (New York: Summit, 1986).

4. "The Silicon Engine: A Timeline of Semiconductors in Computers," Computer History Museum, accessed April 22, 2001, http://www.computerhistory.org/semiconductor/; "The Evolution of a Revolution," Intel, accessed June 2, 2013, http://download.intel.com/pressroom/kits/IntelProcessorHistory.pdf; T. Smith, "Inside Intel's Haswell: What do 1.4 BEELION transistors get you?" *The Register*, June 3, 2013, accessed June 13, 2014, http://www.theregister.co.uk/2013/06/03/feature_inside_haswell_intel_4g_core/.

5. J. Burke, *The Day the Universe Changed* (Boston: Little, Brown, 1985).

6. D. Wakabayashi, "The Point-and-Shoot Camera Faces Its Existential Moment," *Wall Street Journal*, July 30, 2013, accessed June 30, 2014, http://online.wsj.com/news/articles/SB1000142412788732425150457858026371943252.

7. J. Osawa, "Phones Imperil Fancy Cameras," *Wall Street Journal*, November 7, 2013, accessed June 13, 2014, http://online.wsj.com/news/articles/SB1000142405270230467240457918364369623686 8?KEYWORDS=high-end+camera&mg=reno64-wsj.

8. "HTC talks camera tech: DSLR-destroying optical zooming '18 months' away," *Official Vodafone UK blog* (blog), April 18, 2014, accessed June 13, 2014, http://blog.vodafone.co.uk/2014/04/18/htc-talks-camera-tech-optical-zooming/; J. Osawa, "Are Camera Apps Enough for Photo Enthusiasts?" *Wall Street Journal*, November 8, 2013, accessed June 13, 2014, http://blogs.wsj.com/digits/2013/11/08/are-camera-apps-enough-for-photo-enthusiasts/?KEYWORDS=dslr+camera.

9. M. L. Tushman, P. C. Anderson, and C. O'Reilly, "Technology Cycles, Innovation Streams, and Ambidextrous Organizations: Organization Renewal Through Innovation Streams and Strategic Change," in *Managing Strategic Innovation and Change*, ed. M. L. Tushman and P. Anderson (New York: Oxford Press, 1997), 3–23.

10. S. Levy, "Nest's Plan to Stop Brownouts Before They Start," Wired.com, April 22, 2012, accessed June 2, 2013, http://www.wired.com/business/2013/04/nest-energy-services.

11. T. Simonite, "Nest's Smarter Home," *MIT Technology Review*, February 15, 2013, accessed June 2, 2013, http://www.technologyreview.com/featuredstory/511086/how-nests-control-freaks-reinvented-the-thermostat/.

12. "Are Landline Phones Becoming an Endangered Species?" Statistica, March 31, 2014, accessed July 1, 2014, http://www.statista.com/chart/2072/landline-phones-in-the-united-states/.

13. Staff, "Landline Phone Penetration Dwindles as Cell-Only Households Grow," Marketing Charts, June 6, 2012, accessed June 2, 2013, http://www.marketingcharts.com/direct/landline-phone

-penetration-dwindles-as-cell-only-households-grow-22577/.

14. "Wireless and Landline Phones."

15. "AT&T, Verizon Are Leaving Landlines Behind," *Wall Street Journal News Hub*, online video, 17:27, April 8, 2014, accessed June 13, 2014, http://live.wsj.com/video/att-verizon-are-leaving-landlines-behind/7874152B-A635-4092-9B7B-69EB86AE3787.html?KEYWORDS=milestones#!7874152B-A635-4092-9B7B-69EB86AE3787.

16. E. Schlossberg, *Interactive Excellence: Defining and Developing New Standards for the Twenty-First Century* (New York: Ballantine, 1998).

17. W. Abernathy and J. Utterback, "Patterns of Industrial Innovation," *Technology Review* 2 (1978): 40–47.

18. D. Howley, "Wireless Charging Standard Gets One Step Closer," *Laptop Magazine*, February 1, 2014, accessed July 1, 2014, as reported at http://www.techhive.com/article/2096802/wireless-charging-alliances-teaming-up-to-work-toward-a-cable-free-world.html.

19. No author, "Wireless Charging Surge Seen," *Investor's Business Daily*, March 24, 2014, A02.

20. M. Ramsay, "'Real' 4G Standards Ratified by ITU," *Wireless Week*, January 19, 2012, http://wirelessweek.com/News/2012/01/Technologies-Real-4G-Standards-Ratified-ITU-Wireless-Networks/.

21. M. Schilling, "Technological Lockout: An Integrative Model of the Economic and Strategic Factors Driving Technology Success and Failure," *Academy of Management Review* 23 (1998): 267–284; M. Schilling, "Technology Success and Failure in Winner-Take-All Markets: The Impact of Learning Orientation, Timing, and Network Externalities," *Academy of Management Journal* 45 (2002): 387–398.

22. R. Verrier, "Small-town Movie Theaters Threatened by Shift to Digital Cinema," *Los Angeles Times*, May 4, 2013, accessed June 2, 2013, http://articles.latimes.com/print/2013/may/04/entertainment/la-et-ct-last-picture-show-20130504.

23. T. M. Amabile, R. Conti, H. Coon, J. Lazenby, and M. Herron, "Assessing the Work Environment for Creativity," *Academy of Management Journal* 39 (1996): 1154–1184.

24. Ibid.

25. M. Csikszentmihalyi, *Flow: The Psychology of Optimal Experience* (New York: Harper & Row, 1990).

26. L. Emarian, "Creating Culture of IT Innovation Includes Rewarding Failure," *Computer World*, April 6, 2012, accessed June 2, 2013, http://www.computerworld.com/s/article/9225870/Creating_culture_of_IT_innovation_includes_rewarding_failure.

27. A. Ahrendts, "The Experts: How Should Leaders Spur Innovation?" interview by C. Wiens, March 12, 2013, accessed June 13, 2014, http://online.wsj.com/news/articles/SB1000142412788732382670457835292147382531 6?mg=reno64-wsj&url=http%3A%2F%2Fonline.wsj.com%2Farticle%2FSB100014241278873238267045783529214738253316.html.

28. Ibid.

29. Ibid.

30. L. Kwoh, "Memo to Staff: Take More Risks," *Wall Street Journal*, March 20, 2013, accessed June 2, 2013, http://online.wsj.com/article/SB100014241 278 873236396045783703839390447803.html.

31. K. M. Eisenhardt, "Accelerating Adaptive Processes: Product Innovation in the Global Computer Industry," *Administrative Science Quarterly* 40 (1995): 84–110.

32. Ibid.

33. R. Fleming, "Oculus Rift Has Sold Over 85,000 Prototypes," *Digital Trends*, April 16, 2014, accessed June 13, 2014, http://www.digitaltrends.com/gaming/oculus-rift-sold-85000-prototypes/#!YqqBJ.

34. D. Poeter, "Hands on with the Oculus Rift DK2," *PCMag*, March 20, 2014, accessed June 13, 2014, http://www.pcmag.com/article2/0,2817,2455180,00.asp.

35. E. Catmull, "How Pixar Fosters Collective Creativity," *Harvard Business Review*, September 2008, 64–72.

36. D. Roberts, "Sealy Goes to the Mattresses," *Fortune*, September 17, 2012, accessed June 2, 2013, http://management.fortune.cnn.com/2012/09/17/sealy-executive-dream-team/.

37. L. Kraar, "25 Who Help the US Win: Innovators Everywhere Are Generating Ideas to Make America a Stronger Competitor. They Range from a Boss Who Demands the Impossible to a Mathematician with a Mop," *Fortune*, March 22, 1991.

38. M. W. Lawless and P. C. Anderson, "Generational Technological Change: Effects of Innovation and Local Rivalry on Performance," *Academy of Management Journal* 39 (1996): 1185–1217.

39. "USB.org—Hi-Speed FAQ," USB Implementers Forum, accessed July 1, 2014, http://www.usb.org/developers/usb20/faq20/; "USB.org—SuperSpeed USB," USB Implementers Forum, accessed July 1, 2014, http://www.usb.org/developers/ssusb/.

40. A. Vance, "Ansys Aids Innovation with Its Simulation Software," *Bloomberg Businessweek*, March 7, 2013, accessed June 2, 2013, http://www.businessweek.com/articles/2013-03-07/ansys-aids-innovation-with-its-simulation-software.

41. J. Rich, "Twilight Exclusive: Chris Weitz Will Not Direct Third Film, 'Eclipse,'" *Hollywood Insider*, February 21, 2009, accessed July 23, 2010, http://hollywoodinsider.ew.com/2009/02/21/twilight-chris/; G. McIntyre, "On the Set: 'New Moon' on the Rise," *Los Angeles Times*, July 19, 2009, accessed July 23, 2010, http://www.latimes.com/entertainment/news/la-ca-newmoon19-2009jul19,0,3312678,full.story; N. Sperling, "It's Official: Bill Condon Will Direct Twilight's Final Chapter 'Breaking Dawn,'" *Hollywood Insider*, April 28, 2010, accessed July 23, 2010, http://hollywoodinsider.ew.com/2010/04/28/bill-condon-will-direct-twilights-final-chapter-breaking-dawn/.

42. M. Boyle, "How Slim-Fast Lost Out to Weight-Loss Rivals," January 24, 2013, accessed June 3, 2013, http://www.businessweek.com/articles/2013-01-24/how-slim-fast-lost-out-to-weight-loss-rivals.

43. P. Strebel, "Choosing the Right Change Path," *California Management Review* (Winter 1994): 29–51.

44. K. Lewin, *Field Theory in Social Science: Selected Theoretical Papers* (New York: Harper & Brothers, 1951).

45. J. Owen, "Film is finished - this could be its last Oscars," *The Independent*, February 24, 2013, accessed June 13, 2014, http://www.independent.co.uk/arts-entertainment/films/news/film-is-finished—this-could-be-its-last-oscars-8508257.html?printService=print.

46. Lewin, *Field Theory in Social Science*.

47. J. Hansel, "Pulse on Health: A Uniform Policy," PostBulletin.com, March 5, 2012, accessed March 7, 2012, http://www.postbulletin.com/news/stories/display.php?id=1488969.

48. A. B. Fisher, "Making Change Stick," *Fortune*, April 17, 1995, 121.

49. J. P. Kotter and L. A. Schlesinger, "Choosing Strategies for Change," *Harvard Business Review* (March–April 1979): 106–114.

50. S. Giessner, G. Viki, S. Otten, S. Terry, and D. Tauber, "The Challenge of Merging: Merger Patterns, Premerger Status, and Merger Support," *Personality and Social Psychology Bulletin* 32, no. 3 (2006): 339–352.

51. E. Cassano, "How Vince Donnelly Led PMA Companies Through an Acquisition by Involving Everyone," *Smart Business*, February 1, 2012, accessed March 7, 2012, http://www.sbnonline.com/2012/02/how-vince-donnelly-led-pma-companies-through-an-acquisition-by-involving-everyone/.

52. D. Bennett, "Marriage at 30,000 Feet," *Bloomberg Businessweek*, February 6–12, 2012, 58–63.

53. D. Meinert, "An Open Book," *HR Magazine*, April 2013, 42–46.

54. J. P. Kotter, "Leading Change: Why Transformation Efforts Fail," *Harvard Business Review* 73, no. 2 (March–April 1995): 59.

55. P. Smith, "The Nokia insider who knows why it failed warns Apple it could be next," *Financial Review*, September 6, 2013, accessed June 13, 2014, http://www.afr.com/p/technology/next_nokia_insider_who_knows_why_Z8at1lqZLp3mAutUO0ye0H.

56. Ibid.

57. G. Pitts, "A Classic Turnaround—With Some Twists," *The Globe and Mail*, July 7, 2008, B1.

58. P. Burrows, "Stephen Elop's Nokia Adventure," *Bloomberg Businessweek*, June 2, 2011, accessed June 3, 2013, http://www.businessweek.com/magazine/content/11_24/b4232056703101.htm.

59. J. Rossi, "Nokia Releases New Lumia Phone," *Wall Street Journal*, May 14, 2013, accessed June 5, 2013, http://online.wsj.com/article/SB10001424127887323716304578482482212916580.html.

60. Pitts, "A Classic Turnaround."

61. S. Cramm, "A Change of Hearts," *CIO*, April 1, 2003, May 20, 2003, http://www.cio.com/archive/040103/hsleadership.html.

62. J. Scheck, "New Shell CEO Van Beurden Lays Out Turnaround Plan," *Wall Street Journal*, April 27, 2014, accessed July 1, 2014, http://online.wsj.com/news/articles/SB1000142405270230416360457952790186837044?KEYWORDS=Ben+van+Beurden+CEO+Royal+Dutch+Shell&mg=reno64-wsj.

63. R. N. Ashkenas and T. D. Jick, "From Dialogue to Action in GE WorkOut: Developmental Learning in a Change Process," in *Research in Organizational Change and Development*, vol. 6, ed. W. A. Pasmore and R. W. Woodman (Greenwich, CT: JAI Press, 1992), 267–287.

64. T. Stewart, "GE Keeps Those Ideas Coming," *Fortune*, August 12, 1991, 40.

65. W. J. Rothwell, R. Sullivan, and G. M. McLean, *Practicing Organizational Development: A Guide for Consultants* (San Diego, CA: Pfeiffer & Co., 1995).

66. Ibid.

8

1. "Web Table 34. Number of Parent Corporations and Foreign Affiliates, by Region and Economy," *World Investment Report 2011*, United Nations Conference on Trade and Development, accessed June 10, 2013, http://unctad.org/Sections/dite_dir/docs/WIR11_web%20tab%2034.pdf.

2. J. Bennett and R. J. Krishna, "Indian Tire Maker Rolls Cooper into $2.5 Billion Deal," *Wall Street Journal*, June 12, 2013, accessed June 13, 2014, http://online.wsj.com/news/articles/SB10001424127887324188604578541061761314632?KEYWORDS=indian+firm+to+buy+cooper&mg=reno64-wsj.

3. "Ford to Build First Transmission Plant in China," *Boston.com*, May 19, 2011, accessed March 8, 2012, http://articles.boston.com/2011-05-19/business/29561203_1_chongqing-joint-venture-china-association.

4. B. Chen, "Tear Down This Wall—the Chinese Tariff Wall," *Forbes*, July 12, 2012, accessed June 5, 2013, http://www.forbes.com/sites/baizhuchen/2012/07/12/tear-down-this-wall-the-chinese-tariff-wall/.

5. B. Krueger, "A Shoe Tariff with a Big Footprint," *Wall Street Journal*, November 23, 2012, A13.

6. D. Cardwell and K. Bradsher, "US Will Place Tariffs on Chinese Solar Panels," *New York Times*, October 10, 2012, accessed June 5, 2013, http://www.nytimes.com/2012/10/11/business/global/us-sets-tariffs-on-chinese-solar-panels.html?_r=1&.

7. Reuters, "Indonesia Relaxes Limits on Australian Beef Imports," *Reuters*, May 28, 2013, accessed June 6, 2013, http://www.reuters.com/article/2013/05/28/indonesia-beef-australia-idUSL3N0E901O20130528.

8. Reuters, "Mexico Bows to Brazilian Pressure on Auto Exports," *Reuters*, March 15, 2012, accessed June 8, 2013, http://www.reuters.com/article/2012/03/16/mexico-brazil-autos-idUSL2E8EF3G420120316.

9. "Understanding the WTO," *World Trade Organization*, accessed August 5, 2008, http://www.wto.org/english/thewto_e/whatis_e/tif_e/agrm9_e.htm.

10. Reuters, "Russia Blocking US Meat Over Additives, West Sees Protectionism," *Chicago Tribune*, February 8, 2013, accessed June 6, 2013, http://articles.chicagotribune.com/2013-02-08/news/sns-rt-russia-meatl5n0b7d7s-20130208_1_ractopamine-meat-imports-russia-s-wto.

11. J. Wehrman, "Farm Bill's Subsidy for Sugar Under Pressure," *The Columbus Dispatch*, June 20, 2013, accessed July 2, 2014, http://www.dispatch.com/content/stories/local/2013/06/20/farm-bills-subsidy-for-sugar-under-pressure.html.

12. A. Wexler, "Big Sugar Is Set for a Sweet Bailout," *Wall Street Journal*, March 13, 2013, accessed July 2, 2014, http://online.wsj.com/news/articles/SB10001424127887324096404578356740206766164.

13. "GATT/WTO," *Duke Law: Library & Technology*, accessed June 12, 2009, http://www.law.duke.edu/libtech.

14. "IFPI publishes Digital Music Report 2013," *International Federation of the Phonographic Industry*, February 26, 2013, accessed June 8, 2013, http://www.ifpi.org/content/section_resources/dmr2013.html; P. Sonne and M. Colchester, "France, the UK Take Aim at Digital Pirates," *Wall Street Journal*, April 15, 2010, accessed June 9, 2010, http://online.wsj.com/article/SB10001424052702304604204575181820755061494.html.

15. D. Price, "Sizing the Piracy University," *Netnames*, September 2013, accessed July 2, 2014, http://www.netnames.com//sites/default/files/netnames-sizing_piracy_universe-FULLreport-sept2013.pdf.

16. "Shadow Market: 2011 BSA Global Software Piracy Study, Ninth Edition," *BSA | The Software Alliance*, May 15, 2012, accessed June 8, 2013, http://globalstudy.bsa.org/2011/downloads/study_pdf/2011_BSA_Piracy_Study-Standard.pdf.

17. C. Bialik, "Putting a Price Tag on Film Piracy," *Wall Street Journal*, April 5, 2013, accessed June 8, 2013, http://blogs.wsj.com/numbersguy/putting-a-price-tag-on-film-piracy-1228/.

18. "Countries: On the Road to EU Membership," *European Union*, accessed August 11, 2013, http://europa.eu/about-eu/countries/index_en.htm.

19. M. Villarreal and I. Ferguson, "NAFTA at 20: Overview and Trade Effects," *Congressional Research*

Service, February 21, 2013, accessed June 10, 2013, http://www.fas.org/sgp/crs/row/R42965.pdf.

20. Office of the United States Trade Representative, "CAFTA-DR (Dominican Republic-Central America FTA)," accessed June 13, 2014, http://www.ustr.gov/trade-agreements/free-trade-agreements/cafta-dr-dominican-republic-central-america-fta.

21. "UNASUR: Union of South American Nations," *Communidad Andina*, accessed July 2, 2014, http://www.comunidadandina.org/ingles/sudamerican.htm.

22. "Selected Basic ASEAN Indicators," *Association of Southeast Asian Nations*, April 30, 2014, accessed June 13, 2014, http://www.asean.org/images/resources/Statistics/2014/SelectedKey IndicatorAsOfApril/table1_as%20of%20April14_upload.pdf; "Overview of ASEAN-US Dialogue Relations," *Association of Southeast Asian Nations*, accessed July 2, 2014, http://www.asean.org/news/item/overview-of-asean-us-dialogue-relations.

23. "Selected Basic ASEAN Indicators, 2005," *Association of Southeast Asian Nations*, accessed August 6, 2008, http://www.aseansec.org/stat/Table1.pdf; "Top Ten ASEAN Trade Partner Countries/Regions, 2005," *Association of Southeast Asian Nations*, accessed August 6, 2008, http://www.aseansec.org/Stat/Table20.pdf; "ASEAN Free Trade Area (AFTA)," *Association of Southeast Asian Nations*, accessed August 6, 2008, http://www.aseansec.org/12021.htm.

24. "Frequently Asked Questions," *Asia-Pacific Economic Cooperation*, accessed July 2, 2014, http://www.apec.org/FAQ.aspx/; "StatsAPEC—Data for the Asia-Pacific Region—Economic and Social Statistics & Bilateral Trade and Investment Flows," StatsAPEC, accessed July 2, 2014, http://statistics.apec.org/.

25. "Member Economies," *Asia Pacific Economic Cooperation*, accessed August 6, 2008, http://www.apec.org/apec/member_economies/key_websites.html; "Frequently Asked Questions (FAQs)," *Asia-Pacific Economic Cooperation*, accessed August 6, 2008, http://www.apec.org/apec/tools/faqs.html.

26. "Gross National Income Per Capita 2013, Atlas Method and PPP Based," *The World Bank*, April 15, 2013, accessed June 10, 2013, http://data.worldbank.org/data-catalog/GNI-per-capita-Atlas-and-PPP-table; accessed June 13, 2014, http://databank.worldbank.org/data/download/GNIPC.pdf.

27. Ibid.

28. "The Global Competitiveness Report: 2008–2009," *World Economic Forum*, accessed June 14, 2009, http://www.weforum.org/documents/GCR0809/index.html.

29. "Freer Trade Cuts the Cost of Living," *World Trade Organization*, accessed August 6, 2008, http://www.wto.org/english/thewto_e/whatis_e/10ben_e/10b04_e.htm.

30. M. Gao, "Culture Determines Business Models: Analyzing Home Depot's Failure Case in China for International Retailers from a Communication Perspective," *Thunderbird International Business Review*, March/April 2013: 173-191.

31. L. Burkitt, "Home Depot Learns Chinese Prefer 'Do-It-for-Me,'" *Wall Street Journal*, September 14, 2012, accessed June 8, 2013, http://online.wsj.com/article/SB10000872396390444433504577651072911154602.html.

32. Katie Englehart, "Starbucks Go Home," *Macleans*, January 25, 2013, accessed July 2, 2014, http://online.wsj.com/news/articles/SB10001424052702304607104579209971318755960.

33. A. Sundaram and J. S. Black, "The Environment and Internal Organization of Multinational Enterprises," *Academy of Management Review* 17 (1992): 729–757.

34. H. S. James, Jr., and M. Weidenbaum, *When Businesses Cross International Borders: Strategic Alliances & Their Alternatives* (Westport, CT: Praeger Publishers, 1993).

35. P. Marsh, "UK Car Exports Drive Industry's Revival," *Financial Times*, January 17, 2013, accessed June 9, 2013, http://www.ft.com/intl/cms/s/0/cf9261ce-5fc5-11e2-b128-00144 feab49a.html.

36. T. Aeppel, "Oil Shocker: Stung by Soaring Transportation Cost, Factories Bring Jobs Home Again," *Wall Street Journal*, June 13, 2008, A1.

37. K. Schweizer, "'Desperate Housewives' Gets Turkish Twist as Disney Looks Abroad," *Bloomberg Businessweek*, September 18, 2012, accessed June 9, 2013, http://www.businessweek.com/news/2012-09-18/desperate-housewives-gets-turkish-twist-as-disney-looks-abroad.

38. "New Restaurants," *McDonald's*, accessed June 13, 2014, http://www.aboutmcdonalds.com/mcd/franchising/us_franchising/aquiring_a_franchise/new_restaurants.html.

39. A. Lutz, "McDonald's Franchisees Are Furious About How Much It Costs to Operate a Restaurant," *Business Insider*, August 6, 2013, accessed June 13, 2014, http://www.businessinsider.com/mcdonalds-franchise-owners-hold-meeting-2013-8.

40. K. Le Mesurier, "Overseas and Overwhelmed," *BRW*, January 25, 2007, 51.

41. W. Mellor, "McDonald's No Match for KFC in China as Colonel Rules Fast Food," *Bloomberg Businessweek*, January 26, 2011, accessed March 9, 2012, http://www.bloomberg.com/news/2011-01-26/mcdonald-s-no-match-for-kfc-in-china-where-colonel-sanders-rules-fast-food.html.

42. E. Dou, "Hewlett-Packard, Foxconn Launch Joint Server Venture," *Wall Street Journal*, April 30, 2014, accessed June 13, 2014, http://online.wsj.com/news/articles/SB10001424052702033948104579533080961860334?mod=WSJ_hp_LEFTWhatsNewsCollection&mg=reno64-wsj.

43. V. Bajaj, "After a Year of Delays, the First Starbucks Is to Open in Tea-Loving India This Fall," *New York Times*, January 30, 2012, accessed March 9, 2012, http://www.nytimes.com/2012/01/31/business/global/starbucks-to-open-first-indian-store-this-autumn.html.

44. J. R. Hagerty, "Japanese Toilet Maker Lixil Buys American Standard," June 28, 2013, accessed June 13, 2014, http://online.wsj.com/news/articles/SB10001424127887323419604578573121801745426?KEYWORDS=japanese+toilet+maker&mg=reno64-wsj.

45. P. Margot, "Standard Chartered Looks to Get Slimmer," *Wall Street Journal*, March 4, 2014, C3; P. Margot, "Standard Chartered to Sell 2 Korean Units," *Market Watch*, June 16, 2014, accessed July 2, 2014, https://secure.marketwatch.com/story/standard-chartered-to-sell-2-korean-units-2014-06-16.

46. W. Hordes, J. A. Clancy, and J. Baddaley, "A Primer for Global Start-Ups," *Academy of Management Executive*, May 1995, 7–11.

47. P. Dimitratos, J. Johnson, J. Slow, and S. Young, "Micromultinationals: New Types of Firms for the Global Competitive Landscape," *European Management Journal* 21, no. 2 (April 2003): 164; B. M. Oviatt and P. P. McDougall, "Toward a Theory of International New Ventures," *Journal of International Business Studies* (Spring 1994): 45–64; S. Zahra, "A Theory of International New Ventures: A Decade of Research," *Journal of International Business Studies* (January 2005): 20–28.

48. B. Keplesky, "MakerBot's Bre Pettis on the Next Industrial Revolution," *Entrepreneur*, March 9, 2013, accessed June 10, 2013, http://www.entrepreneur.com/blog/printthis/226044; M. Wolf, "How 3D Printing Is Now Helping NASA Get to Space," *Forbes*, January 12, 2013, accessed June 10, 2013, http://www.forbes.com/sites/michaelwolf/2013/01/12/how-3d-printing-is-now-helping-nasa-get-to-space/; "Official International MakerBot Distributors," *MakerBot*, accessed June 10, 2013, http://www.makerbot.com/distributors/.

49. "2013 Worldwide Unit Case Volume Geographic Mix," Coca-Cola, accessed July 2, 2014, http://www.coca-colacompany.com/annual-review/2013/operating_groups.html.

50. "Coca-Cola Single Bottle (20oz/500ml)," *HuMuch?* accessed June 10, 2013, http://www.humuch.com/prices/CocaCola-Single-Bottle-20oz500ml/_____/40.

51. "2010 Annual Report," *The Coca-Cola Company*.

52. "After a Year of Delays."

53. "StarChip Opens New Office in Shanghai, China," *Asia Today*, March 6, 2012, accessed March 9, 2012, http://www.asiatoday.com/pressrelease/starchip-opens-new-office-shanghai-china.

54. "Tax Environment," *NFIA*, accessed June 13, 2014, http://www.nfia.com/tax.html; D. Dzombak, "The Highest Corporate Tax Rates in the World," *The Motley Fool*, March 1, 2014, accessed July 2, 2014, http://www.fool.com/investing/general/2014/03/01/the-highest-corporate-tax-rates-in-the-world.aspx.

55. "Customer Care in the Netherlands," *The Netherlands Foreign Investment Agency*, accessed February 13, 2007, http://www.nfia.com/solutions.php?pageid=11 (content no longer available online).

56. "Foreign Corrupt Business Practices Act," *US Department of Justice*, May 10, 2003, http://www.usdoj.gov/criminal/fraud/.

57. A. Snyder, "European Expansion: How to Shop Around," *Management Review*, November 1, 1993, 16.

58. J. Oetzel, R. Bettis, and M. Zenner, "How Risky Are They?" *Journal of World Business* 36, no. 2 (Summer 2001): 128–145.

59. K. D. Miller, "A Framework for Integrated Risk Management in International Business," *Journal of International Business Studies*, 2nd Quarter 1992, 311.

60. M. Bahree, "Foreign Retailers Regroup in India," *Wall Street Journal*, December 12, 2011, B3.

61. P. Beckett, "Honeywell Chairman: Foreign Firms Scared of India Now," *Wall Street Journal*, May 2, 2012, accessed June 9, 2013, http://online.wsj.com/article/SB100014240527023043743704577379453791550164.html.

62. "Chapter 1: Political Outlook," *UAE Business Forecast Report*, 2007, 1st Quarter, 5–10.

63. R. Roy, "Foreign Online Retailers Ask India to Allow Direct Sales," *Wall Street Journal*, February 12, 2013, accessed June 10, 2013, http://online.wsj.com/article/SB10001424127887324880504578299454251603948.html.

64. G. Hofstede, "The Cultural Relativity of the Quality of Life Concept," *Academy of Management Review* 9 (1984): 389–398; G. Hofstede, "The Cultural Relativity of Organizational Practices and Theories," *Journal of International Business Studies*, Fall 1983, 75–89; G. Hofstede, "The Interaction Between National and Organizational Value Systems," *Journal of Management Studies*, July 1985, 347–357; M. Hoppe, "An Interview with Geert Hofstede," *Academy of Management Executive*, February 2004, 75–79.

65. R. Hodgetts, "A Conversation with Geert Hofstede," *Organizational Dynamics*, Spring 1993, 53–61.

66. T. Lenartowicz and K. Roth, "Does Subculture within a Country Matter? A Cross-Cultural Study of Motivational Domains and Business Performance in Brazil," *Journal of International Business Studies* 32 (2001): 305–325.

67. M. Janssens, J. M. Brett, and F. J. Smith, "Confirmatory Cross-Cultural Research: Testing the Viability of a Corporation-Wide Safety Policy," *Academy of Management Journal* 38 (1995): 364–382.

68. M. Koren, "Why Russians Aren't Smiling at You in Sochi," *National Journal*, February 7, 2014, accessed June 13, 2014, http://www.nationaljournal.com/politics/why-russians-aren-t-smiling-at-you-in-sochi-20140207.

69. J. S. Black, M. Mendenhall, and G. Oddou, "Toward a Comprehensive Model of International Adjustment: An Integration of Multiple Theoretical Perspectives," *Academy of Management Review* 16 (1991): 291–317; R. L. Tung, "American Expatriates Abroad: From Neophytes to Cosmopolitans," *Columbia Journal of World Business*, June 22, 1998, 125; A. Harzing, "The Persistent Myth of High Expatriate Failure Rates," *International Journal of Human Resource Management* 6 (1995): 457–475; A. Harzing, "Are Our Referencing Errors Undermining Our Scholarship and Credibility? The Case of Expatriate Failure Rates," *Journal of Organizational Behavior* 23 (2002): 127–148; N. Forster, "The Persistent Myth of High Expatriate Failure Rates: A Reappraisal," *International Journal of Human Resource Management* 8 (1997): 414–433.

70. J. Black, "The Right Way to Manage Expats," *Harvard Business Review* 77 (March–April 1999): 52; C. Joinson, "No Returns," *HR Magazine*, November 1, 2002, 70.

71. "International assignment perspectives: Critical issues facing the globally mobile workforce," *PricewaterhouseCoopers*, Vol. 5, November 2011, accessed June 13, 2014, http://www.pwc.com/en_US/us/hr-international-assignment-services/publications/assets/ny-12-0258_ias_journal_volume_5_new_images.pdf.

72. R. Feintzeig, "After Stints Abroad, Re-Entry Can Be Hard," *Wall Street Journal*, September 17, 2013, accessed June 14, 2014, http://online.wsj.com/news/articles/SB10001424127887323342404457908 1382781895274?KEYWORDS=after+stints+abroad&mg=reno64-wsj.

73. "Ten Examples of Cross-Cultural Blunders," *UKProEdits*, June 7, 2012, accessed June 10, 2013, http://ukproedits.com/uncategorized/ten-examples-of-cross-cultural-mistakes.

74. J. S. Black and M. Mendenhall, "Cross-Cultural Training Effectiveness: A Review and Theoretical Framework for Future Research," *Academy of Management Review* 15 (1990): 113–136.

75. K. Essick, "Executive Education: Transferees Prep for Life, Work in Far-Flung Lands," *Wall Street Journal*, November 12, 2004, A6.

76. Ibid.

77. P. W. Tam, "Culture Course—'Awareness Training' Helps US Workers Better Know Their Counterparts in India," *Wall Street Journal*, May 25, 2004, B1.

78. S. Hamm, "Aperian: Helping Companies Bridge Cultures," *BusinessWeek*, September 8, 2008, 16.

79. W. Arthur, Jr., and W. Bennett, Jr., "The International Assignee: The Relative Importance of Factors Perceived to Contribute to Success," *Personnel Psychology* 48 (1995): 99–114; B. Cheng, "Home Truths about Foreign Postings; To Make an Overseas Assignment Work, Employers Need More Than an Eager Exec with a Suitcase. They Must Also Motivate the Staffer's Spouse," *BusinessWeek Online*, accessed March 20, 2009, http://www.businessweek.com/careers/content/jul2002/ca20020715_9110.htm.

80. B. Groysberg and R. Abrahams, "A Successful International Assignment Depends on These Factors," *Harvard Business Review* (blog), February 13, 2014, 10:00, accessed June 15, 2014, http://blogs.hbr.org/2014/02/a-successful-international-assignment-depends-on-these-factors/.

81. "OAI: Overseas Assignment Inventory," *Prudential Real Estate and Relocation Services Intercultural Group*, May 11, 2011, http://www.performanceprograms.com/userfiles/image/Cross%20Culture/OAI_Fact_Sheet.pdf.

82. S. P. Deshpande and C. Viswesvaran, "Is Cross-Cultural Training of Expatriate Managers Effective? A Meta-Analysis," *International Journal of Intercultural Relations* 16, no. 3 (1992): 295–310.

83. D. M. Eschbach, G. Parker, and P. Stoeberl, "American Repatriate Employees' Retrospective Assessments of the Effects of Cross-Cultural Training on Their Adaptation to International Assignments," *International Journal of Human Resource Management* 12 (2001): 270–287; "Culture Training: How to Prepare Your Expatriate Employees for Cross-Cultural Work Environments," *Managing Training & Development*, February 1, 2005.

84. J. Areddy, "Deep Inside China, American Family Struggles to Cope," *Wall Street Journal*, August 2, 2005, A1.

9

1. M. Lia, "Thomson Reuters Restructures," *Wall Street Journal*, September 28, 2011, accessed June 12, 2013, http://online.wsj.com/article/SB1000 142405297020413820457659867160182892 8.html; "Annual Review 2013," *Thomson Reuters*, accessed June 16, 2013, http://ar.thomsonreuters.com/financial-performance.html?tab=business-segment-revenue.

2. M. Hammer and J. Champy, *Reengineering the Corporation: A Manifesto for Business Revolution* (New York: Harper & Row, 1993).

3. J. Mick, "Windows 8 Public 'Consumer Preview' Beta Is Live," *Daily Tech*, February 29, 2012, accessed March 11, 2012, http://www.dailytech.com/Windows+8+Public+Consumer +Preview+Beta+is +Live/article24123.htm.

4. J. G. March and H. A. Simon, *Organizations* (New York: John Wiley & Sons, 1958).

5. "Bayer Group: Profile and Organization," *Bayer AG*, accessed March 20, 2009, http://www.bayer.com/bayer-group/profile-and-organization/page2351.htm.

6. "At a Glance," UTC, accessed July 7, 2014, http://www.utc.com/Our-Businesses/Pages/At-A-Glance.aspx#bis.

7. "2013 Annual Report," *United Technologies*, accessed June 16, 2014, http://2013ar.utc.com/assets/pdfs/UTCAR13_FullReport.pdf.

8. "Structure—Group Structure & Corporate Management," *Swisscom AG*, accessed June 16, 2014, http://www.swisscom.ch/en/about/company/structure.html.

9. "Anheiser-Busch InBev 2013 Annual Report," *ABInBev*, accessed June 16, 2014, http://www.ab-inbev.com/pdf/AR13/ABI_AR13_EN_Full.pdf.

10. "Our Top 10 Markets," *AB InBev*, accessed June 16, 2014, http://www.ab-inbev.com/pdf/AR13/AB_InBev_AR_OurTopTenMarkets.pdf.

11. "Anheuser Busch InBev in Russia Key Facts & Figures," *AB InBev*, March 2013, accessed June 16, 2014, http://www.ab-inbev.com/pdf/factsheets/Russia2013.pdf; "Anheuser Busch InBev in Belgium Key Facts & Figures," *AB InBev*, July 2013,

accessed June 16, 2014, http://www.ab-inbev.com/pdf/factsheets/Belgium2013.pdf.

12. Business Wire, "Procter & Gamble Announces Organization Changes," *Motley Fool*, June 5, 2013, accessed July 7, 2014, http://www.fool.com/investing/businesswire/2013/06/05/procter-gamble-announces-organization-changes.aspx; "2013 Annual Report, P&G," *Procter & Gamble*, accessed July 7, 2014, http://www.pg.com/en_US/downloads/investors/annual_reports/2013/2013_Annual Report.pdf.

13. "Corporate Info: Corporate Structure—Four Pillars," *Procter & Gamble*, accessed March 20, 2009, http://www.pg.com/jobs/corporate_structure/four_pillars.jhtml; "P&G Management," *Procter & Gamble*, accessed March 20, 2009, http:// www.pg.com/news/management/bios_photos.jhtml.

14. L. R. Burns, "Adoption and Abandonment of Matrix Management Programs: Effects of Organizational Characteristics and Interorganizational Networks," *Academy of Management Journal* 36 (1993): 106–138.

15. H. Fayol, *General and Industrial Management*, trans. C. Storrs (London: Pitman Publishing, 1949).

16. M. Weber, *The Theory of Social and Economic Organization*, trans. and ed. A. M. Henderson and T. Parsons (New York: Free Press, 1947).

17. Fayol, *General and Industrial Management*.

18. S. Ovide, "American Bill McDermott to Be Sole SAP CEO," *Wall Street Journal*, July 21, 2013; A. Ricadela, "SAP's McDermott Counts on Faster Decision-Making as Sole CEO," *Bloomberg*, May 21, 2014, accessed July 7, 2014, http://www.bloomberg.com/news/2014-05-21/sap-s-mcdermott-seeks-faster-decisions-as-he-starts-as-sole-ceo.html.

19. Lashinsky, "Inside Apple, from Steve Jobs Down to the Janitor: How America's Most Successful—and Most Secretive—Big Company Really Works," *Fortune*, May 23, 2011, 125–134.

20. H. Gayle, "Corner Office: Helene Gayle of CARE, on Managers as Dual citizens," interview by A. Bryant, *New York Times*, June 22, 2013, accessed June 16, 2014, http://www.nytimes.com/2013/06/23/business/helene-gayle-of-care-on-managers-as-dual-citizens.html?_r=1&.

21. E. E. Lawler, S. A. Mohrman, and G. E. Ledford, *Creating High Performance Organizations: Practices and Results of Employee Involvement and Quality Management in Fortune 1000 Companies* (San Francisco: Jossey-Bass, 1995).

22. C. Dawson, "Toyota Overhauls Its R&D Efforts; Japan's Biggest Car Maker Aims for Quicker Decisions, Lower Costs," *Wall Street Journal*, April 9, 2012, http://online.wsj.com/article/SB100014240527 023045877045773335220513778 12.html.

23. S. Curry, "Retention Getters," *Incentive*, April 1, 2005.

24. R. W. Griffin, *Task Design* (Glenview, IL: Scott, Foresman, 1982).

25. F. Herzberg, *Work and the Nature of Man* (Cleveland, OH: World Press, 1966).

26. R. Hackman and G. R. Oldham, *Work Redesign* (Reading, MA: Addison-Wesley, 1980).

27. T. Burns and G. M. Stalker, *The Management of Innovation* (London: Tavistock, 1961).

28. Hammer and Champy, *Reengineering the Corporation*.

29. Ibid.

30. J. D. Thompson, *Organizations in Action* (New York: McGraw-Hill, 1967).

31. D. Pink, "Who Has the Next Big Idea?" *Fast Company*, September 1, 2001, 108.

32. J. B. White, "'Next Big Thing': Re-Engineering Gurus Take Steps to Remodel Their Stalling

Vehicles," *Wall Street Journal Interactive*, November 26, 1996.

33. C. Tuna, "Remembrances: Champion of 'Re-Engineering' Saved Companies, Challenged Thinking," *Wall Street Journal*, September 6, 2008, A12.

34. G. M. Spreitzer, "Individual Empowerment in the Workplace: Dimensions, Measurement, and Validation," *Academy of Management Journal* 38 (1995): 1442–1465.

35. D. Vidalon and P. Denis, "Carrefour Bets on Store Bosses in French Revamp," cNBC, March 12, 2013, accessed July 8, 2014, http://article.wn.com /view/2013/03/12/Carrefour_bets_on_store_bosses _in_French_revamp/.

36. K. W. Thomas and B. A. Velthouse, "Cognitive Elements of Empowerment," *Academy of Management Review* 15 (1990): 666–681.

37. C. Gallo, "How Wegmans, Apple Store and Ritz-Carlton Empower Employees to Offer Best -in-Class Service," *Retail Customer Experience*, December 27, 2012, accessed June 12, 2013, http:// www.retailcustomerexperience.com/article/205849 /How-Wegmans-Apple-Store-and-Ritz-Carlton -empower-employees-to-offer-best-in-class-service.

38. K. D. Backer and S. Miroudot (2013), "Mapping Global Value Chains," *OECD Trade Policy Papers*, No. 159, OECD Publishing, December 19, 2013, accessed July 8, 2014, http:// dx.doi.org/10.1787/5k3v1trgnbr4-en.

39. W. Bulkeley, "New IBM Jobs Can Mean Fewer Jobs Elsewhere," *Wall Street Journal*, March 8, 2004, B1.

40. H. Thomas, "Pharma Companies' Cost Cuts Could Be a Tonic for Quintiles," *Wall Street Journal*, December 21, 2013, B14.

41. C. C. Snow, R. E. Miles, and H. J. Coleman, Jr., "Managing 21st Century Network Organizations," *Organizational Dynamics*, Winter 1992, 5–20.

42. J. H. Sheridan, "The Agile Web: A Model for the Future?" *Industry Week*, March 4, 1996, 31.

10

1. B. Dumaine, "The Trouble with Teams," *Fortune*, September 5, 1994, 86–92.

2. K. C. Stag, E. Salas, and S. M. Fiore, "Best Practices in Cross Training Teams," in *Workforce Cross Training Handbook*, ed. D. A. Nembhard (Boca Raton, FL: CRC Press), 156–175.

3. M. Marks, "The Science of Team Effectiveness," *Psychological Science in the Public Interest* (December 2006): pi–i.

4. J. R. Katzenbach and D. K. Smith, *The Wisdom of Teams* (Boston: Harvard Business School Press, 1993).

5. S. G. Cohen and D. E. Bailey, "What Makes Teams Work: Group Effectiveness Research from the Shop Floor to the Executive Suite," *Journal of Management* 23, no. 3 (1997): 239–290.

6. S. E. Gross, *Compensation for Teams* (New York: American Management Association, 1995); B. L. Kirkman and B. Rosen, "Beyond Self-Management: Antecedents and Consequences of Team Empowerment," *Academy of Management Journal* 42 (1999): 58–74; G. Stalk and T. M. Hout, *Competing Against Time: How Time-Based Competition Is Reshaping Global Markets* (New York: Free Press, 1990); S. C. Wheelwright and K. B. Clark, *Revolutionizing New Product Development* (New York: Free Press, 1992).

7. D. A. Harrison, S. Mohamed, J. E. McGrath, A. T. Florey, and S. W. Vanderstoep, "Time Matters in Team Performance: Effects of Member Familiarity, Entrainment, and Task Discontinuity on Speed and Quality," *Personnel Psychology* 56, no. 3 (August 2003): 633–669.

8. R. Parsons, "Barclays Seeks 'Voice of Customer' for Rebuilding Efforts," *Marketing Week*, September 20, 2013, 12.

9. M. Iqbal, "Blog Archives: Barclays Bank," The Customer & Leadership Blog, May 9, 2014, accessed July 8, 2014, http://thecustomerblog.co.uk /tag/barclays-bank/.

10. R. D. Banker, J. M. Field, R. G. Schroeder, and K. K. Sinha, "Impact of Work Teams on Manufacturing Performance: A Longitudinal Field Study," *Academy of Management Journal* 39 (1996): 867–890.

11. "Entire Organization Rallies to Improve Product Ratings, Sales," *Bazaarvoice*, accessed May 21, 2011, http://www.bazaarvoice.com /resources/case-studies/entire-organization-rallies -improve-product-ratings-sales.

12. J. L. Cordery, W. S. Mueller, and L. M. Smith, "Attitudinal and Behavioral Effects of Autonomous Group Working: A Longitudinal Field Study," *Academy of Management Journal* 34 (1991): 464–476; T. D. Wall, N. J. Kemp, P. R. Jackson, and C. W. Clegg, "Outcomes of Autonomous Workgroups: A Long-Term Field Experiment," *Academy of Management Journal* 29 (1986): 280–304.

13. "Great Little Box Company: A Team Approach to Success," *Industry Canada*, May 7, 2012, accessed June 13, 2013, http://www.ic.gc.ca/eic /site/061.nsf/eng/rd02456.html.

14. R. Liden, S. Wayne, R. Jaworski, and N. Bennett, "Social Loafing: A Field Investigation," *Journal of Management* 30 (2004): 285–304.

15. J. George, "Extrinsic and Intrinsic Origins of Perceived Social Loafing in Organizations," *Academy of Management Journal* 35 (1992): 191–202.

16. T. T. Baldwin, M. D. Bedell, and J. L. Johnson, "The Social Fabric of a Team-Based M.B.A. Program: Network Effects on Student Satisfaction and Performance," *Academy of Management Journal* 40 (1997): 1369–1397.

17. K. H. Price, D. A. Harrison, and J. H. Gavin, "Withholding Inputs in Team Contexts: Member Composition, Interaction Processes, Evaluation Structure and Social Loafing," *Journal of Applied Psychology* 91(6) (2006): 1375–1384.

18. L. P. Tost, F. Gino, and R. P. Larrick, "When Power Makes Others Speechless: The Negative Impact of Leader Power on Team Performance," *Academy of Management Journal* 35, no. 5, October 1, 2013, 1465–1486, accessed June 16, 2014, http:// amj.aom.org/content/56/5/1465.

19. C. Joinson, "Teams at Work," *HR Magazine*, May 1, 1999, 30.

20. R. Wageman, "Critical Success Factors for Creating Superb Self-Managing Teams," *Organizational Dynamics* 26, no. 1 (1997): 49–61.

21. R. Etherington, "Audi Announces New Design Strategy," *Dezeen*, December 19, 2012, accessed June 13, 2013, http://www.dezeen.com/2012/12/19 /audi-announces-new-car-design-strategy/.

22. Kirkman and Rosen, "Beyond Self-Management: Antecedents and Consequences of Team Empowerment."

23. K. Kelly, "Managing Workers Is Tough Enough in Theory. When Human Nature Enters the Picture, It's Worse," *BusinessWeek*, October 21, 1996, 32.

24. S. Easton and G. Porter, "Selecting the Right Team Structure to Work in Your Organization," in *Handbook of Best Practices for Teams*, vol. 1, ed. G. M. Parker (Amherst, MA: Irwin, 1996).

25. S. Wilhelm, "Quadrupling 787 Production Won't Be Easy for Boeing, Just Necessary," *Puget Sound Business Journal*, February 10, 2012, accessed March 12, 2012, http://www.bizjournals .com/seattle/print-edition/2012/02/10/quadrupling -787-production-wont-be.html?page=all.

26. R. M. Yandrick, "A Team Effort: The Promise of Teams Isn't Achieved without Attention to Skills and Training," *HR Magazine*, June 2001, 46(6), 136–144.

27. "Self-Directed Teams Improve On-Time Delivery and Quality," *Manufacturing.net*, June 29, 2012, accessed June 13, 2013, http://www.manufacturing .net/articles/2012/06/self-directed-teams-improve -on-time-delivery-and-quality.

28. R. Williams, "Self-Directed Work Teams: A Competitive Advantage," *Quality Digest*, accessed November 18, 2009, http://www.qualitydigest.com.

29. Yandrick, "A Team Effort."

30. R. J. Recardo, D. Wade, C. A. Mention, and J. Jolly, *Teams* (Houston: Gulf Publishing Co., 1996).

31. D. R. Denison, S. L. Hart, and J. A. Kahn, "From Chimneys to Cross-Functional Teams: Developing and Validating a Diagnostic Model," *Academy of Management Journal* 39, no. 4 (1996): 1005–1023.

32. A. M. Townsend, S. M. DeMarie, and A. R. Hendrickson, "Virtual Teams: Technology and the Workplace of the Future," *Academy of Management Executive* 13, no. 3 (1998): 17–29.

33. F. Rendón, "Understanding the Proliferation of Virtual Teams in the Global Economy," *Huffington Post*, April 28, 2014, accessed June 16, 2014, http://www.huffingtonpost.com/frankie-rendon /understanding-the-prolife_b_5212366.html.

34. J. Hyatt, "MySQL: Workers in 25 Countries with No HQ," *Fortune*, June 1, 2006, accessed August 12, 2008, http://money.cnn.com/2006/05/31 /magazines/fortune/mysql_greatteams_fortune /index.htm.

35. A. M. Townsend, S. M. DeMarie, and A. R. Hendrickson, "Are You Ready for Virtual Teams?" *HR Magazine* 41, no. 9 (1996): 122–126.

36. Townsend, DeMarie, and Hendrickson, "Virtual Teams."

37. W. F. Cascio, "Managing a Virtual Workplace," *Academy of Management Executive* 14 (2000): 81–90.

38. T. Minton-Eversole, "Virtual Teams Used Most by Global Organizations, Survey Says," *Society for Human Resource Management*, July 19, 2012, accessed June 16, 2014, http://www.shrm.org /hrdisciplines/orgempdev/articles/Pages /VirtualTeamsUsedMostbyGlobalOrganizations ,SurveySays.aspx.

39. R. Katz, "The Effects of Group Longevity on Project Communication and Performance," *Administrative Science Quarterly* 27 (1982): 245–282.

40. D. Mankin, S. G. Cohen, and T. K. Bikson, *Teams and Technology: Fulfilling the Promise of the New Organization* (Boston: Harvard Business School Press, 1996).

41. A. P. Ammeter and J. M. Dukerich, "Leadership, Team Building, and Team Member Characteristics in High Performance Project Teams," *Engineering Management* 14, no. 4 (2002, December): 3–11.

42. K. Lovelace, D. Shapiro, and L. Weingart, "Maximizing Cross-Functional New Product Teams' Innovativeness and Constraint Adherence: A Conflict Communications Perspective," *Academy of Management Journal* 44 (2001): 779–793.

43. L. Holpp and H. P. Phillips, "When Is a Team Its Own Worst Enemy?" *Training*, September 1, 1995, 71.

44. S. Asche, "Opinions and Social Pressure," *Scientific American* 193 (1995): 31–35.

45. J. Stephens, "Corner Office: Rah-Rah Isn't for Everyone," interview by A. Bryant, *New York Times*, April 9, 2010, accessed June 11, 2010, http://www.nytimes.com/2010/04/11/business/11corner.html?pagewanted=.

46. S. G. Cohen, G. E. Ledford, and G. M. Spreitzer, "A Predictive Model of Self-Managing Work Team Effectiveness," *Human Relations* 49, no. 5 (1996): 643–676.

47. R. Collett, "How to Improve Product Development Productivity—Lessons from the Checklist Manifesto," *The EE Compendium: The Home of Electronic Engineering and Embedded Systems Programming*, accessed May 22, 2011, http://ee.cleversoul.com/news/lessons-from-the-checklist-manifesto.html.

48. "Institute for Healthcare Improvement: World Health Organization (WHO) Surgical Safety Checklist and Getting Started Kit," World Health Organization, accessed July 9, 2014; http://www.ihi.org/resources/Pages/Tools/WHOSurgicalSafetyChecklistGettingStartedKit.aspx. M. Semel, S. Resch, A. Haynes, L. Funk, A. Bader, W. Berry, T. Weiser, and A. Gawande, "Adopting a Surgical Safety Checklist Could Save Money and Improve the Quality of Care in US Hospitals," *Health Affairs* 29, no. 9 (2010): 1593–1599.

49. K. Bettenhausen and J. K. Murnighan, "The Emergence of Norms in Competitive Decision-Making Groups," *Administrative Science Quarterly* 30 (1985): 350–372.

50. M. E. Shaw, *Group Dynamics* (New York: McGraw Hill, 1981).

51. E. Levenson, "The Power of an Idea," *Fortune*, June 12, 2006, 131.

52. R. E. Silverman, "Tracking Sensors Invade the Workplace," *Wall Street Journal*, March 7, 2013, accessed June 16, 2014, http://online.wsj.com/news/articles/SB10001424127887324034804578344303429080678.

53. S. M. Gully, D. S. Devine, and D. J. Whitney, "A Meta-Analysis of Cohesion and Performance: Effects of Level of Analysis and Task Interdependence," *Small Group Research* 26, no. 4 (1995): 497–520.

54. Ibid.

55. F. Tschan and M. V. Cranach, "Group Task Structure, Processes and Outcomes," in *Handbook of Work Group Psychology*, ed. M. A. West (Chichester, UK: Wiley, 1996).

56. D. E. Yeatts and C. Hyten, *High-Performing Self-Managed Work Teams* (Thousand Oaks, CA: Sage Publications, 1998); H. M. Guttman and R. S. Hawkes, "New Rules for Strategic Development," *Journal of Business Strategy* 25, no. 1 (2004): 34–39.

57. Yeatts and Hyten, *High-Performing Self-Managed Work Teams*; J. Colquitt, R. Noe, and C. Jackson, "Justice in Teams: Antecedents and Consequences of Procedural Justice Climate," *Personnel Psychology*, April 1, 2002, 83.

58. D. S. Kezsbom, "Re-Opening Pandora's Box: Sources of Project Team Conflict in the '90s," *Industrial Engineering* 24, no. 5 (1992): 54–59.

59. A. C. Amason, W. A. Hochwarter, and K. R. Thompson, "Conflict: An Important Dimension in Successful Management Teams," *Organizational Dynamics* 24 (1995): 20.

60. A. C. Amason, "Distinguishing the Effects of Functional and Dysfunctional Conflict on Strategic Decision Making: Resolving a Paradox for Top Management Teams," *Academy of Management Journal* 39, no. 1 (1996): 123–148.

61. K. M. Eisenhardt, J. L. Kahwajy, and L. J. Bourgeois III, "How Management Teams Can Have a Good Fight," *Harvard Business Review* 75, no. 4 (July–August 1997): 77–85.

62. Ibid.

63. C. Nemeth and P. Owens, "Making Work Groups More Effective: The Value of Minority Dissent," in *Handbook of Work Group Psychology*, ed. M. A. West (Chichester, UK: Wiley, 1996).

64. J. M. Levin and R. L. Moreland, "Progress in Small Group Research," *Annual Review of Psychology* 9 (1990): 72–78; S. E. Jackson, "Team Composition in Organizational Settings: Issues in Managing a Diverse Work Force," in *Group Processes and Productivity*, ed. S. Worchel, W. Wood, and J. Simpson (Beverly Hills, CA: Sage, 1992).

65. Eisenhardt, Kahwajy, and Bourgeois, "How Management Teams Can Have a Good Fight."

66. Ibid.

67. B. W. Tuckman, "Development Sequence in Small Groups," *Psychological Bulletin* 63, no. 6 (1965): 384–399.

68. Gross, *Compensation for Teams*.

69. J. F. McGrew, J. G. Bilotta, and J. M. Deeney, "Software Team Formation and Decay: Extending the Standard Model for Small Groups," *Small Group Research* 30, no. 2 (1999): 209–234.

70. J. Case, "What the Experts Forgot to Mention: Management Teams Create New Difficulties, But Succeed for XEL Communication," *Inc.*, September 1, 1993, 66.

71. J. R. Hackman, "The Psychology of Self-Management in Organizations," in *Psychology and Work: Productivity, Change, and Employment*, ed. M. S. Pallak and R. Perloff (Washington, DC: American Psychological Association, 1986), 85–136.

72. A. O'Leary-Kelly, J. J. Martocchio, and D. D. Frink, "A Review of the Influence of Group Goals on Group Performance," *Academy of Management Journal* 37, no. 5 (1994): 1285–1301.

73. A. Zander, "The Origins and Consequences of Group Goals," in *Retrospections on Social Psychology*, ed. L. Festinger (New York: Oxford University Press, 1980), 205–235.

74. M. Erez and A. Somech, "Is Group Productivity Loss the Rule or the Exception? Effects of Culture and Group-Based Motivation," *Academy of Management Journal* 39, no. 6 (1996): 1513–1537.

75. S. Sherman, "Stretch Goals: The Dark Side of Asking for Miracles," *Fortune*, November 13, 1995.

76. J. Muller, "GM's New Goal Is a Stretch: Auto Industry's MVP," *Forbes*, January 31, 2013, accessed June 13, 2013, http://www.forbes.com/sites/joannmuller/2013/01/31/gms-new-goal-seems-a-bit-of-a-stretch-auto-industrys-mvp/.

77. K. R. Thompson, W. A. Hochwarter, and N. J. Mathys, "Stretch Targets: What Makes Them Effective?" *Academy of Management Executive* 11, no. 3 (1997): 48–60.

78. B. Stone, "Inside Google's Secret Lab—Businessweek," May 22, 2013, accessed July 9, 2014, http://www.businessweek.com/articles/2013-05-22/inside-googles-secret-lab.

79. Dumaine, "The Trouble with Teams."

80. G. A. Neuman, S. H. Wagner, and N. D. Christiansen, "The Relationship Between Work-Team Personality Composition and the Job Performance of Teams," *Group & Organization Management* 24, no. 1 (1999): 28–45.

81. M. A. Campion, G. J. Medsker, and A. C. Higgs, "Relations Between Work Group Characteristics and Effectiveness: Implications for Designing Effective Work Groups," *Personnel Psychology* 46, no. 4 (1993): 823–850.

82. B. L. Kirkman and D. L. Shapiro, "The Impact of Cultural Values on Employee Resistance to Teams: Toward a Model of Globalized Self-Managing Work Team Effectiveness," *Academy of Management Review* 22, no. 3 (1997): 730–757.

83. C. Fishman, "Engines of Democracy: The General Electric Plant in Durham, North Carolina Builds Some of the World's Most Powerful Jet Engines. But the Plant's Real Power Lies in the Lessons That It Teaches About the Future of Work and About Workplace Democracy," *Fast Company*, October 1, 1999, 174.

84. J. Bunderson and K. Sutcliffe, "Comparing Alternative Conceptualizations of Functional Diversity in Management Teams: Process and Performance Effects," *Academy of Management Journal* 45 (2002): 875–893.

85. A. Zynga, "The Cognitive Bias Keeping Us from Innovating," *Harvard Business Review* (HBR Blog Network), June 13, 2013 (10:00 a.m.), accessed June 16, 2014, http://blogs.hbr.org/2013/06/the-cognitive-bias-keeping-us-from/#disqus_thread.

86. J. Hackman, "New Rules for Team Building—The Times Are Changing—And So Are the Guidelines for Maximizing Team Performance," *Optimize*, July 1, 2002, 50.

87. Joinson, "Teams at Work."

88. Strozniak, "Teams at Work."

89. Ibid.

90. P. Nicholas, "It's All About Flight or Fight," *Weekend Australian*, March 14, 2009, 1.

91. Wellins, Byham, and Dixon, *Inside Teams*.

92. E. Salas, D. DiazGranados, C. Klein, C. Burke, K. Stagl, G. Goodwin, and S. Halpin, "Does Team Training Improve Team Performance? A Meta-Analysis," *Human Factors* 50, no. 6 (2008): 903–933.

93. S. Caudron, "Tie Individual Pay to Team Success," *Personnel Journal* 73, no. 10 (October 1994): 40.

94. Ibid.

95. Gross, *Compensation for Teams*.

96. G. Ledford, "Three Case Studies on Skill-Based Pay: An Overview," *Compensation & Benefits Review* 23, no. 2 (1991): 11–24.

97. T. Law, "Where Loyalty Is Rewarded," *The Press*, September 29, 2008, Business Day 4.

98. J. R. Schuster and P. K. Zingheim, *The New Pay: Linking Employee and Organizational Performance* (New York: Lexington Books, 1992).

99. Cohen and Bailey, "What Makes Teams Work."

100. R. Allen and R. Kilmann, "Aligning Reward Practices in Support of Total Quality Management," *Business Horizons* 44 (May 2001): 77–85.

11

1. Associated Press, "Employers Ask Job Seekers for Facebook Passwords," *Tampa Bay Times*, March 20, 2012, accessed June 13, 2013, http://www.tampabay.com/news/business/workinglife/employers-ask-job-seekers-for-facebook-passwords/1221041.

2. "Genetic Information Discrimination," U.S. Equal Employment Opportunity Commission, accessed July 9, 2014, http://www.eeoc.gov/laws/types/genetic.cfm.

3. Associated Press, "Hooters Settles Suit, Won't Hire Waiters," *Denver Post*, October 1, 1997, A11.

4. P. S. Greenlaw and J. P. Kohl, "Employer 'Business' and 'Job' Defenses in Civil Rights Actions," *Public Personnel Management* 23, no. 4 (1994): 573.

5. F. Hosier, "OSHA Slaps Company with $1.2M Fine for Training, PPE Violations," *Safety News Alert*, May 31, 2011, accessed March 14, 2012, http://www.safetynewsalert.com/osha-slaps-company-with-1-2m-fine-for-asbestos-violations/.

6. Greenlaw and Kohl, "Employer 'Business' and 'Job' Defenses in Civil Rights Actions."

7. City News Service, "66-Year-Old Man Awarded $26 Million in Age Discrimination Lawsuit," *Los Angeles Daily News*, February 27, 2014, accessed July 9, 2014, http://www.dailynews.com/general-news/20140227/66-year-old-man-awarded-26-million-in-age-discrimination-lawsuit-against-staples.

8. W. Peirce, C. A. Smolinski, and B. Rosen, "Why Sexual Harassment Complaints Fall on Deaf Ears," *Academy of Management Executive* 12, no. 3 (1998): 41–54.

9. R. Gray, "First Student to Pay $150K to Settle Sexual Harassment, Retaliation Suit," *School Transportation News*, February 4, 2011, accessed May 23, 2011, http://www.stnonline.com/home/latest-news/3104-eeoc-orders-first-student-to-pay-150k-to-settle-sexual-harassment-retaliation-suit.

10. E. Francis, "$168 Million Awarded to Woman Harassed in 'Raunchy' Cardiac Surgery Unit," ABC News, March 2, 2012, accessed July 9, 2014, http://abcnews.go.com/US/LegalCenter/168-million-awarded-woman-harassed-raunchy-cardiac-surgery/story?id=15835342&singlePage=true.

11. Peirce, Smolinski, and Rosen, "Why Sexual Harassment Complaints Fall on Deaf Ears."

12. Ibid.

13. E. Larson, "The Economic Costs of Sexual Harassment," *The Freeman* 46, August 1996, accessed August 13, 2008, http://www.thefreemanonline.org/featured/the-economic-costs-of-sexual-harassment/.

14. G. Hyland-Savage, "General Management Perspective on Staffing: The Staffing Commandments," in *On Staffing*, eds. N. C. Bukholder, P. J. Edwards, Jr., and L. Sartain (Hoboken, NJ: Wiley, 2004), 280.

15. R. D. Gatewood and H. S. Field, *Human Resource Selection* (Fort Worth, TX: Dryden Press, 1998).

16. Ibid.

17. E. Gaydos, "Three Awesome Examples of Great Job Descriptions," *TLNT*, August 2, 2012, accessed June 14, 2013, http://www.tlnt.com/2012/08/02/three-awesome-examples-of-great-job-descriptions/.

18. *Griggs v. Duke Power Co.*, 401 US 424, 436 (1971); *Albemarle Paper Co. v. Moody*, 422 US 405 (1975).

19. L. Grensing-Pophal, "Internal Selections," *HR Magazine* 51, no. 12 (2006), http://www.shrm.org/publications/hrmagazine.

20. J. A. Breaugh, *Recruitment: Science and Practice* (Boston: PWSKent, 1992).

21. R. Albergotti, "LinkedIn Wants to Help You Stay at Your Company," *Wall Street Journal* (blog), April 10, 2014, accessed June 17, 2014, http://blogs.wsj.com/atwork/2014/04/10/linkedin-wants-to-help-you-stay-at-your-company/.

22. Ibid.

23. R. Silverman and L. Weber, "An Inside Job: More Firms Opt to Recruit from Within," *Wall Street Journal*, May 29, 2012, accessed June 14, 2013, http://online.wsj.com/article/SB10001424052702303395604577434563715828218.html.

24. L. Klaff, "New Internal Hiring Systems Reduce Cost and Boost Morale," *Workforce Management* 83 (March 2004): 76–79.

25. R. Silverman and L. Weber, "An Inside Job: More Firms Opt to Recruit from Within," *Wall Street Journal*, May 29, 2012, accessed June 14, 2013, http://online.wsj.com/article/SB10001424052702303395604577434563715828218.html.

26. "Virginia M. Rometty," *Forbes*, no date, accessed March 14, 2012, http://people.forbes.com/profile/virginia-m-rometty/4788.

27. J. Dao, "Wal-Mart Plans to Hire Any Veteran Who Wants a Job," *The New York Times*, January 14, 2013, accessed June 14, 2013, http://www.nytimes.com/2013/01/15/us/wal-mart-to-announce-extensive-plan-to-hire-veterans.html?_r=1.

28. J. Breaugh and M. Starke, "Research on Employee Recruitment: So Many Studies, So Many Remaining Questions," *Journal of Management* 26 (2000): 405–434.

29. "Internet Recruitment Report," *NAS Insights*, accessed August 14, 2008, http://www.nasrecruitment.com/talenttips/NASinsights/InternetRecruitingReport06.pdf.

30. K. Maher, "Corporations Cut Middlemen and Do Their Own Recruiting," *Wall Street Journal*, January 14, 2003, B10.

31. E. Glazer, "Virtual Fairs Offer Real Jobs," *Wall Street Journal*, October 31, 2011, B9.

32. C. Gordon, "Getting a Job at Facebook: Inside the 'Meritocratic' Hiring Process," *AOL Jobs*, October 5, 2012, accessed June 14, 2013, http://jobs.aol.com/articles/2012/10/05/want-to-get-a-job-at-facebook-weve-demystified-the-hiring-proc/.

33. C. Camden and B. Wallace, "Job Application Forms: A Hazardous Employment Practice," *Personnel Administrator* 28 (1983): 31–32.

34. J. Valentino-Devries, "Bosses May Use Social Media to Discriminate Against Job Seekers," *Wall Street Journal*, November 20, 2013, accessed July 10, 2014, http://online.wsj.com/news/articles/SB10001424052702303755045792083042551393 92.

35. T. Minton-Eversole, "Background Screens Even More Crucial During Economic Slump," *Society of Human Resource Management*, July 30, 2008, http://www.shrm.org/hrdisciplines/staffingmanagement/articles.

36. S. Adler, "Verifying a Job Candidate's Background: The State of Practice in a Vital Human Resources Activity," *Review of Business* 15, no. 2 (1993/1994): 3–8.

37. W. Woska, "Legal Issues for HR Professionals: Reference Checking/Background Investigations," *Public Personnel Management* 36 (Spring 2007): 79–89.

38. "More Than 70 Percent of HR Professionals Say Reference Checking Is Effective in Identifying Poor Performers," *Society for Human Resource Management*, accessed February 3, 2005, http://www.shrm.org/press_published/CMS_011240.asp.

39. P. Babcock, "Spotting Lies: The High Cost of Careless Hiring," *HR Magazine* 48, no. 10 (October 2003), accessed November 5, 2009, http://findarticles.com/p/articles/mi_m3495/is_10_48/ai_109136217/.

40. E. Leizerman, "Oregon Jury Renders $5.2M Verdict Against Trucking Broker and Driver in Negligent Hiring Case," *PRWeb*, March 6, 2012, accessed June 14, 2013, http://www.prweb.com/releases/2012/3/prweb9258166.htm.

41. M. Le, T. Nguyen, and B. Kleiner, "Legal Counsel: Don't Be Sued for Negligent Hiring," *Nonprofit World*, May 1, 2003, 14–15.

42. "Why It's Critical to Set a Policy on Background Checks for New Hires," *Managing Accounts Payable*, September 2004, 6; J. Schramm, "Future Focus: Background Checking," *HR Magazine* (January 2005), page not available.

43. D. Belkin, "More Job Seekers Scramble to Erase Their Criminal Past," *Wall Street Journal*, November 11, 2009, A1.

44. A. Athavaley, "Job References You Can't Control," *Wall Street Journal*, September 27, 2007, D1.

45. C. Cohen, "Reference Checks," *CA Magazine*, November 2004, 41.

46. Keith J. Winstein, "Inflated Credentials Surface in Executive Suite," *Wall Street Journal*, November 13, 2008, accessed May 30, 2011, http://online.wsj.com/article/SB122652836844922165.html.

47. B. Ellis, "For Hire: Professional Liars for Job Seekers," *CNN Money*, July 17, 2013, accessed July 10, 2014, http://money.cnn.com/2013/07/17/pf/professional-liars/.

48. D. Hambrick and C. Chabris, "What Do SAT and IQ Tests Measure? General Intelligence Predicts School and Life Success," *Slate*, April 14, 2014, accessed July 10, 2014, http://www.slate.com/articles/health_and_science/science/2014/04/what_do_sat_and_iq_tests_measure_general_intelligence_predicts_school_and.html.

49. J. Hunter, "Cognitive Ability, Cognitive Aptitudes, Job Knowledge, and Job Performance," *Journal of Vocational Behavior* 29 (1986): 340–362.

50. F. L. Schmidt, "The Role of General Cognitive Ability and Job Performance: Why There Cannot Be a Debate," *Human Performance* 15 (2002): 187–210.

51. D. Hambrick and C. Chabris, "What Do SAT and IQ Tests Measure? General Intelligence Predicts School and Life Success," *Slate*, April 14, 2014, accessed July 10, 2014, http://www.slate.com/articles/health_and_science/science/2014/04/what_do_sat_and_iq_tests_measure_general_intelligence_predicts_school_and.html.

52. E. E. Cureton, "Comment," in *Research Conference on the Use of Autobiographical Data as Psychological Predictors*, ed. E. R. Henry (Greensboro, NC: The Richardson Foundation, 1965), 13.

53. J. R. Glennon, L. E. Albright, and W. A. Owens, *A Catalog of Life History Items* (Greensboro, NC: The Richardson Foundation, 1966).

54. Gatewood and Field, *Human Resource Selection*.

55. I. Kotlyar and K. Ades, "HR Technology: Assessment Technology Can Help Match the Best Applicant to the Right Job," *HR Magazine* (May 1, 2002): 97.

56. M. S. Taylor and J. A. Sniezek, "The College Recruitment Interview: Topical Content and Applicant Reactions," *Journal of Occupational Psychology* 57 (1984): 157–168.

57. M. Harris, "Reconsidering the Employment Interview: A Review of Recent Literature and Suggestions for Future Research," *Personnel Psychology* (Winter 1989): 691–726.

58. Taylor and Sniezek, "The College Recruitment Interview."

59. R. Burnett, C. Fan, S. J. Motowidlo, and T. DeGroot, "Interview Notes and Validity," *Personnel Psychology* 51, (1998): 375–396; M. A. Campion, D. K. Palmer, and J. E. Campion, "A Review of Structure in the Selection Interview," *Personnel Psychology* 50, no. 3 (1997): 655–702.

60. T. Judge, "The Employment Interview: A Review of Recent Research and Recommendations for Future Research," *Human Resource Management Review* 10, no. 4 (2000): 383–406.

61. J. Cortina, N. Goldstein, S. Payne, K. Davison, and S. Gilliland, "The Incremental Validity of Interview Scores Over and Above Cognitive Ability and Conscientiousness Scores," *Personnel Psychology* 53, no. 2 (2000): 325–351; F. L. Schmidt and

J. E. Hunter, "The Validity and Utility of Selection Methods in Personnel Psychology: Practical and Theoretical Implications of 85 Years of Research Findings," *Psychological Bulletin* 124, no. 2 (1998): 262–274.

62. K. Tyler, "Training Revs Up," *HR Magazine* (April 2005), *Society for Human Resource Management*, accessed March 23, 2009, http://www.shrm.org.

63. "2013 State of the Industry," *ASTD Research*, 2013, accessed June 17, 2014. http://files.astd.org/Research/Infographics/2013_SOIR_Infographic.pdf.

64. The Oil Spill Training Company, accessed August 14, 2008, http://oilspilltraining.com/home/index.asp.

65. D. Belkin and M. Peters, "States Boost Workforce Development to Attract Employers," *Wall Street Journal*, March 21, 2014, accessed June 17, 2014, http://online.wsj.com/news/articles/SB100014240527023032878045794473209432744410?KEYWORDS=states+boost+workforce+development&mg=reno64-wsj.

66. R. King, "The Games Companies Play," *Bloomberg Businessweek*, April 4, 2011, accessed March 14, 2012, http://www.businessweek.com/technology/content/apr2011/tc2011044_943586.htm; "Siemens' Plantville Celebrates One Year, Announces New Site Features," *Siemens*, March 30, 2012, http://www.industry.usa.siemens.com/topics/us/en/pressarchive/2012/pressreleases/Pages/SiemensPlantvilleCelebratesOneYearAnnouncesNewSiteFeatures.aspx.

67. "Westinghouse University Case Study: Aligning a Corporate University to Meet the Needs of the Business," *CORP/U*, May 1, 2012, accessed June 14, 2013, http://www.corpu.com/research/westinghouse-university-aligning-corporate-university-meet-needs-business/; L. Weber, "Fine-Tuning the Perfect Employee—Companies Take to Training Staff, New Hires to Make Up for Low-Skilled Workers," *Wall Street Journal*, December 5, 2011, B9.

68. D. L. Kirkpatrick, "Four Steps to Measuring Training Effectiveness," *Personnel Administrator* 28 (1983): 19–25.

69. L. Bassi, J. Ludwig, D. McMurrer, and M. Van Buren, "Profiting from Learning: Do Firms' Investments in Education and Training Pay Off?" *American Society for Training and Development*, accessed August 14, 2008, http://www.astd.org/NR/rdonlyres/91956A5E-6E57-44DDAE5D-FCFFCDC11C3F/0/ASTD_Profiting_From_Learning.pdf.

70. Just. Daley, "It's Shaping Up to Be a Good Year," *Entrepreneur*, January 2014, 92.

71. S. Culbert, "Get Rid of the Performance Review!" *Wall Street Journal*, June 21, 2012, accessed June 14, 2013, http://online.wsj.com/article/SB12242631887484933.html.

72. D. Murphy, "Are Performance Appraisals Worse Than a Waste of Time? Book Derides Unintended Consequences," *San Francisco Chronicle*, September 9, 2001, W1.

73. K. R. Murphy and J. N. Cleveland, *Understanding Performance Appraisal: Social, Organizational and Goal-Based Perspectives* (Thousand Oaks, CA: Sage, 1995).

74. T. D. Schellhardt, "Annual Agony: It's Time to Evaluate Your Work, and All Involved Are Groaning," *Wall Street Journal*, November 19, 1996, A1.

75. U. J. Wiersma and G. P. Latham, "The Practicality of Behavioral Observation Scales, Behavioral Expectation Scales, and Trait Scales," *Personnel Psychology* 39 (1986): 619–628; U. J. Wiersma, P. T. Van Den Berg, and G. P. Latham, "Dutch Reactions to Behavioral Observation, Behavioral Expectation, and Trait Scales," *Group & Organization Management* 20 (1995): 297–309.

76. D. J. Schleicher, D. V. Day, B. T. Mayes, and R. E. Riggio, "A New Frame for Frame-of-Reference Training: Enhancing the Construct Validity of Assessment Centers," *Journal of Applied Psychology* (August 2002): 735–746.

77. J. Stack, "The Curse of the Annual Performance Review," *Inc.*, March 1, 1997, 39.

78. H. H. Meyer, "A Solution to the Performance Appraisal Feedback Enigma," *Academy of Management Executive* 5, no. 1 (1991): 68–76; G. C. Thornton, "Psychometric Properties of Self-Appraisals of Job Performance," *Personnel Psychology* 33 (1980): 263–271.

79. Thornton, "Psychometric Properties of Self-Appraisals of Job Performance."

80. J. Smither, M. London, R. Flautt, Y. Vargas, and I. Kucine, "Can Working with an Executive Coach Improve Multisource Feedback Ratings Over Time? A Quasi-Experimental Field Study," *Personnel Psychology* (Spring 2003): 21–43.

81. A. Walker and J. Smither, "A Five-Year Study of Upward Feedback: What Managers Do with Their Results Matters," *Personnel Psychology* (Summer 1999): 393–422.

82. J. McGregor, "The Employee Is Always Right," *BusinessWeek*, November 8, 2007, accessed August 14, 2008, http://www.businessweek.com/globalbiz/content/nov2007/gb2007118_541063.htm.

83. K. Chu, "China: A Billion Strong But Short on Workers," *Wall Street Journal*, May 1, 2013, accessed June 14, 2013, http://online.wsj.com/article/SB1000142412788732379810457845515399658318.html.

84. K. Chu, "China Factories Try Karaoke, Speed Dating to Keep Workers," *Wall Street Journal*, May 2, 2013, accessed September 11, 2013, http://online.wsj.com/article/SB10001424127887323798104578452634075519230.html.

85. G. T. Milkovich and J. M. Newman, *Compensation*, 4th ed. (Homewood, IL: Irwin, 1993).

86. M. L. Williams and G. F. Dreher, "Compensation System Attributes and Applicant Pool Characteristics," *Academy of Management Journal* 35, no. 3 (1992): 571–595.

87. J. Quinton, "The Trader Joe's Lesson: How to Pay a Living Wage and Still Make Money in Retail," *The Atlantic*, March 25, 2013, accessed June 14, 2013, http://www.theatlantic.com/business/archive/2013/03/the-trader-joes-lesson-how-to-pay-a-living-wage-and-still-make-money-in-retail/274322/.

88. S. Cooper and C. Debaise, "Best Ways to Pay Your Sales Staff," *Bloomberg Businessweek*, June 5, 2009, accessed September 6, 2010, http://www.businessweek.com/magazine/content/09_66/s0906028668952.htm.

89. J. Blasi, "Southwest Airlines' profit-sharing payout: What capitalism should be," *Fortune*, April 17, 2014, accessed June 17, 2014, http://fortune.com/2014/04/17/southwest-airlines-profit-sharing-payout-what-capitalism-should-be/.

90. M. Josephs, "The Millionaire Truck Driver and Other ESOP Miracles," *Forbes*, April 30, 2014, accessed June 17, 2014, http://www.forbes.com/sites/maryjosephs/2014/04/30/the-millionaire-truck-driver-and-other-esop-miracles/.

91. A. Loten, "Founders Cash Out, But Do Workers Gain?—US Employee-Owned Firms Top 10,000, with More Expected as Owners Retire; Critics Point to Potential Drawbacks," *Wall Street Journal*, April 18, 2013, B4.

92. M. Bloom, "The Performance Effects of Pay Dispersion on Individuals and Organizations," *Academy of Management Journal* 42, no. 1 (1999): 25–40.

93. J. Liberto, "CEOs Earn 354 Times More Than Average Worker," *CNNMoney*, April 15, 2013, accessed June 15, 2013, http://money.cnn.com/2013/04/15/news/economy/ceo-pay-worker/index.html.

94. W. Grossman and R. E. Hoskisson, "CEO Pay at the Crossroads of Wall Street and Main: Toward the Strategic Design of Executive Compensation," *Academy of Management Executive* 12, no. 1 (1998): 43–57.

95. Bloom, "The Performance Effects of Pay Dispersion."

96. M. Bloom and J. Michel, "The Relationships Among Organizational Context, Pay Dispersion, and Managerial Turnover," *Academy of Management Journal* 45 (2002): 33–42.

97. S. Needleman, "Bad Firings Can Hurt Firm's Reputation," *Wall Street Journal*, July 8, 2008, D4.

98. J. Strickland, "Zynga Layoffs: The Aftermath," *Inc*, June 3, 2013, accessed June 17, 2014, http://www.inc.com/julie-strickland/zynga-lay-off-eighteen-percent-staff-close-three-offices.html.

99. A. Rupe, "Horrors from the Bad-Firing File," *Workforce Management*, November 2003, 16.

100. D. Mattel, J. Lublin, and R. Silverman, "Bad Call: How Not to Fire a Worker," *Wall Street Journal*, September 9, 2011, B2.

101. P. Michal-Johnson, *Saying Good-Bye: A Manager's Guide to Employee Dismissal* (Glenview, IL: Scott, Foresman & Co., 1985).

102. M. Bordwin, "Employment Law: Beware of Time Bombs and Shark-Infested Waters," *HR Focus*, April 1, 1995, 19; D. Jones, "Fired Workers Fight Back... and Win; Laws, Juries Shift Protection to Terminated Employees," *USA Today*, April 2, 1998, 01B.

103. "Mass Layoffs in December 2007 and Annual Totals for 2007," *Bureau of Labor Statistics News*, January 24, 2008, accessed August 15, 2008, http://www.bls.gov/news.release/archives/mmls_01242008.pdf.

104. D. McIntyre, "HP to Lay Off 9,000 in Enterprise Services Revamp," *Daily Finance*, June 1, 2010, accessed March 14, 2012, http://www.dailyfinance.com/2010/06/01/hp-layoffs-enterprise-services/; Z. Whittaker, "HP Confirms Layoffs; Cutting 500 Jobs at WebOS Division," *ZDNet*, September 20, 2011, accessed March 14, 2012, http://www.zdnet.com/blog/btl/hp-confirms-layoffs-cutting-500-jobs-at-webos-division/58413.

105. J. Bort, "By Firing 4,000 More People, Cisco Will Have Cut 12,000 Jobs in Two Years," *Business Insider*, August 15, 2013, accessed June 17, 2014, http://www.businessinsider.com/cisco-has-fired-12000-in-last-two-years-2013-8#!KmyxQ.

106. W. F. Cascio, "Employment Downsizing and Its Alternatives: Strategies for Long-Term Success," SHRM Foundation's Effective Practice Guideline Series, Society for Human Resource Management Foundation, accessed July 10, 2014, http://www.shrm.org/about/foundation/products/Documents/Downsizing%20EPG-%20Final.pdf.

107. K. E. Mishra, G. M. Spreitzer, and A. K. Mishra, "Preserving Employee Morale During Downsizing," *Sloan Management Review* 39, no. 2 (1998): 83–95.

108. K. Frieswick, "Until We Meet Again?" *CFO*, October 1, 2001, 41; W. F. Cascio, "Employment Downsizing and Its Alternatives: Strategies for Long-Term Success"; L. Weber and R. Feintzeig, "Assistance for Laid-Off Workers Gets Downsized," *Wall Street Journal*, February 18, 2013, accessed July 10, 2014, http://online.wsj.com/news/articles/SB100014240527023048997045793912540475352652.

109. W. F. Cascio, "Employment Downsizing and Its Alternatives: Strategies for Long-Term Success."

110. J. Hilsenrath, "Adventures in Cost Cutting," *Wall Street Journal*, May 10, 2004, R1.

111. M. Jackson, "Downsized, But Still in the Game: Keeping Up Morale Crucial After Job Cuts," *Boston Globe*, January 11, 2009, G1.

112. J. Ackerman, "Helping Layoff Survivors Cope: Companies Strive to Keep Morale High," *Boston Globe*, December 30, 2001, H1.

113. D. Ferrari, "Designing and Evaluating Early Retirement Programs: The State of Wyoming Experience," *Government Finance Review* 15, no. 1 (1999): 29–31.

114. Hilsenrath, "Adventures in Cost Cutting."

115. J. Lublin and S. Thurm, "How Companies Calculate Odds in Buyout Offers," *Wall Street Journal*, March 27, 2009, B1.

116. M. Willett, "Early Retirement and Phased Retirement Programs for the Public Sector," *Benefits & Compensation Digest*, April 2005, 31.

117. D. R. Dalton, W. D. Todor, and D. M. Krackhardt, "Turnover Overstated: The Functional Taxonomy," *Academy of Management Review* 7 (1982): 117–123.

118. J. R. Hollenbeck and C. R. Williams, "Turnover Functionality versus Turnover Frequency: A Note on Work Attitudes and Organizational Effectiveness," *Journal of Applied Psychology* 71 (1986): 606–611.

119. R. Hastings, "Netflix Culture: Freedom & Responsibility," Netflix, August 1, 2009, accessed July 10, 2014, http://www.slideshare.net/reed2001/culture-1798664#.

120. C. R. Williams, "Reward Contingency, Unemployment, and Functional Turnover," *Human Resource Management Review* 9 (1999): 549–576.

12

1. "Table 6. Percent Distribution of the Projected Population by Race and Hispanic Origin for the United States: 2015 to 2060," U.S. Census Bureau, accessed July 10, 2014, http://www.census.gov/population/projections/data/national/2012/summarytables.html.

2. M. Toosi, "Table 4. Continued- Civilian Labor Force, by Age, Gender, Race, and Ethnicity, 1990, 2000, 2010, and Projected 2020," in "Labor Force Projections to 2020: A More Slowly Growing Workforce," *Monthly Labor Review*, January 2012, 43–64.

3. "Table 3.4. Civilian Labor Force by Age, Sex, Race, and Ethnicity, 1992, 2002, 2012, and Projected 2022 [Numbers in Thousands]," from "Employment Projections: Civilian Labor Force by Age, Sex, Race, and Ethnicity," *Bureau of Labor Statistics*, December 19, 2013, accessed June 17, 2014, http://www.bls.gov/emp/ep_table_304.htm.

4. "Discover McDonald's Around the Globe," *McDonald's*, accessed June 15, 2013, http://www.aboutmcdonalds.com/mcd/country/map.html.

5. O. Putnal, "11 Global McDonald's Menu Items," *Women's Day*, accessed June 15, 2013, http://www.womansday.com/food-recipes/11-global-mcdonalds-menu-items-104999.

6. E. York, "In Speech, McDonald's Thompson Puts Focus on Diversity," *Chicago Tribune*, May 2, 2012, accessed June 15, 2013, http://articles.chicagotribune.com/2012-05-02/business/chi-in-speech-mcdonalds-thompson-puts-focus-on-diversity-20120502_1_diversity-women-and-minority-owned-businesses-mcbites.

7. Equal Employment Opportunity Commission, "Affirmative Action Appropriate Under Title VII of the Civil Rights Act of 1964, as Amended.

Chapter XIV—Equal Employment Opportunity Commission, Part 1608," accessed November 5, 2009, http://www.access.gpo.gov/nara/cfr/waisidx_04/29cfr1608_04.html.

8. Equal Employment Opportunity Commission, "Federal Laws Prohibiting Job Discrimination: Questions and Answers," accessed August 21, 2008, http://www.eeoc.gov/facts/qanda.html.

9. A. P. Carnevale and S. C. Stone, *The American Mosaic: An In-Depth Report on the Future of Diversity at Work* (New York: McGraw-Hill, 1995).

10. T. Roosevelt, "From Affirmative Action to Affirming Diversity," *Harvard Business Review* 68, no. 2 (1990): 107–117.

11. A. M. Konrad and F. Linnehan, "Formalized HRM Structures: Coordinating Equal Employment Opportunity or Concealing Organizational Practices?" *Academy of Management Journal* 38, no. 3 (1995): 787–820; see, for example, *Hopwood v. Texas*, 78 F.3d 932 (5th Cir., March 18, 1996). The U.S. Supreme Court has upheld the principle of affirmative action but has struck down some specific programs.

12. J. Bravin, "Court Backs Affirmative Action Ban—Justices Uphold State Initiative to End Race-Based Admissions, But Are Divided on Broader Issue," *Wall Street Journal*, April 23, 2014, A1.

13. P. Schmidt, "5 More States May Curtail Affirmative Action," *The Chronicle of Higher Education*, October 19, 2007, A1.

14. M. E. Heilman, C. J. Block, and P. Stathatos, "The Affirmative Action Stigma of Incompetence: Effects of Performance Information Ambiguity," *Academy of Management Journal* 40, no. 3 (1997): 603–625.

15. D. Evans, "A Comparison of the Other-Directed Stigmatization Produced by Legal and Illegal Forms of Affirmative Action," *Journal of Applied Psychology* 88, no. 1 (2003): 121–130.

16. E. Orenstein, "The Business Case for Diversity," *Financial Executive*, May 2005, 22–25; G. Robinson and K. Dechant, "Building a Business Case for Diversity," *Academy of Management Executive* 11, no. 3 (1997): 21–31.

17. E. Esen, "2005 Workplace Diversity Practices: Survey Report," *Society for Human Resource Management*, accessed March 24, 2009, http://www.shrm.org/research.

18. Orenstein, "Business Case for Diversity."

19. Esen, "2005 Workplace Diversity Practices: Survey Report."

20. Orenstein, "Business Case for Diversity."

21. K. Wiese, "Judge Approves Merrill Lynch's $160 Million Racial Bias Settlement," *Bloomberg Businessweek*, December 6, 2013, accessed July 11, 2014, http://www.businessweek.com/articles/2013-12-06/judge-approves-merrill-lynchs-160-million-racial-bias-settlement.

22. P. Wright and S. P. Ferris, "Competitiveness Through Management of Diversity: Effects on Stock Price Valuation," *Academy of Management Journal* 38 (1995): 272–285.

23. Ibid.

24. "State & Country QuickFacts," *US Census Bureau*, June 6, 2013, accessed June 15, 2013, http://quickfacts.census.gov/qfd/states/00000.html; J. Humphreys, "The Multicultural Economy 2012," Selig Center for Economic Growth, Terry College of Business, University of Georgia, 2012.

25. S. Murray, "How One Company Put Women in Charge," *Wall Street Journal*, April 1, 2014, accessed July 11, 2014, http://blogs.wsj.com/atwork/2014/04/01/how-one-company-put-women-in-charge/.

26. Anonymous, "Bumpkin Bosses; Schumpeter," *The Economist*, May 10, 2014, 70.

27. W. W. Watson, K. Kumar, and L. K. Michaelsen, "Cultural Diversity's Impact on Interaction Process and Performance: Comparing Homogeneous and Diverse Task Groups," *Academy of Management Journal* 36 (1993): 590–602; K. A. Jehn, G. B. Northcraft, and M. A. Neale, "Why Differences Make a Difference: A Field Study of Diversity, Conflict, and Performance in Workgroups," *Administrative Science Quarterly* 44 (1999): 741–763; E. Kearney, D. Gebert, and S. Voelpel, "When and How Diversity Benefits Teams: The Importance of Team Members' Need for Cognition," *Academy of Management Journal* 52 (2009): 581–598.

28. L. Visconti, "Novartis' David Epstein: A Diverse Team Can 'Accomplish Feats Nobody Thought Possible,'" *DiverstyInc*, February 2, 2013, accessed June 15, 2013, http://www.diversityinc.com/leadership/novartis-david-epstein-a-diverse-team-can-accomplish-feats-nobody-thought-possible/.

29. M. R. Carrell and E. E. Mann, "Defining Workplace Diversity Programs and Practices in Organizations," *Labor Law Journal* 44 (1993): 743–764.

30. D. A. Harrison, K. H. Price, and M. P. Bell, "Beyond Relational Demography: Time and the Effects of Surface- and Deep-Level Diversity on Work Group Cohesion," *Academy of Management Journal* 41 (1998): 96–107.

31. D. Harrison, K. Price, J. Gavin, and A. Florey, "Time, Teams, and Task Performance: Changing Effects of Surface- and Deep-Level Diversity on Group Functioning," *Academy of Management Journal* 45 (2002): 1029–1045.

32. Harrison, Price, and Bell, "Beyond Relational Demography."

33. Ibid.

34. R. Alsop, "Why your grandfather might land a job before you do," *BBC*, October 25, 2013, accessed June 17, 2014, http://www.bbc.com/capital/story/20131024-older-workers-fogey-or-find; E. White, "The New Recruits: Older Workers," *Wall Street Journal*, January 14, 2008, B3.

35. N. Munk, "Finished at Forty: In the New Economy, the Skills That Come with Age Count for Less and Less," *Fortune*, February 1, 1999, 50.

36. "Age Discrimination in Employment Act (includes concurrent charges with Title VII, ADA and EPA) FY 1997 - FY 2013," *US Equal Employment Opportunity Commission*, accessed June 17, 2014, http://www.eeoc.gov/eeoc/statistics/enforcement/adea.cfm.

37. S. R. Rhodes, "Age-Related Differences in Work Attitudes and Behavior," *Psychological Bulletin* 92 (1983): 328–367.

38. T. Ng and D. Feldman, "The Relationship of Age to Ten Dimensions of Job Performance," *Journal of Applied Psychology* 93, no. 2 (2008): 392–423.

39. G. M. McEvoy and W. F. Cascio, "Cumulative Evidence of the Relationship Between Employee Age and Job Performance," *Journal of Applied Psychology* 74 (1989): 11–17; T. Ng and D. Feldman, "The Relationship of Age to Ten Dimensions of Job Performance," *Journal of Applied Psychology* 93, no. 2 (2008): 392–423.

40. S. E. Sullivan and E. A. Duplaga, "Recruiting and Retaining Older Workers for the Millennium," *Business Horizons* 40 (November 12, 1997): 65; E. Townsend, "To Keep Older Workers, Consider New Responsibilities and Guard Against Discrimination," SHRM Foundation, accessed June 17, 2014, http://www.shrm.org/about/foundation/pages/researchthatmatters.aspx.

41. T. Maurer and N. Rafuse, "Learning, Not Litigating: Managing Employee Development and Avoiding Claims of Age Discrimination," *Academy of Management Executive* 15, no. 4 (2001): 110–121.

42. D. Brady, "The Bottom-Line Reasons for Mixing the Young and Old at Work," *Bloomberg Businessweek*, April 10, 2014, accessed July 11, 2014, http://www.businessweek.com/articles/2014-02-10/workplaces-boost-profits-when-young-and-old-workers-mentor-each-other; B. L. Hassell and P. L. Perrewe, "An Examination of Beliefs About Older Workers: Do Stereotypes Still Exist?" *Journal of Organizational Behavior* 16 (1995): 457–468.

43. "Charge Statistics: FY 1997 Through FY 2012," *US Equal Employment Opportunity Commission*, accessed June 15, 2013, http://eeoc.gov/eeoc/statistics/enforcement/charges.cfm.

44. *Women in the Labor Force: A Databook*, US Bureau of Labor Statistics, February 2013, accessed June 15, 2013, http://www.bls.gov/cps/wlf-databook-2012.pdf.

45. *The 2013 State of Women-Owned Businesses Report*, Commissioned by American Express OPEN, with the assistance of the Economic Census Branch of the Company Statistics Division of the US Census Bureau, accessed June 15, 2013, https://c401345.ssl.cf1.rackcdn.com/wp-content/uploads/2013/03/13ADV-WBI-E-StateOfWomenReport_FINAL.pdf.

46. "Chart 1. Women's Earnings as a Percent of Men's, by Age, Full-Time Wage and Salary Workers, 1979-2012 Annual Averages," in "Highlights of Women's Earnings 2012," US Department of Labor, US Bureau of Labor Statistics, October 2013, accessed May 8, 2014, http://www.bls.gov/cps/cpswom2012.pdf.

47. "US Women in Business," *Catalyst*, June 10, 2014, accessed July 11, 2014, http://www.catalyst.org/knowledge/us-women-business-0.

48. R. Molla, "Meet the Women CEOs of the Fortune 500," *Wall Street Journal*, March 7, 2014, accessed July 12, 2014, http://blogs.wsj.com/atwork/2014/03/07/meet-the-women-ceos-of-the-fortune-500/; "Statistical Overview of Women in the Workplace," *Catalyst*, March 3, 2014, accessed June 17, 2014, http://www.catalyst.org/knowledge/statistical-overview-women-workplace.

49. "Women CEOs of the *Fortune* 1000," *Catalyst*, June 10, 2014, accessed June 17, 2014, http://www.catalyst.org/knowledge/women-ceos-fortune-1000.

50. "Statistical Overview of Women in the Workplace."

51. M. Bertrand and K. Hallock, "The Gender Gap in Top Corporate Jobs," *Industrial & Labor Relations Review* 55 (2001): 3–21.

52. J. R. Hollenbeck, D. R. Ilgen, C. Ostroff, and J. B. Vancouver, "Sex Differences in Occupational Choice, Pay, and Worth: A Supply-Side Approach to Understanding the Male-Female Wage Gap," *Personnel Psychology* 40 (1987): 715–744.

53. S. Shellenbarger, "Does Having Kids Dull Career Opportunities?" *WSJ Blogs: The Juggle*, *Wall Street Journal*, April 6, 2011, accessed May 28, 2011, http://blogs.wsj.com/juggle/2011/04/06/does-having-kids-dull-job-ambition/.

54. A. Chaker and H. Stout, "Second Chances: After Years Off, Women Struggle to Revive Careers," *Wall Street Journal*, May 6, 2004, A1.

55. C. Friedersdorf, "Why PepsiCo CEO Indra K. Nooyi Can't Have It All," *The Atlantic*, July 1, 2014, accessed July 12, 2014, http://www.theatlantic.com/business/archive/2014/07/why-pepsico-ceo-indra-k-nooyi-cant-have-it-all/373750/.

56. Department of Industry, Labor and Human Relations, Report of the Governor's Task Force on the Glass Ceiling Commission (Madison, WI: State of Wisconsin, 1993); S. Devillard, S. Sancier, C. Werner, I. Maller, and C. Kossoff, "Women Matter 2013, Gender Diversity in Top Management: Moving Corporate Culture, Moving Boundaries," *McKinsey & Company*, November 2013, 10–11; E. O. Wright and J. Baxter, "The Glass Ceiling Hypothesis: A Reply to Critics," *Gender & Society* 14 (2000): 814–821.

57. M. Fix, G. C. Galster, and R. J. Struyk, "An Overview of Auditing for Discrimination," in *Clear and Convincing Evidence: Measurement of Discrimination in America*, ed. M. Fix and R. Struyk (Washington, DC: Urban Institute Press, 1993), 1–68.

58. S. Devillard, S. Sancier, C. Werner, I. Maller, C. Kossoff, "Women Matter 2013, Gender Diversity in Top Management: Moving Corporate Culture, Moving Boundaries," *McKinsey & Company*, November 2013, 13–14.

59. B. R. Ragins, B. Townsend, and M. Mattis, "Gender Gap in the Executive Suite: CEOs and Female Executives Report on Breaking the Glass Ceiling," *Academy of Management Executive* 12 (1998): 28–42.

60. J. Hoobler, G. Lemmon and S. Wayne, "Women's Managerial Aspirations: An Organizational Development Perspective" *Journal of Management* 40 (2014): 703–730.

61. "Charge Statistics: FY 1997 Through FY 2013," *US Equal Employment Opportunity Commission*, accessed July 12, 2014, http://eeoc.gov/eeoc/statistics/enforcement/charges.cfm.

62. "Ask DiversityInc: Where's the Diversity in Fortune 500 CEOs?" *DiversityInc*, accessed June 17, 2014, http://www.diversityinc.com/diversity-facts/wheres-the-diversity-in-fortune-500-ceos/.

63. "Household Data Annual Averages: Table 11. Employed Persons by Detailed Occupation, Sex, Race, and Hispanic or Latino Ethnicity," in "Labor Force Statistics from the Current Population Survey," *Bureau of Labor Statistics, US Department of Labor*, February 26, 2014, accessed June 17, 2014, http://www.bls.gov/cps/cpsaat11.pdf.

64. D. A. Neal and W. R. Johnson, "The Role of Premarket Factors in Black-White Wage Differences," *Journal of Political Economy* 104, no. 5 (1996): 869–895.

65. Fix, Galster, and Struyk, "An Overview of Auditing for Discrimination."

66. M. Bendick, Jr., C. W. Jackson, and V. A. Reinoso, "Measuring Employment Discrimination Through Controlled Experiments," in *African-Americans and Post-Industrial Labor Markets*, ed. James B. Stewart (New Brunswick, NJ: Transaction Publishers, 1997), 77–100.

67. P. B. Riach and J. Rich, "Measuring Discrimination by Direct Experimental Methods: Seeking Gunsmoke," *Journal of Post Keynesian Economics* 14, no. 2 (Winter 1991–1992): 143–150.

68. A. P. Brief, R. T. Buttram, R. M. Reizenstein, and S. D. Pugh, "Beyond Good Intentions: The Next Steps Toward Racial Equality in the American Workplace," *Academy of Management Executive* 11 (1997): 59–72.

69. L. E. Wynter, "Business & Race: Federal Agencies, Spurred on by Nonprofit Groups, Are Increasingly Embracing the Use of Undercover Investigators to Identify Discrimination in the Marketplace," *Wall Street Journal*, July 1, 1998, B1.

70. "Americans with Disabilities Act Questions and Answers," *US Department of Justice*, accessed July 12, 2014, http://www.ada.gov/qandaeng.htm.

71. M. Brault, "Americans with Disabilities: 2010, Household Economic Studies," in "Current Population Reports," *US Census Bureau*, issued July 2012, 70–131.

72. M. Brault, "Americans with Disabilities: 2010, Household Economic Studies," in "Current Population Reports," US Census Bureau, issued July 2012, 70–131.

73. Louis Harris & Associates, Inc., *Public Attitudes Toward People with Disabilities* (Washington, DC: National Organization on Disability, 1991); Louis Harris & Associates, Inc., *The ICD Survey II: Employing Disabled Americans* (New York: Louis Harris & Associates, Inc., 1987).

74. R. Greenwood and V. A. Johnson, "Employer Perspectives on Workers with Disabilities," *Journal of Rehabilitation* 53 (1987): 37–45.

75. B. Loy, "Accommodation and Compliance Series Workplace Accommodations: Low Cost, High Impact," *Job Accommodation Network*, September 1, 2013, accessed June 17, 2014, https://askjan.org/media/lowcosthighimpact.html.

76. T. E. Narashimhan and G. Babu, "The Chosen Ones," *Business Standard*, March 11, 2012, accessed March 16, 2012, http://www.business-standard.com/india/news/the-chosen-ones/467290/.

77. "Study on the Financing of Assistive Technology Devices and Services for Individuals with Disabilities: A Report to the President and the Congress of the United States," *National Council on Disability*, accessed August 21, 2008, http://www.ncd.gov/newsroom/publications/assistive.html.

78. Ibid.

79. R. B. Cattell, "Personality Pinned Down," *Psychology Today* 7 (1973): 40–46; C. S. Carver and M. F. Scheier, *Perspectives on Personality* (Boston: Allyn & Bacon, 1992).

80. J. M. Digman, "Personality Structure: Emergence of the Five-Factor Model," *Annual Review of Psychology* 41 (1990): 417–440; M. R. Barrick and M. K. Mount, "The Big Five Personality Dimensions and Job Performance: A Meta-Analysis," *Personnel Psychology* 44 (1991): 1–26.

81. R. Cook, "The Changing 'Face' of Your Business: Finding Good People...and Keeping Them Motivated," *PRO Magazine*, March 2005, 43.

82. O. Behling, "Employee Selection: Will Intelligence and Conscientiousness Do the Job?" *Academy of Management Executive* 12 (1998): 77–86.

83. R. S. Dalal, "A Meta-Analysis of the Relationship Between Organizational Citizenship Behavior and Counterproductive Work Behavior," *Journal of Applied Psychology* 90 (2005): 1241–1255.

84. Barrick and Mount, "The Big Five Personality Dimensions and Job Performance"; M. K. Mount and M. R. Barrick, "The Big Five Personality Dimensions: Implications for Research and Practice in Human Resource Management," *Research in Personnel & Human Resources Management* 13 (1995): 153–200; M. K. Mount and M. R. Barrick, "Five Reasons Why the 'Big Five' Article Has Been Frequently Cited," *Personnel Psychology* 51 (1998): 849–857; D. S. Ones, M. K. Mount, M. R. Barrick, and J. E. Hunter, "Personality and Job Performance: A Critique of the Tett, Jackson, and Rothstein (1991) Meta-Analysis," *Personnel Psychology* 47 (1994): 147–156.

85. Mount and Barrick, "Five Reasons Why the 'Big Five' Article Has Been Frequently Cited."

86. J. A. Lopez, "Talking Desks: Personality Types Revealed in State Workstations," *Arizona Republic*, January 7, 1996, D1.

87. "The Diverse Work Force," *Inc.*, January 1993, 33.

88. D. A. Thomas and R. J. Ely, "Making Differences Matter: A New Paradigm for Managing Diversity," *Harvard Business Review* 74 (September-October 1996): 79–90.

89. Esen, "2005 Workplace Diversity Practices: Survey Report."

90. D. A. Thomas and S. Wetlaufer, "A Question of Color: A Debate on Race in the US Workplace," *Harvard Business Review* 75 (September–October 1997): 118–132.

91. E. Esen, "2007 State of Workplace Diversity Management. A Survey Report by the Society for Human Resource Management," 2008.

92. "Oshkosh Corporation—Diversity & Inclusion," Oshkosh, accessed July 12, 2014, http://www.oshkoshcorporation.com/about/diversity.html.

93. J. Espinoza, "Working to Prove Benefits of More Women at the Top," *Wall Street Journal*, February 27, 2011, accessed March 15, 2011, http://online.wsj.com/article/SB10001424052748704150604576166483012821352.html.

94. J. R. Norton and R. E. Fox, *The Change Equation: Capitalizing on Diversity for Effective Organizational Change* (Washington, DC: American Psychological Association, 1997).

95. Ibid.

96. Thomas and Ely, "Making Differences Matter."

97. R. R. Thomas, Jr., *Beyond Race and Gender: Unleashing the Power of Your Total Workforce by Managing Diversity* (New York: AMACOM, 1991).

98. Ibid.

99. T. Cox, Jr., "The Multicultural Organization," *Academy of Management Executive* 5 (1991): 34–47.

100. S. Lubove, "Damned If You Do, Damned If You Don't: Preference Programs Are on the Defensive in the Public Sector, but Plaintiffs' Attorneys and Bureaucrats Keep Diversity Inc. Thriving in Corporate America," *Forbes*, December 15, 1997, 122.

101. L. S. Gottfredson, "Dilemmas in Developing Diversity Programs," in *Diversity in the Workplace*, ed. S. E. Jackson & Associates (New York: Guilford Press, 1992).

102. J. Graham and S. Kerr, "Mentoring," in *Diversity in Engineering: Managing the Workforce of the Future* (Washington, DC: National Academies Press, 2002), accessed June 16, 2013, http://www.nap.edu/openbook.php?record_id=10377&page=99.

103. Rodriguez, "Diversity Finds Its Place."

104. "Diversity at Work: Public Relations Makes a Difference for Global Giants."

105. Carnevale and Stone, *The American Mosaic*.

106. A. Greenwald, B. Nosek, and M. Banaji, "Understanding and Using the Implicit Association Test: I. An Improved Scoring Algorithm," *Journal of Personality & Social Psychology* (August 2003): 197–206; J. S. Lublin, "Bringing Hidden Biases into the Light," *Wall Street Journal*, January 9, 2014, accessed June 17, 2014, http://online.wsj.com/news/articles/SB10001424052702303754404579308562690896896; "The IAT | The Blind Spot," *The Blind Spot*, accessed July 13, 2014, http://spottheblindspot.com/the-iat/.

107. F. Oswald, G. Mitchell, H. Blanton, J. Jaccard, and P. Tetlock, "Predicting Ethnic and Racial Discrimination: A Meta-Analysis of IAT Criterion Studies," *Journal of Personality and Social Psychology* 105 (2013): 171–192.

108. "2010 Corporate Responsibility Report," *Intel*, accessed May 5, 2012, http://csrreportbuilder.intel.com/PDFFiles/CSR_2010_Full-Report.pdf.

109. "Intel Corp.—2012 50 Out Front #16," *Diversity MBA Magazine*, September 16, 2011, accessed March 16, 2012, http://diversitymbamagazine.com/tag/intel.

110. R. Joplin and C. S. Daus, "Challenges of Leading a Diverse Workforce," *Academy of Management Executive* 11 (1997): 32–47.

111. A. Fisher, "Should People Choose Their Own Mentors?" *Fortune*, November 29, 2004, 72.

112. N. Byrnes and R. O. Crocket, "An Historic Succession at Xerox," *Business Week*, June 8, 2009, 18–22.

113. P. Dvorak, "How Executives Are Pushed to Foster Diversity," *Wall Street Journal*, December 18, 2006, accessed March 16, 2012, http://online.wsj.com/article/SB116640764543853102.html?mod=rss_build.

13

1. "State of the Global Workplace: Employee Engagement Insights for Business Leaders Worldwide," Gallup, October 8, 2013, accessed July 13, 2014, http://www.gallup.com/strategicconsulting/164735/state-global-workplace.aspx.

2. P. Campbell and R. D. Pritchard, "Motivation Theory in Industrial and Organizational Psychology," in *Handbook of Industrial and Organizational Psychology*, ed. M. D. Dunnette (Chicago: Rand McNally, 1976).

3. J. Fried, "When the Only Way Up Is Out," *Inc.*, April 2011, 35–36.

4. A. Locke, "The Nature and Causes of Job Satisfaction," in *Handbook of Industrial and Organizational Psychology*, ed. M. D. Dunnette (Chicago: Rand McNally, 1976).

5. H. Maslow, "A Theory of Human Motivation," *Psychological Review* 50 (1943): 370–396.

6. P. Alderfer, *Existence, Relatedness, and Growth: Human Needs in Organizational Settings* (New York: Free Press, 1972).

7. C. McClelland, "Toward a Theory of Motive Acquisition," *American Psychologist* 20 (1965): 321–333; D. C. McClelland and D. H. Burnham, "Power Is the Great Motivator," *Harvard Business Review* 54, no. 2 (1976): 100–110.

8. J. H. Turner, "Entrepreneurial Environments and the Emergence of Achievement Motivation in Adolescent Males," *Sociometry* 33 (1970): 147–165.

9. L. W. Porter, E. E. Lawler III, and J. R. Hackman, *Behavior in Organizations* (New York: McGraw-Hill, 1975).

10. C. Ajila, "Maslow's Hierarchy of Needs Theory: Applicability to the Nigerian Industrial Setting," *IFE Psychology* (1997): 162–174.

11. M. A. Wahba and L. B. Birdwell, "Maslow Reconsidered: A Review of Research on the Need Hierarchy Theory," *Organizational Behavior & Human Performance* 15 (1976): 212–240; J. Rauschenberger, N. Schmitt, and J. E. Hunter, "A Test of the Need Hierarchy Concept by a Markov Model of Change in Need Strength," *Administrative Science Quarterly* 25 (1980): 654–670.

12. E. E. Lawler III and L. W. Porter, "The Effect of Performance on Job Satisfaction," *Industrial Relations* 7 (1967): 20–28.

13. Porter, Lawler, and Hackman, *Behavior in Organizations*.

14. E. White, "Employers Increasingly Favor Bonuses to Raises," *Wall Street Journal*, August 28, 2006, B3.

15. F. Koller, "American Factory Workers Getting $33,029 Yearly Bonuses May Sound Insane, But It's True," *The Motley Fool*, February 1, 2014, accessed July 14, 2014, http://www.fool.com/investing/general/2014/02/01/american-factory-workers-getting-33029-yearly-bonu.aspx.

16. Porter, Lawler, and Hackman, *Behavior in Organizations*.

17. J. McGonigal, "Be a Gamer, Save the World," *Wall Street Journal*, January 22, 2011, C3; IsosMediaCT, "2014 Essential Facts About the Computer and Video Game Industry," *Entertainment Software Association (ESA)*, April 2014, accessed June 18, 2014, http://www.theesa.com/facts/pdfs/ESA_EF_2014.pdf.

18. R. Silverman, "Latest Game Theory: Mixing Work and Play," *Wall Street Journal*, October 10, 2011, accessed June 16, 2013, http://online.wsj.com/article/SB1000142405297020429450457661537178379524848.html.

19. C. Caggiano, "What Do Workers Want?" *Inc.*, November 1992, 101–104; "National Study of the Changing Workforce," *Families & Work Institute*, accessed May 31, 2005, http://www.familiesandwork.org/summary/nscw.pdf.

20. C. Lee, A. Alonso, E. Esen, J. Coombs, and Y. Dong, "Employee Job Satisfaction and Engagement: The Road to Economic Recovery," *Society for Human Resource Management*, May 7, 2014, accessed June 18, 2014, http://www.shrm.org/Research/SurveyFindings/Documents/14-0028%20JobSatEngage_Report_FULL_FNL.pdf.

21. N. Jackson, "5 Ways to Reward Employees When Raises Aren't an Option," *Entrepreneur*, August 24, 2012, accessed June 16, 2013, http://www.entrepreneur.com/article/224249.

22. C. Lee, et. al., "Employee Job Satisfaction and Engagement: The Road to Economic Recovery."

23. J. Laabs, "Satisfy Them with More Than Money," *Personnel Journal* 77, no. 11 (1998): 40.

24. R. Kanfer and P. Ackerman, "Aging, Adult Development, and Work Motivation," *Academy of Management Review* (2004): 440–458.

25. J. Liberto, "CEOs Earn 354 Times More Than Average Worker," *CNNMoney*, April 15, 2013, accessed June 15, 2013, http://money.cnn.com/2013/04/15/news/economy/ceo-pay-worker/index.html.

26. V. Giang, "The 15 Highest-Paid CEOs in America," *Business Insider*, October 26, 2013, accessed June 18, 2014, http://www.businessinsider.com/15-highest-paid-ceos-in-america-2013-10?op=1.

27. L. Culpepper and E. Hurst, "Reporting CEO-to-Employee Pay Ratios: Navigating the Minefield," *Society for Human Resource Management*, November 1, 2010, accessed June 16, 2013, http://www.shrm.org/hrdisciplines/compensation/articles/pages/payratios.aspx.

28. C. T. Kulik and M. L. Ambrose, "Personal and Situational Determinants of Referent Choice," *Academy of Management Review* 17 (1992): 212–237.

29. L. Stevens, "Amazon Vexed by Strikes in Germany," *Wall Street Journal*, June 19, 2013, B1.

30. J. S. Adams, "Toward an Understanding of Inequity," *Journal of Abnormal Social Psychology* 67 (1963): 422–436.

31. S. Choudhury and D. Thoppil, "Toyota Sputters in India—Workers Remain on Strike, Refuse to Sign Code of Conduct," *Wall Street Journal*, March 28, 2014, B4.

32. J. Hagerty, "Anger and Hope Fuel Caterpillar Strikers," *Wall Street Journal*, May 31, 2012, B7.

33. R. A. Cosier and D. R. Dalton, "Equity Theory and Time: A Reformulation," *Academy of Management Review* 8 (1983): 311–319; M. R. Carrell and J. E. Dittrich, "Equity Theory: The Recent Literature, Methodological Considerations, and New Directions," *Academy of Management Review* 3 (1978): 202–209.

34. J. Doom, "American Superconductor Drops on Wider Loss, Lower Forecast," *Bloomberg Businessweek*, February 9, 2012, accessed March 21, 2012, http://www.bloomberg.com/news/2012-02-09/american-superconductor-s-loss-widens-as-sales

-fall-43-percent.html; T. Hoium, "American Superconductor: A Disastrous Year in Review," *The Motley Fool*, December 14, 2011, accessed March 21, 2012, http://www.fool.com/investing /general/2011/12/14/american-superconductor-a -disastrous-year-in-revi.aspx; T. Hoium, "Sinovel Drops the Hammer on American Superconductor," *The Motley Fool*, April 6, 2011, accessed March 21, 2012, http://www.fool.com/investing/general/2011 /04/06/sinovel-drops-the-hammer-on-american -superconducto.aspx.

35. C. Elliott, "When Labor Woes Cause Turbulence for Fliers," *Washington Post*, September 30, 2012, F2; G. Karp, "American Airlines Cancels Flights on Alleged Pilots' 'Sickout,'" *Chicago Tribune*, September 18, 2012, accessed June 16, 2013, http://articles.chicagotribune.com/2012-09-18 /business/chi-american-airlines-cancels-flights-on -pilots-sickout-20120918_1_dennis-tajer-sickout -american-airlines.

36. "Overtime Pay—Wage and Hour Division (WHD)," U.S. Department of Labor, accessed July 15, 2014, http://www.dol.gov/whd/overtime _pay.htm.

37. S. Banjo, "Wal-Mart to Pay $4.8 Million in Back Wages, Damages," *Wall Street Journal*, May 2, 2013, B3.

38. Wage and Hour Division, "2008 Statistical Fact Sheet," *United States Department of Labor*, December, 2008, accessed June 18, 2014, http:// www.dol.gov/whd/statistics/2008FiscalYear.htm.

39. L. Badoux, "Trends in Wage and Hour Litigation Over Unpaid Work Time and the Precautions Employers Should Take," *ADP*, Roseland, NJ, 2012, accessed June 18, 2014, https://www.adp.com /workforce-management/docs/whitepaper /trendsinwageandhourlitigation_05292012.pdf.

40. C. Chen, J. Choi, and S. Chi, "Making Justice Sense of Local-Expatriate Compensation Disparity: Mitigation by Local Referents, Ideological Explanations, and Interpersonal Sensitivity in China-Foreign Joint Ventures," *Academy of Management Journal* (2002): 807–817.

41. K. Bradsher, "Even as Wages Rise, China Exports Grow," *The New York Times*, January 9, 2014, accessed July 15, 2014, http://www.nytimes .com/2014/01/10/business/international/chinese -exports-withstand-rising-labor-costs.html?_r=0; M. Gimein, "If U.S. Wages Rose as Fast as China's, Factories Would Now Pay $50 an Hour," *Bloomberg*, March 27, 2013, accessed July 15, 2014, http://go.bloomberg.com/market-now/2013/03/27 /if-u-s-wages-rose-as-fast-as-chinas-factories-would -pay-50-an-hour/.

42. J. Quigley, "Lenovo CEO to Share $3 Million Bonus with 10,000 Employees," *The Diplomat*, September 3, 2013, accessed July 15, 2014, http:// thediplomat.com/2013/09/lenovo-ceo-to-share -3-million-bonus-with-10000-employees/.

43. Bloomberg News, "Lenovo Chief Yang Shares Bonus with Workers a Second Year," *Bloomberg-Businessweek*, September 2, 2013, accessed July 15, 2014, http://www.businessweek.com/news/2013-09 -01/lenovo-chief-yang-shares-bonus-with-workers -for-second-year.

44. "Apple Supplier Foxconn Cuts Working Hours, Workers Ask Why," *Reuters*, March 30, 2012, accessed May 8, 2012, http://www.reuters .com/article/2012/03/30/us-apple-foxconn-workers -idUSBRE82T0FC20120330; D. Barboza, "Foxconn Plant to Lift Pay Sharply at Factories in China," *New York Times*, February 18, 2012, accessed March 21, 2012, http://www.nytimes.com/2012/02/19 /technology/foxconn-to-raise-salaries-for-workers -by-up-to-25.html; M. Brown, "New Report Details Onerous, Illegal Working Conditions at Foxconn,"

Wired.com, May 6, 2011, accessed March 21, 2012, http://www.wired.com/epicenter/2011/05/foxconn -no-suicide-pledge/; H. Koch, "We Were Not a Very Open Company Before," *Spiegel Online*, May 11, 2011, accessed March 21, 2012, http://www.spiegel .de/international/world/0,1518,761934,00.html.

45. R. Folger and M. A. Konovsky, "Effects of Procedural and Distributive Justice on Reactions to Pay Raise Decisions," *Academy of Management Journal* 32 (1989): 115–130; M. A. Konovsky, "Understanding Procedural Justice and Its Impact on Business Organizations," *Journal of Management* 26 (2000): 489–512.

46. E. Barret-Howard and T. R. Tyler, "Procedural Justice as a Criterion in Allocation Decisions," *Journal of Personality & Social Psychology* 50 (1986): 296–305; Folger and Konovsky, "Effects of Procedural and Distributive Justice on Reactions to Pay Raise Decisions."

47. R. Folger and J. Greenberg, "Procedural Justice: An Interpretive Analysis of Personnel Systems," in *Research in Personnel and Human Resources Management*, vol. 3, ed. K. Rowland and G. Ferris (Greenwich, CT: JAI, 1985); R. Folger, D. Rosenfield, J. Grove, and L. Corkran, "Effects of 'Voice' and Peer Opinions on Responses to Inequity," *Journal of Personality & Social Psychology* 37 (1979): 2253–2261; E. A. Lind and T. R. Tyler, *The Social Psychology of Procedural Justice* (New York: Plenum, 1988); Konovsky, "Understanding Procedural Justice and Its Impact on Business Organizations."

48. V. H. Vroom, *Work and Motivation* (New York: John Wiley & Sons, 1964); L. W. Porter and E. E. Lawler III, *Managerial Attitudes and Performance* (Homewood, IL: Dorsey & Richard D. Irwin, 1968).

49. C. Schultz, "When You Reward, Make It About the Employee—Not the Employer," *TLNT*, May 16, 2012, accessed June 16, 2013, http://www.tlnt.com /2012/05/16/when-you-reward-make-it-about-the -employee-not-the-employer/.

50. S. Miller, "Countering the Employee Recognition Gap," SHRM Library, *Society for Human Resource Management*, February 2006, accessed March 25, 2009, http://www.shrm.org.

51. G. Douglas, "Survey Finds Many Employers Not Satisfied with Their Pay-for-Performance Programs," Bloomberg BNA, December 30, 2013, accessed July 15, 2014, http://www.bna.com/survey -finds-employers-n17179881003/.

52. A. Fox, "Companies Can Benefit When They Disclose Pay Processes to Employees," *HR Magazine*, July 2002, 25.

53. J. Spolsky, "Why I Never Let Employees Negotiate a Raise," *Inc.*, April 1, 2009, accessed February 15, 2010, http://www.inc.com/magazine /20090401/how-hard-could-it-be-employees -negotiate-pay-raises.html.

54. K. W. Thomas and B. A. Velthouse, "Cognitive Elements of Empowerment," *Academy of Management Review* 15 (1990): 666–681.

55. E. L. Thorndike, *Animal Intelligence* (New York: Macmillan, 1911).

56. G. Karp, "United Posts Best On-Time Month of 2012 in November," *Chicago Tribune*, December 3, 2012, accessed June 16, 2013, http://articles .chicagotribune.com/2012-12-03/business/chi-united -posts-best-monthly-ontime-performance-in -november-20121203_1_dispatch-system-software -international-flights-regional-flights.

57. B. F. Skinner, *Science and Human Behavior* (New York: Macmillan, 1954); B. F. Skinner, *Beyond Freedom and Dignity* (New York: Bantam, 1971); B. F. Skinner, *A Matter of Consequences* (New York: New York University Press, 1984).

58. A. M. Dickinson and A. D. Poling, "Schedules of Monetary Reinforcement in Organizational Behavior Management: Latham and Huber Revisited," *Journal of Organizational Behavior Management* 16, no. 1 (1992): 71–91.

59. B. Dolan, "Humana Launches Wellness Platform Vitality," *MobiHealthNews*, July 6, 2011, accessed March 21, 2012, http://mobihealthnews .com/11675/humana-launches-wellness-platform -vitality/; J. McGregor, "Should Companies Penalize Employees Who Smoke?" *Washington Post*, July 7, 2011, accessed March 21, 2012, http:// www.washingtonpost.com/blogs/post-leadership /post/should-companies-penalize-employees-who -smoke/2011/04/01/gIQAENh71H_blog.html; M. Raby, "Humana Offers Incentives for Playing Ubisoft Fitness Games," *Slashgear*, March 14, 2012, accessed March 21, 2012, http://www.slashgear .com/humana-offers-incentives-for-playing-ubisoft -fitness-games-14218455/.

60. L. Kwoh, "Shape Up or Pay Up: Firms Put in New Health Penalties," *Wall Street Journal*, April 6, 2013, A1.

61. D. Fitzgerald, "Staples Defends Executive Bonuses," *Wall Street Journal*, May 26, 2014, accessed July 15, 2014, http://online.wsj.com/news /articles/SB10001424052702304811904579586173 092378940.

62. J. B. Miner, *Theories of Organizational Behavior* (Hinsdale, IL: Dryden, 1980).

63. Dickinson and Poling, "Schedules of Monetary Reinforcement in Organizational Behavior Management."

64. F. Luthans and A. D. Stajkovic, "Reinforce for Performance: The Need to Go Beyond Pay and Even Rewards," *Academy of Management Executive* 13, no. 2 (1999): 49–57.

65. D. Anderson, *Up Your Business! 7 Steps to Fix, Build or Stretch Your Organization* (New York: Wiley, 2003).

66. K. D. Butterfield, L. K. Trevino, and G. A. Ball, "Punishment from the Manager's Perspective: A Grounded Investigation and Inductive Model," *Academy of Management Journal* 39 (1996): 1479–1512.

67. R. D. Arvey and J. M. Ivancevich, "Punishment in Organizations: A Review, Propositions, and Research Suggestions," *Academy of Management Review* 5 (1980): 123–132.

68. R. D. Arvey, G. A. Davis, and S. M. Nelson, "Use of Discipline in an Organization: A Field Study," *Journal of Applied Psychology* 69 (1984): 448–460; M. E. Schnake, "Vicarious Punishment in a Work Setting," *Journal of Applied Psychology* 71 (1986): 343–345.

69. G. A. Yukl and G. P. Latham, "Consequences of Reinforcement Schedules and Incentive Magnitudes for Employee Performance: Problems Encountered in a Field Setting," *Journal of Applied Psychology* 60 (1975): 294–298.

70. E. A. Locke and G. P. Latham, *Goal Setting: A Motivational Technique That Works* (Englewood Cliffs, NJ: Prentice-Hall, 1984); E. A. Locke and G. P. Latham, *A Theory of Goal Setting and Task Performance* (Englewood Cliffs, NJ: Prentice-Hall, 1990).

71. D. Wessel, "Gaming the System to Beat Rush -Hour Traffic," *Wall Street Journal*, July 31, 2013, accessed July 15, 2014, http://online.wsj.com/news /articles/SB10001424127887323997004578639802 367960498.

72. G. Colvin, "The Art of the Self-Managing Team," *Fortune*, December 3, 2012, 22; P. Sangani, "Uber Guru Gary Hamel on Why Old Management Models Need a Major Overhaul," *The Economic Times*, June 14, 2013, accessed June 17, 2013,

http://articles.economictimes.indiatimes.com/2013-06-14/news/39976766_1_gary-hamel-management-guru-innovation.

73. G. P. Latham and E. A. Locke, "Goal Setting—A Motivational Technique That Works," *Organizational Dynamics* 8, no. 2 (1979): 68.

14

1. A. Bryant, "Before the Meeting Adjourns, Tell Me What You'll Do Next," *New York Times*, August 11, 2012, accessed June 17, 2013, http://www.nytimes.com/2012/08/12/business/bill-flemming-of-skanska-usa-building-on-leadership.html?_r=0.

2. W. Bennis, "Why Leaders Can't Lead," *Training & Development Journal* 43, no. 4 (1989).

3. C. Hymnowitz and S. Frier, "Can This IBMer Keep Big Blue's Edge?" *Bloomberg Businessweek*, October 6–November 31, 2011, 31–32.

4. A. Zaleznik, "Managers and Leaders: Are They Different?" *Harvard Business Review* 55 (1977): 76–78; A. Zaleznik, "The Leadership Gap," *Washington Quarterly* 6 (1983): 32–39.

5. S. Grobart, "How Samsung Became the World's No. 1 Smartphone Maker," *Bloomberg Businessweek*, March 28, 2013, accessed June 17, 2013, http://www.businessweek.com/articles/2013-03-28/how-samsung-became-the-worlds-no-dot-1-smartphone-maker.

6. Bennis, "Why Leaders Can't Lead."

7. J. S. Lublin, "Introverted Execs Find Ways to Shine," *Wall Street Journal*, April 14, 2011, accessed March 21, 2012, http://online.wsj.com/article/SB10001424052748703983104576263053775879800.html.

8. D. Jones, "Not All Successful CEOs Are Extroverts," *USA Today*, June 7, 2006, B.1.

9. Ibid.

10. G. Murray, "Caveman Politics," *Psychology Today*, December 15, 2011, accessed June 19, 2014, http://www.psychologytoday.com/blog/caveman-politics/201112/are-you-sure-we-prefer-taller-leaders; G. Murray and J. Schmitz, "Caveman Politics: Evolutionary Leadership Preferences and Physical Stature," *Social Science Quarterly* 92 (2011): 1215-1235.

11. M. Gladwell, "Why Do We Love Tall Men?" Gladwell.com, accessed July 16, 2014, http://gladwell.com/blink/why-do-we-love-tall-men/.

12. R. J. House and R. M Aditya, "The Social Scientific Study of Leadership: Quo Vadis?" *Journal of Management* 23 (1997): 409–473; T. Judge, R. Illies, J. Bono, and M. Gerhardt, "Personality and Leadership: A Qualitative and Quantitative Review," *Journal of Applied Psychology* (August 2002): 765–782; S. A. Kirkpatrick and E. A. Locke, "Leadership: Do Traits Matter?" *Academy of Management Executive* 5, no. 2 (1991): 48–60.

13. House and Aditya, "The Social Scientific Study of Leadership"; Kirkpatrick and Locke, "Leadership: Do Traits Matter?"

14. J. J. Gabarro, *The Dynamics of Taking Charge* (Boston: Harvard Business School Press, 1987).

15. I. Mochari, "The Most Valuable Lesson Jeff Weiner Learned as LinkedIn's CEO," *Inc*, February 7, 2014, accessed June 19, 2014, http://www.inc.com/ilan-mochari/3-tips-fire-fast.html.

16. "Kevin Tsujihara, Chief Executive Officer, Warner Bros.," *Warner Brothers*, accessed June 17, 2013, http://www.warnerbros.com/studio/executives/kevin-tsujihara.html; M. James, "Warner Bros. Names Kevin Tsujihara Chief Executive," *Los Angeles Times*, January 28, 2013, accessed June 17, 2013, http://articles.latimes.com/2013/jan/28/entertainment/la-et-ct-warner-bros-20130128.

17. Kirkpatrick and Locke, "Leadership: Do Traits Matter?"

18. E. A. Fleishman, "The Description of Supervisory Behavior," *Journal of Applied Psychology* 37 (1953): 1–6; L. R. Katz, *New Patterns of Management* (New York: McGraw-Hill, 1961).

19. C. Dawson, "Nissan Drives to Close Gap," *Wall Street Journal*, June 27, 2011, accessed June 17, 2013, http://online.wsj.com/article/SB10001424052702304447804576409472071237288.html; J. Ramsey, "Nissan Announces 'Power 88' Business Plan, All-New Vehicles Every Six Weeks for Six Years," *AutoBlog*, June 27, 2011, accessed June 17, 2013, http://www.autoblog.com/2011/06/27/nissan-announces-power-88-business-plan-all-new-vehicles-ever/.

20. A. Chernoff, "Bosses Listening to Millennial Workers," *CNN*, July 22, 2011, accessed March 22, 2012, http://articles.cnn.com/2011-07-22/living/managing.millennials_1_millennials-social-media-volunteer-work/2?_s=PM:LIVING.

21. P. Weissenberg and M. H. Kavanagh, "The Independence of Initiating Structure and Consideration: A Review of the Evidence," *Personnel Psychology* 25 (1972): 119–130.

22. R. J. House and T. R. Mitchell, "Path-Goal Theory of Leadership," *Journal of Contemporary Business* 3 (1974): 81–97; F. E. Fiedler, "A Contingency Model of Leadership Effectiveness," in *Advances in Experimental Social Psychology*, ed. L. Berkowitz (New York: Academic Press, 1964); V. H. Vroom and P. W. Yetton, *Leadership and Decision Making* (Pittsburgh: University of Pittsburgh Press, 1973); P. Hersey and K. H. Blanchard, The *Management of Organizational Behavior*, 4th ed. (Englewood Cliffs, NJ: Prentice Hall, 1984); S. Kerr and J. M. Jermier, "Substitutes for Leadership: Their Meaning and Measurement," *Organizational Behavior & Human Performance* 22 (1978): 375–403.

23. A. Grant, F. Gino, and D. Hofmann, "The Hidden Advantage of Quiet Bosses," *Harvard Business Review* 88, no. 12 (2010): 28.

24. F. E. Fiedler and M. M. Chemers, *Leadership and Effective Management* (Glenview, IL: Scott, Foresman, 1974); F. E. Fiedler and M. M. Chemers, *Improving Leadership Effectiveness: The Leader Match Concept*, 2nd ed. (New York: Wiley, 1984).

25. A. Davis, "Corner Office: Angus Davis of Swipely, on Working Around Flaws," interview by A. Bryant, *New York Times*, April 24, 2014, accessed June 19, 2014, http://www.nytimes.com/2014/04/25/business/angus-davis-of-swipely-on-working-around-flaws.html.

26. Fiedler and Chemers, *Improving Leadership Effectiveness*.

27. F. E. Fiedler, "The Effects of Leadership Training and Experience: A Contingency Model Interpretation," *Administrative Science Quarterly* 17, no. 4 (1972): 455; F. E. Fiedler, *A Theory of Leadership Effectiveness* (New York: McGraw-Hill, 1967).

28. L. S. Csoka and F. E. Fiedler, "The Effect of Military Leadership Training: A Test of the Contingency Model," *Organizational Behavior & Human Performance* 8 (1972): 395–407.

29. House and Mitchell, "Path-Goal Theory of Leadership."

30. "Up and Coming Leaders," *Entrepreneur*, March 26, 2014, accessed July 17, 2014, http://www.entrepreneur.com/article/231531.

31. M. Tenney, "More Than Money," *Collector*, October 2013, 26-28.

32. House and Mitchell, "Path-Goal Theory of Leadership."

33. B. M. Fisher and J. E. Edwards, "Consideration and Initiating Structure and Their Relationships with Leader Effectiveness: A Meta-Analysis," *Proceedings of the Academy of Management*, August 1988, 201–205.

34. Kotter International, "Leadership Lessons from Domino's Pizza: NFL Draft Edition," *Forbes*, May 12, 2014, accessed June 19, 2014, http://www.forbes.com/sites/johnkotter/2014/05/12/leadership-lessons-from-dominos-pizza-nfl-draft-edition/.

35. L. Faw, "For Domino's, 'Failure Is an Option,'" *Mediapost Agency Daily*, April 14, 2014, accessed July 17, 2014, http://www.mediapost.com/publications/article/223604/for-dominos-failure-is-an-option.html.

36. Domino's TV Commercial, "Failure Is an Option," YouTube.com, 2014, April 15, 2014, accessed July 17, 2014, https://www.youtube.com/watch?v=-NPqOOErP5I.

37. Kotter International, "Innovation Secrets from Domino's Pizza," *Forbes*, March 27, 2012, accessed June 19, 2014, http://www.forbes.com/sites/johnkotter/2012/03/27/innovation-secrets-from-dominos-pizza/.

38. E. Dou, "Asustek Seeks to Challenge Apple in Tablets," *Wall Street Journal*, December 3, 2013, accessed June 18, 2013, http://blogs.wsj.com/digits/2012/12/03/asustek-seeks-to-challenge-apple-in-tablets/; E. Dou, "Asustek to Make Small Windows 8 Tablets," *Wall Street Journal*, May 6, 2013, accessed June 18, 2013, http://online.wsj.com/article/SB10001424127887324326504578466122367669576.html?mod=WSJ_qtoverview_wsjlatest.

39. J. C. Wofford and L. Z. Liska, "Path-Goal Theories of Leadership: A Meta-Analysis," *Journal of Management* 19 (1993): 857–876.

40. House and Aditya, "The Social Scientific Study of Leadership."

41. V. H. Vroom and A. G. Jago, *The New Leadership: Managing Participation in Organizations* (Englewood Cliffs, NJ: Prentice Hall, 1988).

42. C. Fishman, "How Teamwork Took Flight: This Team Built a Commercial Engine—and Self-Managing GE Plant—from Scratch," *Fast Company*, October 1, 1999, 188.

43. Ibid.

44. Ibid.

45. N. Fallon, "Is Your Management Style Hurting Your Team?" *Business News Daily*, May 14, 2014, accessed June 19, 2014, http://www.businessnewsdaily.com/6409-management-styles-strategies.html.

46. G. A. Yukl, *Leadership in Organizations*, 3rd ed. (Englewood Cliffs, NJ: Prentice Hall, 1995).

47. B. M. Bass, *Bass & Stogdill's Handbook of Leadership: Theory, Research, and Managerial Applications* (New York: Free Press, 1990).

48. R. D. Ireland and M. A. Hitt, "Achieving and Maintaining Strategic Competitiveness in the 21st Century: The Role of Strategic Leadership," *Academy of Management Executive* 13, no. 1 (1999): 43–57.

49. R. Dodes, "Barneys, Prada in Tussle," *Wall Street Journal*, February 5, 2011, accessed June 18, 2013, http://online.wsj.com/article/SB10001424052748704570104576124420342774508.html; R. Dodes and C. Passariello, "Luxury Brands Stake Out New Department Store Turf," *Wall Street Journal*, May 4, 2011, accessed June 18, 2013, http://online.wsj.com/article/SB10001424052748704740604576301113906906234.html.

50. P. Thoms and D. B. Greenberger, "Training Business Leaders to Create Positive Organizational Visions of the Future: Is It Successful?" *Academy of Management Journal* (Best Papers & Proceedings 1995): 212–216.

51. M. Weber, *The Theory of Social and Economic Organizations*, trans. R. A. Henderson and T. Parsons (New York: Free Press, 1947).

52. D. A. Waldman and F. J. Yammarino, "CEO Charismatic Leadership: Levels-of-Management and Levels-of-Analysis Effects," *Academy of Management Review* 24, no. 2 (1999): 266–285.

53. K. B. Lowe, K. G. Kroeck, and N. Sivasubramaniam, "Effectiveness Correlates of Transformational and Transactional Leadership: A Meta-Analytic Review of the MLQ Literature," *Leadership Quarterly* 7 (1996): 385–425.

54. J. M. Howell and B. J. Avolio, "The Ethics of Charismatic Leadership: Submission or Liberation?" *Academy of Management Executive* 6, no. 2 (1992): 43–54.

55. G. Colvin, "The Greatest Business Decisions of All Time: Tata Steel," *Fortune*, October 1, 2012, accessed June 18, 2013, http://money.cnn.com/gallery/news/companies/2012/10/01/greatest-business-decisions.fortune/4.html.

56. J. Bunge, "Peregrine Founder Hit with 50 Years," *Wall Street Journal*, February 1, 2013, C1; T. Polansek and R. Schlader, "Peregrine CEO Pleads Guilty to Fraud; To Stay in Jail," *Reuters*, September 17, 2012, accessed June 19, 2013, http://www.reuters.com/article/2012/09/17/us-peregrine-wasendorf-idUSBRE88G16U20120917.

57. D. J. Chandler, "The Perfect Storm of Leaders' Unethical Behavior: A Conceptual Framework," *International Journal of Leadership Studies* 5, no.1 (2009): 69-93.

58. Howell and Avolio, "The Ethics of Charismatic Leadership."

59. B. M. Bass, "From Transactional to Transformational Leadership: Learning to Share the Vision," *Organizational Dynamics* 18 (1990): 19–36.

60. B. M. Bass, *A New Paradigm of Leadership: An Inquiry into Transformational Leadership* (Alexandra, VA: US Army Research Institute for the Behavioral and Social Sciences, 1996).

61. R. Martin, "CEOs Must Model the Behavior for Creating Societal Value," September 26, 2011, accessed July 17, 2014, http://blogs.hbr.org/2011/09/ceos-must-model-the-behavior-a/.

62. CNN Wire Staff, "Network: Leno Took 50% Pay Cut to Reduce 'Tonight Show' Layoffs," CNN, September 8, 2012, accessed July 17, 2014, http://www.cnn.com/2012/09/07/showbiz/jay-leno-tonight-show/; A. Farnham, "Bosses Who Volunteer for Pay Cuts," ABC News, September 11, 2012, accessed July 17, 2014, http://abcnews.go.com/Business/bosses-pay-cuts/story?id=17209062.

63. D. Goldman, "Where Microsoft Geeks Go to 'Do Epic $#!+,'" *CNNMoney*, August 10, 2012, accessed June 18, 2013, http://money.cnn.com/2012/08/10/technology/microsoft-garage/; J. Greene, "Microsoft Opens Garage to Spark Innovation," cNet, July 19, 2011, accessed June 18, 2013, http://news.cnet.com/8301-10805_3-20080542-75/microsoft-opens-garage-to-spark-innovation/.

64. Bass, "From Transactional to Transformational Leadership."

15

1. E. E. Lawler III, L. W. Porter, and A. Tannenbaum, "Manager's Attitudes Toward Interaction Episodes," *Journal of Applied Psychology* 52 (1968): 423–439; H. Mintzberg, *The Nature of Managerial Work* (New York: Harper & Row, 1973).

2. J. D. Maes, T. G. Weldy, and M. L. Icenogle, "A Managerial Perspective: Oral Communication Competency Is Most Important for Business Students in the Workplace," *Journal of Business Communication* 34 (1997): 67–80.

3. E. E. Jones and K. E. Davis, "From Acts to Dispositions: The Attribution Process in Person Perception," in *Advances in Experimental and Social Psychology*, vol. 2, ed. L. Berkowitz (New York: Academic Press, 1965), 219–266; R. G. Lord and J. E. Smith, "Theoretical, Information-Processing, and Situational Factors Affecting Attribution Theory Models of Organizational Behavior," *Academy of Management Review* 8 (1983): 50–60.

4. D. Simons and C. Chabris, "Gorillas in Our Midst: Sustained Inattentional Blindness for Dynamic Events," *Perception* 28 (1999): 1059–1074.

5. J. Zadney and H. B. Gerard, "Attributed Intentions and Informational Selectivity," *Journal of Experimental Social Psychology* 10 (1974): 34–52.

6. M. Beck, "What Cocktail Parties Teach Us," *Wall Street Journal*, April 23, 2012, D1.

7. H. H. Kelly, *Attribution in Social Interaction* (Morristown, NJ: General Learning Press, 1971).

8. J. M. Burger, "Motivational Biases in the Attribution of Responsibility for an Accident: A Meta-Analysis of the Defensive-Attribution Hypothesis," *Psychological Bulletin* 90 (1981): 496–512.

9. D. A. Hofmann and A. Stetzer, "The Role of Safety Climate and Communication in Accident Interpretation: Implications for Learning from Negative Events," *Academy of Management Journal* 41, no. 6 (1998): 644–657.

10. C. Perrow, *Normal Accidents: Living with High-Risk Technologies* (New York: Basic Books, 1984).

11. A. G. Miller and T. Lawson, "The Effect of an Informational Opinion on the Fundamental Attribution Error," *Journal of Personality & Social Psychology* 47 (1989): 873–896; J. M. Burger, "Changes in Attribution Errors Over Time: The Ephemeral Fundamental Attribution Error," *Social Cognition* 9 (1991): 182–193.

12. F. Heider, *The Psychology of Interpersonal Relations* (New York: Wiley, 1958); D. T. Miller and M. Ross, "Self-Serving Biases in Attribution of Causality: Fact or Fiction?" *Psychological Bulletin* 82 (1975): 213–225.

13. J. R. Larson, Jr., "The Dynamic Interplay Between Employees' Feedback-Seeking Strategies and Supervisors' Delivery of Performance Feedback," *Academy of Management Review* 14, no. 3 (1989): 408–422.

14. R. C. Rabin, "15-Minute Visits Take a Toll on the Doctor-Patient Relationship," *Kaiser Health News*, April 21, 2014, accessed June 20, 2014, http://www.kaiserhealthnews.org/Stories/2014/April/21/15-minute-doctor-visits.aspx; S. Wilkins, "The Truth About Those High Patient Satisfaction Scores for Doctor-Patient Communication," *Center For Advancing Health* (Prepared Patient Blog), April 11, 2013, accessed June 20, 2014, http://www.cfah.org/blog/2013/the-truth-about-those-high-patient-satisfaction-scores-for-doctor-patient-communication.

15. Ibid.

16. S. Brownlee, "The Doctor Will See You—If You're Quick," *The Daily Beast*, April 16, 2012, accessed July 19, 2014, http://www.thedailybeast.com/newsweek/2012/04/15/why-your-doctor-has-no-time-to-see-you.html.

17. S. Wilkins, "The Truth About Those High Patient Satisfaction Scores for Doctor-Patient Communication."

18. "The Experts: How to Improve Doctor-Patient Communication," *Wall Street Journal*, April 12, 2013, accessed June 20, 2013, http://online.wsj.com/article/SB1000142412788732405030457841125180590822 8.html.

19. Ibid.

20. S. Wilkins, "The Truth About Those High Patient Satisfaction Scores for Doctor-Patient Communication," Center for Advancing Health (Prepared Patient Blog), April 11, 2013, accessed June 20, 2014, http://www.cfah.org/blog/2013/the-truth-about-those-high-patient-satisfaction-scores-for-doctor-patient-communication.

21. "The Experts: How to Improve Doctor-Patient Communication."

22. Early. Green, "The Origins of Office Speak," *The Atlantic*, April 24, 2014, accessed June 20, 2014, http://www.theatlantic.com/features/archive/2014/04/the-origins-of-office-speak/361135/.

23. C. Hymowitz, "Mind Your Language: To Do Business Today, Consider Delayering," *Wall Street Journal*, March 27, 2006, B1.

24. G. L. Kreps, *Organizational Communication: Theory and Practice* (New York: Longman, 1990).

25. Ibid.

26. J. Jusko, "A Little More Communication," *Industry Week*, March 1, 2010, 19.

27. J. Haden, "Best Way to Make Employees Better at Their Jobs," *Inc.*, July 23, 2012, accessed June 19, 2013, http://www.inc.com/jeff-haden/motivating-employees-with-simple-question.html.

28. A. Truong, "How Jack Dorsey Makes Meetings at Square More Transparent," *FastCompany*, November 5, 2013, accessed June 20, 2014, http://www.fastcompany.com/3021208/fast-feed/how-jack-dorsey-makes-meetings-at-square-transparent.

29. E. Swallow, "How Rumors Could Actually Strengthen Your Company Culture," *Forbes*, March 1, 2013, accessed June 19, 2013, http://www.forbes.com/sites/ericaswallow/2013/03/01/rumor-jar/.

30. J. Sandberg, "Ruthless Rumors and the Managers Who Enable Them," *Wall Street Journal*, October 29, 2003, B1.

31. E. Holm and J. S. Lublin, "Loose Lips Trip Up a Good Hands Executive," *Wall Street Journal*, August 1, 2011, C1.

32. K. Voight, "Office Intelligence," *Asian Wall Street Journal*, January 21, 2005, P1.

33. Davis and O'Connor, "Serial Transmission of Information: A Study of the Grapevine"; C. Hymowitz, "Managing: Spread the Word, Gossip Is Good," *Wall Street Journal*, October 4, 1988, online, page number not available.

34. W. C. Redding, *Communication within the Organization: An Interpretive View of Theory and Research* (New York: Industrial Communication Council, 1972).

35. D. T. Hall, K. L. Otazo, and G. P. Hollenbeck, "Behind Closed Doors: What Really Happens in Executive Coaching," *Organizational Dynamics* 27, no. 3 (1999): 39–53.

36. J. Kelly, "Blowing the Whistle on the Boss," *PR Newswire*, November 15, 2004, http://www.prnewswire.com [content no longer available online].

37. R. McGarvey, "Lords of Discipline," *Entrepreneur Magazine*, January 1, 2000, page number not available.

38. Jack Welch, "'Rank-and-Yank'? That's Not How It's Done," *Wall Street Journal*, November 15, 2013, A.15.

39. N. Goodman, "Jack Welch on How to Manage Employees," *Entrepreneur*, October 5, 2012, accessed July 19, 2014, http://www.entrepreneur.com/blog/224604.

40. C. Hirschman, "Firm Ground: EAP Training for HR and Managers Improves Supervisor-Employee Communication and Helps Organizations Avoid Legal Quagmires," *Employee Benefit*

News, June 13, 2005, http://www.benefitnews.com [content no longer available online].

41. L. V. Gillespie, "Raising A-wear-ness," *Employee Benefit News*, December 1, 2011, accessed March 27, 2012, http://ebn.benefitnews .com/news/hiv-aids-levi-strauss-eap-disease -management-2720149-1.html.

42. A. Mehrabian, "Communication without Words," *Psychology Today* 3 (1968): 53; A. Mehrabian, *Silent Messages* (Belmont, CA: Wadsworth, 1971); R. Harrison, *Beyond Words: An Introduction to Nonverbal Communication* (Upper Saddle River, NJ: Prentice Hall, 1974); A. Mehrabian, *Non-Verbal Communication* (Chicago: Aldine, 1972).

43. M. L. Knapp, *Nonverbal Communication in Human Interaction*, 2nd ed. (New York: Holt, Rinehart & Winston, 1978).

44. H. M. Rosenfeld, "Instrumental Affiliative Functions of Facial and Gestural Expressions," *Journal of Personality & Social Psychology* 24 (1966): 65–72; P. Ekman, "Differential Communication of Affect by Head and Body Cues," *Journal of Personality & Social Psychology* 23 (1965): 726–735; A. Mehrabian, "Significance of Posture and Position in the Communication of Attitude and Status Relationships," *Psychological Bulletin* 71 (1969): 359–372.

45. J. Gottman and R. Levenson, "The Timing of Divorce: Predicting When a Couple Will Divorce over a 14-Year Period," *Journal of Marriage & the Family* 62 (August 2000): 737–745; J. Gottman, R. Levenson, and E. Woodin, "Facial Expressions During Marital Conflict," *Journal of Family Communication* 1, no. 1 (2001): 37–57.

46. S. Shellenbarger, "Just Look Me in the Eye Already," *Wall Street Journal*, May 28, 2013, accessed June 20, 2014, http://online.wsj.com/news /articles/SB10001424127887324809804578511290 822228174.

47. S. Shellenbarger, "Is This How You Really Talk?" *Wall Street Journal*, April 23, 2013, accessed June 20, 2014, http://online.wsj.com/news/articles /SB10001424127887323735604578440851083674898.

48. A. Joyce, "Confidentiality as a Valued Benefit; Loose Lips Can Defeat the Purpose of an Employee Assistance Program," *Washington Post*, May 11, 2003, F05.

49. C. A. Bartlett and S. Ghoshal, "Changing the Role of Top Management: Beyond Systems to People," *Harvard Business Review*, May–June 1995, 132–142.

50. E. Spragins, "Sending the Wrong Message," *Fortune Small Business*, July 1, 2003, 32.

51. J. Fry, "When Talk Isn't Cheap: Is Emailing Colleagues Who Sit Feet Away a Sign of Office Dysfunction, or a Wise Move?" *Wall Street Journal*, November 28, 2005, http://online.wsj.com [content no longer available online].

52. D. F. Larcker, S. Miles, B. Tayan, and M. E. Gutman, "2013 CEO Performance Evaluation Survey," *Stanford Graduate School of Business*, accessed June 20, 2014, http://www.gsb.stanford .edu/cldr/research/surveys/performance.html.

53. "The Joys of Voice Mail," *Inc.*, November 1995, 102.

54. R. G. Nichols, "Do We Know How to Listen? Practical Helps in a Modern Age," in *Communication Concepts and Processes*, ed. J. DeVitor (Englewood Cliffs, NJ: Prentice Hall, 1971); P. V. Lewis, *Organizational Communication: The Essence of Effective Management* (Columbus, OH: Grid Publishing Company, 1975).

55. "Hotel Magnate Bill Marriott on Life's Lessons," *National Public Radio*, April 11, 2013, accessed June 22, 2013, http://www.npr.org/2013 /04/11/176913429/hotel-magnate-bill-marriott-on -lifes-lessons.

56. D. A. Kaplan, "Undercover Employee: A Day on the Job at Three Best Companies," *CNNMoney*, January 20, 2011, accessed March 27, 2012, http:// features.blogs.fortune.cnn.com/2011/01/20 /undercover-employee-a-day-on-the-job-at-three -best-companies/.

57. L. Gurkow, "The Art of Active Listening," *Jerusalem Post*, May 11, 2014, accessed June 20, 2014, http://www.jpost.com/Jewish-World/Judaism /Active-listening-351878.

58. J. Jargon, "Fast-Food Turnaround: Popeyes Louisiana Kitchen CEO Cheryl Bachelder Talks About Her Secret for Repairing Relationships with Angry Franchisees," *Wall Street Journal*, March 10, 2014, R3.

59. Ibid.

60. Atwater, *I Hear You.*

61. C. Edwards, "Death of a Pushy Salesman," *BusinessWeek*, July 3, 2006, 108.

62. J. Sandberg, "Not Communicating with Your Boss? Count Your Blessings," *Wall Street Journal*, May 22, 2007, B1.

63. A. Tugend, "You've Been Doing a Fantastic Job. Just One Thing …," *The New York Times*, April 6, 2013, B5.

64. M. Flatt, "How to Give Feedback That Works," *Inc.*, December 21, 2011, accessed March 27, 2012, http://www.inc.com/michael-flatt/how-to-give -feedback-that-works.html.

65. "Satya Nadella's Email to Employees: Bold Ambition and Our Core," Microsoft, July 18, 2014, accessed July 20, 2014, http://www.microsoft.com /en-us/news/ceo/index.html.

66. Ibid.

67. C. Tuna, "Corporate News: Chambers Vows 'Fix' as Cisco Stumbles," *Wall Street Journal*, April 6, 2011, B2.

68. A. Bryant, "The Memo List: Where Everyone Has an Opinion," *New York Times*, March 10, 2012, accessed March 27, 2012, http://www.nytimes.com /2012/03/11/business/jim-whitehurst-of-red-hat-on -merits-of-an-open-culture.html.

69. D. Pontefract, "The Social C-Suite," *Chief Learning Officer Magazine*, March 13, 2013, accessed July 20, 2014, http://www.clomedia.com /articles/the-social-c-suite.

70. E. W. Morrison, "Organizational Silence: A Barrier to Change and Development in a Pluralistic World," *Academy of Management Review* 25 (2000): 706–725.

71. M. Heffernan, "Encourage Employees to Speak Up," *Inc*, April 9, 2014, accessed July 21, 2014, http://www.inc.com/margaret-heffernan /encourage-employees-to-speak-up.html.

72. R. Willingham, "Jetstar Pilots 'Afraid to Report Risks,'" *The Age*, March 19, 2011, accessed June 17, 2011, http://www.theage.com.au/travel/travel-news /jetstar-pilots-afraid-to-report-risks-20110318 -1c0mi.html.

73. Ibid.

74. "An Inside Look at Corporate Hotlines," Security Director's Report, February 2007, 8.

75. J. Laurie, "Perks at Work; Dealerships Promoting Culture That's Healthy, Motivating and Fun," *Automotive News*, October 18, 2012, accessed June 21, 2013, http://www.autonews.com/apps/pbcs .dll/article?AID=/20121018/RETAIL07/310229898 /dealerships-promoting-culture-thats-healthy -motivating-and-fun; J. LaReau, "Wolfchase Toyota -Scion, Cordova, Tenn.," *Automotive News*, October 18, 2012, accessed June 21, 2013, http://www.autonews .com/apps/pbcs.dll/article?AID=/20121018 /RETAIL07/310229979.

76. C. Hymowitz, "Sometimes, Moving Up Makes It Harder to See What Goes on Below," *Wall Street Journal*, October 15, 2007, B1.

77. A. Bryant, "Every Team Should Have a Devil's Advocate," *New York Times*, December 24, 2011, accessed June 21, 2013, http://www.nytimes.com /2011/12/25/business/ori-hadomi-of-mazor-robotics -on-choosing-devils-advocates.html?pagewanted=all.

78. R. Birch, "How GTE FCU Turned Itself Around After 'Closing Down the Shop,'" *Credit Union Journal*, June 18, 2012, 40.

79. D. Kirkpatrick and D. Roth, "Why There's No Escaping the Blog," *Fortune* (Europe), January 24, 2005, 64.

16

1. R. Leifer and P. K. Mills, "An Information Processing Approach for Deciding Upon Control Strategies and Reducing Control Loss in Emerging Organizations," *Journal of Management* 22 (1996): 113–137.

2. C. Passariello, "Fiercest Match of French Open Tennis Tournament? Raptor vs. Pigeon," *Wall Street Journal*, June 6, 2014, http://online.wsj.com /articles/fiercest-match-of-french-open-tennis -tournament-raptor-vs-pigeon-1402101392, http:// online.wsj.com/news/articles/SB1000142405270230 3442004579123412020578896.

3. J. Bookwalter, "Report: Apple Slows iPhone 5 Production to Address Aluminum Scratches," *TechRadar*, October 10, 2012, accessed June 21, 2013, http://www.techradar.com/us/news/phone -and-communications/mobile-phones/report-apple -slows-iphone-5-production-to-address-aluminum -scratches-1103440.

4. "Our Green Filter," *Green Depot*, accessed June 21, 2013, http://www.greendepot.com /greendepot/dept.asp?dept_id=12; N. Leiber, "With Eco-Friendly Building Supplies, Green Depot Thrives in the Construction Rebound," *Bloomberg Businessweek*, April 11, 2013, accessed June 21, 2013, http://www.businessweek.com /articles/2013-04-11/with-eco-friendly-building -supplies-green-depot-thrives-in-the-construction -rebound.

5. P. Bryan and P. Pane, "Evaluating Fire Service Delivery," *Fire Engineering*, April 2008, 207–210.

6. D. Robb, "Is Big Data Right for Small Business?" *Tech Page One*, June 26, 2014, accessed July 21, 2014, http://techpageone.dell.com/technology /is-big-data-right-for-small-business/.

7. Like. Landro, "Why Hospitals Want Patients to Ask Doctors, 'Have You Washed Your Hands?'" *Wall Street Journal*, September 30, 2013, accessed July 21, 2014, http://online.wsj.com/news/articles/SB1000142 4052702303918804579107202360565642.

8. T. Rosenberg, "An Electronic Eye on Hospital Hand-Washing," *New York Times*, November 24, 2011, http://opinionator.blogs.nytimes.com/2011/11/24 /an-electronic-eye-on-hospital-hand-washing.

9. Ibid.

10. N. Wiener, *Cybernetics; Or Control and Communication in the Animal and the Machine* (New York: Wiley, 1948).

11. Most. Rohde, "Squirrelly Behavior: Critters Shock the System," *Daily Reporter*, January 4, 2011, accessed June 20, 2011, http://dailyreporter .com/2011/01/04/squirrely-behavior-critters-shock -the-system/.

12. J. Mooallem, "Squirrel Power!" *New York Times*, August 31, 2013, accessed June 23, 2014, http://www.nytimes.com/2013/09/01/opinion /sunday/squirrel-power.html?pagewanted=all.

13. Ibid.

14. K. Stack, "Concussion-Sensing Chin Strap Raises Questions," *Wired.com*, March 26, 2012, accessed March 28, 2012, http://www.wired.com/playbook/2012/03/battle-sports-science-impact-indicator/.

15. Leifer and Mills, "An Information Processing Approach."

16. "Minn. Food Company Recalls About 1 Million Eggs in 34 States," *USA Today*, February 3, 2012, accessed March 28, 2012, http://yourlife.usatoday.com/fitness-food/safety/story/2012-02-03/Minn-food-company-recalls-eggs-in-34-states/52951110/1.

17. J. Lauritsen, "Apartment Hires DNA Lab to Tackle Dog Poop Problem," *CBS Minnesota*, May 25, 2012, accessed June 21, 2013, http://minnesota.cbslocal.com/2012/05/25/apartment-hires-dna-lab-to-tackle-dog-poop-problem/.

18. "Average Diesel Cost Falls for Second Straight Week," *HDT Truckinginfo*, May 12, 2014, accessed June 23, 2014, http://www.truckinginfo.com/channel/fuel-smarts/news/story/2014/05/average-diesel-cost-falls-for-second-straight-week.aspx.

19. "Kroger Co. Adopts Westport iCEPACKTM LNG Tank System for Sustainability and Savings," *PRNewswire*, May 6, 2014, accessed June 23, 2014, http://www.prnewswire.com/news-releases/kroger-co-adopts-westport-ice-pack-lng-tank-system-for-sustainability-and-savings-258148831.html.

20. C. Woodyard, "UPS Tries to Save Fuel by Cutting Weight," *USA Today*, June 9, 2011, accessed March 28, 2012, http://www.usatoday.com/money/autos/environment/2011-06-09-ups-vans-save-energy_n.htm.

21. M. Weber, *The Protestant Ethic and the Spirit of Capitalism* (New York: Scribner's, 1958).

22. B. Morris, "Truckers Tire of Government Sleep Rules," *Wall Street Journal*, accessed July 22, 2014, http://online.wsj.com/news/articles/SB10001424052702304672404579182522881942740.

23. D. Gibson, "Angus Barn's Eure: Peyton Manning Check Posting 'Horrible,'" *Triangle Business Journal*, March 7, 2012, accessed March 29, 2012, http://www.bizjournals.com/triangle/blog/2012/03/peyton-leaves-whopper-tip-at-angus-barn.html.

24. L. Scism, "State Farm Is There: As You Drive," *Wall Street Journal*, August 4, 2013, accessed July 22, 2014, http://online.wsj.com/news/articles/SB10001424127887323420604578647950497541958.

25. D. Dahl, "Breaking 3 Workplace Taboos," *Inc.*, March 1, 2011, accessed April 5, 2011, http://www.inc.com/magazine/20110301/breaking-3-workplace-taboos.html; D. Dahl, "A Radical Take on the Virtual Company," *Inc.*, March 1, 2011, accessed April 5, 2011, http://www.inc.com/magazine/20110301/philip-rosedale-on-freelancing-business-processes.html?nav=related.

26. Rajul, "Four Seasons Park Lane Shares Hiring Secrets," London Hotel Insight, January 24, 2011, accessed July 23, 2014, http://londonhotelsinsight.com/2011/01/24/four-seasons-park-lane-shares-hiring-secrets/.

27. "About Four Seasons: Nick Mutton," Four Seasons, accessed July 23, 2014, http://www.fourseasons.com/about_four_seasons/nick-mutton/.

28. A. Kadet, "City News—Metro Money/Jerks Need Not Apply," *Wall Street Journal*, January 18, 2014, accessed July 23, 2014, A16.

29. J. R. Barker, "Tightening the Iron Cage: Concertive Control in Self-Managing Teams," *Administrative Science Quarterly* 38 (1993): 408–437.

30. N. Byrnes, "The Art of Motivation," *BusinessWeek*, May 1, 2006, 56–62.

31. Barker, "Tightening the Iron Cage."

32. C. Manz and H. Sims, "Leading Workers to Lead Themselves: The External Leadership of Self-Managed Work Teams," *Administrative Science Quarterly* 32 (1987): 106–128.

33. J. Slocum and H. A. Sims, "Typology for Integrating Technology, Organization and Job Design," *Human Relations* 33 (1980): 193–212.

34. C. C. Manz and H. P. Sims, Jr., "Self-Management as a Substitute for Leadership: A Social Learning Perspective," *Academy of Management Review* 5 (1980): 361–367.

35. C. Manz and C. Neck, *Mastering Self-Leadership*, 3rd ed. (Upper Saddle River, NJ: Pearson, Prentice Hall, 2004).

36. R. S. Kaplan and D. P. Norton, "Using the Balanced Scorecard as a Strategic Management System," *Harvard Business Review* (January–February 1996): 75–85; R. S. Kaplan and D. P. Norton, "The Balanced Scorecard: Measures That Drive Performance," *Harvard Business Review* (January–February 1992): 71–79.

37. J. Meliones, "Saving Money, Saving Lives," *Harvard Business Review* (November–December 2000): 57–65.

38. S. L. Fawcett, "Fear of Accounts: Improving Managers' Competence and Confidence Through Simulation Exercises," *Journal of European Industrial Training* (February 1996): 17.

39. J. Cole, "New Boeing CFO's Assignment: Signal a Turnaround Quickly," *Wall Street Journal*, January 26, 1999, B1.

40. M. H. Stocks and A. Harrell, "The Impact of an Increase in Accounting Information Level on the Judgment Quality of Individuals and Groups," *Accounting, Organizations & Society* (October–November 1995): 685–700.

41. B. Morris, "Roberto Goizueta and Jack Welch: The Wealth Builders," *Fortune*, December 11, 1995, 80–94.

42. G. Colvin, "America's Best & Worst Wealth Creators: The Real Champions Aren't Always Who You Think. Here's an Eye-Opening Look at Which Companies Produce and Destroy the Most Money for Investors—Plus a New Tool for Spotting Future Winners," *Fortune*, December 18, 2000, 207.

43. "About Herman Miller: Operational Excellence," *Herman Miller*, accessed June 20, 2011, http://www.hermanmiller.com/About-Us/About-Herman-Miller/Operational-Excellence.

44. M. Schurman, "A Herman Miller Primer," *Herman Miller*, accessed June 20, 2011, http://www.hermanmiller.com/MarketFacingTech/hmc/about_us/News_Events_Media/Corporate_Backgrounder.pdf.

45. B. Stewart, *Best-Practice EVA: The Definitive Guide to Measuring and Maximizing Shareholder Value* (New York: Wiley Finance, 2013).

46. "Welcome Complaints," *Office of Consumer and Business Affairs*, Government of South Australia, accessed June 20, 2005, http://www.ocba.sa.gov.au/businessadvice/complaints/03_welcome.html.

47. C. B. Furlong, "12 Rules for Customer Retention," *Bank Marketing* 5 (January 1993): 14.

48. Customer retention graphs, *Vox, Inc.*, accessed August 1, 2009, http://www.voxinc.com/customer-experience-graphs/impact-customer-retention.htm.

49. M. Raphel, "Vanished Customers Are Valuable Customers," *Art Business News*, June 2002, 46.

50. C. A. Reeves and D. A. Bednar, "Defining Quality: Alternatives and Implications," *Academy of Management Review* 19 (1994): 419–445.

51. "Readers' Choice Awards: Top Airlines," *Condé Nast Traveler*, November 2013, accessed June 23, 2014, http://www.cntraveler.com/readers-choice-awards/airlines/best-airlines; "About Us: Singapore Airlines—Our Awards," *Singapore Airlines*, accessed June 23, 2014, http://www.singaporeair.com/en_UK/about-us/sia-history/sia-awards/.

52. S. Holmes, "Creature Comforts at 30,000 Feet," *BusinessWeek*, December 18, 2006, 138.

53. C. Krome, "Kia Optima Earns 'Best Value' Award, Debuts SX Limited," *Autobytel*, February 13, 2012, accessed March 29, 2012, http://www.autobytel.com/kia/optima/2012/news/kia-optima-earns-best-value-award-debuts-sx-limited-109911/.

54. D. R. May and B. L. Flannery, "Cutting Waste with Employee Involvement Teams," *Business Horizons*, September–October 1995, 28–38.

55. J. Carlton, "Some NFL Teams Are Going Green," *Wall Street Journal*, May 18, 2014, accessed June 23, 2014, http://online.wsj.com/news/articles/http://online.wsj.com/news/articles/SB10001424052702304677904579537882691550494.

56. M. Stein, "Talking About Waste with P&G," *Wall Street Journal*, September 12, 2011, R2.

57. A. K. Streeter, "H&M collects your old clothes to make new jeans," *treehugger*, May 30, 2014, accessed June 23, 2014, http://www.treehugger.com/corporate-responsibility/hm-collecting-your-old-clothes-make-new-jeans.html.

58. M. Perella, "How HP and Kyocera Are Applying Circular Economy to Printing," *The Guardian*, May 28, 2014, accessed June 23, 2014, http://www.theguardian.com/sustainable-business/hp-kyocera-circular-economy-printing.

59. L. Downing, "British Retailers Turn Waste into Power," *Bloomberg Businessweek*, June 14, 2012, accessed June 21, 2013, http://www.businessweek.com/articles/2012-06-14/british-retailers-turn-waste-into-power.

60. "The End of the Road: Schools and Computer Recycling," *Intel*, accessed September 5, 2008, http://www.intel.com/education/recycling_computers/recycling.htm.

61. M. Meece, "Giving Those Old Gadgets a Proper Green Burial," *New York Times*, January 6, 2011, accessed March 5, 2011, http://www.nytimes.com/2011/01/06/technology/personaltech/06basics.html?ref=recyclingofwastematerials.

17

1. R. Lenzner, "The Reluctant Entrepreneur," *Forbes*, September 11, 1995, 162–166.

2. "Inflation Calculator | Find US Dollar's Value from 1913-2014," US Inflation Calculator, accessed July 24, 2014, http://www.usinflationcalculator.com/; T. Lee, "Today's iPhone Is More Useful Than $3,000 Worth of Gadgets from a 1991 Radio Shack," *The Washington Post*, January 31, 2014, accessed July 24, 2014, http://www.washingtonpost.com/blogs/the-switch/wp/2014/01/31/todays-iphone-is-more-useful-than-3000-worth-of-gadgets-from-a-1991-radio-shack/.

3. S. Shankland, "Moore's Law: The Rule That Really Matters in Tech," *CNET*, October 15, 2012, accessed June 22, 2013, http://news.cnet.com/8301-11386_3-57526581-76/moores-law-the-rule-that-really-matters-in-tech/.

4. Zacks, "Pandora Listener Hours Up in May—Analyst Blog," *nasdaq.com*, June 5, 2014, accessed June 24, 2014, http://www.nasdaq.com/article/pandora-listener-hours-up-in-may-analyst-blog-cm359420.

5. H. Michael, "Updated Numbers: Beats Music Now Has 250,000 Subscribers," *PhoneArena*, May 29, 2014, accessed July 24, 2014, http://www.phonearena

.com/news/Updated-numbers-Beats-Music-now-has
-250000-subscribers_id56644; H. Karp and A. Barr,
"Apple Taps Tastemakers to Regain Music Mojo,"
Wall Street Journal, May 29, 2014, A1.

6. "Deezer," *Global Listener*, April 2, 2014, accessed
July 23, 2014, http://www.global-listener.com
/deezer-2/; J. Abbruzzese, "Spotify Hits 10 Million
Subscribers," *Mashable*, May 21, 2014, accessed
July 23, 2014, http://mashable.com/2014/05/21
/spotify-10-million-subscribers/; B. Nichols, "Were
Pandora Media's May Metrics Really That Bad?"
Wall St. Cheat Sheet, June 4, 2014, accessed June 24,
2014, http://wallstcheatsheet.com/business/were
-pandora-medias-may-metrics-really-that-bad.html/?a
=viewall.

7. D. A. Fields, "The Myth of First-Mover
Advantage," *Industry Week*, June 12, 2013,
accessed June 24, 2014, http://www.industryweek
.com/innovation/myth-first-mover-advantage.

8. F. Suarez and G. Lanzolla, "The Half-Truth of
First Mover Advantage," *Harvard Business Review*,
April 2005, accessed June 24, 2014, http://hbr.org
/2005/04/the-half-truth-of-first-mover-advantage
/ar/1.

9. S. Rothwell, "British Airways Crews Read Up
on VIPs on iPads," *Bloomberg Businessweek*,
February 15, 2012, accessed April 2, 2012, http://
www.bloomberg.com/news/2012-02-16/british
-airways-crews-tap-into-ipads-for-lowdown-on
-vip-flyers.html.

10. K. Linendoll, "NFL Playbooks: There's an
App for That," *ESPN*, November 6, 2012, accessed
June 22, 2013, http://espn.go.com/blog/playbook
/tech/post/_/id/2808/nfl-teams-prefer-ipads-over
-playbooks.

11. R. Smith, "Find the Best Checkout Line—
Retailers Try to Speed Up; What Works, What
Adds to Shopper Aggravation," *Wall Street Journal*,
December 8, 2011, D1.

12. J. Jargon, "Kroger's New Weapon: Infrared
Cameras—Technology Helps Kroger Reduce Wait
Times to 26 Seconds," *Wall Street Journal*, May 2,
2013, B4.

13. N. Bogart, "Canadian Airline First Air to Live
Stream Black Box Data," *Global News*, May 6,
2014, accessed June 24, 2014, http://globalnews
.ca/news/1314398/canadian-airline-first-air-to-live
-stream-black-box-data/.

14. D. Stacey and G. Raghuvanshi, "Malaysia
Airlines Flight 370: Contractor Will Get 300 Days
to Complete Search," *Wall Street Journal*, June 4,
2014, accessed July 24, 2014, http://online.wsj.com
/articles/contractor-will-get-300-days-to-complete
-malaysia-airlines-flight-370-search-1401849756.

15. A. Pasztor and J. Ostrower, "Missing Malaysia
Jet Adds Fuel to 'Live Black Box' Debate," *Wall
Street Journal*, March 9, 2014, accessed June 24,
2014, http://online.wsj.com/news/articles/SB100014
2405270230402010457942923351 6692014
?KEYWORDS=missing+malaysia+jet+adds
+fuel&mg=reno64-wsj.

16. Bogart, "Canadian Airline First Air to Live
Stream Black Box Data."

17. D. Hernandez, "Artificial Intelligence Is Now
Telling Doctors How to Treat You," *Wired*, June 2,
2014, accessed June 24, 2014, http://www.wired
.com/2014/06/ai-healthcare/.

18. Ibid.

19. Associated Press, "Syrup-makers Go High-Tech
with Wireless Monitoring," *Wall Street Journal*,
April 1, 2014, accessed June 24, 2014, http://online
.wsj.com/article/APe9ecdb54499c4294840e59e
763ef3e38.html?KEYWORDS=monitoring.

20. C. Kang, "Experts: Google Privacy Shift
Will Have Greater Impact on Android Users,"
Washington Post, January 25, 2012, accessed April 2,
2012, http://www.washingtonpost.com/business
/technology/google-sees-profit-in-tracking-users
/2012/01/25/gIQAfDJVRQ_story.html; "Google
Invests $300 Million in Hong Kong Datacenter,"
PCWorld, December 11, 2011, accessed April 2,
2012, http://www.pcworld.com/article/245982
/google_invests_300_million_in_hong_kong
_datacenter.html; S. Grundberg and N. Rolander,
"For Data Center, Google Goes for the Cold,"
Wall Street Journal, September 12, 2011, accessed
April 2, 2012, http://online .wsj.com/article/SB10
0014240531119048361045765605510055 70810.
html; S. Mahtani, "Google to Invest $120 Million
in Singapore Data Center," *Wall Street Journal*,
December 15, 2011, accessed April 2, 2012, http://
online.wsj.com/article/SB10001424052970204026 80
4577099453458240254.html.

21. R. Miller, "Facebook Decloaks, Confirms Plans
for Iowa Server Farm," *Data Center Knowledge*,
April 23, 2013, accessed June 22, 2013, http://www
.datacenterknowledge.com/archives/2013/04/23
/facebook-decloaks-confirms-plans-for-iowa-server
-farm/.

22. E. Dwoskin and G. Bensinger, "Hot New
Thing at the Mall: Heat Maps Track Shoppers,"
Wall Street Journal, December 9, 2013, B1.

23. K. Kamenec, "How Apples iBeacon Could
Upend Retail Shopping," *PC Magazine*, October 24,
2013, accessed July 25, 2014, http://www.pcmag
.com/article2/0,2817,2425052,00.asp.

24. S. Ramachandran, "Netflix Will Pay Comcast
for Speed," *Wall Street Journal*, February 24, 2014,
A1; S. Ramachandran and D. Fitzgerald, "For Web
Firms, Faster Access Comes at a Price," *Wall Street
Journal*, June 19, 2013, B1.

25. S. Lubar, *Infoculture: The Smithsonian Book
of Information Age Inventions* (Boston: Houghton
Mifflin, 1993).

26. Ibid.

27. No author, "Square Deal: Mobile Marketing,"
June 16, 2012, 76.

28. G.M., "They've Got Sklz," *Entrepreneur*,
January 2012, 43.

29. B. Worthen, "Bar Codes on Steroids," *CIO*,
December 15, 2002, 53.

30. B. Barnes, "At Disney Parks, a Bracelet Meant
to Build Loyalty (and Sales)," *New York Times*,
January 7, 2013, accessed June 22, 2013, http://
www.nytimes.com/2013/01/07/business/media
/at-disney-parks-a-bracelet-meant-to-build-loyalty
-and-sales.html?pagewanted=all&_r=0; M. Wilson,
"A $1 Billion Project to Remake the Disney World
Experience, Using RFID," *FastCoDesign*, accessed
June 22, 2013, http://www.fastcodesign.com
/1671616/a-1-billion-project-to-remake-the
-disney-world-experience-using-rfid#1.

31. N. Rubenking, "Hidden Messages," *PC
Magazine*, May 22, 2001, 86.

32. D. Carr, "Giving Viewers What They Want,"
New York Times, February 24, 2013, accessed
June 22, 2013, http:// www.nytimes.com/2013/02/25
/business/media/for-house-of-cards-using-big-data
-to-guarantee-its-popularity.html?pagewanted=all.

33. E. Dwoskin, "How New York's Fire Department
Uses Data Mining," *Wall Street Journal* (Digits blog),
January 24, 2014, 2:12 p.m., accessed June 24, 2014,
http://blogs.wsj.com/digits/2014/01/24/how-new
-yorks-fire-department-uses-data-mining/.

34. Rubenking, "Hidden Messages."

35. C. Duhigg, "How Companies Learn Your
Secrets," *New York Times*, February 16, 2012,
accessed April 3, 2012, http://www.nytimes
.com/2012/02/19/magazine/shopping-habits
.html?pagewanted=all.

36. S. Rosebush and M. Totty, "How Big Data Is
Changing the Whole Equation for Business," *Wall
Street Journal*, March 11, 2013, R1.

37. Ibid.

38. D. Yadron, P. Ziobro, and B. Devlin, "Target
Staff Had Warnings," *Wall Street Journal*,
February 15, 2014, B1; D. Yadron, P. Ziobro,
and C. Levinson, "Target Says Hackers Used
Credentials from Vendor," *Wall Street Journal*,
January 20, 2014, B1.

39. S. Banjo, S. Germano, and D. Johnson, "Traffic
at Target Declines—Transactions Slip 3% to 4% on
Busy Weekend in Wake of Customer Data Breach,"
Wall Street Journal, December 23, 2014, B3.

40. B. Gottesman and K. Karagiannis, "A False Sense
of Security," *PC Magazine*, February 22, 2005, 72.

41. F. J. Derfler, Jr., "Secure Your Network," *PC
Magazine*, June 27, 2000, 183–200.

42. "Authentication," *PC Magazine*, accessed
June 24, 2014, http://www.pcmag.com/encyclopedia
/term/38192/authentication.

43. "Authorization," *PC Magazine*, accessed
June 24, 2014, http://www.pcmag.com/encyclopedia
/term/38202/authorization.

44. L. Seltzer, "Password Crackers," *PC Magazine*,
February 12, 2002, 68.

45. "Two-Factor Authentication," *Information
Security Glossary*, accessed June 28, 2009, http://
www.rsa.com.

46. W. Gordon, "Here's Everywhere You Should
Enable Two-Factor Authentication Right Now,"
LifeHacker, December 10, 2013, accessed July 26,
2014, http://lifehacker.com/5938565/heres
-everywhere-you-should-enable-two-factor
-authentication-right-now; L. Tung, "Google to
Slap Two-Factor Across Apps via Suspicious Logins
Trigger," *ZD Net*, May 15, 2014, accessed June 24,
2014, http://www.zdnet.com/google-to-slap-two
-factor-across-apps-via-suspicious-logins-trigger
-7000029476/.

47. C. Metz "Total Security," *PC Magazine*,
October 1, 2003, B3.

48. J. DeAvila, "Wi-Fi Users, Beware: Hot Spots
Are Weak Spots," *Wall Street Journal*, January 16,
2008, D1.

49. G. A. Fowler, "You Won't Believe How Ador-
able This Kitty Is! Click For More!" *Wall Street
Journal*, March 26, 2013, accessed June 24, 2014,
http://online.wsj.com/news/articles/SB10001424127
887324373204578373011392662962?mg
=reno64-wsj.

50. Ibid.

51. J. van den Hoven, "Executive Support Systems
& Decision Making," *Journal of Systems Management* 47, no. 8 (March–April 1996): 48.

52. D. Hannon, "Colgate-Palmolive Empowers
Senior Leaders with Executive Dashboards,"
InsiderProfiles, April 1, 2011, accessed June 26,
2011, http://insiderprofiles.wispubs.com/article
.aspx?iArticleId=5720.

53. "Intranet," *PC Magazine*, accessed June 24,
2014, http://www.pcmag.com/encyclopedia
/term/45310/intranet.

54. "Accorda Therapeutics Announces Company
Intranet Named One of Ten Best in the World,"
Yahoo! Finance, February 14, 2013, accessed
June 24, 2013, http://finance.yahoo.com/news
/acorda-therapeutics-announces-company
-intranet-120000651.html; K. Kass, "It's Not
Always the Size That Counts in Internal Communication," *Simply-communicate.com*, http://
www.simply-communicate.com/case-studies
/company-profile/it%E2%80%99s-not-always
-size-counts-internal-communication.

55. "Web Services," *PC Magazine*, accessed June 24, 2014, http://www.pcmag.com/encyclopedia/term/54345/web-services.

56. S. Overby, "This Could Be the Start of Something Small," *CIO*, February 15, 2003, 54.

57. "Extranet," *PC Magazine*, accessed June 24, 2014, http://www.pcmag.com/encyclopedia/term/42945/extranet.

58. "Mitsubishi Opens Sales/Training Center; Establishes Online Creative Centers," *Contracting Business.com*, March 27, 2012, accessed April 3, 2012, http://contractingbusiness.com/news/Mitsubishi-training-creative-centers-0328/.

59. M. Hickins, "Hertz Counts on Self-Service Kiosks to Spur Growth," *Wall Street Journal*, May 8, 2012, accessed June 22, 2013, http://blogs.wsj.com/drivers-seat/2012/05/08/hertz-counts-on-self-service-kiosks-to-spur-growth/.

60. S. Hamm, D. Welch, W. Zellner, F. Keenan, and F. Engardio, "Down But Hardly Out: Downturn Be Damned, Companies Are Still Anxious to Expand Online," *BusinessWeek*, March 26, 2001, 126.

61. K. C. Laudon and J. P. Laudon, *Management Information Systems: Organization and Technology* (Upper Saddle River, NJ: Prentice Hall, 1996).

62. J. Borzo, "Software for Symptoms," *Wall Street Journal*, May 23, 2005, R10.

63. Ibid.

64. R. Hernandez, "American Express Authorizer's Assistant," *Business Rules Journal*, August 2001, accessed June 26, 2011, http://bizrules.info/page/art_amexaa.htm.

18

1. N. Shirouzu, "In China, Making Cars on a Budget," *Wall Street Journal*, December 20, 2012, accessed April 9, 2012, http://online.wsj.com/article/SB10001424052748704610904576031293046766076.html?mod=WSJ_business_whatsNews; "Table—China 2011 Car Sales Up 5.2 Percent," *Reuters*, January 16, 2012, accessed April 9, 2012, http://www.reuters.com/article/2012/01/17/autos-china-idUSL3E8CH0V920120117.

2. J. Miller, "Remade in the USA: Indiana Steel Mill Revived with Lessons from Abroad," *Wall Street Journal*, May 21, 2012, A1.

3. G. Polek, "Automation Key to Boeing 777 Production Rate Increase," *AINonline*, June 17, 2013, accessed June 23, 2013, http://www.ainonline.com/aviation-news/paris-air-show/2013-06-17/automation-key-boeing-777-production-rate-increase.

4. Ibid; Web Desk, "Boeing Delivers First 777 Built with Faster Production Rate," *Q13Fox.com*, February 26, 2013, accessed June 23, 2013, http://q13fox.com/2013/02/26/boeing-delivers-first-777-built-with-faster-production-rate/.

5. "Employment Cost Index News Release Text," *Bureau of Labor Statistics*, April 30, 2014, accessed July 27, 2014, http://www.bls.gov/news.release/eci.nr0.htm; "Productivity and Costs: First Quarter 2014, Revised," *Bureau of Labor Statistics*, June 4, 2013, accessed July 27, 2014, http://www.bls.gov/news.release/prod2.nr0.htm.

6. "Historical Income Tables—Families: Table F-23—Families by Total Money Income, Race, and Hispanic Origin of Householder: 1967 to 2012," *US Census Bureau, Current Population Survey, Annual Social and Economic Supplements*, accessed June 9, 2014, http://www.census.gov/hhes/www/income/data/historical/families/.

7. Ibid.

8. The Conference Board Total Economy Data Base, Summary Statistics 1997–2014, "Table 3: Growth of Labor Productivity, Real GDP and Total Hours Worked by Region for Advanced Countries, 1997–2014," *The Conference Board*, accessed July 27, 2014, http://www.conference-board.org/retrievefile.cfm?filename=SummaryTables_Jan20141.pdf&type=subsite.

9. Economic New Release, "Employment Projections, Table 1: Civilian Labor Force by Sex, Age, Race, and Ethnicity, 1992, 2002, 2012, and projected 2022," *Bureau of Labor Statistics*, December 19, 2013, accessed June 25, 2015, http://www.bls.gov/news.release/ecopro.t01.htm.

10. "Charitable Giving Statistics," *National Philanthropic Trust*, accessed June 25, 2014, http://www.nptrust.org/philanthropic-resources/charitable-giving-statistics/.

11. "GDP per Capita by Country 1980-2013: United States," Knoema, accessed July 27, 2014, http://knoema.com/pjeqzh/gdp-per-capita-by-country-1980-2013.

12. "Philanthropy in the American Economy," *Council of Economic Advisers*, February 19, 2002, accessed April 13, 2009, http://clinton4.nara.gov/media/pdf/philanthropy.pdf.

13. M. Perry, "Christmas Shopping 1958 vs. 2012 Illustrates the 'Miracle of the Marketplace' Which Delivers Better and Cheaper Goods," *American Enterprise Institute*, December 28, 2013, accessed July 27, 2014, http://www.aei-ideas.org/2013/12/christmas-shopping-1958-vs-2012-illustrates-the-miracle-of-the-marketplace-which-delivers-better-and-cheaper-goods/.

14. "European Airline Labor Productivity: CAPA Rankings," *CAPA Centre for Aviation*, April 9, 2013, accessed June 23, 2013, http://centreforaviation.com/analysis/european-airline-labour-productivity-capa-rankings-104204.

15. "Productivity (MFP): Frequently Asked Questions," Bureau of Labor Statistics, accessed July 28, 2014, http://www.bls.gov/mfp/mprfaq.htm#1.

16. J. Loehrke and A. Carey, "Report: Average Price of New Car Hits Record in August," *USA Today*, September 5, 2013, accessed July 28, 2014, http://www.usatoday.com/story/money/cars/2013/09/04/record-price-new-car-august/2761341/.

17. C. Woodyard and F. Meier, "GM Makes Big Move Up in J.D. Power Quality Survey," *USA Today*, June 19, 2012, accessed June 23, 2013, http://www.usatoday.com/story/money/cars/2013/06/19/jd-power-initial-quality-survey-gm-ford/2437115/.

18. "Basic Quality Concepts," *American Society for Quality*, accessed August 2, 2009, http://www.asq.org/learn-about-quality/basic-concepts.html.

19. R. E. Markland, S. K. Vickery, and R. A. Davis, "Managing Quality" (Chapter 7), in *Operations Management: Concepts in Manufacturing and Services* (Cincinnati, OH: South-Western College Publishing, 1998).

20. J. Ewoldt, "A Brighter Day for LED Bulbs," *StarTribune*, April 3, 2013, accessed June 23, 2013, http://www.startribune.com/business/201357281.html?refer=y; M. White, "Light Switch: Why You'll Start Using LED Bulbs This Year," *Time*, April 25, 2013, accessed June 23, 2013, http://business.time.com/2013/04/25/light-switch-why-youll-start-using-led-bulbs-this-year/.

21. L. L. Berry and A. Parasuraman, *Marketing Services* (New York: Free Press, 1991).

22. asymco-admin, "The Quantum Leap in Retail," *Asymco*, October 31, 2013, accessed June 25, 2014, http://www.asymco.com/2013/10/31/the-quantum-leap-in-retail/; R. Devine, "Apple Retail Store Numbers Are Up, 30 New Stores for Fiscal 2014," iMore, October 28, 2013, accessed July 28, 2014, http://www.imore.com/apple-retail-store-numbers-are-30-new-stores-fiscal-2014.

23. "Apple, Murphy USA, Tiffany & Co. Top New eMarketer Store Productivity Rankings," *eMarketer Retail*, May 26, 2014, accessed July 28, 2014, http://retail.emarketer.com/apple-murphy-usa-tiffany-co-top-new-emarketer-store-productivity-rankings/.

24. "About ISO," *International Organization for Standardization*, accessed June 25, 2014, http://www.iso.org/iso/home/about.htm.

25. "ISO 9000 Essentials," and "ISO 14000 Essentials," *International Organization for Standardization*, accessed September 12, 2009, http://www.iso.org/iso/iso_catalogue/management_standards/iso_9000_iso_14000.htm.

26. J. Briscoe, S. Fawcett, and R. Todd, "The Implementation and Impact of ISO 9000 Among Small Manufacturing Enterprises," *Journal of Small Business Management* 43 (July 1, 2005): 309.

27. R. Henkoff, "The Hot New Seal of Quality (ISO 9000 Standard of Quality Management)," *Fortune*, June 28, 1993, 116.

28. "Frequently Asked Questions About the Malcolm Baldrige National Quality Award," *National Institute of Standards and Technology*, accessed September 12, 2009, http://www.nist.gov/public_affairs/factsheet/baldfaqs.htm.

29. "Baldrige Award Process Fees," *National Institute of Standards and Technology*, accessed June 25, 2014, http://www.nist.gov/baldrige/enter/award_fees.cfm.

30. "Frequently Asked Questions About the Malcolm Baldrige National Quality Award."

31. Ibid.

32. "Criteria for Performance Excellence," *Baldrige National Quality Program 2008*, accessed September 15, 2008, http://www.quality.nist.gov/PDF_files/2008_Business_Criteria.pdf.

33. Ibid.

34. D. C. Moody, "Beam Integral Part of Prestigious Baldridge Program," *theeasleyprogress.com*, June 4, 2014, accessed June 25, 2014, http://www.theeasleyprogress.com/news/home_top_news/4915403/Beam-integral-part-of-prestigious-Baldridge-Program.

35. J. W. Dean, Jr., and J. Evans, *Total Quality: Management, Organization, and Strategy* (St. Paul, MN: West, 1994).

36. J. W. Dean, Jr., and D. E. Bowen, "Management Theory and Total Quality: Improving Research and Practice Through Theory Development," *Academy of Management Review* 19 (1994): 392–418.

37. "Alaska Airlines Awards and Recognition," Alaska Airlines, accessed June 23, 2013, http://www.alaskaair.com/content/about-us/newsroom/alaska-awards.aspx; M. Kaminsky, "The Weekend Interview with Bill Ayer: An Airline That Makes Money—Really," *Wall Street Journal*, February 4, 2012, A13; T. Maxon, "JetBlue Leads American Customer Satisfaction Index for Second Year," *Dallas Morning News*, June 18, 2012, accessed June 23, 2013, http://aviationblog.dallasnews.com/2013/06/jetblue-leads-american-consumer-satisfaction-index-for-second-year.html/.

38. S. McCartney, "A World Where Flights Aren't Canceled," *Wall Street Journal*, April 2, 2014, accessed July 28, 2014, http://online.wsj.com/news/articles/SB10001424052702303987004579477412359027986.

39. J. Miller, "Remade in the USA: Indiana Steel Mill Revived with Lessons from Abroad," *Wall Street Journal*, May 21, 2012, A1.

40. R. Hallowell, L. A. Schlesinger, and J. Zornitsky, "Internal Service Quality, Customer and Job Satisfaction: Linkages and Implications for Management," *Human Resource Planning* 19 (1996): 20–31; J. L. Heskett, T. O. Jones, G. W. Loveman,

W. E. Sasser, Jr., and L. A. Schlesinger, "Putting the Service-Profit Chain to Work," *Harvard Business Review* (March–April 1994): 164–174.

41. L. Drell, "6 Companies with Awesome Employee Perks," *Mashable Business*, August 7, 2011, accessed April 9, 2012, http://mashable.com/2011/08/07/startup-employee-perks/.

42. J. Paravantis, N. Bouranta, and L. Chitiris, "The Relationship Between Internal and External Service Quality," *International Journal of Contemporary Hospital Management* 21 (2009): 275–293.

43. G. Brewer, "The Ultimate Guide to Winning Customers: The Customer Stops Here," *Sales & Marketing Management* 150 (March 1998): 30; F. F. Reichheld, *The Loyalty Effect: The Hidden Force Behind Growth, Profits, and Lasting Value* (Cambridge, MA: Harvard Business School Press, 2001).

44. J. Heskett, T. Jones, G. Loveman, E. Sasser, and L. Schlesinger, "Putting the Service-Profit Chain to Work," *Harvard Business Review* 86 (July–August 2008): 118–129.

45. L. L. Berry and A. Parasuraman, "Listening to the Customer—The Concept of a Service-Quality Information System," *Sloan Management Review* 38, no. 3 (Spring 1997): 65; C. W. L. Hart, J. L. Heskett, and W. E. Sasser, Jr., "The Profitable Art of Service Recovery," *Harvard Business Review* (July–August 1990): 148–156.

46. A. L. Rodgers, "A 5-Point Plan for Making the Most of Customer Complaints," *Inc.*, January 14, 2014, accessed June 25, 2014, http://www.inc.com/the-build-network/a-5-point-plan-for-making-the-most-of-customer-complaints.html.

47. "Great Customer Service from the Mission Bicycle Company," *37signals.com*, August 16, 2011, accessed April 9, 2012, http://37signals.com/svn/posts/2989-great-customer-service-from-the-mission-bicycle-company.

48. D. E. Bowen and E. E. Lawler III, "The Empowerment of Service Workers: What, Why, How, and When," *Sloan Management Review* 33 (Spring 1992): 31–39; D. E. Bowen and E. E. Lawler III, "Empowering Service Employees," *Sloan Management Review* 36 (Summer 1995): 73–84.

49. Bowen and Lawler, "The Empowerment of Service Workers: What, Why, How, and When."

50. J. Shelly, "Empowering Employees," *Human Resource Executive*, October 2, 2011, accessed April 9, 2012, http://www.hreonline.com/HRE/story.jsp?storyId=533341639.

51. "Customer Service and Business Results: A Survey of Customer Service from Mid-Size Companies," *ZenDesk*, April 2013, accessed July 28, 2014, http://cdn.zendesk.com/resources/whitepapers/Zendesk_WP_Customer_Service_and_Business_Results.pdf.

52. B. Gruel and S. Singh, "Deere's Big Green Profit Machine," *Bloomberg Businessweek*, July 5, 2012, accessed June 23, 2013, http://www.businessweek.com/articles/2012-07-05/deeres-big-green-profit-machine.

53. D. Lavrinc, "Peek Inside Tesla's Robotic Factory," *Wired*, July 16, 2013, accessed June 25, 2014, http://www.wired.com/2013/07/tesla-plant-video/.

54. "Job Shop Hits Bull's Eye with Multitasking," *Manufacturing Engineering* (November 2008): 43–105.

55. J. Bennett and J. Hromadko, "Rare Resin in Shortage After Explosion in Germany; Auto Makers Scramble to Avoid Production Cuts," *Wall Street Journal*, April 18, 2012, B1.

56. S. Ante, "Is This Toy on Your Kid's List? Santa Tried Hard But…," *Wall Street Journal*, December 16, 2011, accessed June 23, 2013, http://online.wsj.com/article/SB10001424052970204844504577100812809564298.html.

57. D. Drickhamer, "Reality Check," *Industry Week*, November 2001, 29.

58. D. Drickhamer, "Zeroing In on World-Class," *Industry Week*, November 2001, 36.

59. "Gartner Announces Rankings of Its 2012 Supply Chain Top 25," *Gartner*, May 22, 2012, accessed June 12, 2013, http://www.gartner.com/newsroom/id/2023116; S. Sage, "Apple Boasts Strongest Manufacturing Supply Chain in the World, Turns Over Inventory in Five Days," *iMore*, June 1, 2012, accessed June 23, 2013, http://www.imore.com/apple-boasts-strongest-supply-chain-world-turns-inventory-days.

60. "Efficient Foodservice Response (EFR)," accessed August 3, 2009, http://www.ifdaonline.org/webarticles.

61. J. R. Henry, "Minimized Setup Will Make Your Packaging Line S.M.I.L.E.," *Packaging Technology & Engineering*, February 1, 1998, 24.

62. J. Donoghue, "The Future Is Now," *Air Transport World*, April 1, 2001, 78; D. Evans, "Aftermarket Outlook," *Aviation Maintenance Magazine*, May 1, 2006, accessed September 13, 2006, http://www.aviationtoday.com.

63. K. Clark, "An Eagle Eye for Inventory," *Chain Store Age*, May 2005, Supplement, 8A.

64. "The Way I Work: Marc Lore of Diapers.com," *Inc.*, September 1, 2009, accessed March 15, 2010, http://www.inc.com/magazine/20090901/the-way-i-work-marc-lore-of-diaperscom.html.

65. E. Powell, Jr., and F. Sahin, "Economic Production Lot Sizing with Periodic Costs and Overtime," *Decision Sciences* 32 (2001): 423–452.

66. "Gartner Announces Rankings of Its 2012 Supply Chain Top 25," *Gartner*, May 22, 2012, accessed June 23, 2013, http://www.gartner.com/newsroom/id/2023116; S. Sage, "Apple Boasts Strongest Manufacturing Supply Chain in the World, Turns Over Inventory in Five Days," *iMore*, June 1, 2012, accessed June 23, 2013, http://www.imore.com/apple-boasts-strongest-supply-chain-world-turns-inventory-days.

67. N. Shirouzu, "Why Toyota Wins Such High Marks on Quality Surveys," *Wall Street Journal*, March 15, 2001, A1.

68. Ibid.

69. G. Gruman, "Supply on Demand; Manufacturers Need to Know What's Selling Before They Can Produce and Deliver Their Wares in the Right Quantities," *Info World*, April 18, 2005, accessed April 15, 2009, http://www.infoworld.com.

Index

A

A-type conflict (affective conflict), 105, 210
AB InBev, 184
ABC, 53
ABC Fine Wine & Spirits, 229
"ABCD" trading houses, 126
AbleData, 258
ABM Industries, 123–124
Above-market wages, 241
Absolute comparisons, 100
Academic journals, 25
Academy of Management Journal, 25
Academy of Management Perspectives, 25
Academy of Management Review, 25
Accenture, 286–287
Acceptance of managerial authority, 38
Accepted goals, 286
Access and legitimacy paradigm, 261
Accommodations for disabilities, 258
Accommodative strategy, 85
Accu-Screen Inc., 227
Ace Hardware, 116, 117
Acer Group, 47
Achievement-oriented leadership, 301, 302
Acorda Therapeutics, 243, 369
Acquisition, 119
Acquisition cost, 357–358
Action plan, 92
Active listening, 326
Acxiom, 357–358
Adaptability, 61
Adaptability screening, 176
Adaptive strategies, 127–128
Additive manufacturing, 385
Adidas, 84
Administrative management, 32–33, 34
Administrative Science Quarterly, 25
Adverse impact, 222
Advocacy groups, 56–57
Adware, 365
Adworkshop, 242
Affective conflict, 105, 210
Affirmative action, 250–251
Affordable Care Act, 75
Agarwal, Ajay, 4
Age discrimination, 253–254
Age Discrimination in Employment Act, 220
Agreeableness, 259

Agricultural commodities, 126
Ahrendts, Angela, 142
Ainsworth, Bill, 131
Air France, 377
AirAsia Japan, 114
Airline industry, 46–47
Airline mergers, 46–47
Airport security, 361
AirTran Airways, 47, 79
al-Farabi, 24
Alaska Airlines, 382–383
Albemarle Paper Co. v. Moody, 224
Alcarcer, Juan, 123
Alderfer's ERG theory, 270, 271
Aldi, 115
Alibaba, 5
All Nippon Airways (ANA), 114
Allaire, Paul A., 265
Allan, Ant, 364
Alliance for Wireless Power (A4WP), 138
Allstate, 321
Alpha House and Betas, 128
Alpha Natural Resources, 303
Altos Research, 125
Amazon, 3, 4, 12, 65, 112, 128, 130, 131, 172, 226, 234, 275, 393
Amazon Instant Video, 53
Amazon MP3, 113
Amazon Prime, 128
Amazon Web Services (AWS), 125
Ambrose, David, 380
AMD Industries, 221
American Airlines, 46, 47, 275, 355
American Express, 372
American Society of Quality, 381
American Standard Brands, 166
American Superconductor, 275
Americans with Disabilities Act, 220
AMP, 176
Analyzers, 128
Anand, Rohini, 266
AnchorFree Hotspot Shield, 367
Ancient Egypt, 24
Ancient Sumer, 23, 24
Anderson, Dave, 285
Andreessen, Marc, 61
Andreessen Horowitz (AH), 61
Android devices, 112
Angus Barn, 340
Ansys, 145
Antivirus software, 366
AOL, 64

AOptix Technologies, 361
APEC, *see* Asia-Pacific Economic Cooperation
Apollo Tyres Ltd., 155
APPLE, 380
Apple, 3, 45, 54, 85, 107, 111–113, 187, 277, 335, 347, 369, 380
Apple App Store, 112
Apple TV, 53
Application forms, 227
Aptitude tests, 229
ArcellorMittal, 375, 383
Archer Daniels Midland, 126
Armstrong, Neil, 96
Armstrong, Tim, 64
Arrivers, 15
Artists Against Fracking (AAF), 56
Artman, Tuomas, 150
As You Sow, 80
ASEAN, *see* Association of Southeast Asian Nations
Asia-Pacific Economic Cooperation (APEC), 161
Assemble-to-order operations, 387
Assembly line, 24
Assessment centers, 231
Assistive technology, 258
Association of Southeast Asian Nations (ASEAN), 160, 161
Association or affinity patterns, 362
Assurance, 380
Asus, 47
Asustek, 301
Atkinson, Cliff, 332
AT&T, 4, 16, 78, 122, 130, 138, 206
Attack, 130, 131
Attention, 314
Attribution theory, 315–316
Aubuchon Hardware, 116
Audi Group, 204
Australian and International Pilots Association, 330
Authentication, 364
Authority, 186–189
Authority and responsibility, 34, 36
Authority-compliance leadership style, 295, 296
Authorization, 364–365
Autonomous work group, 341
Autonomy, 192
Average aggregated inventory, 390
Avis, 242
Avoidance learning, 283

Avoidance strategy, 171
Avon, 96, 223
Awareness training, 264
Axcelis Technologies, 175
Axe, 127
Axis Performance Advisors, 206

B

Bachelder, Cheryl, 326
Background checks, 228–229
Background questions, 232
Badstübner, Achim, 204
Balance sheet, 345
Balanced scorecard, 343–344
Baldridge National Quality Award,
    381–382
Ballmer, Steve, 149
Bank of America, 209
Bank Wiring Room, 37
Bar code, 360
Bar Raisers, 65
Barbarigo, 24
Barclays Bank, 201
Barclays Plc, 124
Bargaining power of buyers, 126
Bargaining power of suppliers, 126
Barnard, Chester, 38
Barnes, Brenda, 292
Barnes & Noble, 130
Barney's, 307
Barrile, Parker, 224
Basic perception process, 313–314
Bassett, Justin, 219
Batch production, 388
Bates, Suzanne, 323
Batra, Raj, 235
Bayod, Marion, 162
BCG matrix, 120–122
"Be Here Now," 64
Beam, Betsy, 382
Beats Music (Apple), 354
Beatty, Sarah, 336
*Becoming a Manager: Mastery of a New
    Identity* (Hill), 17
Bed, Bath, & Beyond, 128
Behavior control, 340
Behavior observation scale (BOS),
    237, 238
Behavioral addition, 63, 64
Behavioral questions, 232
Behavioral substitution, 63, 64
Benchmarking, 336
Bennis, Warren, 291
Berg, Natalie, 90
Berkenstock, Dan, 57
Bernard, Suzanne, 175
Best Buy, 128, 132, 351
Betraying a trust, 16
Bezos, Jeff, 12, 65, 234

BFOQ, *see* Bona fide occupational
    qualification
Bhatt, Paurvi, 322
Big Five personality dimensions,
    259–260
Big Mac index, 169
Bill of materials, 394
Bing, 174
Biographical data (biodata), 230–231
Biometrics, 361, 364
BIS, *see* Business intelligence software
Bish, Walter, 242
Biying, 174
BlackBerry, 45
Blake/Mouton leadership grid, 295, 296
Blinded stage of organizational
    decline, 146
Blog, 331, 333
Bloomberg, Michael, 55
Boeing, 201, 206, 226, 345, 375
Bohlmann, Jaya, 264
Bombardier Aerospace, 175
**Bona fide occupational qualification
    (BFOQ),** 221
Booz Allen Hamilton, 224–225
Borders, 99
BOS, *see* Behavior observation scale
Boston Consulting Group (BCG)
    matrix, 120–122
Bosworth, Andrew, 92
Boukas, Ioannis, 226–227
Bowers, Kim, 10
Box.com, 125
Boycott, 56–57
BPV Capital Management, 62
Brainstorming, 106
Brancucci, Joe, 333
Bratzel, Stefan, 89
Brewer, Howard "Hal," 78
Bribery, 83
Bridgewater Associates, 105
British Airways, 355, 377
Broadcast voice mail, 330
Broker, 199
Brother Jimmy's BBQ, 55
Brown, Gary, 78
Brown, Reginald, Jr., 265
Bryant, Adam, 97
Budget, 345
Budgeting, 98
Bueno, Carlos, 227
Build-to-stock operations, 387
Bunge Ltd., 126
Burberry, 142
Bureau of Labor Statistics website, 69
Bureaucracy, 30, 31
Bureaucratic control, 339–340
Bureaucratic immunity, 213
Bureaucratic management, 30–32
Burger King, 53, 130

Burke, Carolyn, 64
Burns, Ursula, 255, 265
Burns Harbor, 383
Business Confidence Index (Small
    Business Research Board), 50
Business confidence indices, 50
Business intelligence software
    (BIS), 359
Business Plans to Game Plans
    (King), 98
Business Wire, 12
Buyer dependence, 54
Buzzwords, 319
Byron, Kristin, 324

C

C-type conflict (cognitive conflict),
    104, 210
CA Technologies, 78
Cable TV, 53–54
CAD, *see* Computer-aided design
Café Coffee Day, 168
CAFTA-DR, *see* Dominican Republic-
    Central America Free Trade
    Agreement
Campbell Soup Company, 78
Cappelli, Peter, 244
Career path, 225
CareerBuilder.com, 226
Careers and the disABLED, 258
Caregill, 126
Caremark International, 71
Carrefour, 171, 196
Carrying cost, 392
Case studies, 235
Cash cow, 120–121, 122
Cash flow analysis, 344–345
Castro-Wright, Eduardo, 67
Caterpillar, 201, 234
Catmull, Ed, 60, 144
Cato, 24
CBS, 53
Celestica Inc., 149
Center for Auto Safety, 85
Central States Manufacturing, 242
Central tendency error, 237
Centralization of authority, 188
CEO, 6–7
CEO Confidence Index (Conference
    Board), 50
CEO firings, 82–83
CEO pay, 274, 303
Chain of command, 31, 186–187
Challenger, John, 68
Challenging team goals, 213
Champion International, 201
Champy, James, 193
Chandler, Diane, 309
Change agent, 152

Change forces, 147
Change intervention, 148
Change management, 147–153
  anchoring changes in corporation's
    culture, 150–151
  change *vs.* resistance forces, 147
  communicating the vision, 150
  core change coalition, 149
  declaring victory too soon, 150
  General Electric workout, 152
  organizational development,
    152–153
  resistance to change, 147–149
  results-driven change, 151
  sense of urgency, 149
  short-term wins, 150
  vision for change, 150
Changing external environments, 45–48
Character of the rivalry, 124
Charismatic leadership, 307–309, 310
Charlebois, Vic, 356, 357
Checklist Manifesto, The
    (Gawande), 208
Chen, Jerry, 301
Chenab Ltd., 47
Chevy Volt, 86
Chicago Harvester, 24
Chick-fil-A, 53, 263
Chief executive officer (CEO), 6–7
Chief executive officer (CEO) pay,
    274, 303
China
  automobile manufacturers, 375
  polluted water sources, 58
  Yum Brands!, 49
Chipotle, 128
Chopourian, Ani, 222–223
Chouinard, Yvon, 15
Chrysler, 264
Cisco Systems, 125
Citibank, 226
Citigroup, 6
Civil Rights Act of 1964, Title VII,
    220–221, 250
Civil Rights Act of 1991, 51, 220
Clarifying responses, 326, 327
Clark, Jason, 375
Clem, Tim, 10
Cleveland Browns, 65
Client relationships, 192
Clif Bar, 384
Cloak VPN, 367
Closed system, 41
Closure, 315
CLOU, *see* Collegial letter of
    understanding
Cluster chain, 321
Coach luxury retail, 380
Coaching, 153, 235 322
Coca-Cola, 167, 168
Codes of ethics, 76–77

Coercion, 149
Cognitive ability tests, 230
Cognitive conflict, 104, 210
Cognitive map, 59–60
Cognizant, 61
Cohen, Ron, 243, 369
Cohesion, 37
Cohesiveness, 209
Colgate-Palmolive, 368
Collaborative discussion sites, 329, 330
Collectivists, 214
Collegial letter of understanding
    (CLOU), 287
Colleti, Lori Stewart, 244–245
Collins, Jim, 96
Collins, Robert, 219
Colvin, Geoff, 287
Comambault, 32
Combining tasks, 192
Comcast, 359
Commission, 241
Commitment probability rule, 305
Commitment requirement rule, 305
Common Threads Partnership, 86
Communication, 312–333
  attribution theory, 315–316
  basic perception process, 313–314
  coaching/counseling, 322
  defined, 313
  downward, 319–320
  formal communication channels,
    319–320
  giving feedback, 327–328
  grapevine, 320–322
  horizontal, 320
  informal communication channels,
    320–322
  listening, 325–327
  nonverbal, 322–323
  one-on-one, 323–328
  oral, 324
  organization-wide, 328–333
  organizational silence, 330
  perception of others, 315–316
  perception problems, 314–315
  self-perception, 316–317
  upward, 320
  written, 324
Communication cost, 359
Communication medium, 324
Communication process, 317–319
Compagnie de Commentry-
    Fourchambault et Décazeville
    (Comambault), 32
Company code of ethics, 76–77
Company hotlines, 330–331
Company mission, 62
Company-related deviance, 68–69
Compensation
  defined, 240
  pay-level decisions, 241

  pay-structure decisions, 242–243
  pay-variability decisions, 241–242
  teams, 216–217
Competitive advantage, 111
*Competitive Advantage through People:
    Unleashing the Power of the Work
    Force* (Pfeffer), 19
Competitive analysis, 53
Competitive inertia, 114
Competitors, 53
Complex environment, 47
Complex matrix, 186
Component parts inventories, 390
Compressed pay structures, 243
**Compression approach to
    innovation,** 144–146
Compromise, 35
Computer-aided design (CAD), 145
Computer-based learning, 235–236
Conant, Douglas, 260, 292
Concelman, Jim, 322
Concentration of effect, 73
Conceptual skills, 15
Concertive control, 341–342
Concurrent control, 338
Conflict, 104–105, 210–211
Conformance to specifications, 348, 349
Connecticut Spring & Stamping, 206
Connor, Winston, 237
Conscientiousness, 259–260
Consensus, 211
Consideration, 294, 295
**Consistent organizational
    culture,** 62
Constructive conflict and coordination,
    33–35, 36
Constructive feedback, 327–328
Consumer Product Safety Commission
    (CPSC), 55
Continental Airlines, 5, 47
Contingency approach, 40
Contingency management, 41–42
Contingency theory, 296–299
Continuous-flow production, 388
Continuous improvement, 383
**Continuous reinforcement
    schedule,** 284, 286
Control, 36, 334–351
  balanced scorecard, 343–344
  benchmarking, 336
  bureaucratic, 339–340
  concertive, 341–342
  concurrent, 338
  control loss, 338
  corrective action, 337
  customer defections, 347
  defined, 335
  EVA, 345–347
  feedback, 337–338
  feedforward, 338
  financial performance, 344–347

Control (*continued*)
  normative, 340–341
  objective, 340
  quality, 348
  regulation costs, 338
  self-control, 342–343
  standards, 335–336
  waste and pollution minimization, 348–351
Control loss, 338
Control methods, 339–343
Control process, 335–339
Controlling, 6
Conventional level of moral development, 73
Cook, Ian, 260
Cook, Roger, 259
Cookies, 365
Coolidge, Calvin, 89
Cooper Tire & Rubber, 155
Cooperation and acceptance of authority, 38
Cooperative contract, 163–165
Coordination, 36
Corbat, Michael, 6
Corcoran, Patrick, 139
Core capabilities, 115
Core change coalition, 149
Core firms, 116
Corporate antivirus software, 366
Corporate blog, 331
Corporate culture, *see* Organizational culture
Corporate-level strategy, 119–124
Corporate portal, 369
Corrective action, 337
Cortelyou, Bob, 47
Cost leadership, 126
Costco, 351
Cote, David, 171
Cottage workers, 24
Counseling, 153, 322
Country club management, 295, 296
Coury, Robert, 303
Cox, Taylor, 263
Creative work environments, 141–142
Criminal record checks, 229
Crisis stage of organizational decline, 146
Critical mass, 138
Cross, Harold, 371
Cross-functional team, 207
Cross-training, 202, 216
Crutchfield, Kevin, 303
Csikszentmihalyi, Mihaly, 141
CSX Corp., 94
Culbert, Samuel, 236–237
Cultural differences, 172–173, *see also* Global management
Cultural simulations, 175
Culture of play, 64
Culver, John, 165

Cummins Engine, 201
Cuomo, Andrew, 56
Customer, 52–53
Customer defections, 347
Customer departmentalization, 182–183
Customer focus, 382
Customer satisfaction, 20–21, 382
Customs classification, 157
Cutler, Andrew, 62
Cutting and recovery, 124
CVS Caremark, 283
CyberAlert, 12
Cybernetic, 337
Cybernetic control process, 337
Cybernetic feasibility, 339
Cyrus, 24

D

Daimler-Benz, 252
Dairy industry, 47
Dalio, Ray, 105
Daoud, David, 47
Dasra, 86
Data clusters, 363
Data encryption, 366–367
Data mining, 361, 362
Data warehouse, 362
Davis, Angus, 296
Davis, Michelle, 8
Dayforce, 92, 100
De-forming, 212
De-norming, 212
De-storming, 212
Decentralization, 19, 188–189
Decision criteria, 100
Decision making, 98–108
  defined, 98
  Delphi technique, 106
  electronic brainstorming, 106–108
  group, 103–108
  groupthink, 103
  limits, 102–103
  nominal group technique, 105–106
  step 1 (problem definition), 99–100
  step 2 (identify decision criteria), 100
  step 3 (weigh the criteria), 100–101
  step 4 (generate alternative courses of action), 101
  step 5 (evaluate each alternative), 101
  step 6 (compute the optimal decision), 101–102
  structured conflict, 104–105
Decision support system (DSS), 371
Decisional roles, 12–13
Deckers Outdoor, 380
Decoding, 318
Deep-level diversity, 253, 258–260
DeFalco, Louis, 229
Defamation, 229

Defenders, 127
Defensive bias, 315, 316
Defensive strategy, 85
Delegation of authority, 187–188
Dell Computer, 47, 333, 393
Delphi technique, 106
Delta Airlines, 46, 47, 383
Demographics, 51
Denial of service attack, 365
Department of Agriculture, 55
Department of Labor, 55
Departmentalization, 180
Dependent demand system, 394
Derailers, 15, 16
Descriptive Geometry (Monge), 39
Design competition, 138
Design for disassembly, 350
Design iteration, 143
Designing adaptive organizations, *see* Organizational design
Desparate Women, 164
Destructive feedback, 327
DeVaul, Richard, 214
Devil's advocacy, 105
Dialectical inquiry, 105
Diapers.com, 393
Dick's Sporting Goods, 360
Differentiation, 126–127
Differentiation strategy, 169
Difficult goals, 286
DiFonzo, Nicholas, 321
Digital cameras, 136–137
Diocletian, 24
Direct competition, 129–130
Direct foreign investment, 155, 156
Directive leadership, 300–301, 302
DirecTV, 53, 122
Disability, 254, 257–258
Disability discrimination, 255
Discontinuous change, 138
Discretionary responsibilities, 84
Discrimination
  age, 253–254
  disability, 255
  employment, 221–222
  racial and ethnic, 256–257
  sex, 254–256
Discrimination and fairness paradigm, 261
DISH Network, 53
Disney, Walt, 60
Disney Corporation, *see* Walt Disney Company
Disney Institute, 376
Disney World, 361
Disparate treatment, 221
Disposition, 259
Disseminator role, 12
Dissolution stage of organizational decline, 147
Distinctive competence, 115

Distributive justice, 277
Disturbance handler role, 13
Diversification, 119, 123
Diversification *vs.* risk, 121
Diversity, 249, *see also* Workplace diversity
Diversity audits, 265
Diversity pairing, 265
Division of labor, 31, 34
DMG, 13
Do The Math Tour, 82
Documentary training, 175
Dog, 121
Doha Round, 158
Dominant design, 138–140
Domination, 35
Dominican Republic-Central America Free Trade Agreement (CAFTA-DR), 160
Domino's Pizza, 301
Donahoe, John, 118
Donald, Jim, 142
Donnelly, Vince, 148
Dorsey, Jack, 320
Dowd, Rich, 17
Downey, Robert, Jr., 147
Downloading pirated music, 158
Downsizing, 244–245
Downtime, 392
Downward communication, 319–320
Doyle, Patrick, 301
DreamWorks Studios, 54
Dreyfus, 126
drilling down, 319
Drive, 292
"Drive Safe & Save" program (State Farm), 340
D'Souza, Francisco, 61
DSS, *see* Decision support system
Duck N Roll food truck, 58
Duke Children's Hospital, 344
Dulski, Jennifer, 96
Dumpster diving, 69
DuPont Corporation, 223, 264
Dupuy, Christian, 168
Durability, 379
Durosko, Craig, 148–149
DVD-by-mail service, 53
Dweck, Carol, 279
Dynamic environment, 45
Dynegy, 63–64
Dysfunctional turnover, 246

E

E-learning, 235–236
E-readers, 130
EAP, *see* Employee assistance program
Early responders, 131
Early retirement incentive program (ERIP), 245

Easy goals, 286
easyJet, 377
Eaton, 62
eBay, 118
eBay Motors, 118
eBay Now, 118
eBay RedLaser, 118
Economic order quantity (EOQ), 392–393, 394
Economic responsibility, 82–83
Economic value added (EVA), 345–347
Economy, 49–50
EDI, *see* Electronic data interchange
Edison, Thomas, 120
EEOC, *see* Equal Employment Opportunity Commission
Effectiveness, 3
Efficiency, 3
Efficient foodservice response (EFR), 391
Effort and performance, 269–270
80 percent rule, 222
84 Lumber, 116, 117
Einhorn, Richard, 135
EIS, *see* Executive information system
Eisenhower, Dwight D., 325
El Gaucho Luca's Cafe, 58
Elaine Construction, 245
Electronic brainstorming, 106–108
Electronic data interchange (EDI), 369, 370
Electronic health records, 318
Electronic monitoring and distribution services, 12
Electronic scanner, 361
11main.com, 5
Elite SEM, 341
Elop, Stephen, 123, 149, 150
Email, 319, 324
Email snooping, 365
EMC, 175
EMD, 131
Emerson, Monica, 264
Emil, Harry, 310, 311
Emotional stability, 259
Empathy, 380
Emphatic listening, 326–327
Employee assistance program (EAP), 322
Employee-centered leadership, 294
Employee involvement, 61
Employee involvement team, 205–206
Employee participation, 148, 152
Employee referrals, 226
Employee satisfaction, 20–21, 385
Employee selection, 65, 227–232
Employee separation, 241
Employee shrinkage, 68–69
Employee stock ownership plan (ESOP), 242

Employee termination, 243–244
Employee turnover, 246
Employment discrimination, 221–222
Employment interview, 211, 228, 232, 233
Employment issues, *see* Human resource management
Employment legislation, 219–223
Employment references, 228–229
Employment security, 19
Empowering workers, 195, 386
Empowerment, 195–196, 281
Enabling Profitable Growth in the Food-Prepared-Away-From-Home Industries, 391
Encoding, 317
Eni S.p.A., 68
Entrepreneur role, 13
Environment Protection Agency (EPA), 55
Environmental change, 45
Environmental complexity, 47
Environmental scanning, 57–58, 115
Environmental uncertainty, 48
EOQ, *see* Economic order quantity
Epstein, David, 85, 252
Equal Employment Opportunity Commission (EEOC), 52, 55, 220, 221, 250, 264
Equal Pay Act, 220
Equity theory, 274–278
    changing the referent, 276
    components, 274–275
    correcting major inequities, 276–277
    decreasing/withholding inputs, 275
    defined, 274
    fair decision-making processes, 277–278
    increasing outcomes, 275
    rationalizing/distorting outcomes, 276
    reducing employee inputs, 277
ERG theory, 270, 271
ERIP, *see* Early retirement incentive program
ESOP, *see* Employee stock ownership plan
Esprit de corps, 34
Ethical behavior, 67
Ethical charismatics, 308, 309
Ethical climate, 78–80
Ethical decision making, 74–76, 79
Ethical intensity, 72–73
Ethical responsibility, 83–84
Ethics, 67–80
    charismatic leadership, 308, 309
    codes of ethics, 76–77
    defined, 67
    ethical climate, 78–80
    ethical intensity, 72–73
    ethics training, 77–78
    hiring ethical employees, 76
    model of ethical decision making, 79

Ethics (*continued*)
  moral development, 73–74
  principles of ethical decision making,
    74–76
  punishing ethics violators, 80
  state of ethics today, 67
  U.S. Sentencing Guidelines, 69–71
  whistleblowing, 79–80
  workplace deviance, 68–69
Ethics code, 76–77
Ethics compliance program, 71
Ethics training, 77–78
Eure, Van, 340
Euro, 159
Euro RSCG Worldwide PR, 294–295
European Cities Monitor (Cushman &
    Wakefield), 101, 102, 169
European Union (EU), 159
EVA, *see* Economic value added
Evaluation apprehension, 106–107
Evercan, 351
Evonik Industries AG, 389
**Executive information system
    (EIS),** 368
Executive Order 11246, 250
Expatriate, 174–177
Expectancy, 278
Expectancy theory, 278–281
Experiential approach to innovation,
    142–144
Experiential exercises, 235
Expert system, 371–372
Export Now, 163
Exporting, 163
Extended Stay America, 142
External attribution, 315
External blog, 333
External environment, 45
External pressures, 53
External recruiting, 225–227
Externals, 302
Extinction, 283
Extranet, 370
Extraversion, 259
Extrinsic rewards, 271
Exxon Mobile, 81

F

Facebook, 92, 93, 227, 320, 358–359
Fadell, Tony, 138
"Failure Is an Option" advertising
    campaign (Domino's), 301
Fair Labor Standards Act (FLSA)
    violations, 275, 276
Fairness, 274
Family and Medical Leave Act, 51, 220
Fandango, 360
Fandray, Dayton, 79
Farmville, 363
Farmville 2, 363

Fast food industry, 189
Faulty action stage of organizational
    decline, 146
Fayol, Henri, 4, 30, 32–33, 34
Fayol's 14 principles of management, 34
Fear, 278
Federal Communications Commission
    (FCC), 55
Federal employment laws, 219–221
Federal News Service, 12
Federal regulatory agencies and com-
    missions, 55
Federal Reserve System, 55
Federal Trade Commission (FTC), 55
FedEx, 206
Feedback, 192
Feedback channels, 192
Feedback control, 337–338
Feedback to sender, 318
Feedforward control, 338
Felice, Sergio, 51
Feminine cultures, 172, 173
Fiat, 95
FICO, 8
"Fiction of superior authority," 38
Fiedler's contingency theory, 296–299
Field simulation training, 175–176
Figurehead role, 11
Films and videos, 235
Final assembly, 390
Financial performance, 344–347
Financial ratios, 345
Finished goods inventories, 390
Firewall, 366
Firing employees, 243–244
Firm-level strategy, 128–132
First Air, 356, 357
First-line manager, 9
First-mover advantage, 354–355
First Student, 222
**Fixed interval reinforcement
    schedule,** 284
Fixed ratio reinforcement schedule,
    284
Flemming, Bill, 291
Flexible manufacturing, 388–389
Flexon, Bob, 63, 64
Flextronics International, 240
Flickinger, Burt, 126
Flow, 141
FLSA violations, 275, 276
FLYHTStream, 357
Focus strategy, 127
Fog Creek Software, 281
Follett, Mary Parker, 33–35, 36
Food and Drug Administration (FDA),
    55, 56
Food industry, 391
Food trucks, 58
Football concussions, 338
Ford, Bill, 13

Ford, Henry, 24
Ford Focus Electric, 387
Ford Motor Company, 13, 24, 53, 155,
    201, 336, 363
Foreign Corrupt Practices Act, 83
Foreign direct investment, 155, 156
Formal authority system, 302
Formal communication channel,
    319–320
Forming, 211
Four-fifths (or 80 percent) rule, 222
Four Seasons Hotels, 341
Fox, 53
Foxconn, 85, 277, 335
Fracking, 56, 81
Frady, Kelly, 242
Frame-of-reference training, 238
Franchise, 164
Franchising, 164–165
Freame, John, 124
Frederickson, Valerie, 65
Free trade, 176
Freedom, 142
Freetextbooks.com, 272
French Open tennis tournament, 335
Frequent informal meetings, 332
Fresh & Easy stores, 90
Fried, Jason, 269, 386
Friedland, Jonathan, 362
Friedman, Milton, 80
Friesen, Candy, 327
Fry, Jason, 324
Fugere, Danielle, 81
Functional departmentalization,
    180–181
Functional turnover, 246
Functions of the Executive, The
    (Barnard), 38
Fundamental attribution error, 316
Fung, Sandra, 202
Furlong, Tom, 359

G

Gainsharing, 217
Gales, Jean-Marc, 51
Gallo, Carmine, 196
Gallo, Cheryl, 339
Gamification, 272
Gantt, Henry, 29–30
Gantt chart, 29–30
Garage (Microsoft), 310
Garlinghouse, Brad, 64
GATT, *see* General Agreement on
    Tariffs and Trade
Gawande, Atul, 208
Gayle, Helen, 187
Gazelle.com, 351
GE Aircraft Engines, 303
**General Agreement on Tariffs and
    Trade (GATT),** 158

General and Industrial Management (Fayol), 30, 34
General Electric (GE), 120, 131, 201, 293, 385
General Electric workout, 152
General environment
  defined, 48
  economy, 49–50
  political/legal component, 51–52
  sociocultural component, 50–51
  technological component, 50
General goals, 286
General Motors (GM), 84–85, 87, 213, 336, 375, 387
Generational change, 145
Genetic Information Nondiscrimination Act, 220
Geographic departmentalization, 183–184
Getting to Yes: Negotiating Agreement without Giving In (Fisher et al.), 35
Ghazali, 24
Ghosn, Carlos, 294
Gibson, Kristen, 127
Gibson, Riley, 64
Gilbreth, Frank, 28
Gilbreth, Lillian, 29
Gilbreth's motion studies, 27–29
Gino, Francesca, 240
GitHub, 10
Giving feedback, 327–328
Giving of orders, 36
Gladwell, Malcolm, 292
Glass ceiling, 254
Glee, 164
Global business, 155
Global consistency, 162
Global joint venture, 165
Global management, 154–177
  cooperative contracts, 163–165
  cultural differences, 172–173
  direct foreign investment, 155, 156
  expatriates, 174–177
  exporting, 163
  franchising, 164–165
  GATT, 158
  global consistency, 162
  global new ventures, 166–167
  growth potential of foreign markets, 167–168
  licensing, 164
  local adaptation, 162
  multinational corporations, 155
  office/manufacturing location, 168–170
  overseas assignments, 174–177
  political risk, 170–172
  regional trading zones, 158–161
  strategic alliances, 165
  trade agreements, 157–161
  trade barriers, 156–157

wholly owned affiliates, 166
world's best cities for business, 170
WTO, 158, 159
Global new ventures, 166–167
Global positioning satellite (GPS), 45
Global sourcing, 56
Glocer, Thomas, 179
Goal, 286
Goal acceptance, 286
Goal commitment, 92
Goal congruence rule, 305
Goal difficulty, 286
Goal setting
  diversity, 264
  planning, 91
  teams, 212–214
Goal-setting theory, 286–289
Goal specificity, 286
Gobillot, Lori, 5
GoDaddy.com, 125
Goizueta, Roberto, 345
Golden, Jocelyn, 227
"Good boy, nice girl" stage, 73
Google, 57, 112, 347, 358, 366
Google Authentication, 366
Google X, 213–214
Gossip chain, 321
Gould, Thomas, 124
Government import standards, 157
GPS, *see* Global positioning satellite
Graco, 32
Grand strategy, 122–124
Grapevine, 320–322
Grapevine communication networks, 321
Graphic rating scale (GRS), 237, 238
Grauch, Fred, 389
Grauch Enterprises, 389
Grazier, Peter, 216
Great Little Box Company (GLBC), 202
"Great person" theory, 292
Grech, Pippa, 356
Green Depot, 336
Griggs v. Duke Power Co., 224
Grocery stores, 392
GROHE Group, 166
Groleau, Mike, 258
Group decision making, 103–108
Group discussions, 235
Group dynamics and cohesion, 37
Groupon, 7
Groupthink, 103, 203
Growth strategy, 122–123
Gupta, Kamlesh, 171
Gutenberg, Johannes, 40

H

Hachette, 3
Haden, Jeff, 11
Hadomi, Ori, 332

Haines, Ray, 263
Halo error, 237
Hammer, Michael, 147, 193
Hammergren, John H., 274
Hammurabi, 24
"Hand Hygiene Saves Lives," 336
Hand-to-mouth inventory, 39
Hansell, Jordan, 11
Hardee's, 53
Harford, Tim, 328
Harker, Susan, 65
HarperCollins, 3
Harvard Business Review, 25
Hasbro, 115
Hawthorne effect, 35
Hawthorne Studies, 35–38
Hayase, Hiroshi, 54
Hayes, Phillip, 157
Hazard Analysis and Critical Control Points program, 55
HCL Technologies, 240
Health insurance (employee benefit), 273
H.E.A.R.D., 376
Heard, Tyler, 331
Hearing, 325
Hee, Lee Kun, 291
Henson, Maureen, 224
Herman Miller, 346
Hernandez, Manny, 340
Hershey's, 77
Hertz Rent-a-Car, 371
Hewlett-Packard (HP), 47, 54, 125
Heyl Logistics, 228–229
Hicks, Wayland, 265
Hierarchical pay structures, 242–243
Hierarchy of needs, 270, 271
Higher-order needs, 271
Hilgert, Ray, 322
Hill, Linda, 17
Hinshaw, Scott, 301
Hirai, Kazuo, 114, 186
Hire.com, 226
Historical overview, 23–38
  administrative management, 32–33, 34
  bureaucratic management, 30–32
  constructive conflict and coordination, 33–35, 36
  cooperation and acceptance of authority, 38
  Gantt chart, 29–30
  Hawthorne Studies, 35–38
  motion studies, 27–29
  scientific management, 25–57
  timeline (5000 BCE - 1525), 24
Hitchcock, Steven, 206
HIV Connect (Levi Strauss), 322
H&M, 350
Hofstede, Geert, 172, 173
Hofstede's five cultural dimensions, 172, 173

Holding cost, 392
Holmes, Ryan, 330
Home Depot, 116, 117, 162
Home improvement industry, 116
Honda, 53, 375
Honesty, 293
Honeywell International, 171
Hong Kong, 83
Hooters, 221
Horizontal ambition, 269
Horizontal communication, 320
Hormel Foods, 122
Horowitz, Ben, 61
Horvitz, Eric, 357
Hosmer, La Rue, 74
Hospital patient infections, 336
Hostile work environment, 222
HotJobs.com, 226
House of Cards, 128, 361–362
HRIS, *see* Human resource information system
HRM, *see* Human resource management
HTC, 45
Huawei Enterprises, 11
Hulu, 53
Human Equation: Building Profits by Putting People First, The (Pfeffer), 19
Human Problems of an Industrial Civilization, The (Mayo), 35
Human resource information system (HRIS), 227
Human resource management (HRM), 218–246
  adverse impact, 222
  compensation, 240–243
  defined, 219
  discrimination, 221–222
  downsizing, 244–245
  employee turnover, 246
  employment legislation, 219–223
  four-fifths rule, 222
  interviews, 228, 232, 233
  job analysis, 223–224
  layoffs, 244–245
  onboarding, 240
  overview (exhibit), 219
  performance appraisal, 236–240
  privacy issues, 219, 228
  recruiting, 223–227
  retirement, 245–246
  safety standards, 221
  selection, 227–232
  sexual harassment, 222–223
  terminating employees, 243–244
  training, 233–236
Human skills, 14–15
Humana, 283
HumanaVitality, 283
Humor, 211

Hutchins, David, 341
Hybrid car batteries, 140
Hydraulic fracturing, 56
Hyland-Savage, Gail, 223
Hymowitz, Carol, 319
Hyundai, 53, 89

I

"I" (pronoun), 325
IAT, *see* Implicit Association Test
IBM, 54, 78
IBM Credit, 193–194
Ice, Jim, 236
iCloud, 113
Idealized influence, 310
IKEA, 255
Illegally downloading music, 158
Immediate feedback, 328
Immelt, Jeff, 293
Imperfectly imitable resources, 112
Implicit Association Test (IAT), 264–265
Impoverished management, 295, 296
In-basket exercise, 231
Inaction stage of organizational decline, 146
Incentives, 26
Income statement, 345
Incremental change, 140
Independent demand system, 394
India
  global retailers, 171
  social responsibility, 86
Individualism, 172, 173
Individualism-collectivism, 214
Individualists, 214
Individualized consideration, 311
Industrial Revolution, 24
Industry-level strategy, 124–128
Industry regulation, 55–56
Informal communication channel (grapevine), 320–322
Informal meetings, 332
Information, 354, *see also* Managing information
Informational roles, 11–12
Initial assembly, 390
Initiating structure, 294, 295
Innovation, *see* Organizational innovation
Innovation streams, 136–140
Inputs, 274
Inspirational motivation, 310
Installation & Services Technologies, 241
Instrumental exchange stage, 73
Instrumentality, 279
Integrative conflict resolution, 35
Integrity, 293
Integrity test, 76
Intel, 136, 265
Intellectual stimulation, 310
Intelligence praise, 279

Interactive Excellence (Schlossberg), 138
InterContinental Hotels, 363
Intermittent reinforcement schedule, 284
Internal attribution, 315
Internal blog, 333
Internal environment, 60
Internal motivation, 190
Internal recruiting, 224–225
Internal service quality, 384
Internals, 301–302
International assignments, 174–177
International Telecommunication Union (ITU), 139
International Telegraph Convention, 139
Internet job listings, 226
Internet training, 235–236
Interorganizational process, 196
Interpersonal communication process, 317–319
Interpersonal roles, 10–11
Interpersonal skills, 215
Interpretation, 314
Interval reinforcement schedule, 284
Interview, 228, 232, 233
Intranet, 368–369
Intraorganizational process, 193
Intrinsic rewards, 271–272
Intuit, 336
Intuitive Research and Technology Corp., 78
Inventory, 39, 389–394
Inventory management, 392–394
Inventory records, 394
Inventory turnover, 391
iPad, 111, 112
iPhone, 45
iPhone 5, 335
Iqbal, Maz, 201
Irani, J. J., 308
Iron Man 3 (film), 13
ISO 9000, 380–381
ISO 14000, 380–381
iTunes, 53, 113

J

Japanese farmers, 176
Japanese-style role-playing games (JRPGs), 6
Jargon, 319
JCM, *see* Job characteristics model
JCPenney, 82–83
J.D. Power survey of initial car quality, 378
Jetstar Airways, 330
JIT inventory system, *see* Just-in-time (JIT) inventory system
Job analysis, 223–224
Job-centered leadership, 294

Job characteristics model (JCM), 190–192
Job description, 223, 225
Job design, 189–192
Job enlargement, 190
Job enrichment, 190
Job evaluation, 241
Job interview, 211, 228, 232, 233
Job performance, 269–270
Job posting, 224
Job rotation, 190
Job satisfaction, 20–21
Job shop, 389
Job specialization, 189
Job specifications, 223
Jobs, Steve, 60, 107, 210
John Deere 8R tractor, 387
Johnson, Doug, 203
Johnson, Ron, 82
Joint venture, 165
Jonath, Franklin, 9
Jones, Bruce, 376
Journal of Applied Psychology, 25
J.P. Morgan, 84
Jubelirer, Matt, 310, 311
Junglee.com, 172
Juniper Research, 372
**Just-in-time (JIT) inventory
    system,** 393
Justus, J.R., 62

K

Kamath, Suresh, 258
Kanban, 393
Karabasevic, Dejan, 275
Kasten, Thomas, 195
Katz, Joel, 78
Kaur, Daljit, 356
Keeper Test, 246
Kennedy, John F., 96
Kenny, David, 53
Kerr, Orin, 219
Keystone XL pipeline, 82
Keystroke monitoring, 365
KFC, 49, 165
KFC China, 165
Kia, 53
Kia Optima, 348
Kiel, Dana, 322
Kilburg, Richard, 17
Kim, Charlie, 300
Kimberly-Clark, 141, 252
Kindle Paperwhite, 130
Kinesics, 323
King, Aaron, 242
King, Jan, 98
Kirshner, Ben, 341
"Kiss of Yes," 147
Knowledge, 371
Kodak, 90

Kohlberg, Lawrence, 73–74
Kohlberg's stages of moral development, 73–74
Komatsu, 97
Korn/Ferry International, 229
Korver-Swanson, Louise, 175
Kotter, John, 149, 150
Kroc, Ray, 89
Kroger, 339, 356
Kyocera, 350–351

L

Labor laws, 221
Labor productivity, 377
Lacher, Joseph, 321
Lafley, A. G., 310
Lampa, Henrik, 350
Landline telephones, 138
Large-system interventions, 152–153
Larsen, Laurel, 176
Laser Soft Info Systems, 258
Late responders, 131
Latif, Muhammad, 47
Lauzon, Armand, 152
Lavin, Frank, 163
Law and order stage, 73–74
Lawler, Edward, 214
Layoffs, 244–245
Le, Amy, 58
Leader information rule, 305
Leader-member relations, 297, 298
Leader role, 11
Leaderless group discussion, 231
Leadership, 290–311
    behaviors, 294–296
    Blake/Mouton leadership grid,
        295, 296
    charismatic, 307–309
    defined, 291
    extroversion/intraversion, 292
    Fiedler's contingency theory, 296–299
    Follett, 36
    leaders/managers, compared,
        291–292
    normative decision theory, 303–307
    path-goal theory, 299–302
    powerful leaders, 144
    strategic, 307
    trait theory, 292–294
    transactional, 311
    transformational, 309–311
    visionary, 307–311
Leadership behaviors, 294–296
Leadership style, 296
Leadership traits, 292–294
Leading, 5–6
Leahy, Terry, 90
Learned needs theory, 270, 271
Learning and effectiveness paradigm,
    262–263

Least Preferred Coworker (LPC) scale,
    297–299
Lebowitz, Josh, 55
Lectures, 235
Lee, Angela, 277
Lee, Hope, 58
Lee Kun Hee, 291
Legal environment, 51–52
Legal responsibility, 83
Leniency error, 237
Lennon, Sean, 56
Leno, Jay, 310
Lenovo, 277
Leonard, Stew, 347
Levi Strauss, 195, 322
Lewin, Kurt, 148
Liaison role, 11
Licensing, 164
Lincoln Electric, 271
Line authority, 187
Line-flow production, 388
Line function, 187
LinkedIn, 227
Linton, Tom, 240
Lintz, Janice Schacter, 135
Listen360, 52
Listening, 325–327
LiveNation, 360
Lixil, 166
Local adaptation, 162
Locke, Edwin, 26, 92
Locomotive manufacturing, 131
Locus of control, 301–302
Long-haul truckers, 339–340
Long-term orientation, 172, 173
Lore, Mark, 393
Löscher, Peter, 13
Lost efficiency, 392
LoveMachine, 340
Low-cost strategy, 169
Lower-order needs, 271
Lowe's, 116, 117
Lozano, Bobby, 351
LPC scale, 297–299
Luby's, 130
Lufthansa, 377
Luthans, Fred, 285
Lyne, 330

M

Ma, Jack, 5
Maastricht Treaty of Europe, 159, 160
Macaroni Grill, 52
Machiavelli, Niccolo, 24
Mackay, Harvey, 211
Mackey, John, 310
Macmillan, 3
Maersk Line, 83
Magna-Tiles, 390–391
Magnitude of consequences, 72

Make-to-order operations, 386–387
Make-to-stock operations, 387–388
MakerBot, 167
Malaysia Airlines Flight 370 crash, 356
Malicious scripts and applets, 365
Management
  academic journals, 25
  contingency, 41–42
  defined, 3
  functions, 4–6
  historical overview. *see* Historical
    overview
  information, 39–40
  operations, 37–38
  systems, 40–41
  transition to, 17–19
Management by objectives, 97
Management functions, 4–6
Management skills, 13–15
Management style, 19
Manager
  customer satisfaction, 20–21
  extraversion/introversion, 260
  kinds, 6–10
  leader, compared, 291–292
  legal risk, 52
  mistakes, 15–17
  roles, 10–13
  skills, 13–15
  what to avoid doing, 11
Managerial directives/orders, 38
Managerial roles, 10–13
Managing information, 39–40, 352–372
  accurate information, 356
  acquisition cost, 357–358
  capturing information, 360–361
  communication cost, 359
  competitive advantage, 355–356
  complete information, 356–357
  external access and sharing, 369–371
  first-mover advantage, 354–355
  internal access and sharing, 368–369
  processing cost, 358
  processing information, 361–363
  protecting information, 363–368
  raw data/information, contrasted, 354
  relevant information, 357
  retrieval cost, 359
  security threats, 363–368
  sharing knowledge and expertise,
    371–372
  storage cost, 358–359
  timely information, 357
Mandi, Jack, 68
Manning, Peyton, 340
Manthey, Brian, 338
Manufacturing flexibility, 388
Manufacturing operations, 386–389
Maple syrup production, 357
Marathe, Paraag, 350
March Madness office pools, 68

Marchionne, Sergio, 95
Mariwalla, Kavita, 357
Market commonality, 129, 131
Marks, Michael, 54
Married with Children, 164
Married women (with children) who
  work, 50, 51
Marriott, Bill, 325, 326
Martens, Phil, 8
Martin, Roger, 310
Martinson, Eileen, 5
Marvel Studios, 13
Masculine cultures, 172, 173
Maslow's hierarchy of needs, 270, 271
Mason, Andrew, 7
**Materials requirement planning
  (MRP),** 393–394
Matrix departmentalization, 184–186
Matsuda, Yosuke, 6
Maximize, 103
Mayo, Elton, 35, 37
Mayo Clinic, 147
Mazor Robotics, 332
MBC Group, 164
McAfee, Andrew, 142
McCafé, 130
McClelland's learned needs theory,
  270, 271
McDermott, Bill, 187
McDonald, James, 227
McDonald's, 53, 129, 130, 164, 189,
  190, 250, 348, 381
McDonald's drive-through window
  job, 192
McGee, Tom, 265
McKee, Keith, 215
McNamara, Steve, 45
Meadowbrook Maple Syrup, 357
Mechanistic organization, 193
Media advocacy, 56
Medical mistakes, 319
Medici family, 40
Meggy, Robert, 202
Mehta, Manish, 333
Meliones, Jon, 344
Memo List (Red Hat), 61, 62, 329
Mental or physical disabilities, 257–258
Mentoring, 235, 264, 265
Menzies, Kate, 162
Merck, 197
Mercy General Hospital, 222–223
Mergers and acquisitions, 62, 123
Merit-based promotion, 31
Merrill, Douglas, 104
Merrill Lynch, 252
Metropolitan Life Insurance, 359
Michael Foods, 338
Michaels, David, 79
Michelin, 283
Microblogging, 333
Microsoft, 47, 179, 180, 310, 319, 329

Microsoft-Nokia tie up, 123
Microsoft Surface, 111
Middle East, 171
Middle management, 96
Middle manager, 8–9
Middle-of-the-road management, 295, 296
Midvale Steel Company, 25
Milestones, 143–144
Milwaukee Mutual Insurance, 216
Minnesota Clerical Test, 230
Minority domination, 203, 210
Minority experiences for top
  executives, 266
Mintzberg, Henry, 10, 12, 90
Mission, 96
Mission Bicycle Company, 386
Mission statement, 62
Misunderstanding and distrust, 147
MIT Sloan Management Review, 25
Mitsubishi Electric Cooling &
  Heating, 370
Mittal, Lakshmi, 383
Mobile boarding pass, 360
Mobile payment scams, 372
Modernizing Medicine, 357
Modular organization, 196–197
Mohawk Industries, 283
Mohrman, Susan, 216
Mollick, Ethan, 9
Moltz, Barry, 386
Monge, Gaspard, 39
Monitor role, 12
Monster.com, 226
Moore, Gordon, 353
Moorehead, Scott, 320
Moore's law, 353
Moral development, 73–74
More, Thomas, 24
Morning Star, 287
Morrissey, Helena, 262
Motion study, 28
Motivation, 268–289
  defined, 269
  effort and performance, 269–270
  equity theory, 274–278
  expectancy theory, 278–281
  extrinsic/intrinsic rewards, 271–272
  goal-setting theory, 286–289
  manager's role, 272–273
  need satisfaction, 270–271
  overview (exhibit), 288
  question to ask, 289
  reinforcement theory, 281–286
  teams, 213
  what does not work, 278
Motivation to manage, 15
Motorola, 45
Moufarrige, Taine, 216
MRP, *see* Materials requirement
  planning (MRP)
Mucci, Martin, 80

Muhlhauser, Craig, 149, 150
Mulcahy, Anne, 265
Multifactor productivity, 377
Multifunctional teams, 144
Multinational corporation, 155
Murphy, Robert, 107
Music streaming, 354
Muslim Consumers Association of
    Malaysia (MCAM), 57
Mutton, Nick, 341
Myers, Stacy, 215
Mylan, 303
MySpace, 354

N

Nadella, Satya, 123, 329
NAFTA, *see* North American Free
    Trade Agreement
Nagamori, Sigenobu, 137
NASA, 96
National Center for Employee Owner-
    ship, 242
National culture, 172
National Labor Relations Board
    (NLRB), 55, 221
National Rehabilitation Information
    Center, 258
Natural Resources Defense Council, 82
Natural work units, 192
Nayar, Vineet, 3
NBC, 53
Nebuchadnezzar, 24
Need satisfaction, 270–271
Needs, 270
Needs assessment, 233
Negative reinforcement, 283
Negligent hiring, 228–229
Negotiator role, 13
Nest, 137–138
Nestlé, 58, 123
Net operating profit after taxes
    (NOPAT), 345
Net Optics, 320–321
Netbooks, 112
Netflix, 53, 128, 246, 359, 361–362
NetJets, 11
Netscape, 354
New York City Fire Department, 362
Newegg.com, 351
News Corporation, 84
Newton Investment Management, 262
Next Jump, 300
Nickel, Bobby, 221
Nickerson, Barry, 245
Nicol, Ron, 245
Nicor National, 386
Nike, 385
9/11 terrorist attacks, 46
Nissan, 53, 294, 375
Nissan Power 88, 294

Noise, 319
Nokia, 122, 149, 150
Nokia Siemens, 122
Nominal group technique, 105–106
Nonfinancial rewards, 217
Nonsubstitutable resources, 112–113
Nontariff barriers, 157
Nonverbal communication, 322–323
Nook Simple Touch, 130
Nook Touch with Glowlight, 130
Nooyi, Indra, 255, 292
NOPAT, *see* Net operating profit after
    taxes
Nordstrom, 358
Normative control, 340–341
Normative decision theory, 303–307
Norming, 211–212
Norms, 208–209
**North American Free Trade Agree-
    ment (NAFTA),** 159, 160
North Shore University Hospital, 337
Northwest Airlines, 47
Norwex, 127
Novartis, 85
Novartis Oncology, 252
Novelis, 8, 91, 351
Nowogrodski, Avinoam, 9, 10
Nucor, 341
Nuovo, Frank, 149
Nutella, 196
Nye, Dan, 229

O

O/I ratio, 275
Obama, Barack, 75
Objective control, 340
Objective performance measures, 237
Occupational Safety and Health Act
    (OSHA), 221
Occupational Safety and Health Admin-
    istration (OSHA), 55, 79, 221
Ocean Spray, 202
Oculus Rift virtual reality, 93
Oculus VR, 93, 143
Odagiri, Yoshinori, 114
OECD, *see* Organization for Economic
    Cooperation and Development
Office Depot, 54
Official Harmonized Tariff Schedule, 157
Older workers, 253–254
OMGPOP, 243
Omidyar, Pierre, 118
On-the-job training, 235
Onboarding, 240
"100 Best" companies, 20, 21
One-on-one communication, 323–328
Online discussion forums, 329
Ono, Yoko, 56
Open system, 41
Openness to experience, 260

Operational plans, 97–98
Operations management, 38–39,
    374–394
    defined, 375
    inventory, 389–394
    manufacturing operations, 386–389
    productivity, 375–378
    quality, 378–383
    service operations, 383–386
Opportunistic behavior, 54
Optical character recognition, 361
Optimal decision, 101–102
Options-based planning, 93
Oracle, 125
Oral communication, 324
Orange Is the New Black, 128
Orbis International, 208
Ordering cost, 391
Organic organization, 193
Organization, 314
Organization for Economic Cooperation
    and Development (OECD), 49
Organization-wide communication,
    328–333
Organizational change, *see* Change
    management
Organizational culture, 60–65, 150
    changing the culture, 62–65
    creating the culture, 60–61
    culture of play, 64
    defined, 60
    keys to success, 61–62
    levels, 63
    maintaining the culture, 61
Organizational decline, 146–147
Organizational design, 178–199
    authority, 186–189
    chain of command, 186–187
    customer departmentalization,
        182–183
    degree of centralization, 188–189
    delegation of authority, 187–188
    empowerment, 195–196
    functional departmentalization,
        180–181
    geographic departmentalization,
        183–184
    job design, 189–192
    line *vs.* staff authority, 187
    matrix departmentalization, 184–186
    mechanistic *vs.* organic organization,
        193
    modular organization, 196–197
    product departmentalization,
        181–182
    reengineering, 193–195
    virtual organization, 197–199
Organizational development, 152
Organizational development interven-
    tions, 152–153
Organizational encouragement, 141

Organizational environment, 44–60
  acting on threats and opportunities, 58–60
  changing external environments, 45–48
  environmental scanning, 57–58
  general environment, 48–52
  interpreting environmental factors, 58
  simple/complex environment, 47
  specific environment, 52–57
  stable/dynamic environment, 45
  uncertainty, 48
Organizational heroes, 61
Organizational innovation, 135–146
  compression approach, 144–146
  creative work environments, 141–142
  defined, 135
  discontinuous change, 138
  dominant design, 138–140
  experiential approach, 142–144
  innovation streams, 136–140
  managing innovation, 140–146
  planning for incremental innovation, 145
  technological discontinuity, 137–138
  technological lockout, 139
  technological substitution, 138
  technology cycles, 135–136
Organizational mission, 95, 96
Organizational plurality, 262
Organizational process, 179
Organizational silence, 330
Organizational stakeholder, 80, 81
Organizational stories, 61
Organizational strategy, 110–132
  adaptive strategies, 127–128
  corporate-level strategies, 119–124
  firm-level strategies, 128–132
  grand strategies, 122–124
  industry-level strategies, 124–128
  need for strategic change, 113–115
  Porter's five industry forces, 124–126
  portfolio strategy, 119–122
  positioning strategies, 126–127
  situational analysis, 115–117
  strategic alternatives, 117–119
Organizational structure, 179, *see also* Organizational design
Organizing, 5
Oriental Trading Company (OTC), 201–202
OSHA, *see* Occupational Safety and Health Administration
OshKosh, 261
Outcome/input (O/I) ratio, 274
Outcomes, 274
Outplacement services, 244
Output control, 340
Overlapping steps, 145
Overreward, 275
Overseas assignment inventory (OAI), 176

Overseas assignments, 174–177
Overt integrity test, 76
Overtime pay, 275

P

Pacific Resources International, 240
"Packet sniffer" software, 367
pain points, 319
Panama Canal, 58
Panamax ships, 58
Pandora, 354
Panera, 128
Panizza, Ruben, 368
Paralanguage, 323
Paraphrasing responses, 326, 327
Parikh, Jay, 359
Parker, Peter, 35
Partial productivity, 377
Participative leadership, 301, 302
Password, 364
Password cracking software, 365
Patagonia, 15, 86
Patent Trial and Appeal Board, 139
Path-goal theory, 299–302
Patience & Nicholson (P&N), 217
Pauzié, Laurent, 162
Pay-level decisions, 241
Pay-structure decisions, 242–243
Pay-variability decisions, 241–242
Paychex, 79, 80
PCs, 47
Peach Aviation, 114
Pearce, Terry, 327
Penguin, 3
Pennebaker, James, 325
People power, 19–21
Perceived ability, 301
Perception, 313
Perception of others, 315–316
Perception problems, 314–315
Perceptual filters, 313
Peregrine Financial Group, 308
Performance appraisal, 236–240
Performance feedback, 93, 286–287
Performance tests, 231
Performing, 212
Persistence, 89, 293
Person-focused interventions, 153
Personal aggression, 69
Personal computer (PC) business, 47
Personality, 259–260
Personality-based integrity test, 76
Peterman, Mark, 279
Pettine, Mike, 65
Pettis, Bre, 167
Pfeffer, Jeffrey, 19, 123
Phased retirement, 246
Phillips, Juanita, 78
Phishing, 365
Piecework, 241

Pineau-Boddison, Sandra, 148
Pixar and Disney Animation Studios, 143–144
Pizza Hut, 49
Plagiarism, 143
Plank, Kevin, 61
Planned readings, 235
Planning, 4–5, 89–98
  action plan, 92
  advantages/disadvantages, 89–90
  budgeting, 98
  defined, 4, 89
  double-edged sword, 90
  goal commitment, 92
  maintaining flexibility, 93–94
  operational plans, 97–98
  options-based, 93
  setting goals, 91
  single-use plans, 97
  standing plans, 97–98
  strategic plans, 95
  tactical plans, 96
  top-to-bottom, 95
  tracking progress, 92–93
Plantville, 235, 236
Plassat, Georges, 196
Platek, Allen, 144
Play-Doh, 388
PlayerLync (NFL), 356
Playstation 4 video game console, 114
PMA Companies, 148
Polaroid, 242
Policies, 97
Policy uncertainty, 160
Political deviance, 69
Political risk, 170–172
Political uncertainty, 160
Politics and legal environment, 51–52
Pomerenke, Melody, 338
Pooled interdependence, 195
PooPrints.com, 338
Pop-up stores, 198
Popeyes Louisiana Kitchen, 326
Porras, Jerry, 96
Porter, Barbara, 386
Porter, Michael, 124, 126
Porter's five industry forces, 124–126
Portfolio strategy, 119–122
Position power, 298
Positioning strategies, 126–127
Positive reinforcement, 282
Post messengers, 40
Post Panamax ships, 58
Postconventional level of moral development, 74
Power, 36
Power distance, 172, 173
Power Matters Alliance (PMA), 138
Powerful leader, 144
Prabhakar, Balaji, 287
Prada, 307

Praise, 278, 279
Preconventional level of moral development, 73
Predictive patterns, 363
Pregnancy Discrimination Act, 220
Presenteeism, 97
Price Check app, 131, 132
Primary stakeholder, 81
Primary work group, 302
Prime lending rate, 48
Prime Music (Amazon), 354
Principle of distributive justice, 75
Principle of government requirements, 75
Principle of individual rights, 75
Principle of long-term self-interest, 74
Principle of personal virtue, 75
Principle of religious injunctions, 75
Principle of utilitarian benefits, 76
Principles of Scientific Management, The (Taylor), 26
Pringles potato chips, 119
Private investigators, 229
Proactive customer monitoring, 53
Proactive strategy, 85
Probability of effect, 72
Problem, 99
Problem definition, 99–100
Problem-oriented feedback, 328
Problem structure rule, 305
Procedural justice, 277
Procedures, 98
Processing cost, 358
Processing information, 361–363
Procter & Gamble, 119, 184–186, 201, 226, 252
Product boycott, 56–57
Product departmentalization, 181–182
Product failure, 379
Product piracy, 158
Product prototype, 143
Product reliability, 379
Production blocking, 106
Production deviance, 68
Productivity, 375–378
Profit and loss statement, 345
Profit sharing, 242
Progress Energy, 245
Progressive Insurance, 226
Project team, 207–208
Promotion from within, 224
Pronoun "I," 325
Property deviance, 68
Prospectors, 127
Protecting information, 363–368
Protectionism, 156
Proximal goals, 92
Proximity of effect, 73
Prudential Relocation Management, 176
Pruning roses, 124

Public communications, 56
Public key encryption, 367
Puckett, John, 212
Punctuated equilibrium theory, 46
Punishment, 283, 285
Punishment and obedience stage, 73
Purchasing power, 167
Purpose statement, 95–96
Pyramid of King Khufu, 24

Q

QR code, 360
Qualification-based hiring, 31
Quality, 378–383
  Baldridge National Quality Award, 381–382
  conformance to specifications, 348, 349
  defined, 379
  excellence, 348, 349
  ISO certification, 380–381
  quality-related characteristics, 379–380
  TQM, 382–383
  value, 349
Quality rule, 305
Qualtrics, 97
Question mark, 120
Quid pro quo sexual harassment, 222
QuikTrip, 241
Quota, 157
QWERTY keyboard, 139

R

Race IAT, 265
Racial and ethnic discrimination, 256–257
Radha Krisna Store, 171
Radio frequency identification (RFID) tags, 45, 360–361
Rake, Michael, 124
Rancy, François, 139
Rangaswamy, Satish, 275
Rare resources, 112
Rate buster, 26
Rater training, 238
Ratio reinforcement schedule, 284
Rational decision making, 98
Raw data, 354
Raw material inventories, 389–390
Raytheon, 266
Reactive customer monitoring, 52
Reactive strategy, 84
Reactors, 128
Reciprocal interdependence, 195
Recovery, 124
Recruiting, 223–227
Recycle, reclaim, reuse, 336, 350
Red Hat, 61–62, 329
Red Lobster, 129
Redberg, Rita, 318

Redbox, 128
Redbox Instant, 128
Reddit, 224
Reengineering, 193–195
Reengineering the Corporation (Hammer/Champy), 193
Referents, 274
Reflecting feelings, 327
Refreezing, 148
Regional trading zones, 158–161
Regulation costs, 338
Regulatory agencies, 55–56
Reinforcement, 281
Reinforcement contingencies, 281, 282
Reinforcement theory, 281–286
  administering punishment at appropriate time, 285–286
  components, 282–283
  defined, 281
  reinforcing wrong behaviors, 285
  schedules of reinforcement, 283–285, 286
Reinforcing the wrong behaviors, 285
Related diversification, 122
Relationship behavior, 54
Relationship-oriented leader, 297, 299
Relative comparisons, 100
"Reply all" (email), 319
Resistance forces, 147
Resistance to change, 147–149
Resource allocator role, 13
Resource scarcity, 47
Resource similarity, 129, 131
Resources, 111
Response, 130, 131
Responsiveness, 380
Results-driven change, 151
Résumé, 227
Retention, 314
Retirement, 245–246
Retrenchment strategy, 124
Retrieval cost, 359
RFID tags, *see* Radio frequency identification (RFID) tags
Richter, David, 141
rightsizing, 319
Ringlemann, Maximillian, 203
Risk-avoiding strategy, 117
Risk management, 53
Risk-seeking strategy, 117
Ritz-Carlton Hotels, 196
Roach, Stephen, 196
Roberts, Russell, 80
Robinson, Jonathan, 272–273
Rodriguezmacedo Rivera, Jose Luis, 84
Roku, 53
Role-playing, 235
Rollnick, William, 83
Rometty, Virginia, 225, 291
Rootkit, 365

Ropes courses, 37
Rosedale, Philip, 340
Rosedale Estates North, 338–339
Ross, Angus, 51
RouteOne, 369
Rover.com, 240
Royal Dutch Shell, 62, 151
Rubin, Jeff, 163
Rules and regulations, 98
Runyon, Chuck, 236
Russia, 174
Ryanair, 377

S

S-curve pattern of innovation,
   135–136
Safeguard Scientifics, 11
Saks Fifth Avenue, 194
Salesforce.com, 125
Salzman, Marian, 294, 295
Samsung, 45, 54, 291, 393
San Francisco 49ers, 349
Sanghavi, Deval, 86
SAP, 187
Sarbanes-Oxley Act, 79
Satisficing, 103
Scalar chain, 34
Scandinavian Airlines, 377
Scavenger hunts, 37
Scharlau, Ed, 340
Schedule of reinforcement, 238–285,
   281, 286
Schlage Lock Company, 96
Schlesinger, Jill, 122
Schlossberg, Edwin, 138
Scholastic Aptitude Test (SAT), 229
Schultz, Carol, 278
Scientific management, 25–57
Scioto Downs Racino, 258
Scott, Cheryl, 165
Seafood processors, 55
Sealy Company, 144
Sears, 394
Seattle's Best Coffee, 130
Secondary firms, 116
Secondary stakeholder, 81
Secure sockets layer (SSL)
   encryption, 367
Securities and Exchange Commission
   (SEC), 55
Security threats, 363–368
Selection, 65, 227–232
Selection tests, 229–232
Selective hiring, 19
Selective perception, 314
Self-confidence, 293
Self-control (self-management),
   342–343
Self-designing team, 206
Self-managed team, 19

Self-management, 342–343
Self-managing team, 206
Self-perception, 316–317
Self-service kiosk, 371
Self-serving bias, 316
Semi-autonomous work group, 206
Semistructured interview, 232
Semistructured questions, 232
September 11 terrorist attacks, 46
Sequence patterns, 363
Sequential design process, 145
Sequential interdependence, 195
Servcorp, 216
Service capability, 385
Service operations, 383–386
Service-profit chain, 384–385
Service recovery, 385–386
Service recovery strategy, 376
Service reliability, 379
Serviceability, 379
Setup cost, 391–392
Severance payments, 244
Sex discrimination, 254–256
Sexual harassment, 222–223
Shadow-strategy task force, 116
Shaikh, Jim, 145
Shareholder model, 80
Sharing information, 19
Sharing knowledge and expertise,
   371–372
Sharp, Isadore, 341
Shaw, Bob, 321
Sheikh Abdul Kareem Khadaied, 57
Shen, Jerry, 301
Shilmover, Fred, 336
Short-term/long-term orientation,
   172, 173
Shortening development time, 145
Siemens, 13, 235
Silva, Camy, 58
Silva, Pablo, 58
Silverman, Craig, 243
Simon, William, 226
Simon & Schuster, 3
Simonsen, Michael, 125
Simple environment, 47
Simple matrix, 186
Simulations and games, 235
Singapore Airlines, 348
Single-use plans, 97
Sinovel, 275
Situational (SWOT) analysis,
   115–117
Situational favorableness, 297–298
Situational questions, 232
Skanska USA Building, 291
Skill-based pay, 217
Skill variety, 191
Skills-based diversity training, 264
Skybox, 57
Slack resources, 93

Sladek, Carol, 98
Slim-Fast, 146
Small-group interventions, 153
S.M.A.R.T. goals, 91
Smartphones, 137
Smith, James C., 187
Smith, Rick, 217
Smith, Ryan, 12
Snabe, Jim, 187
Social consensus, 72
Social contract stage, 74
Social integration, 253, 258
Social loafing, 203, 213
Social responsibility, 80–87
   defined, 80
   discretionary responsibilities, 84
   economic performance, and, 86–87
   economic responsibility, 82–83
   ethical responsibility, 83–84
   India, in, 86
   legal responsibility, 83
   shareholder model, 80
   social responsiveness, 84–85
   stakeholder model, 80–82
Social responsiveness, 84–85
Sociocultural considerations, 50–51
Sociotechnical systems, 153
Sodexho Alliance, 266
Sodexo, 264
Soldiering, 25
Sony, 97, 114
Sorkin, Eric, 357
Southwest Airlines, 47, 343, 344
Spam, 365
Specialized jobs, 189
Specific ability tests (aptitude tests),
   229
Specific environment, 52–57
   advocacy groups, 56–57
   competitor component, 53–54
   customer component, 52–53
   defined, 48
   industry regulation component,
      55–56
   supplier component, 54
Specific feedback, 328
Specific goals, 286
Specific team goals, 213
Spencer, Dale, 339
Sperry Software, 319
Spokesperson role, 12
Spolsky, Joel, 281
Spotify, 113
Springer, Jon, 126
Sprint, 130
Spyware, 365
Square, 320
Square Enix, 6
Squirrel-related power outage, 338
SSL encryption, *see* Secure sockets layer
   (SSL) encryption

Stability strategy, 123–124
Stable environment, 45
Staff authority, 187
Staff function, 187
Stakeholder, 80, 81
Stakeholder model, 80–82
Standard Chartered PLC, 166
Standardization, 189
Standards, 335–336
Standing plans, 97–98
Staples, 221, 283
Star, 120
Starbucks, 3, 162, 360
Starbucks-Tata joint venture, 165, 166, 168
StarChip, 168
State Farm Insurance, 340
Status differences, 19
Stealing ideas, 143
Steinhafel, Gregg, 13
Stephens, Jilly, 208
Stevens, Ann, 97
Stew Leonard's grocery store chain, 347
Stock options, 242
Stockout, 390
Stockout cost, 392
Storage cost, 392
Storage cost, 358–359
Storming, 211
Storytelling, 332
Strategic alliances, 165
Strategic dissonance, 114
Strategic group, 116
Strategic leadership, 307
Strategic Management Journal, 25
Strategic objective, 96
Strategic plans, 95
Strategic reference point theory, 117–119
Strategic reference points, 117–119
Strategy, see Organizational strategy
Strategy-making process, 113–119
Stretch goals, 213
Strickland, Don, 90
Structural accommodation, 213
Structured conflict, 104–105
Structured interviews, 232, 233
Stum, David, 273
Subjective performance measures, 237, 238
Suboptimization, 343
Subordinate conflict rule, 305
Subordinate information rule, 305
Subordination of individual interests to the general interest, 34
Subsidies, 157
Subsystem, 40
Subway, 130
Sugar processors, 157
Sumerians, 23, 24
Summarizing responses, 326, 327

Summit Entertainment, 145
Sun Design Home Remodeling Specialists, 148
Sun Tzu, 24
Sunhee Moon, 359
Supermarket industry, 392
Supervised data mining, 362
Supervisory encouragement, 142
Supplier involvement, 145
Suppliers, 54
Supportive leadership, 301, 302
Surface-level diversity, 252–258
Surprise visits, 332
Survey feedback, 153, 331
Sustainable competitive advantage, 112
Sweden garbage problem, 342
Sweethearting, 69
Swipely, 296
Swisscom AG, 182, 183
SWOT analysis, 115–117
Symantec, 366
Symbian, 150
Symmantec, 83
Synapse (Acorda Therapeutics), 369
sync up, 319
Synergy, 41
Syrian Economic Army, 320
System, 40
Systems management, 40–41
Systems view of organizations, 41

T

T-Mobile, 131
Tablet computers, 111
Tactical plans, 96
Tamme, Jacob, 356
Tap Track system, 357
Target, 13, 96–97, 115, 363
Tariff, 156
Task identity, 191
Task interdependence, 194–195
Task-oriented leader, 297, 299
Task significance, 191–192
Task structure, 297, 298, 302
Tata-Starbucks joint venture, 165, 166, 168
Tata Steel, 308
Tax haven, 168
Taxi industry, 45
Taylor, Frederick W., 25–57
Taylor's four principles of scientific management, 26
Team, see Teams and teamwork
Team autonomy continuum, 205
Team building, 153
Team cohesiveness, 209
Team compensation and recognition, 216–217
Team conflict, 210–211

Team diversity, 215
Team goals, 212–214
Team leader, 9–10
Team level, 215
Team management, 295, 296
Team norms, 208–209
Team outing, 216
Team player inventory, 214
Team size, 209–210
Team training, 215–216
Teambuilding exercises, 37
Teambuilding Inc., 216
Teams and teamwork, 200–217
  advantages/disadvantages of teams, 201–203
  autonomy, 204–206
  cohesiveness, 209
  compensation, 216–217
  conflict, 210–211
  consensus, 211
  cross-functional team, 207
  customer satisfaction, 201
  goal setting, 212–214
  individualism-collectivism, 214
  job satisfaction, 202
  minority domination, 203, 210
  motivation, 213
  project team, 207–208
  stages of team development, 211–212
  team diversity, 215
  team level, 215
  team norms, 208–209
  team size, 209–210
  training, 215–216
  virtual team, 207
  when to use teams, 203–204
Teamwork, 383
Technical skills, 14
Technical training, 216
Technological discontinuity, 137–138
Technological innovation, see Organizational innovation
Technological lockout, 139
Technological substitution, 138
Technology, 50, 136
Technology cycle, 135–136
Televised/videotaped speeches and meetings, 329
Temporal immediacy, 73
Terminating employees, 243–244
Terramar Sports, 84
Tesco, 90, 171
Tesla Motors, 96
Tesla Motors' Model S, 388
Tesla Roadster, 96
Testing, 143
Texas Industries, 223
The Cellular Connection, 320
The Weather Co. (The Weather Channel), 53

Theory of Social and Economic Organization, The (Weber), 30, 31
"Think Different" campaign (Apple), 107
37signals.com, 269, 386
Thomas, David, 262, 265
Thompson, Don, 250
Thomson Reuters, 179, 186, 187
Thornbrugh, Mike, 241
Threat of new entrants, 125
Threat of substitute products or services, 125
Threats and opportunities, 58–60
3D design software, 145
3D printing, 385
3M, 119, 122, 127, 201, 206, 391
350.org, 82
360-degree feedback, 239, 240
Ticketless travel, 370–371
TicketMaster, 360
Tiffany & Co., 380
Time study, 28
Time Warner, 84
Title VII of 1964 Civil Rights Act, 220–221, 250
Together We Are Safe, 8
Top manager, 6–7
Toshiba, 54
Total quality management (TQM), 382–383
Toyota, 53, 140, 189, 275, 393
Toys "R" Us, 198
TQM, *see* Total quality management
Trade agreements, 157–161
Trade barriers, 156–157
Traditional work group, 205
Training, 233–236
  competitive advantage, 19
  defined, 233
  determining training needs, 233–234
  diversity training and practices, 264–266
  ethics, 77–78
  methods, 234–236
  objectives, 235
  OD intervention, 153
  overseas assignments, 174–176
  rater, 238
  teams, 215–216
Trainor, Russ, 356
Trait theory, 292–294
Traits, 292
Transactional leadership, 311
Transformational leadership, 309–311
Transition to management, 17–19
Transparency, 340
Trojan horse, 365
Trucking industry, 339–340
True Point, 320

Trust falls, 37
TSMC (Taiwan Semiconductor Manufacturing Company), 54
Tsuchiya, Tsugio, 137
Tsujihara, Kevin, 294
Twilight movie franchise, 145
Twitter, 320, 333
Two-factor authentication, 366

U

Uber, 45, 125–126
Ubisoft, 283
Unaccepted goals, 286
UNASUR, *see* Union of South American Nations
Uncertainty, 48
Uncertainty avoidance, 172, 173
Under Armour, 60
Underreward, 274–275
Unethical charismatics, 308, 309
Unfreezing, 148
Uniform Guidelines on Employment Selection Procedures, 221, 224
Uniformed Services Employment and Reemployment Rights Act, 220
Unilever, 85, 146
Union of South American Nations (UNASUR), 160–161
Union Pacific, 94
Unit goal setting, 153
United Airlines, 5, 46, 47, 242, 281
United Airlines-Continental Airlines merger, 148
United Technologies Corporation (UTC), 181, 182
Unity of command, 34, 187
Unity of direction, 34
Universal principle stage, 74
Unrelated diversification, 120
unsiloing, 319
Unstructured interviews, 232
Unsupervised data mining, 362
UPS, 72–76, 339
Upward communication, 320
Uruguay Round, 158
U.S. Air Force, 230
U.S. Airways, 46, 47
U.S. Sentencing Commission Guidelines for Organizations, 69–71
U.S. Steel, 54
USB slots, 145

V

Valence, 278
Valuable resources, 112
Value, 348
van Beurden, Ben, 151
Variable interval reinforcement schedule, 284

Variable ratio reinforcement schedule, 284
Variation, 383
VC firms, *see* Venture capital (VC) firms
Venetians, 24
Venture capital (VC) firms, 61
Verizon, 128, 130, 138
Verschatse, Ludwig, 335
Vertesi, Janet, 367
Vertical loading, 192
Vestibule training, 235
Viacom, 84
Virtual organization, 197–199
Virtual organization agreement, 199
Virtual private network (VPN), 367
Virtual reality headsets, 93, 143
Virtual team, 207
Virus, 365, 366
Visible artifacts, 64
Vision, 95, 150
Visionary leadership, 307–311
Vlastelica, John, 65
Voice messaging (voice mail), 329–330
Voluntary export restraints, 157
Volunteerism, 78
VPN, *see* Virtual private network
Vroom-Yetton-Jago model, 303

W

Wages, 19
Walgreens, 254
Walk-ins, 226
Walk the talk, 150
Walmart, 56, 83–84, 115, 171, 275, 358, 369
Walt Disney Company, 13, 84, 96, 164
Wardell, Chuck, 229
Warner Bros. Entertainment, 294
Wasendorf, Russell, Sr., 308
Waste and pollution minimization, 348–351
Waste disposal, 351
Waste prevention and reduction, 349–350
Waste treatment, 351
WeatherFX, 53
Web services, 369, 370
Weber, Max, 30–32, 307, 339
Weimerskirch, Arnold, 381
Weiner, Jeff, 293
Weiner, Russell, 301
Weirton Steel Corp., 242
Wendy's, 53, 128, 130
West, Mike, 62
Western Electric Company, 35
Westinghouse Electric, 236
Westinghouse University, 236
Wetzel, Andy, 301
Whistleblowing, 79–80
White hat hackers, 368

Whitehorn, Symon, 137
Whitehurst, Jim, 61, 62, 329
Whitney, Eli, 39
Whole Foods, 282–283, 310
Wholly owned affiliates, 166
Wi-Fi alliance, 368
Wilson, Thomas, 321
WinCo, 126
Windows 8 operating system, 47
Winkler, Howard, 77
Wipro, 240
Wireless carriers, 130–131
Wireless networks, 367–368
Wireless Power Consortium (WPC), 138
Wizz Air, 377
Wladawsky-Berger, Irving, 89
Wolfchase Toyota-Scion, 331
Women
  glass ceiling, 254
  high-level positions, 256
  married women (with children) who work, 50, 51
  pay inequality, 255
  sex discrimination, 254–256
Wong, Simon, 5
Wood, Andrew, 146
Wood, Melissa, 146
Woodward, Richard, 330
Work group encouragement, 142
Work-in-process inventories, 390
Work sample tests, 231

Work team, 201, *see also* Teams and teamwork
Workforce Central, 92
Workforce Ready, 92
Workforce scheduling, 92
Workplace deviance, 68–69
Workplace diversity, 248–266
  affirmative action, 250–251
  age, 253–254
  attracting/retaining talented workers, 252
  cost savings, 251–252
  deep-level diversity, 258–260
  diversity paradigms, 261–263
  diversity principles, 263–264
  diversity training and practices, 264–266
  driving business growth, 252
  mental or physical disabilities, 257–258
  personality, 259–260
  race and ethnicity, 256–257
  sex, 254–256
  surface-level diversity, 252–258
Workplace violence, 69
World Trade Organization (WTO), 158, 159
World Vision, 69
World's best cities for business, 170
Worm, 365
Written communication, 324
Wrongful discharge, 244

Wrongful termination lawsuits, 52
WTO, *see* World Trade Organization

Xenophon, 24
Xerox, 265
Xu, William, 11

Yahoo!, 354
Yamaha, 394
Yammer, 330
Your Shape: Fitness Evolved 2012 (Xbox), 283
YouTube, 53
Yuanqing, Yang, 277
Yum! Brands, 49, 165

Z

Zappos.com, 234
Zarrilli, Stephen, 11
Zellers, 97
ZenBox, 125
Zetlin, Minda, 278
Zichermann, Gabe, 272
Zone of indifference, 38
Zynga, 243, 363
Zynga, Andy, 215

A GUIDE FOR NEW MANAGERS: SIX STEPS TO BECOME A SUCCESSFUL MANAGER

—ED MUZIO

If you've recently been hired as a manager, you know the dirty secret: Management positions come with surprisingly little guidance. Whether you were promoted internally or brought in from outside, you were probably expected to hit the ground running, toward only the vaguest of goals.

Many of the problems new managers experience stem from that secret. They are faced with an ill-defined job and equally intense pressure from above and below. Plus, as the pivot points in the information revolution, they are barraged with queries about the work of their groups.

It's easy to see why capable, well-meaning managers resort to micromanagement, detachment, grandstanding, or sheer blockheadedness in an effort to find some sort of stability for themselves and their employees.

How can you avoid these pitfalls? The following six steps will help you define your purpose as manager:

1. DEFINE YOUR OWN JOB CLEARLY.

If you're a new manager, this is your first and most important step. You need a memorable, meaningful definition, something that you can figuratively (or literally) write across your bathroom mirror so that you see it every morning.

I suggest "engender useful output." Your primary responsibility as a manager is to maximize the likelihood that your employees will be productive; your task is to create an environment in which employee output is clearly defined and realistically achievable. If you're not doing that, then it doesn't matter what data you're gathering, which employees you're monitoring, or whose ear you're bending. You may be busy, you may be stressed, and you may look managerial, but you're not doing your job.

2. DEFINE YOUR GROUP'S OUTPUT.

To engender output you must first define it. This task is easier said than done. Today's workplace changes quickly, and managers at all levels are expected to turn the work of their groups on a dime. Your own manager may not be terribly clear on long range company plans, so neither of you may fully understand how the work of your group will change in the next quarter, month, or even week.

Uncertainty about the future is not an excuse for lack of productivity in the present. If your plan is to wait around until everything is known before doing anything, you might as well lock the doors and go home for good! Things will change again and again, and only by delivering on current plans will you and your company learn what works, and what changes to make next. Besides, the definition of your group's required output is the definition of YOUR required output as manager. Defining it is one part good management practice and one part career survival.

3. SEEK MOMENTARY CLARITY RATHER THAN PERMANENT ANSWERS.

Speak with your leaders about what your group can reasonably produce right now and then agree to task your group with producing it right now. Make it clear that unless you hear otherwise, until the next scheduled check-in you will follow the current plan. Then, verbally summarize the output you are committing to engender in about 90 seconds. During follow-up discussions with your management, use that mini-commercial as a way to gently remind them what you are working on so that they can edit your understanding if needed.

When changes, do come, don't fight them. Welcome the new information, openly revise your understanding of what you need to produce, and clearly explain the time and resources you need to accomplish the change. If you can't turn the boat in an hour, say so. It's far better to be up front when something isn't possible than to agree to it under duress but fail to deliver.

4. BECOME AN EXPERT IN DEFINING AND COMMUNICATING EXPECTATIONS.

Of course, your definition is only half the story. To engender output from your group, you need to convert from the commitment you made as manager into what each of your employees must do individually.

Contrary to popular opinion, this doesn't mean telling your employees what to do. It means teaching them to discuss what they are doing themselves—to create their own 90-second mini-commercials—and then working with them on a shared understanding of what's needed. You haven't successfully taught an employee his or her expected output until you hear that person say it to you spontaneously, in a way that matches your own understanding. Then you know it's happening.

This also means your employees must be in the habit of speaking openly about what they are doing. To get honesty, avoid using discussions about current objectives as pop quizzes! When you need to adjust an employee's understanding of his or her work, frame your conversation as being about expectations for the future and defining how to succeed. Don't let it degrade into how the employee should already know these things. Remember: When your employees don't know what they're supposed to be doing, it's at least as likely to be your fault as theirs.

5. KEEP TALKING ABOUT OUTPUT.

A VSO, or *verbalized summary objective statement*, is a kind of mini-commercial in which you state the output you're trying to deliver at the moment. It should take about 90 seconds and should list about 5–7 output goals that together cover about 80% of what you are working on. It's yours to change, adjust, and modify whenever you see fit. It's also yours to use as your introduction whenever you're talking to people in or about your workplace. Use VSOs with your management and teach your employees to use them with you.

Why? Your VSO trains people as to what to expect—and not expect—from you. It provides an avenue for a manager to edit an employee's understanding of the job, and a basis for you to accept or decline requests for additional work. As time goes by, and you deliver on your VSO, you also increase your credibility within the organization as people see that you are following through on your commitments.

6. KEEP AT IT.

Management is like exercise: it's often difficult, you're never done, and it requires self-discipline.

Get in the habit of having conversations with superiors about the output needed from your group and discussions with your employees about their individual contributions to that output. Then remind yourself that your job is to maximize the chances that your employees will produce. This won't make management easy, but it's the first step in making you better at it.

AUTHOR BIO

Edward G. Muzio, CEO of Group Harmonics, is the author of the award winning books *Make Work Great: Supercharge Your Team, Reinvent the Culture, and Gain Influence One Person at a Time* and *Four Secrets to Liking Your Work: You May Not Need to Quit to Get the Job You Want*. An expert in workplace improvement and its relationship to individual enjoyment, Muzio has been featured on Fox Business Network, CBS, and other national media. For more information visit *Make Work Great* and follow the author on Facebook.

WHAT'S INSIDE:

Key topics in this chapter: definition of management, four functions of management, kinds of managers, Mintzberg's managerial roles, management skills, what makes successful and unsuccessful managers, the transition from employee to manager, and how good management increases a company's competitive advantage.

CHAPTER OUTLINE

1-1 **Management Is... 3**

1-2 **Management Functions 4**
1-2a Planning 4
1-2b Organizing 5
1-2c Leading 5
1-2d Controlling 6

1-3 **Kinds of Managers 6**
1-3a Top Managers 6
1-3b Middle Managers 8
1-3c First-Line Managers 9
1-3d Team Leaders 9

1-4 **Managerial Roles 10**
1-4a Interpersonal Roles 10
1-4b Informational Roles 11
1-4c Decisional Roles 12

1-5 **What Companies Look for in Managers 13**

1-6 **Mistakes Managers Make 15**

1-7 **The Transition to Management: The First Year 17**

1-8 **Competitive Advantage Through People 19**

LEARNING OUTCOMES

1-1 Describe what management is.

1-2 Explain the four functions of management.

1-3 Describe different kinds of managers.

1-4 Explain the major roles and subroles that managers perform in their jobs.

1-5 Explain what companies look for in managers.

1-6 Discuss the top mistakes that managers make in their jobs.

1-7 Describe the transition that employees go through when they are promoted to management.

1-8 Explain how and why companies can create competitive advantage through people.

VIDEO

*Profile on Camp Bow Wow

Run time: approximately 10 minutes

Sue Ryan, a Camp Bow Wow franchisee from Colorado, knows the ins and outs of managing a care center for pets. To help launch her business a few years ago, Ryan recruited experienced pet care worker Candace Stathis, who came on as a camp counselor. Ryan soon recognized that Stathis was a star performer with a natural ability to work with clients and pets alike, and today, Stathis serves as the camp's general manager. At Camp Bow Wow, store managers have distinct roles from camp counselors. Whereas counselors typically take care of dogs, answer phones, and book reservations, managers must know how to run all operations and mange people as well. To keep the camp running as efficiently as possible, Stathis maintains a strict daily schedule for doggie baths, nail trimmings, feedings, and play time.

Ask your students:

1. List the four functions of management and explain which might be most needed for the Camp Bow Wow leaders highlighted in the video.

2. Which activities at Camp Bow Wow require high efficiency? Which activities require high effectiveness?

3. List two activities that leaders at Camp Bow Wow perform daily, and identify which of the managerial roles discussed in the chapter figure prominently for each.

INSTRUCTOR PREP 1

TERMS

Management 3

Efficiency 3

Effectiveness 3

Planning 4

Organizing 5

Leading 5

Controlling 6

Top managers 6

Middle managers 8

First-line managers 9

Team leaders 9

Figurehead role 11

Leader role 11

Liaison role 11

Monitor role 12

Disseminator role 12

Spokesperson role 12

Entrepreneur role 13

Disturbance handler role 13

Resource allocator role 13

Negotiator role 13

Technical skills 14

Human skills 14

Conceptual skills 15

Motivation to manage 15

NEW TO MGMT8

(by section)

1-1 New examples on Starbucks and Amazon

1-2a New example on Alibaba

1-2c New example on Sparta Systems

1-3a New examples on Novelis and new feature box on Square Enix

1-3b New examples on life as a middle manager and the Wharton School of Business

1-3d New examples about great leaders

1-4a New examples on CST Brands and Huawei Enterprises

1-4b New example on Amazon

1-4c New example on Target and Ford

1-6 New example about failing to delegate

1-7 New feature box on being a new CFO

DISCUSSION QUESTIONS

1. There is no formal code of conduct for managers. Given the regularity with which business scandals are reported in the press, do you think a code should be developed?

2. Do you think one (or more) of Mintzberg's roles is more important than the others? Why or why not?

3. Which of the top ten mistakes that managers make do you think is the most serious or the most likely to cause derailment on its own?

GROUP ACTIVITY

"SAYING NO TO AN INVESTOR"

Divide the class into groups of three to five students and give each group the following scenario:

You are the senior management team at Honest Tea, a company dedicated to providing healthy drinks that use all organic and unprocessed ingredients. The company proudly displays its commitment by including a label on all of its products that says, "No High Fructose Corn Syrup," a sweetener that has been criticized for increasing obesity, diabetes symptoms, and liver disease.

However, one of your biggest investors, Coca-Cola, is disturbed by the label, which it sees as a criticism of its own products, most of which use high fructose corn syrup. So, senior managers from Coca-Cola ask your company to either change the label or get rid of it. While all of you are deeply committed to Honest Tea's mission, you're also concerned about not angering Coca-Cola, which owns 40 percent of your company.

Questions

1. How is this decision emblematic of a manager's role as a liaison?

2. How would your team respond to Coca-Cola's request?

Source: E. Olson, "Can Honest Tea Say No to Coke, Its Biggest Investor?" *New York Times*, July 7, 2010, accessed July 10, 2010, http://www.nytimes.com/2010/07/08/business /smallbusiness/08sbiz.html?dbk.

ASSIGNMENTS

Have students go to the website of Stephenville, Texas, at http://www .ci.stephenville.tx.us. There is a link at the site labeled "City Government" that shows the organizational chart of the city government. Instruct students to determine who would be considered 1) top management, 2) middle management, and 3) first-level management. Ask students if they think team managers could also be used in this city government.

Large Section

Assign the electronic case homework and quiz on *Netflix*.

ADDITIONAL RESOURCES

A selection of materials can be found in the Instructor Manual.

WHAT'S INSIDE:

Key topics in this chapter: origins of management and key management theorists and the different schools of management thought, including scientific management, bureaucratic and administrative management, human relations management, and operations, information, systems, and contingency management.

LEARNING OUTCOMES

2-1 Explain the origins of management.

2-2 Explain the history of scientific management.

2-3 Discuss the history of bureaucratic and administrative management.

2-4 Explain the history of human relations management.

2-5 Discuss the history of operations, information, systems, and contingency management.

CHAPTER OUTLINE

2-1 The Origins of Management 23
  2-1a Management Ideas and Practices Throughout History 23
  2-1b Why We Need Managers Today 23

2-2 Scientific Management 25
  2-2a Father of Scientific Management: Frederick W. Taylor 25
  2-2b Motion Studies: Frank and Lillian Gilbreth 27
  2-2c Charts: Henry Gantt 29

2-3 Bureaucratic and Administrative Management 30
  2-3a Bureaucratic Management: Max Weber 30
  2-3b Administrative Management: Henri Fayol 32

2-4 Human Relations Management 33
  2-4a Constructive Conflict and Coordination: Mary Parker Follett 33
  2-4b Hawthorne Studies: Elton Mayo 35
  2-4c Cooperation and Acceptance of Authority: Chester Barnard 38

VIDEO

*Profile on Barcelona Restaurant Group

Run time: approximately 10 minutes

Andy Pforzheimer is himself a renowned chef and the co-owner of Barcelona Restaurant Group, a collection of seven wine and tapas bars in Connecticut and Georgia. When customers dine at any of Pforzheimer's restaurants, they experience the local color and personal touch of a neighborhood eatery. The wait staff is personable and strives to get to know customers' tastes. Delivering this unique dining experience requires a unique approach to management. The company gives employees the freedom and control they need to impress customers. It recruits self-confident individuals who can take ownership over the establishment and its success. Further, Pforzheimer is adamant that his staff be mature and willing to take responsibility for their work and success.

Ask your students:

1. What aspects of restaurant work are especially challenging to wait staff, and how does Barcelona's approach to management help employees overcome the downsides of the job?

2. What steps do the leaders of Barcelona Restaurant Group take to ensure cooperation and acceptance of authority from their employees?

3. Would the management style of Barcelona Restaurant Group best be described as scientific management or contingency management?

NEW TO MGMT8

(by section)

Because this chapter addresses the history of management, the content has remained intact from *MGMT6*.

DISCUSSION QUESTIONS

1. Managers have been around only since the nineth century. Does that mean that the origin of management also dates to that time? Explain.

2. Managers who have unchecked power, authority, and autonomy are more likely to engage in unethical and illegal behaviors. How can companies check the power of managers without resorting to micromanaging.

INSTRUCTOR PREP 2

2-5 Operations, Information, Systems, and Contingency Management 38

2-5a Operations Management 38

2-5b Information Management 39

2-5c Systems Management 40

2-5d Contingency Management 41

TERMS

Scientific management 25

Soldiering 25

Rate buster 26

Motion study 28

Time study 28

Gantt chart 29

Bureaucracy 30

Domination 35

Compromise 35

Integrative conflict resolution 35

Organization 38

System 40

Subsystems 40

Synergy 41

Closed systems 41

Open systems 41

Contingency approach 42

GROUP ACTIVITY

"TOUGH LOVE?"

Divide the class into groups of three to five students and give each group the following scenario:

All 305 employees of a Mott's apple juice plant have been on strike for more than three months. They are protesting the fact that the company wants to make severe cuts in pay and benefits—a reduction of wages by $3,000 per year, a pension freeze, a reduction in 401(k) contributions, and a decrease in the health insurance subsidy.

While cuts in pay and benefits are nothing new during recessions, what is unusual in this case is that Mott's parent company, Dr. Pepper Snapple Group, is more profitable than ever. In the last year, its net income was $550 million, a dramatic improvement from the previous year, when it lost $312 million. Because of this success, employees are accusing the company of being greedy. The company, meanwhile, defends the cuts by arguing that its current labor costs are considerably higher than those of other local companies. The average pay at the Mott's plant is $21 per hour, while other factories and transportation companies in the area pay closer to $14 per hour.

Questions

1. How could you help steer negotiations between labor and management so that the conflict between them is healthy and productive? Is that even possible?

2. Is the company justified in trying to cut costs even when it has made a huge profit? Are the employees justified in not working to protest what they perceive as unfair cuts?

Source: S. Greenhouse, "In Mott's Strike, More Than Pay at Stake," *New York Times*, August 17, 2010, accessed August 20, 2010, http://www.nytimes.com/2010/08/18/business/18motts.html?_r=2&adxnnl=1&adxnnlx=1285063223-w2+X3nxQPGJVMXG0FhiuDQ.

ASSIGNMENTS

Ask students to read the first three chapters of *Cheaper by the Dozen*, written by Frank Gilbreth Jr. and his sister Ernestine Gilbreth Carey about their parents, specifically, their father, Frank Gilbreth. Ask students to respond to the following questions: What management theories are described in the book? How did the Gilbreths apply their theories in their family situation? How did their family situation inspire new management ideas?

Large Section

Assign the electronic case homework and quiz on *ISG Steelton*.

ADDITIONAL RESOURCES

A selection of materials can be found in the Instructor Manual.

WHAT'S INSIDE:

Key topics in this chapter: effect of changing environments on organizations, four components of the general environment, five components of the specific environment, a three-step process to make sense of a company's changing environment, and creation of organizational cultures that foster success.

LEARNING OUTCOMES

3-1 Discuss how changing environments affect organizations.

3-2 Describe the four components of the general environment.

3-3 Explain the five components of the specific environment.

3-4 Describe the process that companies use to make sense of their changing environments.

3-5 Explain how organizational cultures are created and how they can help companies be successful.

CHAPTER OUTLINE

3-1 Changing Environments 45
  3-1a Environmental Change 45
  3-1b Environmental Complexity 47
  3-1c Resource Scarcity 47
  3-1d Uncertainty 48

3-2 General Environment 48
  3-2a Economy 49
  3-2b Technological Component 50
  3-2c Sociocultural Component 50
  3-2d Political/Legal Component 51

3-3 Specific Environment 52
  3-3a Customer Component 52
  3-3b Competitor Component 53
  3-3c Supplier Component 54
  3-3d Industry Regulation Component 55
  3-3e Advocacy Groups 56

3-4 Making Sense of Changing Environments 57
  3-4a Environmental Scanning 57
  3-4b Interpreting Environmental Factors 58
  3-4c Acting on Threats and Opportunities 58

VIDEO

*Profile on Camp Bow Wow

Run time: approximately 10 minutes

In ten years, Camp Bow Wow has grown from a single kennel in Denver, Colorado, to a $40 million business, with more than 150 locations. The transition from a small family business to a national chain, however, required a shift from a family-based culture to a business- and performancebased culture. A key element of Camp Bow Wow's culture is the staff's deep emotional connection with animals. The connection is immediately apparent at corporate headquarters, where offices are bustling with employees and pets alike. According to founder Heidi Ganahal, "What we do is focus on what's important to us, and that's the animals."

Ask your students:

1. What aspects of Camp Bow Wow's corporate culture reflect the surface level of the organizational culture? What aspects reflect the values and beliefs? What aspects reflect the unconsciously held assumptions and beliefs?

2. Why did Camp Bow Wow have to change its culture when it became a national franchise?

3. What impact does Heidi Ganahl's personal story have on employees at Camp Bow Wow?

NEW TO MGMT8

(by section)

3-1   New example on Uber and new feature box on risk management

3-1c   New example on Chenab Ltd.

3-2   New example on Yum! Brands

3-2a   New example on the Organization for Economic Cooperation and Development

3-2c   New example on the European auto sector

3-2d   New wrongful termination statistics

3-3a   New example on The Weather Co.

3-3c   New examples on Apple, Samsung, and Dreamworks, and new feature box on Walmart

3-3e   New example on Cadbury

3-4a   New example on Skybox

INSTRUCTOR PREP 3

3-5 Organizational Cultures: Creation, Success, and Change 60
3-5a Creation and Maintenance of Organizational Cultures 60
3-5b Successful Organizational Cultures 61
3-5c Changing Organizational Cultures 62

TERMS

External environments 45
Environmental change 45
Stable environment 45
Dynamic environment 45
Punctuated equilibrium theory 46
Environmental complexity 47
Simple environment 47
Complex environment 47
Resource scarcity 47
Uncertainty 48
General environment 48
Specific environment 48
Business confidence indices 50
Technology 50
Competitors 53
Competitive analysis 53
Suppliers 54
Supplier dependence 54
Buyer dependence 54
Opportunistic behavior 54
Relationship behavior 54
Industry regulation 55
Advocacy groups 56
Public communications 56
Media advocacy 56
Product boycott 56
Environmental scanning 57
Cognitive maps 59
Internal environment 60
Organizational culture 60
Organizational stories 61
Organizational heroes 61
Company mission 62
Consistent organizational culture 62
Behavioral addition 63
Behavioral substitution 63
Visible artifacts 64

3-4b New example on the Panama Canal

3-5a New examples on Steve Jobs, Walt Disney, Andreesen Horowitz, and Cognizant

3-5b New example on BPV Capital Management and new feature box on Eaton

3-5c New examples on the Cleveland Browns and Amazon

DISCUSSION QUESTIONS

1. What forces determine how a company conducts its business?

2. How important is it to you to know all the details when you're involved in something? Under what conditions do you find uncertainty stressful? Under what conditions do you find uncertainty energizing?

3. Where should a manager draw the line with regard to giving and receiving gifts? How much is too much?

GROUP ACTIVITY

"DESIGN A NEW OFFICE"

Divide the class into groups of three to five students and give each group the following scenario:

In just three short years, your graphic design firm has grown rapidly—from three full-time employees to nearly 100. So it seems like the ideal time to build a new office facility, one that will accommodate all of the new employees and provide room for future growth. Employees want space to meet with other colleagues and bounce around ideas. They also want some quiet space where they can think creatively. They want a place that is comfortable but not so casual that people come to work wearing shorts and sandals. Most of all, they want a place that will help stir creativity and innovation, the lifeblood of your company.

As a team, your task is to create an office design that reflects the company culture that your employees want to cultivate.

ASSIGNMENTS

Ask students to collect stories about the founder of a large business, such as Walmart or Starbucks. Ask them to write a paper focusing on who the founders are, what vision they created, and how they may still influence the culture of the organization.

Large Section

Assign the electronic case homework and quiz on *Waste Management*.

ADDITIONAL RESOURCES

A selection of materials can be found in the Instructor Manual.

WHAT'S INSIDE:

Key topics in this chapter: common kinds of workplace deviance, US Sentencing Commission Guidelines for Organizations, ethical decision making, socially responsible organizations, and effects of social responsibility on an organization's economic performance.

CHAPTER OUTLINE

4-1 Workplace Deviance 67

4-2 U.S. Sentencing Commission Guidelines for Organizations 69
4-2a Who, What, and Why? 69
4-2b Determining the Punishment 69

4-3 Influences on Ethical Decision Making 72
4-3a Ethical Intensity of the Decision 72
4-3b Moral Development 73
4-3c Principles of Ethical Decision Making 74

4-4 Practical Steps to Ethical Decision Making 76
4-4a Selecting and Hiring Ethical Employees 76
4-4b Codes of Ethics 76
4-4c Ethics Training 77
4-4d Ethical Climate 78

4-5 To Whom Are Organizations Socially Responsible? 80

4-6 For What Are Organizations Socially Responsible? 82

4-7 Responses to Demands for Social Responsibility 84

4-8 Social Responsibility and Economic Performance 86

LEARNING OUTCOMES

4-1 Identify common kinds of workplace deviance.

4-2 Describe the US Sentencing Commission Guidelines for Organizations and explain how they both encourage ethical behavior and punish unethical behavior by businesses.

4-3 Describe what influences ethical decision making.

4-4 Explain what practical steps managers can take to improve ethical decision making.

4-5 Explain to whom organizations are socially responsible.

4-6 Explain for what organizations are socially responsible.

4-7 Explain how organizations can respond to societal demands for social responsibility.

4-8 Explain whether social responsibility hurts or helps an organization's economic performance.

VIDEO

*Profile on Theo Chocolate

Run time: approximately 10 minutes

Joe Whinney exudes a sense of mission in everything he does. After a trip to cacao farms in Central America, Whinney decided to build the first organic fair trade chocolate factory in the United States. By building the first sustainable chocolate maker in the nation, Whinney hoped to help solve social and environmental issues by operating a profitable and ethical business. While Theo Chocolate is finding good success in the organic foods industry, perhaps the most exciting thing for "Theonistas" is that the company is being hailed as a voice for change. Employees say they have gained a loyal following for their efforts in the developing world, and business success has opened up new opportunities for sharing their vision of a better world.

Ask your students:

1. Which of the four strategies for responding to social responsibility best reflects Theo Chocolate?

2. How does Theo Chocolate's business practices reflect the stakeholder model of social responsibility?

3. What would happen if fair trade goals conflicted with a company's primary responsibility to be profitable?

INSTRUCTOR PREP 4

TERMS

Ethics 67

Ethical behavior 67

Workplace deviance 68

Production deviance 68

Property deviance 68

Employee shrinkage 68

Political deviance 69

Personal aggression 69

Ethical intensity 72

Magnitude of consequences 72

Social consensus 72

Probability of effect 72

Temporal immediacy 73

Proximity of effect 73

Concentration of effect 73

Preconventional level of moral development 73

Conventional level of moral development 73

Postconventional level of moral development 74

Principle of long-term self-interest 74

Principle of religious injunctions 75

Principle of government requirements 75

Principle of individual rights 75

Principle of personal virtue 75

Principle of distributive justice 75

Principle of utilitarian benefits 76

Overt integrity test 76

Personality-based integrity test 76

Whistleblowing 79

Social responsibility 80

Shareholder model 80

Stakeholder model 80

Stakeholders 80

NEW TO MGMT8

(by section)

4-1   Updated statistics on ethics in business and workplace deviance

4-2a   New example on World Vision

4-3   New example on UPS

4-4   New data on ethics training

4-4c   New examples on Southern Co. and Intuitive Research and Technology Corp.

4-4d   New statistics on ethical climate; new examples on the Supreme Court and Paychex

4-5   New example on Exxon Mobil

4-6   New examples on Symantec and Walmart

4-7   New examples on General Motors, Novartis, and Unilever; new feature box on social responsibility in India

DISCUSSION QUESTIONS

1. Is workplace deviance a fact of life for companies, or can it be mitigated? Explain.

2. If you can't hire entirely ethical employees, can you teach employees to act more ethically than they might be inclined? How?

3. Would you be willing to pay more for products made by socially responsible companies? How much more?

Primary stakeholder 81

Secondary stakeholder 81

Economic responsibility 82

Legal responsibility 83

Ethical responsibility 83

GROUP ACTIVITY

"ETHICS DEBATE"

Divide the class into thirds (or into six groups, if your class is large). One third (or two groups) will represent a major tobacco company like R.J. Reynolds or Altria. The second third will represent an anti-smoking activist group. The last third will represent the US government. The topic that will be debated is: Should tobacco companies cease and desist all advertising in the United States? Each group should thoroughly research the issues, write a position statement, and come prepared to debate in class. An especially interesting way to divide students would be to include smokers in the anti-smoking group and nonsmokers in the group representing tobacco companies.

ASSIGNMENTS

Ask students to read Johnson & Johnson's credo at http://www.jnj.com /sites/default/files/pdf/jnj_ourcredo _english_us_8.5x11_cmyk.pdf. Have them identify the four major groups of stakeholders referred to in the credo. They should also describe each group and indicate how important it is to the company. Finally, ask students: What is the reasoning behind the order in which the stakeholders are listed?

Large Section

Assign the electronic case homework and quiz on *American Express*.

ADDITIONAL RESOURCES

A selection of materials can be found in the Instructor Manual.

Discretionary responsibilities 84

Social responsiveness 84

Reactive strategy 84

Defensive strategy 85

Accommodative strategy 85

Proactive strategy 85

WHAT'S INSIDE:

Key topics in this chapter: benefits and pitfalls of planning, five steps to making a plan that works, planning at all management levels, steps and limits to rational decision making and group decisions, and group decision-making techniques.

LEARNING OUTCOMES

5-1 Discuss the benefits and pitfalls of planning.

5-2 Describe how to make a plan that works.

5-3 Discuss how companies can use plans at all management levels, from top to bottom.

5-4 Explain the steps and limits to rational decision making.

5-5 Explain how group decisions and group decision-making techniques can improve decision making.

CHAPTER OUTLINE

5-1 Benefits and Pitfalls of Planning 89
5-1a Benefits of Planning 89
5-1b Pitfalls of Planning 90

5-2 How to Make a Plan That Works 90
5-2a Setting Goals 91
5-2b Developing Commitment to Goals 92
5-2c Developing Effective Action Plans 92
5-2d Tracking Progress 92
5-2e Maintaining Flexibility 93

5-3 Planning from Top to Bottom 94
5-3a Starting at the Top 95
5-3b Bending in the Middle 96
5-3c Finishing at the Bottom 97

5-4 Steps and Limits to Rational Decision Making 98
5-4a Define the Problem 99
5-4b Identify Decision Criteria 100
5-4c Weigh the Criteria 100
5-4d Generate Alternative Courses of Action 101
5-4e Evaluate Each Alternative 101
5-4f Compute the Optimal Decision 101
5-4g Limits to Rational Decision Making 102

VIDEO

*Profile on Plant Fantasies

Run time: approximately 9 minutes

Teresa Carleo, owner of Plant Fantasies, is the gardener for such well-known New York City properties as the Trump Organization, John Jay College, and Jack Resnick & Sons. In landscaping, success often boils down to big decisions over little details. While some decisions involve plant colors and types, others involve complex negotiation with people, such as when Plant Fantasies builds designs created by outside landscape architects. Despite Carleo's confidence in her own decision making, the Plant Fantasies owner understands the benefits of empowering others. But regardless of who makes decisions, Carleo expects all her employees to share her high standards for quality.

Ask your students:

1. Did Plant Fantasies owner Teresa Carleo follow the rational decision-making process to launch Plant Fantasies? Explain.

2. List an example of a programmed decision at Plant Fantasies. Identify a nonprogrammed decision at Plant Fantasies.

NEW TO MGMT8

(by section)

5-1a New example on ID3

5-2a New example on Novelis

5-2e New example on Union Pacific and new feature box on scheduling

5-3a New examples on Jennifer Dulski and Tesla and new feature box on Apple

5-3c New example on "presenteeism"

5-4a New example on Guitar Center

5-5 New statistics on usage of teams

5-5b New example on ZestFinance

DISCUSSION QUESTIONS

1. What processes do you go through to make a decision? Is it the same for all levels of decisions?

2. What do you personally think is the biggest obstacle to making good decisions?

3. Do you think it is easier to make decisions as an individual or as part of a group?

INSTRUCTOR PREP 5

TERMS

Planning 89

S.M.A.R.T. goals 91

Goal commitment 92

Action plan 92

Proximal goals 92

Distal goals 93

Options-based planning 93

Slack resources 93

Strategic plans 95

Purpose statement 95

Strategic objective 96

Tactical plans 96

Management by objectives 97

Operational plans 97

Single-use plans 97

Standing plans 97

Policies 97

Procedures 98

Rules and regulations 98

Budgeting 98

Decision making 98

Rational decision making 98

Problem 99

Decision criteria 100

Absolute comparisons 100

Relative comparisons 100

Maximize 103

Satisficing 103

Groupthink 103

C-type conflict (cognitive conflict) 104

A-type conflict (affective conflict) 105

Devil's advocacy 105

Dialectical inquiry 105

Nominal group technique 105

Delphi technique 106

Brainstorming 106

Electronic brainstorming 106

Production blocking 106

Evaluation apprehension 106

5-5 **Using Groups to Improve Decision Making** 103

5-5a Advantages and Pitfalls of Group Decision Making 103

5-5b Structured Conflict 104

5-5c Nominal Group Technique 105

5-5d Delphi Technique 106

5-5e Electronic Brainstorming 106

GROUP ACTIVITY

"DISASTER PLANNING"

Divide the class into small groups and assign them the task of creating a disaster response plan for their company. Their plan should be general enough so that it is applicable to a variety of disaster situations (e.g., hurricane, tornado, earthquake, fire). It should also be as comprehensive as possible, so that it details how the company will handle issues like disruptions in operations, employee and family notifications, supplier/customer relationships, and working with government responders. The students may also want to consider how their company will respond to the physical and material needs of the larger community.

ASSIGNMENTS

Have students research a company that is currently facing a big dilemma. The dilemma can be ethical, financial, political, etc. Students should thoroughly study the problem, research potential solutions, and use the rational decision-making process to decide what should be done.

Have groups work through the decision of where to live as a new college student. Each group should generate a list of decision criteria, weight the criteria in both absolute and relative fashion, and then generate a list of alternatives.

Large Section

Assign the electronic case homework and quiz on *Dupont*.

ADDITIONAL RESOURCES

A selection of materials can be found in the Instructor Manual.

WHAT'S INSIDE:

Key topics in this chapter: components of sustainable competitive advantage; steps in the strategy-making process; and corporate-, industry-, and firm-level strategies, including portfolio strategy and Porter's five industry forces.

LEARNING OUTCOMES

6-1 Specify the components of sustainable competitive advantage, and explain why it is important.

6-2 Describe the steps involved in the strategy-making process.

6-3 Explain the different kinds of corporate-level strategies.

6-4 Describe the different kinds of industry-level strategies.

6-5 Explain the components and kinds of firm-level strategies.

CHAPTER OUTLINE

6-1 Sustainable Competitive Advantage 111

6-2 Strategy-Making Process 113
6-2a Assessing the Need for Strategic Change 113
6-2b Situational Analysis 115
6-2c Choosing Strategic Alternatives 117

6-3 Corporate-Level Strategies 119
6-3a Portfolio Strategy 119
6-3b Grand Strategies 122

6-4 Industry-Level Strategies 124
6-4a Five Industry Forces 124
6-4b Positioning Strategies 126
6-4c Adaptive Strategies 127

6-5 Firm-Level Strategies 128
6-5a Direct Competition 129
6-5b Strategic Moves of Direct Competition 130

VIDEO

*Profile on Theo Chocolate

Run time: approximately 9 minutes

When Theo Chocolate first started its production, the company offered an exotic line of dark chocolate and milk chocolate bars and truffles. These early treats had unusual names such as the 3400 Phinney Bar, and they were wrapped in artistic watercolor packaging with whimsical cover designs. Though the chocolate was well received by critics and organic food enthusiasts, it was not popular with mainstream consumers. Founder Joe Whinney began working on a new strategy, creating classic milk chocolate bars as a gateway product that would attract consumers more easily. The end result is that Theo now offers two distinct product lines for two different market segments—the Classic line of milk chocolate bars for mainstream customers, and Fantasy Flavors for more adventurous eaters.

Ask your students:

1. Evaluate Theo's new strategy in light of the company's strengths, weaknesses, opportunities, and threats.

2. Using the BCG matrix, explain Theo's decision to offer a classic line of chocolate bars after having limited success with Fantasy Flavor chocolates.

3. Which of the three competitive strategies—differentiation, cost leadership, or focus—do you think is right for Theo Chocolate? Explain.

NEW TO MGMT8

(by section)

6-1 Updated statistics on the Apple iPad and Microsoft Surface tablets

6-2b Updated statistics on hardware retailers

6-3b New examples on AT&T and Barclays Plc

6-4a New example on Altos Research

6-4b New examples on WinCo Foods and Norwex and new feature box on the Dangers of Diversification

6-4c Updated examples on video streaming services and new feature box on Amazon

6-5b New example on wireless carriers and update to Kindle vs. Nook

INSTRUCTOR PREP 6

TERMS

Resources 111

Competitive advantage 111

Sustainable competitive advantage 112

Valuable resource 112

Rare resource 112

Imperfectly imitable resource 112

Nonsubstitutable resource 112

Competitive inertia 114

Strategic dissonance 114

Situational (SWOT) analysis 115

Distinctive competence 115

Core capabilities 115

Shadow-strategy task force 116

Strategic group 116

Core firms 116

Secondary firms 116

Strategic reference points 117

Corporate-level strategy 119

Diversification 119

Portfolio strategy 119

Acquisition 119

Unrelated diversification 120

BCG matrix 120

Star 120

Question mark 120

Cash cow 120

Dog 121

Related diversification 122

Grand strategy 122

Growth strategy 122

Stability strategy 123

Retrenchment strategy 124

Recovery 124

Industry-level strategy 124

Character of the rivalry 124

Threat of new entrants 125

Threat of substitute products or services 125

Bargaining power of suppliers 126

Bargaining power of buyers 126

Cost leadership 126

Differentiation 126

Focus strategy 127

Defenders 127

Prospectors 127

Analyzers 128

Reactors 128

Firm-level strategy 129

Direct competition 129

Market commonality 129

Resource similarity 129

Attack 130

Response 130

DISCUSSION QUESTIONS

1. Ask students to respond to this statement: Sustainable competitive advantage only functions well as a theory and is impossible in practice.

2. Do you do any benchmarking in order to boost your performance as a student, an athlete, or hobbyist of any sort? What do you do and how does it help?

GROUP ACTIVITY

"INDUSTRY ANALYSIS"

Divide the class into small groups. Each group should select a company that participates in an industry that has at least three other competitors. Groups should (1) identify the strategic group in which the company participates, (2) conduct analyses of the five industry forces, (3) determine which company uses which positioning strategy, and (4) determine which company uses which adaptive strategy. The groups should present their findings to the class.

ASSIGNMENTS

Ask students to do some basic research about Kodak, a company that faces an uncertain future due to the ubiquitous nature of digital photography. Ask students to assess the company's strengths, weaknesses, opportunities, and threats given the rapid changes in the digital age.

Large Section

Assign the electronic case homework and quiz on *The Walt Disney Company*.

ADDITIONAL RESOURCES

A selection of materials can be found in the Instructor Manual.

INSTRUCTOR PREP

Innovation and Change

WHAT'S INSIDE:

Key topics in this chapter: the importance of innovation, methods to effectively manage organizational innovation, organizational decline, and methods to better manage change.

CHAPTER OUTLINE

7-1 Why Innovation Matters 135
    7-1a Technology Cycles 135
    7-1b Innovation Streams 136

7-2 Managing Innovation 140
    7-2a Managing Sources of Innovation 140
    7-2b Experiential Approach: Managing Innovation during Discontinuous Change 142
    7-2c Compression Approach: Managing Innovation during Incremental Change 144

7-3 Organizational Decline: The Risk of Not Changing 146

7-4 Managing Change 147
    7-4a Managing Resistance to Change 148
    7-4b What Not to Do When Leading Change 149
    7-4c Change Tools and Techniques 151

LEARNING OUTCOMES

7-1 Explain why innovation matters to companies.

7-2 Discuss the different methods that managers can use to effectively manage innovation in their organizations.

7-3 Discuss why not changing can lead to organizational decline.

7-4 Discuss the different methods that managers can use to better manage change as it occurs.

VIDEO

*Profile on Holden Outerwear

Run time: approximately 10 minutes

Founded in 2002 by professional snowboarder Mikey LeBlanc, Holden Outerwear has given traditional baggy outerwear a complete style makeover. Unlike ski-apparel brands that focus on utility at the expense of looking good, Holden pants and jackets possess features that are inspired by runway brands like Marc Jacobs and G-Star, as Holden is always looking to bring new elements of style to the slopes. Holden has the attention of everyone in its industry. Retailers wait eagerly to see LeBlanc's newest collections, and competitors from Burton and Salomon to Bonfire and Walmart borrow heavily from Holden's collections. LeBlanc doesn't worry too much about the rampant plagiarism that goes on in his industry. As he sees it, imitation is the highest form of flattery. Plus, Holden's business is based on finding the next big thing. When it comes to style, Holden is the leader, never the follower.

Ask your students:

1. Identify the type of change that Holden's leaders are managing on a daily basis.

2. What resistance has Holden encountered while introducing innovative garment designs? How was it able to overcome that resistance?

NEW TO MGMT8

(by section)

7-1a Updated stats on processor chips

7-1b New examples on DSLR cameras, wireless charging devices, and AT&T and Verizon

7-2 New feature box on the Patent Trial and Appeal Board

7-2a New example on Burberry

7-2b New examples on Oculus Rift

7-2c New example on USB devices

7-4 New example on film vs. digital recording

7-4b New example on Nokia

7-4c New example on Royal Dutch Shell

INSTRUCTOR PREP 7

TERMS

Organizational innovation 135

Technology cycle 135

S-curve pattern of innovation 135

Innovation streams 137

Technological discontinuity 137

Discontinuous change 138

Technological substitution 138

Design competition 138

Dominant design 138

Technological lockout 139

Incremental change 140

Creative work environments 141

Flow 141

Experiential approach to innovation 142

Design iteration 143

Product prototype 143

Testing 143

Milestones 143

Multifunctional teams 144

Compression approach to innovation 144

Generational change 145

Organizational decline 146

Change forces 147

Resistance forces 147

Resistance to change 147

Unfreezing 148

Change intervention 148

Refreezing 148

Coercion 149

Results-driven change 151

General Electric workout 152

Organizational development 152

Change agent 152

DISCUSSION QUESTIONS

1. Why do people tend to resist change? What problems can that tendency create for managers? What do you think managers can do to reduce resistance?

2. Which kind of people tend to be more innovative in a given field: those who are knowledgeable or those who are inexperienced in the field? Why?

3. How do you think work environment influences the innovation process? Explain.

GROUP ACTIVITY

"CREATIVE LEARNING ENVIRONMENTS"

Divide the class into small groups (four to five students). Using the "creative work environment" model in Exhibit 7.3, have each group come up with ideas about innovations in higher education that might arise by paying attention to the following components of a creative work environment: (1) challenging work, (2) organizational encouragement, (3) supervisory encouragement, (4) work group encouragement, and (5) freedom. Groups should also list any organizational impediments to innovation in higher education. Instructors may wish to reformat this activity as a discussion of how to make public education more creative.

ASSIGNMENTS

Have students draft a response to the following statement: Egalitarian companies are more innovative.

Have students use the Internet to find high-tech companies that are known for innovation and change. Ask them to identify the characteristics of these companies that make them so adept at innovation.

Large Section

Assign the electronic case homework and quiz on *3M*.

ADDITIONAL RESOURCES

A selection of materials can be found in the Instructor Manual.

WHAT'S INSIDE:

Key topics in this chapter: trade rules and agreements for global business, standardized and adapted business procedures, global business organizations, favorable business climates, adaptation to cultural differences, and preparation for international assignments.

CHAPTER OUTLINE

8-1 Global Business, Trade Rules, and Trade Agreements 155
  8-1a The Impact of Global Business 155
  8-1b Trade Barriers 156
  8-1c Trade Agreements 157
  8-1d Consumers, Trade Barriers, and Trade Agreements 161

8-2 Consistency or Adaptation? 161

8-3 Forms for Global Business 163
  8-3a Exporting 163
  8-3b Cooperative Contracts 163
  8-3c Strategic Alliances 165
  8-3d Wholly Owned Affiliates (Build or Buy) 166
  8-3e Global New Ventures 166

8-4 Finding the Best Business Climate 167
  8-4a Growing Markets 167
  8-4b Choosing an Office/ Manufacturing Location 168
  8-4c Minimizing Political Risk 170

8-5 Becoming Aware of Cultural Differences 172

8-6 Preparing for an International Assignment 174
  8-6a Language and Cross-Cultural Training 174
  8-6b Spouse, Family, and Dual-Career Issues 176

LEARNING OUTCOMES

8-1 Discuss the impact of global business and the trade rules and agreements that govern it.

8-2 Explain why companies choose to standardize or adapt their business procedures.

8-3 Explain the different ways that companies can organize to do business globally.

8-4 Explain how to find a favorable business climate.

8-5 Discuss the importance of identifying and adapting to cultural differences.

8-6 Explain how to successfully prepare workers for international assignments.

VIDEO

*Profile on Holden Outerwear

Run time: approximately 10 minutes

Like so many other American brands, Holden Outwear apparel is made in China. While the company would like to manufacture in the United States, government regulations, labor costs, and high corporate tax rates are too heavy a burden. Availability of materials is another factor, as many of the pieces that Holden needs, like buttons, snaps, and fabrics, would still have to be brought in from Asia. For any company that sources materials and labor overseas, shipping is a vital concern. In the early years, Holden used nearly a dozen shippers to transport garments from China. To increase efficiency and reduce costs, the company coordinated shipping through a single distribution hub in China, so that just two companies now handle all of Holden's shipping.

Ask your students:

1. Which stage of globalization characterizes Holden Outerwear's international involvement?

2. Identify Holden's primary approach to entering the international market. What are the benefits of this entry strategy?

3. What are the challenges of international management for leaders at Holden?

NEW TO MGMT8

(by section)

8-1 Updated statistics and data throughout section and new example on Apollo Tyres

8-1b New example on U.S. sugar subsidies

8-1c Updated statistics on Internet piracy and trade agreements

8-1d Updated statistics on per capita earnings

8-2 Updated examples on Home Depot and Starbucks

8-3b Updated statistics on McDonald's franchises

8-3c New examples on HP and merging cultures

INSTRUCTOR PREP 8

TERMS

Global business 155

Multinational corporation 155

Direct foreign investment 155

Trade barriers 156

Protectionism 156

Tariff 156

Nontariff barriers 157

Quota 157

Voluntary export restraints 157

Government import standard 157

Subsidies 157

Customs classification 157

General Agreement on Tariffs and Trade (GATT) 158

World Trade Organization (WTO) 158

Regional trading zones 158

Maastricht Treaty of Europe 159

North American Free Trade Agreement (NAFTA) 159

Dominican Republic-Central America Free Trade Agreement (CAFTA-DR) 160

Union of South American Nations (UNASUR) 160

Association of Southeast Asian Nations (ASEAN) 161

Asia-Pacific Economic Cooperation (APEC) 161

Global consistency 162

Local adaptation 162

Exporting 163

Cooperative contract 163

Licensing 164

Franchise 164

Strategic alliance 165

Joint venture 165

Wholly owned affiliates 166

Global new ventures 167

Purchasing power 167

Political uncertainty 170

Policy uncertainty 170

National culture 172

Expatriate 174

8-3d   New examples on Lixil and Standard Chartered PLC

8-4a   Updated statistics on Coke and the Big Mac Index

8-4b   New example on Ireland tax rates

8-6   New example on the Russian culture and updated statistics on international assignments

8-6b   New example on the Harvard Business Review

DISCUSSION QUESTIONS

1. Have you lived, worked, or studied abroad? Where? What was the biggest difference between your host culture and your native culture?

2. Can any company go global? Why or why not?

GROUP ACTIVITY

"OUTSOURCE OR NOT?"

Divide the class into groups of three to five students and give each group the following scenario:

Super Sized Cycles specializes in making larger bicycles for overweight riders. Thanks to Internet sales, the company has increased sales every year. However, profits have been razor thin. The problem is that the company currently obtains parts from U.S.-based companies. Though this allows for individualized customer service, it is also expensive, as each bike costs roughly $1,250 to produce. If, however, Super Sized Cycles were to source materials from Taiwan, it could pay just $400 to $500 for each bike.

Questions:

1. What are the advantages and disadvantages of working with U.S. suppliers? Of working with foreign suppliers?

2. What would be the best option for insuring the continued success of Super Sized Cycles?

Source: J. Grossmann, "Make Bikes in the US, or Go Abroad to Cut Costs?" *New York Times*, June 2, 2010, accessed June 9, 2011, http://www.nytimes.com/2010/06/03/business/smallbusiness/03sbiz.html.

ASSIGNMENTS

Assign students to audit an introductory foreign language class on campus. Instruct students to attend a class on a language they do not speak. You may need to create a note that students can give to the language instructor asking permission to sit in for one or more class sessions as a way to gain exposure to a new language. Ask students what difficulties they had in being in a foreign language environment. What tools, resources, or training do they think would be most helpful for adapting to such situations?

Large Section

Assign the electronic case homework and quiz on *Groupon*.

ADDITIONAL RESOURCES

A selection of materials can be found in the Instructor Manual.

INSTRUCTOR PREP
Designing Adaptive Organizations

9

WHAT'S INSIDE:

Key topics in this chapter: departmentalization approach to organizational structure, organizational authority, the job characteristics model, methods for job design, reengineering, and modular and virtual organizations.

CHAPTER OUTLINE

9-1 Departmentalization 179
9-1a Functional Departmentalization 180
9-1b Product Departmentalization 181
9-1c Customer Departmentalization 182
9-1d Geographic Departmentalization 183
9-1e Matrix Departmentalization 184

9-2 Organizational Authority 186
9-2a Chain of Command 186
9-2b Line versus Staff Authority 187
9-2c Delegation of Authority 187
9-2d Degree of Centralization 188

9-3 Job Design 189
9-3a Job Specialization 189
9-3b Job Rotation, Enlargement, and Enrichment 190
9-3c Job Characteristics Model 190

9-4 Intraorganizational Processes 192
9-4a Reengineering 193
9-4b Empowerment 195

9-5 Interorganizational Processes 196
9-5a Modular Organizations 196
9-5b Virtual Organizations 197

LEARNING OUTCOMES

9-1 Describe the departmentalization approach to organizational structure.

9-2 Explain organizational authority.

9-3 Discuss the different methods for job design.

9-4 Explain the methods that companies are using to redesign internal organizational processes (i.e., intraorganizational processes).

9-5 Describe the methods that companies are using to redesign external organizational processes (i.e., interorganizational processes).

VIDEO

*Profile on Modern Shed

Run time: approximately 10 minutes

Modern Shed, based in Seattle, builds paneled dwellings for use as studio spaces, home offices, pool houses, project sheds, guesthouses, and more. Like the sheds, the company is built to be adaptive, scalable, and suited to the needs of the environment. Modern Shed counts only twelve to fourteen full-time employees. But at times, its output rivals that of a large builder, thanks to collaboration with outside sales reps and a dealer network comprised of thirty-five independent contractors. According to company founder Ryan Smith, the logical process of building sheds from smaller-scale structures to larger ones is a metaphor for how modern organizations should be built. "You can use the analogy for organizations and people as well as structures," Smith states. "If you go too big you don't understand it; you have to start small."

Ask your students:

1. Describe how Modern Shed functions as a modular organization.

2. What are the advantages and disadvantages of Modern Shed's organizational structure?

NEW TO MGMT8

(by section)

9-1 Updates to Thomson Reuters example

9-1b Updates to UTC data

9-1c Updates to Swisscom

9-1d Updates to AB InBev data

9-1e Updates to P&G example

9-2a New example on SAP

9-2c New example on CARE U.S.A.

9-4b New example on Carrefour

9-5 New example on Nutella

9-5a New example on Merck

INSTRUCTOR PREP 9

TERMS

Organizational structure 179

Organizational process 179

Departmentalization 180

Functional departmentalization 180

Product departmentalization 181

Customer departmentalization 182

Geographic departmentalization 183

Matrix departmentalization 184

Simple matrix 186

Complex matrix 186

Authority 186

Chain of command 186

Unity of command 187

Line authority 187

Staff authority 187

Line function 187

Staff function 187

Delegation of authority 187

Centralization of authority 188

Decentralization 188

Standardization 189

Job design 189

Job specialization 189

Job rotation 190

Job enlargement 190

Job enrichment 190

Job characteristics model (JCM) 190

Internal motivation 190

Skill variety 191

Task identity 191

Task significance 191

Autonomy 192

Feedback 192

Mechanistic organization 193

Organic organization 193

Intraorganizational process 193

Reengineering 193

Task interdependence 194

Pooled interdependence 195

Sequential interdependence 195

Reciprocal interdependence 195

Empowering workers 195

Empowerment 196

Interorganizational process 196

Modular organization 197

Virtual organization 197

DISCUSSION QUESTIONS

1. What do you think determines how a company decides to structure itself?

2. Have you ever seen (or done) a job and thought, "If only they did *this*, it would be faster, better, easier, etc.?" Describe the situation.

3. Can a company outsource core business activities and still be successful? Explain your reasoning.

GROUP ACTIVITY

"ORGANIZATIONAL STRUCTURE"

Divide the class into small groups. Each group should create a company and clearly identify what business it is in. Then, each group should come up with an organizational design that they believe would provide their company with the best potential for growth. Each group should present their organizational design and explain why they believe their choice of design is ideal for their company.

ASSIGNMENTS

Ask students to come up with some ideas on how job rotation, job enlargement, and job enrichment could be used with the following jobs: a janitor in a large cleaning company, a secretary in an insurance company, a fifth-grade teacher, a paralegal who does nothing but research, and an intern for the state governor.

Large Section

Assign the electronic case homework and quiz on *Eli Lilly*.

ADDITIONAL RESOURCES

A selection of materials can be found in the Instructor Manual.

WHAT'S INSIDE:

Key topics in this chapter: advantages and disadvantages of using teams, different kinds of teams, the team autonomy continuum, characteristics of work teams, and work-team effectiveness.

LEARNING OUTCOMES

10-1 Explain the good and bad of using teams.

10-2 Recognize and understand the different kinds of teams.

10-3 Understand the general characteristics of work teams.

10-4 Explain how to enhance work team effectiveness.

CHAPTER OUTLINE

10-1 The Good and Bad of Using Teams 201
10-1a The Advantages of Teams 201
10-1b The Disadvantages of Teams 203
10-1c When to Use Teams 203

10-2 Kinds of Teams 204
10-2a Autonomy, the Key Dimension 204
10-2b Special Kinds of Teams 206

10-3 Work Team Characteristics 208
10-3a Team Norms 208
10-3b Team Cohesiveness 209
10-3c Team Size 209
10-3d Team Conflict 210
10-3e Stages of Team Development 211

10-4 Enhancing Work Team Effectiveness 212
10-4a Setting Team Goals and Priorities 212
10-4b Selecting People for Teamwork 214
10-4c Team Training 215
10-4d Team Compensation and Recognition 216

MULTIMEDIA

PPT—The Highlights

Slide 10   Team Norms

Slide 14   Having a Good Fight

Slide 17   Stretch Goals

Slide 21   Team Compensation

VIDEO

*Profile on Holden Outerwear

Run time: approximately 10 minutes

At Holden Outerwear, it's all about teamwork. Founder Mikey LeBlanc believes that teamwork is critical to the company's position as an innovation leader. Holden's use of teams is something that emerged out of necessity. For much of the company's brief history, managers worked independently on design projects. But as the company grew, LeBlanc needed more designers, and he began looking to outside freelancers for help. Nikki Brush, a design and development manager at Holden, remembers when she was first brought on as a freelancer. Today she is a full-time manager at the company. The switch from freelancer to in-house manager has been positive for Brush, although her role on the team has changed. Even so, she is happier working inside the firm. Not only does she now know where Holden is going, but she also helps set the course.

Ask your students:

1. What type of team did Nikki Brush participate in when she was a freelancer? What type of team does she participate in as a full-time employee at Holden?

2. What are the advantages and disadvantages of using teams at Holden? What can managers do to help avoid the disadvantages?

3. What steps do the leaders of Holden take to ensure that their workgroups have high levels of cohesion?

NEW TO MGMT8

(by section)

10-1a   New example on Barclays

10-1b   New minority domination example

10-2b   New data on virtual teams and obstacles to virtual teams

10-3b   New example on Bank of America

10-4a   New example on Google X

10-4b   New example on Nine Sigma International

INSTRUCTOR PREP 10

KEY TERMS

Work team 201

Cross-training 202

Social loafing 203

Traditional work group 205

Employee involvement team 205

Semi-autonomous work group 206

Self-managing team 206

Self-designing team 206

Cross-functional team 207

Virtual team 207

Project team 207

Norms 208

Cohesiveness 209

Forming 211

Storming 211

Norming 211

Performing 212

De-norming 212

De-storming 212

De-forming 212

Structural accommodation 213

Bureaucratic immunity 213

Individualism-collectivism 214

Team level 215

Team diversity 215

Interpersonal skills 215

Skill-based pay 217

Gainsharing 217

DISCUSSION QUESTIONS

1. Have you ever been on a team with a slacker? Have you ever been the slacker?

2. Have you ever been on a team that was particularly cohesive? How did that team perform? In contrast, have you ever participated on a team that was fragmented? How was that experience?

GROUP ACTIVITY

"TWO (OR MORE) HEADS ARE BETTER THAN ONE"

Write the word management *on the board and ask students to make as many words out of that word as possible. (For example, the words* man, gem, *and* age.) *Have students work individually and avoid sharing information. After five minutes, divide the class into groups of four or five and have them do the same exercise in groups. How many more words did the highest-scoring team find than the highest-scoring individual? The point of the exercise is to prove that teams have higher performance than individuals.*

ASSIGNMENTS

Divide the class into small groups. Each group should thoroughly research a particular team that they believe has been successful. Each group should cover the following in the research: (1) What are the characteristics of this model team? (2) What difficulties has it encountered? (3) How did the team overcome these difficulties? (4) How was the team successful? Groups should come to class prepared to discuss their research.

Large Section

Assign the electronic case homework and quiz on *Cessna*.

ADDITIONAL RESOURCES

A selection of materials can be found in the Instructor Manual.

WHAT'S INSIDE:

Key topics in this chapter: employment laws; recruiting; selection techniques and procedures; training needs and methods; performance appraisal and feedback; compensation strategies; and employee separations, including termination, downsizing, retirement, and turnover.

LEARNING OUTCOMES

11-1 Explain how different employment laws affect human resource practice.

11-2 Explain how companies use recruiting to find qualified job applicants.

11-3 Describe the selection techniques and procedures that companies use when deciding which applicants should receive job offers.

11-4 Describe how to determine training needs and select the appropriate training methods.

11-5 Discuss how to use performance appraisal to give meaningful performance feedback.

11-6 Describe basic compensation strategies and discuss the four kinds of employee separations.

CHAPTER OUTLINE

11-1 Employment Legislation 219
 11-1a Federal Employment Laws 219
 11-1b Adverse Impact and Employment Discrimination 221
 11-1c Sexual Harassment 222

11-2 Recruiting 223
 11-2a Job Analysis and Recruiting 223
 11-2b Internal Recruiting 224
 11-2c External Recruiting 225

11-3 Selection 227
 11-3a Application Forms and Résumés 227
 11-3b References and Background Checks 228
 11-3c Selection Tests 229
 11-3d Interviews 232

11-4 Training 233
 11-4a Determining Training Needs 233
 11-4b Training Methods 234
 11-4c Evaluating Training 236

11-5 Performance Appraisal 236
 11-5a Accurately Measuring Job Performance 237
 11-5b Sharing Performance Feedback 238

11-6 Compensation and Employee Separation 240
 11-6a Compensation Decisions 241
 11-6b Terminating Employees 243
 11-6c Downsizing 244
 11-6d Retirement 245
 11-6e Employee Turnover 246

VIDEO

*Profile on Barcelona Restaurant Group

Run time: approximately 10 minutes

At the Barcelona Restaurant Group, turnover among wait staff is 60 to 70 percent. One way that Barcelona tries to reduce turnover is to select the right people using a three-stage recruitment process. First, leaders conduct twenty-minute interviews with dozens of candidates. Next, applicants are asked to spend $100 at a Barcelona restaurant and write an essay about the event. The third step is "the trail," when job candidates command the floor, interact with wait staff and customers, and demonstrate job skills. Approximately one-fourth of the candidates who go on a trail can expect to be hired. At the end of the day, according to Scott Lawton, the company's chief operating officer, people either possess the necessary intelligence and skills to run a restaurant or they don't. The industry doesn't have much time for learning curves, and the success or failure of any establishment depends on the performance of competent, self-motivated employees.

Ask your students:

1. List the three main activities of human resource management (HRM) and identify which activity is examined at length in the video.

2. Of the various steps in Barcelona's employee selection process, the job interview is the most brief. Do you agree with the company's approach to interviewing? Why or why not?

3. Describe Barcelona's three-stage process for matching job applicants with its organizational objectives, and explain how each stage reveals the fit between job applicants and the needs of the restaurant.

INSTRUCTOR PREP 11

TERMS

Human resource management (HRM) 219

Bona fide occupational qualification (BFOQ) 221

Disparate treatment 221

Adverse impact 222

Four-fifths (or 80 percent) rule 222

Sexual harassment 222

Quid pro quo sexual harassment 222

Hostile work environment 222

Recruiting 223

Job analysis 223

Job description 223

Job specifications 223

Internal recruiting 224

External recruiting 225

Selection 227

Validation 227

Human resource information system (HRIS) 227

Employment references 228

Background checks 228

Specific ability tests (aptitude tests) 229

Cognitive ability tests 230

Biographical data (biodata) 230

Work sample tests 231

Assessment centers 231

Interview 232

Unstructured interviews 232

Structured interviews 232

Training 233

Needs assessment 233

Performance appraisal 236

Objective performance measures 237

Subjective performance measures 237

Behavior observation scales (BOSs) 237

Rater training 238

360-degree feedback 239

NEW TO MGMT8

(by section)

11-1a   Updates to employment labor laws; GINA added to Exhibit 11.2

11-1b   New example on Staples

11-1c   New example on Mercy General Hospital

11-2b   New example on LinkedIn

11-3a   New example on social media as a screening tool; updates to Exhibit 11.4

11-3b   New example on private investigators

11-4   Updated data on training; new feature box on onboarding

11-4a   Updated feature box on Amazon

11-4b   New example on Caterpillar

11-6a   New examples on Southwest Airlines and Central States Manufacturing

11-6b   New example on Zynga

11-6c   New example on Cisco; updated data on outplacement services

DISCUSSION QUESTIONS

1. How many of you have been to a job fair? Based on what you experienced, do you think it is hard to find qualified workers? Why or why not?

2. What advantages can you see in hiring nearly half of a company's managers from outside the company? What advantages are there to promoting internal talent?

GROUP ACTIVITY

"INTERVIEW"

Divide the class into groups of three or four students and ask each group to prepare to interview an entry-level candidate. Each group should decide if the interview will be structured, unstructured, or semistructured and why. The groups that have chosen structured or semistructured interviews should come up with a list of questions that they will ask. Groups that chose unstructured interviews should create a plan for how they will spend the interview time. Finally, each group should create a list of what they are looking for in the ideal candidate.

ASSIGNMENTS

Have students find Internet sites of three companies that deal with outplacement of terminated employees. They should write a one-paragraph summary of the services that each firm offers.

Large Section

Assign the electronic case homework and quiz on *Nick's Pizza & Pub*.

ADDITIONAL RESOURCES

A selection of materials can be found in the Instructor Manual.

Compensation 240

Employee separation 241

Job evaluation 241

Piecework 241

Commission 241

Profit sharing 242

Employee stock ownership plan (ESOP) 242

Stock options 242

Wrongful discharge 244

Downsizing 244

Outplacement services 244

Early retirement incentive programs (ERIPs) 245

Phased retirement 246

Employee turnover 246

Functional turnover 246

Dysfunctional turnover 246

WHAT'S INSIDE:

Key topics in this chapter: affirmative action versus diversity, surface-level diversity, deep-level diversity, and diversity paradigms and principles.

CHAPTER OUTLINE

12-1 Diversity: Differences That Matter 249
12-1a Diversity Is Not Affirmative Action 250
12-1b Diversity Makes Good Business Sense 251

12-2 Surface-Level Diversity 252
12-2a Age 253
12-2b Sex 254
12-2c Race/Ethnicity 256
12-2d Mental or Physical Disabilities 257

12-3 Deep-Level Diversity 258

12-4 Managing Diversity 260
12-4a Diversity Paradigms 261
12-4b Diversity Principles 263
12-4c Diversity Training and Practices 264

LEARNING OUTCOMES

12-1 Describe diversity and explain why it matters.

12-2 Understand the special challenges that the dimensions of surface-level diversity pose for managers.

12-3 Explain how the dimensions of deep-level diversity affect individual behavior and interactions in the workplace.

12-4 Explain the basic principles and practices that can be used to manage diversity.

VIDEO

*Profile on Mitchell Gold + Bob Williams

Run time: approximately 10 minutes

When Mitchell Gold and Bob Williams started their furniture company in 1989, they had a vision for how they wanted to run things. They would guarantee comfort, minimize costs, enact rigorous controls, and produce the styles they liked for their own homes. They had one other important goal: to foster a diverse workplace where employees could labor unburdened by stress, worry, or discrimination. The company has clear nondiscrimination policies and extensive diversity training, and it ensures that all employees receive the same benefits, regardless of race, gender, or religion. As employees have come to recognize, Mitchell Gold + Bob Williams is a diversity trendsetter. The company's founders envisioned a workplace where individuals felt safe and respected, and now, some twenty years later, the business is reaping rewards of diversity. With more than $100 million in annual sales, it's clear that people-focused business strategies are paying off.

Ask your students:

1. What are advantages and disadvantages of diversity at Mitchell Gold + Bob Williams?

2. How does MG + BW's approach to diversity reflect the learning and effectiveness paradigm?

3. How might a commitment to diversity at MG + BW help managers with globalization?

NEW TO MGMT8

(by section)

12-1	Updated statistics throughout section
12-1a	New example on the Supreme Court
12-1b	New examples on Merrill Lynch and Kimberly-Clark
12-2	Updated statistics throughout section
12-2a	Updated examples on beliefs about older workers
12-2b	New examples on Indra Nooyi and strategies for encouraging advancement
12-4a	New example on OshKosh
12-4c	Updated example on IAT

INSTRUCTOR PREP 12

TERMS

Diversity 249

Affirmative action 250

Surface-level diversity 252

Deep-level diversity 253

Social integration 253

Age discrimination 253

Sex discrimination 254

Glass ceiling 254

Racial and ethnic discrimination 256

Disability 257

Disability discrimination 257

Disposition 259

Personality 259

Extraversion 259

Emotional stability 259

Agreeableness 259

Conscientiousness 259

Openness to experience 260

Organizational plurality 262

Skills-based diversity training 264

Awareness training 264

Diversity audits 265

Diversity pairing 265

DISCUSSION QUESTIONS

1. What is the difference between diversity and affirmative action?

2. Diversity is about having a variety of differences. What kind of differences are we talking about?

3. Can you think of a legitimate situation in which hiring for diversity should be limited or avoided? If so, what? Would that have more to do with surface- or deep-level diversity?

GROUP ACTIVITY

"CREATING A MORE DIVERSE COMPANY"

Divide the class into small groups. Each group is to create a detailed plan for their company to increase diversity at all levels of the organization, from entry-level employees to executive leadership. The plan should include information about how to recruit, develop, and train minorities, and how to deal with various cultural issues that an organization faces as it looks to increase diversity.

ASSIGNMENTS

Instruct students to take the free online Myers-Briggs Type Indicator (MBTI) test at http://www.humanmetrics.com/cgi-win/JTypes2.asp. This is a seventy-two-question test that should take no longer than ten to fifteen minutes to complete. Have students submit the test and find out what MBTI types they are. Ask students to read about their types and then ask the following questions: What are some of the strengths of your personality style as it involves the workplace? What are some weaknesses?

Ask students to go to the website of the Americans with Disabilities Act (ADA) at the Department of Justice at http://www.dol.gov/dol/topic/disability/ada.htm and answer the following questions: What specific rights does the ADA protect? What are some new or proposed regulations within the ADA?

Large Section

Assign the electronic case homework and quiz on the *Circuit Court, Macomb County, Michigan*.

ADDITIONAL RESOURCES

A selection of materials can be found in the Instructor Manual.

INSTRUCTOR PREP 13
Motivation

WHAT'S INSIDE:

Key topics in this chapter: basics of motivation, and motivation theories, including equity, expectancy, reinforcement, and goal-setting theories; a model that integrates all these theories concludes the chapter.

CHAPTER OUTLINE

13-1 Basics of Motivation 269
13-1a Effort and Performance 269
13-1b Need Satisfaction 270
13-1c Extrinsic and Intrinsic Rewards 271
13-1d Motivating with the Basics 272

13-2 Equity Theory 274
13-2a Components of Equity Theory 274
13-2b How People React to Perceived Inequity 275
13-2c Motivating with Equity Theory 276

13-3 Expectancy Theory 278
13-3a Components of Expectancy Theory 278
13-3b Motivating with Expectancy Theory 279

13-4 Reinforcement Theory 281
13-4a Components of Reinforcement Theory 282
13-4b Schedules for Delivering Reinforcement 283
13-4c Motivating with Reinforcement Theory 285

13-5 Goal-Setting Theory 286
13-5a Components of Goal-Setting Theory 286
13-5b Motivating with Goal-Setting Theory 287

13-6 Motivating with the Integrated Model 289

LEARNING OUTCOMES

13-1 Explain the basics of motivation.

13-2 Use equity theory to explain how employees' perceptions of fairness affect motivation.

13-3 Use expectancy theory to describe how workers' expectations about rewards, effort, and the link between rewards and performance influence motivation.

13-4 Explain how reinforcement theory works and how it can be used to motivate.

13-5 Describe the components of goal-setting theory and how managers can use them to motivate workers.

13-6 Discuss how the entire motivation model can be used to motivate workers.

VIDEO

*Profile on LivingSocial Escapes

Run time: approximately 10 minutes

LivingSocial Escapes, which offers a range of outdoor excursions, demands high commitment from employees. When hiring new workers, founder Bram Levy offers only the most basic outline of job responsibilities. "Think about the brand and what we're trying to develop," Levy tells new recruits. "Now take it and formulate what you think will be best and run with it." The employees must then come up with creative ideas and execute them. Though demanding, this approach to motivation has great benefits for employees, since employees can share in the financial rewards—even part-time guides get special bonuses if trips are profitable.

Ask your students:

1. Which needs in Maslow's hierarchy are most important to the employees who work for LivingSocial Escapes, and how can managers use this information to develop a highly motivated workforce?

2. According to equity theory, how might a LivingSocial Escapes guide react if he or she feels underpaid or unappreciated?

3. What outcomes or rewards possess high valence for managers and guides who work at LivingSocial Escapes?

NEW TO MGMT8

(by section)

13-1 New Gallup employee engagement statistics

13-1b Updated instructions for the motivation model

13-1c New example on Lincoln Electric, new SHRM survey, new feature box on rewards, and updated game industry statistics

13-1d Updated SHRM survey statistics

13-2 Updated CEO pay statistics

WWW.CENGAGE.COM/LOGIN

INSTRUCTOR PREP 13

TERMS

Motivation 269

Needs 270

Extrinsic reward 271

Intrinsic reward 271

Equity theory 274

Inputs 274

Outcomes 274

Referents 274

Outcome/input (O/I) ratio 274

Underreward 274

Overreward 275

Distributive justice 277

Procedural justice 277

Expectancy theory 278

Valence 278

Expectancy 278

Instrumentality 279

Reinforcement theory 281

Reinforcement 281

Reinforcement contingencies 281

Schedule of reinforcement 281

Positive reinforcement 282

Negative reinforcement 283

Punishment 283

Extinction 283

Continuous reinforcement schedule 284

Intermittent reinforcement schedule 284

Fixed interval reinforcement schedule 284

Variable interval reinforcement schedule 284

Fixed ratio reinforcement schedule 284

Variable ratio reinforcement schedule 284

Goal 286

Goal-setting theory 286

Goal specificity 286

Goal difficulty 286

Goal acceptance 286

Performance feedback 286

13-2a New examples on Amazon and Toyota

13-2b Updated Department of Labor statistics

13-2c New example on Lenovo

13-3b New Mercer's Pay for Performance Survey

13-4a New example on Staples

13-4c New feature box on the Right Kind of Praise

13-5b New example on Accenture

DISCUSSION QUESTIONS

1. How do you, personally, try to restore equity when you perceive you have been treated unfairly?

2. Do you think that behavior is a function of its consequences? Explain.

GROUP ACTIVITY

"SURVIVOR GUILT"

Divide the class into groups of three to five students and give each group the following scenario:

Last month, because of increasing losses, management concluded that the only way to save the company would be through layoffs. In just four days, one-third of the entire company was let go. What no one expected, however, were the negative effects of the layoffs on those who still had their jobs. They were afraid that the layoffs wouldn't end with one round. They were worried that they would be asked to do much more work for not much more money. But most of all, they felt guilty, since they still had jobs while their friends would have to struggle through unemployment.

How would you motivate the workers in this company to do their best?

ASSIGNMENTS

This project begins with students making a list of financial, non-financial, and social rewards that can be tied to performance in college. Then, have students create a short survey in which they ask respondents to rank the attractiveness of each reward on the list, with 1 being "not motivating at all" and 10 being "very motivating." If you are using this as an individual project, instruct students to administer the survey to at least twenty-five students and compile the results.

Large Section

Assign the electronic case homework and quiz on *SAS*.

ADDITIONAL RESOURCES

A selection of materials can be found in the Instructor Manual.

WHAT'S INSIDE:

Key topics in this chapter: definition of leadership, traits and behaviors of effective leaders, and three major situational approaches to leadership— contingency theory, path-goal theory, and normative decision theory; also introduced are the topics of visionary, charismatic, and transformational leadership.

CHAPTER OUTLINE

14-1 Leaders versus Managers 291

14-2 Who Leaders Are and What Leaders Do 292
  14-2a Leadership Traits 292
  14-2b Leadership Behaviors 294

14-3 Putting Leaders in the Right Situation: Fiedler's Contingency Theory 296
  14-3a Leadership Style: Least Preferred Coworker 297
  14-3b Situational Favorableness 297
  14-3c Matching Leadership Styles to Situations 298

14-4 Adapting Leader Behavior: Path-Goal Theory 299
  14-4a Leadership Styles 300
  14-4b Subordinate and Environmental Contingencies 301
  14-4c Outcomes 302

14-5 Adapting Leader Behavior: Normative Decision Theory 303
  14-5a Decision Styles 303
  14-5b Decision Quality and Acceptance 303

14-6 Visionary Leadership 307
  14-6a Charismatic Leadership 307
  14-6b Transformational Leadership 309

LEARNING OUTCOMES

14-1 Explain what leadership is.

14-2 Describe who leaders are and what effective leaders do.

14-3 Explain Fiedler's contingency theory.

14-4 Describe how path-goal theory works.

14-5 Explain the normative decision theory.

14-6 Explain how visionary leadership (i.e., charismatic or transformational leadership) helps leaders achieve strategic leadership.

VIDEO

*Profile on Camp Bow Wow

Run time: approximately 10 minutes

While consistency and conformity are critical to the success of any chain, Camp Bow Wow seeks creative input from the franchisees who bought in to the system. To maintain a standard business template while encouraging fresh ideas, founder Heidi Ganahl keeps a door open for anyone who wants to meet and offer feedback. The policy has produced many visible improvements to the company, such as the new Tea Cup Pup Lounge, a play zone for small dogs. Since franchise companies attract hundreds of independent business owners into the system, Ganahl has to work with many strong leaders, which requires two-way cooperation and respect. She also has to manage personal relationships and keep every individual focused on business

Ask your students:

1. Does Camp Bow Wow CEO Heidi Ganahl possess qualities associated with contemporary leadership?

2. In what way is Heidi Ganahl's leadership charismatic and visionary? Give examples.

3. Where does Heidi Ganahl's leadership fall on the Leadership Grid discussed in the chapter? Explain.

NEW TO MGMT8

(by section)

14-2a New feature box on leadership succession at GE; new examples on perception of traits and LinkedIn

14-3 New examples on pizza franchises and Angus Davis

14-4 New example on Next Jump

14-4a New example on Domino's Pizza

14-5b New quote by John Canfield

14-6a New examples on A.G. Lafley, John Mackey, and Jay Leno

INSTRUCTOR PREP 14

TERMS

Leadership 291

Trait theory 292

Traits 292

Initiating structure 294

Consideration 294

Leadership style 296

Contingency theory 296

Situational favorableness 297

Leader-member relations 297

Task structure 297

Position power 298

Path-goal theory 299

Directive leadership 300

Supportive leadership 301

Participative leadership 301

Achievement-oriented leadership 301

Normative decision theory 303

Strategic leadership 307

Visionary leadership 307

Charismatic leadership 307

Ethical charismatics 308

Unethical charismatics 308

Transformational leadership 309

Transactional leadership 311

DISCUSSION QUESTIONS

1. Have you ever been in a position in which you were required to lead? What were your primary goals? Who did you turn to for help and why?

2. Do you think leadership qualities have to be inborn, or do you think they can be developed?

GROUP ACTIVITY

"A LEADER EMERGES"

Divide the class into groups of three to five people. Assign one person in each group to take notes and not participate in the exercise. This student should take notes on (1) who emerges as the leader, (2) what leadership style is used, and (3) how decision making is conducted in the group. Give the groups the following scenario:

You and your group have just uncovered a genie's lamp. You rub it and—surprise!—a genie appears. The genie states that he will grant three wishes, but you all have to agree on these wishes . . . you are not allowed to divide the wishes between individuals in the group.

Brainstorm a list of about ten wishes your group would like to make. Narrow this list down to the three that you are allowed. Provide reasons for these to be your final choices. At the end of the exercise, the note-taker should report to the class what happened in the exercise.

ASSIGNMENTS

Ask each student to thoroughly research a particular person they believe to be a strong leader. Students' research should include the trait theory of leadership and at least one other leadership theory. Students should cite specific examples of behaviors exhibited by the leaders. The research should culminate in a paper or presentation to the class.

Large Section

Assign the electronic case homework and quiz on *Apple*.

ADDITIONAL RESOURCES

A selection of materials can be found in the Instructor Manual.

WHAT'S INSIDE:

Key topics in this chapter: perception, attribution, and communication problems; organizational communication; coaching and counseling; nonverbal communication; and organization-wide communication.

CHAPTER OUTLINE

15-1 Perception and Communication Problems 313
15-1a Basic Perception Process 313
15-1b Perception Problems 314
15-1c Perceptions of Others 315
15-1d Self-Perception 316

15-2 Kinds of Communication 317
15-2a The Communication Process 317
15-2b Formal Communication Channels 319
15-2c Informal Communication Channels 320
15-2d Coaching and Counseling: One-on-One Communication 322
15-2e Nonverbal Communication 322

15-3 Managing One-on-One Communication 323
15-3a Choosing the Right Communication Medium 324
15-3b Listening 325
15-3c Giving Feedback 327

15-4 Managing Organization-Wide Communication 328
15-4a Improving Transmission: Getting the Message Out 329
15-4b Improving Reception: Hearing What Others Feel and Think 330

LEARNING OUTCOMES

15-1 Explain the role that perception plays in communication and communication problems.

15-2 Describe the communication process and the various kinds of communication in organizations.

15-3 Explain how managers can manage effective one-on-one communication.

15-4 Describe how managers can manage effective organization-wide communication.

VIDEO

*Profile on Plant Fantasies

Run time: approximately 10 minutes

In a day when companies use Twitter and Facebook to communicate, Teresa Carleo of Plant Fantasies is a genuine throwback. She doesn't use social media or email. At first glance, Carleo's preference for traditional communication methods seems out of touch with twenty-first century technologies. Far from being neo-Luddites, however, the leaders at Plant Fantasies demand communication that works—and that means matching the right communication methods with the right business situations. For example, some tasks at Plant Fantasies involve installing and maintaining gardens. Other situations require collaboration with landscape designers. Still others involve speaking with clients. Not all communication channels are equally suited for each situation; tweeting may be effective in one situation yet hopelessly inappropriate within another setting. Teresa Carleo insists on making a personal connection with customers. After a friend's hand-written note recently touched her in a unique way, the Plant Fantasies founder decided to launch a personal letter-writing campaign to clients.

Ask your students:

1. Why would Teresa Carleo favor face-to-face communication over email when dealing with customers?

2. Why would Carleo prefer to use electronic communication methods for certain types of communication within the company?

3. In the video, Carleo says that she worries that at times she communicates too much. What steps could she take to confirm that her messages are being heard and understood by others?

NEW TO MGMT8

(by section)

15-1d New feature box on the use of pronouns

15-2a New examples on hospitalization studies and jargon; updated statistics on doctor listening; new feature box on telling stories

15-2b New example on Square

15-2d New example on Jack Welch

15-3b New example on Popeyes Louisiana Chicken and new study from Stanford Business School

15-3c New example on Tim Harford

INSTRUCTOR PREP 15

TERMS

Communication 313

Perception 313

Perceptual filters 313

Selective perception 314

Closure 315

Attribution theory 315

Defensive bias 315

Fundamental attribution error 316

Self-serving bias 316

Encoding 317

Decoding 318

Feedback to sender 318

Noise 319

Jargon 319

Formal communication channel 319

Downward communication 319

Upward communication 320

Horizontal communication 320

Informal communication channel (grapevine) 320

Coaching 322

Counseling 322

Nonverbal communication 322

Kinesics 323

Paralanguage 323

Communication medium 324

Hearing 325

Listening 325

Active listening 326

Empathetic listening 326

Destructive feedback 327

Constructive feedback 327

Online discussion forums 329

Televised/videotaped speeches and meetings 329

Organizational silence 330

Company hotlines 330

Survey feedback 331

Blog 333

15-4a   New examples on Microsoft and HootSuite

15-4b   New statistics on reporting problems at work

DISCUSSION QUESTIONS

1. Does good listening have to involve verbally responding to the speaker?

2. Do you read blogs or post on one? What makes a good (or bad) blog? Do blogs have a place in the corporate environment? Why or why not?

GROUP ACTIVITY

"DELIVERING BAD NEWS"

Divide the class into groups of three to five students and give each group the following scenario:

As a manager, it's easy to deliver good news, whether it's rising stock prices, increased profit, or reviewing the outstanding performance of a stellar employee. It's a completely different story to deliver bad news, like declining revenue, which must be delivered in an honest but sensitive way.

In your groups, create an outline for how you would communicate the bad news in each of the following scenarios:

1. In spite of heavy investments into new technology, you must report to shareholders that your company's profits have fallen 20 percent.

2. An employee who has been with the company for thirty-five years has been performing under standards for the last seven years. After much consideration, managers have decided that he should be let go. It's been left to you to inform the employee.

ASSIGNMENTS

Assign students to go to the website of any well-known company and evaluate its external communication on the following attributes: (1) How user-friendly is the website? (2) What kinds of information are communicated? (3) Does the website allow people to communicate with corporate officers? (4) How honest is the company regarding information, especially negative information? and (5) How would you rate the website overall on its communication (on a scale of 1 to 10, with 10 being excellent)?

Large Section

Assign the electronic case homework and quiz on *Google*.

ADDITIONAL RESOURCES

A selection of materials can be found in the Instructor Manual.

WHAT'S INSIDE:

Key topics in this chapter: basic control process; different methods for achieving control; the balanced scorecard; and control of organizational behaviors, processes, and outcomes; this chapter also has a Financial Review Card for students.

CHAPTER OUTLINE

16-1 The Control Process 335
16-1a Standards 335
16-1b Comparison to Standards 336
16-1c Corrective Action 337
16-1d Dynamic, Cybernetic Process 337
16-1e Feedback, Concurrent, and Feedforward Control 337
16-1f Control Isn't Always Worthwhile or Possible 338

16-2 Control Methods 339
16-2a Bureaucratic Control 339
16-2b Objective Control 340
16-2c Normative Control 340
16-2d Concertive Control 341
16-2e Self-Control 342

16-3 What to Control? 343
16-3a The Balanced Scorecard 343
16-3b The Financial Perspective: Controlling Budgets, Cash Flows, and Economic Value Added 344
16-3c The Customer Perspective: Controlling Customer Defections 347
16-3d The Internal Perspective: Controlling Quality 348
16-3e The Innovation and Learning Perspective: Controlling Waste and Pollution 348

LEARNING OUTCOMES

16-1 Describe the basic control process.

16-2 Discuss the various methods that managers can use to maintain control.

16-3 Describe the behaviors, processes, and outcomes that today's managers are choosing to control in their organizations.

VIDEO

*Profile on Barcelona Restaurant Group

Run time: approximately 7 minutes

CEO Andy Pforzheimer and his COO, Scott, rely on technology to be able to control the many facets of their restaurants. Email, texts, video loops, and secret shopper reports allow them to provide a great experience for their customers. In addition, they have a desire to know what is going on in their restaurant and to do so by probing and holding weekly meetings to discuss financial figures, shopper reports, and comment cards from their customers. They make an effort to bring their staff together to discuss their needs, points of improvement, and an opportunity to collaborate for the betterment of their group. At the end of the day, they want to provide a great experience for customers and do so while keeping their self-respect and maintaining a highly successful business/operation.

Ask your students:

1. Using all available resources to review your company's performance is vital. Where does the COO, Scott, claim he gets this information from?

2. What is the purpose of the weekly "war room" meetings that are held with the executives, general managers, and chefs?

3. What are the two things that Andy Pforzheimer says are at stake at the end of the day when it comes to his company's success?

NEW TO MGMT8

(by section)

16-1 New example on the French Open

16-1a New example on Intuit

16-1b New example on the Center for Disease Control

16-1e Updated example on squirrels

16-2 New example on Kroger

16-2a New example on the U.S. Department of Transportation

16-2b New example on State Farm Insurance

16-2c New examples on the Four Seasons and Elite SEM

16-2d Updated example on Conde Nast Traveler

16-3e New examples on the San Francisco 49ers, H&M, and Kyocera; new feature box on Novelis

INSTRUCTOR PREP 16

TERMS

Control 335

Standards 335

Benchmarking 336

Cybernetic 337

Feedback control 337

Concurrent control 338

Feedforward control 338

Control loss 338

Regulation costs 338

Cybernetic feasibility 339

Bureaucratic control 339

Objective control 340

Behavior control 340

Output control 340

Normative control 340

Concertive control 341

Self-control (self-management) 342

Balanced scorecard 343

Suboptimization 343

Cash flow analysis 344

Balance sheets 345

Income statements 345

Financial ratios 345

Budgets 345

Economic value added (EVA) 345

Customer defections 347

Value 348

DISCUSSION QUESTIONS

1. Do you use a personal budget? Chapter 5 discussed budgets as plans for allocating resources. How do you think budgets can be used as control tools?

2. What do you think about this statement: "Self-control is the preferred control method"?

GROUP ACTIVITY

"THE PROBLEM WITH CUPS"

Divide the class into groups of three to five students and give each group the following scenario:

Starbucks has always strived to take leadership in environmental issues, whether it was by encouraging customers to compost used coffee grounds or offering free coffee drinks to customers who brought in their own reusable mugs. But the company faces a major problem that has few solutions—cups. Across all of its stores, Starbucks uses more than 3 billion paper cups every year, most of which end up in the trash. Though the company would love to recycle these cups, it can't, since most processors don't have a process for recycling paper cups that are lined with plastic, as the Starbucks cups are. The plastic lining also prevents the cups from being composted.

Questions

1. How can Starbucks maintain its commitment to reducing waste as it keeps sending paper cups to landfills?

2. What steps do you think Starbucks could take to reduce the number of paper cups it uses?

Source: A. Kamenetz, "The Starbucks Cup Dilemma," *Fast Company*, October 20, 2010, accessed January 4, 2011, http://www.fastcompany .com/magazine/150/a-story-of -starbucks-and-the-limits-of-corporate-sustainability.html.

ASSIGNMENTS

One behavior in businesses related to control is employee use of the Internet. Ask students to evaluate whether control in this area is worthwhile and which kind of control method is appropriate. Are there companies for which it would be more important to implement strict Internet-use controls? Which companies and why?

Large Section

Assign the electronic case homework and quiz on *Caterpillar*.

ADDITIONAL RESOURCES

A selection of materials can be found in the Instructor Manual.

Basic Accounting Tools for Controlling Financial Performance

Steps for a Basic Cash Flow Analysis

1. Forecast sales (steady, up, or down).
2. Project changes in anticipated cash inflows (as a result of changes).
3. Project anticipated cash outflows (as a result of changes).
4. Project net cash flows by combining anticipated cash inflows and outflows.

Parts of a Basic Balance Sheet (Assets = Liabilities + Owner's Equity)

1. Assets
   a. Current assets (cash, short-term investment, marketable securities, accounts receivable, etc.)
   b. Fixed assets (land, buildings, machinery, equipment, etc.)
2. Liabilities
   a. Current liabilities (accounts payable, notes payable, taxes payable, etc.)
   b. Long-term liabilities (long-term debt, deferred income taxes, etc.)
3. Owner's Equity
   a. Preferred stock and common stock
   b. Additional paid-in capital
   c. Retained earnings

Basic Income Statement

SALES REVENUE
− sales returns and allowances
+ other income
= NET REVENUE
− cost of goods sold (beginning inventory, costs of goods purchased, ending inventory)
= GROSS PROFIT
− total operating expenses (selling, general, and administrative expenses)
= INCOME FROM OPERATIONS
− interest expense
= PRETAX INCOME
− income taxes
= NET INCOME

Common Kinds of Budgets

Revenue Budgets—used to project or forecast future sales.	• Accuracy of projection depends on economy, competitors, sales force estimates, etc. • Determined by estimating future sales volume and sales prices for all products and services.
Expense Budgets—used within departments and divisions to determine how much will be spent on various supplies, projects, or activities.	• One of the first places that companies look for cuts when trying to lower expenses.
Profit Budgets—used by profit centers, which have "profit and loss" responsibility.	• Profit budgets combine revenue and expense budgets into one budget. • Typically used in large businesses with multiple plants and divisions.
Cash Budgets—used to forecast how much cash a company will have on hand to meet expenses.	• Similar to cash-flow analyses. • Used to identify cash shortfalls, which must be covered to pay bills, or cash excesses, which should be invested for a higher return.
Capital Expenditure Budgets—used to forecast large, long-lasting investments in equipment, buildings, and property.	• Help managers identify funding that will be needed to pay for future expansion or strategic moves designed to increase competitive advantage.
Variable Budgets—used to project costs across varying levels of sales and revenues.	• Important because it is difficult to accurately predict sales revenue and volume. • Lead to more accurate budgeting with respect to labor, materials, and administrative expenses, which vary with sales volume and revenues. • Build flexibility into the budgeting process.

Common Financial Ratios

Ratios	Formula	What It Means	When to Use
Liquidity Ratios			
Current Ratio	$\dfrac{\text{Current Assets}}{\text{Current Liabilities}}$	• Whether you have enough assets on hand to pay for short-term bills and obligations. • Higher is better. • Recommended level is two times as many current assets as current liabilities.	• Track monthly and quarterly. • Basic measure of your company's health.
Quick (Acid Test) Ratio	$\dfrac{(\text{Current Assets} - \text{Inventories})}{\text{Current Liabilities}}$	• Stricter than current ratio. • Whether you have enough (i.e., cash) to pay short-term bills and obligations. • Higher is better. • Recommended level is one or higher.	• Track monthly. • Also calculate quick ratio with potential customers to evaluate whether they're likely to pay you in a timely manner.
Leverage Ratios			
Debt to Equity	$\dfrac{\text{Total Liabilities}}{\text{Total Equity}}$	• Indicates how much the company is leveraged (in debt) by comparing what is owed (liabilities) to what is owned (equity). • Lower is better. A high debt-to-equity ratio could indicate that the company has too much debt. • Recommended level depends on industry.	• Track monthly. • Lenders often use this to determine the creditworthiness of a business (i.e., whether to approve additional loans).
Debt Coverage	$\dfrac{(\text{Net Profit} + \text{Noncash Expense})}{\text{Debt}}$	• Indicates how well cash flow covers debt payments. • Higher is better.	• Track monthly. • Lenders look at this ratio to determine if there is adequate cash to make loan payments.
Efficiency Ratios			
Inventory Turnover	$\dfrac{\text{Cost of Goods Sold}}{\text{Average Value of Inventory}}$	• Whether you're making efficient use of inventory. • Higher is better, indicating that inventory (dollars) isn't purchased (spent) until needed. • Recommended level depends on industry.	• Track monthly by using a twelve-month rolling average.
Average Collections Period	$\dfrac{\text{Accounts Receivable}}{(\text{Annual Net Credit Sales} \div 365)}$	• Shows on average how quickly your customers are paying their bills. • Recommended level is no more than fifteen days longer than credit terms. If credit is net thirty days, then average should not be longer than forty-five days.	• Track monthly. • Use to determine how long company's money is being tied up in customer credit.
Profitability Ratios			
Gross Profit Margin	$\dfrac{\text{Gross Profit}}{\text{Total Sales}}$	• Shows how efficiently a business is using its materials and labor in the production process. • Higher is better, indicating that a profit can be made if fixed costs are controlled.	• Track monthly. • Analyze when unsure about product or service pricing. • Low margin compared to competitors means you're underpricing.
Return on Equity	$\dfrac{\text{Net Income}}{\text{Owner's Equity}}$	• Shows what was earned on your investment in the business during a particular period. Often called "return on investment." • Higher is better.	• Track quarterly and annually. • Use to compare to what you might have earned on the stock market, bonds, or government Treasury bills during the same period.

WHAT'S INSIDE:

Key topics in this chapter: strategic importance of information; characteristics of useful information (i.e., its value and costs); capturing, processing, and protecting information; data mining; and accessing and sharing information and knowledge.

LEARNING OUTCOMES

17-1 Explain the strategic importance of information.

17-2 Describe the characteristics of useful information (i.e., its value and costs).

17-3 Explain the basics of capturing, processing, and protecting information.

17-4 Describe how companies can access and share information and knowledge.

CHAPTER OUTLINE

17-1 Strategic Importance of Information 353

17-1a First-Mover Advantage 354

17-1b Sustaining Competitive Advantage 355

17-2 Characteristics and Costs of Useful Information 356

17-2a Accurate Information 356

17-2b Complete Infovrmation 356

17-2c Relevant Information 357

17-2d Timely Information 357

17-2e Acquisition Costs 357

17-2f Processing Costs 358

17-2g Storage Costs 358

17-2h Retrieval Costs 359

17-2i Communication Costs 359

17-3 Capturing, Processing, and Protecting Information 359

17-3a Capturing Information 360

17-3b Processing Information 361

17-3c Protecting Information 363

17-4 Accessing and Sharing Information and Knowledge 368

17-4a Internal Access and Sharing 368

17-4b External Access and Sharing 369

17-4c Sharing Knowledge and Expertise 371

VIDEO

*Profile on Numi Organic Tea

Run time: approximately 10 minutes

When Brian Durkee shows up at Numi Organic Tea every day to work as the director of operations, he's on a mission to make Numi a worldwide leader in sustainable supply chain management. Setting up and maintaining an efficient enterprise resource planning (ERP) system turned out to be much easier than converting Chinese suppliers to profoundly different farming methods and ways of doing business. Numi had just begun to implement an ERP system with integrated inventory management and accounting when Durkee joined the company. In this video, Durkee explains how Numi is dedicated to sustainable supply chain management, eliminating waste, and using recycled materials.

Ask your students:

1. What kinds of challenges does Numi face in managing information?

2. Why was it no longer sufficient for Numi to use programs like Excel and QuickBooks to manage its information?

3. What are some of the advantages Durkee mentions that have come with using the ERP system?

NEW TO MGMT8

(by section)

17-1 Update to Moore's Law and new example on the iPhone

17-1a New example on Pandora

17-2b New example on airline black boxes

17-2c New example on Modernizing Medicine

17-2d New example on Meadowbrook Maple Syrup

17-2h New example on Sunhee Moon

17-3a New example on QR codes

17-3b New example on the New York City Fire Department; new feature box on Hiding from Big Data

17-3c New examples on Target, Google Apps, VPN service providers, and "white hat hackers"; updated feature box on biometric data

INSTRUCTOR PREP 17

TERMS

Moore's law 353

Raw data 354

Information 354

First-mover advantage 354

Acquisition cost 357

Processing cost 358

Storage cost 358

Retrieval cost 359

Communication cost 359

Bar code 360

Radio frequency identification (RFID) tags 360

Electronic scanner 361

Optical character recognition 361

Processing information 361

Data mining 361

Data warehouse 362

Supervised data mining 362

Unsupervised data mining 362

Association or affinity patterns 362

Sequence patterns 363

Predictive patterns 363

Data clusters 363

Protecting information 363

Authentication 364

Authorization 364

Two-factor authentication 366

Firewall 366

Virus 366

Data encryption 366

Virtual private network (VPN) 367

Secure sockets layer (SSL) encryption 367

Executive information system (EIS) 368

Intranets 368

Corporate portal 369

Electronic data interchange (EDI) 369

Web services 369

Extranets 370

Knowledge 371

Decision support system (DSS) 371

Expert system 371

DISCUSSION QUESTIONS

1. Do you think having the latest and greatest technology is the best way for a company to gain a competitive advantage? Explain.

2. How long can Moore's law continue to apply? Can computing costs go nearly to zero? What are the implications of lower computing costs?

3. What technology is currently used in the classroom that enhances the instructor's ability to provide information and the students' ability to receive information? What technology is not available that would improve information sharing in the classroom?

GROUP ACTIVITY

"TECHNOLOGY CASE STUDY"

Divide the class into small groups. Each group should research a real company (local, national, or global) and list ten ways in which the company uses technology. This project should culminate in a paper and/or presentation given to the entire class.

ASSIGNMENTS

Ask students to do a comprehensive comparison of Amazon.com and Barnes & Noble that covers (1) the number of titles in stock; (2) the prices; (3) delivery options, including shipping prices; (4) the number of international titles in stock; (5) the ease of searching for titles; and (6) anything else that would be important to them as customers. Does Amazon, which was founded in 1995, still have the first-mover advantage? Which online bookstore would students be more likely to use? Why?

Large Section

Assign the electronic case homework and quiz on *Delta Airlines*.

ADDITIONAL RESOURCES

A selection of materials can be found in the Instructor Manual.

WHAT'S INSIDE:

Key topics in this chapter: basics of operations management, productivity measurements, quality awards and certifications, service operations and service recovery, manufacturing operations, inventory management, and economic order quantity.

LEARNING OUTCOMES

18-1 Discuss the kinds of productivity and their importance in managing operations.

18-2 Explain the role that quality plays in managing operations.

18-3 Explain the essentials of managing a service business.

18-4 Describe the different kinds of manufacturing operations.

18-5 Explain why and how companies should manage inventory levels.

CHAPTER OUTLINE

18-1 Productivity 375
18-1a Why Productivity Matters 375
18-1b Kinds of Productivity 377

18-2 Quality 378
18-2a Quality-Related Characteristics for Products and Services 379
18-2b ISO 9000 and 14000 380
18-2c Baldrige National Quality Award 381
18-2d Total Quality Management 382

18-3 Service Operations 383
18-3a The Service-Profit Chain 384
18-3b Service Recovery and Empowerment 385

18-4 Manufacturing Operations 386
18-4a Amount of Processing in Manufacturing Operations 386
18-4b Flexibility of Manufacturing Operations 388

18-5 Inventory 389
18-5a Types of Inventory 389
18-5b Measuring Inventory 390
18-5c Costs of Maintaining an Inventory 391
18-5d Managing Inventory 392

VIDEO

*Profile on Barcelona Restaurant Group

Run time: approximately 10 minutes

At Barcelona Restaurant Group, quality is defined not just by the food but also by the service that the waitstaff delivers. The company's restaurants are renowned for providing a personal touch to diners. And while managers are responsible for watching over wait times, bussing, and cleanliness, it is up to each individual employee to deliver a consistently excellent experience. To ensure consistent quality across the board, Barcelona uses five "feedback loops" that gauge restaurant performance: a "secret shopper" program, credit card rewards for customers who complete surveys, customer comment cards, emails, and surveillance cameras. In addition to these loops, the owners and general managers walk the floor constantly to advise wait staff and gather feedback from customers. There's plenty at stake if Barcelona fails to control its performance. Co-founder Andy Pforzheimer notes that disappointing one's customers is the quickest way to kill a business. However, failure is about more than losing money: it's also about losing face.

Ask your students:

1. How does Barcelona Restaurant Group's approach to customer service fulfill the quality-related characteristics of services?

2. How does Barcelona Restaurant Group's approach to customer service fulfill the three aspects of total quality management?

3. Discuss how Barcelona Restaurant Group implements service recovery and service empowerment.

NEW TO MGMT8

(by section)

18-1 New example on ArcellorMittal

18-1a Updated statistics throughout section

18-2 Updated information on J.D. Power and Associates

18-2a Updated statistics on the Apple Store

18-2c New example on Baldrige Award examiners; updated statistics on the Baldrige Award

18-2d New examples on airline quality standards and ArcellorMittal

18-3b Updated customer service statistics; new feature box on the Disney Institute

INSTRUCTOR PREP 18

TERMS

Operations management 375

Productivity 375

Partial productivity 377

Multifactor productivity 377

Quality 379

ISO 9000 380

ISO 14000 380

Total quality management (TQM) 382

Customer focus 382

Customer satisfaction 382

Continuous improvement 383

Variation 383

Teamwork 383

Internal service quality 384

Service recovery 385

Make-to-order operation 386

Assemble-to-order operation 387

Make-to-stock operation 387

Manufacturing flexibility 388

Continuous-flow production 388

Line-flow production 388

Batch production 388

Job shops 389

Inventory 389

Raw material inventories 389

Component parts inventories 390

Work-in-process inventories 390

Finished goods inventories 390

Average aggregate inventory 390

Stockout 390

Inventory turnover 391

Ordering cost 391

Setup cost 391

Holding cost 392

Stockout cost 392

Economic order quantity (EOQ) 392

Just-in-time (JIT) inventory system 393

Kanban 393

Materials requirement planning (MRP) 393

Independent demand system 394

Dependent demand system 394

18-4   New feature box on additive manufacturing

18-4b   New example on Tesla Motors

18-5   New example on Gustin Jeans

DISCUSSION QUESTIONS

1. How productive are you on a scale of 1 to 10, with 10 being extremely productive? What keeps you from being even more productive?

2. Is the customer always right? When would you protect your frontline employees? What types of customers would you not want?

GROUP ACTIVITY

"QUALITY SERVICE"

Divide the class into small groups. Have each group select a type of retailer that it wants to research (such as deep-discount stores or computer stores) and visit at least three different examples of that type of store. An example would be to do research on deep-discount stores and visit Walmart, Kmart, and Target. At least one student in the group should buy something from the store and then fill out a survey that was written in advance on the quality of customer service using the characteristics of quality service discussed in the chapter. Results should be presented in class.

ASSIGNMENTS

Use an article search database at your library and find three articles on inventory control systems used by different companies. Instruct students to contrast and compare the systems in a three-page paper.

Large Section

Assign the electronic case homework and quiz on *Louis Vuitton*.

ADDITIONAL RESOURCES

A selection of materials can be found in the Instructor Manual.